CORPORATE AND PARTNERSHIP INCOME TAX CODE AND REGULATIONS

SELECTED SECTIONS

2019–2020 Edition

STEVEN A. BANK

Paul Hastings Professor of Business Law
UCLA School of Law

KIRK J. STARK

Barrall Family Professor of Tax Law and Policy
UCLA School of Law

FOUNDATION
PRESS

© 2002–2004 FOUNDATION PRESS
© 2005–2012 by THOMSON REUTERS/FOUNDATION PRESS
© 2013 LEG, Inc. d/b/a West Academic Publishing
© 2014–2018 LEG, Inc. d/b/a West Academic
© 2019 LEG, Inc. d/b/a West Academic
     444 Cedar Street, Suite 700
     St. Paul, MN 55101
     1-877-888-1330

Printed in the United States of America

ISBN: 978-1-64242-914-5

PREFACE

As the title suggests, this volume provides the user with certain "Selected Sections" of the Internal Revenue Code pertaining to the tax treatment of corporations, partnerships, and related entities. It is designed for use in connection with courses covering corporate and partnership taxation and is not intended to be a complete reference. It includes the provisions of the Internal Revenue Code and Treasury Regulations most commonly covered in courses such as corporate taxation, partnership taxation, and the combined taxation of business enterprises course, as well as some generally applicable individual income tax provisions that professors might ask students to refer to in a business entity tax course. In order to keep the volume lean to make it user-friendly for both teachers and students, it does not include provisions covering more specialized subjects such as insurance, real estate investment trusts, or international aspects of the taxation of business enterprises. Ellipsis marks are utilized to indicate where material has been excluded from a provision of the Code or Regulations. Temporary regulations are generally included, but proposed regulations are not. The text of the volume is current through March 31, 2019.

STEVEN A. BANK
KIRK J. STARK

June 2019

Contents

CORPORATE AND PARTNERSHIP INCOME TAX CODE AND REGULATIONS

SELECTED SECTIONS

2019–2020 Edition

SUBTITLE A—INCOME TAXES

Current Through March 31, 2019

Chapter 1—Normal Taxes or Surtaxes

Subchapter A—Determination of Tax Liability

Part I—Tax on Individuals

§ 1. Tax imposed

(a) Married individuals filing joint returns and surviving spouses.—There is hereby imposed on the taxable income of—

(1) every married individual (as defined in section 7703) who makes a single return jointly with his spouse under section 6013, and

(2) every surviving spouse (as defined in section 2(a)),

a tax determined in accordance with the following table:

If taxable income is:	The tax is:
Not over $36,900	15% of taxable income.
Over $36,900 but not over $89,150	$5,535, plus 28% of the excess over $36,900.
Over $89,150 but not over $140,000	$20,165, plus 31% of the excess over $89,150.
Over $140,000 but not over $250,000	$35,928.50, plus 36% of the excess over $140,000.
Over $250,000	$75,528.50, plus 39.6% of the excess over $250,000.

* * *

(c) Unmarried individuals (other than surviving spouses and heads of households).—There is hereby imposed on the taxable income of every individual (other than a surviving spouse as defined in section 2(a) or the head of a household as defined in section 2(b)) who is not a married individual (as defined in section 7703) a tax determined in accordance with the following table:

If taxable income is:	The tax is:
Not over $22,100	15% of taxable income.
Over $22,100 but not over $53,500	$3,315, plus 28% of the excess over $22,100.
Over $53,500 but not over $115,000	$12,107, plus 31% of the excess over $53,500.
Over $115,000 but not over $250,000	$31,172, plus 36% of the excess over $115,000.
Over $250,000	$79,772, plus 39.6% of the excess over $250,000.

* * *

(e) Estates and trusts.—There is hereby imposed on the taxable income of—

(1) every estate, and

(2) every trust,

taxable under this subsection a tax determined in accordance with the following table:

If taxable income is:	The tax is:
Not over $1,500	15% of taxable income.
Over $1,500 but not over $3,500	$225, plus 28% of the excess over $1,500.
Over $3,500 but not over $5,500	$785, plus 31% of the excess over $3,500.
Over $5,500 but not over $7,500	$1,405, plus 36% of the excess over $5,500.
Over $7,500	$2,125, plus 39.6% of the excess over $7,500.

* * *

(h) Maximum capital gains rate.—

(1) In general.—If a taxpayer has a net capital gain for any taxable year, the tax imposed by this section for such taxable year shall not exceed the sum of—

(A) a tax computed at the rates and in the same manner as if this subsection had not been enacted on the greater of—

(i) taxable income reduced by the net capital gain; or

(ii) the lesser of—

(I) the amount of taxable income taxed at a rate below 25 percent; or

(II) taxable income reduced by the adjusted net capital gain,

(B) 0 percent of so much of the adjusted net capital gain (or, if less, taxable income) as does not exceed the excess (if any) of—

(i) the amount of taxable income which would (without regard to this paragraph) be taxed at a rate below 25 percent, over

(ii) the taxable income reduced by the adjusted net capital gain;

(C) 15 percent of the lesser of—

(i) so much of the adjusted net capital gain (or, if less, taxable income) as exceeds the amount on which a tax is determined under subparagraph (B), or

(ii) the excess of—

(I) the amount of taxable income which would (without regard to this paragraph) be taxed at a rate below 39.6 percent, over

(II) the sum of the amounts on which a tax is determined under subparagraphs (A) and (B),

(D) 20 percent of the adjusted net capital gain (or, if less, taxable income) in excess of the sum of the amounts on which tax is determined under subparagraphs (B) and (C),

(E) 25 percent of the excess (if any) of—

(i) the unrecaptured section 1250 gain (or, if less, the net capital gain (determined without regard to paragraph (11))), over

(ii) the excess (if any) of—

(I) the sum of the amount on which tax is determined under subparagraph (A) plus the net capital gain, over

(II) taxable income; and

(F) 28 percent of the amount of taxable income in excess of the sum of the amounts on which tax is determined under the preceding subparagraphs of this paragraph.

(2) Net capital gain taken into account as investment income.—For purposes of this subsection, the net capital gain for any taxable year shall be reduced (but not below zero) by the amount which the taxpayer takes into account as investment income under section 163(d)(4)(B)(iii).

(3) Adjusted net capital gain.—For purposes of this subsection, the term "adjusted net capital gain" means the sum of—

(A) net capital gain (determined without regard to paragraph (11)) reduced (but not below zero) by the sum of—

   (i) unrecaptured section 1250 gain, and

   (ii) 28-percent rate gain, plus

(B) qualified dividend income (as defined in paragraph (11)).

(4) 28 percent rate gain.—For purposes of this subsection, the term "28-percent rate gain" means the excess (if any) of—

(A) the sum of—

   (i) collectibles gain; and

   (ii) section 1202 gain, over

(B) the sum of—

   (i) collectibles loss;

   (ii) the net short-term capital loss; and

   (iii) the amount of long-term capital loss carried under section 1212(b)(1)(B) to the taxable year.

(5) Collectibles gain and loss.—For purposes of this subsection—

(A) In general.—The terms "collectibles gain" and "collectibles loss" mean gain or loss (respectively) from the sale or exchange of a collectible (as defined in section 408(m) without regard to paragraph (3) thereof) which is a capital asset held for more than 1 year but only to the extent such gain is taken into account in computing gross income and such loss is taken into account in computing taxable income.

(B) Partnerships, etc.—For purposes of subparagraph (A), any gain from the sale of an interest in a partnership, S corporation, or trust which is attributable to unrealized appreciation in the value of collectibles shall be treated as gain from the sale or exchange of a collectible. Rules similar to the rules of section 751 shall apply for purposes of the preceding sentence.

(6) Unrecaptured section 1250 gain.—For purposes of this subsection—

(A) In general.—The term "unrecaptured section 1250 gain" means the excess (if any) of—

   (i) the amount of long-term capital gain (not otherwise treated as ordinary income) which would be treated as ordinary income if section 1250(b)(1) included all depreciation and the applicable percentage under section 1250(a) were 100 percent, over

(ii) the excess (if any) of—

(I) the amount described in paragraph (4)(B); over

(II) the amount described in paragraph (4)(A).

(B) **Limitation with respect to section 1231 property.**—The amount described in subparagraph (A)(i) from sales, exchanges, and conversions described in section 1231(a)(3)(A) for any taxable year shall not exceed the net section 1231 gain (as defined in section 1231(c)(3)) for such year.

(7) **Section 1202 gain**

For purposes of this subsection, the term "section 1202 gain" means the excess of—

(A) the gain which would be excluded from gross income under section 1202 but for the percentage limitation in section 1202(a), over

(B) the gain excluded from gross income under section 1202.

(8) **Coordination with recapture of net ordinary losses under section 1231.**—If any amount is treated as ordinary income under section 1231(c), such amount shall be allocated among the separate categories of net section 1231 gain (as defined in section 1231(c)(3)) in such manner as the Secretary may by forms or regulations prescribe.

(9) **Regulations.**—The Secretary may prescribe such regulations as are appropriate (including regulations requiring reporting) to apply this subsection in the case of sales and exchanges by pass-thru entities and of interests in such entities.

(10) **Pass-thru entity defined.**—For purposes of this subsection, the term "pass-thru entity" means—

(A) a regulated investment company;

(B) a real estate investment trust;

(C) an S corporation;

(D) a partnership;

(E) an estate or trust;

(F) a common trust fund; and

(G) a qualified electing fund (as defined in section 1295).

(11) **Dividends taxed as net capital gain.**—

(A) **In general.**—For purposes of this subsection, the term 'net capital gain' means net capital gain (determined without regard to this paragraph) increased by qualified dividend income.

(B) **Qualified dividend income.**—For purposes of this paragraph—

(i) **In general.**—The term 'qualified dividend income' means dividends received during the taxable year from—

(I) domestic corporations, and

(II) qualified foreign corporations.

(ii) **Certain dividends excluded.**—Such term shall not include—

(I) any dividend from a corporation which for the taxable year of the corporation in which the distribution is made, or the preceding taxable year, is a corporation exempt from tax under section 501 or 521,

(II) any amount allowed as a deduction under section 591 (relating to deduction for dividends paid by mutual savings banks, etc.), and

(III) any dividend described in section 404(k).

(iii) **Coordination with section 246(c).**—Such term shall not include any dividend on any share of stock—

(I) with respect to which the holding period requirements of section 246(c) are not met (determined by substituting in section 246(c) "60 days" for "45 days" each place it appears and by substituting "121-day period" for "91-day period"), or

(II) to the extent that the taxpayer is under an obligation (whether pursuant to a short sale or otherwise) to make related payments with respect to positions in substantially similar or related property.

(C) Qualified foreign corporations.—

(i) **In general.**—Except as otherwise provided in this paragraph, the term 'qualified foreign corporation' means any foreign corporation if—

(I) such corporation is incorporated in a possession of the United States, or

(II) such corporation is eligible for benefits of a comprehensive income tax treaty with the United States which the Secretary determines is satisfactory for purposes of this paragraph and which includes an exchange of information program.

(ii) **Dividends on stock readily tradable on United States securities market.**—A foreign corporation not otherwise treated as a qualified foreign corporation under clause (i) shall be so treated with respect to any dividend paid by such corporation if the stock with respect to which such dividend is paid is readily tradable on an established securities market in the United States.

(iii) **Exclusion of dividends of certain foreign corporations.**—Such term shall not include any foreign corporation which for the taxable year of the corporation in which the dividend was paid, or the preceding taxable year, is a passive foreign investment company (as defined in section 1297).

(iv) **Coordination with foreign tax credit limitation.**—Rules similar to the rules of section 904(b)(2)(B) shall apply with respect to the dividend rate differential under this paragraph.

(D) Special rules.—

(i) **Amounts taken into account as investment income.**—Qualified dividend income shall not include any amount which the taxpayer takes into account as investment income under section 163(d)(4)(B).

(ii) **Extraordinary dividends.**—If an individual receives, with respect to any share of stock, qualified dividend income from 1 or more dividends which are extraordinary dividends (within the meaning of section 1059(c)), any loss on the sale or exchange of such share shall, to the extent of such dividends, be treated as long-term capital loss.

(iii) Treatment of dividends from regulated investment companies and real estate investment trusts.—A dividend received from a regulated investment company or a real estate investment trust shall be subject to the limitations prescribed in sections 854 and 857.

(i) Rate reductions after 2000.—

(1) 10-percent rate bracket.—

(A) In general.—In the case of taxable years beginning after December 31, 2000—

(i) the rate of tax under subsections (a), (b), (c), and (d) on taxable income not over the initial bracket amount shall be 10 percent, and

(ii) the 15 percent rate of tax shall apply only to taxable income over the initial bracket amount but not over the maximum dollar amount for the 15-percent rate bracket.

(B) Initial bracket amount.—For purposes of this paragraph, the initial bracket amount is—

(i) $14,000 in the case of subsection (a),

(ii) $10,000 in the case of subsection (b), and

(iii) 1/2 the amount applicable under clause (i) (after adjustment, if any, under subparagraph (C)) in the case of subsections (c) and (d).

(C) Inflation adjustment.—In prescribing the tables under subsection (f) which apply with respect to taxable years beginning in calendar years after 2003—

(i) the cost-of-living adjustment shall be determined under subsection (f)(3) by substituting "2002" for "1992" in subparagraph (B) thereof, and

(ii) the adjustments under clause (i) shall not apply to the amount referred to in subparagraph (B)(iii).

If any amount after adjustment under the preceding sentence is not a multiple of $50, such amount shall be rounded to the next lowest multiple of $50.

(2) 25-, 28-, and 33-percent rate brackets—The tables under subsections (a), (b), (c), (d), and (e) shall be applied—

(A) by substituting "25%" for "28%" each place it appears (before the application of subparagraph (B)),

(B) by substituting "28%" for "31%" each place it appears, and

(C) by substituting "33%" for "36%" each place it appears.

(3) Modifications to income tax brackets for high-income taxpayers

(A) 35-percent rate bracket—In the case of taxable years beginning after December 31, 2012—

(i) the rate of tax under subsections (a), (b), (c), and (d) on a taxpayer's taxable income in the highest rate bracket shall be 35 percent to the extent such income does not exceed an amount equal to the excess of—

(I) the applicable threshold, over

(II) the dollar amount at which such bracket begins, and

(ii) the 39.6 percent rate of tax under such subsections shall apply only to the taxpayer's taxable income in such bracket in excess of the amount to which clause (i) applies.

(B) **Applicable threshold**—For purposes of this paragraph, the term "applicable threshold" means—

(i) $450,000 in the case of subsection (a),

(ii) $425,000 in the case of subsection (b),

(iii) $400,000 in the case of subsection (c), and

(iv) 1/2 the amount applicable under clause (i) (after adjustment, if any, under subparagraph (C)) in the case of subsection (d).

(C) **Inflation adjustment**—For purposes of this paragraph, with respect to taxable years beginning in calendar years after 2013, each of the dollar amounts under clauses (i), (ii), and (iii) of subparagraph (B) shall be adjusted in the same manner as under paragraph (1)(C)(i), except that subsection (f)(3)(B) shall be applied by substituting "2012" for "1992".

(4) **Adjustment of tables**—The Secretary shall adjust the tables prescribed under subsection (f) to carry out this subsection.

(j) **Modifications for taxable years 2018 through 2025.**—

(1) **In general.**—In the case of a taxable year beginning after December 31, 2017, and before January 1, 2026—

(A) subsection (i) shall not apply, and

(B) this section (other than subsection (i)) shall be applied as provided in paragraphs (2) through (6).

(2) **Rate tables.**—

(A) **Married individuals filing joint returns and surviving spouses.**—The following table shall be applied in lieu of the table contained in subsection (a):

If taxable income is:	The tax is:
Not over $19,050	10% of taxable income.
Over $19,050 but not over $77,400	$1,905, plus 12% of the excess over $19,050.
Over $77,400 but not over $165,000	$8,907, plus 22% of the excess over $77,400.
Over $165,000 but not over $315,000	$28,179, plus 24% of the excess over $165,000.
Over $315,000 but not over $400,000	$64,179, plus 32% of the excess over $315,000.
Over $400,000 but not over $600,000	$91,379, plus 35% of the excess over $400,000.
Over $600,000	$161,379, plus 37% of the excess over $600,000.

(B) **Heads of household.**—The following table shall be applied in lieu of the table contained in subsection (b):

If taxable income is:	The tax is:
Not over $13,600	10% of taxable income.
Over $13,600 but not over $51,800	$1,360, plus 12% of the excess over $13,600.
Over $51,800 but not over $82,500	$5,944, plus 22% of the excess over $51,800.

Over $82,500 but not over $157,500 ....$12,698, plus 24% of the excess over $82,500.

Over $157,500 but not over $200,000 ....$30,698, plus 32% of the excess over $157,500.

Over $200,000 but not over $500,000 ....$44,298, plus 35% of the excess over $200,000.

Over $500,000...$149,298, plus 37% of the excess over $500,000.

(C) **Unmarried individuals other than surviving spouses and heads of household.**—The following table shall be applied in lieu of the table contained in subsection (c):

If taxable income is:	The tax is:
Not over $9,525	10% of taxable income.
Over $9,525 but not over $38,700	$952.50, plus 12% of the excess over $9,525.
Over $38,700 but not over $82,500	$4,453.50, plus 22% of the excess over $38,700.
Over $82,500 but not over $157,500	$14,089.50, plus 24% of the excess over $82,500.
Over $157,500 but not over $200,000	$32,089.50, plus 32% of the excess over $157,500.
Over $200,000 but not over $500,000	$45,689.50, plus 35% of the excess over $200,000.
Over $500,000...	$150,689.50, plus 37% of the excess over $500,000.

(D) **Married individuals filing separate returns.**—The following table shall be applied in lieu of the table contained in subsection (d):

If taxable income is:	The tax is:
Not over $9,525	10% of taxable income.
Over $9,525 but not over $38,700	$952.50, plus 12% of the excess over $9,525.
Over $38,700 but not over $82,500	$4,453.50, plus 22% of the excess over $38,700.
Over $82,500 but not over $157,500	$14,089.50, plus 24% of the excess over $82,500.
Over $157,500 but not over $200,000	$32,089.50, plus 32% of the excess over $157,500.
Over $200,000 but not over $300,000	$45,689.50, plus 35% of the excess over $200,000.
Over $300,000...	$80,689.50, plus 37% of the excess over $300,000.

(E) **Estates and trusts.**—The following table shall be applied in lieu of the table contained in subsection (e):

If taxable income is:	The tax is:
Not over $2,550	10% of taxable income.
Over $2,550 but not over $9,150	$255, plus 24% of the excess over $2,550.
Over $9,150 but not over $12,500	$1,839, plus 35% of the excess over $9,150.
Over $12,500...	$3,011.50, plus 37% of the excess over $12,500.

(F) **References to rate tables.**—Any reference in this title to a rate of tax under subsection (c) shall be treated as a reference to the corresponding rate bracket under subparagraph (C) of this paragraph, except that the reference in section 3402(q)(1) to the third lowest rate of tax applicable under subsection (c) shall be treated as a reference to the fourth lowest rate of tax under subparagraph (C).

(3) Adjustments.—

(A) **No adjustment in 2018.**—The tables contained in paragraph (2) shall apply without adjustment for taxable years beginning after December 31, 2017, and before January 1, 2019.

(B) **Subsequent years.**—For taxable years beginning after December 31, 2018, the Secretary shall prescribe tables which shall apply in lieu of the tables contained in paragraph (2) in the same manner as under paragraphs (1) and (2) of subsection (f) (applied without regard to clauses (i) and (ii) of subsection (f)(2)(A)), except that in prescribing such tables—

(i) subsection (f)(3) shall be applied by substituting 'calendar year 2017' for 'calendar year 2016' in subparagraph (A)(ii) thereof,

(ii) subsection (f)(7)(B) shall apply to any unmarried individual other than a surviving spouse or head of household, and

(iii) subsection (f)(8) shall not apply.

(4) Special rules for certain children with unearned income.—

(A) In general.—In the case of a child to whom subsection (g) applies for the taxable year, the rules of subparagraphs (B) and (C) shall apply in lieu of the rule under subsection (g)(1).

(B) Modifications to applicable rate brackets.— In determining the amount of tax imposed by this section for the taxable year on a child described in subparagraph (A), the income tax table otherwise applicable under this subsection to the child shall be applied with the following modifications:

(i) 24-percent bracket.—The maximum taxable income which is taxed at a rate below 24 percent shall not be more than the sum of—

(I) the earned taxable income of such child, plus

(II) the minimum taxable income for the 24-percent bracket in the table under paragraph (2)(E) (as adjusted under paragraph (3)) for the taxable year.

(ii) 35-percent bracket.—The maximum taxable income which is taxed at a rate below 35 percent shall not be more than the sum of—

(I) the earned taxable income of such child, plus

(II) the minimum taxable income for the 35-percent bracket in the table under paragraph (2)(E) (as adjusted under paragraph (3)) for the taxable year.

(iii) 37-percent bracket.—The maximum taxable income which is taxed at a rate below 37 percent shall not be more than the sum of—

(I) the earned taxable income of such child, plus

(II) the minimum taxable income for the 37-percent bracket in the table under paragraph (2)(E) (as adjusted under paragraph (3)) for the taxable year.

(C) Coordination with capital gains rates.—For purposes of applying section 1(h) (after the modifications under paragraph (5)(A))—

(i) the maximum zero rate amount shall not be more than the sum of—

(I) the earned taxable income of such child, plus

(II) the amount in effect under paragraph (5)(B)(i)(IV) for the taxable year, and

(ii) the maximum 15-percent rate amount shall not be more than the sum of—

(I) the earned taxable income of such child, plus

(II) the amount in effect under paragraph (5)(B)(ii)(IV) for the taxable year.

(D) Earned taxable income.—For purposes of this paragraph, the term 'earned taxable income' means, with respect to any child for any taxable year, the taxable income of such child reduced (but not below zero) by the net unearned income (as defined in subsection (g)(4)) of such child.

(5) Application of current income tax brackets to capital gains brackets.—

(A) In general.—Section 1(h)(1) shall be applied—

(i) by substituting 'below the maximum zero rate amount' for 'which would (without regard to this paragraph) be taxed at a rate below 25 percent' in subparagraph (B)(i), and

(ii) by substituting 'below the maximum 15-percent rate amount' for 'which would (without regard to this paragraph) be taxed at a rate below 39.6 percent' in subparagraph (C)(ii)(I).

(B) Maximum amounts defined.—For purposes of applying section 1(h) with the modifications described in subparagraph (A)—

(i) Maximum zero rate amount.—The maximum zero rate amount shall be—

(I) in the case of a joint return or surviving spouse, $77,200,

(II) in the case of an individual who is a head of household (as defined in section 2(b)), $51,700,

(III) in the case of any other individual (other than an estate or trust), an amount equal to 1/2 of the amount in effect for the taxable year under subclause (I), and

(IV) in the case of an estate or trust, $2,600.

(ii) Maximum 15-percent rate amount.—The maximum 15-percent rate amount shall be—

(I) in the case of a joint return or surviving spouse, $479,000 (1/2 such amount in the case of a married individual filing a separate return),

(II) in the case of an individual who is the head of a household (as defined in section 2(b)), $452,400,

(III) in the case of any other individual (other than an estate or trust), $425,800, and

(IV) in the case of an estate or trust, $12,700.

(C) Inflation adjustment.—In the case of any taxable year beginning after 2018, each of the dollar amounts in clauses (i) and (ii) of subparagraph (B) shall be increased by an amount equal to—

(i) such dollar amount, multiplied by

(ii) the cost-of-living adjustment determined under subsection (f)(3) for the calendar year in which the taxable year begins, determined by substituting 'calendar year 2017' for 'calendar year 2016' in subparagraph (A)(ii) thereof. If any increase under this subparagraph is not a multiple of $50, such increase shall be rounded to the next lowest multiple of $50.

* * *

Part II — Tax on Corporations

§ 11. Tax imposed.

(a) Corporations in general. A tax is hereby imposed for each taxable year on the taxable income of every corporation.

(b) Amount of tax.—The amount of the tax imposed by subsection (a) shall be 21 percent of taxable income.

(c) Exceptions. Subsection (a) shall not apply to a corporation subject to a tax imposed by—

(1) section 594 (relating to mutual savings banks conducting life insurance business),

(2) subchapter L (sec. 801 and following, relating to insurance companies), or

(3) subchapter M (sec. 851 and following, relating to regulated investment companies and real estate investment trusts).

(d) Foreign corporations. In the case of a foreign corporation, the taxes imposed by subsection (a) and section 55 shall apply only as provided by section 882.

* * *

Subchapter B — Computation of Taxable Income

Part I — Definition of Gross Income

§ 83. Property transferred in connection with performance of services.

(a) General rule.—If, in connection with the performance of services, property is transferred to any person other than the person for whom such services are performed, the excess of—

(1) the fair market value of such property (determined without regard to any restriction other than a restriction which by its terms will never lapse) at the first time the rights of the person having the beneficial interest in such property are transferable or are not subject to a substantial risk of forfeiture, whichever occurs earlier, over

(2) the amount (if any) paid for such property,

shall be included in the gross income of the person who performed such services in the first taxable year in which the rights of the person having the beneficial interest in such property are transferable or are not subject to a substantial risk of forfeiture, whichever is applicable. The preceding sentence shall not apply if such person sells or otherwise disposes of such property in an arm's length transaction before his rights in such property become transferable or not subject to a substantial risk of forfeiture.

(b) Election to include in gross income in year of transfer.—

(1) In general.—Any person who performs services in connection with which property is transferred to any person may elect to include in his gross income, for the taxable year in which such property is transferred, the excess of—

(A) the fair market value of such property at the time of transfer (determined without regard to any restriction other than a restriction which by its terms will never lapse), over

(B) the amount (if any) paid for such property.

11

If such election is made, subsection (a) shall not apply with respect to the transfer of such property, and if such property is subsequently forfeited, no deduction shall be allowed in respect of such forfeiture.

(2) Election.—An election under paragraph (1) with respect to any transfer of property shall be made in such manner as the Secretary prescribes and shall be made not later than 30 days after the date of such transfer. Such election may not be revoked except with the consent of the Secretary.

(c) Special rules.—For purposes of this section—

(1) Substantial risk of forfeiture.—The rights of a person in property are subject to a substantial risk of forfeiture if such person's rights to full enjoyment of such property are conditioned upon the future performance of substantial services by any individual.

(2) Transferability of property.—The rights of a person in property are transferable only if the rights in such property of any transferee are not subject to a substantial risk of forfeiture.

(3) Sales which may give rise to suit under Section 16(b) of the Securities Exchange Act of 1934.—So long as the sale of property at a profit could subject a person to suit under section 16(b) of the Securities Exchange Act of 1934, such person's rights in such property are—

(A) subject to a substantial risk of forfeiture, and

(B) not transferable.

(4) For purposes of determining an individual's basis in property transferred in connection with the performance of services, rules similar to the rules of section 72(w) shall apply.

(d) Certain restrictions which will never lapse.—

(1) Valuation.—In the case of property subject to a restriction which by its terms will never lapse, and which allows the transferee to sell such property only at a price determined under a formula, the price so determined shall be deemed to be the fair market value of the property unless established to the contrary by the Secretary, and the burden of proof shall be on the Secretary with respect to such value.

(2) Cancellation.—If, in the case of property subject to a restriction which by its terms will never lapse, the restriction is canceled, then, unless the taxpayer establishes—

(A) that such cancellation was not compensatory, and

(B) that the person, if any, who would be allowed a deduction if the cancellation were treated as compensatory, will treat the transaction as not compensatory, as evidenced in such manner as the Secretary shall prescribe by regulations,

the excess of the fair market value of the property (computed without regard to the restrictions) at the time of cancellation over the sum of—

(C) the fair market value of such property (computed by taking the restriction into account) immediately before the cancellation, and

(D) the amount, if any, paid for the cancellation,

shall be treated as compensation for the taxable year in which such cancellation occurs.

(e) Applicability of section.—This section shall not apply to—

(1) a transaction to which section 421 applies,

(2) a transfer to or from a trust described in section 401(a) or a transfer under an annuity plan which meets the requirements of section 404(a)(2),

(3) the transfer of an option without a readily ascertainable fair market value,

(4) the transfer of property pursuant to the exercise of an option with a readily ascertainable fair market value at the date of grant, or

(5) group-term life insurance to which section 79 applies.

(f) **Holding period.**—In determining the period for which the taxpayer has held property to which subsection (a) applies, there shall be included only the period beginning at the first time his rights in such property are transferable or are not subject to a substantial risk of forfeiture, whichever occurs earlier.

(g) **Certain exchanges.**—If property to which subsection (a) applies is exchanged for property subject to restrictions and conditions substantially similar to those to which the property given in such exchange was subject, and if section 354, 355, 356, or 1036 (or so much of section 1031 as relates to section 1036) applied to such exchange, or if such exchange was pursuant to the exercise of a conversion privilege—

(1) such exchange shall be disregarded for purposes of subsection (a), and

(2) the property received shall be treated as property to which subsection (a) applies.

(h) **Deduction by employer.**—In the case of a transfer of property to which this section applies or a cancellation of a restriction described in subsection (d), there shall be allowed as a deduction under section 162, to the person for whom were performed the services in connection with which such property was transferred, an amount equal to the amount included under subsection (a), (b), or (d)(2) in the gross income of the person who performed such services. Such deduction shall be allowed for the taxable year of such person in which or with which ends the taxable year in which such amount is included in the gross income of the person who performed such services.

* * *

§ 108. Income from discharge of indebtedness.

(a) Exclusion from gross income.—

(1) **In general**—Gross income does not include any amount which (but for this subsection) would be includible in gross income by reason of the discharge (in whole or in part) of indebtedness of the taxpayer if—

(A) the discharge occurs in a title 11 case,

(B) the discharge occurs when the taxpayer is insolvent,

(C) the indebtedness discharged is qualified farm indebtedness, or

(D) in the case of a taxpayer other than a C corporation, the indebtedness discharged is qualified real property business indebtedness.

* * *

(2) Coordination of exclusions.—

(A) Title 11 exclusion takes precedence.—Subparagraphs (B), (C), and (D) of paragraph (1) shall not apply to a discharge which occurs in a title 11 case.

(B) Insolvency exclusion takes precedence over qualified farm exclusion and qualified real property business exclusion.—Subparagraphs (C) and (D) of paragraph (1) shall not apply to a discharge to the extent the taxpayer is insolvent.

* * *

(3) Insolvency exclusion limited to amount of insolvency.—In the case of a discharge to which paragraph (1)(B) applies, the amount excluded under paragraph (1)(B) shall not exceed the amount by which the taxpayer is insolvent.

(b) Reduction of tax attributes.—

(1) In general.—The amount excluded from gross income under subparagraph (A), (B), or (C) of subsection (a)(1) shall be applied to reduce the tax attributes of the taxpayer as provided in paragraph (2).

(2) Tax attributes affected; order of reduction.—Except as provided in paragraph (5), the reduction referred to in paragraph (1) shall be made in the following tax attributes in the following order:

(A) NOL.—Any net operating loss for the taxable year of the discharge, and any net operating loss carryover to such taxable year.

(B) General business credit.—Any carryover to or from the taxable year of a discharge of an amount for purposes for determining the amount allowable as a credit under section 38 (relating to general business credit).

(C) Minimum tax credit.—The amount of the minimum tax credit available under section 53(b) as of the beginning of the taxable year immediately following the taxable year of the discharge.

(D) Capital loss carryovers.—Any net capital loss for the taxable year of the discharge, and any capital loss carryover to such taxable year under section 1212.

(E) Basis reduction.—

(i) In general.—The basis of the property of the taxpayer.

(ii) Cross reference.—For provisions for making the reduction described in clause (i), see section 1017.

(F) Passive activity loss and credit carryovers.—Any passive activity loss or credit carryover of the taxpayer under section 469(b) from the taxable year of the discharge.

(G) Foreign tax credit carryovers.—Any carryover to or from the taxable year of the discharge for purposes of determining the amount of the credit allowable under section 27.

(3) Amount of reduction.—

(A) In general.—Except as provided in subparagraph (B), the reductions described in paragraph (2) shall be one dollar for each dollar excluded by subsection (a).

(B) Credit carryover reduction.—The reductions described in subparagraphs (B), (C), and (G) shall be 33 1/3 cents for each dollar excluded by subsection (a). The reduction described in subparagraph (F) in any passive activity credit carryover shall be 33 1/3 cents for each dollar excluded by subsection (a).

(4) Ordering rules.—

(A) Reductions made after determination of tax for year.—The reductions described in paragraph (2) shall be made after the determination of the tax imposed by this chapter for the taxable year of the discharge.

(B) Reductions under subparagraph (A) or (D) of paragraph (2).—The reductions described in subparagraph (A) or (D) of paragraph (2) (as the case may be) shall be made first in the loss for the taxable year of the discharge and then in the carryovers to such taxable year in the order of the taxable years from which each such carryover arose.

(C) Reductions under subparagraphs (B) and (G) of paragraph (2).—The reductions described in subparagraphs (B) and (G) of paragraph (2) shall be made in the order in which carryovers are taken into account under this chapter for the taxable year of the discharge.

(5) Election to apply reduction first against depreciable property.—

(A) In general.—The taxpayer may elect to apply any portion of the reduction referred to in paragraph (1) to the reduction under section 1017 of the basis of the depreciable property of the taxpayer.

(B) Limitation.—The amount to which an election under subparagraph (A) applies shall not exceed the aggregate adjusted bases of the depreciable property held by the taxpayer as of the beginning of the taxable year following the taxable year in which the discharge occurs.

(C) Other tax attributes not reduced.—Paragraph (2) shall not apply to any amount to which an election under this paragraph applies.

(c) Treatment of discharge of qualified real property business indebtedness.—

(1) Basis reduction.—

(A) In general.—The amount excluded from gross income under subparagraph (D) of subsection (a)(1) shall be applied to reduce the basis of the depreciable real property of the taxpayer.

(B) Cross reference.—For provisions making the reduction described in subparagraph (A), see section 1017.

(2) Limitations.—

(A) Indebtedness in excess of value.—The amount excluded under subparagraph (D) of subsection (a)(1) with respect to any qualified real property business indebtedness shall not exceed the excess (if any) of—

(**i**) the outstanding principal amount of such indebtedness (immediately before the discharge), over

(**ii**) the fair market value of the real property described in paragraph (3)(A) (as of such time), reduced by the outstanding principal amount of any other qualified real property business indebtedness secured by such property (as of such time).

(B) Overall limitation.—The amount excluded under subparagraph (D) of subsection (a)(1) shall not exceed the aggregate adjusted bases of depreciable real property (determined after any reductions under subsections (b) and (g)) held by the taxpayer immediately before the discharge (other than depreciable real property acquired in contemplation of such discharge).

(3) Qualified real property business indebtedness.—The term "qualified real property business indebtedness" means indebtedness which—

(A) was incurred or assumed by the taxpayer in connection with real property used in a trade or business and is secured by such real property,

(B) was incurred or assumed before January 1, 1993, or if incurred or assumed on or after such date, is qualified acquisition indebtedness, and

(C) with respect to which such taxpayer makes an election to have this paragraph apply.

Such term shall not include qualified farm indebtedness. Indebtedness under subparagraph (B) shall include indebtedness resulting from the refinancing of indebtedness under subparagraph (B) (or this sentence), but only to the extent it does not exceed the amount of the indebtedness being refinanced.

(4) Qualified acquisition indebtedness.—For purposes of paragraph (3)(B), the term "qualified acquisition indebtedness" means, with respect to any real property described in paragraph (3)(A), indebtedness incurred or assumed to acquire, construct, reconstruct, or substantially improve such property.

(5) Regulations.—The Secretary shall issue such regulations as are necessary to carry out this subsection, including regulations preventing the abuse of this subsection through cross-collateralization or other means.

(d) Meaning of terms; special rules relating to certain provisions.—

(1) Indebtedness of taxpayer.—For purposes of this section, the term "indebtedness of the taxpayer" means any indebtedness—

(A) for which the taxpayer is liable, or

(B) subject to which the taxpayer holds property.

(2) Title 11 case.—For purposes of this section, the term "title 11 case" means a case under title 11 of the United States Code (relating to bankruptcy), but only if the taxpayer is under the jurisdiction of the court in such case and the discharge of indebtedness is granted by the court or is pursuant to a plan approved by the court.

(3) Insolvent.—For purposes of this section, the term "insolvent" means the excess of liabilities over the fair market value of assets. With respect to any discharge, whether or not the taxpayer is insolvent, and the amount by which the taxpayer is insolvent, shall be determined on the basis of the taxpayer's assets and liabilities immediately before the discharge.

(4) Repealed.

(5) Depreciable property.—The term "depreciable property" has the same meaning as when used in section 1017.

(6) Certain provisions to be applied at partner level.—In the case of a partnership, subsections (a), (b), (c) and (g) shall be applied at the partner level.

(7) Special rules for S corporation.—

(A) Certain provisions to be applied at corporate level.—In the case of an S corporation, subsections (a), (b), (c), and (g) shall be applied at the corporate level, including by not taking into account under section 1366(a) any amount excluded under subsection (a) of this section.

(B) Reduction in carryover of disallowed losses and deductions.—In the case of an S corporation, for purposes of subparagraph (A) of subsection (b)(2), any loss or deduction which is disallowed for the taxable year of the discharge under section 1366(d)(1) shall be treated as a net operating loss for such taxable year. The preceding sentence shall not apply to any discharge to the extent that subsection (a)(1)(D) applies to such discharge.

(C) Coordination with basis adjustments under section 1367(b)(2).—For purposes of subsection (e)(6), a shareholder's adjusted basis in indebtedness of an S corporation shall be determined without regard to any adjustments made under section 1367(b)(2).

(8) Reductions of tax attributes in title 11 cases of individuals to be made by estate.—In any case under chapter 7 or 11 of title 11 of the United States Code to which section 1398 applies, for purposes of paragraphs (1) and (5) of subsection (b) the estate (and not the individual) shall be treated as the taxpayer. The preceding sentence shall not apply for purposes of applying section 1017 to property transferred by the estate to the individual.

(9) Time for making election, etc.—

(A) Time.—An election under paragraph (5) of subsection (b) or under paragraph (3)(C) of subsection (c) shall be made on the taxpayer's return for the taxable year in which the discharge occurs or at such other time as may be permitted in regulations prescribed by the Secretary.

(B) Revocation only with consent.—An election referred to in subparagraph (A), once made, may be revoked only with the consent of the Secretary.

(C) Manner.—An election referred to in subparagraph (A) shall be made in such manner as the Secretary may by regulations prescribe.

(10) Cross reference.—For provision that no reduction is to be made in the basis of exempt property of an individual debtor, see section 1017(c)(1).

(e) General rules for discharge of indebtedness (including discharges not in title 11 cases or insolvency).—For purposes of this title—

(1) No other insolvency exception.—Except as otherwise provided in this section, there shall be no insolvency exception from the general rule that gross income includes income from the discharge of indebtedness.

(2) Income not realized to extent of lost deductions.—No income shall be realized from the discharge of indebtedness to the extent that payment of the liability would have given rise to a deduction.

(3) Adjustments for unamortized premium and discount.—The amount taken into account with respect to any discharge shall be properly adjusted for unamortized premium and unamortized discount with respect to the indebtedness discharged.

(4) Acquisition of indebtedness by person related to debtor.—

(A) Treated as acquisition by debtor.—For purposes of determining income of the debtor from discharge of indebtedness, to the extent provided in regulations prescribed by the Secretary, the acquisition of outstanding indebtedness by a person bearing a relationship to the debtor specified in section 267(b) or 707(b)(1) from a person who does not bear such a relationship to the debtor shall be treated as the acquisition of such indebtedness by the debtor. Such regulations shall provide for such adjustments in the treatment of any subsequent transactions involving the indebtedness as may be appropriate by reason of the application of the preceding sentence.

(B) Members of family.—For purposes of this paragraph, sections 267(b) and 707(b) (1) shall be applied as if section 267(c)(4) provided that the family of an individual consists of the individual's spouse, the individual's children, grandchildren, and parents, and any spouse of the individual's children or grandchildren.

(C) Entities under common control treated as related.—For purposes of this paragraph, two entities which are treated as a single employer under subsection (b) or (c) of section 414 shall be treated as bearing a relationship to each other which is described in section 267(b).

(5) Purchase-money debt reduction for solvent debtor treated as price reduction.—If—

(A) the debt of a purchaser of property to the seller of such property which arose out of the purchase of such property is reduced,

(B) such reduction does not occur—

(i) in a title 11 case, or

(ii) when the purchaser is insolvent, and

(C) but for this paragraph, such reduction would be treated as income to the purchaser from the discharge of indebtedness,

then such reduction shall be treated as a purchase price adjustment.

(6) Indebtedness contributed to capital.—Except as provided in regulations, for purposes of determining income of the debtor from discharge of indebtedness, if a debtor corporation acquires its indebtedness from a shareholder as a contribution to capital—

(A) section 118 shall not apply, but

(B) such corporation shall be treated as having satisfied the indebtedness with an amount of money equal to the shareholder's adjusted basis in the indebtedness.

(7) Recapture of gain on subsequent sale of stock.—

(A) In general.—If a creditor acquires stock of a debtor corporation in satisfaction of such corporation's indebtedness, for purposes of section 1245—

(i) such stock (and any other property the basis of which is determined in whole or in part by reference to the adjusted basis of such stock) shall be treated as section 1245 property,

(ii) the aggregate amount allowed to the creditor—

(I) as deductions under subsection (a) or (b) of section 166 (by reason of the worthlessness or partial worthlessness of the indebtedness), or

(II) as an ordinary loss on the exchange,

shall be treated as an amount allowed as a deduction for depreciation, and

(iii) an exchange of such stock qualifying under section 354(a), 355(a), or 356(a) shall be treated as an exchange to which section 1245(b)(3) applies.

The amount determined under clause (ii) shall be reduced by the amount (if any) included in the creditor's gross income on the exchange.

(B) Special rule for cash basis taxpayers.—In the case of any creditor who computes his taxable income under the cash receipts and disbursements method, proper adjustment shall be made in the amount taken into account under clause (ii) of subparagraph (A) for any amount which was not included in the creditor's gross income but which would have been included in such gross income if such indebtedness had been satisfied in full.

(C) Stock of parent corporation.—For purposes of this paragraph, stock of a corporation in control (within the meaning of section 368(c)) of the debtor corporation shall be treated as stock of the debtor corporation.

(D) Treatment of successor corporation.—For purposes of this paragraph, the term "debtor corporation" includes a successor corporation.

(E) Partnership rule.—Under regulations prescribed by the Secretary, rules similar to the rules of the foregoing subparagraphs of this paragraph shall apply with respect to the indebtedness of a partnership.

(8) Indebtedness satisfied by corporate stock or partnership interest.—For purposes of determining income of a debtor from discharge of indebtedness, if—

(A) a debtor corporation transfers stock, or

(B) a debtor partnership transfers a capital or profits interest in such partnership,

to a creditor in satisfaction of its recourse or nonrecourse indebtedness, such corporation or partnership shall be treated as having satisfied the indebtedness with an amount of money equal to the fair market value of the stock or interest. In the case of any partnership, any discharge of indebtedness income recognized under this paragraph shall be included in the distributive shares of taxpayers which were the partners in the partnership immediately before such discharge.

(9) Discharge of indebtedness income not taken into account in determining whether entity meets REIT qualifications.—Any amount included in gross income by reason of the discharge of indebtedness shall not be taken into account for purposes of paragraphs (2) and (3) of section 856(c).

(10) Indebtedness satisfied by issuance of debt instrument.—

(A) In general.—For purposes of determining income of a debtor from discharge of indebtedness, if a debtor issues a debt instrument in satisfaction of indebtedness, such debtor shall be treated as having satisfied the indebtedness with an amount of money equal to the issue price of such debt instrument.

(B) Issue price.—For purposes of subparagraph (A), the issue price of any debt instrument shall be determined under sections 1273 and 1274. For purposes of the preceding sentence, section 1273(b)(4) shall be applied by reducing the stated redemption price of any instrument by the portion of such stated redemption price which is treated as interest for purposes of this chapter.

* * *

§ 118. Contributions to the capital of a corporation

(a) General rule.—In the case of a corporation, gross income does not include any contribution to the capital of the taxpayer.

(b) Exceptions.—For purposes of subsection (a), the term 'contribution to the capital of the taxpayer' does not include—

(1) any contribution in aid of construction or any other contribution as a customer or potential customer, and

(2) any contribution by any governmental entity or civic group (other than a contribution made by a shareholder as such).

* * *

(e) Cross references

(1) For basis of property acquired by a corporation through a contribution to its capital, see section 362.

* * *

Part VI—Itemized Deductions for Individuals and Corporations

§ 163. Interest

(a) General rule.—There shall be allowed as a deduction all interest paid or accrued within the taxable year on indebtedness.

* * *

(j) Limitation on business interest.—

(1) In general.—The amount allowed as a deduction under this chapter for any taxable year for business interest shall not exceed the sum of—

(A) the business interest income of such taxpayer for such taxable year,

(B) 30 percent of the adjusted taxable income of such taxpayer for such taxable year, plus

(C) the floor plan financing interest of such taxpayer for such taxable year.

The amount determined under subparagraph (B) shall not be less than zero.

(2) Carryforward of disallowed business interest.—The amount of any business interest not allowed as a deduction for any taxable year by reason of paragraph (1) shall be treated as business interest paid or accrued in the succeeding taxable year.

(3) Exemption for certain small businesses.—In the case of any taxpayer (other than a tax shelter prohibited from using the cash receipts and disbursements method of accounting under section 448(a)(3)) which meets the gross receipts test of section 448(c) for any taxable year, paragraph (1) shall not apply to such taxpayer for such taxable year. In the case of any taxpayer which is not a corporation or a partnership, the gross receipts test of section 448(c) shall be applied in the same manner as if such taxpayer were a corporation or partnership.

(4) Application to partnerships, etc.—

(A) In general.—In the case of any partnership—

(i) this subsection shall be applied at the partnership level and any deduction for business interest shall be taken into account in determining the non-separately stated taxable income or loss of the partnership, and

(ii) the adjusted taxable income of each partner of such partnership—

(I) shall be determined without regard to such partner's distributive share of any items of income, gain, deduction, or loss of such partnership, and

(II) shall be increased by such partner's distributive share of such partnership's excess taxable income.

For purposes of clause (ii)(II), a partner's distributive share of partnership excess taxable income shall be determined in the same manner as the partner's distributive share of nonseparately stated taxable income or loss of the partnership.

(B) Special rule for carryforwards.—

(i) In general.—The amount of any business interest not allowed as a deduction to a partnership for any taxable year by reason of paragraph (1) for any taxable year—

(I) shall not be treated under paragraph (2) as business interest paid or accrued by the partnership in the succeeding taxable year, and

(II) shall, subject to clause (ii), be treated as excess business interest which is allocated to each partner in the same manner as the non-separately stated taxable income or loss of the partnership.

(ii) Treatment of excess business interest allocated to partners.—If a partner is allocated any excess business interest from a partnership under clause (i) for any taxable year—

(I) such excess business interest shall be treated as business interest paid or accrued by the partner in the next succeeding taxable year in which the partner is allocated excess taxable income from such partnership, but only to the extent of such excess taxable income, and

(II) any portion of such excess business interest remaining after the application of subclause (I) shall, subject to the limitations of subclause (I), be treated as business interest paid or accrued in succeeding taxable years.

For purposes of applying this paragraph, excess taxable income allocated to a partner from a partnership for any taxable year shall not be taken into account under paragraph (1)(A) with respect to any business interest other than excess business interest from the partnership until all such excess business interest for such taxable year and all preceding taxable years has been treated as paid or accrued under clause (ii).

(iii) Basis adjustments.—

(I) In general.—The adjusted basis of a partner in a partnership interest shall be reduced (but not below zero) by the amount of excess business interest allocated to the partner under clause (i)(II).

(II) Special rule for dispositions.—If a partner disposes of a partnership interest, the adjusted basis of the partner in the partnership interest shall be increased immediately before the disposition by the amount of the excess (if any) of the amount of the basis reduction under subclause (I) over the portion of any excess business interest allocated to the partner under clause (i)(II) which has previously been treated under clause (ii) as business interest paid or accrued by the partner.

The preceding sentence shall also apply to transfers of the partnership interest (including by reason of death) in a transaction in which gain is not recognized in whole or in part. No deduction shall be allowed to the transferor or transferee under this chapter for any excess business interest resulting in a basis increase under this subclause.

(C) Excess taxable income.—The term 'excess taxable income' means, with respect to any partnership, the amount which bears the same ratio to the partnership's adjusted taxable income as—

(i) the excess (if any) of—

(I) the amount determined for the partnership under paragraph (1)(B), over

(II) the amount (if any) by which the business interest of the partnership, reduced by the floor plan financing interest, exceeds the business interest income of the partnership, bears to

(ii) the amount determined for the partnership under paragraph (1)(B).

(D) Application to S corporations.—Rules similar to the rules of subparagraphs (A) and (C) shall apply with respect to any S corporation and its shareholders.

(5) Business interest.—For purposes of this subsection, the term 'business interest' means any interest paid or accrued on indebtedness properly allocable to a trade or business. Such term shall not include investment interest (within the meaning of subsection (d)).

(6) Business interest income.—For purposes of this sub-section, the term 'business interest income' means the amount of interest includible in the gross income of the taxpayer for the taxable year which is properly allocable to a trade or business. Such term shall not include investment income (within the meaning of subsection (d)).

(7) Trade or business.—For purposes of this subsection—

(A) In general.—The term 'trade or business' shall not include—

(i) the trade or business of performing services as an employee,

(ii) any electing real property trade or business,

(iii) any electing farming business, or

(iv) the trade or business of the furnishing or sale of—

(I) electrical energy, water, or sewage disposal services,

(II) gas or steam through a local distribution system, or

(III) transportation of gas or steam by pipeline, if the rates for such furnishing or sale, as the case may be, have been established or approved by a State or political subdivision thereof, by any agency or instrumentality of the United States, by a public service or public utility commission or other similar body of any State or political subdivision thereof, or by the governing or ratemaking body of an electric cooperative.

(B) Electing real property trade or business.—For purposes of this paragraph, the term 'electing real property trade or business' means any trade or business which is described in section 469(c)(7)(C) and which makes an election under this subparagraph. Any such election shall be made at such time and in such manner as the Secretary shall prescribe, and, once made, shall be irrevocable.

(C) Electing farming business.—For purposes of this paragraph, the term 'electing farming business' means—

(i) a farming business (as defined in section 263A(e)(4)) which makes an election under this subparagraph, or

(ii) any trade or business of a specified agricultural or horticultural cooperative (as defined in section 199A(g)(2)) with respect to which the cooperative makes an election under this subparagraph.

Any such election shall be made at such time and in such manner as the Secretary shall prescribe, and, once made, shall be irrevocable.

(8) Adjusted taxable income.—For purposes of this sub-section, the term 'adjusted taxable income' means the taxable income of the taxpayer—

(A) computed without regard to—

(i) any item of income, gain, deduction, or loss which is not properly allocable to a trade or business,

(ii) any business interest or business interest income,

(iii) the amount of any net operating loss deduction under section 172,

(iv) the amount of any deduction allowed under section 199A, and

(v) in the case of taxable years beginning before January 1, 2022, any deduction allowable for depreciation, amortization, or depletion, and

(B) computed with such other adjustments as provided by the Secretary.

(9) Floor plan financing interest defined.—For purposes of this subsection—

(A) In general.—The term 'floor plan financing interest' means interest paid or accrued on floor plan financing indebtedness.

(B) Floor plan financing indebtedness.—The term floor plan financing indebtedness' means indebtedness—

(i) used to finance the acquisition of motor vehicles held for sale or lease, and

(ii) secured by the inventory so acquired.

(C) **Motor vehicle.**—The term 'motor vehicle' means a motor vehicle that is any of the following:

(i) Any self-propelled vehicle designed for transporting persons or property on a public street, highway, or road.

(ii) A boat.

(iii) Farm machinery or equipment.

* * *

§ 172. Net operating loss deduction.—

(a) **Deduction allowed.**—There shall be allowed as a deduction for the taxable year an amount equal to the lesser of—

(1) the aggregate of the net operating loss carryovers to such year, plus the net operating loss carrybacks to such year, or

(2) 80 percent of taxable income computed without regard to the deduction allowable under this section.

For purposes of this subtitle, the term 'net operating loss deduction' means the deduction allowed by this subsection.

(b) **Net operating loss carrybacks and carryovers**

(1) **Years to which loss may be carried**

(A) **General rule**—Except as otherwise provided in this paragraph, a net operating loss for any taxable year—

(i) shall not be a net operating loss carryback to any taxable year preceding the taxable year of such loss, and

(ii) shall be a net operating loss carryover to each taxable year following the taxable year of the loss.

(B) **Farming losses.**—

(i) **In general.**—In the case of any portion of a net operating loss for the taxable year which is a farming loss with respect to the taxpayer, such loss shall be a net operating loss carryback to each of the 2 taxable years preceding the taxable year of such loss.

(ii) **Farming loss.**—For purposes of this section, the term 'farming loss' means the lesser of—

(I) the amount which would be the net operating loss for the taxable year if only income and deductions attributable to farming businesses (as defined in section 263A(e)(4)) are taken into account, or

(II) the amount of the net operating loss for such taxable year.

(iii) Coordination with paragraph (2).—For purposes of applying paragraph (2), a farming loss for any taxable year shall be treated as a separate net operating loss for such taxable year to be taken into account after the remaining portion of the net operating loss for such taxable year.

(iv) Election.—Any taxpayer entitled to a 2-year carryback under clause (i) from any loss year may elect not to have such clause apply to such loss year. Such election shall be made in such manner as prescribed by the Secretary and shall be made by the due date (including extensions of time) for filing the taxpayer's return for the taxable year of the net operating loss. Such election, once made for any taxable year, shall be irrevocable for such taxable year.

(2) Amount of carrybacks and carryovers—The entire amount of the net operating loss for any taxable year (hereinafter in this section referred to as the "loss year") shall be carried to the earliest of the taxable years to which (by reason of paragraph (1)) such loss may be carried. The portion of such loss which shall be carried to each of the other taxable years shall be the excess, if any, of the amount of such loss over the sum of the taxable income for each of the prior taxable years to which such loss may be carried. For purposes of the preceding sentence, the taxable income for any such prior taxable year shall—

(A) be computed with the modifications specified in subsection (d) other than paragraphs (1), (4), and (5) thereof, and by determining the amount of the net operating loss deduction without regard to the net operating loss for the loss year or for any taxable year thereafter,

(B) not be considered to be less than zero, and

(C) not exceed the amount determined under subsection (a)(2) for such prior taxable year.

(3) Election to waive carryback.—Any taxpayer entitled to a carryback period under paragraph (1) may elect to relinquish the entire carryback period with respect to a net operating loss for any taxable year. Such election shall be made in such manner as may be prescribed by the Secretary, and shall be made by the due date (including extensions of time) for filing the taxpayer's return for the taxable year of the net operating loss for which the election is to be in effect. Such election, once made for any taxable year, shall be irrevocable for such taxable year.

* * *

(c) Net operating loss defined.—For purposes of this section, the term "net operating loss" means the excess of the deductions allowed by this chapter over the gross income. Such excess shall be computed with the modifications specified in subsection (d).

(d) Modifications.—The modifications referred to in this section are as follows:

(1) Net operating loss deduction.—No net operating loss deduction shall be allowed.

(2) Capital gains and losses of taxpayers other than corporations.—In the case of a taxpayer other than a corporation—

(A) the amount deductible on account of losses from sales or exchanges of capital assets shall not exceed the amount includable on account of gains from sales or exchanges of capital assets; and

(B) the exclusion provided by section 1202 shall not be allowed.

(3) Deduction for personal exemptions.—No deduction shall be allowed under section 151 (relating to personal exemptions). No deduction in lieu of any such deduction shall be allowed.

(4) Nonbusiness deductions of taxpayers other than corporations.—In the case of a taxpayer other than a corporation, the deductions allowable by this chapter which are not attributable to a taxpayer's trade or business shall be allowed only to the extent of the amount of the gross income not derived from such trade or business. For purposes of the preceding sentence—

(A) any gain or loss from the sale or other disposition of—

(i) property, used in the trade or business, of a character which is subject to the allowance for depreciation provided in section 167, or

(ii) real property used in the trade or business, shall be treated as attributable to the trade or business;

(B) the modifications specified in paragraphs (1), (2)(B), and (3) shall be taken into account;

(C) any deduction allowable under section 165(c)(3) (relating to casualty losses) shall not be taken into account; and

(D) any deduction allowed under section 404 to the extent attributable to contributions which are made on behalf of an individual who is an employee within the meaning of section 401(c)(1) shall not be treated as attributable to the trade or business of such individual.

(5) Computation of deduction for dividends received, etc.—The deductions allowed by sections 243 (relating to dividends received by corporations) and 245 (relating to dividends received from certain foreign corporations) shall be computed without regard to section 246(b) (relating to limitation on aggregate amount of deductions).

(6) Modifications related to real estate investment trusts—In the case of any taxable year for which part II of subchapter M (relating to real estate investment trusts) applies to the taxpayer—

(A) the net operating loss for such taxable year shall be computed by taking into account the adjustments described in section 857(b)(2) (other than the deduction for dividends paid described in section 857(b)(2)(B));

(B) where such taxable year is a "prior taxable year" referred to in paragraph (2) of subsection (b), the term "taxable income" in such paragraph shall mean "real estate investment trust taxable income" (as defined in section 857(b)(2));

(C) subsection (a)(2) shall be applied by substituting 'real estate investment trust taxable income (as defined in section 857(b)(2) but without regard to the deduction for dividends paid (as defined in section 561))' for 'taxable income."

(7) Manufacturing deduction.—The deduction under section 199 shall not be allowed.

(8) Qualified business income deduction.—The deduction under section 199A shall not be allowed.

* * *

(e) Law applicable to computations.—In determining the amount of any net operating loss carryback or carryover to any taxable year, the necessary computations involving any other taxable year shall be made under the law applicable to such other taxable year.

* * *

§ 199A. Qualified business income

(a) In general.—In the case of a taxpayer other than a corporation, there shall be allowed as a deduction for any taxable year an amount equal to the sum of—

(1) the lesser of—

(A) the combined qualified business income amount of the taxpayer, or

(B) an amount equal to 20 percent of the excess (if any) of—

(i) the taxable income of the taxpayer for the taxable year, over

(ii) the sum of any net capital gain (as defined in section 1(h)), plus the aggregate amount of the qualified cooperative dividends, of the taxpayer for the taxable year, plus

(2) the lesser of—

(A) 20 percent of the aggregate amount of the qualified cooperative dividends of the taxpayer for the taxable year, or

(B) taxable income (reduced by the net capital gain (as so defined)) of the taxpayer for the taxable year.

The amount determined under the preceding sentence shall not exceed the taxable income (reduced by the net capital gain (as so defined)) of the taxpayer for the taxable year.

(b) Combined qualified business income amount.—For purposes of this section—

(1) In general.—The term 'combined qualified business income amount' means, with respect to any taxable year, an amount equal to—

(A) the sum of the amounts determined under paragraph (2) for each qualified trade or business carried on by the taxpayer, plus

(B) 20 percent of the aggregate amount of the qualified REIT dividends and qualified publicly traded partnership income of the taxpayer for the taxable year.

(2) Determination of deductible amount for each trade or business.—The amount determined under this paragraph with respect to any qualified trade or business is the lesser of—

(A) 20 percent of the taxpayer's qualified business income with respect to the qualified trade or business, or

(B) the greater of—

(i) 50 percent of the W-2 wages with respect to the qualified trade or business, or

(ii) the sum of 25 percent of the W-2 wages with respect to the qualified trade or business, plus 2.5 percent of the unadjusted basis immediately after acquisition of all qualified property.

(3) Modifications to limit based on taxable income.—

(A) Exception from limit.—In the case of any taxpayer whose taxable income for the taxable year does not exceed the threshold amount, paragraph (2) shall be applied without regard to subparagraph (B).

(B) Phase-in limit for certain taxpayers.—

(i) In general.—If—

(I) the taxable income of a taxpayer for any taxable year exceeds the threshold amount, but does not exceed the sum of the threshold amount plus $50,000 ($100,000 in the case of a joint return), and

(II) the amount determined under paragraph (2)(B) (determined without regard to this subparagraph) with respect to any qualified trade or business carried on by the taxpayer is less than the amount determined under paragraph (2)(A) with respect such trade or business,

then paragraph (2) shall be applied with respect to such trade or business without regard to subparagraph (B) thereof and by reducing the amount determined under subparagraph (A) thereof by the amount determined under clause (ii).

(ii) Amount of reduction.—The amount determined under this subparagraph is the amount which bears the same ratio to the excess amount as—

(I) the amount by which the taxpayer's taxable income for the taxable year exceeds the threshold amount, bears to

(II) $50,000 ($100,000 in the case of a joint return).

(iii) Excess amount.—For purposes of clause (ii), the excess amount is the excess of—

(I) the amount determined under paragraph (2)(A) (determined without regard to this paragraph), over

(II) the amount determined under paragraph (2)(B) (determined without regard to this paragraph).

(4) Wages etc.—

(A) In general.—The term 'W-2 wages' means, with respect to any person for any taxable year of such person, the amounts described in paragraphs (3) and (8) of section 6051(a) paid by such person with respect to employment of employees by such person during the calendar year ending during such taxable year.

(B) Limitation to wages attributable to qualified business income.—Such term shall not include any amount which is not properly allocable to qualified business income for purposes of subsection (c)(1).

(C) Return requirement.—Such term shall not include any amount which is not properly included in a return filed with the Social Security Administration on or before the 60th day after the due date (including extensions) for such return.

(5) Acquisitions, dispositions, and short taxable years.—The Secretary shall provide for the application of this subsection in cases of a short taxable year or where the taxpayer acquires, or disposes of, the major portion of a trade or business or the major portion of a separate unit of a trade or business during the taxable year.

(6) Qualified property.—For purposes of this section:

(A) In general.—The term 'qualified property' means, with respect to any qualified trade or business for a taxable year, tangible property of a character subject to the allowance for depreciation under section 167—

(i) which is held by, and available for use in, the qualified trade or business at the close of the taxable year,

(ii) which is used at any point during the taxable year in the production of qualified business income, and

(iii) the depreciable period for which has not ended before the close of the taxable year.

(B) Depreciable period.—The term 'depreciable period' means, with respect to qualified property of a taxpayer, the period beginning on the date the property was first placed in service by the taxpayer and ending on the later of—

(i) the date that is 10 years after such date, or

(ii) the last day of the last full year in the applicable recovery period that would apply to the property under section 168 (determined without regard to subsection (g) thereof).

(c) Qualified business income.—For purposes of this section—

(1) In general.—The term 'qualified business income' means, for any taxable year, the net amount of qualified items of income, gain, deduction, and loss with respect to any qualified trade or business of the taxpayer. Such term shall not include any qualified REIT dividends, qualified cooperative dividends, or qualified publicly traded partnership income.

(2) Carryover of losses.—If the net amount of qualified income, gain, deduction, and loss with respect to qualified trades or businesses of the taxpayer for any taxable year is less than zero, such amount shall be treated as a loss from a qualified trade or business in the succeeding taxable year.

(3) Qualified items of income, gain, deduction, and loss.—For purposes of this subsection—

(A) In general.—The term 'qualified items of income, gain, deduction, and loss' means items of income, gain, deduction, and loss to the extent such items are—

(i) effectively connected with the conduct of a trade or business within the United States (within the meaning of section 864(c), determined by substituting 'qualified trade or business (within the meaning of section 199A)' for 'nonresident alien individual or a foreign corporation' or for 'a foreign corporation' each place it appears), and

(ii) included or allowed in determining taxable income for the taxable year.

(B) Exceptions.—The following investment items shall not be taken into account as a qualified item of income, gain, deduction, or loss:

(i) Any item of short-term capital gain, short-term capital loss, long-term capital gain, or long-term capital loss.

(ii) Any dividend, income equivalent to a dividend, or payment in lieu of dividends described in section 954(c)(1)(G).

(iii) Any interest income other than interest income which is properly allocable to a trade or business.

(iv) Any item of gain or loss described in subparagraph (C) or (D) of section 954(c)(1) (applied by substituting 'qualified trade or business' for 'controlled foreign corporation').

(v) Any item of income, gain, deduction, or loss taken into account under section 954(c)(1)(F) (determined without regard to clause (ii) thereof and other than items attributable to notional principal contracts entered into in transactions qualifying under section 1221(a)(7)).

(vi) Any amount received from an annuity which is not received in connection with the trade or business.

(vii) Any item of deduction or loss properly allocable to an amount described in any of the preceding clauses.

(4) Treatment of reasonable compensation and guaranteed payments.—Qualified business income shall not include—

(A) reasonable compensation paid to the taxpayer by any qualified trade or business of the taxpayer for services rendered with respect to the trade or business,

(B) any guaranteed payment described in section 707(c) paid to a partner for services rendered with respect to the trade or business, and

(C) to the extent provided in regulations, any payment described in section 707(a) to a partner for services rendered with respect to the trade or business.

(d) Qualified trade or business.—For purposes of this section—

(1) In general.—The term 'qualified trade or business' means any trade or business other than—

(A) a specified service trade or business, or

(B) the trade or business of performing services as an employee.

(2) Specified service trade or business.—The term 'specified service trade or business' means any trade or business—

(A) which is described in section 1202(e)(3)(A) (applied without regard to the words 'engineering, architecture,') or which would be so described if the term 'employees or owners' were substituted for 'employees' therein, or

(B) which involves the performance of services that consist of investing and investment management, trading, or dealing in securities (as defined in section 475(c)(2)), partnership interests, or commodities (as defined in section 475(e)(2)).

(3) Exception for specified service business based on taxpayer's income.—

(A) In general.—If, for any taxable year, the taxable income of any taxpayer is less than the sum of the threshold amount plus $50,000 ($100,000 in the case of a joint return), then—

(i) any specified service trade or business of the taxpayer shall not fail to be treated as a qualified trade or business due to paragraph (1)(A), but

(ii) only the applicable percentage of qualified items of income, gain, deduction, or loss, and the W-2 wages and the unadjusted basis immediately after acquisition of qualified property, of the taxpayer allocable to such specified service trade or business shall be taken into account in computing the qualified business income, W-2 wages, and the unadjusted basis immediately after acquisition of qualified property of the taxpayer for the taxable year for purposes of applying this section.

(B) Applicable percentage.—For purposes of subparagraph (A), the term 'applicable percentage' means, with respect to any taxable year, 100 percent reduced (not below zero) by the percentage equal to the ratio of—

(i) the taxable income of the taxpayer for the taxable year in excess of the threshold amount, bears to

(ii) $50,000 ($100,000 in the case of a joint return).

(e) Other definitions.—For purposes of this section—

(1) Taxable income.—Taxable income shall be computed without regard to the deduction allowable under this section.

(2) Threshold amount.—

(A) In general.—The term 'threshold amount' means $157,500 (200 percent of such amount in the case of a joint return).

(B) Inflation adjustment.—In the case of any taxable year beginning after 2018, the dollar amount in subparagraph (A) shall be increased by an amount equal to—

(i) such dollar amount, multiplied by

(ii) the cost-of-living adjustment determined under section 1(f)(3) for the calendar year in which the taxable year begins, determined by substituting 'calendar year 2017' for 'calendar year 2016' in subparagraph (A)(ii) thereof.

The amount of any increase under the preceding sentence shall be rounded as provided in section 1(f)(7).

(3) Qualified REIT dividend.—The term 'qualified REIT dividend' means any dividend from a real estate investment trust received during the taxable year which—

(A) is not a capital gain dividend, as defined in section 857(b)(3), and

(B) is not qualified dividend income, as defined in section 1(h)(11).

(4) Qualified cooperative dividend.—The term 'qualified cooperative dividend' means any patronage dividend (as defined in section 1388(a)), any per-unit retain allocation (as defined in section 1388(f)), and any qualified written notice of allocation (as defined in section 1388(c)), or any similar amount received from an organization described in subparagraph (B)(ii), which—

(A) is includible in gross income, and "(B) is received from—

(i) an organization or corporation described in section 501(c)(12) or 1381(a), or

(ii) an organization which is governed under this title by the rules applicable to cooperatives under this title before the enactment of subchapter T.

(5) Qualified Publicly Traded Partnership Income.—The term 'qualified publicly traded partnership income' means, with respect to any qualified trade or business of a taxpayer, the sum of—

(A) the net amount of such taxpayer's allocable share of each qualified item of income, gain, deduction, and loss (as defined in subsection (c)(3) and determined after the application of subsection (c)(4)) from a publicly traded partnership (as defined in section 7704(a)) which is not treated as a corporation under section 7704(c), plus

(B) any gain recognized by such taxpayer upon disposition of its interest in such partnership to the extent such gain is treated as an amount realized from the sale or exchange of property other than a capital asset under section 751(a).

(f) Special rules.—

(1) Application to partnership and S corporations.—

(A) In general.—In the case of a partnership or S corporation—

(i) this section shall be applied at the partner or shareholder level,

(ii) each partner or shareholder shall take into account such person's allocable share of each qualified item of income, gain, deduction, and loss, and

(iii) each partner or shareholder shall be treated for purposes of subsection (b) as having W-2 wages and unadjusted basis immediately after acquisition of qualified property for the taxable year in an amount equal to such person's allocable share of the W-2 wages and the unadjusted basis immediately after acquisition of qualified property of the partnership or S corporation for the taxable year (as determined under regulations prescribed by the Secretary).

For purposes of clause (iii), a partner's or shareholder's allocable share of W-2 wages shall be determined in the same manner as the partner's or shareholder's allocable share of wage expenses. For purposes of such clause, partner's or shareholder's allocable share of the unadjusted basis immediately after acquisition of qualified property shall be determined in the same manner as the partner's or shareholder's allocable share of depreciation. For purposes of this subparagraph, in the case of an S corporation, an allocable share shall be the shareholder's pro rata share of an item.

(B) Application to trusts and estates.—Rules similar to the rules under section 199(d)(1)(B)(i) (as in effect on December 1, 2017) for the apportionment of W-2 wages shall apply to the apportionment of W-2 wages and the apportionment of unadjusted basis immediately after acquisition of qualified property under this section.

(C) Treatment of trade and businesses in Puerto Rico.—

(i) In general.—In the case of any taxpayer with qualified business income from sources within the commonwealth of Puerto Rico, if all such income is taxable under section 1 for such taxable year, then for purposes of determining the qualified business income of such taxpayer for such taxable year, the term 'United States' shall include the Commonwealth of Puerto Rico.

(ii) Special rule for applying limit.—In the case of any taxpayer described in clause (i), the determination of W-2 wages of such taxpayer with respect to any qualified trade or business conducted in Puerto Rico shall be made without regard to any exclusion under section 3401(a)(8) for remuneration paid for services in Puerto Rico.

(2) Coordination with minimum tax.—For purposes of determining alternative minimum taxable income under section 55, qualified business income shall be determined without regard to any adjustments under sections 56 through 59.

(3) Deduction limited to income taxes.—The deduction under subsection (a) shall only be allowed for purposes of this chapter.

(4) Regulations.—The Secretary shall prescribe such regulations as are necessary to carry out the purposes of this section, including regulations—

(A) for requiring or restricting the allocation of items and wages under this section and such reporting requirements as the Secretary determines appropriate, and

(B) for the application of this section in the case of tiered entities.

(g) Deduction allowed to specified agricultural or horticultural cooperatives.—

(1) In general.—In the case of any taxable year of a specified agricultural or horticultural cooperative beginning after December 31, 2017, there shall be allowed a deduction in an amount equal to the lesser of—

(A) 20 percent of the excess (if asssssny) of—

(i) the gross income of a specified agricultural or horticultural cooperative, over

(ii) the qualified cooperative dividends (as defined in subsection (e)(4)) paid during the taxable year for the taxable year, or

(B) the greater of—

(i) 50 percent of the W-2 wages of the cooperative with respect to its trade or business, or

(ii) the sum of 25 percent of the W-2 wages of the cooperative with respect to its trade or business, plus 2.5 percent of the unadjusted basis immediately after acquisition of all qualified property of the cooperative.

(2) Limitation.—The amount determined under paragraph (1) shall not exceed the taxable income of the specified agricultural or horticultural for the taxable year.

(3) Specified agricultural or horticultural cooperative.—For purposes of this subsection, the term 'specified agricultural or horticultural cooperative' means an organization to which part I of subchapter T applies which is engaged in—

(A) the manufacturing, production, growth, or extraction in whole or significant part of any agricultural or horticultural product,

(B) the marketing of agricultural or horticultural products which its patrons have so manufactured, produced, grown, or extracted, or

(C) the provision of supplies, equipment, or services to farmers or to organizations described in subparagraph (A) or (B).

(h) Anti-abuse rules.—The Secretary shall—

(1) apply rules similar to the rules under section 179(d)(2) in order to prevent the manipulation of the depreciable period of qualified property using transactions between related parties, and

(2) prescribe rules for determining the unadjusted basis immediately after acquisition of qualified property acquired in like-kind exchanges or involuntary conversions.

(i) Termination.—This section shall not apply to taxable years beginning after December 31, 2025.

* * *

Part VIII—Special Deductions for Corporations

§ 241. Allowance of special deductions.

In addition to the deductions provided in part VI (sec. 161 and following), there shall be allowed as deductions in computing taxable income the items specified in this part.

§ 243. Dividends received by corporations.

(a) General rule—In the case of a corporation, there shall be allowed as a deduction an amount equal to the following percentages of the amount received as dividends from a domestic corporation which is subject to taxation under this chapter:

(1) 50 percent, in the case of dividends other than dividends described in paragraph (2) or (3);

(2) 100 percent, in the case of dividends received by a small business investment company operating under the Small Business Investment Act of 1958 (15 U.S.C. 661 and following); and

(3) 100 percent, in the case of qualifying dividends (as defined in subsection (b)(1)).

(b) Qualifying dividends

(1) In general—For purposes of this section, the term "qualifying dividend" means any dividend received by a corporation—

(A) if at the close of the day on which such dividend is received, such corporation is a member of the same affiliated group as the corporation distributing such dividend, and

(B) if—

(i) such dividend is distributed out of the earnings and profits of a taxable year of the distributing corporation which ends after December 31, 1963, for which an election under section 1562 was not in effect, and on each day of which the distributing corporation and the corporation receiving the dividend were members of such affiliated group, or

(ii) such dividend is paid by a corporation with respect to which an election under section 936 is in effect for the taxable year in which such dividend is paid.

(2) Affiliated group—For purposes of this subsection:

(A) In general—The term "affiliated group" has the meaning given such term by section 1504(a), except that for such purposes sections 1504(b)(2), 1504(b)(4), and 1504(c) shall not apply.

* * *

(c) Increased percentage from 20-percent owned corporations

(1) In general—In the case of any dividend received from a "20-percent owned corporation", subsection (a)(1) shall be applied by substituting "65 percent" for "50 percent."

(2) 20-percent owned corporation—For purposes of this section, the term "20-percent owned corporation" means any corporation if 20 percent or more of the stock of such corporation (by vote and value) is owned by the taxpayer. For purposes of the preceding sentence, stock described in section 1504(a)(4) shall not be taken into account.

* * *

§ 246. Rules applying to deductions for dividends received.

(a) Deduction not allowed for dividends from certain corporations.—

(1) In general.—The deductions allowed by sections 243 and 245 shall not apply to any dividend from a corporation which, for the taxable year of the corporation in which the distribution is made, or for the next preceding taxable year of the corporation, is a corporation exempt from tax under section 501 (relating to certain charitable, etc., organizations) or section 521 (relating to farmers' cooperative associations).

* * *

(b) Limitation on aggregate amount of deductions.—

(1) General rule—Except as provided in paragraph (2), the aggregate amount of the deductions allowed by section 199A, 243(a)(1) and subsection (a) or (b) of section 245 shall not exceed the percentage determined under paragraph (3) of the taxable income computed without regard to the deductions allowed by sections 172, 199, 243(a)(1), and subsection (a) or (b) of section 245, without regard to any adjustment under section 1059, and without regard to any capital loss carryback to the taxable year under section 1212(a)(1).

(2) Effect of net operating loss.—Paragraph (1) shall not apply for any taxable year for which there is a net operating loss (as determined under section 172).

(3) Special rules.—The provisions of paragraph (1) shall be applied—

(A) first separately with respect to dividends from 20-percent owned corporations (as defined in section 243(c)(2)) and the percentage determined under this paragraph shall be 65 percent, and

(B) then separately with respect to dividends not from 20-percent owned corporations and the percentage determined under this paragraph shall be 50 percent and the taxable income shall be reduced by the aggregate amount of dividends from 20-percent owned corporations (as so defined)

(c) Exclusion of certain dividends.—

(1) In general.—No deduction shall be allowed under section 243, 245, or 245A, in respect of any dividend on any share of stock—

(A) which is held by the taxpayer for 45 days or less during the 91-day period beginning on the date which is 45 days before the date on which such share becomes ex-dividend with respect to such dividend, or

35

(B) to the extent that the taxpayer is under an obligation (whether pursuant to a short sale or otherwise) to make related payments with respect to positions in substantially similar or related property.

(2) 90-day rule in the case of certain preference dividends—In the case of stock having preference in dividends, if the taxpayer receives dividends with respect to such stock which are attributable to a period or periods aggregating in excess of 366 days, paragraph (1)(A) shall be applied—

(A) by substituting "90 days" for "45 days" each place it appears, and

(B) by substituting "181-day period" for "91-day period".

(3) Determination of holding periods—For purposes of this subsection, in determining the period for which the taxpayer has held any share of stock—

(A) the day of disposition, but not the day of acquisition, shall be taken into account, and

(B) paragraph (4) of section 1223 shall not apply.

(4) Holding period reduced for periods where risk of loss diminished

The holding periods determined for purposes of this subsection shall be appropriately reduced (in the manner provided in regulations prescribed by the Secretary) for any period (during such periods) in which—

(A) the taxpayer has an option to sell, is under a contractual obligation to sell, or has made (and not closed) a short sale of, substantially identical stock or securities,

(B) the taxpayer is the grantor of an option to buy substantially identical stock or securities, or

(C) under regulations prescribed by the Secretary, a taxpayer has diminished his risk of loss by holding 1 or more other positions with respect to substantially similar or related property.

The preceding sentence shall not apply in the case of any qualified covered call (as defined in section 1092(c)(4) but without regard to the requirement that gain or loss with respect to the option not be ordinary income or loss), other than a qualified covered call option to which section 1092(f) applies.

* * *

§ 246A. Dividends received deduction reduced where portfolio stock is debt financed.

(a) General rule.—In the case of any dividend on debt-financed portfolio stock, there shall be substituted for the percentage which (but for this subsection) would be used in determining the amount of the deduction allowable under section 243 or 245(a) a percentage equal to the product of—

(1) 50 percent (65 percent in the case of any dividend from a 20-percent owned corporation as defined in section 243(c)(2)), and

(2) 100 percent minus the average indebtedness percentage.

(b) Section not to apply to dividends for which 100 percent dividends received deduction allowable.—Subsection (a) shall not apply to—

(1) qualifying dividends (as defined in section 243(b) without regard to section 243(d)(4)), and

(2) dividends received by a small business investment company operating under the Small Business Investment Act of 1958.

(c) Debt financed portfolio stock.—For purposes of this section—

(1) In general.—The term "debt financed portfolio stock" means any portfolio stock if at some time during the base period there is portfolio indebtedness with respect to such stock.

(2) Portfolio stock.—The term "portfolio stock" means any stock of a corporation unless—

(A) as of the beginning of the ex-dividend date, the taxpayer owns stock of such corporation—

(i) possessing at least 50 percent of the total voting power of the stock of such corporation, and

(ii) having a value equal to at least 50 percent of the total value of the stock of such corporation, or

(B) as of the beginning of the ex-dividend date—

(i) the taxpayer owns stock of such corporation which would meet the requirements of subparagraph (A) if "20 percent" were substituted for "50 percent" each place it appears in such subparagraph, and

(ii) stock meeting the requirements of subparagraph (A) is owned by 5 or fewer corporate shareholders.

* * *

(4) Treatment of certain preferred stock.—For purposes of determining whether the requirements of subparagraph (A) or (B) of paragraph (2) or of subparagraph (A) of paragraph (3) are met, stock described in section 1504(a)(4) shall not be taken into account.

(d) Average indebtedness percentage.—For purposes of this section—

(1) In general.—Except as provided in paragraph (2), the term "average indebtedness percentage" means the percentage obtained by dividing—

(A) the average amount (determined under regulations prescribed by the Secretary) of the portfolio indebtedness with respect to the stock during the base period, by

(B) the average amount (determined under regulations prescribed by the Secretary) of the adjusted basis of the stock during the base period.

(2) Special rule where stock not held throughout base period.—In the case of any stock which was not held by the taxpayer throughout the base period, paragraph (1) shall be applied as if the base period consisted only of that portion of the base period during which the stock was held by the taxpayer.

(3) Portfolio indebtedness.—

(A) In general.—The term "portfolio indebtedness" means any indebtedness directly attributable to investment in the portfolio stock.

(B) Certain amounts received from short sale treated as indebtedness.—For purposes of subparagraph (A), any amount received from a short sale shall be treated as indebtedness for the period beginning on the day on which such amount is received and ending on the day the short sale is closed.

(4) Base period.—The term "base period" means, with respect to any dividend, the shorter of—

    (A) the period beginning on the ex-dividend date for the most recent previous dividend on the stock and ending on the day before the ex-dividend date for the dividend involved, or

    (B) the 1-year period ending on the day before the ex-dividend date for the dividend involved.

(e) Reduction in dividends received deduction not to exceed allocable interest.—Under regulations prescribed by the Secretary, any reduction under this section in the amount allowable as a deduction under section 243 or 245 with respect to any dividend shall not exceed the amount of any interest deduction (including any deductible short sale expense) allocable to such dividend.

* * *

§ 248. Organizational expenditures.

(a) Election to deduct.—If a corporation elects the application of this subsection (in accordance with regulations prescribed by the Secretary) with respect to any organizational expenditures—

    (1) the corporation shall be allowed a deduction for the taxable year in which the corporation begins business in an amount equal to the lesser of—

        (A) the amount of organizational expenditures with respect to the taxpayer, or

        (B) $5,000, reduced (but not below zero) by the amount by which such organizational expenditures exceed $50,000, and

    (2) the remainder of such organizational expenditures shall be allowed as a deduction ratably over the 180-month period beginning with the month in which the corporation begins business.

(b) Organizational expenditures defined.—The term "organizational expenditures" means any expenditure which—

    (1) is incident to the creation of the corporation;

    (2) is chargeable to capital account; and

    (3) is of a character which, if expended incident to the creation of a corporation having a limited life, would be amortizable over such life.

(c) Time for and scope of election.—The election provided by subsection (a) may be made for any taxable year, but only if made not later than the time prescribed by law for filing the return for such taxable year (including extensions thereof).

* * *

Part IX—Items Not Deductible

§ 267. Losses, expenses, and interest with respect to transactions between related taxpayers.

(a) In general.

(1) Deduction for losses disallowed. No deduction shall be allowed in respect of any loss from the sale or exchange of property, directly or indirectly, between persons specified in any of the paragraphs of subsection (b). The preceding sentence shall not apply to any loss of the distributing corporation (or the distributee) in the case of a distribution in complete liquidation.

(2) Matching of deduction and payee income item in the case of expenses and interest. If—

(A) by reason of the method of accounting of the person to whom the payment is to be made, the amount thereof is not (unless paid) includible in the gross income of such person, and

(B) at the close of the taxable year of the taxpayer for which (but for this paragraph) the amount would be deductible under this chapter, both the taxpayer and the person to whom the payment is to be made are persons specified in any of the paragraphs of subsection (b),

then any deduction allowable under this chapter in respect of such amount shall be allowable as of the day as of which such amount is includible in the gross income of the person to whom the payment is made (or, if later, as of the day on which it would be so allowable but for this paragraph). For purposes of this paragraph, in the case of a personal service corporation (within the meaning of section 441(i)(2)), such corporation and any employee-owner (within the meaning of section 269A(b)(2), as modified by section 441(i)(2)) shall be treated as persons specified in subsection (b).

(3) Payments to foreign persons.—

(A) In general.—The Secretary shall by regulations apply the matching principle of paragraph (2) in cases in which the person to whom the payment is to be made is not a United States person.

(B) Special rule for certain foreign entities.—

(i) In general.—Notwithstanding subparagraph (A), in the case of any item payable to a controlled foreign corporation (as defined in section 957) or a passive foreign investment company (as defined in section 1297), a deduction shall be allowable to the payor with respect to such amount for any taxable year before the taxable year in which paid only to the extent that an amount attributable to such item is includible (determined without regard to properly allocable deductions and qualified deficits under section 952(c)(1)(B)) during such prior taxable year in the gross income of a United States person who owns (within the meaning of section 958(a)) stock in such corporation.

(ii) Secretarial authority.—The Secretary may by regulation exempt transactions from the application of clause (i), including any transaction which is entered into by a payor in the ordinary course of a trade or business in which the payor is predominantly engaged and in which the payment of the accrued amounts occurs within 8 1/2 months after accrual or within such other period as the Secretary may prescribe.

* * *

(b) Relationships. The persons referred to in subsection (a) are:

(1) Members of a family, as defined in subsection (c)(4);

(2) An individual and a corporation more than 50 percent in value of the outstanding stock of which is owned, directly or indirectly, by or for such individual;

(3) Two corporations which are members of the same controlled group (as defined in subsection (f));

(4) A grantor and a fiduciary of any trust;

(5) A fiduciary of a trust and a fiduciary of another trust, if the same person is a grantor of both trusts;

(6) A fiduciary of a trust and a beneficiary of such trust;

(7) A fiduciary of a trust and a beneficiary of another trust, if the same person is a grantor of both trusts;

(8) A fiduciary of a trust and a corporation more than 50 percent in value of the outstanding stock of which is owned, directly or indirectly, by or for the trust or by or for a person who is a grantor of the trust;

(9) A person and an organization to which section 501 (relating to certain educational and charitable organizations which are exempt from tax) applies and which is controlled directly or indirectly by such person or (if such person is an individual) by members of the family of such individual;

(10) A corporation and a partnership if the same persons own—

(A) more than 50 percent in value of the outstanding stock of the corporation, and

(B) more than 50 percent of the capital interest, or the profits interest, in the partnership;

(11) An S corporation and another S corporation if the same persons own more than 50 percent in value of the outstanding stock of each corporation;

(12) An S corporation and a C corporation, if the same persons own more than 50 percent in value of the outstanding stock of each corporation; or

(13) Except in the case of a sale or exchange in satisfaction of a pecuniary bequest, an executor of an estate and a beneficiary of such estate.

(c) Constructive ownership of stock. For purposes of determining, in applying subsection (b), the ownership of stock—

(1) Stock owned, directly or indirectly, by or for a corporation, partnership, estate, or trust shall be considered as being owned proportionately by or for its shareholders, partners, or beneficiaries;

(2) An individual shall be considered as owning the stock owned, directly or indirectly, by or for his family;

(3) An individual owning (otherwise than by the application of paragraph (2)) any stock in a corporation shall be considered as owning the stock owned, directly or indirectly, by or for his partner;

(4) The family of an individual shall include only his brothers and sisters (whether by the whole or half blood), spouse, ancestors, and lineal descendants; and

(5) Stock constructively owned by a person by reason of the application of paragraph (1) shall, for the purpose of applying paragraph (1), (2), or (3), be treated as actually owned by such person, but stock constructively owned by an individual by reason of the application of paragraph (2) or (3) shall not be treated as owned by him for the purpose of again applying either of such paragraphs in order to make another the constructive owner of such stock.

(d) Amount of gain where loss previously disallowed. If—

(1) in the case of a sale or exchange of property to the taxpayer a loss sustained by the transferor is not allowable to the transferor as a deduction by reason of subsection (a)(1) and

(2) the taxpayer sells or otherwise disposes of such property (or of other property the basis of which in his hands is determined directly or indirectly by reference to such property) at a gain,

then such gain shall be recognized only to the extent that it exceeds so much of such loss as is properly allocable to the property sold or otherwise disposed of by the taxpayer. This subsection shall not apply if the loss sustained by the transferor is not allowable to the transferor as a deduction by reason of section 1091 (relating to wash sales).

(e) Special rules for pass-thru entities.

(1) In general. In the case of any amount paid or incurred by, to, or on behalf of, a pass-thru entity, for purposes of applying subsection (a)(2)—

(A) such entity,

(B) in the case of—

(i) a partnership, any person who owns (directly or indirectly) any capital interest or profits interest of such partnership, or

(ii) an S corporation, any person who owns (directly or indirectly) any of the stock of such corporation,

(C) any person who owns (directly or indirectly) any capital interest or profits interest of a partnership in which such entity owns (directly or indirectly) any capital interest or profits interest, and

(D) any person related (within the meaning of subsection (b) of this section or section 707(b)(1)) to a person described in subparagraph (B) or (C), shall be treated as persons specified in a paragraph of subsection (b). Subparagraph (C) shall apply to a transaction only if such transaction is related either to the operations of the partnership described in such subparagraph or to an interest in such partnership.

(2) Pass-thru entity. For purposes of this section, the term "pass-thru entity" means—

(A) a partnership, and

(B) an S corporation.

(3) Constructive ownership in the case of partnerships. For purposes of determining ownership of a capital interest or profits interest of a partnership, the principles of subsection (c) shall apply, except that—

    (A) paragraph (3) of subsection (c) shall not apply, and

    (B) interests owned (directly or indirectly) by or for a C corporation shall be considered as owned by or for any shareholder only if such shareholder owns (directly or indirectly) 5 percent or more in value of the stock of such corporation.

(4) Subsection (a)(2) not to apply to certain guaranteed payments of partnerships. In the case of any amount paid or incurred by a partnership, subsection (a)(2) shall not apply to the extent that section 707(c) applies to such amount.

(5) Exception for certain expenses and interest of partnerships owning low-income housing.

    (A) In general. This subsection shall not apply with respect to qualified expenses and interest paid or incurred by a partnership owning low-income housing to—

        (i) any qualified 5-percent or less partner of such partnership, or

        (ii) any person related (within the meaning of subsection (b) of this section or section 707(b)(1)) to any qualified 5-percent or less partner of such partnership.

    (B) Qualified 5-percent or less partner. For purposes of this paragraph, the term "qualified 5-percent or less partner" means any partner who has (directly or indirectly) an interest of 5 percent or less in the aggregate capital and profits interests of the partnership but only if—

        (i) such partner owned the low-income housing at all times during the 2-year period ending on the date such housing was transferred to the partnership, or

        (ii) such partnership acquired the low-income housing pursuant to a purchase, assignment, or other transfer from the Department of Housing and Urban Development or any State or local housing authority.

For purposes of the preceding sentence, a partner shall be treated as holding any interest in the partnership which is held (directly or indirectly) by any person related (within the meaning of subsection (b) of this section or section 707(b)(1)) to such partner.

    (C) Qualified expenses and interest. For purpose of this paragraph, the term "qualified expenses and interest" means any expense or interest incurred by the partnership with respect to low-income housing held by the partnership but—

        (i) only if the amount of such expense or interest (as the case may be) is unconditionally required to be paid by the partnership not later than 10 years after the date such amount was incurred, and

        (ii) in the case of such interest, only if such interest is incurred at an annual rate not in excess of 12 percent.

    (D) Low-income housing. For purposes of this paragraph, the term "low-income housing" means—

        (i) any interest in property described in clause (i), (ii), (iii), or (iv) of section 1250(a)(1)(B), and

(ii) any interest in a partnership owning such property.

(6) Cross reference. For additional rules relating to partnerships, see section 707(b).

(f) Controlled group defined; special rules applicable to controlled groups.

(1) Controlled group defined. For purposes of this section, the term "controlled group" has the meaning given to such term by section 1563(a), except that—

(A) "more than 50 percent" shall be substituted for "at least 80 percent" each place it appears in section 1563(a), and

(B) the determination shall be made without regard to subsections (a)(4) and (e)(3)(C) of section 1563.

(2) Deferral (rather than denial) of loss from sale or exchange between members. In the case of any loss from the sale or exchange of property which is between members of the same controlled group and to which subsection (a)(1) applies (determined without regard to this paragraph but with regard to paragraph (3))—

(A) subsections (a)(1) and (d) shall not apply to such loss, but

(B) such loss shall be deferred until the property is transferred outside such controlled group and there would be recognition of loss under consolidated return principles or until such other time as may be prescribed in regulations.

(3) Loss deferral rules not to apply in certain cases.

(A) Transfer to DISC. For purposes of applying subsection (a)(1), the term "controlled group" shall not include a DISC.

(B) Certain sales of inventory. Except to the extent provided in regulations prescribed by the Secretary, subsection (a)(1) shall not apply to the sale or exchange of property between members of the same controlled group (or persons described in subsection (b)(10)) if—

(i) such property in the hands of the transferor is property described in section 1221(1),

(ii) such sale or exchange is in the ordinary course of the transferor's trade or business,

(iii) such property in the hands of the transferee is property described in section 1221(1), and

(iv) the transferee or the transferor is a foreign corporation.

(C) Certain foreign currency losses. To the extent provided in regulations, subsection (a)(1) shall not apply to any loss sustained by a member of a controlled group on the repayment of a loan made to another member of such group if such loan is payable in a foreign currency or is denominated in such a currency and such loss is attributable to a reduction in value of such foreign currency.

(D) redemptions by fund-of-funds regulated investment companies. Except to the extent provided in regulations prescribed by the Secretary, subsection (a)(1) shall not apply to any distribution in redemption of stock of a regulated investment company if—

(i) such company issues only stock which is redeemable upon the demand of the stockholder, and

(ii) such redemption is upon the demand of another regulated investment company.

(4) Determination of relationship resulting in disallowance of loss, for purposes of other provisions. For purposes of any other section of this title which refers to a relationship which would result in a disallowance of losses under this section, deferral under paragraph (2) shall be treated as disallowance.

(g) Coordination with section 1041. Subsection (a)(1) shall not apply to any transfer described in section 1041(a) (relating to transfers of property between spouses or incident to divorce).

§ 269. Acquisitions made to evade or avoid income tax.

(a) In general.—If—

(1) any person or persons acquire, or acquired directly or indirectly, control of a corporation, or

(2) any corporation acquires, or acquired directly or indirectly, property of another corporation, not controlled, directly or indirectly, immediately before such acquisition, by such acquiring corporation or its stockholders, the basis of which property, in the hands of the acquiring corporation, is determined by reference to the basis in the hands of the transferor corporation, and the principal purpose for which such acquisition was made is evasion or avoidance of Federal income tax by securing the benefit of a deduction, credit, or other allowance which such person or corporation would not otherwise enjoy, then the Secretary may disallow such deduction, credit, or other allowance. For purposes of paragraphs (1) and (2), control means the ownership of stock possessing at least 50 percent of the total combined voting power of all classes of stock entitled to vote or at least 50 percent of the total value of shares of all classes of stock of the corporation.

(b) Certain liquidations after qualified stock purchases.—

(1) In general.—If—

(A) there is a qualified stock purchase by a corporation of another corporation,

(B) an election is not made under section 338 with respect to such purchase,

(C) the acquired corporation is liquidated pursuant to a plan of liquidation adopted not more than 2 years after the acquisition date, and

(D) the principal purpose for such liquidation is the evasion or avoidance of Federal income tax by securing the benefit of a deduction, credit, or other allowance which the acquiring corporation would not otherwise enjoy, then the Secretary may disallow such deduction, credit, or other allowance.

(2) Meaning of terms.—For purposes of paragraph (1), the terms "qualified stock purchase" and "acquisition date" have the same respective meanings as when used in section 338.

(c) Power of Secretary to allow deduction, etc., in part.—In any case to which subsection (a) or (b) applies the Secretary is authorized—

(1) to allow as a deduction, credit, or allowance any part of any amount disallowed by such subsection, if he determines that such allowance will not result in the evasion or avoidance of Federal income tax for which the acquisition was made; or

(2) to distribute, apportion, or allocate gross income, and distribute, apportion, or allocate the deductions, credits, or allowances the benefit of which was sought to be secured, between or among the corporations, or properties, or parts thereof, involved, and to allow such deductions, credits, or allowances so distributed, apportioned, or allocated, but to give effect to such allowance only to such extent as he determines will not result in the evasion or avoidance of Federal income tax for which the acquisition was made; or

(3) to exercise his powers in part under paragraph (1) and in part under paragraph (2).

§ 269A. Personal service corporations formed or availed of to avoid or evade income tax.

(a) General rule.—If—

(1) substantially all of the services of a personal service corporation are performed for (or on behalf of) 1 other corporation, partnership, or other entity, and

(2) the principal purpose for forming, or availing of, such personal service corporation is the avoidance or evasion of Federal income tax by reducing the income of, or securing the benefit of any expense, deduction, credit, exclusion, or other allowance for, any employee-owner which would not otherwise be available,

then the Secretary may allocate all income, deductions, credits, exclusions, and other allowances between such personal service corporation and its employee-owners, if such allocation is necessary to prevent avoidance or evasion of Federal income tax or clearly to reflect the income of the personal service corporation or any of its employee-owners.

(b) Definitions.—For purposes of this section—

(1) Personal service corporation.—

The term "personal service corporation" means a corporation the principal activity of which is the performance of personal services and such services are substantially performed by employee-owners.

(2) Employee-owner.—

The term "employee-owner" means any employee who owns, on any day during the taxable year, more than 10 percent of the outstanding stock of the personal service corporation. For purposes of the preceding sentence, section 318 shall apply, except that "5 percent" shall be substituted for "50 percent" in section 318(a)(2)(C).

(3) Related persons.—

All related persons (within the meaning of section 144(a)(3)) shall be treated as 1 entity.

Subchapter C—Corporate Distributions and Adjustments

Part I—Distributions by Corporations

Subpart A—Effects on Recipients

§ 301. Distributions of property.

(a) In general.—Except as otherwise provided in this chapter, a distribution of property (as defined in section 317(a)) made by a corporation to a shareholder with respect to its stock shall be treated in the manner provided in subsection (c).

(b) Amount distributed.—

(1) General rule.—For purposes of this section, the amount of any distribution shall be the amount of money received, plus the fair market value of the other property received.

(2) Reduction for liabilities.—The amount of any distribution determined under paragraph (1) shall be reduced (but not below zero) by—

(A) the amount of any liability of the corporation assumed by the shareholder in connection with the distribution, and

(B) the amount of any liability to which the property received by the shareholder is subject immediately before, and immediately after, the distribution.

(3) Determination of fair market value.—For purposes of this section, fair market value shall be determined as of the date of the distribution.

(c) Amount taxable.—In the case of a distribution to which subsection (a) applies—

(1) Amount constituting dividend.—That portion of the distribution which is a dividend (as defined in section 316) shall be included in gross income.

(2) Amount applied against basis.—That portion of the distribution which is not a dividend shall be applied against and reduce the adjusted basis of the stock.

(3) Amount in excess of basis.—

(A) In general.—Except as provided in subparagraph (B), that portion of the distribution which is not a dividend, to the extent that it exceeds the adjusted basis of the stock, shall be treated as gain from the sale or exchange of property.

(B) Distributions out of increase in value accrued before March 1, 1913.—That portion of the distribution which is not a dividend, to the extent that it exceeds the adjusted basis of the stock and to the extent that it is out of increase in value accrued before March 1, 1913, shall be exempt from tax.

(d) Basis.—The basis of property received in a distribution to which subsection (a) applies shall be the fair market value of such property.

(e) Special rule for certain distributions received by 20 percent corporate shareholder.—

(1) In general.—Except to the extent otherwise provided in regulations, solely for purposes of determining the taxable income of any 20 percent corporate shareholder (and its adjusted basis in the stock of the distributing corporation), section 312 shall be applied with respect to the distributing corporation as if it did not contain subsections (k) and (n) thereof.

(2) 20 percent corporate shareholder.—For purposes of this subsection, the term "20 percent corporate shareholder" means, with respect to any distribution, any corporation which owns (directly or through the application of section 318)—

(A) stock in the corporation making the distribution possessing at least 20 percent of the total combined voting power of all classes of stock entitled to vote, or

(B) at least 20 percent of the total value of all stock of the distributing corporation (except nonvoting stock which is limited and preferred as to dividends),

but only if, but for this subsection, the distributee corporation would be entitled to a deduction under section 243, 244, or 245 with respect to such distribution.

(3) Application of section 312(n)(7) not affected.—The reference in paragraph (1) to subsection (n) of section 312 shall be treated as not including a reference to paragraph (7) of such subsection.

(4) Regulations.—The Secretary shall prescribe such regulations as may be necessary or appropriate to carry out the purposes of this subsection.

(f) Special rules.—

(1) For distributions in redemption of stock, see section 302.

(2) For distributions in complete liquidation, see part II (sec. 331 and following).

(3) For distributions in corporate organizations and reorganizations, see part III (sec. 351 and following).

(4) For taxation of dividends received by individuals at capital gains rates, see section 1(h)(11).

§ 302. Distributions in redemption of stock.

(a) General rule.—If a corporation redeems its stock (within the meaning of section 317(b)), and if paragraph (1), (2), (3), (4), or (5) of subsection (b) applies, such redemption shall be treated as a distribution in part or full payment in exchange for the stock.

(b) Redemptions treated as exchanges.—

(1) Redemptions not equivalent to dividends.—Subsection (a) shall apply if the redemption is not essentially equivalent to a dividend.

(2) Substantially disproportionate redemption of stock.—

(A) In general.—Subsection (a) shall apply if the distribution is substantially disproportionate with respect to the shareholder.

(B) Limitation.—This paragraph shall not apply unless immediately after the redemption the shareholder owns less than 50 percent of the total combined voting power of all classes of stock entitled to vote.

(C) Definitions.—For purposes of this paragraph, the distribution is substantially disproportionate if—

(i) the ratio which the voting stock of the corporation owned by the shareholder immediately after the redemption bears to all of the voting stock of the corporation at such time, is less than 80 percent of—

(ii) the ratio which the voting stock of the corporation owned by the shareholder immediately before the redemption bears to all of the voting stock of the corporation at such time.

For purposes of this paragraph, no distribution shall be treated as substantially disproportionate unless the shareholder's ownership of the common stock of the corporation (whether voting or nonvoting) after and before redemption also meets the 80 percent requirement of the preceding sentence. For purposes of the preceding sentence, if there is more than one class of common stock, the determinations shall be made by reference to fair market value.

(D) **Series of redemptions.**—This paragraph shall not apply to any redemption made pursuant to a plan the purpose or effect of which is a series of redemptions resulting in a distribution which (in the aggregate) is not substantially disproportionate with respect to the shareholder.

(3) **Termination of shareholder's interest.**—Subsection (a) shall apply if the redemption is in complete redemption of all of the stock of the corporation owned by the shareholder.

(4) **Redemption from noncorporate shareholder in partial liquidation.**—Subsection (a) shall apply to a distribution if such distribution is—

(A) in redemption of stock held by a shareholder who is not a corporation, and

(B) in partial liquidation of the distributing corporation.

(5) **Redemptions by certain regulated investment companies.**—Except to the extent provided in regulations prescribed by the Secretary, subsection (a) shall apply to any distribution in redemption of stock of a publicly offered regulated investment company (within the meaning of section 67(c)(2)(B)) if—

(A) such redemption is upon the demand of the stockholder, and

(B) such company issues only stock which is redeemable upon the demand of the stockholder.

(6) **Application of paragraphs.**—In determining whether a redemption meets the requirements of paragraph (1), the fact that such redemption fails to meet the requirements of paragraph (2), (3), or (4) shall not be taken into account. If a redemption meets the requirements of paragraph (3) and also the requirements of paragraph (1), (2), or (4), then so much of subsection (c)(2) as would (but for this sentence) apply in respect of the acquisition of an interest in the corporation within the 10-year period beginning on the date of the distribution shall not apply.

(c) **Constructive ownership of stock.**—

(1) **In general.**—Except as provided in paragraph (2) of this subsection, section 318(a) shall apply in determining the ownership of stock for purposes of this section.

(2) **For determining termination of interest.**—

(A) In the case of a distribution described in subsection (b)(3), section 318(a)(1) shall not apply if—

(i) immediately after the distribution the distributee has no interest in the corporation (including an interest as officer, director, or employee), other than an interest as a creditor,

(ii) the distributee does not acquire any such interest (other than stock acquired by bequest or inheritance) within 10 years from the date of such distribution, and

(iii) the distributee, at such time and in such manner as the Secretary by regulations prescribes, files an agreement to notify the Secretary of any acquisition described in clause (ii) and to retain such records as may be necessary for the application of this paragraph.

If the distributee acquires such an interest in the corporation (other than by bequest or inheritance) within 10 years from the date of the distribution, then the periods of limitation provided in sections 6501 and 6502 on the making of an assessment and the collection by levy or a proceeding in court shall, with respect to any deficiency (including interest and additions to the tax) resulting from such acquisition, include one year immediately following the date on which the distributee (in accordance with regulations prescribed by the Secretary) notifies the Secretary of such acquisition; and such assessment and collection may be made notwithstanding any provision of law or rule of law which otherwise would prevent such assessment and collection.

(B) Subparagraph (A) of this paragraph shall not apply if—

(i) any portion of the stock redeemed was acquired, directly or indirectly, within the 10-year period ending on the date of the distribution by the distributee from a person the ownership of whose stock would (at the time of distribution) be attributable to the distributee under section 318(a), or

(ii) any person owns (at the time of the distribution) stock the ownership of which is attributable to the distributee under section 318(a) and such person acquired any stock in the corporation, directly or indirectly, from the distributee within the 10-year period ending on the date of the distribution, unless such stock so acquired from the distributee is redeemed in the same transaction.

The preceding sentence shall not apply if the acquisition (or, in the case of clause (ii), the disposition) by the distributee did not have as one of its principal purposes the avoidance of Federal income tax.

(C) Special rule for waivers by entities.—

(i) In general.—Subparagraph (A) shall not apply to a distribution to any entity unless—

(I) such entity and each related person meet the requirements of clauses (i), (ii), and (iii) of subparagraph (A), and

(II) each related person agrees to be jointly and severally liable for any deficiency (including interest and additions to tax) resulting from an acquisition described in clause (ii) of subparagraph (A).

In any case to which the preceding sentence applies, the second sentence of subparagraph (A) and subparagraph (B)(ii) shall be applied by substituting "distributee or any related person" for "distributee" each place it appears.

(ii) Definitions.—For purposes of this subparagraph—

(I) the term "entity" means a partnership, estate, trust, or corporation; and

(II) the term "related person" means any person to whom ownership of stock in the corporation is (at the time of the distribution) attributable under section 318(a)(1) if such stock is further attributable to the entity under section 318(a)(3).

(d) Redemptions treated as distributions of property.—Except as otherwise provided in this subchapter, if a corporation redeems its stock (within the meaning of section 317(b)), and if subsection (a) of this section does not apply, such redemption shall be treated as a distribution of property to which section 301 applies.

(e) Partial liquidation defined.—

(1) In general.—For purposes of subsection (b)(4), a distribution shall be treated as in partial liquidation of a corporation if—

(A) the distribution is not essentially equivalent to a dividend (determined at the corporate level rather than at the shareholder level), and

(B) the distribution is pursuant to a plan and occurs within the taxable year in which the plan is adopted or within the succeeding taxable year.

(2) Termination of business.—The distributions which meet the requirements of paragraph (1)(A) shall include (but shall not be limited to) a distribution which meets the requirements of subparagraphs (A) and (B) of this paragraph:

(A) The distribution is attributable to the distributing corporation's ceasing to conduct, or consists of the assets of, a qualified trade or business.

(B) Immediately after the distribution, the distributing corporation is actively engaged in the conduct of a qualified trade or business.

(3) Qualified trade or business.—For purposes of paragraph (2), the term "qualified trade or business" means any trade or business which—

(A) was actively conducted throughout the 5-year period ending on the date of the redemption, and

(B) was not acquired by the corporation within such period in a transaction in which gain or loss was recognized in whole or in part.

(4) Redemption may be pro rata.—Whether or not a redemption meets the requirements of subparagraphs (A) and (B) of paragraph (2) shall be determined without regard to whether or not the redemption is pro rata with respect to all of the shareholders of the corporation.

(5) Treatment of certain pass-thru entities.—For purposes of determining under subsection (b)(4) whether any stock is held by a shareholder who is not a corporation, any stock held by a partnership, estate, or trust shall be treated as if it were actually held proportionately by its partners or beneficiaries.

(f) Cross references.—For special rules relating to redemption—

(1) Death taxes.—Of stock to pay death taxes, see section 303.

(2) Section 306 stock.—Of section 306 stock, see section 306.

(3) Liquidations.—Of stock in complete liquidation, see section 331.

§ 303. Distributions in redemption of stock to pay death taxes.

(a) In general.—A distribution of property to a shareholder by a corporation in redemption of part or all of the stock of such corporation which (for Federal estate tax purposes) is included in determining the gross estate of a decedent, to the extent that the amount of such distribution does not exceed the sum of—

(1) the estate, inheritance, legacy, and succession taxes (including any interest collected as a part of such taxes) imposed because of such decedent's death, and

(2) the amount of funeral and administration expenses allowable as deductions to the estate under section 2053 (or under section 2106 in the case of the estate of a decedent non-resident, not a citizen of the United States),

shall be treated as a distribution in full payment in exchange for the stock so redeemed.

(b) Limitations on application of subsection (a).—

(1) Period for distribution.—Subsection (a) shall apply only to amounts distributed after the death of the decedent and—

(A) within the period of limitations provided in section 6501(a) for the assessment of the Federal estate tax (determined without the application of any provision other than section 6501(a)), or within 90 days after the expiration of such period,

(B) if a petition for redetermination of a deficiency in such estate tax has been filed with the Tax Court within the time prescribed in section 6213, at any time before the expiration of 60 days after the decision of the Tax Court becomes final, or

(C) if an election has been made under section 6166 and if the time prescribed by this subparagraph expires at a later date than the time prescribed by subparagraph (B) of this paragraph, within the time determined under section 6166 for the payment of the installments.

(2) Relationship of stock to decedent's estate.—

(A) In general.—Subsection (a) shall apply to a distribution by a corporation only if the value (for Federal estate tax purposes) of all of the stock of such corporation which is included in determining the value of the decedent's gross estate exceeds 35 percent of the excess of—

(i) the value of the gross estate of such decedent, over

(ii) the sum of the amounts allowable as a deduction under section 2053 or 2054.

(B) Special rule for stock in 2 or more corporations.—For purposes of subparagraph (A), stock of 2 or more corporations, with respect to each of which there is included in determining the value of the decedent's gross estate 20 percent or more in value of the outstanding stock, shall be treated as the stock of a single corporation. For purposes of the 20-percent requirement of the preceding sentence, stock which, at the decedent's death, represents the surviving spouse's interest in property held by the decedent and the surviving spouse as community property or as joint tenants, tenants by the entirety, or tenants in common shall be treated as having been included in determining the value of the decedent's gross estate.

(3) Relationship of shareholder to estate tax.—Subsection (a) shall apply to a distribution by a corporation only to the extent that the interest of the shareholder is reduced directly (or through a binding obligation to contribute) by any payment of an amount described in paragraph (1) or (2) of subsection (a).

(4) Additional requirements for distributions made more than 4 years after decedent's death.—In the case of amounts distributed more than 4 years after the date of the decedent's death, subsection (a) shall apply to a distribution by a corporation only to the extent of the lesser of—

(A) the aggregate of the amounts referred to in paragraph (1) or (2) of subsection (a) which remained unpaid immediately before the distribution, or

(B) the aggregate of the amounts referred to in paragraph (1) or (2) of subsection (a) which are paid during the 1-year period beginning on the date of such distribution.

(c) Stock with substituted basis.—If—

(1) a shareholder owns stock of a corporation (referred to in this subsection as "new stock") the basis of which is determined by reference to the basis of stock of a corporation (referred to in this subsection as "old stock"),

(2) the old stock was included (for Federal estate tax purposes) in determining the gross estate of a decedent, and

(3) subsection (a) would apply to a distribution of property to such shareholder in redemption of the old stock,

then, subject to the limitations specified in subsection (b), subsection (a) shall apply in respect of a distribution in redemption of the new stock.

(d) Special rules for generation-skipping transfers.—Where stock in a corporation is the subject of a generation-skipping transfer (within the meaning of section 2611(a)) occurring at the same time as and as a result of the death of an individual—

(1) the stock shall be deemed to be included in the gross estate of such individual;

(2) taxes of the kind referred to in subsection (a)(1) which are imposed because of the generation-skipping transfer shall be treated as imposed because of such individual's death (and for this purpose the tax imposed by section 2601 shall be treated as an estate tax);

(3) the period of distribution shall be measured from the date of the generation-skipping transfer; and

(4) the relationship of stock to the decedent's estate shall be measured with reference solely to the amount of the generation-skipping transfer.

§ 304. Redemption through use of related corporations.

(a) Treatment of certain stock purchases.—

(1) Acquisition by related corporation (other than subsidiary).—For purposes of sections 302 and 303, if—

(A) one or more persons are in control of each of two corporations, and

(B) in return for property, one of the corporations acquires stock in the other corporation from the person (or persons) so in control,

then (unless paragraph (2) applies) such property shall be treated as a distribution in redemption of the stock of the corporation acquiring such stock. To the extent that such distribution is treated as a distribution to which section 301 applies, the transferor and the acquiring corporation shall be treated in the same manner as if the transferor had transferred the stock so acquired to the acquiring corporation in exchange for stock of the acquiring corporation in a transaction to which section 351(a) applies, and then the acquiring corporation had redeemed the stock it was treated as issuing in such transaction.

(2) Acquisition by subsidiary.—For purposes of sections 302 and 303, if—

(A) in return for property, one corporation acquires from a shareholder of another corporation stock in such other corporation, and

(B) the issuing corporation controls the acquiring corporation,

then such property shall be treated as a distribution in redemption of the stock of the issuing corporation.

(b) Special rules for application of subsection (a).—

(1) Rule for determinations under section 302(b).—In the case of any acquisition of stock to which subsection (a) of this section applies, determinations as to whether the acquisition is, by reason of section 302(b), to be treated as a distribution in part or full payment in exchange for the stock shall be made by reference to the stock of the issuing corporation. In applying section 318(a) (relating to constructive ownership of stock) with respect to section 302(b) for purposes of this paragraph, sections 318(a)(2)(C) and 318(a)(3)(C) shall be applied without regard to the 50 percent limitation contained therein.

(2) Amount constituting dividend.—In the case of any acquisition of stock to which subsection (a) applies, the determination of the amount which is a dividend (and the source thereof) shall be made as if the property were distributed—

(A) by the acquiring corporation to the extent of its earnings and profits, and

(B) then by the issuing corporation to the extent of its earnings and profits.

(3) Coordination with section 351.—

(A) Property treated as received in redemption.—Except as otherwise provided in this paragraph, subsection (a) (and not section 351 and not so much of sections 357 and 358 as relates to section 351) shall apply to any property received in a distribution described in subsection (a).

(B) Certain assumptions of liability, etc.—

(i) In general.—In the case of an acquisition described in section 351, subsection (a) shall not apply to any liability—

(I) assumed by the acquiring corporation, or

(II) to which the stock is subject,

if such liability was incurred by the transferor to acquire the stock. For purposes of the preceding sentence, the term "stock" means stock referred to in paragraph (1)(B) or (2)(A) of subsection (a).

(ii) Extension of obligations, etc.—For purposes of clause (i), an extension, renewal, or refinancing of a liability which meets the requirements of clause (i) shall be treated as meeting such requirements.

(iii) Clause (i) does not apply to stock acquired from related person except where complete termination.—Clause (i) shall apply only to stock acquired by the transferor from a person—

(I) none of whose stock is attributable to the transferor under section 318(a) (other than paragraph (4) thereof), or

(II) who satisfies rules similar to the rules of section 302(c)(2) with respect to both the acquiring and the issuing corporations (determined as if such person were a distributee of each such corporation).

* * *

(4) Treatment of certain intragroup transactions.—

(A) In general.—In the case of any transfer described in subsection (a) of stock from 1 member of an affiliated group to another member of such group, proper adjustments shall be made to—

(i) the adjusted basis of any intragroup stock, and

(ii) the earnings and profits of any member of such group,

to the extent necessary to carry out the purposes of this section.

(B) Definitions.—For purposes of this paragraph—

(i) Affiliated group.—The term "affiliated group" has the meaning given such term by section 1504(a).

(ii) Intragroup stock.—The term "intragroup stock" means any stock which—

(I) is in a corporation which is a member of an affiliated group, and

(II) is held by another member of such group.

* * *

(c) Control.—

(1) In general.—For purposes of this section, control means the ownership of stock possessing at least 50 percent of the total combined voting power of all classes of stock entitled to vote, or at least 50 percent of the total value of shares of all classes of stock. If a person (or persons) is in control (within the meaning of the preceding sentence) of a corporation which in turn owns at least 50 percent of the total combined voting power of all stock entitled to vote of another corporation, or owns at least 50 percent of the total value of the shares of all classes of stock of another corporation, then such person (or persons) shall be treated as in control of such other corporation.

(2) Stock acquired in the transaction.—For purposes of subsection (a)(1)—

(A) General rule.—Where 1 or more persons in control of the issuing corporation transfer stock of such corporation in exchange for stock of the acquiring corporation, the stock of the acquiring corporation received shall be taken into account in determining whether such person or persons are in control of the acquiring corporation.

(B) Definition of control group.—Where 2 or more persons in control of the issuing corporation transfer stock of such corporation to the acquiring corporation and, after the transfer, the transferors are in control of the acquiring corporation, the person or persons in control of each corporation shall include each of the persons who so transfer stock.

(3) Constructive ownership.—

(A) In general.—Section 318(a) (relating to constructive ownership of stock) shall apply for purposes of determining control under this section.

(B) Modification of 50-percent limitations in section 318.—For purposes of subparagraph (A)—

(i) paragraph (2)(C) of section 318(a) shall be applied by substituting "5 percent" for "50 percent", and

(ii) paragraph (3)(C) of section 318(a) shall be applied—

(I) by substituting "5 percent" for "50 percent", and

(II) in any case where such paragraph would not apply but for subclause (I), by considering a corporation as owning the stock (other than stock in such corporation) owned by or for any shareholder of such corporation in that proportion which the value of the stock which such shareholder owned in such corporation bears to the value of all stock in such corporation.

§ 305. Distributions of stock and stock rights.

(a) General rule.—Except as otherwise provided in this section, gross income does not include the amount of any distribution of the stock of a corporation made by such corporation to its shareholders with respect to its stock.

(b) Exceptions.—Subsection (a) shall not apply to a distribution by a corporation of its stock, and the distribution shall be treated as a distribution of property to which section 301 applies—

(1) Distributions in lieu of money.—If the distribution is, at the election of any of the shareholders (whether exercised before or after the declaration thereof), payable either—

(A) in its stock, or

(B) in property.

(2) Disproportionate distributions.—If the distribution (or a series of distributions of which such distribution is one) has the result of—

(A) the receipt of property by some shareholders, and

(B) an increase in the proportionate interests of other shareholders in the assets or earnings and profits of the corporation.

(3) Distributions of common and preferred stock.—If the distribution (or a series of distributions of which such distribution is one) has the result of—

(A) the receipt of preferred stock by some common shareholders, and

(B) the receipt of common stock by other common shareholders.

(4) Distributions on preferred stock.—If the distribution is with respect to preferred stock, other than an increase in the conversion ratio of convertible preferred stock made solely to take account of a stock dividend or stock split with respect to the stock into which such convertible stock is convertible.

(5) Distributions of convertible preferred stock.—If the distribution is of convertible preferred stock, unless it is established to the satisfaction of the Secretary that such distribution will not have the result described in paragraph (2).

(c) Certain transactions treated as distributions.—For purposes of this section and section 301, the Secretary shall prescribe regulations under which a change in conversion ratio, a change in redemption price, a difference between redemption price and issue price, a redemption which is treated as a distribution to which section 301 applies, or any transaction (including a recapitalization) having a similar effect on the interest of any shareholder shall be treated as a distribution with respect to any shareholder whose proportionate interest in the earnings and profits or assets of the corporation is increased by such change, difference, redemption, or similar transaction. Regulations prescribed under the preceding sentence shall provide that—

(1) where the issuer of stock is required to redeem the stock at a specified time or the holder of stock has the option to require the issuer to redeem the stock, a redemption premium resulting from such requirement or option shall be treated as reasonable only if the amount of such premium does not exceed the amount determined under the principles of section 1273(a)(3),

(2) a redemption premium shall not fail to be treated as a distribution (or series of distributions) merely because the stock is callable, and

(3) in any case in which a redemption premium is treated as a distribution (or series of distributions), such premium shall be taken into account under principles similar to the principles of section 1272(a).

(d) Definitions.—

(1) Rights to acquire stock.—For purposes of this section, the term "stock" includes rights to acquire such stock.

(2) Shareholders.—For purposes of subsections (b) and (c), the term "shareholder" includes a holder of rights or of convertible securities.

(e) Treatment of purchaser of stripped preferred stock.—

(1) In general.—If any person purchases after April 30, 1993, any stripped preferred stock, then such person, while holding such stock, shall include in gross income amounts equal to the amounts which would have been so includible if such stripped preferred stock were a bond issued on the purchase date and having original issue discount equal to the excess, if any, of—

(A) the redemption price for such stock, over

(B) the price at which such person purchased such stock.

The preceding sentence shall also apply in the case of any person whose basis in such stock is determined by reference to the basis in the hands of such purchaser.

(2) Basis adjustments.—Appropriate adjustments to basis shall be made for amounts includible in gross income under paragraph (1).

(3) Tax treatment of person stripping stock.—If any person strips the rights to 1 or more dividends from any stock described in paragraph (5)(B) and after April 30, 1993, disposes of such dividend rights, for purposes of paragraph (1), such person shall be treated as having purchased the stripped preferred stock on the date of such disposition for a purchase price equal to such person's adjusted basis in such stripped preferred stock.

(4) Amounts treated as ordinary income.—Any amount included in gross income under paragraph (1) shall be treated as ordinary income.

(5) Stripped preferred stock.—For purposes of this subsection—

(A) In general.—The term "stripped preferred stock" means any stock described in subparagraph (B) if there has been a separation in ownership between such stock and any dividend on such stock which has not become payable.

(B) Description of stock.—Stock is described in this subsection if such stock—

(i) is limited and preferred as to dividends and does not participate in corporate growth to any significant extent, and

(ii) has a fixed redemption price.

(6) Purchase.—For purposes of this subsection, the term "purchase" means—

(A) any acquisition of stock, where

(B) the basis of such stock is not determined in whole or in part by the reference to the adjusted basis of such stock in the hands of the person from whom acquired.

(7) Cross reference.—For treatment of stripped interests in certain accounts or entities holding preferred stock, see section 1286(f).

(f) Cross references.—For special rules—

(1) Relating to the receipt of stock and stock rights in corporate organizations and reorganizations, see part III (sec. 351 and following).

(2) In the case of a distribution which results in a gift, see section 2501 and following.

(3) In the case of a distribution which has the effect of the payment of compensation, see section 61(a)(1).

§ 306. Dispositions of certain stock.

(a) General rule.—If a shareholder sells or otherwise disposes of section 306 stock (as defined in subsection (c))—

(1) Dispositions other than redemptions.—If such disposition is not a redemption (within the meaning of section 317(b))—

(A) The amount realized shall be treated as ordinary income. This subparagraph shall not apply to the extent that—

(i) the amount realized, exceeds

(ii) such stock's ratable share of the amount which would have been a dividend at the time of distribution if (in lieu of section 306 stock) the corporation had distributed money in an amount equal to the fair market value of the stock at the time of distribution.

(B) Any excess of the amount realized over the sum of—

(i) the amount treated under subparagraph (A) as ordinary income, plus

(ii) the adjusted basis of the stock,

shall be treated as gain from the sale of such stock.

(C) No loss shall be recognized.

(D) **Treatment as dividend.**—For purposes of section 1(h)(11) and such other provisions as the Secretary may specify, any amount treated as ordinary income under this paragraph shall be treated as a dividend received from the corporation.

(2) **Redemption.**—If the disposition is a redemption, the amount realized shall be treated as a distribution of property to which section 301 applies.

(b) **Exceptions.**—Subsection (a) shall not apply—

(1) **Termination of shareholder's interest, etc.—**

(A) **Not in redemption.**—If the disposition—

(i) is not a redemption;

(ii) is not, directly or indirectly, to a person the ownership of whose stock would (under section 318(a)) be attributable to the shareholder; and

(iii) terminates the entire stock interest of the shareholder in the corporation (and for purposes of this clause, section 318(a) shall apply).

(B) **In redemption.**—If the disposition is a redemption and paragraph (3) or (4) of section 302(b) applies.

(2) **Liquidations.**—If the section 306 stock is redeemed in a distribution in complete liquidation to which part II (sec. 331 and following) applies.

(3) **Where gain or loss is not recognized.**—To the extent that, under any provision of this subtitle, gain or loss to the shareholder is not recognized with respect to the disposition of the section 306 stock.

(4) **Transactions not in avoidance.**—If it is established to the satisfaction of the Secretary—

(A) that the distribution, and the disposition or redemption, or

(B) in the case of a prior or simultaneous disposition (or redemption) of the stock with respect to which the section 306 stock disposed of (or redeemed) was issued, that the disposition (or redemption) of the section 306 stock,

was not in pursuance of a plan having as one of its principal purposes the avoidance of Federal income tax.

(c) **Section 306 stock defined.—**

(1) **In general.**—For purposes of this subchapter, the term "section 306 stock" means stock which meets the requirements of subparagraph (A), (B), or (C) of this paragraph.

(A) **Distributed to seller.**—Stock (other than common stock issued with respect to common stock) which was distributed to the shareholder selling or otherwise disposing of such stock if, by reason of section 305(a), any part of such distribution was not includible in the gross income of the shareholder.

(B) Received in a corporate reorganization or separation.—Stock which is not common stock and—

(i) which was received, by the shareholder selling or otherwise disposing of such stock, in pursuance of a plan of reorganization (within the meaning of section 368(a)), or in a distribution or exchange to which section 355 (or so much of section 356 as relates to section 355) applied, and

(ii) with respect to the receipt of which gain or loss to the shareholder was to any extent not recognized by reason of part III, but only to the extent that either the effect of the transaction was substantially the same as the receipt of a stock dividend, or the stock was received in exchange for section 306 stock.

For purposes of this section, a receipt of stock to which the foregoing provisions of this subparagraph apply shall be treated as a distribution of stock.

(C) Stock having transferred or substituted basis.—Except as otherwise provided in subparagraph (B), stock the basis of which (in the hands of the shareholder selling or otherwise disposing of such stock) is determined by reference to the basis (in the hands of such shareholder or any other person) of section 306 stock.

(2) Exception where no earnings and profits.—For purposes of this section, the term "section 306 stock" does not include any stock no part of the distribution of which would have been a dividend at the time of the distribution if money had been distributed in lieu of the stock.

(3) Certain stock acquired in section 351 exchange.—The term "section 306 stock" also includes any stock which is not common stock acquired in an exchange to which section 351 applied if receipt of money (in lieu of the stock) would have been treated as a dividend to any extent. Rules similar to the rules of section 304(b)(2) shall apply—

(A) for purposes of the preceding sentence, and

(B) for purposes of determining the application of this section to any subsequent disposition of stock which is section 306 stock by reason of an exchange described in the preceding sentence.

(4) Application of attribution rules for certain purposes.—For purposes of paragraphs (1)(B)(ii) and (3), section 318(a) shall apply. For purposes of applying the preceding sentence to paragraph (3), the rules of section 304(c)(3)(B) shall apply.

(d) Stock rights.—For purposes of this section—

(1) stock rights shall be treated as stock, and

(2) stock acquired through the exercise of stock rights shall be treated as stock distributed at the time of the distribution of the stock rights, to the extent of the fair market value of such rights at the time of the distribution.

(e) Convertible stock.—For purposes of subsection (c)—

(1) if section 306 stock was issued with respect to common stock and later such section 306 stock is exchanged for common stock in the same corporation (whether or not such exchange is pursuant to a conversion privilege contained in the section 306 stock), then (except as provided in paragraph (2)) the common stock so received shall not be treated as section 306 stock; and

(2) common stock with respect to which there is a privilege of converting into stock other than common stock (or into property), whether or not the conversion privilege is contained in such stock, shall not be treated as common stock.

* * *

(g) Change in terms and conditions of stock.—If a substantial change is made in the terms and conditions of any stock, then, for purposes of this section—

(1) the fair market value of such stock shall be the fair market value at the time of the distribution or at the time of such change, whichever such value is higher;

(2) such stock's ratable share of the amount which would have been a dividend if money had been distributed in lieu of stock shall be determined as of the time of distribution or as of the time of such change, whichever such ratable share is higher; and

(3) subsection (c)(2) shall not apply unless the stock meets the requirements of such subsection both at the time of such distribution and at the time of such change.

§ 307. Basis of stock and stock rights acquired in distributions.

(a) General rule.—If a shareholder in a corporation receives its stock or rights to acquire its stock (referred to in this subsection as "new stock") in a distribution to which section 305(a) applies, then the basis of such new stock and of the stock with respect to which it is distributed (referred to in this section as "old stock"), respectively, shall, in the shareholder's hands, be determined by allocating between the old stock and the new stock the adjusted basis of the old stock. Such allocation shall be made under regulations prescribed by the Secretary.

(b) Exception for certain stock rights.—

(1) In general.—If—

(A) a corporation distributes rights to acquire its stock to a shareholder in a distribution to which section 305(a) applies, and

(B) the fair market value of such rights at the time of the distribution is less than 15 percent of the fair market value of the old stock at such time,

then subsection (a) shall not apply and the basis of such rights shall be zero, unless the taxpayer elects under paragraph (2) of this subsection to determine the basis of the old stock and of the stock rights under the method of allocation provided in subsection (a).

(2) Election.—The election referred to in paragraph (1) shall be made in the return filed within the time prescribed by law (including extensions thereof) for the taxable year in which such rights were received. Such election shall be made in such manner as the Secretary may by regulations prescribe, and shall be irrevocable when made.

* * *

Subpart B—Effects on Corporation

§ 311. Taxability of corporation on distribution.

(a) General rule.—Except as provided in subsection (b), no gain or loss shall be recognized to a corporation on the distribution (not in complete liquidation) with respect to its stock of—

(1) its stock (or rights to acquire its stock), or

(2) property.

(b) Distributions of appreciated property.—

(1) In general.—If—

    (A) a corporation distributes property (other than an obligation of such corporation) to a shareholder in a distribution to which subpart A applies, and

    (B) the fair market value of such property exceeds its adjusted basis (in the hands of the distributing corporation),

then gain shall be recognized to the distributing corporation as if such property were sold to the distributee at its fair market value.

(2) Treatment of liabilities.—Rules similar to the rules of section 336(b) shall apply for purposes of this subsection.

(3) Special rule for certain distributions of partnership or trust interests.—If the property distributed consists of an interest in a partnership or trust, the Secretary may by regulations provide that the amount of the gain recognized under paragraph (1) shall be computed without regard to any loss attributable to property contributed to the partnership or trust for the principal purpose of recognizing such loss on the distribution.

§ 312. Effect on earnings and profits

(a) General rule—Except as otherwise provided in this section, on the distribution of property by a corporation with respect to its stock, the earnings and profits of the corporation (to the extent thereof) shall be decreased by the sum of—

(1) the amount of money,

(2) the principal amount of the obligations of such corporation (or, in the case of obligations having original issue discount, the aggregate issue price of such obligations), and

(3) the adjusted basis of the other property, so distributed.

(b) Distributions of appreciated property—On the distribution by a corporation, with respect to its stock, of any property (other than an obligation of such corporation) the fair market value of which exceeds the adjusted basis thereof—

(1) the earnings and profits of the corporation shall be increased by the amount of such excess, and

(2) subsection (a)(3) shall be applied by substituting "fair market value" for "adjusted basis".

For purposes of this subsection and subsection (a), the adjusted basis of any property is its adjusted basis as determined for purposes of computing earnings and profits.

(c) Adjustments for liabilities—In making the adjustments to the earnings and profits of a corporation under subsection (a) or (b), proper adjustment shall be made for—

(1) the amount of any liability to which the property distributed is subject, and

(2) the amount of any liability of the corporation assumed by a shareholder in connection with the distribution.

(d) Certain distributions of stock and securities

(1) In general—The distribution to a distributee by or on behalf of a corporation of its stock or securities, of stock or securities in another corporation, or of property, in a distribution to which this title applies, shall not be considered a distribution of the earnings and profits of any corporation—

(A) if no gain to such distributee from the receipt of such stock or securities, or property, was recognized under this title, or

(B) if the distribution was not subject to tax in the hands of such distributee by reason of section 305(a).

(2) Stock or securities—For purposes of this subsection, the term "stock or securities" includes rights to acquire stock or securities.

* * *

(f) Effect on earnings and profits of gain or loss and of receipt of tax-free distributions

(1) Effect on earnings and profits of gain or loss—The gain or loss realized from the sale or other disposition (after February 28, 1913) of property by a corporation—

(A) for the purpose of the computation of the earnings and profits of the corporation, shall (except as provided in subparagraph (B)) be determined by using as the adjusted basis the adjusted basis (under the law applicable to the year in which the sale or other disposition was made) for determining gain, except that no regard shall be had to the value of the property as of March 1, 1913; but

(B) for purposes of the computation of the earnings and profits of the corporation for any period beginning after February 28, 1913, shall be determined by using as the adjusted basis the adjusted basis (under the law applicable to the year in which the sale or other disposition was made) for determining gain.

Gain or loss so realized shall increase or decrease the earnings and profits to, but not beyond, the extent to which such a realized gain or loss was recognized in computing taxable income under the law applicable to the year in which such sale or disposition was made. Where, in determining the adjusted basis used in computing such realized gain or loss, the adjustment to the basis differs from the adjustment proper for the purpose of determining earnings and profits, then the latter adjustment shall be used in determining the increase or decrease above provided. For purposes of this subsection, a loss with respect to which a deduction is disallowed under section 1091 (relating to wash sales of stock or securities), or the corresponding provision of prior law, shall not be deemed to be recognized.

(2) Effect on earnings and profits of receipt of tax-free distributions—Where a corporation receives (after February 28, 1913) a distribution from a second corporation which (under the law applicable to the year in which the distribution was made) was not a taxable dividend to the shareholders of the second corporation, the amount of such distribution shall not increase the earnings and profits of the first corporation in the following cases:

(A) no such increase shall be made in respect of the part of such distribution which (under such law) is directly applied in reduction of the basis of the stock in respect of which the distribution was made; and

62

(**B**) no such increase shall be made if (under such law) the distribution causes the basis of the stock in respect of which the distribution was made to be allocated between such stock and the property received (or such basis would, but for section 307(b), be so allocated).

* * *

(h) Allocation in certain corporate separations and reorganizations

(**1**) **Section 355**—In the case of a distribution or exchange to which section 355 (or so much of section 356 as relates to section 355) applies, proper allocation with respect to the earnings and profits of the distributing corporation and the controlled corporation (or corporations) shall be made under regulations prescribed by the Secretary.

(**2**) **Section 368(a)(1)(C) or (D)**—In the case of a reorganization described in subparagraph (C) or (D) of section 368(a)(1), proper allocation with respect to the earnings and profits of the acquired corporation shall, under regulations prescribed by the Secretary, be made between the acquiring corporation and the acquired corporation (or any corporation which had control of the acquired corporation before the reorganization).

* * *

(n) Adjustments to earnings and profits to more accurately reflect economic gain and loss

For purposes of computing the earnings and profits of a corporation, the following adjustments shall be made:

* * *

(5) Installment sales

In the case of any installment sale, earnings and profits shall be computed as if the corporation did not use the installment method.

* * *

(7) Redemptions

If a corporation distributes amounts in a redemption to which section 302(a) or 303 applies, the part of such distribution which is properly chargeable to earnings and profits shall be an amount which is not in excess of the ratable share of the earnings and profits of such corporation accumulated after February 28, 1913, attributable to the stock so redeemed.

* * *

Subpart C—Definitions; Constructive Ownership of Stock

§ 316. Dividend defined.

(a) **General rule.**—For purposes of this subtitle, the term "dividend" means any distribution of property made by a corporation to its shareholders—

(**1**) out of its earnings and profits accumulated after February 28, 1913, or

(2) out of its earnings and profits of the taxable year (computed as of the close of the taxable year without diminution by reason of any distributions made during the taxable year), without regard to the amount of the earnings and profits at the time the distribution was made.

Except as otherwise provided in this subtitle, every distribution is made out of earnings and profits to the extent thereof, and from the most recently accumulated earnings and profits. To the extent that any distribution is, under any provision of this subchapter, treated as a distribution of property to which section 301 applies, such distribution shall be treated as a distribution of property for purposes of this subsection.

(b) Special rules.—

(1) Certain insurance company dividends.— The definition in subsection (a) shall not apply to the term "dividend" as used in subchapter L in any case where the reference is to dividends of insurance companies paid to policyholders as such.

(2) Distributions by personal holding companies.—

(A) In the case of a corporation which—

(i) under the law applicable to the taxable year in which the distribution is made, is a personal holding company (as defined in section 542), or

(ii) for the taxable year in respect of which the distribution is made under section 563(b) (relating to dividends paid after the close of the taxable year), or section 547 (relating to deficiency dividends), or the corresponding provisions of prior law, is a personal holding company under the law applicable to such taxable year,

the term "dividend" also means any distribution of property (whether or not a dividend as defined in subsection (a)) made by the corporation to its shareholders, to the extent of its undistributed personal holding company income (determined under section 545 without regard to distributions under this paragraph) for such year.

(B) For purposes of subparagraph (A), the term "distribution of property" includes a distribution in complete liquidation occurring within 24 months after the adoption of a plan of liquidation, but—

(i) only to the extent of the amounts distributed to distributees other than corporate shareholders, and

(ii) only to the extent that the corporation designates such amounts as a dividend distribution and duly notifies such distributees of such designation, under regulations prescribed by the Secretary, but

(iii) not in excess of the sum of such distributees' allocable share of the undistributed personal holding company income for such year, computed without regard to this subparagraph or section 562(b).

* * *

§ 317. Other definitions.

(a) Property.— For purposes of this part, the term "property" means money, securities, and any other property; except that such term does not include stock in the corporation making the distribution (or rights to acquire such stock).

(b) Redemption of stock.—For purposes of this part, stock shall be treated as redeemed by a corporation if the corporation acquires its stock from a shareholder in exchange for property, whether or not the stock so acquired is cancelled, retired, or held as treasury stock.

§ 318. Constructive ownership of stock.

(a) General rule.—For purposes of those provisions of this subchapter to which the rules contained in this section are expressly made applicable—

(1) Members of family.—

(A) In general.—An individual shall be considered as owning the stock owned, directly or indirectly, by or for—

(i) his spouse (other than a spouse who is legally separated from the individual under a decree of divorce or separate maintenance), and

(ii) his children, grandchildren, and parents.

(B) Effect of adoption.—For purposes of subparagraph (A)(ii), a legally adopted child of an individual shall be treated as a child of such individual by blood.

(2) Attribution from partnerships, estates, trusts, and corporations.—

(A) From partnerships and estates.—Stock owned, directly or indirectly, by or for a partnership or estate shall be considered as owned proportionately by its partners or beneficiaries.

(B) From trusts.—

(i) Stock owned, directly or indirectly, by or for a trust (other than an employees' trust described in section 401(a) which is exempt from tax under section 501(a)) shall be considered as owned by its beneficiaries in proportion to the actuarial interest of such beneficiaries in such trust.

(ii) Stock owned, directly or indirectly, by or for any portion of a trust of which a person is considered the owner under subpart E of part I of subchapter J (relating to grantors and others treated as substantial owners) shall be considered as owned by such person.

(C) From corporations.—If 50 percent or more in value of the stock in a corporation is owned, directly or indirectly, by or for any person, such person shall be considered as owning the stock owned, directly or indirectly, by or for such corporation, in that proportion which the value of the stock which such person so owns bears to the value of all the stock in such corporation.

(3) Attribution to partnerships, estates, trusts, and corporations.—

(A) To partnerships and estates.—Stock owned, directly or indirectly, by or for a partner or a beneficiary of an estate shall be considered as owned by the partnership or estate.

(B) To trusts.—

(i) Stock owned, directly or indirectly, by or for a beneficiary of a trust (other than an employees' trust described in section 401(a) which is exempt from tax under section 501(a)) shall be considered as owned by the trust, unless such beneficiary's interest in the trust is a remote contingent interest. For purposes of this clause, a contingent interest of a beneficiary in a trust shall be considered remote if, under the maximum exercise of discretion by the trustee in favor of such beneficiary, the value of such interest, computed actuarially, is 5 percent or less of the value of the trust property.

(**ii**) Stock owned, directly or indirectly, by or for a person who is considered the owner of any portion of a trust under subpart E of part I of subchapter J (relating to grantors and others treated as substantial owners) shall be considered as owned by the trust.

(**C**) **To corporations.**—If 50 percent or more in value of the stock in a corporation is owned, directly or indirectly, by or for any person, such corporation shall be considered as owning the stock owned, directly or indirectly, by or for such person.

(**4**) **Options.**—If any person has an option to acquire stock, such stock shall be considered as owned by such person. For purposes of this paragraph, an option to acquire such an option, and each one of a series of such options, shall be considered as an option to acquire such stock.

(**5**) **Operating rules.**—

(**A**) **In general.**—Except as provided in subparagraphs (B) and (C), stock constructively owned by a person by reason of the application of paragraph (1), (2), (3), or (4), shall, for purposes of applying paragraphs (1), (2), (3), and (4), be considered as actually owned by such person.

(**B**) **Members of family.**—Stock constructively owned by an individual by reason of the application of paragraph (1) shall not be considered as owned by him for purposes of again applying paragraph (1) in order to make another the constructive owner of such stock.

(**C**) **Partnerships, estates, trusts, and corporations.**—Stock constructively owned by a partnership, estate, trust, or corporation by reason of the application of paragraph (3) shall not be considered as owned by it for purposes of applying paragraph (2) in order to make another the constructive owner of such stock.

(**D**) **Option rule in lieu of family rule.**—For purposes of this paragraph, if stock may be considered as owned by an individual under paragraph (1) or (4), it shall be considered as owned by him under paragraph (4).

(**E**) **S corporation treated as partnership.**—For purposes of this subsection—

(**i**) an S corporation shall be treated as a partnership, and

(**ii**) any shareholder of the S corporation shall be treated as a partner of such partnership.

The preceding sentence shall not apply for purposes of determining whether stock in the S corporation is constructively owned by any person.

(**b**) **Cross references.**—For provisions to which the rules contained in subsection (a) apply, see—

(**1**) section 302 (relating to redemption of stock);

(**2**) section 304 (relating to redemption by related corporations);

(3) section 306(b)(1)(A) (relating to disposition of section 306 stock);

(4) section 338(h)(3) (defining purchase);

(5) section 382(*l*)(3) (relating to special limitations on net operating loss carryovers);

* * *

Part II—Corporate Liquidations

Subpart A—Effects on Recipients

§ 331. Gain or loss to shareholders in corporate liquidations.

(a) Distributions in complete liquidation treated as exchanges.—Amounts received by a shareholder in a distribution in complete liquidation of a corporation shall be treated as in full payment in exchange for the stock.

(b) Nonapplication of section 301.—Section 301 (relating to effects on shareholder of distributions of property) shall not apply to any distribution of property (other than a distribution referred to in paragraph (2)(B) of section 316(b)) in complete liquidation.

(c) Cross reference.—For general rule for determination of the amount of gain or loss recognized, see section 1001.

§ 332. Complete liquidations of subsidiaries.

(a) General rule.—No gain or loss shall be recognized on the receipt by a corporation of property distributed in complete liquidation of another corporation.

(b) Liquidations to which section applies.—For purposes of this section, a distribution shall be considered to be in complete liquidation only if—

(1) the corporation receiving such property was, on the date of the adoption of the plan of liquidation, and has continued to be at all times until the receipt of the property, the owner of stock (in such other corporation) meeting the requirements of section 1504(a)(2); and either

(2) the distribution is by such other corporation in complete cancellation or redemption of all its stock, and the transfer of all the property occurs within the taxable year; in such case the adoption by the shareholders of the resolution under which is authorized the distribution of all the assets of such corporation in complete cancellation or redemption of all its stock shall be considered an adoption of a plan of liquidation, even though no time for the completion of the transfer of the property is specified in such resolution; or

(3) such distribution is one of a series of distributions by such other corporation in complete cancellation or redemption of all its stock in accordance with a plan of liquidation under which the transfer of all the property under the liquidation is to be completed within 3 years from the close of the taxable year during which is made the first of the series of distributions under the plan, except that if such transfer is not completed within such period, or if the taxpayer does not continue qualified under paragraph (1) until the completion of such transfer, no distribution under the plan shall be considered a distribution in complete liquidation.

If such transfer of all the property does not occur within the taxable year, the Secretary may require of the taxpayer such bond, or waiver of the statute of limitations on assessment and collection, or both, as he may deem necessary to insure, if the transfer of the property is not completed within such 3-year period, or if the taxpayer does not continue qualified under paragraph (1) until the completion of such transfer, the assessment and collection of all income taxes then imposed by law for such taxable year or subsequent taxable years, to the extent attributable to property so received. A distribution otherwise constituting a distribution in complete liquidation within the meaning of this subsection shall not be considered as not constituting such a distribution merely because it does not constitute a distribution or liquidation within the meaning of the corporate law under which the distribution is made; and for purposes of this subsection a transfer of property of such other corporation to the taxpayer shall not be considered as not constituting a distribution (or one of a series of distributions) in complete cancellation or redemption of all the stock of such other corporation, merely because the carrying out of the plan involves (A) the transfer under the plan to the taxpayer by such other corporation of property, not attributable to shares owned by the taxpayer, on an exchange described in section 361, and (B) the complete cancellation or redemption under the plan, as a result of exchanges described in section 354, of the shares not owned by the taxpayer.

(c) Deductible liquidating distributions of regulated investment companies and real estate investment trusts.—If a corporation receives a distribution from a regulated investment company or a real estate investment trust which is considered under subsection (b) as being in complete liquidation of such company or trust, then, notwithstanding any other provision of this chapter [26 U.S.C.A. § 1 et seq.], such corporation shall recognize and treat as a dividend from such company or trust an amount equal to the deduction for dividends paid allowable to such company or trust by reason of such distribution.

(d) Recognition of gain on liquidation of certain holding companies.—

(1) In general.—In the case of any distribution to a foreign corporation in complete liquidation of an applicable holding company—

(A) subsection (a) and section 331 shall not apply to such distribution, and

(B) such distribution shall be treated as a distribution to which section 301 applies.

(2) Applicable holding company.—For purposes of this subsection:

(A) In general.—The term "applicable holding company" means any domestic corporation—

(i) which is a common parent of an affiliated group,

(ii) stock of which is directly owned by the distributee foreign corporation,

(iii) substantially all of the assets of which consist of stock in other members of such affiliated group, and

(iv) which has not been in existence at all times during the 5 years immediately preceding the date of the liquidation.

(B) Affiliated group.—For purposes of this subsection, the term "affiliated group" has the meaning given such term by section 1504(a) (without regard to paragraphs (2) and (4) of section 1504(b)).

(3) Coordination with Subpart F.—If the distributee of a distribution described in paragraph (1) is a controlled foreign corporation (as defined in section 957), then notwithstanding paragraph (1) or subsection (a), such distribution shall be treated as a distribution to which section 331 applies.

(4) Regulations.—The Secretary shall provide such regulations as appropriate to prevent the abuse of this subsection, including regulations which provide, for the purposes of clause (iv) of paragraph (2)(A), that a corporation is not in existence for any period unless it is engaged in the active conduct of a trade or business or owns a significant ownership interest in another corporation so engaged.

§ 334. Basis of property received in liquidations.

(a) General rule.—If property is received in a distribution in complete liquidation, and if gain or loss is recognized on receipt of such property, then the basis of the property in the hands of the distributee shall be the fair market value of such property at the time of the distribution.

(b) Liquidation of subsidiary.—

(1) In general. If property is received by a corporate distributee in a distribution in a complete liquidation to which section 332 applies (or in a transfer described in section 337(b)(1)), the basis of such property in the hands of such distributee shall be the same as it would be in the hands of the transferor; except that, in the hands of such distributee—

(A) the basis of such property shall be the fair market value of the property at the time of the distribution in any case in which gain or loss is recognized by the liquidating corporation with respect to such property, and

(B) the basis of any property described in section 362(e)(1)(B) shall be the fair market value of the property at the time of the distribution in any case in which such distributee's aggregate adjusted basis of such property would (but for this subparagraph) exceed the fair market value of such property immediately after such liquidation.

(2) Corporate distributee.—For purposes of this subsection, the term "corporate distributee" means only the corporation which meets the stock ownership requirements specified in section 332(b).

Subpart B—Effects on Corporation

§ 336. Gain or loss recognized on property distributed in complete liquidation.

(a) General rule.—Except as otherwise provided in this section or section 337, gain or loss shall be recognized to a liquidating corporation on the distribution of property in complete liquidation as if such property were sold to the distributee at its fair market value.

(b) Treatment of liabilities.—If any property distributed in the liquidation is subject to a liability or the shareholder assumes a liability of the liquidating corporation in connection with the distribution, for purposes of subsection (a) and section 337, the fair market value of such property shall be treated as not less than the amount of such liability.

(c) Exception for liquidations which are part of a reorganization.—For provision providing that this subpart does not apply to distributions in pursuance of a plan of reorganization, see section 361(c)(4).

(d) Limitations on recognition of loss.—

(1) No loss recognized in certain distributions to related persons.—

(A) In general.—No loss shall be recognized to a liquidating corporation on the distribution of any property to a related person (within the meaning of section 267) if—

(i) such distribution is not pro rata, or

(ii) such property is disqualified property.

(B) Disqualified property.—For purposes of subparagraph (A), the term "disqualified property" means any property which is acquired by the liquidating corporation in a transaction to which section 351 applied, or as a contribution to capital, during the 5-year period ending on the date of the distribution. Such term includes any property if the adjusted basis of such property is determined (in whole or in part) by reference to the adjusted basis of property described in the preceding sentence.

(2) Special rule for certain property acquired in certain carryover basis transactions.—

(A) In general.—For purposes of determining the amount of loss recognized by any liquidating corporation on any sale, exchange, or distribution of property described in subparagraph (B), the adjusted basis of such property shall be reduced (but not below zero) by the excess (if any) of—

(i) the adjusted basis of such property immediately after its acquisition by such corporation, over

(ii) the fair market value of such property as of such time.

(B) Description of property.—

(i) **In general.**—For purposes of subparagraph (A), property is described in this subparagraph if—

(I) such property is acquired by the liquidating corporation in a transaction to which section 351 applied or as a contribution to capital, and

(II) the acquisition of such property by the liquidating corporation was part of a plan a principal purpose of which was to recognize loss by the liquidating corporation with respect to such property in connection with the liquidation.

Other property shall be treated as so described if the adjusted basis of such other property is determined (in whole or in part) by reference to the adjusted basis of property described in the preceding sentence.

(ii) **Certain acquisitions treated as part of plan.**—For purposes of clause (i), any property described in clause (i)(I) acquired by the liquidated corporation after the date 2 years before the date of the adoption of the plan of complete liquidation shall, except as provided in regulations, be treated as acquired as part of a plan described in clause (i)(II).

(C) Recapture in lieu of disallowance.—The Secretary may prescribe regulations under which, in lieu of disallowing a loss under subparagraph (A) for a prior taxable year, the gross income of the liquidating corporation for the taxable year in which the plan of complete liquidation is adopted shall be increased by the amount of the disallowed loss.

(3) Special rule in case of liquidation to which section 332 applies.—In the case of any liquidation to which section 332 applies, no loss shall be recognized to the liquidating corporation on any distribution in such liquidation. The preceding sentence shall apply to any distribution to the 80-percent distributee only if subsection (a) or (b)(1) of section 337 applies to such distribution.

(e) Certain stock sales and distributions may be treated as asset transfers. — Under regulations prescribed by the Secretary, if —

(1) a corporation owns stock in another corporation meeting the requirements of section 1504(a)(2), and

(2) such corporation sells, exchanges, or distributes all of such stock,

an election may be made to treat such sale, exchange, or distribution as a disposition of all of the assets of such other corporation, and no gain or loss shall be recognized on the sale, exchange, or distribution of such stock.

§ 337. Nonrecognition for property distributed to parent in complete liquidation of subsidiary.

(a) In general. — No gain or loss shall be recognized to the liquidating corporation on the distribution to the 80-percent distributee of any property in a complete liquidation to which section 332 applies.

(b) Treatment of indebtedness of subsidiary, etc. —

(1) Indebtedness of subsidiary to parent. — If —

(A) a corporation is liquidated in a liquidation to which section 332 applies, and

(B) on the date of the adoption of the plan of liquidation, such corporation was indebted to the 80-percent distributee,

for purposes of this section and section 336, any transfer of property to the 80-percent distributee in satisfaction of such indebtedness shall be treated as a distribution to such distributee in such liquidation.

* * *

(c) 80-percent distributee. — For purposes of this section, the term "80-percent distributee" means only the corporation which meets the 80-percent stock ownership requirements specified in section 332(b). For purposes of this section, the determination of whether any corporation is an 80-percent distributee shall be made without regard to any consolidated return regulation.

* * *

§ 338. Certain stock purchases treated as asset acquisitions.

(a) General rule. — For purposes of this subtitle, if a purchasing corporation makes an election under this section (or is treated under subsection (e) as having made such an election), then, in the case of any qualified stock purchase, the target corporation —

(1) shall be treated as having sold all of its assets at the close of the acquisition date at fair market value in a single transaction, and

(2) shall be treated as a new corporation which purchased all of the assets referred to in paragraph (1) as of the beginning of the day after the acquisition date.

(b) Basis of assets after deemed purchase. —

(1) In general.—For purposes of subsection (a), the assets of the target corporation shall be treated as purchased for an amount equal to the sum of—

(A) the grossed-up basis of the purchasing corporation's recently purchased stock, and

(B) the basis of the purchasing corporation's nonrecently purchased stock.

(2) Adjustment for liabilities and other relevant items.—The amount described in paragraph (1) shall be adjusted under regulations prescribed by the Secretary for liabilities of the target corporation and other relevant items.

(3) Election to step-up the basis of certain target stock.—

(A) **In general.**—Under regulations prescribed by the Secretary, the basis of the purchasing corporation's nonrecently purchased stock shall be the basis amount determined under subparagraph (B) of this paragraph if the purchasing corporation makes an election to recognize gain as if such stock were sold on the acquisition date for an amount equal to the basis amount determined under subparagraph (B).

(B) **Determination of basis amount.**—For purposes of subparagraph (A), the basis amount determined under this subparagraph shall be an amount equal to the grossed-up basis determined under subparagraph (A) of paragraph (1) multiplied by a fraction—

(i) the numerator of which is the percentage of stock (by value) in the target corporation attributable to the purchasing corporation's nonrecently purchased stock, and

(ii) the denominator of which is 100 percent minus the percentage referred to in clause (i).

(4) Grossed-up basis.—For purposes of paragraph (1), the grossed-up basis shall be an amount equal to the basis of the corporation's recently purchased stock, multiplied by a fraction—

(A) the numerator of which is 100 percent, minus the percentage of stock (by value) in the target corporation attributable to the purchasing corporation's nonrecently purchased stock, and

(B) the denominator of which is the percentage of stock (by value) in the target corporation attributable to the purchasing corporation's recently purchased stock.

(5) Allocation among assets.—The amount determined under paragraphs (1) and (2) shall be allocated among the assets of the target corporation under regulations prescribed by the Secretary.

(6) Definitions of recently purchased stock and nonrecently purchased stock.—For purposes of this subsection—

(A) **Recently purchased stock.**—The term "recently purchased stock" means any stock in the target corporation which is held by the purchasing corporation on the acquisition date and which was purchased by such corporation during the 12-month acquisition period.

(B) **Nonrecently purchased stock.**—The term "nonrecently purchased stock" means any stock in the target corporation which is held by the purchasing corporation on the acquisition date and which is not recently purchased stock.

[(c) Repealed.]

(d) Purchasing corporation; target corporation; qualified stock purchase.—For purposes of this section—

(1) Purchasing corporation.—The term "purchasing corporation" means any corporation which makes a qualified stock purchase of stock of another corporation.

(2) Target corporation.—The term "target corporation" means any corporation the stock of which is acquired by another corporation in a qualified stock purchase.

(3) Qualified stock purchase.—The term "qualified stock purchase" means any transaction or series of transactions in which stock (meeting the requirements of section 1504(a)(2)) of 1 corporation is acquired by another corporation by purchase during the 12-month acquisition period.

(e) Deemed election where purchasing corporation acquires asset of target corporation.—

(1) In general.—A purchasing corporation shall be treated as having made an election under this section with respect to any target corporation if, at any time during the consistency period, it acquires any asset of the target corporation (or a target affiliate).

(2) Exceptions.—Paragraph (1) shall not apply with respect to any acquisition by the purchasing corporation if—

(A) such acquisition is pursuant to a sale by the target corporation (or the target affiliate) in the ordinary course of its trade or business,

(B) the basis of the property acquired is determined wholly by reference to the adjusted basis of such property in the hands of the person from whom acquired,

(C) such acquisition was before September 1, 1982, or

(D) such acquisition is described in regulations prescribed by the Secretary and meets such conditions as such regulations may provide.

(3) Anti-avoidance rule.—Whenever necessary to carry out the purpose of this subsection and subsection (f), the Secretary may treat stock acquisitions which are pursuant to a plan and which meet the requirements of section 1504(a)(2) as qualified stock purchases.

(f) Consistency required for all stock acquisitions from same affiliated group.—If a purchasing corporation makes qualified stock purchases with respect to the target corporation and 1 or more target affiliates during any consistency period, then (except as otherwise provided in subsection (e))—

(1) any election under this section with respect to the first such purchase shall apply to each other such purchase, and

(2) no election may be made under this section with respect to the second or subsequent such purchase if such an election was not made with respect to the first such purchase.

(g) Election.—

(1) When made.—Except as otherwise provided in regulations, an election under this section shall be made not later than the 15th day of the 9th month beginning after the month in which the acquisition date occurs.

(2) Manner.—An election by the purchasing corporation under this section shall be made in such manner as the Secretary shall by regulations prescribe.

(3) Election irrevocable.—An election by a purchasing corporation under this section, once made, shall be irrevocable.

(h) Definitions and special rules.—For purposes of this section—

(1) 12-month acquisition period.—The term "12-month acquisition period" means the 12-month period beginning with the date of the first acquisition by purchase of stock included in a qualified stock purchase (or, if any of such stock was acquired in an acquisition which is a purchase by reason of subparagraph (C) of paragraph (3), the date on which the acquiring corporation is first considered under section 318(a) (other than paragraph (4) thereof) as owning stock owned by the corporation from which such acquisition was made).

(2) Acquisition date.—The term "acquisition date" means, with respect to any corporation, the first day on which there is a qualified stock purchase with respect to the stock of such corporation.

(3) Purchase.—

    (A) In general.—The term "purchase" means any acquisition of stock, but only if—

        (i) the basis of the stock in the hands of the purchasing corporation is not determined (I) in whole or in part by reference to the adjusted basis of such stock in the hands of the person from whom acquired, or (II) under section 1014(a) (relating to property acquired from a decedent),

        (ii) the stock is not acquired in an exchange to which section 351, 354, 355, or 356 applies and is not acquired in any other transaction described in regulations in which the transferor does not recognize the entire amount of the gain or loss realized on the transaction, and

        (iii) the stock is not acquired from a person the ownership of whose stock would, under section 318(a) (other than paragraph (4) thereof), be attributed to the person acquiring such stock.

    (B) Deemed purchase under subsection (a).—The term "purchase" includes any deemed purchase under subsection (a)(2). The acquisition date for a corporation which is deemed purchased under subsection (a)(2) shall be determined under regulations prescribed by the Secretary.

    (C) Certain stock acquisitions from related corporations.—

        (i) In general.—Clause (iii) of subparagraph (A) shall not apply to an acquisition of stock from a related corporation if at least 50 percent in value of the stock of such related corporation was acquired by purchase (within the meaning of subparagraphs (A) and (B)).

        (ii) Certain distributions.—Clause (i) of subparagraph (A) shall not apply to an acquisition of stock described in clause (i) of this subparagraph if the corporation acquiring such stock—

            (I) made a qualified stock purchase of stock of the related corporation, and

            (II) made an election under this section (or is treated under subsection (e) as having made such an election) with respect to such qualified stock purchase.

        (iii) Related corporation defined.—For purposes of this subparagraph, a corporation is a related corporation if stock owned by such corporation is treated (under section 318(a) other than paragraph (4) thereof) as owned by the corporation acquiring the stock.

(4) Consistency period.—

(A) In general.—Except as provided in subparagraph (B), the term "consistency period" means the period consisting of—

(i) the 1-year period before the beginning of the 12-month acquisition period for the target corporation,

(ii) such acquisition period (up to and including the acquisition date), and

(iii) the 1-year period beginning on the day after the acquisition date.

(B) Extension where there is plan.—The period referred to in subparagraph (A) shall also include any period during which the Secretary determines that there was in effect a plan to make a qualified stock purchase plus 1 or more other qualified stock purchases (or asset acquisitions described in subsection (e)) with respect to the target corporation or any target affiliate.

(5) Affiliated group.—The term "affiliated group" has the meaning given to such term by section 1504(a) (determined without regard to the exceptions contained in section 1504(b)).

(6) Target affiliate.—

(A) In general.—A corporation shall be treated as a target affiliate of the target corporation if each of such corporations was, at any time during so much of the consistency period as ends on the acquisition date of the target corporation, a member of an affiliated group which had the same common parent.

* * *

(8) Acquisitions by affiliated group treated as made by 1 corporation.—Except as provided in regulations prescribed by the Secretary, stock and asset acquisitions made by members of the same affiliated group shall be treated as made by 1 corporation.

(9) Target not treated as member of affiliated group.—Except as otherwise provided in paragraph (10) or in regulations prescribed under this paragraph, the target corporation shall not be treated as a member of an affiliated group with respect to the sale described in subsection (a)(1).

(10) Elective recognition of gain or loss by target corporation, together with nonrecognition of gain or loss on stock sold by selling consolidated group.—

(A) In general.—Under regulations prescribed by the Secretary, an election may be made under which if—

(i) the target corporation was, before the transaction, a member of the selling consolidated group, and

(ii) the target corporation recognizes gain or loss with respect to the transaction as if it sold all of its assets in a single transaction,

then the target corporation shall be treated as a member of the selling consolidated group with respect to such sale, and (to the extent provided in regulations) no gain or loss will be recognized on stock sold or exchanged in the transaction by members of the selling consolidated group.

(B) Selling consolidated group.—For purposes of subparagraph (A), the term "selling consolidated group" means any group of corporations which (for the taxable period which includes the transaction)—

    (i) includes the target corporation, and

    (ii) files a consolidated return.

To the extent provided in regulations, such term also includes any affiliated group of corporations which includes the target corporation (whether or not such group files a consolidated return).

(C) Information required to be furnished to the Secretary.—Under regulations, where an election is made under subparagraph (A), the purchasing corporation and the common parent of the selling consolidated group shall, at such times and in such manner as may be provided in regulations, furnish to the Secretary the following information:

    (i) The amount allocated under subsection (b)(5) to goodwill or going concern value.

    (ii) Any modification of the amount described in clause (i).

    (iii) Any other information as the Secretary deems necessary to carry out the provisions of this paragraph.

(11) Elective formula for determining fair market value.—For purposes of subsection (a)(1), fair market value may be determined on the basis of a formula provided in regulations prescribed by the Secretary which takes into account liabilities and other relevant items.

* * *

(15) Combined deemed sale return.—Under regulations prescribed by the Secretary, a combined deemed sale return may be filed by all target corporations acquired by a purchasing corporation on the same acquisition date if such target corporations were members of the same selling consolidated group (as defined in subparagraph (B) of paragraph (10)).

* * *

(i) Regulations.—The Secretary shall prescribe such regulations as may be necessary or appropriate to carry out the purposes of this section, including—

(1) regulations to ensure that the purpose of this section to require consistency of treatment of stock and asset sales and purchases may not be circumvented through the use of any provision of law or regulations (including the consolidated return regulations) and

(2) regulations providing for the coordination of the provisions of this section with the provision of this title relating to foreign corporations and their shareholders.

* * *

Subpart D—Definition and Special Rule

§ 346. Definition and special rule.

(a) Complete liquidation.—For purposes of this subchapter, a distribution shall be treated as in complete liquidation of a corporation if the distribution is one of a series of distributions in redemption of all of the stock of the corporation pursuant to a plan.

(b) Transactions which might reach same result as partial liquidations.—The Secretary shall prescribe such regulations as may be necessary to ensure that the purposes of subsections (a) and (b) of section 222 of the Tax Equity and Fiscal Responsibility Act of 1982 (which repeal the special tax treatment for partial liquidations) may not be circumvented through the use of section 355, 351, or any other provision of law or regulations (including the consolidated return regulations).

Part III—Corporate Organizations and Reorganizations

Subpart A—Corporate Organizations

§ 351. Transfer to corporation controlled by transferor.

(a) General rule.—No gain or loss shall be recognized if property is transferred to a corporation by one or more persons solely in exchange for stock in such corporation and immediately after the exchange such person or persons are in control (as defined in section 368(c)) of the corporation.

(b) Receipt of property.—If subsection (a) would apply to an exchange but for the fact that there is received, in addition to the stock permitted to be received under subsection (a), other property or money, then—

    (1) gain (if any) to such recipient shall be recognized, but not in excess of—

        (A) the amount of money received, plus

        (B) the fair market value of such other property received; and

    (2) no loss to such recipient shall be recognized.

(c) Special rules where distribution to shareholders.—

    (1) In general.—In determining control for purposes of this section, the fact that any corporate transferor distributes part or all of the stock in the corporation which it receives in the exchange to its shareholders shall not be taken into account.

    (2) Special rule for section 355.—If the requirements of section 355 (or so much of section 356 as relates to section 355) are met with respect to a distribution described in paragraph (1), then, solely for purposes of determining the tax treatment of the transfers of property to the controlled corporation by the distributing corporation, the fact that the shareholders of the distributing corporation dispose of part or all of the distributed stock, or the fact that the corporation whose stock was distributed issues additional stock, shall not be taken into account in determining control for purposes of this section.

(d) Services, certain indebtedness, and accrued interest not treated as property.—For purposes of this section, stock issued for—

    (1) services,

    (2) indebtedness of the transferee corporation which is not evidenced by a security, or

    (3) interest on indebtedness of the transferee corporation which accrued on or after the beginning of the transferor's holding period for the debt,

shall not be considered as issued in return for property.

(e) Exceptions.—This section shall not apply to—

(1) Transfer of property to an investment company.—A transfer of property to an investment company. For purposes of the preceding sentence, the determination of whether a company is an investment company shall be made—

　(A) by taking into account all stock and securities held by the company, and

　(B) by treating as stock and securities—

　　(i) money,

　　(ii) stocks and other equity interests in a corporation, evidences of indebtedness, options, forward or futures contracts, notional principal contracts and derivatives,

　　(iii) any foreign currency,

　　(iv) any interest in a real estate investment trust, a common trust fund, a regulated investment company, a publicly-traded partnership (as defined in section 7704(b)) or any other equity interest (other than in a corporation) which pursuant to its terms or any other arrangement is readily convertible into, or exchangeable for, any asset described in any preceding clause, this clause or clause (v) or (viii),

　　(v) except to the extent provided in regulations prescribed by the Secretary, any interest in a precious metal, unless such metal is used or held in the active conduct of a trade or business after the contribution,

　　(vi) except as otherwise provided in regulations prescribed by the Secretary, interests in any entity if substantially all of the assets of such entity consist (directly or indirectly) of any assets described in any preceding clause or clause (viii),

　　(vii) to the extent provided in regulations prescribed by the Secretary, any interest in any entity not described in clause (vi), but only to the extent of the value of such interest that is attributable to assets listed in clauses (i) through (v) or clause (viii), or

　　(viii) any other asset specified in regulations prescribed by the Secretary.

The Secretary may prescribe regulations that, under appropriate circumstances, treat any asset described in clauses (i) through (v) as not so listed.

(2) Title 11 or similar case.—A transfer of property of a debtor pursuant to a plan while the debtor is under the jurisdiction of a court in a title 11 or similar case (within the meaning of section 368(a)(3)(A)), to the extent that the stock received in the exchange is used to satisfy the indebtedness of such debtor.

(f) Treatment of controlled corporation.—If—

　(1) property is transferred to a corporation (hereinafter in this subsection referred to as the "controlled corporation") in an exchange with respect to which gain or loss is not recognized (in whole or in part) to the transferor under this section, and

　(2) such exchange is not in pursuance of a plan of reorganization,

section 311 shall apply to any transfer in such exchange by the controlled corporation in the same manner as if such transfer were a distribution to which subpart A of part I applies.

(g) Nonqualified preferred stock not treated as stock.—

　(1) In general.—In the case of a person who transfers property to a corporation and receives nonqualified preferred stock—

(A) subsection (a) shall not apply to such transferor, and

(B) if (and only if) the transferor receives stock other than nonqualified preferred stock—

(i) subsection (b) shall apply to such transferor; and

(ii) such nonqualified preferred stock shall be treated as other property for purposes of applying subsection (b).

(2) **Nonqualified preferred stock.**—For purposes of paragraph (1)—

(A) **In general.**—The term "nonqualified preferred stock" means preferred stock if—

(i) the holder of such stock has the right to require the issuer or a related person to redeem or purchase the stock,

(ii) the issuer or a related person is required to redeem or purchase such stock,

(iii) the issuer or a related person has the right to redeem or purchase the stock and, as of the issue date, it is more likely than not that such right will be exercised, or

(iv) the dividend rate on such stock varies in whole or in part (directly or indirectly) with reference to interest rates, commodity prices, or other similar indices.

(B) **Limitations.**—Clauses (i), (ii), and (iii) of subparagraph (A) shall apply only if the right or obligation referred to therein may be exercised within the 20-year period beginning on the issue date of such stock and such right or obligation is not subject to a contingency which, as of the issue date, makes remote the likelihood of the redemption or purchase.

(C) **Exceptions for certain rights or obligations.**—

(i) **In general.**—A right or obligation shall not be treated as described in clause (i), (ii), or (iii) of subparagraph (A) if—

(I) it may be exercised only upon the death, disability, or mental incompetency of the holder, or

(II) in the case of a right or obligation to redeem or purchase stock transferred in connection with the performance of services for the issuer or a related person (and which represents reasonable compensation), it may be exercised only upon the holder's separation from service from the issuer or a related person.

(ii) **Exception.**—Clause (i)(I) shall not apply if the stock relinquished in the exchange, or the stock acquired in the exchange is in—

(I) a corporation if any class of stock in such corporation or a related party is readily tradable on an established securities market or otherwise, or

(II) any other corporation if such exchange is part of a transaction or series of transactions in which such corporation is to become a corporation described in subclause (I).

(3) **Definitions.**—For purposes of this subsection—

(A) **Preferred stock.**—The term "preferred stock" means stock which is limited and preferred as to dividends and does not participate in corporate growth to any significant extent. Stock shall not be treated as participating in corporate growth to any significant extent unless there is a real and meaningful likelihood of the shareholder actually participating in the earnings and growth of the corporation.

(B) Related person.—A person shall be treated as related to another person if they bear a relationship to such other person described in section 267(b) or 707(b).

(4) Regulations.—The Secretary may prescribe such regulations as may be necessary or appropriate to carry out the purposes of this subsection and sections 354(a)(2)(C), 355(a)(3)(D), and 356(e). The Secretary may also prescribe regulations, consistent with the treatment under this subsection and such sections, for the treatment of nonqualified preferred stock under other provisions of this title.

(h) Cross references.—

(1) For special rule where another party to the exchange assumes a liability, see section 357.

(2) For the basis of stock or property received in an exchange to which this section applies, see sections 358 and 362.

(3) For special rule in the case of an exchange described in this section but which results in a gift, see section 2501 and following.

(4) For special rule in the case of an exchange described in this section but which has the effect of the payment of compensation by the corporation or by a transferor, see section 61(a)(1).

(5) For coordination of this section with section 304, see section 304(b)(3).

Subpart B—Effects on Shareholders and Security Holders

§ 354. Exchanges of stock and securities in certain reorganizations.

(a) General rule.—

(1) In general.—No gain or loss shall be recognized if stock or securities in a corporation a party to a reorganization are, in pursuance of the plan of reorganization, exchanged solely for stock or securities in such corporation or in another corporation a party to the reorganization.

(2) Limitations.—

(A) Excess principal amount.—Paragraph (1) shall not apply if—

(i) the principal amount of any such securities received exceeds the principal amount of any such securities surrendered, or

(ii) any such securities are received and no such securities are surrendered.

(B) Property attributable to accrued interest.—Neither paragraph (1) nor so much of section 356 as relates to paragraph (1) shall apply to the extent that any stock (including nonqualified preferred stock, as defined in section 351(g)(2)), securities, or other property received is attributable to interest which has accrued on securities on or after the beginning of the holder's holding period.

(C) Nonqualified preferred stock.—

(i) In general.—Nonqualified preferred stock (as defined in section 351(g)(2)) received in exchange for stock other than nonqualified preferred stock (as so defined) shall not be treated as stock or securities.

(ii) Recapitalizations of family-owned corporations.—

(I) In general.—Clause (i) shall not apply in the case of a recapitalization under section 368(a)(1)(E) of a family-owned corporation.

(II) Family-owned corporation.—For purposes of this clause, except as provided in regulations, the term "family-owned corporation" means any corporation which is described in clause (i) of section 447(d)(2)(C) throughout the 8-year period beginning on the date which is 5 years before the date of the recapitalization. For purposes of the preceding sentence, stock shall not be treated as owned by a family member during any period described in section 355(d)(6)(B).

(III) Extension of statute of limitations.—The statutory period for the assessment of any deficiency attributable to a corporation failing to be a family-owned corporation shall not expire before the expiration of 3 years after the date the Secretary is notified by the corporation (in such manner as the Secretary may prescribe) of such failure, and such deficiency may be assessed before the expiration of such 3-year period notwithstanding the provisions of any other law or rule of law which would otherwise prevent such assessment.

(3) Cross references.—

(A) For treatment of the exchange if any property is received which is not permitted to be received under this subsection (including an excess principal amount of securities received over securities surrendered, but not including nonqualified preferred stock and property to which paragraph (2)(B) applies), see section 356.

(B) For treatment of accrued interest in the case of an exchange described in paragraph (2)(B), see section 61.

(b) Exception.—

(1) In general.—Subsection (a) shall not apply to an exchange in pursuance of a plan of reorganization within the meaning of subparagraph (D) or (G) of section 368(a)(1), unless—

(A) the corporation to which the assets are transferred acquires substantially all of the assets of the transferor of such assets; and

(B) the stock, securities, and other properties received by such transferor, as well as the other properties of such transferor, are distributed in pursuance of the plan of reorganization.

(2) Cross reference.—For special rules for certain exchanges in pursuance of plans of reorganization within the meaning of subparagraph (D) or (G) of section 368(a)(1), see section 355.

* * *

§ 355. Distribution of stock and securities of a controlled corporation.

(a) Effect on distributees.—

(1) General rule.—If—

(A) a corporation (referred to in this section as the "distributing corporation")—

    (i) distributes to a shareholder, with respect to its stock, or

    (ii) distributes to a security holder, in exchange for its securities,

solely stock or securities of a corporation (referred to in this section as "controlled corporation") which it controls immediately before the distribution,

(B) the transaction was not used principally as a device for the distribution of the earnings and profits of the distributing corporation or the controlled corporation or both (but the mere fact that subsequent to the distribution stock or securities in one or more of such corporations are sold or exchanged by all or some of the distributees (other than pursuant to an arrangement negotiated or agreed upon prior to such distribution) shall not be construed to mean that the transaction was used principally as such a device),

(C) the requirements of subsection (b) (relating to active businesses) are satisfied, and

(D) as part of the distribution, the distributing corporation distributes—

    (i) all of the stock and securities in the controlled corporation held by it immediately before the distribution, or

    (ii) an amount of stock in the controlled corporation constituting control within the meaning of section 368(c), and it is established to the satisfaction of the Secretary that the retention by the distributing corporation of stock (or stock and securities) in the controlled corporation was not in pursuance of a plan having as one of its principal purposes the avoidance of Federal income tax,

then no gain or loss shall be recognized to (and no amount shall be includible in the income of) such shareholder or security holder on the receipt of such stock or securities.

(2) Non pro rata distributions, etc.—Paragraph (1) shall be applied without regard to the following:

(A) whether or not the distribution is pro rata with respect to all of the shareholders of the distributing corporation,

(B) whether or not the shareholder surrenders stock in the distributing corporation, and

(C) whether or not the distribution is in pursuance of a plan of reorganization (within the meaning of section 368(a)(1)(D)).

(3) Limitations.—

(A) Excess principal amount.—Paragraph (1) shall not apply if—

    (i) the principal amount of the securities in the controlled corporation which are received exceeds the principal amount of the securities which are surrendered in connection with such distribution, or

    (ii) securities in the controlled corporation are received and no securities are surrendered in connection with such distribution.

(B) Stock acquired in taxable transactions within 5 years treated as boot.—For purposes of this section (other than paragraph (1)(D) of this subsection) and so much of section 356 as relates to this section, stock of a controlled corporation acquired by the distributing corporation by reason of any transaction—

(i) which occurs within 5 years of the distribution of such stock, and

(ii) in which gain or loss was recognized in whole or in part, shall not be treated as stock of such controlled corporation, but as other property.

(C) **Property attributable to accrued interest.**—Neither paragraph (1) nor so much of section 356 as relates to paragraph (1) shall apply to the extent that any stock (including nonqualified preferred stock, as defined in section 351(g)(2)), securities, or other property received is attributable to interest which has accrued on securities on or after the beginning of the holder's holding period.

(D) **Nonqualified preferred stock.**—Nonqualified preferred stock (as defined in section 351(g)(2)) received in a distribution with respect to stock other than nonqualified preferred stock (as so defined) shall not be treated as stock or securities.

(4) Cross references.—

(A) For treatment of the exchange if any property is received which is not permitted to be received under this subsection (including an excess principal amount of securities received over securities surrendered, but not including nonqualified preferred stock and property to which paragraph (3)(C) applies), see section 356.

(B) For treatment of accrued interest in the case of an exchange described in paragraph (3)(C), see section 61.

(b) Requirements as to active business.—

(1) In general.—Subsection (a) shall apply only if either—

(A) the distributing corporation, and the controlled corporation (or, if stock of more than one controlled corporation is distributed, each of such corporations), is engaged immediately after the distribution in the active conduct of a trade or business, or

(B) immediately before the distribution, the distributing corporation had no assets other than stock or securities in the controlled corporations and each of the controlled corporations is engaged immediately after the distribution in the active conduct of a trade or business.

(2) Definition.—For purposes of paragraph (1), a corporation shall be treated as engaged in the active conduct of a trade or business if and only if—

(A) it is engaged in the active conduct of a trade or business,

(B) such trade or business has been actively conducted throughout the 5-year period ending on the date of the distribution,

(C) such trade or business was not acquired within the period described in subparagraph (B) in a transaction in which gain or loss was recognized in whole or in part, and

(D) control of a corporation which (at the time of acquisition of control) was conducting such trade or business—

(i) was not acquired by any distributee corporation directly (or through 1 or more corporations, whether through the distributing corporation or otherwise) within the period described in subparagraph (B) and was not acquired by the distributing corporation directly (or through 1 or more corporations) within such period, or

(ii) was so acquired by any such corporation within such period, but, in each case in which such control was so acquired, it was so acquired, only by reason of transactions in which gain or loss was not recognized in whole or in part, or only by reason of such transactions combined with acquisitions before the beginning of such period.

For purposes of subparagraph (D), all distributee corporations which are members of the same affiliated group (as defined in section 1504(a) without regard to section 1504(b)) shall be treated as 1 distributee corporation.

(3) Special rules for determining active conduct in the case of affiliated groups.—

(A) In general.—For purposes of determining whether a corporation meets the requirements of paragraph (2)(A), all members of such corporation's separate affiliated group shall be treated as one corporation.

(B) Separate affiliated group.—For purposes of this paragraph, the term 'separate affiliated group' means, with respect to any corporation, the affiliated group which would be determined under section 1504(a) if such corporation were the common parent and section 1504(b) did not apply.

(C) Treatment of trade or business conducted by acquired member.—If a corporation became a member of a separate affiliated group as a result of one or more transactions in which gain or loss was recognized in whole or in part, any trade or business conducted by such corporation (at the time that such corporation became such a member) shall be treated for purposes of paragraph (2) as acquired in a transaction in which gain or loss was recognized in whole or in part.

(D) Regulations.—The Secretary shall prescribe such regulations as are necessary or appropriate to carry out the purposes of this paragraph, including regulations which provide for the proper application of subparagraphs (B), (C), and (D) of paragraph (2), and modify the application of subsection (a)(3)(B), in connection with the application of this paragraph.

(c) Taxability of corporation on distribution.—

(1) In general.—Except as provided in paragraph (2), no gain or loss shall be recognized to a corporation on any distribution to which this section (or so much of section 356 as relates to this section) applies and which is not in pursuance of a plan of reorganization.

(2) Distribution of appreciated property.—

(A) In general.—If—

(i) in a distribution referred to in paragraph (1), the corporation distributes property other than qualified property, and

(ii) the fair market value of such property exceeds its adjusted basis (in the hands of the distributing corporation),

then gain shall be recognized to the distributing corporation as if such property were sold to the distributee at its fair market value.

(B) Qualified property.—For purposes of subparagraph (A), the term "qualified property" means any stock or securities in the controlled corporation.

(C) Treatment of liabilities.—If any property distributed in the distribution referred to in paragraph (1) is subject to a liability or the shareholder assumes a liability of the distributing corporation in connection with the distribution, then, for purposes of subparagraph (A), the fair market value of such property shall be treated as not less than the amount of such liability.

(3) Coordination with sections 311 and 336(a).—Sections 311 and 336(a) shall not apply to any distribution referred to in paragraph (1).

(d) Recognition of gain on certain distributions of stock or securities in controlled corporation.—

(1) In general.—In the case of a disqualified distribution, any stock or securities in the controlled corporation shall not be treated as qualified property for purposes of subsection (c)(2) of this section or section 361(c)(2).

(2) Disqualified distribution.—For purposes of this subsection, the term "disqualified distribution" means any distribution to which this section (or so much of section 356 as relates to this section) applies if, immediately after the distribution—

    (A) any person holds disqualified stock in the distributing corporation which constitutes a 50-percent or greater interest in such corporation, or

    (B) any person holds disqualified stock in the controlled corporation (or, if stock of more than 1 controlled corporation is distributed, in any controlled corporation) which constitutes a 50-percent or greater interest in such corporation.

(3) Disqualified stock.—For purposes of this subsection, the term "disqualified stock" means—

    (A) any stock in the distributing corporation acquired by purchase during the 5-year period ending on the date of the distribution, and

    (B) any stock in any controlled corporation—

        (i) acquired by purchase during the 5-year period ending on the date of the distribution, or

        (ii) received in the distribution to the extent attributable to distributions on—

            (I) stock described in subparagraph (A), or

            (II) any securities in the distributing corporation acquired by purchase during the 5-year period ending on the date of the distribution.

(4) 50-percent or greater interest.—For purposes of this subsection, the term "50-percent or greater interest" means stock possessing at least 50 percent of the total combined voting power of all classes of stock entitled to vote or at least 50 percent of the total value of shares of all classes of stock.

(5) Purchase.—For purposes of this subsection—

    (A) In general.—Except as otherwise provided in this paragraph, the term "purchase" means any acquisition but only if—

        (i) the basis of the property acquired in the hands of the acquirer is not determined (I) in whole or in part by reference to the adjusted basis of such property in the hands of the person from whom acquired, or (II) under section 1014(a), and

(ii) the property is not acquired in an exchange to which section 351, 354, 355, or 356 applies.

(B) Certain section 351 exchanges treated as purchases.—The term "purchase" includes any acquisition of property in an exchange to which section 351 applies to the extent such property is acquired in exchange for—

(i) any cash or cash item,

(ii) any marketable stock or security, or

(iii) any debt of the transferor.

(C) Carryover basis transactions.—If—

(i) any person acquires property from another person who acquired such property by purchase (as determined under this paragraph with regard to this subparagraph), and

(ii) the adjusted basis of such property in the hands of such acquirer is determined in whole or in part by reference to the adjusted basis of such property in the hands of such other person,

such acquirer shall be treated as having acquired such property by purchase on the date it was so acquired by such other person.

(6) Special rule where substantial diminution of risk.—

(A) In general.—If this paragraph applies to any stock or securities for any period, the running of any 5-year period set forth in subparagraph (A) or (B) of paragraph (3) (whichever applies) shall be suspended during such period.

(B) Property to which suspension applies.—This paragraph applies to any stock or securities for any period during which the holder's risk of loss with respect to such stock or securities, or with respect to any portion of the activities of the corporation, is (directly or indirectly) substantially diminished by—

(i) an option,

(ii) a short sale,

(iii) any special class of stock, or

(iv) any other device or transaction.

(7) Aggregation rules.—

(A) In general.—For purposes of this subsection, a person and all persons related to such person (within the meaning of section 267(b) or 707(b)(1)) shall be treated as one person.

(B) Persons acting pursuant to plans or arrangements.—If two or more persons act pursuant to a plan or arrangement with respect to acquisitions of stock or securities in the distributing corporation or controlled corporation, such persons shall be treated as one person for purposes of this subsection.

(8) Attribution from entities.—

(A) In general.—Paragraph (2) of section 318(a) shall apply in determining whether a person holds stock or securities in any corporation (determined by substituting "10 percent" for "50 percent" in subparagraph (C) of such paragraph (2) and by treating any reference to stock as including a reference to securities).

(B) Deemed purchase rule.—If—

(i) any person acquires by purchase an interest in any entity, and

(ii) such person is treated under subparagraph (A) as holding any stock or securities by reason of holding such interest, such stock or securities shall be treated as acquired by purchase by such person on the later of the date of the purchase of the interest in such entity or the date such stock or securities are acquired by purchase by such entity.

(9) Regulations.—The Secretary shall prescribe such regulations as may be necessary to carry out the purposes of this subsection, including—

(A) regulations to prevent the avoidance of the purposes of this subsection through the use of related persons, intermediaries, pass-thru entities, options, or other arrangements, and

(B) regulations modifying the definition of the term "purchase".

(e) Recognition of gain on certain distributions of stock or securities in connection with acquisitions.—

(1) General rule.—If there is a distribution to which this subsection applies, any stock or securities in the controlled corporation shall not be treated as qualified property for purposes of subsection (c)(2) of this section or section 361(c)(2).

(2) Distributions to which subsection applies.—

(A) In general.—This subsection shall apply to any distribution—

(i) to which this section (or so much of section 356 as relates to this section) applies, and

(ii) which is part of a plan (or series of related transactions) pursuant to which 1 or more persons acquire directly or indirectly stock representing a 50-percent or greater interest in the distributing corporation or any controlled corporation.

(B) Plan presumed to exist in certain cases.—If 1 or more persons acquire directly or indirectly stock representing a 50-percent or greater interest in the distributing corporation or any controlled corporation during the 4-year period beginning on the date which is 2 years before the date of the distribution, such acquisition shall be treated as pursuant to a plan described in subparagraph (A)(ii) unless it is established that the distribution and the acquisition are not pursuant to a plan or series of related transactions.

(C) Certain plans disregarded.—A plan (or series of related transactions) shall not be treated as described in subparagraph (A)(ii) if, immediately after the completion of such plan or transactions, the distributing corporation and all controlled corporations are members of a single affiliated group (as defined in section 1504 without regard to subsection (b) thereof).

(D) Coordination with subsection (d).—This subsection shall not apply to any distribution to which subsection (d) applies.

(3) Special rules relating to acquisitions.—

(A) Certain acquisitions not taken into account.—Except as provided in regulations, the following acquisitions shall not be taken into account in applying paragraph (2) (A)(ii):

(i) The acquisition of stock in any controlled corporation by the distributing corporation.

(ii) The acquisition by a person of stock in any controlled corporation by reason of holding stock or securities in the distributing corporation.

(iii) The acquisition by a person of stock in any successor corporation of the distributing corporation or any controlled corporation by reason of holding stock or securities in such distributing or controlled corporation.

(iv) The acquisition of stock in the distributing corporation or any controlled corporation to the extent that the percentage of stock owned directly or indirectly in such corporation by each person owning stock in such corporation immediately before the acquisition does not decrease.

This subparagraph shall not apply to any acquisition if the stock held before the acquisition was acquired pursuant to a plan (or series of related transactions) described in paragraph (2)(A)(ii).

(B) Asset acquisitions.—Except as provided in regulations, for purposes of this subsection, if the assets of the distributing corporation or any controlled corporation are acquired by a successor corporation in a transaction described in subparagraph (A), (C), or (D) of section 368(a)(1) or any other transaction specified in regulations by the Secretary, the shareholders (immediately before the acquisition) of the corporation acquiring such assets shall be treated as acquiring stock in the corporation from which the assets were acquired.

(4) Definition and special rules.—For purposes of this subsection—

(A) 50-percent or greater interest.—The term "50-percent or greater interest" has the meaning given such term by subsection (d)(4).

(B) Distributions in title 11 or similar case.—Paragraph (1) shall not apply to any distribution made in a title 11 or similar case (as defined in section 368(a)(3)).

(C) Aggregation and attribution rules.—

(i) **Aggregation.**—The rules of paragraph (7)(A) of subsection (d) shall apply.

(ii) **Attribution.**—Section 318(a)(2) shall apply in determining whether a person holds stock or securities in any corporation. Except as provided in regulations, section 318(a)(2)(C) shall be applied without regard to the phrase "50 percent or more in value" for purposes of the preceding sentence.

(D) Successors and predecessors.—For purposes of this subsection, any reference to a controlled corporation or a distributing corporation shall include a reference to any predecessor or successor of such corporation.

(E) Statute of limitations.—If there is a distribution to which paragraph (1) applies—

(i) the statutory period for the assessment of any deficiency attributable to any part of the gain recognized under this subsection by reason of such distribution shall not expire before the expiration of 3 years from the date the Secretary is notified by the taxpayer (in such manner as the Secretary may by regulations prescribe) that such distribution occurred, and

(ii) such deficiency may be assessed before the expiration of such 3-year period notwithstanding the provisions of any other law or rule of law which would otherwise prevent such assessment.

(5) Regulations.—The Secretary shall prescribe such regulations as may be necessary to carry out the purposes of this subsection, including regulations—

(A) providing for the application of this subsection where there is more than 1 controlled corporation,

(B) treating 2 or more distributions as 1 distribution where necessary to prevent the avoidance of such purposes, and

(C) providing for the application of rules similar to the rules of subsection (d)(6) where appropriate for purposes of paragraph (2)(B).

(f) Section not to apply to certain intragroup distributions.—Except as provided in regulations, this section (or so much of section 356 as relates to this section) shall not apply to the distribution of stock from 1 member of an affiliated group (as defined in section 1504(a)) to another member of such group if such distribution is part of a plan (or series of related transactions) described in subsection (e)(2)(A)(ii) (determined after the application of subsection (e)).

(g) Section not to apply to distributions involving disqualified investment corporations.—

(1) In general.—This section (and so much of section 356 as relates to this section) shall not apply to any distribution which is part of a transaction if—

(A) either the distributing corporation or controlled corporation is, immediately after the transaction, a disqualified investment corporation, and

(B) any person holds, immediately after the transaction, a 50-percent or greater interest in any disqualified investment corporation, but only if such person did not hold such an interest in such corporation immediately before the transaction.

(2) Disqualified investment corporations.—For purposes of this subsection—

(A) In general.—The term "disqualified investment corporation" means any distributing or controlled corporation if the fair market value of the investment assets of the corporation is—

(i) in the case of distributions after the end of the 1-year period beginning on the date of the enactment of this subsection, $2/3$ or more of the fair market value of all assets of the corporation, and

(ii) in the case of distributions during such 1-year period, $3/4$ or more of the fair market value of all assets of the corporation.

(B) Investment assets.—

(i) **In general.**—Except as otherwise provided in this subparagraph, the term "investment assets" means—

(I) cash,

(II) any stock or securities in a corporation,

(III) any interest in a partnership,

(IV) any debt instrument or other evidence of indebtedness,

(V) any option, forward or futures contract, notional principal contract, or derivative,

(VI) foreign currency, or

(VII) any similar asset.

(ii) Exception for assets used in active conduct of certain financial trades or businesses.—Such term shall not include any asset which is held for use in the active and regular conduct of—

(I) a lending or finance business (within the meaning of section 954(h)(4)),

(II) a banking business through a bank (as defined in section 581), a domestic building and loan association (within the meaning of section 7701(a)(19)), or any similar institution specified by the Secretary, or

(III) an insurance business if the conduct of the business is licensed, authorized, or regulated by an applicable insurance regulatory body. This clause shall only apply with respect to any business if substantially all of the income of the business is derived from persons who are not related (within the meaning of section 267(b) or 707(b)(1)) to the person conducting the business.

(iii) Exception for securities marked to market.—Such term shall not include any security (as defined in section 475(c)(2)) which is held by a dealer in securities and to which section 475(a) applies.

(iv) Stock or securities in a 20-percent controlled entity.—

(I) In general.—Such term shall not include any stock and securities in, or any asset described in subclause (IV) or (V) of clause (i) issued by, a corporation which is a 20-percent controlled entity with respect to the distributing or controlled corporation.

(II) Look-thru rule.—The distributing or controlled corporation shall, for purposes of applying this subsection, be treated as owning its ratable share of the assets of any 20-percent controlled entity.

(III) 20-percent controlled entity.—For purposes of this clause, the term "20-percent controlled entity" means, with respect to any distributing or controlled corporation, any corporation with respect to which the distributing or controlled corporation owns directly or indirectly stock meeting the requirements of section 1504(a)(2), except that such section shall be applied by substituting "20 percent" for "80 percent" and without regard to stock described in section 1504(a)(4).

(v) Interests in certain partnerships.—

(I) In general.—Such term shall not include any interest in a partnership, or any debt instrument or other evidence of indebtedness, issued by the partnership, if 1 or more of the trades or businesses of the partnership are (or, without regard to the 5-year requirement under subsection (b)(2)(B), would be) taken into account by the distributing or controlled corporation, as the case may be, in determining whether the requirements of subsection (b) are met with respect to the distribution.

(II) Look-thru rule.—The distributing or controlled corporation shall, for purposes of applying this subsection, be treated as owning its ratable share of the assets of any partnership described in subclause (I).

(3) 50-percent or greater interest.—For purposes of this subsection—

(A) In general.—The term "50-percent or greater interest" has the meaning given such term by subsection (d)(4).

(B) Attribution rules.—The rules of section 318 shall apply for purposes of determining ownership of stock for purposes of this paragraph.

(4) Transaction.—For purposes of this subsection, the term "transaction" includes a series of transactions.

(5) Regulations.—The Secretary shall prescribe such regulations as may be necessary to carry out, or prevent the avoidance of, the purposes of this subsection, including regulations—

(A) to carry out, or prevent the avoidance of, the purposes of this subsection in cases involving—

(i) the use of related persons, intermediaries, pass-thru entities, options, or other arrangements, and

(ii) the treatment of assets unrelated to the trade or business of a corporation as investment assets if, prior to the distribution, investment assets were used to acquire such unrelated assets,

(B) which in appropriate cases exclude from the application of this subsection a distribution which does not have the character of a redemption which would be treated as a sale or exchange under section 302, and

(C) which modify the application of the attribution rules applied for purposes of this subsection.

* * *

§ 356. Receipt of additional consideration.

(a) Gain on exchanges.—

(1) Recognition of gain.—If—

(A) section 354 or 355 would apply to an exchange but for the fact that

(B) the property received in the exchange consists not only of property permitted by section 354 or 355 to be received without the recognition of gain but also of other property or money,

then the gain, if any, to the recipient shall be recognized, but in an amount not in excess of the sum of such money and the fair market value of such other property.

(2) Treatment as dividend.—If an exchange is described in paragraph (1) but has the effect of the distribution of a dividend (determined with the application of section 318(a)), then there shall be treated as a dividend to each distributee such an amount of the gain recognized under paragraph (1) as is not in excess of his ratable share of the undistributed earnings and profits of the corporation accumulated after February 28, 1913. The remainder, if any, of the gain recognized under paragraph (1) shall be treated as gain from the exchange of property.

(b) Additional consideration received in certain distributions.—If—

(1) section 355 would apply to a distribution but for the fact that

(2) the property received in the distribution consists not only of property permitted by section 355 to be received without the recognition of gain, but also of other property or money, then an amount equal to the sum of such money and the fair market value of such other property shall be treated as a distribution of property to which section 301 applies.

(c) Loss.—If—

(1) section 354 would apply to an exchange, or section 355 would apply to an exchange or distribution, but for the fact that

(2) the property received in the exchange or distribution consists not only of property permitted by section 354 or 355 to be received without the recognition of gain or loss, but also of other property or money,

then no loss from the exchange or distribution shall be recognized.

(d) Securities as other property.—For purposes of this section—

(1) In general.—Except as provided in paragraph (2), the term "other property" includes securities.

(2) Exceptions.—

(A) Securities with respect to which nonrecognition of gain would be permitted.—The term "other property" does not include securities to the extent that, under section 354 or 355, such securities would be permitted to be received without the recognition of gain.

(B) Greater principal amount in section 354 exchange.—If—

(i) in an exchange described in section 354 (other than subsection (c) thereof), securities of a corporation a party to the reorganization are surrendered and securities of any corporation a party to the reorganization are received, and

(ii) the principal amount of such securities received exceeds the principal amount of such securities surrendered,

then, with respect to such securities received, the term "other property" means only the fair market value of such excess. For purposes of this subparagraph and subparagraph (C), if no securities are surrendered, the excess shall be the entire principal amount of the securities received.

(C) Greater principal amount in section 355 transaction.—If, in an exchange or distribution described in section 355, the principal amount of the securities in the controlled corporation which are received exceeds the principal amount of the securities in the distributing corporation which are surrendered, then, with respect to such securities received, the term "other property" means only the fair market value of such excess.

(e) Nonqualified preferred stock treated as other property.—For purposes of this section—

(1) In general.—Except as provided in paragraph (2), the term "other property" includes nonqualified preferred stock (as defined in section 351(g)(2)).

(2) Exception.—The term "other property" does not include nonqualified preferred stock (as so defined) to the extent that, under section 354 or 355, such preferred stock would be permitted to be received without the recognition of gain.

(f) Exchanges for section 306 stock.—Notwithstanding any other provision of this section, to the extent that any of the other property (or money) is received in exchange for section 306 stock, an amount equal to the fair market value of such other property (or the amount of such money) shall be treated as a distribution of property to which section 301 applies.

(g) Transactions involving gift or compensation.—

For special rules for a transaction described in section 354, 355, or this section, but which—

(1) results in a gift, see section 2501 and following, or

(2) has the effect of the payment of compensation, see section 61(a)(1).

§ 357. Assumption of liability.

(a) General rule.—Except as provided in subsections (b) and (c), if—

(1) the taxpayer receives property which would be permitted to be received under section 351 or 361 without the recognition of gain if it were the sole consideration, and

(2) as part of the consideration, another party to the exchange assumes a liability of the taxpayer

then such assumption shall not be treated as money or other property, and shall not prevent the exchange from being within the provisions of section 351 or 361, as the case may be.

(b) Tax avoidance purpose.—

(1) In general.—If, taking into consideration the nature of the liability and the circumstances in the light of which the arrangement for the assumption was made, it appears that the principal purpose of the taxpayer with respect to the assumption described in subsection (a)—

(A) was a purpose to avoid Federal income tax on the exchange, or

(B) if not such purpose, was not a bona fide business purpose,

then such assumption (in the total amount of the liability assumed pursuant to such exchange) shall, for purposes of section 351 or 361 (as the case may be), be considered as money received by the taxpayer on the exchange.

(2) Burden of proof.—In any suit or proceeding where the burden is on the taxpayer to prove such assumption is not to be treated as money received by the taxpayer, such burden shall not be considered as sustained unless the taxpayer sustains such burden by the clear preponderance of the evidence.

(c) Liabilities in excess of basis.—

(1) In general.—In the case of an exchange—

(A) to which section 351 applies, or

(B) to which section 361 applies by reason of a plan of reorganization within the meaning of section 368(a)(1)(D) with respect to which stock or securities of the corporation to which the assets are transferred are distributed in a transaction which qualifies under section 355,

if the sum of the amount of the liabilities assumed exceeds the total of the adjusted basis of the property transferred pursuant to such exchange, then such excess shall be considered as a gain from the sale or exchange of a capital asset or of property which is not a capital asset, as the case may be.

(2) Exceptions.—Paragraph (1) shall not apply to any exchange—

(A) to which subsection (b)(1) of this section applies, or

(B) which is pursuant to a plan of reorganization within the meaning of section 368(a)(1)(G) where no former shareholder of the transferor corporation receives any consideration for his stock.

(3) Certain liabilities excluded.—

(A) In general.—If a taxpayer transfers, in an exchange to which section 351 applies, a liability the payment of which either—

(i) would give rise to a deduction, or

(ii) would be described in section 736(a),

then, for purposes of paragraph (1), the amount of such liability shall be excluded in determining the amount of liabilities assumed

(B) Exception.—Subparagraph (A) shall not apply to any liability to the extent that the incurrence of the liability resulted in the creation of, or an increase in, the basis of any property.

(d) Determination of amount of liability assumed.—

(1) In general.—For purposes of this section, section 358(d), section 362(d), section 368(a)(1)(C), and section 368(a)(2)(B), except as provided in regulations—

(A) a recourse liability (or portion thereof) shall be treated as having been assumed if, as determined on the basis of all facts and circumstances, the transferee has agreed to, and is expected to, satisfy such liability (or portion), whether or not the transferor has been relieved of such liability; and

(B) except to the extent provided in paragraph (2), a nonrecourse liability shall be treated as having been assumed by the transferee of any asset subject to such liability.

(2) Exception for nonrecourse liability.—The amount of the nonrecourse liability treated as described in paragraph (1)(B) shall be reduced by the lesser of—

(A) the amount of such liability which an owner of other assets not transferred to the transferee and also subject to such liability has agreed with the transferee to, and is expected to, satisfy; or

(B) the fair market value of such other assets (determined without regard to section 7701(g)).

(3) Regulations.—The Secretary shall prescribe such regulations as may be necessary to carry out the purposes of this subsection and section 362(d). The Secretary may also prescribe regulations which provide that the manner in which a liability is treated as assumed under this subsection is applied, where appropriate, elsewhere in this title.

§ 358. Basis to distributees.

(a) General rule.—In the case of an exchange to which section 351, 354, 355, 356, or 361 applies—

(1) Nonrecognition property.—The basis of the property permitted to be received under such section without the recognition of gain or loss shall be the same as that of the property exchanged—

(A) decreased by—

(i) the fair market value of any other property (except money) received by the taxpayer,

(ii) the amount of any money received by the taxpayer, and

(iii) the amount of loss to the taxpayer which was recognized on such exchange, and

(B) increased by—

(i) the amount which was treated as a dividend, and

(ii) the amount of gain to the taxpayer which was recognized on such exchange (not including any portion of such gain which was treated as a dividend).

(2) Other property.—The basis of any other property (except money) received by the taxpayer shall be its fair market value.

(b) Allocation of basis.—

(1) In general.—Under regulations prescribed by the Secretary, the basis determined under subsection (a)(1) shall be allocated among the properties permitted to be received without the recognition of gain or loss.

(2) Special rule for section 355.—In the case of an exchange to which section 355 (or so much of section 356 as relates to section 355) applies, then in making the allocation under paragraph (1) of this subsection, there shall be taken into account not only the property so permitted to be received without the recognition of gain or loss, but also the stock or securities (if any) of the distributing corporation which are retained, and the allocation of basis shall be made among all such properties.

* * *

(c) Section 355 transactions which are not exchanges.—For purposes of this section, a distribution to which section 355 (or so much of section 356 as relates to section 355) applies shall be treated as an exchange, and for such purposes the stock and securities of the distributing corporation which are retained shall be treated as surrendered, and received back, in the exchange.

(d) Assumption of liability.—

(1) In general.—Where, as part of the consideration to the taxpayer, another party to the exchange assumed a liability of the taxpayer, such assumption shall, for purposes of this section, be treated as money received by the taxpayer on the exchange.

(2) Exception.—Paragraph (1) shall not apply to the amount of any liability excluded under section 357(c)(3).

(e) Exception.—This section shall not apply to property acquired by a corporation by the exchange of its stock or securities (or the stock or securities of a corporation which is in control of the acquiring corporation) as consideration in whole or in part for the transfer of the property to it.

(f) Definition of nonrecognition property in case of section 361 exchange.—For purposes of this section, the property permitted to be received under section 361 without the recognition of gain or loss shall be treated as consisting only of stock or securities in another corporation a party to the reorganization.

(g) Adjustments in intragroup transactions involving section 355.—In the case of a distribution to which section 355 (or so much of section 356 as relates to section 355) applies and which involves the distribution of stock from 1 member of an affiliated group (as defined in section 1504(a) without regard to subsection (b) thereof) to another member of such group, the Secretary may, notwithstanding any other provision of this section, provide adjustments to the adjusted basis of any stock which—

(1) is in a corporation which is a member of such group, and

(2) is held by another member of such group, to appropriately reflect the proper treatment of such distribution.

(h) Special rules for assumption of liabilities to which subsection (d) does not apply.

(1) In general.—If after application of the other provisions of this section to an exchange or series of exchanges, the basis of property to which subsection (a)(1) applies exceeds the fair market value of such property, then such basis shall be reduced (but not below such fair market value) by the amount (determined as of the date of the exchange) of any liability—

(A) which is assumed by another person as part of the exchange, and

(B) with respect to which subsection (d)(1) does not apply to the assumption.

(2) Exceptions.—Except as provided by the Secretary, paragraph (1) shall not apply to any liability if—

(A) the trade or business with which the liability is associated is transferred to the person assuming the liability as part of the exchange, or

(B) substantially all of the assets with which the liability is associated are transferred to the person assuming the liability as part of the exchange.

(3) Liability.—For purposes of this subsection, the term "liability" shall include any fixed or contingent obligation to make payment, without regard to whether the obligation is otherwise taken into account for purposes of this title.

Subpart C—Effects on Corporations

§ 361. Nonrecognition of gain or loss to corporations; treatment of distributions.

(a) General rule.—No gain or loss shall be recognized to a corporation if such corporation is a party to a reorganization and exchanges property, in pursuance of the plan of reorganization, solely for stock or securities in another corporation a party to the reorganization.

(b) Exchanges not solely in kind.—

(1) Gain.—If subsection (a) would apply to an exchange but for the fact that the property received in exchange consists not only of stock or securities permitted by subsection (a) to be received without the recognition of gain, but also of other property or money, then—

(A) Property distributed.—If the corporation receiving such other property or money distributes it in pursuance of the plan of reorganization, no gain to the corporation shall be recognized from the exchange, but

(B) Property not distributed.—If the corporation receiving such other property or money does not distribute it in pursuance of the plan of reorganization, the gain, if any, to the corporation shall be recognized.

The amount of gain recognized under subparagraph (B) shall not exceed the sum of the money and the fair market value of the other property so received which is not so distributed.

(2) Loss.—If subsection (a) would apply to an exchange but for the fact that the property received in exchange consists not only of property permitted by subsection (a) to be received without the recognition of gain or loss, but also of other property or money, then no loss from the exchange shall be recognized.

(3) Treatment of transfers to creditors.—For purposes of paragraph (1), any transfer of the other property or money received in the exchange by the corporation to its creditors in connection with the reorganization shall be treated as a distribution in pursuance of the plan of reorganization. The Secretary may prescribe such regulations as may be necessary to prevent avoidance of tax through abuse of the preceding sentence or subsection (c)(3). In the case of a reorganization described in section 368(a)(1)(D) with respect to which stock or securities of the corporation to which the assets are transferred are distributed in a transaction which qualifies under section 355, this paragraph shall apply only to the extent that the sum of the money and the fair market value of other property transferred to such creditors does not exceed the adjusted bases of such assets transferred.

(c) Treatment of distributions.—

(1) In general.—Except as provided in paragraph (2), no gain or loss shall be recognized to a corporation a party to a reorganization on the distribution to its shareholders of property in pursuance of the plan of reorganization.

(2) Distributions of appreciated property.—

(A) In general.—If—

(i) in a distribution referred to in paragraph (1), the corporation distributes property other than qualified property, and

(ii) the fair market value of such property exceeds its adjusted basis (in the hands of the distributing corporation), then gain shall be recognized to the distributing corporation as if such property were sold to the distributee at its fair market value.

(B) Qualified property.—For purposes of this subsection, the term "qualified property" means—

(i) any stock in (or right to acquire stock in) the distributing corporation or obligation of the distributing corporation, or

(ii) any stock in (or right to acquire stock in) another corporation which is a party to the reorganization or obligation of another corporation which is such a party if such stock (or right) or obligation is received by the distributing corporation in the exchange.

(C) Treatment of liabilities.—If any property distributed in the distribution referred to in paragraph (1) is subject to a liability or the shareholder assumes a liability of the distributing corporation in connection with the distribution, then, for purposes of subparagraph (A), the fair market value of such property shall be treated as not less than the amount of such liability.

(3) Treatment of certain transfers to creditors.—For purposes of this subsection, any transfer of qualified property by the corporation to its creditors in connection with the reorganization shall be treated as a distribution to its shareholders pursuant to the plan of reorganization.

(4) Coordination with other provisions.—Section 311 and subpart B of part II of this subchapter shall not apply to any distribution referred to in paragraph (1).

(5) Cross reference.—For provision providing for recognition of gain in certain distributions, see section 355(d).

§ 362. Basis to corporations.

(a) Property acquired by issuance of stock or as paid-in surplus.—If property was acquired by a corporation—

(1) in connection with a transaction to which section 351 (relating to transfer of property to corporation controlled by transferor) applies, or

(2) as paid-in surplus or as a contribution to capital, then the basis shall be the same as it would be in the hands of the transferor, increased in the amount of gain recognized to the transferor on such transfer.

(b) Transfers to corporations.—If property was acquired by a corporation in connection with a reorganization to which this part applies, then the basis shall be the same as it would be in the hands of the transferor, increased in the amount of gain recognized to the transferor on such transfer. This subsection shall not apply if the property acquired consists of stock or securities in a corporation a party to the reorganization, unless acquired by the exchange of stock or securities of the transferee (or of a corporation which is in control of the transferee) as the consideration in whole or in part for the transfer.

(c) Special rule for certain contributions to capital.—

(1) Property other than money.—Notwithstanding subsection (a)(2), if property other than money—

(A) is acquired by a corporation as a contribution to capital, and

(B) is not contributed by a shareholder as such, then the basis of such property shall be zero.

(2) Money.—Notwithstanding subsection (a)(2), if money—

(A) is received by a corporation as a contribution to capital, and

(B) is not contributed by a shareholder as such,

then the basis of any property acquired with such money during the 12-month period beginning on the day the contribution is received shall be reduced by the amount of such contribution. The excess (if any) of the amount of such contribution over the amount of the reduction under the preceding sentence shall be applied to the reduction (as of the last day of the period specified in the preceding sentence) of the basis of any other property held by the taxpayer. The particular properties to which the reductions required by this paragraph shall be allocated shall be determined under regulations prescribed by the Secretary.

(d) Limitation on basis increase attributable to assumption of liability.—

(1) In general.—In no event shall the basis of any property be increased under subsection (a) or (b) above the fair market value of such property (determined without regard to section 7701(g)) by reason of any gain recognized to the transferor as a result of the assumption of a liability.

(2) Treatment of gain not subject to tax.—Except as provided in regulations, if—

(A) gain is recognized to the transferor as a result of an assumption of a nonrecourse liability by a transferee which is also secured by assets not transferred to such transferee; and

(B) no person is subject to tax under this title on such gain, then, for purposes of determining basis under subsections (a) and (b), the amount of gain recognized by the transferor as a result of the assumption of the liability shall be determined as if the liability assumed by the transferee equaled such transferee's ratable portion of such liability determined on the basis of the relative fair market values (determined without regard to section 7701(g)) of all of the assets subject to such liability.

(e) Limitations on built-in losses.—

(1) Limitation on importation of built-in losses.—

(A) In general.—If in any transaction described in subsection (a) or (b) there would (but for this subsection) be an importation of a net built-in loss, the basis of each property described in subparagraph (B) which is acquired in such transaction shall (notwithstanding subsections (a) and (b)) be its fair market value immediately after such transaction.

(B) Property described.—For purposes of subparagraph (A), property is described in this subparagraph if—

(i) gain or loss with respect to such property is not subject to tax under this subtitle in the hands of the transferor immediately before the transfer, and

(ii) gain or loss with respect to such property is subject to such tax in the hands of the transferee immediately after such transfer.

In any case in which the transferor is a partnership, the preceding sentence shall be applied by treating each partner in such partnership as holding such partner's proportionate share of the property of such partnership.

(C) Importation of net built-in loss.—For purposes of subparagraph (A), there is an importation of a net built-in loss in a transaction if the transferee's aggregate adjusted bases of property described in subparagraph (B) which is transferred in such transaction would (but for this paragraph) exceed the fair market value of such property immediately after such transaction.

(2) Limitation on transfer of built-in losses in section 351 transactions.—

(A) In general.—If—

(i) property is transferred by a transferor in any transaction which is described in subsection (a) and which is not described in paragraph (1) of this subsection, and

(ii) the transferee's aggregate adjusted bases of such property so transferred would (but for this paragraph) exceed the fair market value of such property immediately after such transaction,

then, notwithstanding subsection (a), the transferee's aggregate adjusted bases of the property so transferred shall not exceed the fair market value of such property immediately after such transaction.

(B) Allocation of basis reduction.—The aggregate reduction in basis by reason of subparagraph (A) shall be allocated among the property so transferred in proportion to their respective built-in losses immediately before the transaction.

(C) Election to apply limitation to transferor's stock basis.—

(i) In general.—If the transferor and transferee of a transaction described in subparagraph (A) both elect the application of this subparagraph—

(I) subparagraph (A) shall not apply, and

(II) the transferor's basis in the stock received for property to which subparagraph (A) does not apply by reason of the election shall not exceed its fair market value immediately after the transfer.

(ii) Election.—An election under clause (i) shall be included with the return of tax for the taxable year in which the transaction occurred, shall be in such form and manner as the Secretary may prescribe, and, once made, shall be irrevocable.

Subpart D—Special Rule; Definitions

§ 368. Definitions relating to corporate reorganizations.

(a) Reorganization.—

(1) In general.—For purposes of parts I and II and this part, the term "reorganization" means—

(A) a statutory merger or consolidation;

(B) the acquisition by one corporation, in exchange solely for all or a part of its voting stock (or in exchange solely for all or a part of the voting stock of a corporation which is in control of the acquiring corporation), of stock of another corporation if, immediately after the acquisition, the acquiring corporation has control of such other corporation (whether or not such acquiring corporation had control immediately before the acquisition);

(C) the acquisition by one corporation, in exchange solely for all or a part of its voting stock (or in exchange solely for all or a part of the voting stock of a corporation which is in control of the acquiring corporation), of substantially all of the properties of another corporation, but in determining whether the exchange is solely for stock the assumption by the acquiring corporation of a liability of the other, shall be disregarded;

(D) a transfer by a corporation of all or a part of its assets to another corporation if immediately after the transfer the transferor, or one or more of its shareholders (including persons who were shareholders immediately before the transfer), or any combination thereof, is in control of the corporation to which the assets are transferred; but only if, in pursuance of the plan, stock or securities of the corporation to which the assets are transferred are distributed in a transaction which qualifies under section 354, 355, or 356;

(E) a recapitalization;

(F) a mere change in identity, form, or place of organization of one corporation, however effected; or

(G) a transfer by a corporation of all or part of its assets to another corporation in a title 11 or similar case; but only if, in pursuance of the plan, stock or securities of the corporation to which the assets are transferred are distributed in a transaction which qualifies under section 354, 355, or 356.

(2) Special rules relating to paragraph (1).—

(A) Reorganizations described in both paragraph (1)(C) and paragraph (1)(D).— If a transaction is described in both paragraph (1)(C) and paragraph (1)(D), then, for purposes of this subchapter (other than for purposes of subparagraph (C)), such transaction shall be treated as described only in paragraph (1)(D).

(B) Additional consideration in certain paragraph (1)(C) cases.—If—

(i) one corporation acquires substantially all of the properties of another corporation,

(ii) the acquisition would qualify under paragraph (1)(C) but for the fact that the acquiring corporation exchanges money or other property in addition to voting stock, and

(iii) the acquiring corporation acquires, solely for voting stock described in paragraph (1)(C), property of the other corporation having a fair market value which is at least 80 percent of the fair market value of all of the property of the other corporation,

then such acquisition shall (subject to subparagraph (A) of this paragraph) be treated as qualifying under paragraph (1)(C). Solely for the purpose of determining whether clause (iii) of the preceding sentence applies, the amount of any liability assumed by the acquiring corporation shall be treated as money paid for the property.

(C) Transfers of assets or stock to subsidiaries in certain paragraph (1)(A), (1)(B), (1)(C), and (1)(G) cases.—A transaction otherwise qualifying under paragraph (1)(A), (1)(B), or (1)(C) shall not be disqualified by reason of the fact that part or all of the assets or stock which were acquired in the transaction are transferred to a corporation controlled by the corporation acquiring such assets or stock. A similar rule shall apply to a transaction otherwise qualifying under paragraph (1)(G) where the requirements of subparagraphs (A) and (B) of section 354(b)(1) are met with respect to the acquisition of the assets.

(D) Use of stock of controlling corporation in paragraph (1)(A) and (1)(G) cases.—The acquisition by one corporation, in exchange for stock of a corporation (referred to in this subparagraph as "controlling corporation") which is in control of the acquiring corporation, of substantially all of the properties of another corporation shall not disqualify a transaction under paragraph (1)(A) or (1)(G) if—

(i) no stock of the acquiring corporation is used in the transaction, and

(ii) in the case of a transaction under paragraph (1)(A), such transaction would have qualified under paragraph (1)(A) had the merger been into the controlling corporation.

(E) Statutory merger using voting stock of corporation controlling merged corporation.—A transaction otherwise qualifying under paragraph (1)(A) shall not be disqualified by reason of the fact that stock of a corporation (referred to in this subparagraph as the "controlling corporation") which before the merger was in control of the merged corporation is used in the transaction, if—

(i) after the transaction, the corporation surviving the merger holds substantially all of its properties and of the properties of the merged corporation (other than stock of the controlling corporation distributed in the transaction); and

(ii) in the transaction, former shareholders of the surviving corporation exchanged, for an amount of voting stock of the controlling corporation, an amount of stock in the surviving corporation which constitutes control of such corporation.

* * *

(G) Distribution requirement for paragraph (1)(C).—

(i) **In general.**—A transaction shall fail to meet the requirements of paragraph (1)(C) unless the acquired corporation distributes the stock, securities, and other properties it receives, as well as its other properties, in pursuance of the plan of reorganization. For purposes of the preceding sentence, if the acquired corporation is liquidated pursuant to the plan of reorganization, any distribution to its creditors in connection with such liquidation shall be treated as pursuant to the plan of reorganization.

(ii) **Exception.**—The Secretary may waive the application of clause (i) to any transaction subject to any conditions the Secretary may prescribe.

(H) Special rules for determining whether certain transactions are qualified under paragraph (1)(D).—For purposes of determining whether a transaction qualifies under paragraph (1)(D)—

(i) in the case of a transaction with respect to which the requirements of subparagraphs (A) and (B) of section 354(b)(1) are met, the term "control" has the meaning given such term by section 304(c), and

(ii) in the case of a transaction with respect to which the requirements of section 355 (or so much of section 356 as relates to section 355) are met, the fact that the shareholders of the distributing corporation dispose of part or all of the distributed stock, or the fact that the corporation whose stock was distributed issues additional stock, shall not be taken into account.

* * *

(3) Additional rules relating to title 11 and similar cases.—

(A) Title 11 or similar case defined.—For purposes of this part, the term "title 11 or similar case" means—

(i) a case under title 11 of the United States Code, or

(ii) a receivership, foreclosure, or similar proceeding in a Federal or State court.

(B) Transfer of assets in a title 11 or similar case.—In applying paragraph (1)(G), a transfer of the assets of a corporation shall be treated as made in a title 11 or similar case if and only if—

(i) any party to the reorganization is under the jurisdiction of the court in such case, and

(ii) the transfer is pursuant to a plan of reorganization approved by the court.

(C) Reorganizations qualifying under paragraph (1)(G) and another provision.—If a transaction would (but for this subparagraph) qualify both—

(i) under subparagraph (G) of paragraph (1), and

(ii) under any other subparagraph of paragraph (1) or under section 332 or 351,

then, for purposes of this subchapter (other than section 357(c)(1)), such transaction shall be treated as qualifying only under subparagraph (G) of paragraph (1).

* * *

(E) Application of paragraph (2)(E)(ii).—In the case of a title 11 or similar case, the requirement of clause (ii) of paragraph (2)(E) shall be treated as met if—

(i) no former shareholder of the surviving corporation received any consideration for his stock, and

(ii) the former creditors of the surviving corporation exchanged, for an amount of voting stock of the controlling corporation, debt of the surviving corporation which had a fair market value equal to 80 percent or more of the total fair market value of the debt of the surviving corporation.

(b) Party to a reorganization.—For purposes of this part, the term "a party to a reorganization" includes—

(1) a corporation resulting from a reorganization, and

(2) both corporations, in the case of a reorganization resulting from the acquisition by one corporation of stock or properties of another.

In the case of a reorganization qualifying under paragraph (1)(B) or (1)(C) of subsection (a), if the stock exchanged for the stock or properties is stock of a corporation which is in control of the acquiring corporation, the term "a party to a reorganization" includes the corporation so controlling the acquiring corporation. In the case of a reorganization qualifying under paragraph

(1)(A), (1)(B), (1)(C), or (1)(G) of subsection (a) by reason of paragraph (2)(C) of subsection (a), the term "a party to a reorganization" includes the corporation controlling the corporation to which the acquired assets or stock are transferred. In the case of a reorganization qualifying under paragraph (1)(A) or (1)(G) of subsection (a) by reason of paragraph (2)(D) of that subsection, the term "a party to a reorganization" includes the controlling corporation referred to in such paragraph (2)(D). In the case of a reorganization qualifying under subsection (a)(1)(A) by reason of subsection (a)(2)(E), the term "party to a reorganization" includes the controlling corporation referred to in subsection (a)(2)(E).

(c) **Control defined.**—For purposes of part I (other than section 304), part II, this part, and part V, the term "control" means the ownership of stock possessing at least 80 percent of the total combined voting power of all classes of stock entitled to vote and at least 80 percent of the total number of shares of all other classes of stock of the corporation.

Part V—Carryovers

§ 381. Carryovers in certain corporate acquisitions.

(a) **General rule.**—In the case of the acquisition of assets of a corporation by another corporation—

(1) in a distribution to such other corporation to which section 332 (relating to liquidations of subsidiaries) applies; or

(2) in a transfer to which section 361 (relating to nonrecognition of gain or loss to corporations) applies, but only if the transfer is in connection with a reorganization described in subparagraph (A), (C), (D), (F), or (G) of section 368(a)(1),

the acquiring corporation shall succeed to and take into account, as of the close of the day of distribution or transfer, the items described in subsection (c) of the distributor or transferor corporation, subject to the conditions and limitations specified in subsections (b) and (c). For purposes of the preceding sentence, a reorganization shall be treated as meeting the requirements of subparagraph (D) or (G) of section 368(a)(1) only if the requirements of subparagraphs (A) and (B) of section 354(b)(1) are met.

(b) **Operating rules.**—Except in the case of an acquisition in connection with a reorganization described in subparagraph (F) of section 368(a)(1)—

(1) The taxable year of the distributor or transferor corporation shall end on the date of distribution or transfer.

(2) For purposes of this section, the date of distribution or transfer shall be the day on which the distribution or transfer is completed; except that, under regulations prescribed by the Secretary, the date when substantially all of the property has been distributed or transferred may be used if the distributor or transferor corporation ceases all operations, other than liquidating activities, after such date.

(3) The corporation acquiring property in a distribution or transfer described in subsection (a) shall not be entitled to carry back a net operating loss or a net capital loss for a taxable year ending after the date of distribution or transfer to a taxable year of the distributor or transferor corporation.

(c) **Items of the distributor or transferor corporation.**—The items referred to in subsection (a) are:

(1) Net operating loss carryovers.—The net operating loss carryovers determined under section 172, subject to the following conditions and limitations:

(A) The taxable year of the acquiring corporation to which the net operating loss carryovers of the distributor or transferor corporation are first carried shall be the first taxable year ending after the date of distribution or transfer.

(B) In determining the net operating loss deduction, the portion of such deduction attributable to the net operating loss carryovers of the distributor or transferor corporation to the first taxable year of the acquiring corporation ending after the date of distribution or transfer shall be limited to an amount which bears the same ratio to the taxable income (determined without regard to a net operating loss deduction) of the acquiring corporation in such taxable year as the number of days in the taxable year after the date of distribution or transfer bears to the total number of days in the taxable year.

(C) For the purpose of determining the amount of the net operating loss carryovers under section 172(b)(2), a net operating loss for a taxable year (hereinafter in this subparagraph referred to as the "loss year") of a distributor or transferor corporation which ends on or before the end of a loss year of the acquiring corporation shall be considered to be a net operating loss for a year prior to such loss year of the acquiring corporation. For the same purpose, the taxable income for a "prior taxable year" (as the term is used in section 172(b)(2)) shall be computed as provided in such section; except that, if the date of distribution or transfer is on a day other than the last day of a taxable year of the acquiring corporation—

(i) such taxable year shall (for the purpose of this subparagraph only) be considered to be 2 taxable years (hereinafter in this subparagraph referred to as the "pre-acquisition part year" and the "post-acquisition part year");

(ii) the pre-acquisition part year shall begin on the same day as such taxable year begins and shall end on the date of distribution or transfer;

(iii) the post-acquisition part year shall begin on the day following the date of distribution or transfer and shall end on the same day as the end of such taxable year;

(iv) the taxable income for such taxable year (computed with the modifications specified in section 172(b)(2)(A) but without a net operating loss deduction) shall be divided between the pre-acquisition part year and the post-acquisition part year in proportion to the number of days in each;

(v) the net operating loss deduction for the pre-acquisition part year shall be determined as provided in section 172(b)(2)(B), but without regard to a net operating loss year of the distributor or transferor corporation; and

(vi) the net operating loss deduction for the post-acquisition part year shall be determined as provided in section 172(b)(2)(B).

(2) Earnings and profits.—In the case of a distribution or transfer described in subsection (a)—

(A) the earnings and profits or deficit in earnings and profits, as the case may be, of the distributor or transferor corporation shall, subject to subparagraph (B), be deemed to have been received or incurred by the acquiring corporation as of the close of the date of the distribution or transfer; and

(B) a deficit in earnings and profits of the distributor, transferor, or acquiring corporation shall be used only to offset earnings and profits accumulated after the date of transfer. For this purpose, the earnings and profits for the taxable year of the acquiring corporation in which the distribution or transfer occurs shall be deemed to have been accumulated after such distribution or transfer in an amount which bears the same ratio to the undistributed earnings and profits of the acquiring corporation for such taxable year (computed without regard to any earnings and profits received from the distributor or transferor corporation, as described in subparagraph (A) of this paragraph) as the number of days in the taxable year after the date of distribution or transfer bears to the total number of days in the taxable year.

(3) Capital loss carryover.—The capital loss carryover determined under section 1212, subject to the following conditions and limitations:

(A) The taxable year of the acquiring corporation to which the capital loss carryover of the distributor or transferor corporation is first carried shall be the first taxable year ending after the date of distribution or transfer.

(B) The capital loss carryover shall be a short-term capital loss in the taxable year determined under subparagraph (A) but shall be limited to an amount which bears the same ratio to the capital gain net income (determined without regard to a short-term capital loss attributable to capital loss carryover), if any, of the acquiring corporation in such taxable year as the number of days in the taxable year after the date of distribution or transfer bears to the total number of days in the taxable year.

(C) For purposes of determining the amount of such capital loss carryover to taxable years following the taxable year determined under subparagraph (A), the capital gain net income in the taxable year determined under subparagraph (A) shall be considered to be an amount equal to the amount determined under subparagraph (B).

(4) Method of accounting.—The acquiring corporation shall use the method of accounting used by the distributor or transferor corporation on the date of distribution or transfer unless different methods were used by several distributor or transferor corporations or by a distributor or transferor corporation and the acquiring corporation. If different methods were used, the acquiring corporation shall use the method or combination of methods of computing taxable income adopted pursuant to regulations prescribed by the Secretary.

(5) Inventories.—In any case in which inventories are received by the acquiring corporation, such inventories shall be taken by such corporation (in determining its income) on the same basis on which such inventories were taken by the distributor or transferor corporation, unless different methods were used by several distributor or transferor corporations or by a distributor or transferor corporation and the acquiring corporation. If different methods were used, the acquiring corporation shall use the method or combination of methods of taking inventory adopted pursuant to regulations prescribed by the Secretary.

(6) Method of computing depreciation allowance.—The acquiring corporation shall be treated as the distributor or transferor corporation for purposes of computing the depreciation allowance under sections 167 and 168 on property acquired in a distribution or transfer with respect to so much of the basis in the hands of the acquiring corporation as does not exceed the adjusted basis in the hands of the distributor or transferor corporation.

[(7) Repealed.]

(8) Installment method.—If the acquiring corporation acquires installment obligations (the income from which the distributor or transferor corporation reports on the installment basis under section 453) the acquiring corporation shall, for purposes of section 453, be treated as if it were the distributor or transferor corporation.

(9) Amortization of bond discount or premium.—If the acquiring corporation assumes liability for bonds of the distributor or transferor corporation issued at a discount or premium, the acquiring corporation shall be treated as the distributor or transferor corporation after the date of distribution or transfer for purposes of determining the amount of amortization allowable or includible with respect to such discount or premium.

(10) Treatment of certain mining development and exploration expenses of distributor or transferor corporation.—The acquiring corporation shall be entitled to deduct, as if it were the distributor or transferor corporation, expenses deferred under section 616 (relating to certain development expenditures) if the distributor or transferor corporation has so elected.

(11) Contributions to pension plans, employees' annuity plans, and stock bonus and profit-sharing plans.—The acquiring corporation shall be considered to be the distributor or transferor corporation after the date of distribution or transfer for the purpose of determining the amounts deductible under section 404 with respect to pension plans, employees' annuity plans, and stock bonus and profit-sharing plans.

(12) Recovery of tax benefit items.—If the acquiring corporation is entitled to the recovery of any amounts previously deducted by (or allowable as credits to) the distributor or transferor corporation, the acquiring corporation shall succeed to the treatment under section 111 which would apply to such amounts in the hands of the distributor or transferor corporation.

(13) Involuntary conversions under section 1033.—The acquiring corporation shall be treated as the distributor or transferor corporation after the date of distribution or transfer for purposes of applying section 1033.

(14) Dividend carryover to personal holding company.—The dividend carryover (described in section 564) to taxable years ending after the date of distribution or transfer.

[(15) Repealed.]

(16) Certain obligations of distributor or transferor corporation.—If the acquiring corporation—

(A) assumes an obligation of the distributor or transferor corporation which, after the date of the distribution or transfer, gives rise to a liability, and

(B) such liability, if paid or accrued by the distributor or transferor corporation, would have been deductible in computing its taxable income,

the acquiring corporation shall be entitled to deduct such items when paid or accrued, as the case may be, as if such corporation were the distributor or transferor corporation. A corporation which would have been an acquiring corporation under this section if the date of distribution or transfer had occurred on or after the effective date of the provisions of this subchapter applicable to a liquidation or reorganization, as the case may be, shall be entitled, even though the date of distribution or transfer occurred before such effective date, to apply this paragraph with respect to amounts paid or accrued in taxable years beginning after December 31, 1953, on account of such obligations of the distributor or transferor corporation. This paragraph shall not apply if such obligations are reflected in the amount of stock, securities, or property transferred by the acquiring corporation to the transferor corporation for the property of the transferor corporation.

(17) Deficiency dividend of personal holding company.—If the acquiring corporation pays a deficiency dividend (as defined in section 547(d)) with respect to the distributor or transferor corporation, such distributor or transferor corporation shall, with respect to such payments, be entitled to the deficiency dividend deduction provided in section 547.

(18) Percentage depletion on extraction of ores or minerals from the waste or residue of prior mining.—The acquiring corporation shall be considered to be the distributor or transferor corporation for the purpose of determining the applicability of section 613(c)(3) (relating to extraction of ores or minerals from the ground).

(19) Charitable contributions in excess of prior years' limitations.—Contributions made in the taxable year ending on the date of distribution or transfer and the 4 prior taxable years by the distributor or transferor corporation in excess of the amount deductible under section 170(b)(2) for such taxable years shall be deductible by the acquiring corporation for its taxable years which begin after the date of distribution or transfer, subject to the limitations imposed in section 170(b)(2). In applying the preceding sentence, each taxable year of the distributor or transferor corporation beginning on or before the date of distribution or transfer shall be treated as a prior taxable year with reference to the acquiring corporation's taxable years beginning after such date.

(20) Carryforward of disallowed business interest.—The carryover of disallowed business interest described in section 163(j)(2) to taxable years ending after the date of distribution or transfer.

* * *

§ 382. Limitation on net operating loss carryforwards and certain built-in losses following ownership change.

(a) General rule.—The amount of the taxable income of any new loss corporation for any post-change year which may be offset by pre-change losses shall not exceed the section 382 limitation for such year.

(b) Section 382 limitation.—For purposes of this section—

(1) In general.—Except as otherwise pr ovided in this section, the section 382 limitation for any post-change year is an amount equal to—

(A) the value of the old loss corporation, multiplied by

(B) the long-term tax-exempt rate.

(2) Carryforward of unused limitation.—If the section 382 limitation for any post-change year exceeds the taxable income of the new loss corporation for such year which was offset by pre-change losses, the section 382 limitation for the next post-change year shall be increased by the amount of such excess.

(3) Special rule for post-change year which includes change date.—In the case of any post-change year which includes the change date—

(A) Limitation does not apply to taxable income before change.—Subsection (a) shall not apply to the portion of the taxable income for such year which is allocable to the period in such year on or before the change date. Except as provided in subsection (h)(5) and in regulations, taxable income shall be allocated ratably to each day in the year.

(B) Limitation for period after change.—For purposes of applying the limitation of subsection (a) to the remainder of the taxable income for such year, the section 382 limitation shall be an amount which bears the same ratio to such limitation (determined without regard to this paragraph) as—

(i) the number of days in such year after the change date, bears to

(ii) the total number of days in such year.

(c) Carryforwards disallowed if continuity of business requirements not met.—

(1) In general.—Except as provided in paragraph (2), if the new loss corporation does not continue the business enterprise of the old loss corporation at all times during the 2-year period beginning on the change date, the section 382 limitation for any post-change year shall be zero.

(2) Exception for certain gains.—The section 382 limitation for any post-change year shall not be less than the sum of—

(A) any increase in such limitation under—

(i) subsection (h)(1)(A) for recognized built-in gains for such year, and

(ii) subsection (h)(1)(C) for gain recognized by reason of an election under section 338, plus

(B) any increase in such limitation under subsection (b)(2) for amounts described in subparagraph (A) which are carried forward to such year.

(d) Pre-change loss and post-change year.—For purposes of this section—

(1) Pre-change loss.—The term "pre-change loss" means—

(A) any net operating loss carryforward of the old loss corporation to the taxable year ending with the ownership change or in which the change date occurs, and

(B) the net operating loss of the old loss corporation for the taxable year in which the ownership change occurs to the extent such loss is allocable to the period in such year on or before the change date.

Except as provided in subsection (h)(5) and in regulations, the net operating loss shall, for purposes of subparagraph (B), be allocated ratably to each day in the year.

(2) Post-change year.—The term "post-change year" means any taxable year ending after the change date.

(3) Application to carryforward of disallowed interest.—The term 'pre-change loss' shall include any carryover of disallowed interest described in section 163(j)(2) under rules similar to the rules of paragraph (1).

(e) Value of old loss corporation.—For purposes of this section—

(1) In general.—Except as otherwise provided in this subsection, the value of the old loss corporation is the value of the stock of such corporation (including any stock described in section 1504(a)(4)) immediately before the ownership change.

(2) Special rule in the case of redemption or other corporate contraction.—If a redemption or other corporate contraction occurs in connection with an ownership change, the value under paragraph (1) shall be determined after taking such redemption or other corporate contraction into account.

* * *

(f) Long-term tax-exempt rate.—For purposes of this section—

(1) In general.—The long-term tax-exempt rate shall be the highest of the adjusted Federal long-term rates in effect for any month in the 3-calendar-month period ending with the calendar month in which the change date occurs.

(2) Adjusted Federal long-term rate.—For purposes of paragraph (1), the term "adjusted Federal long-term rate" means the Federal long-term rate determined under section 1274(d), except that—

(A) paragraphs (2) and (3) thereof shall not apply, and

(B) such rate shall be properly adjusted for differences between rates on long-term taxable and tax-exempt obligations.

(g) Ownership change.—For purposes of this section—

(1) In general.—There is an ownership change if, immediately after any owner shift involving a 5-percent shareholder or any equity structure shift—

(A) the percentage of the stock of the loss corporation owned by 1 or more 5-percent shareholders has increased by more than 50 percentage points, over

(B) the lowest percentage of stock of the loss corporation (or any predecessor corporation) owned by such shareholders at any time during the testing period.

(2) Owner shift involving 5-percent shareholder.—There is an owner shift involving a 5-percent shareholder if—

(A) there is any change in the respective ownership of stock of a corporation, and

(B) such change affects the percentage of stock of such corporation owned by any person who is a 5-percent shareholder before or after such change.

(3) Equity structure shift defined.—

(A) In general.—The term "equity structure shift" means any reorganization (within the meaning of section 368). Such term shall not include—

(i) any reorganization described in subparagraph (D) or (G) of section 368(a)(1) unless the requirements of section 354(b)(1) are met, and

(ii) any reorganization described in subparagraph (F) of section 368(a)(1).

(B) Taxable reorganization-type transactions, etc.—To the extent provided in regulations, the term "equity structure shift" includes taxable reorganization-type transactions, public offerings, and similar transactions.

(4) Special rules for application of subsection.—

(A) Treatment of less than 5-percent shareholders.—Except as provided in subparagraphs (B)(i) and (C), in determining whether an ownership change has occurred, all stock owned by shareholders of a corporation who are not 5-percent shareholders of such corporation shall be treated as stock owned by 1 5-percent shareholder of such corporation.

(B) Coordination with equity structure shifts.—For purposes of determining whether an equity structure shift (or subsequent transaction) is an ownership change—

(i) Less than 5-percent shareholders.—Subparagraph (A) shall be applied separately with respect to each group of shareholders (immediately before such equity structure shift) of each corporation which was a party to the reorganization involved in such equity structure shift.

(ii) Acquisitions of stock.—Unless a different proportion is established, acquisitions of stock after such equity structure shift shall be treated as being made proportionately from all shareholders immediately before such acquisition.

(C) Coordination with other owner shifts.—Except as provided in regulations, rules similar to the rules of subparagraph (B) shall apply in determining whether there has been an owner shift involving a 5-percent shareholder and whether such shift (or subsequent transaction) results in an ownership change.

(D) Treatment of worthless stock.—If any stock held by a 50-percent shareholder is treated by such shareholder as becoming worthless during any taxable year of such shareholder and such stock is held by such shareholder as of the close of such taxable year, for purposes of determining whether an ownership change occurs after the close of such taxable year, such shareholder—

(i) shall be treated as having acquired such stock on the 1st day of his 1st succeeding taxable year, and

(ii) shall not be treated as having owned such stock during any prior period.

For purposes of the preceding sentence, the term "50-percent shareholder" means any person owning 50 percent or more of the stock of the corporation at any time during the 3-year period ending on the last day of the taxable year with respect to which the stock was so treated.

(h) Special rules for built-in gains and losses and section 338 gains.—For purposes of this section—

(1) In general.—

(A) Net unrealized built-in gain.—

(i) In general.—If the old loss corporation has a net unrealized built-in gain, the section 382 limitation for any recognition period taxable year shall be increased by the recognized built-in gains for such taxable year.

(ii) Limitation.—The increase under clause (i) for any recognition period taxable year shall not exceed—

(I) the net unrealized built-in gain, reduced by

(II) recognized built-in gains for prior years ending in the recognition period.

(B) Net unrealized built-in loss.—

(i) In general.—If the old loss corporation has a net unrealized built-in loss, the recognized built-in loss for any recognition period taxable year shall be subject to limitation under this section in the same manner as if such loss were a pre-change loss.

(ii) Limitation.—Clause (i) shall apply to recognized built-in losses for any recognition period taxable year only to the extent such losses do not exceed—

(I) the net unrealized built-in loss, reduced by

(II) recognized built-in losses for prior taxable years ending in the recognition period.

(C) Special rules for certain section 338 gains.—If an election under section 338 is made in connection with an ownership change and the net unrealized built-in gain is zero by reason of paragraph (3)(B), then, with respect to such change, the section 382 limitation for the post-change year in which gain is recognized by reason of such election shall be increased by the lesser of—

(i) the recognized built-in gains by reason of such election, or

(ii) the net unrealized built-in gain (determined without regard to paragraph (3)(B)).

(2) Recognized built-in gain and loss.—

(A) Recognized built-in gain.—The term "recognized built-in gain" means any gain recognized during the recognition period on the disposition of any asset to the extent the new loss corporation establishes that—

(i) such asset was held by the old loss corporation immediately before the change date, and

(ii) such gain does not exceed the excess of—

(I) the fair market value of such asset on the change date, over

(II) the adjusted basis of such asset on such date.

(B) Recognized built-in loss.—The term "recognized built-in loss" means any loss recognized during the recognition period on the disposition of any asset except to the extent the new loss corporation establishes that—

(i) such asset was not held by the old loss corporation immediately before the change date, or

(ii) such loss exceeds the excess of—

(I) the adjusted basis of such asset on the change date, over

(II) the fair market value of such asset on such date.

Such term includes any amount allowable as depreciation, amortization, or depletion for any period within the recognition period except to the extent the new loss corporation establishes that the amount so allowable is not attributable to the excess described in clause (ii).

(3) Net unrealized built-in gain and loss defined.—

(A) Net unrealized built-in gain and loss.—

(i) In general.—The terms "net unrealized built-in gain" and "net unrealized built-in loss" mean, with respect to any old loss corporation, the amount by which—

(I) the fair market value of the assets of such corporation immediately before an ownership change is more or less, respectively, than

(II) the aggregate adjusted basis of such assets at such time.

(ii) Special rule for redemptions or other corporate contractions.—If a redemption or other corporate contraction occurs in connection with an ownership change, to the extent provided in regulations, determinations under clause (i) shall be made after taking such redemption or other corporate contraction into account.

(B) Threshold requirement.—

(i) In general.—If the amount of the net unrealized built-in gain or net unrealized built-in loss (determined without regard to this subparagraph) of any old loss corporation is not greater than the lesser of—

(I) 15 percent of the amount determined for purposes of subparagraph (A)(i)(I), or

(II) $10,000,000, the net unrealized built-in gain or net unrealized built-in loss shall be zero.

(ii) Cash and cash items not taken into account.—In computing any net unrealized built-in gain or net unrealized built-in loss under clause (i), except as provided in regulations, there shall not be taken into account—

(I) any cash or cash item, or

(II) any marketable security which has a value which does not substantially differ from adjusted basis.

(4) Disallowed loss allowed as a carryforward.—If a deduction for any portion of a recognized built-in loss is disallowed for any post-change year, such portion—

(A) shall be carried forward to subsequent taxable years under rules similar to the rules for the carrying forward of net operating losses (or to the extent the amount so disallowed is attributable to capital losses, under rules similar to the rules for the carrying forward of net capital losses), but

(B) shall be subject to limitation under this section in the same manner as a pre-change loss.

(5) Special rules for post-change year which includes change date.—For purposes of subsection (b)(3)—

(A) in applying subparagraph (A) thereof, taxable income shall be computed without regard to recognized built-in gains to the extent such gains increased the section 382 limitation for the year (or recognized built-in losses to the extent such losses are treated as pre-change losses), and gain described in paragraph (1)(C), for the year, and

(B) in applying subparagraph (B) thereof, the section 382 limitation shall be computed without regard to recognized built-in gains, and gain described in paragraph (1)(C), for the year.

(6) Treatment of certain built-in items.—

(A) Income items.—Any item of income which is properly taken into account during the recognition period but which is attributable to periods before the change date shall be treated as a recognized built-in gain for the taxable year in which it is properly taken into account.

(B) Deduction items.—Any amount which is allowable as a deduction during the recognition period (determined without regard to any carryover) but which is attributable to periods before the change date shall be treated as a recognized built-in loss for the taxable year for which it is allowable as a deduction.

(C) Adjustments.—The amount of the net unrealized built-in gain or loss shall be properly adjusted for amounts which would be treated as recognized built-in gains or losses under this paragraph if such amounts were properly taken into account (or allowable as a deduction) during the recognition period.

(7) Recognition period, etc.—

(A) Recognition period.—The term "recognition period" means, with respect to any ownership change, the 5-year period beginning on the change date.

(B) Recognition period taxable year.—The term "recognition period taxable year" means any taxable year any portion of which is in the recognition period.

(8) Determination of fair market value in certain cases.—If 80 percent or more in value of the stock of a corporation is acquired in 1 transaction (or in a series of related transactions during any 12-month period), for purposes of determining the net unrealized built-in loss, the fair market value of the assets of such corporation shall not exceed the grossed up amount paid for such stock properly adjusted for indebtedness of the corporation and other relevant items.

(9) Tax-free exchanges or transfers.—The Secretary shall prescribe such regulations as may be necessary to carry out the purposes of this subsection where property held on the change date was acquired (or is subsequently transferred) in a transaction where gain or loss is not recognized (in whole or in part).

(i) Testing period.—For purposes of this section—

(1) 3-year period.—Except as otherwise provided in this section, the testing period is the 3-year period ending on the day of any owner shift involving a 5-percent shareholder or equity structure shift.

(2) Shorter period where there has been recent ownership change.—If there has been an ownership change under this section, the testing period for determining whether a 2nd ownership change has occurred shall not begin before the 1st day following the change date for such earlier ownership change.

(3) Shorter period where all losses arise after 3-year period begins.—The testing period shall not begin before the earlier of the 1st day of the 1st taxable year from which there is a carryforward of a loss or of an excess credit to the 1st post-change year or the taxable year in which the transaction being tested occurs. Except as provided in regulations, this paragraph shall not apply to any loss corporation which has a net unrealized built-in loss (determined after application of subsection (h)(3)(B)).

(j) Change date.—For purposes of this section, the change date is—

(1) in the case where the last component of an ownership change is an owner shift involving a 5-percent shareholder, the date on which such shift occurs, and

(2) in the case where the last component of an ownership change is an equity structure shift, the date of the reorganization.

(k) Definitions and special rules.—For purposes of this section—

(1) Loss corporation.—The term "loss corporation" means a corporation entitled to use a net operating loss carryover or having a net operating loss for the taxable year in which the ownership change occurs. Such term shall include any corporation entitled to use a carryforward of disallowed interest described in section 381(c)(20). Except to the extent provided in regulations, such term includes any corporation with a net unrealized built-in loss.

(2) Old loss corporation.—The term "old loss corporation" means any corporation—

(A) with respect to which there is an ownership change, and

(B) which (before the ownership change) was a loss corporation.

(3) New loss corporation.—The term "new loss corporation" means a corporation which (after an ownership change) is a loss corporation. Nothing in this section shall be treated as implying that the same corporation may not be both the old loss corporation and the new loss corporation.

(4) Taxable income.—Taxable income shall be computed with the modifications set forth in section 172(d).

(5) Value.—The term "value" means fair market value.

(6) Rules relating to stock.—

(A) Preferred stock.—Except as provided in regulations and subsection (e), the term "stock" means stock other than stock described in section 1504(a)(4).

(B) Treatment of certain rights, etc.—The Secretary shall prescribe such regulations as may be necessary—

(i) to treat warrants, options, contracts to acquire stock, convertible debt interests, and other similar interests as stock, and

(ii) to treat stock as not stock.

(C) Determinations on basis of value.—Determinations of the percentage of stock of any corporation held by any person shall be made on the basis of value.

(7) 5-percent shareholder.—The term "5-percent shareholder" means any person holding 5 percent or more of the stock of the corporation at any time during the testing period.

(l) Certain additional operating rules.—For purposes of this section—

(1) Certain capital contributions not taken into account.—

(A) In general.—Any capital contribution received by an old loss corporation as part of a plan a principal purpose of which is to avoid or increase any limitation under this section shall not be taken into account for purposes of this section.

(B) Certain contributions treated as part of plan.—For purposes of subparagraph (A), any capital contribution made during the 2-year period ending on the change date shall, except as provided in regulations, be treated as part of a plan described in subparagraph (A).

(2) Ordering rules for application of section.—

(A) Coordination with section 172(b) carryover rules.—In the case of any pre-change loss for any taxable year (hereinafter in this subparagraph referred to as the "loss year") subject to limitation under this section, for purposes of determining under the 2nd sentence of section 172(b)(2) the amount of such loss which may be carried to any taxable year, taxable income for any taxable year shall be treated as not greater than—

(i) the section 382 limitation for such taxable year, reduced by

(ii) the unused pre-change losses for taxable years preceding the loss year. Similar rules shall apply in the case of any credit or loss subject to limitation under section 383.

(B) Ordering rule for losses carried from same taxable year.—In any case in which—

(i) a pre-change loss of a loss corporation for any taxable year is subject to a section 382 limitation, and

(ii) a net operating loss of such corporation from such taxable year is not subject to such limitation, taxable income shall be treated as having been offset first by the loss subject to such limitation.

(3) Operating rules relating to ownership of stock.—

(A) Constructive ownership.—Section 318 (relating to constructive ownership of stock) shall apply in determining ownership of stock, except that—

(i) paragraphs (1) and (5)(B) of section 318(a) shall not apply and an individual and all members of his family described in paragraph (1) of section 318(a) shall be treated as 1 individual for purposes of applying this section,

(ii) paragraph (2) of section 318(a) shall be applied—

(I) without regard to the 50-percent limitation contained in subparagraph (C) thereof, and

(II) except as provided in regulations, by treating stock attributed thereunder as no longer being held by the entity from which attributed,

(iii) paragraph (3) of section 318(a) shall be applied only to the extent provided in regulations,

(iv) except to the extent provided in regulations, an option to acquire stock shall be treated as exercised if such exercise results in an ownership change, and

(v) in attributing stock from an entity under paragraph (2) of section 318(a), there shall not be taken into account—

(I) in the case of attribution from a corporation, stock which is not treated as stock for purposes of this section, or

(II) in the case of attribution from another entity, an interest in such entity similar to stock described in subclause (I).

A rule similar to the rule of clause (iv) shall apply in the case of any contingent purchase, warrant, convertible debt, put, stock subject to a risk of forfeiture, contract to acquire stock, or similar interests.

(B) Stock acquired by reason of death, gift, divorce, separation, etc.—If—

(i) the basis of any stock in the hands of any person is determined—

(I) under section 1014 (relating to property acquired from a decedent),

(II) section 1015 (relating to property acquired by a gift or transfer in trust), or

(III) section 1041(b)(2) (relating to transfers of property between spouses or incident to divorce),

(ii) stock is received by any person in satisfaction of a right to receive a pecuniary bequest, or

(iii) stock is acquired by a person pursuant to any divorce or separation instrument (within the meaning of section 71(b)(2)),

such person shall be treated as owning such stock during the period such stock was owned by the person from whom it was acquired.

(C) Certain changes in percentage ownership which are attributable to fluctuations in value not taken into account.—Except as provided in regulations, any change in proportionate ownership which is attributable solely to fluctuations in the relative fair market values of different classes of stock shall not be taken into account.

(4) Reduction in value where substantial nonbusiness assets.—

(A) In general.—If, immediately after an ownership change, the new loss corporation has substantial nonbusiness assets, the value of the old loss corporation shall be reduced by the excess (if any) of—

(i) the fair market value of the nonbusiness assets of the old loss corporation, over

(ii) the nonbusiness asset share of indebtedness for which such corporation is liable.

(B) Corporation having substantial nonbusiness assets.—For purposes of subparagraph (A)—

(i) In general.—The old loss corporation shall be treated as having substantial nonbusiness assets if at least 1/3 of the value of the total assets of such corporation consists of nonbusiness assets.

* * *

(C) Nonbusiness assets.—For purposes of this paragraph, the term "nonbusiness assets" means assets held for investment.

(D) Nonbusiness asset share.—For purposes of this paragraph, the nonbusiness asset share of the indebtedness of the corporation is an amount which bears the same ratio to such indebtedness as—

(i) the fair market value of the nonbusiness assets of the corporation, bears to

(ii) the fair market value of all assets of such corporation.

(E) Treatment of subsidiaries.—For purposes of this paragraph, stock and securities in any subsidiary corporation shall be disregarded and the parent corporation shall be deemed to own its ratable share of the subsidiary's assets. For purposes of the preceding sentence, a corporation shall be treated as a subsidiary if the parent owns 50 percent or more of the combined voting power of all classes of stock entitled to vote, and 50 percent or more of the total value of shares of all classes of stock.

(5) Title 11 or similar case.—

(A) In general.—Subsection (a) shall not apply to any ownership change if—

(i) the old loss corporation is (immediately before such ownership change) under the jurisdiction of the court in a title 11 or similar case, and

(ii) the shareholders and creditors of the old loss corporation (determined immediately before such ownership change) own (after such ownership change and as a result of being shareholders or creditors immediately before such change) stock of the new loss corporation (or stock of a controlling corporation if also in bankruptcy) which meets the requirements of section 1504(a)(2) (determined by substituting "50 percent" for "80 percent" each place it appears).

(B) Reduction for interest payments to creditors becoming shareholders.—In any case to which subparagraph (A) applies, the pre-change losses and excess credits (within the meaning of section 383(a)(2)) which may be carried to a post-change year shall be computed as if no deduction was allowable under this chapter for the interest paid or accrued by the old loss corporation on indebtedness which was converted into stock pursuant to title 11 or similar case during—

(i) any taxable year ending during the 3-year period preceding the taxable year in which the ownership change occurs, and

(ii) the period of the taxable year in which the ownership change occurs on or before the change date.

(C) Coordination with section 108.—In applying section 108(e)(8) to any case to which subparagraph (A) applies, there shall not be taken into account any indebtedness for interest described in subparagraph (B).

(D) Section 382 limitation zero if another change within 2 years.—If, during the 2-year period immediately following an ownership change to which this paragraph applies, an ownership change of the new loss corporation occurs, this paragraph shall not apply and the section 382 limitation with respect to the 2nd ownership change for any post-change year ending after the change date of the 2nd ownership change shall be zero.

(E) Only certain stock taken into account.—For purposes of subparagraph (A)(ii), stock transferred to a creditor shall be taken into account only to the extent such stock is transferred in satisfaction of indebtedness and only if such indebtedness—

(i) was held by the creditor at least 18 months before the date of the filing of the title 11 or similar case, or

(ii) arose in the ordinary course of the trade or business of the old loss corporation and is held by the person who at all times held the beneficial interest in such indebtedness.

(F) **Title 11 or similar case.**—For purposes of this paragraph, the term "title 11 or similar case" has the meaning given such term by section 368(a)(3)(A).

(G) **Election not to have paragraph apply.**—A new loss corporation may elect, subject to such terms and conditions as the Secretary may prescribe, not to have the provisions of this paragraph apply.

(6) **Special rule for insolvency transactions.**—If paragraph (5) does not apply to any reorganization described in subparagraph (G) of section 368(a)(1) or any exchange of debt for stock in a title 11 or similar case (as defined in section 368(a)(3)(A)), the value under subsection (e) shall reflect the increase (if any) in value of the old loss corporation resulting from any surrender or cancellation of creditors' claims in the transaction.

(7) **Coordination with alternative minimum tax.**—The Secretary shall by regulation provide for the application of this section to the alternative tax net operating loss deduction under section 56(d).

(8) **Predecessor and successor entities.**—Except as provided in regulations, any entity and any predecessor or successor entities of such entity shall be treated as 1 entity.

(m) **Regulations.**—The Secretary shall prescribe such regulations as may be necessary or appropriate to carry out the purposes of this section and section 383, including (but not limited to) regulations—

(1) providing for the application of this section and section 383 where an ownership change with respect to the old loss corporation is followed by an ownership change with respect to the new loss corporation, and

(2) providing for the application of this section and section 383 in the case of a short taxable year,

(3) providing for such adjustments to the application of this section and section 383 as is necessary to prevent the avoidance of the purposes of this section and section 383, including the avoidance of such purposes through the use of related persons, pass-thru entities, or other intermediaries,

(4) providing for the application of subsection (g)(4) where there is only 1 corporation involved, and

(5) providing, in the case of any group of corporations described in section 1563(a) (determined by substituting "50 percent" for "80 percent" each place it appears and determined without regard to paragraph (4) thereof), appropriate adjustments to value, built-in gain or loss, and other items so that items are not omitted or taken into account more than once.

(n) **Special rule for certain ownership changes.**—

(1) **In general.**—The limitation contained in subsection (a) shall not apply in the case of an ownership change which is pursuant to a restructuring plan of a taxpayer which—

(A) is required under a loan agreement or a commitment for a line of credit entered into with the Department of the Treasury under the Emergency Economic Stabilization Act of 2008, and

(B) is intended to result in a rationalization of the costs, capitalization, and capacity with respect to the manufacturing workforce of, and suppliers to, the taxpayer and its subsidiaries.

(2) Subsequent acquisitions.—Paragraph (1) shall not apply in the case of any subsequent ownership change unless such ownership change is described in such paragraph.

(3) Limitation based on control in corporation.—

(A) In general.—Paragraph (1) shall not apply in the case of any ownership change if, immediately after such ownership change, any person (other than a voluntary employees' beneficiary association under section 501(c)(9)) owns stock of the new loss corporation possessing 50 percent or more of the total combined voting power of all classes of stock entitled to vote, or of the total value of the stock of such corporation.

(B) Treatment of related persons.—

(i) In general.—Related persons shall be treated as a single person for purposes of this paragraph.

(ii) Related persons.—For purposes of clause (i), a person shall be treated as related to another person if—

(I) such person bears a relationship to such other person described in section 267(b) or 707(b), or

(II) such persons are members of a group of persons acting in concert.'.

* * *

§ 383. Special limitations on certain excess credits, etc.

(a) Excess credits.—

(1) In general.—Under regulations, if an ownership change occurs with respect to a corporation, the amount of any excess credit for any taxable year which may be used in any post-change year shall be limited to an amount determined on the basis of the tax liability which is attributable to so much of the taxable income as does not exceed the section 382 limitation for such post-change year to the extent available after the application of section 382 and subsections (b) and (c) of this section.

(2) Excess credit.—For purposes of paragraph (1), the term "excess credit" means—

(A) any unused general business credit of the corporation under section 39, and

(B) any unused minimum tax credit of the corporation under section 53.

(b) Limitation on net capital loss.—If an ownership change occurs with respect to a corporation, the amount of any net capital loss under section 1212 for any taxable year before the 1st post-change year which may be used in any post-change year shall be limited under regulations which shall be based on the principles applicable under section 382. Such regulations shall provide that any such net capital loss used in a post-change year shall reduce the section 382 limitation which is applied to pre-change losses under section 382 for such year.

* * *

(d) Pro ration rules for year which includes change.—For purposes of this section, rules similar to the rules of subsections (b)(3) and (d)(1)(B) of section 382 shall apply.

(e) Definitions.—Terms used in this section shall have the same respective meanings as when used in section 382, except that appropriate adjustments shall be made to take into account that the limitations of this section apply to credits and net capital losses.

§ 384. Limitation on use of preacquisition losses to offset built-in gains.

(a) General rule.—If—

(1)(A) a corporation acquires directly (or through 1 or more other corporations) control of another corporation, or

(B) the assets of a corporation are acquired by another corporation in a reorganization described in subparagraph (A), (C), or (D) of section 368(a)(1), and

(2) either of such corporations is a gain corporation,

income for any recognition period taxable year (to the extent attributable to recognized built-in gains) shall not be offset by any preacquisition loss (other than a preacquisition loss of the gain corporation).

(b) Exception where corporations under common control.—

(1) In general.—Subsection (a) shall not apply to the preacquisition loss of any corporation if such corporation and the gain corporation were members of the same controlled group at all times during the 5-year period ending on the acquisition date.

(2) Controlled group.—For purposes of this subsection, the term "controlled group" means a controlled group of corporations (as defined in section 1563(a)); except that—

(A) "more than 50 percent" shall be substituted for "at least 80 percent" each place it appears,

(B) the ownership requirements of section 1563(a) must be met both with respect to voting power and value, and

(C) the determination shall be made without regard to subsection (a)(4) of section 1563.

(3) Shorter period where corporations not in existence for 5 years.—If either of the corporations referred to in paragraph (1) was not in existence throughout the 5-year period referred to in paragraph (1), the period during which such corporation was in existence (or if both, the shorter of such periods) shall be substituted for such 5-year period.

(c) Definitions.—For purposes of this section—

(1) Recognized built-in gain.—

(A) In general.—The term "recognized built-in gain" means any gain recognized during the recognition period on the disposition of any asset except to the extent the gain corporation (or, in any case described in subsection (a)(1)(B), the acquiring corporation) establishes that—

(i) such asset was not held by the gain corporation on the acquisition date, or

(ii) such gain exceeds the excess (if any) of—

(I) the fair market value of such asset on the acquisition date, over

(II) the adjusted basis of such asset on such date.

(B) Treatment of certain income items.—Any item of income which is properly taken into account for any recognition period taxable year but which is attributable to periods before the acquisition date shall be treated as a recognized built-in gain for the taxable year in which it is properly taken into account and shall be taken into account in determining the amount of the net unrealized built-in gain.

(C) Limitation.—The amount of the recognized built-in gains for any recognition period taxable year shall not exceed—

(i) the net unrealized built-in gain, reduced by

(ii) the recognized built-in gains for prior years ending in the recognition period which (but for this section) would have been offset by preacquisition losses.

(2) Acquisition date.—The term "acquisition date" means

(A) in any case described in subsection (a)(1)(A), the date on which the acquisition of control occurs, or

(B) in any case described in subsection (a)(1)(B), the date of the transfer in the reorganization.

(3) Preacquisition loss.—

(A) In general.—The term "preacquisition loss" means—

(i) any net operating loss carryforward to the taxable year in which the acquisition date occurs, and

(ii) any net operating loss for the taxable year in which the acquisition date occurs to the extent such loss is allocable to the period in such year on or before the acquisition date.

Except as provided in regulations, the net operating loss shall, for purposes of clause (ii), be allocated ratably to each day in the year.

(B) Treatment of recognized built-in loss.—In the case of a corporation with a net unrealized built-in loss, the term "preacquisition loss" includes any recognized built-in loss.

(4) Gain corporation.—The term "gain corporation" means any corporation with a net unrealized built-in gain.

(5) Control.—The term "control" means ownership of stock in a corporation which meets the requirements of section 1504(a)(2).

(6) Treatment of members of same group.—Except as provided in regulations and except for purposes of subsection (b), all corporations which are members of the same affiliated group immediately before the acquisition date shall be treated as 1 corporation. To the extent provided in regulations, section 1504 shall be applied without regard to subsection (b) thereof for purposes of the preceding sentence.

(7) Treatment of predecessors and successors.—Any reference in this section to a corporation shall include a reference to any predecessor or successor thereof.

(8) Other definitions.—Except as provided in regulations, the terms "net unrealized built-in gain", "net unrealized built-in loss", "recognized built-in loss", "recognition period", and "recognition period taxable year", have the same respective meanings as when used in section 382(h), except that the acquisition date shall be taken into account in lieu of the change date.

(d) Limitation also to apply to excess credits or net capital losses.—Rules similar to the rules of subsection (a) shall also apply in the case of any excess credit (as defined in section 383(a)(2)) or net capital loss.

(e) Ordering rules for net operating losses, etc.—

(1) Carryover rules.—If any preacquisition loss may not offset a recognized built-in gain by reason of this section, such gain shall not be taken into account in determining under section 172(b)(2) the amount of such loss which may be carried to other taxable years. A similar rule shall apply in the case of any excess credit or net capital loss limited by reason of subsection (d).

(2) Ordering rule for losses carried from same taxable year.—In any case in which—

(A) a preacquisition loss for any taxable year is subject to limitation under subsection (a), and

(B) a net operating loss from such taxable year is not subject to such limitation,

taxable income shall be treated as having been offset 1st by the loss subject to such limitation.

(f) Regulations.—The Secretary shall prescribe such regulations as may be necessary to carry out the purposes of this section, including regulations to ensure that the purposes of this section may not be circumvented through—

(1) the use of any provision of law or regulations (including subchapter K of this chapter), or

(2) contributions of property to a corporation.

Part VI—Treatment of Certain Corporate Interests as Stock or Indebtedness

§ 385. Treatment of certain interests in corporations as stock or indebtedness.

(a) Authority to prescribe regulations.—The Secretary is authorized to prescribe such regulations as may be necessary or appropriate to determine whether an interest in a corporation is to be treated for purposes of this title as stock or indebtedness (or as in part stock and in part indebtedness).

(b) Factors.—The regulations prescribed under this section shall set forth factors which are to be taken into account in determining with respect to a particular factual situation whether a debtor-creditor relationship exists or a corporation-shareholder relationship exists. The factors so set forth in the regulations may include among other factors:

(1) whether there is a written unconditional promise to pay on demand or on a specified date a sum certain in money in return for an adequate consideration in money or money's worth, and to pay a fixed rate of interest,

(2) whether there is subordination to or preference over any indebtedness of the corporation,

(3) the ratio of debt to equity of the corporation,

(4) whether there is convertibility into the stock of the corporation, and

(5) the relationship between holdings of stock in the corporation and holdings of the interest in question.

(c) Effect of classification by issuer.—

(1) In general.—The characterization (as of the time of issuance) by the issuer as to whether an interest in a corporation is stock or indebtedness shall be binding on such issuer and on all holders of such interest (but shall not be binding on the Secretary).

(2) Notification of inconsistent treatment.—Except as provided in regulations, paragraph (1) shall not apply to any holder of an interest if such holder on his return discloses that he is treating such interest in a manner inconsistent with the characterization referred to in paragraph (1).

(3) Regulations.—The Secretary is authorized to require such information as the Secretary determines to be necessary to carry out the provisions of this subsection.

Subchapter E—Accounting Periods and Methods of Accounting

Part II—Methods of Accounting

§ 453. Installment Method—

(a) General rule—Except as otherwise provided in this section, income from an installment sale shall be taken into account for purposes of this title under the installment method.

(b) Installment sale defined—For purposes of this section—

(1) In general—The term "installment sale" means a disposition of property where at least 1 payment is to be received after the close of the taxable year in which the disposition occurs.

(2) Exceptions—The term "installment sale" does not include—

(A) Dealer dispositions—Any dealer disposition (as defined in subsection (*l*)).

(B) Inventories of personal property—A disposition of personal property of a kind which is required to be included in the inventory of the taxpayer if on hand at the close of the taxable year.

(c) Installment method defined—For purposes of this section, the term "installment method" means a method under which the income recognized for any taxable year from a disposition is that proportion of the payments received in that year which the gross profit (realized or to be realized when payment is completed) bears to the total contract price.

* * *

§ 461. General rule for taxable year of deduction

(a) General rule.—The amount of any deduction or credit allowed by this subtitle shall be taken for the taxable year which is the proper taxable year under the method of accounting used in computing taxable income.

* * *

(1) Limitation.—In the case of taxable year of a taxpayer other than a corporation beginning after December 31, 2017, and before January 1, 2026—

(A) subsection (j) (relating to limitation on excess farm losses of certain taxpayers) shall not apply, and

(B) any excess business loss of the taxpayer for the taxable year shall not be allowed.

(2) Disallowed loss carryover.—Any loss which is disallowed under paragraph (1) shall be treated as a net operating loss carryover to the following taxable year under section 172.

(3) Excess business loss.—For purposes of this subsection—

(A) In general.—The term 'excess business loss' means the excess (if any) of—

(i) the aggregate deductions of the taxpayer for the taxable year which are attributable to trades or businesses of such taxpayer (determined without regard to whether or not such deductions are disallowed for such taxable year under paragraph (1)), over

(ii) the sum of—

(I) the aggregate gross income or gain of such taxpayer for the taxable year which is attributable to such trades or businesses, plus

(II) $250,000 (200 percent of such amount in the case of a joint return).

(B) Adjustment for inflation.—In the case of any taxable year beginning after December 31, 2018, the $250,000 amount in subparagraph (A)(ii)(II) shall be increased by an amount equal to—

(i) such dollar amount, multiplied by

(ii) the cost-of-living adjustment determined under section 1(f)(3) for the calendar year in which the taxable year begins, determined by substituting '2017' for '2016' in subparagraph (A)(ii) thereof.

If any amount as increased under the preceding sentence is not a multiple of $1,000, such amount shall be rounded to the nearest multiple of $1,000.

(4) Application of subsection in case of partnerships and S corporations.—In the case of a partnership or S corporation—

(A) this subsection shall be applied at the partner or shareholder level, and

(B) each partner's or shareholder's allocable share of the items of income, gain, deduction, or loss of the partnership or S corporation for any taxable year from trades or businesses attributable to the partnership or S corporation shall be taken into account by the partner or shareholder in applying this subsection to the taxable year of such partner or shareholder with or within which the taxable year of the partnership or S corporation ends.

For purposes of this paragraph, in the case of an S corporation, an allocable share shall be the shareholder's pro rata share of an item.

(5) Additional reporting.—The Secretary shall prescribe such additional reporting requirements as the Secretary determines necessary to carry out the purposes of this subsection.

(6) Coordination with section 469.—This subsection shall be applied after the application of section 469.

* * *

Part III—Adjustments

§ 481. Adjustments required by changes in method of accounting.

(a) General rule—In computing the taxpayer's taxable income for any taxable year (referred to in this section as the "year of the change")—

(1) if such computation is under a method of accounting different from the method under which the taxpayer's taxable income for the preceding taxable year was computed, then

(2) there shall be taken into account those adjustments which are determined to be necessary solely by reason of the change in order to prevent amounts from being duplicated or omitted, except there shall not be taken into account any adjustment in respect of any taxable year to which this section does not apply unless the adjustment is attributable to a change in the method of accounting initiated by the taxpayer.

* * *

(d) Adjustments attributable to conversion from S corporation to C corporation.—

(1) In general.—In the case of an eligible terminated S corporation, any adjustment required by subsection (a)(2) which is attributable to such corporation's revocation described in paragraph (2)(A)(ii) shall be taken into account ratably during the 6-taxable year period beginning with the year of change.

(2) Eligible terminated S corporation.—For purposes of this subsection, the term 'eligible terminated S corporation' means any C corporation—

(A) which—

(i) was an S corporation on the day before the date of the enactment of the Tax Cuts and Jobs Act, and

(ii) during the 2-year period beginning on the date of such enactment makes a revocation of its election under section 1362(a), and

(B) the owners of the stock of which, determined on the date such revocation is made, are the same owners (and in identical proportions) as on the date of such enactment.

§ 482. Allocation of income and deductions among taxpayers.

In any case of two or more organizations, trades, or businesses (whether or not incorporated, whether or not organized in the United States, and whether or not affiliated) owned or controlled directly or indirectly by the same interests, the Secretary may distribute, apportion, or allocate gross income, deductions, credits, or allowances between or among such organizations, trades, or businesses, if he determines that such distribution, apportionment, or allocation is necessary in order to prevent evasion of taxes or clearly to reflect the income of any of such organizations, trades, or businesses. In the case of any transfer (or license) of intangible property (within the meaning of section 936(h)(3)(B)), the income with respect to such transfer or license shall be commensurate with the income attributable to the intangible.

Subchapter G—Corporations Used to Avoid Income Tax on Shareholders

Part I—Corporations Improperly Accumulating Surplus

§ 531. Imposition of accumulated earnings tax.

In addition to other taxes imposed by this chapter, there is hereby imposed for each taxable year on the accumulated taxable income (as defined in section 535) of each corporation described in section 532, an accumulated earnings tax equal to 20 percent of the accumulated taxable income.

§ 532. Corporations subject to accumulated earnings tax.

(a) **General rule.**—The accumulated earnings tax imposed by section 531 shall apply to every corporation (other than those described in subsection (b)) formed or availed of for the purpose of avoiding the income tax with respect to its shareholders or the shareholders of any other corporation, by permitting earnings and profits to accumulate instead of being divided or distributed.

(b) **Exceptions.**—The accumulated earnings tax imposed by section 531 shall not apply to—

(1) a personal holding company (as defined in section 542),

* * *

(3) a corporation exempt from tax under subchapter F (section 501 and following), or

* * *

(c) **Application determined without regard to number of shareholders.**—The application of this part to a corporation shall be determined without regard to the number of shareholders of such corporation.

§ 533. Evidence of purpose to avoid income tax.

(a) **Unreasonable accumulation determinative of purpose.**—For purposes of section 532, the fact that the earnings and profits of a corporation are permitted to accumulate beyond the reasonable needs of the business shall be determinative of the purpose to avoid the income tax with respect to shareholders, unless the corporation by the preponderance of the evidence shall prove to the contrary.

(b) **Holding or investment company.**—The fact that any corporation is a mere holding or investment company shall be prima facie evidence of the purpose to avoid the income tax with respect to shareholders.

§ 534. Burden of proof.

(a) General rule.—In any proceeding before the Tax Court involving a notice of deficiency based in whole or in part on the allegation that all or any part of the earnings and profits have been permitted to accumulate beyond the reasonable needs of the business, the burden of proof with respect to such allegation shall—

(1) if notification has not been sent in accordance with subsection (b), be on the Secretary, or

(2) if the taxpayer has submitted the statement described in subsection (c), be on the Secretary with respect to the grounds set forth in such statement in accordance with the provisions of such subsection.

(b) Notification by Secretary.—Before mailing the notice of deficiency referred to in subsection (a), the Secretary may send by certified mail or registered mail a notification informing the taxpayer that the proposed notice of deficiency includes an amount with respect to the accumulated earnings tax imposed by section 531.

(c) Statement by taxpayer.—Within such time (but not less than 30 days) after the mailing of the notification described in subsection (b) as the Secretary may prescribe by regulations, the taxpayer may submit a statement of the grounds (together with facts sufficient to show the basis thereof) on which the taxpayer relies to establish that all or any part of the earnings and profits have not been permitted to accumulate beyond the reasonable needs of the business.

* * *

§ 535. Accumulated taxable income.

(a) Definition.—For purposes of this subtitle, the term "accumulated taxable income" means the taxable income, adjusted in the manner provided in subsection (b), minus the sum of the dividends paid deduction (as defined in section 561) and the accumulated earnings credit (as defined in subsection (c)).

(b) Adjustments to taxable income.—For purposes of subsection (a), taxable income shall be adjusted as follows:

(1) Taxes.—There shall be allowed as a deduction Federal income and excess profits taxes and income, war profits, and excess profits taxes of foreign countries and possessions of the United States (to the extent not allowable as a deduction under section 275(a)(4)), accrued during the taxable year or deemed to be paid by a domestic corporation under section 902(a) or 960(a)(1) for the taxable year, but not including the accumulated earnings tax imposed by section 531, the personal holding company tax imposed by section 541, or the taxes imposed by corresponding sections of a prior income tax law.

(2) Charitable contributions.—The deduction for charitable contributions provided under section 170 shall be allowed without regard to section 170(b)(2).

(3) Special deductions disallowed.—The special deductions for corporations provided in part VIII (except section 248) of subchapter B (section 241 and following, relating to the deduction for dividends received by corporations, etc.) shall not be allowed.

(4) Net operating loss.—The net operating loss deduction provided in section 172 shall not be allowed.

(5) Capital losses.—

(A) In general.—Except as provided in subparagraph (B), there shall be allowed as a deduction an amount equal to the net capital loss for the taxable year (determined without regard to paragraph (7)(A)).

(B) Recapture of previous deductions for capital gains.—The aggregate amount allowable as a deduction under subparagraph (A) for any taxable year shall be reduced by the lesser of—

(i) the nonrecaptured capital gains deductions, or

(ii) the amount of the accumulated earnings and profits of the corporation as of the close of the preceding taxable year.

(C) Nonrecaptured capital gains deductions.—For purposes of subparagraph (B), the term "nonrecaptured capital gains deductions" means the excess of—

(i) the aggregate amount allowable as a deduction under paragraph (6) for preceding taxable years beginning after July 18, 1984, over

(ii) the aggregate of the reductions under subparagraph (B) for preceding taxable years.

(6) Net capital gains.—

(A) In general.—There shall be allowed as a deduction—

(i) the net capital gain for the taxable year (determined with the application of paragraph (7)), reduced by

(ii) the taxes attributable to such net capital gain.

(B) Attributable taxes.—For purposes of subparagraph (A), the taxes attributable to the net capital gain shall be an amount equal to the difference between—

(i) the taxes imposed by this subtitle (except the tax imposed by this part) for the taxable year, and

(ii) such taxes computed for such year without including in taxable income the net capital gain for the taxable year (determined without the application of paragraph (7)).

(7) Capital loss carryovers.—

(A) Unlimited carryforward.—The net capital loss for any taxable year shall be treated as a short-term capital loss in the next taxable year.

(B) Section 1212 inapplicable.—No allowance shall be made for the capital loss carryback or carryforward provided in section 1212.

(8) Special rules for mere holding or investment companies.—In the case of a mere holding or investment company—

(A) Capital loss deduction, etc., not allowed.—Paragraphs (5) and (7)(A) shall not apply.

(B) Deduction for certain offsets.—There shall be allowed as a deduction the net short-term capital gain for the taxable year to the extent such gain does not exceed the amount of any capital loss carryover to such taxable year under section 1212 (determined without regard to paragraph (7)(B)).

(C) Earnings and profits.—For purposes of subchapter C, the accumulated earnings and profits at any time shall not be less than they would be if this subsection had applied to the computation of earnings and profits for all taxable years beginning after July 18, 1984.

* * *

(c) Accumulated earnings credit.—

(1) General rule.—For purposes of subsection (a), in the case of a corporation other than a mere holding or investment company the accumulated earnings credit is (A) an amount equal to such part of the earnings and profits for the taxable year as are retained for the reasonable needs of the business, minus (B) the deduction allowed by subsection (b)(6). For purposes of this paragraph, the amount of the earnings and profits for the taxable year which are retained is the amount by which the earnings and profits for the taxable year exceed the dividends paid deduction (as defined in section 561) for such year.

(2) Minimum credit.—

(A) In general.—The credit allowable under paragraph (1) shall in no case be less than the amount by which $250,000 exceeds the accumulated earnings and profits of the corporation at the close of the preceding taxable year.

(B) Certain service corporations.—In the case of a corporation the principal function of which is the performance of services in the field of health, law, engineering, architecture, accounting, actuarial science, performing arts, or consulting, subparagraph (A) shall be applied by substituting "$150,000" for "$250,000".

(3) Holding and investment companies.—In the case of a corporation which is a mere holding or investment company, the accumulated earnings credit is the amount (if any) by which $250,000 exceeds the accumulated earnings and profits of the corporation at the close of the preceding taxable year.

(4) Accumulated earnings and profits.—For purposes of paragraphs (2) and (3), the accumulated earnings and profits at the close of the preceding taxable year shall be reduced by the dividends which under section 563(a) (relating to dividends paid after the close of the taxable year) are considered as paid during such taxable year.

* * *

§ 537. Reasonable needs of the business.

(a) General rule.—For purposes of this part, the term "reasonable needs of the business" includes—

(1) the reasonably anticipated needs of the business,

(2) the section 303 redemption needs of the business, and

(3) the excess business holdings redemption needs of the business.

(b) Special rules.—For purposes of subsection (a)—

(1) Section 303 redemption needs.—The term "section 303 redemption needs" means, with respect to the taxable year of the corporation in which a shareholder of the corporation died or any taxable year thereafter, the amount needed (or reasonably anticipated to be needed) to make a redemption of stock included in the gross estate of the decedent (but not in excess of the maximum amount of stock to which section 303(a) may apply).

* * *

(3) Obligations incurred to make redemptions.—In applying paragraphs (1) and (2), the discharge of any obligation incurred to make a redemption described in such paragraphs shall be treated as the making of such redemption.

* * *

(4) Product liability loss reserves.—The accumulation of reasonable amounts for the payment of reasonably anticipated product liability losses (as defined in section 172(f)), as determined under regulations prescribed by the Secretary, shall be treated as accumulated for the reasonably anticipated needs of the business.

(5) No inference as to prior taxable years.—The application of this part to any taxable year before the first taxable year specified in paragraph (1) shall be made without regard to the fact that distributions in redemption coming within the terms of such paragraphs were subsequently made.

Part II—Personal Holding Companies

§ 541. Imposition of personal holding company tax.

In addition to other taxes imposed by this chapter, there is hereby imposed for each taxable year on the undistributed personal holding company income (as defined in section 545) of every personal holding company (as defined in section 542) a personal holding company tax equal to 20 percent of the undistributed personal holding company income.

§ 542. Definition of personal holding company.

(a) General rule.—For purposes of this subtitle, the term "personal holding company" means any corporation (other than a corporation described in subsection (c)) if—

(1) Adjusted ordinary gross income requirement.—At least 60 percent of its adjusted ordinary gross income (as defined in section 543(b)(2)) for the taxable year is personal holding company income (as defined in section 543(a)), and

(2) Stock ownership requirement.—At any time during the last half of the taxable year more than 50 percent in value of its outstanding stock is owned, directly or indirectly, by or for not more than 5 individuals

* * *

(c) Exceptions.—The term "personal holding company" as defined in subsection (a) does not include—

(1) a corporation exempt from tax under subchapter F (sec. 501 and following);

(2) a bank as defined in section 581, or a domestic building and loan association within the meaning of section 7701(a)(19);

(3) a life insurance company;

(4) a surety company;

* * *

(6) a lending or finance company if—

(A) 60 percent or more of its ordinary gross income (as defined in section 543(b)(1)) is derived directly from the active and regular conduct of a lending or finance business;

(B) the personal holding company income for the taxable year (computed without regard to income described in subsection (d)(3) and income derived directly from the active and regular conduct of a lending or finance business, and computed by including as personal holding company income the entire amount of the gross income from rents, royalties, produced film rents, and compensation for use of corporate property by shareholders) is not more than 20 percent of the ordinary gross income;

(C) the sum of the deductions which are directly allocable to the active and regular conduct of its lending or finance business equals or exceeds the sum of—

(i) 15 percent of so much of the ordinary gross income derived therefrom as does not exceed $500,000, plus

(ii) 5 percent of so much of the ordinary gross income derived therefrom as exceeds $500,000; and

(D) the loans to a person who is a shareholder in such company during the taxable year by or for whom 10 percent or more in value of its outstanding stock is owned directly or indirectly (including, in the case of an individual, stock owned by members of his family as defined in section 544(a)(2)), outstanding at any time during such year do not exceed $5,000 in principal amount;

* * *

§ 543. Personal holding company income.

(a) General rule.—For purposes of this subtitle, the term "personal holding company income" means the portion of the adjusted ordinary gross income which consists of:

(1) Dividends, etc.—Dividends, interest, royalties (other than mineral, oil, or gas royalties or copyright royalties), and annuities. This paragraph shall not apply to—

(A) interest constituting rent (as defined in subsection (b)(3)),

* * *

(C) active business computer software royalties (within the meaning of subsection (d)), and

(D) interest received by a broker or dealer (within the meaning of section 3(a)(4) or (5) of the Securities and Exchange Act of 1934) in connection with—

(i) any securities or money market instruments held as property described in section 1221(1),

(ii) margin accounts, or

(iii) any financing for a customer secured by securities or money market instruments.

(2) Rents.—The adjusted income from rents; except that such adjusted income shall not be included if—

(A) such adjusted income constitutes 50 percent or more of the adjusted ordinary gross income, and

(B) the sum of—

(i) the dividends paid during the taxable year (determined under section 562),

(ii) the dividends considered as paid on the last day of the taxable year under section 563(c) (as limited by the second sentence of section 563(b)), and

(iii) the consent dividends for the taxable year (determined under section 565), equals or exceeds the amount, if any, by which the personal holding company income for the taxable year (computed without regard to this paragraph and paragraph (6), and computed by including as personal holding company income copyright royalties and the adjusted income from mineral, oil, and gas royalties) exceeds 10 percent of the ordinary gross income.

* * *

(b) Definitions.—For purposes of this part—

(1) Ordinary gross income.—The term "ordinary gross income" means the gross income determined by excluding—

(A) all gains from the sale or other disposition of capital assets, and

(B) all gains (other than those referred to in subparagraph (A)) from the sale or other disposition of property described in section 1231(b).

(2) Adjusted ordinary gross income.—The term "adjusted ordinary gross income" means the ordinary gross income adjusted as follows:

(A) Rents.—From the gross income from rents (as defined in the second sentence of paragraph (3) of this subsection) subtract the amount allowable as deductions for—

(i) exhaustion, wear and tear, obsolescence, and amortization of property other than tangible personal property which is not customarily retained by any one lessee for more than three years,

(ii) property taxes,

(iii) interest, and

(iv) rent,

to the extent allocable, under regulations prescribed by the Secretary, to such gross income from rents. The amount subtracted under this subparagraph shall not exceed such gross income from rents.

* * *

(C) Interest.—There shall be excluded—

(i) interest received on a direct obligation of the United States held for sale to customers in the ordinary course of trade or business by a regular dealer who is making a primary market in such obligations, and

(ii) interest on a condemnation award, a judgment, and a tax refund.

* * *

§ 544. Rules for determining stock ownership.

(a) Constructive ownership.—For purposes of determining whether a corporation is a personal holding company, insofar as such determination is based on stock ownership under section 542(a)(2), section 543(a)(7), section 543(a)(6), or section 543(a)(4)—

(1) Stock not owned by individual.—Stock owned, directly or indirectly, by or for a corporation, partnership, estate, or trust shall be considered as being owned proportionately by its shareholders, partners, or beneficiaries.

(2) Family and partnership ownership.—An individual shall be considered as owning the stock owned, directly or indirectly, by or for his family or by or for his partner. For purposes of this paragraph, the family of an individual includes only his brothers and sisters (whether by the whole or half blood), spouse, ancestors, and lineal descendants.

(3) Options.—If any person has an option to acquire stock, such stock shall be considered as owned by such person. For purposes of this paragraph, an option to acquire such an option, and each one of a series of such options, shall be considered as an option to acquire such stock.

(4) Application of family-partnership and option rules.—Paragraphs (2) and (3) shall be applied—

(A) for purposes of the stock ownership requirement provided in section 542(a)(2), if, but only if, the effect is to make the corporation a personal holding company;

(B) for purposes of section 543(a)(7) (relating to personal service contracts), of section 543(a)(6) (relating to use of property by shareholders), or of section 543(a)(4) (relating to copyright royalties), if, but only if, the effect is to make the amounts therein referred to includible under such paragraph as personal holding company income.

(5) Constructive ownership as actual ownership.—Stock constructively owned by a person by reason of the application of paragraph (1) or (3) shall, for purposes of applying paragraph (1) or (2), be treated as actually owned by such person; but stock constructively owned by an individual by reason of the application of paragraph (2) shall not be treated as owned by him for purposes of again applying such paragraph in order to make another the constructive owner of such stock.

(6) Option rule in lieu of family and partnership rule.—If stock may be considered as owned by an individual under either paragraph (2) or (3) it shall be considered as owned by him under paragraph (3).

* * *

§ 545. Undistributed personal holding company income.

(a) Definition.—For purposes of this part, the term "undistributed personal holding company income" means the taxable income of a personal holding company adjusted in the manner provided in subsections (b), (c), and (d), minus the dividends paid deduction as defined in section 561. * * *

(b) Adjustments to taxable income.—For the purposes of subsection (a), the taxable income shall be adjusted as follows:

(1) Taxes.—There shall be allowed as a deduction Federal income and excess profits taxes and income, war profits and excess profits taxes of foreign countries and possessions of the United States (to the extent not allowable as a deduction under section 275(a)(4)), accrued during the taxable year or deemed to be paid by a domestic corporation under section 902(a) or 960(a)(1) for the taxable year, but not including the accumulated earnings tax imposed by section 531, the personal holding company tax imposed by section 541, or the taxes imposed by corresponding sections of a prior income tax law.

(2) Charitable contributions.—The deduction for charitable contributions provided under section 170 shall be allowed, but in computing such deduction the limitations in section 170(b)(1)(A), (B), (D), and (E) shall apply, and section 170(b)(2) and (d)(1) shall not apply. For purposes of this paragraph, the term "contribution base" when used in section 170(b)(1) means the taxable income computed with the adjustments (other than the 10-percent limitation) provided in section 170(b)(2) and (d)(1) and without deduction of the amount disallowed under paragraph (6) of this subsection.

(3) Special deductions disallowed.—The special deductions for corporations provided in part VIII (except section 248) of subchapter B (section 241 and following, relating to the deduction for dividends received by corporations, etc.) shall not be allowed.

(4) Net operating loss.—The net operating loss deduction provided in section 172 shall not be allowed, but there shall be allowed as a deduction the amount of the net operating loss (as defined in section 172(c)) for the preceding taxable year computed without the deductions provided in part VIII (except section 248) of subchapter B.

(5) Net capital gains.—There shall be allowed as a deduction the net capital gain for the taxable year, minus the taxes imposed by this subtitle attributable to such net capital gain. The taxes attributable to such net capital gain shall be an amount equal to the difference between—

(A) the taxes imposed by this subtitle (except the tax imposed by this part) for such year, and

(B) such taxes computed for such year without including such net capital gain in taxable income.

(6) Expenses and depreciation applicable to property of the taxpayer.—The aggregate of the deductions allowed under section 162 (relating to trade or business expenses) and section 167 (relating to depreciation), which are allocable to the operation and maintenance of property owned or operated by the corporation, shall be allowed only in an amount equal to the rent or other compensation received for the use of, or the right to use, the property, unless it is established (under regulations prescribed by the Secretary) to the satisfaction of the Secretary—

(A) that the rent or other compensation received was the highest obtainable, or, if none was received, that none was obtainable;

(B) that the property was held in the course of a business carried on bona fide for profit; and

(C) either that there was reasonable expectation that the operation of the property would result in a profit, or that the property was necessary to the conduct of the business.

* * *

§ 547. Deduction for deficiency dividends.

(a) General rule.—If a determination (as defined in subsection (c)) with respect to a taxpayer establishes liability for personal holding company tax imposed by section 541 (or by a corresponding provision of a prior income tax law) for any taxable year, a deduction shall be allowed to the taxpayer for the amount of deficiency dividends (as defined in subsection (d)) for the purpose of determining the personal holding company tax for such year, but not for the purpose of determining interest, additional amounts, or assessable penalties computed with respect to such personal holding company tax.

(b) Rules for application of section.—

(1) Allowance of deduction.—The deficiency dividend deduction shall be allowed as of the date the claim for the deficiency dividend deduction is filed.

(2) Credit or refund.—If the allowance of a deficiency dividend deduction results in an overpayment of personal holding company tax for any taxable year, credit or refund with respect to such overpayment shall be made as if on the date of the determination 2 years remained before the expiration of the period of limitation on the filing of claim for refund for the taxable year to which the overpayment relates. No interest shall be allowed on a credit or refund arising from the application of this section.

(c) Determination.—For purposes of this section, the term "determination" means—

(1) a decision by the Tax Court or a judgment, decree, or other order by any court of competent jurisdiction, which has become final;

(2) a closing agreement made under section 7121; or

(3) under regulations prescribed by the Secretary, an agreement signed by the Secretary and by, or on behalf of, the taxpayer relating to the liability of such taxpayer for personal holding company tax.

(d) Deficiency dividends.—

(1) Definition.—For purposes of this section, the term "deficiency dividends" means the amount of the dividends paid by the corporation on or after the date of the determination and before filing claim under subsection (e), which would have been includible in the computation of the deduction for dividends paid under section 561 for the taxable year with respect to which the liability for personal holding company tax exists, if distributed during such taxable year. No dividends shall be considered as deficiency dividends for purposes of subsection (a) unless distributed within 90 days after the determination.

(2) Effect on dividends paid deduction.—

(A) For taxable year in which paid.—Deficiency dividends paid in any taxable year (to the extent of the portion thereof taken into account under subsection (a) in determining personal holding company tax) shall not be included in the amount of dividends paid for such year for purposes of computing the dividends paid deduction for such year and succeeding years.

(B) **For prior taxable year.**—Deficiency dividends paid in any taxable year (to the extent of the portion thereof taken into account under subsection (a) in determining personal holding company tax) shall not be allowed for purposes of section 563(b) in the computation of the dividends paid deduction for the taxable year preceding the taxable year in which paid.

(e) **Claim required.**—No deficiency dividend deduction shall be allowed under subsection (a) unless (under regulations prescribed by the Secretary) claim therefor is filed within 120 days after the determination.

(f) **Suspension of statute of limitations and stay of collection.**—

(1) **Suspension of running of statute.**—If the corporation files a claim, as provided in subsection (e), the running of the statute of limitations provided in section 6501 on the making of assessments, and the bringing of distraint or a proceeding in court for collection, in respect of the deficiency and all interest, additional amounts, or assessable penalties, shall be suspended for a period of 2 years after the date of the determination.

(2) **Stay of collection.**—In the case of any deficiency with respect to the tax imposed by section 541 established by a determination under this section—

(A) the collection of the deficiency and all interest, additional amounts, and assessable penalties shall, except in cases of jeopardy, be stayed until the expiration of 120 days after the date of the determination, and

(B) if claim for deficiency dividend deduction is filed under subsection (e), the collection of such part of the deficiency as is not reduced by the deduction for deficiency dividends provided in subsection (a) shall be stayed until the date the claim is disallowed (in whole or in part), and if disallowed in part collection shall be made only with respect to the part disallowed.

No distraint or proceeding in court shall be begun for the collection of an amount the collection of which is stayed under subparagraph (A) or (B) during the period for which the collection of such amount is stayed.

(g) **Deduction denied in case of fraud, etc.**—No deficiency dividend deduction shall be allowed under subsection (a) if the determination contains a finding that any part of the deficiency is due to fraud with intent to evade tax, or to wilful failure to file an income tax return within the time prescribed by law or prescribed by the Secretary in pursuance of law.

Part IV—Deduction for Dividends Paid

§ 561. Definition of deduction for dividends paid.

(a) **General rule.**—The deduction for dividends paid shall be the sum of—

(1) the dividends paid during the taxable year,

(2) the consent dividends for the taxable year (determined under section 565), and

(3) in the case of a personal holding company, the dividend carryover described in section 564.

(b) **Special rules applicable.**—In determining the deduction for dividends paid, the rules provided in section 562 (relating to rules applicable in determining dividends eligible for dividends paid deduction) and section 563 (relating to dividends paid after the close of the taxable year) shall be applicable.

§ 562. Rules applicable in determining dividends eligible for dividends paid deduction.

(a) General rule.—For purposes of this part, the term "dividend" shall, except as otherwise provided in this section, include only dividends described in section 316 (relating to definition of dividends for purposes of corporate distributions).

(b) Distributions in liquidation.—

(1) Except in the case of a personal holding company described in section 542—

(A) in the case of amounts distributed in liquidation, the part of such distribution which is properly chargeable to earnings and profits accumulated after February 28, 1913, shall be treated as a dividend for purposes of computing the dividends paid deduction, and

(B) in the case of a complete liquidation occurring within 24 months after the adoption of a plan of liquidation, any distribution within such period pursuant to such plan shall, to the extent of the earnings and profits (computed without regard to capital losses) of the corporation for the taxable year in which such distribution is made, be treated as a dividend for purposes of computing the dividends paid deduction.

For purposes of subparagraph (A), a liquidation includes a redemption of stock to which section 302 applies. Except to the extent provided in regulations, the preceding sentence shall not apply in the case of any mere holding or investment company which is not a regulated investment company.

(2) In the case of a complete liquidation of a personal holding company, occurring within 24 months after the adoption of a plan of liquidation, the amount of any distribution within such period pursuant to such plan shall be treated as a dividend for purposes of computing the dividends paid deduction, to the extent that such amount is distributed to corporate distributees and represents such corporate distributees' allocable share of the undistributed personal holding company income for the taxable year of such distribution computed without regard to this paragraph and without regard to subparagraph (B) of section 316(b)(2).

(c) Preferential dividends.—

(1) In general.—Except in the case of a publicly offered regulated investment company (as defined in section 67(c)(2)(B)) or a publicly offered REIT, the amount of any distribution shall not be considered as a dividend for purposes of computing the dividends paid deduction, unless such distribution is pro rata, with no preference to any share of stock as compared with other shares of the same class, and with no preference to one class of stock as compared with another class except to the extent that the former is entitled (without reference to waivers of their rights by shareholders) to such preference. In the case of a distribution by a regulated investment company (other than a publicly offered regulated investment company (as so defined)) to a shareholder who made an initial investment of at least $10,000,000 in such company, such distribution shall not be treated as not being pro rata or as being preferential solely by reason of an increase in the distribution by reason of reductions in administrative expenses of the company.

(2) Publicly Offered REIT.—For purposes of this subsection, the term 'publicly offered REIT' means a real estate investment trust which is required to file annual and periodic reports with the Securities and Exchange Commission under the Securities Exchange Act of 1934.

(d) Distributions by a member of an affiliated group.—In the case where a corporation which is a member of an affiliated group of corporations filing or required to file a consolidated return for a taxable year is required to file a separate personal holding company schedule for such taxable year, a distribution by such corporation to another member of the affiliated group shall be considered as a dividend for purposes of computing the dividends paid deduction if such distribution would constitute a dividend under the other provisions of this section to a recipient which is not a member of an affiliated group.

(e) Special rules for real estate investment trusts.—

(1) Determination of earnings and profits for purposes of dividend paid deduction—In the case of a real estate investment trust, in determining the amount of dividends under section 316 for purposes of computing the dividends paid deduction, the earnings and profits of such trust for any taxable year beginning after December 31, 1980, shall be increased by the total amount of gain (if any) on the sale or exchange of real property by such trust during such taxable year.

(2) Authority to provide alternative remedies for certain failures.—In the case of a failure of a distribution by a real estate investment trust to comply with the requirements of subsection (c), the Secretary may provide an appropriate remedy to cure such failure in lieu of not considering the distribution to be a dividend for purposes of computing the dividends paid deduction if—

(A) the Secretary determines that such failure is inadvertent or is due to reasonable cause and not due to willful neglect, or

(B) such failure is of a type of failure which the Secretary has identified for purposes of this paragraph as being described in subparagraph (A).

§ 563. Rules relating to dividends paid after close of taxable year.

(a) Accumulated earnings tax.—In the determination of the dividends paid deduction for purposes of the accumulated earnings tax imposed by section 531, a dividend paid after the close of any taxable year and on or before the 15th day of the third month following the close of such taxable year shall be considered as paid during such taxable year.

(b) Personal holding company tax.—In the determination of the dividends paid deduction for purposes of the personal holding company tax imposed by section 541, a dividend paid after the close of any taxable year and on or before the 15th day of the third month following the close of such taxable year shall, to the extent the taxpayer elects in its return for the taxable year, be considered as paid during such taxable year. The amount allowed as a dividend by reason of the application of this subsection with respect to any taxable year shall not exceed either—

(1) The undistributed personal holding company income of the corporation for the taxable year, computed without regard to this subsection, or

(2) 20 percent of the sum of the dividends paid during the taxable year, computed without regard to this subsection.

(c) Dividends considered as paid on last day of taxable year.—For the purpose of applying section 562(a), with respect to distributions under subsection (a) or (b) of this section, a distribution made after the close of a taxable year and on or before the 15th day of the third month following the close of the taxable year shall be considered as made on the last day of such taxable year.

* * *

§ 564. Dividend carryover.

(a) General rule.—For purposes of computing the dividends paid deduction under section 561, in the case of a personal holding company the dividend carryover for any taxable year shall be the dividend carryover to such taxable year, computed as provided in subsection (b), from the two preceding taxable years.

(b) Computation of dividend carryover.—The dividend carryover to the taxable year shall be determined as follows:

(1) For each of the 2 preceding taxable years there shall be determined the taxable income computed with the adjustments provided in section 545 (whether or not the taxpayer was a personal holding company for either of such preceding taxable years), and there shall also be determined for each such year the deduction for dividends paid during such year as provided in section 561 (but determined without regard to the dividend carryover to such year).

(2) There shall be determined for each such taxable year whether there is an excess of such taxable income over such deduction for dividends paid or an excess of such deduction for dividends paid over such taxable income, and the amount of each such excess.

(3) If there is an excess of such deductions for dividends paid over such taxable income for the first preceding taxable year, such excess shall be allowed as a dividend carryover to the taxable year.

(4) If there is an excess of such deduction for dividends paid over such taxable income for the second preceding taxable year, such excess shall be reduced by the amount determined in paragraph (5), and the remainder of such excess shall be allowed as a dividend carryover to the taxable year.

(5) The amount of the reduction specified in paragraph (4) shall be the amount of the excess of the taxable income, if any, for the first preceding taxable year over such deduction for dividends paid, if any, for the first preceding taxable year.

§ 565. Consent dividends.

(a) General rule.—If any person owns consent stock (as defined in subsection (f)(1)) in a corporation on the last day of the taxable year of such corporation, and such person agrees, in a consent filed with the return of such corporation in accordance with regulations prescribed by the Secretary, to treat as a dividend the amount specified in such consent, the amount so specified shall, except as provided in subsection (b), constitute a consent dividend for purposes of section 561 (relating to the deduction for dividends paid).

(b) Limitations.—A consent dividend shall not include—

(1) an amount specified in a consent which, if distributed in money, would constitute, or be part of, a distribution which would be disqualified for purposes of the dividends paid deduction under section 562(c) (relating to preferential dividends), or

(2) an amount specified in a consent which would not constitute a dividend (as defined in section 316) if the total amounts specified in consents filed by the corporation had been distributed in money to shareholders on the last day of the taxable year of such corporation.

(c) Effect of consent.—The amount of a consent dividend shall be considered, for purposes of this title—

(1) as distributed in money by the corporation to the shareholder on the last day of the taxable year of the corporation, and

(2) as contributed to the capital of the corporation by the shareholder on such day.

(d) Consent dividends and other distributions.—If a distribution by a corporation consists in part of consent dividends and in part of money or other property, the entire amount specified in the consents and the amount of such money or other property shall be considered together for purposes of applying this title.

(e) Nonresident aliens and foreign corporations.—In the case of a consent dividend which, if paid in money would be subject to the provisions of section 1441 (relating to withholding of tax on nonresident aliens) or section 1442 (relating to withholding of tax on foreign corporations), this section shall not apply unless the consent is accompanied by money, or such other medium of payment as the Secretary may by regulations authorize, in an amount equal to the amount that would be required to be deducted and withheld under sections 1441 or 1442 if the consent dividend had been, on the last day of the taxable year of the corporation, paid to the shareholder in money as a dividend. The amount accompanying the consent shall be credited against the tax imposed by this subtitle on the shareholder.

(f) Definitions.—

(1) Consent stock.—Consent stock, for purposes of this section, means the class or classes of stock entitled, after the payment of preferred dividends, to a share in the distribution (other than in complete or partial liquidation) within the taxable year of all the remaining earnings and profits, which share constitutes the same proportion of such distribution regardless of the amount of such distribution.

(2) Preferred dividends.—Preferred dividends, for purposes of this section, means a distribution (other than in complete or partial liquidation), limited in amount, which must be made on any class of stock before a further distribution (other than in complete or partial liquidation) of earnings and profits may be made within the taxable year.

Subchapter K—Partners and Partnerships

Part I—Determination of Tax Liability

§ 701. Partners, not partnership, subject to tax.

A partnership as such shall not be subject to the income tax imposed by this chapter. Persons carrying on business as partners shall be liable for income tax only in their separate or individual capacities.

§ 702. Income and credits of partner.

(a) General rule.—In determining his income tax, each partner shall take into account separately his distributive share of the partnership's—

(1) gains and losses from sales or exchanges of capital assets held for not more than 1 year,

(2) gains and losses from sales or exchanges of capital assets held for more than 1 year,

(3) gains and losses from sales or exchanges of property described in section 1231 (relating to certain property used in a trade or business and involuntary conversions),

(4) charitable contributions (as defined in section 170(c)),

(5) dividends with respect to which section (1)(h)(11) or part VIII of subchapter B applies,

(6) taxes, described in section 901, paid or accrued to foreign countries and to possessions of the United States,

(7) other items of income, gain, loss, deduction, or credit, to the extent provided by regulations prescribed by the Secretary, and

(8) taxable income or loss, exclusive of items requiring separate computation under other paragraphs of this subsection.

(b) Character of items constituting distributive share.—The character of any item of income, gain, loss, deduction, or credit included in a partner's distributive share under paragraphs (1) through (7) of subsection (a) shall be determined as if such item were realized directly from the source from which realized by the partnership, or incurred in the same manner as incurred by the partnership.

(c) Gross income of a partner.—In any case where it is necessary to determine the gross income of a partner for purposes of this title, such amount shall include his distributive share of the gross income of the partnership.

(d) Cross reference.—For rules relating to procedures for determining the tax treatment of partnership items see subchapter C of chapter 63 (section 6221 and following).

§ 703. Partnership computations.

(a) Income and deductions.—The taxable income of a partnership shall be computed in the same manner as in the case of an individual except that—

(1) the items described in section 702(a) shall be separately stated, and

(2) the following deductions shall not be allowed to the partnership:

(A) the deductions for personal exemptions provided in section 151,

(B) the deduction for taxes provided in section 164(a) with respect to taxes, described in section 901, paid or accrued to foreign countries and to possessions of the United States,

(C) the deduction for charitable contributions provided in section 170,

(D) the net operating loss deduction provided in section 172,

(E) the additional itemized deductions for individuals provided in part VII of subchapter B (sec. 211 and following), and

(F) the deduction for depletion under section 611 with respect to oil and gas wells.

(b) Elections of the partnership.—Any election affecting the computation of taxable income derived from a partnership shall be made by the partnership, except that any election under—

(1) subsection (b)(5) or (c)(3) of section 108 (relating to income from discharge of indebtedness),

(2) section 617 (relating to deduction and recapture of certain mining exploration expenditures), or

(3) section 901 (relating to taxes of foreign countries and possessions of the United States), shall be made by each partner separately.

* * *

§ 704. Partner's distributive share.

(a) **Effect of partnership agreement.**—A partner's distributive share of income, gain, loss, deduction, or credit shall, except as otherwise provided in this chapter, be determined by the partnership agreement.

(b) **Determination of distributive share.**—A partner's distributive share of income, gain, loss, deduction, or credit (or item thereof) shall be determined in accordance with the partner's interest in the partnership (determined by taking into account all facts and circumstances), if—

(1) the partnership agreement does not provide as to the partner's distributive share of income, gain, loss, deduction, or credit (or item thereof), or

(2) the allocation to a partner under the agreement of income, gain, loss, deduction, or credit (or item thereof) does not have substantial economic effect.

(c) **Contributed property.**—

(1) **In general.**—Under regulations prescribed by the Secretary—

(A) income, gain, loss, and deduction with respect to property contributed to the partnership by a partner shall be shared among the partners so as to take account of the variation between the basis of the property to the partnership and its fair market value at the time of contribution,

(B) if any property so contributed is distributed (directly or indirectly) by the partnership (other than to the contributing partner) within 7 years of being contributed—

(i) the contributing partner shall be treated as recognizing gain or loss (as the case may be) from the sale of such property in an amount equal to the gain or loss which would have been allocated to such partner under subparagraph (A) by reason of the variation described in subparagraph (A) if the property had been sold at its fair market value at the time of the distribution,

(ii) the character of such gain or loss shall be determined by reference to the character of the gain or loss which would have resulted if such property had been sold by the partnership to the distributee, and

(iii) appropriate adjustments shall be made to the adjusted basis of the contributing partner's interest in the partnership and to the adjusted basis of the property distributed to reflect any gain or loss recognized under this subparagraph, and

(C) if any property so contributed has a built-in loss—

(i) such built-in loss shall be taken into account only in determining the amount of items allocated to the contributing partner, and

(ii) except as provided in regulations, in determining the amount of items allocated to other partners, the basis of the contributed property in the hands of the partnership shall be treated as being equal to its fair market value at the time of contribution.

For purposes of subparagraph (C), the term "built-in loss" means the excess of the adjusted basis of the property (determined without regard to subparagraph (C)(ii)) over its fair market value at the time of contribution.

(2) Special rule for distributions where gain or loss would not be recognized outside partnerships.—Under regulations prescribed by the Secretary, if—

(A) property contributed by a partner (hereinafter referred to as the "contributing partner") is distributed by the partnership to another partner, and

(B) other property of a like kind (within the meaning of section 1031) is distributed by the partnership to the contributing partner not later than the earlier of—

(i) the 180th day after the date of the distribution described in subparagraph (A), or

(ii) the due date (determined with regard to extensions) for the contributing partner's return of the tax imposed by this chapter for the taxable year in which the distribution described in subparagraph (A) occurs,

then to the extent of the value of the property described in subparagraph (B), paragraph (1)(B) shall be applied as if the contributing partner had contributed to the partnership the property described in subparagraph (B).

(3) Other rules.—Under regulations prescribed by the Secretary, rules similar to the rules of paragraph (1) shall apply to contributions by a partner (using the cash receipts and disbursements method of accounting) of accounts payable and other accrued but unpaid items. Any reference in paragraph (1) or (2) to the contributing partner shall be treated as including a reference to any successor of such partner.

(d) Limitation on allowance of losses.—

(1) In general.—A partner's distributive share of partnership loss (including capital loss) shall be allowed only to the extent of the adjusted basis of such partner's interest in the partnership at the end of the partnership year in which such loss occurred.

(2) Carryover.—Any excess of such loss over such basis shall be allowed as a deduction at the end of the partnership year in which such excess is repaid to the partnership.

(3) Special rules.—

(A) In general.—In determining the amount of any loss under paragraph (1), there shall be taken into account the partner's distributive share of amounts described in paragraphs (4) and (6) of section 702(a).

(B) Exception.—In the case of a charitable contribution of property whose fair market value exceeds its adjusted basis, subparagraph (A) shall not apply to the extent of the partner's distributive share of such excess.

(e) Partnership interests created by gift.—

(1) Distributive share of donee includible in gross income.—In the case of any partnership interest created by gift, the distributive share of the donee under the partnership agreement shall be includible in his gross income, except to the extent that such share is determined without allowance of reasonable compensation for services rendered to the partnership by the donor, and except to the extent that the portion of such share attributable to donated capital is proportionately greater than the share of the donor attributable to the donor's capital. The distributive share of a partner in the earnings of the partnership shall not be diminished because of absence due to military service.

(2) Purchase of interest by member of family.—For purposes of this subsection, an interest purchased by one member of a family from another shall be considered to be created by gift from the seller, and the fair market value of the purchased interest shall be considered to be donated capital. The "family" of any individual shall include only his spouse, ancestors, and lineal descendants, and any trusts for the primary benefit of such persons.

(f) Cross reference.—For rules in the case of the sale, exchange, liquidation, or reduction of a partner's interest, see section 706(c)(2).

§ 705. Determination of basis of partner's interest.

(a) General rule.—The adjusted basis of a partner's interest in a partnership shall, except as provided in subsection (b), be the basis of such interest determined under section 722 (relating to contributions to a partnership) or section 742 (relating to transfers of partnership interests)—

(1) increased by the sum of his distributive share for the taxable year and prior taxable years of—

(A) taxable income of the partnership as determined under section 703(a),

(B) income of the partnership exempt from tax under this title, and

(C) the excess of the deductions for depletion over the basis of the property subject to depletion;

(2) decreased (but not below zero) by distributions by the partnership as provided in section 733 and by the sum of his distributive share for the taxable year and prior taxable years of—

(A) losses of the partnership, and

(B) expenditures of the partnership not deductible in computing its taxable income and not properly chargeable to capital account; and

(3) decreased (but not below zero) by the amount of the partner's deduction for depletion for any partnership oil and gas property to the extent such deduction does not exceed the proportionate share of the adjusted basis of such property allocated to such partner under section 613A(c)(7)(D).

(b) Alternative rule.—The Secretary shall prescribe by regulations the circumstances under which the adjusted basis of a partner's interest in a partnership may be determined by reference to his proportionate share of the adjusted basis of partnership property upon a termination of the partnership.

§ 706. Taxable years of partner and partnership.

(a) Year in which partnership income is includible.—In computing the taxable income of a partner for a taxable year, the inclusions required by section 702 and section 707(c) with respect to a partnership shall be based on the income, gain, loss, deduction, or credit of the partnership for any taxable year of the partnership ending within or with the taxable year of the partner.

(b) Taxable year.—

(1) Partnership's taxable year.—

(A) Partnership treated as taxpayer.—The taxable year of a partnership shall be determined as though the partnership were a taxpayer.

(B) Taxable year determined by reference to partners.—Except as provided in subparagraph (C), a partnership shall not have a taxable year other than—

(i) the majority interest taxable year (as defined in paragraph (4)),

(ii) if there is no taxable year described in clause (i), the taxable year of all the principal partners of the partnership, or

(iii) if there is no taxable year described in clause (i) or (ii), the calendar year unless the Secretary by regulations prescribes another period.

(C) Business purpose.—A partnership may have a taxable year not described in subparagraph (B) if it establishes, to the satisfaction of the Secretary, a business purpose therefor. For purposes of this subparagraph, any deferral of income to partners shall not be treated as a business purpose.

(2) Partner's taxable year.—A partner may not change to a taxable year other than that of a partnership in which he is a principal partner unless he establishes, to the satisfaction of the Secretary, a business purpose therefor.

(3) Principal partner.—For the purpose of this subsection, a principal partner is a partner having an interest of 5 percent or more in partnership profits or capital.

(4) Majority interest taxable year; limitation on required changes.—

(A) Majority interest taxable year defined.—For purposes of paragraph (1)(B)(i)—

(i) In general.—The term "majority interest taxable year" means the taxable year (if any) which, on each testing day, constituted the taxable year of 1 or more partners having (on such day) an aggregate interest in partnership profits and capital of more than 50 percent.

(ii) Testing days.—The testing days shall be—

(I) the 1st day of the partnership taxable year (determined without regard to clause (i)), or

(II) the days during such representative period as the Secretary may prescribe.

(B) Further change not required for 3 years.—Except as provided in regulations necessary to prevent the avoidance of this section, if, by reason of paragraph (1)(B)(i), the taxable year of a partnership is changed, such partnership shall not be required to change to another taxable year for either of the 2 taxable years following the year of change.

(5) Application with other sections.—Except as provided in regulations, for purposes of determining the taxable year to which a partnership is required to change by reason of this subsection, changes in taxable years of other persons required by this subsection, section 441(i), section 584(i), section 644, or section 1378(a) shall be taken into account.

(c) Closing of partnership year.—

(1) General rule.—Except in the case of a termination of a partnership and except as provided in paragraph (2) of this subsection, the taxable year of a partnership shall not close as the result of the death of a partner, the entry of a new partner, the liquidation of a partner's interest in the partnership, or the sale or exchange of a partner's interest in the partnership.

(2) Treatment of dispositions.—

(A) Disposition of entire interest.—The taxable year of a partnership shall close with respect to a partner whose entire interest in the partnership terminates (whether by reason of death, liquidation, or otherwise).

(B) Disposition of less than entire interest.—The taxable year of a partnership shall not close (other than at the end of a partnership's taxable year as determined under subsection (b)(1)) with respect to a partner who sells or exchanges less than his entire interest in the partnership or with respect to a partner whose interest is reduced (whether by entry of a new partner, partial liquidation of a partner's interest, gift, or otherwise).

(d) Determination of distributive share when partner's interest changes.—

(1) In general.—Except as provided in paragraphs (2) and (3), if during any taxable year of the partnership there is a change in any partner's interest in the partnership, each partner's distributive share of any item of income, gain, loss, deduction, or credit of the partnership for such taxable year shall be determined by the use of any method prescribed by the Secretary by regulations which takes into account the varying interests of the partners in the partnership during such taxable year.

(2) Certain cash basis items prorated over period to which attributable.—

(A) In general.—If during any taxable year of the partnership there is a change in any partner's interest in the partnership, then (except to the extent provided in regulations) each partner's distributive share of any allocable cash basis item shall be determined—

(i) by assigning the appropriate portion of such item to each day in the period to which it is attributable, and

(ii) by allocating the portion assigned to any such day among the partners in proportion to their interests in the partnership at the close of such day.

(B) Allocable cash basis item.—For purposes of this paragraph, the term "allocable cash basis item" means any of the following items with respect to which the partnership uses the cash receipts and disbursements method of accounting:

(i) Interest.

(ii) Taxes.

(iii) Payments for services or for the use of property.

(iv) Any other item of a kind specified in regulations prescribed by the Secretary as being an item with respect to which the application of this paragraph is appropriate to avoid significant misstatements of the income of the partners.

(C) Items attributable to periods not within taxable year.—If any portion of any allocable cash basis item is attributable to—

(i) any period before the beginning of the taxable year, such portion shall be assigned under subparagraph (A)(i) to the first day of the taxable year, or

(ii) any period after the close of the taxable year, such portion shall be assigned under subparagraph (A)(i) to the last day of the taxable year.

(D) Treatment of deductible items attributable to prior periods.—If any portion of a deductible cash basis item is assigned under subparagraph (C)(i) to the first day of any taxable year—

(i) such portion shall be allocated among persons who are partners in the partnership during the period to which such portion is attributable in accordance with their varying interests in the partnership during such period, and

(ii) any amount allocated under clause (i) to a person who is not a partner in the partnership on such first day shall be capitalized by the partnership and treated in the manner provided for in section 755.

(3) Items attributable to interest in lower tier partnership prorated over entire taxable year.—If—

(A) during any taxable year of the partnership there is a change in any partner's interest in the partnership (hereinafter in this paragraph referred to as the "upper tier partnership"), and

(B) such partnership is a partner in another partnership (hereinafter in this paragraph referred to as the "lower tier partnership"), then (except to the extent provided in regulations) each partner's distributive share of any item of the upper tier partnership attributable to the lower tier partnership shall be determined by assigning the appropriate portion (determined by applying principles similar to the principles of subparagraphs (C) and (D) of paragraph (2)) of each such item to the appropriate days during which the upper tier partnership is a partner in the lower tier partnership and by allocating the portion assigned to any such day among the partners in proportion to their interests in the upper tier partnership at the close of such day.

(4) Taxable year determined without regard to subsection (c)(2)(A).—For purposes of this subsection, the taxable year of a partnership shall be determined without regard to subsection (c)(2)(A).

§ 707. Transactions between partner and partnership.

(a) Partner not acting in capacity as partner.—

(1) In general.—If a partner engages in a transaction with a partnership other than in his capacity as a member of such partnership, the transaction shall, except as otherwise provided in this section, be considered as occurring between the partnership and one who is not a partner.

(2) Treatment of payments to partners for property or services.—Under regulations prescribed by the Secretary—

(A) Treatment of certain services and transfers of property.—If—

(i) a partner performs services for a partnership or transfers property to a partnership,

(ii) there is a related direct or indirect allocation and distribution to such partner, and (**iii**) the performance of such services (or such transfer) and the allocation and distribution, when viewed together, are properly characterized as a transaction occurring between the partnership and a partner acting other than in his capacity as a member of the partnership,

such allocation and distribution shall be treated as a transaction described in paragraph (1).

(**B**) **Treatment of certain property transfers.**—If—

(**i**) there is a direct or indirect transfer of money or other property by a partner to a partnership,

(**ii**) there is a related direct or indirect transfer of money or other property by the partnership to such partner (or another partner), and

(**iii**) the transfers described in clauses (i) and (ii), when viewed together, are properly characterized as a sale or exchange of property,

such transfers shall be treated either as a transaction described in paragraph (1) or as a transaction between 2 or more partners acting other than in their capacity as members of the partnership.

(**b**) **Certain sales or exchanges of property with respect to controlled partnerships.**—

(**1**) **Losses disallowed.**—No deduction shall be allowed in respect of losses from sales or exchanges of property (other than an interest in the partnership), directly or indirectly, between—

(**A**) a partnership and a person owning, directly or indirectly, more than 50 percent of the capital interest, or the profits interest, in such partnership, or

(**B**) two partnerships in which the same persons own, directly or indirectly, more than 50 percent of the capital interests or profits interests.

In the case of a subsequent sale or exchange by a transferee described in this paragraph, section 267(d) shall be applicable as if the loss were disallowed under section 267(a)(1). For purposes of section 267(a)(2), partnerships described in subparagraph (B) of this paragraph shall be treated as persons specified in section 267(b).

(**2**) **Gains treated as ordinary income.**—In the case of a sale or exchange, directly or indirectly, of property, which in the hands of the transferee, is property other than a capital asset as defined in section 1221—

(**A**) between a partnership and a person owning, directly or indirectly, more than 50 percent of the capital interest, or profits interest, in such partnership, or

(**B**) between two partnerships in which the same persons own, directly or indirectly, more than 50 percent of the capital interest or profits interests, any gain recognized shall be considered as ordinary income.

(**3**) **Ownership of a capital or profits interest.**—For purposes of paragraphs (1) and (2) of this subsection, the ownership of a capital or profits interest in a partnership shall be determined in accordance with the rules for constructive ownership of stock provided in section 267(c) other than paragraph (3) of such section.

(**c**) **Guaranteed payments.**—To the extent determined without regard to the income of the partnership, payments to a partner for services or the use of capital shall be considered as made to one who is not a member of the partnership, but only for the purposes of section 61(a) (relating to gross income) and, subject to section 263, for purposes of section 162(a) (relating to trade or business expenses).

§ 708. Continuation of partnership.

(a) General rule.—For purposes of this subchapter, an existing partnership shall be considered as continuing if it is not terminated.

(b) Termination.—

(1) General rule.—For purposes of subsection (a), a partnership shall be considered as terminated only if no part of any business, financial operation, or venture of the partnership continues to be carried on by any of its partners in a partnership.

(2) Special rules.—

(A) Merger or consolidation.—In the case of the merger or consolidation of two or more partnerships, the resulting partnership shall, for purposes of this section, be considered the continuation of any merging or consolidating partnership whose members own an interest of more than 50 percent in the capital and profits of the resulting partnership.

(B) Division of a partnership.—In the case of a division of a partnership into two or more partnerships, the resulting partnerships (other than any resulting partnership the members of which had an interest of 50 percent or less in the capital and profits of the prior partnership) shall, for purposes of this section, be considered a continuation of the prior partnership.

§ 709. Treatment of organization and syndication fees.

(a) General rule.—Except as provided in subsection (b), no deduction shall be allowed under this chapter to the partnership or to any partner for any amounts paid or incurred to organize a partnership or to promote the sale of (or to sell) an interest in such partnership.

(b) Deduction of organization fees.—

(1) Allowance of deduction.—If a taxpayer elects the application of this subsection (in accordance with regulations prescribed by the Secretary) with respect to any organizational expenses—

(A) the taxpayer shall be allowed a deduction for the taxable year in which the partnership begins business in an amount equal to the lesser of—

(i) the amount of organizational expenses with respect to the partnership, or

(ii) $5,000, reduced (but not below zero) by the amount by which such organizational expenses exceed $50,000, and

(B) the remainder of such organizational expenses shall be allowed as a deduction ratably over the 180-month period beginning with the month in which the partnership begins business.

(2) Dispositions before close of amortization period.—In any case in which a partnership is liquidated before the end of the period to which paragraph (1)(B) applies, any deferred expenses attributable to the partnership which were not allowed as a deduction by reason of this section may be deducted to the extent allowable under section 165.

(3) Organizational expenses defined.—The organizational expenses to which paragraph (1) applies, are expenditures which—

(A) are incident to the creation of the partnership;

(B) are chargeable to capital account; and

(C) are of a character which, if expended incident to the creation of a partnership having an ascertainable life, would be amortized over such life.

§§ 710–720. [Reserved for future use.]

Part II—Contributions, Distributions, and Transfers

Subpart A—Contributions to a Partnership

§ 721. Nonrecognition of gain or loss on contribution.

(a) General rule.—No gain or loss shall be recognized to a partnership or to any of its partners in the case of a contribution of property to the partnership in exchange for an interest in the partnership.

(b) Special rule.—Subsection (a) shall not apply to gain realized on a transfer of property to a partnership which would be treated as an investment company (within the meaning of section 351) if the partnership were incorporated.

(c) Regulations relating to certain transfers to partnerships.—The Secretary may provide by regulations that subsection (a) shall not apply to gain realized on the transfer of property to a partnership if such gain, when recognized, will be includible in the gross income of a person other than a United States person.

(d) Transfers of intangibles.—For regulatory authority to treat intangibles transferred to a partnership as sold, see section 367(d)(3).

§ 722. Basis of contributing partner's interest.

The basis of an interest in a partnership acquired by a contribution of property, including money, to the partnership shall be the amount of such money and the adjusted basis of such property to the contributing partner at the time of the contribution increased by the amount (if any) of gain recognized under section 721(b) to the contributing partner at such time.

§ 723. Basis of property contributed to partnership.

The basis of property contributed to a partnership by a partner shall be the adjusted basis of such property to the contributing partner at the time of the contribution increased by the amount (if any) of gain recognized under section 721(b) to the contributing partner at such time.

§ 724. Character of gain or loss on contributed unrealized receivables, inventory items, and capital loss property.

(a) Contributions of unrealized receivables.—In the case of any property which—

(1) was contributed to the partnership by a partner, and

(2) was an unrealized receivable in the hands of such partner immediately before such contribution, any gain or loss recognized by the partnership on the disposition of such property shall be treated as ordinary income or ordinary loss, as the case may be.

(b) Contributions of inventory items.—In the case of any property which—

(1) was contributed to the partnership by a partner, and

(2) was an inventory item in the hands of such partner immediately before such contribution,

any gain or loss recognized by the partnership on the disposition of such property during the 5-year period beginning on the date of such contribution shall be treated as ordinary income or ordinary loss, as the case may be.

(c) Contributions of capital loss property.—In the case of any property which—

(1) was contributed by a partner to the partnership, and

(2) was a capital asset in the hands of such partner immediately before such contribution,

any loss recognized by the partnership on the disposition of such property during the 5-year period beginning on the date of such contribution shall be treated as a loss from the sale of a capital asset to the extent that, immediately before such contribution, the adjusted basis of such property in the hands of the partner exceeded the fair market value of such property.

(d) Definitions.—For purposes of this section—

(1) Unrealized receivable.—The term "unrealized receivable" has the meaning given such term by section 751(c) (determined by treating any reference to the partnership as referring to the partner).

(2) Inventory item.—The term "inventory item" has the meaning given such term by section 751(d) (determined by treating any reference to the partnership as referring to the partner and by applying section 1231 without regard to any holding period therein provided).

(3) Substituted basis property.—

(A) In general.—If any property described in subsection (a), (b), or (c) is disposed of in a nonrecognition transaction, the tax treatment which applies to such property under such subsection shall also apply to any substituted basis property resulting from such transaction. A similar rule shall also apply in the case of a series of non-recognition transactions.

(B) Exception for stock in C corporation.—Subparagraph (A) shall not apply to any stock in a C corporation received in an exchange described in section 351.

§§ 725–730. [Reserved for future use.]

Subpart B—Distributions by a Partnership

§ 731. Extent of recognition of gain or loss on distribution.

(a) Partners.—In the case of a distribution by a partnership to a partner—

(1) gain shall not be recognized to such partner, except to the extent that any money distributed exceeds the adjusted basis of such partner's interest in the partnership immediately before the distribution, and

(2) loss shall not be recognized to such partner, except that upon a distribution in liquidation of a partner's interest in a partnership where no property other than that described in subparagraph (A) or (B) is distributed to such partner, loss shall be recognized to the extent of the excess of the adjusted basis of such partner's interest in the partnership over the sum of—

(A) any money distributed, and

(B) the basis to the distributee, as determined under section 732, of any unrealized receivables (as defined in section 751(c)) and inventory (as defined in section 751(d)).

Any gain or loss recognized under this subsection shall be considered as gain or loss from the sale or exchange of the partnership interest of the distributee partner.

(b) Partnerships.—No gain or loss shall be recognized to a partnership on a distribution to a partner of property, including money.

(c) Treatment of marketable securities.—

(1) In general.—For purposes of subsection (a)(1) and section 737—

(A) the term "money" includes marketable securities, and

(B) such securities shall be taken into account at their fair market value as of the date of the distribution.

(2) Marketable securities.—For purposes of this subsection:

(A) In general.—The term "marketable securities" means financial instruments and foreign currencies which are, as of the date of the distribution, actively traded (within the meaning of section 1092(d)(1)).

(B) Other property.—Such term includes—

(i) any interest in—

(I) a common trust fund, or

(II) a regulated investment company which is offering for sale or has outstanding any redeemable security (as defined in section 2(a)(32) of the Investment Company Act of 1940) of which it is the issuer,

(ii) any financial instrument which, pursuant to its terms or any other arrangement, is readily convertible into, or exchangeable for, money or marketable securities,

(iii) any financial instrument the value of which is determined substantially by reference to marketable securities,

(iv) except to the extent provided in regulations prescribed by the Secretary, any interest in a precious metal which, as of the date of the distribution, is actively traded (within the meaning of section 1092(d)(1)) unless such metal was produced, used, or held in the active conduct of a trade or business by the partnership,

(v) except as otherwise provided in regulations prescribed by the Secretary, interests in any entity if substantially all of the assets of such entity consist (directly or indirectly) of marketable securities, money, or both, and

(vi) to the extent provided in regulations prescribed by the Secretary, any interest in an entity not described in clause (v) but only to the extent of the value of such interest which is attributable to marketable securities, money, or both.

(C) Financial instrument.—The term "financial instrument" includes stocks and other equity interests, evidences of indebtedness, options, forward or futures contracts, notional principal contracts, and derivatives.

(3) Exceptions.—

(A) In general.—Paragraph (1) shall not apply to the distribution from a partnership of a marketable security to a partner if—

(i) the security was contributed to the partnership by such partner, except to the extent that the value of the distributed security is attributable to marketable securities or money contributed (directly or indirectly) to the entity to which the distributed security relates,

(ii) to the extent provided in regulations prescribed by the Secretary, the property was not a marketable security when acquired by such partnership, or

(iii) such partnership is an investment partnership and such partner is an eligible partner thereof.

(B) Limitation on gain recognized.—In the case of a distribution of marketable securities to a partner, the amount taken into account under paragraph (1) shall be reduced (but not below zero) by the excess (if any) of—

(i) such partner's distributive share of the net gain which would be recognized if all of the marketable securities of the same class and issuer as the distributed securities held by the partnership were sold (immediately before the transaction to which the distribution relates) by the partnership for fair market value, over

(ii) such partner's distributive share of the net gain which is attributable to the marketable securities of the same class and issuer as the distributed securities held by the partnership immediately after the transaction, determined by using the same fair market value as used under clause (i).

Under regulations prescribed by the Secretary, all marketable securities held by the partnership may be treated as marketable securities of the same class and issuer as the distributed securities.

(C) Definitions relating to investment partnerships.—For purposes of subparagraph (A)(iii):

(i) Investment partnership.—The term "investment partnership" means any partnership which has never been engaged in a trade or business and substantially all of the assets (by value) of which have always consisted of—

(I) money,

(II) stock in a corporation,

(III) notes, bonds, debentures, or other evidences of indebtedness,

(IV) interest rate, currency, or equity notional principal contracts,

(V) foreign currencies,

(VI) interests in or derivative financial instruments (including options, forward or futures contracts, short positions, and similar financial instruments) in any asset described in any other subclause of this clause or in any commodity traded on or subject to the rules of a board of trade or commodity exchange,

(VII) other assets specified in regulations prescribed by the Secretary, or

(VIII) any combination of the foregoing.

(ii) Exception for certain activities.—A partnership shall not be treated as engaged in a trade or business by reason of—

(I) any activity undertaken as an investor, trader, or dealer in any asset described in clause (i), or

(II) any other activity specified in regulations prescribed by the Secretary.

(iii) Eligible partner.—

(I) In general.—The term "eligible partner" means any partner who, before the date of the distribution, did not contribute to the partnership any property other than assets described in clause (i).

(II) Exception for certain nonrecognition transactions.—The term "eligible partner" shall not include the transferor or transferee in a nonrecognition transaction involving a transfer of any portion of an interest in a partnership with respect to which the transferor was not an eligible partner.

(iv) Look-thru of partnership tiers.—Except as otherwise provided in regulations prescribed by the Secretary—

(I) a partnership shall be treated as engaged in any trade or business engaged in by, and as holding (instead of a partnership interest) a proportionate share of the assets of, any other partnership in which the partnership holds a partnership interest, and

(II) a partner who contributes to a partnership an interest in another partnership shall be treated as contributing a proportionate share of the assets of the other partnership. If the preceding sentence does not apply under such regulations with respect to any interest held by a partnership in another partnership, the interest in such other partnership shall be treated as if it were specified in a subclause of clause (i).

(4) Basis of securities distributed.—

(A) In general.—The basis of marketable securities with respect to which gain is recognized by reason of this subsection shall be—

(i) their basis determined under section 732, increased by

(ii) the amount of such gain.

(B) Allocation of basis increase.—Any increase in basis attributable to the gain described in subparagraph (A)(ii) shall be allocated to marketable securities in proportion to their respective amounts of unrealized appreciation before such increase.

(5) Subsection disregarded in determining basis of partner's interest in partnership and of basis of partnership property.—Sections 733 and 734 shall be applied as if no gain were recognized, and no adjustment were made to the basis of property, under this subsection.

(6) Character of gain recognized.—In the case of a distribution of a marketable security which is an unrealized receivable (as defined in section 751(c)) or an inventory item (as defined in section 751(d)), any gain recognized under this subsection shall be treated as ordinary income to the extent of any increase in the basis of such security attributable to the gain described in paragraph (4)(A)(ii).

(7) Regulations.—The Secretary shall prescribe such regulations as may be necessary or appropriate to carry out the purposes of this subsection, including regulations to prevent the avoidance of such purposes.

(d) Exceptions.—This section shall not apply to the extent otherwise provided by section 736 (relating to payments to a retiring partner or a deceased partner's successor in interest), section 751 (relating to unrealized receivables and inventory items), and section 737 (relating to recognition of precontribution gain in case of certain distributions).

§ 732. Basis of distributed property other than money.

(a) Distributions other than in liquidation of a partner's interest.—

(1) General rule.—The basis of property (other than money) distributed by a partnership to a partner other than in liquidation of the partner's interest shall, except as provided in paragraph (2), be its adjusted basis to the partnership immediately before such distribution.

(2) Limitation.—The basis to the distributee partner of property to which paragraph (1) is applicable shall not exceed the adjusted basis of such partner's interest in the partnership reduced by any money distributed in the same transaction.

(b) Distributions in liquidation.—The basis of property (other than money) distributed by a partnership to a partner in liquidation of the partner's interest shall be an amount equal to the adjusted basis of such partner's interest in the partnership reduced by any money distributed in the same transaction.

(c) Allocation of basis.—

(1) In general.—The basis of distributed properties to which subsection (a)(2) or (b) is applicable shall be allocated—

(A)(i) first to any unrealized receivables (as defined in section 751(c)) and inventory items (as defined in section 751(d)) in an amount equal to the adjusted basis of each such property to the partnership, and

(ii) if the basis to be allocated is less than the sum of the adjusted bases of such properties to the partnership, then, to the extent any decrease is required in order to have the adjusted bases of such properties equal the basis to be allocated, in the manner provided in paragraph (3), and

(B) to the extent of any basis remaining after the allocation under subparagraph (A), to other distributed properties—

(i) first by assigning to each such other property such other property's adjusted basis to the partnership, and

(ii) then, to the extent any increase or decrease in basis is required in order to have the adjusted bases of such other distributed properties equal such remaining basis, in the manner provided in paragraph (2) or (3), whichever is appropriate.

(2) Method of allocating increase.—Any increase required under paragraph (1)(B) shall be allocated among the properties—

(A) first to properties with unrealized appreciation in proportion to their respective amounts of unrealized appreciation before such increase (but only to the extent of each property's unrealized appreciation), and

(B) then, to the extent such increase is not allocated under subparagraph (A), in proportion to their respective fair market values.

(3) Method of allocating decrease.—Any decrease required under paragraph (1)(A) or (1)(B) shall be allocated—

(A) first to properties with unrealized depreciation in proportion to their respective amounts of unrealized depreciation before such decrease (but only to the extent of each property's unrealized depreciation), and

(B) then, to the extent such decrease is not allocated under subparagraph (A), in proportion to their respective adjusted bases (as adjusted under subparagraph (A)).

(d) Special partnership basis to transferee.—For purposes of subsections (a), (b), and (c), a partner who acquired all or a part of his interest by a transfer with respect to which the election provided in section 754 is not in effect, and to whom a distribution of property (other than money) is made with respect to the transferred interest within 2 years after such transfer, may elect, under regulations prescribed by the Secretary, to treat as the adjusted partnership basis of such property the adjusted basis such property would have if the adjustment provided in section 743(b) were in effect with respect to the partnership property. The Secretary may by regulations require the application of this subsection in the case of a distribution to a transferee partner, whether or not made within 2 years after the transfer, if at the time of the transfer the fair market value of the partnership property (other than money) exceeded 110 percent of its adjusted basis to the partnership.

(e) Exception.—This section shall not apply to the extent that a distribution is treated as a sale or exchange of property under section 751(b) (relating to unrealized receivables and inventory items).

(f) Corresponding adjustment to basis of assets of a distributed corporation controlled by a corporate partner.—

(1) In general.—If—

(A) a corporation (hereafter in this subsection referred to as the 'corporate partner') receives a distribution from a partnership of stock in another corporation (hereafter in this subsection referred to as the 'distributed corporation'),

(B) the corporate partner has control of the distributed corporation immediately after the distribution or at any time thereafter, and

(C) the partnership's adjusted basis in such stock immediately before the distribution exceeded the corporate partner's adjusted basis in such stock immediately after the distribution,

then an amount equal to such excess shall be applied to reduce (in accordance with subsection (c)) the basis of property held by the distributed corporation at such time (or, if the corporate partner does not control the distributed corporation at such time, at the time the corporate partner first has such control).

(2) Exception for certain distributions before control acquired.—Paragraph (1) shall not apply to any distribution of stock in the distributed corporation if—

(A) the corporate partner does not have control of such corporation immediately after such distribution, and

(B) the corporate partner establishes to the satisfaction of the Secretary that such distribution was not part of a plan or arrangement to acquire control of the distributed corporation.

(3) Limitations on basis reduction.—

(A) **In general.**—The amount of the reduction under paragraph (1) shall not exceed the amount by which the sum of the aggregate adjusted bases of the property and the amount of money of the distributed corporation exceeds the corporate partner's adjusted basis in the stock of the distributed corporation.

(B) **Reduction not to exceed adjusted basis of property.**—No reduction under paragraph (1) in the basis of any property shall exceed the adjusted basis of such property (determined without regard to such reduction).

(4) Gain recognition where reduction limited.—If the amount of any reduction under paragraph (1) (determined after the application of paragraph (3)(A)) exceeds the aggregate adjusted bases of the property of the distributed corporation—

(A) such excess shall be recognized by the corporate partner as long-term capital gain, and

(B) the corporate partner's adjusted basis in the stock of the distributed corporation shall be increased by such excess.

(5) Control.—For purposes of this subsection, the term "control" means ownership of stock meeting the requirements of section 1504(a)(2).

(6) Indirect distributions.—For purposes of paragraph (1), if a corporation acquires (other than in a distribution from a partnership) stock the basis of which is determined (by reason of being distributed from a partnership) in whole or in part by reference to subsection (a)(2) or (b), the corporation shall be treated as receiving a distribution of such stock from a partnership.

(7) Special rule for stock in controlled corporation.—If the property held by a distributed corporation is stock in a corporation which the distributed corporation controls, this subsection shall be applied to reduce the basis of the property of such controlled corporation. This subsection shall be reapplied to any property of any controlled corporation which is stock in a corporation which it controls.

(8) Regulations.—The Secretary shall prescribe such regulations as may be necessary to carry out the purposes of this subsection, including regulations to avoid double counting and to prevent the abuse of such purposes.

§ 733. Basis of distributee partner's interest.

In the case of a distribution by a partnership to a partner other than in liquidation of a partner's interest, the adjusted basis to such partner of his interest in the partnership shall be reduced (but not below zero) by—

(1) the amount of any money distributed to such partner, and

(2) the amount of the basis to such partner of distributed property other than money, as determined under section 732.

§ 734. Adjustment to basis of undistributed partnership property where section 754 election or substantial basis reduction.

(a) General rule.—The basis of partnership property shall not be adjusted as the result of a distribution of property to a partner unless the election, provided in section 754 (relating to optional adjustment to basis of partnership property), is in effect with respect to such partnership or unless there is a substantial basis reduction.

(b) Method of adjustment.—In the case of a distribution of property to a partner, a partnership, with respect to which the election provided in section 754 is in effect or unless there is a substantial basis reduction, shall—

(1) increase the adjusted basis of partnership property by—

(A) the amount of any gain recognized to the distributee partner with respect to such distribution under section 731(a)(1), and

(B) in the case of distributed property to which section 732(a)(2) or (b) applies, the excess of the adjusted basis of the distributed property to the partnership immediately before the distribution (as adjusted by section 732(d)) over the basis of the distributed property to the distributee, as determined under section 732, or

(2) decrease the adjusted basis of partnership property by—

(A) the amount of any loss recognized to the distributee partner with respect to such distribution under section 731(a)(2), and

(B) in the case of distributed property to which section 732(b) applies, the excess of the basis of the distributed property to the distributee, as determined under section 732, over the adjusted basis of the distributed property to the partnership immediately before such distribution (as adjusted by section 732(d)).

Paragraph (1)(B) shall not apply to any distributed property which is an interest in another partnership with respect to which the election provided in section 754 is not in effect.

(c) Allocation of basis.—The allocation of basis among partnership properties where subsection (b) is applicable shall be made in accordance with the rules provided in section 755.

(d) Substantial basis reduction.—

(1) **In general.**—For purposes of this section, there is a substantial basis reduction with respect to a distribution if the sum of the amounts described in subparagraphs (A) and (B) of subsection (b)(2) exceeds $250,000.

(2) **Regulations.**—For regulations to carry out this subsection, see section 743(d)(2).

(e) Exception for securitization partnerships.—For purposes of this section, a securitization partnership (as defined in section 743(f)) shall not be treated as having a substantial basis reduction with respect to any distribution of property to a partner.

§ 735. Character of gain or loss on disposition of distributed property.

(a) Sale or exchange of certain distributed property.—

(1) **Unrealized receivables.**—Gain or loss on the disposition by a distributee partner of unrealized receivables (as defined in section 751(c)) distributed by a partnership, shall be considered as ordinary income or as ordinary loss, as the case may be.

(2) Inventory items.—Gain or loss on the sale or exchange by a distributee partner of inventory items (as defined in section 751(d)) distributed by a partnership shall, if sold or exchanged within 5 years from the date of the distribution, be considered as ordinary income or as ordinary loss, as the case may be.

(b) Holding period for distributed property.—In determining the period for which a partner has held property received in a distribution from a partnership (other than for purposes of subsection (a)(2)), there shall be included the holding period of the partnership, as determined under section 1223, with respect to such property.

(c) Special rules.—

(1) Waiver of holding periods contained in section 1231.—For purposes of this section, section 751(d) (defining inventory item) shall be applied without regard to any holding period in section 1231(b).

(2) Substituted basis property.—

(A) In general.—If any property described in subsection (a) is disposed of in a non-recognition transaction, the tax treatment which applies to such property under such subsection shall also apply to any substituted basis property resulting from such transaction. A similar rule shall also apply in the case of a series of nonrecognition transactions.

(B) Exception for stock in C corporation.—Subparagraph (A) shall not apply to any stock in a C corporation received in an exchange described in section 351.

§ 736. Payments to a retiring partner or a deceased partner's successor in interest.

(a) Payments considered as distributive share or guaranteed payment.—Payments made in liquidation of the interest of a retiring partner or a deceased partner shall, except as provided in subsection (b), be considered—

(1) as a distributive share to the recipient of partnership income if the amount thereof is determined with regard to the income of the partnership, or

(2) as a guaranteed payment described in section 707(c) if the amount thereof is determined without regard to the income of the partnership.

(b) Payments for interest in partnership.—

(1) General rule.—Payments made in liquidation of the interest of a retiring partner or a deceased partner shall, to the extent such payments (other than payments described in paragraph (2)) are determined, under regulations prescribed by the Secretary, to be made in exchange for the interest of such partner in partnership property, be considered as a distribution by the partnership and not as a distributive share or guaranteed payment under subsection (a).

(2) Special rules.—For purposes of this subsection, payments in exchange for an interest in partnership property shall not include amounts paid for—

(A) unrealized receivables of the partnership (as defined in section 751(c)), or

(B) good will of the partnership, except to the extent that the partnership agreement provides for a payment with respect to good will.

(3) Limitation on application of paragraph (2).—Paragraph (2) shall apply only if—

(A) capital is not a material income-producing factor for the partnership, and

(B) the retiring or deceased partner was a general partner in the partnership.

(c) [Deleted.]

§ 737. Recognition of precontribution gain in case of certain distributions to contributing partner.

(a) General rule.—In the case of any distribution by a partnership to a partner, such partner shall be treated as recognizing gain in an amount equal to the lesser of—

(1) the excess (if any) of (A) the fair market value of property (other than money) received in the distribution over (B) the adjusted basis of such partner's interest in the partnership immediately before the distribution reduced (but not below zero) by the amount of money received in the distribution, or

(2) the net precontribution gain of the partner.

Gain recognized under the preceding sentence shall be in addition to any gain recognized under section 731. The character of such gain shall be determined by reference to the proportionate character of the net precontribution gain.

(b) Net precontribution gain.—For purposes of this section, the term "net precontribution gain" means the net gain (if any) which would have been recognized by the distributee partner under section 704(c)(1)(B) if all property which—

(1) had been contributed to the partnership by the distributee partner within 7 years of the distribution, and

(2) is held by such partnership immediately before the distribution,

had been distributed by such partnership to another partner.

(c) Basis rules.—

(1) Partner's interest.—The adjusted basis of a partner's interest in a partnership shall be increased by the amount of any gain recognized by such partner under subsection (a). For purposes of determining the basis of the distributed property (other than money), such increase shall be treated as occurring immediately before the distribution.

(2) Partnership's basis in contributed property.—Appropriate adjustments shall be made to the adjusted basis of the partnership in the contributed property referred to in subsection (b) to reflect gain recognized under subsection (a).

(d) Exceptions.—

(1) Distributions of previously contributed property.—If any portion of the property distributed consists of property which had been contributed by a distributee partner to the partnership, such property shall not be taken into account under subsection (a)(1) and shall not be taken into account in determining the amount of the net precontribution gain. If the property distributed consists of an interest in an entity, the preceding sentence shall not apply to the extent that the value of such interest is attributable to property contributed to such entity after such interest had been contributed to the partnership.

(2) Coordination with section 751.—This section shall not apply to the extent section 751(b) applies to such distribution.

(e) Marketable securities treated as money.—For treatment of marketable securities as money for purposes of this section, see section 731(c).

Subpart C—Transfers of Interest in a Partnership

§ 741. Recognition and character of gain or loss on sale or exchange.

In the case of a sale or exchange of an interest in a partnership, gain or loss shall be recognized to the transferor partner. Such gain or loss shall be considered as gain or loss from the sale or exchange of a capital asset, except as otherwise provided in section 751 (relating to unrealized receivables and inventory items).

§ 742. Basis of transferee partner's interest.

The basis of an interest in a partnership acquired other than by contribution shall be determined under part II of subchapter O (sec. 1011 and following).

§ 743. Special rules where section 754 election or substantial built-in loss.

(a) General rule.—The basis of partnership property shall not be adjusted as the result of a transfer of an interest in a partnership by sale or exchange or on the death of a partner unless the election provided by section 754 (relating to optional adjustment to basis of partnership property) is in effect with respect to such partnership or unless the partnership has a substantial built-in loss immediately after such transfer.

(b) Adjustment to basis of partnership property.—In the case of a transfer of an interest in a partnership by sale or exchange or upon the death of a partner, a partnership with respect to which the election provided in section 754 is in effect or which has a substantial built-in loss immediately after such transfer shall—

(1) increase the adjusted basis of the partnership property by the excess of the basis to the transferee partner of his interest in the partnership over his proportionate share of the adjusted basis of the partnership property, or

(2) decrease the adjusted basis of the partnership property by the excess of the transferee partner's proportionate share of the adjusted basis of the partnership property over the basis of his interest in the partnership.

Under regulations prescribed by the Secretary, such increase or decrease shall constitute an adjustment to the basis of partnership property with respect to the transferee partner only. A partner's proportionate share of the adjusted basis of partnership property shall be determined in accordance with his interest in partnership capital and, in the case of property contributed to the partnership by a partner, section 704(c) (relating to contributed property) shall apply in determining such share. In the case of an adjustment under this subsection to the basis of partnership property subject to depletion, any depletion allowable shall be determined separately for the transferee partner with respect to his interest in such property.

(c) Allocation of basis.—The allocation of basis among partnership properties where subsection (b) is applicable shall be made in accordance with the rules provided in section 755.

(d) Substantial built-in loss.—

(1) **In general.**—For purposes of this section, a partnership has a substantial built-in loss with respect to a transfer of an interest in the partnership if—

(**A**) the partnership's adjusted basis in the partnership property exceeds by more than $250,000 the fair market value of such property, or

(**B**) the transferee partner would be allocated a loss of more than $250,000 if the partnership assets were sold for cash equal to their fair market value immediately after such transfer.

(**2**) **Regulations.**—The Secretary shall prescribe such regulations as may be appropriate to carry out the purposes of paragraph (1) and section 734(d), including regulations aggregating related partnerships and disregarding property acquired by the partnership in an attempt to avoid such purposes.

(**e**) **Alternative rules for electing investment partnerships.**—

(**1**) **No adjustment of partnership basis.**—For purposes of this section, an electing investment partnership shall not be treated as having a substantial built-in loss with respect to any transfer occurring while the election under paragraph (6)(A) is in effect.

(**2**) **Loss deferral for transferee partner.**—In the case of a transfer of an interest in an electing investment partnership, the transferee partner's distributive share of losses (without regard to gains) from the sale or exchange of partnership property shall not be allowed except to the extent that it is established that such losses exceed the loss (if any) recognized by the transferor (or any prior transferor to the extent not fully offset by a prior disallowance under this paragraph) on the transfer of the partnership interest.

(**3**) **No reduction in partnership basis.**—Losses disallowed under paragraph (2) shall not decrease the transferee partner's basis in the partnership interest.

(**4**) **Certain basis reductions treated as losses.**—In the case of a transferee partner whose basis in property distributed by the partnership is reduced under section 732(a)(2), the amount of the loss recognized by the transferor on the transfer of the partnership interest which is taken into account under paragraph (2) shall be reduced by the amount of such basis reduction.

(**5**) **Electing investment partnership.**—For purposes of this subsection, the term "electing investment partnership" means any partnership if—

(**A**) the partnership makes an election to have this subsection apply,

(**B**) the partnership would be an investment company under section 3(a)(1)(A) of the Investment Company Act of 1940 but for an exemption under paragraph (1) or (7) of section 3(c) of such Act,

(**C**) such partnership has never been engaged in a trade or business,

(**D**) substantially all of the assets of such partnership are held for investment,

(**E**) at least 95 percent of the assets contributed to such partnership consist of money,

(**F**) no assets contributed to such partnership had an adjusted basis in excess of fair market value at the time of contribution,

(**G**) all partnership interests of such partnership are issued by such partnership pursuant to a private offering before the date which is 24 months after the date of the first capital contribution to such partnership,

(**H**) the partnership agreement of such partnership has substantive restrictions on each partner's ability to cause a redemption of the partner's interest, and

(I) the partnership agreement of such partnership provides for a term that is not in excess of 15 years.

The election described in subparagraph (A), once made, shall be irrevocable except with the consent of the Secretary.

(6) Regulations.—The Secretary shall prescribe such regulations as may be appropriate to carry out the purposes of this subsection, including regulations for applying this subsection to tiered partnerships.

(f) Exception for securitization partnerships.—

(1) No adjustment of partnership basis.—For purposes of this section, a securitization partnership shall not be treated as having a substantial built-in loss with respect to any transfer.

(2) Securitization partnership.—For purposes of paragraph (1), the term "securitization partnership" means any partnership the sole business activity of which is to issue securities which provide for a fixed principal (or similar) amount and which are primarily serviced by the cash flows of a discrete pool (either fixed or revolving) of receivables or other financial assets that by their terms convert into cash in a finite period, but only if the sponsor of the pool reasonably believes that the receivables and other financial assets comprising the pool are not acquired so as to be disposed of.

§§ 744–750. [Reserved for future use.]

Subpart D—Provisions Common to Other Subparts

§ 751. Unrealized receivables and inventory items.

(a) Sale or exchange of interest in partnership.—The amount of any money, or the fair market value of any property, received by a transferor partner in exchange for all or a part of his interest in the partnership attributable to—

(1) unrealized receivables of the partnership, or

(2) inventory items of the partnership,

shall be considered as an amount realized from the sale or exchange of property other than a capital asset.

(b) Certain distributions treated as sales or exchanges.—

(1) General rule.—To the extent a partner receives in a distribution—

(A) partnership property which is—

(i) unrealized receivables, or

(ii) inventory items which have appreciated substantially in value,

in exchange for all or a part of his interest in other partnership property (including money), or

(B) partnership property (including money) other than property described in subparagraph (A)(i) or (ii) in exchange for all or a part of his interest in partnership property described in subparagraph (A)(i) or (ii), such transactions shall, under regulations prescribed by the Secretary, be considered as a sale or exchange of such property between the distributee and the partnership (as constituted after the distribution).

(2) Exceptions.—Paragraph (1) shall not apply to—

(A) a distribution of property which the distributee contributed to the partnership, or

(B) payments, described in section 736(a), to a retiring partner or successor in interest of a deceased partner.

(3) Substantial appreciation.—For purposes of paragraph (1)—

(A) In general.—Inventory items of the partnership shall be considered to have appreciated substantially in value if their fair market value exceeds 120 percent of the adjusted basis to the partnership of such property.

(B) Certain property excluded.—For purposes of subparagraph (A), there shall be excluded any inventory property if a principal purpose for acquiring such property was to avoid the provisions of this subsection relating to inventory items.

(c) Unrealized receivables.—For purposes of this subchapter, the term "unrealized receivables" includes, to the extent not previously includible in income under the method of accounting used by the partnership, any rights (contractual or otherwise) to payment for—

(1) goods delivered, or to be delivered, to the extent the proceeds therefrom would be treated as amounts received from the sale or exchange of property other than a capital asset, or

(2) services rendered, or to be rendered.

For purposes of this section and sections 731, 732, and 741 (but not for purposes of section 736), such term also includes mining property (as defined in section 617(f)(2)), stock in a DISC (as described in section 992(a)), section 1245 property (as defined in section 1245(a)(3)), stock in certain foreign corporations (as described in section 1248), section 1250 property (as defined in section 1250(c)), farm land (as defined in section 1252(a)), franchises, trademarks, or trade names (referred to in section 1253(a)), and an oil, gas, or geothermal property (described in section 1254) but only to the extent of the amount which would be treated as gain to which section 617(d)(1), 995(c), 1245(a), 1248(a), 1250(a), 1252(a), 1253(a), or 1254(a) would apply if (at the time of the transaction described in this section or section 731, 732, or 741, as the case may be) such property had been sold by the partnership at its fair market value. For purposes of this section and sections 731, 732, and 741 (but not for purposes of section 736), such term also includes any market discount bond (as defined in section 1278) and any short-term obligation (as defined in section 1283) but only to the extent of the amount which would be treated as ordinary income if (at the time of the transaction described in this section or section 731, 732, or 741, as the case may be) such property had been sold by the partnership.

(d) Inventory items.—For purposes of this subchapter, the term "inventory items" means—

(1) property of the partnership of the kind described in section 1221(a)(1),

(2) any other property of the partnership which, on sale or exchange by the partnership, would be considered property other than a capital asset and other than property described in section 1231, and

(3) any other property held by the partnership which, if held by the selling or distributee partner, would be considered property of the type described in paragraph (1) or (2).

(e) Limitation on tax attributable to deemed sales of section 1248 stock.—For purposes of applying this section and sections 731 and 741 to any amount resulting from the reference to section 1248(a) in the second sentence of subsection (c), in the case of an individual, the tax attributable to such amount shall be limited in the manner provided by subsection (b) of section 1248 (relating to gain from certain sales or exchanges of stock in certain foreign corporation).

(f) Special rules in the case of tiered partnerships, etc.—In determining whether property of a partnership is—

(1) an unrealized receivable, or

(2) an inventory item,

such partnership shall be treated as owning its proportionate share of the property of any other partnership in which it is a partner. Under regulations, rules similar to the rules of the preceding sentence shall also apply in the case of interests in trusts.

§ 752. Treatment of certain liabilities.

(a) Increase in partner's liabilities.—Any increase in a partner's share of the liabilities of a partnership, or any increase in a partner's individual liabilities by reason of the assumption by such partner of partnership liabilities, shall be considered as a contribution of money by such partner to the partnership.

(b) Decrease in partner's liabilities.—Any decrease in a partner's share of the liabilities of a partnership, or any decrease in a partner's individual liabilities by reason of the assumption by the partnership of such individual liabilities, shall be considered as a distribution of money to the partner by the partnership.

(c) Liability to which property is subject.—For purposes of this section, a liability to which property is subject shall, to the extent of the fair market value of such property, be considered as a liability of the owner of the property.

(d) Sale or exchange of an interest.—In the case of a sale or exchange of an interest in a partnership, liabilities shall be treated in the same manner as liabilities in connection with the sale or exchange of property not associated with partnerships.

§ 753. Partner receiving income in respect of decedent.

The amount includible in the gross income of a successor in interest of a deceased partner under section 736(a) shall be considered income in respect of a decedent under section 691.

§ 754. Manner of electing optional adjustment to basis of partnership property.

If a partnership files an election, in accordance with regulations prescribed by the Secretary, the basis of partnership property shall be adjusted, in the case of a distribution of property, in the manner provided in section 734 and, in the case of a transfer of a partnership interest, in the manner provided in section 743. Such an election shall apply with respect to all distributions of property by the partnership and to all transfers of interests in the partnership during the taxable year with respect to which such election was filed and all subsequent taxable years. Such election may be revoked by the partnership, subject to such limitations as may be provided by regulations prescribed by the Secretary.

§ 755. Rules for allocation of basis.

(a) General rule.—Any increase or decrease in the adjusted basis of partnership property under section 734(b) (relating to the optional adjustment to the basis of undistributed partnership property) or section 743(b) (relating to the optional adjustment to the basis of partnership property in the case of a transfer of an interest in a partnership) shall, except as provided in subsection (b), be allocated—

(1) in a manner which has the effect of reducing the difference between the fair market value and the adjusted basis of partnership properties, or

(2) in any other manner permitted by regulations prescribed by the Secretary.

(b) **Special rule.**—In applying the allocation rules provided in subsection (a), increases or decreases in the adjusted basis of partnership property arising from a distribution of, or a transfer of an interest attributable to, property consisting of—

(1) capital assets and property described in section 1231(b), or

(2) any other property of the partnership,

shall be allocated to partnership property of a like character except that the basis of any such partnership property shall not be reduced below zero. If, in the case of a distribution, the adjustment to basis of property described in paragraph (1) or (2) is prevented by the absence of such property or by insufficient adjusted basis for such property, such adjustment shall be applied to subsequently acquired property of a like character in accordance with regulations prescribed by the Secretary.

(c) **No allocation of basis decrease to stock of corporate partner.**—In making allocation under subsection (a) of any decrease in the adjusted basis of partnership property under section 734(b)—

(1) no allocation may be made to stock in a corporation (or any person related (within the meaning of sections 267(b) and 707(b)(1)) to such corporation) which is a partner in the partnership, and

(2) any amount not allocable to stock by reason of paragraph (1) shall be allocated under subsection (a) to other partnership property.

Gain shall be recognized to the partnership to the extent that the amount required to be allocated under paragraph (2) to other partnership property exceeds the aggregate adjusted basis of such other property immediately before the allocation required by paragraph (2).

§§ 756–760. [Reserved for future use.]

Part III—Definitions

§ 761. Terms defined.

(a) **Partnership.**—For purposes of this subtitle, the term "partnership" includes a syndicate, group, pool, joint venture, or other unincorporated organization through or by means of which any business, financial operation, or venture is carried on, and which is not, within the meaning of this title, a corporation or a trust or estate. Under regulations the Secretary may, at the election of all the members of an unincorporated organization, exclude such organization from the application of all or part of this subchapter, if it is availed of—

(1) for investment purposes only and not for the active conduct of a business,

(2) for the joint production, extraction, or use of property, but not for the purpose of selling services or property produced or extracted, or

(3) by dealers in securities for a short period for the purpose of underwriting, selling, or distributing a particular issue of securities,

if the income of the members of the organization may be adequately determined without the computation of partnership taxable income.

(b) Partner.—For purposes of this subtitle, the term "partner" means a member of a partnership. In the case of a capital interest in a partnership in which capital is a material income-producing factor, whether a person is a partner with respect to such interest shall be determined without regard to whether such interest was derived by gift from any other person.

(c) Partnership agreement.—For purposes of this subchapter, a partnership agreement includes any modifications of the partnership agreement made prior to, or at, the time prescribed by law for the filing of the partnership return for the taxable year (not including extensions) which are agreed to by all the partners, or which are adopted in such other manner as may be provided by the partnership agreement.

(d) Liquidation of a partner's interest.—For purposes of this subchapter, the term "liquidation of a partner's interest" means the termination of a partner's entire interest in a partnership by means of a distribution, or a series of distributions, to the partner by the partnership.

(e) Distributions of partnership interests treated as exchanges.—Except as otherwise provided in regulations, for purposes of—

(1) section 708 (relating to continuation of partnership),

(2) section 743 (relating to optional adjustment to basis of partnership property), and

(3) any other provision of this subchapter specified in regulations prescribed by the Secretary,

any distribution of an interest in a partnership (not otherwise treated as an exchange) shall be treated as an exchange.

(f) Qualified joint venture.—

(1) In general.—In the case of a qualified joint venture conducted by a husband and wife who file a joint return for the taxable year, for purposes of this title—

(A) such joint venture shall not be treated as a partnership,

(B) all items of income, gain, loss, deduction, and credit shall be divided between the spouses in accordance with their respective interests in the venture, and

(C) each spouse shall take into account such spouse's respective share of such items as if they were attributable to a trade or business conducted by such spouse as a sole proprietor.

(2) Qualified joint venture.—For purposes of paragraph (1), the term 'qualified joint venture' means any joint venture involving the conduct of a trade or business if—

(A) the only members of such joint venture are a husband and wife,

(B) both spouses materially participate (within the meaning of section 469(h) without regard to paragraph (5) thereof) in such trade or business, and

(C) both spouses elect the application of this subsection.

(g) Cross reference.—For rules in the case of the sale, exchange, liquidation, or reduction of a partner's interest, see sections 704(b) and 706(c)(2).

Part IV—Special Rules for Electing Large Partnerships

§ 771. Application of subchapter to electing large partnerships.

The preceding provisions of this subchapter to the extent inconsistent with the provisions of this part shall not apply to an electing large partnership and its partners.

§ 772. Simplified flow-through.

(a) General rule.—In determining the income tax of a partner of an electing large partnership, such partner shall take into account separately such partner's distributive share of the partnership's—

(1) taxable income or loss from passive loss limitation activities,

(2) taxable income or loss from other activities,

(3) net capital gain (or net capital loss)—

(A) to the extent allocable to passive loss limitation activities, and

(B) to the extent allocable to other activities,

(4) tax-exempt interest,

(5) applicable net AMT adjustment separately computed for—

(A) passive loss limitation activities, and

(B) other activities,

(6) general credits,

(7) low-income housing credit determined under section 42,

(8) rehabilitation credit determined under section 47,

(9) foreign income taxes, and

(10) other items to the extent that the Secretary determines that the separate treatment of such items is appropriate.

(b) Separate computations.—In determining the amounts required under subsection (a) to be separately taken into account by any partner, this section and section 773 shall be applied separately with respect to such partner by taking into account such partner's distributive share of the items of income, gain, loss, deduction, or credit of the partnership.

(c) Treatment at partner level.—

(1) **In general.**—Except as provided in this subsection, rules similar to the rules of section 702(b) shall apply to any partner's distributive share of the amounts referred to in subsection (a).

(2) **Income or loss from passive loss limitation activities.**—For purposes of this chapter, any partner's distributive share of any income or loss described in subsection (a)(1) shall be treated as an item of income or loss (as the case may be) from the conduct of a trade or business which is a single passive activity (as defined in section 469). A similar rule shall

apply to a partner's distributive share of amounts referred to in paragraphs (3)(A) and (5)(A) of subsection (a).

(3) Income or loss from other activities.—

(A) In general.—For purposes of this chapter, any partner's distributive share of any income or loss described in subsection (a)(2) shall be treated as an item of income or expense (as the case may be) with respect to property held for investment.

(B) Deductions for loss not subject to section 67.—The deduction under section 212 for any loss described in subparagraph (A) shall not be treated as a miscellaneous itemized deduction for purposes of section 67.

(4) Treatment of net capital gain or loss.—For purposes of this chapter, any partner's distributive share of any gain or loss described in subsection (a)(3) shall be treated as a longterm capital gain or loss, as the case may be.

(5) Minimum tax treatment.—In determining the alternative minimum taxable income of any partner, such partner's distributive share of any applicable net AMT adjustment shall be taken into account in lieu of making the separate adjustments provided in sections 56, 57, and 58 with respect to the items of the partnership. Except as provided in regulations, the applicable net AMT adjustment shall be treated, for purposes of section 53, as an adjustment or item of tax preference not specified in section 53(d)(1)(B)(ii).

(6) General credits.—A partner's distributive share of the amount referred to in paragraph (6) of subsection (a) shall be taken into account as a current year business credit.

(d) Operating rules.—For purposes of this section—

(1) Passive loss limitation activity.—The term "passive loss limitation activity" means—

(A) any activity which involves the conduct of a trade or business, and

(B) any rental activity.

For purposes of the preceding sentence, the term "trade or business" includes any activity treated as a trade or business under paragraph (5) or (6) of section 469(c).

(2) Tax-exempt interest.—The term "tax-exempt interest" means interest excludable from gross income under section 103.

(3) Applicable net AMT adjustment.—

(A) In general.—The applicable net AMT adjustment is—

(i) with respect to taxpayers other than corporations, the net adjustment determined by using the adjustments applicable to individuals, and

(ii) with respect to corporations, the net adjustment determined by using the adjustments applicable to corporations.

(B) Net adjustment.—The term "net adjustment" means the net adjustment in the items attributable to passive loss activities or other activities (as the case may be) which would result if such items were determined with the adjustments of sections 56, 57, and 58.

(4) Treatment of certain separately stated items.—

(A) Exclusion for certain purposes.—In determining the amounts referred to in paragraphs (1) and (2) of subsection (a), any net capital gain or net capital loss (as the case may be), and any item referred to in subsection (a)(11), shall be excluded.

(B) Allocation rules.—The net capital gain shall be treated—

(i) as allocable to passive loss limitation activities to the extent the net capital gain does not exceed the net capital gain determined by only taking into account gains and losses from sales and exchanges of property used in connection with such activities, and

(ii) as allocable to other activities to the extent such gain exceeds the amount allocated under clause (i).

A similar rule shall apply for purposes of allocating any net capital loss.

(C) Net capital loss.—The term "net capital loss" means the excess of the losses from sales or exchanges of capital assets over the gains from sales or exchange of capital assets.

(5) General credits.—The term "general credits" means any credit other than the low-income housing credit, the rehabilitation credit, and the foreign tax credit.

(6) Foreign income taxes.—The term "foreign income taxes" means taxes described in section 901 which are paid or accrued to foreign countries and to possessions of the United States.

(e) Special rule for unrelated business tax.—In the case of a partner which is an organization subject to tax under section 511, such partner's distributive share of any items shall be taken into account separately to the extent necessary to comply with the provisions of section 512(c) (1).

(f) Special rules for applying passive loss limitations.—If any person holds an interest in an electing large partnership other than as a limited partner—

(1) paragraph (2) of subsection (c) shall not apply to such partner, and

(2) such partner's distributive share of the partnership items allocable to passive loss limitation activities shall be taken into account separately to the extent necessary to comply with the provisions of section 469.

The preceding sentence shall not apply to any items allocable to an interest held as a limited partner.

§ 773. Computations at partnership level.

(a) General rule.—

(1) Taxable income.—The taxable income of an electing large partnership shall be computed in the same manner as in the case of an individual except that—

(A) the items described in section 772(a) shall be separately stated, and

(B) the modifications of subsection (b) shall apply.

(2) Elections.—All elections affecting the computation of the taxable income of an electing large partnership or the computation of any credit of an electing large partnership shall be made by the partnership; except that the election under section 901, and any election under section 108, shall be made by each partner separately.

(3) Limitations, etc.—

(A) In general.—Except as provided in subparagraph (B), all limitations and other provisions affecting the computation of the taxable income of an electing large partnership or the computation of any credit of an electing large partnership shall be applied at the partnership level (and not at the partner level).

(B) Certain limitations applied at partner level.—The following provisions shall be applied at the partner level (and not at the partnership level):

(i) Section 68 (relating to overall limitation on itemized deductions).

(ii) Sections 49 and 465 (relating to at risk limitations).

(iii) Section 469 (relating to limitation on passive activity losses and credits).

(iv) Any other provision specified in regulations.

(4) Coordination with other provisions.—Paragraphs (2) and (3) shall apply notwithstanding any other provision of this chapter other than this part.

(b) Modifications to determination of taxable income.—In determining the taxable income of an electing large partnership—

(1) Certain deductions not allowed.—The following deductions shall not be allowed:

(A) The deduction for personal exemptions provided in section 151.

(B) The net operating loss deduction provided in section 172.

(C) The additional itemized deductions for individuals provided in part VII of subchapter B (other than section 212 thereof).

(2) Charitable deductions.—In determining the amount allowable under section 170, the limitation of section 170(b)(2) shall apply.

(3) Coordination with section 67.—In lieu of applying section 67, 70 percent of the amount of the miscellaneous itemized deductions shall be disallowed.

(c) Special rules for income from discharge of indebtedness.—If an electing large partnership has income from the discharge of any indebtedness—

(1) such income shall be excluded in determining the amounts referred to in section 772(a), and

(2) in determining the income tax of any partner of such partnership—

(A) such income shall be treated as an item required to be separately taken into account under section 772(a), and

(B) the provisions of section 108 shall be applied without regard to this part.

§ 774. Other modifications.

(a) Treatment of certain optional adjustments, etc.—In the case of an electing large partnership—

(1) computations under section 773 shall be made without regard to any adjustment under section 743(b) or 108(b), but

(2) a partner's distributive share of any amount referred to in section 772(a) shall be appropriately adjusted to take into account any adjustment under section 743(b) or 108(b) with respect to such partner.

(b) Credit recapture determined at partnership level.—

(1) In general.—In the case of an electing large partnership—

(A) any credit recapture shall be taken into account by the partnership, and

(B) the amount of such recapture shall be determined as if the credit with respect to which the recapture is made had been fully utilized to reduce tax.

(2) Method of taking recapture into account.—An electing large partnership shall take into account a credit recapture by reducing the amount of the appropriate current year credit to the extent thereof, and if such recapture exceeds the amount of such current year credit, the partnership shall be liable to pay such excess.

(3) Dispositions not to trigger recapture.—No credit recapture shall be required by reason of any transfer of an interest in an electing large partnership.

(4) Credit recapture.—For purposes of this subsection, the term "credit recapture" means any increase in tax under section 42(j) or 50(a).

(c) Partnership not terminated by reason of change in ownership.—Subparagraph (B) of section 708(b)(1) shall not apply to an electing large partnership.

(d) Partnership entitled to certain credits.—The following shall be allowed to an electing large partnership and shall not be taken into account by the partners of such partnership:

(1) The credit provided by section 34.

(2) Any credit or refund under section 852(b)(3)(D) or 857(b)(3)(D).

(e) Treatment of REMIC residuals.—For purposes of applying section 860E(e)(6) to any electing large partnership—

(1) all interests in such partnership shall be treated as held by disqualified organizations,

(2) in lieu of applying subparagraph (C) of section 860E(e)(6), the amount subject to tax under section 860E(e)(6) shall be excluded from the gross income of such partnership, and

(3) subparagraph (D) of section 860E(e)(6) shall not apply.

(f) Special rules for applying certain installment sale rules.—In the case of an electing large partnership—

(1) the provisions of sections 453(l)(3) and 453A shall be applied at the partnership level, and

(2) in determining the amount of interest payable under such sections, such partnership shall be treated as subject to tax under this chapter at the highest rate of tax in effect under section 1 or 11.

§ 775. Electing large partnership defined.

(a) **General rule.**—For purposes of this part—

(1) **In general.**—The term "electing large partnership" means, with respect to any partnership taxable year, any partnership if—

(A) the number of persons who were partners in such partnership in the preceding partnership taxable year equaled or exceeded 100, and

(B) such partnership elects the application of this part. To the extent provided in regulations, a partnership shall cease to be treated as an electing large partnership for any partnership taxable year if in such taxable year fewer than 100 persons were partners in such partnership.

(2) **Election.**—The election under this subsection shall apply to the taxable year for which made and all subsequent taxable years unless revoked with the consent of the Secretary.

(b) **Special rules for certain service partnerships.**—

(1) **Certain partners not counted.**—For purposes of this section, the term "partner" does not include any individual performing substantial services in connection with the activities of the partnership and holding an interest in such partnership, or an individual who formerly performed substantial services in connection with such activities and who held an interest in such partnership at the time the individual performed such services.

(2) **Exclusion.**—For purposes of this part, an election under subsection (a) shall not be effective with respect to any partnership if substantially all the partners of such partnership—

(A) are individuals performing substantial services in connection with the activities of such partnership or are personal service corporations (as defined in section 269A(b)) the owner-employees (as defined in section 269A(b)) of which perform such substantial services,

(B) are retired partners who had performed such substantial services, or

(C) are spouses of partners who are performing (or had previously performed) such substantial services.

(3) **Special rule for lower tier partnerships.**—For purposes of this subsection, the activities of a partnership shall include the activities of any other partnership in which the partnership owns directly an interest in the capital and profits of at least 80 percent.

(c) **Exclusion of commodity pools.**—For purposes of this part, an election under subsection (a) shall not be effective with respect to any partnership the principal activity of which is the buying and selling of commodities (not described in section 1221(1)), or options, futures, or forwards with respect to such commodities.

(d) **Secretary may rely on treatment on return.**—If, on the partnership return of any partnership, such partnership is treated as an electing large partnership, such treatment shall be binding on such partnership and all partners of such partnership but not on the Secretary.

§ 776. Special rules for partnerships holding oil and gas properties.

(a) **Computation of percentage depletion.**—In the case of an electing large partnership, except as provided in subsection (b)—

(1) the allowance for depletion under section 611 with respect to any partnership oil or gas property shall be computed at the partnership level without regard to any provision of section 613A requiring such allowance to be computed separately by each partner,

(2) such allowance shall be determined without regard to the provisions of section 613A(c) limiting the amount of production for which percentage depletion is allowable and without regard to paragraph (1) of section 613A(d), and

(3) paragraph (3) of section 705(a) shall not apply.

(b) Treatment of certain partners.—

(1) In general.—In the case of a disqualified person, the treatment under this chapter of such person's distributive share of any item of income, gain, loss, deduction, or credit attributable to any partnership oil or gas property shall be determined without regard to this part. Such person's distributive share of any such items shall be excluded for purposes of making determinations under sections 772 and 773.

(2) Disqualified person.—For purposes of paragraph (1), the term "disqualified person" means, with respect to any partnership taxable year—

(A) any person referred to in paragraph (2) or (4) of section 613A(d) for such person's taxable year in which such partnership taxable year ends, and

(B) any other person if such person's average daily production of domestic crude oil and natural gas for such person's taxable year in which such partnership taxable year ends exceeds 500 barrels.

(3) Average daily production.—For purposes of paragraph (2), a person's average daily production of domestic crude oil and natural gas for any taxable year shall be computed as provided in section 613A(c)(2)—

(A) by taking into account all production of domestic crude oil and natural gas (including such person's proportionate share of any production of a partnership),

(B) by treating 6,000 cubic feet of natural gas as a barrel of crude oil, and

(C) by treating as 1 person all persons treated as 1 taxpayer under section 613A(c)(8) or among whom allocations are required under such section.

§ 777. Regulations.

The Secretary shall prescribe such regulations as may be appropriate to carry out the purposes of this part.

§§ 778–800. [Reserved for future use.]

Subchapter O—Gain or Loss on Disposition of Property

Part I—Determination of Amount of and Recognition of Gain or Loss

§ 1001. Determination of amount of and recognition of gain or loss.

(a) Computation of gain or loss.—The gain from the sale or other disposition of property shall be the excess of the amount realized therefrom over the adjusted basis provided in section

1011 for determining gain, and the loss shall be the excess of the adjusted basis provided in such section for determining loss over the amount realized.

(b) Amount realized.—The amount realized from the sale or other disposition of property shall be the sum of any money received plus the fair market value of the property (other than money) received. In determining the amount realized—

(**1**) there shall not be taken into account any amount received as reimbursement for real property taxes which are treated under section 164(d) as imposed on the purchaser, and

(**2**) there shall be taken into account amounts representing real property taxes which are treated under section 164(d) as imposed on the taxpayer if such taxes are to be paid by the purchaser.

(c) Recognition of gain or loss.—Except as otherwise provided in this subtitle, the entire amount of the gain or loss, determined under this section, on the sale or exchange of property shall be recognized.

* * *

Part II—Basis Rules of General Application

§ 1011. Adjusted basis for determining gain or loss.

(**a**) **General rule.**—The adjusted basis for determining the gain or loss from the sale or other disposition of property, whenever acquired, shall be the basis (determined under section 1012 or other applicable sections of this subchapter and subchapters C (relating to corporate distributions and adjustments), K (relating to partners and partnerships), and P (relating to capital gains and losses)), adjusted as provided in section 1016.

(**b**) **Bargain sale to a charitable organization.**—If a deduction is allowable under section 170 (relating to charitable contributions) by reason of a sale, then the adjusted basis for determining the gain from such sale shall be that portion of the adjusted basis which bears the same ratio to the adjusted basis as the amount realized bears to the fair market value of the property.

§ 1012. Basis of property—cost.

The basis of property shall be the cost of such property, except as otherwise provided in this subchapter and subchapters C (relating to corporate distributions and adjustments), K (relating to partners and partnerships), and P (relating to capital gains and losses). The cost of real property shall not include any amount in respect of real property taxes which are treated under section 164(d) as imposed on the taxpayer.

* * *

§ 1014. Basis of property acquired from a decedent.

(**a**) **In general.**—Except as otherwise provided in this section, the basis of property in the hands of a person acquiring the property from a decedent or to whom the property passed from a decedent shall, if not sold, exchanged, or otherwise disposed of before the decedent's death by such person, be—

(**1**) the fair market value of the property at the date of the decedent's death,

(2) in the case of an election under either section 2032, its value at the applicable valuation date prescribed by those sections,

(3) in the case of an election under section 2032A, its value determined under such section, or

(4) to the extent of the applicability of the exclusion described in section 2031(c), the basis in the hands of the decedent.

* * *

§ 1015. Basis of property acquired by gifts and transfers in trust.

(a) Gifts after December 31, 1920.—If the property was acquired by gift after December 31, 1920, the basis shall be the same as it would be in the hands of the donor or the last preceding owner by whom it was not acquired by gift, except that if such basis (adjusted for the period before the date of the gift as provided in section 1016) is greater than the fair market value of the property at the time of the gift, then for the purpose of determining loss the basis shall be such fair market value. If the facts necessary to determine the basis in the hands of the donor or the last preceding owner are unknown to the donee, the Secretary shall, if possible, obtain such facts from such donor or last preceding owner, or any other person cognizant thereof. If the Secretary finds it impossible to obtain such facts, the basis in the hands of such donor or last preceding owner shall be the fair market value of such property as found by the Secretary as of the date or approximate date at which, according to the best information that the Secretary is able to obtain, such property was acquired by such donor or last preceding owner.

* * *

§ 1016. Adjustments to basis.

(a) General rule.—Proper adjustment in respect of the property shall in all cases be made—

(1) for expenditures, receipts, losses, or other items, properly chargeable to capital account, but no such adjustment shall be made—

(A) for taxes or other carrying charges described in section 266, or

(B) for expenditures described in section 173 (relating to circulation expenditures),

for which deductions have been taken by the taxpayer in determining taxable income for the taxable year or prior taxable years;

(2) in respect of any period since February 28, 1913, for exhaustion, wear and tear, obsolescence, amortization, and depletion, to the extent of the amount—

(A) allowed as deductions in computing taxable income under this subtitle or prior income tax laws, and

(B) resulting (by reason of the deductions so allowed) in a reduction for any taxable year of the taxpayer's taxes under this subtitle (other than chapter 2, relating to tax on self-employment income), or prior income, war-profits, or excess-profits tax laws,

but not less than the amount allowable under this subtitle or prior income tax laws. Where no method has been adopted under section 167 (relating to depreciation deduction), the amount allowable shall be determined under the straight line method.

* * *

Part III—Common Nontaxable Exchanges

§ 1031. Exchange of real property held for productive use or investment.
(a) Nonrecognition of gain or loss from exchanges solely in kind.—

(1) In general.—No gain or loss shall be recognized on the exchange of real property held for productive use in a trade or business or for investment if such real property is exchanged solely for real property of like kind which is to be held either for productive use in a trade or business or for investment.

(2) Exception.—This subsection shall not apply to any exchange or real property held primarily for sale.

(3) Requirement that property be identified and that exchange be completed not more than 180 days after transfer of exchanged property

For purposes of this subsection, any property received by the taxpayer shall be treated as property which is not like-kind property if—

(A) such property is not identified as property to be received in the exchange on or before the day which is 45 days after the date on which the taxpayer transfers the property relinquished in the exchange, or

(B) such property is received after the earlier of—

(i) the day which is 180 days after the date on which the taxpayer transfers the property relinquished in the exchange, or

(ii) the due date (determined with regard to extension) for the transferor's return of the tax imposed by this chapter for the taxable year in which the transfer of the relinquished property occurs.

(b) Gain from exchanges not solely in kind.—If an exchange would be within the provisions of subsection (a), of section 1035(a), of section 1036(a), or of section 1037(a), if it were not for the fact that the property received in exchange consists not only of property permitted by such provisions to be received without the recognition of gain, but also of other property or money, then the gain, if any, to the recipient shall be recognized, but in an amount not in excess of the sum of such money and the fair market value of such other property.

(c) Loss from exchanges not solely in kind.—If an exchange would be within the provisions of subsection (a), of section 1035(a), of section 1036(a), or of section 1037(a), if it were not for the fact that the property received in exchange consists not only of property permitted by such provisions to be received without the recognition of gain or loss, but also of other property or money, then no loss from the exchange shall be recognized.

(d) Basis.—If property was acquired on an exchange described in this section, section 1035(a), section 1036(a), or section 1037(a), then the basis shall be the same as that of the property exchanged, decreased in the amount of any money received by the taxpayer and increased in the amount of gain or decreased in the amount of loss to the taxpayer that was recognized on such exchange. If the property so acquired consisted in part of the type of property permitted by this section, section 1035(a), section 1036(a), or section 1037(a), to be received without the recognition of gain or loss, and in part of other property, the basis provided in this subsection shall be allocated between the properties (other than money) received, and for the purpose of the allocation there shall be assigned to such other property an amount equivalent to its fair market value at the date of the exchange. For purposes of this section, section 1035(a), and section 1036(a), where as part of the consideration to the taxpayer another party to the exchange assumed a liability of the taxpayer or acquired from the taxpayer property subject to a liability, such assumption or acquisition (in the amount of the liability) shall be considered as money received by the taxpayer on the exchange.

* * *

§ 1032. Exchange of stock for property.

(a) Nonrecognition of gain or loss.—No gain or loss shall be recognized to a corporation on the receipt of money or other property in exchange for stock (including treasury stock) of such corporation. No gain or loss shall be recognized by a corporation with respect to any lapse or acquisition of an option to buy or sell its stock (including treasury stock).

(b) Basis.—For basis of property acquired by a corporation in certain exchanges for its stock, see section 362.

* * *

§ 1036. Stock for stock of same corporation.

(a) General rule.—No gain or loss shall be recognized if common stock in a corporation is exchanged solely for common stock in the same corporation, or if preferred stock in a corporation is exchanged solely for preferred stock in the same corporation.

(b) Nonqualified preferred stock not treated as stock.—For purposes of this section, nonqualified preferred stock (as defined in section 351(g)(2)) shall be treated as property other than stock.

(c) Cross references.—(1) For rules relating to recognition of gain or loss where an exchange is not solely in kind, see subsections (b) and (c) of section 1031.

(2) For rules relating to the basis of property acquired in an exchange described in subsection (a), see subsection (d) of section 1031.

Part IV—Special Rules

§ 1059. Corporate shareholder's basis in stock reduced by nontaxed portion of extraordinary dividends.

(a) General rule.—If any corporation receives any extraordinary dividend with respect to any share of stock and such corporation has not held such stock for more than 2 years before the dividend announcement date—

(1) Reduction in basis.—The basis of such corporation in such stock shall be reduced (but not below zero) by the nontaxed portion of such dividends.

(2) Amounts in excess of basis.—If the nontaxed portion of such dividends exceeds such basis, such excess shall be treated as gain from the sale or exchange of such stock for the taxable year in which the extraordinary dividend is received.

(b) Nontaxed portion.—For purposes of this section—

(1) In general.—The nontaxed portion of any dividend is the excess (if any) of—

(A) the amount of such dividend, over

(B) the taxable portion of such dividend.

(2) Taxable portion.—The taxable portion of any dividend is—

(A) the portion of such dividend includible in gross income, reduced by

(B) the amount of any deduction allowable with respect to such dividend under section 243, 244, or 245.

(c) Extraordinary dividend defined.—For purposes of this section—

(1) In general.—The term "extraordinary dividend" means any dividend with respect to a share of stock if the amount of such dividend equals or exceeds the threshold percentage of the taxpayer's adjusted basis in such share of stock.

(2) Threshold percentage.—The term "threshold percentage" means—

(A) 5 percent in the case of stock which is preferred as to dividends, and

(B) 10 percent in the case of any other stock.

(3) Aggregation of dividends.—

(A) Aggregation within 85-day period.—All dividends—

(i) which are received by the taxpayer (or a person described in subparagraph (C)) with respect to any share of stock, and

(ii) which have ex-dividend dates within the same period of 85 consecutive days, shall be treated as 1 dividend.

(B) Aggregation within 1 year where dividends exceed 20 percent of adjusted basis.—All dividends—

(i) which are received by the taxpayer (or a person described in subparagraph (C)) with respect to any share of stock, and

(ii) which have ex-dividend dates during the same period of 365 consecutive days,

shall be treated as extraordinary dividends if the aggregate of such dividends exceeds 20 percent of the taxpayer's adjusted basis in such stock (determined without regard to this section).

(C) Substituted basis transactions.—In the case of any stock, a person is described in this subparagraph if—

(i) the basis of such stock in the hands of such person is determined in whole or in part by reference to the basis of such stock in the hands of the taxpayer, or

(ii) the basis of such stock in the hands of the taxpayer is determined in whole or in part by reference to the basis of such stock in the hands of such person.

(4) Fair market value determination.—If the taxpayer establishes to the satisfaction of the Secretary the fair market value of any share of stock as of the day before the ex-dividend date, the taxpayer may elect to apply paragraphs (1) and (3) by substituting such value for the taxpayer's adjusted basis.

(d) Special rules.—For purposes of this section—

(1) Time for reduction.—Any reduction in basis under subsection (a)(1) shall be treated as occurring at the beginning of the ex-dividend date of the extraordinary dividend to which the reduction relates.

(2) Distributions in kind.—To the extent any dividend consists of property other than cash, the amount of such dividend shall be treated as the fair market value of such property (as of the date of the distribution) reduced as provided in section 301(b)(2).

(3) Determination of holding period.—For purposes of determining the holding period of stock under subsection (a), rules similar to the rules of paragraphs (3) and (4) of section 246(c) shall apply; except that "2 years" shall be substituted for the number of days specified in subparagraph (B) of section 246(c)(3).

(4) Ex-dividend date.—The term "ex-dividend date" means the date on which the share of stock becomes ex-dividend.

(5) Dividend announcement date.—The term "dividend announcement date" means, with respect to any dividend, the date on which the corporation declares, announces, or agrees to the amount or payment of such dividend, whichever is the earliest.

(6) Exception where stock held during entire existence of corporation.—

(A) In general.—Subsection (a) shall not apply to any extraordinary dividend with respect to any share of stock of a corporation if—

(i) such stock was held by the taxpayer during the entire period such corporation was in existence, and

(ii) except as provided in regulations, no earnings and profits of such corporation were attributable to transfers of property from (or earnings and profits of) a corporation which is not a qualified corporation.

(B) Qualified corporation.—For purposes of subparagraph (A), the term "qualified corporation" means any corporation (including a predecessor corporation)—

(i) with respect to which the taxpayer holds directly or indirectly during the entire period of such corporation's existence at least the same ownership interest as the taxpayer holds in the corporation distributing the extraordinary dividend, and

(ii) which has no earnings and profits—

(I) which were earned by, or

(II) which are attributable to gain on property which accrued during a period the corporation holding the property was,

a corporation not described in clause (i).

(C) Application of paragraph.—This paragraph shall not apply to any extraordinary dividend to the extent such application is inconsistent with the purposes of this section.

(e) Special rules for certain distributions.—

(1) Treatment of partial liquidations and certain redemptions.—Except as otherwise provided in regulations—

(A) Redemptions.—In the case of any redemption of stock—

    (i) which is part of a partial liquidation (within the meaning of section 302(e)) of the redeeming corporation,

    (ii) which is not pro rata as to all shareholders, or

    (iii) which would not have been treated (in whole or in part) as a dividend if—

        (I) any options had not been taken into account under section 318(a)(4), or

        (II) section 304(a) had not applied,

any amount treated as a dividend with respect to such redemption shall be treated as an extraordinary dividend to which paragraphs (1) and (2) of subsection (a) apply without regard to the period the taxpayer held such stock. In the case of a redemption described in clause (iii), only the basis in the stock redeemed shall be taken into account under subsection (a).

    (B) Reorganizations, etc.—An exchange described in section 356 which is treated as a dividend shall be treated as a redemption of stock for purposes of applying subparagraph (A).

(2) Qualifying dividends.—

    (A) In general.—Except as provided in regulations, the term "extraordinary dividend" does not include any qualifying dividend (within the meaning of section 243).

    (B) Exception.—Subparagraph (A) shall not apply to any portion of a dividend which is attributable to earnings and profits which—

    (i) were earned by a corporation during a period it was not a member of the affiliated group, or

    (ii) are attributable to gain on property which accrued during a period the corporation holding the property was not a member of the affiliated group.

(3) Qualified preferred dividends.—

    (A) In general.—In the case of 1 or more qualified preferred dividends with respect to any share of stock—

    (i) this section shall not apply to such dividends if the taxpayer holds such stock for more than 5 years, and

    (ii) if the taxpayer disposes of such stock before it has been held for more than 5 years, the aggregate reduction under subsection (a)(1) with respect to such dividends shall not be greater than the excess (if any) of—

        (I) the qualified preferred dividends paid with respect to such stock during the period the taxpayer held such stock, over

        (II) the qualified preferred dividends which would have been paid during such period on the basis of the stated rate of return.

    (B) Rate of return.—For purposes of this paragraph—

    (i) Actual rate of return.—The actual rate of return shall be the rate of return for the period for which the taxpayer held the stock, determined—

        (I) by only taking into account dividends during such period, and

(II) by using the lesser of the adjusted basis of the taxpayer in such stock or the liquidation preference of such stock.

(ii) Stated rate of return.—The stated rate of return shall be the annual rate of the qualified preferred dividend payable with respect to any share of stock (expressed as a percentage of the amount described in clause (i)(II)).

(C) Definitions and special rules.—For purposes of this paragraph—

(i) Qualified preferred dividend.—The term "qualified preferred dividend" means any fixed dividend payable with respect to any share of stock which—

(I) provides for fixed preferred dividends payable not less frequently than annually, and

(II) is not in arrears as to dividends at the time the taxpayer acquires the stock.

Such term shall not include any dividend payable with respect to any share of stock if the actual rate of return on such stock exceeds 15 percent.

(ii) Holding period.—In determining the holding period for purposes of subparagraph (A)(ii), subsection (d)(3) shall be applied by substituting "5 years" for "2 years".

(f) Treatment of dividends on certain preferred stock.—

(1) In general.—Any dividend with respect to disqualified preferred stock shall be treated as an extraordinary dividend to which paragraphs (1) and (2) of subsection (a) apply without regard to the period the taxpayer held the stock.

(2) Disqualified preferred stock.—For purposes of this subsection, the term "disqualified preferred stock" means any stock which is preferred as to dividends if—

(A) when issued, such stock has a dividend rate which declines (or can reasonably be expected to decline) in the future,

(B) the issue price of such stock exceeds its liquidation rights or its stated redemption price, or

(C) such stock is otherwise structured—

(i) to avoid the other provisions of this section, and

(ii) to enable corporate shareholders to reduce tax through a combination of dividend received deductions and loss on the disposition of the stock.

(g) Regulations.—The Secretary shall prescribe such regulations as may be appropriate to carry out the purposes of this section, including regulations—

(1) providing for the application of this section in the case of stock dividends, stock splits, reorganizations, and other similar transactions, in the case of stock held by pass-thru entities, and in the case of consolidated groups, and

(2) providing that the rules of subsection (f) shall apply in the case of stock which is not preferred as to dividends in cases where stock is structured to avoid the purposes of this section.

§ 1061. Partnership interests held in connection with performance of services.

(a) In general.—If one or more applicable partnership interests are held by a taxpayer at any time during the taxable year, the excess (if any) of—

(1) the taxpayer's net long-term capital gain with respect to such interests for such taxable year, over

(2) the taxpayer's net long-term capital gain with respect to such interests for such taxable year computed by applying paragraphs (3) and (4) of sections 1222 by substituting '3 years' for '1 year',

shall be treated as short-term capital gain, notwithstanding section 83 or any election in effect under section 83(b).

(b) Special rule.—To the extent provided by the Secretary, subsection (a) shall not apply to income or gain attributable to any asset not held for portfolio investment on behalf of third party investors.

(c) Applicable partnership interest.—For purposes of this section—

(1) In general.—Except as provided in this paragraph or paragraph (4), the term 'applicable partnership interest' means any interest in a partnership which, directly or indirectly, is transferred to (or is held by) the taxpayer in connection with the performance of substantial services by the taxpayer, or any other related person, in any applicable trade or business. The previous sentence shall not apply to an interest held by a person who is employed by another entity that is conducting a trade or business (other than an applicable trade or business) and only provides services to such other entity.

(2) Applicable trade or business.—The term 'applicable trade or business' means any activity conducted on a regular, continuous, and substantial basis which, regardless of whether the activity is conducted in one or more entities, consists, in whole or in part, of—

(A) raising or returning capital, and

(B) either—

(i) investing in (or disposing of) specified assets (or identifying specified assets for such investing or disposition), or

(ii) developing specified assets.

(3) Specified asset.—The term 'specified asset' means securities (as defined in section 475(c)(2) without regard to the last sentence thereof), commodities (as defined in section 475(e)(2)), real estate held for rental or investment, cash or cash equivalents, options or derivative contracts with respect to any of the foregoing, and an interest in a partnership to nt of the partnership's proportionate interest in any of the foregoing.

(4) Exceptions.—The term 'applicable partnership interest' shall not include—

(A) any interest in a partnership directly or indirectly held by a corporation, or

(B) any capital interest in the partnership which provides the taxpayer with a right to share in partnership capital commensurate with—

(i) the amount of capital contributed (determined at the time of receipt of such partnership interest), or

(ii) the value of such interest subject to tax under section 83 upon the receipt or vesting of such interest.

(5) Third party investor.—The term 'third party investor' means a person who—

(A) holds an interest in the partnership which does not constitute property held in connection with an applicable trade or business; and

(B) is not (and has not been) actively engaged, and is (and was) not related to a person so engaged, in (directly or indirectly) providing substantial services described in paragraph (1) for such partnership or any applicable trade or business.

(d) Transfer of applicable partnership interest to related person.—

(1) In general.—If a taxpayer transfers any applicable partnership interest, directly or indirectly, to a person related to the taxpayer, the taxpayer shall include in gross income (as short term capital gain) the excess (if any) of—

(A) so much of the taxpayer's long-term capital gains with respect to such interest for such taxable year attributable to the sale or exchange of any asset held for not more than 3 years as is allocable to such interest, over

(B) any amount treated as short term capital gain under subsection (a) with respect to the transfer of such interest.

(2) Related person.—For purposes of this paragraph, a person is related to the taxpayer if—

(A) the person is a member of the taxpayer's family within the meaning of section 318(a)(1), or

(B) the person performed a service within the current calendar year or the preceding three calendar years in any applicable trade or business in which or for which the taxpayer performed a service.

(e) Reporting.—The Secretary shall require such reporting (at the time and in the manner prescribed by the Secretary) as is necessary to carry out the purposes of this section.

(f) Regulations.—The Secretary shall issue such regulations or other guidance as is necessary or appropriate to carry out the purposes of this section.

Subchapter P—Capital Gains and Losses

Part I—Treatment of Capital Gains

§ 1201. Alternative tax for corporations.

(a) General rule.—If for any taxable year a corporation has a net capital gain and any rate of tax imposed by section 11, 511, or 831(a) or (b) (whichever is applicable) exceeds 35 percent (determined without regard to the last 2 sentences of section 11(b)(1)), then, in lieu of any such tax, there is hereby imposed a tax (if such tax is less than the tax imposed by such sections) which shall consist of the sum of—

(1) a tax computed on the taxable income reduced by the amount of the net capital gain, at the rates and in the manner as if this subsection had not been enacted, plus

(2) a tax of 35 percent of the net capital gain (or, if less, taxable income).

* * *

§ 1202. 50-percent exclusion for gain from certain small business stock.

(a) Exclusion.—(1) In general.—In the case of a taxpayer other than a corporation, gross income shall not include 50 percent of any gain from the sale or exchange of qualified small business stock held for more than 5 years.

* * *

(4) 100 percent exclusion for stock acquired during certain periods in 2011, 2012, 2013, 2014, and thereafter.—In the case of qualified small business stock acquired after the date of the enactment of the Creating Small Business Jobs Act of 2010—

(A) Paragraph (1) shall be applied by substituting "100 percent" for "50 percent",

* * *

(b) Per-issuer limitation on taxpayer's eligible gain.—

(1) In general.—If the taxpayer has eligible gain for the taxable year from 1 or more dispositions of stock issued by any corporation, the aggregate amount of such gain from dispositions of stock issued by such corporation which may be taken into account under subsection (a) for the taxable year shall not exceed the greater of—

(A) $10,000,000 reduced by the aggregate amount of eligible gain taken into account under subsection (a) for prior taxable years and attributable to dispositions of stock issued by such corporation, or

(B) 10 times the aggregate adjusted bases of qualified small business stock issued by such corporation and disposed of by the taxpayer during the taxable year.

For purposes of subparagraph (B), the adjusted basis of any stock shall be determined without regard to any addition to basis after the date on which such stock was originally issued.

(2) Eligible gain.—For purposes of this subsection, the term "eligible gain" means any gain from the sale or exchange of qualified small business stock held for more than 5 years.

(3) Treatment of married individuals.—

(A) Separate returns.—In the case of a separate return by a married individual, paragraph (1)(A) shall be applied by substituting "$5,000,000" for "$10,000,000".

(B) Allocation of exclusion.—In the case of any joint return, the amount of gain taken into account under subsection (a) shall be allocated equally between the spouses for purposes of applying this subsection to subsequent taxable years.

(C) Marital status.—For purposes of this subsection, marital status shall be determined under section 7703.

(c) Qualified small business stock.—For purposes of this section—

(1) In general.—Except as otherwise provided in this section, the term "qualified small business stock" means any stock in a C corporation which is originally issued after the date of the enactment of the Revenue Reconciliation Act of 1993, if—

(A) as of the date of issuance, such corporation is a qualified small business, and

(B) except as provided in subsections (f) and (h), such stock is acquired by the taxpayer at its original issue (directly or through an underwriter)—

(i) in exchange for money or other property (not including stock), or

(ii) as compensation for services provided to such corporation (other than services performed as an underwriter of such stock).

(2) Active business requirement; etc.—

(A) **In general.**—Stock in a corporation shall not be treated as qualified small business stock unless, during substantially all of the taxpayer's holding period for such stock, such corporation meets the active business requirements of subsection (e) and such corporation is a C corporation.

* * *

(d) Qualified small business.—For purposes of this section—

(1) In general.—The term "qualified small business" means any domestic corporation which is a C corporation if—

(A) the aggregate gross assets of such corporation (or any predecessor thereof) at all times on or after the date of the enactment of the Revenue Reconciliation Act of 1993, and before the issuance did not exceed $50,000,000,

(B) the aggregate gross assets of such corporation immediately after the issuance (determined by taking into account amounts received in the issuance) does not exceed $50,000,000, and

(C) such corporation agrees to submit such reports to the Secretary and to shareholders as the Secretary may require to carry out the purposes of this section.

* * *

(e) Active business requirement.—

(1) In general.—For purposes of subsection (c)(2), the requirements of this subsection are met by a corporation for any period if during such period—

(A) at least 80 percent (by value) of the assets of such corporation are used by such corporation in the active conduct of 1 or more qualified trades or businesses, and

(B) such corporation is an eligible corporation.

(2) Special rule for certain activities.—For purposes of paragraph (1), if, in connection with any future qualified trade or business, a corporation is engaged in—

(A) start-up activities described in section 195(c)(1)(A),

(B) activities resulting in the payment or incurring of expenditures which may be treated as research and experimental expenditures under section 174, or

(C) activities with respect to in-house research expenses described in section 41(b)(4), assets used in such activities shall be treated as used in the active conduct of a qualified trade or business. Any determination under this paragraph shall be made without regard to whether a corporation has any gross income from such activities at the time of the determination.

(3) Qualified trade or business.—For purposes of this subsection, the term "qualified trade or business" means any trade or business other than—

(A) any trade or business involving the performance of services in the fields of health, law, engineering, architecture, accounting, actuarial science, performing arts, consulting, athletics, financial services, brokerage services, or any other trade or business where the principal asset of such trade or business is the reputation or skill of 1 or more of its employees,

(B) any banking, insurance, financing, leasing, investing, or similar business,

(C) any farming business (including the business of raising or harvesting trees),

(D) any business involving the production or extraction of products of a character with respect to which a deduction is allowable under section 613 or 613A, and

(E) any business of operating a hotel, motel, restaurant, or similar business.

* * *

(6) Working capital.—For purposes of paragraph (1)(A), any assets which—

(A) are held as a part of the reasonably required working capital needs of a qualified trade or business of the corporation, or

(B) are held for investment and are reasonably expected to be used within 2 years to finance research and experimentation in a qualified trade or business or increases in working capital needs of a qualified trade or business,

shall be treated as used in the active conduct of a qualified trade or business. For periods after the corporation has been in existence for at least 2 years, in no event may more than 50 percent of the assets of the corporation qualify as used in the active conduct of a qualified trade or business by reason of this paragraph.

(7) Maximum real estate holdings.—A corporation shall not be treated as meeting the requirements of paragraph (1) for any period during which more than 10 percent of the total value of its assets consists of real property which is not used in the active conduct of a qualified trade or business. For purposes of the preceding sentence, the ownership of, dealing in, or renting of real property shall not be treated as the active conduct of a qualified trade or business.

(8) Computer software royalties.—For purposes of paragraph (1), rights to computer software which produces active business computer software royalties (within the meaning of section 543(d)(1)) shall be treated as an asset used in the active conduct of a trade or business.

* * *

Part II—Treatment of Capital Losses

§ 1211. Limitation on capital losses.

(a) Corporations.—In the case of a corporation, losses from sales or exchanges of capital assets shall be allowed only to the extent of gains from such sales or exchanges.

(b) Other taxpayers.—In the case of a taxpayer other than a corporation, losses from sales or exchanges of capital assets shall be allowed only to the extent of the gains from such sales or exchanges, plus (if such losses exceed such gains) the lower of—

(1) $3,000 ($1,500 in the case of a married individual filing a separate return), or

(2) the excess of such losses over such gains.

§ 1212. Capital loss carrybacks and carryovers.

(a) Corporations.—

(1) In general.—If a corporation has a net capital loss for any taxable year (hereinafter in this paragraph referred to as the "loss year"), the amount thereof shall be—

(A) a capital loss carryback to each of the 3 taxable years preceding the loss year, but only to the extent—

(i) such loss is not attributable to a foreign expropriation capital loss, and

(ii) the carryback of such loss does not increase or produce a net operating loss (as defined in section 172(c)) for the taxable year to which it is being carried back;

(B) except as provided in subparagraph (C), a capital loss carryover to each of the 5 taxable years succeeding the loss year; and

(C) a capital loss carryover to each of the 10 taxable years succeeding the loss year, but only to the extent such loss is attributable to a foreign expropriation loss,

and shall be treated as a short-term capital loss in each such taxable year. The entire amount of the net capital loss for any taxable year shall be carried to the earliest of the taxable years to which such loss may be carried, and the portion of such loss which shall be carried to each of the other taxable years to which such loss may be carried shall be the excess, if any, of such loss over the total of the capital gain net income for each of the prior taxable years to which such loss may be carried. For purposes of the preceding sentence, the capital gain net income for any such prior taxable year shall be computed without regard to the net capital loss for the loss year or for any taxable year thereafter. In the case of any net capital loss which cannot be carried back in full to a preceding taxable year by reason of clause (ii) of subparagraph (A), the capital gain net income for such prior taxable year shall in no case be treated as greater than the amount of such loss which can be carried back to such preceding taxable year upon the application of such clause (ii).

* * *

(b) Other taxpayers.—

(1) In general.—If a taxpayer other than a corporation has a net capital loss for any taxable year—

(A) the excess of the net short-term capital loss over the net long-term capital gain for such year shall be a short-term capital loss in the succeeding taxable year, and

(B) the excess of the net long-term capital loss over the net short-term capital gain for such year shall be a long-term capital loss in the succeeding taxable year.

(2) Treatment of amounts allowed under section 1211(b)(1) or (2).—

(A) In general.—For purposes of determining the excess referred to in subparagraph (A) or (B) of paragraph (1), there shall be treated as a short-term capital gain in the taxable year an amount equal to the lesser of—

(i) the amount allowed for the taxable year under paragraph (1) or (2) of section 1211(b), or

(ii) the adjusted taxable income for such taxable year.

(B) Adjusted taxable income.—For purposes of subparagraph (A), the term "adjusted taxable income" means taxable income increased by the sum of—

(i) the amount allowed for the taxable year under paragraph (1) or (2) of section 1211(b), and

(ii) the deduction allowed for such year under section 151 or any deduction in lieu thereof.

For purposes of the preceding sentence, any excess of the deductions allowed for the taxable year over the gross income for such year shall be taken into account as negative taxable income.

* * *

Part III—General Rules for Determining Capital Gains and Losses

§ 1221. Capital asset defined.

(a) In general.—For purposes of this subtitle, the term "capital asset" means property held by the taxpayer (whether or not connected with his trade or business), but does not include—

(1) stock in trade of the taxpayer or other property of a kind which would properly be included in the inventory of the taxpayer if on hand at the close of the taxable year, or property held by the taxpayer primarily for sale to customers in the ordinary course of his trade or business;

(2) property, used in his trade or business, of a character which is subject to the allowance for depreciation provided in section 167, or real property used in his trade or business;

(3) a patent, invention, model or design (whether or not patented), a secret formula or process, a copyright, a literary, musical, or artistic composition, a letter or memorandum, or similar property, held by—

(A) a taxpayer whose personal efforts created such property,

(B) in the case of a letter, memorandum, or similar property, a taxpayer for whom such property was prepared or produced, or

(C) a taxpayer in whose hands the basis of such property is determined, for purposes of determining gain from a sale or exchange, in whole or part by reference to the basis of such property in the hands of a taxpayer described in subparagraph (A) or (B);

(4) accounts or notes receivable acquired in the ordinary course of trade or business for services rendered or from the sale of property described in paragraph (1);

(5) a publication of the United States Government (including the Congressional Record) which is received from the United States Government or any agency thereof, other than by purchase at the price at which it is offered for sale to the public, and which is held by—

(A) a taxpayer who so received such publication, or

(B) a taxpayer in whose hands the basis of such publication is determined, for purposes of determining gain from a sale or exchange, in whole or in part by reference to the basis of such publication in the hands of a taxpayer described in subparagraph (A);

(6) any commodities derivative financial instrument held by a commodities derivatives dealer, unless—

    (A) it is established to the satisfaction of the Secretary that such instrument has no connection to the activities of such dealer as a dealer, and

    (B) such instrument is clearly identified in such dealer's records as being described in subparagraph (A) before the close of the day on which it was acquired, originated, or entered into (or such other time as the Secretary may by regulations prescribe);

(7) any hedging transaction which is clearly identified as such before the close of the day on which it was acquired, originated, or entered into (or such other time as the Secretary may by regulations prescribe); or

(8) supplies of a type regularly used or consumed by the taxpayer in the ordinary course of a trade or business of the taxpayer.

(b) Definitions and Special Rules.—

* * *

(2) Hedging transaction.—

    (A) In general.—For purposes of this section, the term "hedging transaction" means any transaction entered into by the taxpayer in the normal course of the taxpayer's trade or business primarily—

        (i) to manage risk of price changes or currency fluctuations with respect to ordinary property which is held or to be held by the taxpayer,

        (ii) to manage risk of interest rate or price changes or currency fluctuations with respect to borrowings made or to be made, or ordinary obligations incurred or to be incurred, by the taxpayer, or

        (iii) to manage such other risks as the Secretary may prescribe in regulations.

* * *

§ 1222. Other terms relating to capital gains and losses.

For purposes of this subtitle—

    (1) Short-term capital gain.—The term "short-term capital gain" means gain from the sale or exchange of a capital asset held for not more than 1 year, if and to the extent such gain is taken into account in computing gross income.

    (2) Short-term capital loss.—The term "short-term capital loss" means loss from the sale or exchange of a capital asset held for not more than 1 year, if and to the extent that such loss is taken into account in computing taxable income.

    (3) Long-term capital gain.—The term "long-term capital gain" means gain from the sale or exchange of a capital asset held for more than 1 year, if and to the extent such gain is taken into account in computing gross income.

    (4) Long-term capital loss.—The term "long-term capital loss" means loss from the sale or exchange of a capital asset held for more than 1 year, if and to the extent that such loss is taken into account in computing taxable income.

(5) Net short-term capital gain.—The term "net short-term capital gain" means the excess of short-term capital gains for the taxable year over the short-term capital losses for such year.

(6) Net short-term capital loss.—The term "net short-term capital loss" means the excess of short-term capital losses for the taxable year over the short-term capital gains for such year.

(7) Net long-term capital gain.—The term "net long-term capital gain" means the excess of long-term capital gains for the taxable year over the long-term capital losses for such year.

(8) Net long-term capital loss.—The term "net long-term capital loss" means the excess of long-term capital losses for the taxable year over the long-term capital gains for such year.

(9) Capital gain net income.—The term "capital gain net income" means the excess of the gains from sales or exchanges of capital assets over the losses from such sales or exchanges.

(10) Net capital loss.—The term "net capital loss" means the excess of the losses from sales or exchanges of capital assets over the sum allowed under section 1211. In the case of a corporation, for the purpose of determining losses under this paragraph, amounts which are short-term capital losses under section 1212 shall be excluded.

(11) Net capital gain.—The term "net capital gain" means the excess of the net long-term capital gain for the taxable year over the net short-term capital loss for such year.

§ 1223. Holding period of property.

For purposes of this subtitle—

(1) In determining the period for which the taxpayer has held property received in an exchange, there shall be included the period for which he held the property exchanged if, under this chapter, the property has, for the purpose of determining gain or loss from a sale or exchange, the same basis in whole or in part in his hands as the property exchanged, and, in the case of such exchanges, the property exchanged at the time of such exchange was a capital asset as defined in section 1221 or property described in section 1231. For purposes of this paragraph—

(A) an involuntary conversion described in section 1033 shall be considered an exchange of the property converted for the property acquired, and

(B) a distribution to which section 355 (or so much of section 356 as relates to section 355) applies shall be treated as an exchange.

(2) In determining the period for which the taxpayer has held property however acquired there shall be included the period for which such property was held by any other person, if under this chapter such property has, for the purpose of determining gain or loss from a sale or exchange, the same basis in whole or in part in his hands as it would have in the hands of such other person.

(3) In determining the period for which the taxpayer has held stock or securities the acquisition of which (or the contract or option to acquire which) resulted in the nondeductibility (under section 1091 relating to wash sales) of the loss from the sale or other disposition of substantially identical stock or securities, there shall be included the period for which he held the stock or securities the loss from the sale or other disposition of which was not deductible.

(4) In determining the period for which the taxpayer has held stock or rights to acquire stock received on a distribution, if the basis of such stock or rights is determined under section 307, there shall (under regulations prescribed by the Secretary) be included the period for which he held the stock in the distributing corporation before the receipt of such stock or rights upon such distribution.

(5) In determining the period for which the taxpayer has held stock or securities acquired from a corporation by the exercise of rights to acquire such stock or securities, there shall be included only the period beginning with the date on which the right to acquire was exercised.

* * *

(9) In the case of a person acquiring property from a decedent or to whom property passed from a decedent (within the meaning of section 1014(b)), if—

(A) the basis of such property in the hands of such person is determined under section 1014, and

(B) such property is sold or otherwise disposed of by such person within 1 year after the decedent's death,

then such person shall be considered to have held such property for more than 1 year.

* * *

§ 1231. Property used in the trade or business and involuntary conversions—
(a) General rule—
(1) Gains exceed losses—If—

(A) the section 1231 gains for any taxable year, exceed

(B) the section 1231 losses for such taxable year, such gains and losses shall be treated as long-term capital gains or long-term capital losses, as the case may be.

(2) Gains do not exceed losses—If—

(A) the section 1231 gains for any taxable year, do not exceed

(B) the section 1231 losses for such taxable year, such gains and losses shall not be treated as gains and losses from sales or exchanges of capital assets.

(3) Section 1231 gains and losses—For purposes of this subsection—

(A) Section 1231 gain—The term "section 1231 gain" means—

(i) any recognized gain on the sale or exchange of property used in the trade or business, and

(ii) any recognized gain from the compulsory or involuntary conversion (as a result of destruction in whole or in part, theft or seizure, or an exercise of the power of requisition or condemnation or the threat or imminence thereof) into other property or money of—

(I) property used in the trade or business, or

(II) any capital asset which is held for more than 1 year and is held in connection with a trade or business or a transaction entered into for profit.

(B) Section 1231 loss—The term "section 1231 loss" means any recognized loss from a sale or exchange or conversion described in subparagraph (A).

(4) Special rules—For purposes of this subsection—

(A) In determining under this subsection whether gains exceed losses—

(i) the section 1231 gains shall be included only if and to the extent taken into account in computing gross income, and

(ii) the section 1231 losses shall be included only if and to the extent taken into account in computing taxable income, except that section 1211 shall not apply.

(B) Losses (including losses not compensated for by insurance or otherwise) on the destruction, in whole or in part, theft or seizure, or requisition or condemnation of—

(i) property used in the trade or business, or

(ii) capital assets which are held for more than 1 year and are held in connection with a trade or business or a transaction entered into for profit, shall be treated as losses from a compulsory or involuntary conversion.

(C) In the case of any involuntary conversion (subject to the provisions of this subsection but for this sentence) arising from fire, storm, shipwreck, or other casualty, or from theft, of any—

(i) property used in the trade or business, or

(ii) any capital asset which is held for more than 1 year and is held in connection with a trade or business or a transaction entered into for profit, this subsection shall not apply to such conversion (whether resulting in gain or loss) if during the taxable year the recognized losses from such conversions exceed the recognized gains from such conversions.

(b) Definition of property used in the trade or business—For purposes of this section—

(1) General rule—The term "property used in the trade or business" means property used in the trade or business, of a character which is subject to the allowance for depreciation provided in section 167, held for more than 1 year, and real property used in the trade or business, held for more than 1 year, which is not—

(A) property of a kind which would properly be includible in the inventory of the taxpayer if on hand at the close of the taxable year,

(B) property held by the taxpayer primarily for sale to customers in the ordinary course of his trade or business,

(C) a patent, invention, model or design (whether or not patented), a secret formula or process, a copyright, a literary, musical, or artistic composition, a letter or memorandum, or similar property, held by a taxpayer described in paragraph (3) of section 1221(a), or

(D) a publication of the United States Government (including the Congressional Record) which is received from the United States Government, or any agency thereof, other than by purchase at the price at which it is offered for sale to the public, and which is held by a taxpayer described in paragraph (5) of section 1221(a).

* * *

(c) Recapture of net ordinary losses—

(1) In general

The net section 1231 gain for any taxable year shall be treated as ordinary income to the extent such gain does not exceed the non-recaptured net section 1231 losses.

(2) Non-recaptured net section 1231 losses—For purposes of this subsection, the term "non-recaptured net section 1231 losses" means the excess of—

(A) the aggregate amount of the net section 1231 losses for the 5 most recent preceding taxable years beginning after December 31, 1981, over

(B) the portion of such losses taken into account under paragraph (1) for such preceding taxable years.

(3) Net section 1231 gain—For purposes of this subsection, the term "net section 1231 gain" means the excess of—

(A) the section 1231 gains, over

(B) the section 1231 losses.

(4) Net section 1231 loss—For purposes of this subsection, the term "net section 1231 loss" means the excess of—

(A) the section 1231 losses, over

(B) the section 1231 gains.

(5) Special rules—For purposes of determining the amount of the net section 1231 gain or loss for any taxable year, the rules of paragraph (4) of subsection (a) shall apply.

§ 1239. Gain from sale of depreciable property between certain related taxpayers.

(a) Treatment of gain as ordinary income.—In the case of a sale or exchange of property, directly or indirectly, between related persons, any gain recognized to the transferor shall be treated as ordinary income if such property is, in the hands of the transferee, of a character which is subject to the allowance for depreciation provided in section 167.

(b) Related persons.—For purposes of subsection (a), the term "related persons" means—

(1) a person and all entities which are controlled entities with respect to such person,

(2) a taxpayer and any trust in which such taxpayer (or his spouse) is a beneficiary, unless such beneficiary's interest in the trust is a remote contingent interest (within the meaning of section 318(a)(3)(B)(i)), and

(3) except in the case of a sale or exchange in satisfaction of a pecuniary bequest, an executor of an estate and a beneficiary of such estate.

(c) Controlled entity defined.—

(1) General rule.—For purposes of this section, the term "controlled entity" means, with respect to any person—

(A) a corporation more than 50 percent of the value of the outstanding stock of which is owned (directly or indirectly) by or for such person,

(B) a partnership more than 50 percent of the capital interest or profits interest in which is owned (directly or indirectly) by or for such person, and

(C) any entity which is a related person to such person under paragraph (3), (10), (11), or (12) of section 267(b).

(2) Constructive ownership.—For purposes of this section, ownership shall be determined in accordance with rules similar to the rules under section 267(c) (other than paragraph (3) thereof).

(d) Employer and related employee association.—For purposes of subsection (a), the term "related person" also includes—

(1) an employer and any person related to the employer (within the meaning of subsection (b)), and

(2) a welfare benefit fund (within the meaning of section 419(e)) which is controlled directly or indirectly by persons referred to in paragraph (1).

(e) Patent applications treated as depreciable property.—For purposes of this section, a patent application shall be treated as property which, in the hands of the transferee, is of a character which is subject to the allowance for depreciation provided in section 167.

* * *

§ 1242. Losses on small business investment company stock.

If—

(1) a loss is on stock in a small business investment company operating under the Small Business Investment Act of 1958, and

(2) such loss would (but for this section) be a loss from the sale or exchange of a capital asset,

then such loss shall be treated as an ordinary loss. For purposes of section 172 (relating to the net operating loss deduction) any amount of loss treated by reason of this section as an ordinary loss shall be treated as attributable to a trade or business of the taxpayer.

§ 1243. Loss of small business investment company.

In the case of a small business investment company operating under the Small Business Investment Act of 1958, if—

(1) a loss is on stock received pursuant to the conversion privilege of convertible debentures acquired pursuant to section 304 of the Small Business Investment Act of 1958, and

(2) such loss would (but for this section) be a loss from the sale or exchange of a capital asset,

then such loss shall be treated as an ordinary loss.

§ 1244. Losses on small business stock.

(a) General rule.—In the case of an individual, a loss on section 1244 stock issued to such individual or to a partnership which would (but for this section) be treated as a loss from the sale or exchange of a capital asset shall, to the extent provided in this section, be treated as an ordinary loss.

(b) Maximum amount for any taxable year.—For any taxable year the aggregate amount treated by the taxpayer by reason of this section as an ordinary loss shall not exceed—

(1) $50,000, or

(2) $100,000, in the case of a husband and wife filing a joint return for such year under section 6013.

(c) Section 1244 stock defined.—

(1) In general.—For purposes of this section, the term "section 1244 stock" means stock in a domestic corporation if—

(A) at the time such stock is issued, such corporation was a small business corporation,

(B) such stock was issued by such corporation for money or other property (other than stock and securities), and

(C) such corporation, during the period of its 5 most recent taxable years ending before the date the loss on such stock was sustained, derived more than 50 percent of its aggregate gross receipts from sources other than royalties, rents, dividends, interests, annuities, and sales or exchanges of stocks or securities.

(2) Rules for application of paragraph (1)(c).—

(A) Period taken into account with respect to new corporations.—For purposes of paragraph (1)(C), if the corporation has not been in existence for 5 taxable years ending before the date the loss on the stock was sustained, there shall be substituted for such 5-year period—

(i) the period of the corporation's taxable years ending before such date, or

(ii) if the corporation has not been in existence for 1 taxable year ending before such date, the period such corporation has been in existence before such date.

(B) Gross receipts from sales of securities.—For purposes of paragraph (1)(C), gross receipts from the sales or exchanges of stock or securities shall be taken into account only to the extent of gains therefrom.

(C) Nonapplication where deductions exceed gross income.—Paragraph (1)(C) shall not apply with respect to any corporation if, for the period taken into account for purposes of paragraph (1)(C), the amount of the deductions allowed by this chapter (other than by sections 172, 243, and 245) exceeds the amount of gross income.

(3) Small business corporation defined.—

(A) In general.—For purposes of this section, a corporation shall be treated as a small business corporation if the aggregate amount of money and other property received by the corporation for stock, as a contribution to capital, and as paid-in surplus, does not exceed $1,000,000. The determination under the preceding sentence shall be made as of the time of the issuance of the stock in question but shall include amounts received for such stock and for all stock theretofore issued.

(B) Amount taken into account with respect to property.—For purposes of subparagraph (A), the amount taken into account with respect to any property other than money shall be the amount equal to the adjusted basis to the corporation of such property for determining gain, reduced by any liability to which the property was subject or which was assumed by the corporation. The determination under the preceding sentence shall be made as of the time the property was received by the corporation.

* * *

§ 1245. Gain from dispositions of certain depreciable property—

(a) General rule

(1) Ordinary income—Except as otherwise provided in this section, if section 1245 property is disposed of the amount by which the lower of—

(A) the recomputed basis of the property, or

(B) (i) in the case of a sale, exchange, or involuntary conversion, the amount realized, or

    (ii) in the case of any other disposition, the fair market value of such property,

exceeds the adjusted basis of such property shall be treated as ordinary income. Such gain shall be recognized notwithstanding any other provision of this subtitle.

(2) Recomputed basis—For purposes of this section—

(A) In general—The term "recomputed basis" means, with respect to any property, its adjusted basis recomputed by adding thereto all adjustments reflected in such adjusted basis on account of deductions (whether in respect of the same or other property) allowed or allowable to the taxpayer or to any other person for depreciation or amortization.

(B) Taxpayer may establish amount allowed—For purposes of subparagraph (A), if the taxpayer can establish by adequate records or other sufficient evidence that the amount allowed for depreciation or amortization for any period was less than the amount allowable, the amount added for such period shall be the amount allowed.

(C) Certain deductions treated as amortization—Any deduction allowable under section 179, 179A, 179B, 179C, 179D, 179E, 181, 190, 193, or 194 shall be treated as if it were a deduction allowable for amortization.

(3) Section 1245 property—For purposes of this section, the term "section 1245 property" means any property which is or has been property of a character subject to the allowance for depreciation provided in section 167 and is either—

(A) personal property,

(B) other property (not including a building or its structural components) but only if such other property is tangible and has an adjusted basis in which there are reflected adjustments described in paragraph (2) for a period in which such property (or other property)—

    (i) was used as an integral part of manufacturing, production, or extraction or of furnishing transportation, communications, electrical energy, gas, water, or sewage disposal services,

    (ii) constituted a research facility used in connection with any of the activities referred to in clause (i), or

(iii) constituted a facility used in connection with any of the activities referred to in clause (i) for the bulk storage of fungible commodities (including commodities in a liquid or gaseous state),

(C) so much of any real property (other than any property described in subparagraph (B)) which has an adjusted basis in which there are reflected adjustments for amortization under section 169, 179, 179A, 179B, 179C, 179D, 179E, 185, 188 (as in effect before its repeal by the Revenue Reconciliation Act of 1990), 190, 193, or 194,

(D) a single purpose agricultural or horticultural structure (as defined in section 168 (i)(13)),

(E) a storage facility (not including a building or its structural components) used in connection with the distribution of petroleum or any primary product of petroleum, or

(F) any railroad grading or tunnel bore (as defined in section 168 (e)(4)).

(b) Exceptions and limitations

(1) **Gifts**—Subsection (a) shall not apply to a disposition by gift.

(2) **Transfers at death**—Except as provided in section 691 (relating to income in respect of a decedent), subsection (a) shall not apply to a transfer at death.

(3) **Certain tax-free transactions**—If the basis of property in the hands of a transferee is determined by reference to its basis in the hands of the transferor by reason of the application of section 332, 351, 361, 721, or 731, then the amount of gain taken into account by the transferor under subsection (a)(1) shall not exceed the amount of gain recognized to the transferor on the transfer of such property (determined without regard to this section). Except as provided in paragraph (6), this paragraph shall not apply to a disposition to an organization (other than a cooperative described in section 521) which is exempt from the tax imposed by this chapter.

(4) **Like kind exchanges; involuntary conversions, etc.**—If property is disposed of and gain (determined without regard to this section) is not recognized in whole or in part under section 1031 or 1033, then the amount of gain taken into account by the transferor under subsection (a)(1) shall not exceed the sum of—

(A) the amount of gain recognized on such disposition (determined without regard to this section), plus

(B) the fair market value of property acquired which is not section 1245 property and which is not taken into account under subparagraph (A).

(5) Property distributed by a partnership to a partner

(A) **In general**—For purposes of this section, the basis of section 1245 property distributed by a partnership to a partner shall be deemed to be determined by reference to the adjusted basis of such property to the partnership.

(B) **Adjustments added back**—In the case of any property described in subparagraph (A), for purposes of computing the recomputed basis of such property the amount of the adjustments added back for periods before the distribution by the partnership shall be—

(i) the amount of the gain to which subsection (a) would have applied if such property had been sold by the partnership immediately before the distribution at its fair market value at such time, reduced by

(ii) the amount of such gain to which section 751 (b) applied.

* * *

Subchapter S—Tax Treatment of S Corporations and Their Shareholders

Part I—In General

§ 1361. S Corporation defined.

(a) S Corporation defined.—

(1) In general.—For purposes of this title, the term "S corporation" means, with respect to any taxable year, a small business corporation for which an election under section 1362(a) is in effect for such year.

(2) C corporation.—For purposes of this title, the term "C corporation" means, with respect to any taxable year, a corporation which is not an S corporation for such year.

(b) Small business corporation.—

(1) In general.—For purposes of this subchapter, the term "small business corporation" means a domestic corporation which is not an ineligible corporation and which does not—

(A) have more than 100 shareholders,

(B) have as a shareholder a person (other than an estate, a trust described in subsection (c)(2), or an organization described in subsection (c)(6)) who is not an individual,

(C) have a nonresident alien as a shareholder, and

(D) have more than 1 class of stock.

(2) Ineligible corporation defined.—For purposes of paragraph (1), the term "ineligible corporation" means any corporation which is—

(A) a financial institution which uses the reserve method of accounting for bad debts described in section 585,

(B) an insurance company subject to tax under subchapter L,

(C) a corporation to which an election under section 936 applies, or

(D) a DISC or former DISC.

(3) Treatment of certain wholly owned subsidiaries.—

(A) In general.—Except as provided in regulations prescribed by the Secretary and in the case of information returns required under part III of subchapter A of chapter 61, for purposes of this title—

(i) a corporation which is a qualified subchapter S subsidiary shall not be treated as a separate corporation, and

(ii) all assets, liabilities, and items of income, deduction, and credit of a qualified subchapter S subsidiary shall be treated as assets, liabilities, and such items (as the case may be) of the S corporation.

(B) Qualified subchapter S subsidiary.—For purposes of this paragraph, the term "qualified subchapter S subsidiary" means any domestic corporation which is not an ineligible corporation (as defined in paragraph (2)), if—

(i) 100 percent of the stock of such corporation is held by the S corporation, and

(ii) the S corporation elects to treat such corporation as a qualified subchapter S subsidiary.

(C) Treatment of terminations of qualified subchapter S subsidiary status.—

(i) In general.—For purposes of this title, if any corporation which was a qualified subchapter S subsidiary ceases to meet the requirements of subparagraph (B), such corporation shall be treated as a new corporation acquiring all of its assets (and assuming all of its liabilities) immediately before such cessation from the S corporation in exchange for its stock.

(ii) Termination by reason of sale of stock.—If the failure to meet the requirements of subparagraph (B) is by reason of the sale of stock of a corporation which is a qualified subchapter S subsidiary, the sale of such stock shall be treated as if—

(I) the sale were a sale of an undivided interest in the assets of such corporation (based on the percentage of the corporation's stock sold), and

(II) the sale were followed by an acquisition by such corporation of all of its assets (and the assumption by such corporation of all of its liabilities) in a transaction to which section 351 applies.

(D) Election after termination.—If a corporation's status as a qualified subchapter S subsidiary terminates, such corporation (and any successor corporation) shall not be eligible to make—

(i) an election under subparagraph (B)(ii) to be treated as a qualified subchapter S subsidiary, or

(ii) an election under section 1362(a) to be treated as an S corporation, before its 5th taxable year which begins after the 1st taxable year for which such termination was effective, unless the Secretary consents to such election.

* * *

(c) Special rules for applying subsection (b).—

(1) Members of a family treated as 1 shareholder.—

(A) In general.—For purposes of subsection (b)(1)(A), there shall be treated as one shareholder—

(i) a husband and wife (and their estates), and

(ii) all members of a family (and their estates).

(B) Members of a family

For purposes of this paragraph—

(i) In general.—The term "members of a family" means a common ancestor, any lineal descendant of such common ancestor, and any spouse or former spouse of such common ancestor or any such lineal descendant.

(ii) Common ancestor.—An individual shall not be considered to be a common ancestor if, on the applicable date, the individual is more than 6 generations removed from the youngest generation of shareholders who would (but for this subparagraph) be members of the family. For purposes of the preceding sentence, a spouse (or former spouse) shall be treated as being of the same generation as the individual to whom such spouse is (or was) married.

(iii) Applicable date.—The term "applicable date" means the latest of—

(I) the date the election under section 1362 (a) is made,

(II) the earliest date that an individual described in clause (i) holds stock in the S corporation, or

(III) October 22, 2004.

(C) Effect of adoption, etc.

Any legally adopted child of an individual, any child who is lawfully placed with an individual for legal adoption by the individual, and any eligible foster child of an individual (within the meaning of section 152 (f)(1)(C)), shall be treated as a child of such individual by blood.

(2) Certain trusts permitted as shareholders.—

(A) In general.—For purposes of subsection (b)(1)(B), the following trusts may be shareholders:

(i) A trust all of which is treated (under subpart E of part I of subchapter J of this chapter) as owned by an individual who is a citizen or resident of the United States.

(ii) A trust which was described in clause (i) immediately before the death of the deemed owner and which continues in existence after such death, but only for the 2-year period beginning on the day of the deemed owner's death.

(iii) A trust with respect to stock transferred to it pursuant to the terms of a will, but only for the 2-year period beginning on the day on which such stock is transferred to it.

(iv) A trust created primarily to exercise the voting power of stock transferred to it.

(v) An electing small business trust.

* * *

(B) Treatment as shareholders.—For purposes of subsection (b)(1)—

(i) In the case of a trust described in clause (i) of subparagraph (A), the deemed owner shall be treated as the shareholder.

(ii) In the case of a trust described in clause (ii) of subparagraph (A), the estate of the deemed owner shall be treated as the shareholder.

(iii) In the case of a trust described in clause (iii) of subparagraph (A), the estate of the testator shall be treated as the shareholder.

(iv) In the case of a trust described in clause (iv) of subparagraph (A), each beneficiary of the trust shall be treated as a shareholder.

(v) In the case of a trust described in clause (v) of subparagraph (A), each potential current beneficiary of such trust shall be treated as a shareholder; except that, if for any period there is no potential current beneficiary of such trust, such trust shall be treated as the shareholder during such period. This clause shall not apply for purposes of subsection (b)(1)(C).

* * *

(3) Estate of individual in bankruptcy may be shareholder.—For purposes of subsection (b)(1)(B), the term "estate" includes the estate of an individual in a case under title 11 of the United States Code.

(4) Differences in common stock voting rights disregarded.—For purposes of subsection (b)(1)(D), a corporation shall not be treated as having more than 1 class of stock solely because there are differences in voting rights among the shares of common stock.

(5) Straight debt safe harbor.—

(A) In general.—For purposes of subsection (b)(1)(D), straight debt shall not be treated as a second class of stock.

(B) Straight debt defined.—For purposes of this paragraph, the term "straight debt" means any written unconditional promise to pay on demand or on a specified date a sum certain in money if—

(i) the interest rate (and interest payment dates) are not contingent on profits, the borrower's discretion, or similar factors,

(ii) there is no convertibility (directly or indirectly) into stock, and

(iii) the creditor is an individual (other than a nonresident alien), an estate, a trust described in paragraph (2), or a person which is actively and regularly engaged in the business of lending money.

(C) Regulations.—The Secretary shall prescribe such regulations as may be necessary or appropriate to provide for the proper treatment of straight debt under this subchapter and for the coordination of such treatment with other provisions of this title.

(6) Certain exempt organizations permitted as shareholders.—For purposes of subsection (b)(1)(B), an organization which is—

(A) described in section 401(a) or 501(c)(3), and

(B) exempt from taxation under section 501(a),

may be a shareholder in an S corporation.

(d) Special rule for qualified subchapter S trust.—

(1) In general.—In the case of a qualified subchapter S trust with respect to which a beneficiary makes an election under paragraph (2)—

(A) such trust shall be treated as a trust described in subsection (c)(2)(A)(i),

(B) for purposes of section 678(a), the beneficiary of such trust shall be treated as the owner of that portion of the trust which consists of stock in an S corporation with respect to which the election under paragraph (2) is made, and

(C) for purposes of applying sections 465 and 469 to the beneficiary of the trust, the disposition of the S corporation stock by the trust shall be treated as a disposition by such beneficiary.

(2) Election.—

(A) In general.— A beneficiary of a qualified subchapter S trust (or his legal representative) may elect to have this subsection apply.

(B) Manner and time of election.—

(i) Separate election with respect to each corporation.— An election under this paragraph shall be made separately with respect to each corporation the stock of which is held by the trust.

(ii) Elections with respect to successive income beneficiaries.— If there is an election under this paragraph with respect to any beneficiary, an election under this paragraph shall be treated as made by each successive beneficiary unless such beneficiary affirmatively refuses to consent to such election.

(iii) Time, manner, and form of election.— Any election, or refusal, under this paragraph shall be made in such manner and form, and at such time, as the Secretary may prescribe.

(C) Election irrevocable.— An election under this paragraph, once made, may be revoked only with the consent of the Secretary.

(D) Grace period.— An election under this paragraph shall be effective up to 15 days and 2 months before the date of the election.

(3) Qualified subchapter S trust.— For purposes of this subsection, the term "qualified subchapter S trust" means a trust—

(A) the terms of which require that—

(i) during the life of the current income beneficiary, there shall be only 1 income beneficiary of the trust,

(ii) any corpus distributed during the life of the current income beneficiary may be distributed only to such beneficiary,

(iii) the income interest of the current income beneficiary in the trust shall terminate on the earlier of such beneficiary's death or the termination of the trust, and

(iv) upon the termination of the trust during the life of the current income beneficiary, the trust shall distribute all of its assets to such beneficiary, and

(B) all of the income (within the meaning of section 643(b)) of which is distributed (or required to be distributed) currently to 1 individual who is a citizen or resident of the United States.

A substantially separate and independent share of a trust within the meaning of section 663(c) shall be treated as a separate trust for purposes of this subsection and subsection (c).

(4) Trust ceasing to be qualified.—

(A) Failure to meet requirements of paragraph (3)(A).—If a qualified subchapter S trust ceases to meet any requirement of paragraph (3)(A), the provisions of this subsection shall not apply to such trust as of the date it ceases to meet such requirement.

(B) Failure to meet requirements of paragraph (3)(B).—If any qualified subchapter S trust ceases to meet any requirement of paragraph (3)(B) but continues to meet the requirements of paragraph (3)(A), the provisions of this subsection shall not apply to such trust as of the first day of the first taxable year beginning after the first taxable year for which it failed to meet the requirements of paragraph (3)(B).

(e) Electing small business trust defined.—

(1) Electing small business trust.—For purposes of this section—

(A) In general.—Except as provided in subparagraph (B), the term "electing small business trust" means any trust if—

(i) such trust does not have as a beneficiary any person other than (I) an individual, (II) an estate, or (III) an organization described in paragraph (2), (3), (4), or (5) of section 170(c), or (IV) an organization described in section 170(c)(1) which holds a contingent interest in such trust and is not a potential current beneficiary,

(ii) no interest in such trust was acquired by purchase, and

(iii) an election under this subsection applies to such trust.

(B) Certain trusts not eligible.—The term "electing small business trust" shall not include—

(i) any qualified subchapter S trust (as defined in subsection (d)(3)) if an election under subsection (d)(2) applies to any corporation the stock of which is held by such trust,

(ii) any trust exempt from tax under this subtitle, and

(iii) any charitable remainder annuity trust or charitable remainder unitrust (as defined in section 664(d)).

(C) Purchase.—For purposes of subparagraph (A), the term "purchase" means any acquisition if the basis of the property acquired is determined under section 1012.

(2) Potential current beneficiary.—For purposes of this section, the term "potential current beneficiary" means, with respect to any period, any person who at any time during such period is entitled to, or at the discretion of any person may receive, a distribution from the principal or income of the trust (determined without regard to any power of appointment to the extent such power remains unexercised at the end of such period). If a trust disposes of all of the stock which it holds in an S corporation, then, with respect to such corporation, the term "potential current beneficiary" does not include any person who first met the requirements of the preceding sentence during the 1-year period ending on the date of such disposition.

(3) Election.—An election under this subsection shall be made by the trustee. Any such election shall apply to the taxable year of the trust for which made and all subsequent taxable years of such trust unless revoked with the consent of the Secretary.

(4) Cross reference.—For special treatment of electing small business trusts, see section 641(c).

(f) Restricted bank director stock.—

(1) In general.—Restricted bank director stock shall not be taken into account as outstanding stock of the S corporation in applying this subchapter (other than section 1368(f)).

(2) Restricted bank director stock.—For purposes of this subsection, the term 'restricted bank director stock' means stock in a bank (as defined in section 581) or a depository institution holding company (as defined in section 3(w)(1) of the Federal Deposit Insurance Act (12 U.S.C. 1813(w)(1)), if such stock—

(A) is required to be held by an individual under applicable Federal or State law in order to permit such individual to serve as a director, and

(B) is subject to an agreement with such bank or company (or a corporation which controls (within the meaning of section 368(c)) such bank or company) pursuant to which the holder is required to sell back such stock (at the same price as the individual acquired such stock) upon ceasing to hold the office of director.

(3) Cross reference.—For treatment of certain distributions with respect to restricted bank director stock, see section 1368(f).

(g) Special rule for bank required to change from the reserve method of accounting on becoming S corporation.—In the case of a bank which changes from the reserve method of accounting for bad debts described in section 585 or 593 for its first taxable year for which an election under section 1362(a) is in effect, the bank may elect to take into account any adjustments under section 481 by reason of such change for the taxable year immediately preceding such first taxable year.

§ 1362. Election; revocation; termination.

(a) Election.—

(1) In general.—Except as provided in subsection (g), a small business corporation may elect, in accordance with the provisions of this section, to be an S corporation.

(2) All shareholders must consent to election.—An election under this subsection shall be valid only if all persons who are shareholders in such corporation on the day on which such election is made consent to such election.

(b) When made.—

(1) In general.—An election under subsection (a) may be made by a small business corporation for any taxable year—

(A) at any time during the preceding taxable year, or

(B) at any time during the taxable year and on or before the 15th day of the 3d month of the taxable year.

(2) Certain elections made during 1st 2 1/2 months treated as made for next taxable year.—If—

(A) an election under subsection (a) is made for any taxable year during such year and on or before the 15th day of the 3d month of such year, but

(B) either—

(i) on 1 or more days in such taxable year before the day on which the election was made the corporation did not meet the requirements of subsection (b) of section 1361, or

(ii) 1 or more of the persons who held stock in the corporation during such taxable year and before the election was made did not consent to the election,

then such election shall be treated as made for the following taxable year.

(3) Election made after 1st 2 1/2 months treated as made for following taxable year.—If—

(A) a small business corporation makes an election under subsection (a) for any taxable year, and

(B) such election is made after the 15th day of the 3d month of the taxable year and on or before the 15th day of the 3rd month of the following taxable year, then such election shall be treated as made for the following taxable year.

(4) Taxable years of 2 1/2 months or less.—For purposes of this subsection, an election for a taxable year made not later than 2 months and 15 days after the first day of the taxable year shall be treated as timely made during such year.

(5) Authority to treat late elections, etc., as timely.—If—

(A) an election under subsection (a) is made for any taxable year (determined without regard to paragraph (3)) after the date prescribed by this subsection for making such election for such taxable year or no such election is made for any taxable year, and

(B) the Secretary determines that there was reasonable cause for the failure to timely make such election, the Secretary may treat such an election as timely made for such taxable year (and paragraph (3) shall not apply).

(c) Years for which effective.—An election under subsection (a) shall be effective for the taxable year of the corporation for which it is made and for all succeeding taxable years of the corporation, until such election is terminated under subsection (d).

(d) Termination.—

(1) By revocation.—

(A) In general.—An election under subsection (a) may be terminated by revocation.

(B) More than one-half of shares must consent to revocation.—An election may be revoked only if shareholders holding more than one-half of the shares of stock of the corporation on the day on which the revocation is made consent to the revocation.

(C) When effective.—Except as provided in subparagraph (D)—

(i) a revocation made during the taxable year and on or before the 15th day of the 3d month thereof shall be effective on the 1st day of such taxable year, and

(ii) a revocation made during the taxable year but after such 15th day shall be effective on the 1st day of the following taxable year.

(D) Revocation may specify prospective date.—If the revocation specifies a date for revocation which is on or after the day on which the revocation is made, the revocation shall be effective on and after the date so specified.

(2) By corporation ceasing to be small business corporation.—

(A) In general.—An election under subsection (a) shall be terminated whenever (at any time on or after the 1st day of the 1st taxable year for which the corporation is an S corporation) such corporation ceases to be a small business corporation.

(B) When effective.—Any termination under this paragraph shall be effective on and after the date of cessation.

(3) Where passive investment income exceeds 25 percent of gross receipts for 3 consecutive taxable years and corporation has accumulated earnings and profits.—

(A) Termination.—

(i) In general.—An election under subsection (a) shall be terminated whenever the corporation—

(I) has accumulated earnings and profits at the close of each of 3 consecutive taxable years, and

(II) has gross receipts for each of such taxable years more than 25 percent of which are passive investment income.

(ii) When effective.—Any termination under this paragraph shall be effective on and after the first day of the first taxable year beginning after the third consecutive taxable year referred to in clause (i).

(iii) Years taken into account.—A prior taxable year shall not be taken into account under clause (i) unless the corporation was an S corporation for such taxable year.

(B) Gross receipts from the sales of certain assets.—For purposes of this paragraph—

(i) in the case of dispositions of capital assets (other than stock and securities), gross receipts from such dispositions shall be taken into account only to the extent of the capital gain net income therefrom, and

(ii) in the case of sales or exchanges of stock or securities, gross receipts shall be taken into account only to the extent of the gains therefrom.

(C) Passive investment income defined.—

(i) In general.—Except as otherwise provided in this subparagraph, the term 'passive investment income' means gross receipts derived from royalties, rents, dividends, interest, and annuities.

(ii) Exception for interest on notes from sales of inventory.—The term 'passive investment income' shall not include interest on any obligation acquired in the ordinary course of the corporation's trade or business from its sale of property described in section 1221(a)(1).

(iii) Treatment of certain lending or finance companies.—If the S corporation meets the requirements of section 542(c)(6) for the taxable year, the term 'passive investment income' shall not include gross receipts for the taxable year which are derived directly from the active and regular conduct of a lending or finance business (as defined in section 542(d)(1)).

(iv) Treatment of certain dividends.—If an S corporation holds stock in a C corporation meeting the requirements of section 1504(a)(2), the term 'passive investment income' shall not include dividends from such C corporation to the extent such dividends are attributable to the earnings and profits of such C corporation derived from the active conduct of a trade or business.

(v) Exception for banks, etc.—In the case of a bank (as defined in section 581) or a depository institution holding company (as defined in section 3(w)(1) of the Federal Deposit Insurance Act (12 U.S.C. 1813(w)(1)), the term 'passive investment income' shall not include—

(I) interest income earned by such bank or company, or

(II) dividends on assets required to be held by such bank or company, including stock in the Federal Reserve Bank, the Federal Home Loan Bank, or the Federal Agricultural Mortgage Bank or participation certificates issued by a Federal Intermediate Credit Bank.

(e) Treatment of S termination year.—

(1) In general.—In the case of an S termination year, for purposes of this title—

(A) S short year.—The portion of such year ending before the 1st day for which the termination is effective shall be treated as a short taxable year for which the corporation is an S corporation.

(B) C short year.—The portion of such year beginning on such 1st day shall be treated as a short taxable year for which the corporation is a C corporation.

(2) Pro rata allocation.—Except as provided in paragraph (3) and subparagraphs (C) and (D) of paragraph (6), the determination of which items are to be taken into account for each of the short taxable years referred to in paragraph (1) shall be made—

(A) first by determining for the S termination year—

(i) the amount of each of the items of income, loss, deduction, or credit described in section 1366(a)(1)(A), and

(ii) the amount of the nonseparately computed income or loss, and

(B) then by assigning an equal portion of each amount determined under subparagraph (A) to each day of the S termination year.

(3) Election to have items assigned to each short taxable year under normal tax accounting rules.—

(A) In general.—A corporation may elect to have paragraph (2) not apply.

(B) Shareholders must consent to election.—An election under this subsection shall be valid only if all persons who are shareholders in the corporation at any time during the S short year and all persons who are shareholders in the corporation on the first day of the C short year consent to such election.

(4) S termination year.—For purposes of this subsection, the term 'S termination year' means any taxable year of a corporation (determined without regard to this subsection) in which a termination of an election made under subsection (a) takes effect (other than on the 1st day thereof).

(5) Tax for C short year determined on annualized basis.—

(A) In general.—The taxable income for the short year described in subparagraph (B) of paragraph (1) shall be placed on an annual basis by multiplying the taxable income for such short year by the number of days in the S termination year and by dividing the result by the number of days in the short year. The tax shall be the same part of the tax computed on the annual basis as the number of days in such short year is of the number of days in the S termination year.

(B) Section 443(d)(2) to apply.—Subsection (d) of section 443 shall apply to the short taxable year described in subparagraph (B) of paragraph (1).

(6) Other special rules.—For purposes of this title—

(A) Short years treated as 1 year for carryover purposes.—The short taxable year described in subparagraph (A) of paragraph (1) shall not be taken into account for purposes of determining the number of taxable years to which any item may be carried back or carried forward by the corporation.

(B) Due date for S year.—The due date for filing the return for the short taxable year described in subparagraph (A) of paragraph (1) shall be the same as the due date for filing the return for the short taxable year described in subparagraph (B) of paragraph (1) (including extensions thereof).

(C) Paragraph (2) not to apply to items resulting from section 338.—Paragraph (2) shall not apply with respect to any item resulting from the application of section 338.

(D) Pro rata allocation for S termination year not to apply if 50-percent change in ownership.—Paragraph (2) shall not apply to an S termination year if there is a sale or exchange of 50 percent or more of the stock in such corporation during such year.

(f) Inadvertent invalid elections or terminations.—If—

(1) an election under subsection (a), section 1361(b)(3)(B)(ii), or section 1361(c)(1)(A) (ii) by any corporation—

(A) was not effective for the taxable year for which made (determined without regard to subsection (b)(2)) by reason of a failure to meet the requirements of section 1361(b) or to obtain shareholder consents, or

(B) was terminated under paragraph (2) or (3) of subsection (d), section 1361(b)(3)(C), or section 1361(c)(1)(D)(iii),

(2) the Secretary determines that the circumstances resulting in such ineffectiveness or termination were inadvertent,

(3) no later than a reasonable period of time after discovery of the circumstances resulting in such ineffectiveness or termination, steps were taken—

(A) so that the corporation for which the election was made or the termination occurred is a small business corporation or a qualified subchapter S subsidiary, as the case may be, or

(B) to acquire the required shareholder consents, and

(4) the corporation for which the election was made or the termination occurred, and each person who was a shareholder in such corporation at any time during the period specified pursuant to this subsection, agrees to make such adjustments (consistent with the treatment of such corporation as an S corporation or a qualified subchapter S subsidiary, as the case may be) as may be required by the Secretary with respect to such period,

then, notwithstanding the circumstances resulting in such ineffectiveness or termination, such corporation shall be treated as an S corporation or a qualified subchapter S subsidiary, as the case may be during the period specified by the Secretary.

(g) Election after termination.—If a small business corporation has made an election under subsection (a) and if such election has been terminated under subsection (d), such corporation (and any successor corporation) shall not be eligible to make an election under subsection (a) for any taxable year before its 5th taxable year which begins after the 1st taxable year for which such termination is effective, unless the Secretary consents to such election.

§ 1363. Effect of Election on Corporation.

(a) General rule.—Except as otherwise provided in this subchapter, an S corporation shall not be subject to the taxes imposed by this chapter.

(b) Computation of corporation's taxable income.—The taxable income of an S corporation shall be computed in the same manner as in the case of an individual, except that—

(1) the items described in section 1366(a)(1)(A) shall be separately stated,

(2) the deductions referred to in section 703(a)(2) shall not be allowed to the corporation,

(3) section 248 shall apply, and

(4) section 291 shall apply if the S corporation (or any predecessor) was a C corporation for any of the 3 immediately preceding taxable years.

(c) Elections of the S Corporation.—

(1) In general.—Except as provided in paragraph (2), any election affecting the computation of items derived from an S corporation shall be made by the corporation.

(2) Exceptions.—In the case of an S corporation, elections under the following provisions shall be made by each shareholder separately—

(A) section 617 (relating to deduction and recapture of certain mining exploration expenditures), and

(B) section 901 (relating to taxes of foreign countries and possessions of the United States).

(d) Recapture of LIFO benefits.—

(1) In general.—If—

(A) an S corporation was a C corporation for the last taxable year before the first taxable year for which the election under section 1362(a) was effective, and

(B) the corporation inventoried goods under the LIFO method for such last taxable year, the LIFO recapture amount shall be included in the gross income of the corporation for such last taxable year (and appropriate adjustments to the basis of inventory shall be made to take into account the amount included in gross income under this paragraph).

(2) Additional tax payable in installments.—

(A) In general.—Any increase in the tax imposed by this chapter by reason of this subsection shall be payable in 4 equal installments.

(B) Date for payment of installments.—The first installment under subparagraph (A) shall be paid on or before the due date (determined without regard to extensions) for the return of the tax imposed by this chapter for the last taxable year for which the corporation was a C corporation and the 3 succeeding installments shall be paid on or before the due date (as so determined) for the corporation's return for the 3 succeeding taxable years.

(C) No interest for period of extension.—Notwithstanding section 6601(b), for purposes of section 6601, the date prescribed for the payment of each installment under this paragraph shall be determined under this paragraph.

(3) LIFO recapture amount.—For purposes of this subsection, the term 'LIFO recapture amount' means the amount (if any) by which—

(A) the inventory amount of the inventory asset under the first-in, first-out method authorized by section 471, exceeds

(B) the inventory amount of such assets under the LIFO method.

For purposes of the preceding sentence, inventory amounts shall be determined as of the close of the last taxable year referred to in paragraph (1).

(4) Other definitions.—For purposes of this subsection—

(A) LIFO method.—The term 'LIFO method' means the method authorized by section 472.

(B) Inventory assets.—The term 'inventory assets' means stock in trade of the corporation, or other property of a kind which would properly be included in the inventory of the corporation if on hand at the close of the taxable year.

(C) Method of determining inventory amount.—The inventory amount of assets under a method authorized by section 471 shall be determined—

(i) if the corporation uses the retail method of valuing inventories under section 472, by using such method, or

(ii) if clause (i) does not apply, by using cost or market, whichever is lower.

(D) Not treated as member of affiliated group.—Except as provided in regulations, the corporation referred to in paragraph (1) shall not be treated as a member of an affiliated group with respect to the amount included in gross income under paragraph (1).

Part II—Tax Treatment of Shareholders

§ 1366. Pass-thru of items to shareholders.

(a) Determination of shareholder's tax liability.—

(1) In general.—In determining the tax under this chapter of a shareholder for the shareholder's taxable year in which the taxable year of the S corporation ends (or for the final taxable year of a shareholder who dies, or of a trust or estate which terminates, before the end of the corporation's taxable year), there shall be taken into account the shareholder's pro rata share of the corporation's

(A) items of income (including tax-exempt income), loss, deduction, or credit the separate treatment of which could affect the liability for tax of any shareholder, and

(B) nonseparately computed income or loss.

For purposes of the preceding sentence, the items referred to in subparagraph (A) shall include amounts described in paragraph (4) or (6) of section 702(a).

(2) Nonseparately computed income or loss defined.—For purposes of this subchapter, the term 'nonseparately computed income or loss' means gross income minus the deductions allowed to the corporation under this chapter, determined by excluding all items described in paragraph (1)(A).

(b) Character passed thru.—The character of any item included in a shareholder's pro rata share under paragraph (1) of subsection (a) shall be determined as if such item were realized directly from the source from which realized by the corporation, or incurred in the same manner as incurred by the corporation.

(c) Gross income of a shareholder.—In any case where it is necessary to determine the gross income of a shareholder for purposes of this title, such gross income shall include the shareholder's pro rata share of the gross income of the corporation.

(d) Special rules for losses and deductions.—

(1) Cannot exceed shareholder's basis in stock and debt.—The aggregate amount of losses and deductions taken into account by a shareholder under subsection (a) for any taxable year shall not exceed the sum of

(A) the adjusted basis of the shareholder's stock in the S corporation (determined with regard to paragraphs (1) and (2)(A) of section 1367(a) for the taxable year), and

(B) the shareholder's adjusted basis of any indebtedness of the S corporation to the shareholder (determined without regard to any adjustment under paragraph (2) of section 1367(b) for the taxable year).

(2) Indefinite carryover of disallowed losses and deductions.—

(A) In general.—Except as provided in subparagraph (B), any loss or deduction which is disallowed for any taxable year by reason of paragraph (1) shall be treated as incurred by the corporation in the succeeding taxable year with respect to that shareholder.

(B) Transfers of stock between spouses or incident to divorce.—In the case of any transfer described in section 1041(a) of stock of an S corporation, any loss or deduction described in subparagraph (A) with respect such stock shall be treated as incurred by the corporation in the succeeding taxable year with respect to the transferee.

(3) Carryover of disallowed losses and deductions to post-termination transition period.—

(A) In general.—If for the last taxable year of a corporation for which it was an S corporation a loss or deduction was disallowed by reason of paragraph (1), such loss or deduction shall be treated as incurred by the shareholder on the last day of any post-termination transition period.

(B) Cannot exceed shareholder's basis in stock.—The aggregate amount of losses and deductions taken into account by a shareholder under subparagraph (A) shall not exceed the adjusted basis of the shareholder's stock in the corporation (determined at the close of the last day of the post-termination transition period and without regard to this paragraph).

(C) Adjustment in basis of stock.—The shareholder's basis in the stock of the corporation shall be reduced by the amount allowed as a deduction by reason of this paragraph.

(D) At-risk limitations.—To the extent that any increase in adjusted basis described in subparagraph (B) would have increased the shareholder's amount at risk under section 465 if such increase had occurred on the day preceding the commencement of the post-termination transition period, rules similar to the rules described in subparagraphs (A) through (C) shall apply to any losses disallowed by reason of section 465(a).

(e) Treatment of family group.—If an individual who is a member of the family (within the meaning of section 704(e)(3)) of one or more shareholders of an S corporation renders services for the corporation or furnishes capital to the corporation without receiving reasonable compensation therefor, the Secretary shall make such adjustments in the items taken into account by such individual and such shareholders as may be necessary in order to reflect the value of such services or capital.

(f) Special rules.—

(1) Subsection (a) not to apply to credit allowable under section 34.—Subsection (a) shall not apply with respect to any credit allowable under section 34 (relating to certain uses of gasoline and special fuels).

(2) Treatment of tax imposed on built-in gains.—If any tax is imposed under section 1374 for any taxable year on an S corporation, for purposes of subsection (a), the amount so imposed shall be treated as a loss sustained by the S corporation during such taxable year. The character of such loss shall be determined by allocating the loss proportionately among the recognized built-in gains giving rise to such tax.

(3) Reduction in pass-thru for tax imposed on excess net passive income.—If any tax is imposed under section 1375 for any taxable year on an S corporation, for purposes of subsection (a), each item of passive investment income shall be reduced by an amount which bears the same ratio to the amount of such tax as—

(A) the amount of such item, bears to

(B) the total passive investment income for the taxable year.

§ 1367. Adjustments to basis of stock of shareholders, etc.

(a) General rule.—

(1) Increases in basis.—The basis of each shareholder's stock in an S corporation shall be increased for any period by the sum of the following items determined with respect to that shareholder for such period:

(A) the items of income described in subparagraph (A) of section 1366(a)(1),

(B) any nonseparately computed income determined under subparagraph (B) of section 1366(a)(1), and

(C) the excess of the deductions for depletion over the basis of the property subject to depletion.

(2) Decreases in basis.—The basis of each shareholder's stock in an S corporation shall be decreased for any period (but not below zero) by the sum of the following items determined with respect to the shareholder for such period:

(A) distributions by the corporation which were not includible in the income of the shareholder by reason of section 1368,

(B) the items of loss and deduction described in subparagraph (A) of section 1366(a)(1),

(C) any nonseparately computed loss determined under subparagraph (B) of section 1366(a)(1),

(D) any expense of the corporation not deductible in computing its taxable income and not properly chargeable to capital account, and

(E) the amount of the shareholder's deduction for depletion for any oil and gas property held by the S corporation to the extent such deduction does not exceed the proportionate share of the adjusted basis of such property allocated to such shareholder under section 613A(c)(11)(B).

The decrease under subparagraph (B) by reason of a charitable contribution (as defined in section 170(c)) of property shall be the amount equal to the shareholder's pro rata share of the adjusted basis of such property.

(b) Special rules.—

(1) Income items.—An amount which is required to be included in the gross income of a shareholder and shown on his return shall be taken into account under subparagraph (A) or (B) of subsection (a)(1) only to the extent such amount is included in the shareholder's gross income on his return, increased or decreased by any adjustment of such amount in a redetermination of the shareholder's tax liability.

(2) Adjustments in basis of indebtedness.—

(A) Reduction of basis.—If for any taxable year the amounts specified in subparagraphs (B), (C), (D), and (E) of subsection (a)(2) exceed the amount which reduces the shareholder's basis to zero, such excess shall be applied to reduce (but not below zero) the shareholder's basis in any indebtedness of the S corporation to the shareholder.

(B) Restoration of basis.—If for any taxable year beginning after December 31, 1982, there is a reduction under subparagraph (A) in the shareholder's basis in the indebtedness of an S corporation to a shareholder, any net increase (after the application of paragraphs (1) and (2) of subsection (a)) for any subsequent taxable year shall be applied to restore such reduction in basis before any of it may be used to increase the shareholder's basis in the stock of the S corporation.

(3) Coordination with sections 165(g) and 166(d).—This section and section 1366 shall be applied before the application of sections 165(g) and 166(d) to any taxable year of the shareholder or the corporation in which the security or debt becomes worthless.

(4) Adjustments in case of inherited stock.—

(A) In general.—If any person acquires stock in an S corporation by reason of the death of a decedent or by bequest, devise, or inheritance, section 691 shall be applied with respect to any item of income of the S corporation in the same manner as if the decedent had held directly his pro rata share of such item.

(B) Adjustments to basis.—The basis determined under section 1014 of any stock in an S corporation shall be reduced by the portion of the value of the stock which is attributable to items constituting income in respect of the decedent.

§ 1368. Distributions.

(a) General rule.—A distribution of property made by an S corporation with respect to its stock to which (but for this subsection) section 301(c) would apply shall be treated in the manner provided in subsection (b) or (c), whichever applies.

(b) S corporation having no earnings and profits.—In the case of a distribution described in subsection (a) by an S corporation which has no accumulated earnings and profits—

(1) Amount applied against basis.—The distribution shall not be included in gross income to the extent that it does not exceed the adjusted basis of the stock.

(2) Amount in excess of basis.—If the amount of the distribution exceeds the adjusted basis of the stock, such excess shall be treated as gain from the sale or exchange of property.

(c) S corporation having earnings and profits.—In the case of a distribution described in subsection (a) by an S corporation which has accumulated earnings and profits—

(1) Accumulated adjustments account.—That portion of the distribution which does not exceed the accumulated adjustments account shall be treated in the manner provided by subsection (b).

(2) Dividend.—That portion of the distribution which remains after the application of paragraph (1) shall be treated as a dividend to the extent it does not exceed the accumulated earnings and profits of the S corporation.

(3) Treatment of remainder.—Any portion of the distribution remaining after the application of paragraph (2) of this subsection shall be treated in the manner provided by subsection (b).

Except to the extent provided in regulations, if the distributions during the taxable year exceed the amount in the accumulated adjustments account at the close of the taxable year, for purposes of this subsection, the balance of such account shall be allocated among such distributions in proportion to their respective sizes.

(d) Certain adjustments taken into account.—Subsections (b) and (c) shall be applied by taking into account (to the extent proper)—

(1) the adjustments to the basis of the shareholder's stock described in section 1367, and

(2) the adjustments to the accumulated adjustments account which are required by subsection (e)(1).

In the case of any distribution made during any taxable year, the adjusted basis of the stock shall be determined with regard to the adjustments provided in paragraph (1) of section 1367(a) for the taxable year.

(e) Definitions and special rules.—For purposes of this section—

(1) Accumulated adjustments account.—

(A) In general.—Except as otherwise provided in this paragraph, the term "accumulated adjustments account" means an account of the S corporation which is adjusted for the S period in a manner similar to the adjustments under section 1367 (except that no adjustment shall be made for income (and related expenses) which is exempt from tax under this title and the phrase "(but not below zero)" shall be disregarded in section 1367(a)(2)) and no adjustment shall be made for Federal taxes attributable to any taxable year in which the corporation was a C corporation.

(B) Amount of adjustment in the case of redemptions.—In the case of any redemption which is treated as an exchange under section 302(a) or 303(a), the adjustment in the accumulated adjustments account shall be an amount which bears the same ratio to the balance in such account as the number of shares redeemed in such redemption bears to the number of shares of stock in the corporation immediately before such redemption.

(C) Net loss for year disregarded.—

(i) In general.—In applying this section to distributions made during any taxable year, the amount in the accumulated adjustments account as of the close of such taxable year shall be determined without regard to any net negative adjustment for such taxable year.

(ii) Net negative adjustment.—For purposes of clause (i), the term "net negative adjustment" means, with respect to any taxable year, the excess (if any) of—

(I) the reductions in the account for the taxable year (other than for distributions), over

(II) the increases in such account for such taxable year.

(2) S period.—The term 'S period' means the most recent continuous period during which the corporation has been an S corporation. Such period shall not include any taxable year beginning before January 1, 1983.

(3) Election to distribute earnings first.—

(A) In general.—An S corporation may, with the consent of all of its affected shareholders, elect to have paragraph (1) of subsection (c) not apply to all distributions made during the taxable year for which the election is made.

(B) Affected shareholder.—For purposes of subparagraph (A), the term 'affected shareholder' means any shareholder to whom a distribution is made by the S corporation during the taxable year.

(f) Restricted bank director stock.—If a director receives a distribution (not in part or full payment in exchange for stock) from an S corporation with respect to any restricted bank director stock (as defined in section 1361(f)), the amount of such distribution—

(1) shall be includible in gross income of the director, and

(2) shall be deductible by the corporation for the taxable year of such corporation in which or with which ends the taxable year in which such amount in included in the gross income of the director.

Part III—Special Rules

§ 1371. Coordination with subchapter C.

(a) Application of subchapter C rules.—Except as otherwise provided in this title, and except to the extent inconsistent with this subchapter, subchapter C shall apply to an S corporation and its shareholders.

(b) No carryover between C year and S year.—

(1) From C year to S year.—No carryforward, and no carryback, arising for a taxable year for which a corporation is a C corporation may be carried to a taxable year for which such corporation is an S corporation.

(2) No carryover from S year.—No carryforward, and no carryback, shall arise at the corporate level for a taxable year for which a corporation is an S corporation.

(3) Treatment of S year as elapsed year.—Nothing in paragraphs (1) and (2) shall prevent treating a taxable year for which a corporation is an S corporation as a taxable year for purposes of determining the number of taxable years to which an item may be carried back or carried forward.

(c) Earnings and profits.—

(1) In general.—Except as provided in paragraphs (2) and (3) and subsection (d)(3), no adjustment shall be made to the earnings and profits of an S corporation.

(2) Adjustments for redemptions, liquidations, reorganizations, divisives, etc.—In the case of any transaction involving the application of subchapter C to any S corporation, proper adjustment to any accumulated earnings and profits of the corporation shall be made.

(3) Adjustments in case of distributions treated as dividends under section 1368(c) (2).—Paragraph (1) shall not apply with respect to that portion of a distribution which is treated as a dividend under section 1368(c)(2).

(d) Coordination with investment credit recapture.—

(1) No recapture by reason of election.—Any election under section 1362 shall be treated as a mere change in the form of conducting a trade or business for purposes of the second sentence of section 50(a)(4).

(2) Corporation continues to be liable.—Notwithstanding an election under section 1362, an S corporation shall continue to be liable for any increase in tax under section 49(b) or 50(a) attributable to credits allowed for taxable years for which such corporation was not an S corporation.

(3) Adjustment to earnings and profits for amount of recapture.—Paragraph (1) of subsection (c) shall not apply to any increase in tax under section 49(b) or 50(a) for which the S corporation is liable.

(e) Cash distributions during post-termination transition period.—

(1) In general.—Any distribution of money by a corporation with respect to its stock during a post-termination transition period shall be applied against and reduce the adjusted basis of the stock, to the extent that the amount of the distribution does not exceed the accumulated adjustments account (within the meaning of section 1368(e)).

(2) Election to distribute earnings first.—An S corporation may elect to have paragraph (1) not apply to all distributions made during a post-termination transition period described in section 1377(b)(1)(A). Such election shall not be effective unless all shareholders of the S corporation to whom distributions are made by the S corporation during such post-termination transition period consent to such election.

(f) Cash distributions following post-termination period.—In the case of a distribution of money by an eligible terminated S corporation (as defined in section 481(d)) after the post-termination transition period, the accumulated adjustments account shall be allocated to such distribution, and the distribution shall be chargeable to accumulated earnings and profits, in the same ratio as the amount of such accumulated adjustments account of such accumulated earnings and profits.

§ 1372. Partnership rules to apply for fringe benefit purposes.

(a) General rule.—For purposes of applying the provisions of this subtitle which relate to employee fringe benefits—

(1) the S corporation shall be treated as a partnership, and

(2) any 2-percent shareholder of the S corporation shall be treated as a partner of such partnership.

(b) 2-percent shareholder defined.—For purposes of this section, the term "2-percent shareholder" means any person who owns (or is considered as owning within the meaning of section 318) on any day during the taxable year of the S corporation more than 2 percent of the outstanding stock of such corporation or stock possessing more than 2 percent of the total combined voting power of all stock of such corporation.

§ 1373. Foreign income.

(a) S corporation treated as partnership, etc.—For purposes of subparts A and F of part III, and part V, of subchapter N (relating to income from sources without the United States)

(1) an S corporation shall be treated as a partnership, and

(2) the shareholders of such corporation shall be treated as partners of such partnership.

(b) Recapture of overall foreign loss.—For purposes of section 904(f) (relating to recapture of overall foreign loss), the making or termination of an election to be treated as an S corporation shall be treated as a disposition of the business.

§ 1374. Tax imposed on certain built-in gains.

(a) General rule.—If for any taxable year beginning in the recognition period an S corporation has a net recognized built-in gain there is hereby imposed a tax (computed under subsection (b)) on the income of such corporation for such taxable year.

(b) Amount of tax.—

(1) In general.—The amount of the tax imposed by subsection (a) shall be computed by applying the highest rate of tax specified in section 11(b) to the net recognized built-in gain of the S corporation for the taxable year.

(2) Net operating loss carryforwards from C years allowed.—Notwithstanding section 1371(b)(1), any net operating loss carryforward arising in a taxable year for which the corporation was a C corporation shall be allowed for purposes of this section as a deduction against the net recognized built-in gain of the S corporation for the taxable year. For purposes of determining the amount of any such loss which may be carried to subsequent taxable years, the amount of the net recognized built-in gain shall be treated as taxable income. Rules similar to the rules of the preceding sentences of this paragraph shall apply in the case of a capital loss carryforward arising in a taxable year for which the corporation was a C corporation.

(3) Credits.—

(A) In general.—Except as provided in subparagraph (B), no credit shall be allowable under part IV of subchapter A of this chapter (other than under section 34) against the tax imposed by subsection (a).

(B) Business credit carryforwards from C years allowed.—Notwithstanding section 1371(b)(1), any business credit carryforward under section 39 arising in a taxable year for which the corporation was a C corporation shall be allowed as a credit against the tax imposed by subsection (a) in the same manner as if it were imposed by section 11. A similar rule shall apply in the case of the minimum tax credit under section 53 to the extent attributable to taxable years for which the corporation was a C corporation.

(4) Coordination with section 1201(a).—For purposes of section 1201(a)—

(A) the tax imposed by subsection (a) shall be treated as if it were imposed by section 11, and

(B) the amount of the net recognized built in gain shall be treated as the taxable income.

(c) Limitations.—

(1) Corporations which were always S corporations.—Subsection (a) shall not apply to any corporation if an election under section 1362(a) has been in effect with respect to such corporation for each of its taxable years. Except as provided in regulations, an S corporation and any predecessor corporation shall be treated as 1 corporation for purposes of the preceding sentence.

(2) Limitation on amount of net recognized built-in gain.—The amount of the net recognized built-in gain taken into account under this section for any taxable year shall not exceed the excess (if any) of—

(A) the net unrealized built-in gain, over

(B) the net recognized built-in gain for prior taxable years beginning in the recognition period.

(d) Definitions and special rules.—For purposes of this section—

(1) Net unrealized built-in gain.—The term "net unrealized built-in gain" means the amount (if any) by which—

(A) the fair market value of the assets of the S corporation as of the beginning of its 1st taxable year for which an election under section 1362(a) is in effect, exceeds

(B) the aggregate adjusted bases of such assets at such time.

(2) Net recognized built-in gain.—

(A) In general.—The term "net recognized built-in gain" means, with respect to any taxable year in the recognition period, the lesser of

(i) the amount which would be the taxable income of the S corporation for such taxable year if only recognized built-in gains and recognized built-in losses were taken into account, or

(ii) such corporation's taxable income for such taxable year (determined as provided in section 1375(b)(1)(B)).

(B) Carryover.—If, for any taxable year, the amount referred to in clause (i) of subparagraph (A) exceeds the amount referred to in clause (ii) of subparagraph (A), such excess shall be treated as a recognized built-in gain in the succeeding taxable year. The preceding sentence shall apply only in the case of a corporation treated as an S corporation by reason of an election made on or after March 31, 1988.

(3) Recognized built-in gain.—The term "recognized built-in gain" means any gain recognized during the recognition period on the disposition of any asset except to the extent that the S corporation establishes that—

(A) such asset was not held by the S corporation as of the beginning of the 1st taxable year for which it was an S corporation, or

(B) such gain exceeds the excess (if any) of—

(i) the fair market value of such asset as of the beginning of such 1st taxable year, over

(ii) the adjusted basis of the asset as of such time.

(4) Recognized built-in losses.—The term "recognized built-in loss" means any loss recognized during the recognition period on the disposition of any asset to the extent that the S corporation establishes that

(A) such asset was held by the S corporation as of the beginning of the 1st taxable year referred to in paragraph (3), and

(B) such loss does not exceed the excess of

(i) the adjusted basis of such asset as of the beginning of such 1st taxable year, over

(ii) the fair market value of such asset as of such time.

(5) Treatment of certain built-in items.—

(A) Income items.—Any item of income which is properly taken into account during the recognition period but which is attributable to periods before the 1st taxable year for which the corporation was an S corporation shall be treated as a recognized built-in gain for the taxable year in which it is properly taken into account.

(B) Deduction items.—Any amount which is allowable as a deduction during the recognition period (determined without regard to any carryover) but which is attributable to periods before the 1st taxable year referred to in subparagraph (A) shall be treated as a recognized built-in loss for the taxable year for which it is allowable as a deduction.

(C) Adjustment to net unrealized built-in gain.—The amount of the net unrealized built-in gain shall be properly adjusted for amounts which would be treated as recognized built-in gains or losses under this paragraph if such amounts were properly taken into account (or allowable as a deduction) during the recognition period.

(6) Treatment of certain property.—If the adjusted basis of any asset is determined (in whole or in part) by reference to the adjusted basis of any other asset held by the S corporation as of the beginning of the 1st taxable year referred to in paragraph (3)—

(A) such asset shall be treated as held by the S corporation as of the beginning of such 1st taxable year, and

(B) any determination under paragraph (3)(B) or (4)(B) with respect to such asset shall be made by reference to the fair market value and adjusted basis of such other asset as of the beginning of such 1st taxable year.

(7) Recognition period.—

(A) In general.—The term 'recognition period' means the 5-year period beginning with the 1st day of the 1st taxable year for which the corporation was an S corporation. For purposes of applying this section to any amount includible in income by reason of distributions to shareholders pursuant to section 593(e), the preceding sentence shall be applied without regard to the phrase '5-year'.

(B) Installment sales.—If an S corporation sells an asset and reports the income from the sale using the installment method under section 453, the treatment of all payments received shall be governed by the provisions of this paragraph applicable to the taxable year in which such sale was made.—

* * *

(8) Treatment of transfer of assets from C corporation to S corporation.—

(A) In general.—Except to the extent provided in regulations, if

(i) an S corporation acquires any asset, and

(ii) the S corporation's basis in such asset is determined (in whole or in part) by reference to the basis of such asset (or any other property) in the hands of a C corporation,

then a tax is hereby imposed on any net recognized built-in gain attributable to any such assets for any taxable year beginning in the recognition period. The amount of such tax shall be determined under the rules of this section as modified by subparagraph (B).

(B) Modifications.—For purposes of this paragraph, the modifications of this subparagraph are as follows:

(i) In general.—The preceding paragraphs of this subsection shall be applied by taking into account the day on which the assets were acquired by the S corporation in lieu of the beginning of the 1st taxable year for which the corporation was an S corporation.

(ii) Subsection (c)(1) not to apply.—Subsection (c)(1) shall not apply.

(9) Reference to 1st taxable year.—Any reference in this section to the 1st taxable year for which the corporation was an S corporation shall be treated as a reference to the 1st taxable year for which the corporation was an S corporation pursuant to its most recent election under section 1362.

(e) Regulations.—The Secretary shall prescribe such regulations as may be necessary to carry out the purposes of this section including regulations providing for the appropriate treatment of successor corporations.

§ 1375. Tax imposed when passive investment income of corporation having accumulated earnings and profits exceeds 25 percent of gross receipts.

(a) General rule.—If for the taxable year an S corporation has—

(1) accumulated earnings and profits at the close of such taxable year, and

(2) gross receipts more than 25 percent of which are passive investment income,

then there is hereby imposed a tax on the income of such corporation for such taxable year. Such tax shall be computed by multiplying the excess net passive income by the highest rate of tax specified in section 11(b).

(b) Definitions.—For purposes of this section—

(1) Excess net passive income.—

(A) In general.—Except as provided in subparagraph (B), the term "excess net passive income" means an amount which bears the same ratio to the net passive income for the taxable year as

(i) the amount by which the passive investment income for the taxable year exceeds 25 percent of the gross receipts for the taxable year, bears to

(ii) the passive investment income for the taxable year.

(B) Limitation.—The amount of the excess net passive income for any taxable year shall not exceed the amount of the corporation's taxable income for such taxable year as determined under section 63(a)—

(i) without regard to the deductions allowed by part VIII of subchapter B (other than the deduction allowed by section 248, relating to organization expenditures), and

(ii) without regard to the deduction under section 172.

(2) Net passive income.—The term "net passive income" means—

(A) passive investment income, reduced by

(B) the deductions allowable under this chapter which are directly connected with the production of such income (other than deductions allowable under section 172 and part VIII of subchapter B).

(3) Passive investment income, etc.—The terms "passive investment income" and "gross receipts" have the same respective meanings as when used in paragraph (3) of section 1362(d).

(4) Coordination with section 1374.—Notwithstanding paragraph (3), the amount of passive investment income shall be determined by not taking into account any recognized built-in gain or loss of the S corporation for any taxable year in the recognition period. Terms used in the preceding sentence shall have the same respective meanings as when used in section 1374.

(c) Credits not allowable.—No credit shall be allowed under part IV of subchapter A of this chapter (other than section 34) against the tax imposed by subsection (a).

(d) Waiver of tax in certain cases.—If the S corporation establishes to the satisfaction of the Secretary that—

(1) it determined in good faith that it had no subchapter C earnings and profits at the close of a taxable year, and

(2) during a reasonable period of time after it was determined that it did have subchapter C earnings and profits at the close of such taxable year such earnings and profits were distributed,

the Secretary may waive the tax imposed by subsection (a) for such taxable year.

Part IV—Definitions; Miscellaneous

§ 1377. Definitions and special rule.

(a) Pro rata share.—For purposes of this subchapter—

(1) In general.—Except as provided in paragraph (2), each shareholder's pro rata share of any item for any taxable year shall be the sum of the amounts determined with respect to the shareholder—

(A) by assigning an equal portion of such item to each day of the taxable year, and

(B) then by dividing that portion pro rata among the shares outstanding on such day.

(2) Election to terminate year.—

(A) In general.—Under regulations prescribed by the Secretary, if any shareholder terminates the shareholder's interest in the corporation during the taxable year and all affected shareholders and the corporation agree to the application of this paragraph, paragraph (1) shall be applied to the affected shareholders as if the taxable year consisted of 2 taxable years the first of which ends on the date of the termination.

(B) Affected shareholders.—For purposes of subparagraph (A), the term "affected shareholders" means the shareholder whose interest is terminated and all shareholders to whom such shareholder has transferred shares during the taxable year. If such shareholder has transferred shares to the corporation, the term 'affected shareholders' shall include all persons who are shareholders during the taxable year.

(b) Post-termination transition period.—

(1) In general.—For purposes of this subchapter, the term "post-termination transition period" means—

(A) the period beginning on the day after the last day of the corporation's last taxable year as an S corporation and ending on the later of—

(i) the day which is 1 year after such last day, or

(ii) the due date for filing the return for such last year as an S corporation (including extensions),

(B) the 120-day period beginning on the date of any determination pursuant to an audit of the taxpayer which follows the termination of the corporation's election and which adjusts a subchapter S item of income, loss, or deduction of the corporation arising during the S period (as defined in section 1368(e)(2)), and

(C) the 120-day period beginning on the date of a determination that the corporation's election under section 1362(a) had terminated for a previous taxable year.

(2) Determination defined.—For purposes of paragraph (1), the term "determination" means—

(A) a determination as defined in section 1313(a), or

(B) an agreement between the corporation and the Secretary that the corporation failed to qualify as an S corporation.

(3) Special rules for audit related post-termination transition periods.—

(A) No application to carryovers.—Paragraph (1)(B) shall not apply for purposes of section 1366(d)(3).

(B) Limitation on application to distributions.—Paragraph (1)(B) shall apply to a distribution described in section 1371(e) only to the extent that the amount of such distribution does not exceed the aggregate increase (if any) in the accumulated adjustments account (within the meaning of section 1368(e)) by reason of the adjustments referred to in such paragraph.

(c) Manner of making elections, etc.—Any election under this subchapter, and any revocation under section 1362(d)(1), shall be made in such manner as the Secretary shall by regulations prescribe.

§ 1378. Taxable year of S corporation.

(a) General rule.—For purposes of this subtitle, the taxable year of an S corporation shall be a permitted year.

(b) Permitted year defined.—For purposes of this section, the term "permitted year" means a taxable year which—

(1) is a year ending December 31, or

(2) is any other accounting period for which the corporation establishes a business purpose to the satisfaction of the Secretary.

For purposes of paragraph (2), any deferral of income to shareholders shall not be treated as a business purpose.

§ 1379. Transitional rules on enactment.

(a) Old elections.—Any election made under section 1372(a) (as in effect before the enactment of the Subchapter S Revision Act of 1982) shall be treated as an election made under section 1362.

(b) References to prior law included.—Any references in this title to a provision of this subchapter shall, to the extent not inconsistent with the purposes of this subchapter, include a reference to the corresponding provision as in effect before the enactment of the Subchapter S Revision Act of 1982.

(c) Distributions of undistributed taxable income.—If a corporation was an electing small business corporation for the last preenactment year, subsections (f) and (d) of section 1375 (as in effect before the enactment of the Subchapter S Revision Act of 1982) shall continue to apply with respect to distributions of undistributed taxable income for any taxable year beginning before January 1, 1983.

(d) Carryforwards.—If a corporation was an electing small business corporation for the last preenactment year and is an S corporation for the 1st postenactment year, any carryforward to the 1st postenactment year which arose in a taxable year for which the corporation was an electing small business corporation shall be treated as arising in the 1st postenactment year.

(e) Preenactment and postenactment years defined.—For purposes of this subsection

(1) Last preenactment year.—The term "last preenactment year" means the last taxable year of a corporation which begins before January 1, 1983.

(2) 1st postenactment year.—The term "1st postenactment year" means the 1st taxable year of a corporation which begins after December 31, 1982.

Chapter 6—Consolidated Returns

Subchapter A—Returns and Payment of Tax

§ 1501. Privilege to file consolidated returns.

An affiliated group of corporations shall, subject to the provisions of this chapter, have the privilege of making a consolidated return with respect to the income tax imposed by chapter 1 for the taxable year in lieu of separate returns. The making of a consolidated return shall be upon the condition that all corporations which at any time during the taxable year have been members of the affiliated group consent to all the consolidated return regulations prescribed under section 1502 prior to the last day prescribed by law for the filing of such return. The making of a consolidated return shall be considered as such consent. In the case of a corporation which is a member of the affiliated group for a fractional part of the year, the consolidated return shall include the income of such corporation for such part of the year as it is a member of the affiliated group.

§ 1502. Regulations.

The Secretary shall prescribe such regulations as he may deem necessary in order that the tax liability of any affiliated group of corporations making a consolidated return and of each corporation in the group, both during and after the period of affiliation, may be returned, determined, computed, assessed, collected, and adjusted, in such manner as clearly to reflect the income-tax liability and the various factors necessary for the determination of such liability, and in order to prevent avoidance of such tax liability. In carrying out the preceding sentence, the Secretary may prescribe rules that are different from the provisions of chapter 1 that would apply if such corporations filed separate returns.

§ 1503. Computation and payment of tax.

(a) General rule.—In any case in which a consolidated return is made or is required to be made, the tax shall be determined, computed, assessed, collected, and adjusted in accordance with the regulations under section 1502 prescribed before the last day prescribed by law for the filing of such return.

* * *

(e) Special rule for determining adjustments to basis.—

(1) In general.—Solely for purposes of determining gain or loss on the disposition of intragroup stock and the amount of any inclusion by reason of an excess loss account, in determining the adjustments to the basis of such intragroup stock on account of the earnings and profits of any member of an affiliated group for any consolidated year (and in determining the amount in such account)—

(A) such earnings and profits shall be determined as if section 312 were applied for such taxable year (and all preceding consolidated years of the member with respect to such group) without regard to subsections (k) and (n) thereof, and

(B) earnings and profits shall not include any amount excluded from gross income under section 108 to the extent the amount so excluded was not applied to reduce tax attributes (other than basis in property).

(2) Definitions.—For purposes of this subsection—

(A) Intragroup stock.—The term "intragroup stock" means any stock which—

(i) is in a corporation which is or was a member of an affiliated group of corporations, and

(ii) is held by another corporation which is or was a member of such group.

Such term includes any other property the basis of which is determined (in whole or in part) by reference to the basis of stock described in the preceding sentence.

(B) Consolidated year.—The term "consolidated year" means any taxable year for which the affiliated group makes a consolidated return.

(C) Application of section 312(n)(7) not affected.—The reference in paragraph (1) to subsection (n) of section 312 shall be treated as not including a reference to paragraph (7) of such subsection.

(3) Adjustments.—Under regulations prescribed by the Secretary, proper adjustments shall be made in the application of paragraph (1)—

(A) in the case of any property acquired by the corporation before consolidation, for the difference between the adjusted basis of such property for purposes of computing taxable income and its adjusted basis for purposes of computing earnings and profits, and

(B) in the case of any property, for any basis adjustment under section 50(c).

(4) Elimination of election to reduce basis of indebtedness.—Nothing in the regulations prescribed under section 1502 shall permit any reduction in the amount otherwise included in gross income by reason of an excess loss account if such reduction is on account of a reduction in the basis of indebtedness.

(f) Limitation on use of group losses to offset income of subsidiary paying preferred dividends.—

(1) In general.—In the case of any subsidiary distributing during any taxable year dividends on any applicable preferred stock—

(A) no group loss item shall be allowed to reduce the disqualified separately computed income of such subsidiary for such taxable year, and

(B) no group credit item shall be allowed against the tax imposed by this chapter on such disqualified separately computed income.

(2) Group items.—For purposes of this subsection—

(A) Group loss item.—The term "group loss item" means any of the following items of any other member of the affiliated group which includes the subsidiary:

    (i) Any net operating loss and any net operating loss carryover or carryback under section 172.

    (ii) Any loss from the sale or exchange of any capital asset and any capital loss carryover or carryback under section 1212.

(B) Group credit item.—The term "group credit item" means any credit allowable under part IV of subchapter A of chapter 1 (other than section 34) to any other member of the affiliated group which includes the subsidiary and any carryover or carryback of any such credit.

(3) Other definitions.—For purposes of this subsection—

(A) Disqualified separately computed income.—The term "disqualified separately computed income" means the portion of the separately computed taxable income of the subsidiary which does not exceed the dividends distributed by the subsidiary during the taxable year on applicable preferred stock.

(B) Separately computed taxable income.—The term "separately computed taxable income" means the separate taxable income of the subsidiary for the taxable year determined—

    (i) by taking into account gains and losses from the sale or exchange of a capital asset and section 1231 gains and losses,

    (ii) without regard to any net operating loss or capital loss carryover or carryback, and

    (iii) with such adjustments as the Secretary may prescribe.

(C) Subsidiary.—The term "subsidiary" means any corporation which is a member of an affiliated group filing a consolidated return other than the common parent.

(D) Applicable preferred stock.—The term "applicable preferred stock" means stock described in section 1504(a)(4) in the subsidiary which is—

    (i) issued after November 17, 1989, and

    (ii) held by a person other than a member of the same affiliated group as the subsidiary.

(4) Regulations.—The Secretary shall prescribe such regulations as may be necessary or appropriate to carry out the provisions of this subsection, including regulations—

(A) to prevent the avoidance of this subsection through the transfer of built-in losses to the subsidiary,

(B) to provide rules for cases in which the subsidiary owns (directly or indirectly) stock in another member of the affiliated group, and

(C) to provide for the application of this subsection where dividends are not paid currently, where the redemption and liquidation rights of the applicable preferred stock exceed the issue price for such stock, or where the stock is otherwise structured to avoid the purposes of this subsection.

§ 1504. Definitions.

(a) Affiliated group defined.—For purposes of this subtitle—

(1) In general.—The term "affiliated group" means—

(A) 1 or more chains of includible corporations connected through stock ownership with a common parent corporation which is an includible corporation, but only if—

(B)(i) the common parent owns directly stock meeting the requirements of paragraph (2) in at least 1 of the other includible corporations, and

(ii) stock meeting the requirements of paragraph (2) in each of the includible corporations (except the common parent) is owned directly by 1 or more of the other includible corporations.

(2) 80-percent voting and value test.—The ownership of stock of any corporation meets the requirements of this paragraph if it—

(A) possesses at least 80 percent of the total voting power of the stock of such corporation, and

(B) has a value equal to at least 80 percent of the total value of the stock of such corporation.

(3) 5 years must elapse before reconsolidation.—

(A) In general.—If—

(i) a corporation is included (or required to be included) in a consolidated return filed by an affiliated group, and

(ii) such corporation ceases to be a member of such group, with respect to periods after such cessation, such corporation (and any successor of such corporation) may not be included in any consolidated return filed by the affiliated group (or by another affiliated group with the same common parent or a successor of such common parent) before the 61st month beginning after its first taxable year in which it ceased to be a member of such affiliated group.

(B) Secretary may waive application of subparagraph (A).—The Secretary may waive the application of subparagraph (A) to any corporation for any period subject to such conditions as the Secretary may prescribe.

(4) Stock not to include certain preferred stock.—For purposes of this subsection, the term "stock" does not include any stock which—

(A) is not entitled to vote,

(B) is limited and preferred as to dividends and does not participate in corporate growth to any significant extent,

(C) has redemption and liquidation rights which do not exceed the issue price of such stock (except for a reasonable redemption or liquidation premium), and

(D) is not convertible into another class of stock.

(5) Regulations.—The Secretary shall prescribe such regulations as may be necessary or appropriate to carry out the purposes of this subsection, including (but not limited to) regulations—

(**A**) which treat warrants, obligations convertible into stock, and other similar interests as stock, and stock as not stock,

(**B**) which treat options to acquire or sell stock as having been exercised,

(**C**) which provide that the requirements of paragraph (2)(B) shall be treated as met if the affiliated group, in reliance on a good faith determination of value, treated such requirements as met,

(**D**) which disregard an inadvertent ceasing to meet the requirements of paragraph (2)(B) by reason of changes in relative values of different classes of stock,

(**E**) which provide that transfers of stock within the group shall not be taken into account in determining whether a corporation ceases to be a member of an affiliated group, and

(**F**) which disregard changes in voting power to the extent such changes are disproportionate to related changes in value.

(**b**) **Definition of "includible corporation".**—As used in this chapter, the term "includible corporation" means any corporation except—

(**1**) Corporations exempt from taxation under section 501.

(**2**) Insurance companies subject to taxation under section 801.

(**3**) Foreign corporations.

(**4**) Corporations with respect to which an election under section 936 (relating to possession tax credit) is in effect for the taxable year.

(**5**) Repealed.

(**6**) Regulated investment companies and real estate investment trusts subject to tax under subchapter M of chapter 1.

(**7**) A DISC (as defined in section 992(a)(1)).

(**8**) An S corporation.

* * *

Subchapter B—Related Rules

Part I—In General

§ 1551. Disallowance of the benefits of the graduated corporate rates and accumulated earnings credit.

(a) **In general.**—If—

(**1**) any corporation transfers, directly or indirectly, all or part of its property (other than money) to a transferee corporation, or

(**2**) five or fewer individuals who are in control of a corporation transfer, directly or indirectly, property (other than money) to a transferee corporation,

and the transferee corporation was created for the purpose of acquiring such property or was not actively engaged in business at the time of such acquisition, and if after such transfer the transferor or transferors are in control of such transferee corporation during any part of the taxable year of such transferee corporation, then for such taxable year of such transferee corporation the Secretary may (except as may be otherwise determined under subsection (c)) disallow the benefits of the rates contained in section 11(b) which are lower than the highest rate specified in such section, or the accumulated earnings credit provided in paragraph (2) or (3) of section 535(c), unless such transferee corporation shall establish by the clear preponderance of the evidence that the securing of such benefits or credit was not a major purpose of such transfer.

(b) Control.—For purposes of subsection (a), the term "control" means—

(1) With respect to a transferee corporation described in subsection (a)(1), the ownership by the transferor corporation, its shareholders, or both, of stock possessing at least 80 percent of the total combined voting power of all classes of stock entitled to vote or at least 80 percent of the total value of shares of all classes of the stock; or

(2) With respect to each corporation described in subsection (a)(2), the ownership by the five or fewer individuals described in such subsection of stock possessing—

(A) at least 80 percent of the total combined voting power of all classes of stock entitled to vote or at least 80 percent of the total value of shares of all classes of the stock of each corporation, and

(B) more than 50 percent of the total combined voting power of all classes of stock entitled to vote or more than 50 percent of the total value of shares of all classes of stock of each corporation, taking into account the stock ownership of each such individual only to the extent such stock ownership is identical with respect to each such corporation.

For purposes of this subsection, section 1563(e) shall apply in determining the ownership of stock.

(c) Authority of the Secretary under this section.—The provisions of section 269(c), and the authority of the Secretary under such section, shall, to the extent not inconsistent with the provisions of this section, be applicable to this section.

§ 1552. Earnings and profits.

(a) General rule.—Pursuant to regulations prescribed by the Secretary the earnings and profits of each member of an affiliated group required to be included in a consolidated return for such group filed for a taxable year shall be determined by allocating the tax liability of the group for such year among the members of the group in accord with whichever of the following methods the group shall elect in its first consolidated return filed for such a taxable year:

(1) The tax liability shall be apportioned among the members of the group in accordance with the ratio which that portion of the consolidated taxable income attributable to each member of the group having taxable income bears to the consolidated taxable income.

(2) The tax liability of the group shall be allocated to the several members of the group on the basis of the percentage of the total tax which the tax of such member if computed on a separate return would bear to the total amount of the taxes for all members of the group so computed.

(3) The tax liability of the group (excluding the tax increases arising from the consolidation) shall be allocated on the basis of the contribution of each member of the group to the consolidated taxable income of the group. Any tax increases arising from the consolidation shall be distributed to the several members in direct proportion to the reduction in tax liability resulting to such members from the filing of the consolidated return as measured by the difference between their tax liabilities determined on a separate return basis and their tax liabilities based on their contributions to the consolidated taxable income.

(4) The tax liability of the group shall be allocated in accord with any other method selected by the group with the approval of the Secretary.

(b) Failure to elect.—If no election is made in such first return, the tax liability shall be allocated among the several members of the group pursuant to the method prescribed in subsection (a)(1).

Part II—Certain Controlled Corporations

§ 1561. Limitations on certain multiple tax benefits in the case of certain controlled corporations.

(a) In general.—The component members of a controlled group of corporations on a December 31 shall, for their taxable years which include such December 31, be limited for purposes of this subtitle to one $250,000 ($150,000 if any component member is a corporation described in section 535(c)(2)(B)) amount for purposes of computing the accumulated earnings credit under section 535(c)(2) and (3). Such amount shall be divided equally among the component members of such group on such December 31 unless the Secretary prescribes regulations permitting an unequal allocation of such amount.

* * *

§ 1563. Definitions and special rules.

(a) Controlled group of corporations.—For purposes of this part, the term "controlled group of corporations" means any group of—

(1) Parent-subsidiary controlled group.—One or more chains of corporations connected through stock ownership with a common parent corporation if—

(A) stock possessing at least 80 percent of the total combined voting power of all classes of stock entitled to vote or at least 80 percent of the total value of shares of all classes of stock of each of the corporations, except the common parent corporation, is owned (within the meaning of subsection (d)(1)) by one or more of the other corporations; and

(B) the common parent corporation owns (within the meaning of subsection (d)(1)) stock possessing at least 80 percent of the total combined voting power of all classes of stock entitled to vote or at least 80 percent of the total value of shares of all classes of stock of at least one of the other corporations, excluding, in computing such voting power or value, stock owned directly by such other corporations.

(2) Brother-sister controlled group.—Two or more corporations if 5 or fewer persons who are individuals, estates, or trusts own (within the meaning of subsection (d)(2)) stock possessing more than 50 percent of the total combined voting power of all classes of stock entitled to vote or more than 50 percent of the total value of shares of all classes of stock of each corporation, taking into account the stock ownership of each such person only to the extent such stock ownership is identical with respect to each such corporation.

(3) Combined group.—Three or more corporations each of which is a member of a group of corporations described in paragraph (1) or (2), and one of which—

(A) is a common parent corporation included in a group of corporations described in paragraph (1), and also

(B) is included in a group of corporations described in paragraph (2).

* * *

(b) Component member.—

(1) General rule.—For purposes of this part, a corporation is a component member of a controlled group of corporations on a December 31 of any taxable year (and with respect to the taxable year which includes such December 31) if such corporation—

(A) is a member of such controlled group of corporations on the December 31 included in such year and is not treated as an excluded member under paragraph (2), or

(B) is not a member of such controlled group of corporations on the December 31 included in such year but is treated as an additional member under paragraph (3).

(2) Excluded members.—A corporation which is a member of a controlled group of corporations on December 31 of any taxable year shall be treated as an excluded member of such group for the taxable year including such December 31 if such corporation—

(A) is a member of such group for less than one-half the number of days in such taxable year which precede such December 31,

(B) is exempt from taxation under section 501(a) (except a corporation which is subject to tax on its unrelated business taxable income under section 511) for such taxable year,

(C) is a foreign corporation subject to tax under section 881 for such taxable year,

* * *

(3) Additional members.—A corporation which

(A) was a member of a controlled group of corporations at any time during a calendar year,

(B) is not a member of such group on December 31 of such calendar year, and

(C) is not described, with respect to such group, in subparagraph (B), (C), (D), or (E) of paragraph (2),

shall be treated as an additional member of such group on December 31 for its taxable year including such December 31 if it was a member of such group for one-half (or more) of the number of days in such taxable year which precede such December 31.

(4) Overlapping groups.—If a corporation is a component member of more than one controlled group of corporations with respect to any taxable year, such corporation shall be treated as a component member of only one controlled group. The determination as to the group of which such corporation is a component member shall be made under regulations prescribed by the Secretary which are consistent with the purposes of this part.

(c) Certain stock excluded.—

(1) General rule.—For purposes of this part, the term "stock" does not include—

(A) nonvoting stock which is limited and preferred as to dividends,

(B) treasury stock, and

(C) stock which is treated as "excluded stock" under paragraph (2).

(2) Stock treated as "excluded stock".—

(A) Parent-subsidiary controlled group.—For purposes of subsection (a)(1), if a corporation (referred to in this paragraph as "parent corporation") owns (within the meaning of subsections (d)(1) and (e)(4)), 50 percent or more of the total combined voting power of all classes of stock entitled to vote or 50 percent or more of the total value of shares of all classes of stock in another corporation (referred to in this paragraph as "subsidiary corporation"), the following stock of the subsidiary corporation shall be treated as excluded stock—

(i) stock in the subsidiary corporation held by a trust which is part of a plan of deferred compensation for the benefit of the employees of the parent corporation or the subsidiary corporation,

(ii) stock in the subsidiary corporation owned by an individual (within the meaning of subsection (d)(2)) who is a principal stockholder or officer of the parent corporation. For purposes of this clause, the term "principal stockholder" of a corporation means an individual who owns (within the meaning of subsection (d)(2)) 5 percent or more of the total combined voting power of all classes of stock entitled to vote or 5 percent or more of the total value of shares of all classes of stock in such corporation,

(iii) stock in the subsidiary corporation owned (within the meaning of subsection (d)(2)) by an employee of the subsidiary corporation if such stock is subject to conditions which run in favor of such parent (or subsidiary) corporation and which substantially restrict or limit the employee's right (or if the employee constructively owns such stock, the direct owner's right) to dispose of such stock, or

(iv) stock in the subsidiary corporation owned (within the meaning of subsection (d)(2)) by an organization (other than the parent corporation) to which section 501 (relating to certain educational and charitable organizations which are exempt from tax) applies and which is controlled directly or indirectly by the parent corporation or subsidiary corporation, by an individual, estate, or trust that is a principal stockholder (within the meaning of clause (ii)) of the parent corporation, by an officer of the parent corporation, or by any combination thereof.

(B) Brother-sister controlled group.—For purposes of subsection (a)(2), if 5 or fewer persons who are individuals, estates, or trusts (referred to in this subparagraph as "common owners") own (within the meaning of subsection (d)(2)), 50 percent or more of the total combined voting power of all classes of stock entitled to vote or 50 percent or more of the total value of shares of all classes of stock in a corporation, the following stock of such corporation shall be treated as excluded stock—

(i) stock in such corporation held by an employees' trust described in section 401(a) which is exempt from tax under section 501(a), if such trust is for the benefit of the employees of such corporation,

(ii) stock in such corporation owned (within the meaning of subsection (d)(2)) by an employee of the corporation if such stock is subject to conditions which run in favor of any of such common owners (or such corporation) and which substantially restrict or limit the employee's right (or if the employee constructively owns such stock, the direct owner's right) to dispose of such stock. If a condition which limits or restricts the employee's right (or the direct owner's right) to dispose of such stock also applies to the stock held by any of the common owners pursuant to a bona fide reciprocal stock purchase arrangement, such condition shall not be treated as one which restricts or limits the employee's right to dispose of such stock, or

(iii) stock in such corporation owned (within the meaning of subsection (d)(2)) by an organization to which section 501 (relating to certain educational and charitable organizations which are exempt from tax) applies and which is controlled directly or indirectly by such corporation, by an individual, estate, or trust that is a principal stockholder (within the meaning of subparagraph (A)(ii)) of such corporation, by an officer of such corporation, or by any combination thereof.

(d) Rules for determining stock ownership.—

(1) Parent-subsidiary controlled group.—For purposes of determining whether a corporation is a member of a parent-subsidiary controlled group of corporations (within the meaning of subsection (a)(1)), stock owned by a corporation means—

(A) stock owned directly by such corporation, and

(B) stock owned with the application of paragraphs (1), (2), and (3) of subsection (e).

(2) Brother-sister controlled group.—For purposes of determining whether a corporation is a member of a brother-sister controlled group of corporations (within the meaning of subsection (a)(2)), stock owned by a person who is an individual, estate, or trust means—

(A) stock owned directly by such person, and

(B) stock owned with the application of subsection (e).

(e) Constructive ownership.—

(1) Options.—If any person has an option to acquire stock, such stock shall be considered as owned by such person. For purposes of this paragraph, an option to acquire such an option, and each one of a series of such options, shall be considered as an option to acquire such stock.

(2) Attribution from partnerships.—Stock owned, directly or indirectly, by or for a partnership shall be considered as owned by any partner having an interest of 5 percent or more in either the capital or profits of the partnership in proportion to his interest in capital or profits, whichever such proportion is the greater.

(3) Attribution from estates or trusts.—

(A) Stock owned, directly or indirectly, by or for an estate or trust shall be considered as owned by any beneficiary who has an actuarial interest of 5 percent or more in such stock, to the extent of such actuarial interest. For purposes of this subparagraph, the actuarial interest of each beneficiary shall be determined by assuming the maximum exercise of discretion by the fiduciary in favor of such beneficiary and the maximum use of such stock to satisfy his rights as a beneficiary.

(B) Stock owned, directly or indirectly, by or for any portion of a trust of which a person is considered the owner under subpart E of part I of subchapter J (relating to grantors and others treated as substantial owners) shall be considered as owned by such person.

(C) This paragraph shall not apply to stock owned by any employees' trust described in section 401(a) which is exempt from tax under section 501(a).

(4) Attribution from corporations.—Stock owned, directly or indirectly, by or for a corporation shall be considered as owned by any person who owns (within the meaning of subsection (d)) 5 percent or more in value of its stock in that proportion which the value of the stock which such person so owns bears to the value of all the stock in such corporation.

(5) Spouse.—An individual shall be considered as owning stock in a corporation owned, directly or indirectly, by or for his spouse (other than a spouse who is legally separated from the individual under a decree of divorce whether interlocutory or final, or a decree of separate maintenance), except in the case of a corporation with respect to which each of the following conditions is satisfied for its taxable year—

(A) The individual does not, at any time during such taxable year, own directly any stock in such corporation;

(B) The individual is not a director or employee and does not participate in the management of such corporation at any time during such taxable year;

(C) Not more than 50 percent of such corporation's gross income for such taxable year was derived from royalties, rents, dividends, interest, and annuities; and

(D) Such stock in such corporation is not, at any time during such taxable year, subject to conditions which substantially restrict or limit the spouse's right to dispose of such stock and which run in favor of the individual or his children who have not attained the age of 21 years.

(6) Children, grandchildren, parents, and grandparents.—

(A) Minor children.—An individual shall be considered as owning stock owned, directly or indirectly, by or for his children who have not attained the age of 21 years, and, if the individual has not attained the age of 21 years, the stock owned, directly or indirectly, by or for his parents.

(B) Adult children and grandchildren.—An individual who owns (within the meaning of subsection (d)(2), but without regard to this subparagraph) more than 50 percent of the total combined voting power of all classes of stock entitled to vote or more than 50 percent of the total value of shares of all classes of stock in a corporation shall be considered as owning the stock in such corporation owned, directly or indirectly, by or for his parents, grandparents, grandchildren, and children who have attained the age of 21 years.

(C) Adopted child.—For purposes of this section, a legally adopted child of an individual shall be treated as a child of such individual by blood.

(f) Other definitions and rules.—

(1) Employee defined.—For purposes of this section the term "employee" has the same meaning such term is given by paragraphs (1) and (2) of section 3121(d).

(2) Operating rules.—

(A) In general.—Except as provided in subparagraph (B), stock constructively owned by a person by reason of the application of paragraph (1), (2), (3), (4), (5), or (6) of subsection (e) shall, for purposes of applying such paragraphs, be treated as actually owned by such person.

(B) Members of family.—Stock constructively owned by an individual by reason of the application of paragraph (5) or (6) of subsection (e) shall not be treated as owned by him for purposes of again applying such paragraphs in order to make another the constructive owner of such stock.

(3) Special rules.—For purposes of this section—

(A) If stock may be considered as owned by a person under subsection (e)(1) and under any other paragraph of subsection (e), it shall be considered as owned by him under subsection (e)(1).

(B) If stock is owned (within the meaning of subsection (d)) by two or more persons, such stock shall be considered as owned by the person whose ownership of such stock results in the corporation being a component member of a controlled group. If by reason of the preceding sentence, a corporation would (but for this sentence) become a component member of two controlled groups, it shall be treated as a component member of one controlled group. The determination as to the group of which such corporation is a component member shall be made under regulations prescribed by the Secretary which are consistent with the purposes of this part.

(C) If stock is owned by a person within the meaning of subsection (d) and such ownership results in the corporation being a component member of a controlled group, such stock shall not be treated as excluded stock under subsection (c)(2), if by reason of treating such stock as excluded stock the result is that such corporation is not a component member of a controlled group of corporations.

* * *

SUBTITLE F—PROCEDURE AND ADMINISTRATION

Chapter 68—Additions to the Tax, Additional Amounts, and Assessable Penalties

§ 6662. Imposition of accuracy-related penalty on underpayments

(a) Imposition of penalty.—If this section applies to any portion of an underpayment of tax required to be shown on a return, there shall be added to the tax an amount equal to 20 percent of the portion of the underpayment to which this section applies.

* * *

(d) Substantial understatement of income tax

(1) Substantial understatement

(A) In general—For purposes of this section, there is a substantial understatement of income tax for any taxable year if the amount of the understatement for the taxable year exceeds the greater of—

(i) 10 percent of the tax required to be shown on the return for the taxable year, or

(ii) $5,000.

* * *

(C) Special rule for taxpayers claiming section 199A deduction.—In the case of any taxpayer who claims the deduction allowed under section 199A for the taxable year, subparagraph (A) shall be applied by substituting '5 percent' for '10 percent.'

Chapter 79—Definitions

§ 7701. Definitions.

(a) When used in this title, where not otherwise distinctly expressed or manifestly incompatible with the intent thereof—

(1) Person.—The term 'person' shall be construed to mean and include an individual, a trust, estate, partnership, association, company or corporation.

(2) Partnership and partner.—The term 'partnership' includes a syndicate, group, pool, joint venture, or other unincorporated organization, through or by means of which any business, financial operation, or venture is carried on, and which is not, within the meaning of this title, a trust or estate or a corporation; and the term 'partner' includes a member in such a syndicate, group, pool, joint venture, or organization.

(3) Corporation.—The term 'corporation' includes associations, joint-stock companies, and insurance companies.

* * *

(7) Stock.—The term "stock" includes shares in an association, joint-stock company, or insurance company.

(8) Shareholder.—The term "shareholder" includes a member in an association, joint-stock company, or insurance company.

* * *

(23) Taxable year.—The term "taxable year" means the calendar year, or the fiscal year ending during such calendar year, upon the basis of which the taxable income is computed under subtitle A. "Taxable year" means, in the case of a return made for a fractional part of a year under the provisions of subtitle A or under regulations prescribed by the Secretary, the period for which such return is made.

(24) Fiscal year.—The term "fiscal year" means an accounting period of 12 months ending on the last day of any month other than December.

* * *

(26) Trade or business.—The term "trade or business" includes the performance of the functions of a public office.

* * *

(42) Substituted basis property.—The term "substituted basis property" means property which is—

    (A) transferred basis property, or

    (B) exchanged basis property.

(43) Transferred basis property.—The term "transferred basis property" means property having a basis determined under any provision of subtitle A (or under any corresponding provision of prior income tax law) providing that the basis shall be determined in whole or in part by reference to the basis in the hands of the donor, grantor, or other transferor.

(44) Exchanged basis property.—The term "exchanged basis property" means property having a basis determined under any provision of subtitle A (or under any corresponding provision of prior income tax law) providing that the basis shall be determined in whole or in part by reference to other property held at any time by the person for whom the basis is to be determined.

(45) Nonrecognition transaction.—The term "nonrecognition transaction" means any disposition of property in a transaction in which gain or loss is not recognized in whole or in part for purposes of subtitle A.

* * *

(*o*) Clarification of economic substance doctrine.—

(1) Application of doctrine.—In the case of any transaction to which the economic substance doctrine is relevant, such transaction shall be treated as having economic substance only if—

    (A) the transaction changes in a meaningful way (apart from Federal income tax effects) the taxpayer's economic position, and

    (B) the taxpayer has a substantial purpose (apart from Federal income tax effects) for entering into such transaction.

(2) Special rule where taxpayer relies on profit potential.—

(A) In general.—The potential for profit of a transaction shall be taken into account in determining whether the requirements of subparagraphs (A) and (B) of paragraph (1) are met with respect to the transaction only if the present value of the reasonably expected pre-tax profit from the transaction is substantial in relation to the present value of the expected net tax benefits that would be allowed if the transaction were respected.

(B) Treatment of fees and foreign taxes.—Fees and other transaction expenses shall be taken into account as expenses in determining pre-tax profit under subparagraph (A). The Secretary shall issue regulations requiring foreign taxes to be treated as expenses in determining pre-tax profit in appropriate cases.

(3) State and local tax benefits.—For purposes of paragraph (1), any State or local income tax effect which is related to a Federal income tax effect shall be treated in the same manner as a Federal income tax effect.

(4) Financial accounting benefits.—For purposes of paragraph (1)(B), achieving a financial accounting benefit shall not be taken into account as a purpose for entering into a transaction if the origin of such financial accounting benefit is a reduction of Federal income tax.

(5) Definitions and special rules.—For purposes of this subsection—

(A) Economic substance doctrine.—The term 'economic substance doctrine' means the common law doctrine under which tax benefits under subtitle A with respect to a transaction are not allowable if the transaction does not have economic substance or lacks a business purpose.

(B) Exception for personal transactions of individuals.—In the case of an individual, paragraph (1) shall apply only to transactions entered into in connection with a trade or business or an activity engaged in for the production of income.

(C) Determination of application of doctrine not affected.—The determination of whether the economic substance doctrine is relevant to a transaction shall be made in the same manner as if this subsection had never been enacted.

(D) Transaction.—The term 'transaction' includes a series of transactions.

* * *

§ 7704. Certain publicly traded partnerships treated as corporations.

(a) General rule.—For purposes of this title, except as provided in subsection (c), a publicly traded partnership shall be treated as a corporation.

(b) Publicly traded partnership.—For purposes of this section, the term "publicly traded partnership" means any partnership if—

(1) interests in such partnership are traded on an established securities market, or

(2) interests in such partnership are readily tradable on a secondary market (or the substantial equivalent thereof).

(c) Exception for partnerships with passive-type income.—

(1) In general.—Subsection (a) shall not apply to any publicly traded partnership for any taxable year if such partnership met the gross income requirements of paragraph (2) for such taxable year and each preceding taxable year beginning after December 31, 1987, during which the partnership (or any predecessor) was in existence. For purposes of the preceding sentence, a partnership shall not be treated as being in existence during any period before the 1st taxable year in which such partnership (or a predecessor) was a publicly traded partnership.

(2) Gross income requirements.—A partnership meets the gross income requirements of this paragraph for any taxable year if 90 percent or more of the gross income of such partnership for such taxable year consists of qualifying income.

(3) Exception not to apply to certain partnerships which could qualify as regulated investment companies.—This subsection shall not apply to any partnership which would be described in section 851(a) if such partnership were a domestic corporation. To the extent provided in regulations, the preceding sentence shall not apply to any partnership a principal activity of which is the buying and selling of commodities (not described in section 1221(1)), or options, futures, or forwards with respect to commodities.

(d) Qualifying income.—For purposes of this section—

(1) In general.—Except as otherwise provided in this subsection, the term "qualifying income" means—

(A) interest,

(B) dividends,

(C) real property rents,

(D) gain from the sale or other disposition of real property (including property described in section 1221(1)),

(E) income and gains derived from the exploration, development, mining or production, processing, refining, transportation (including pipelines transporting gas, oil, or products thereof), or the marketing of any mineral or natural resource (including fertilizer, geothermal energy, and timber),

(F) any gain from the sale or disposition of a capital asset (or property described in section 1231(b)) held for the production of income described in any of the foregoing subparagraphs of this paragraph, and

(G) in the case of a partnership described in the second sentence of subsection (c) (3), income and gains from commodities (not described in section 1221(1)) or futures, forwards, and options with respect to commodities.

For purposes of subparagraph (E), the term "mineral or natural resource" means any product of a character with respect to which a deduction for depletion is allowable under section 611; except that such term shall not include any product described in subparagraph (A) or (B) of section 613(b)(7).

(2) Certain interest not qualified.—Interest shall not be treated as qualifying income if—

(A) such interest is derived in the conduct of a financial or insurance business, or

(B) such interest would be excluded from the term "interest" under section 856(f).

(3) Real property rent.—The term "real property rent" means amounts which would qualify as rent from real property under section 856(d) if—

(**A**) such section were applied without regard to paragraph (2)(C) thereof (relating to independent contractor requirements), and

(**B**) stock owned, directly or indirectly, by or for a partner would not be considered as owned under section 318(a)(3)(A) by the partnership unless 5 percent or more (by value) of the interests in such partnership are owned, directly or indirectly, by or for such partner.

(4) Certain income qualifying under regulated investment company or real estate trust provisions.—The term "qualifying income" also includes any income which would qualify under section 851(b)(2) or 856(c)(2).

(5) Special rule for determining gross income from certain real property sales.—In the case of the sale or other disposition of real property described in section 1221(1), gross income shall not be reduced by inventory costs.

(e) Inadvertent terminations.—If—

(**1**) a partnership fails to meet the gross income requirements of subsection (c)(2),

(**2**) the Secretary determines that such failure was inadvertent,

(**3**) no later than a reasonable time after the discovery of such failure, steps are taken so that such partnership once more meets such gross income requirements, and

(**4**) such partnership agrees to make such adjustments (including adjustments with respect to the partners) or to pay such amounts as may be required by the Secretary with respect to such period, then, notwithstanding such failure, such entity shall be treated as continuing to meet such gross income requirements for such period.

(f) Effect of becoming corporation.—As of the 1st day that a partnership is treated as a corporation under this section, for purposes of this title, such partnership shall be treated as—

(**1**) transferring all of its assets (subject to its liabilities) to a newly formed corporation in exchange for the stock of the corporation, and

(**2**) distributing such stock to its partners in liquidation of their interests in the partnership.

(g) Exception for electing 1987 partnerships.—

(**1**) **In general.**—Subsection (a) shall not apply to an electing 1987 partnership.

(**2**) **Electing 1987 partnership.**—For purposes of this subsection, the term 'electing 1987 partnership' means any publicly traded partnership if—

(**A**) such partnership is an existing partnership (as defined in section 10211(c)(2) of the Revenue Reconciliation Act of 1987),

(**B**) subsection (a) has not applied (and without regard to subsection (c)(1) would not have applied) to such partnership for all prior taxable years beginning after December 31, 1987, and before January 1, 1998, and

(**C**) such partnership elects the application of this subsection, and consents to the application of the tax imposed by paragraph (3), for its first taxable year beginning after December 31, 1997.

A partnership which, but for this sentence, would be treated as an electing 1987 partnership shall cease to be so treated (and the election under subparagraph (C) shall cease to be in effect) as of the 1st day after December 31, 1997, on which there has been an addition of a substantial new line of business with respect to such partnership.

(3) Additional tax on electing partnerships.—

(A) Imposition of tax.—There is hereby imposed for each taxable year on the income of each electing 1987 partnership a tax equal to 3.5 percent of such partnership's gross income for the taxable year from the active conduct of trades and businesses by the partnership.

(B) Adjustments in the case of tiered partnerships.—For purposes of this paragraph, in the case of a partnership which is a partner in another partnership, the gross income referred to in subparagraph (A) shall include the partnership's distributive share of the gross income of such other partnership from the active conduct of trades and businesses of such other partnership. A similar rule shall apply in the case of lower-tiered partnerships.

(C) Treatment of tax.—For purposes of this title, the tax imposed by this paragraph shall be treated as imposed by chapter 1 other than for purposes of determining the amount of any credit allowable under chapter 1 and shall be paid by the partnership. Section 6655 shall be applied to such partnership with respect to such tax in the same manner as if the partnership were a corporation, such tax were imposed by section 11, and references in such section to taxable income were references to the gross income referred to in subparagraph (A).

(4) Election.—An election and consent under this subsection shall apply to the taxable year for which made and all subsequent taxable years unless revoked by the partnership. Such revocation may be made without the consent of the Secretary, but, once so revoked, may not be reinstated.

TREASURY REGULATIONS

Current Through March 31, 2019

Computation of Taxable Income

§ 1.83–1 Property transferred in connection with the performance of services.

(a) Inclusion in gross income—(1) General rule. Section 83 provides rules for the taxation of property transferred to an employee or independent contractor (or beneficiary thereof) in connection with the performance of services by such employee or independent contractor. In general, such property is not taxable under section 83(a) until it has been transferred (as defined in § 1.83–3(a)) to such person and become substantially vested (as defined in § 1.83–3(b)) in such person. In that case, the excess of—

(i) The fair market value of such property (determined without regard to any lapse restriction, as defined in § 1.83–3(i)) at the time that the property becomes substantially vested, over

(ii) The amount (if any) paid for such property,

shall be included as compensation in the gross income of such employee or independent contractor for the taxable year in which the property becomes substantially vested. Until such property becomes substantially vested, the transferor shall be regarded as the owner of such property, and any income from such property received by the employee or independent contractor (or beneficiary thereof) or the right to the use of such property by the employee or independent contractor constitutes additional compensation and shall be included in the gross income of such employee or independent contractor for the taxable year in which such income is received or such use is made available. This paragraph applies to a transfer of property in connection with the performance of services even though the transferor is not the person for whom such services are performed.

* * *

(b) Subsequent sale, forfeiture, or other disposition of nonvested property. (1) If substantially nonvested property (that has been transferred in connection with the performance of services) is subsequently sold or otherwise disposed of to a third party in an arm's length transaction while still substantially nonvested, the person who performed such services shall realize compensation in an amount equal to the excess of—

(i) The amount realized on such sale or other disposition, over

(ii) The amount (if any) paid for such property.

Such amount of compensation is includible in his gross income in accordance with his method of accounting. Two preceding sentences also apply when the person disposing of the property has received it in a non-arm's length transaction described in paragraph (c) of this section. In addition, section 83(a) and paragraph (a) of this section shall thereafter cease to apply with respect to such property.

(2) If substantially nonvested property that has been transferred in connection with the performance of services to the person performing such services is forfeited while still substantially nonvested and held by such person, the difference between the amount paid (if any) and the amount received upon forfeiture (if any) shall be treated as an ordinary gain or loss. This paragraph (b)(2) does not apply to property to which § 1.83–2(a) applies.

(3) This paragraph (b) shall not apply to, and no gain shall be recognized on, any sale, forfeiture, or other disposition described in this paragraph to the extent that any property received in exchange therefor is substantially nonvested. Instead, section 83 and this section shall apply with respect to such property received (as if it were substituted for the property disposed of).

(c) Dispositions of nonvested property not at arm's length. If substantially nonvested property (that has been transferred in connection with the performance of services) is disposed of in a transaction which is not at arm's length and the property remains substantially nonvested, the person who performed such services realizes compensation equal in amount to the sum of any money and the fair market value of any substantially vested property received in such disposition. Such amount of compensation is includible in his gross income in accordance with his method of accounting. However, such amount of compensation shall not exceed the fair market value of the property disposed of at the time of disposition (determined without regard to any lapse restriction), reduced by the amount paid for such property. In addition, section 83 and these regulations shall continue to apply with respect to such property, except that any amount previously includible in gross income under this paragraph (c) shall thereafter be treated as an amount paid for such property. For example, if in 1971 an employee pays $50 for a share of stock which has a fair market value of $100 and is substantially nonvested at that time and later in 1971 (at a time when the property still has a fair market value of $100 and is still substantially nonvested) the employee disposes of, in a transaction not at arm's length, the share of stock to his wife for $10, the employee realizes compensation of $10 in 1971. If in 1972, when the share of stock has a fair market value of $120, it becomes substantially vested, the employee realizes additional compensation in 1972 in the amount of $60 (the $120 fair market value of the stock less both the $50 price paid for the stock and the $10 taxed as compensation in 1971). For purposes of this paragraph, if substantially nonvested property has been transferred to a person other than the person who performed the services, and the transferee dies holding the property while the property is still substantially nonvested and while the person who performed the services is alive, the transfer which results by reason of the death of such transferee is a transfer not at arm's length.

(d) Certain transfers upon death. If substantially nonvested property has been transferred in connection with the performance of services and the person who performed such services dies while the property is still substantially nonvested, any income realized on or after such death with respect to such property under this section is income in respect of a decedent to which the rules of section 691 apply. In such a case the income in respect of such property shall be taxable under section 691 (except to the extent not includible under section 101(b)) to the estate or beneficiary of the person who performed the services, in accordance with section 83 and the regulations thereunder. However, if an item of income is realized upon such death before July 21, 1978, because the property became substantially vested upon death, the person responsible for filing decedent's income tax return for decedent's last taxable year may elect to treat such item as includible in gross income for decedent's last taxable year by including such item in gross income on the return or amended return filed for decedent's last taxable year.

(e) Forfeiture after substantial vesting. If a person is taxable under section 83(a) when the property transferred becomes substantially vested and thereafter the person's beneficial interest in such property is nevertheless forfeited pursuant to a lapse restriction, any loss incurred by such person (but not by a beneficiary of such person) upon such forfeiture shall be an ordinary loss to the extent the basis in such property has been increased as a result of the recognition of income by such person under section 83(a) with respect to such property.

(f) Examples. The provisions of this section may be illustrated by the following examples:

Example (1). On November 1, 1978, X corporation sells to E, an employee, 100 shares of X corporation stock at $10 per share. At the time of such sale the fair market value of the X corporation stock is $100 per share. Under the terms of the sale each share of stock is subject to a substantial risk of forfeiture which will not lapse until November 1, 1988. Evidence of this restriction is stamped on the face of E's stock certificates, which are therefore nontransferable (within the meaning of § 1.83–3(d)). Since in 1978 E's stock is substantially nonvested, E does not include any of such amount in his gross income as compensation in 1978. On November 1, 1988, the fair market value of the X corporation stock is $250 per share. Since the X corporation stock becomes substantially vested in 1988, E must include $24,000 (100 shares of X corporation stock x $250 fair market value per share less $10 price paid by E for each share) as compensation for 1988. Dividends paid by X to E on E's stock after it was transferred to E on November 1, 1973, are taxable to E as additional compensation during the period E's stock is substantially nonvested and are deductible as such by X.

Example (2). Assume the facts are the same as in example (1), except that on November 1, 1985, each share of stock of X corporation in E's hands could as a matter of law be transferred to a bona fide purchaser who would not be required to forfeit the stock if the risk of forfeiture materialized. In the event, however, that the risk materializes, E would be liable in damages to X. On November 1, 1985, the fair market value of the X corporation stock is $230 per share. Since E's stock is transferable within the meaning of § 1.83–3(d) in 1985, the stock is substantially vested and E must include $22,000 (100 shares of X corporation

stock x $230 fair market value per share less $10 price paid by E for each share) as compensation for 1985.

Example (3). Assume the facts are the same as in example (1) except that, in 1984 E sells his 100 shares of X corporation stock in an arm's length sale to I, an investment company, for $120 per share. At the time of this sale each share of X corporation's stock has a fair market value of $200. Under paragraph (b) of this section, E must include $11,000 (100 shares of X corporation stock x $120 amount realized per share less $10 price paid by E per share) as compensation for 1984 notwithstanding that the stock remains nontransferable and is still subject to a substantial risk of forfeiture at the time of such sale. Under § 1.83–4(b)(2), I's basis in the X corporation stock is $120 per share.

§ 1.83–2 Election to include in gross income in year of transfer.

(a) In general. If property is transferred (within the meaning of § 1.83–3(a)) in connection with the performance of services, the person performing such services may elect to include in gross income under section 83(b) the excess (if any) of the fair market value of the property at the time of transfer (determined without regard to any lapse restriction, as defined in § 1.83–3(i)) over the amount (if any) paid for such property, as compensation for services. The fact that the transferee has paid full value for the property transferred, realizing no bargain element in the transaction, does not preclude the use of the election as provided for in this section. If this election is made, the substantial vesting rules of section 83(a) and the regulations thereunder do not apply with respect to such property, and except as otherwise provided in section 83(d)(2) and the regulations thereunder (relating to the cancellation of a nonlapse restriction), any subsequent appreciation in the value of the property is not taxable as compensation to the person who performed the services. Thus, property with respect to which this election is made shall be includible in gross income as of the time of transfer, even though such property is substantially nonvested (as defined in § 1.83–3(b)) at the time of transfer, and no compensation will be includible in gross income when such property becomes substantially vested (as defined in § 1.83–3(b)). In computing the gain or loss from the subsequent sale or exchange of such property, its basis shall be the amount paid for the property increased by the amount included in gross income under section 83(b). If property for which a section 83(b) election is in effect is forfeited while substantially nonvested, such forfeiture shall be treated as a sale or exchange upon which there is realized a loss equal to the excess (if any) of—

(1) The amount paid (if any) for such property, over,

(2) The amount realized (if any) upon such forfeiture.

If such property is a capital asset in the hands of the taxpayer, such loss shall be a capital loss. A sale or other disposition of the property that is in substance a forfeiture, or is made in contemplation of a forfeiture, shall be treated as a forfeiture under the two immediately preceding sentences.

(b) Time for making election. Except as provided in the following sentence, the election referred to in paragraph (a) of this section shall be filed not later than 30 days after the date the property was transferred (or, if later, January 29, 1970) and may be filed prior to the date of transfer. Any statement filed before February 15, 1970, which was amended not later than February 16, 1970, in order to make it conform to the requirements of paragraph (e) of this section, shall be deemed a proper election under section 83(b).

(c) Manner of making election. The election referred to in paragraph (a) of this section is made by filing one copy of a written statement with the internal revenue office with which the person who performed the services files his return.

(d) Additional copies. The person who performed the services shall also submit a copy of the statement referred to in paragraph (c) of this section to the person for whom the services are performed. In addition, if the person who performs the services and the transferee of such property are not the same person, the person who performs the services shall submit a copy of such statement to the transferee of the property.

(e) Content of statement. The statement shall be signed by the person making the election and shall indicate that it is being made under section 83(b) of the Code, and shall contain the following information:

(1) The name, address and taxpayer identification number of the taxpayer;

(2) A description of each property with respect to which the election is being made;

(3) The date or dates on which the property is transferred and the taxable year (for example, "calendar year 1970" or "fiscal year ending May 31, 1970") for which such election was made;

(4) The nature of the restriction or restrictions to which the property is subject;

(5) The fair market value at the time of transfer (determined without regard to any lapse restriction, as defined in § 1.83–3(i)) of each property with respect to which the election is being made;

(6) The amount (if any) paid for such property; and

(7) With respect to elections made after July 21, 1978, a statement to the effect that copies have been furnished to other persons as provided in paragraph (d) of this section.

(f) Revocability of election. An election under section 83(b) may not be revoked except with the consent of the Commissioner. Consent will be granted only in the case where the transferee is under a mistake of fact as to the underlying transaction and must be requested within 60 days of the date on which the mistake of fact first became known to the person who made the election. In any event, a mistake as to the value, or decline in the value, of the property with respect to which an election under section 83(b) has been made or a failure to perform an act contemplated at the time of transfer of such property does not constitute a mistake of fact.

§ 1.83–3 Meaning and use of certain terms.

(a) Transfer — (1) In general. For purposes of section 83 and the regulations thereunder, a transfer of property occurs when a person acquires a beneficial ownership interest in such property (disregarding any lapse restriction, as defined in § 1.83–3(i)). For special rules applying to the transfer of a life insurance contract (or an undivided interest therein) that is part of a split-dollar life insurance arrangement (as defined in § 1.61–22(b)(1) or (2)), see § 1.61–22(g).

(2) Option. The grant of an option to purchase certain property does not constitute a transfer of such property. However, see § 1.83–7 for the extent to which the grant of the option itself is subject to section 83. In addition, if the amount paid for the transfer of property is an indebtedness secured by the transferred property, on which there is no personal liability to pay all or a substantial part of such indebtedness, such transaction may be in substance the same as the grant of an option. The determination of the substance of the transaction shall be based upon all the facts and circumstances. The factors to be taken into account include the type of property involved, the extent to which the risk that the property will decline in value has been transferred, and the likelihood that the purchase price will, in fact, be paid. See also § 1.83–4(c) for the treatment of forgiveness of indebtedness that has constituted an amount paid.

(3) Requirement that property be returned. Similarly, no transfer may have occurred where property is transferred under conditions that require its return upon the happening of an event that is certain to occur, such as the termination of employment. In such a case, whether there is, in fact, a transfer depends upon all the facts and circumstances. Factors which indicate that no transfer has occurred are described in paragraph (a)(4), (5), and (6) of this section.

(4) Similarity to option. An indication that no transfer has occurred is the extent to which the conditions relating to a transfer are similar to an option.

(5) Relationship to fair market value. An indication that no transfer has occurred is the extent to which the consideration to be paid the transferee upon surrendering the property does not approach the fair market value of the property at the time of surrender. For purposes of paragraph (a)(5) and (6) of this section, fair market value includes fair market value determined under the rules of § 1.83–5(a)(1), relating to the valuation of property subject to nonlapse restrictions. Therefore, the existence of a nonlapse restriction referred to in § 1.83–5(a)(1) is not a factor indicating no transfer has occurred.

(6) Risk of loss. An indication that no transfer has occurred is the extent to which the transferee does not incur the risk of a beneficial owner that the value of the property at the time of transfer will decline substantially. Therefore, for purposes of this (6), risk of decline in property value is not limited to the risk that any amount paid for the property may be lost.

(7) Examples. The provisions of this paragraph may be illustrated by the following examples:

Example (1). On January 3, 1971, X corporation sells for $500 to S, a salesman of X, 10 shares of stock in X corporation with a fair market value of $1,000. The stock is nontransferable and subject to return to the corporation (for $500) if S's sales do not reach a certain level by December 31, 1971. Disregarding the restriction concerning S's sales (since the restriction is a lapse restriction), S's interest in the stock is that of a beneficial owner and therefore a transfer occurs on January 3, 1971.

Example (2). On November 17, 1972, W sells to E 100 shares of stock in W corporation with a fair market value of $10,000 in exchange for a $10,000 note without personal liability. The note requires E to make yearly payments of $2,000 commencing in 1973. E collects the dividends, votes the stock and pays the interest on the note. However, he makes no payments toward the face amount of the note. Because E has no personal liability on the note, and since E is making no payments towards the face amount of the note, the likelihood of E paying the full purchase price is in substantial doubt. As a result E has not incurred the risks of a beneficial owner that the value of the stock will decline. Therefore, no transfer of the stock has occurred on November 17, 1972, but an option to purchase the stock has been granted to E.

Example (3). On January 3, 1971, X corporation purports to transfer to E, an employee, 100 shares of stock in X corporation. The X stock is subject to the sole restriction that E must sell such stock to X on termination of employment for any reason for an amount which is equal to the excess (if any) of the book value of the X stock at termination of employment over book value on January 3, 1971. The stock is not transferable by E and the restrictions on transfer are stamped on the certificate. Under these facts and circumstances, there is no transfer of the X stock within the meeting of section 83.

Example (4). Assume the same facts as in example (3) except that E paid $3,000 for the stock and that the restriction required E upon termination of employment to sell the stock to M for the total amount of dividends that have been declared on the stock since September 2, 1971, or $3,000 whichever is higher. Again, under the facts and circumstances, no transfer of the X stock has occurred.

Example (5). On July 4, 1971, X corporation purports to transfer to G, an employee, 100 shares of X stock. The stock is subject to the sole restriction that upon termination of employment G must sell the stock to X for the greater of its fair market value at such time or $100, the amount G paid for the stock. On July 4, 1971 the X stock has a fair market value of $100. Therefore, G does not incur the risk of a beneficial owner that the value of the stock at the time of transfer ($100) will decline substantially. Under these facts and circumstances, no transfer has occurred.

(b) Substantially vested and substantially nonvested property. For purposes of section 83 and the regulations thereunder, property is substantially nonvested when it is subject to a substantial risk of forfeiture, within the meaning of paragraph (c) of this section, and is nontransferable, within the meaning of paragraph (d) of this section. Property is substantially vested for such purposes when it is either transferable or not subject to a substantial risk of forfeiture.

(c) Substantial risk of forfeiture—(1) In general. For purposes of section 83 and the regulations thereunder, whether a risk of forfeiture is substantial or not depends upon the facts and circumstances. A substantial risk of forfeiture exists where rights in property that are transferred are conditioned, directly or indirectly, upon the future performance (or refraining from performance) of substantial services by any person, or the occurrence of a condition related to a purpose of the transfer, and the possibility of forfeiture is substantial if such condition is not satisfied.

Property is not transferred subject to a substantial risk of forfeiture to the extent that the employer is required to pay the fair market value of a portion of such property to the employee upon the return of such property. The risk that the value of property will decline during a certain period of time does not constitute a substantial risk of forfeiture. A nonlapse restriction, standing by itself, will not result in a substantial risk of forfeiture.

(2) Illustrations of substantial risks of forfeiture. The regularity of the performance of services and the time spent in performing such services tend to indicate whether services required by a condition are substantial. The fact that the person performing services has the right to decline to perform such services without forfeiture may tend to establish that services are insubstantial. Where stock is transferred to an underwriter prior to a public offering and the full enjoyment of such stock is expressly or impliedly conditioned upon the successful completion of the underwriting, the stock is subject to a substantial risk of forfeiture. Where an employee receives property from an employer subject to a requirement that it be returned if the total earnings of the employer do not increase, such property is subject to a substantial risk of forfeiture. On the other hand, requirements that the property be returned to the employer if the employee is discharged for cause or for committing a crime will not be considered to result in a substantial risk of forfeiture. An enforceable requirement that the property be returned to the employer if the employee accepts a job with a competing firm will not ordinarily be considered to result in a substantial risk of forfeiture unless the particular facts and circumstances indicate to the contrary. Factors which may be taken into account in determining whether a covenant not to compete constitutes a substantial risk of forfeiture are the age of the employee, the availability of alternative employment opportunities, the likelihood of the employee's obtaining such other employment, the degree of skill possessed by the employee, the employee's health, and the practice (if any) of the employer to enforce such covenants. Similarly, rights in property transferred to a retiring employee subject to the sole requirement that it be returned unless he renders consulting services upon the request of his former employer will not be considered subject to a substantial risk of forfeiture unless he is in fact expected to perform substantial services.

(3) Enforcement of forfeiture condition. In determining whether the possibility of forfeiture is substantial in the case of rights in property transferred to an employee of a corporation who owns a significant amount of the total combined voting power or value of all classes of stock of the employer corporation or of its parent corporation, there will be taken into account (i) the employee's relationship to other stockholders and the extent of their control, potential control and possible loss of control of the corporation, (ii) the position of the employee in the corporation and the extent to which he is subordinate to other employees, (iii) the employee's relationship to the officers and directors of the corporation, (iv) the person or persons who must approve the employee's discharge, and (v) past actions of the employer in enforcing the provisions of the restrictions. For example, if an employee would be considered as having received rights in property subject to a substantial risk of forfeiture, but for the fact that the employee owns 20 percent of the single class of stock in the transferor corporation, and if the remaining 80 percent of the class of stock is owned by an unrelated individual (or members of such an individual's family) so that the possibility of the corporation enforcing a restriction on such rights is substantial, then such rights are subject to a substantial risk of forfeiture. On the other hand, if 4 percent of the voting power of all the stock of a corporation is owned by the president of such corporation and the remaining stock is so diversely held by the public that the president, in effect, controls the corporation, then the possibility of the corporation enforcing a restriction on rights in property transferred to the president is not substantial, and such rights are not subject to a substantial risk of forfeiture.

(4) Examples. The rules contained in paragraph (c)(1) of this section may be illustrated by the following examples. In each example it is assumed that, if the conditions on transfer are not satisfied, the forfeiture provision will be enforced.

Example (1). On November 1, 1971, corporation X transfers in connection with the performance of services to E, an employee, 100 shares of corporation X stock for $90 per share. Under the terms of the transfer, E will be subject to a binding commitment to resell the stock to corporation X at $90 per share if he leaves the employment of corporation X for any reason prior to the expiration of a 2-year period from the date of such transfer. Since E must perform substantial services for corporation X and will not be paid more than $90 for the stock, regardless of its value, if he fails to perform such services during such 2-year period, E's rights in the stock are subject to a substantial risk of forfeiture during such period.

Example (2). On November 10, 1971, corporation X transfers in connection with the performance of services to a trust for the benefit of employees, $100x. Under the terms of the trust any child of an employee who is an enrolled full-time student at an accredited educational institution as a candidate for a degree will receive an annual grant of cash for each academic year the student completes as a student in good standing, up to a maximum of four years. E, an employee, has a child who is enrolled as a full-time student at an accredited college as a candidate for a degree. Therefore, E has a beneficial interest in the assets of the trust equalling the value of four cash grants. Since E's child must complete one year of college in order to receive a cash grant, E's interest in the trust assets are subject to a substantial risk of forfeiture to the extent E's child has not become entitled to any grants.

Example (3). On November 25, 1971, corporation X gives to E, an employee, in connection with his performance of services to corporation X, a bonus of 100 shares of corporation X stock. Under the terms of the bonus arrangement E is obligated to return the corporation X stock to corporation X if he ter-

minates his employment for any reason. However, for each year occurring after November 25, 1971, during which E remains employed with corporation X, E ceases to be obligated to return 10 shares of the corporation X stock. Since in each year occurring after November 25, 1971, for which E remains employed he is not required to return 10 shares of corporation X's stock, E's rights in 10 shares each year for 10 years cease to be subject to a substantial risk of forfeiture for each year he remains so employed.

* * *

(e) Property. For purposes of section 83 and the regulations thereunder, the term "property" includes real and personal property other than either money or an unfunded and unsecured promise to pay money or property in the future. The term also includes a beneficial interest in assets (including money) which are transferred or set aside from the claims of creditors of the transferor, for example, in a trust or escrow account. See, however, § 1.83–8(a) with respect to employee trusts and annuity plans subject to section 402(b) and section 403(c). In the case of a transfer of a life insurance contract, retirement income contract, endowment contract, or other contract providing life insurance protection, only the cash surrender value of the contract is considered to be property. Notwithstanding the previous sentence, in the case of a transfer of a life insurance contract, retirement income contract, endowment contract, or other contract providing life insurance protection, or any undivided interest therein, that is part of a split-dollar life insurance arrangement (as defined in § 1.61–22(b)(1) or (2)) that is entered into, or materially modified (within the meaning of § 1.61–22(j)(2)), after September 17, 2003, the policy cash value and all other rights under such contract (including any supplemental agreements thereto and whether or not guaranteed), other than current life insurance protection, are treated as property for purposes of this section. Where rights in a contract providing life insurance protection are substantially nonvested, see § 1.83–1(a)(2) for rules relating to taxation of the cost of life insurance protection.

(f) Property transferred in connection with the performance of services. Property transferred to an employee or an independent contractor (or beneficiary thereof) in recognition of the performance of, or the refraining from performance of, services is considered transferred in connection with the performance of services within the meaning of section 83. The existence of other persons entitled to buy stock on the same terms and conditions as an employee, whether pursuant to a public or private offering may, however, indicate that in such circumstances a transfer to the employee is not in recognition of the performance of, or the refraining from performance of, services. The transfer of property is subject to section 83 whether such transfer is in respect of past, present, or future services.

(g) Amount paid. For purposes of section 83 and the regulations thereunder, the term "amount paid" refers to the value of any money or property paid for the transfer of property to which section 83 applies, and does not refer to any amount paid for the right to use such property or to receive the income therefrom. Such value does not include any stated or unstated interest payments. For rules regarding the calculation of the amount of unstated interest payments, see § 1.483–1(c). When section 83 applies to the transfer of property pursuant to the exercise of an option, the term "amount paid" refers to any amount paid for the grant of the option plus any amount paid as the exercise price of the option. For rules regarding the forgiveness of indebtedness treated as an amount paid, see § 1.83–4(c).

(h) Nonlapse restriction. For purposes of section 83 and the regulations thereunder, a restriction which by its terms will never lapse (also referred to as a "nonlapse restriction") is a permanent limitation on the transferability of property—

(1) Which will require the transferee of the property to sell, or offer to sell, such property at a price determined under a formula, and

(2) Which will continue to apply to and be enforced against the transferee or any subsequent holder (other than the transferor).

A limitation subjecting the property to a permanent right of first refusal in a particular person at a price determined under a formula is a permanent nonlapse restriction. Limitations imposed by registration requirements of State or Federal security laws or similar laws imposed with respect to sales or other dispositions of stock or securities are not nonlapse restrictions. An obligation to resell or to offer to sell property transferred in connection with the performance of services to a specific person or persons at its fair market value at the time of such sale is not a nonlapse restriction. See § 1.83–5(c) for examples of nonlapse restrictions.

(i) Lapse restriction. For purposes of section 83 and the regulations thereunder, the term "lapse restriction" means a restriction other than a nonlapse restriction as defined in paragraph (h) of this section, and includes (but is not limited to) a restriction that carries a substantial risk of forfeiture.

(j) Sales which may give rise to suit under section 16(b) of the Securities Exchange Act of 1934—(1) In general. For purposes of section 83 and the regulations thereunder if the sale of property at a profit within six months after the purchase of the property could subject a person to suit under section 16(b) of the Securities Exchange Act of 1934, the person's rights in the property are treated as subject to a substantial risk of forfeiture and as not transferable until the earlier of (i) the expiration of such six-month period, or (ii) the first day on which the sale of such property at a profit will not subject the person to suit under section 16(b) of the Securities Exchange Act of 1934. However, whether an option is "transferable by the optionee" for purposes of § 1.83–7(b)

(2)(i) is determined without regard to section 83(c)(3) and this paragraph (j).

(2) Examples. The provisions of this paragraph may be illustrated by the following examples:

Example (1). On January 1, 1983, X corporation sells to P, a beneficial owner of 12% of X corporation stock, in connection with P's performance of services, 100 shares of X corporation stock at $10 per share. At the time of the sale the fair market value of the X corporation stock is $100 per share. P, as a beneficial owner of more than 10% of X corporation stock, is liable to suit under section 16(b) of the Securities Exchange Act of 1934 for recovery of any profit from any sale and purchase or purchase and sale of X corporation stock within a six-month period, but no other restrictions apply to the stock. Because the section 16(b) restriction is applicable to P, P's rights in the 100 shares of stock purchased on January 1, 1983, are treated as subject to a substantial risk of forfeiture and as not transferable through June 29, 1983. P chooses not to make an election under section 83(b) and therefore does not include any amount with respect to the stock purchase in gross income as compensation on the date of purchase. On June 30, 1983, the fair market value of X corporation stock is $250 per share. P must include $24,000 (100 shares of X corporation stock x $240 ($250 fair market value per share less $10 price paid by P for each share)) in gross income as compensation on June 30, 1983. If, in this example, restrictions other than section 16(b) applied to the stock, such other restrictions (but not section 16(b)) would be taken into account in determining whether the stock is subject to a substantial risk of forfeiture and is nontransferable for periods after June 29, 1983.

Example (2). Assume the same facts as in example (1) except that P is not an insider on or after May 1, 1983, and the section 16(b) restriction does not apply beginning on that date. On May 1, 1983, P must include in gross income as compensation the difference between the fair market value of the stock on that date and the amount paid for the stock.

Example (3). Assume the same facts as in example (1) except that on June 1, 1983, X corporation sells to P an additional 100 shares of X corporation stock at $20 per share. At the time of the sale the fair market value of the X corporation stock is $150 per share. On June 30, 1983, P must include $24,000 in gross income as compensation with respect to the January 1, 1983 purchase. On November 30, 1983, the fair market value of X corporation stock is $200 per share. Accordingly, on that date P must include $18,000 (100 shares of X corporation stock x $180 ($200 fair market value per share less $20 price paid by P for each share)) in gross income as compensation with respect to the June 1, 1983 purchase.

* * *

§ 1.83–4 Special rules.

(a) Holding period. Under section 83(f), the holding period of transferred property to which section 83(a) applies shall begin just after such property is substantially vested. However, if the person who has performed the services in connection with which property is transferred has made an election under section 83(b), the holding period of such property shall begin just after the date such property is transferred. If property to which section 83 and the regulations thereunder apply is transferred at arm's length, the holding period of such property in the hands of the transferee shall be determined in accordance with the rules provided in section 1223.

(b) Basis. (1) Except as provided in paragraph (b)(2) of this section, if property to which section 83 and the regulations thereunder apply is acquired by any person (including a person who acquires such property in a subsequent transfer which is not at arm's length), while such property is still substantially nonvested, such person's basis for the property shall reflect any amount paid for such property and any amount includible in the gross income of the person who performed the services (including any amount so includible as a result of a disposition by the person who acquired such property.) Such basis shall also reflect any adjustments to basis provided under sections 1015 and 1016.

(2) If property to which § 1.83–1 applies is transferred at arm's length, the basis of the property in the hands of the transferee shall be determined under section 1012 and the regulations thereunder.

(c) Forgiveness of indebtedness treated as an amount paid. If an indebtedness that has been treated as an amount paid under § 1.83–1(a)(1)(ii) is subsequently cancelled, forgiven or satisfied for an amount less than the amount of such indebtedness, the amount that is not, in fact, paid shall be includible in the gross income of the service provider in the taxable year in which such cancellation, forgiveness or satisfaction occurs.

§ 1.83–5 Restrictions that will never lapse.

(a) Valuation. For purposes of section 83 and the regulations thereunder, in the case of property subject to a nonlapse restriction (as defined in § 1.83–3(h)), the price determined under the formula price will be considered to be the fair market value of the property unless established to the contrary by the Commissioner, and the burden of proof shall be on the commissioner with respect to such value. If stock in a corporation is subject to a nonlapse restriction which requires the transferee to sell such stock only at a formula price based on book value, a reasonable multiple of earnings or a reasonable combination thereof, the price so determined will ordinarily be regarded as determinative of the fair market value of such property for purposes of section 83. However, in certain circumstances the formula price will not be considered to be the fair market value of property subject to such a formula price restriction, even though the formula price restriction is a substantial factor in determining such value. For example, where the formula

price is the current book value of stock, the book value of the stock at some time in the future may be a more accurate measure of the value of the stock than the current book value of the stock for purposes of determining the fair market value of the stock at the time the stock becomes substantially vested.

(b) Cancellation—(1) In general. Under section 83(d)(2), if a nonlapse restriction imposed on property that is subject to section 83 is cancelled, then, unless the taxpayer establishes—

(i) That such cancellation was not compensatory, and

(ii) That the person who would be allowed a deduction, if any, if the cancellation were treated as compensatory, will treat the transaction as not compensatory, as provided in paragraph (c)(2) of this section, the excess of the fair market value of such property (computed without regard to such restriction) at the time of cancellation, over the sum of—

(iii) The fair market value of such property (computed by taking the restriction into account) immediately before the cancellation, and

(iv) The amount, if any, paid for the cancellation, shall be treated as compensation for the taxable year in which such cancellation occurs. Whether there has been a noncompensatory cancellation of a nonlapse restriction under section 83(d)(2) depends upon the particular facts and circumstances. Ordinarily the fact that the employee or independent contractor is required to perform additional services or that the salary or payment of such a person is adjusted to take the cancellation into account indicates that such cancellation has a compensatory purpose. On the other hand, the fact that the original purpose of a restriction no longer exists may indicate that the purpose of such cancellation is noncompensatory. Thus, for example, if a so-called "buy-sell" restriction was imposed on a corporation's stock to limit ownership of such stock and is being cancelled in connection with a public offering of the stock, such cancellation will generally be regarded as noncompensatory. However, the mere fact that the employer is willing to forego a deduction under section 83(h) is insufficient evidence to establish a noncompensatory cancellation of a nonlapse restriction. The refusal by a corporation or shareholder to repurchase stock of the corporation which is subject to a permanent right of first refusal will generally be treated as a cancellation of a nonlapse restriction. The preceding sentence shall not apply where there is no nonlapse restriction, for example, where the price to be paid for the stock subject to the right of first refusal is the fair market value of the stock. Section 83(d)(2) and this (1) do not apply where immediately after the cancellation of a nonlapse restriction the property is still substantially nonvested and no section 83(b) election has been made with respect to such property. In such a case the rules of section 83(a) and § 1.83–1 shall apply to such property.

(2) Evidence of noncompensatory cancellation. In addition to the information necessary to establish the factors described in paragraph (b)(1) of this section, the taxpayer shall request the employer to furnish the taxpayer with a written statement indicating that the employer will not treat the cancellation of the nonlapse restriction as a compensatory event, and that no deduction will be taken with respect to such cancellation. The taxpayer shall file such written statement with his income tax return for the taxable year in which or with which such cancellation occurs.

(c) Examples. The provisions of this section may be illustrated by the following examples:

Example (1). On November 1, 1971, X corporation whose shares are closely held and not regularly traded, transfers to E, an employee, 100 shares of X corporation stock subject to the condition that, if he desires to dispose of such stock during the period of his employment, he must resell the stock to his employer

at its then existing book value. In addition, E or E's estate is obligated to offer to sell the stock at his retirement or death to his employer at its then existing book value. Under these facts and circumstances, the restriction to which the shares of X corporation stock are subject is a nonlapse restriction. Consequently, the fair market value of the X stock is includible in E's gross income as compensation for taxable year 1971. However, in determining the fair market value of the X stock, the book value formula price will ordinarily be regarded as being determinative of such value.

Example (2). Assume the facts are the same as in example (1), except that the X stock is subject to the condition that if E desires to dispose of the stock during the period of his employment he must resell the stock to his employer at a multiple of earnings per share that is in this case a reasonable approximation of value at the time of transfer to E. In addition, E or E's estate is obligated to offer to sell the stock at his retirement or death to his employer at the same multiple of earnings. Under these facts and circumstances, the restriction to which the X corporation stock is subject is a nonlapse restriction. Consequently, the fair market value of the X stock is includible in E's gross income for taxable year 1971. However, in determining the fair market value of the X stock, the multiple-of-earnings formula price will ordinarily be regarded as determinative of such value.

Example (3). On January 4, 1971, X corporation transfers to E, an employee, 100 shares of stock in X corporation. Each such share of stock is subject to an agreement between X and E whereby E agrees that such shares are to be held solely for investment purposes and not for resale (a so-called investment letter restriction). E's rights in such stock are substantially vested upon transfer, causing the fair market value of each share of X corporation stock to be includible in E's gross income as compensation for taxable year 1971. Since such an investment letter restriction does not constitute a nonlapse restriction, in determining the fair market value of each share, the investment letter restriction is disregarded.

Example (4). On September 1, 1971, X corporation transfers to B, an independent contractor, 500 shares of common stock in X corporation in exchange for B's agreement to provide services in the construction of an office building on property owned by X corporation. X corporation has 100 shares of preferred stock outstanding and an additional 500 shares of common stock outstanding. The preferred stock has a liquidation value of $1,000x, which is equal to the value of all assets owned by X. Therefore, the book value of the common stock in X corporation is $0. Under the terms of the transfer, if B wishes to dispose of the stock, B must offer to sell the stock to X for 150 percent of the then existing book value of B's common stock. The stock is also subject to a substantial risk of forfeiture until B performs the agreed-upon services. B makes a timely election under section 83(b) to include the value of the stock in gross income in 1971. Under these facts and circumstances, the restriction to which the shares of X corporation common stock are subject is a nonlapse restriction. In determining the fair market value of the X common stock at the time of transfer, the book value formula price would ordinarily be regarded as determinative of such value. However, the fair market value of X common stock at the time of transfer, subject to the book value restriction, is greater than $0 since B was willing to agree to provide valuable personal services in exchange for the stock. In determining the fair market value of the stock, the expected book value after construction of the office building would be given great weight. The likelihood of completion of construction would be a factor in determining the expected book value after completion of construction.

§ 1.83–6 Deduction by employer.

(a) Allowance of deduction—(1) General rule. In the case of a transfer of property in connection with the performance of services, or a compensatory cancellation of a nonlapse restriction described in section 83(d) and § 1.83–5, a deduction is allowable under section 162 or 212 to the person for whom the services were performed. The amount of the deduction is equal to the amount included as compensation in the gross income of the service provider under section 83(a), (b), or (d) (2), but only to the extent the amount meets the requirements of section 162 or 212 and the regulations thereunder. The deduction is allowed only for the taxable year of that person in which or with which ends the taxable year of the service provider in which the amount is included as compensation. For purposes of this paragraph, any amount excluded from gross income under section 79 or section 101(b) or subchapter N is considered to have been included in gross income.

(2) Special rule. For purposes of paragraph (a)(1) of this section, the service provider is deemed to have included the amount as compensation in gross income if the person for whom the services were performed satisfies in a timely manner all requirements of section 6041 or section 6041A, and the regulations thereunder, with respect to that amount of compensation. For purposes of the preceding sentence, whether a person for whom services were performed satisfies all requirements of section 6041 or section 6041A, and the regulations thereunder, is determined without regard to § 1.6041–3(c) (exception for payments to corporations). In the case of a disqualifying disposition of stock described in section 421(b), an employer that otherwise satisfies all requirements of section 6041 and the regulations thereunder will be considered to have done so timely for purposes of this paragraph (a)(2) if Form W-2 or Form W-2c, as appropriate, is furnished to the employee or former employee, and is filed with the federal government, on or before the date on which the employer files the tax return claiming the deduction relating to the disqualifying disposition.

(3) Exceptions. Where property is substantially vested upon transfer, the deduction shall be allowed to such person in accordance with his method of accounting (in conformity with sections 446 and 461). In the case of a transfer to an employee benefit plan described in § 1.162–10(a) or a transfer to an employees' trust or annuity plan described in section 404(a)(5) and the regulations thereunder, section 83(h) and this section do not apply.

(4) Capital expenditure, etc. No deduction is allowed under section 83(h) to the extent that the transfer of property constitutes a capital expenditure, an item of deferred expense, or an amount properly includible in the value of inventory items. In the case of a capital expenditure, for example, the basis of the property to which such capital expenditure relates shall be increased at the same time and to the same extent as any amount includible in the employee's gross income in respect of such transfer. Thus, for example, no deduction is allowed to a corporation in respect of a transfer of its stock to a promoter upon its organization, notwithstanding that such promoter must include the value of such stock in his gross income in accordance with the rules under section 83.

(5) Transfer of life insurance contract (or an undivided interest therein)—(i) General rule. In the case of a transfer of a life insurance contract (or an undivided interest therein) described in § 1.61–22(c)(3) in connection with the performance of services, a deduction is allowable under paragraph (a)(1) of this section to the person for whom the services were performed. The amount of the deduction, if allowable, is equal to the sum of the amount included as compensation in the gross income of the service provider under § 1.61–22(g)(1) and the amount determined under § 1.61–22(g)(1)(ii).

(ii) Effective date—(A) General rule— Paragraph (a)(5)(i) of this section applies to any split-dollar life insurance arrangement (as defined in § 1.61–22(b)(1) or (2)) entered into after September 17, 2003. For purposes of this

paragraph (a)(5), an arrangement is entered into as determined under § 1.61–22(j)(1)(ii).

(B) Modified arrangements treated as new arrangements. If an arrangement entered into on or before September 17, 2003 is materially modified (within the meaning of § 1.61–22(j)(2)) after September 17, 2003, the arrangement is treated as a new arrangement entered into on the date of the modification.

(6) Effective date. Paragraphs (a)(1) and (2) of this section apply to deductions for taxable years beginning on or after January 1, 1995. However, taxpayers may also apply paragraphs (a)(1) and (2) of this section when claiming deductions for taxable years beginning before that date if the claims are not barred by the statute of limitations. Paragraphs (a)(3) and (4) of this section are effective as set forth in § 1.83–8(b).

(b) Recognition of gain or loss. Except as provided in section 1032, at the time of a transfer of property in connection with the performance of services the transferor recognizes gain to the extent that the transferor receives an amount that exceeds the transferor's basis in the property. In addition, at the time a deduction is allowed under section 83(h) and paragraph (a) of this section, gain or loss is recognized to the extent of the difference between (1) the sum of the amount paid plus the amount allowed as a deduction under section 83(h), and (2) the sum of the taxpayer's basis in the property plus any amount recognized pursuant to the previous sentence.

(c) Forfeitures. If, under section 83(h) and paragraph (a) of this section, a deduction, an increase in basis, or a reduction of gross income was allowable (disregarding the reasonableness of the amount of compensation) in respect of a transfer of property and such property is subsequently forfeited, the amount of such deduction, increase in basis or reduction of gross income shall be includible in the gross income of the person to whom it was allowable for the taxable year of forfeiture. The basis of such property in the hands of the person to whom it is forfeited shall include any such amount includible in the gross income of such person, as well as any amount such person pays upon forfeiture.

(d) Special rules for transfers by shareholders—(1) Transfers. If a shareholder of a corporation transfers property to an employee of such corporation or to an independent contractor (or to a beneficiary thereof), in consideration of services performed for the corporation, the transaction shall be considered to be a contribution of such property to the capital of such corporation by the shareholder, and immediately thereafter a transfer of such property by the corporation to the employee or independent contractor under paragraphs (a) and (b) of this section. For purposes of this (1), such a transfer will be considered to be in consideration for services performed for the corporation if either the property transferred is substantially nonvested at the time of transfer or an amount is includible in the gross income of the employee or independent contractor at the time of transfer under § 1.83–1(a)(1) or § 1.83–2(a). In the case of such a transfer, any money or other property paid to the shareholder for such stock shall be considered to be paid to the corporation and transferred immediately thereafter by the corporation to the shareholder as a distribution to which section 302 applies. For special rules that may apply to a corporation's transfer of its own stock to any person in consideration of services performed for another corporation or partnership, see § 1.1032–3. The preceding sentence applies to transfers of stock and amounts paid for such stock occurring on or after May 16, 2000.

(2) Forfeiture. If, following a transaction described in paragraph (d)(1) of this section, the transferred property is forfeited to the shareholder, paragraph (c) of this section shall apply both with respect to the shareholder and with respect to the corporation. In addition, the corporation shall in the taxable year of forfeiture be allowed a loss (or realize a gain) to offset any gain (or loss) realized under paragraph (b) of this section. For example, if a shareholder transfers property to an employee of the corporation as compensation, and as a result the shareholder's basis of $200x in such property is allocated to his stock in such corporation and such corporation recognizes a short-term capital gain of $800x, and is allowed a deduction of $1,000x on such transfer, upon a subsequent forfeiture of the property to the shareholder, the shareholder shall take $200x into gross income, and the corporation shall take $1,000x into gross income and be allowed a short-term capital loss of $800x.

(e) Options. [Reserved]

(f) Reporting requirements. [Reserved]

§ 1.83–7 Taxation of nonqualified stock options.

(a) In general. If there is granted to an employee or independent contractor (or beneficiary thereof) in connection with the performance of services, an option to which section 421 (relating generally to certain qualified and other options) does not apply, section 83(a) shall apply to such grant if the option has a readily ascertainable fair market value (determined in accordance with paragraph (b) of this section) at the time the option is granted. The person who performed such services realizes compensation upon such grant at the time and in the amount determined under section 83(a). If section 83(a) does not apply to the grant of such an option because the option does not have a readily ascertainable fair market value at the time of grant, sections 83(a) and 83(b) shall apply at the time the option is exercised or otherwise disposed of, even though the fair market value of such option may have become readily ascertainable before such time. If the option is exercised, sections 83(a) and 83(b) apply to the transfer of property pursuant to such exercise, and the employee or independent contractor realizes compensation upon such transfer at the time and in the amount determined under section 83(a) or 83(b). If the option is sold or otherwise disposed of in an arm's length transaction, sections 83(a) and 83(b) apply to the transfer of money or other property received in the same manner as sections 83(a) and 83(b) would have applied to the transfer of property pursuant to an exercise of the option. The preceding sentence does not apply to a sale or other disposition of the option to a person related to the service provider that occurs on or after July 2, 2003. For this purpose, a person is related to the service provider if—

(1) The person and the service provider bear a relationship to each other that is specified in section 267(b) or 707(b)(1), subject to the modifications that the language "20 percent" is used instead of "50 percent" each place it appears in sections 267(b) and 707(b)(1), and section 267(c)(4) is applied as if the family of an individual includes the spouse of any member of the family; or

(2) The person and the service provider are engaged in trades or businesses under common control (within the meaning of section 52(a) and (b)); provided that a person is not related to the service provider if the person is the service recipient with respect to the option or the grantor of the option.

(b) Readily ascertainable defined—(1) Actively traded on an established market. Options have a value at the time they are granted, but that value is ordinarily not readily ascertainable unless the option is actively traded on an established market. If an option is actively traded on an established market, the fair market value of such option is readily ascertainable for purposes of this section by applying the rules of valuation set forth in § 20.2031–2.

(2) Not actively traded on an established market. When an option is not actively traded on an established market, it does not have a readily ascertainable fair market value unless its fair market value can otherwise be measured with reasonable accuracy. For purposes of this section, if an option is not actively traded on an established market, the option does not have a readily ascertainable fair market value when granted unless the taxpayer can show that all of the following conditions exist:

(i) The option is transferable by the optionee;

(ii) The option is exercisable immediately in full by the optionee;

(iii) The option or the property subject to the option is not subject to any restriction or condition (other than a lien or other condition to secure the payment of the purchase price) which has a significant effect upon the fair market value of the option; and

(iv) The fair market value of the option privilege is readily ascertainable in accordance with paragraph (b)(3) of this section.

(3) Option privilege. The option privilege in the case of an option to buy is the opportunity to benefit during the option's exercise period from any increase in the value of property subject to the option during such period, without risking any capital. Similarly, the option privilege in the case of an option to sell is the opportunity to benefit during the exercise period from a decrease in the value of property subject to the option. For example, if at some time during the exercise period of an option to buy, the fair market value of the property subject to the option is greater than the option's exercise price, a profit may be realized by exercising the option and immediately selling the property so acquired for its higher fair market value. Irrespective of whether any such gain may be realized immediately at the time an option is granted, the fair market value of an option to buy includes the value of the right to benefit from any future increase in the value of the property subject to the option (relative to the option exercise price), without risking any capital. Therefore, the fair market value of an option is not merely the difference that may exist at a particular time between the option's exercise price and the value of the property subject to the option, but also includes the value of the option privilege for the remainder of the exercise period. Accordingly, for purposes of this section, in determining whether the fair market value of an option is readily ascertainable, it is necessary to consider whether the value of the entire option privilege can be measured with reasonable accuracy. In determining whether the value of the option privilege is readily ascertainable, and in determining the amount of such value when such value is readily ascertainable, it is necessary to consider—

(i) Whether the value of the property subject to the option can be ascertained;

(ii) The probability of any ascertainable value of such property increasing or decreasing; and

(iii) The length of the period during which the option can be exercised.

(c) Reporting requirements. [Reserved]

* * *

§ 1.83–8 Applicability of section and transitional rules.

(a) Scope of section 83. Section 83 is not applicable to—

(1) A transaction concerning an option to which section 421 applies;

(2) A transfer to or from a trust described in section 401(a) for the benefit of employees or their beneficiaries, or a transfer under an annuity plan that meets the requirements of section 404(a)(2) for the benefit of employees or their beneficiaries;

(3) The transfer of an option without a readily ascertainable fair market value (as defined in § 1.83–7(b)(1)); or

(4) The transfer of property pursuant to the exercise of an option with a readily ascertainable fair market value at the date of grant. Section 83 applies to a transfer to or from a trust or under an annuity plan for the benefit of employees, independent contractors, or their beneficiaries (except as provided in paragraph (a)(2) of this section), but to the extent a transfer is subject to section 402(b) or 403(c), section 83 applies to such a transfer only as provided for in section 402(b) or 403(c).

(b) Transitional rules—(1) In general. Except as otherwise provided in this paragraph, section 83 and the regulations thereunder shall apply to property transferred after June 30, 1969.

(2) Binding written contracts. Section 83 and the regulations thereunder shall not apply to property transferred pursuant to a binding written contract entered into before April 22, 1969. For purposes of this paragraph, a binding written contract means only a written contract under which the employee or independent contractor has an enforceable right to compel the transfer of property or to obtain damages upon the breach of such contract. A contract which provides that a person's right to such property is contingent upon the happening of an event (including the passage of time) may satisfy the requirements of this paragraph. However, if the event itself, or the determination of whether the event has occurred, rests with the board of directors or any other individual or group acting on behalf of the employer (other than an arbitrator), the contract will not be treated as giving the person an enforceable right for purposes of this paragraph.

The fact that the board of directors has the power (either expressly or impliedly) to terminate employment of an officer pursuant to a contract that contemplates the completion of services over a fixed or ascertainable period does not negate the existence of a binding written contract. Nor will the binding nature of the contract be negated by a provision in such contract which allows the employee or independent contractor to terminate the contract for any year and receive cash instead of property if such election would cause a substantial penalty, such as a forfeiture of part or all of the property received in connection with the performance of services in an earlier year.

* * *

(4) Certain written plans. Section 83 shall not apply to property transferred (whether or not by the exercise of an option) before May 1, 1970, pursuant to a written plan adopted and approved before July 1, 1969. A plan is to be considered as having been adopted and approved before July 1, 1969, only if prior to such date the transferor of the property undertook an ascertainable course of conduct which under applicable State law does not require further approval by the board of directors or the stockholders of any corporation. For example, if a corporation transfers property to an employee in connection with the performance of services pursuant to a plan adopted and approved before July 1, 1969, by the board of directors of such corporation, it is not necessary that the stockholders have adopted or approved such plan if State law does not require such approval. However, such approval is necessary if required by the articles of incorporation or the bylaws or if, by its terms, such plan will not become effective without such approval.

(5) Certain options granted pursuant to a binding written contract. Section 83 shall not apply to property transferred before January 1, 1973, upon the exercise of an option granted pursuant to a binding written contract (as defined in paragraph (b)(2) of this section) entered into before April 22, 1969, between a corporation and the transferor of such property requiring the transferor to grant options to employees of such corporation (or a subsidiary of such corporation) to purchase a determinable number of shares of stock of such corporation, but only if the transferee was an employee of such corporation (or a subsidiary of such corporation) on or before April 22, 1969.

(6) Certain tax free exchanges. Section 83 shall not apply to property transferred in exchange for (or pursuant to the exercise of a conversion privilege contained in) property transferred before July 1, 1969, or in exchange for property to which section 83 does not apply (by reason of paragraphs (1), (2), (3), or (4) of section 83(i)), if section 354, 355, 356, or 1036 (or so much of section 1031 as relates to section 1036) applies, or if gain or loss is not otherwise required to be recognized upon the exercise of such conversion privilege, and if the property received in such exchange is subject to restrictions and conditions substantially similar to those to which the property given in such exchange was subject.

* * *

§ 1.108–7 Reduction of attributes.

* * *

(d) Special rules for S corporations— (1) In general. If an S corporation excludes COD income from gross income under section 108(a)(1)(A), (B), or (C), the amount excluded shall be applied to reduce the S corporation's tax attributes under paragraph (a)(1) of this section. For purposes of paragraph (a)(1)(i) of this section, the aggregate amount of the shareholders' losses or deductions that are disallowed for the taxable year of the discharge under section 1366(d)(1), including disallowed losses or deductions of a shareholder that transfers all of the shareholder's stock in the S corporation during the taxable year of the discharge, is treated as the net operating loss tax attribute (deemed NOL) of the S corporation for the taxable year of the discharge.

(2) Allocation of excess losses or deductions—(i) In general. If the amount of an S corporation's deemed NOL exceeds the amount of the S corporation's COD income that is excluded from gross income under section 108(a)(1)(A), (B), or (C), the excess deemed NOL shall be allocated to the shareholder or shareholders of the S corporation as a loss or deduction that is disallowed under section 1366(d) for the taxable year of the discharge.

(ii) Multiple shareholders—(A) In general. If an S corporation has multiple shareholders, to determine the amount of the S corporation's excess deemed NOL to be allocated to each shareholder under paragraph (d)(2)(i) of this section, calculate with respect to each shareholder the shareholder's excess amount. The shareholder's excess amount is the amount (if any) by which the shareholder's losses or deductions disallowed under section 1366(d)(1) (before any reduction under paragraph (a)(1) of this section) exceed the amount of COD income that would have been taken into account by that shareholder under section 1366(a) had the COD income not been excluded under section 108(a).

(B) Shareholders with a shareholder's excess amount. Each shareholder that has a shareholder's excess amount, as determined under paragraph (d)(2)(ii)(A) of this section, is allocated an amount equal to the S corporation's excess deemed NOL multiplied by a fraction, the numerator of which is the shareholder's excess amount and the denominator of which is the sum of all shareholders' excess amounts.

(C) Shareholders with no shareholder's excess amount. If a shareholder does not have a shareholder's excess amount as determined in paragraph (d)(2)(ii)(A) of this section, none of the S corporation's excess deemed NOL shall be allocated to that shareholder.

(iii) Terminating shareholder. Any amount of the S corporation's excess deemed NOL allocated under paragraph (d)(2) of this section to a shareholder that had transferred all of the shareholder's stock in the corporation during the taxable year of the discharge is permanently disallowed under § 1.1366–2(a)(6), unless the transfer of stock is described in section 1041(a). If the transfer of stock is described in section 1041(a), the amount of the S corporation's excess deemed NOL allocated to the transferor under paragraph (d)(2) of this section shall be treated as a loss or deduction incurred by the corporation in the succeeding taxable year with respect to the transferee. See section 1366(d)(2)(B).

(3) Character of excess losses or deductions allocated to a shareholder. The character of an S corporation's excess deemed NOL that is allocated to a shareholder under paragraph (d)(2) of this section consists of a proportionate amount of each item of the shareholder's loss or deduction that is disallowed for the taxable year of the discharge under section 1366(d)(1).

(4) Information requirements. If an S corporation excludes COD income from gross income under section 108(a) for a taxable year, each shareholder of the S corporation during the taxable year of the discharge must report to the S corporation the amount of the shareholder's losses and deductions that are disallowed for the taxable year of the discharge under section 1366(d)(1), even if that amount is zero. If a shareholder fails to report the amount of the shareholder's losses and deductions that are disallowed for the taxable year of the discharge under section 1366(d)(1) to the S corporation, or if the S corporation knows that the amount reported by the shareholder is inaccurate, or if the information, as reported, appears to be incomplete or incorrect, the S corporation may rely on its own books and records, as well as other information available to the S corporation, to determine the amount of the shareholder's losses and deductions that are disallowed for the taxable year of the discharge under section 1366(d)(1), provided that the S corporation knows or reasonably believes that its information presents an accurate reflection of the shareholder's disallowed losses and deductions under section 1366(d)(1). The S corporation must report to each shareholder the amount of the S corporation's excess deemed NOL that is allocated to that shareholder under paragraph (d)(2) of this section, even if that amount is zero, in accordance with applicable forms and instructions.

(e) * * *

Example (5). (i) Facts. During the entire calendar year 2009, A, B, and C each own equal shares of stock in X, a calendar year S corporation. As of December 31, 2009, A, B, and C each have a zero stock basis and X does not have any indebtedness to A, B, or C. For the 2009 taxable year, X excludes from gross income $45,000 of COD income under section 108(a)(1)(A). The COD income (had it not been excluded) would have been allocated $15,000 to A, $15,000 to B, and $15,000 to C under section 1366(a). For the 2009 taxable year, X has $30,000 of losses and deductions that X passes through pro rata to A, B, and C in the amount of $10,000 each. The losses and deductions that pass through to A, B, and C are disallowed under section 1366(d)(1). In addition, B has $10,000 of section 1366(d) losses from prior years and C has $20,000 of section 1366(d) losses from prior years. A's ($10,000), B's ($20,000) and C's ($30,000) combined $60,000 of disallowed losses and deductions for the taxable year of the discharge are treated as a current year net operating loss tax attribute of X under section 108(d)(7)(B) (deemed NOL) for purposes of the section 108(b) reduction of tax attributes.

(ii) Allocation. Under section 108(b)(2)(A), X's $45,000 of excluded COD income reduces the $60,000 deemed NOL to $15,000. Therefore, X has a $15,000 excess net operating loss (excess deemed NOL) to allocate to its shareholders. Under paragraph (d)(2)(ii)(C) of this section, none of the $15,000 excess deemed NOL is allocated to A because A's section 1366(d) losses and deductions immediately prior to the section 108(b)(2)(A) reduction ($10,000) do not exceed A's share of the excluded COD income for 2008 ($15,000). Thus, A has no shareholder's excess amount. Each of B's and C's respective section 1366(d) losses and deductions immediately prior to the section 108(b)(2)(A) reduction exceed each of B's and C's respective shares of the excluded COD income for 2008. B's excess amount is $5,000 ($20,000 − $15,000) and C's excess amount is $15,000 ($30,000 − $15,000). Therefore, the total of all shareholders' excess amounts is $20,000. Under paragraph (d)(2) of this section, X will allocate $3,750 of the $15,000 excess deemed NOL to B ($15,000 × $5,000 / $20,000) and $11,250 of the $15,000 excess deemed NOL to C ($15,000 x $15,000

/ $20,000). These amounts are treated as losses and deductions disallowed under section 1366(d)(1) for the taxable year of the discharge. Accordingly, at the beginning of 2010, A has no section 1366(d)(2) carryovers, B has $3,750 of carryovers, and C has $11,250 of carryovers.

(iii) Character. Immediately prior to the section 108(b)(2)(A) reduction, B's $20,000 of section 1366(d) losses and deductions consisted of $8,000 of long-term capital losses, $7,000 of section 1231 losses, and $5,000 of ordinary losses. After the section 108(b)(2)(A) tax attribute reduction, X will allocate $3,750 of the excess deemed NOL to B. Under paragraph (d)(3) of this section, the $3,750 excess deemed NOL allocated to B consists of $1,500 of longterm capital losses (($8,000 / $20,000) x $3,750), $1,312.50 of section 1231 losses (($7,000 / $20,000) x $3,750), and $937.50 of ordinary losses (($5,000 / $20,000) x $3,750). As a result, at the beginning of 2010, B's $3,750 of section 1366(d)(2) carryovers consist of $1,500 of longterm capital losses, $1,312.50 of section 1231 losses, and $937.50 of ordinary losses.

Example (6). (i) A and B each own 50 percent of the shares of stock in X, a calendar year S corporation. On March 1, 2009, X realizes $12,000 of COD income and excludes this amount from gross income under section 108(a)(1)(A) for X's 2009 taxable year. On June 30, 2009, A sells all of her shares of stock in X to C in a transfer not described in section 1041(a). X does not make a terminating election under section 1377(a)(2). The COD income (had it not been excluded) would have been allocated $3,000 to A, $6,000 to B, and $3,000 to C under section 1366(a). Prior to the section 108(b)(2)(A) reduction, for the taxable year of the discharge the shareholders have disallowed losses and deductions under section 1366(d) (including disallowed losses carried over to the current year under section 1366(d)(2)) in the following amounts: A − $5,000, B − $13,000, and C − $2,000. The combined

$20,000 of disallowed losses and deductions for the taxable year of the discharge are treated as a current year net operating loss tax attribute of X under section 108(d)(7)(B) (deemed NOL).

(ii) Under section 108(b)(2)(A), X's $12,000 of excluded COD income reduces the $20,000 deemed NOL to $8,000. Therefore, X has an $8,000 excess net operating loss (excess deemed NOL) to allocate to its shareholders. Under paragraph (d)(2)(ii)(C) of this section, none of the $8,000 excess deemed NOL is allocated to C because C's section 1366(d) losses and deductions immediately prior to the section 108(b)(2)(A) reduction ($2,000) do not exceed C's share of the excluded COD income for 2008 ($3,000). However, each of A's and B's respective section 1366(d) losses and deductions immediately prior to the section 108(b)(2)(A) reduction exceed each of A's and B's respective shares of the excluded COD income for 2009. A's excess amount is $2,000 ($5,000 – $3,000) and B's excess amount is $7,000 ($13,000 – $6,000). Therefore, the total of all shareholders' excess amounts is $9,000. Under paragraph (d)(2) of this section, X will allocate $1,777.78 of the $8,000 excess deemed NOL to A ($8,000 x $2,000 / $9,000) and $6,222.22 of the $8,000 excess deemed NOL to B ($8,000 x $7,000 / $9,000). However, because A transferred all of her shares of stock in X in a transaction not described in section 1041(a), A's $1,777.78 of section 1366(d) losses and deductions are permanently disallowed under paragraph (d)(2)(iii) of this section. Accordingly, at the beginning of 2010, B has $6,222.22 of section 1366(d)(2) carryovers and C has no section 1366(d)(2) carryovers.

Example (7). The facts are the same as in Example 6, except that X, with the consent of A and C, makes a terminating election under section 1377(a)(2) upon A's sale of her stock in X to C. Therefore, the COD income (had it not been excluded) would have been allocated $6,000 to A, $6,000 to B, and $0 to C.

Under paragraph (d)(2)(ii)(C) of this section, none of the $8,000 excess deemed NOL is allocated to A because A's section 1366(d) losses and deductions immediately prior to the section 108(b)(2)(A) reduction ($5,000) do not exceed A's share of the excluded COD income for 2009 ($6,000). However, each of B's and C's respective section 1366(d) losses and deductions immediately prior to the section 108(b)(2)(A) reduction exceed each of B's and C's respective shares of the excluded COD income for 2009. B's excess amount is $7,000 ($13,000 – $6,000), C's excess amount is $2,000 ($2,000 – $0). Therefore, the total of all shareholders' excess amounts is $9,000. Under paragraph (d)(2) of this section, X will allocate $6,222.22 of the $8,000 excess deemed NOL to B ($8,000 x $7,000 / $9,000) and $1,777.78 of the $8,000 excess deemed NOL to C. Accordingly, at the beginning of 2010, B has $6,222.22 of section 1366(d)(2) carryovers and C has $1,777.78 of section 1366(d)(2) carryovers.

(f) Effective/applicability date—(1) Paragraphs (a), (b), (c), and Examples 1, 2, 3, and 4 of paragraph (e) of this section apply to discharges of indebtedness occurring on or after May 10, 2004.

(2) Paragraph (d) and Examples 5, 6, and 7 of paragraph (e) of this section apply to discharges of indebtedness occurring on or after October 30, 2009. Paragraph (d)(2)(iii) of this section applies on and after July 23, 2014. * * *

§ 1.199A–1 Operational rules.

(a) Overview—(1) In general. This section provides operational rules for calculating the section 199A(a) qualified business income deduction (section 199A deduction) under section 199A of the Internal Revenue Code (Code). This section refers to the rules in §§ 1.199A–2 through 1.199A–6. This paragraph (a) provides an overview of this section. Paragraph (b) of this section provides definitions that apply for purposes of section 199A and §§ 1.199A–1 through 1.199A–6. Paragraph (c) of this section provides computational rules and examples for individuals whose taxable income does not exceed the threshold amount. Paragraph (d) of this section provides computational rules and examples for individuals whose taxable income exceeds the threshold amount. Paragraph (e) of this section provides special rules for purposes of section 199A and §§ 1.199A–1 through 1.199A–6. This section and §§ 1.199A–2 through 1.199A–6 do not apply for purposes of calculating the deduction in section 199A(g) for specified agricultural and horticultural cooperatives.

(2) Usage of term individual. For purposes of applying the rules of §§ 1.199A–1 through 1.199A–6, a reference to an individual includes a reference to a trust (other than a grantor trust) or an estate to the extent that the section 199A deduction is determined by the trust or estate under the rules of § 1.199A–6.

(b) Definitions. For purposes of section 199A and §§ 1.199A–1 through 1.199A–6, the following definitions apply:

(1) *Aggregated trade or business* means two or more trades or businesses that have been aggregated pursuant to § 1.199A–4.

(2) *Applicable percentage* means, with respect to any taxable year, 100 percent reduced (not below zero) by the percentage equal to the ratio that the taxable income of the individual for the taxable year in excess of the threshold amount, bears to $50,000 (or $100,000 in the case of a joint return).

(3) *Net capital gain* means *net capital gain* as defined in section 1222(11) plus any *qualified dividend income* (as defined in section 1(h)(11)(B)) for the taxable year.

(4) *Phase-in range* means a range of taxable income between the threshold amount and the threshold amount plus $50,000 (or $100,000 in the case of a joint return).

(5) *Qualified business income (QBI)* means the net amount of qualified items of income, gain, deduction, and loss with respect

to any trade or business (or aggregated trade or business) as determined under the rules of § 1.199A–3(b).

(6) *QBI component* means the amount determined under paragraph (d)(2) of this section.

(7) *Qualified PTP income* is defined in § 1.199A–3(c)(3).

(8) *Qualified REIT dividends* are defined in § 1.199A–3(c)(2).

(9) *Reduction amount* means, with respect to any taxable year, the excess amount multiplied by the ratio that the taxable income of the individual for the taxable year in excess of the threshold amount, bears to $50,000 (or $100,000 in the case of a joint return). For purposes of this paragraph (b)(9), the *excess amount* is the amount by which 20 percent of QBI exceeds the greater of 50 percent of W-2 wages or the sum of 25 percent of W-2 wages plus 2.5 percent of the UBIA of qualified property.

(10) *Relevant passthrough entity (RPE)* means a partnership (other than a PTP) or an S corporation that is owned, directly or indirectly, by at least one individual, estate, or trust. Other passthrough entities including common trust funds as described in § 1.6032–T and religious or apostolic organizations described in section 501(d) are also treated as RPEs if the entity files a Form 1065, *U.S. Return of Partnership Income*, and is owned, directly or indirectly, by at least one individual, estate, or trust. A trust or estate is treated as an RPE to the extent it passes through QBI, W-2 wages, UBIA of qualified property, qualified REIT dividends, or qualified PTP income.

(11) *Specified service trade or business (SSTB)* means a specified service trade or business as defined in § 1.199A–5(b).

(12) *Threshold amount* means, for any taxable year beginning before 2019, $157,500 (or $315,000 in the case of a taxpayer filing a joint return). In the case of any taxable year beginning after 2018, the threshold amount is the dollar amount in the preceding sentence increased by an amount equal to such dollar amount, multiplied by the cost-of-living adjustment determined under section 1(f)(3) of the Code for the calendar year in which the taxable year begins, determined by substituting "calendar year 2017" for "calendar year 2016" in section 1(f)(3)(A)(ii). The amount of any increase under the preceding sentence is rounded as provided in section 1(f)(7) of the Code.

(13) *Total QBI amount* means the net total QBI from all trades or businesses (including the individual's share of QBI from trades or business conducted by RPEs).

(14) *Trade or business* means a trade or business that is a trade or business under section 162 (a section 162 trade or business) other than the trade or business of performing services as an employee. In addition, rental or licensing of tangible or intangible property (rental activity) that does not rise to the level of a section 162 trade or business is nevertheless treated as a trade or business for purposes of section 199A, if the property is rented or licensed to a trade or business conducted by the individual or an RPE which is commonly controlled under § 1.199A–4(b)(1)(i) (regardless of whether the rental activity and the trade or business are otherwise eligible to be aggregated under § 1.199A–4(b)(1)).

(15) *Unadjusted basis immediately after acquisition of qualified property* (*UBIA of qualified property*) is defined in § 1.199A–2(c).

(16) *W-2 wages* means W-2 wages of a trade or business (or aggregated trade or business) properly allocable to QBI as determined under § 1.199A–2(b).

(c) Computation of the section 199A deduction for individuals with taxable income not exceeding threshold amount—(1) In general. The section 199A deduction is determined for individuals with taxable income for the taxable year that does not exceed the threshold amount by adding 20 percent of the total QBI amount (including the individual's share of QBI from an RPE and QBI attributable to an SSTB) and 20 percent of the combined amount of qualified REIT dividends and qualified PTP income (including the individual's share of qualified REIT dividends and qualified PTP income from RPEs and qualified PTP income attributable to an SSTB). That sum is then compared to 20 percent of the amount by which the individual's taxable income exceeds net capital gain. The lesser of these two amounts is the individual's section 199A deduction.

(2) Carryover rules—(i) Negative total QBI amount. If the total QBI amount is less than zero, the portion of the individual's section 199A deduction related to QBI is zero for the taxable year. The negative total QBI amount is treated as negative QBI from a separate trade or business in the succeeding taxable years of the individual for purposes of section 199A and this section. This carryover rule does not affect the deductibility of the loss for purposes of other provisions of the Code.

(ii) Negative combined qualified REIT dividends/qualified PTP income. If the combined amount of REIT dividends and qualified PTP income is less than zero, the portion of the individual's section 199A deduction related to qualified REIT dividends and qualified PTP income is zero for the taxable year. The negative combined amount must be carried forward and used to offset the combined amount of REIT dividends and qualified PTP income in the succeeding taxable years of the individual for purposes of section 199A and this section. This carryover rule does not affect the deductibility of the loss for purposes of other provisions of the Code.

(3) Examples. The following examples illustrate the provisions of this paragraph (c). For purposes of these examples, unless indicated otherwise, assume that all of the trades or businesses are trades or businesses as defined in paragraph (b)(14) of this section and all of the tax items are effectively connected to a trade or business within the United States within the meaning of section 864(c). Total taxable income does not include the section 199A deduction.

(i) Example (1). A, an unmarried individual, owns and operates a computer repair shop as a sole proprietorship. The business generates $100,000 in net taxable income from operations in 2018. A has no capital gains or losses. After allowable deductions not relating to the business, A's total taxable income for 2018 is $81,000. The business's QBI is $100,000, the net amount of its qualified items of income, gain, deduction, and loss. A's section 199A deduction for 2018 is equal to $16,200, the lesser of 20% of A's QBI from the business ($100,000 x 20% = $20,000) and 20% of A's total taxable income for the taxable year ($81,000 x 20% = $16,200).

(ii) Example (2). Assume the same facts as in *Example 1* of paragraph (c)(3)(i) of this section, except that A also has $7,000 in net capital gain for 2018 and that, after allowable deductions not relating to the business, A's taxable income for 2018 is $74,000. A's taxable income minus net capital gain is $67,000 ($74,000 – $7,000). A's section 199A deduction is equal to $13,400, the lesser of 20% of A's QBI from the business ($100,000 x 20% = $20,000) and 20% of A's total taxable income minus net capital gain for the taxable year ($67,000 x 20% = $13,400).

(iii) Example (3). B and C are married and file a joint individual income tax return. B earns $50,000 in wages as an employee of an unrelated company in 2018. C owns 100% of the shares of X, an S corporation that provides landscaping services. X generates $100,000 in net income from operations in 2018. X pays C $150,000 in wages in 2018. B and C have no capital gains or losses. After allowable deductions not related to X, B and C's total taxable income for 2018 is $270,000. B's and C's wages are not considered to be income from a trade or business for purposes of the section 199A deduction. Because X is an S corpora-

tion, its QBI is determined at the S corporation level. X's QBI is $100,000, the net amount of its qualified items of income, gain, deduction, and loss. The wages paid by X to C are considered to be a qualified item of deduction for purposes of determining X's QBI. The section 199A deduction with respect to X's QBI is then determined by C, X's sole shareholder, and is claimed on the joint return filed by B and C. B and C's section 199A deduction is equal to $20,000, the lesser of 20% of C's QBI from the business ($100,000 x 20% = $20,000) and 20% of B and C's total taxable income for the taxable year ($270,000 x 20% = $54,000).

(iv) Example (4). Assume the same facts as in *Example 3* of paragraph (c)(3)(iii) of this section except that B also earns $1,000 in qualified REIT dividends and $500 in qualified PTP income in 2018, increasing taxable income to $271,500. B and C's section 199A deduction is equal to $20,300, the lesser of:

(A) 20% of C's QBI from the business ($100,000 x 20% = $20,000) plus 20% of B's combined qualified REIT dividends and qualified PTP income ($1500 x 20% = $300); and

(B) 20% of B and C's total taxable for the taxable year ($271,500 x 20% = $54,300).

(d) Computation of the section 199A deduction for individuals with taxable income above threshold amount—(1) In general. The section 199A deduction is determined for individuals with taxable income for the taxable year that exceeds the threshold amount by adding the QBI component described in paragraph (d)(2) of this section and the qualified REIT dividends/qualified PTP income component described in paragraph (d)(3) of this section (including the individual's share of qualified REIT dividends and qualified PTP income from RPEs). That sum is then compared to 20 percent of the amount by which the individual's taxable income exceeds net capital gain. The lesser of these two amounts is the individual's section 199A deduction.

(2) QBI component. An individual with taxable income for the taxable year that exceeds the threshold amount determines the QBI component using the following computational rules, which are to be applied in the order they appear.

(i) SSTB exclusion. If the individual's taxable income is within the phase-in range, then only the applicable percentage of QBI, W-2 wages, and UBIA of qualified property for each SSTB is taken into account for all purposes of determining the individual's section 199A deduction, including the application of the netting and carryover rules described in paragraph (d)(2)(iii) of this section. If the individual's taxable income exceeds the phase-in range, then none of the individual's share of QBI, W-2 wages, or UBIA of qualified property attributable to an SSTB may be taken into account for purposes of determining the individual's section 199A deduction.

(ii) Aggregated trade or business. If an individual chooses to aggregate trades or businesses under the rules of § 1.199A–4, the individual must combine the QBI, W-2 wages, and UBIA of qualified property of each trade or business within an aggregated trade or business prior to applying the netting and carryover rules described in paragraph (d)(2)(iii) of this section and the W-2 wage and UBIA of qualified property limitations described in paragraph (d)(2)(iv) of this section.

(iii) Netting and carryover—(A) Netting. If an individual's QBI from at least one trade or business (including an aggregated trade or business) is less than zero, the individual must offset the QBI attributable to each trade or business (or aggregated trade or business) that produced net positive QBI with the QBI from each trade or business (or aggregated trade or business) that produced net negative QBI in proportion to the relative amounts of net QBI in the trades or businesses (or aggregated trades or businesses) with positive QBI. The adjusted QBI is then used in paragraph (d)(2)(iv) of this section. The W-2 wages and

UBIA of qualified property from the trades or businesses (including aggregated trades or businesses) that produced net negative QBI are not taken into account for purposes of this paragraph (d) and are not carried over to the subsequent year.

(B) Carryover of negative total QBI amount. If an individual's QBI from all trades or businesses (including aggregated trades or businesses) combined is less than zero, the QBI component is zero for the taxable year. This negative amount is treated as negative QBI from a separate trade or business in the succeeding taxable years of the individual for purposes of section 199A and this section. This carryover rule does not affect the deductibility of the loss for purposes of other provisions of the Code. The W-2 wages and UBIA of qualified property from the trades or businesses (including aggregated trades or businesses) that produced net negative QBI are not taken into account for purposes of this paragraph (d) and are not carried over to the subsequent year.

(iv) QBI component calculation—(A) General rule. Except as provided in paragraph (d)(2)(iv)(B) of this section, the QBI component is the sum of the amounts determined under this paragraph (d)(2)(iv)(A) for each trade or business (or aggregated trade or business). For each trade or business (or aggregated trade or business) (including trades or businesses operated through RPEs) the individual must determine the lesser of—

(1) 20 percent of the QBI for that trade or business (or aggregated trade or business); or

(2) The greater of—

(i) 50 percent of W-2 wages with respect to that trade or business (or aggregated trade or business); or

(ii) The sum of 25 percent of W-2 wages with respect to that trade or business (or aggregated trade or business) plus 2.5 percent of the UBIA of qualified property with respect to that trade or business (or aggregated trade or business).

(B) Taxpayers with taxable income within phase-in range. If the individual's taxable income is within the phase-in range and the amount determined under paragraph (d)(2)(iv)(A)(*2*) of this section for a trade or business (or aggregated trade or business) is less than the amount determined under paragraph (d)(2)(iv)(A)(*1*) of this section for that trade or business (or aggregated trade or business), the amount determined under paragraph (d)(2)(iv)(A) of this section for such trade or business (or aggregated trade or business) is modified. Instead of the amount determined under paragraph (d)(2)(iv)(A)(*2*) of this section, the QBI component for the trade or business (or aggregated trade or business) is the amount determined under paragraph (d)(2)(iv)(A)(*1*) of this section reduced by the reduction amount as defined in paragraph (b)(9) of this section. This reduction amount does not apply if the amount determined in paragraph (d)(2)(iv)(A)(*2*) of this section is greater than the amount determined under paragraph (d)(2)(iv)(A)(*1*) of this section (in which circumstance the QBI component for the trade or business (or aggregated trade or business) will be the unreduced amount determined in paragraph (d)(2)(iv)(A)(*1*) of this section).

(3) Qualified REIT dividends/qualified PTP income component—(i) In general. The qualified REIT dividend/qualified PTP income component is 20 percent of the combined amount of qualified REIT dividends and qualified PTP income received by the individual (including the individual's share of qualified REIT dividends and qualified PTP income from RPEs).

(ii) SSTB exclusion. If the individual's taxable income is within the phase-in range, then only the applicable percentage of qualified PTP income generated by an SSTB is taken into account for purposes of determining the individual's section 199A deduction, including the determination of the combined amount of qualified REIT dividends and qualified PTP income described in paragraph (d)

(1) of this section. If the individual's taxable income exceeds the phase-in range, then none of the individual's share of qualified PTP income generated by an SSTB may be taken into account for purposes of determining the individual's section 199A deduction.

(iii) Negative combined qualified REIT dividends/qualified PTP income. If the combined amount of REIT dividends and qualified PTP income is less than zero, the portion of the individual's section 199A deduction related to qualified REIT dividends and qualified PTP income is zero for the taxable year. The negative combined amount must be carried forward and used to offset the combined amount of REIT dividends/qualified PTP income in the succeeding taxable years of the individual for purposes of section 199A and this section. This carryover rule does not affect the deductibility of the loss for purposes of other provisions of the Code.

(4) Examples. The following examples illustrate the provisions of this paragraph (d). For purposes of these examples, unless indicated otherwise, assume that all of the trades or businesses are trades or businesses as defined in paragraph (b)(14) of this section, none of the trades or businesses are SSTBs as defined in paragraph (b)(11) of this section and § 1.199A–5(b); and all of the tax items associated with the trades or businesses are effectively connected to a trade or business within the United States within the meaning of section 864(c). Also assume that the taxpayers report no capital gains or losses or other tax items not specified in the examples. Total taxable income does not include the section 199A deduction.

(i) Example 1. D, an unmarried individual, operates a business as a sole proprietorship. The business generates $1,000,000 of QBI in 2018. Solely for purposes of this example, assume that the business paid no wages and holds no qualified property for use in the business. After allowable deductions unrelated to the business, D's total taxable income for

2018 is $980,000. Because D's taxable income exceeds the applicable threshold amount, D's section 199A deduction is subject to the W-2 wage and UBIA of qualified property limitations. D's section 199A deduction is limited to zero because the business paid no wages and held no qualified property.

(ii) Example 2. Assume the same facts as in *Example 1* of paragraph (d)(4)(i) of this section, except that D holds qualified property with a UBIA of $10,000,000 for use in the trade or business. D reports $4,000,000 of QBI for 2020. After allowable deductions unrelated to the business, D's total taxable income for 2020 is $3,980,000. Because D's taxable income is above the threshold amount, the QBI component of D's section 199A deduction is subject to the W-2 wage and UBIA of qualified property limitations. Because the business has no W-2 wages, the QBI component of D's section 199A deduction is limited to the lesser of 20% of the business's QBI or 2.5% of its UBIA of qualified property. Twenty percent of the $4,000,000 of QBI is $800,000. Two and one-half percent of the $10,000,000 UBIA of qualified property is $250,000. The QBI component of D's section 199A deduction is thus limited to $250,000. D's section 199A deduction is equal to the lesser of:

(A) 20% of the QBI from the business as limited ($250,000); or

(B) 20% of D's taxable income ($3,980,000 x 20% = $796,000). Therefore, D's section 199A deduction for 2020 is $250,000.

(iii) Example 3. E, an unmarried individual, is a 30% owner of LLC, which is classified as a partnership for Federal income tax purposes. In 2018, the LLC has a single trade or business and reports QBI of $3,000,000. The LLC pays total W-2 wages of $1,000,000, and its total UBIA of qualified property is $100,000. E is allocated 30% of all items of the partnership. For the 2018 taxable year, E reports $900,000 of QBI from the LLC. After allowable deductions unrelated to LLC, E's taxable income is $880,000. Because E's

taxable income is above the threshold amount, the QBI component of E's section 199A deduction will be limited to the lesser of 20% of E's share of LLC's QBI or the greater of the W-2 wage or UBIA of qualified property limitations. Twenty percent of E's share of QBI of $900,000 is $180,000. The W-2 wage limitation equals 50% of E's share of the LLC's wages ($300,000) or $150,000. The UBIA of qualified property limitation equals $75,750, the sum of 25% of E's share of LLC's wages ($300,000) or $75,000 plus 2.5% of E's share of UBIA of qualified property ($30,000) or $750. The greater of the limitation amounts ($150,000 and $75,750) is $150,000. The QBI component of E's section 199A deduction is thus limited to $150,000, the lesser of 20% of QBI ($180,000) and the greater of the limitations amounts ($150,000). E's section 199A deduction is equal to the lesser of 20% of the QBI from the business as limited ($150,000) or 20% of E's taxable income ($880,000 x 20% = $176,000). Therefore, E's section 199A deduction is $150,000 for 2018.

* * *

(v) Example 5: Phase-in range. (A) B and C are married and file a joint individual income tax return. B is a shareholder in M, an entity taxed as an S corporation for Federal income tax purposes that conducts a single trade or business. M holds no qualified property. B's share of the M's QBI is $300,000 in 2018. B's share of the W-2 wages from M in 2018 is $40,000. C earns wage income from employment by an unrelated company. After allowable deductions unrelated to M, B and C's taxable income for 2018 is $375,000. B and C are within the phase-in range because their taxable income exceeds the applicable threshold amount, $315,000, but does not exceed the threshold amount plus $100,000, or $415,000. Consequently, the QBI component of B and C's section 199A deduction may be limited by the W-2 wage and UBIA of qualified property limitations but the limitations will be phased in.

(B) Because M does not hold qualified property, only the W-2 wage limitation must be calculated. In order to apply the W-2 wage limitation, B and C must first determine 20% of B's share of M's QBI. Twenty percent of B's share of M's QBI of $300,000 is $60,000. Next, B and C must determine 50% of B's share of M's W-2 wages. Fifty percent of B's share of M's W-2 wages of $40,000 is $20,000. Because 50% of B's share of M's W-2 wages ($20,000) is less than 20% of B's share of M's QBI ($60,000), B and C must determine the QBI component of their section 199A deduction by reducing 20% of B's share of M's QBI by the reduction amount.

(C) B and C are 60% through the phase-in range (that is, their taxable income exceeds the threshold amount by $60,000 and their phase-in range is $100,000). B and C must determine the excess amount, which is the excess of 20% of B's share of M's QBI, or $60,000, over 50% of B's share of M's W-2 wages, or $20,000. Thus, the excess amount is $40,000. The reduction amount is equal to 60% of the excess amount, or $24,000. Thus, the QBI component of B and C's section 199A deduction is equal to $36,000, 20% of B's $300,000 share M's QBI (that is, $60,000), reduced by $24,000. B and C's section 199A deduction is equal to the lesser of 20% of the QBI from the business as limited ($36,000) or 20% of B and C's taxable income ($375,000 x 20% = $75,000). Therefore, B and C's section 199A deduction is $36,000 for 2018.

(vi) Example 6. (A) Assume the same facts as in *Example 5* of paragraph (d)(4)(v) of this section, except that M is engaged in an SSTB. Because B and C are within the phase-in range, B must reduce the QBI and W-2 wages allocable to B from M to the applicable percentage of those items. B and C's applicable percentage is 100% reduced by the percentage equal to the ratio that their taxable income for the taxable year ($375,000) exceeds their threshold amount ($315,000), or $60,000, bears to $100,000. Their applicable percentage

is 40%. The applicable percentage of B's QBI is ($300,000 x 40% =) $120,000, and the applicable percentage of B's share of W-2 wages is ($40,000 x 40% =) $16,000. These reduced numbers must then be used to determine how B's section 199A deduction is limited.

(B) B and C must apply the W-2 wage limitation by first determining 20% of B's share of M's QBI as limited by paragraph (d)(4)(vi)(A) of this section. Twenty percent of B's share of M's QBI of $120,000 is $24,000. Next, B and C must determine 50% of B's share of M's W-2 wages. Fifty percent of B's share of M's W-2 wages of $16,000 is $8,000. Because 50% of B's share of M's W-2 wages ($8,000) is less than 20% of B's share of M's QBI ($24,000), B and C's must determine the QBI component of their section 199A deduction by reducing 20% of B's share of M's QBI by the reduction amount.

(C) B and C are 60% through the phase-in range (that is, their taxable income exceeds the threshold amount by $60,000 and their phase-in range is $100,000). B and C must determine the excess amount, which is the excess of 20% of B's share of M's QBI, as adjusted in paragraph (d)(4)(vi)(A) of this section or $24,000, over 50% of B's share of M's W-2 wages, as adjusted in paragraph (d)(4)(vi)(A) of this section, or $8,000. Thus, the excess amount is $16,000. The reduction amount is equal to 60% of the excess amount or $9,600. Thus, the QBI component of B and C's section 199A deduction is equal to $14,400, 20% of B's share M's QBI of $24,000, reduced by $9,600. B and C's section 199A deduction is equal to the lesser of 20% of the QBI from the business as limited ($14,400) or 20% of B's and C's taxable income ($375,000 x 20% = $75,000). Therefore, B and C's section 199A deduction is $14,400 for 2018.

* * *

(e) Special rules—(1) Effect of deduction. In the case of a partnership or S corporation, section 199A is applied at the partner or shareholder level. The rules of subchapter

K and subchapter S of the Code apply in their entirety for purposes of determining each partner's or shareholder's share of QBI, W-2 wages, UBIA of qualified property, qualified REIT dividends, and qualified PTP income or loss. The section 199A deduction has no effect on the adjusted basis of a partner's interest in the partnership, the adjusted basis of a shareholder's stock in an S corporation, or an S corporation's accumulated adjustments account.

(2) Disregarded entities. An entity with a single owner that is treated as disregarded as an entity separate from its owner under any provision of the Code is disregarded for purposes of section 199A and §§ 1.199A–1 through 1.199A–6.

* * *

(6) Imposition of accuracy-related penalty on underpayments. For rules related to the imposition of the accuracy-related penalty on underpayments for taxpayers who claim the deduction allowed under section 199A, see section 6662(d)(1)(C).

* * *

§ 1.199A–3 Qualified business income, qualified REIT dividends, and qualified PTP income.

(a) In general. This section provides rules on the determination of a trade or business's qualified business income (QBI), as well as the determination of qualified real estate investment trust (REIT) dividends and qualified publicly traded partnership (PTP) income. The provisions of this section apply solely for purposes of section 199A of the Internal Revenue Code (Code). Paragraph (b) of this section provides rules for the determination of QBI. Paragraph (c) of this section provides rules for the determination of qualified REIT dividends and qualified PTP income. QBI must be determined and reported for each trade or business by the individual or relevant passthrough entity (RPE) that directly conducts the trade or business before applying the aggregation rules of § 1.199A–4.

(b) Definition of qualified business income—(1) In general. For purposes of this section, the term *qualified business income* or *QBI* means, for any taxable year, the net amount of qualified items of income, gain, deduction, and loss with respect to any trade or business of the taxpayer as described in paragraph (b)(2) of this section, provided the other requirements of this section and section 199A are satisfied (including, for example, the exclusion of income not effectively connected with a United States trade or business).

(i) Section 751 gain. With respect to a partnership, if section 751(a) or (b) applies, then gain or loss attributable to assets of the partnership giving rise to ordinary income under section 751(a) or (b) is considered attributable to the trades or businesses conducted by the partnership, and is taken into account for purposes of computing QBI.

(ii) Guaranteed payments for the use of capital. Income attributable to a guaranteed payment for the use of capital is not considered to be attributable to a trade or business, and thus is not taken into account for purposes of computing QBI except to the extent properly allocable to a trade or business of the recipient. The partnership's deduction associated with the guaranteed payment will be taken into account for purposes of computing QBI if such deduction is properly allocable to the trade or business and is otherwise deductible for Federal income tax purposes.

(iii) Section 481 adjustments. Section 481 adjustments (whether positive or negative) are taken into account for purposes of computing QBI to the extent that the requirements of this section and section 199A are otherwise satisfied, but only if the adjustment arises in taxable years ending after December 31, 2017.

(iv) Previously disallowed losses. Generally, previously disallowed losses or deductions (including under sections 465, 469, 704(d), and 1366(d)) allowed in the taxable year are taken into account for purposes of computing QBI. These losses shall be used, for purposes of section 199A and these regulations, in order from the oldest to the most recent on a first-in, first-out (FIFO) basis. However, losses or deductions that were disallowed, suspended, limited, or carried over from taxable years ending before January 1, 2018 (including under sections 465, 469, 704(d), and 1366(d)), are not taken into account in a later taxable year for purposes of computing QBI.

(v) Net operating losses. Generally, a net operating loss deduction under section 172 is not considered with respect to a trade or business and therefore, is not taken into account in computing QBI. However, an excess business loss under section 461(*l*) is treated as a net operating loss carryover to the following taxable year and is taken into account for purposes of computing QBI in the subsequent taxable year in which it is deducted.

(vi) Other deductions. Generally, deductions attributable to a trade or business are taken into account for purposes of computing QBI to the extent that the requirements of section 199A and this section are otherwise satisfied. For purposes of section 199A only, deductions such as the deductible portion of the tax on self-employment income under section 164(f), the self-employed health insurance deduction under section 162(*l*), and the deduction for contributions to qualified retirement plans under section 404 are considered attributable to a trade or business to the extent that the individual's gross income from the trade or business is taken into account in calculating the allowable deduction, on a proportionate basis to the gross income received from the trade or business.

(2) Qualified items of income, gain, deduction, and loss—(i) In general. The term *qualified items of income, gain, deduction, and loss* means items of gross income, gain, deduction, and loss to the extent such items are—

(A) Effectively connected with the conduct of a trade or business within the United States (within the meaning of section 864(c), determined by substituting "trade or business (within the meaning of section 199A)" for "nonresident alien individual or a foreign corporation" or for "a foreign corporation" each place it appears); and

(B) Included or allowed in determining taxable income for the taxable year.

(ii) Items not taken into account. Notwithstanding paragraph (b)(2)(i) of this section and in accordance with section 199A(c)(3)(B) and (c)(4), the following items are not taken into account as qualified items of income, gain, deduction, or loss and thus are not included in determining QBI:

(A) Any item of short-term capital gain, short-term capital loss, long-term capital gain, or long-term capital loss, including any item treated as one of such items under any other provision of the Code. This provision does not apply to the extent an item is treated as anything other than short-term capital gain, short-term capital loss, long-term capital gain, or long-term capital loss.

(B) Any dividend, income equivalent to a dividend, or payment in lieu of dividends described in section 954(c)(1)(G). Any amount described in section 1385(a)(1) is not treated as described in this clause.

(C) Any interest income other than interest income which is properly allocable to a trade or business. For purposes of section 199A and this section, interest income attributable to an investment of working capital, reserves, or similar accounts is not properly allocable to a trade or business.

(D) Any item of gain or loss described in section 954(c)(1)(C) (transactions in commodities) or section 954(c)(1)(D) (excess foreign currency gains) applied in each case by substituting "trade or business (within the meaning of section 199A)" for "controlled foreign corporation."

(E) Any item of income, gain, deduction, or loss described in section 954(c)(1)(F) (income from notional principal contracts) determined without regard to section 954(c)(1)(F)(ii) and other than items attributable to notional principal contracts entered into in transactions qualifying under section 1221(a)(7).

(F) Any amount received from an annuity which is not received in connection with the trade or business.

(G) Any qualified REIT dividends as defined in paragraph (c)(2) of this section or qualified PTP income as defined in paragraph (c)(3) of this section.

(H) Reasonable compensation received by a shareholder from an S corporation. However, the S corporation's deduction for such reasonable compensation will reduce QBI if such deduction is properly allocable to the trade or business and is otherwise deductible for Federal income tax purposes.

(I) Any guaranteed payment described in section 707(c) received by a partner for services rendered with respect to the trade or business, regardless of whether the partner is an individual or an RPE. However, the partnership's deduction for such guaranteed payment will reduce QBI if such deduction is properly allocable to the trade or business and is otherwise deductible for Federal income tax purposes.

(J) Any payment described in section 707(a) received by a partner for services rendered with respect to the trade or business, regardless of whether the partner is an individual or an RPE. However, the partnership's deduction for such payment will reduce QBI if such deduction is properly allocable to the trade or business and is otherwise deductible for Federal income tax purposes.

* * *

(4) Wages. Expenses for all wages paid (or incurred in the case of an accrual method taxpayer) must be taken into account in computing QBI (if the requirements of this section and section 199A are satisfied) regardless of the application of the W-2 wage limitation described in § 1.199A–1(d)(2)(iv).

(5) Allocation of items among directly-conducted trades or businesses. If an individual or an RPE directly conducts multiple trades or businesses, and has items of QBI that are properly attributable to more than one trade or business, the individual or RPE must allocate those items among the several trades or businesses to which they are attributable using a reasonable method based on all the facts and circumstances. The individual or RPE may use a different reasonable method with respect to different items of income, gain, deduction, and loss. The chosen reasonable method for each item must be consistently applied from one taxable year to another and must clearly reflect the income and expenses of each trade or business. The overall combination of methods must also be reasonable based on all facts and circumstances. The books and records maintained for a trade or business must be consistent with any allocations under this paragraph (b)(5).

(c) Qualified REIT Dividends and Qualified PTP Income—(1) In general. Qualified REIT dividends and qualified PTP income are the sum of qualified REIT dividends as defined in paragraph (c)(2) of this section earned directly or through an RPE and the net amount of qualified PTP income as defined in paragraph (c)(3) of this section earned directly or through an RPE.

(2) Qualified REIT dividend—(i) The term *qualified REIT dividend* means any dividend from a REIT received during the taxable year which—

(A) Is not a capital gain dividend, as defined in section 857(b)(3); and

(B) Is not qualified dividend income, as defined in section 1(h)(11).

(ii) The term qualified REIT dividend does not include any REIT dividend received with respect to any share of REIT stock—

(A) That is held by the shareholder for 45 days or less (taking into account the principles of section 246(c)(3) and (4)) during the 91-day period beginning on the date which is 45 days before the date on which such share becomes ex-dividend with respect to such dividend; or

(B) To the extent that the shareholder is under an obligation (whether pursuant to a short sale or otherwise) to make related payments with respect to positions in substantially similar or related property.

(3) Qualified PTP income—(i) In general. The term *qualified PTP income* means the sum of—

(A) The net amount of such taxpayer's allocable share of income, gain, deduction, and loss from a PTP as defined in section 7704(b) that is not taxed as a corporation under section 7704(a); plus

(B) Any gain or loss attributable to assets of the PTP giving rise to ordinary income under section 751(a) or (b) that is considered attributable to the trades or businesses conducted by the partnership.

(ii) Special rules. The rules applicable to the determination of QBI described in paragraph (b) of this section also apply to the determination of a taxpayer's allocable share of income, gain, deduction, and loss from a PTP. An individual's allocable share of income from a PTP, and any section 751 gain or loss is qualified PTP income only to the extent the items meet the qualifications of section 199A and this section, including the requirement that the item is included or allowed in determining taxable income for the taxable year, and the requirement that the item be effectively connected with the conduct of a trade or business within the United States. For example, if an individual owns an interest in a PTP, and for the taxable year is allocated a distributive share of net loss which is disallowed under the passive activity rules of section 469, such loss is not taken into account for purposes of section 199A. The specified service trade or business limitations described in §§ 1.199A–1(d)(3) and 1.199A–5 also apply to income earned from a PTP. Furthermore, each PTP is required

to determine its qualified PTP income for each trade or business and report that information to its owners as described in § 1.199A–6(b)(3).

(d) [Reserved]

(e) Applicability date—(1) General rule. Except as provided in paragraph (e)(2) of this section, the provisions of this section apply to taxable years ending after February 8, 2019.

(2) Exceptions—(i) Anti-abuse rules. The provisions of paragraph (c)(2)(ii) of this section apply to taxable years ending after December 22, 2017.

(ii) Non-calendar year RPE. For purposes of determining QBI, W-2 wages, UBIA of qualified property, and the aggregate amount of qualified REIT dividends and qualified PTP income if an individual receives any of these items from an RPE with a taxable year that begins before January 1, 2018, and ends after December 31, 2017, such items are treated as having been incurred by the individual during the individual's taxable year in which or with which such RPE taxable year ends.

§ 1.199A–4 Aggregation.

(a) Scope and purpose. An individual or RPE may be engaged in more than one trade or business. Except as provided in this section, each trade or business is a separate trade or business for purposes of applying the limitations described in § 1.199A–1(d)(2)(iv). This section sets forth rules to allow individuals and RPEs to aggregate trades or businesses, treating the aggregate as a single trade or business for purposes of applying the limitations described in § 1.199A–1(d)(2)(iv). Trades or businesses may be aggregated only to the extent provided in this section, but aggregation by taxpayers is not required.

(b) Aggregation rules—(1) General rule. Trades or businesses may be aggregated only if an individual or RPE can demonstrate that—

(i) The same person or group of persons, directly or by attribution under sections 267(b) or 707(b), owns 50 percent or more of each trade or business to be aggregated, meaning in the case of such trades or businesses owned by an S corporation, 50 percent or more of the issued and outstanding shares of the corporation, or, in the case of such trades or businesses owned by a partnership, 50 percent or more of the capital or profits in the partnership;

(ii) The ownership described in paragraph (b)(1)(i) of this section exists for a majority of the taxable year, including the last day of the taxable year, in which the items attributable to each trade or business to be aggregated are included in income;

(iii) All of the items attributable to each trade or business to be aggregated are reported on returns with the same taxable year, not taking into account short taxable years;

(iv) None of the trades or businesses to be aggregated is a *specified service trade or business* (SSTB) as defined in § 1.199A–5; and

(v) The trades or businesses to be aggregated satisfy at least two of the following factors (based on all of the facts and circumstances):

(A) The trades or businesses provide products, property, or services that are the same or customarily offered together.

(B) The trades or businesses share facilities or share significant centralized business elements, such as personnel, accounting, legal, manufacturing, purchasing, human resources, or information technology resources.

(C) The trades or businesses are operated in coordination with, or reliance upon, one or more of the businesses in the aggregated group (for example, supply chain interdependencies).

* * *

(c) Reporting and consistency requirements—(1) Individuals. Once an individual chooses to aggregate two or more trades or businesses, the individual must consistently report the aggregated trades or businesses in all subsequent taxable years. A failure to aggregate will not be considered to be an aggregation for purposes of this rule. An individual

that fails to aggregate may not aggregate trades or businesses on an amended return (other than an amended return for the 2018 taxable year). However, an individual may add a newly created or newly acquired (including through non-recognition transfers) trade or business to an existing aggregated trade or business (including the aggregated trade or business of an RPE) if the requirements of paragraph (b)(1) of this section are satisfied. In a subsequent year, if there is a significant change in facts and circumstances such that an individual's prior aggregation of trades or businesses no longer qualifies for aggregation under the rules of this section, then the trades or businesses will no longer be aggregated within the meaning of this section, and the individual must reapply the rules in paragraph (b)(1) of this section to determine a new permissible aggregation (if any). An individual also must report aggregated trades or businesses of an RPE in which the individual holds a direct or indirect interest.

* * *

(3) RPEs. Once an RPE chooses to aggregate two or more trades or businesses, the RPE must consistently report the aggregated trades or businesses in all subsequent taxable years. A failure to aggregate will not be considered to be an aggregation for purposes of this rule. An RPE that fails to aggregate may not aggregate trades or businesses on an amended return (other than an amended return for the 2018 taxable year). However, an RPE may add a newly created or newly acquired (including through non-recognition transfers) trade or business to an existing aggregated trade or business (other than the aggregated trade or business of a lower-tier RPE) if the requirements of paragraph (b)(1) of this section are satisfied. In a subsequent year, if there is a significant change in facts and circumstances such that an RPE's prior aggregation of trades or businesses no longer qualifies for aggregation under the rules of this section, then the trades or businesses will no longer be aggregated within the meaning of this section, and the RPE must reapply the rules in paragraph (b)(1) of this section to determine a new permissible aggregation (if any). An RPE also must report aggregated trades or businesses of a lower-tier RPE in which the RPE holds a direct or indirect interest.

* * *

(d) **Examples.** The following examples illustrate the principles of this section. For purposes of these examples, assume the taxpayer is a United States citizen, all individuals and RPEs use a calendar taxable year, there are no ownership changes during the taxable year, all trades or businesses satisfy the requirements under section 162, all tax items are effectively connected to a trade or business within the United States within the meaning of section 864(c), and none of the trades or businesses is an SSTB within the meaning of § 1.199A–5. Except as otherwise specified, a single capital letter denotes an individual taxpayer.

(1) **Example 1—(i) Facts.** A wholly owns and operates a catering business and a restaurant through separate disregarded entities. The catering business and the restaurant share centralized purchasing to obtain volume discounts and a centralized accounting office that performs all of the bookkeeping, tracks and issues statements on all of the receivables, and prepares the payroll for each business. A maintains a website and print advertising materials that reference both the catering business and the restaurant. A uses the restaurant kitchen to prepare food for the catering business. The catering business employs its own staff and owns equipment and trucks that are not used or associated with the restaurant.

(ii) **Analysis.** Because the restaurant and catering business are held in disregarded entities, A will be treated as operating each of these businesses directly and thereby satisfies paragraph (b)(1)(i) of this section. Under paragraph (b)(1)(v) of this section, A satisfies the following factors: paragraph (b)(1)(v)(A) of this section is met as both businesses offer prepared food to customers; and paragraph (b)

(1)(v)(B) of this section is met because the two businesses share the same kitchen facilities in addition to centralized purchasing, marketing, and accounting. Having satisfied paragraphs (b)(1)(i) through (v) of this section, A may treat the catering business and the restaurant as a single trade or business for purposes of applying § 1.199A–1(d).

(2) **Example 2—(i) Facts.** Assume the same facts as in *Example 1* of paragraph (d)(1) of this section, but the catering and restaurant businesses are owned in separate partnerships and A, B, C, and D each own a 25% interest in each of the two partnerships. A, B, C, and D are unrelated.

(ii) **Analysis.** Because under paragraph (b) (1)(i) of this section A, B, C, and D together own more than 50% of each of the two partnerships, they may each treat the catering business and the restaurant as a single trade or business for purposes of applying § 1.199A–1(d).

(3) **Example 3—(i) Facts.** W owns a 75% interest in S1, an S corporation, and a 75% interest in PRS, a partnership. S1 manufactures clothing and PRS is a retail pet food store. W manages S1 and PRS.

(ii) **Analysis.** W owns more than 50% of the stock of S1 and more than 50% of PRS thereby satisfying paragraph (b)(1)(i) of this section. Although W manages both S1 and PRS, W is not able to satisfy the requirements of paragraph (b)(1)(v) of this section as the two businesses do not provide goods or services that are the same or customarily offered together; there are no significant centralized business elements; and no facts indicate that the businesses are operated in coordination with, or reliance upon, one another. W must treat S1 and PRS as separate trades or businesses for purposes of applying § 1.199A–1(d).

* * *

§ 1.199A–5 Specified service trades or businesses and the trade or business of performing services as an employee.

(a) **Scope and effect—(1) Scope.** This section provides guidance on specified service trades or businesses (SSTBs) and the trade or business of performing services as an employee. This paragraph (a) describes the effect of a trade or business being an SSTB and the trade or business of performing services as an employee. Paragraph (b) of this section provides definitional guidance on SSTBs. Paragraph (c) of this section provides special rules related to SSTBs. Paragraph (d) of this section provides guidance on the trade or business of performing services as an employee. The provisions of this section apply solely for purposes of section 199A of the Internal Revenue Code (Code).

(2) **Effect of being an SSTB.** If a trade or business is an SSTB, no qualified business income (QBI), W-2 wages, or unadjusted basis immediately after acquisition (UBIA) of qualified property from the SSTB may be taken into account by any individual whose taxable income exceeds the phase-in range as defined in § 1.199A–1(b)(4), even if the item is derived from an activity that is not itself a specified service activity. The SSTB limitation also applies to income earned from a publicly traded partnership (PTP). If a trade or business conducted by a relevant passthrough entity (RPE) or PTP is an SSTB, this limitation applies to any direct or indirect individual owners of the business, regardless of whether the owner is passive or participated in any specified service activity. However, the SSTB limitation does not apply to individuals with taxable income below the threshold amount as defined in § 1.199A–1(b)(12). A phase-in rule, provided in § 1.199A–1(d)(2), applies to individuals with taxable income within the phase-in range, allowing them to take into account a certain "applicable percentage" of QBI, W-2 wages, and UBIA of qualified property from an SSTB. The phase-in rule also applies to income earned from a PTP. A direct or indirect owner of a trade or business engaged in the performance of a specified service is engaged in the performance of the specified service for purposes of section 199A and this section, regardless of whether the owner is passive or participated in the specified service activity.

(3) **Trade or business of performing services as an employee.** The trade or business of performing services as an employee is not a trade or business for purposes of section 199A and the regulations thereunder. Therefore, no items of income, gain, deduction, or loss from the trade or business of performing services as an employee constitute QBI within the meaning of section 199A and § 1.199A–3. No taxpayer may claim a section 199A deduction for wage income, regardless of the amount of taxable income.

(b) **Definition of specified service trade or business.** Except as provided in paragraph (c)(1) of this section, the term *specified service trade or business (SSTB)* means any of the following:

(1) **Listed SSTBs.** Any trade or business involving the performance of services in one or more of the following fields:

(i) *Health* as described in paragraph (b)(2)(ii) of this section;

(ii) *Law* as described in paragraph (b)(2)(iii) of this section;

(iii) *Accounting* as described in paragraph (b)(2)(iv) of this section;

(iv) *Actuarial science* as described in paragraph (b)(2)(v) of this section;

(v) *Performing arts* as described in paragraph (b)(2)(vi) of this section;

(vi) *Consulting* as described in paragraph (b)(2)(vii) of this section;

(vii) *Athletics* as described in paragraph (b)(2)(viii) of this section;

(viii) *Financial services* as described in paragraph (b)(2)(ix) of this section;

(ix) *Brokerage services* as described in paragraph (b)(2)(x) of this section;

(x) *Investing and investment management* as described in paragraph (b)(2)(xi) of this section;

(xi) *Trading* as described in paragraph (b)(2)(xii) of this section;

(xii) *Dealing in securities (as defined in section 475(c)(2)), partnership interests, or commodities (as defined in section 475(e)(2))* as described in paragraph (b)(2)(xiii) of this section; or

(xiii) *Any trade or business where the principal asset of such trade or business is the reputation or skill of one or more of its employees or owners* as defined in paragraph (b)(2)(xiv) of this section.

(2) Additional rules for applying section 199A(d)(2) and paragraph (b) of this section—(i) In general—(A) No effect on other tax rules. This paragraph (b)(2) provides additional rules for determining whether a business is an SSTB within the meaning of section 199A(d)(2) and paragraph (b) of this section only. The rules of this paragraph (b)(2) apply solely for purposes of section 199A and therefore may not be taken into account for purposes of applying any provision of law or regulation other than section 199A and the regulations thereunder, except to the extent such provision expressly refers to section 199A(d) or this section.

(B) Hedging transactions. Income, deduction, gain or loss from a *hedging transaction* (as defined in § 1.1221–2(b)) entered into by an individual or RPE in the normal course of the individual's or RPE's trade or business is treated as income, deduction, gain, or loss from that trade or business for purposes of this paragraph (b)(2). See also § 1.446–4.

(ii) Meaning of services performed in the field of health. For purposes of section 199A(d)(2) and paragraph (b)(1)(i) of this section only, the *performance of services in the field of health* means the provision of medical services by individuals such as physicians, pharmacists, nurses, dentists, veterinarians, physical therapists, psychologists, and other similar healthcare professionals performing services in their capacity as such. The performance of services in the field of health does not include the provision of services not directly related to a medical services field, even though the services provided may purportedly relate to the health of the service recipient. For example, the performance of services in the field of health does not include the operation of health clubs or health spas that provide physical exercise or conditioning to their customers, payment processing, or the research, testing, and manufacture and/or sales of pharmaceuticals or medical devices.

(iii) Meaning of services performed in the field of law. For purposes of section 199A(d)(2) and paragraph (b)(1)(ii) of this section only, the *performance of services in the field of law* means the performance of legal services by individuals such as lawyers, paralegals, legal arbitrators, mediators, and similar professionals performing services in their capacity as such. The performance of services in the field of law does not include the provision of services that do not require skills unique to the field of law; for example, the provision of services in the field of law does not include the provision of services by printers, delivery services, or stenography services.

(iv) Meaning of services performed in the field of accounting. For purposes of section 199A(d)(2) and paragraph (b)(1)(iii) of this section only, the *performance of services in the field of accounting* means the provision of services by individuals such as accountants, enrolled agents, return preparers, financial auditors, and similar professionals performing services in their capacity as such.

(v) Meaning of services performed in the field of actuarial science. For purposes of section 199A(d)(2) and paragraph (b)(1)(iv) of this section only, the *performance of services in the field of actuarial science* means the provision of services by individuals such as actuaries and similar professionals performing services in their capacity as such.

(vi) Meaning of services performed in the field of performing arts. For purposes of section 199A(d)(2) and paragraph (b)(1)(v) of this section only, the *performance of services in the field of the performing arts* means the performance of services by individuals who participate in the creation of performing arts, such as actors, singers, musicians, entertainers, directors, and similar professionals performing services in their capacity as such. The performance of services in the field of performing arts does not include the provision of services that do not require skills unique to the creation of performing arts, such as the maintenance and operation of equipment or facilities for use in the performing arts. Similarly, the performance of services in the field of the performing arts does not include the provision of services by persons who broadcast or otherwise disseminate video or audio of performing arts to the public.

(vii) Meaning of services performed in the field of consulting. For purposes of section 199A(d)(2) and paragraph (b)(1)(vi) of this section only, the *performance of services in the field of consulting* means the provision of professional advice and counsel to clients to assist the client in achieving goals and solving problems. Consulting includes providing advice and counsel regarding advocacy with the intention of influencing decisions made by a government or governmental agency and all attempts to influence legislators and other government officials on behalf of a client by lobbyists and other similar professionals performing services in their capacity as such. The performance of services in the field of consulting does not include the performance of services other than advice and counsel, such as sales (or economically similar services) or the provision of training and educational courses. For purposes of the preceding sentence, the determination of whether a person's services

are sales or economically similar services will be based on all the facts and circumstances of that person's business. Such facts and circumstances include, for example, the manner in which the taxpayer is compensated for the services provided. Performance of services in the field of consulting does not include the performance of consulting services embedded in, or ancillary to, the sale of goods or performance of services on behalf of a trade or business that is otherwise not an SSTB (such as typical services provided by a building contractor) if there is no separate payment for the consulting services. Services within the fields of architecture and engineering are not treated as consulting services.

(viii) Meaning of services performed in the field of athletics. For purposes of section 199A(d)(2) and paragraph (b)(1)(vii) of this section only, the *performance of services in the field of athletics* means the performance of services by individuals who participate in athletic competition such as athletes, coaches, and team managers in sports such as baseball, basketball, football, soccer, hockey, martial arts, boxing, bowling, tennis, golf, skiing, snowboarding, track and field, billiards, and racing. The performance of services in the field of athletics does not include the provision of services that do not require skills unique to athletic competition, such as the maintenance and operation of equipment or facilities for use in athletic events. Similarly, the performance of services in the field of athletics does not include the provision of services by persons who broadcast or otherwise disseminate video or audio of athletic events to the public.

(ix) Meaning of services performed in the field of financial services. For purposes of section 199A(d)(2) and paragraph (b)(1)(viii) of this section only, the *performance of services in the field of financial services* means the provision of financial services to clients including managing wealth, advising clients with respect to finances, developing retirement plans, developing wealth transition plans, the provision of advisory and other similar services regarding valuations, mergers, acquisitions, dispositions, restructurings (including in title 11 of the Code or similar cases), and raising financial capital by underwriting, or acting as a client's agent in the issuance of securities and similar services. This includes services provided by financial advisors, investment bankers, wealth planners, retirement advisors, and other similar professionals performing services in their capacity as such. Solely for purposes of section 199A, the performance of services in the field of financial services does not include taking deposits or making loans, but does include arranging lending transactions between a lender and borrower.

(x) Meaning of services performed in the field of brokerage services. For purposes of section 199A(d)(2) and paragraph (b)(1)(ix) of this section only, the *performance of services in the field of brokerage services* includes services in which a person arranges transactions between a buyer and a seller with respect to securities (as defined in section 475(c)(2)) for a commission or fee. This includes services provided by stock brokers and other similar professionals, but does not include services provided by real estate agents and brokers, or insurance agents and brokers.

(xi) Meaning of the provision of services in investing and investment management. For purposes of section 199A(d)(2) and paragraph (b)(1)(x) of this section only, the *performance of services that consist of investing and investment management* refers to a trade or business involving the receipt of fees for providing investing, asset management, or investment management services, including providing advice with respect to buying and selling investments. The performance of services of investing and investment management does not include directly managing real property.

(xii) Meaning of the provision of services in trading. For purposes of section 199A(d)(2) and paragraph (b)(1)(xi) of this section only, the *performance of services that consist*

of trading means a trade or business of trading in securities (as defined in section 475(c)(2)), commodities (as defined in section 475(e)(2)), or partnership interests. Whether a person is a trader in securities, commodities, or partnership interests is determined by taking into account all relevant facts and circumstances, including the source and type of profit that is associated with engaging in the activity regardless of whether that person trades for the person's own account, for the account of others, or any combination thereof.

(xiii) Meaning of the provision of services in dealing—(A) Dealing in securities. For purposes of section 199A(d)(2) and paragraph (b)(1)(xii) of this section only, *the performance of services that consist of dealing in securities (as defined in section 475(c)(2))* means regularly purchasing securities from and selling securities to customers in the ordinary course of a trade or business or regularly offering to enter into, assume, offset, assign, or otherwise terminate positions in securities with customers in the ordinary course of a trade or business. Solely for purposes of the preceding sentence, the performance of services to originate a loan is not treated as the purchase of a security from the borrower in determining whether the lender is dealing in securities.

(B) Dealing in commodities. For purposes of section 199A(d)(2) and paragraph (b)(1)(xii) of this section only, *the performance of services that consist of dealing in commodities (as defined in section 475(e)(2))* means regularly purchasing commodities from and selling commodities to customers in the ordinary course of a trade or business or regularly offering to enter into, assume, offset, assign, or otherwise terminate positions in commodities with customers in the ordinary course of a trade or business. Solely for purposes of the preceding sentence, gains and losses from qualified active sales as defined in paragraph (b)(2)(xiii)(B)(*1*) of this section are not taken into account in determining whether a person is engaged in the trade or business of dealing in commodities.

(1) Qualified active sale. The term *qualified active sale* means the sale of commodities in the active conduct of a commodities business as a producer, processor, merchant, or handler of commodities if the trade or business is as an active producer, processor, merchant or handler of commodities. A hedging transaction described in paragraph (b)(2)(i)(B) of this section is treated as a qualified active sale. The sale of commodities held by a trade or business other than in its capacity as an active producer, processor, merchant, or handler of commodities is not a qualified active sale. For example, the sale by a trade or business of commodities that were held for investment or speculation would not be a qualified active sale.

(2) Active conduct of a commodities business. For purposes of paragraph (b)(2)(xiii)(B)(*1*) of this section, a trade or business is engaged in the active conduct of a commodities business as a producer, processor, merchant, or handler of commodities only with respect to commodities for which each of the conditions described in paragraphs (b)(2)(xiii)(B)(*3*) through (*5*) of this section are satisfied.

(3) Directly holds commodities as inventory or similar property. The commodities trade or business holds the commodities directly, and not through an agent or independent contractor, as inventory or similar property. The term inventory or similar property means property that is stock in trade of the trade or business or other property of a kind that would properly be included in the inventory of the trade or business if on hand at the close of the taxable year, or property held by the trade or business primarily for sale to customers in the ordinary course of its trade or business.

(4) Directly incurs substantial expenses in the ordinary course. The commodities trade or business incurs substantial expenses in the ordinary course of the commodities trade or business from engaging in one or more of the following activities directly, and not through an agent or independent contractor—

(i) Substantial activities in the production of the commodities, including planting, tending or harvesting crops, raising or slaughtering livestock, or extracting minerals;

(ii) Substantial processing activities prior to the sale of the commodities, including the blending and drying of agricultural commodities, or the concentrating, refining, mixing, crushing, aerating or milling of commodities; or

(iii) Significant activities as described in paragraph (b)(2)(xiii)(B)(*5*) of this section.

(5) Significant activities for purposes of paragraph (b)(2)(xiii)(B)(4)(iii) of this section. The commodities trade or business performs significant activities with respect to the commodities that consists of—

(i) The physical movement, handling and storage of the commodities, including preparation of contracts and invoices, arranging transportation, insurance and credit, arranging for receipt, transfer or negotiation of shipping documents, arranging storage or warehousing, and dealing with quality claims;

(ii) Owning and operating facilities for storage or warehousing; or

(iii) Owning, chartering, or leasing vessels or vehicles for the transportation of the commodities.

(C) Dealing in partnership interests. For purposes of section 199A(d)(2) and paragraph (b)(1)(xii) of this section only, *the performance of services that consist of dealing in partnership interests* means regularly purchasing partnership interests from and selling partnership interests to customers in the ordinary course of a trade or business or regularly offering to enter into, assume, offset, assign, or otherwise terminate positions in partnership interests with customers in the ordinary course of a trade or business.

(xiv) Meaning of trade or business where the principal asset of such trade or business is the reputation or skill of one or more employees or owners. For purposes of section 199A(d)(2) and paragraph (b)(1)(xiii) of this section only, the term *any trade or business where the principal asset of such trade or business is the reputation or skill of one or more of its employees or owners* means any trade or business that consists of any of the following (or any combination thereof):

(A) A trade or business in which a person receives fees, compensation, or other income for endorsing products or services;

(B) A trade or business in which a person licenses or receives fees, compensation, or other income for the use of an individual's image, likeness, name, signature, voice, trademark, or any other symbols associated with the individual's identity; or

(C) Receiving fees, compensation, or other income for appearing at an event or on radio, television, or another media format.

(D) For purposes of paragraphs (b)(2)(xiv)(A) through (C) of this section, the term *fees, compensation, or other income* includes the receipt of a partnership interest and the corresponding distributive share of income, deduction, gain, or loss from the partnership, or the receipt of stock of an S corporation and the corresponding income, deduction, gain, or loss from the S corporation stock.

(3) Examples. The following examples illustrate the rules in paragraphs (a) and (b) of this section. The examples do not address all types of services that may or may not qualify as specified services. Unless otherwise provided, the individual in each example has taxable income in excess of the threshold amount.

(i) Example 1. B is a board-certified pharmacist who contracts as an independent contractor with X, a small medical facility in a rural area. X employs one full time pharmacist, but contracts with B when X's needs exceed the capacity of its full-time staff. When engaged by X, B is responsible for receiving and reviewing orders from physicians providing medical care at the facility; making recommendations on dosing and alternatives to the ordering physician; performing inoculations, checking for drug interactions, and filling pharmaceutical orders for patients receiving care at X. B is engaged in the performance of services in the field of health within the meaning of section 199A(d)(2) and paragraphs (b)(1)(i) and (b)(2)(ii) of this section.

(ii) Example 2. X is the operator of a residential facility that provides a variety of services to senior citizens who reside on campus. For residents, X offers standard domestic services including housing management and maintenance, meals, laundry, entertainment, and other similar services. In addition, X contracts with local professional healthcare organizations to offer residents a range of medical and health services provided at the facility, including skilled nursing care, physical and occupational therapy, speech-language pathology services, medical social services, medications, medical supplies and equipment used in the facility, ambulance transportation to the nearest supplier of needed services, and dietary counseling. X receives all of its income from residents for the costs associated with residing at the facility. Any health and medical services are billed directly by the healthcare providers to the senior citizens for those professional healthcare services even though those services are provided at the facility. X does not perform services in the field of health within the meaning of section 199A(d)(2) and paragraphs (b)(1)(i) and (b)(2)(ii) of this section.

(iii) Example 3. Y operates specialty surgical centers that provide outpatient medical procedures that do not require the patient to remain overnight for recovery or observation following the procedure. Y is a private organization that owns a number of facilities throughout the country. For each facility, Y ensures compliance with state and Federal laws for medical facilities and manages the facility's operations and performs all administrative functions. Y does not employ physicians, nurses, and medical assistants, but enters into agreements with other professional medical organizations or directly with the medical professionals to perform the procedures and provide all medical care. Patients are billed by Y for the facility costs relating to their procedure and by the healthcare professional or their affiliated organization for the actual costs of the procedure conducted by the physician and medical support team. Y does not perform services in the field of health within the meaning of section 199A(d)(2) and paragraphs (b)(1)(i) and (b)(2)(ii) of this section.

(iv) Example 4. Z is the developer and the only provider of a patented test used to detect a particular medical condition. Z accepts test orders only from health care professionals (Z's clients), does not have contact with patients, and Z's employees do not diagnose, treat, or manage any aspect of patient care. A, who manages Z's testing operations, is the only employee with an advanced medical degree. All other employees are technical support staff and not healthcare professionals. Z's workers are highly educated, but the skills the workers bring to the job are not often useful for Z's testing methods. In order to perform the duties required by Z, employees receive more than a year of specialized training for working with Z's test, which is of no use to other employers. Upon completion of an ordered test, Z analyses the results and provides its clients a report summarizing the findings. Z does not discuss the report's results, or the patient's diagnosis or treatment with any health care provider or the patient. Z is not informed by the healthcare provider as to the healthcare provider's diagnosis or treatment. Z is not providing services in the field of health within the meaning of section 199A(d)(2) and paragraphs (b)(1)(i) and (b)(2)(ii) of this section or where the principal asset of the trade or business is the reputation or skill of one or more of its employees within the meaning of paragraphs (b)(1)(xiii) and (b)(2)(xiv) of this section.

(v) Example 5. A, a singer and songwriter, writes and records a song. A is paid a mechanical royalty when the song is licensed or streamed. A is also paid a performance royalty when the recorded song is played publicly. A is engaged in the performance of services in an SSTB in the field of performing arts within the meaning of section 199A(d)(2) or paragraphs (b)(1)(v) and (b)(2)(vi) of this section. The royalties that A receives for the song are not eligible for a deduction under section 199A.

(vi) Example 6. B is a partner in Movie LLC, a partnership. Movie LLC is a film production company. Movie LLC plans and coordinates film production. Movie LLC shares in the profits of the films that it produces. Therefore, Movie LLC is engaged in the performance of services in an SSTB in the field of performing arts within the meaning of section 199A(d)(2) or paragraphs (b)(1)(v) and (b)(2)(vi) of this section. B is a passive owner in Movie LLC and does not provide any services with respect to Movie LLC. However, because Movie LLC is engaged in an SSTB in the field of performing arts, B's distributive share of the income, gain, deduction, and loss with respect to Movie LLC is not eligible for a deduction under section 199A.

(vii) Example 7. C is a partner in Partnership, which solely owns and operates a professional sports team. Partnership employs athletes and sells tickets and broadcast rights for games in which the sports team competes. Partnership sells the broadcast rights to Broadcast LLC, a separate trade or business. Broadcast LLC solely broadcasts the games. Partnership is engaged in the performance of services in an SSTB in the field of athletics within the meaning of section 199A(d)(2) or paragraphs (b)(1)(vii) and (b)(2)(viii) of this section. The tickets sales and the sale of the broadcast rights are both the performance of services in the field of athletics. C is a passive owner in Partnership and C does not provide any services with respect to Partnership or the sports team. However, because Partnership is engaged in an

SSTB in the field of athletics, C's distributive share of the income, gain, deduction, and loss with respect to Partnership is not eligible for a deduction under section 199A. Broadcast LLC is not engaged in the performance of services in an SSTB in the field of athletics.

(viii) Example 8. D is in the business of providing services that assist unrelated entities in making their personnel structures more efficient. D studies its client's organization and structure and compares it to peers in its industry. D then makes recommendations and provides advice to its client regarding possible changes in the client's personnel structure, including the use of temporary workers. D does not provide any temporary workers to its clients and D's compensation and fees are not affected by whether D's clients used temporary workers. D is engaged in the performance of services in an SSTB in the field of consulting within the meaning of section 199A(d)(2) or paragraphs (b)(1)(vi) and (b)(2)(vii) of this section.

(ix) Example 9. E is an individual who owns and operates a temporary worker staffing firm primarily focused on the software consulting industry. Business clients hire E to provide temporary workers that have the necessary technical skills and experience with a variety of business software to provide consulting and advice regarding the proper selection and operation of software most appropriate for the business they are advising. E does not have a technical software engineering background and does not provide software consulting advice herself. E reviews resumes and refers candidates to the client when the client indicates a need for temporary workers. E does not evaluate her clients' needs about whether the client needs workers and does not evaluate the clients' consulting contracts to determine the type of expertise needed. Rather, the client provides E with a job description indicating the required skills for the upcoming consulting project. E is paid a fixed fee for each temporary worker actually hired by the client and receives a bonus if that worker is hired permanently within a year of referral. E's fee is not contingent on the profits of its clients. E is not considered to be engaged in the performance of services in the field of consulting within the meaning of section 199A(d)(2) or (b)(1)(vi) and (b)(2)(vii) of this section.

(x) Example 10. F is in the business of licensing software to customers. F discusses and evaluates the customer's software needs with the customer. The taxpayer advises the customer on the particular software products it licenses. F is paid a flat price for the software license. After the customer licenses the software, F helps to implement the software. F is engaged in the trade or business of licensing software and not engaged in an SSTB in the field of consulting within the meaning of section 199A(d)(2) or paragraphs (b)(1)(vi) and (b)(2)(vii) of this section.

(xi) Example 11. G is in the business of providing services to assist clients with their finances. G will study a particular client's financial situation, including, the client's present income, savings, and investments, and anticipated future economic and financial needs. Based on this study, G will then assist the client in making decisions and plans regarding the client's financial activities. Such financial planning includes the design of a personal budget to assist the client in monitoring the client's financial situation, the adoption of investment strategies tailored to the client's needs, and other similar services. G is engaged in the performance of services in an SSTB in the field of financial services within the meaning of section 199A(d)(2) or paragraphs (b)(1)(viii) and (b)(2)(ix) of this section.

(xii) Example 12. H is in the business of franchising a brand of personal financial planning offices, which generally provide personal wealth management, retirement planning, and other financial advice services to customers for a fee. H does not provide financial planning services itself. H licenses the right to use the business tradename, other branding intellectual property, and a marketing plan to third-party financial planner franchisees that operate the franchised locations and provide all services to customers. In exchange, the franchisees compensate H based on a fee structure, which includes a one-time fee to acquire the franchise. H is not engaged in the performance of services in the field of financial services within the meaning of section 199A(d)(2) or paragraphs (b)(1)(viii) and (b)(2)(ix) of this section.

(xiii) Example 13. J is in the business of executing transactions for customers involving various types of securities or commodities generally traded through organized exchanges or other similar networks. Customers place orders with J to trade securities or commodities based on the taxpayer's recommendations. J's compensation for its services typically is based on completion of the trade orders. J is engaged in an SSTB in the field of brokerage services within the meaning of section 199A(d)(2) or paragraphs (b)(1)(ix) and (b)(2)(x) of this section.

(xiv) Example 14. K owns 100% of Corp, an S corporation, which operates a bicycle sales and repair business. Corp has 8 employees, including K. Half of Corp's net income is generated from sales of new and used bicycles and related goods, such as helmets, and bicycle-related equipment. The other half of Corp's net income is generated from bicycle repair services performed by K and Corp's other employees. Corp's assets consist of inventory, fixtures, bicycle repair equipment, and a leasehold on its retail location. Several of the employees and G have worked in the bicycle business for many years, and have acquired substantial skill and reputation in the field. Customers often consult with the employees on the best bicycle for purchase. K is in the business of sales and repairs of bicycles and is not engaged in an SSTB within the meaning of section 199A(d)(2) or paragraphs (b)(1)(xiii) and (b)(2)(xiv) of this section.

(xv) Example 15. L is a well-known chef and the sole owner of multiple restaurants each of which is owned in a disregarded entity. Due to L's skill and reputation as a chef, L receives an endorsement fee of $500,000 for the use of L's name on a line of cooking utensils and cookware. L is in the trade or business of being a chef and owning restaurants and such trade or business is not an SSTB. However, L is also in the trade or business of receiving endorsement income. L's trade or business consisting of the receipt of the endorsement fee for L's skill and/or reputation is an SSTB within the meaning of section 199A(d)(2) or paragraphs (b)(1)(xiii) and (b)(2)(xiv) of this section.

(xvi) Example 16. M is a well-known actor. M entered into a partnership with Shoe Company, in which M contributed her likeness and the use of her name to the partnership in exchange for a 50% interest in the partnership and a guaranteed payment. M's trade or business consisting of the receipt of the partnership interest and the corresponding distributive share with respect to the partnership interest for M's likeness and the use of her name is an SSTB within the meaning of section 199A(d)(2) or paragraphs (b)(1)(xiii) and (b)(2)(xiv) of this section.

(c) Special rules—(1) De minimis rule— (i) Gross receipts of $25 million or less. For a trade or business with gross receipts of $25 million or less for the taxable year, a trade or business is not an SSTB if less than 10 percent of the gross receipts of the trade or business are attributable to the performance of services in a field described in paragraph (b) of this section. For purposes of determining whether this 10 percent test is satisfied, the performance of any activity incident to the actual performance of services in the field is considered the performance of services in that field.

(ii) Gross receipts of greater than $25 million. For a trade or business with gross receipts of greater than $25 million for the taxable year, the rules of paragraph (c)(1)(i) of this section are applied by substituting "5 percent" for "10 percent" each place it appears.

(iii) Examples. The following examples illustrate the provisions of paragraph (c)(1) of this section.

(A) Example 1. Landscape LLC sells lawn care and landscaping equipment and also provides advice and counsel on landscape design for large office parks and residential buildings. The landscape design services include advice on the selection and placement of trees, shrubs, and flowers and are considered to be the performance of services in the field of consulting under paragraphs (b)(1)(vi) and (b)(2)(vii) of this section. Landscape LLC separately invoices for its landscape design services and does not sell the trees, shrubs, or flowers it recommends for use in the landscape design. Landscape LLC maintains one set of books and records and treats the equipment sales and design services as a single trade or business for purposes of sections 162 and 199A. Landscape LLC has gross receipts of $2 million. $250,000 of the gross receipts is attributable to the landscape design services, an SSTB. Because the gross receipts from the consulting services exceed 10 percent of Landscape LLC's total gross receipts, the entirety of Landscape LLC's trade or business is considered an SSTB.

(B) Example 2. Animal Care LLC provides veterinarian services performed by licensed staff and also develops and sells its own line of organic dog food at its veterinarian clinic and online. The veterinarian services are considered to be the performance of services in the field of health under paragraphs (b)(1)(i) and (b)(2)(ii) of this section. Animal Care LLC separately invoices for its veterinarian services and the sale of its organic dog food. Animal Care LLC maintains separate books and records for its veterinarian clinic and its development and sale of its dog food. Animal Care LLC also has separate employees who are unaffiliated with the veterinary clinic and who only work on the formulation, marketing, sales, and distribution of the organic dog food products. Animal Care LLC treats its veterinary practice and the dog food development and sales as separate trades or businesses for purposes of section 162 and 199A. Animal Care LLC has gross receipts of $3,000,000. $1,000,000 of the gross receipts is attributable to the veterinary services, an SSTB. Although the gross receipts from the services in the field of health exceed 10 percent of Animal Care LLC's total gross receipts, the dog food development and sales business is not considered an SSTB due to the fact that the veterinary practice and the dog food development and sales are separate trades or businesses under section 162.

(2) Services or property provided to an SSTB—(i) In general. If a trade or business provides property or services to an SSTB within the meaning of this section and there is 50 percent or more common ownership of the trades or businesses, that portion of the trade or business of providing property or services to the 50 percent or more commonly-owned SSTB will be treated as a separate SSTB with respect to the related parties.

(ii) 50 percent or more common ownership. For purposes of paragraph (c)(2)(i) and (ii) of this section, 50 percent or more common ownership includes direct or indirect ownership by related parties within the meaning of sections 267(b) or 707(b).

(iii) Examples. The following examples illustrate the provisions of paragraph (c)(2) of this section.

(A) Example 1. Law Firm is a partnership that provides legal services to clients, owns its own office building and employs its own administrative staff. Law Firm divides into three partnerships. Partnership 1 performs legal services to clients. Partnership 2 owns the office building and rents the entire building to Partnership 1. Partnership 3 employs the administrative staff and through a contract with Partnership 1 provides administrative services to Partnership 1 in exchange for fees. All three of the partnerships are owned by the same people (the original owners of Law Firm). Because Partnership 2 provides all of its property to Partnership 1, and Partnership 3 provides all of its services to Partnership 1, Partnerships 2 and 3 will each be treated as an SSTB under paragraph (c)(2) of this section.

(B) Example 2. Assume the same facts as in Example 1 of this paragraph (c)(2), except that Partnership 2, which owns the office building, rents 50 percent of the building to Partnership 1, which provides legal services, and the other 50 percent to various unrelated third party tenants. Because Partnership 2 is owned by the same people as Partnership 1, the portion of Partnership 2's leasing activity related to the lease of the building to Partnership 1 will be treated as a separate SSTB. The remaining 50 percent of Partnership 2's leasing activity will not be treated as an SSTB.

(d) Trade or business of performing services as an employee—(1) In general. The trade or business of performing services as an employee is not a trade or business for purposes of section 199A and the regulations thereunder. Therefore, no items of income, gain, deduction, and loss from the trade or business of performing services as an employee constitute QBI within the meaning of section 199A and § 1.199A–3. Except as provided in paragraph (d)(3) of this section, income from the trade or business of performing services as an employee refers to all wages (within the meaning of section 3401(a)) and other income earned in a capacity as an employee, including payments described in § 1.6041–2(a)(1) (other than payments to individuals described in section 3121(d)(3)) and § 1.6041–2(b)(1).

(2) Employer's Federal employment tax classification of employee immaterial. For purposes of determining whether wages are earned in a capacity as an employee as provided in paragraph (d)(1) of this section, the treatment of an employee by an employer as anything other than an employee for Federal employment tax purposes is immaterial. Thus, if a worker should be properly classified as an employee, it is of no consequence that the employee is treated as a non-employee by the employer for Federal employment tax purposes.

(3) Presumption that former employees are still employees—(i) Presumption. Solely for purposes of section 199A(d)(1)(B) and paragraph (d)(1) of this section, an individual that was properly treated as an employee for Federal employment tax purposes by the person to which he or she provided services and who is subsequently treated as other than an employee by such person with regard to the provision of substantially the same services directly or indirectly to the person (or a related person), is presumed, for three years after ceasing to be treated as an employee for Federal employment tax purposes, to be in the trade or business of performing services as an employee with regard to such services. As provided in paragraph (d)(3)(ii) of this section, this presumption may be rebutted upon a showing by the individual that, under Federal tax law, regulations, and principles (including common-law employee classification rules), the individual is performing services in a capacity other than as an employee. This presumption applies regardless of whether the individual provides services directly or indirectly through an entity or entities.

(ii) Rebuttal of presumption. Upon notice from the IRS, an individual rebuts the presumption in paragraph (d)(3)(i) of this section by providing records, such as contracts or partnership agreements, that provide sufficient evidence to corroborate the individual's status as a non-employee.

(iii) Examples. The following examples illustrate the provision of paragraph (d)(3) of this section. Unless otherwise provided, the individual in each example has taxable income in excess of the threshold amount.

(A) Example 1. A is employed by PRS, a partnership for Federal tax purposes, as a full-time employee and is treated as such for Federal employment tax purposes. A quits his job for PRS and enters into a contract with PRS under which A provides substantially the same services that A previously provided to PRS in A's capacity as an employee. Because A was treated as an employee for services he provided to PRS, and now is no longer treated as an employee with regard to such services, A is presumed (solely for purposes of section 199A(d)(1)(B) and paragraphs (a)(3) and (d) of this section) to be in the trade or business of performing services as an employee with regard to his services performed for PRS. Unless the presumption is rebutted with a showing that, under Federal tax law, regulations, and principles (including the common-law employee classification rules), A is not an employee, any amounts paid by PRS to A with respect to such services will not be QBI for purposes of section 199A. The presumption would apply even if, instead of contracting directly with PRS, A formed a disregarded entity, or a passthrough entity, and the entity entered into the contract with PRS.

(B) Example 2. C is an attorney employed as an associate in a law firm (Law Firm 1) and was treated as such for Federal employment tax purposes. C and the other associates in Law Firm 1 have taxable income below the threshold amount. Law Firm 1 terminates its employment relationship with C and its other associates. C and the other former associates form a new partnership, Law Firm 2, which contracts to perform legal services for Law Firm 1. Therefore, in form, C is now a partner in Law Firm 2 which earns income from providing legal services to Law Firm 1. C continues to provide substantially the same legal services to Law Firm 1 and its clients. Because C was previously treated as an employee for services she provided to Law Firm 1, and now is no longer treated as an employee with regard to such services, C is presumed (solely for purposes of section 199A(d)(1)(B) and paragraphs (a)(3) and (d) of this section) to be in the trade or business of performing services as an employee with respect to the services C provides to Law Firm 1 indirectly through Law Firm 2. Unless the presumption

is rebutted with a showing that, under Federal tax law, regulations, and principles (including common-law employee classification rules), C's distributive share of Law Firm 2 income (including any guaranteed payments) will not be QBI for purposes of section 199A. The results in this example would not change if, instead of contracting with Law Firm 1, Law Firm 2 was instead admitted as a partner in Law Firm 1.

(C) Example 3. E is an engineer employed as a senior project engineer in an engineering firm, Engineering Firm. Engineering Firm is a partnership for Federal tax purposes and structured such that after 10 years, senior project engineers are considered for partner if certain career milestones are met. After 10 years, E meets those career milestones and is admitted as a partner in Engineering Firm. As a partner in Engineering Firm, E shares in the net profits of Engineering Firm, and also otherwise satisfies the requirements under Federal tax law, regulations, and principles (including common-law employee classification rules) to be respected as a partner. E is presumed (solely for purposes of section 199A(d)(1)(B) and paragraphs (a)(3) and (d) of this section) to be in the trade or business of performing services as an employee with respect to the services E provides to Engineering Firm. However, E is able to rebut the presumption by showing that E became a partner in Engineering Firm as a career milestone, shares in the overall net profits in Engineering Firm, and otherwise satisfies the requirements under Federal tax law, regulations, and principles (including common-law employee classification rules) to be respected as a partner.

(D) Example 4. F is a financial advisor employed by a financial advisory firm, Advisory Firm, a partnership for Federal tax purposes, as a fulltime employee and is treated as such for Federal employment tax purposes. F has taxable income below the threshold amount. Advisory Firm is a partnership and offers F the opportunity to be admitted as a partner. F elects to be admitted as a partner to Advisory Firm and is admitted as a partner to Advisory Firm. As a partner in Advisory Firm, F shares in the net profits of Advisory Firm, is obligated to Advisory Firm in ways that F was not previously obligated as an employee, is no longer entitled to certain benefits available only to employees of Advisory Firm, and has materially modified his relationship with Advisory Firm. F's share of net profits is not subject to a floor or capped at a dollar amount. F is presumed (solely for purposes of section 199A(d)(1)(B) and paragraphs (a)(3) and (d) of this section) to be in the trade or business of performing services as an employee with respect to the services F provides to Advisory Firm. However, F is able to rebut the presumption by showing that F became a partner in Advisory Firm by sharing in the profits of Advisory Firm, materially modifying F's relationship with Advisory Firm, and otherwise satisfying the requirements under Federal tax law, regulations, and principles (including common-law employee classification rules) to be respected as a partner.

(e) Applicability date—(1) General rule. Except as provided in paragraph (e)(2) of this section, the provisions of this section apply to taxable years ending after February 8, 2019.

(2) Exceptions-(i) Anti-abuse rules. The provisions of paragraphs (c)(2) and (d)(3) of this section apply to taxable years ending after December 22, 2017.

(ii) Non-calendar year RPE. For purposes of determining QBI, W-2 wages, UBIA of qualified property, and the aggregate amount of qualified REIT dividends and qualified PTP income, if an individual receives any of these items from an RPE with a taxable year that begins before January 1, 2018, and ends after December 31, 2017, such items are treated as having been incurred by the individual during the individual's taxable year in which or with which such RPE taxable year ends.

* * *

Corporate Distributions and Adjustments

§ 1.301–1 Rules applicable with respect to distributions of money and other property.

(a) General. Section 301 provides the general rule for treatment of distributions on or after June 22, 1954, of property by a corporation to a shareholder with respect to its stock. The term "property" is defined in section 317(a). Such distributions, except as otherwise provided in this chapter, shall be treated as provided in section 301(c). Under section 301(c), distributions may be included in gross income, applied against and reduce the adjusted basis of the stock, or treated as gain from the sale or exchange of property. The amount of the distributions to which section 301 applies is determined in accordance with the provisions of section 301(b). The basis of property received in a distribution to which section 301 applies is determined in accordance with the provisions of section 301(d). Accordingly, except as otherwise provided in this chapter, a distribution on or after June 22, 1954, of property by a corporation to a shareholder with respect to its stock shall be included in gross income to the extent the amount distributed is considered a dividend under section 316.

(b) Time of inclusion in gross income and of determination of fair market value. A distribution made by a corporation to its shareholders shall be included in the gross income of the distributees when the cash or other property is unqualifiedly made subject to their demands. However, if such distribution is a distribution other than in cash, the fair market value of the property shall be determined as of the date of distribution without regard to whether such date is the same as that on which the distribution is includible in gross income. For example, if a corporation distributes a taxable dividend in property (the adjusted basis of which exceeds its fair market value on December 31, 1955) on December 31, 1955, which is received by, or unqualifiedly made subject to the demand of, its shareholders on January 2, 1956, the amount to be included in the gross income of the shareholders will be the fair market value of such property on December 31, 1955, although such amount will not be includible in the gross income of the shareholders until January 2, 1956.

(c) Application of section to shareholders. Section 301 is not applicable to an amount paid by a corporation to a shareholder unless the amount is paid to the shareholder in his capacity as such.

(d) Distributions to corporate shareholders. (1) If the shareholder is a corporation, the amount of any distribution to be taken into account under section 301(c) shall be:

(i) The amount of money distributed,

(ii) An amount equal to the fair market value of any property distributed which consists of any obligations of the distributing corporation, stock of the distributing corporation treated as property under section 305(b), or rights to acquire such stock treated as property under section 305(b), plus

(iii) In the case of a distribution not described in subdivision (iv) of this subparagraph, an amount equal to (a) the fair market value of any other property distributed or, if lesser, (b) the adjusted basis of such other property in the hands of the distributing corporation (determined immediately before the distribution and increased for any gain recognized to the distributing corporation * * *

* * *

(2) In the case of a distribution the amount of which is determined by reference to the adjusted basis described in subparagraph (1)(iii) (b) of this paragraph:

(i) That portion of the distribution which is a dividend under section 301(c)(1) may not exceed such adjusted basis, or

(ii) If the distribution is not out of earnings and profits, the amount of the reduction in basis of the shareholder's stock, and the amount of any gain resulting from such distribution, are to be determined by reference to such adjusted basis of the property which is distributed.

* * *

(e) Adjusted basis. In determining the adjusted basis of property distributed in the hands of the distributing corporation immediately before the distribution for purposes of section 301(b)(1)(B)(ii), (b)(1)(C)(i), and (d) (2)(B), the basis to be used shall be the basis for determining gain upon a sale or exchange.

(f) Examples. The application of this section (except paragraph (n)) may be illustrated by the following examples:

Example (1). On January 1, 1955, A, an individual owned all of the stock of Corporation M with an adjusted basis of $2,000. During 1955, A received distributions from Corporation M totaling $30,000, consisting of $10,000 in cash and listed securities having a basis in the hands of Corporation M and a fair market value on the date distributed of $20,000. Corporation M's taxable year is the calendar year. As of December 31, 1954, Corporation M had earnings and profits accumulated in the amount of $26,000, and it had no earnings and profits and no deficit for 1955. Of the $30,000 received by A, $26,000 will be treated as an ordinary dividend; the remaining $4,000 will be applied against the adjusted basis of his stock; the $2,000 in excess of the adjusted basis of his stock will be treated as gain from the sale or exchange of property (under section 301(c) (3)(A)). If A subsequently sells his stock in Corporation M, the basis for determining gain or loss on the sale will be zero.

Example (2). The facts are the same as in Example 1 with the exceptions that the shareholder of Corporation M is Corporation W and that the securities which were distributed had an adjusted basis to Corporation M of

$15,000. The distribution received by Corporation W totals $25,000 consisting of $10,000 in cash and securities with an adjusted basis of $15,000. The total $25,000 will be treated as a dividend to Corporation W since the earnings and profits of Corporation M ($26,000) are in excess of the amount of the distribution.

* * *

(g) Reduction for liabilities—(1) General rule. For the purpose of section 301, no reduction shall be made for the amount of any liability, unless the liability is assumed by the shareholder within the meaning of section 357(d).

(2) No reduction below zero. Any reduction pursuant to paragraph (g)(1) of this section shall not cause the amount of the distribution to be reduced below zero.

(3) Effective dates—(i) In general. This paragraph (g) applies to distributions occurring after January 4, 2001.

(ii) Retroactive application. This paragraph (g) also applies to distributions made on or before January 4, 2001, if the distribution is made as part of a transaction described in, or substantially similar to, the transaction in Notice 99–59 (1999–2 C.B. 761), including transactions designed to reduce gain (see § 601.601(d)(2) of this chapter). For rules for distributions on or before January 4, 2001 (other than distributions on or before that date to which this paragraph (g) applies), see rules in effect on January 4, 2001 (see § 1.301–1(g) as contained in 26 CFR Part 1 revised April 1, 2001).

* * *

(j) Transfers for less than fair market value. If property is transferred by a corporation to a shareholder which is not a corporation for an amount less than its fair market value in a sale or exchange, such shareholder shall be treated as having received a distribution to which section 301 applies. In such case, the amount of the distribution shall be the difference between the amount paid for the property and its fair market value. If property is trans-

ferred in a sale or exchange by a corporation to a shareholder which is a corporation, for an amount less than its fair market value and also less than its adjusted basis, such shareholder shall be treated as having received a distribution to which section 301 applies, and—

(1) Where the fair market value of the property equals or exceeds its adjusted basis in the hands of the distributing corporation the amount of the distribution shall be the excess of the adjusted basis (increased by the amount of gain recognized under section 311(b), (c), or (d), or under section 341(f), 617(d), 1245(a), 1250(a), 1251(c), 1252(a), or 1254(a) to the distributing corporation) over the amount paid for the property;

(2) Where the fair market value of the property is less than its adjusted basis in the hands of the distributing corporation, the amount of the distribution shall be the excess of such fair market value over the amount paid for the property.

* * *

(k) Application of rule respecting transfers for less than fair market value. The application of paragraph (j) of this section may be illustrated by the following examples:

Example (1). On January 1, 1955, A, an individual shareholder of corporation X, purchased property from that corporation for $20. The fair market value of such property was $100, and its basis in the hands of corporation X was $25. The amount of the distribution determined under section 301(b) is $80. If A were a corporation, the amount of the distribution would be $5 (assuming that sections 311(b) and (c), 1245(a), and 1250(a) do not apply), the excess of the basis of the property in the hands of corporation X over the amount received therefor. The basis of such property to corporation A would be $25. If the basis of the property in the hands of corporation X were $10, the corporate shareholder, A, would not receive a distribution. The basis of such property to corporation A would be $20. Whether or not A is a corporation, the excess of the amount paid over the basis of the property in the hands of corporation X ($20 over $10) would be a taxable gain to corporation X.

* * *

(*l*) **Transactions treated as distributions.** A distribution to shareholders with respect to their stock is within the terms of section 301 although it takes place at the same time as another transaction if the distribution is in substance a separate transaction whether or not connected in a formal sense. This is most likely to occur in the case of a recapitalization, a reincorporation, or a merger of a corporation with a newly organized corporation having substantially no property. For example, if a corporation having only common stock outstanding, exchanges one share of newly issued common stock and one bond in the principal amount of $10 for each share of outstanding common stock, the distribution of the bonds will be a distribution of property (to the extent of their fair market value) to which section 301 applies, even though the exchange of common stock for common stock may be pursuant to a plan of reorganization under the terms of section 368(a)(1)(E) (recapitalization) and even though the exchange of common stock for common stock may be tax free by virtue of section 354.

(**m**) **Cancellation of indebtedness.** The cancellation of indebtedness of a shareholder by a corporation shall be treated as a distribution of property.

* * *

§ 1.302–1 General.

(**a**) Under section 302(d), unless otherwise provided in subchapter C, chapter 1 of the Code, a distribution in redemption of stock shall be treated as a distribution of property to which section 301 applies if the distribution is not within any of the provisions of section 302(b). A distribution in redemption of stock shall be considered a distribution in part or full payment in exchange for the stock under sec-

tion 302(a) provided paragraph (1), (2), (3), or (4) of section 302(b) applies. Section 318(a) (relating to constructive ownership of stock) applies to all redemptions under section 302 except that in the termination of a shareholder's interest certain limitations are placed on the application of section 318(a)(1) by section 302(c)(2). The term "redemption of stock" is defined in section 317(b).* * *

* * *

§ 1.302–2 Redemptions not taxable as dividends.

(**a**) **In general.** The fact that a redemption fails to meet the requirements of paragraph (2), (3) or (4) of section 302(b) shall not be taken into account in determining whether the redemption is not essentially equivalent to a dividend under section 302(b)(1). See, however, paragraph (b) of this section. For example, if a shareholder owns only nonvoting stock of a corporation which is not section 306 stock and which is limited and preferred as to dividends and in liquidation, and one-half of such stock is redeemed, the distribution will ordinarily meet the requirements of paragraph (1) of section 302(b) but will not meet the requirements of paragraph (2), (3) or (4) of such section. The determination of whether or not a distribution is within the phrase "essentially equivalent to a dividend" (that is, having the same effect as a distribution without any redemption of stock) shall be made without regard to the earnings and profits of the corporation at the time of the distribution. For example, if A owns all the stock of a corporation and the corporation redeems part of his stock at a time when it has no earnings and profits, the distribution shall be treated as a distribution under section 301 pursuant to section 302(d).

(**b**) **Redemption not essentially equivalent to a dividend—(1) In general.** The question whether a distribution in redemption of stock of a shareholder is not essentially equivalent to a dividend under section 302(b) (1) depends upon the facts and circumstances of each case. One of the facts to be considered in making this determination is the constructive stock ownership of such shareholder under section 318(a). All distributions in pro rata redemptions of a part of the stock of a corporation generally will be treated as distributions under section 301 if the corporation has only one class of stock outstanding. However, for distributions in partial liquidation, see section 302(e). The redemption of all of one class of stock (except section 306 stock) either at one time or in a series of redemptions generally will be considered as a distribution under section 301 if all classes of stock outstanding at the time of the redemption are held in the same proportion. Distributions in redemption of stock may be treated as distributions under section 301 regardless of the provisions of the stock certificate and regardless of whether all stock being redeemed was acquired by the stockholders from whom the stock was redeemed by purchase or otherwise.

* * *

(c) Basis adjustments. In any case in which an amount received in redemption of stock is treated as a distribution of a dividend, proper adjustment of the basis of the remaining stock will be made with respect to the stock redeemed. (For adjustments to basis required for certain redemptions of corporate shareholders that are treated as extraordinary dividends, see section 1059 and the regulations thereunder.) The following examples illustrate the application of this rule:

Example (1). A, an individual, purchased all of the stock of Corporation X for $100,000. In 1955 the corporation redeems half of the stock for $150,000, and it is determined that this amount constitutes a dividend. The remaining stock of Corporation X held by A has a basis of $100,000.

Example (2). H and W, husband and wife, each own half of the stock of Corporation X. All of the stock was purchased by H for $100,000 cash. In 1950 H gave one-half of the stock to W, the stock transferred having a value

in excess of $50,000. In 1955 all of the stock of H is redeemed for $150,000, and it is determined that the distribution to H in redemption of his shares constitutes the distribution of a dividend. Immediately after the transaction, W holds the remaining stock of Corporation X with a basis of $100,000.

Example (3). The facts are the same as in Example (2) with the additional facts that the outstanding stock of Corporation X consists of 1,000 shares and all but 10 shares of the stock of H is redeemed. Immediately after the transaction, H holds 10 shares of the stock of Corporation X with a basis of $50,000, and W holds 500 shares with a basis of $50,000.

* * *

§ 1.302–3 Substantially disproportionate redemption.

(a) Section 302(b)(2) provides for the treatment of an amount received in redemption of stock as an amount received in exchange for such stock if—

(1) Immediately after the redemption the shareholder owns less than 50 percent of the total combined voting power of all classes of stock as provided in section 302(b)(2)(B),

(2) The redemption is a substantially disproportionate redemption within the meaning of section 302(b)(2)(C), and

(3) The redemption is not pursuant to a plan described in section 302(b)(2)(D).

Section 318(a) (relating to constructive ownership of stock) shall apply both in making the disproportionate redemption test and in determining the percentage of stock ownership after the redemption. The requirements under section 302(b)(2) shall be applied to each shareholder separately and shall be applied only with respect to stock which is issued and outstanding in the hands of the shareholders. Section 302(b)(2) only applies to a redemption of voting stock or to a redemption of both voting stock and other stock. Section 302(b)(2) does not apply to the redemption solely of nonvoting stock (common or preferred). However, if a redemption is treated as an exchange to a particular shareholder under the terms of section 302(b)(2), such section will apply to the simultaneous redemption of nonvoting preferred stock (which is not section 306 stock) owned by such shareholder and such redemption will also be treated as an exchange. Generally, for purposes of this section, stock which does not have voting rights until the happening of an event, such as a default in the payment of dividends on preferred stock, is not voting stock until the happening of the specified event. Subsection 302(b)(2)(D) provides that a redemption will not be treated as substantially disproportionate if made pursuant to a plan the purpose or effect of which is a series of redemptions which result in the aggregate in a distribution which is not substantially disproportionate. Whether or not such a plan exists will be determined from all the facts and circumstances.

(b) The application of paragraph (a) of this section is illustrated by the following example:

Example. Corporation M has outstanding 400 shares of common stock of which A, B, C and D each own 100 shares or 25 percent. No stock is considered constructively owned by A, B, C or D under section 318. Corporation M redeems 55 shares from A, 25 shares from B, and 20 shares from C. For the redemption to be disproportionate as to any shareholder, such shareholder must own after the redemptions less than 20 percent (80 percent of 25 percent) of the 300 shares of stock then outstanding. After the redemptions, A owns 45 shares (15 percent), B owns 75 shares (25 percent), and C owns 80 shares (26 2/3 percent). The distribution is disproportionate only with respect to A.

§ 1.302–4 Termination of shareholder's interest.

Section 302(b)(3) provides that a distribution in redemption of all of the stock of the corporation owned by a shareholder shall be treated as a distribution in part or full payment in exchange for the stock of such shareholder. In determining whether all of the stock of the shareholder has been redeemed, the general rule of section 302(c)(1) requires that the rules of constructive ownership provided in section 318(a) shall apply. Section 302(c)(2), however, provides that section 318(a)(1) (relating to constructive ownership of stock owned by members of a family) shall not apply where the specific requirements of section 302(c)(2) are met. The following rules shall be applicable in determining whether the specific requirements of section 302(c)(2) are met:

(a) Statement. The agreement specified in section 302(c)(2)(A)(iii) shall be in the form of a statement entitled, "STATEMENT PURSUANT TO SECTION 302(c)(2)(A)(iii) BY [INSERT NAME AND TAXPAYER IDENTIFICATION NUMBER (IF ANY) OF TAXPAYER OR RELATED PERSON, AS THE CASE MAY BE], A DISTRIBUTEE (OR RELATED PERSON) OF [INSERT NAME AND EMPLOYER IDENTIFICATION NUMBER (IF ANY) OF DISTRIBUTING CORPORATION]." The distributee must include such statement on or with the distributee's first return for the taxable year in which the distribution described in section 302(b)(3) occurs. If the distributee is a controlled foreign corporation (within the meaning of section 957), each United States shareholder (within the meaning of section 951(b)) with respect thereto must include this statement on or with its return. The distributee must represent in the statement—

(1) THE DISTRIBUTEE (OR RELATED PERSON) HAS NOT ACQUIRED, OTHER THAN BY BEQUEST OR INHERITANCE, ANY INTEREST IN THE CORPORATION (AS DESCRIBED IN SECTION 302(c)(2)(A)(i)) SINCE THE DISTRIBUTION; and

(2) THE DISTRIBUTEE (OR RELATED PERSON) WILL NOTIFY THE INTERNAL REVENUE SERVICE OF ANY ACQUISITION, OTHER THAN BY BEQUEST OR INHERITANCE, OF SUCH AN INTEREST IN THE CORPORATION WITHIN 30 DAYS

AFTER THE ACQUISITION, IF THE ACQUISITION OCCURS WITHIN 10 YEARS FROM THE DATE OF THE DISTRIBUTION.

(b) Substantiation information. The distributee who files an agreement under section 302(c)(2)(A)(iii) shall retain copies of income tax returns and any other records indicating fully the amount of tax which would have been payable had the redemption been treated as a distribution subject to section 301.

(c) Stock of parent, subsidiary or successor corporation redeemed. If stock of a parent corporation is redeemed, section 302(c)(2) (A), relating to acquisition of an interest in the corporation within 10 years after termination shall be applied with reference to an interest both in the parent corporation and any subsidiary of such parent corporation. If stock of a parent corporation is sold to a subsidiary in a transaction described in section 304, section 302(c)(2)(A) shall be applicable to the acquisition of an interest in such subsidiary corporation or in the parent corporation. If stock of a subsidiary corporation is redeemed, section 302(c)(2)(A) shall be applied with reference to an interest both in such subsidiary corporation and its parent. Section 302(c)(2)(A) shall also be applied with respect to an interest in a corporation which is a successor corporation to the corporation the interest in which has been terminated.

(d) Redeemed shareholder as creditor. For the purpose of section 302(c)(2)(A)(i), a person will be considered to be a creditor only if the rights of such person with respect to the corporation are not greater or broader in scope than necessary for the enforcement of his claim. Such claim must not in any sense be proprietary and must not be subordinate to the claims of general creditors. An obligation in the form of a debt may thus constitute a proprietary interest. For example, if under the terms of the instrument the corporation may discharge the principal amount of its obligation to a person by payments, the amount or certainty of which are dependent upon the earnings of the corporation, such a person is not a creditor of the corporation. Furthermore, if under the terms of the instrument the rate of purported interest is dependent upon earnings, the holder of such instrument may not, in some cases, be a creditor.

(e) Acquisition of assets pursuant to creditor's rights. In the case of a distributee to whom section 302(b)(3) is applicable, who is a creditor after such transaction, the acquisition of the assets of the corporation in the enforcement of the rights of such creditor shall not be considered an acquisition of an interest in the corporation for purposes of section 302(c)(2) unless stock of the corporation, its parent corporation, or, in the case of a redemption of stock of a parent corporation, of a subsidiary of such corporation is acquired.

(f) Constructive ownership rules applicable. In determining whether an entire interest in the corporation has been terminated under section 302(b)(3), under all circumstances paragraphs (2), (3), (4), and (5) of section 318(a) (relating to constructive ownership of stock) shall be applicable.

(g) Avoidance of Federal income tax. Section 302(c)(2)(B) provides that section 302(c)(2)(A) shall not apply—

(1) If any portion of the stock redeemed was acquired directly or indirectly within the 10-year period ending on the date of the distribution by the distributee from a person, the ownership of whose stock would (at the time of distribution) be attributable to the distributee under section 318(a), or

(2) If any person owns (at the time of the distribution) stock, the ownership of which is attributable to the distributee under section 318(a), such person acquired any stock in the corporation directly or indirectly from the distributee within the 10-year period ending on the date of the distribution, and such stock so acquired from the distributee is not redeemed in the same transaction, unless the acquisition (described in subparagraph (1) of this paragraph) or the disposition by the distributee (described in subparagraph (2) of this paragraph) did not have as one of its principal purposes the avoidance of Federal income tax. A transfer of stock by the transferor, within the 10-year period ending on the date of the distribution, to a person whose stock would be attributable to the transferor shall not be deemed to have as one of its principal purposes the avoidance of Federal income tax merely because the transferee is in a lower income tax bracket than the transferor.

(h) Effective/applicability date. Paragraph (a) of this section applies to any taxable year beginning on or after May 30, 2006. * * *

§ 1.304–1. General.

(a) * * * section 304 is applicable where a shareholder sells stock of one corporation to a related corporation as defined in section 304. Sales to which section 304 is applicable shall be treated as redemptions subject to sections 302 and 303.

* * *

§ 1.304–2. Acquisition by related corporation (other than subsidiary).

(a) If a corporation, in return for property, acquires stock of another corporation from one or more persons, and the person or persons from whom the stock was acquired were in control of both such corporations before the acquisition, then such property shall be treated as received in redemption of stock of the acquiring corporation. The stock received by the acquiring corporation shall be treated as a contribution to the capital of such corporation. See section 362(a) for determination of the basis of such stock. The transferor's basis for his stock in the acquiring corporation shall be increased by the basis of the stock surrendered by him. (But see below in this paragraph for subsequent reductions of basis in certain cases.) As to each person transferring stock, the amount received shall be treated as a distribu-

tion of property under section 302(d), unless as to such person such amount is to be treated as received in exchange for the stock under the terms of section 302(a) or section 303. In applying section 302(b), reference shall be had to the shareholder's ownership of stock in the issuing corporation and not to his ownership of stock in the acquiring corporation (except for purposes of applying section 318(a)). In determining control and applying section 302(b), section 318(a) (relating to the constructive ownership of stock) shall be applied without regard to the 50-percent limitation contained in section 318(a)(2)(C) and (3)(C). A series of redemptions referred to in section 302(b)(2) (D) shall include acquisitions by either of the corporations of stock of the other and stock redemptions by both corporations. If section 302(d) applies to the surrender of stock by a shareholder, his basis for his stock in the acquiring corporation after the transaction (increased as stated above in this paragraph) shall not be decreased except as provided in section 301. If section 302(d) does not apply, the property received shall be treated as received in a distribution in payment in exchange for stock of the acquiring corporation under section 302(a), which stock has a basis equal to the amount by which the shareholder's basis for his stock in the acquiring corporation was increased on account of the contribution to capital as provided for above in this paragraph. Accordingly, such amount shall be applied in reduction of the shareholder's basis for his stock in the acquiring corporation. Thus, the basis of each share of the shareholder's stock in the acquiring corporation will be the same as the basis of such share before the entire transaction. The holding period of the stock which is considered to have been redeemed shall be the same as the holding period of the stock actually surrendered.

* * *

(b) In any case in which two or more persons, in the aggregate, control two corporations, section 304(a)(1) will apply to sales by such persons of stock in either corporation to the other (whether or not made simultaneously) provided the sales by each of such persons are related to each other. The determination of whether the sales are related to each other shall be dependent upon the facts and circumstances surrounding all of the sales. For this purpose, the fact that the sales may occur during a period of one or more years (such as in the case of a series of sales by persons who together control each of such corporations immediately prior to the first of such sales and immediately subsequent to the last of such sales) shall be disregarded, provided the other facts and circumstances indicate related transactions.

(c) Examples. The application of section 304(a)(1) may be illustrated by the following examples:

Example (1). Corporation X and corporation Y each have outstanding 200 shares of common stock. One-half of the stock of each corporation is owned by an individual, A, and one-half by another individual, B, who is unrelated to A. On or after August 31, 1964, A sells 30 shares of corporation X stock to corporation Y for $50,000, such stock having an adjusted basis of $10,000 to A. After the sale, A is considered as owning corporation X stock as follows: (i) 70 shares directly, and (ii) 15 shares constructively, since by virtue of his 50-percent ownership of Y he constructively owns 50 percent of the 30 shares owned directly by Y. Since A's percentage of ownership of X's voting stock after the sale (85 out of 200 shares, or 42.5%) is not less than 80 percent of his percentage of ownership of X's voting stock before the sale (100 out of 200 shares, or 50%), the transfer is not "substantially disproportionate" as to him as provided in section 302(b)(2). Under these facts, and assuming that section 302(b)(1) is not applicable, the entire $50,000 is treated as a dividend to A to the extent of the earnings and profits of corporation Y. The basis of the corporation X stock to corporation Y is $10,000, its adjusted basis to A. The amount of $10,000 is added to the basis of the stock of corporation Y in the hands of A.

Example (2). The facts are the same as in *Example (1)* except that A sells 80 shares of corporation X stock to corporation Y, and the sale occurs before August 31, 1964. After the sale, A is considered as owning corporation X stock as follows: (i) 20 shares directly, and (ii) 90 shares indirectly, since by virtue of his 50-percent ownership of Y he constructively owns 50 percent of the 80 shares owned directly by Y and 50 percent of the 100 shares attributed to Y because they are owned by Y's stockholder, B. Since after the sale A owns a total of more than 50 percent of the voting power of all of the outstanding stock of X (110 out of 200 shares, or 55%), the transfer is not "substantially disproportionate" as to him as provided in section 302(b)(2).

Example (3). Corporation X and corporation Y each have outstanding 100 shares of common stock. A, an individual, owns one-half the stock of corporation X, and C owns one-half the stock of corporation Y. A, B, and C are unrelated. A sells 30 shares of the stock of corporation X to corporation Y for $50,000, such stock having an adjusted basis of $10,000 to him. After the sale, A is considered as owning 35 shares of the stock of corporation X (20 shares directly and 15 constructively because one-half of the 30 shares owned by corporation Y are attributed to him). Since before the sale he owned 50 percent of the stock of corporation X and after the sale he owned directly and constructively only 35 percent of such stock, the redemption is substantially disproportionate as to him pursuant to the provisions of section 302(b)(2). He, therefore, realizes a gain of $40,000 ($50,000 minus $10,000). If the stock surrendered is a capital asset, such gain is long-term or short-term capital gain depending on the period of time that such stock was held. The basis to A for the stock of corporation Y is not changed as a result of the entire transaction. The basis to corporation Y for the stock of corporation X is $50,000, i.e., the basis of the transferor ($10,000), increased in the amount of gain recognized to the transferor ($40,000) on the transfer.

Example (4). Corporation X and corporation Y each have outstanding 100 shares of common stock. H, an individual, W, his wife, S, his son, and G, his grandson, each own 25 shares of stock of each corporation. H sells all of his 25 shares of stock of corporation X to corporation Y. Since both before and after the transaction H owned directly and constructively 100 percent of the stock of corporation X, and assuming that section 302(b)(1) is not applicable, the amount received by him for his stock of corporation X is treated as a dividend to him to the extent of the earnings and profits of corporation Y.

§ 1.304–3. Acquisition by a subsidiary.

(a) If a subsidiary acquires stock of its parent corporation from a shareholder of the parent corporation, the acquisition of such stock shall be treated as though the parent corporation had redeemed its own stock. For the purpose of this section, a corporation is a parent corporation if it meets the 50 percent ownership requirements of section 304(c). The determination whether the amount received shall be treated as an amount received in payment in exchange for the stock shall be made by applying section 303, or by applying section 302(b) with reference to the stock of the issuing parent corporation. If such distribution would have been treated as a distribution of property (pursuant to section 302(d)) under section 301, the entire amount of the selling price of the stock shall be treated as a dividend to the seller to the extent of the earnings and profits of the parent corporation determined as if the distribution had been made to it of the property that the subsidiary exchanged for the stock. In such cases, the transferor's basis for his remaining stock in the parent corporation will be determined by including the amount of the basis of the stock of the parent corporation sold to the subsidiary.

(b) Section 304(a)(2) may be illustrated by the following example:

Example. Corporation M has outstanding 100 shares of common stock which are owned as follows: B, 75 shares, C, son of B, 20 shares, and D, daughter of B, 5 shares. Corporation M owns the stock of Corporation X. B sells his 75 shares of Corporation M stock to Corporation X. Under section 302(b)(3) this is a termination of B's entire interest in Corporation M and the full amount received from the sale of his stock will be treated as payment in exchange for this stock, provided he fulfills the requirements of section 302(c)(2) (relating to an acquisition of an interest in the corporations).

§ 1.304–4. Special rule for the use of related corporations to avoid the application of section 304.

(a) Scope and purpose. This section applies to determine the amount of a property distribution constituting a dividend (and the source thereof) under section 304(b)(2), for certain transactions involving controlled corporations. The purpose of this section is to prevent the avoidance of the application of section 304 to a controlled corporation.

(b) Amount and source of dividend. For purposes of determining the amount constituting a dividend (and source thereof) under section 304(b)(2), the following rules shall apply:

(1) Deemed acquiring corporation. A corporation (deemed acquiring corporation) shall be treated as acquiring for property the stock of a corporation (issuing corporation) acquired for property by another corporation (acquiring corporation) that is controlled by the deemed acquiring corporation, if a principal purpose for creating, organizing, or funding the acquiring corporation by any means (including through capital contributions or debt) is to avoid the application of section 304 to the deemed acquiring corporation. See paragraph (c) Example 1 of this section for an illustration of this paragraph.

(2) Deemed issuing corporation. The acquiring corporation shall be treated as acquiring for property the stock of a corporation (deemed issuing corporation) controlled by the issuing corporation if, in connection with the acquisition for property of stock of the issuing corporation by the acquiring corporation, the issuing corporation acquired stock of the deemed issuing corporation with a principal purpose of avoiding the application of section 304 to the deemed issuing corporation. See paragraph (c) Example 2 of this section for an illustration of this paragraph.

(c) Examples. The rules of this section are illustrated by the following examples:

Example (1). (i) Facts. P, a domestic corporation, wholly owns CFC1, a controlled foreign corporation with substantial accumulated earnings and profits. CFC1 is organized in Country X, which imposes a high rate of tax on the income of CFC1. P also wholly owns CFC2, a controlled foreign corporation with accumulated earnings and profits of $200x. CFC2 is organized in Country Y, which imposes a low rate of tax on the income of CFC2. P wishes to own all of its foreign corporations in a direct chain and to repatriate the cash of CFC2. In order to avoid having to obtain Country X approval for the acquisition of CFC1 (a Country X corporation) by CFC2 (a Country Y corporation) and to avoid the dividend distribution from CFC2 to P that would result if CFC2 were the acquiring corporation, P causes CFC2 to form CFC3 in Country X and to contribute $100x to CFC3. CFC3 then acquires all of the stock of CFC1 from P for $100x.

(ii) Result. Because a principal purpose for creating, organizing, or funding CFC3 (acquiring corporation) is to avoid the application of section 304 to CFC2 (deemed acquiring corporation), under paragraph (b)(1) of this section, for purposes of determining the amount of the $100x distribution constituting a dividend (and source thereof) under section 304(b)(2), CFC2 shall be treated as acquiring the stock of CFC1 (issuing corporation) from P for $100x. As a result, P receives a $100x distribution out of the earnings and profits of CFC2 to which section 301(c)(1) applies.

Example (2). (i) Facts. P, a domestic corporation, wholly owns CFC1, a controlled foreign corporation with substantial accumulated earnings and profits. The CFC1 stock has a basis of $100x. CFC1 is organized in Country X. P also wholly owns CFC2, a controlled foreign corporation with zero accumulated earnings and profits. CFC2 is organized in Country Y. P wishes to own all of its foreign corporations in a direct chain and to repatriate the cash of CFC2. In order to avoid having to obtain Country X approval for the acquisition of CFC1 (a Country X corporation) by CFC2 (a Country Y corporation) and to avoid a dividend distribution from CFC1 to P, P forms a new corporation (CFC3) in Country X and transfers the stock of CFC1 to CFC3 in exchange for CFC3 stock. P then transfers the stock of CFC3 to CFC2 in exchange for $100x.

(ii) Result. Because a principal purpose for the transfer of the stock of CFC1 (deemed issuing corporation) by P to CFC3 (issuing corporation) is to avoid the application of section 304 to CFC1, under paragraph (b)(2) of this section, for purposes of determining the amount of the $100x distribution constituting a dividend (and source thereof) under section 304(b)(2), CFC2 (acquiring corporation) shall be treated as acquiring the stock of CFC1 from P for $100x . As a result, P receives a $100x distribution out of the earnings and profits of CFC1 to which section 301(c)(1) applies.

* * *

§ 1.304–5 Control.

(a) Control requirement in general. Section 304(c)(1) provides that, for purposes of section 304, control means the ownership of stock possessing at least 50 percent of the total combined voting power of all classes of stock entitled to vote or at least 50 percent of the total value of shares of all classes of stock. Section 304(c)(3) makes section 318(a) (relating to constructive ownership of stock), as modified by section 304(c)(3)(B), applicable to section 304 for purposes of determining control under section 304(c)(1).

(b) Effect of section 304(c)(2)(B). (1) In general. In determining whether the control test with respect to both the issuing and acquiring corporations is satisfied, section 304(a)(1) considers only the person or persons that—

(i) Control the issuing corporation before the transaction;

(ii) Transfer issuing corporation stock to the acquiring corporation for property; and

(iii) Control the acquiring corporation thereafter.

(2) Application. Section 317 defines property to include money, securities, and any other property except stock (or stock rights) in the distributing corporation. However, section 304(c)(2)(B) provides a special rule to extend the relevant group of persons to be tested for control of both the issuing and acquiring corporations to include the person or persons that do not acquire property, but rather solely stock from the acquiring corporation in the transaction. Section 304(c)(2)(B) provides that if two or more persons in control of the issuing corporation transfer stock of such corporation to the acquiring corporation, and if the transferors are in control of the acquiring corporation after the transfer, the person or persons in control of each corporation include each of those transferors. Because the purpose of section 304(c)(2)(B) is to include in the relevant control group the person or persons that retain or acquire acquiring corporation stock in the transaction, only the person or persons transferring stock of the issuing corporation that retain or acquire any proprietary interest in the acquiring corporation are taken into account for purposes of applying section 304(c)(2)(B).

(3) Example. This section may be illustrated by the following example.

Example. (a) A, the owner of 20% of T's only class of stock, transfers that stock to P solely in exchange for all of the P stock. Pursuant to the same transaction, P, solely in ex-change for cash, acquires the remaining 80% of the T stock from T's other shareholder, B, who is unrelated to A and P.

(b) Although A and B together were in control of T (the issuing corporation) before the transaction and A and B each transferred T stock to P (the acquiring corporation), sections 304(a)(1) and (c)(2)(B) do not apply to B because B did not retain or acquire any proprietary interest in P in the transaction. Section 304(a)(1) also does not apply to A because A (or any control group of which A was a member) did not control T before the transaction and P after the transaction.

* * *

§ 1.305–1 Stock dividends.

(a) In general. Under section 305, a distribution made by a corporation to its shareholders in its stock or in rights to acquire its stock is not included in gross income except as provided in section 305(b) and the regulations promulgated under the authority of section 305(c). A distribution made by a corporation to its shareholders in its stock or rights to acquire its stock which would not otherwise be included in gross income by reason of section 305 shall not be so included merely because such distribution was made out of Treasury stock or consisted of rights to acquire Treasury stock. See section 307 for rules as to basis of stock and stock rights acquired in a distribution.

(b) Amount of distribution. (1) In general, where a distribution of stock or rights to acquire stock of a corporation is treated as a distribution of property to which section 301 applies by reason of section 305(b), the amount of the distribution, in accordance with section 301(b) and § 1.301–1, is the fair market value of such stock or rights on the date of distribution. See example (1) of § 1.305–2(b).

(2) Where a corporation which regularly distributes its earnings and profits, such as a regulated investment company, declares a dividend pursuant to which the shareholders may elect to receive either money or stock of the distributing corporation of equivalent value, the amount of the distribution of the stock received by any shareholder electing to receive stock will be considered to equal the amount of the money which could have been received instead. See example (2) of § 1.305–2(b).

(3) For rules for determining the amount of the distribution where certain transactions, such as changes in conversion ratios or periodic redemptions, are treated as distributions under section 305(c), see examples (6), (8), (9), and (15) of § 1.305–3(e).

* * *

(d) Definitions. (1) For purposes of this section and § § 1.305–2 through 1.305–7, the term "stock" includes rights or warrants to acquire such stock.

(2) For purposes of §§ 1.305–2 through 1.305–7, the term "shareholder" includes a holder of rights or warrants or a holder of convertible securities.

§ 1.305–2 Distributions in lieu of money.

(a) In general. Under section 305(b)(1), if any shareholder has the right to an election or option with respect to whether a distribution shall be made either in money or any other property, or in stock or rights to acquire stock of the distributing corporation, then, with respect to all shareholders, the distribution of stock or rights to acquire stock is treated as a distribution of property to which section 301 applies regardless of—

(1) Whether the distribution is actually made in whole or in part in stock or in stock rights;

(2) Whether the election or option is exercised or exercisable before or after the declaration of the distribution;

(3) Whether the declaration of the distribution provides that the distribution will be made in one medium unless the shareholder specifically requests payment in the other;

(4) Whether the election governing the nature of the distribution is provided in the declaration of the distribution or in the corporate charter or arises from the circumstances of the distribution; or

(5) Whether all or part of the shareholders have the election.

(b) Examples. The application of section 305(b)(1) may be illustrated by the following examples:

Example (1). (i) Corporation X declared a dividend payable in additional shares of its common stock to the holders of its outstanding common stock on the basis of two additional shares for each share held on the record date but with the provision that, at the election of any shareholder made within a specified period prior to the distribution date, he may receive one additional share for each share held on the record date plus $12 principal amount of securities of corporation Y owned by corporation X. The fair market value of the stock of corporation X on the distribution date was $10 per share. The fair market value of $12 principal amount of securities of corporation Y on the distribution date was $11 but such securities had a cost basis to corporation X of $9.

(ii) The distribution to all shareholders of one additional share of stock of corporation X (with respect to which no election applies) for each share outstanding is not a distribution to which section 301 applies.

(iii) The distribution of the second share of stock of corporation X to those shareholders who do not elect to receive securities of corporation Y is a distribution of property to which section 301 applies, whether such shareholders are individuals or corporations. The amount of the distribution to which section 301 applies is $10 per share of stock of corporation X held on the record date (the fair market value of the stock of corporation X on the distribution date).

* * *

(v) In the case of the individual shareholders of corporation X who elects to receive such securities, the amount of the distribution to which section 301 applies is $11 per share of stock of corporation X held on the record date (the fair market value of the $12 principal amount of securities of corporation Y on the distribution date).

(vi) In the case of the corporate shareholders of corporation X electing to receive such securities, the amount of the distribution to which section 301 applies is $9 per share of stock of corporation X held on the record date (the basis of the securities of corporation Y in the hands of corporation X).

Example (2). On January 10, 1970, corporation X, a regulated investment company, declared a dividend of $1 per share on its common stock payable on February 11, 1970, in cash or in stock of corporation X of equivalent value determined as of January 22, 1970, at the election of the shareholder made on or before January 22, 1970. The amount of the distribution to which section 301 applies is $1 per share whether the shareholder elects to take cash or stock and whether the shareholder is an individual or a corporation. Such amount will also be used in determining the dividend paid deduction of corporation X and the reduction in earnings and profits of corporation X.

§ 1.305–3 Disproportionate distributions.

(a) In general. Under section 305(b)(2), a distribution (including a deemed distribution) by a corporation of its stock or rights to acquire its stock is treated as a distribution of property to which section 301 applies if the distribution (or a series of distributions of which such distribution is one) has the result of (1) the receipt of money or other property by some shareholders, and (2) an increase in the proportionate interests of other shareholders in the assets or earnings and profits of the corporation. Thus, if a corporation has two classes of common stock outstanding and cash dividends are paid on one class and stock div-

idends are paid on the other class, the stock dividends are treated as distributions to which section 301 applies.

(b) Special rules. (1) As used in section 305(b)(2), the term "a series of distributions" encompasses all distributions of stock made or deemed made by a corporation which have the result of the receipt of cash or property by some shareholders and an increase in the proportionate interests of other shareholders.

(2) In order for a distribution of stock to be considered as one of a series of distributions it is not necessary that such distribution be pursuant to a plan to distribute cash or property to some shareholders and to increase the proportionate interests of other shareholders. It is sufficient if there is an actual or deemed distribution of stock (of which such distribution is one) and as a result of such distribution or distributions some shareholders receive cash or property and other shareholders increase their proportionate interests. For example, if a corporation pays quarterly stock dividends to one class of common shareholders and annual cash dividends to another class of common shareholders the quarterly stock dividends constitute a series of distributions of stock having the result of the receipt of cash or property by some shareholders and an increase in the proportionate interests of other shareholders. This is so whether or not the stock distributions and the cash distributions are steps in an overall plan or are independent and unrelated. Accordingly, all the quarterly stock dividends are distributions to which section 301 applies.

(3) There is no requirement that both elements of section 305(b)(2) (i.e., receipt of cash or property by some shareholders and an increase in proportionate interests of other shareholders) occur in the form of a distribution or series of distributions as long as the result of a distribution or distributions of stock is that some shareholders' proportionate interests increase and other shareholders in fact receive cash or property. Thus, there is no requirement that the shareholders receiving cash or property acquire the cash or property by way of a corporate distribution with respect to their shares, so long as they receive such cash or property in their capacity as shareholders, if there is a stock distribution which results in a change in the proportionate interests of some shareholders and other shareholders receive cash or property. However, in order for a distribution of property to meet the requirement of section 305(b)(2), such distribution must be made to a shareholder in his capacity as a shareholder, and must be a distribution to which section 301, 356(a)(2), 871(a)(1)(A), 881(a)(1), 852(b), or 857(b) applies. (Under section 305(d)(2), the payment of interest to a holder of a convertible debenture is treated as a distribution of property to a shareholder for purposes of section 305(b)(2).) For example if a corporation makes a stock distribution to its shareholders and, pursuant to a prearranged plan with such corporation, a related corporation purchases such stock from those shareholders who want cash, in a transaction to which section 301 applies by virtue of section 304, the requirements of section 305(b)(2) are satisfied. In addition, a distribution of property incident to an isolated redemption of stock (for example, pursuant to a tender offer) will not cause section 305(b)(2) to apply even though the redemption distribution is treated as a distribution of property to which section 301, 871(a)(1)(A), 881(a)(1), or 356(a)(2) applies.

(4) Where the receipt of cash or property occurs more than 36 months following a distribution or series of distributions of stock, or where a distribution or series of distributions of stock is made more than 36 months following the receipt of cash or property, such distribution or distributions will be presumed not to result in the receipt of cash or property by some shareholders and an increase in the proportionate interest of other shareholders, unless the receipt of cash or property and the distribution or series of distributions of stock are made pursuant to a plan. For example, if, pursuant to a plan, a corporation pays cash dividends to some shareholders on January 1,

1971 and increases the proportionate interests of other shareholders on March 1, 1974, such increases in proportionate interests are distributions to which section 301 applies.

(5) In determining whether a distribution or a series of distributions has the result of a disproportionate distribution, there shall be treated as outstanding stock of the distributing corporation (i) any right to acquire such stock (whether or not exercisable during the taxable year), and (ii) any security convertible into stock of the distributing corporation (whether or not convertible during the taxable year).

(6) In cases where there is more than one class of stock outstanding, each class of stock is to be considered separately in determining whether a shareholder has increased his proportionate interest in the assets or earnings and profits of a corporation. The individual shareholders of a class of stock will be deemed to have an increased interest if the class of stock as a whole has an increased interest in the corporation.

(c) Distributions of cash in lieu of fractional shares. (1) Section 305(b)(2) will not apply if—

(i) A corporation declares a dividend payable in stock of the corporation and distributes cash in lieu of fractional shares to which shareholders would otherwise be entitled, or

(ii) Upon a conversion of convertible stock or securities a corporation distributes cash in lieu of fractional shares to which shareholders would otherwise be entitled.

Provided the purpose of the distribution of cash is to save the corporation the trouble, expense, and inconvenience of issuing and transferring fractional shares (or scrip representing fractional shares), or issuing full shares representing the sum of fractional shares, and not to give any particular group of shareholders an increased interest in the assets or earnings and profits of the corporation. For purposes of paragraph (c)(1)(i) of this section, if the total amount of cash distributed in lieu of fractional shares is 5 percent or less of the total fair market value of the stock distributed (determined as of the date of declaration), the distribution shall be considered to be for such valid purpose.

(2) In a case to which subparagraph (1) of this paragraph applies, the transaction will be treated as though the fractional shares were distributed as part of the stock distribution and then were redeemed by the corporation. The treatment of the cash received by a shareholder will be determined under section 302.

* * *

(e) Examples. The application of section 305(b)(2) to distributions of stock and section 305(c) to deemed distributions of stock may be illustrated by the following examples:

Example (1). Corporation X is organized with two classes of common stock, class A and class B. Each share of stock is entitled to share equally in the assets and earnings and profits of the corporation. Dividends may be paid in stock or in cash on either class of stock without regard to the medium of payment of dividends on the other class. A dividend is declared on the class A stock payable in additional shares of class A stock and a dividend is declared on class B stock payable in cash. Since the class A shareholders as a class will have increased their proportionate interests in the assets and earnings and profits of the corporation and the class B shareholders will have received cash, the additional shares of class A stock are distributions of property to which section 301 applies. This is true even with respect to those shareholders who may own class A stock and class B stock in the same proportion.

Example (2). Corporation Y is organized with two classes of stock, class A common, and class B, which is nonconvertible and limited and preferred as to dividends. A dividend is declared upon the class A stock payable in additional shares of class A stock and a dividend is declared on the class B stock payable in cash. The distribution of class A stock is not one to which section 301 applies because the distribution does not increase the proportionate interests of the class A shareholders as a class.

Example (3). Corporation K is organized with two classes of stock, class A common, and class B, which is nonconvertible preferred stock. A dividend is declared upon the class A stock payable in shares of class B stock and a dividend is declared on the class B stock payable in cash. Since the class A shareholders as a class have an increased interest in the assets and earnings and profits of the corporation, the stock distribution is treated as a distribution to which section 301 applies. If, however, a dividend were declared upon the class A stock payable in a new class of preferred stock that is subordinated in all respects to the class B stock, the distribution would not increase the proportionate interests of the class A shareholders in the assets or earnings and profits of the corporation and would not be treated as a distribution to which section 301 applies.

Example (4). (i) Corporation W has one class of stock outstanding, class A common. The corporation also has outstanding interest paying securities convertible into class A common stock which have a fixed conversion ratio that is not subject to full adjustment in the event stock dividends or rights are distributed to the class A shareholders. Corporation W distributes to the class A shareholders rights to acquire additional shares of class A stock. During the year, interest is paid on the convertible securities.

(ii) The stock rights and convertible securities are considered to be outstanding stock of the corporation and the distribution increases the proportionate interests of the class A shareholders in the assets and earnings and profits of the corporation. Therefore, the distribution is treated as a distribution to which section 301 applies. The same result would follow if, instead of convertible securities, the corporation had outstanding convertible stock. If, however, the conversion ratio of the securities or stock were fully adjusted to reflect the distribution of rights to the class A shareholders, the rights to acquire class A stock would not increase the proportionate interests of the class A shareholders in the assets and earnings and profits of the corporation and would not be treated as a distribution to which section 301 applies.

Example (5). (i) Corporation S is organized with two classes of stock, class A common and class B convertible preferred. The class B is fully protected against dilution in the event of a stock dividend or stock split with respect to the class A stock; however, no adjustment in the conversion ratio is required to be made until the stock dividends equal 3 percent of the common stock issued and outstanding on the date of the first such stock dividend except that such adjustment must be made no later than 3 years after the date of the stock dividend. Cash dividends are paid annually on the class B stock.

(ii) Corporation S pays a 1 percent stock dividend on the class A stock in 1970. In 1971, another 1 percent stock dividend is paid and in 1972 another 1 percent stock dividend is paid. The conversion ratio of the class B stock is increased in 1972 to reflect the three stock dividends paid on the class A stock. The distributions of class A stock are not distributions to which section 301 applies because they do not increase the proportionate interests of the class A shareholders in the assets and earnings and profits of the corporation.

Example (6). (i) Corporation M is organized with two classes of stock outstanding, class A and class B. Each class B share may be converted, at the option of the holder, into class A shares. During the first year, the conversion ratio is one share of class A stock for each share of class B stock. At the beginning of each subsequent year, the conversion ratio is increased by 0.05 share of class A stock for each share of class B stock. Thus, during the second year, the conversion ratio would be 1.05 shares of class A stock for each share of

class B stock, during the third year, the ratio would be 1.10 shares, etc.

(ii) M pays an annual cash dividend on the class A stock. At the beginning of the second year, when the conversion ratio is increased to 1.05 shares of class A stock for each share of class B stock, a distribution of 0.05 shares of class A stock is deemed made under section 305(c) with respect to each share of class B stock, since the proportionate interests of the class B shareholders in the assets or earnings and profits of M are increased and the transaction has the effect described in section 305(b)(2). Accordingly, sections 305(b)(2) and 301 apply to the transaction.

* * *

Example (10). Corporation P has 1,000 shares of stock outstanding. T owns 700 shares of the P stock and G owns 300 shares of the P stock. In a single and isolated redemption to which section 301 applies, the corporation redeems 150 shares of T's stock. Since this is an isolated redemption and is not a part of a periodic redemption plan, G is not treated as having received a deemed distribution under section 305(c) to which sections 305(b)(2) and 301 apply even though he has an increased proportionate interest in the assets and earnings and profits of the corporation.

Example (11). Corporation Q is a large corporation whose sole class of stock is widely held. However, the four largest shareholders are officers of the corporation and each owns 8 percent of the outstanding stock. In 1974, in a distribution to which section 301 applies, the corporation redeems 1.5 percent of the stock from each of the four largest shareholders in preparation for their retirement. From 1970 through 1974, the corporation distributes annual stock dividends to its shareholders. No other distributions were made to these shareholders. Since the 1974 redemptions are isolated and are not part of a plan for periodically redeeming the stock of the corporation, the shareholders receiving stock dividends will not be treated as having received a distribution under section 305(b)(2) even though they have an increased proportionate interest in the assets and earnings and profits of the corporation and whether or not the redemptions are treated as distributions to which section 301 applies.

Example (12). Corporation R has 2,000 shares of class A stock outstanding. Five shareholders own 300 shares each and five shareholders own 100 shares each. In preparation for the retirement of the five major shareholders, corporation R, in a single and isolated transaction, has a recapitalization in which each share of class A stock may be exchanged either for five shares of new class B nonconvertible preferred stock plus 0.4 share of new class C common stock, or for two shares of new class C common stock. As a result of the exchanges, each of the five major shareholders receives 1,500 shares of class B nonconvertible preferred stock and 120 shares of class C common stock. The remaining shareholders each receives 200 shares of class C common stock. None of the exchanges are within the purview of section 305.

* * *

Example (15). (i) Facts. Corporation V is organized with two classes of stock, class A common and class B convertible preferred. The class B stock is issued for $100 per share and is convertible at the holder's option into class A at a fixed ratio that is not subject to full adjustment in the event stock dividends or rights are distributed to the class A shareholders. The class B stock pays no dividends but it is mandatorily redeemable in 10 years for $200. Under sections 305(c) and 305(b)(4), the entire redemption premium (i.e., the excess of the redemption price over the issue price) is deemed to be a distribution of preferred stock on preferred stock which is taxable as a distribution of property under section 301. This amount is considered to be distributed over the 10-year period under principles similar to the principles of section 1272(a). During the year, the corporation declares a dividend on

the class A stock payable in additional shares of class A stock.

(ii) Analysis. The distribution on the class A stock is a distribution to which sections 305(b)(2) and 301 apply since it increases the proportionate interests of the class A shareholders in the assets and earnings and profits of the corporation and the class B shareholders have received property (i.e., the constructive distribution described above). If, however, the conversion ratio of the class B stock were subject to full adjustment to reflect the distribution of stock to class A shareholders, the distribution of stock dividends on the class A stock would not increase the proportionate interest of the class A shareholders in the assets and earnings and profits of the corporation and such distribution would not be a distribution to which section 301 applies.

§ 1.305–4 Distributions of common and preferred stock.

(a) In general. Under section 305(b)(3), a distribution (or a series of distributions) by a corporation which results in the receipt of preferred stock (whether or not convertible into common stock) by some common shareholders and the receipt of common stock by other common shareholders is treated as a distribution of property to which section 301 applies. For the meaning of the term "a series of distribution," see subparagraphs (1) through (6) of § 1.305–3(b).

(b) Examples. The application of section 305(b)(3) may be illustrated by the following examples:

Example (1). Corporation X is organized with two classes of common stock, class A and class B. Dividends may be paid in stock or in cash on either class of stock without regard to the medium of payment of dividends on the other class. A dividend is declared on the class A stock payable in additional shares of class A stock and a dividend is declared on class B stock payable in newly authorized class C stock which is nonconvertible and limited and preferred as to dividends. Both the distribution of class A shares and the distribution of new class C shares are distributions to which section 301 applies.

Example (2). Corporation Y is organized with one class of stock, class A common. During the year the corporation declares a dividend on the class A stock payable in newly authorized class B preferred stock which is convertible into class A stock no later than 6 months from the date of distribution at a price that is only slightly higher than the market price of class A stock on the date of distribution. Taking into account the dividend rate, redemption provisions, the marketability of the convertible stock, and the conversion price, it is reasonable to anticipate that within a relatively short period of time some shareholders will exercise their conversion rights and some will not. Since the distribution can reasonably be expected to result in the receipt of preferred stock by some common shareholders and the receipt of common stock by other common shareholders, the distribution is a distribution of property to which section 301 applies.

§ 1.305–5 Distributions on preferred stock.

(a) **In general.** Under section 305(b)(4), a distribution by a corporation of its stock (or rights to acquire its stock) made (or deemed made under section 305(c)) with respect to its preferred stock is treated as a distribution of property to which section 301 applies unless the distribution is made with respect to convertible preferred stock to take into account a stock dividend, stock split, or any similar event (such as the sale of stock at less than the fair market value pursuant to a rights offering) which would otherwise result in the dilution of the conversion right. For purposes of the preceding sentence, an adjustment in the conversion ratio of convertible preferred stock made solely to take into account the distribution by a closed end regulated investment company of a capital gain dividend with respect to the stock into which such stock is convertible shall not be considered a "similar event." The term

"preferred stock" generally refers to stock which, in relation to other classes of stock outstanding, enjoys certain limited rights and privileges (generally associated with specified dividend and liquidation priorities) but does not participate in corporate growth to any significant extent. The distinguishing feature of "preferred stock" for the purposes of section 305(b)(4) is not its privileged position as such, but that such privileged position is limited, and that such stock does not participate in corporate growth to any significant extent. However, a right to participate which lacks substance will not prevent a class of stock from being treated as preferred stock. Thus, stock which enjoys a priority as to dividends and on liquidation but which is entitled to participate, over and above such priority, with another less privileged class of stock in earnings and profits and upon liquidation, may nevertheless be treated as preferred stock for purposes of section 305 if, taking into account all the facts and circumstances, it is reasonable to anticipate at the time a distribution is made (or is deemed to have been made) with respect to such stock that there is little or no likelihood of such stock actually participating in current and anticipated earnings and upon liquidation beyond its preferred interest. Among the facts and circumstances to be considered are the prior and anticipated earnings per share, the cash dividends per share, the book value per share, the extent of preference and of participation of each class, both absolutely and relative to each other, and any other facts which indicate whether or not the stock has a real and meaningful probability of actually participating in the earnings and growth of the corporation. The determination of whether stock is preferred for purposes of section 305 shall be made without regard to any right to convert such stock into another class of stock of the corporation. The term "preferred stock", however, does not include convertible debentures.

(b) **Redemption premium—(1) In general.** If a corporation issues preferred stock that may be redeemed under the circumstances described in this paragraph (b) at a price higher than the issue price, the difference (the redemption premium) is treated under section 305(c) as a constructive distribution (or series of constructive distributions) of additional stock on preferred stock that is taken into account under principles similar to the principles of section 1272(a). However, constructive distribution treatment does not result under this paragraph (b) if the redemption premium does not exceed a de minimis amount, as determined under the principles of section 1273(a)(3). For purposes of this paragraph (b), preferred stock that may be acquired by a person other than the issuer (the third person) is deemed to be redeemable under the circumstances described in this paragraph (b), and references to the issuer include the third person, if—

(i) This paragraph (b) would apply to the stock if the third person were the issuer; and

(ii) Either—

(A) The acquisition of the stock by the third person would be treated as a redemption for federal income tax purposes (under section 304 or otherwise); or

(B) The third person and the issuer are members of the same affiliated group (having the meaning for this purpose given the term by section 1504(a), except that section 1504(b) shall not apply) and a principal purpose of the arrangement for the third person to acquire the stock is to avoid the application of section 305 and paragraph (b)(1) of this section.

(2) Mandatory redemption or holder put. Paragraph (b)(1) of this section applies to stock if the issuer is required to redeem the stock at a specified time or the holder has the option (whether or not currently exercisable) to require the issuer to redeem the stock. However, paragraph (b)(1) of this section will not apply if the issuer's obligation to redeem or the holder's ability to require the issuer to redeem is subject to a contingency that is beyond the legal or practical control of either the holder or the holders as a group (or through a relat-

ed party within the meaning of section 267(b) or 707(b)), and that, based on all of the facts and circumstances as of the issue date, renders remote the likelihood of redemption. For purposes of this paragraph, a contingency does not include the possibility of default, insolvency, or similar circumstances, or that a redemption may be precluded by applicable law which requires that the issuer have a particular level of capital, surplus, or similar items. A contingency also does not include an issuer's option to require earlier redemption of the stock. For rules applicable if stock may be redeemed at more than one time, see paragraph (b)(4) of this section.

Example (5). (i) Facts. (A) Corporation Y is a domestic corporation with only common stock outstanding. On January 1, 1996, Y issues 100 shares of its 10% preferred stock to a holder. The holder is unrelated to Y both before and after the stock issuance. The issue price of the preferred stock is $100 per share. The preferred stock is—

(1) Callable at the option of Y on or before January 1, 2001, at a price of $105 per share plus any accrued but unpaid dividends; and

(2) Mandatorily redeemable on January 1, 2006, at a price of $100 per share plus any accrued but unpaid dividends.

(B) The preferred stock provides that if Y fails to exercise its option to call the preferred stock on or before January 1, 2001, the holder will be entitled to appoint a majority of Y's directors. Based on all of the facts and circumstances as of the issue date, Y is likely to have the legal and financial capacity to exercise its right to redeem. There are no other facts and circumstances as of the issue date that would affect whether Y will call the preferred stock on or before January 1, 2001.

(ii) Analysis. Under paragraph (b)(3)(i) of this section, paragraph (b)(1) of this section applies because, by virtue of the change of control provision and the absence of any contrary facts, it is more likely than not that Y will

exercise its option to call the preferred stock on or before January 1, 2001. The safe harbor rule of paragraph (b)(3)(ii) of this section does not apply because the provision that failure to call will cause the holder to gain control of the corporation is a plan, arrangement, or agreement that effectively requires or is intended to compel Y to redeem the preferred stock. Under paragraph (b)(4) of this section, the constructive distribution occurs over the period ending on January 1, 2001. Redemption is most likely to occur on that date, because that is the date on which the corporation minimizes the rate of return to the holder while preventing the holder from gaining control. The de minimis exception of paragraph (b)(1) of this section does not apply because the $5 per share difference between the redemption price and the issue price exceeds the amount determined under the principles of section 1273(a)(3) (5 x. 0025 x $105 = $1.31). Accordingly, $5 per share, the difference between the redemption price and the issue price, is treated as a constructive distribution received by the holder on an economic accrual basis over the five-year period ending on January 1, 2001, under principles similar to the principles of section 1272(a).

§ 1.305–6 Distributions of convertible preferred.

(a) **In general.** (1) Under section 305(b)(5), a distribution by a corporation of its convertible preferred stock or rights to acquire such stock made or considered as made with respect to its stock is treated as a distribution of property to which section 301 applies unless the corporation establishes that such distribution will not result in a disproportionate distribution as described in § 1.305–3.

(2) The distribution of convertible preferred stock is likely to result in a disproportionate distribution when both of the following conditions exist: (i) The conversion right must be exercised within a relatively short period of time after the date of distribution of the stock; and (ii) taking into account such factors as the dividend rate, the redemption provisions, the

marketability of the convertible stock, and the conversion price, it may be anticipated that some shareholders will exercise their conversion rights and some will not. On the other hand, where the conversion right may be exercised over a period of many years and the dividend rate is consistent with market conditions at the time of distribution of the stock, there is no basis for predicting at what time and the extent to which the stock will be converted and it is unlikely that a disproportionate distribution will result.

(b) **Examples.** The application of section 305(b)(5) may be illustrated by the following examples:

Example (1). Corporation Z is organized with one class of stock, class A common. During the year the corporation declares a dividend on the class A stock payable in newly authorized class B preferred stock which is convertible into class A stock for a period of 20 years from the date of issuance. Assuming dividend rates are normal in light of existing conditions so that there is no basis for predicting the extent to which the stock will be converted, the circumstances will ordinarily be sufficient to establish that a disproportionate distribution will not result since it is impossible to predict the extent to which the class B stock will be converted into class A stock. Accordingly, the distribution of class B stock is not one to which section 301 applies.

Example (2). Corporation X is organized with one class of stock, class A common. During the year the corporation declares a dividend on the class A stock payable in newly authorized redeemable class C preferred stock which is convertible into class A common stock no later than 4 months from the date of distribution at a price slightly higher than the market price of class A stock on the date of distribution. By prearrangement with corporation X, corporation Y, an insurance company, agrees to purchase class C stock from any shareholder who does not wish to convert. By reason of this prearrangement, it is anticipated that the shareholders will either sell the class C stock to the insurance company (which expects to retain the shares for investment purposes) or will convert. As a result, some of the shareholders exercise their conversion privilege and receive additional shares of class A stock, while other shareholders sell their class C stock to corporation Y and receive cash. The distribution is a distribution to which section 301 applies since it results in the receipt of property by some shareholders and an increase in the proportionate interests of other shareholders.

§ 1.305–7 Certain transactions treated as distributions.

(a) **In general.** Under section 305(c), a change in conversion ratio, a change in redemption price, a difference between redemption price and issue price, a redemption which is treated as a distribution to which section 301 applies, or any transaction (including a recapitalization) having a similar effect on the interest of any shareholder may be treated as a distribution with respect to any shareholder whose proportionate interest in the earnings and profits or assets of the corporation is increased by such change, difference, redemption, or similar transaction. In general, such change, difference, redemption, or similar transaction will be treated as a distribution to which sections 305(b) and 301 apply where—

(1) The proportionate interest of any shareholder in the earnings and profits or assets of the corporation deemed to have made such distribution is increased by such change, difference, redemption, or similar transaction; and

(2) Such distribution has the result described in paragraph (2), (3), (4), or (5) of section 305(b).

Where such change, difference, redemption, or similar transaction is treated as a distribution under the provisions of this section, such distribution will be deemed made with respect to any shareholder whose interest in the earnings and profits or assets of the distrib-

uting corporation is increased thereby. Such distribution will be deemed to be a distribution of the stock of such corporation made by the corporation to such shareholder with respect to his stock. Depending upon the facts presented, the distribution may be deemed to be made in common or preferred stock. For example, where a redemption premium exists with respect to a class of preferred stock under the circumstances described in § 1.305–5(b) and the other requirements of this section are also met, the distribution will be deemed made with respect to such preferred stock, in stock of the same class. Accordingly, the preferred shareholders are considered under sections 305(b)(4) and 305(c) to have received a distribution of preferred stock to which section 301 applies. See the examples in § § 1.305–3(e) and 1.305–5(d) for further illustrations of the application of section 305(c).

* * *

§ 1.306–1 General.

(a) Section 306 provides, in general, that the proceeds from the sale or redemption of certain stock (referred to as "section 306 stock") shall be treated either as ordinary income or as a distribution of property to which section 301 applies. Section 306 stock is defined in section 306(c) and is usually preferred stock received either as a nontaxable dividend or in a transaction in which no gain or loss is recognized. Section 306(b) lists certain circumstances in which the special rules of section 306(a) shall not apply.

(b)(1) If a shareholder sells or otherwise disposes of section 306 stock (other than by redemption or within the exceptions listed in section 306(b)), the entire proceeds received from such disposition shall be treated as ordinary income to the extent that the fair market value of the stock sold, on the date distributed to the shareholder, would have been a dividend to such shareholder had the distributing corporation distributed cash in lieu of stock. Any excess of the amount received over the sum of the amount treated as ordinary income plus the adjusted basis of the stock disposed of, shall be treated as gain from the sale of a capital asset or noncapital asset as the case may be. No loss shall be recognized. No reduction of earnings and profits results from any disposition of stock other than a redemption. The term "disposition" under section 306(a)(1) includes, among other things, pledges of stock under certain circumstances, particularly where the pledgee can look only to the stock itself as its security.

(2) Section 306(a)(1) may be illustrated by the following examples:

Example (1). On December 15, 1954, A and B owned equally all of the stock of Corporation X which files its income tax return on a calendar year basis. On that date Corporation X distributed pro rata 100 shares of preferred stock as a dividend on its outstanding common stock. On December 15, 1954, the preferred stock had a fair market value of $10,000. On December 31, 1954, the earnings and profits of Corporation X were $20,000. The 50 shares of preferred stock so distributed to A had an allocated basis to him of $10 per share or a total of $500 for the 50 shares. Such shares had a fair market value of $5,000 when issued. A sold the 50 shares of preferred stock on July 1, 1955, for $6,000. Of this amount $5,000 will be treated as ordinary income; $500 ($6,000 minus $5,500) will be treated as gain from the sale of a capital or noncapital asset as the case may be.

Example (2). The facts are the same as in Example 1 except that A sold his 50 shares of preferred stock for $5,100. Of this amount $5,000 will be treated as ordinary income. No loss will be allowed. There will be added back to the basis of the common stock of Corporation X with respect to which the preferred stock was distributed, $400, the allocated basis of $500 reduced by the $100 received.

Example (3). The facts are the same as in example 1 except that A sold 25 of his shares of preferred stock for $2,600. Of this amount

$2,500 will be treated as ordinary income. No loss will be allowed. There will be added back to the basis of the common stock of Corporation X with respect to which the preferred stock was distributed, $150, the allocated basis of $250 reduced by the $100 received.

(c) The entire amount received by a shareholder from the redemption of section 306 stock shall be treated as a distribution of property under section 301.

§ 1.306–2 Exception.

(a) If a shareholder terminates his entire stock interest in a corporation—

(1) By a sale or other disposition within the requirements of section 306(b)(1)(A), or

(2) By redemption under section 302(b)(3) (through the application of section 306(b)(1)(B)),

the amount received from such disposition shall be treated as an amount received in part or full payment for the stock sold or redeemed. In the case of a sale, only the stock interest need be terminated. In determining whether an entire stock interest has been terminated under section 306(b)(1)(A), all of the provisions of section 318(a) (relating to constructive ownership of stock) shall be applicable. In determining whether a shareholder has terminated his entire interest in a corporation by a redemption of his stock under section 302(b)(3), all of the provisions of section 318(a) shall be applicable unless the shareholder meets the requirements of section 302(c)(2) (relating to termination of all interest in the corporation). If the requirements of section 302(c)(2) are met, section 318(a)(1) (relating to members of a family) shall be inapplicable. Under all circumstances paragraphs (2), (3), (4), and (5) of section 318(a) shall be applicable.

(b) Section 306(a) does not apply to—

(1) Redemptions of section 306 stock pursuant to a partial or complete liquidation of a corporation to which part II (section 331 and

following), subchapter C, chapter 1 of the Code applies,

(2) Exchanges of section 306 stock solely for stock in connection with a reorganization or in an exchange under section 351, 355, or section 1036 (relating to exchanges of stock for stock in the same corporation) to the extent that gain or loss is not recognized to the shareholder as the result of the exchange of the stock (see paragraph (d) of § 1.306–3 relative to the receipt of other property), and

(3) A disposition or redemption, if it is established to the satisfaction of the Commissioner that the distribution, and the disposition or redemption, was not in pursuance of a plan having as one of its principal purposes the avoidance of Federal income tax. However, in the case of a prior or simultaneous disposition (or redemption) of the stock with respect to which the section 306 stock disposed of (or redeemed) was issued, it is not necessary to establish that the distribution was not in pursuance of such a plan. For example, in the absence of such a plan and of any other facts the first sentence of this subparagraph would be applicable to the case of dividends and isolated dispositions of section 306 stock by minority shareholders. Similarly, in the absence of such a plan and of any other facts, if a shareholder received a distribution of 100 shares of section 306 stock on his holdings of 100 shares of voting common stock in a corporation and sells his voting common stock before he disposes of his section 306 stock, the subsequent disposition of his section 306 stock would not ordinarily be considered a disposition one of the principal purposes of which is the avoidance of Federal income tax.

§ 1.306–3 Section 306 stock defined.

(a) For the purpose of subchapter C, chapter 1 of the Code, the term "section 306 stock" means stock which meets the requirements of section 306(c)(1). Any class of stock distributed to a shareholder in a transaction in which no amount is includible in the income of the shareholder or no gain or loss is recognized may be section 306 stock, if a distribution of money by the distributing corporation in lieu of such stock would have been a dividend in whole or in part. However, except as provided in section 306(g), if no part of a distribution of money by the distributing corporation in lieu of such stock would have been a dividend, the stock distributed will not constitute section 306 stock.

(b) For the purpose of section 306, rights to acquire stock shall be treated as stock. Such rights shall not be section 306 stock if no part of the distribution would have been a dividend if money had been distributed in lieu of the rights. When stock is acquired by the exercise of rights which are treated at section 306 stock, the stock acquired is section 306 stock. Upon the disposition of such stock (other than by redemption or within the exceptions listed in section 306(b)), the proceeds received from the disposition shall be treated as ordinary income to the extent that the fair market value of the stock rights, on the date distributed to the shareholder, would have been a dividend to the shareholder had the distributing corporation distributed cash in lieu of stock rights. Any excess of the amount realized over the sum of the amount treated as ordinary income plus the adjusted basis of the stock, shall be treated as gain from the sale of the stock.

(c) Section 306(c)(1)(A) provides that section 306 stock is any stock (other than common issued with respect to common) distributed to the shareholder selling or otherwise disposing thereof if, under section 305(a) (relating to distributions of stock and stock rights) any part of the distribution was not included in the gross income of the distributee.

(d) Section 306(c)(1)(B) includes in the definition of section 306 stock any stock except common stock, which is received by a shareholder in connection with a reorganization under section 368 or in a distribution or exchange under section 355 (or so much of section 356 as relates to section 355) provided the effect of the transaction is substantially the same as the receipt of a stock dividend, or the stock is received in exchange for section 306 stock. If, in a transaction to which section 356 is applicable, a shareholder exchanges section 306 stock for stock and money or other property, the entire amount of such money and of the fair market value of the other property (not limited to the gain recognized) shall be treated as a distribution of property to which section 301 applies. Common stock received in exchange for section 306 stock in a recapitalization shall not be considered section 306 stock. Ordinarily, section 306 stock includes stock which is not common stock received in pursuance of a plan of reorganization (within the meaning of section 368(a)) or received in a distribution or exchange to which section 355 (or so much of section 356 as relates to section 355) applies if cash received in lieu of such stock would have been treated as a dividend under section 356(a)(2) or would have been treated as a distribution to which section 301 applies by virtue of section 356(b) or section 302(d). The application of the preceding sentence is illustrated by the following examples:

Example (1). Corporation A, having only common stock outstanding, is merged in a statutory merger (qualifying as a reorganization under section 368(a)) with Corporation B. Pursuant to such merger, the shareholders of Corporation A received both common and preferred stock in Corporation B. The preferred stock received by such shareholders is section 306 stock.

Example (2). X and Y each own one-half of the 2,000 outstanding shares of preferred stock and one-half of the 2,000 outstanding shares of common stock of Corporation C. Pursuant to a reorganization within the meaning of section 368(a)(1)(E) (recapitalization) each shareholder exchanges his preferred stock for preferred stock of a new issue which is not substantially different from the preferred stock previously held. Unless the preferred stock exchanged was itself section 306 stock the preferred stock received is not section 306 stock.

(e) Section 306(c)(1)(C) includes in the definition of section 306 stock any stock (except as provided in section 306(c)(1)(B)) the basis of which in the hands of the person disposing of such stock, is determined by reference to section 306 stock held by such shareholder or any other person. Under this paragraph common stock can be section 306 stock. Thus, if a person owning section 306 stock in Corporation A transfers it to Corporation B which is controlled by him in exchange for common stock of Corporation B in a transaction to which section 351 is applicable, the common stock so received by him would be section 306 stock and subject to the provisions of section 306(a) on its disposition. In addition, the section 306 stock transferred is section 306 stock in the hands of Corporation B, the transferee. Section 306 stock transferred by gift remains section 306 stock in the hands of the donee. Stock received in exchange for section 306 stock under section 1036(a) (relating to exchange of stock for stock in the same corporation) or under so much of section 1031(b) as relates to section 1036(a) becomes section 306 stock and acquires, for purposes of section 306, the characteristics of the section 306 stock exchanged. The entire amount of the fair market value of the other property received in such transaction shall be considered as received upon a disposition (other than a redemption) to which section 306(a) applies. Section 306 stock ceases to be so classified if the basis of such stock is determined by reference to its fair market value on the date of the decedent-stockholder's death or the optional valuation date under section 1014.

(f) If section 306 stock which was distributed with respect to common stock is exchanged for common stock in the same corporation (whether or not such exchange is pursuant to a conversion privilege contained in section 306 stock), such common stock shall not be section 306 stock. This paragraph applies to exchanges not coming within the purview of section 306(c)(1)(B). Common stock which is convertible into stock other than common stock or into property, shall not be considered common stock. It is immaterial whether the conversion privilege is contained in the stock or in some type of collateral agreement.

(g) If there is a substantial change in the terms and conditions of any stock, then, for the purpose of this section —

(1) The fair market value of such stock shall be the fair market value at the time of distribution or the fair market value at the time of such change, whichever is higher;

(2) Such stock's ratable share of the amount which would have been a dividend if money had been distributed in lieu of stock shall be determined by reference to the time of distribution or by reference to the time of such change, whichever ratable share is higher; and

(3) Section 306(c)(2) shall be inapplicable if there would have been a dividend to any extent if money had been distributed in lieu of the stock either at the time of the distribution or at the time of such change.

* * *

§ 1.307–1 General.

(a) If a shareholder receives stock or stock rights as a distribution on stock previously held and under section 305 such distribution is not includible in gross income then, except as provided in section 307(b) and § 1.307–2, the basis of the stock with respect to which the distribution was made shall be allocated between the old and new stocks or rights in proportion to the fair market values of each on the date of distribution. If a shareholder receives stock or stock rights as a distribution on stock previously held and pursuant to section 305 part of the distribution is not includible in gross income, then (except as provided in section 307(b) and § 1.307–2) the basis of the stock with respect to which the distribution is made shall be allocated between (1) the old stock and (2) that part of the new stock or rights which is not includible in gross income, in proportion to the fair market values of each

on the date of distribution. The date of distribution in each case shall be the date the stock or the rights are distributed to the stockholder and not the record date. The general rule will apply with respect to stock rights only if such rights are exercised or sold.

(b) The application of paragraph (a) of this section is illustrated by the following example:

Example. A taxpayer in 1947 purchased 100 shares of common stock at $100 per share and in 1954 by reason of the ownership of such stock acquired 100 rights entitling him to subscribe to 100 additional shares of such stock at $90 a share. Immediately after the issuance of the rights, each of the shares of stock in respect of which the rights were acquired had a fair market value, ex-rights, of $110 and the rights had a fair market value of $19 each. The basis of the rights and the common stock for the purpose of determining the basis for gain or loss on a subsequent sale or exercise of the rights or a sale of the old stock is computed as follows:

100 (shares) × $100 = $10,000, cost of old stock (stock in respect of which the rights were acquired).

100 (shares) × $110 = $11,000, market value of old stock.

100 (rights) × $19 = $1,900, market value of rights.

11,000/12,900 of $10,000 = $8,527.13, cost of old stock apportioned to such stock.

1,900/12,900 of $10,000 = $1,472.87, cost of old stock apportioned to rights.

If the rights are sold, the basis for determining gain or loss will be $14.7287 per right. If the rights are exercised, the basis of the new stock acquired will be the subscription price paid therefor ($90) plus the basis of the rights exercised ($14.7287 each) or $104.7287 per share. The remaining basis of the old stock for the purpose of determining gain or loss on a subsequent sale will be $85.2713 per share.

§ 1.307–2 Exception.

The basis of rights to buy stock which are excluded from gross income under section 305(a), shall be zero if the fair market value of such rights on the date of distribution is less than 15 percent of the fair market value of the old stock on that date, unless the shareholder elects to allocate part of the basis of the old stock to the rights as provided in paragraph (a) of § 1.307–1. The election shall be made by a shareholder with respect to all the rights received by him in a particular distribution in respect of all the stock of the same class owned by him in the issuing corporation at the time of such distribution. Such election to allocate basis to rights shall be in the form of a statement attached to the shareholder's return for the year in which the rights are received. This election, once made, shall be irrevocable with respect to the rights for which the election was made. Any shareholder making such an election shall retain a copy of the election and of the tax return with which it was filed, in order to substantiate the use of an allocated basis upon a subsequent disposition of the stock acquired by exercise.

§ 1.312–1 Adjustment to earnings and profits reflecting distributions by corporations.

(a) In general, on the distribution of property by a corporation with respect to its stock, its earnings, and profits (to the extent thereof) shall be decreased by—

(1) The amount of money,

(2) The principal amount of the obligations of such corporation issued in such distribution, and

(3) The adjusted basis of other property.

* * *

(b) The adjustment provided in section 312(a)(3) with respect to a distribution of property (other than money or its own obligations) shall be made notwithstanding the fact that such property has appreciated or depreciated in value since acquisition.

(c) The application of this section may be illustrated by the following examples:

Example (1). Corporation A distributes to its sole shareholder property with a value of $10,000 and a basis of $5,000. It has $12,500

in earnings and profits. The reduction in earnings and profits by reason of such distribution is $5,000. Such is the reduction even though the amount of $10,000 is includible in the income of the shareholder (other than a corporation) as a dividend.

Example (2). The facts are the same as in example (1) above except that the property has a basis of $15,000 and the earnings and profits of the corporation are $20,000. The reduction in earnings and profits is $15,000. Such is the reduction even though only the amount of $10,000 is includible in the income of the shareholder as a dividend.

(d) In the case of a distribution of stock or rights to acquire stock a portion of which is includible in income by reason of section 305(b), the earnings and profits shall be reduced by the fair market value of such portion. No reduction shall be made if a distribution of stock or rights to acquire stock is not includible in income under the provisions of section 305.

(e) No adjustment shall be made in the amount of the earnings and profits of the issuing corporation upon a disposition of section 306 stock unless such disposition is a redemption.

* * *

§ 1.312–3 Liabilities.

The amount of any reductions in earnings and profits described in section 312(a) or (b) shall be (a) reduced by the amount of any liability to which the property distributed was subject and by the amount of any other liability of the corporation assumed by the shareholder in connection with such distribution, and (b) increased by the amount of gain recognized to the corporation under section 311(b), (c), or (d), or under section 341(f), 617(d), 1250(a), 1251(c), 1252(a), or 1254(a).

§ 1.312–6 Earnings and profits.

(a) In determining the amount of earnings and profits (whether of the taxable year, or accumulated since February 28, 1913, or accumulated before March 1, 2013), due consideration must be given to the facts, and, while mere bookkeeping entries increasing or decreasing surplus will not be conclusive, the amount of the earnings and profits in any case will be dependent upon the method of accounting properly employed in computing taxable income (or net income, as the case may be). For instance, a corporation keeping its books and filing its income tax returns under subchapter E, chapter 1 of the Code, on the cash receipts and disbursements basis may not use the accrual basis in determining earnings and profits. * * *

(b) Among the items entering into the computation of corporate earnings and profits for a particular period are all income exempted by statute, income not taxable by the Federal Government under the Constitution, as well as all items includible in gross income under section 61 or corresponding provisions of prior revenue acts. Gains and losses within the purview of section 1002 or corresponding provisions of prior revenue acts are brought into the earnings and profits at the time and to the extent such gains and losses are recognized under that section. Interest on State bonds and certain other obligations, although not taxable when received by a corporation, is taxable to the same extent as other dividends when distributed to shareholders in the form of dividends.

* * *

§ 1.312–10 Allocation of earnings in certain corporate separations.

(a) If one corporation transfers part of its assets constituting an active trade or business to another corporation in a transaction to which section 368(a)(1)(D) applies and immediately thereafter the stock and securities of the controlled corporation are distributed in a distribution or exchange to which section 355 (or so much of section 356 as relates to section 355) applies, the earnings and profits of the distributing corporation immediately before the transaction shall be allocated between the distributing corporation and the controlled corporation. In the case of a newly created controlled corporation, such allocation generally shall be made in proportion to the fair market value of the business or businesses (and interests in any other properties) retained by the distributing corporation and the business or businesses (and interests in any other properties) of the controlled corporation immediately after the transaction. In a proper case, allocation shall be made between the distributing corporation and the controlled corporation in proportion to the net basis of the assets transferred and of the assets retained or by such other method as may be appropriate under the facts and circumstances of the case. The term "net basis" means the basis of the assets less liabilities assumed or liabilities to which such assets are subject. The part of the earnings and profits of the taxable year of the distributing corporation in which the transaction occurs allocable to the controlled corporation shall be included in the computation of the earnings and profits of the first taxable year of the controlled corporation ending after the date of the transaction.

(b) If a distribution or exchange to which section 355 applies (or so much of section 356 as relates to section 355) is not in pursuance of a plan meeting the requirements of a reorganization as defined in section 368(a)(1)(D), the earnings and profits of the distributing corporation shall be decreased by the lesser of the following amounts:

(1) The amount by which the earnings and profits of the distributing corporation would have been decreased if it had transferred the stock of the controlled corporation to a new corporation in a reorganization to which section 368(a)(1)(D) applied and immediately thereafter distributed the stock of such new corporation or,

(2) The net worth of the controlled corporation. (For this purpose the term "net worth" means the sum of the basis of all of the properties plus cash minus all liabilities.) If the earnings and profits of the controlled corporation immediately before the transaction are less than the amount of the decrease in earnings and profits of the distributing corporation (including a case in which the controlled corporation has a deficit) the earnings and profits of the controlled corporation, after the transaction, shall be equal to the amount of such decrease.

If the earnings and profits of the controlled corporation immediately before the transaction are more than the amount of the decrease in the earnings and profits of the distributing corporation, they shall remain unchanged.

(c) In no case shall any part of a deficit of a distributing corporation within the meaning of section 355 be allocated to a controlled corporation.

§ 1.312–11 Effect on earnings and profits of certain other tax-free exchanges, tax-free distributions, and tax-free transfers from one corporation to another.

(a) In a transfer described in section 381(a), the acquiring corporation, as defined in § 1.381(a)–1(b)(2), and only that corporation, succeeds to the earnings and profits of the distributor or transferor corporation (within the meaning of § 1.381(a)–1(a)). Except as provided in § 1.312–10, in all other cases in which property is transferred from one corporation to another, no allocation of the earnings and profits of the transferor is made to the transferee.

* * *

§ 1.316–1 Dividends.

(a)(1) The term "dividend" for the purpose of subtitle A of the Code comprises any distribution of property as defined in section 317 in the ordinary course of business, even though extraordinary in amount, made by a domestic or foreign corporation to its shareholders out of either—

(i) Earnings and profits accumulated since February 28, 1913, or

(ii) Earnings and profits of the taxable year computed without regard to the amount of the earnings and profits (whether of such year or accumulated since February 28, 1913) at the time the distribution was made.

The earnings and profits of the taxable year shall be computed as of the close of such year, without diminution by reason of any distributions made during the taxable year. For the purpose of determining whether a distribution constitutes a dividend, it is unnecessary to ascertain the amount of the earnings and profits accumulated since February 28, 1913, if the earnings and profits of the taxable year are equal to or in excess of the total amount of the distributions made within such year.

(2) Where a corporation distributes property to its shareholders on or after June 22, 1954, the amount of the distribution which is a dividend to them may not exceed the earnings and profits of the distributing corporation.

(3) The rule of (2) above may be illustrated by the following example:

Example. X and Y, individuals, each own one-half of the stock of Corporation A which has earnings and profits of $10,000. Corporation A distributes property having a basis of $6,000 and a fair market value of $16,000 to its shareholders, each shareholder receiving property with a basis of $3,000 and with a fair market value of $8,000 in a distribution to which section 301 applies. The amount taxable to each shareholder as a dividend under section 301(c) is $5,000.

* * *

(e) The application of section 316 may be illustrated by the following examples:

Example (1). At the beginning of the calendar year 1955, Corporation M had an operating deficit of $200,000 and the earnings and profits for the year amounted to $100,000. Beginning on March 16, 1955, the corporation made quarterly distributions of $25,000 during the taxable year to its shareholders. Each distribution is a taxable dividend in full, irrespective of the actual or the pro rata amount of the earnings and profits on hand at any of the dates of distribution, since the total distributions made during the year ($100,000) did not exceed the total earnings and profits of the year ($100,000).

* * *

§ 1.316–2 Sources of distribution in general.

(a) For the purpose of income taxation every distribution made by a corporation is made out of earnings and profits to the extent thereof and from the most recently accumulated earnings and profits. In determining the source of a distribution, consideration should be given first, to the earnings and profits of the taxable year; second, to the earnings and profits accumulated since February 28, 1913, only in the case where, and to the extent that, the distributions made during the taxable year are not regarded as out of the earnings and profits of that year; third, to the earnings and profits accumulated before March 1, 1913, only after all the earnings and profits of the taxable year and all the earnings and profits accumulated since February 28, 1913, have been distributed; and, fourth, to sources other than earnings and profits only after the earnings and profits have been distributed.

(b) If the earnings and profits of the taxable year (computed as of the close of the year without diminution by reason of any distributions made during the year and without regard to the amount of earnings and profits at the time of the distribution) are sufficient in amount to cover all the distributions made during that year, then each distribution is a taxable dividend. See § 1.316–1. If the distributions made during the taxable year consist only of money and exceed the earnings and profits of such year, then that proportion of each distribution which the total of the earnings and profits of the year bears to the total distributions made during the year shall be regarded as out of the earnings and profits of that year. The portion of each such distribution which is not regarded as out of earnings and profits of the taxable year shall be considered a taxable dividend to the extent of the earnings and profits accumulated since February 28, 1913, and available on the date of the distribution. In any case in which it is necessary to determine the amount of earnings and profits accumulated since February 28, 1913, and the actual earnings and profits to the date of a distribution within any taxable year (whether beginning before January 1, 1936, or, in the case of an operating deficit, on or after that date) cannot be shown, the earnings and profits for the year (or accounting period, if less than a year) in which the distribution was made shall be prorated to the date of the distribution not counting the date on which the distribution was made.

(c) The provisions of the section may be illustrated by the following example:

Example. At the beginning of the calendar year 1955, Corporation M had $12,000 in earnings and profits accumulated since February 28, 1913. Its earnings and profits for 1955 amounted to $30,000. During the year it made quarterly cash distributions of $15,000 each. Of each of the four distributions made, $7,500 (that portion of $15,000 which the amount of $30,000, the total earnings and profits of the taxable year, bears to $60,000, the total distributions made during the year) was paid out of the earnings and profits of the taxable year; and of the first and second distributions, $7,500 and $4,500, respectively, were paid out of the earnings and profits accumulated after February 28, 1913, and before the taxable year, as follows:

Distributions during 1955				
Date	Amount	Portion out of earnings and profits of the taxable year	Portion out of earnings accumulated since Feb. 28, 1913, and before the taxable year	Taxable amt. of each distribution
March 10	$15,000	$7,500	$7,500	$15,000
June 10	15,000	7,500	4,500	12,000
September 10	15,000	7,500	—	7,500
December 10	15,000	7,500	—	7,500
Total amount taxable as dividends			42,000	

§ 1.318–1 Constructive ownership of stock; introduction.

(a) For the purposes of certain provisions of chapter 1 of the Code, section 318(a) provides that stock owned by a taxpayer includes stock constructively owned by such taxpayer under the rules set forth in such section. An individual is considered to own the stock owned, directly or indirectly, by or for his spouse (other than a spouse who is legally separated from the individual under a decree of divorce or separate maintenance), and by or for his children, grandchildren, and parents. Under section 318(a)(2) and (3), constructive ownership rules are established for partnerships and partners, estates and beneficiaries, trusts and beneficiaries, and corporations and stockholders. If any person has an option to acquire stock, such stock is considered as owned by such person. The term "option" includes an option to acquire such an option and each of a series of such options.

(b) In applying section 318(a) to determine the stock ownership of any person for any one purpose—

(1) A corporation shall not be considered to own its own stock by reason of section 318(a)(3)(C);

(2) In any case in which an amount of stock owned by any person may be included in the computation more than one time, such stock shall be included only once, in the manner in which it will impute to the person concerned the largest total stock ownership; and

(3) In determining the 50-percent requirement of section 318(a)(2)(C) and (3)(C), all of the stock owned actually and constructively by the person concerned shall be aggregated.

§ 1.318–2 Application of general rules.

(a) The application of paragraph (b) of § 1.318–1 may be illustrated by the following examples:

Example (1). H, an individual, owns all of the stock of corporation A. Corporation A is not considered to own the stock owned by H in corporation A.

Example (2). H, an individual, his wife, W, and his son, S, each own one-third of the stock of the Green Corporation. For purposes of determining the amount of stock owned by H, W, or S for purposes of section 318(a)(2)(C) and (3)(C), the amount of stock held by the other members of the family shall be added pursuant to paragraph (b)(3) of § 1.318–1 in applying the 50-percent requirement of such section. H, W, or S, as the case may be, is for this purpose deemed to own 100 percent of the stock of the Green Corporation.

(b) The application of section 318(a)(1), relating to members of a family, may be illustrated by the following example:

Example. An individual, H, his wife, W, his son, S, and his grandson (S's son), G, own the

100 outstanding shares of stock of a corporation, each owning 25 shares. H, W, and S are each considered as owning 100 shares. G is considered as owning only 50 shares, that is, his own and his father's.

(c) The application of section 318(a)(2) and (3), relating to partnerships, trusts and corporations, may be illustrated by the following examples:

Example (1). A, an individual, has a 50 percent interest in a partnership. The partnership owns 50 of the 100 outstanding shares of stock of a corporation, the remaining 50 shares being owned by A. The partnership is considered as owning 100 shares. A is considered as owning 75 shares.

Example (2). A testamentary trust owns 25 of the outstanding 100 shares of stock of a corporation. A, an individual, who holds a vested remainder in the trust having a value, computed actuarially equal to 4 percent of the value of the trust property, owns the remaining 75 shares. Since the interest of A in the trust is a vested interest rather than a contingent interest (whether or not remote), the trust is considered as owning 100 shares. A is considered as owning 76 shares.

Example (3). The facts are the same as in (2), above, except that A's interest in the trust is a contingent remainder. A is considered as owning 76 shares. However, since A's interest in the trust is a remote contingent interest, the trust is not considered as owning any of the shares owned by A.

Example (4). A and B, unrelated individuals, own 70 percent and 30 percent, respectively, in value of the stock of Corporation M. Corporation M owns 50 of the 100 outstanding shares of stock of Corporation O, the remaining 50 shares being owned by A. Corporation M is considered as owning 100 shares of Corporation O, and A is considered as owning 85 shares.

Example (5). A and B, unrelated individuals, own 70 percent and 30 percent, respective-

ly, of the stock of corporation M. A, B, and corporation M all own stock of corporation O. Since B owns less than 50 percent in value of the stock of corporation M, neither B nor corporation M constructively owns the stock of corporation O owned by the other. However, for purposes of certain sections of the Code, such as sections 304 and 856(d), the 50-percent limitation of section 318(a)(2)(C) and (3) (C) is disregarded or is reduced to less than 30 percent. For such purposes, B constructively owns his proportionate share of the stock of corporation O owned directly by corporation M, and corporation M constructively owns the stock of corporation O owned by B.

§1.318–3 Estates, trusts, and options.

* * *

(c) The application of section 318(a) relating to options may be illustrated by the following example:

Example. A and B, unrelated individuals, own all of the 100 outstanding shares of stock of a corporation, each owning 50 shares. A has an option to acquire 25 of B's shares and has an option to acquire a further option to acquire the remaining 25 of B's shares. A is considered as owning the entire 100 shares of stock of the corporation.

§1.318–4 Constructive ownership as actual ownership; exceptions.

(a) In general. Section 318(a)(5)(A) provides that, except as provided in section 318(a) (5)(B) and (C), stock constructively owned by a person by reason of the application of section 318(a)(1), (2), (3), or (4) shall be considered as actually owned by such person for purposes of applying section 318(a)(1), (2), (3), and (4). For example, if a trust owns 50 percent of the stock of corporation X, stock of corporation Y owned by corporation X which is attributed to the trust may be further attributed to the beneficiaries of the trust.

(b) Constructive family ownership. Section 318(a)(5)(B) provides that stock constructively owned by an individual by reason of ownership by a member of his family shall not be considered as owned by him for purposes of making another family member the constructive owner of such stock under section 318(a)(1). For example, if F and his two sons, A and B, each own one-third of the stock of a corporation, under section 318(a)(1), A is treated as owning constructively the stock owned by his father but is not treated as owning the stock owned by B. Section 318(a)(5)(B) prevents the attribution of the stock of one brother through the father to the other brother, an attribution beyond the scope of section 318(a)(1) directly.

(c) **Reattribution.** (1) Section 318(a)(5)(C) provides that stock constructively owned by a partnership, estate, trust, or corporation by reason of the application of section 318(a)(3) shall not be considered as owned by it for purposes of applying section 318(a)(2) in order to make another the constructive owner of such stock. For example, if two unrelated individuals are beneficiaries of the same trust, stock held by one which is attributed to the trust under section 318(a)(3) is not reattributed from the trust to the other beneficiary. However, stock constructively owned by reason of section 318(a)(2) may be reattributed under section 318(a)(3). Thus, for example, if all the stock of corporations X and Y is owned by A, stock of corporation Z held by X is attributed to Y through A.

(2) Section 318(a)(5)(C) does not prevent reattribution under section 318(a)(2) of stock constructively owned by an entity under section 318(a)(3) if the stock is also constructively owned by the entity under section 318(a)(4). For example, if individuals A and B are beneficiaries of a trust and the trust has an option to buy stock from A, B is considered under section 318(a)(2)(B) as owning a proportionate part of such stock.

* * *

§ 1.331–1 Corporate liquidations.

(a) **In general.** Section 331 contains rules governing the extent to which gain or loss is recognized to a shareholder receiving a distribution in complete or partial liquidation of a corporation. Under section 331(a)(1), it is provided that amounts distributed in complete liquidation of a corporation shall be treated as in full payment in exchange for the stock. Under section 331(a)(2), it is provided that amounts distributed in partial liquidation of a corporation shall be treated as in full or part payment in exchange for the stock. For this purpose, the term partial liquidation shall have the meaning ascribed in section 346. If section 331 is applicable to the distribution of property by a corporation, section 301 (relating to the effects on a shareholder of distributions of property) has no application other than to a distribution in complete liquidation to which section 316(b)(2)(B) applies. See paragraph (b)(2) of § 1.316–1.

(b) **Gain or loss.** The gain or loss to a shareholder from a distribution in partial or complete liquidation is to be determined under section 1001 by comparing the amount of the distribution with the cost or other basis of the stock. The gain or loss will be recognized to the extent provided in section 1002 and will be subject to the provisions of parts I, II, and III (section 1201 and following), subchapter P, chapter 1 of the Code.

(c) **Recharacterization.** A liquidation which is followed by a transfer to another corporation of all or part of the assets of the liquidating corporation or which is preceded by such a transfer may, however, have the effect of the distribution of a dividend or of a transaction in which no loss is recognized and gain is recognized only to the extent of "other property." See sections 301 and 356.

* * *

(e) **Example.** The provisions of this section may be illustrated by the following example:

Example. A, an individual who makes his income tax returns on the calendar year basis, owns 20 shares of stock of the P Corporation, a domestic corporation, 10 shares of which were acquired in 1951 at a cost of $1,500 and the remainder of 10 shares in December 1954 at a cost of $2,900. He receives in April 1955 a distribution of $250 per share in complete liquidation, or $2,500 on the 10 shares acquired in 1951, and $2,500 on the 10 shares acquired in December 1954. The gain of $1,000 on the shares acquired in 1951 is a long-term capital gain to be treated as provided in parts I, II, and III (section 1201 and following), subchapter P, chapter 1 of the Code. The loss of $400 on the shares acquired in 1954 is a short-term capital loss to be treated as provided in parts I, II, and III (section 1201 and following), subchapter P, chapter 1 of the Code.* * *

§ 1.332–1 Distributions in liquidation of subsidiary corporation; general.

Under the general rule prescribed by section 331 for the treatment of distributions in liquidation of a corporation, amounts received by one corporation in complete liquidation of another corporation are treated as in full payment in exchange for stock in such other corporation, and gain or loss from the receipt of such amounts is to be determined as provided in section 1001. Section 332 excepts from the general rule property received, under certain specifically described circumstances, by one corporation as a distribution in complete liquidation of the stock of another corporation and provides for the nonrecognition of gain or loss in those cases which meet the statutory requirements. See section 334(b) for the basis for determining gain or loss from the subsequent sale of property received upon complete liquidations such as described in this section. * * *

§ 1.332–2 Requirements for nonrecognition of gain or loss.

(a) The nonrecognition of gain or loss under section 332 is limited to the receipt of property by a corporation that is the actual owner of stock (in the liquidating corporation) meeting the requirements of section 1504(a)(2). The recipient corporation must have been the owner of the specified amount of such stock on the date of the adoption of the plan of liquidation and have continued so to be at all times until the receipt of the property. If the recipient corporation does not continue qualified with respect to the ownership of stock of the liquidating corporation and if the failure to continue qualified occurs at any time prior to the completion of the transfer of all the property, the provisions for the nonrecognition of gain or loss do not apply to any distribution received under the plan.

(b) Section 332 applies only to those cases in which the recipient corporation receives at least partial payment for the stock which it owns in the liquidating corporation. If section 332 is not applicable, see section 165(g) relative to allowance of losses on worthless securities.

(c) To constitute a distribution in complete liquidation within the meaning of section 332, the distribution must be (1) made by the liquidating corporation in complete cancellation or redemption of all of its stock in accordance with a plan of liquidation, or (2) one of a series of distributions in complete cancellation or redemption of all its stock in accordance with a plan of liquidation. Where there is more than one distribution, it is essential that a status of liquidation exist at the time the first distribution is made under the plan and that such status continue until the liquidation is completed. Liquidation is completed when the liquidating corporation and the receiver or trustees in liquidation are finally divested of all the property (both tangible and intangible). A status of liquidation exists when the corporation ceases to be a going concern and its activities are merely for the purpose of winding up its affairs, paying its debts, and distributing any remaining balance to its shareholders. A liquidation may be completed prior to the actual dissolution of the liquidating corporation. However, legal dissolution of the corporation is not required. Nor will the mere retention of a nominal amount of assets for the sole purpose of preserving the corporation's legal existence disqualify the transaction. * * *

(d) If a transaction constitutes a distribution in complete liquidation within the meaning of the Internal Revenue Code of 1954 and satisfies the requirements of section 332, it is not material that it is otherwise described under the local law. If a liquidating corporation distributes all of its property in complete liquidation and if pursuant to the plan for such complete liquidation a corporation owning the specified amount of stock in the liquidating corporation receives property constituting amounts distributed in complete liquidation within the meaning of the Code and also receives other property attributable to shares not owned by it, the transfer of the property to the recipient corporation shall not be treated, by reason of the receipt of such other property, as not being a distribution (or one of a series of distributions) in complete cancellation or redemption of all of the stock of the liquidating corporation within the meaning of section 332, even though for purposes of those provisions relating to corporate reorganizations the amount received by the recipient corporation in excess of its ratable share is regarded as acquired upon the issuance of its stock or securities in a tax-free exchange as described in section 361 and the cancellation or redemption of the stock not owned by the recipient corporation is treated as occurring as a result of a tax-free exchange described in section 354.

(e) The application of these rules may be illustrated by the following example:

Example. On September 1, 1954, the M Corporation had outstanding capital stock consisting of 3,000 shares of common stock, par value $100 a share, and 1,000 shares of preferred stock, par value $100 a share, which preferred stock was limited and preferred as to dividends and had no voting rights. On that date, and thereafter until the date of dissolution of the M Corporation, the O Corporation owned 2,500 shares of common stock of the M Corporation. By statutory merger consummated on October 1, 1954, pursuant to a plan of liquidation adopted on September 1, 1954, the M Corporation was merged into the O Corporation, the O Corporation under the plan issuing stock which was received by the other holders of the stock of the M Corporation. The receipt by the O Corporation of the properties of the M Corporation is a distribution received by the O Corporation in complete liquidation of the M Corporation within the meaning of section 332, and no gain or loss is recognized as the result of the receipt of such properties.

* * *

§ 1.332–5 Distribution in liquidation as affecting minority interests.

Upon the liquidation of a corporation in pursuance of a plan of complete liquidation, the gain or loss of minority shareholders shall be determined without regard to section 332, since it does not apply to that part of distributions in liquidation received by minority shareholders.

* * *

§ 1.332–7 Indebtedness of subsidiary to parent.

If section 332(a) is applicable to the receipt of the subsidiary's property in complete liquidation, then no gain or loss shall be recognized to the subsidiary upon the transfer of such properties even though some of the properties are transferred in satisfaction of the subsidiary's indebtedness to its parent. See section 337(b)(1),However, any gain or loss realized by the parent corporation on such satisfaction of indebtedness, shall be recognized to the parent corporation at the time of the liquidation. For example, if the parent corporation purchased its subsidiary's bonds at a discount and upon liquidation of the subsidiary the parent corporation receives payment for the face amount of such bonds, gain shall be recognized to the parent corporation. Such gain shall be measured by the difference between the cost or other basis of the bonds to the parent and the amount received in payment of the bonds.

* * *

§ 1.336–1 General principles, nomenclature, and definitions for a section 336(e) election.

(a) Overview—(1) In general. Section 336(e) authorizes the promulgation of regulations under which, in certain circumstances, a sale, exchange, or distribution of the stock of a corporation may be treated as an asset sale. This section and §§1.336–2 through 1.336–5 provide the rules for and consequences of making such election. This section provides the definitions and nomenclature. Generally, except to the extent inconsistent with section 336(e), the results of section 336(e) should coincide with those of section 338(h)(10). Accordingly, to the extent not inconsistent with section 336(e) or these regulations, the principles of section 338 and the regulations under section 338 apply for purposes of these regulations. For example, §1.338(h)(10)–1(d)(8), concerning the availability of the section 453 installment method, may apply with respect to section 336(e).

(2) Consistency rules. In general, the principles of §1.338–8, concerning asset and stock consistency, apply with respect to section 336(e). However, for this purpose, the application of §1.338–8(b)(1) is modified such that §1.338–8(b)(1)(iii) applies to an asset if the asset is owned, immediately after its acquisition and on the disposition date, by a person or by a related person (as defined in §1.336–1(b)(12)) to a person that acquires, by sale, exchange, distribution, or any combination thereof, five percent or more, by value, of the stock of target in the qualified stock disposition.

(b) Definitions. For purposes of §§1.336–1 through 1.336–5 (except as otherwise provided):

(1) Seller. The term *seller* means any domestic corporation that makes a qualified stock disposition of stock of another corporation. Seller includes both a transferor and a distributor of target stock. Generally, all members of a consolidated group that dispose of target stock are treated as a single seller. See §1.336–2(g)(2).

(2) Purchaser. The term *purchaser* means one or more persons that acquire or receive the stock of another corporation in a qualified stock disposition. A purchaser includes both a transferee and a distributee of target stock.

(3) Target; S corporation target; old target; new target. The term *target* means any domestic corporation the stock of which is sold, exchanged, or distributed in a qualified stock disposition. An *S corporation target* is a target that is an S corporation immediately before the disposition date; any other target is a *non-S corporation target*. Except as the context otherwise requires, a reference to target includes a reference to an S corporation target. In the case of a transaction not described in section 355(d)(2) or (e)(2), *old target* refers to target for periods ending on or before the close of target's disposition date and *new target* refers to target for subsequent periods. In the case of a transaction described in section 355(d)(2) or (e)(2), *old target* refers to target for periods ending on or before the disposition date as well as for subsequent periods.

(4) S corporation shareholders. *S corporation shareholders* are the S corporation target's shareholders. Unless otherwise provided, a reference to S corporation shareholders refers both to S corporation shareholders who dispose of and those who do not dispose of their S corporation target stock.

(5) Disposed of; disposition—(i) In general. The term *disposed of* refers to a transfer of stock in a disposition. The term *disposition* means any sale, exchange, or distribution of stock, but only if—

(A) The basis of the stock in the hands of the purchaser is not determined in whole or in part by reference to the adjusted basis of such stock in the hands of the person from whom the stock is acquired or under section 1014(a) (relating to property acquired from a decedent);

(B) Except as provided in paragraph (b)(5)(ii) of this section, the stock is not sold, exchanged, or distributed in a transaction to which section 351, 354, 355, or 356 applies and is not sold, exchanged, or distributed in any transaction described in regulations in which the transferor does not recognize the entire amount of the gain or loss realized in the transaction; and

(C) The stock is not sold, exchanged, or distributed to a related person.

(ii) Exception for disposition of stock in certain section 355 transactions. Notwithstanding paragraph (b)(5)(i)(B) of this section, a distribution of stock to a person who is not a related person in a transaction in which the full amount of stock gain would be recognized pursuant to section 355(d)(2) or (e)(2) shall be considered a disposition.

(iii) Transactions with related persons. In determining whether stock is sold, exchanged, or distributed to a related person, the principles of section 338(h)(3)(C) and §1.338–3(b)(3) shall apply.

(iv) No consideration paid. Stock in target may be considered disposed of if, under general principles of tax law, seller is considered to sell, exchange, or distribute stock of target notwithstanding that no amount may be paid for (or allocated to) the stock.

(v) Disposed of stock reacquired by certain persons. Stock disposed of by seller to another person under this section that is reacquired by seller or a member of seller's consolidated group during the 12-month disposition period shall not be considered as disposed of.

Similarly, stock disposed of by an S corporation shareholder to another person under this section that is reacquired by the S corporation shareholder or by a person related (within the meaning of paragraph (b)(12) of this section) to the S corporation shareholder during the 12-month disposition period shall not be considered as disposed of.

(6) Qualified stock disposition—(i) In general. The term *qualified stock disposition* means any transaction or series of transactions in which stock meeting the requirements of section 1504(a)(2) of a domestic corporation is either sold, exchanged, or distributed, or any combination thereof, by another domestic corporation or by the S corporation shareholders in a disposition, within the meaning of paragraph (b)(5) of this section, during the 12-month disposition period.

(ii) Overlap with qualified stock purchase—(A) In general. Except as provided in paragraph (b)(6)(ii)(B) of this section, a transaction satisfying the definition of a qualified stock disposition under paragraph (b)(6)(i) of this section, which also qualifies as a qualified stock purchase (as defined in section 338(d)(3)), will not be treated as a qualified stock disposition.

(B) Exception. If, as a result of the deemed sale of old target's assets pursuant to a section 336(e) election, there would be, but for paragraph (b)(6)(ii)(A) of this section, a qualified stock disposition of the stock of a subsidiary of target, then paragraph (b)(6)(ii)(A) shall not apply to the disposition of the stock of the subsidiary.

(7) 12-month disposition period. The term *12-month disposition period* means the 12-month period beginning with the date of the first sale, exchange, or distribution of stock included in a qualified stock disposition.

(8) Disposition date. The term *disposition date* means, with respect to any corporation, the first day on which there is a qualified stock disposition with respect to the stock of such corporation.

(9) Disposition date assets. *Disposition date assets* are the assets of target held at the beginning of the day after the disposition date (but see §1.338–1(d) (regarding certain transactions on the disposition date)).

(10) Domestic corporation. The term *domestic corporation* has the same meaning as in §1.338–2(c)(9).

(11) Section 336(e) election. A section 336(e) election is an election to apply section 336(e) to target. A section 336(e) election is made by making an election for target under §1.336–2(h).

(12) Related persons. Two persons are related if stock of a corporation owned by one of the persons would be attributed under section 318(a), other than section 318(a)(4), to the other. However, neither section 318(a)(2)(A) nor section 318(a)(3)(A) apply to attribute stock ownership from a partnership to a partner, or from a partner to a partnership, if such partner owns, directly or indirectly, interests representing less than five percent of the value of the partnership.

(13) Liquidation. Any reference to a liquidation is treated as a reference to the transfer described in §1.336–2(b)(1)(iii) notwithstanding its ultimate characterization for Federal income tax purposes.

(14) Deemed asset disposition. The deemed sale of old target's assets is, without regard to its characterization for Federal income tax purposes, referred to as the deemed asset disposition.

(15) Deemed disposition tax consequences. Deemed disposition tax consequences refers to, in the aggregate, the Federal income tax consequences (generally, the income, gain, deduction, and loss) of the deemed asset disposition. Deemed disposition tax consequences also refers to the Federal income tax consequences of the transfer of a particular asset in the deemed asset disposition.

(16) 80-percent purchaser. An 80-percent purchaser is any purchaser that, after application of the attribution rules of section 318(a), other than section 318(a)(4), owns 80 percent or more of the voting power or value of target stock.

(17) Recently disposed stock. The term *recently disposed stock* means any stock in target that is not held by seller, a member of seller's consolidated group, or an S corporation shareholder immediately after the close of the disposition date and that was disposed of by seller, a member of seller's consolidated group, or an S corporation shareholder during the 12-month disposition period.

(18) Nonrecently disposed stock. The term *nonrecently disposed stock* means stock in target that is held on the disposition date by a purchaser or a person related (as described in §1.336–1(b)(12)) to the purchaser who owns, on the disposition date, with the application of section 318(a), other than section 318(a)(4), at least 10 percent of the total voting power or value of the stock of target and that is not recently disposed stock.

(c) Nomenclature. For purposes of §§1.336–1 through 1.336–5, except as otherwise provided, Parent, Seller, Target, Sub, S Corporation Target, and Target Subsidiary are domestic corporations and A, B, C, and D are individuals, none of whom are related to Parent, Seller, Target, Sub, S Corporation Target, Target Subsidiary, or each other.

§ 1.336–2 Availability, mechanics, and consequences of section 336(e) election.

(a) Availability of election. A section 336(e) election is available if seller or S corporation shareholder(s) dispose of stock of another corporation (target) in a qualified stock disposition (as defined in §1.336–1(b)(6)). A section 336(e) election is irrevocable. A section 336(e) election is not available for transactions described in section 336(e) that do not constitute qualified stock dispositions.

(b) Deemed transaction—(1) Dispositions not described in section 355(d)(2) or (e)(2)—(i) Old target—deemed asset disposition—(A) In general. This paragraph (b)(1) provides the Federal income tax consequences of a section 336(e) election made with respect to a qualified stock disposition not described, in whole or in part, in section 355(d)(2) or (e)(2). For the Federal income tax consequences of a section 336(e) election made with respect to a qualified stock disposition described, in whole or in part, in section 355(d)(2) or (e)(2), see paragraph (b)(2) of this section. In general, if a section 336(e) election is made, seller (or S corporation shareholders) are treated as not having sold, exchanged, or distributed the stock disposed of in the qualified stock disposition. Instead, old target is treated as selling its assets to an unrelated person in a single transaction at the close of the disposition date (but before the deemed liquidation described in paragraph (b)(1)(iii) of this section) in exchange for the aggregate deemed asset disposition price (ADADP) as determined under §1.336–3. ADADP is allocated among the disposition date assets in the same manner as the aggregate deemed sale price (ADSP) is allocated under §§1.338–6 and 1.338–7 in order to determine the amount realized from each of the sold assets. Old target realizes the deemed disposition tax consequences from the deemed asset disposition before the close of the disposition date while old target is owned by seller or the S corporation shareholders. If old target is an S corporation target, old target's S election continues in effect through the close of the disposition date (including the time of the deemed asset disposition and the deemed liquidation) notwithstanding section 1362(d)(2)(B). Also, if old target is an S corporation target (but not a qualified subchapter S subsidiary), any direct or indirect subsidiaries of old target that old target has elected to treat as qualified subchapter S subsidiaries under section 1361(b)(3) remain qualified subchapter S subsidiaries through the close of the disposition date.

(B) Gains and losses—(1) Gains. Except as provided in §1.338(h)(10)–1(d)(8) (regarding the installment method), old target shall recognize all of the gains realized on the deemed asset disposition.

(2) Losses—(i) In general. Except as provided in paragraphs (b)(1)(i)(B)(2)(*ii*), (*iii*), and (*iv*) of this section, old target shall recognize all of the losses realized on the deemed asset disposition.

(ii) Stock distributions. Notwithstanding paragraphs (b)(1)(i)(A) and (b)(1)(iii)(A) of this section, for purposes of determining the amount of target's losses that are disallowed on the deemed asset disposition, seller is still treated as selling, exchanging, or distributing its target stock disposed of in the 12-month disposition period. If target's losses realized on the deemed sale of all of its assets exceed target's gains realized (a net loss), the portion of such net loss attributable to a distribution of target stock during the 12-month disposition period is disallowed. The total amount of disallowed loss and the allocation of disallowed loss is determined in the manner provided in paragraphs (b)(1)(i)(B)(2)(*iii*) and (*iv*) of this section.

* * *

(ii) New target—deemed purchase. New target is treated as acquiring all of its assets from an unrelated person in a single transaction at the close of the disposition date (but before the deemed liquidation) in exchange for an amount equal to the adjusted grossed-up basis (AGUB) as determined under §1.336–4. New target allocates the consideration deemed paid in the transaction in the same manner as new target would under §§1.338–6 and 1.338–7 in order to determine the basis in each of the purchased assets. If new target qualifies as a small business corporation within the meaning of section 1361(b) and wants to be an S corporation, a new election under section 1362(a) must be made. Notwithstanding paragraph (b)(1)(iii) of this section (deemed liquidation of old target), new target remains liable for the tax liabilities of old target (including the tax liability for the deemed disposition tax consequences). For example, new target remains liable for the tax liabilities of the members of any consolidated group that are attributable to taxable years in which those corporations and old target joined in the same consolidated return. See §1.1502–6(a).

(iii) Old target and seller—deemed liquidation—(A) In general. If old target is an S corporation, S corporation shareholders (whether or not they sell or exchange their stock) take their *pro rata* share of the deemed disposition tax consequences into account under section 1366 and increase or decrease their basis in target stock under section 1367. Old target and seller (or S corporation shareholders) are treated as if, before the close of the disposition date, after the deemed asset disposition described in paragraph (b)(1)(i)(A) of this section, and while target is owned by seller or S corporation shareholders, old target transferred all of the consideration deemed received from new target in the deemed asset disposition to seller or S corporation shareholders, any S corporation election for old target terminated, and old target ceased to exist. The transfer from old target to seller or S corporation shareholders is characterized for Federal income tax purposes in the same manner as if the parties had actually engaged in the transactions deemed to occur because of this section and taking into account other transactions that actually occurred or are deemed to occur. For example, the transfer may be treated as a distribution in pursuance of a plan of reorganization, a distribution in complete cancellation or redemption of all of its stock, one of a series of distributions in complete cancellation or redemption of all of its stock in accordance with a plan of liquidation, or part of a circular flow of cash. In most cases, the transfer will be treated as a distribution in complete liquidation to which sections 331 or 332 and sections 336 or 337 apply.

* * *

(iv) Seller—distribution of target stock. In the case of a distribution of target stock in a qualified stock disposition, seller (the distributor) is deemed to purchase from an unrelated person, on the disposition date, immediately after the deemed liquidation of old target, the amount of stock distributed in the qualified stock disposition (new target stock) and to have distributed such new target stock to its shareholders. Seller recognizes no gain or loss on the distribution of such stock.

(v) Seller—retention of target stock. If seller or an S corporation shareholder retains any target stock after the disposition date, seller or the S corporation shareholder is treated as purchasing the stock so retained from an unrelated person (new target stock) on the day after the disposition date for its fair market value. The holding period for the retained stock starts on the day after the disposition date. For purposes of this paragraph (b)(1)(v), the fair market value of all of the target stock equals the grossed-up amount realized on the sale, exchange, or distribution of recently disposed stock of target (see §1.336–3(c)).

(2) Dispositions described in section 355(d)(2) or (e)(2)—(i) Old target—deemed asset disposition—(A) In general. This paragraph (b)(2) provides the Federal income tax consequences of a section 336(e) election made with respect to a qualified stock disposition resulting, in whole or in part, from a disposition described in section 355(d)(2) or (e)(2). Old target is treated as selling its assets to an unrelated person in a single transaction at the close of the disposition date in exchange for the ADADP as determined under §1.336–3. ADADP is allocated among the disposition date assets in the same manner as ADSP is allocated under §§1.338–6 and 1.338–7 in order to determine the amount realized from each of the sold assets. Old target realizes the deemed disposition tax consequences from the deemed asset disposition before the close of the disposition date while old target is owned by seller.

(1) Old target not deemed to liquidate. In general, unlike a section 338(h)(10) election or a section 336(e) election made with respect to a qualified stock disposition not described, in whole or in part, in section 355(d)(2) or (e)(2), old target is not deemed to liquidate after the deemed asset disposition.

(2) Exception. If an election is made under §1.1502–13(f)(5)(ii)(E), then solely for purposes of §1.1502–13(f)(5)(ii)(C), immediately after the deemed asset disposition of old target, old target is deemed to liquidate into seller.

(B) Gains and losses—(1) Gains. Except as provided in §1.338(h)(10)–1(d)(8) (regarding the installment method), old target shall recognize all of the gains realized on the deemed asset disposition.

(2) Losses—(i) In general. Except as provided in paragraphs (b)(2)(i)(B)(*2*)(*ii*), (*iii*), and (*iv*) of this section, old target shall recognize all of the losses realized on the deemed asset disposition.

(ii) Stock distributions. If target's losses realized on the deemed sale of all of its assets exceed target's gains realized (a net loss), the portion of such net loss attributable to a distribution of target stock during the 12-month disposition period is disallowed. The total amount of disallowed loss and the allocation of disallowed loss is determined in the manner provided in paragraphs (b)(2)(i)(B)(*2*)(*iii*) and (*iv*) of this section.

* * *

(c) Purchaser. Generally, the making of a section 336(e) election will not affect the Federal income tax consequences to which purchaser would have been subject with respect to the acquisition of target stock if a section 336(e) election was not made. Thus, notwithstanding §§1.336–2(b)(1)(i)(A), 1.336–2(b)(1)(iv), and 1.336–2(b)(2)(iii)(A), purchaser will still be treated as having purchased, received in an exchange, or received in a distribution, the stock of target so acquired on the date actually acquired. However, see section 1223(1)

(B) with respect to the holding period for stock acquired pursuant to a distribution qualifying under section 355 (or so much of section 356 that relates to section 355). The Federal income tax consequences of the deemed asset disposition and liquidation of target may affect purchaser's consequences. For example, if seller distributes the stock of target to its shareholders in a qualified stock disposition for which a section 336(e) election is made, any increase in seller's earnings and profits as a result of old target's deemed asset disposition and liquidation into seller may increase the amount of a distribution to the shareholders constituting a dividend under section 301(c)(1).

(d) Minority shareholders—(1) In general. This paragraph (d) describes the treatment of shareholders of old target other than seller, a member of seller's consolidated group, and S corporation shareholders (whether or not they sell or exchange their stock of target). A shareholder to which this paragraph (d) applies is referred to as a minority shareholder.

(2) Sale, exchange, or distribution of target stock by a minority shareholder. A minority shareholder recognizes gain or loss (as permitted under the general principles of tax law) on its sale, exchange, or distribution of target stock.

(3) Retention of target stock by a minority shareholder. A minority shareholder who retains its target stock does not recognize gain or loss under this section with respect to its shares of target stock. The minority shareholder's basis and holding period for that target stock are not affected by the section 336(e) election. Notwithstanding this treatment of the minority shareholder, if a section 336(e) election is made, target will still be treated as disposing of all of its assets in the deemed asset disposition.

(e) Treatment consistent with an actual asset disposition. Except as otherwise provided, no provision in this section shall produce a Federal income tax result under subtitle A of the Internal Revenue Code that would not occur if the parties had actually engaged in the transactions deemed to occur because of this section, taking into account other transactions that actually occurred or are deemed to occur. See §1.338–1(a)(2) regarding the application of other rules of law.

(f) Treatment of target under other provisions of the Internal Revenue Code. The provisions §1.338–1(b) apply with respect to the treatment of new target after a section 336(e) election, treating any reference to section 338 or 338(h)(10) as a reference to section 336(e).

* * *

§ 1.337–1 Nonrecognition for property distributed to parent in complete liquidation of subsidiary.

(a) General rule. If sections 332(a) and 337 are applicable with respect to the receipt of a subsidiary's property in complete liquidation, no gain or loss is recognized to the liquidating subsidiary with respect to such property (including property distributed with respect to indebtedness, see section 337(b)(1) and § 1.332–7), except as provided in section 337(b)(2) (distributions to certain tax-exempt distributees), section 367(e)(2) (distributions to foreign corporations), and section 897(d) (distributions of U.S. real property interests by foreign corporations).

(b) Applicability date. This section applies to any taxable year beginning on or after March 28, 2016.

§ 1.338–1 General principles; status of old target and new target.

(a) In general—(1) Deemed transaction. Elections are available under section 338 when a purchasing corporation acquires the stock of another corporation (the target) in a qualified stock purchase. One type of election, under section 338(g), is available to the purchasing corporation. Another type of election, under section 338(h)(10), is, in more limited circumstances, available jointly

to the purchasing corporation and the sellers of the stock. (Rules concerning eligibility for these elections are contained in §§ 1.338–2, 1.338–3, and 1.338(h)(10)–1.) However, if, as a result of the deemed purchase of old target's assets pursuant to a section 336(e) election, there would be both a qualified stock purchase and a qualified stock disposition (as defined in §1.336–1(b)(6)) of the stock of a subsidiary of target, neither a section 338(g) election nor a section 338(h)(10) election may be made with respect to the qualified stock purchase of the subsidiary. Instead, a section 336(e) election may be made with respect to such purchase. See §1.336–1(b)(6)(ii). Although target is a single corporation under corporate law, if a section 338 election is made, then two separate corporations, old target and new target, generally are considered to exist for purposes of subtitle A of the Internal Revenue Code. Old target is treated as transferring all of its assets to an unrelated person in exchange for consideration that includes the discharge of its liabilities (see § 1.1001–2(a)), and new target is treated as acquiring all of its assets from an unrelated person in exchange for consideration that includes the assumption of those liabilities. (Such transaction is, without regard to its characterization for Federal income tax purposes, referred to as the deemed asset sale and the income tax consequences thereof as the deemed sale tax consequences.) If a section 338(h)(10) election is made, old target is deemed to liquidate following the deemed asset sale.

* * *

§ 1.338–3 Qualification for the section 338 election.

(a) Scope. This section provides rules on whether certain acquisitions of stock are qualified stock purchases and on other miscellaneous issues under section 338.

(b) Rules relating to qualified stock purchases—(1) Purchasing corporation requirement. An individual cannot make a qualified stock purchase of target. Section 338(d)(3) requires, as a condition of a qualified stock purchase, that a corporation purchase the stock of target. If an individual forms a corporation (new P) to acquire target stock, new P can make a qualified stock purchase of target if new P is considered for tax purposes to purchase the target stock. Facts that may indicate that new P does not purchase the target stock include new P's merging downstream into target, liquidating, or otherwise disposing of the target stock following the purported qualified stock purchase.

(2) Purchase. The term *purchase* has the same meaning as in section 338(h)(3). Stock in a target (or target affiliate) may be considered purchased if, under general principles of tax law, the purchasing corporation is considered to own stock of the target (or target affiliate) meeting the requirements of section 1504(a)(2), notwithstanding that no amount may be paid for (or allocated to) the stock.

(3) Acquisitions of stock from related corporations—(i) In general. Stock acquired by a purchasing corporation from a related corporation (R) is generally not considered acquired by purchase. See section 338(h)(3)(A)(iii).

(ii) Time for testing relationship. For purposes of section 338(h)(3)(A)(iii), a purchasing corporation is treated as related to another person if the relationship specified in section 338(h)(3)(A)(iii) exists—

(A) In the case of a single transaction, immediately after the purchase of target stock;

(B) In the case of a series of acquisitions otherwise constituting a qualified stock purchase within the meaning of section 338(d)(3), immediately after the last acquisition in such series; and

(C) In the case of a series of transactions effected pursuant to an integrated plan to dispose of target stock, immediately after the last transaction in such series.

(iii) Cases where section 338(h)(3)(C) applies—acquisitions treated as purchases. If section 338(h)(3)(C) applies and the purchasing corporation is treated as acquiring stock by purchase from R, solely for purposes of determining when the stock is considered acquired, target stock acquired from R is considered to have been acquired by the purchasing corporation on the day on which the purchasing corporation is first considered to own that stock under section 318(a) (other than section 318(a)(4)).

(iv) Examples. The following examples illustrate this paragraph (b)(3):

Example (1). (i) S is the parent of a group of corporations that are engaged in various businesses. Prior to January 1, Year 1, S decided to discontinue its involvement in one line of business. To accomplish this, S forms a new corporation, Newco, with a nominal amount of cash. Shortly thereafter, on January 1, Year 1, S transfers all the stock of the subsidiary conducting the unwanted business (T) to Newco in exchange for 100 shares of Newco common stock and a Newco promissory note. Prior to January 1, Year 1, S and Underwriter (U) had entered into a binding agreement pursuant to which U would purchase 60 shares of Newco common stock from S and then sell those shares in an Initial Public Offering (IPO). On January 6, Year 1, the IPO closes.

(ii) Newco's acquisition of T stock is one of a series of transactions undertaken pursuant to one integrated plan. The series of transactions ends with the closing of the IPO and the transfer of all the shares of stock in accordance with the agreements. Immediately after the last transaction effected pursuant to the plan, S owns 40 percent of Newco, which does not give rise to a relationship described in section 338(h)(3)(A)(iii). See § 1.338–3(b)(3)(ii)(C). Accordingly, S and Newco are not related for purposes of section 338(h)(3)(A)(iii).

(iii) Further, because Newco's basis in the T stock is not determined by reference to S's basis in the T stock and because the transaction

is not an exchange to which section 351, 354, 355, or 356 applies, Newco's acquisition of the T stock is a purchase within the meaning of section 338(h)(3).

Example (2). (i) On January 1 of Year 1, P purchases 75 percent in value of the R stock. On that date, R owns 4 of the 100 shares of T stock. On June 1 of Year 1, R acquires an additional 16 shares of T stock. On December 1 of Year 1, P purchases 70 shares of T stock from an unrelated person and 12 of the 20 shares of T stock held by R.

(ii) Of the 12 shares of T stock purchased by P from R on December 1 of Year 1, 3 of those shares are deemed to have been acquired by P on January 1 of Year 1, the date on which 3 of the 4 shares of T stock held by R on that date were first considered owned by P under section 318(a)(2)(C) (i.e., 4 × .75). The remaining 9 shares of T stock purchased by P from R on December 1 of Year 1 are deemed to have been acquired by P on June 1 of Year 1, the date on which an additional 12 of the 20 shares of T stock owned by R on that date were first considered owned by P under section 318(a)(2)(C) (i.e., (20 × .75)–3). Because stock acquisitions by P sufficient for a qualified stock purchase of T occur within a 12-month period (i.e., 3 shares constructively on January 1 of Year 1, 9 shares constructively on June 1 of Year 1, and 70 shares actually on December 1 of Year 1), a qualified stock purchase is made on December 1 of Year 1.

Example (3). (i) On February 1 of Year 1, P acquires 25 percent in value of the R stock from B (the sole shareholder of P). That R stock is not acquired by purchase. See section 338(h)(3)(A)(iii). On that date, R owns 4 of the 100 shares of T stock. On June 1 of Year 1, P purchases an additional 25 percent in value of the R stock, and on January 1 of Year 2, P purchases another 25 percent in value of the R stock. On June 1 of Year 2, R acquires an additional 16 shares of the T stock. On December 1 of Year 2, P purchases 68 shares of the T stock from an unrelated person and 12 of the 20 shares of the T stock held by R.

(ii) Of the 12 shares of the T stock purchased by P from R on December 1 of Year 2, 2 of those shares are deemed to have been acquired by P on June 1 of Year 1, the date on which 2 of the 4 shares of the T stock held by R on that date were first considered owned by P under section 318(a)(2)(C) (i.e., 4 ×. 5). For purposes of this attribution, the R stock need not be acquired by P by purchase. See section 338(h)(1). (By contrast, the acquisition of the T stock by P from R does not qualify as a purchase unless P has acquired at least 50 percent in value of the R stock by purchase. Section 338(h)(3)(C)(i).) Of the remaining 10 shares of the T stock purchased by P from R on December 1 of Year 2, 1 of those shares is deemed to have been acquired by P on January 1 of Year 2, the date on which an additional 1 share of the 4 shares of the T stock held by R on that date was first considered owned by P under section 318(a)(2)(C) (i.e., (4 ×. 75)–2). The remaining 9 shares of the T stock purchased by P from R on December 1 of Year 2, are deemed to have been acquired by P on June 1 of Year 2, the date on which an additional 12 shares of the T stock held by R on that date were first considered owned by P under section 318(a)(2)(C) (i.e., (20 ×. 75)–3). Because a qualified stock purchase of T by P is made on December 1 of Year 2 only if all 12 shares of the T stock purchased by P from R on that date are considered acquired during a 12-month period ending on that date (so that, in conjunction with the 68 shares of the T stock P purchased on that date from the unrelated person, 80 of T's 100 shares are acquired by P during a 12-month period) and because 2 of those 12 shares are considered to have been acquired by P more than 12 months before December 1 of Year 2 (i.e., on June 1 of Year 1), a qualified stock purchase is not made. (Under § 1.338–8(j)(2), for purposes of applying the consistency rules, P is treated as making a qualified stock purchase of T if, pursuant to an arrangement, P purchases T stock satisfying

the requirements of section 1504(a)(2) over a period of more than 12 months.)

Example (4). Assume the same facts as in *Example 3,* except that on February 1 of Year 1, P acquires 25 percent in value of the R stock by purchase. The result is the same as in *Example 3.*

(4) Acquisition date for tiered targets—(i) Stock sold in deemed asset sale. If an election under section 338 is made for target, old target is deemed to sell target's assets and new target is deemed to acquire those assets. Under section 338(h)(3)(B), new target's deemed purchase of stock of another corporation is a purchase for purposes of section 338(d)(3) on the acquisition date of target. If new target's deemed purchase causes a qualified stock purchase of the other corporation and if a section 338 election is made for the other corporation, the acquisition date for the other corporation is the same as the acquisition date of target. However, the deemed sale and purchase of the other corporation's assets is considered to take place after the deemed sale and purchase of target's assets.

(ii) Example. The following example illustrates this paragraph (b)(4):

Example. A owns all of the T stock. T owns 50 of the 100 shares of X stock. The other 50 shares of X stock are owned by corporation Y, which is unrelated to A, T, or P. On January 1 of Year 1, P makes a qualified stock purchase of T from A and makes a section 338 election for T. On December 1 of Year 1, P purchases the 50 shares of X stock held by Y. A qualified stock purchase of X is made on December 1 of Year 1, because the deemed purchase of 50 shares of X stock by new T because of the section 338 election for T and the actual purchase of 50 shares of X stock by P are treated as purchases made by one corporation. Section 338(h)(8). For purposes of determining whether those purchases occur within a 12-month acquisition period as required by section 338(d)(3), T is deemed to purchase its X stock on T's acquisition date, i.e., January 1 of Year 1.

(5) Effect of redemptions—(i) General rule. Except as provided in this paragraph (b)(5), a qualified stock purchase is made on the first day on which the percentage ownership requirements of section 338(d)(3) are satisfied by reference to target stock that is both—

(A) Held on that day by the purchasing corporation; and

(B) Purchased by the purchasing corporation during the 12-month period ending on that day.

(ii) Redemptions from persons unrelated to the purchasing corporation. Target stock redemptions from persons unrelated to the purchasing corporation that occur during the 12-month acquisition period are taken into account as reductions in target's outstanding stock for purposes of determining whether target stock purchased by the purchasing corporation in the 12-month acquisition period satisfies the percentage ownership requirements of section 338(d)(3).

(iii) Redemptions from the purchasing corporation or related persons during 12-month acquisition period—(A) General rule. For purposes of the percentage ownership requirements of section 338(d)(3), a redemption of target stock during the 12-month acquisition period from the purchasing corporation or from any person related to the purchasing corporation is not taken into account as a reduction in target's outstanding stock.

(B) Exception for certain redemptions from related corporations. A redemption of target stock during the 12-month acquisition period from a corporation related to the purchasing corporation is taken into account as a reduction in target's outstanding stock to the extent that the redeemed stock would have been considered purchased by the purchasing corporation (because of section 338(h)(3)(C)) during the 12-month acquisition period if the redeemed stock had been acquired by the purchasing corporation from the related corporation on the day of the redemption. See paragraph (b)(3) of this section.

(iv) Examples. The following examples illustrate this paragraph (b)(5):

Example (1). QSP on stock purchase date; redemption from unrelated person during 12-month period. A owns all 100 shares of T stock. On January 1 of Year 1, P purchases 40 shares of the T stock from A. On July 1 of Year 1, T redeems 25 shares from A. On December 1 of Year 1, P purchases 20 shares of the T stock from A. P makes a qualified stock purchase of T on December 1 of Year 1, because the 60 shares of T stock purchased by P within the 12-month period ending on that date satisfy the 80-percent ownership requirements of section 338(d)(3) (i.e., 60/75 shares), determined by taking into account the redemption of 25 shares.

Example (2). QSP on stock redemption date; redemption from unrelated person during 12-month period. The facts are the same as in *Example 1*, except that P purchases 60 shares of T stock on January 1 of Year 1 and none on December 1 of Year 1. P makes a qualified stock purchase of T on July 1 of Year 1, because that is the first day on which the T stock purchased by P within the preceding 12-month period satisfies the 80-percent ownership requirements of section 338(d)(3) (i.e., 60/75 shares), determined by taking into account the redemption of 25 shares.

Example (3). Redemption from purchasing corporation not taken into account. On December 15 of Year 1, T redeems 30 percent of its stock from P. The redeemed stock was held by P for several years and constituted P's total interest in T. On December 1 of Year 2, P purchases the remaining T stock from A. P does not make a qualified stock purchase of T on December 1 of Year 2. For purposes of the 80-percent ownership requirements of section 338(d)(3), the redemption of P's T stock on December 15 of Year 1 is not taken into account as a reduction in T's outstanding stock.

Example (4). Redemption from related person taken into account. On January 1 of Year 1, P purchases 60 of the 100 shares of X stock.

On that date, X owns 40 of the 100 shares of T stock. On April 1 of Year 1, T redeems X's T stock and P purchases the remaining 60 shares of T stock from an unrelated person. For purposes of the 80-percent ownership requirements of section 338(d)(3), the redemption of the T stock from X (a person related to P) is taken into account as a reduction in T's outstanding stock. If P had purchased the 40 redeemed shares from X on April 1 of Year 1, all 40 of the shares would have been considered purchased (because of section 338(h)(3)(C)(i)) during the 12-month period ending on April 1 of Year 1 (24 of the 40 shares would have been considered purchased by P on January 1 of Year 1 and the remaining 16 shares would have been considered purchased by P on April 1 of Year 1). See paragraph (b)(3) of this section. Accordingly, P makes a qualified stock purchase of T on April 1 of Year 1, because the 60 shares of T stock purchased by P on that date satisfy the 80-percent ownership requirements of section 338(d)(3) (i.e., 60/60 shares), determined by taking into account the redemption of 40 shares.

(c) Effect of post-acquisition events on eligibility for section 338 election—(1) Post-acquisition elimination of target. (i) The purchasing corporation may make an election under section 338 for target even though target is liquidated on or after the acquisition date. If target liquidates on the acquisition date, the liquidation is considered to occur on the following day and immediately after new target's deemed purchase of assets. The purchasing corporation may also make an election under section 338 for target even though target is merged into another corporation, or otherwise disposed of by the purchasing corporation provided that, under the facts and circumstances, the purchasing corporation is considered for tax purposes as the purchaser of the target stock. See § 1.338(h)(10)–1T(c)(2) for special rules concerning section 338(h)(10) elections in certain multi-step transactions.

(ii) The following examples illustrate this paragraph (c)(1):

Example (1). On January 1 of Year 1, P purchases 100 percent of the outstanding common stock of T. On June 1 of Year 1, P sells the T stock to an unrelated person. Assuming that P is considered for tax purposes as the purchaser of the T stock, P remains eligible, after June 1 of Year 1, to make a section 338 election for T that results in a deemed asset sale of T's assets on January 1 of Year 1.

Example (2). On January 1 of Year 1, P makes a qualified stock purchase of T. On that date, T owns the stock of T1. On March 1 of Year 1, T sells the T1 stock to an unrelated person. On April 1 of Year 1, P makes a section 338 election for T. Notwithstanding that the T1 stock was sold on March 1 of Year 1, the section 338 election for T on April 1 of Year 1 results in a qualified stock purchase by T of T1 on January 1 of Year 1. See paragraph (b)(4)(i) of this section.

(2) Post-acquisition elimination of the purchasing corporation. An election under section 338 may be made for target after the acquisition of assets of the purchasing corporation by another corporation in a transaction described in section 381(a), provided that the purchasing corporation is considered for tax purposes as the purchaser of the target stock. The acquiring corporation in the section 381(a) transaction may make an election under section 338 for target.

(d) Consequences of post-acquisition elimination of target where section 338 election not made—(1) Scope. The rules of this paragraph (d) apply to the transfer of target assets to the purchasing corporation (or another member of the same affiliated group as the purchasing corporation) (the transferee) following a qualified stock purchase of target stock, if the purchasing corporation does not make a section 338 election for target. Notwithstanding the rules of this paragraph (d), section 354(a) (and so much of section 356 as relates to section 354) cannot apply to any person other than the purchasing corporation or another member of the same affiliated group as the purchasing corporation unless the transfer of target assets is pursuant to a reorganization as determined without regard to this paragraph (d).

(2) Continuity of interest. By virtue of section 338, in determining whether the continuity of interest requirement of § 1.368–1(b) is satisfied on the transfer of assets from target to the transferee, the purchasing corporation's target stock acquired in the qualified stock purchase represents an interest on the part of a person who was an owner of the target's business enterprise prior to the transfer that can be continued in a reorganization.

(3) Control requirement. By virtue of section 338, the acquisition of target stock in the qualified stock purchase will not prevent the purchasing corporation from qualifying as a shareholder of the target transferor for the purpose of determining whether, immediately after the transfer of target assets, a shareholder of the transferor is in control of the corporation to which the assets are transferred within the meaning of section 368(a)(1)(D).

(4) Solely for voting stock requirement. By virtue of section 338, the acquisition of target stock in the qualified stock purchase for consideration other than voting stock will not prevent the subsequent transfer of target assets from satisfying the solely for voting stock requirement for purposes of determining if the transfer of target assets qualifies as a reorganization under section 368(a)(1)(C).

(5) Example. The following example illustrates this paragraph (d):

Example. (i) Facts. P, T, and X are domestic corporations. T and X each operate a trade or business. A and K, individuals unrelated to P, own 85 and 15 percent, respectively, of the stock of T. P owns all of the stock of X. The total adjusted basis of T's property exceeds the sum of T's liabilities plus the amount of liabilities to which T's property is subject. P purchases all of A's T stock for cash in a qualified stock purchase. P does not make an election under section 338(g) with respect to its acquisition of T stock. Shortly after the acquisition date, and as part of the same plan, T merges under applicable state law into X in a transaction that, but for the question of continuity of interest, satisfies all the requirements of section 368(a)(1)(A). In the merger, all of T's assets are transferred to X. P and K receive X stock in exchange for their T stock. P intends to retain the stock of X indefinitely.

(ii) Status of transfer as a reorganization. By virtue of section 338, for the purpose of determining whether the continuity of interest requirement of § 1.368–1(b) is satisfied, P's T stock acquired in the qualified stock purchase represents an interest on the part of a person who was an owner of T's business enterprise prior to the transfer that can be continued in a reorganization through P's continuing ownership of X. Thus, the continuity of interest requirement is satisfied and the merger of T into X is a reorganization within the meaning of section 368(a)(1)(A). Moreover, by virtue of section 338, the requirement of section 368(a)(1)(D) that a target shareholder control the transferee immediately after the transfer is satisfied because P controls X immediately after the transfer. In addition, all of T's assets are transferred to X in the merger and P and K receive the X stock exchanged therefor in pursuance of the plan of reorganization. Thus, the merger of T into X is also a reorganization within the meaning of section 368(a)(1)(D).

(iii) Treatment of T and X. Under section 361(a), T recognizes no gain or loss in the merger. Under section 362(b), X's basis in the assets received in the merger is the same as the basis of the assets in T's hands. X succeeds to and takes into account the items of T as provided in section 381.

(iv) Treatment of P. By virtue of section 338, the transfer of T assets to X is a reorganization. Pursuant to that reorganization, P exchanges its T stock solely for stock of X, a party to the reorganization. Because P is the purchasing corporation, section 354 applies to P's exchange of T stock for X stock in the merger of T into X. Thus, P recognizes no gain or loss on the exchange. Under section 358, P's basis in the X stock received in the exchange is the same as the basis of P's T stock exchanged therefor.

(v) Treatment of K. Because K is not the purchasing corporation (or an affiliate thereof), section 354 cannot apply to K's exchange of T stock for X stock in the merger of T into X unless the transfer of T's assets is pursuant to a reorganization as determined without regard to this paragraph (d). Under general principles of tax law applicable to reorganizations, the continuity of interest requirement is not satisfied because P's stock purchase and the merger of T into X are pursuant to an integrated transaction in which A, the owner of 85 percent of the stock of T, received solely cash in exchange for A's T stock. See, e.g., § 1.368–1(e)(1)(i); *Yoc Heating* v. *Commissioner,* 61 T.C. 168 (1973); *Kass* v. *Commissioner,* 60 T.C. 218 (1973), aff'd, 491 F.2d 749 (3d Cir. 1974). Thus, the requisite continuity of interest under § 1.368–1(b) is lacking and section 354 does not apply to K's exchange of T stock for X stock. K recognizes gain or loss, if any, pursuant to section 1001(c) with respect to its T stock.

§ 1.338–4 Aggregate deemed sale price; various aspects of taxation of the deemed asset sale.

(a) Scope. This section provides rules under section 338(a)(1) to determine the aggregate deemed sale price (ADSP) for target. ADSP is the amount for which old target is deemed to have sold all of its assets in the deemed asset sale. ADSP is allocated among target's assets in accordance with § 1.338–6 to determine the amount for which each asset is deemed to have been sold. When a subsequent increase or decrease is required under general principles of tax law with respect to an element of ADSP, the redetermined ADSP is allocated among target's assets in accordance with § 1.338–7.

This § 1.338–4 also provides rules regarding the recognition of gain or loss on the deemed sale of target affiliate stock. Notwithstanding section 338(h)(6)(B)(ii), stock held by a target affiliate in a foreign corporation or in a corporation that is a DISC or that is described in section 1248(e) is not excluded from the operation of section 338.

(b) Determination of ADSP—(1) General rule. ADSP is the sum of—

(i) The grossed-up amount realized on the sale to the purchasing corporation of the purchasing corporation's recently purchased target stock (as defined in section 338(b)(6)(A)); and

(ii) The liabilities of old target.

(2) Time and amount of ADSP—(i) Original determination. ADSP is initially determined at the beginning of the day after the acquisition date of target. General principles of tax law apply in determining the timing and amount of the elements of ADSP.

(ii) Redetermination of ADSP. ADSP is redetermined at such time and in such amount as an increase or decrease would be required, under general principles of tax law, for the elements of ADSP. For example, ADSP is redetermined because of an increase or decrease in the amount realized for recently purchased stock or because liabilities not originally taken into account in determining ADSP are subsequently taken into account. Increases or decreases with respect to the elements of ADSP result in the reallocation of ADSP among target's assets under § 1.338–7.

(iii) Example. The following example illustrates this paragraph (b)(2):

Example. In Year 1, T, a manufacturer, purchases a customized delivery truck from X with purchase money indebtedness having a stated principal amount of $100,000. P acquires all of the stock of T in Year 3 for $700,000 and makes a section 338 election for T. Assume T has no liabilities other than its purchase money indebtedness to X. In Year 4, when T is neither insolvent nor in a title 11 case, T and X agree to reduce the amount of the purchase money indebtedness to $80,000. Assume further that the reduction would be a purchase price reduction under section 108(e)(5). T and X's agreement to reduce the amount of the purchase money indebtedness would not, under general principles of tax law that would apply if the deemed asset sale had actually occurred, change the amount of liabilities of old target taken into account in determining its amount realized. Accordingly, ADSP is not redetermined at the time of the reduction. See § 1.338–5(b)(2)(iii) *Example 1* for the effect on AGUB.

(c) Grossed-up amount realized on the sale to the purchasing corporation of the purchasing corporation's recently purchased target stock—(1) Determination of amount. The grossed-up amount realized on the sale to the purchasing corporation of the purchasing corporation's recently purchased target stock is an amount equal to—

(i) The amount realized on the sale to the purchasing corporation of the purchasing corporation's recently purchased target stock determined as if the selling shareholder(s) were required to use old target's accounting methods and characteristics and the installment method were not available and determined without regard to the selling costs taken into account under paragraph (c)(1)(iii) of this section;

(ii) Divided by the percentage of target stock (by value, determined on the acquisition date) attributable to that recently purchased target stock;

(iii) Less the selling costs incurred by the selling shareholders in connection with the sale to the purchasing corporation of the purchasing corporation's recently purchased target stock that reduce their amount realized on the sale of the stock (e.g., brokerage commissions and any similar costs to sell the stock).

(2) Example. The following example illustrates this paragraph (c):

Example. T has two classes of stock outstanding, voting common stock and preferred stock described in section 1504(a)(4). On March 1 of Year 1, P purchases 40 percent of the outstanding T stock from S1 for $500, 20 percent of the outstanding T stock from S2 for $225, and 20 percent of the outstanding T stock from S3 for $275. On that date, the fair market value of all the T voting common stock is $1,250 and the preferred stock $750. S1, S2, and S3 incur $40, $35, and $25 respectively of selling costs. S1 continues to own the remaining 20 percent of the outstanding T stock. The grossed-up amount realized on the sale to P of P's recently purchased T stock is calculated as follows: The total amount realized (without regard to selling costs) is $1,000 (500 + 225 + 275). The percentage of T stock by value on the acquisition date attributable to the recently purchased T stock is 50% (1,000/(1,250 + 750)). The selling costs are $100 (40 + 35 + 25). The grossed-up amount realized is $1,900 (1,000/.5 – 100).

(d) Liabilities of old target—(1) In general. In general, the liabilities of old target are measured as of the beginning of the day after the acquisition date. (But see § 1.338–1(d) (regarding certain transactions on the acquisition date).) In order to be taken into account in ADSP, a liability must be a liability of target that is properly taken into account in amount realized under general principles of tax law that would apply if old target had sold its assets to an unrelated person for consideration that included the discharge of its liabilities. See § 1.1001–2(a). Such liabilities may include liabilities for the tax consequences resulting from the deemed sale.

(2) Time and amount of liabilities. The time for taking into account liabilities of old target in determining ADSP and the amount of the liabilities taken into account is determined as if old target had sold its assets to an unrelated person for consideration that included the discharge of the liabilities by the unrelated person. For example, if no amount of a target liability is properly taken into account in amount realized as of the beginning of the day after the acquisition date, the liability is not initially taken into account in determining ADSP (although it may be taken into account at some later date).

(e) Deemed sale tax consequences. Gain or loss on each asset in the deemed sale is computed by reference to the ADSP allocated to that asset. ADSP is allocated under the rules of § 1.338–6. Though deemed sale tax consequences may increase or decrease ADSP by creating or reducing a tax liability, the amount of the tax liability itself may be a function of the size of the deemed sale tax consequences. Thus, these determinations may require trial and error computations.

(f) Other rules apply in determining ADSP. ADSP may not be applied in such a way as to contravene other applicable rules. For example, a capital loss cannot be applied to reduce ordinary income in calculating the tax liability on the deemed sale for purposes of determining ADSP.

(g) Examples. The following examples illustrate this section. For purposes of the examples in this paragraph (g), unless otherwise stated, T is a calendar year taxpayer that files separate returns and that has no loss, tax credit, or other carryovers to Year 1. Depreciation for Year 1 is not taken into account. T has no liabilities other than the Federal income tax liability resulting from the deemed asset sale, and the T shareholders have no selling costs. Assume that T's tax rate for any ordinary income or net capital gain resulting from the deemed sale of assets is 34 percent and that any capital loss is offset by capital gain. On July 1 of Year 1, P purchases all of the stock of T and makes a section 338 election for T. The examples are as follows:

Example (1). One class. (i) On July 1 of Year 1, T's only asset is an item of section 1245 property with an adjusted basis to T of $50,400, a recomputed basis of $80,000, and a fair market value of $100,000. P purchases all of the T stock for $75,000, which also equals the amount realized for the stock determined as if the selling shareholder(s) were required to use old target's accounting methods and characteristics.

(ii) ADSP is determined as follows (for purposes of this section (g), G is the grossed-up amount realized on the sale to P of P's recently purchased T stock, L is T's liabilities other than T's tax liability for the deemed sale tax consequences, TR is the applicable tax rate, and B is the adjusted basis of the asset deemed sold):

$$ADSP = G + L + TR \times (ADSP - B)$$

$$ADSP = (\$75,000/1) + \$0 + .34 \times (ADSP - \$50,400)$$

$$ADSP = \$75,000 + .34ADSP - \$17,136.$$
$$66ADSP = \$57,864$$

$$ADSP = \$87,672.72$$

(iii) Because ADSP for T ($87,672.72) does not exceed the fair market value of T's asset ($100,000), a Class V asset, T's entire ADSP is allocated to that asset. Thus, T's deemed sale results in $37,272.72 of taxable income (consisting of $29,600 of ordinary income and $7,672.72 of capital gain).

(iv) The facts are the same as in paragraph (i) of this *Example 1,* except that on July 1 of Year 1, P purchases only 80 of the 100 shares of T stock for $60,000. The grossed-up amount realized on the sale to P of P's recently purchased T stock (G) is $75,000 ($60,000/.8). Consequently, ADSP and the deemed sale tax consequences are the same as in paragraphs (ii) and (iii) of this *Example 1.*

(v) The facts are the same as in paragraph (i) of this *Example 1,* except that T also has goodwill (a Class VII asset) with an appraised value of $10,000. The results are the same as in paragraphs (ii) and (iii) of this *Example 1.* Because ADSP does not exceed the fair market value of the Class V asset, no amount is allocated to the Class VII asset (goodwill).

Example (2). More than one class. (i) P purchases all of the T stock for $140,000, which also equals the amount realized for the stock determined as if the selling shareholder(s) were required to use old target's accounting methods and characteristics. On July 1 of Year 1, T has liabilities (not including the tax liability for the deemed sale tax consequences) of $50,000, cash (a Class I asset) of $10,000, actively traded securities (a Class II asset) with a basis of $4,000 and a fair market value of $10,000, goodwill (a Class VII asset) with a basis of $3,000, and the following Class V assets:

Asset	Basis	FMV	Ratio of asset FMV to total Class V FMV
Land	$5,000	$35,000	.14
Building	10,000	50,000	.20
Equipment A (Recomputed basis $80,000)	5,000	90,000	.36
Equipment B (Recomputed basis $20,000)	10,000	75,000	.30
Totals	$30,000	$250,000	1.00

(ii) ADSP exceeds $20,000. Thus, $10,000 of ADSP is allocated to the cash and $10,000 to the actively traded securities. The amount allocated to an asset (other than a Class VII asset) cannot exceed its fair market value (however, the fair market value of any property subject to nonrecourse indebtedness is treated as being not less than the amount of such indebtedness; see § 1.338–6(a)(2)). See § 1.338–6(c)(1) (relating to fair market value limitation).

(iii) The portion of ADSP allocable to the Class V assets is preliminarily determined as follows (in the formula, the amount allocated to the Class I assets is referred to as I and the amount allocated to the Class II assets as II):

$$ADSPV = (G - (I + II)) + L + TR \times [(II - BII) + (ADSPV - BV)]$$

$$ADSPV = (\$140,000 - (\$10,000 + \$10,000))$$

+ $50,000 + .34 × [($10,000 − $4,000) + (ADSPV − ($5,000 + $10,000 + $5,000 + $10,000))]

ADSPV = $161,840 + .34ADSPV

.66 ADSPV = $161,840

ADSPV = $245,212.12

(iv) Because, under the preliminary calculations of ADSP, the amount to be allocated to the Class I, II, III, IV, V, and VI assets does not exceed their aggregate fair market value, no ADSP amount is allocated to goodwill. Accordingly, the deemed sale of the goodwill results in a capital loss of $3,000. The portion of ADSP allocable to the Class V assets is finally determined by taking into account this loss as follows:

ADSPV = (G − (I + II)) + L + T R × [(II − BII) + (ADSPV − BV) + (ADSPVII − B VII)]

ADSPV = ($140,000 − ($10,000 + $10,000)) + $50,000 + .34 × [($10,000 − $4,000) + (ADSPV − $30,000) + ($0 − $3,000)]

ADSPV = $160,820 +. 34ADSPV

.66 ADSPV = $160,820

ADSPV = $243,666.67

(v) The allocation of ADSPV among the Class V assets is in proportion to their fair market values, as follows:

Asset	ADSP	Gain
Land	$34,113.33	$29,113.33 (capital gain).
Building	48,733.34	38,733.34 (capital gain).
Equipment A	87,720.00	82,720.00 (75,000 ordinary income; 7,720 capital gain).
Equipment B	73,100.00	63,100.00 (10,000 ordinary income; 53,100 capital gain).
Totals	243,666.67	213,666.67

Example (3). More than one class. (i) The facts are the same as in *Example 2,* except that P purchases the T stock for $150,000, rather than $140,000. The amount realized for the

stock determined as if the selling shareholder(s) were required to use old target's accounting methods and characteristics is also $150,000.

(ii) As in *Example 2,* ADSP exceeds $20,000. Thus, $10,000 of ADSP is allocated to the cash and $10,000 to the actively traded securities.

(iii) The portion of ADSP allocable to the Class V assets as preliminarily determined under the formula set forth in paragraph (iii) of *Example 2* is $260,363.64. The amount allocated to the Class V assets cannot exceed their aggregate fair market value ($250,000). Thus, preliminarily, the ADSP amount allocated to Class V assets is $250,000.

(iv) Based on the preliminary allocation, the ADSP is determined as follows (in the formula, the amount allocated to the Class I assets is referred to as I, the amount allocated to the Class II assets as II, and the amount allocated to the Class V assets as V):

ADSP = G + L + TR × [(II − BII) + (V − BV) + (ADSP − (I + II + V + BVII))]

ADSP = $150,000 + $50,000 + .34 × [($10,000 − $4,000) + ($250,000 − $30,000) + (ADSP − ($10,000 + $10,000 + $250,000 + $3,000))]

ADSP = $200,000 + .34ADSP − $15,980. 66ADSP = $184,020

ADSP = $278,818.18

(v) Because ADSP as determined exceeds the aggregate fair market value of the Class I, II, III, IV, V, and VI assets, the $250,000 amount preliminarily allocated to the Class V assets is appropriate. Thus, the amount of ADSP allocated to Class V assets equals their aggregate fair market value ($250,000), and the allocated ADSP amount for each Class V asset is its fair market value. Further, because there are no Class VI assets, the allocable ADSP amount for the Class VII asset (goodwill) is $8,818.18 (the excess of ADSP over

the aggregate ADSP amounts for the Class I, II, III, IV, V and VI assets).

Example (4). Amount allocated to T1 stock. (i) The facts are the same as in *Example 2,* except that T owns all of the T1 stock (instead of the building), and T1's only asset is the building. The T1 stock and the building each have a fair market value of $50,000, and the building has a basis of $10,000. A section 338 election is made for T1 (as well as T), and T1 has no liabilities other than the tax liability for the deemed sale tax consequences. T is the common parent of a consolidated group filing a final consolidated return described in § 1.338–10(a)(1).

(ii) ADSP exceeds $20,000. Thus, $10,000 of ADSP is allocated to the cash and $10,000 to the actively traded securities.

(iii) Because T does not recognize any gain on the deemed sale of the T1 stock under paragraph (h)(2) of this section, appropriate adjustments must be made to reflect accurately the fair market value of the T and T1 assets in determining the allocation of ADSP among T's Class V assets (including the T1 stock). In preliminarily calculating ADSPV in this case, the T1 stock can be disregarded and, because T owns all of the T1 stock, the T1 asset can be treated as a T asset. Under this assumption, ADSPV is $243,666.67. See paragraph (iv) of *Example 2.*

(iv) Because the portion of the preliminary ADSP allocable to Class V assets ($243,666.67) does not exceed their fair market value ($250,000), no amount is allocated to Class VII assets for T. Further, this amount ($243,666.67) is allocated among T's Class V assets in proportion to their fair market values. See paragraph (v) of *Example 2.* Tentatively, $48,733.34 of this amount is allocated to the T1 stock.

(v) The amount tentatively allocated to the T1 stock, however, reflects the tax incurred on the deemed sale of the T1 asset equal to $13,169.34 (.34 × ($48,733.34 − $10,000)).

Thus, the ADSP allocable to the Class V assets of T, and the ADSP allocable to the T1 stock, as preliminarily calculated, each must be reduced by $13,169.34. Consequently, these amounts, respectively, are $230,497.33 and $35,564.00. In determining ADSP for T1, the grossed-up amount realized on the deemed sale to new T of new T's recently purchased T1 stock is $35,564.00.

(vi) The facts are the same as in paragraph (i) of this *Example 4,* except that the T1 building has a $12,500 basis and a $62,500 value, all of the outstanding T1 stock has a $62,500 value, and T owns 80 percent of the T1 stock. In preliminarily calculating ADSPV, the T1 stock can be disregarded but, because T owns only 80 percent of the T1 stock, only 80 percent of T1 asset basis and value should be taken into account in calculating T's ADSP. By taking into account 80 percent of these amounts, the remaining calculations and results are the same as in paragraphs (ii), (iii), (iv), and (v) of this *Example 4,* except that the grossed-up amount realized on the sale of the recently purchased T1 stock is $44,455.00 ($35,564.00/0.8).

(h) Deemed sale of target affiliate stock — (1) Scope. This paragraph (h) prescribes rules relating to the treatment of gain or loss realized on the deemed sale of stock of a target affiliate when a section 338 election (but not a section 338(h)(10) election) is made for the target affiliate. For purposes of this paragraph (h), the definition of domestic corporation in § 1.338–2(c)(9) is applied without the exclusion therein for DISCs, corporations described in section 1248(e), and corporations to which an election under section 936 applies.

(2) In general. Except as otherwise provided in this paragraph (h), if a section 338 election is made for target, target recognizes no gain or loss on the deemed sale of stock of a target affiliate having the same acquisition date and for which a section 338 election is made if—

(i) Target directly owns stock in the target affiliate satisfying the requirements of section 1504(a)(2);

(ii) Target and the target affiliate are members of a consolidated group filing a final consolidated return described in § 1.338–10(a)(1); or

(iii) Target and the target affiliate file a combined return under § 1.338–10(a)(4).

(3) Deemed sale of foreign target affiliate by a domestic target. A domestic target recognizes gain or loss on the deemed sale of stock of a foreign target affiliate. For the proper treatment of such gain or loss, see, e.g., sections 1246, 1248, 1291 *et seq.*, and 338(h)(16) and § 1.338–9.

(4) Deemed sale producing effectively connected income. A foreign target recognizes gain or loss on the deemed sale of stock of a foreign target affiliate to the extent that such gain or loss is effectively connected (or treated as effectively connected) with the conduct of a trade or business in the United States.

(5) Deemed sale of insurance company target affiliate electing under section 953(d). A domestic target recognizes gain (but not loss) on the deemed sale of stock of a target affiliate that has in effect an election under section 953(d) in an amount equal to the lesser of the gain realized or the earnings and profits described in section 953(d)(4)(B).

(6) Deemed sale of DISC target affiliate. A foreign or domestic target recognizes gain (but not loss) on the deemed sale of stock of a target affiliate that is a DISC or a former DISC (as defined in section 992(a)) in an amount equal to the lesser of the gain realized or the amount of accumulated DISC income determined with respect to such stock under section 995(c). Such gain is included in gross income as a dividend as provided in sections 995(c)(2) and 996(g).

(7) Anti-stuffing rule. If an asset the adjusted basis of which exceeds its fair market value is contributed or transferred to a target

affiliate as transferred basis property (within the meaning of section 7701(a)(43)) and a purpose of such transaction is to reduce the gain (or increase the loss) recognized on the deemed sale of such target affiliate's stock, the gain or loss recognized by target on the deemed sale of stock of the target affiliate is determined as if such asset had not been contributed or transferred.

(8) Examples. The following examples illustrate this paragraph (h):

Example (1). (i) P makes a qualified stock purchase of T and makes a section 338 election for T. T's sole asset, all of the T1 stock, has a basis of $50 and a fair market value of $150. T's deemed purchase of the T1 stock results in a qualified stock purchase of T1 and a section 338 election is made for T1. T1's assets have a basis of $50 and a fair market value of $150.

(ii) T realizes $100 of gain on the deemed sale of the T1 stock, but the gain is not recognized because T directly owns stock in T1 satisfying the requirements of section 1504(a)(2) and a section 338 election is made for T1.

(iii) T1 recognizes gain of $100 on the deemed sale of its assets.

Example (2). The facts are the same as in *Example 1,* except that P does not make a section 338 election for T1. Because a section 338 election is not made for T1, the $100 gain realized by T on the deemed sale of the T1 stock is recognized.

Example (3). (i) P makes a qualified stock purchase of T and makes a section 338 election for T. T owns all of the stock of T1 and T2. T's deemed purchase of the T1 and T2 stock results in a qualified stock purchase of T1 and T2 and section 338 elections are made for T1 and T2. T1 and T2 each own 50 percent of the vote and value of T3 stock. The deemed purchases by T1 and T2 of the T3 stock result in a qualified stock purchase of T3 and a section 338 election is made for T3. T is the common parent of a consolidated group and all of the deemed asset sales are reported on the T group's final consolidated return. See § 1.338–10(a)(1).

(ii) Because T, T1, T2 and T3 are members of a consolidated group filing a final consolidated return, no gain or loss is recognized by T, T1 or T2 on their respective deemed sales of target affiliate stock.

Example (4). (i) T's sole asset, all of the FT1 stock, has a basis of $25 and a fair market value of $150. FT1's sole asset, all of the FT2 stock, has a basis of $75 and a fair market value of $150. FT1 and FT2 each have $50 of accumulated earnings and profits for purposes of section 1248(c) and (d). FT2's assets have a basis of $125 and a fair market value of $150, and their sale would not generate subpart F income under section 951. The sale of the FT2 stock or assets would not generate income effectively connected with the conduct of a trade or business within the United States. FT1 does not have an election in effect under section 953(d) and neither FT1 nor FT2 is a passive foreign investment company.

(ii) P makes a qualified stock purchase of T and makes a section 338 election for T. T's deemed purchase of the FT1 stock results in a qualified stock purchase of FT1 and a section 338 election is made for FT1. Similarly, FT1's deemed purchase of the FT2 stock results in a qualified stock purchase of FT2 and a section 338 election is made for FT2.

(iii) T recognizes $125 of gain on the deemed sale of the FT1 stock under paragraph (h)(3) of this section. FT1 does not recognize $75 of gain on the deemed sale of the FT2 stock under paragraph (h)(2) of this section. FT2 recognizes $25 of gain on the deemed sale of its assets. The $125 gain T recognizes on the deemed sale of the FT1 stock is included in T's income as a dividend under section 1248, because FT1 and FT2 have sufficient earnings and profits for full recharacterization ($50 of accumulated earnings and profits in FT1, $50 of accumulated earnings and profits in FT2, and $25 of deemed sale earnings and profits in FT2). Section 1.338–9(b). For purposes of

sections 901 through 908, the source and foreign tax credit limitation basket of $25 of the recharacterized gain on the deemed sale of the FT1 stock is determined under section 338(h)(16).

§ 1.338–5 Adjusted grossed-up basis.

(a) Scope. This section provides rules under section 338(b) to determine the adjusted grossed-up basis (AGUB) for target. AGUB is the amount for which new target is deemed to have purchased all of its assets in the deemed purchase under section 338(a)(2). AGUB is allocated among target's assets in accordance with § 1.338–6 to determine the price at which the assets are deemed to have been purchased. When a subsequent increase or decrease with respect to an element of AGUB is required under general principles of tax law, redetermined AGUB is allocated among target's assets in accordance with § 1.338–7.

(b) Determination of AGUB—(1) General rule. AGUB is the sum of—

(i) The grossed-up basis in the purchasing corporation's recently purchased target stock;

(ii) The purchasing corporation's basis in nonrecently purchased target stock; and

(iii) The liabilities of new target.

(2) Time and amount of AGUB—(i) Original determination. AGUB is initially determined at the beginning of the day after the acquisition date of target. General principles of tax law apply in determining the timing and amount of the elements of AGUB.

(ii) Redetermination of AGUB. AGUB is redetermined at such time and in such amount as an increase or decrease would be required, under general principles of tax law, with respect to an element of AGUB. For example, AGUB is redetermined because of an increase or decrease in the amount paid or incurred for recently purchased stock or nonrecently purchased stock or because liabilities not originally taken into account in determining AGUB are subsequently taken into account. An increase or decrease to one element of AGUB also may cause an increase or decrease to another element of AGUB. For example, if there is an increase in the amount paid or incurred for recently purchased stock after the acquisition date, any increase in the basis of nonrecently purchased stock because a gain recognition election was made is also taken into account when AGUB is redetermined. Increases or decreases with respect to the elements of AGUB result in the reallocation of AGUB among target's assets under § 1.338–7.

(iii) Examples. The following examples illustrate this paragraph (b)(2):

Example (1). In Year 1, T, a manufacturer, purchases a customized delivery truck from X with purchase money indebtedness having a stated principal amount of $100,000. P acquires all of the stock of T in Year 3 for $700,000 and makes a section 338 election for T. Assume T has no liabilities other than its purchase money indebtedness to X. In Year 4, when T is neither insolvent nor in a title 11 case, T and X agree to reduce the amount of the purchase money indebtedness to $80,000. Assume that the reduction would be a purchase price reduction under section 108(e)(5). T and X's agreement to reduce the amount of the purchase money indebtedness would, under general principles of tax law that would apply if the deemed asset sale had actually occurred, change the amount of liabilities of old target taken into account in determining its basis. Accordingly, AGUB is redetermined at the time of the reduction. See paragraph (e)(2) of this section. Thus the purchase price reduction affects the basis of the truck only indirectly, through the mechanism of §§ 1.338–6 and 1.338–7. See § 1.338–4(b)(2)(iii) *Example* for the effect on ADSP.

Example (2). T, an accrual basis taxpayer, is a chemical manufacturer. In Year 1, T is obligated to remediate environmental contamination at the site of one of its plants. Assume that all the events have occurred that establish the fact of the liability and the amount of the liability can be determined with reasonable accuracy but economic performance has not occurred with respect to the liability within the meaning of section 461(h). P acquires all of the stock of T in Year 1 and makes a section 338 election for T. Assume that, if a corporation unrelated to T had actually purchased T's assets and assumed T's obligation to remediate the contamination, the corporation would not satisfy the economic performance requirements until Year 5. Under section 461(h), the assumed liability would not be treated as incurred and taken into account in basis until that time. The incurrence of the liability in Year 5 under the economic performance rules is an increase in the amount of liabilities properly taken into account in basis and results in the redetermination of AGUB. (Respecting ADSP, compare § 1.461–4(d)(5), which provides that economic performance occurs for old T as the amount of the liability is properly taken into account in amount realized on the deemed asset sale. Thus ADSP is not redetermined when new T satisfies the economic performance requirements.)

(c) Grossed-up basis of recently purchased stock. The purchasing corporation's grossed-up basis of recently purchased target stock (as defined in section 338(b)(6)(A)) is an amount equal to—

(1) The purchasing corporation's basis in recently purchased target stock at the beginning of the day after the acquisition date determined without regard to the acquisition costs taken into account in paragraph (c)(3) of this section;

(2) Multiplied by a fraction, the numerator of which is 100 minus the number that is the percentage of target stock (by value, determined on the acquisition date) attributable to the purchasing corporation's nonrecently purchased target stock, and the denominator of which is the number equal to the percentage of target stock (by value, determined on the acquisition date) attributable to the purchasing corporation's recently purchased target stock;

(3) Plus the acquisition costs the purchasing corporation incurred in connection with its purchase of the recently purchased stock that are capitalized in the basis of such stock (e.g., brokerage commissions and any similar costs incurred by the purchasing corporation to acquire the stock).

(d) Basis of nonrecently purchased stock; gain recognition election—(1) No gain recognition election. In the absence of a gain recognition election under section 338(b)(3) and this section, the purchasing corporation retains its basis in the nonrecently purchased stock.

(2) Procedure for making gain recognition election. A gain recognition election may be made for nonrecently purchased stock of target (or a target affiliate) only if a section 338 election is made for target (or the target affiliate). The gain recognition election is made by attaching a gain recognition statement to a timely filed Form 8023 for target. The gain recognition statement must contain the information specified in the form and its instructions. The gain recognition election is irrevocable. If a section 338(h)(10) election is made for target, see § 1.338(h)(10)–1(d)(1) (providing that the purchasing corporation is automatically deemed to have made a gain recognition election for its nonrecently purchased T stock).

(3) Effect of gain recognition election—(i) In general. If the purchasing corporation makes a gain recognition election, then for all purposes of the Internal Revenue Code—

(A) The purchasing corporation is treated as if it sold on the acquisition date the nonrecently purchased target stock for the basis amount determined under paragraph (d)(3)(ii) of this section; and

(B) The purchasing corporation's basis on the acquisition date in nonrecently purchased target stock immediately following the deemed sale in paragraph (d)(3)(i)(A) of this section is the basis amount.

(ii) Basis amount. The basis amount is equal to the amount in paragraphs (c)(1) and (2) of this section (the purchasing corporation's grossed-up basis in recently purchased target stock at the beginning of the day after the acquisition date determined without regard to the acquisition costs taken into account in paragraph (c)(3) of this section) multiplied by a fraction the numerator of which is the percentage of target stock (by value, determined on the acquisition date) attributable to the purchasing corporation's nonrecently purchased target stock and the denominator of which is 100 percent minus the numerator amount. Thus, if target has a single class of outstanding stock, the purchasing corporation's basis in each share of nonrecently purchased target stock after the gain recognition election is equal to the average price per share of the purchasing corporation's recently purchased target stock.

(iii) Losses not recognized. Only gains (unreduced by losses) on the nonrecently purchased target stock are recognized.

(iv) Stock subject to election. The gain recognition election applies to—

(A) All nonrecently purchased target stock; and

(B) Any nonrecently purchased stock in a target affiliate having the same acquisition date as target if such target affiliate stock is held by the purchasing corporation on such date.

(e) Liabilities of new target—(1) In general. The liabilities of new target are the liabilities of target as of the beginning of the day after the acquisition date (but see § 1.338–1(d) (regarding certain transactions on the acquisition date)). In order to be taken into account in AGUB, a liability must be a liability of target that is properly taken into account in basis under general principles of tax law that would apply if new target had acquired its assets from an unrelated person for consideration that included discharge of the liabilities of that unrelated person. Such liabilities may include liabilities for the tax consequences resulting from the deemed sale.

(2) Time and amount of liabilities. The time for taking into account liabilities of old target in determining AGUB and the amount of the liabilities taken into account is determined as if new target had acquired its assets from an unrelated person for consideration that included the discharge of its liabilities.

(3) Interaction with deemed sale tax consequences. In general, see § 1.338–4(e). Although ADSP and AGUB are not necessarily linked, if an increase in the amount realized for recently purchased stock of target is taken into account after the acquisition date, and if the tax on the deemed sale tax consequences is a liability of target, any increase in that liability is also taken into account in redetermining AGUB.

(f) Adjustments by the Internal Revenue Service. In connection with the examination of a return, the Commissioner may increase (or decrease) AGUB under the authority of section 338(b)(2) and allocate such amounts to target's assets under the authority of section 338(b)(5) so that AGUB and the basis of target's assets properly reflect the cost to the purchasing corporation of its interest in target's assets. Such items may include distributions from target to the purchasing corporation, capital contributions from the purchasing corporation to target during the 12-month acquisition period, or acquisitions of target stock by the purchasing corporation after the acquisition date from minority shareholders. See also § 1.338–1(d) (regarding certain transactions on the acquisition date).

(g) Examples. The following examples illustrate this section. For purposes of the examples in this paragraph (g), T has no liabilities other than the tax liability for the deemed sale tax consequences, T shareholders incur no costs in selling the T stock, and P incurs no costs in acquiring the T stock. The examples are as follows:

Example (1). (i) Before July 1 of Year 1, P purchases 10 of the 100 shares of T stock for $5,000. On July 1 of Year 2, P purchases 80 shares of T stock for $60,000 and makes a section 338 election for T. As of July 1 of Year 2, T's only asset is raw land with an adjusted basis to T of $50,400 and a fair market value of $100,000. T has no loss or tax credit carryovers to Year 2. T's marginal tax rate for any ordinary income or net capital gain resulting from the deemed asset sale is 34 percent. The 10 shares purchased before July 1 of Year 1 constitute nonrecently purchased T stock with respect to P's qualified stock purchase of T stock on July 1 of Year 2.

(ii) The ADSP formula as applied to these facts is the same as in § 1.338–4(g) *Example 1*. Accordingly, the ADSP for T is $87,672.72. The existence of nonrecently purchased T stock is irrelevant for purposes of the ADSP formula, because that formula treats P's nonrecently purchased T stock in the same manner as T stock not held by P.

(iii) The total tax liability resulting from T's deemed asset sale, as calculated under the ADSP formula, is $12,672.72.

(iv) If P does not make a gain recognition election, the AGUB of new T's assets is $85,172.72, determined as follows (In the following formula below, GRP is the grossed-up basis in P's recently purchased T stock, BNP is P's basis in nonrecently purchased T stock, L is T's liabilities, and X is P's acquisition costs for the recently purchased T stock):

AGUB = GRP + BNP + L + X

AGUB = $60,000 × [(1 − .1)/.8] + $5,000 + $12,672.72 + 0

AGUB = $85,172.72

(v) If P makes a gain recognition election, the AGUB of new T's assets is $87,672.72, determined as follows:

AGUB = $60,000 × [(1 − .1)/.8] + $60,000 × [(1 −. 1)/.8] × [.1/(1 − .1)] + $12,672.72

AGUB = $87,672.72

(vi) The calculation of AGUB if P makes a gain recognition election may be simplified as follows:

AGUB = $60,000/.8 + $12,672.72

AGUB = $87,672.72

(vii) As a result of the gain recognition election, P's basis in its nonrecently purchased T stock is increased from $5,000 to $7,500 (i.e., $60,000 × [(1 − .1)/.8] × [.1/(1 − .1)]). Thus, P recognizes a gain in Year 2 with respect to its nonrecently purchased T stock of $2,500 (i.e., $7,500 − $5,000).

Example (2). On January 1 of Year 1, P purchases one-third of the T stock. On March 1 of Year 1, T distributes a dividend to all of its shareholders. On April 15 of Year 1, P purchases the remaining T stock and makes a section 338 election for T. In appropriate circumstances, the Commissioner may decrease the AGUB of T to take into account the payment of the dividend and properly reflect the fair market value of T's assets deemed purchased.

Example (3). (i) T's sole asset is a building worth $100,000. At this time, T has 100 shares of stock outstanding. On August 1 of Year 1, P purchases 10 of the 100 shares of T stock for $8,000. On June 1 of Year 2, P purchases 50 shares of T stock for $50,000. On June 15 of Year 2, P contributes a tract of land to the capital of T and receives 10 additional shares of T stock as a result of the contribution. Both the basis and fair market value of the land at that time are $10,800. On June 30 of Year 2, P purchases the remaining 40 shares of T stock for $40,000 and makes a section 338 election for T. The AGUB of T is $108,800.

(ii) To prevent the shifting of basis from the contributed property to other assets of T, the Commissioner may allocate $10,800 of the AGUB to the land, leaving $98,000 to be allocated to the building. See paragraph (f) of this section. Otherwise, applying the allocation rules of § 1.338–6 would, on these facts, result in an allocation to the recently contributed land of an amount less than its value of $10,800, with the difference being allocated to the building already held by T.

§ 1.338–6 Allocation of ADSP and AGUB among target assets.

(a) Scope—(1) In general. This section prescribes rules for allocating ADSP and AGUB among the acquisition date assets of a target for which a section 338 election is made.

(2) Fair market value—(i) In general. Generally, the fair market value of an asset is its gross fair market value (i.e., fair market value determined without regard to mortgages, liens, pledges, or other liabilities). However, for purposes of determining the amount of old target's deemed sale tax consequences, the fair market value of any property subject to a nonrecourse indebtedness will be treated as being not less than the amount of such indebtedness. (For purposes of the preceding sentence, a liability that was incurred because of the acquisition of the property is disregarded to the extent that such liability was not taken into account in determining old target's basis in such property.)

(ii) Transaction costs. Transaction costs are not taken into account in allocating ADSP or AGUB to assets in the deemed sale (except indirectly through their effect on the total ADSP or AGUB to be allocated).

(iii) Internal Revenue Service authority. In connection with the examination of a return, the Internal Revenue Service may challenge the taxpayer's determination of the fair market value of any asset by any appropriate method and take into account all factors, including any lack of adverse tax interests between the parties.

(b) General rule for allocating ADSP and AGUB—(1) Reduction in the amount of consideration for Class I assets. Both ADSP and AGUB, in the respective allocation of each, are first reduced by the amount of Class I assets. Class I assets are cash and general deposit accounts (including savings and checking accounts) other than certificates of deposit held in banks, savings and loan associations, and other depository institutions. If the amount of Class I assets exceeds AGUB, new target will immediately realize ordinary income in an amount equal to such excess. The amount of ADSP or AGUB remaining after the reduction is to be allocated to the remaining acquisition date assets.

(2) Other assets—(i) In general. Subject to the limitations and other rules of paragraph (c) of this section, ADSP and AGUB (as reduced by the amount of Class I assets) are allocated among Class II acquisition date assets of target in proportion to the fair market values of such Class II assets at such time, then among Class III assets so held in such proportion, then among Class IV assets so held in such proportion, then among Class V assets so held in such proportion, then among Class VI assets so held in such proportion, and finally to Class VII assets. If an asset is described below as includible in more than one class, then it is included in such class with the lower or lowest class number (for instance, Class III has a lower class number than Class IV).

(ii) Class II assets. Class II assets are actively traded personal property within the meaning of section 1092(d)(1) and § 1.1092(d)–1 (determined without regard to section 1092(d)(3)). In addition, Class II assets include certificates of deposit and foreign currency even if they are not actively traded personal property. Class II assets do not include stock of target affiliates, whether or not of a class that is actively traded, other than actively traded stock described in section 1504(a)(4). Examples of Class II assets include U.S. government securities and publicly traded stock.

(iii) Class III assets. Class III assets are assets that the taxpayer marks to market at least annually for Federal income tax purposes and debt instruments (including accounts receivable). However, Class III assets do not include—

(A) Debt instruments issued by persons related at the beginning of the day following the acquisition date to the target under section 267(b) or 707;

(B) Contingent debt instruments subject to § 1.1275–4, § 1.483–4, or section 988, unless the instrument is subject to the non-contingent bond method of § 1.1275–4(b) or is described in § 1.988–2(b)(2)(i)(B)(2); and

(C) Debt instruments convertible into the stock of the issuer or other property.

(iv) Class IV assets. Class IV assets are stock in trade of the taxpayer or other property of a kind that would properly be included in the inventory of taxpayer if on hand at the close of the taxable year, or property held by the taxpayer primarily for sale to customers in the ordinary course of its trade or business.

(v) Class V assets. Class V assets are all assets other than Class I, II, III, IV, VI, and VII assets.

(vi) Class VI assets. Class VI assets are all section 197 intangibles, as defined in section 197, except goodwill and going concern value.

(vii) Class VII assets. Class VII assets are goodwill and going concern value (whether or not the goodwill or going concern value qualifies as a section 197 intangible).

(3) Other items designated by the Internal Revenue Service. Similar items may be added to any class described in this paragraph (b) by designation in the Internal Revenue Bulletin by the Internal Revenue Service (see § 601.601(d)(2) of this chapter).

(c) Certain limitations and other rules for allocation to an asset—(1) Allocation not to exceed fair market value. The amount of ADSP or AGUB allocated to an asset (other than Class VII assets) cannot exceed the fair market value of that asset at the beginning of the day after the acquisition date.

(2) Allocation subject to other rules. The amount of ADSP or AGUB allocated to an asset is subject to other provisions of the Internal

Revenue Code or general principles of tax law in the same manner as if such asset were transferred to or acquired from an unrelated person in a sale or exchange. For example, if the deemed asset sale is a transaction described in section 1056(a) (relating to basis limitation for player contracts transferred in connection with the sale of a franchise), the amount of AGUB allocated to a contract for the services of an athlete cannot exceed the limitation imposed by that section. As another example, section 197(f)(5) applies in determining the amount of AGUB allocated to an amortizable section 197 intangible resulting from an assumption-reinsurance transaction.

(3) Special rule for allocating AGUB when purchasing corporation has nonrecently purchased stock—(i) Scope. This paragraph (c)(3) applies if at the beginning of the day after the acquisition date—

(A) The purchasing corporation holds nonrecently purchased stock for which a gain recognition election under section 338(b)(3) and § 1.338–5(d) is not made; and

(B) The hypothetical purchase price determined under paragraph (c)(3)(ii) of this section exceeds the AGUB determined under § 1.338–5(b).

(ii) Determination of hypothetical purchase price. Hypothetical purchase price is the AGUB that would result if a gain recognition election were made.

(iii) Allocation of AGUB. Subject to the limitations in paragraphs (c)(1) and (2) of this section, the portion of AGUB (after reduction by the amount of Class I assets) to be allocated to each Class II, III, IV, V, VI, and VII asset of target held at the beginning of the day after the acquisition date is determined by multiplying—

(A) The amount that would be allocated to such asset under the general rules of this section were AGUB equal to the hypothetical purchase price; by

(B) A fraction, the numerator of which is actual AGUB (after reduction by the amount of Class I assets) and the denominator of which is the hypothetical purchase price (after reduction by the amount of Class I assets).

(4) Liabilities taken into account in determining amount realized on subsequent disposition. In determining the amount realized on a subsequent sale or other disposition of property deemed purchased by new target, § 1.1001–2(a)(3) shall not apply to any liability that was taken into account in AGUB.

(d) Examples. The following examples illustrate §§ 1.338–4, 1.338–5, and this section:

Example (1). (i) T owns 90 percent of the outstanding T1 stock. P purchases 100 percent of the outstanding T stock for $2,000. There are no acquisition costs. P makes a section 338 election for T and, as a result, T1 is considered acquired in a qualified stock purchase. A section 338 election is made for T1. The grossed-up basis of the T stock is $2,000 (i.e., $2,000 + 1/1).

(ii) The liabilities of T as of the beginning of the day after the acquisition date (including the tax liability for the deemed sale tax consequences) that would, under general principles of tax law, properly be taken into account at that time, are as follows:

Liabilities (nonrecourse mortgage plus unsecured liabilities)	$700
Taxes Payable	300
Total	1,000

(iii) The AGUB of T is determined as follows:

Grossed-up basis	$2,000
Total liabilities	1,000
AGUB	3,000

(iv) Assume that ADSP is also $3,000.

(v) Assume that, at the beginning of the day after the acquisition date, T's cash and the fair

market values of T's Class II, III, IV, and V assets are as follows:

Asset class	Asset	Fair market value
I	Cash	$ 200
II	Portfolio of actively traded securities	300
III	Accounts receivable	600
IV	Inventory	300
V	Building	800
V	Land	200
V	Investment in T1	450
	Total	2,850

*Amount.

(vi) Under paragraph (b)(1) of this section, the amount of ADSP and AGUB allocable to T's Class II, III, IV, and V assets is reduced by the amount of cash to $2,800, i.e., $3,000 – $200. $300 of ADSP and of AGUB is then allocated to actively traded securities. $600 of ADSP and of AGUB is then allocated to accounts receivable. $300 of ADSP and of AGUB is then allocated to the inventory. Since the remaining amount of ADSP and of AGUB is $1,600 (i.e., $3,000 – ($200 + $300 + $600 + $300)), an amount which exceeds the sum of the fair market values of T's Class V assets, the amount of ADSP and of AGUB allocated to each Class V asset is its fair market value:

Building...800

Land 200

Investment in T1 450

Total 1,450

(vii) T has no Class VI assets. The amount of ADSP and of AGUB allocated to T's Class VII assets (goodwill and going concern value) is $150, i.e., $1,600 – $1,450.

(viii) The grossed-up basis of the T1 stock is $500, i.e., $450 × 1/.9.

(ix) The liabilities of T1 as of the beginning of the day after the acquisition date (including the tax liability for the deemed sale tax consequences) that would, under general principles of tax law, properly be taken into account at that time, are as follows:

General Liabilities....................................$100

Taxes Payable...20

Total 120

(x) The AGUB of T1 is determined as follows:

Grossed-up basis of T1 Stock $500

Liabilities 120

AGUB 620

(xi) Assume that ADSP is also $620.

(xii) Assume that at the beginning of the day after the acquisition date, T1's cash and the fair market values of its Class IV and VI assets are as follows:

Asset class	Asset	Fair market value
I	Cash	*$ 50
IV	Inventory	200
VI	Patent	350
	Total	600

*Amount.

(xiii) The amount of ADSP and of AGUB allocable to T1's Class IV and VI assets is first reduced by the $50 of cash.

(xiv) Because the remaining amount of ADSP and of AGUB ($570) is an amount which exceeds the fair market value of T1's only Class IV asset, the inventory, the amount allocated to the inventory is its fair market value ($200). After that, the remaining amount of ADSP and of AGUB ($370) exceeds the fair market value of T1's only Class VI asset, the patent. Thus, the amount of ADSP and of AGUB allocated to the patent is its fair market value ($350).

(xv) The amount of ADSP and of AGUB allocated to T1's Class VII assets (goodwill and going concern value) is $20, i.e., $570 – $550.

* * *

§ 1.338–8 Asset and stock consistency.

(a) Introduction—(1) Overview. This section implements the consistency rules of sections 338(e) and (f). Under this section, no election under section 338 is deemed made or required with respect to target or any target affiliate. Instead, the person acquiring an asset may have a carryover basis in the asset.

(2) General application. The consistency rules generally apply if the purchasing corporation acquires an asset directly from target during the target consistency period and target is a subsidiary in a consolidated group. In such a case, gain from the sale of the asset is reflected under the investment adjustment provisions of the consolidated return regulations in the basis of target stock and may reduce gain from the sale of the stock. See § 1.1502–32 (investment adjustment provisions). Under the consistency rules, the purchasing corporation generally takes a carryover basis in the asset, unless a section 338 election is made for target. Similar rules apply if the purchasing corporation acquires an asset directly from a lower-tier target affiliate if gain from the sale is reflected under the investment adjustment provisions in the basis of target stock.

(3) Extensions of the general rules. If an arrangement exists, paragraph (f) of this section generally extends the carryover basis rule to certain cases in which the purchasing corporation acquires assets indirectly from target (or a lower-tier target affiliate). To prevent avoidance of the consistency rules, paragraph (j) of this section also may extend the consistency period or the 12-month acquisition period and may disregard the presence of conduits.

(4) Application where certain dividends are paid. Paragraph (g) of this section extends the carryover basis rule to certain cases in which dividends are paid to a corporation that is not a member of the same consolidated group as the distributing corporation. Generally, this rule applies where a 100 percent dividends received deduction is used in conjunction with asset dispositions to achieve an effect similar to that available under the investment adjustment provisions of the consolidated return regulations.

(5) Application to foreign target affiliates. Paragraph (h) of this section extends the carryover basis rule to certain cases involving target affiliates that are controlled foreign corporations.

(6) Stock consistency. This section limits the application of the stock consistency rules to cases in which the rules are necessary to prevent avoidance of the asset consistency rules. Following the general treatment of a section 338(h)(10) election, a sale of a corporation's stock is treated as a sale of the corporation's assets if a section 338(h)(10) election is made. Because gain from this asset sale may be reflected in the basis of the stock of a higher-tier target, the carryover basis rule may apply to the assets.

(b) Consistency for direct acquisitions—(1) General rule. The basis rules of paragraph (d) of this section apply to an asset if—

(i) The asset is disposed of during the target consistency period;

(ii) The basis of target stock, as of the target acquisition date, reflects gain from the disposition of the asset (see paragraph (c) of this section); and

(iii) The asset is owned, immediately after its acquisition and on the target acquisition date, by a corporation that acquires stock of target in the qualified stock purchase (or by an affiliate of an acquiring corporation).

(2) Section 338(h)(10) elections. For purposes of this section, if a section 338(h)(10) election is made for a corporation acquired in a qualified stock purchase—

(i) The acquisition is treated as an acquisition of the corporation's assets (see § 1.338(h)(10)–1); and

(ii) The corporation is not treated as target.

(c) Gain from disposition reflected in basis of target stock. For purposes of this section:

(1) General rule. Gain from the disposition of an asset is reflected in the basis of a corporation's stock if the gain is taken into account under § 1.1502–32, directly or indirectly, in determining the basis of the stock, after applying section 1503(e) and other provisions of the Internal Revenue Code.

(2) Gain not reflected if section 338 election made for target. Gain from the disposition of an asset that is otherwise reflected in the basis of target stock as of the target acquisition date is not considered reflected in the basis of target stock if a section 338 election is made for target.

(3) Gain reflected by reason of distributions. Gain from the disposition of an asset is not considered reflected in the basis of target stock merely by reason of the receipt of a distribution from a target affiliate that is not a member of the same consolidated group as the distributee. See paragraph (g) of this section for the treatment of dividends eligible for a 100 percent dividends received deduction.

(4) Controlled foreign corporations. For a limitation applicable to gain of a target affiliate that is a controlled foreign corporation, see paragraph (h)(2) of this section.

(5) Gain recognized outside the consolidated group. Gain from the disposition of an asset by a person other than target or a target affiliate is not reflected in the basis of a corporation's stock unless the person is a conduit, as defined in paragraph (j)(4) of this section.

(d) Basis of acquired assets—(1) Carryover basis rule. If this paragraph (d) applies to an asset, the asset's basis immediately after its acquisition is, for all purposes of the Internal Revenue Code, its adjusted basis immediately before its disposition.

(2) Exceptions to carryover basis rule for certain assets. The carryover basis rule of paragraph (d)(1) of this section does not apply to the following assets—

(i) Any asset disposed of in the ordinary course of a trade or business (see section 338(e)(2)(A));

(ii) Any asset the basis of which is determined wholly by reference to the adjusted basis of the asset in the hands of the person that disposed of the asset (see section 338(e)(2)(B));

(iii) Any debt or equity instrument issued by target or a target affiliate (*see* paragraph (h)(3) of this section for an exception relating to the stock of a target affiliate that is a controlled foreign corporation);

(iv) Any asset the basis of which immediately after its acquisition would otherwise be less than its adjusted basis immediately before its disposition; and

(v) Any asset identified by the Internal Revenue Service in a revenue ruling or revenue procedure.

(3) Exception to carryover basis rule for de minimis assets. The carryover basis rules of this section do not apply to an asset if the asset is not disposed of as part of the same arrangement as the acquisition of target and the aggregate amount realized for all assets otherwise subject to the carryover basis rules of this section does not exceed $250,000.

(4) Mitigation rule—(i) General rule. If the carryover basis rules of this section apply to an asset and the asset is transferred to a domestic corporation in a transaction to which section 351 applies or as a contribution to capital and no gain is recognized, the transferor's basis in the stock of the transferee (but not the transferee's basis in the asset) is determined without taking into account the carryover basis rules of this section.

(ii) Time for transfer. This paragraph (d)(4) applies only if the asset is transferred before the due date (including extensions) for the transferor's income tax return for the year that includes the last date for which a section 338 election may be made for target.

(e) Examples—(1) In general. For purposes of the examples in this section, unless otherwise stated, the basis of each asset is the same for determining earnings and profits and taxable income, the exceptions to paragraph (d)(1) of this section do not apply, the taxable year of all persons is the calendar year, and the following facts apply: S is the common parent of a consolidated group that includes T, T1, T2, and T3; S owns all of the stock of T and T3; and T owns all of the stock of T1, which owns all of the stock of T2. B is unrelated to the S group and owns all of the stock of P, which owns all of the stock of P1. Y and Y1 are partnerships that are unrelated to the S group but may be related to the P group. Z is a corporation that is not related to any of the other parties.

[Graphic Omitted.]

(2) Direct acquisitions. Paragraphs (b), (c), and (d) of this section may be illustrated by the following examples:

Example (1). Asset acquired from target by purchasing corporation. *(a)* On February 1 of Year 1, T sells an asset to P1 and recognizes gain. T's gain from the disposition of the asset is taken into account under § 1.1502–32 in determining S's basis in the T stock. On January 1 of Year 2, P1 makes a qualified stock purchase of T from S. No section 338 election is made for T.

(b) T disposed of the asset during its consistency period, gain from the asset disposition is reflected in the basis of the T stock as of T's acquisition date (January 1 of Year 2), and the asset is owned both immediately after the asset disposition (February 1 of Year 1) and on T's acquisition date by P1, the corporation that acquired T stock in the qualified stock purchase. Consequently, under paragraph (b) of this section, paragraph (d)(1) of this section applies to the asset and P1's basis in the asset is T's

adjusted basis in the asset immediately before the sale to P1.

Example (2). Gain from section 338(h)(10) election reflected in stock basis. *(a)* On February 1 of Year 1, P1 makes a qualified stock purchase of T2 from T1. A section 338(h)(10) election is made for T2 and T2 recognizes gain on each of its assets. T2's gain is taken into account under § 1.1502–32 in determining S's basis in the T stock. On January 1 of Year 2, P1 makes a qualified stock purchase of T from S. No section 338 election is made for T.

(b) Under paragraph (b)(2) of this section, the acquisition of the T2 stock is treated as an acquisition of T2's assets on February 1 of Year 1, because a section 338(h)(10) election is made for T2. The gain recognized by T2 under section 338(h)(10) is reflected in S's basis in the T stock as of T's acquisition date. Because the other requirements of paragraph (b) of this section are satisfied, paragraph (d)(1) of this section applies to the assets and new T2's basis in its assets is old T2's adjusted basis in the assets immediately before the disposition.

Example (3). Corporation owning asset ceases affiliation with corporation purchasing target before target acquisition date. *(a)* On February 1 of Year 1, T sells an asset to P1 and recognizes gain. On December 1 of Year 1, P disposes of all of the P1 stock while P1 still owns the asset. On January 1 of Year 2, P makes a qualified stock purchase of T from S. No section 338 election is made for T.

(b) Immediately after T's disposition of the asset, the asset is owned by P1 which is affiliated on that date with P, the corporation that acquired T stock in the qualified stock purchase. However, the asset is owned by a corporation (P1) that is no longer affiliated with P on T's acquisition date. Although the other requirements of paragraph (b) of this section are satisfied, the requirements of paragraph (b)(1)(iii) of this section are not satisfied. Consequently, the basis rules of paragraph (d) of this section do not apply to the asset by reason of P1's acquisition.

(c) If P acquires all of the Z stock and P1 transfers the asset to Z on or before T's acquisition date (January 1 of Year 2), the asset is owned by an affiliate of P both on February 1 of Year 1 (P1) and on January 1 of Year 2 (Z). Consequently, all of the requirements of paragraph (b) of this section are satisfied and paragraph (d)(1) of this section applies to the asset and P1's basis in the asset is T's adjusted basis in the asset immediately before the sale to P1.

Example (4). Gain reflected in stock basis notwithstanding offsetting loss or distribution. *(a)* On April 1 of Year 1, T sells an asset to P1 and recognizes gain. In Year 1, T distributes an amount equal to the gain. On March 1 of Year 2, P makes a qualified stock purchase of T from S. No section 338 election is made for T.

(b) Although, as a result of the distribution, there is no adjustment with respect to the T stock under § 1.1502–32 for Year 1, T's gain from the disposition of the asset is considered reflected in S's basis in the T stock. The gain is considered to have been taken into account under § 1.1502–32 in determining the adjustments to S's basis in the T stock because S's basis in the T stock is different from what it would have been had there been no gain.

(c) If T distributes an amount equal to the gain on February 1 of Year 2, rather than in Year 1, the results would be the same because S's basis in the T stock is different from what it would have been had there been no gain. If the distribution in Year 2 is by reason of an election under § 1.1502–32(f)(2), the results would be the same.

(d) If, in Year 1, T does not make a distribution and the S group does not file a consolidated return, but, in Year 2, the S group does file a consolidated return and makes an election under § 1.1502–32(f)(2) for T, the results would be the same. S's basis in the T stock is different from what it would have been had there been no gain. Paragraph (c)(3) of this section (gain not considered reflected by reason of distributions) does not apply to the deemed distribution under the election because S and T are members of the same consolidated group. If T distributes an amount equal to the gain in Year 2 and no election is made under § 1.1502–32(f)(2), the results would be the same.

(e) If, in Year 1, T incurs an unrelated loss in an amount equal to the gain, rather than distributing an amount equal to the gain, the results would be the same because the gain is taken into account under § 1.1502–32 in determining S's basis in the T stock.

Example (5). Gain of a target affiliate reflected in stock basis after corporate reorganization. *(a)* On February 1 of Year 1, T3 sells an asset to P1 and recognizes gain. On March 1 of Year 1, S contributes the T3 stock to T in a transaction qualifying under section 351. On January 15 of Year 2, P1 makes a qualified stock purchase of T from S. No section 338 election is made for T.

(b) T3's gain from the asset sale is taken into account under § 1.1502–32 in determining S's basis in the T3 stock. Under section 358, the gain that is taken into account under § 1.1502–32 in determining S's basis in the T3 stock is also taken into account in determining S's basis in the T stock following S's contribution of the T3 stock to T. Consequently, under paragraph (b) of this section, paragraph (d) (1) of this section applies to the asset and P1's basis in the asset is T3's adjusted basis in the asset immediately before the sale to P1.

(c) If on March 1 of Year 1, rather than S contributing the T3 stock to T, S causes T3 to merge into T in a transaction qualifying under section 368(a)(1)(D), the results would be the same.

Example (6). Gain not reflected if election under section 338 made. *(a)* On February 1 of Year 1, T1 sells an asset to P1 and recognizes gain. On January 1 of Year 2, P1 makes a qualified stock purchase of T1 from T. A section 338 election (but not a section 338(h)(10) election) is made for T1.

(b) Under paragraph (c)(2) of this section, because a section 338 election is made for T1,

T's basis in the T1 stock is considered not to reflect gain from the disposition. Consequently, the requirement of paragraph (b)(1)(ii) of this section is not satisfied. Thus, P1's basis in the asset is not determined under paragraph (d) of this section. Although the section 338 election for T1 results in a qualified stock purchase of T2, the requirement of paragraph (b)(1)(ii) of this section is not satisfied with respect to T2, whether or not a section 338 election is made for T2.

(c) If, on January 1 of Year 2, P1 makes a qualified stock purchase of T from S and a section 338 election for T, rather than T1, S's basis in the T stock is considered not to reflect gain from T1's disposition of the asset. However, the section 338 election for T results in a qualified stock purchase of T1. Because the gain is reflected in T's basis in the T1 stock, the requirements of paragraph (b) of this section are satisfied. Consequently, P1's basis in the asset is determined under paragraph (d)(1) of this section unless a section 338 election is also made for T1.

(f) Extension of consistency to indirect acquisitions—(1) Introduction. If an arrangement exists (see paragraph (j)(5) of this section), this paragraph (f) generally extends the consistency rules to indirect acquisitions that have the same effect as direct acquisitions. For example, this paragraph (f) applies if, pursuant to an arrangement, target sells an asset to an unrelated person who then sells the asset to the purchasing corporation.

(2) General rule. This paragraph (f) applies to an asset if, pursuant to an arrangement—

(i) The asset is disposed of during the target consistency period;

(ii) The basis of target stock as of, or at any time before, the target acquisition date reflects gain from the disposition of the asset; and

(iii) The asset ownership requirements of paragraph (b)(1)(iii) of this section are not satisfied, but the asset is owned, at any time

during the portion of the target consistency period following the target acquisition date, by—

(A) A corporation—

(1) The basis of whose stock, as of, or at any time before, the target acquisition date, reflects gain from the disposition of the asset; and

(2) That is affiliated, at any time during the target consistency period, with a corporation that acquires stock of target in the qualified stock purchase; or

(B) A corporation that at the time it owns the asset is affiliated with a corporation described in paragraph (f)(2)(iii)(A) of this section.

(3) Basis of acquired assets. If this paragraph (f) applies to an asset, the principles of the basis rules of paragraph (d) of this section apply to the asset as of the date, following the disposition with respect to which gain is reflected in the basis of target's stock, that the asset is first owned by a corporation described in paragraph (f)(2)(iii) of this section. If the principles of the carryover basis rule of paragraph (d)(1) of this section apply to an asset, the asset's basis also is reduced (but not below zero) by the amount of any reduction in its basis occurring after the disposition with respect to which gain is reflected in the basis of target's stock.

(4) Examples. This paragraph (f) may be illustrated by the following examples:

Example (1). Acquisition of asset from unrelated party by purchasing corporation. (a) On February 1 of Year 1, T sells an asset to Z and recognizes gain. On February 15 of Year 1, P1 makes a qualified stock purchase of T from S. No section 338 election is made for T. P1 buys the asset from Z on March 1 of Year 1, before Z has reduced the basis of the asset through depreciation or otherwise.

(b) Paragraph (b) of this section does not apply to the asset because the asset ownership requirements of paragraph (b)(1)(iii) of

this section are not satisfied. However, the asset ownership requirements of paragraph (f)(2)(iii) of this section are satisfied because, during the portion of T's consistency period following T's acquisition date, the asset is owned by P1 while it is affiliated with T. Consequently, paragraph (f) of this section applies to the asset if there is an arrangement for T to dispose of the asset during T's consistency period, for the gain to be reflected in S's basis in the T stock as of T's acquisition date, and for P1 to own the asset during the portion of T's consistency period following T's acquisition date. If the arrangement exists, under paragraph (f)(3) of this section, P1's basis in the asset is determined as of March 1 of Year 1, under the principles of paragraph (d) of this section. Consequently, P1's basis in the asset is T's adjusted basis in the asset immediately before the sale to Z.

(c) If P1 acquires the asset from Z on January 15 of Year 2 (rather than on March 1 of Year 1), and Z's basis in the asset has been reduced through depreciation at the time of the acquisition, P1's basis in the asset as of January 15 of Year 2 would be T's adjusted basis in the asset immediately before the sale to Z, reduced (but not below zero) by the amount of the depreciation. Z's basis and depreciation are determined without taking into account the basis rules of paragraph (d) of this section.

(d) If P, rather than P1, acquires the asset from Z, the results would be the same.

(e) If, on March 1 of Year 1, P1 acquires the Z stock, rather than acquiring the asset from Z, paragraph (f) of this section would apply to the asset if an arrangement exists. However, under paragraph (f)(3) of this section, Z's basis in the asset would be determined as of February 1 of Year 1, the date the asset is first owned by a corporation (Z) described in paragraph (f)(2)(iii) of this section. Consequently, Z's basis in the asset as of February 1 of Year 1, determined under the principles of paragraph (d) of this section, would be T's adjusted basis in the asset immediately before the sale to Z.

Example (2). Acquisition of asset from target by target affiliate. (a) On February 1 of Year 1, T contributes an asset to T1 in a transaction qualifying under section 351 and in which T recognizes gain under section 351(b) that is deferred under § 1.1502–13. On March 1 of Year 1, P1 makes a qualified stock purchase of T from S and, pursuant to § 1.1502–13, the deferred gain is taken into account by T immediately before T ceases to be a member of the S group. No section 338 election is made for T.

(b) Paragraph (b) of this section does not apply to the asset because the asset ownership requirements of paragraph (b)(1)(iii) of this section are not satisfied.

(c) T1 is not described in paragraph (f)(2)(iii)(A) of this section because the basis of the T1 stock does not reflect gain from the disposition of the asset. Although, under section 358(a)(1)(B)(ii), T's basis in the T1 stock is increased by the amount of the gain, the gain is not taken into account directly or indirectly under § 1.1502–32 in determining T's basis in the T1 stock.

(d) T1 is described in paragraph (f)(2)(iii)(B) of this section because, during the portion of T's consistency period following T's acquisition date, T1 owns the asset while it is affiliated with T, a corporation described in paragraph (f)(2)(iii)(A) of this section. Consequently, paragraph (f) of this section applies to the asset if there is an arrangement. Under paragraph (j)(5) of this section, the fact that, at the time T1 acquires the asset from T, T1 is related (within the meaning of section 267(b)) to T indicates that an arrangement exists.

Example (3). Acquisition of asset from target and indirect acquisition of target stock. (a) On February 1 of Year 1, T sells an asset to P1 and recognizes gain. On March 1 of Year 1, Z makes a qualified stock purchase of T from S. No section 338 election is made for T. On January 1 of Year 2, P1 acquires the T stock from Z other than in a qualified stock purchase.

(b) The asset ownership requirements of paragraph (b)(1)(iii) of this section are not satisfied because the asset was never owned by Z, the corporation that acquired T stock in the qualified stock purchase (or by a corporation that was affiliated with Z at the time it owned the asset). However, because the asset is owned by P1 while it is affiliated with T during the portion of T's consistency period following T's acquisition date, paragraph (f) of this section applies to the asset if there is an arrangement. If there is an arrangement, the principles of the carryover basis rule of paragraph (d)(1) of this section apply to determine P1's basis in the asset unless Z makes a section 338 election for T. See paragraph (c)(2) of this section.

(c) If P1 also makes a qualified stock purchase of T from Z, the results would be the same. If there is an arrangement, the principles of the carryover basis rule of paragraph (d)(1) of this section apply to determine P1's basis in the asset unless Z makes a section 338 election for T. However, these principles apply to determine P1's basis in the asset if P1, but not Z, makes a section 338 election for T. The basis of the T stock no longer reflects, as of T's acquisition date by P1, the gain from the disposition of the asset.

(d) Assume Z purchases the T stock other than in a qualified stock purchase and P1 makes a qualified stock purchase of T from Z. Paragraph (b) of this section does not apply to the asset because gain from the disposition of the asset is not reflected in the basis of T's stock as of T's acquisition date (January 1 of Year 2). However, because the gain is reflected in S's basis in the T stock before T's acquisition date and the asset is owned by P1 while it is affiliated with T during the portion of T's consistency period following T's acquisition date, paragraph (f) of this section applies to the asset if there is an arrangement. If there is an arrangement, the principles of the carryover basis rule of paragraph (d)(1) of this section apply to determine P1's basis in the asset even if P1 makes a section 338 election for T. The

basis of the T stock no longer reflects, as of T's acquisition date, the gain from the disposition of the asset.

Example (4). Asset acquired from target affiliate by corporation that becomes its affiliate. *(a)* On February 1 of Year 1, T1 sells an asset to P1 and recognizes gain. On February 15 of Year 1, Z makes a qualified stock purchase of T from S. No section 338 election is made for T. On June 1 of Year 1, P1 acquires the T1 stock from T, other than in a qualified stock purchase.

(b) The asset ownership requirements of paragraph (b)(1)(iii) of this section are not satisfied because the asset was never owned by Z, the corporation that acquired T stock in the qualified stock purchase (or by a corporation that was affiliated with Z at the time it owned the asset).

(c) P1 is not described in paragraph (f)(2)(iii)(A) of this section because gain from the disposition of the asset is not reflected in the basis of the P1 stock.

(d) P1 is described in paragraph (f)(2)(iii)(B) of this section because the asset is owned by P1 while P1 is affiliated with T1 during the portion of T's consistency period following T's acquisition date. T1 becomes affiliated with Z, the corporation that acquired T stock in the qualified stock purchase, during T's consistency period, and, as of T's acquisition date, the basis of T1's stock reflects gain from the disposition of the asset. Consequently, paragraph (f) of this section applies to the asset if there is an arrangement.

Example (5). De minimis rules. (a) On February 1 of Year 1, T sells an asset to P and recognizes gain. On February 15 of Year 1, T1 sells an asset to Z and recognizes gain. The aggregate amount realized by T and T1 on their respective sales of assets is not more than $250,000. On March 1 of Year 1, T3 sells an asset to P and recognizes gain. On April 1 of Year 1, P makes a qualified stock purchase of T from S. No section 338 election is made for T.

On June 1 of Year 1, P1 buys from Z the asset sold by T1.

(b) Under paragraph (b) of this section, the basis rules of paragraph (d) of this section apply to the asset sold by T. Under paragraph (f) of this section, the principles of the basis rules of paragraph (d) of this section apply to the asset sold by T1 if there is an arrangement. Because T3's gain is not reflected in the basis of the T stock, the basis rules of this section do not apply to the asset sold by T3.

(c) The de minimis rule of paragraph (d)(3) of this section applies to an asset if the asset is not disposed of as part of the same arrangement as the acquisition of T and the aggregate amount realized for all assets otherwise subject to the carryover basis rules does not exceed $250,000. The aggregate amount realized by T and T1 does not exceed $250,000. (The asset sold by T3 is not taken into account for purposes of the de minimis rule.) Thus, the de minimis rule applies to the asset sold by T if the asset is not disposed of as part of the same arrangement as the acquisition of T.

(d) If, under paragraph (f) of this section, the principles of the carryover basis rules of paragraph (d)(1) of this section otherwise apply to the asset sold by T1 because of an arrangement, the de minimis rules of this section do not apply to the asset because of the arrangement.

(e) Assume on June 1 of Year 1, Z acquires the T1 stock from T, other than in a qualified stock purchase, rather than P1 buying the T1 asset, and paragraph (f) of this section applies because there is an arrangement. Because the asset was disposed of and the T1 stock was acquired as part of the arrangement, the de minimis rules of this section do not apply to the asset.

(g) Extension of consistency if dividends qualifying for 100 percent dividends received deduction are paid — (1) General rule for direct acquisitions from target. Unless a section 338 election is made for target, the ba-

sis rules of paragraph (d) of this section apply to an asset if—

(i) Target recognizes gain (whether or not deferred) on disposition of the asset during the portion of the target consistency period that ends on the target acquisition date;

(ii) The asset is owned, immediately after the asset disposition and on the target acquisition date, by a corporation that acquires stock of target in the qualified stock purchase (or by an affiliate of an acquiring corporation); and

(iii) During the portion of the target consistency period that ends on the target acquisition date, the aggregate amount of dividends paid by target, to which section 243(a)(3) applies, exceeds the greater of—

(A) $250,000; or

(B) 125 percent of the yearly average amount of dividends paid by target, to which section 243(a)(3) applies, during the three calendar years immediately preceding the year in which the target consistency period begins (or, if shorter, the period target was in existence).

(2) Other direct acquisitions having same effect. The basis rules of paragraph (d) of this section also apply to an asset if the effect of a transaction described in paragraph (g)(1) of this section is achieved through any combination of disposition of assets and payment of dividends to which section 243(a)(3) applies (or any other dividends eligible for a 100 percent dividends received deduction). See paragraph (h)(4) of this section for additional rules relating to target affiliates that are controlled foreign corporations.

(3) Indirect acquisitions. The principles of paragraph (f) of this section also apply for purposes of this paragraph (g).

(4) Examples. This paragraph (g) may be illustrated by the following examples:

Example (1). Asset acquired from target paying dividends to which section 243(a)(3) applies. (a) The S group does not file a consolidated return. In Year 1, Year 2, and Year 3, T pays dividends to S to which section 243(a)(3) applies of $200,000, $250,000, and $300,000, respectively. On February 1 of Year 4, T sells an asset to P and recognizes gain. On January 1 of Year 5, P makes a qualified stock purchase of T from S. No section 338 election is made for T. During the portion of T's consistency period that ends on T's acquisition date, T pays S dividends to which section 243(a)(3) applies of $1,000,000.

(b) Under paragraph (g)(1) of this section, paragraph (d) of this section applies to the asset. T recognizes gain on disposition of the asset during the portion of T's consistency period that ends on T's acquisition date, the asset is owned by P immediately after the disposition and on T's acquisition date, and T pays dividends described in paragraph (g)(1)(iii) of this section. Consequently, under paragraph (d)(1) of this section, P's basis in the asset is T's adjusted basis in the asset immediately before the sale to P.

(c) If T is a controlled foreign corporation, the results would be the same if T pays dividends in the amount described in paragraph (g)(1)(iii) of this section that qualify for a 100 percent dividends received deduction. See sections 243(e) and 245.

(d) If S and T3 file a consolidated return in which T, T1, and T2 do not join, the results would be the same because the dividends paid by T are still described in paragraph (g)(1)(iii) of this section.

(e) If T, T1, and T2 file a consolidated return in which S and T3 do not join, the results would be the same because the dividends paid by T are still described in paragraph (g)(1)(iii) of this section.

Example (2). Asset disposition by target affiliate achieving same effect. (a) The S group does not file a consolidated return. On February 1 of Year 1, T2 sells an asset to P and recognizes gain. T pays dividends to S described in paragraph (g)(1)(iii) of this section. On January 1 of Year 2, P makes a qualified stock

purchase of T from S. No section 338 election is made for T.

(b) Paragraph (g)(1) of this section does not apply to the asset because T did not recognize gain on the disposition of the asset. However, under paragraph (g)(2) of this section, because the asset disposition by T2 and the dividends paid by T achieve the effect of a transaction described in paragraph (g)(1) of this section, the carryover basis rule of paragraph (d)(1) of this section applies to the asset. The effect was achieved because T2 is a lower-tier affiliate of T and the dividends paid by T to S reduce the value to S of T and its lower-tier affiliates.

(c) If T2 is a controlled foreign corporation, the results would be the same because T2 is a lower-tier affiliate of T and the dividends paid by T to S reduce the value to S of T and its lower-tier affiliates.

(d) If P buys an asset from T3, rather than T2, the asset disposition and the dividends do not achieve the effect of a transaction described in paragraph (g)(1) of this section because T3 is not a lower-tier affiliate of T. Thus, the basis rules of paragraph (d) of this section do not apply to the asset. The results would be the same whether or not P also acquires the T3 stock (whether or not in a qualified stock purchase).

Example (3). Dividends by target affiliate achieving same effect. (a) The S group does not file a consolidated return. On February 1 of Year 1, T1 sells an asset to P and recognizes gain. On January 1 of Year 2, P makes a qualified stock purchase of T from S. No section 338 election is made for T. T does not pay dividends to S described in paragraph (g)(1)(iii) of this section. However, T1 pays dividends to T that would be described in paragraph (g)(1)(iii) of this section if T1 were a target.

(b) Paragraph (g)(1) of this section does not apply to the asset because T did not recognize gain on the disposition of the asset and did not pay dividends described in paragraph (g)(1)(iii) of this section. Further, paragraph (g)(2)

of this section does not apply because the dividends paid by T1 to T do not reduce the value to S of T and its lower-tier affiliates.

(c) If both S and T own T1 stock and T1 pays dividends to S that would be described in paragraph (g)(1)(iii) of this section if T1 were a target, paragraph (g)(2) of this section would apply because the dividends paid by T1 to S reduce the value to S of T and its lower-tier affiliates. If T, rather than T1, sold the asset to P, the results would be the same. Further, if T and T1 pay dividends to S that, only when aggregated, would be described in paragraph (g)(1)(iii) of this section (if they were all paid by T), the results would be the same.

Example (4). Gain reflected by reason of dividends. *(a)* S and T file a consolidated return in which T1 and T2 do not join. On February 1 of Year 1, T1 sells an asset to P and recognizes gain. On January 1 of Year 2, P makes a qualified stock purchase of T from S. No section 338 election is made for T. T1 pays dividends to T that would be described in paragraph (g)(1)(iii) of this section if T1 were a target.

(b) The requirements of paragraph (b) of this section are not satisfied because, under paragraph (c)(3) of this section, gain from T1's sale is not reflected in S's basis in the T stock by reason of the dividends paid by T1 to T.

(c) Although the dividends paid by T1 to T do not reduce the value to S of T and its lower-tier affiliates, paragraph (g)(2) of this section applies because the dividends paid by T1 to T are taken into account under § 1.1502–32 in determining S's basis in the T stock. Consequently, the carryover basis rule of paragraph (d)(1) of this section applies to the asset.

(h) Consistency for target affiliates that are controlled foreign corporations—(1) In general. This paragraph (h) applies only if target is a domestic corporation. For additional rules that may apply with respect to controlled foreign corporations, see paragraph (g) of this section. The definitions and nomenclature of § 1.338–2(b) and (c) and paragraph (e) of this section apply for purposes of this section.

(2) Income or gain resulting from asset dispositions—(i) General rule. Income or gain of a target affiliate that is a controlled foreign corporation from the disposition of an asset is not reflected in the basis of target stock under paragraph (c) of this section unless the income or gain results in an inclusion under section 951(a)(1)(A), 951(a)(1)(C), 1291 or 1293.

(ii) Basis of controlled foreign corporation stock. If, by reason of paragraph (h)(2)(i) of this section, the carryover basis rules of this section apply to an asset, no increase in basis in the stock of a controlled foreign corporation under section 961(a) or 1293(d)(1), or under regulations issued pursuant to section 1297(b)(5), is allowed to target or a target affiliate to the extent the increase is attributable to income or gain described in paragraph (h)(2)(i) of this section. A similar rule applies to the basis of any property by reason of which the stock of the controlled foreign corporation is considered owned under section 958(a)(2) or 1297(a).

(iii) Operating rule. For purposes of this paragraph (h)(2)—

(A) If there is an income inclusion under section 951(a)(1)(A) or (C), the shareholder's income inclusion is first attributed to the income or gain of the controlled foreign corporation from the disposition of the asset to the extent of the shareholder's pro rata share of such income or gain; and

(B) Any income or gain under section 1293 is first attributed to the income or gain from the disposition of the asset to the extent of the shareholder's pro rata share of the income or gain.

(iv) Increase in asset or stock basis—(A) If the carryover basis rules under paragraph (h)(2)(i) of this section apply to an asset, and the purchasing corporation disposes of the asset to an unrelated party in a taxable transaction and recognizes and includes in its U.S. gross income or the U.S. gross income of its shareholders the greater of the income or gain from the disposition of the asset by the selling controlled foreign corporation that was reflected in the basis of the target stock under paragraph (c) of this section, or the gain recognized on the asset by the purchasing corporation on the disposition of the asset, then the purchasing corporation or the target or a target affiliate, as appropriate, shall increase the basis of the selling controlled foreign corporation stock subject to paragraph (h)(2)(ii) of this section, as of the date of the disposition of the asset by the purchasing corporation, by the amount of the basis increase that was denied under paragraph (h)(2)(ii) of this section. The preceding sentence shall apply only to the extent that the controlled foreign corporation stock is owned (within the meaning of section 958(a)) by a member of the purchasing corporation's affiliated group.

(B) If the carryover basis rules under paragraph (h)(2)(i) of this section apply to an asset, and the purchasing corporation or the target or a target affiliate, as appropriate, disposes of the stock of the selling controlled foreign corporation to an unrelated party in a taxable transaction and recognizes and includes in its U.S. gross income or the U.S. gross income of its shareholders the greater of the gain equal to the basis increase that was denied under paragraph (h)(2)(ii) of this section, or the gain recognized in the stock by the purchasing corporation or by the target or a target affiliate, as appropriate, on the disposition of the stock, then the purchasing corporation shall increase the basis of the asset, as of the date of the disposition of the stock of the selling controlled foreign corporation by the purchasing corporation or by the target or a target affiliate, as appropriate, by the amount of the basis increase that was denied pursuant to paragraph (h)(2)(i) of this section. The preceding sentence shall apply only to the extent that the asset is owned (within the meaning of section 958(a)) by a member of the purchasing corporation's affiliated group.

(3) Stock issued by target affiliate that is a controlled foreign corporation. The exception to the carryover basis rules of this section provided in paragraph (d)(2)(iii) of this section does not apply to stock issued by a target affiliate that is a controlled foreign corporation. After applying the carryover basis rules of this section to the stock, the basis in the stock is increased by the amount treated as a dividend under section 1248 on the disposition of the stock (or that would have been so treated but for section 1291), except to the extent the basis increase is attributable to the disposition of an asset in which a carryover basis is taken under this section.

(4) Certain distributions—(i) General rule. In the case of a target affiliate that is a controlled foreign corporation, paragraph (g) of this section applies with respect to the target affiliate by treating any reference to a dividend to which section 243(a)(3) applies as a reference to any amount taken into account under § 1.1502–32 in determining the basis of target stock that is—

(A) A dividend;

(B) An amount treated as a dividend under section 1248 (or that would have been so treated but for section 1291); or

(C) An amount included in income under section 951(a)(1)(B).

(ii) Basis of controlled foreign corporation stock. If the carryover basis rules of this section apply to an asset, the basis in the stock of the controlled foreign corporation (or any property by reason of which the stock is considered owned under section 958(a)(2)) is reduced (but not below zero) by the sum of any amounts that are treated, solely by reason of the disposition of the asset, as a dividend, amount treated as a dividend under section 1248 (or that would have been so treated but for section 1291), or amount included in income under section 951(a)(1)(B). For this purpose, any dividend, amount treated as a dividend under section 1248 (or that would have been so treated but for section 1291), or amount included in income under section 951(a)(1)(B) is considered attributable first to earnings and profits resulting from the disposition of the asset.

(iii) Increase in asset or stock basis—(A) If the carryover basis rules under paragraphs (g) and (h)(4)(i) of this section apply to an asset, and the purchasing corporation disposes of the asset to an unrelated party in a taxable transaction and recognizes and includes in its U.S. gross income or the U.S. gross income of its shareholders the greater of the gain equal to the basis increase denied in the asset pursuant to paragraphs (g) and (h)(4)(i) of this section, or the gain recognized on the asset by the purchasing corporation on the disposition of the asset, then the purchasing corporation or the target or a target affiliate, as appropriate, shall increase the basis of the selling controlled foreign corporation stock subject to paragraph (h)(4)(ii) of this section, as of the date of the disposition of the asset by the purchasing corporation, by the amount of the basis reduction under paragraph (h)(4)(ii) of this section. The preceding sentence shall apply only to the extent that the controlled foreign corporation stock is owned (within the meaning of section 958(a)) by a member of the purchasing corporation's affiliated group.

(B) If the carryover basis rules under paragraphs (g) and (h)(4)(i) of this section apply to an asset, and the purchasing corporation or the target or a target affiliate, as appropriate, disposes of the stock of the selling controlled foreign corporation to an unrelated party in a taxable transaction and recognizes and includes in its U.S. gross income or the U.S. gross income of its shareholders the greater of the amount of the basis reduction under paragraph (h)(4)(ii) of this section, or the gain recognized in the stock by the purchasing corporation or by the target or a target affiliate, as appropriate, on the disposition of the stock, then the purchasing corporation shall increase the basis

of the asset, as of the date of the disposition of the stock of the selling controlled foreign corporation by the purchasing corporation or by the target or a target affiliate, as appropriate, by the amount of the basis increase that was denied pursuant to paragraphs (g) and (h)(4)(i) of this section. The preceding sentence shall apply only to the extent that the asset is owned (within the meaning of section 958(a)) by a member of the purchasing corporation's affiliated group.

(5) Examples. This paragraph (h) may be illustrated by the following examples:

Example (1). Stock of target affiliate that is a CFC. (a) The S group files a consolidated return; however, T2 is a controlled foreign corporation. On December 1 of Year 1, T1 sells the T2 stock to P and recognizes gain. On January 2 of Year 2, P makes a qualified stock purchase of T from S. No section 338 election is made for T.

(b) Under paragraph (b)(1) of this section, paragraph (d) of this section applies to the T2 stock. Under paragraph (h)(3) of this section, paragraph (d)(2)(iii) of this section does not apply to the T2 stock. Consequently, paragraph (d)(1) of this section applies to the T2 stock. However, after applying paragraph (d)(1) of this section, P's basis in the T2 stock is increased by the amount of T1's gain on the sale of the T2 stock that is treated as a dividend under section 1248. Because P has a carryover basis in the T2 stock, the T2 stock is not considered purchased within the meaning of section 338(h)(3) and no section 338 election may be made for T2.

Example (2). Stock of target affiliate CFC; inclusion under subpart F. (a) The S group files a consolidated return; however, T2 is a controlled foreign corporation. On December 1 of Year 1, T2 sells an asset to P and recognizes subpart F income that results in an inclusion in T1's gross income under section 951(a)(1)(A). On January 2 of Year 2, P makes a qualified stock purchase of T from S. No section 338 election is made for T.

(b) Because gain from the disposition of the asset results in an inclusion under section 951(a)(1)(A), the gain is reflected in the basis of the T stock as of T's acquisition date. See paragraph (h)(2)(i) of this section. Consequently, under paragraph (b)(1) of this section, paragraph (d)(1) of this section applies to the asset. In addition, under paragraph (h)(2)(ii) of this section, T1's basis in the T2 stock is not increased under section 961(a) by the amount of the inclusion that is attributable to the sale of the asset.

(c) If, in addition to making a qualified stock purchase of T, P acquires the T2 stock from T1 on January 1 of Year 2, the results are the same for the asset sold by T2. In addition, under paragraph (h)(2)(ii) of this section, T1's basis in the T2 stock is not increased by the amount of the inclusion that is attributable to the gain on the sale of the asset. Further, under paragraph (h)(3) of this section, paragraph (d)(1) of this section applies to the T2 stock. However, after applying paragraph (d) (1) of this section, P's basis in the T2 stock is increased by the amount of T1's gain on the sale of the T2 stock that is treated as a dividend under section 1248. Finally, because P has a carryover basis in the T2 stock, the T2 stock is not considered purchased within the meaning of section 338(h)(3) and no section 338 election may be made for T2.

(d) If P makes a qualified stock purchase of T2 from T1, rather than of T from S, and T1's gain on the sale of T2 is treated as a dividend under section 1248, under paragraph (h)(1) of this section, paragraphs (h)(2) and (3) of this section do not apply because there is no target that is a domestic corporation. Consequently, the carryover basis rules of paragraph do not apply to the asset sold by T2 or the T2 stock.

Example (3). Gain reflected by reason of section 1248 dividend; gain from non-subpart F asset. (a) The S group files a consolidated return; however, T2 is a controlled foreign corporation. In Years 1 through 4, T2 does not pay any dividends to T1 and no amount is included in T1's income under section 951(a)(1)(B). On December 1 of Year 4, T2 sells an asset with a basis of $400,000 to P for $900,000. T2's gain of $500,000 is not subpart F income. On December 15 of Year 4, T1 sells T2, in which it has a basis of $600,000, to P for $1,600,000. Under section 1248, $800,000 of T1's gain of $1,000,000 is treated as a dividend. However, in the absence of the sale of the asset by T2 to P, only $300,000 would have been treated as a dividend under section 1248. On December 30 of Year 4, P makes a qualified stock purchase of T1 from T. No section 338 election is made for T1.

(b) Under paragraph (h)(4) of this section, paragraph (g)(2) of this section applies by reference to the amount treated as a dividend under section 1248 on the disposition of the T2 stock. Because the amount treated as a dividend is taken into account in determining T's basis in the T1 stock under § 1.1502–32, the sale of the T2 stock and the deemed dividend have the effect of a transaction described in paragraph (g)(1) of this section. Consequently, paragraph (d)(1) of this section applies to the asset sold by T2 to P and P's basis in the asset is $400,000 as of December 1 of Year 4.

(c) Under paragraph (h)(3) of this section, paragraph (d)(1) of this section applies to the T2 stock and P's basis in the T2 stock is $600,000 as of December 15 of Year 4. Under paragraphs (h)(3) and (4)(ii) of this section, however, P's basis in the T2 stock is increased by $300,000 (the amount of T1's gain treated as a dividend under section 1248 ($800,000), other than the amount treated as a dividend solely as a result of the sale of the asset by T2 to P ($500,000)) to $900,000.

(i) [Reserved.]

(j) Anti-avoidance rules. For purposes of this section—

(1) Extension of consistency period. The target consistency period is extended to include any continuous period that ends on, or begins on, any day of the consistency period during which a purchasing corporation, or any person related, within the meaning of section 267(b) or 707(b)(1), to a purchasing corporation, has an arrangement—

(i) To purchase stock of target; or

(ii) To own an asset to which the carryover basis rules of this section apply, taking into account the extension.

(2) Qualified stock purchase and 12-month acquisition period. The 12-month acquisition period is extended if, pursuant to an arrangement, a corporation acquires by purchase stock of another corporation satisfying the requirements of section 1504(a)(2) over a period of more than 12 months.

(3) Acquisitions by conduits—(i) Asset ownership—(A) General rule. A corporation is treated as owning any portion of an asset attributed to the corporation from a conduit under section 318(a) (treating any asset as stock for this purpose), for purposes of—

(1) The asset ownership requirements of this section; and

(2) Determining whether a controlled foreign corporation is a target affiliate for purposes of paragraph (h) of this section.

(B) Application of carryover basis rule. If the basis rules of this section apply to the asset, the basis rules of this section apply to the entire asset (not just the portion for which ownership is attributed).

(ii) Stock acquisitions—(A) Purchase by conduit. A corporation is treated as purchasing stock of another corporation attributed to the corporation from a conduit under section 318(a) on the day the stock is purchased by the conduit. The corporation is not treated as purchasing the stock, however, if the conduit purchased the stock more than two years before the date the stock is first attributed to the corporation.

(B) Purchase of conduit by corporation. If a corporation purchases an interest in a conduit (treating the interest as stock for this purpose), the corporation is treated as purchasing on that date any stock owned by a conduit on that date and attributed to the corporation under section 318(a) with respect to the interest in the conduit that was purchased.

(C) Purchase of conduit by conduit. If a conduit (the *first* conduit) purchases an interest in a second conduit (treating the interest as stock for this purpose), the first conduit is treated as purchasing on that date any stock owned by a conduit on that date and attributed to the first conduit under section 318(a) with respect to the interest in the second conduit that was purchased.

(4) Conduit. A person (other than a corporation) is a conduit as to a corporation if—

(i) The corporation would be treated under section 318(a)(2)(A) and (B) (attribution from partnerships, estates, and trusts) as owning any stock owned by the person; and

(ii) The corporation, together with its affiliates, would be treated as owning an aggregate of at least 50 percent of the stock owned by the person.

(5) Existence of arrangement. The existence of an arrangement is determined under all the facts and circumstances. For an arrangement to exist, there need not be an enforceable, written, or unconditional agreement, and all the parties to the transaction need not have participated in each step of the transaction. One factor indicating the existence of an arrangement is the participation of a related party. For this purpose, persons are related if they are related within the meaning of section 267(b) or 707(b)(1).

(6) Predecessor and successor—(i) Persons. A reference to a person (including target, target affiliate, and purchasing corporation) includes, as the context may require, a reference to a predecessor or successor. For this purpose, a predecessor is a transferor or distributor of assets to a person (the successor) in a transaction—

(A) To which section 381(a) applies; or

(B) In which the successor's basis for the assets is determined, directly or indirectly, in whole or in part, by reference to the basis of the transferor or distributor.

(ii) Assets. A reference to an asset (the first asset) includes, as the context may require, a reference to any asset the basis of which is determined, directly or indirectly, in whole or in part, by reference to the first asset.

(7) Examples. This paragraph (j) may be illustrated by the following examples:

Example (1). Asset owned by conduit treated as owned by purchaser of target stock. (a) P owns a 60-percent interest in Y. On March 1 of Year 1, T sells an asset to Y and recognizes gain. On January 1 of Year 2, P makes a qualified stock purchase of T from S. No section 338 election is made for T.

(b) Under paragraph (j)(4) of this section, Y is a conduit with respect to P. Consequently, under paragraph (j)(3)(i)(A) of this section, P is treated as owning 60% of the asset on March 1 of Year 1 and January 1 of Year 2. Because P is treated as owning part or all of the asset both immediately after the asset disposition and on T's acquisition date, paragraph (b) of this section applies to the asset. Consequently, paragraph (d)(1) of this section applies to the asset and Y's basis in the asset is T's adjusted basis in the asset immediately before the sale to Y.

Example (2). Corporation whose stock is owned by conduit treated as affiliate. (a) P owns an 80-percent interest in Y. Y owns all of the stock of Z. On March 1 of Year 1, T sells an asset to Z and recognizes gain. On January 1 of Year 2, P makes a qualified stock purchase of T from S. No section 338 election is made for T.

(b) Under paragraph (j)(4) of this section, Y is a conduit with respect to P. Consequently, under paragraph (j)(3)(i)(A) of this section, P is treated as owning 80% of the Z stock and Z is therefore treated as an affiliate of P for purposes of applying the asset ownership requirements of paragraph (b)(1)(iii) of this section. Because Z, an affiliate of P, owns the asset

both immediately after the asset disposition and on T's acquisition date, paragraph (b) of this section applies to the asset, and the asset's basis is determined under paragraph (d) of this section.

(c) If, instead of owning an 80-percent interest in Y, P owned a 79-percent interest in Y, Z would not be treated as an affiliate of P and paragraph (b) of this section would not apply to the asset.

Example (3). Qualified stock purchase by reason of stock purchase by conduit. (a) P owns a 90-percent interest in Y. Y owns a 60-percent interest in Y1. On February 1 of Year 2, T sells an asset to P and recognizes gain. On January 1 of Year 3, P purchases 70% of the T stock from S and Y1 purchases the remaining 30% of the T stock from S.

(b) Under paragraph (j)(3)(ii)(A) of this section, P is treated as purchasing on January 1 of Year 3, the 16.2% of the T stock that is attributed to P from Y and Y1 under section 318(a). Thus, for purposes of this section, P is treated as making a qualified stock purchase of T on January 1 of Year 3, paragraph (b) of this section applies to the asset, and the asset's basis is determined under paragraph (d) of this section. However, because P is not treated as having made a qualified stock purchase of T for purposes of making an election under section 338, no election can be made for T.

(c) If Y1 purchases 20% of the T stock from S on December 1 of Year 1, rather than 30% on January 1 of Year 3, P would be treated as purchasing 10.8% of the T stock on December 1 of Year 1. Thus, if paragraph (j)(2) of this section (relating to extension of the 12-month acquisition period) does not apply, P would not be treated as making a qualified stock purchase of T, because P is not treated as purchasing T stock satisfying the requirements of section 1504(a)(2) within a 12-month period.

Example (4). Successor asset. (a) On February 1 of Year 1, T sells stock of X to P1 and recognizes gain. On December 1 of Year 1, P1 exchanges its X stock for stock in new X in a reorganization qualifying under section 368(a)(1)(F). On January 1 of Year 2, P1 makes a qualified stock purchase of T from S. No section 338 election is made for T.

(b) The asset ownership requirements of paragraph (b)(1)(iii) of this section are satisfied because, under paragraph (j)(6)(ii) of this section, P1 is treated as owning the X stock on T's acquisition date. P1 is treated as owning the X stock on that date because P1 owns the new X stock and P1's basis in the new X stock is determined by reference to P1's basis in the X stock. Consequently, under paragraph (d)(1) of this section, P1's basis in the X stock on February 1 of Year 1 is T's adjusted basis in the X stock immediately before the sale to P1.

§ 1.338(h)(10)–1 Deemed asset sale and liquidation.

(a) Scope. This section prescribes rules for qualification for a section 338(h)(10) election and for making a section 338(h)(10) election. This section also prescribes the consequences of such election. The rules of this section are in addition to the rules of §§ 1.338–1 through 1.338–10 and, in appropriate cases, apply instead of the rules of §§ 1.338–1 through 1.338–10.

(b) Definitions—(1) Consolidated target. A consolidated target is a target that is a member of a consolidated group within the meaning of § 1.1502–1(h) on the acquisition date and is not the common parent of the group on that date.

(2) Selling consolidated group. A selling consolidated group is the consolidated group of which the consolidated target is a member on the acquisition date.

(3) Selling affiliate; affiliated target. A selling affiliate is a domestic corporation that owns on the acquisition date an amount of stock in a domestic target, which amount of stock is described in section 1504(a)(2), and does not join in filing a consolidated return with the target. In such case, the target is an affiliated target.

(4) S corporation target. An S corporation target is a target that is an S corporation immediately before the acquisition date.

(5) S corporation shareholders. S corporation shareholders are the S corporation target's shareholders. Unless otherwise indicated, a reference to S corporation shareholders refers both to S corporation shareholders who do and those who do not sell their target stock.

(6) Liquidation. Any reference in this section to a liquidation is treated as a reference to the transfer described in paragraph (d)(4) of this section notwithstanding its ultimate characterization for Federal income tax purposes.

(c) Section 338(h)(10) election—(1) In general. A section 338(h)(10) election may be made for T if P acquires stock meeting the requirements of section 1504(a)(2) from a selling consolidated group, a selling affiliate, or the S corporation shareholders in a qualified stock purchase.

(2) Availability of section 338(h)(10) election in certain multi-step transactions. Notwithstanding anything to the contrary in § 1.338–3(c)(1)(i), a section 338(h)(10) election may be made for T where P's acquisition of T stock, viewed independently, constitutes a qualified stock purchase and, after the stock acquisition, T merges or liquidates into P (or another member of the affiliated group that includes P), whether or not, under relevant provisions of law, including the step transaction doctrine, the acquisition of the T stock and the merger or liquidation of T qualify as a reorganization described in section 368(a). If a section 338(h)(10) election is made in a case where the acquisition of T stock followed by a merger or liquidation of T into P qualifies as a reorganization described in section 368(a), for all Federal tax purposes, P's acquisition of T stock is treated as a qualified stock purchase and is not treated as part of a reorganization described in section 368(a).

(3) Simultaneous joint election requirement. A section 338(h)(10) election is made jointly by P and the selling consolidated group (or the selling affiliate or the S corporation shareholders) on Form 8023 in accordance with the instructions to the form. S corporation shareholders who do not sell their stock must also consent to the election. The section 338(h)(10) election must be made not later than the 15th day of the 9th month beginning after the month in which the acquisition date occurs.

(4) Irrevocability. A section 338(h)(10) election is irrevocable. If a section 338(h)(10) election is made for T, a section 338 election is deemed made for T.

(5) Effect of invalid election. If a section 338(h)(10) election for T is not valid, the section 338 election for T is also not valid.

(d) Certain consequences of section 338(h)(10) election. For purposes of subtitle A of the Internal Revenue Code (except as provided in § 1.338–1(b)(2)), the consequences to the parties of making a section 338(h)(10) election for T are as follows:

(1) P. P is automatically deemed to have made a gain recognition election for its non-recently purchased T stock, if any. The effect of a gain recognition election includes a taxable deemed sale by P on the acquisition date of any nonrecently purchased target stock. See § 1.338–5(d).

(2) New T. The AGUB for new T's assets is determined under § 1.338–5 and is allocated among the acquisition date assets under §§ 1.338–6 and 1.338–7. Notwithstanding paragraph (d)(4) of this section (deemed liquidation of old T), new T remains liable for the tax liabilities of old T (including the tax liability for the deemed sale tax consequences). For example, new T remains liable for the tax liabilities of the members of any consolidated group that are attributable to taxable years in which those corporations and old T joined in the same consolidated return. See § 1.1502–6(a).

(3) Old T—deemed sale—(i) In general. Old T is treated as transferring all of its assets to an unrelated person in exchange for consideration that includes the discharge of its liabilities in a single transaction at the close of the acquisition date (but before the deemed liquidation). See § 1.338–1(a) regarding the tax characterization of the deemed asset sale. Except as provided in § 1.338(h)(10)–1(d)(8) (regarding the installment method), old T recognizes all of the gain realized on the deemed transfer of its assets in consideration for the ADSP. ADSP for old T is determined under § 1.338–4 and allocated among the acquisition date assets under §§ 1.338–6 and 1.338–7. Old T realizes the deemed sale tax consequences from the deemed asset sale before the close of the acquisition date while old T is a member of the selling consolidated group (or owned by the selling affiliate or owned by the S corporation shareholders). If T is an affiliated target, or an S corporation target, the principles of §§ 1.338–2(c)(10) and 1.338–10(a)(1), (5), and (6)(i) apply to the return on which the deemed sale tax consequences are reported. When T is an S corporation target, T's S election continues in effect through the close of the acquisition date (including the time of the deemed asset sale and the deemed liquidation) notwithstanding section 1362(d)(2)(B). Also, when T is an S corporation target (but not a qualified subchapter S subsidiary), any direct and indirect subsidiaries of T which T has elected to treat as qualified subchapter S subsidiaries under section 1361(b)(3) remain qualified subchapter S subsidiaries through the close of the acquisition date.

(ii) Tiered targets. In the case of parent-subsidiary chains of corporations making elections under section 338(h)(10), the deemed asset sale of a parent corporation is considered to precede that of its subsidiary. See § 1.338–3(b)(4)(i).

(4) Old T and selling consolidated group, selling affiliate, or S corporation shareholders—deemed liquidation; tax characteri-

zation—**(i) In general.** Old T is treated as if, before the close of the acquisition date, after the deemed asset sale in paragraph (d)(3) of this section, and while old T is a member of the selling consolidated group (or owned by the selling affiliate or owned by the S corporation shareholders), it transferred all of its assets to members of the selling consolidated group, the selling affiliate, or S corporation shareholders and ceased to exist. The transfer from old T is characterized for Federal income tax purposes in the same manner as if the parties had actually engaged in the transactions deemed to occur because of this section and taking into account other transactions that actually occurred or are deemed to occur. For example, the transfer may be treated as a distribution in pursuance of a plan of reorganization, a distribution in complete cancellation or redemption of all its stock, one of a series of distributions in complete cancellation or redemption of all its stock in accordance with a plan of liquidation, or part of a circular flow of cash. In most cases, the transfer will be treated as a distribution in complete liquidation to which section 336 or 337 applies.

(ii) Tiered targets. In the case of parent-subsidiary chains of corporations making elections under section 338(h)(10), the deemed liquidation of a subsidiary corporation is considered to precede the deemed liquidation of its parent.

(5) Selling consolidated group, selling affiliate, or S corporation shareholders—(i) In general. If T is an S corporation target, S corporation shareholders (whether or not they sell their stock) take their pro rata share of the deemed sale tax consequences into account under section 1366 and increase or decrease their basis in T stock under section 1367. Members of the selling consolidated group, the selling affiliate, or S corporation shareholders are treated as if, after the deemed asset sale in paragraph (d)(3) of this section and before the close of the acquisition date, they received the assets transferred by old T in the transaction described in paragraph (d)(4)(i) of this section. In most cases, the transfer will be treated as a distribution in complete liquidation to which section 331 or 332 applies.

(ii) Basis and holding period of T stock not acquired. A member of the selling consolidated group (or the selling affiliate or an S corporation shareholder) retaining T stock is treated as acquiring the stock so retained on the day after the acquisition date for its fair market value. The holding period for the retained stock starts on the day after the acquisition date. For purposes of this paragraph, the fair market value of all of the T stock equals the grossed-up amount realized on the sale to P of P's recently purchased target stock. See § 1.338–4(c).

(iii) T stock sale. Members of the selling consolidated group (or the selling affiliate or S corporation shareholders) recognize no gain or loss on the sale or exchange of T stock included in the qualified stock purchase (although they may recognize gain or loss on the T stock in the deemed liquidation).

(6) Nonselling minority shareholders other than nonselling S corporation shareholders—(i) In general. This paragraph (d) (6) describes the treatment of shareholders of old T other than the following: Members of the selling consolidated group, the selling affiliate, S corporation shareholders (whether or not they sell their stock), and P. For a description of the treatment of S corporation shareholders, see paragraph (d)(5) of this section. A shareholder to which this paragraph (d)(6) applies is called a minority shareholder.

(ii) T stock sale. A minority shareholder recognizes gain or loss on the shareholder's sale or exchange of T stock included in the qualified stock purchase.

(iii) T stock not acquired. A minority shareholder does not recognize gain or loss under this section with respect to shares of T stock retained by the shareholder. The shareholder's basis and holding period for that T stock is not affected by the section 338(h)(10) election.

(7) Consolidated return of selling consolidated group. If P acquires T in a qualified stock purchase from a selling consolidated group—

(i) The selling consolidated group must file a consolidated return for the taxable period that includes the acquisition date;

(ii) A consolidated return for the selling consolidated group for that period may not be withdrawn on or after the day that a section 338(h)(10) election is made for T; and

(iii) Permission to discontinue filing consolidated returns cannot be granted for, and cannot apply to, that period or any of the immediately preceding taxable periods during which consolidated returns continuously have been filed.

(8) Availability of the section 453 installment method. Solely for purposes of applying sections 453, 453A, and 453B, and the regulations thereunder (the installment method) to determine the consequences to old T in the deemed asset sale and to old T (and its shareholders, if relevant) in the deemed liquidation, the rules in paragraphs (d)(1) through (7) of this section are modified as follows:

(i) In deemed asset sale. Old T is treated as receiving in the deemed asset sale new T installment obligations, the terms of which are identical (except as to the obligor) to P installment obligations issued in exchange for recently purchased stock of T. Old T is treated as receiving in cash all other consideration in the deemed asset sale other than the assumption of, or taking subject to, old T liabilities. For example, old T is treated as receiving in cash any amounts attributable to the grossing-up of amount realized under § 1.338–4(c). The amount realized for recently purchased stock taken into account in determining ADSP is adjusted (and, thus, ADSP is redetermined) to reflect the amounts paid under an installment obligation for the stock when the total payments

under the installment obligation are greater or less than the amount realized.

(ii) In deemed liquidation. Old T is treated as distributing in the deemed liquidation the new T installment obligations that it is treated as receiving in the deemed asset sale. The members of the selling consolidated group, the selling affiliate, or the S corporation shareholders are treated as receiving in the deemed liquidation the new T installment obligations that correspond to the P installment obligations they actually received individually in exchange for their recently purchased stock. The new T installment obligations may be recharacterized under other rules. See for example § 1.453–11(a)(2) which, in certain circumstances, treats the new T installment obligations deemed distributed by old T as if they were issued by new T in exchange for the stock in old T owned by members of the selling consolidated group, the selling affiliate, or the S corporation shareholders. The members of the selling consolidated group, the selling affiliate, or the S corporation shareholders are treated as receiving all other consideration in the deemed liquidation in cash.

(9) Treatment consistent with an actual asset sale. No provision in section 338(h)(10) or this section shall produce a Federal income tax result under subtitle A of the Internal Revenue Code that would not occur if the parties had actually engaged in the transactions deemed to occur because of this section and taking into account other transactions that actually occurred or are deemed to occur. See, however, § 1.338–1(b)(2) for certain exceptions to this rule.

(e) Examples. The following examples illustrate the provisions of this section:

Example (1). (i) S1 owns all of the T stock and T owns all of the stock of T1 and T2. S1 is the common parent of a consolidated group that includes T, T1, and T2. P makes a qualified stock purchase of all of the T stock from S1. S1 joins with P in making a section 338(h)(10) election for T and for the deemed purchase of T1. A section 338 election is not made for T2.

(ii) S1 does not recognize gain or loss on the sale of the T stock and T does not recognize gain or loss on the sale of the T1 stock because section 338(h)(10) elections are made for T and T1. Thus, for example, gain or loss realized on the sale of the T or T1 stock is not taken into account in earnings and profits. However, because a section 338 election is not made for T2, T must recognize any gain or loss realized on the deemed sale of the T2 stock. See § 1.338–4(h).

(iii) The results would be the same if S1, T, T1, and T2 are not members of any consolidated group, because S1 and T are selling affiliates.

Example (2). *(i)* S and T are solvent corporations. S owns all of the outstanding stock of T. S and P agree to undertake the following transaction: T will distribute half its assets to S, and S will assume half of T's liabilities. Then, P will purchase the stock of T from S. S and P will jointly make a section 338(h)(10) election with respect to the sale of T. The corporations then complete the transaction as agreed.

(ii) Under section 338(a), the assets present in T at the close of the acquisition date are deemed sold by old T to new T. Under paragraph (d)(4) of this section, the transactions described in paragraph (d) of this section are treated in the same manner as if they had actually occurred. Because S and P had agreed that, after T's actual distribution to S of part of its assets, S would sell T to P pursuant to an election under section 338(h)(10), and because paragraph (d)(4) of this section deems T subsequently to have transferred all its assets to its shareholder, T is deemed to have adopted a plan of complete liquidation under section 332. T's actual transfer of assets to S is treated as a distribution pursuant to that plan of complete liquidation.

Example (3). *(i)* S1 owns all of the outstanding stock of both T and S2. All three are

corporations. S1 and P agree to undertake the following transaction. T will transfer substantially all of its assets and liabilities to S2, with S2 issuing no stock in exchange therefor, and retaining its other assets and liabilities. Then, P will purchase the stock of T from S1. S1 and P will jointly make a section 338(h)(10) election with respect to the sale of T. The corporations then complete the transaction as agreed.

(ii) Under section 338(a), the remaining assets present in T at the close of the acquisition date are deemed sold by old T to new T. Under paragraph (d)(4) of this section, the transactions described in this section are treated in the same manner as if they had actually occurred. Because old T transferred substantially all of its assets to S2, and is deemed to have distributed all its remaining assets and gone out of existence, the transfer of assets to S2, taking into account the related transfers, deemed and actual, qualifies as a reorganization under section 368(a)(1)(D). Section 361(c)(1) and not section 332 applies to T's deemed liquidation.

Example (4). *(i)* T owns two assets: an actively traded security (Class II) with a fair market value of $100 and an adjusted basis of $100, and inventory (Class IV) with a fair market value of $100 and an adjusted basis of $100. T has no liabilities. S is negotiating to sell all the stock in T to P for $100 cash and contingent consideration. Assume that under generally applicable tax accounting rules, P's adjusted basis in the T stock immediately after the purchase would be $100, because the contingent consideration is not taken into account. Thus, under the rules of § 1.338–5, AGUB would be $100. Under the allocation rules of § 1.338–6, the entire $100 would be allocated to the Class II asset, the actively traded security, and no amount would be allocated to the inventory. P, however, plans immediately to cause T to sell the inventory, but not the actively traded security, so it requests that, prior to the stock sale, S cause T to create a new subsidiary, Newco, and contribute the actively traded security to the capital of Newco. Because the stock in Newco, which would not be actively traded, is a Class V asset, under the rules of § 1.338–6 $100 of AGUB would be allocated to the inventory and no amount of AGUB would be allocated to the Newco stock. Newco's own AGUB, $0 under the rules of § 1.338–5, would be allocated to the actively traded security. When P subsequently causes T to sell the inventory, T would realize no gain or loss instead of realizing gain of $100.

(ii) Assume that, if the T stock had not it-self been sold but T had instead sold both its inventory and the Newco stock to P, T would for tax purposes be deemed instead to have sold both its inventory and actively traded se-curity directly to P, with P deemed then to have created Newco and contributed the actively traded security to the capital of Newco. Sec-tion 338, if elected, generally recharacterizes a stock sale as a deemed sale of assets. However, paragraph (d)(9) of this section states, in gen-eral, that no provision of section 338(h)(10) or the regulations thereunder shall produce a Federal income tax result under subtitle A of the Internal Revenue Code that would not oc-cur if the parties had actually engaged in the transactions deemed to occur by virtue of the section 338(h)(10) election, taking into ac-count other transactions that actually occurred or are deemed to occur. Hence, the deemed sale of assets under section 338(h)(10) should be treated as one of the inventory and actively traded security themselves, not of the inven-tory and Newco stock. The anti-abuse rule of § 1.338–1(c) does not apply, because the sub-stance of the deemed sale of assets is a sale of the inventory and the actively traded security themselves, not of the inventory and the New-co stock. Otherwise, the anti-abuse rule might apply.

Example (5). (i) T, a member of a sell-ing consolidated group, has only one class of stock, all of which is owned by S1. On March 1 of Year 2, S1 sells its T stock to P for $80,000, and joins with P in making a sec-tion 338(h)(10) election for T. There are no selling costs or acquisition costs. On March 1 of Year 2, T owns land with a $50,000 basis and $75,000 fair market value and equipment with a $30,000 adjusted basis, $70,000 recom-puted basis, and $60,000 fair market value. T also has a $40,000 liability. S1 pays old T's allocable share of the selling group's consoli-dated tax liability for Year 2 including the tax liability for the deemed sale tax consequences (a total of $13,600).

(ii) ADSP of $120,000 ($80,000 + $40,000 + 0) is allocated to each asset as follows:

Assets	Basis	FMV	Fraction	Allocable ADSP
Land	$50,000	$75,000	5/9	$66,667
Equipment	30,000	60,000	4/9	53,333
Total	80,000	135,000	1	120,000

(iii) Under paragraph (d)(3) of this section, old T has gain on the deemed sale of $40,000 (consisting of $16,667 of capital gain and $23,333 of ordinary income).

(iv) Under paragraph (d)(5)(iii) of this sec-tion, S1 recognizes no gain or loss upon its sale of the old T stock to P. S1 also recognizes no gain or loss upon the deemed liquidation of T. See paragraph (d)(4) of this section and section 332.

(v) P's basis in new T stock is P's cost for the stock, $80,000. See section 1012.

(vi) Under § 1.338–5, the AGUB for new T is $120,000, i.e., P's cost for the old T stock ($80,000) plus T's liability ($40,000). This AGUB is allocated as basis among the new T assets under §§ 1.338–6 and 1.338–7.

Example (6). (i) The facts are the same as in Example 5, except that S1 sells 80 percent of the old T stock to P for $64,000, rather than 100 percent of the old T stock for $80,000.

(ii) The consequences to P, T, and S1 are the same as in Example 5, except that:

(A) P's basis for its 80-percent interest in the new T stock is P's $64,000 cost for the stock. See section 1012.

(B) Under § 1.338–5, the AGUB for new T is $120,000 (i.e., $64,000/.8 + $40,000 + $0).

(C) Under paragraph (d)(4) of this section, S1 recognizes no gain or loss with respect to the retained stock in T. See section 332.

(D) Under paragraph (d)(5)(ii) of this section, the basis of the T stock retained by S1 is $16,000 (i.e., $120,000 $40,000 (the ADSP amount for the old T assets over the sum of new T's liabilities immediately after the acquisition date) ".20 (the proportion of T stock retained by S1)).

Example (7). (i) The facts are the same as in Example 6, except that K, a shareholder unrelated to T or P, owns the 20 percent of the T stock that is not acquired by P in the qualified stock purchase. K's basis in its T stock is $5,000.

(ii) The consequences to P, T, and S1 are the same as in Example 6.

(iii) Under paragraph (d)(6)(iii) of this section, K recognizes no gain or loss, and K's basis in its T stock remains at $5,000.

Example (8). (i) The facts are the same as in Example 5, except that the equipment is held by T1, a wholly-owned subsidiary of T, and a section 338(h)(10) election is also made for T1. The T1 stock has a fair market value of $60,000. T1 has no assets other than the equipment and no liabilities. S1 pays old T's and old T1's allocable shares of the selling group's consolidated tax liability for Year 2 including the tax liability for T and T1's deemed sale tax consequences.

(ii) ADSP for T is $120,000, allocated $66,667 to the land and $53,333 to the stock. Old T's deemed sale results in $16,667 of capital gain on its deemed sale of the land. Under paragraph (d)(5)(iii) of this section, old T does not recognize gain or loss on its deemed sale of the T1 stock. See section 332.

(iii) ADSP for T1 is $53,333 (i.e., $53,333 + $0 + $0). On the deemed sale of the equip-

ment, T1 recognizes ordinary income of $23,333.

(iv) Under paragraph (d)(5)(iii) of this section, S1 does not recognize gain or loss upon its sale of the old T stock to P.

Example (9). (i) The facts are the same as in Example 8, except that P already owns 20 percent of the T stock, which is nonrecently purchased stock with a basis of $6,000, and that P purchases the remaining 80 percent of the T stock from S1 for $64,000.

(ii) The results are the same as in Example 8, except that under paragraph (d)(1) of this section and § 1.338–5(d), P is deemed to have made a gain recognition election for its nonrecently purchased T stock. As a result, P recognizes gain of $10,000 and its basis in the nonrecently purchased T stock is increased from $6,000 to $16,000. P's basis in all the T stock is $80,000 (i.e., $64,000 + $16,000). The computations are as follows:

(A) P's grossed-up basis for the recently purchased T stock is $64,000 * * *

(B) P's basis amount for the nonrecently purchased T stock is $16,000 * * *

(C) The gain recognized on the nonrecently purchased stock is $10,000 * * *

Example (10). (i) T is an S corporation whose sole class of stock is owned 40 percent each by A and B and 20 percent by C. T, A, B, and C all use the cash method of accounting. A and B each has an adjusted basis of $10,000 in the stock. C has an adjusted basis of $5,000 in the stock. A, B, and C hold no installment obligations to which section 453A applies. On March 1 of Year 1, A sells its stock to P for $40,000 in cash and B sells its stock to P for a $25,000 note issued by P and real estate having a fair market value of $15,000. The $25,000 note, due in full in Year 7, is not publicly traded and bears adequate stated interest. A and B have no selling expenses. T's sole asset is real estate, which has a value of $110,000 and an adjusted basis of $35,000. Also, T's real estate is encumbered by long-outstanding purchase-money indebtedness of $10,000. The real estate does not have built-in gain subject to section 1374. A, B, and C join with P in making a section 338(h)(10) election for T.

(ii) Solely for purposes of application of sections 453, 453A, and 453B, old T is considered in its deemed asset sale to receive back from new T the $25,000 note (considered issued by new T) and $75,000 of cash (total consideration of $80,000 paid for all the stock sold, which is then divided by .80 in the grossing-up, with the resulting figure of $100,000 then reduced by the amount of the installment note). Absent an election under section 453(d), gain is reported by old T under the installment method.

(iii) In applying the installment method to old T's deemed asset sale, the contract price for old T's assets deemed sold is $100,000, the $110,000 selling price reduced by the indebtedness of $10,000 to which the assets are subject. (The $110,000 selling price is itself the sum of the $80,000 grossed-up in paragraph (ii) above to $100,000 and the $10,000 liability.) Gross profit is $75,000 ($110,000 selling price – old T's basis of $35,000). Old T's gross profit ratio is 0.75 (gross profit of $75,000 / $100,000 contract price). Thus, $56,250 (0.75 × the $75,000 cash old T is deemed to receive in Year 1) is Year 1 gain attributable to the sale, and $18,750 ($75,000 – $56,250) is recovery of basis.

(iv) In its liquidation, old T is deemed to distribute the $25,000 note to B, since B actually sold the stock partly for that consideration. To the extent of the remaining liquidating distribution to B, it is deemed to receive, along with A and C, the balance of old T's liquidating assets in the form of cash. Under section 453(h), B, unless it makes an election under section 453(d), is not required to treat the receipt of the note as a payment for the T stock; P's payment of the $25,000 note in Year 7 to B is a payment for the T stock. Because section 453(h) applies to B, old T's deemed liquidating distribution of the note is, under

section 453B(h), not treated as a taxable disposition by old T.

(v) Under section 1366, A reports 40 percent, or $22,500, of old T's $56,250 gain recognized in Year 1. Under section 1367, this increases A's $10,000 adjusted basis in the T stock to $32,500. Next, in old T's deemed liquidation, A is considered to receive $40,000 for its old T shares, causing it to recognize an additional $7,500 gain in Year 1.

(vi) Under section 1366, B reports 40 percent, or $22,500, of old T's $56,250 gain recognized in Year 1. Under section 1367, this increases B's $10,000 adjusted basis in its T stock to $32,500. Next, in old T's deemed liquidation, B is considered to receive the $25,000 note and $15,000 of other consideration. Applying section 453, including section 453(h), to the deemed liquidation, B's selling price and contract price are both $40,000. Gross profit is $7,500 ($40,000 selling price B's basis of $32,500). B's gross profit ratio is 0.1875 (gross profit of $7,500 / $40,000 contract price). Thus, $2,812.50 (0.1875 × $15,000) is Year 1 gain attributable to the deemed liquidation. In Year 7, when the $25,000 note is paid, B has $4,687.50 (0.1875 × $25,000) of additional gain.

(vii) Under section 1366, C reports 20 percent, or $11,250, of old T's $56,250 gain recognized in Year 1. Under section 1367, this increases C's $5,000 adjusted basis in its T stock to $16,250. Next, in old T's deemed liquidation, C is considered to receive $20,000 for its old T shares, causing it to recognize an additional $3,750 gain in Year 1. Finally, under paragraph (d)(5)(ii) of this section, C is considered to acquire its stock in T on the day after the acquisition date for $20,000 (fair market value = grossed-up amount realized of $100,000 × 20%). C's holding period in the stock deemed received in new T begins at that time.

Example (11). Stock acquisition followed by upstream merger—without section 338(h) (10) election. (i) P owns all the stock of Y, a newly formed subsidiary. S owns all the stock of T. Each of P, S, T and Y is a domestic corporation. P acquires all of the T stock in a statutory merger of Y into T, with T surviving. In the merger, S receives consideration consisting of 50% P voting stock and 50% cash. Viewed independently of any other step, P's acquisition of T stock constitutes a qualified stock purchase. As part of the plan that includes P's acquisition of the T stock, T subsequently merges into P. Viewed independently of any other step, T's merger into P qualifies as a liquidation described in section 332. Absent the application of paragraph (c)(2) of this section, the step transaction doctrine would apply to treat P's acquisition of the T stock and T's merger into P as an acquisition by P of T's assets in a reorganization described in section 368(a). P and S do not make a section 338(h)(10) election with respect to P's purchase of the T stock.

(ii) Because P and S do not make an election under section 338(h)(10) for T, P's acquisition of the T stock and T's merger into P is treated as part of a reorganization described in section 368(a).

Example (12). Stock acquisition followed by upstream merger—with section 338(h)(10) election. (i) The facts are the same as in Example 11 except that P and S make a joint election under section 338(h)(10) for T.

(ii) Pursuant to paragraph (c)(2) of this section, as a result of the election under section 338(h)(10), for all Federal tax purposes, P's acquisition of the T stock is treated as a qualified stock purchase and P's acquisition of the T stock is not treated as part of a reorganization described in section 368(a).

Example (13). Stock acquisition followed by brother-sister merger—with section 338(h) (10) election. (i) The facts are the same as in Example 12, except that, following P's acquisition of the T stock, T merges into X, a domestic corporation that is a wholly owned subsidiary of P. Viewed independently of any other step, T's merger into X qualifies as a reorganization described in section 368(a). Absent the application of paragraph (c)(2) of this section, the step transaction doctrine would apply to treat P's acquisition of the T stock and T's merger into X as an acquisition by X of T's assets in a reorganization described in section 368(a).

(ii) Pursuant to paragraph (c)(2) of this section, as a result of the election under section 338(h)(10), for all Federal tax purposes, P's acquisition of T stock is treated as a qualified stock purchase and P's acquisition of T stock is not treated as part of a reorganization described in section 368(a).

Example (14). Stock acquisition that does not qualify as a qualified stock purchase followed by upstream merger. (i) The facts are the same as in Example 11, except that, in the statutory merger of Y into T, S receives only P voting stock.

(ii) Pursuant to § 1.338–3(c)(1)(i) and paragraph (c)(2) of this section, no election under section 338(h)(10) can be made with respect to P's acquisition of the T stock because, pursuant to relevant provisions of law, including the step transaction doctrine, that acquisition followed by T's merger into P is treated as a reorganization described in section 368(a)(1) (A), and that acquisition, viewed independently of T's merger into P, does not constitute a qualified stock purchase under section 338(d) (3). Accordingly, P's acquisition of the T stock and T's merger into P is treated as a reorganization described in section 368(a).

(f) Inapplicability of provisions. The provisions of section 6043, § 1.331–1(d) and § 1.332–6 (relating to information returns and recordkeeping requirements for corporate liquidations) do not apply to the deemed liquidation of old T under paragraph (d)(4) of this section.

(g) Required information. The Commissioner may exercise the authority granted in section 338(h)(10)(C)(iii) to require provision of any information deemed necessary to carry out the provisions of section 338(h)(10) by requiring submission of information on any tax reporting form.

(h) Effective date. This section is applicable to stock acquisitions occurring on or after July 5, 2006. * * *

§ 1.346–1 Partial liquidation.

(a) General. This section defines a partial liquidation. If amounts are distributed in partial liquidation such amounts are treated under section 331(a)(2) as received in part or full payment in exchange for the stock. A distribution is treated as in partial liquidation of a corporation if:

(1) The distribution is one of a series of distributions in redemption of all of the stock of the corporation pursuant to a plan of complete liquidation, or

(2) The distribution:

(i) Is not essentially equivalent to a dividend,

(ii) Is in redemption of a part of the stock of the corporation pursuant to a plan, and

(iii) Occurs within the taxable year in which the plan is adopted or within the succeeding taxable year.

An example of a distribution which will qualify as a partial liquidation under subparagraph (2) of this paragraph and section 346(a) is a distribution resulting from a genuine contraction of the corporate business such as the distribution of unused insurance proceeds recovered as a result of a fire which destroyed part of the business causing a cessation of a part of its activities. On the other hand, the distribution of funds attributable to a reserve for an expansion program which has been abandoned does not qualify as a partial liquidation within the meaning of section 346(a). A distribution to which section 355 applies (or so much of section 356 as relates to section 355) is not a distribution in partial liquidation within the meaning of section 346(a).

(b) Special requirements on termination of business. A distribution which occurs within the taxable year in which the plan is adopted or within the succeeding taxable year and which meets the requirements of subsection (b) of section 346 falls within paragraph (a)(2) of this section and within section 346(a)(2). The requirements which a distribution must meet to fall within subsection (b) of section 346 are:

(1) Such distribution is attributable to the corporation's ceasing to conduct, or consists of assets of, a trade or business which has been actively conducted throughout the five-year period immediately before the distribution, which trade or business was not acquired by the corporation within such period in a transaction in which gain or loss was recognized in whole or in part, and

(2) Immediately after such distribution by the corporation it is actively engaged in the conduct of a trade or business, which trade or business was actively conducted throughout the five-year period ending on the date of such distribution and was not acquired by the corporation within such period in a transaction in which gain or loss was recognized in whole or in part.

A distribution shall be treated as having been made in partial liquidation pursuant to section 346(b) if it consists of the proceeds of the sale of the assets of a trade or business which has been actively conducted for the five-year period and has been terminated, or if it is a distribution in kind of the assets of such a business, or if it is a distribution in kind of some of the assets of such a business and of the proceeds of the sale of the remainder of the assets of such a business. In general, a distribution which will qualify under section 346(b) may consist of, but is not limited to:

(i) Assets (other than inventory or property described in subdivision (ii) of this subparagraph) used in the trade or business throughout the five-year period immediately before the distribution (for this purpose an asset shall be considered used in the trade or business during the period of time the asset which it replaced was so used), or

(ii) Proceeds from the sale of assets described in subdivision (i) of this subparagraph, and, in addition,

(iii) The inventory of such trade or business or property held primarily for sale to customers in the ordinary course of business, if:

(*a*) The items constituting such inventory or such property were substantially similar to the items constituting such inventory or property during the five-year period immediately before the distribution, and

(*b*) The quantity of such items on the date of distribution was not substantially in excess of the quantity of similar items regularly on hand in the conduct of such business during such five-year period, or

(iv) Proceeds from the sale of inventory or property described in subdivision (iii) of this subparagraph, if such inventory or property is sold in bulk in the course of termination of such trade or business and if with respect to such inventory the conditions of subdivision (iii)(a) and (b) of this subparagraph would have been met had such inventory or property been distributed on the date of such sale.

(c) **Active conduct of a trade or business.** For the purpose of section 346(b)(1), a corporation shall be deemed to have actively conducted a trade or business immediately before the distribution, if:

(1) In the case of a business the assets of which have been distributed in kind, the business was operated by such corporation until the date of distribution, or

(2) In the case of a business the proceeds of the sale of the assets of which are distributed, such business was actively conducted until the date of sale and the proceeds of such sale were distributed as soon thereafter as reasonably possible.

The term "active conduct of a trade or busi-

ness" shall have the same meaning in this section as in [§ 1.355–3(b)(2)]

§ 1.346–2 Treatment of certain redemptions.

If a distribution in a redemption of stock qualifies as a distribution in part or full payment in exchange for the stock under both section 302(a) and this section, then only this section shall be applicable. None of the limitations of section 302 shall be applicable to such redemption.

§ 1.346–3 Effect of certain sales.

The determination of whether assets sold in connection with a partial liquidation are sold by the distributing corporation or by the shareholder is a question of fact to be determined under the facts and circumstances of each case.

§ 1.351–1 Transfer to corporation controlled by transferor.

(a) **In general—(1) Nonrecognition of gain or loss.** Section 351(a) provides, in general, for the nonrecognition of gain or loss upon the transfer by one or more persons of property to a corporation solely in exchange for stock in such corporation, if immediately after the exchange, such person or persons are in control of the corporation to which the property was transferred. As used in section 351, the phrase "one or more persons" includes individuals, trusts, estates, partnerships, associations, companies, or corporations. To be in control of the transferee corporation, such person or persons must own immediately after the transfer stock possessing at least 80 percent of the total combined voting power of all classes of stock entitled to vote and at least 80 percent of the total number of shares of all other classes of stock of such corporation (see section 368(c)). In determining control under this section, the fact that any corporate transferor distributes part or all of the stock which it receives in the exchange to its shareholders shall not be taken into account. The phrase "immediately after the exchange" does not necessarily require simultaneous exchanges by two or more persons, but comprehends a situation where the rights of the parties have been previously defined and the execution of the agreement proceeds with an expedition consistent with orderly procedure. For purposes of this section, stock rights and stock warrants are not included in the term *stock*.

(i) Stock will not be treated as issued for property if it is issued for services rendered or to be rendered to or for the benefit of the issuing corporation; and

(ii) Stock will not be treated as issued for property if it is issued for property which is of relatively small value in comparison to the value of the stock already owned (or to be received for services) by the person who transferred such property and the primary purpose of the transfer is to qualify under this section the exchanges of property by other persons transferring property.

* * *

(2) **Application.** The application of section 351(a) is illustrated by the following examples:

Example (1). C owns a patent right worth $25,000 and D owns a manufacturing plant worth $75,000. C and D organize the R Corporation with an authorized capital stock of $100,000. C transfers his patent right to the R Corporation for $25,000 of its stock and D transfers his plant to the new corporation for $75,000 of its stock. No gain or loss to C or D is recognized.

Example (2). B owns certain real estate which cost him $50,000 in 1930, but which has a fair market value of $200,000 in 1955. He transfers the property to the N Corporation in 1955 for 78 percent of each class of stock of the corporation having a fair market value of $200,000, the remaining 22 percent of the stock of the corporation having been issued by the corporation in 1940 to other persons for

cash. B realized a taxable gain of $150,000 on this transaction.

Example (3). E, an individual, owns property with a basis of $10,000 but which has a fair market value of $18,000. E also had rendered services valued at $2,000 to Corporation F. Corporation F has outstanding 100 shares of common stock all of which are held by G. Corporation F issues 400 shares of its common stock (having a fair market value of $20,000) to E in exchange for his property worth $18,000 and in compensation for the services he has rendered worth $2,000. Since immediately after the transaction, E owns 80 percent of the outstanding stock of Corporation F, no gain is recognized upon the exchange of the property for the stock. However, E realized $2,000 of ordinary income as compensation for services rendered to Corporation F.

(3) **Underwritings of stock — (i) In general.** For the purpose of section 351, if a person acquires stock of a corporation from an underwriter in exchange for cash in a qualified underwriting transaction, the person who acquires stock from the underwriter is treated as transferring cash directly to the corporation in exchange for stock of the corporation and the underwriter is disregarded. A qualified underwriting transaction is a transaction in which a corporation issues stock for cash in an underwriting in which either the underwriter is an agent of the corporation or the underwriter's ownership of the stock is transitory.

* * *

(b) **Multiple transferors — (1) Disproportionate transfers.** When property is transferred to a corporation by two or more persons in exchange for stock, as described in paragraph (a) of this section, and the stock received is disproportionate to the transferor's prior interest in such property, the entire transaction will be given tax effect in accordance with its true nature, and the transaction may be treated as if the stock had first been received in proportion and then some of such stock had been used to make gifts (section 2501 and following), to pay compensation (sections 61(a) (1) and 83(a)), or to satisfy obligations of the transferor of any kind.

(2) Application. The application of paragraph (b)(1) of this section may be illustrated as follows:

Example (1). Individuals A and B, father and son, organize a corporation with 100 shares of common stock to which A transfers property worth $8,000 in exchange for 20 shares of stock, and B transfers property worth $2,000 in exchange for 80 shares of stock. No gain or loss will be recognized under section 351. However, if it is determined that A in fact made a gift to B, such gift will be subject to tax under section 2501 and following. Similarly, if B had rendered services to A (such services having no relation to the assets transferred or to the business of the corporation) and the disproportion in the amount of stock received constituted the payment of compensation by A to B, B will be taxable upon the fair market value of the 60 shares of stock received as compensation for services rendered, and A will realize gain or loss upon the difference between the basis to him of the 60 shares and their fair market value at the time of the exchange.

Example (2). Individuals C and D each transferred, to a newly organized corporation, property having a fair market value of $4,500 in exchange for the issuance by the corporation of 45 shares of its capital stock to each transferor. At the same time, the corporation issued to E, an individual, 10 shares of its capital stock in payment for organizational and promotional services rendered by E for the benefit of the corporation. E transferred no property to the corporation. C and D were under no obligation to pay for E's services. No gain or loss is recognized to C or D. E received compensation taxable as ordinary income to the extent of the fair market value of the 10 shares of stock received by him.

* * *

§ 1.351–2 Receipt of property.

(a) If an exchange would be within the provisions of section 351(a) if it were not for the fact that the property received in exchange consists not only of property permitted by such subsection to be received without the recognition of gain, but also of other property or money, then the gain, if any, to the recipient shall be recognized, but in an amount not in excess of the sum of such money and the fair market value of such other property. No loss to the recipient shall be recognized.

* * *

§ 1.354–1 Exchanges of stock and securities in certain reorganizations.

(a) Section 354 provides that under certain circumstances no gain or loss is recognized to a shareholder who surrenders his stock in exchange for other stock or to a security holder who surrenders his securities in exchange for stock. Section 354 also provides that under certain circumstances a security holder may surrender securities and receive securities in the same principal amount or in a lesser principal amount without the recognition of gain or loss to him. The exchanges to which section 354 applies must be pursuant to a plan of reorganization as provided in section 368(a) and the stock and securities surrendered as well as the stock and securities received must be those of a corporation which is a party to the reorganization. Section 354 does not apply to exchanges pursuant to a reorganization described in section 368(a)(1)(D) unless the transferor corporation—

(1) Transfers all or substantially all of its assets to a single corporation, and

(2) Distributes all of its remaining properties (if any) and the stock, securities and other properties received in the exchange to its shareholders or security holders in pursuance of the plan of reorganization. The fact that properties retained by the transferor corporation, or received in exchange for the properties transferred in the reorganization, are used to satisfy existing liabilities not represented by securities and which were incurred in the ordinary course of business before the reorganization does not prevent the application of section 354 to an exchange pursuant to a plan of reorganization defined in section 368(a)(1)(D).

(b) Except as provided in section 354(c) and (d), section 354 is not applicable to an exchange of stock or securities if a greater principal amount of securities is received than the principal amount of securities the recipient surrenders, or if securities are received and the recipient surrenders no securities. See, however, section 356 and regulations pertaining to such section. See also section 306 with respect to the receipt of preferred stock in a transaction to which section 354 is applicable.

* * *

(d) The rules of section 354 may be illustrated by the following examples:

Example (1). Pursuant to a reorganization under section 368(a) to which Corporations T and W are parties, A, a shareholder in Corporation T, surrenders all his common stock in Corporation T in exchange for common stock of Corporation W. No gain or loss is recognized to A.

Example (2). Pursuant to a reorganization under section 368(a) to which Corporations X and Y are parties, B, a shareholder in Corporation X, surrenders all his stock in X for stock and securities in Y. Section 354 does not apply to this exchange. See, however, section 356.

Example (3). C, a shareholder in Corporation Z surrenders all his stock in Corporation Z in exchange for securities in Corporation Z. Whether or not this exchange is in connection with a recapitalization under section 368(a)(1) (E), section 354 does not apply. See, however, section 302.

Example (4). The facts are the same as in Example 3 of this paragraph (d), except that C receives solely rights to acquire stock in Corporation Z. Section 354 does not apply.

(e) Except as provided in § 1.356–6, for purposes of section 354, the term securities includes rights issued by a party to the reorganization to acquire its stock. For purposes of this section and section 356(d)(2)(B), a right to acquire stock has no principal amount. For this purpose, rights to acquire stock has the same meaning as it does under sections 305 and 317(a). Other Internal Revenue Code provisions governing the treatment of rights to acquire stock may also apply to certain exchanges occurring in connection with a reorganization. See, for example, sections 83 and 421 through 424 and the regulations thereunder.

(f) See § 1.356–7(a) and (b) for the treatment of nonqualified preferred stock (as defined in section 351(g)(2)) received in certain exchanges for nonqualified preferred stock or preferred stock. See § 1.356–7(c) for the treatment of preferred stock received in certain exchanges for common or preferred stock described in section 351(g)(2)(C)(i)(II).

§ 1.355–1 Distribution of stock and securities of a controlled corporation.

* * *

(b) Application of section. Section 355 provides for the separation, without recognition of gain or loss to (or the inclusion in income of) the shareholders and security holders, of one or more existing businesses formerly operated, directly or indirectly, by a single corporation (the "distributing corporation"). It applies only to the separation of existing businesses that have been in active operation for at least five years (or a business that has been in active operation for at least five years into separate businesses), and which, in general, have been owned, directly or indirectly, for at least five years by the distributing corporation. A separation is achieved through the distribution by the distributing corporation of stock, or stock and securities, of one or more subsidiaries (the "controlled corporations") to its shareholders with respect to its stock or to its security holders in exchange for its securities.

The controlled corporations may be preexisting or newly created subsidiaries. Throughout the regulations under section 355, the term "distribution" refers to a distribution by the distributing corporation of stock, or stock and securities, of one or more controlled corporations, unless the context indicates otherwise. Section 355 contemplates the continued operation of the business or businesses existing prior to the separation. See § 1.355–4 for types of distributions that may qualify under section 355, including pro rata distributions and non pro rata distributions.

(c) Stock rights. Except as provided in § 1.356–6, for purposes of section 355, the term securities includes rights issued by the distributing corporation or the controlled corporation to acquire the stock of that corporation. For purposes of this section and section 356(d)(2)(B), a right to acquire stock has no principal amount. For this purpose, rights to acquire stock has the same meaning as it does under sections 305 and 317(a). Other Internal Revenue Code provisions governing the treatment of rights to acquire stock may also apply to certain distributions occurring in connection with a transaction described in section 355. See, for example, sections 83 and 421 through 424 and the regulations thereunder. This paragraph (c) applies to distributions occurring on or after March 9, 1998.

(d) Nonqualified preferred stock. See § 1.356–7(a) and (b) for the treatment of nonqualified preferred stock (as defined in section 351(g)(2)) received in certain exchanges for (or in certain distributions with respect to) nonqualified preferred stock or preferred stock. See § 1.356–7(c) for the treatment of the receipt of preferred stock in certain exchanges for (or in certain distributions with respect to) common or preferred stock described in section 351(g)(2)(C)(i)(II).

§ 1.355–2 Limitations.

(a) Property distributed. Section 355 applies to a distribution only if the property dis-

tributed consists solely of stock, or stock and securities, of a controlled corporation. If additional property (including an excess principal amount of securities received over securities surrendered) is received, see section 356.

(b) Independent business purpose—(1) Independent business purpose requirement. Section 355 applies to a transaction only if it is carried out for one or more corporate business purposes. A transaction is carried out for a corporate business purpose if it is motivated, in whole or substantial part, by one or more corporate business purposes. The potential for the avoidance of Federal taxes by the distributing or controlled corporations (or a corporation controlled by either) is relevant in determining the extent to which an existing corporate business purpose motivated the distribution. The principal reason for this business purpose requirement is to provide nonrecognition treatment only to distributions that are incident to readjustments of corporate structures required by business exigencies and that effect only readjustments of continuing interests in property under modified corporate forms. This business purpose requirement is independent of the other requirements under section 355.

(2) Corporate business purpose. A corporate business purpose is a real and substantial non Federal tax purpose germane to the business of the distributing corporation, the controlled corporation, or the affiliated group (as defined in § 1.355–3(b)(4)(iv)) to which the distributing corporation belongs. A purpose of reducing non Federal taxes is not a corporate business purpose if (i) the transaction will effect a reduction in both Federal and non Federal taxes because of similarities between Federal tax law and the tax law of the other jurisdiction and (ii) the reduction of Federal taxes is greater than or substantially coextensive with the reduction of non Federal taxes. See examples (7) and (8) of paragraph (b)(5) of this section. A shareholder purpose (for example, the personal planning purposes of a shareholder) is not a corporate business purpose. Depending upon the facts of a particular case, however, a shareholder purpose for a transaction may be so nearly coextensive with a corporate business purpose as to preclude any distinction between them. In such a case, the transaction is carried out for one or more corporate business purposes. See example (2) of paragraph (b)(5) of this section.

(3) **Business purpose for distribution.** The distribution must be carried out for one or more corporate business purposes. See example (3) of paragraph (b)(5) of this section. If a corporate business purpose can be achieved through a nontaxable transaction that does not involve the distribution of stock of a controlled corporation and which is neither impractical nor unduly expensive, then, for purposes of paragraph (b)(1) of this section, the separation is not carried out for that corporate business purpose. See examples (3) and (4) of paragraph (b)(5) of this section. For rules with respect to the requirement of a business purpose for a transfer of assets to a controlled corporation in connection with a reorganization described in section 368(a)(1)(D), See § 1.368–1(b).

(4) **Business purpose as evidence of non-device.** The corporate business purpose or purposes for a transaction are evidence that the transaction was not used principally as a device for the distribution of earnings and profits within the meaning of section 355(a)(1)(B). See paragraph (d)(3)(ii) of this section.

(5) **Examples.** The provisions of this paragraph (b) may be illustrated by the following examples:

Example (1). Corporation X is engaged in the production, transportation, and refining of petroleum products. In 1985, X acquires all of the properties of corporation Z, which is also engaged in the production, transportation, and refining of petroleum products. In 1991, as a result of antitrust litigation, X is ordered to divest itself of all of the properties acquired from Z. X transfers those properties to new corporation Y and distributes the stock of Y pro rata to X's shareholders. In view of the divestiture

order, the distribution is carried out for a corporate business purpose. See paragraph (b)(1) of this section.

Example (2). Corporation X is engaged in two businesses: The manufacture and sale of furniture and the sale of jewelry. The businesses are of equal value. The outstanding stock of X is owned equally by unrelated individuals A and B. A is more interested in the furniture business, while B is more interested in the jewelry business. A and B decide to split up the businesses and go their separate ways. A and B anticipate that the operations of each business will be enhanced by the separation because each shareholder will be able to devote his undivided attention to the business in which he is more interested and more proficient. Accordingly, X transfers the jewelry business to new corporation Y and distributes the stock of Y to B in exchange for all of B's stock in X. The distribution is carried out for a corporate business purpose, notwithstanding that it is also carried out in part for shareholder purposes. See paragraph (b)(2) of this section.

Example (3). Corporation X is engaged in the manufacture and sale of toys and the manufacture and sale of candy. The shareholders of X wish to protect the candy business from the risks and vicissitudes of the toy business. Accordingly, X transfers the toy business to new corporation Y and distributes the stock of Y to X's shareholders. Under applicable law, the purpose of protecting the candy business from the risks and vicissitudes of the toy business is achieved as soon as X transfers the toy business to Y. Therefore, the distribution is not carried out for a corporate business purpose. See paragraph (b)(3) of this section.

Example (4). Corporation X is engaged in a regulated business in State T. X owns all of the stock of corporation Y, a profitable corporation that is not engaged in a regulated business. Commission C sets the rates that X may charge its customers, based on its total income. C has recently adopted rules according to which the total income of a corporation includes the income of a business if, and only if, the business is operated, directly or indirectly, by the corporation. Total income, for this purpose, includes the income of a wholly owned subsidiary corporation but does not include the income of a parent or "brother/sister" corporation. Under C's new rule, X's total income includes the income of Y, with the result that X has suffered a reduction of the rates that it may charge its customers. It would not be impractical or unduly expensive to create in a nontaxable transaction (such as a transaction qualifying under section 351) a holding company to hold the stock of X and Y. X distributes the stock of Y to X's shareholders. The distribution is not carried out for the purpose of increasing the rates that X may charge its customers because that purpose could be achieved through a nontaxable transaction, the creation of a holding company, that does not involve the distribution of stock of a controlled corporation and which is neither impractical nor unduly expensive. See paragraph (b)(3) of this section.

Example (5). The facts are the same as in example (4), except that C has recently adopted rules according to which the total income of a corporation includes not only the income included in example (3), but also the income of any member of the affiliated group to which the corporation belongs. In order to avoid a reduction in the rates that it may charge its customers, X distributes the stock of Y to X's shareholders. The distribution is carried out for a corporate business purpose. See paragraph (b)(3) of this section.

Example (6). (i) Corporation X owns all of the one class of stock of corporation Y. X distributes the stock of Y pro rata to its five shareholders, all of whom are individuals, for the sole purpose of enabling X and/or Y to elect to become an S corporation. The distribution does not meet the corporate business purpose requirement. See paragraph (b)(1) and (2) of this section.

(ii) The facts are the same as in Example 6(i), except that the business of Y is operated

as a division of X. X transfers this division to new corporation Y and distributes the stock of Y pro rata to its shareholders, all of whom are individuals, for the sole purpose of enabling X and/or Y to elect to become an S corporation. The distribution does not meet the corporate business purpose requirement. See paragraph (b)(1) and (2) of this section.

Example (7). The facts are the same as in example (6)(i), except that the distribution is made to enable X to elect to become an S corporation both for Federal tax purposes and for purposes of the income tax imposed by State M. State M has tax law provisions similar to subchapter S of the Internal Revenue Code of 1986. An election to be an S corporation for Federal tax purposes will effect a substantial reduction in Federal taxes that is greater than the reduction of State M taxes pursuant to an election to be an S corporation for State M purposes. The purpose of reducing State M taxes is not a corporate business purpose. The distribution does not meet the corporate business purpose requirements. See paragraph (b)(1) and (2) of this section.

Example (8). The facts are the same as Example (7), except that the distribution also is made to enable A, a key employee of Y, to acquire stock of Y without investing in X. A is considered to be critical to the success of Y and he has indicated that he will seriously consider leaving the company if he is not given the opportunity to purchase a significant amount of stock of Y. As a matter of state law, Y could not issue stock to the employee while it was a subsidiary of X. As in Example (7), the purpose of reducing State M taxes is not a corporate business purpose. In order to determine whether the issuance of stock to the key employee, in fact, motivated the distribution of the Y stock, the potential avoidance of Federal taxes is a relevant factor to take into account. If the facts and circumstances establish that the distribution was substantially motivated by the need to issue stock to the employee, the distribution will meet the corporate business purpose requirement.

(c) Continuity of interest requirement—(1) Requirement. Section 355 applies to a separation that effects only a readjustment of continuing interests in the property of the distributing and controlled corporations. In this regard section 355 requires that one or more persons who, directly or indirectly, were the owners of the enterprise prior to the distribution or exchange own, in the aggregate, an amount of stock establishing a continuity of interest in each of the modified corporate forms in which the enterprise is conducted after the separation. This continuity of interest requirement is independent of the other requirements under section 355.

(2) Examples.

Example (1). For more than five years, corporation X has been engaged directly in one business, and indirectly in a different business through its wholly owned subsidiary, S. The businesses are equal in value. At all times, the outstanding stock of X has been owned equally by unrelated individuals A and B. For valid business reasons, A and B cause X to distribute all of the stock of S to B in exchange for all of B's stock in X. After the transaction, A owns all the stock of X and B owns all the stock of S. The continuity of interest requirement is met because one or more persons who were the owners of X prior to the distribution (A and B) own, in the aggregate, an amount of stock establishing a continuity of interest in each of X and S after the distribution.

Example (2). Assume the same facts as in Example (1), except that pursuant to a plan to acquire a stock interest in X without acquiring, directly or indirectly, an interest in S, C purchased one-half of the X stock owned by A and immediately thereafter X distributed all of the S stock to B in exchange for all of B's stock in X. After the transactions, A owns 50 percent of X and B owns 100 percent of S. The distribution by X of all of the stock of S to B in exchange for all of B's stock in X will sat-

isfy the continuity of interest requirement for section 355 because one or more persons who were the owners of X prior to the distribution (A and B) own, in the aggregate, an amount of stock establishing a continuity of interest in each of X and S after the distribution.

Example (3). Assume the same facts as in Examples (1) and (2), except that C purchased all of the X stock owned by A. After the transactions, neither A nor B own any of the stock of X, and B owns all the stock of S. The continuity of interest requirement is not met because the owners of X prior to the distribution (A and B) do not, in the aggregate, own an amount of stock establishing a continuity of interest in each of X and S after the distribution, i.e., although A and B collectively have retained 50 percent of their equity interest in the former combined enterprise, they have failed to continue to own the minimum stock interest in the distributing corporation, X, that would be required in order to meet the continuity of interest requirement.

Example (4). Assume the same facts as in Examples (1) and (2), except that C purchased 80 percent of the X stock owned by A. After the transactions, A owns 20 percent of the stock of X, B owns no X stock, and B owns 100 percent of the S stock. The continuity of interest requirement is not met because the owners of X prior to the distribution (A and B) do not, in the aggregate, have a continuity of interest in each of X and S after the distribution, i.e., although A and B collectively have retained 60 percent of their equity interest in the former combined enterprise, the 20 percent interest of A in X is less than the minimum equity interest in the distributing corporation, X, that would be required in order to meet the continuity of interest requirement.

(d) Device for distribution of earnings and profits—(1) In general. Section 355 does not apply to a transaction used principally as a device for the distribution of the earnings and profits of the distributing corporation, the controlled corporation, or both (a "device").

Section 355 recognizes that a tax-free distribution of the stock of a controlled corporation presents a potential for tax avoidance by facilitating the avoidance of the dividend provisions of the Code through the subsequent sale or exchange of stock of one corporation and the retention of the stock of another corporation. A device can include a transaction that effects a recovery of basis. In this paragraph (d), "exchange" includes transactions, such as redemptions, treated as exchanges under the Code. Generally, the determination of whether a transaction was used principally as a device will be made from all of the facts and circumstances, including, but not limited to, the presence of the device factors specified in paragraph (d)(2) of this section ("evidence of device"), and the presence of the nondevice factors specified in paragraph (d)(3) of this section ("evidence of nondevice"). However, if a transaction is specified in paragraph (d)(5) of this section, then it is ordinarily considered not to have been used principally as a device.

(2) **Device factors—(i) In general.** The presence of any of the device factors specified in this subparagraph (2) is evidence of device. The strength of this evidence depends on the facts and circumstances.

(ii) **Pro rata distribution.** A distribution that is pro rata or substantially pro rata among the shareholders of the distributing corporation presents the greatest potential for the avoidance of the dividend provisions of the Code and, in contrast to other types of distributions, is more likely to be used principally as a device. Accordingly, the fact that a distribution is pro rata or substantially pro rata is evidence of device.

(iii) **Subsequent sale or exchange of stock—(A) In general.** A sale or exchange of stock of the distributing or the controlled corporation after the distribution (a "subsequent sale or exchange") is evidence of device. Generally, the greater the percentage of the stock sold or exchanged after the distribution, the stronger the evidence of device. In addition,

the shorter the period of time between the distribution and the sale or exchange, the stronger the evidence of device.

(B) **Sale or exchange negotiated or agreed upon before the distribution.** A subsequent sale or exchange pursuant to an arrangement negotiated or agreed upon before the distribution is substantial evidence of device.

(C) **Sale or exchange not negotiated or agreed upon before the distribution.** A subsequent sale or exchange not pursuant to an arrangement negotiated or agreed upon before the distribution is evidence of device.

(D) **Negotiated or agreed upon before the distribution.** For purposes of this subparagraph (2), a sale or exchange is always pursuant to an arrangement negotiated or agreed upon before the distribution if enforceable rights to buy or sell existed before the distribution. If a sale or exchange was discussed by the buyer and the seller before the distribution and was reasonably to be anticipated by both parties, then the sale or exchange will ordinarily be considered to be pursuant to an arrangement negotiated or agreed upon before the distribution.

(E) **Exchange in pursuance of a plan of reorganization.** For purposes of this subparagraph (2), if stock is exchanged for stock in pursuance of a plan of reorganization, and either no gain or loss or only an insubstantial amount of gain is recognized on the exchange, then the exchange is not treated as a subsequent sale or exchange, but the stock received in the exchange is treated as the stock surrendered in the exchange. For this purpose, gain treated as a dividend pursuant to sections 356(a)(2) and 316 shall be disregarded.

(iv) **Nature and use of assets—(A) In general.** The determination of whether a transaction was used principally as a device will take into account the nature, kind, amount, and use of the assets of the distributing and the controlled corporations (and corporations controlled by them) immediately after the transaction.

(B) Assets not used in a trade or business meeting the requirement of section 355(b). The existence of assets that are not used in a trade or business that satisfies the requirements of section 355(b) is evidence of device. For this purpose, assets that are not used in a trade or business that satisfies the requirements of section 355(b) include, but are not limited to, cash and other liquid assets that are not related to the reasonable needs of a business satisfying such section. The strength of the evidence of device depends on all the facts and circumstances, including, but not limited to, the ratio for each corporation of the value of assets not used in a trade or business that satisfies the requirements of section 355(b) to the value of its business that satisfies such requirements. A difference in the ratio described in the preceding sentence for the distributing and controlled corporation is ordinarily not evidence of device if the distribution is not pro rata among the shareholders of the distributing corporation and such difference is attributable to a need to equalize the value of the stock distributed and the value of the stock or securities exchanged by the distributees.

(C) Related function. There is evidence of device if a business of either the distributing or controlled corporation (or a corporation controlled by it) is (1) a "secondary business" that continues as a secondary business for a significant period after the separation, and (2) can be sold without adversely affecting the business of the other corporation (or a corporation controlled by it). A secondary business is a business of either the distributing or controlled corporation, if its principal function is to serve the business of the other corporation (or a corporation controlled by it). A secondary business can include a business transferred to a newly-created subsidiary or a business which serves a business transferred to a newly-created subsidiary. The activities of the secondary business may consist of providing property

or performing services. Thus, in example (11) of § 1.355–3(c), evidence of device would be presented if the principal function of the coal mine (satisfying the requirements of the steel business) continued after the separation and the coal mine could be sold without adversely affecting the steel business. Similarly, in example (10) of § 1.355–3(c), evidence of device would be presented if the principal function of the sales operation after the separation is to sell the output from the manufacturing operation and the sales operation could be sold without adversely affecting the manufacturing operation.

(3) Nondevice factors—(i) In general. The presence of any of the nondevice factors specified in this subparagraph (3) is evidence of nondevice. The strength of this evidence depends on all of the facts and circumstances.

(ii) Corporate business purpose. The corporate business purpose for the transaction is evidence of nondevice. The stronger the evidence of device (such as the presence of the device factors specified in paragraph (d)(2) of this section), the stronger the corporate business purpose required to prevent the determination that the transaction was used principally as a device. Evidence of device presented by the transfer or retention of assets not used in a trade or business that satisfies the requirements of section 355(b) can be outweighed by the existence of a corporate business purpose for those transfers or retentions. The assessment of the strength of a corporate business purpose will be based on all of the facts and circumstances, including, but not limited to, the following factors:

(A) The importance of achieving the purpose to the success of the business;

(B) The extent to which the transaction is prompted by a person not having a proprietary interest in either corporation, or by other outside factors beyond the control of the distributing corporation; and

(C) The immediacy of the conditions prompting the transaction.

(iii) Distributing corporation publicly traded and widely held. The fact that the distributing corporation is publicly traded and has no shareholder who is directly or indirectly the beneficial owner of more than five percent of any class of stock is evidence of nondevice.

(iv) Distribution to domestic corporate shareholders. The fact that the stock of the controlled corporation is distributed to one or more domestic corporations that, if section 355 did not apply, would be entitled to a deduction under section 243(a)(1) available to corporations meeting the stock ownership requirements of section 243(c), or a deduction under section 243(a)(2) or (3) or 245(b) is evidence of nondevice.

(4) Examples. The provisions of paragraph (d)(1) through (3) of this section may be illustrated by the following examples:

Example (1). Individual A owns all of the stock of corporation X, which is engaged in the warehousing business. X owns all of the stock of corporation Y, which is engaged in the transportation business. X employs individual B, who is extremely knowledgeable of the warehousing business in general and the operations of X in particular. B has informed A that he will seriously consider leaving the company if he is not given the opportunity to purchase a significant amount of stock of X. Because of his knowledge and experience, the loss of B would seriously damage the business of X. B cannot afford to purchase any significant amount of stock of X as long as X owns Y. Accordingly, X distributes the stock of Y to A and A subsequently sells a portion of his X stock to B. However, X could have issued additional shares to B sufficient to give B an equivalent ownership interest in X. There is no other evidence of device or evidence of nondevice. In light of the fact that X could have issued additional shares to B, the sale of X stock by A is substantial evidence of device. The transaction is considered to have been used principally as a device. See paragraph (d)(1), (2)(ii), (iii)(A), (B), and (D), and (3)(i) and (ii) of this section.

Example (2). Corporation X owns and operates a fast food restaurant in State M and owns all of the stock of corporation Y, which owns and operates a fast food restaurant in State N. X and Y operate their businesses under franchises granted by D and E, respectively. X owns cash and marketable securities that exceed the reasonable needs of its business but whose value is small relative to the value of its business. E has recently changed its franchise policy and will no longer grant or renew franchises to subsidiaries (or other members of the same affiliated group) of corporations operating businesses under franchises granted by its competitors. Thus, Y will lose its franchise if it remains a subsidiary of X. The franchise is about to expire. Accordingly, X distributes the stock of Y pro rata among X's shareholders. X retains its business and transfers cash and marketable securities to Y in an amount proportional to the value of Y's business. There is no other evidence of device or evidence of nondevice. The transfer by X to Y and the retention by X of cash and marketable securities is relatively weak evidence of device because after the transfer X and Y hold cash and marketable securities in amounts proportional to the values of their businesses. The fact that the distribution is pro rata is evidence of device. A strong corporate business purpose is relatively strong evidence of nondevice. Accordingly, the transaction is considered not to have been used principally as a device. See paragraph (d)(1), (2)(ii), (iv)(A) and (B), and (3)(i) and (ii)(A), (B), and (C) of this section.

Example (3). Corporation X is engaged in a regulated business in State M and owns all of the stock of corporation Y, which is not engaged in a regulated business in State M. State M has recently amended its laws to provide that affiliated corporations operating in M may not conduct both regulated and unregulated businesses. X transfers cash not related to the reasonable needs of the business of X or Y to Y and then distributes the stock of Y pro rata among X's shareholders. As a result of the transfer of cash, the ratio of the value of its assets not used in a trade or business that satisfies the requirements of section 355(b) to the value of its business is substantially greater for Y than for X. There is no other evidence of device or evidence of nondevice. The transfer of cash by X to Y is relatively strong evidence of device because after the transfer Y holds disproportionately many assets that are not used in a trade or business that satisfies the requirements of section 355(b). The fact that the distribution is pro rata is evidence of device. The strong business purpose is relatively strong evidence of nondevice, but it does not pertain to the transfer. Accordingly, the transaction is considered to have been used principally as a device. See paragraph (d)(1), (2)(ii), (iv)(A) and (B), and (3) and (i) and (ii) of this section.

Example (4). The facts are the same as in example (3), except that, instead of transferring cash to Y, X purchases operating assets unrelated to the business of Y and transfers them to Y prior to the distribution. There is no other evidence of device or evidence of nondevice. The transaction is considered to have been used principally as a device. See paragraph (d)(1), (2)(ii), (iv)(A) and (B), and (3)(i) and (ii) of this section.

(5) Transactions ordinarily not considered as a device—(i) In general. This subparagraph (5) specifies three distributions that ordinarily do not present the potential for tax avoidance described in paragraph (d)(1) of this section. Accordingly, such distributions are ordinarily considered not to have been used principally as a device, notwithstanding the presence of any of the device factors described in paragraph (d)(2) of this section. A transaction described in paragraph (d)(5)(iii) or (iv) of this section is not protected by this subparagraph (5) from a determination that it was used principally as a device if it involves the distribution of the stock of more than one controlled corporation and facilitates the avoidance of the

dividend provisions of the Code through the subsequent sale or exchange of stock of one corporation and the retention of the stock of another corporation.

(ii) Absence of earnings and profits. A distribution is ordinarily considered not to have been used principally as a device if—

(A) The distributing and controlled corporations have no accumulated earnings and profits at the beginning of their respective taxable years,

(B) The distributing and controlled corporations have no current earnings and profits as of the date of the distribution, and

(C) No distribution of property by the distributing corporation immediately before the separation would require recognition of gain resulting in current earnings and profits for the taxable year of the distribution.

(iii) Section 303(a) transactions. A distribution is ordinarily considered not to have been used principally as a device if, in the absence of section 355, with respect to each shareholder distributee, the distribution would be a redemption to which section 303(a) applied.

(iv) Section 302(a) transactions. A distribution is ordinarily considered not to have been used principally as a device if, in the absence of section 355, with respect to each shareholder distributee, the distribution would be a redemption to which section 302(a) applied. For purposes of the preceding sentence, section 302(c)(2)(A)(ii) and (iii) shall not apply.

(v) Examples. The provisions of this subparagraph (5) may be illustrated by the following examples:

Example (1). The facts are the same as in example (3) of paragraph (d)(4) of this section, except that X and Y had no accumulated earnings and profits at the beginning of its taxable year, X and Y have no current earnings and profits as of the date of the distribution, and no distribution of property by X immediately before the separation would require recognition of gain that would result in earnings and profits for the taxable year of the distribution. The transaction is considered not to have been used principally as a device. See paragraph (d)(5)(i) and (ii) of this section.

Example (2). Corporation X is engaged in three businesses: a hotel business, a restaurant business, and a rental real estate business. Individuals A, B, and C own all of the stock of X. X transfers the restaurant business to new corporation Y and transfers the rental real estate business to new corporation Z. X then distributes the stock of Y and Z pro rata between B and C in exchange for all of their stock in X. In the absence of section 355, the distribution would be a redemption to which section 302(a) applied. Since this distribution involves the stock of more than one controlled corporation and facilitates the avoidance of the dividend provisions of the Code through the subsequent sale or exchange of stock in one corporation and the retention of the stock of another corporation, it is not protected by paragraph (d)(5)(i) and (iv) of this section from a determination that it was used principally as a device. Thus, the determination of whether the transaction was used principally as a device must be made from all the facts and circumstances, including the presence of the device factors and nondevice factors specified in paragraph (d)(2) and (3) of this section.

(e) Stock and securities distributed—(1) In general. Section 355 applies to a distribution only if the distributing corporation distributes—

(i) All of the stock and securities of the controlled corporation that it owns, or

(ii) At least an amount of the stock of the controlled corporation that constitutes control as defined in section 368(c). In such a case, all, or any part, of the securities of the controlled corporation may be distributed, and paragraph (e)(2) of this section shall apply.

(2) Additional rules. Where a part of either the stock or the securities of the controlled corporation is retained under paragraph (e)(1)(ii) of this section, it must be established to the satisfaction of the Commissioner that the retention by the distributing corporation was not in pursuance of a plan having as one of its principal purposes the avoidance of Federal income tax. Ordinarily, the corporate business purpose or purposes for the distribution will require the distribution of all of the stock and securities of the controlled corporation. If the distribution of all of the stock and securities of a controlled corporation would be treated to any extent as a distribution of "other property" under section 356, this fact tends to establish that the retention of stock or securities is in pursuance of a plan having as one of its principal purposes the avoidance of Federal income tax.

(f) Principal amount of securities—(1) Securities received. Section 355 does not apply to a distribution if, with respect to any shareholder or security holder, the principal amount of securities received exceeds the principal amount of securities surrendered, or securities are received but no securities are surrendered. In such cases, see section 356.

(2) Only stock received. If only stock is received in a distribution to which section 355(a)(1)(A) applies, the principal amount of the securities surrendered, if any, and the par value or stated value of the stock surrendered, if any, are not relevant to the application of that section.

(g) [Reserved]. For further guidance see § 1.355–2T(g).

(2) Example. Paragraph (g)(1) of this section may be illustrated by the following example:

(g) Recently acquired controlled stock under section 355(a)(3)(B)—(1) Other property. Except as provided in paragraph (g)(2) of this section, for purposes of section 355(a)(1)(A), section 355(c), and so much of section 356 as relates to section 355, stock of a controlled corporation acquired by the DSAG in a taxable transaction (as defined in paragraph (g)(4) of this section) within the five-year period ending on the date of the distribution (pre-distribution period) shall not be treated as stock of the controlled corporation but shall be treated as "other property." Transfers of controlled corporation stock that is owned by the DSAG immediately before and immediately after the transfer are disregarded and are not acquisitions for purposes of this paragraph (g)(1).

(2) Exceptions. Paragraph (g)(1) of this section does not apply to an acquisition of stock of the controlled corporation—

(i) If the controlled corporation is a DSAG member at any time after the acquisition (but prior to the distribution); or

(ii) Described in § 1.355–3(b)(4)(iii).

(3) DSAG. For purposes of this paragraph (g), a DSAG is the distributing corporation's separate affiliated group (the affiliated group which would be determined under section 1504(a) if such corporation werc the common parent and section 1504(b) did not apply) that consists of the distributing corporation as the common parent and all corporations affiliated with the distributing corporation through stock ownership described in section 1504(a)(1)(B) (regardless of whether the corporations are includible corporations under section 1504(b)). For purposes of paragraph (g)(1) of this section, any reference to the DSAG is a reference to the distributing corporation if it is not the common parent of a separate affiliated group.

(4) Taxable transaction—(i) Generally. For purposes of this paragraph (g), a taxable transaction is a transaction in which gain or loss was recognized in whole or in part.

(ii) Dunn Trust and predecessor issues. [Reserved].

(5) Examples. The following examples illustrate this paragraph (g). Assume that C, D, P, and S are corporations, X is an unrelated individual, each of the transactions is unrelated

to any other transaction and, but for the issue of whether C stock is treated as "other property" under section 355(a)(3)(B), the distributions satisfy all of the requirements of section 355. No inference should be drawn from any of these examples as to whether any requirements of section 355 other than section 355(a)(3)(B), as specified, are satisfied. Furthermore, the following definitions apply:

(i) Purchase is an acquisition that is a taxable transaction.

(ii) Section 368(c) stock is stock constituting control within the meaning of section 368(c).

(iii) Section 1504(a)(2) stock is stock meeting the requirements of section 1504(a)(2).

Example (1). Hot stock. For more than five years, D has owned section 368(c) stock but not section 1504(a)(2) stock of C. In year 6, D purchases additional C stock from X. However, D does not own section 1504(a)(2) stock of C after the year 6 purchase. If D distributes all of its C stock within five years after the year 6 purchase, for purposes of section 355(a)(1)(A), section 355(c), and so much of section 356 as relates to section 355, the C stock purchased in year 6 would be treated as "other property." See paragraph (g)(1) of this section.

Example (2). C becomes a DSAG member. For more than five years, D has owned section 368(c) stock but not section 1504(a)(2) stock of C. In year 6, D purchases additional C stock from X such that D's total ownership of C is section 1504(a)(2) stock. If D distributes all of its C stock within five years after the year 6 purchase, the distribution of the C stock purchased in year 6 would not be treated as "other property" because C becomes a DSAG member. See paragraph (g)(2)(i) of this section. The result would be the same if D did not own any C stock prior to year 6 and D purchased all of the C stock in year 6. See paragraph (g)(2)(i) of this section. Similarly, if D did not own any C stock prior to year 6, D purchased 20 percent of the C stock in year 6, and then acquired all of the remaining C stock in year 7, the C stock purchased in year 6 and the C stock acquired in year 7 (even if purchased) would not be treated as "other property" because C becomes a DSAG member. See paragraph (g)(2)(i) of this section.

Example (3). Intra-SAG transaction. For more than five years, D has owned all of the stock of S. D and S, in the aggregate, have owned section 368(c) stock but not section 1504(a)(2) stock of C. Therefore, D and S are DSAG members, but C is not. In year 6, D purchases S's C stock. If D distributes all of its C stock within five years after the year 6 purchase, the distribution of the C stock purchased in year 6 would not be treated as "other property." D's purchase of the C stock from S is disregarded for purposes of paragraph (g)(1) of this section because that C stock was owned by the DSAG immediately before and immediately after the purchase. See paragraph (g)(1) of this section.

Example (4). Affiliate exception. For more than five years, P has owned 90 percent of the sole outstanding class of the stock of D and a portion of the stock of C, and X has owned the remaining 10 percent of the D stock. Throughout this period, D has owned section 368(c) stock but not section 1504(a)(2) stock of C. In year 6, D purchases P's C stock. However, D does not own section 1504(a)(2) stock of C after the year 6 purchase. If D distributes all of its C stock to X in exchange for X's D stock within five years after the year 6 purchase, the distribution of the C stock purchased in year 6 would not be treated as "other property" because the C stock was purchased from a member (P) of the affiliated group (as defined in § 1.355–3(b)(4)(iv)) of which D is a member, and P did not purchase that C stock within the pre-distribution period. See paragraph (g)(2)(ii) of this section.

(h) Active conduct of a trade or business. Section 355 applies to a distribution only if the requirements of § 1.355–3 (relating to the active conduct of a trade or business) are satisfied.

(i) Effective/applicability date. Paragraphs (g)(1) through (g)(5) of this section apply to distributions occurring after October 20, 2011. * * *

§ 1.355–3 Active conduct of a trade or business.

(a) General requirements—(1) Application of section 355. Under section 355(b)(1), a distribution of stock, or stock and securities, of a controlled corporation qualifies under section 355 only if—

(i) The distributing and the controlled corporations are each engaged in the active conduct of a trade or business immediately after the distribution (section 355(b)(1)(A)), or

(ii) Immediately before the distribution, the distributing corporation had no assets other than stock or securities of the controlled corporations, and each of the controlled corporations is engaged in the active conduct of a trade or business immediately after the distribution (section 355(b)(1)(B)). A de minimis amount of assets held by the distributing corporation shall be disregarded for purposes of this paragraph (a)(1)(ii).

(2) Examples. Paragraph (a)(1) of this section may be illustrated by the following examples:

Example (1). Prior to the distribution, corporation X is engaged in the active conduct of a trade or business and owns all of the stock of corporation Y, which also is engaged in the active conduct of a trade or business. X distributes all of the stock of Y to X's shareholders, and each corporation continues the active conduct of its trade or business. The active business requirement of section 355(b)(1)(A) is satisfied.

Example (2). The facts are the same as in example (1), except that X transfers all of its assets other than the stock of Y to a new corporation in exchange for all of the stock of the new corporation and then distributes the stock of both controlled corporations to X's shareholders. The active business requirement of section 355(b)(1)(B) is satisfied.

(b) Active conduct of a trade or business defined—(1) In general. Section 355(b)(2) provides rules for determining whether a corporation is treated as engaged in the active conduct of a trade or business for purposes of section 355(b)(1). Under section 355(b)(2)(A), a corporation is treated as engaged in the active conduct of a trade or business if it is itself engaged in the active conduct of a trade or business or if substantially all of its assets consist of the stock, or stock and securities, of a corporation or corporations controlled by it (immediately after the distribution) each of which is engaged in the active conduct of a trade or business.

(2) Active conduct of a trade or business immediately after distribution—(i) In general. For purposes of section 355(b), a corporation shall be treated as engaged in the "active conduct of a trade or business" immediately after the distribution if the assets and activities of the corporation satisfy the requirements and limitations described in paragraph (b)(2)(ii), (iii), and (iv) of this section.

(ii) Trade or business. A corporation shall be treated as engaged in a trade or business immediately after the distribution if a specific group of activities are being carried on by the corporation for the purpose of earning income or profit, and the activities included in such group include every operation that forms a part of, or a step in, the process of earning income or profit. Such group of activities ordinarily must include the collection of income and the payment of expenses.

(iii) Active conduct. For purposes of section 355(b), the determination whether a trade or business is actively conducted will be made from all of the facts and circumstances. Generally, the corporation is required itself to perform active and substantial management and operational functions. Generally, activi-

ties performed by the corporation itself do not include activities performed by persons outside the corporation, including independent contractors. A corporation may satisfy the requirements of this subdivision (iii) through the activities that it performs itself, even though some of its activities are performed by others. Separations of real property all or substantially all of which is occupied prior to the distribution by the distributing or the controlled corporation (or by any corporation controlled directly or indirectly by either of those corporations) will be carefully scrutinized with respect to the requirements of section 355(b) and this § 1.355–3.

(iv) Limitations. The active conduct of a trade or business does not include—

(A) The holding for investment purposes of stock, securities, land, or other property, or

(B) The ownership and operation (including leasing) of real or personal property used in a trade or business, unless the owner performs significant services with respect to the operation and management of the property.

(3) Active conduct for five-year period preceding distribution. Under section 355(b)(2)(B), a trade or business that is relied upon to meet the requirements of section 355(b) must have been actively conducted throughout the five-year period ending on the date of the distribution. For purposes of this subparagraph (3)—

(i) Activities which constitute a trade or business under the tests described in paragraph (b)(2) of this section shall be treated as meeting the requirement of the preceding sentence if such activities were actively conducted throughout the 5-year period ending on the date of distribution, and

(ii) The fact that a trade or business underwent change during the five-year period preceding the distribution (for example, by the addition of new or the dropping of old products, changes in production capacity, and the like) shall be disregarded, provided that the changes are not of such a character as to constitute the acquisition of a new or different business. In particular, if a corporation engaged in the active conduct of one trade or business during that five-year period purchased, created, or otherwise acquired another trade or business in the same line of business, then the acquisition of that other business is ordinarily treated as an expansion of the original business, all of which is treated as having been actively conducted during that five-year period, unless that purchase, creation, or other acquisition effects a change of such a character as to constitute the acquisition of a new or different business.

* * *

(c) **Examples.** The following examples illustrate section 355(b)(2)(A) and (B) and paragraph (b)(1), (2), and (3) of this section. However, a transaction that satisfies these active business requirements will qualify under section 355 only if it satisfies the other requirements of section 355(a) and (b).

Example (1). Corporation X is engaged in the manufacture and sale of soap and detergents and also owns investment securities. X transfers the investment securities to new subsidiary Y and distributes the stocks of Y to X's sharcholders. Y does not satisfy the requirements of section 355(b) because the holding of investment securities does not constitute the active conduct of a trade or business. See paragraph (b)(2)(iv)(A) of this section.

Example (2). Corporation X owns, manages, and derives rental income from an office building and also owns vacant land. X transfers the land to new subsidiary Y and distributes the stock of Y to X's shareholders. Y will subdivide the land, install streets and utilities, and sell the developed lots to various homebuilders. Y does not satisfy the requirements of section 355(b) because no significant development activities were conducted with respect to the land during the five-year period ending on the date of the distribution. See paragraph (b)(3) of this section.

Example (3). Corporation X owns land on which it conducts a ranching business. Oil has been discovered in the area, and it is apparent that oil may be found under the land on which the ranching business is conducted. X has engaged in no significant activities in connection with its mineral rights. X transfers its mineral rights to new subsidiary Y and distributes the stock of Y to X's shareholders. Y will actively pursue the development of the oil producing potential of the property. Y does not satisfy the requirements of section 355(b) because X engaged in no significant exploitation activities with respect to the mineral rights during the five-year period ending on the date of the distribution. See paragraph (b)(3) of this section.

Example (4). For more than five years, corporation X has conducted a single business of constructing sewage disposal plants and other facilities. X transfers one-half of its assets to new subsidiary Y. These assets include a contract for the construction of a sewage disposal plant in State M, construction equipment, cash, and other tangible assets. X retains a contract for the construction of a sewage disposal plant in State N, construction equipment, cash, and other intangible assets. X then distributes the stock of Y to one of X's shareholders in exchange for all of his stock of X. X and Y both satisfy the requirements of section 355(b). See paragraph (b)(3)(i) of this section.

Example (5). For the past six years, corporation X has owned and operated two factories devoted to the production of edible pork skins. The entire output of one factory is sold to one customer, C, while the output of the second factory is sold to C and a number of other customers. To eliminate errors in packaging, X opens a new factory. Thereafter, orders from C are processed and packaged at the two original factories, while the new factory handles only orders from other customers. Eight months after opening the new factory, X transfers it and related business assets to new subsidiary Y and distributes the stock of Y to X's shareholders. X and Y both satisfy the requirements of section 355(b). See paragraph (b)(3)(i) and (ii) of this section.

Example (6). Corporation X has owned and operated a men's retail clothing store in the downtown area of the City of G for nine years and has owned and operated another men's retail clothing store in a suburban area of G for seven years. X transfers the store building, fixtures, inventory, and other assets related to the operations of the suburban store to new subsidiary Y. X also transfers to Y the delivery trucks and delivery personnel that formerly served both stores. Henceforth, X will contract with a local public delivery service to make its deliveries. X retains the warehouses that formerly served both stores. Henceforth, Y will lease warehouse space from an unrelated public warehouse company. X then distributes the stock of Y to X's shareholders. X and Y both satisfy the requirements of section 355(b). See paragraph (b)(3)(i) of this section.

Example (7). For the past nine years, corporation X has owned and operated a department store in the downtown area of the City of G. Three years ago, X acquired a parcel of land in a suburban area of G and constructed a new department store on it. X transfers the suburban store and related business assets to new subsidiary Y and distributes the stock of Y to X's shareholders. After the distribution, each store has its own manager and is operated independently of the other store. X and Y both satisfy the requirements of section 355(b). See paragraph (b)(3)(i) and (ii) of this section.

Example (8). For the past six years, corporation X has owned and operated hardware stores in several states. Two years ago, X purchased all of the assets of a hardware store in State M, where X had not previously conducted business. X transfers the State M store and related business assets to new subsidiary Y and distributes the stock of Y to X's shareholders. After the distribution, the State M store has its own manager and is operated independently of the other stores. X and Y both satisfy the

requirements of section 355(b). See paragraph (b)(3)(i) and (ii) of this section.

Example (9). For the past eight years, corporation X has engaged in the manufacture and sale of household products. Throughout this period, X has maintained a research department for use in connection with its manufacturing activities. The research department has 30 employees actively engaged in the development of new products. X transfers the research department to new subsidiary Y and distributes the stock of Y to X's shareholders. After the distribution, Y continues its research operations on a contractual basis with several corporations, including X. X and Y both satisfy the requirements of section 355(b). See paragraph (b)(3)(i) of this section. The result in this example is the same if, after the distribution, Y continues its research operations but furnishes its services only to X. See paragraph (b)(3)(i) of this section. However, see § 1.355–2(d)(2)(iv)(C) (related function device factor) for possible evidence of device.

Example (10). For the past six years, corporation X has processed and sold meat products. X derives income from no other source. X separates the sales function from the processing function by transferring the business assets related to the sales function and cash for working capital to new subsidiary Y. X then distributes the stock of Y to X's shareholders. After the distribution, Y purchases for resale the meat products processed by X. X and Y both satisfy the requirements of section 355(b). See paragraph (b)(3)(i) of this section. However, see § 1.355–2(d)(2)(iv)(C) (related function device factor) for possible evidence of device.

Example (11). For the past eight years, corporation X has been engaged in the manufacture and sale of steel and steel products. X owns all of the stock of corporation Y, which, for the past six years, has owned and operated a coal mine for the sole purpose of supplying X's coal requirements in the manufacture of steel. X distributes the stock of Y to X's shareholders. X and Y both satisfy the requirements of section 355(b). See paragraph (b)(3)(i) of this section. However, see § 1.355–2(d)(2)(iv)(C) (related function device factor) for possible evidence of device.

Example (12). For the past seven years, corporation X, a bank, has owned an eleven-story office building, the ground floor of which X has occupied in the conduct of its banking business. The remaining ten floors are rented to various tenants. Throughout this seven-year period, the building has been managed and maintained by employees of the bank. X transfers the building to new subsidiary Y and distributes the stock of Y to X's shareholders. Henceforth, Y will manage the building, negotiate leases, seek new tenants, and repair and maintain the building. X and Y both satisfy the requirements of section 355(b). See paragraph (b)(3) of this section.

Example (13). For the past nine years, corporation X, a bank, has owned a two-story building, the ground floor and one half of the second floor of which X has occupied in the conduct of its banking business. The other half of the second floor has been rented as storage space to a neighboring retail merchant. X transfers the building to new subsidiary Y and distributes the stock of Y to X's shareholders. After the distribution, X leases from Y the space in the building that it formerly occupied. Under the lease, X will repair and maintain its portion of the building and pay property taxes and insurance. Y does not satisfy the requirements of section 355(b) because it is not engaged in the active conduct of a trade or business immediately after the distribution. See paragraph (b)(2)(iv)(A) of this section. This example does not address the question of whether the activities of X with respect to the building prior to the separation would constitute the active conduct of a trade or business.

§ 1.355–4 Non pro rata distributions, etc.

Section 355 provides for nonrecognition of gain or loss with respect to a distribution whether or not (a) the distribution is pro rata with respect to all of the shareholders of the distributing corporation, (b) the distribution is pursuant to a plan of reorganization within the meaning of section 368(a)(1)(D), or (c) the shareholder surrenders stock in the distributing corporation. Under section 355, the stock of a controlled corporation may consist of common stock or preferred stock. (See, however, section 306 and the regulations thereunder.) Section 355 does not apply, however, if the substance of a transaction is merely an exchange between shareholders or security holders of stock or securities in one corporation for stock or securities in another corporation. For example, if two individuals, A and B, each own directly 50 percent of the stock of corporation X and 50 percent of the stock of corporation Y, section 355 would not apply to a transaction in which A and B transfer all of their stock of X and Y to a new corporation Z, for all of the stock of Z, and Z then distributes the stock of X to A and the stock of Y to B.

§ 1.355–6 Recognition of gain on certain distributions of stock or securities in controlled corporation.

(a) Conventions—(1) Examples. For purposes of the examples in this section, unless otherwise stated, assume that P, S, T, X, Y, N, HC, D, D1, D2, D3, and C are corporations, A and B are individuals, shareholders are not treated as one person under section 355(d)(7), stock has been owned for more than five years and section 355(d)(6) and paragraph (e)(4) of this section do not apply, no election under section 338 (if available) is made, and all transactions described are respected under general tax principles, including the step transaction doctrine. No inference should be drawn from any example as to whether any requirements of section 355 other than those of section 355(d), as specified, are satisfied.

(2) Five-year period. For purposes of this section, the term five-year period means the five-year period (determined after applying section 355(d)(6) and paragraph (e)(4) of this section) ending on the date of the distribution,

but in no event beginning earlier than October 10, 1990.

(3) Distributing securities. For purposes of determining if stock of any controlled corporation received in the distribution is disqualified stock described in section 355(d)(3)(B)(ii)(II) (relating to a distribution of controlled corporation stock on any securities in the distributing corporation acquired by purchase during the five-year period), references in this section to stock of a corporation that is or becomes a distributing corporation includes securities of the corporation. Similarly, a reference to stock in paragraph (c)(4) of this section (relating to a plan or arrangement) includes securities.

(4) Marketable securities. Unless otherwise stated, any reference in this section to marketable stock includes marketable securities.

(b) General rules and purposes of section 355(d)—(1) Disqualified distributions in general. In the case of a disqualified distribution, any stock or securities in the controlled corporation shall not be treated as qualified property for purposes of section 355(c)(2) or 361(c)(2). In general, a disqualified distribution is any distribution to which section 355 (or so much of section 356 as relates thereto) applies if, immediately after the distribution—

(i) Any person holds disqualified stock in the distributing corporation that constitutes a 50 percent or greater interest in such corporation; or

(ii) Any person holds disqualified stock in the controlled corporation (or, if stock of more than one controlled corporation is distributed, in any controlled corporation) that constitutes a 50 percent or greater interest in such corporation.

(2) Disqualified stock—(i) In general. Disqualified stock is—

(A) Any stock in the distributing corporation acquired by purchase during the five-year period; and

(B) Any stock in any controlled corporation—

(1) Acquired by purchase during the five-year period; or

(2) Received in the distribution to the extent attributable to distributions on any stock in the distributing corporation acquired by purchase during the five-year period.

(ii) Purchase. For the definition of a purchase for purposes of section 355(d) and this section, see section 355(d)(5) and paragraph (d) of this section.

(iii) Exceptions—(A) Purchase eliminated. Stock (or an interest in another entity) that is acquired by purchase (including stock (or another interest) that is treated as acquired by purchase under paragraph (e)(2), (3), or (4) of this section) ceases to be acquired by that purchase if (and when) the basis resulting from the purchase is eliminated. For purposes of this paragraph (b)(2)(iii), basis resulting from the purchase is basis in the stock (or in an interest in another entity) that is directly purchased during the five-year period or that is treated as acquired by purchase during such period under paragraph (e)(2), (3), or (4) of this section.

(B) Deemed purchase eliminated. Stock (or an interest in another entity) that is deemed purchased under section 355(d)(8) or paragraph (e)(1) of this section shall cease to be treated as purchased if (and when) the basis resulting from the purchase that effects the deemed purchase is eliminated.

(C) Elimination of basis—(1) General rule. Basis in the stock of a corporation (or in an interest in another entity) is eliminated if (and when) it would no longer be taken into account by any person in determining gain or loss on a sale or exchange of any stock of such corporation (or an interest in the other entity). Basis is not eliminated, however, if it is allocated between stock of two corporations under § 1.358–2(a).

(2) Special rule for transferred and exchanged basis property. Basis of stock (or an interest in another entity) resulting from a purchase (the first purchase) is eliminated if (and when) such stock (or other interest) is subsequently transferred to another person in an exchange or other transfer to which paragraph (e)(2) or (3) of this section applies (the second purchase). The elimination of basis in stock (or in another interest) resulting from the first purchase, however, does not eliminate the basis resulting from the second purchase in the stock (or other interest) that is treated as acquired by purchase by the acquirer in a transaction to which paragraph (e)(2) of this section applies or by the person making the exchange in a transaction to which paragraph (e)(3) of this section applies.

(3) **Special rule for Split-offs and Split-ups.** Under section 355(d)(3)(B)(ii) and paragraph (b)(2)(i)(B)(2) of this section, disqualified stock includes controlled corporation stock received in exchange for distributing corporation stock acquired by purchase. Solely for purposes of determining whether controlled corporation stock received in a distribution in exchange for distributing corporation stock is disqualified stock described in that section and paragraph immediately after the distribution, paragraph (b)(2)(iii)(C)(2) of this section does not apply to the exchange to eliminate basis resulting from a purchase of that distributing corporation stock (notwithstanding that paragraph (e)(3) of this section applies to the exchange).

(D) Special rule if basis allocated between two corporations. If the shareholder of a distributing corporation, pursuant to § 1.358–2, allocates basis resulting from a purchase between the stock of two or more corporations then, following such allocation, the determination of whether such basis has been eliminated shall be made separately with respect to the stock of each such corporation.

(3) Certain distributions not disqualified distributions because purposes of section 355(d) not violated—(i) In general. Notwithstanding the provisions of section 355(d)

(2) and this paragraph (b), a distribution is not a disqualified distribution if the distribution does not violate the purposes of section 355(d) as provided in this paragraph (b)(3). A distribution does not violate the purposes of section 355(d) if the effect of the distribution is neither—

(A) To increase ownership (combined direct and indirect) in the distributing corporation or any controlled corporation by a disqualified person; nor

(B) To provide a disqualified person with a purchased basis in the stock of any controlled corporation.

(ii) Disqualified person. A disqualified person is any person (taking into account section 355(d)(7) and paragraph (c)(4) of this section) that, immediately after a distribution, holds (directly or indirectly under section 355(d)(8) and paragraph (e)(1) of this section) disqualified stock in the distributing corporation or controlled corporation that—

(A) The person—

(*1*) Acquired by purchase under section 355(d)(5) or (8) and paragraphs (d) and (e) of this section during the five-year period, or

(*2*) Received in the distribution to the extent attributable to distributions on any stock in the distributing corporation acquired by purchase under section 355(d)(5) or (8) and paragraphs (d) and (e) of this section by that person during the five-year period; and

(B) Constitutes a 50 percent or greater interest in such corporation (under section 355(d)(4) and paragraph (c) of this section).

(iii) Purchased basis. In general, a purchased basis is basis in controlled corporation stock that is disqualified stock. However, basis in controlled corporation stock that is disqualified stock will not be treated as purchased basis if the controlled corporation stock and any distributing corporation stock with respect to which the controlled corporation stock is distributed are treated as acquired by purchase solely under the attribution rules of section 355(d)(8) and paragraph (e)(1) of this section. The prior sentence will not apply, however, if the distributing corporation stock is treated as acquired by purchase under the attribution rules as a result of the acquisition of an interest in a partnership (the purchased partnership), and following the distribution, the controlled corporation stock is directly held by the purchased partnership (or a chain of partnerships that includes the purchased partnership).

(iv) Increase in interest because of payment of cash in lieu of fractional shares. Any increase in direct or indirect ownership in the distributing corporation or any controlled corporation by a disqualified person because of a payment of cash in lieu of issuing fractional shares will be disregarded for purposes of paragraph (b)(3)(i)(A) of this section if the payment of the cash is solely to avoid the expense and inconvenience of issuing fractional share interests, and does not represent separately bargained for consideration.

(v) Other exceptions. The Commissioner may provide by guidance published in the Internal Revenue Bulletin that other distributions are not disqualified distributions because they do not violate the purposes of section 355(d).

(vi) Examples. The following examples illustrate this paragraph (b)(3):

Example (1). Stock distributed in spin-off; no purchased basis. D owns all of the stock of D1, and D1 owns all the stock of C. A purchases 60 percent of the D stock for cash. Within five years of A's purchase, D1 distributes the C stock to D. A is treated as having purchased 60 percent of the stock of both D1 and C on the date A purchases 60 percent of the D stock under the attribution rules of section 355(d)(8) and paragraph (e)(1) of this section. The C stock received by D is attributable to a distribution on purchased D1 stock under section 355(d)(3)(B)(ii). Accordingly, the D1 and C stock each is disqualified stock under section 355(d)(3) and paragraph (b)(2) of this section, and A is a disqualified person under paragraph

(b)(3)(ii) of this section. However, the purposes of section 355(d) under paragraph (b)(3)(i) of this section are not violated. A did not increase direct or indirect ownership in D1 or C. In addition, D's basis in the C stock is not a purchased basis under paragraph (b)(3)(iii) of this section because both the D1 and the C stock are treated as acquired by purchase solely under the attribution rules of section 355(d)(8) and paragraph (e)(1) of this section. Accordingly, D1's distribution of the C stock to D is not a disqualified distribution under section 355(d)(2) and paragraph (b)(1) of this section.

Example (2). Stock distributed in spin-off; purchased basis. The facts are the same as *Example 1,* except that D immediately further distributes the C stock to its shareholders (including A) pro rata. The D and C stock each is disqualified stock under section 355(d)(3) and paragraph (b)(2) of this section, and A is a disqualified person under paragraph (b)(3)(ii) of this section. The purposes of section 355(d) under paragraph (b)(3)(i) of this section are violated. A did not increase direct or indirect ownership in D or C. However, A's basis in the C stock is a purchased basis under paragraph (b)(3)(iii) of this section because the D stock is not treated as acquired by purchase solely under the attribution rules of section 355(d)(8) and paragraph (e)(1) of this section. Accordingly, the further distribution is a disqualified distribution under section 355(d)(2) and paragraph (b)(1) of this section.

Example (3). Stock distributed in split-off with ownership increase; purchased basis. The facts are the same as *Example 1,* except that D immediately further distributes the C stock to A in exchange for A's purchased stock in D. The C stock received by A is attributable to a distribution on purchased D stock under section 355(d)(3)(B)(ii), and A's basis in the C stock is determined by reference to the adjusted basis of A's purchased D stock under paragraph (e)(3) of this section. (Under paragraph (b)(2)(iii)(B)(*3*) of this section, the basis resulting from A's purchase of D stock is not eliminated solely for purposes of determining if the C stock acquired by A is disqualified stock immediately after the distribution, notwithstanding that paragraph (e)(3) of this section applies to the exchange.) Accordingly, the D stock and the C stock each is disqualified stock under section 355(d)(3) and paragraph (b)(2) of this section, and A is a disqualified person under paragraph (b)(3)(ii) of this section. The purposes of section 355(d) under paragraph (b)(3)(i) of this section are violated because A increased its ownership in C from a 60 percent indirect interest to a 100 percent direct interest, and because A's basis in the C stock is a purchased basis under paragraph (b)(3)(iii) of this section. Accordingly, the further distribution is a disqualified distribution under section 355(d)(2) and paragraph (b)(1) of this section.

Example (4). Stock distributed in spin-off; purchased basis. D1 owns all the stock of C. D purchases all of the stock of D1 for cash. Within five years of D's purchase of D1, P acquires all of the stock of D1 from D in a section 368(a)(1)(B) reorganization that is not a reorganization under section 368(a)(1)(A) by reason of section 368(a)(2)(E), and D1 distributes all of its C stock to P. P is treated as having acquired the D1 stock by purchase on the date D acquired it under the transferred basis rule of section 355(d)(5)(C) and paragraph (e)(2) of this section. P is treated as having purchased all of the C stock on the date D purchased the D1 stock under the attribution rules of section 355(d)(8) and paragraph (e)(1) of this section, and the C stock received by P is attributable to a distribution on purchased D1 stock under section 355(d)(3)(B)(ii). Accordingly, the D1 and C stock each is disqualified stock under section 355(d)(3) and paragraph (b)(2) of this section, and P is a disqualified person under paragraph (b)(3)(ii) of this section. The purposes of section 355(d) under paragraph (b)(3)(i) of this section are violated. P did not increase direct or indirect ownership in D1 or C. However, P's basis in the C stock is a purchased basis under paragraph (b)(3)(iii) of this

section because the D1 stock is not treated as acquired by purchase solely under the attribution rules of section 355(d)(8) and paragraph (e)(1) of this section. Accordingly, D1's distribution of the C stock to P is a disqualified distribution under section 355(d)(2) and paragraph (b)(1) of this section.

* * *

(4) Anti-avoidance rule—(i) In general. Notwithstanding any provision of section 355(d) or this section, the Commissioner may treat any distribution as a disqualified distribution under section 355(d)(2) and paragraph (b)(1) of this section if the distribution or another transaction or transactions are engaged in or structured with a principal purpose to avoid the purposes of section 355(d) or this section with respect to the distribution. Without limiting the preceding sentence, the Commissioner may determine that the existence of a related person, intermediary, pass-through entity, or similar person (an intermediary) should be disregarded, in whole or in part, if the intermediary is formed or availed of with a principal purpose to avoid the purposes of section 355(d) or this section.

(ii) Example. The following example illustrates this paragraph (b)(4):

Example. Post-distribution redemption. B wholly owns D, which wholly owns C. With a principal purpose to avoid the purposes of section 355(d), A, B, D, and C engage in the following transactions. A purchases 45 of 100 shares of the only class of D stock. Within five years after A's purchase, D distributes all of its 100 shares in C to A and B pro rata. D then redeems 20 shares of B's D stock, and C redeems 20 shares of B's C stock. After the redemption, A owns 45 shares and B owns 35 shares in each of D and C. Under paragraph (b)(4)(i) of this section, the Commissioner may treat A as owning disqualified stock in D and C that constitutes a 50 percent or greater interest in D and C immediately after the distribution. Under that treatment, the distribution is a disqualified distribution under section 355(d)(2) and paragraph (b)(1) of this section.

(c) Whether a person holds a 50 percent or greater interest—(1) In general. Under section 355(d)(4), 50 percent or greater interest means stock possessing at least 50 percent of the total combined voting power of all classes of stock entitled to vote or at least 50 percent of the total value of shares of all classes of stock.

(2) Valuation. For purposes of section 355(d)(4) and this section, all shares of stock within a single class are considered to have the same value. But see paragraph (c)(3)(vii) (A) of this section (determination of whether it is reasonably certain that an option will be exercised).

* * *

(4) Plan or arrangement—(i) In general. Under section 355(d)(7)(B), if two or more persons act pursuant to a plan or arrangement with respect to acquisitions of stock in the distributing corporation or controlled corporation, those persons are treated as one person for purposes of section 355(d).

(ii) Understanding. For purposes of section 355(d)(7)(B), two or more persons who are (or will after an acquisition become) shareholders (or are treated as shareholders under paragraph (c)(3)(ii) of this section) act pursuant to a plan or arrangement with respect to an acquisition of stock only if they have a formal or informal understanding among themselves to make a coordinated acquisition of stock. A principal element in determining if such an understanding exists is whether the investment decision of each person is based on the investment decision of one or more other existing or prospective shareholders. However, the participation by creditors in formulating a plan for an insolvency workout or a reorganization in a title 11 or similar case (whether as members of a creditors' committee or otherwise) and the receipt of stock by creditors in satisfaction of indebtedness pursuant to the workout or re-

organization do not cause the creditors to be considered as acting pursuant to a plan or arrangement.

(iii) Examples. The following examples illustrate paragraph (c)(4)(ii) of this section:

Example (1). D has 1,000 shares of common stock outstanding. A group of 20 unrelated individuals who previously owned no D stock (the Group) agree among themselves to acquire 50 percent or more of D's stock. The Group is not a person under section 7701(a) (1). Subsequently, pursuant to their understanding, the members of the Group purchase 600 shares of D common stock from the existing D shareholders (a total of 60 percent of the D stock), with each member purchasing 30 shares. Under paragraph (c)(4)(ii) of this section, the members of the Group have a formal or informal understanding among themselves to make a coordinated acquisition of stock. Their interests are therefore aggregated under section 355(d)(7)(B), and they are treated as one person that purchased 600 shares of D's stock for purposes of section 355(d).

Example (2). D has 1,000 shares of outstanding stock owned by unrelated individuals. D's management is concerned that D may become subject to a takeover bid. In separate meetings, D's management meets with potential investors who own no stock and are friendly to management to convince them to acquire D's stock based on an understanding that D will assemble a group that in the aggregate will acquire more than 50 percent of D's stock. Subsequently, 15 of these investors each purchases four percent of D's outstanding stock. Under paragraph (c)(4)(ii) of this section, the 15 investors have a formal or informal understanding among themselves to make a coordinated acquisition of stock. Their interests are therefore aggregated under section 355(d)(7) (B), and they are treated as one person that purchased 600 shares of D stock for purposes of section 355(d).

Example (3). (i) D has 1,000 shares of outstanding stock owned by unrelated individuals. An investment advisor advises its clients that it believes D's stock is undervalued and recommends that they acquire D stock. Acting on the investment advisor's recommendation, 20 unrelated individuals each purchases 30 shares of the outstanding D stock. Each client's decision was not based on the investment decisions made by one or more other clients. Because there is no formal or informal understanding among the clients to make a coordinated acquisition of D stock, their interests are not aggregated under section 355(d)(7)(B) and they are treated as making separate purchases.

(ii) The facts are the same as in paragraph (i) of this *Example 3*, except that the investment advisor is also the underwriter (without regard to whether it is a firm commitment or best efforts underwriting) for a primary or secondary offering of D stock. The result is the same.

(iii) The facts are the same as in paragraph (i) of this *Example 3*, except that, instead of an investment advisor recommending that clients purchase D stock, the trustee of several trusts qualified under section 401(a) sponsored by unrelated corporations causes each trust to purchase the D stock. The result is the same, provided that the trustee's investment decision made on behalf of each trust was not based on the investment decision made on behalf of one or more of the other trusts.

(iv) Exception—(A) Subsequent disposition. If two or more persons do not act pursuant to a plan or arrangement within the meaning of this paragraph (c)(4) with respect to an acquisition of stock in a corporation (the first corporation), a subsequent acquisition in which such persons exchange their stock in the first corporation for stock in another corporation (the second corporation) in a transaction in which the basis of the second corporation's stock in the hands of such persons is determined in whole or in part by reference to the basis of their stock in the first corporation, will not result in such persons being treated as one person, even if the acquisition of the second

corporation's stock is pursuant to a plan or arrangement.

(B) Example. The following example illustrates this paragraph (c)(4)(iv):

Example. In an initial public offering of D stock on Date 1, 100 investors independently purchase one percent each of the D stock. Two years later, D merges into P (in a reorganization described in section 368(a)(1)(A)) and, pursuant to the plan of reorganization, the D shareholders exchange their D stock for 50 percent of the stock of P. The D shareholders approve the plan by a two-thirds vote, as required by state law. Under section 358(a), each shareholder's basis in its P stock is determined by reference to the basis of the D stock it purchased. Under paragraph (e)(3) of this section, the former D shareholders are treated as purchasing their P stock on Date 1. The investors do not become a single person under paragraph (c)(4) of this section with respect to the deemed purchase of the P stock on Date 1 by virtue of their acquisition of the P stock pursuant to the merger on Date 2.

(d) Purchase—(1) In general—(i) Definition of purchase under section 355(d)(5) (A). Under section 355(d)(5)(A), except as otherwise provided in section 355(d)(5)(B) and (C), a *purchase* means any acquisition, but only if—

(A) The basis of the property acquired in the hands of the acquirer is not determined—

(*1*) In whole or in part by reference to the adjusted basis of such property in the hands of the person from whom acquired; or

(*2*) Under section 1014(a); and

(B) The property is not acquired in an exchange to which section 351, 354, 355, or 356 applies.

(ii) Section 355 distributions. Paragraph (d)(1)(i)(B) of this section includes all section 355 distributions, whether in exchange (in whole or in part) for stock or pro rata.

(iii) Example. The following example illustrates this paragraph (d)(1):

Example. Section 304(a)(1) acquisition. A, who owns all of the stock of P and T, sells the T stock to P for cash. The T stock is not marketable stock under section 355(d)(5)(B)(ii) and paragraph (d)(3)(ii) of this section. A is treated under section 304(a)(1) as receiving a distribution in redemption of the P stock. Under section 302(d), the deemed redemption is treated as a section 301 distribution. Assume that under sections 304(b)(2) and 301(c)(1), all of the distribution is a dividend. A and P are treated in the same manner as if A had transferred the T stock to P in exchange for stock of P in a transaction to which section 351(a) applies, and P had then redeemed the stock P was treated as issuing in the transaction. Under section 362(a), P's basis in the T stock is determined by reference to A's adjusted basis in the T stock, and there is no basis increase in the T stock because A recognizes no gain on the deemed transfer. Accordingly, P's acquisition of the T stock from A is not a purchase by P under section 355(d)(5)(A)(i)(I) and paragraphs (d)(1)(i)(A)(*1*) and (d)(2)(i)(B) of this section.

(2) Exceptions to definition of purchase under section 355(d)(5)(A). The following acquisitions are not treated as purchases under section 355(d)(5)(A):

(i) Acquisition of stock in a transaction which includes other property or money— (A) Transferors and shareholders of transferor or distributing corporations—(1) In general. An acquisition of stock permitted to be received by a transferor of property without the recognition of gain under section 351(a), or permitted to be received without the recognition of gain under section 354, 355, or 356 is not a purchase to the extent section 358(a)(1) applies to determine the recipient's basis in the stock received, whether or not the recipient recognizes gain under section 351(b) or 356. But see paragraph (e)(3) of this section (interest received in exchange for purchased interest

in exchanged basis transaction treated as purchased).

(2) Exception. To the extent there is received in the exchange or distribution, in addition to stock described in paragraph (d)(2)(i)(A)(*1*) of this section, stock that is other property under section 351(b) or 356(a)(1), the stock is treated as purchased on the date of the exchange or distribution for purposes of section 355(d).

(B) Transferee corporations—(1) In general. An acquisition of stock by a corporation is not a purchase to the extent section 334(b) or 362(a) or (b) applies to determine the corporation's basis in the stock received. But see section 355(d)(5)(C) and paragraph (e)(2) of this section (purchased property transferred in transferred basis transaction is treated as purchased by transferee).

(2) Exception. If a corporation acquires stock, the stock is treated as purchased on the date of the stock acquisition for purposes of section 355(d)—

(*i*) If the liquidating corporation recognizes gain or loss with respect to the transferred stock as described in section 334(b)(1); or

(*ii*) To the extent the basis of the transferred stock is increased through the recognition of gain by the transferor under section 362(a) or (b).

(C) Examples. The following examples illustrate this paragraph (d)(2)(i):

Example (1). (i) A owns all the stock of T. T merges into D in a transaction qualifying under section 368(a)(1)(A), with A exchanging all of the T stock for D stock and $100 cash. Under section 356(a)(1), A recognizes $100 of the realized gain on the transaction. Under section 358(a)(1), A's basis in the D stock equals A's basis in the T stock, decreased by the $100 received and increased by the gain recognized, also $100. Under paragraph (d)(2)(i)(A) of this section, A is not treated as having purchased the D stock for purposes of section 355(d)(5).

(ii) The facts are the same as in paragraph (i) of this *Example 1,* except that rather than D stock and $100 cash, A receives D stock and stock in C, a corporation not a party to the reorganization, with a fair market value of $100. Under section 358(a)(2), A's basis in the C stock is its fair market value, or $100. Under paragraph (d)(2)(i)(A)(2) of this section, A is treated as having purchased the C stock, but not the D stock, for purposes of section 355(d)(5).

Example (2). A purchases all of the stock of D, which is not marketable stock, on Date 1 for $90. Within five years of A's purchase, on Date 2, A contributes the D stock to P in exchange for P stock worth $90 and $10 cash in a transaction qualifying under section 351. A recognizes a gain of $10 as a result of the transfer. Under section 362(a), P's basis in D is $100. P is treated as having purchased 90 percent ($90 worth) of the D stock on Date 1 under section 355(d)(5)(C) and paragraph (e)(2) of this section and as having purchased 10 percent ($10 worth) of the D stock on Date 2 under paragraph (d)(2)(i)(B)(2)(*ii*) of this section.

(ii) Acquisition of stock in a distribution to which section 305(a) applies. An acquisition of stock in a distribution qualifying under section 305(a) is not a purchase to the extent section 307(a) applies to determine the recipient's basis. However, to the extent the distribution is of rights to acquire stock, see paragraph (c)(3) of this section for rules regarding options, warrants, convertible obligations, and other similar interests.

(iii) Section 1036(a) exchange. An exchange of stock qualifying under section 1036(a) is not a purchase by either party to the exchange to the extent the basis of the property acquired equals that of the property exchanged under section 1031(d).

(iv) Section 338 elections—(A) In general. Stock acquired in a qualified stock purchase with respect to which a section 338 election (or a section 338(h)(10) election) is made

is not treated as a purchase for purposes of section 355(d)(5)(A). However, any stock (or an interest in another entity) held by old target that is treated as purchased by new target is treated as acquired by purchase for purposes of section 355(d)(5)(A) unless a section 338 election or section 338(h)(10) election also is made for that stock. See § 1.338–2T(c) for the definitions of section 338 election, section 338(h)(10) election, old target, and new target.

(B) Example. The following example illustrates this paragraph (d)(2)(iv):

Example. T owns all of the stock of S and no other assets. X acquires all of the T stock from the T shareholders for cash and makes an election under section 338. Under section 338(a) and (b), T, as Old T, is treated as having sold all of its assets at fair market value and purchased the assets as a new corporation, New T, as of the beginning of the day after the acquisition date. Under paragraph (d)(2)(iv)(A) of this section, X is not treated as having purchased the T stock. Absent a section 338 election or a section 338(h)(10) election with respect to S, New T is treated as having purchased all of the S stock under section 355(d)(5)(A).

(v) Partnership distributions—(A) Section 732(b). An acquisition of stock (or an interest in another entity) in a liquidation of a partner's interest in a partnership in which basis is determined pursuant to section 732(b) is a purchase at the time of the liquidation.

(B) Section 734(b). If the adjusted basis of stock (or an interest in another entity) held by a partnership is increased under section 734(b), a proportionate amount of the stock (or other interest) will be treated as purchased at the time of the basis adjustment, determined by reference to the amount of the basis adjustment (but not in excess of the fair market value of the stock (or other interest) at the time of the adjustment) over the fair market value of the stock (or other interest) at the time of the adjustment.

(3) Certain section 351 exchanges treated as purchases—(i) In general—(A) Treatment of stock received by transferor. Under section 355(d)(5)(B), a purchase includes any acquisition of property in an exchange to which section 351 applies to the extent the property is acquired in exchange for any cash or cash item, any marketable stock, or any debt of the transferor. The property treated as acquired by purchase is the property received by the transferor in the exchange.

(B) Multiple classes of stock. If the transferor in a transaction described in section 355(d)(5)(B) receives stock or securities of more than one class, or receives both stock and securities, then the amount of stock or securities purchased is determined in a manner that corresponds to the allocation of basis to the stock or securities under section 358. See § 1.358–2(b).

(ii) Cash item, marketable stock. For purposes of section 355(d)(5)(B) and this paragraph (d)(3), either or both of the terms cash item and marketable stock include personal property within the meaning of section 1092(d)(1) and § 1.1092(d)–1, without giving effect to section 1092(d)(3).

(iii) Exception for certain acquisitions— (A) In general. Except to the extent provided in paragraph (e)(3) of this section (interest received in exchange for purchased interest in exchanged basis transaction treated as purchased), an acquisition of stock in a corporation in a section 351 transaction by one or more persons in exchange for an amount of stock in another corporation (the transferred corporation) that meets the requirements of section 1504(a)(2) is not a purchase by the transferor or transferors, regardless of whether the stock of the transferred corporation is marketable stock under section 355(d)(5)(B)(ii) and paragraph (d)(3)(ii) of this section.

(B) Example. The following example illustrates this paragraph (d)(3)(iii):

Example. D's two classes of stock, voting common and nonvoting preferred, are both widely held and publicly traded. The nonvoting preferred stock is stock described in section 1504(a)(4). Assume that all of the D stock is marketable stock under section 355(d)(5)(B)(ii) and paragraph (d)(3)(ii) of this section. D's board of directors proposes that, for valid business purposes, D's common stock should be held by a holding company, HC, but its preferred stock should not be transferred to HC. As proposed, the D common shareholders exchange their D stock solely for HC common stock in a section 351(a) transaction. The D preferred shareholders retain their stock. HC acquires an amount of D stock that meets the requirements of section 1504(a)(2). Although the D common stock was marketable stock in the hands of the D shareholders immediately before the transfer, and the D nonvoting preferred stock is marketable stock after the transfer, the D shareholders are not treated as having acquired the HC stock by purchase (except to the extent the exchanged basis rule of paragraph (e)(3) of this section may apply to treat HC stock as purchased on the date the exchanged D stock was purchased).

(iv) Exception for assets transferred as part of an active trade or business—(A) In general. Except to the extent provided in paragraph (e)(3) of this section, an acquisition not described in paragraph (d)(3)(iii) of this section of stock in exchange for any cash or cash item, any marketable stock, or any debt of the transferor in a section 351 transaction is not a purchase if—

(1) The transferor is engaged in the active conduct of a trade or business under paragraph (d)(3)(iv)(B) of this section and the transferred items (including debt incurred in the ordinary course of the trade or business) are used in the trade or business;

(2) The transferred items do not exceed the reasonable needs of the trade or business under paragraph (d)(3)(iv)(C) of this section;

(3) The transferor transfers the items as part of the trade or business; and

(4) The transferee continues the active conduct of the trade or business.

(B) Active conduct of a trade or business. For purposes of this paragraph (d)(3)(iv), whether, with respect to the trade or business at issue, the transferor and transferee are engaged in the active conduct of a trade or business is determined under § 1.355–3(b)(2) and (3), except that—

(1) Conduct is tested before the transfer (with respect to the transferor) and after the transfer (with respect to the transferee) rather than immediately after a distribution; and

(2) The trade or business need not have been conducted for five years before its transfer, but it must have been conducted for a sufficient period of time to establish that it is a viable and ongoing trade or business.

(C) Reasonable needs of the trade or business. For purposes of this paragraph (d)(3)(iv), the reasonable needs of the trade or business include only the amount of cash or cash items, marketable stock, or debt of the transferor that a prudent business person apprised of all relevant facts would consider necessary for the present and reasonably anticipated future needs of the business. Transferred items may be considered necessary for reasonably anticipated future needs only if the transferor and transferee have specific, definite, and feasible plans for their use. Those plans must require that items intended for anticipated future needs rather than present needs be used as expeditiously as possible consistent with the business purpose for retention of the items. Future needs are not reasonably anticipated if they are uncertain or vague or where the execution of the plan for their use is substantially postponed. The reasonable needs of a trade or business are generally its needs at the time of the transfer of the business including the items. However, for purposes of applying section 355(d) to a distribution, events and conditions after the transfer and through the date immediately after the distribution (including whether plans for the use of transferred items have been consummated or substantially postponed) may be considered to determine whether at the time of the transfer the items were necessary for the present and reasonably anticipated future needs of the business.

(D) Consideration of all facts and circumstances. All facts and circumstances are considered in determining whether this paragraph (d)(3)(iv) applies.

(E) Successive transfers. A transfer of assets does not fail to meet the requirements of paragraph (d)(3)(iv)(A)(*4*) of this section solely because the transferee transfers the assets directly (or indirectly through other members) to another member of the transferee's affiliated group, as defined in § 1.355–3(b)(4)(iv) (the final transferee), if the requirements of paragraphs (d)(3)(iv)(A)(*1*), (*2*), (*3*) and (*4*) of this section would be met if the transferor had transferred the assets directly to the final transferee.

(v) Exception for transfer between members of the same affiliated group—(A) In general. Except to the extent provided in paragraph (e)(3) of this section, an acquisition of stock (whether actual or constructive) not described in paragraphs (d)(3)(iii) and (iv) of this section in exchange for any cash or cash item, marketable stock, or debt of the transferor in a section 351 transaction is not a purchase if—

(1) The transferor corporation or corporations and the transferee corporation (whether formed in the transaction or already existing) are members of the same affiliated group as defined in section 1504(a) before the section 351 transaction (if the transferee corporation is in existence before the transaction);

(2) The cash or cash item, marketable stock or debt of the transferor are not included in assets that are acquired (or treated as acquired) by the transferor (or another member of the transferor's affiliated group) from a nonmember in a related transaction in which section

362(a) or (b) applies to determine the basis in the acquired assets; and

(3) The transferor corporation or corporations, the transferee corporation, and any distributed controlled corporation of the transferee corporation do not cease to be members of such affiliated group in any transaction pursuant to a plan that includes the section 351 transaction (including any distribution of a controlled corporation by the transferee corporation). But see paragraph (b)(4) of this section where the transfer is made for a principal purpose to avoid the purposes of section 355(d).

* * *

(4) **Triangular asset reorganizations—(i) Definition.** A triangular asset reorganization is a reorganization that qualifies under—

(A) Section 368(a)(1)(A) or (G) by reason of section 368(a)(2)(D);

(B) Section 368(a)(1)(A) by reason of section 368(a)(2)(E) (regardless of whether section 368(a)(3)(E) applies), unless the transaction also qualifies as either a section 351 transfer or a reorganization under section 368(a)(1)(B); or

(C) Section 368(a)(1)(C), and stock of the controlling corporation rather than the acquiring corporation is exchanged for the acquired corporation's properties.

(ii) **Treatment.** Notwithstanding section 355(d)(5)(A), for purposes of section 355(d), the controlling corporation in a triangular asset reorganization is treated as having—

(A) Acquired the assets of the acquired corporation (and as having assumed any liabilities assumed by the controlling corporation's subsidiary corporation or to which the acquired corporation's assets were subject (the acquired liabilities)) in a transaction in which the controlling corporation's basis in the acquired corporation's assets was determined under section 362(b); and

(B) Transferred the acquired assets and acquired liabilities to its subsidiary corporation in a section 351 transfer.

(iii) **Example.** The following example illustrates this paragraph (d)(4):

Example. Forward triangular reorganization. P forms S with $25 of cash and T merges into S in a reorganization qualifying under section 368(a)(1)(A) by reason of section 368(a)(2)(D) in which the T shareholders receive $70 of P stock and $15 of cash in exchange for their T stock. T is not a common parent of a consolidated group of corporations. The remaining $10 of cash with which P formed S will not be used in the acquired business. T's assets consist only of assets part of and used in its business with a value of $80, and $5 of cash that is not part of or used in T's business. T has no liabilities. S will use T's business assets in T's business (which will become S's business), but will invest the $5 of cash in an unrelated passive investment. Under paragraph (d)(4)(ii) of this section, P is treated as acquiring the T assets in a transaction in which P's basis in the T assets was determined under section 362(b) and contributing them to S in a section 351 transfer. Under paragraph (d)(3)(v) of this section, $10 (of the total $25) of cash contributed by P to S upon S's formation is not treated as a purchase of S stock. The $15 (of the total $25) of cash contributed by P to S upon S's formation that is paid to T's shareholders is not treated as a purchase of S stock. The exception in paragraph (d)(3)(v) of this section does not apply to the $5 of cash from T's business because P is treated as having acquired T's assets in a related transaction in which section 362(b) applies to determine P's basis in such assets. Accordingly, P is treated under section 355(d)(5)(B) and paragraph (d)(3)(iv) of this section as having purchased $5 of the S stock, but is not deemed to have purchased the remaining $80 of the S stock.

(5) **Reverse triangular reorganizations other than triangular asset reorganizations—(i) In general.** Except as provided in

paragraph (d)(5)(ii) of this section, if a transaction qualifies as a reorganization under section 368(a)(1)(A) by reason of section 368(a)(2)(E) and also as either a reorganization under section 368(a)(1)(B) or a section 351 transfer, then either section 355(d)(5)(B) (and paragraphs (d)(3)(i) through (iv) of this section) or 355(d)(5)(C) (and paragraph (e)(2) of this section) applies. Regardless of which method the controlling corporation employs to determine its basis in the surviving corporation stock under § 1.358–6(c)(2)(ii) or § 1.1502–30(b), the total amount of surviving corporation stock treated as purchased by the controlling corporation will equal the higher of—

(A) The amount of surviving corporation stock that would be treated as purchased (on the date of the deemed section 351 transfer) by the controlling corporation if the controlling corporation acquired the surviving corporation's assets and assumed its liabilities in a transaction in which the controlling corporation's basis in the surviving corporation assets was determined under section 362(b), and then transferred the acquired assets and liabilities to the surviving corporation in a section 351 transfer (see §§ 1.358–6(c)(1) and (2)(ii)(A), and 1.1502–30(b)); or

(B) The amount of surviving corporation stock that would be treated as purchased (on the date the surviving corporation shareholders purchased their surviving corporation stock) if the controlling corporation acquired the stock of the surviving corporation in a transaction in which the basis in the surviving corporation's stock was determined under section 362(b) (see §§ 1.358–6(c)(2)(ii)(B) and 1.1502–30(b)).

(ii) Letter ruling and closing agreement. If a controlling corporation obtains a letter ruling and enters into a closing agreement under section 7121 in which it agrees to determine its basis in surviving corporation stock under § 1.358–6(c)(2)(ii)(A), or under § 1.1502–30(b) by applying § 1.358–6(c)(2)(ii)(A) (deemed asset acquisition and trans-

fer by controlling corporation), then section 355(d)(5)(B) and paragraphs (d)(3)(i) through (iv) of this section apply, and section 355(d)(5)(C) and paragraph (e)(2) of this section do not apply. If a controlling corporation obtains a letter ruling and enters into a closing agreement under section 7121 under which it agrees to determine its basis in surviving corporation stock under § 1.358–6(c)(2)(ii)(B), or under § 1.1502–30(b) by applying § 1.358–6(c)(2)(ii)(B) (deemed stock acquisition), then section 355(d)(5)(C) and paragraph (e)(2) of this section apply, and section 355(d)(5)(B) and paragraphs (d)(3)(i) through (iv) of this section do not apply.

(iii) Example. The following example illustrates this paragraph (d)(5):

Example. Reverse triangular reorganization; purchase. (i) A purchases 60 percent of the stock of D on Date 1. D owns no cash items, marketable stock, or transferor debt, but holds cash that is not part of or used in D's trade or business under paragraph (d)(3)(iv) of this section and that represents 20 percent of D's value. On Date 2, P forms S, and S merges into D in a reorganization qualifying under section 368(a)(1)(B) and under section 368(a)(1)(A) by reason of section 368(a)(2)(E). In the reorganization, P acquires all of the D stock in exchange solely for P stock. After Date 2, and within five years after Date 1, D distributes its wholly owned subsidiary C to P. P does not obtain a letter ruling and enter into a closing agreement under paragraph (d)(5)(ii) of this section. P would acquire 20 percent of the D stock by purchase on Date 2 under paragraph (d)(5)(i)(A) of this section by operation of section 355(d)(5)(B) and paragraph (d)(3)(iv) of this section. The exception in paragraph (d)(3)(v) of this section does not apply because D was not affiliated with P before the transaction in which the section 351 transfer is deemed to occur and D's assets are treated as acquired by P in a related transaction in which section 362(b) applies to determine P's basis in the D assets. P would acquire 60 percent of the D stock by purchase on Date 1 under paragraph (d)(5)(i)(B) of this section because, under the transferred basis rule of section 355(d)(5)(C) and paragraph (e)(2) of this section, P is treated as though P purchased the D stock on the date A purchased it. Accordingly, under paragraph (d)(5)(i) of this section, P is treated as acquiring the higher amount (60 percent) by purchase on Date 1. D's distribution of C to P is a disqualified distribution under section 355(d)(2) and paragraph (b)(1) of this section. In addition, A is treated as acquiring the P stock by purchase on Date 1 under paragraph (e)(3) of this section because A's basis in the P stock is determined by reference to A's basis in the D stock.

(ii) The facts are the same as in paragraph (i) of this *Example,* except that P obtains a letter ruling and enters into a closing agreement under which it agrees to determine its basis in the D stock under § 1.358–6(c)(2)(ii)(A). Under paragraph (d)(5)(ii) of this section, section 355(d)(5)(B) (and paragraphs (d)(3)(i) through (iv) of this section) applies, and section 355(d)(5)(C) (and paragraph (e)(2) of this section) does not apply. Accordingly, P is treated as acquiring only 20 percent of the D stock by purchase on Date 2. D's distribution of C to P is not a disqualified distribution under section 355(d)(2) and paragraph (b)(1) of this section.

(6) Treatment of group structure changes—(i) In general. Notwithstanding section 355(d)(5)(A), for purposes of section 355(d), if a corporation succeeds another corporation as the common parent of a consolidated group in a group structure change to which § 1.1–31 applies, the new common parent is treated as having acquired the assets and assumed the liabilities of the former common parent in a transaction in which the new common parent's basis in the former common parent's assets was determined under section 362(b), and then transferred the acquired assets and liabilities to the former common parent (or, if the former common parent does not survive, to the new common parent's subsidiary) in a section 351

transfer, with the new common parent and former common parent being treated as not in the same affiliated group at the time of the transfer for purposes of applying paragraph (d)(3)(v) of this section (notwithstanding § 1.1502–31(c)(2)).

(ii) Adjustments to basis of higher-tier members. A higher-tier member that indirectly owns all or part of the former common parent's stock after a group structure change is treated as having purchased the stock of an immediate subsidiary to the extent that the higher-tier member's basis in the subsidiary is increased under § 1.1502–31(d)(4).

(iii) Example. The following example illustrates this paragraph (d)(6):

Example. P is the common parent of a consolidated group, and T is the common parent of another group. P has owned S for more than five years, and the fair market value of the S stock is $50. T's assets consist only of non-marketable stock of direct and indirect wholly owned subsidiaries with a value of $50, assets used in its business with a value of $50, and $50 of marketable stock that is not part of or used in T's business. T has no liabilities. T merges into S with the T shareholders receiving solely P stock with a value of $150 in exchange for their T stock in a section 368(a)(2)(D) reorganization. S will use T's business assets in T's business (which will become S's business), but will hold the $50 of marketable stock for investment purposes. Assume that the transaction is a reverse acquisition under § 1.1502–75(d)(3) because the T shareholders, as a result of owning T stock, own more than 50 percent of the value of P's stock immediately after the transaction. Thus, the transaction is a group structure change under § 1.1502–33(f)(1). Under paragraph (d)(6) of this section, P is treated as having acquired the assets of T in a transaction in which P's basis in the T assets was determined under section 362(b), and then transferred the acquired assets to S in a section 351 transfer, with P and T being treated as not in the same affiliated group at the time of the transfer solely for purposes of paragraph (d)(3)(v) of this section. The exception in paragraph (d)(3)(v) of this section (transfers within an affiliated group) does not apply. Accordingly, P is treated under section 355(d)(5)(B) and paragraph (d)(3)(iv) of this section as having purchased $50 of the S stock (attributable to the marketable stock), but is not deemed to have purchased the remaining $150 of the S stock.

(7) Special rules for triangular asset reorganizations, other reverse triangular reorganizations, and group structure changes. The amount of acquiring subsidiary, surviving corporation, or former common parent stock that is treated as purchased under paragraph (c)(4), (5)(i)(A), or (6) of this section (by operation of section 355(d)(5)(B) and paragraphs (d)(3)(i) through (iv) of this section) is adjusted to reflect any basis adjustment under—

(i) Section 1.358–6(c)(2)(i)(B) and (C) (reduction of basis adjustment in reverse triangular reorganization where controlling corporation acquires less than all of the surviving corporation stock), § 1.1502–30(b) (applying § 1.358–6(c)(2)(i)(B) and (C) to a consolidated group), and § 1.1502–31(d)(2)(ii) (reduction of basis adjustment in group structure change where new common parent acquires less than all of the former common parent stock); or

(ii) Section 1.358–6(d) (reduction of basis adjustment in any triangular reorganization to the extent controlling corporation does not provide consideration), § 1.1502–30(b) (applying § 1.358–6(d) (except § 1.358–6(d)(2)) to a consolidated group), and § 1.1502–31(d)(1) (reduction of basis adjustment in group structure change to the extent new common parent does not provide consideration).

(e) Deemed purchase and timing rules—(1) Attribution and aggregation—(i) In general. Under section 355(d)(8)(B), if any person acquires by purchase an interest in any entity, and the person is treated under section 355(d)(8)(A) as holding any stock by reason of holding the interest, the stock shall be treated as acquired by purchase on the later of the date of the purchase of the interest in the entity or the date the stock is acquired by purchase by such entity.

(ii) Purchase of additional interest. If a person and an entity are treated as a single person under section 355(d)(7), and the person later purchases an additional interest in the entity, the person is treated as purchasing on the date of the later purchase the amount of stock attributed from the entity to the person under section 355(d)(8)(A) as a result of the additional interest.

(iii) Purchase between persons treated as one person. If two persons are treated as one person under section 355(d)(7), and one later purchases stock from the other, the date of the later purchase is used for purposes of determining when the five-year period commences.

(iv) Purchase by a person already treated as holding stock under section 355(d)(8)(A). If a person who is already treated as holding stock under section 355(d)(8)(A) later directly purchases such stock, the date of the later direct purchase is used for purposes of determining when the five-year period commences.

(v) Examples. The following examples illustrate this paragraph (e)(1):

Example (1). On Date 1, A purchases 10 percent of the stock of P, which has held 100 percent of the stock of T for more than five years at the time of A's purchase. A is deemed to have purchased 10 percent of P's T stock on Date 1. If A later purchases an additional 41 percent of the stock of P on Date 2, A is deemed to have purchased an additional 41 percent of P's T stock on Date 2. Because A and P are now related persons under section 267(b), they are treated as one person under section 355(d)(7)(A), and A is treated as owning all of P's T stock. A is treated as acquiring 51 percent of the T stock by purchase at the times of A's respective purchases of P stock on Date 1 and Date 2. The remaining 49 percent of T stock is treated as acquired when P acquired the T stock, more than five years before Date 1. If P distributes T after Date 2 and within five years after Date 1, the distribution will be a disqualified distribution under section 355(d)(2) and paragraph (b)(1) of this section.

* * *

(2) Transferred basis rule. If any person acquires property from another person who acquired the property by purchase (determined with regard to section 355(d)(5) and paragraphs (d) and (e)(2), (3) and (4) of this section, but without regard to section 355(d)(8) and paragraph (e)(1) of this section), and the adjusted basis of the property in the hands of the acquirer is determined in whole or in part by reference to the adjusted basis of the property in the hands of the other person, the acquirer is treated as having acquired the property by purchase on the date it was so acquired by the other person. The rule in this paragraph (e)(2) applies, for example, where stock of a corporation acquired by purchase is subsequently acquired in a section 351 transfer or a reorganization qualifying under section 368(a)(1)(B), but does not apply if the stock of a former common parent is acquired in a group structure change to which § 1.1–31 applies. But see paragraph (d)(2)(i)(B)(2) of this section for situations where the stock is treated as purchased on the date of a transfer.

(3) Exchanged basis rule—(i) In general. If any person acquires an interest in an entity (the first interest) by purchase (determined with regard to section 355(d)(5) and paragraphs (d) and (e)(2), (3) and (4) of this section, but without regard to section 355(d)(8) and paragraph (e)(1) of this section), and the first interest is exchanged for an interest in the same or another entity (the second interest) where the adjusted basis of the second interest is determined in whole or in part by reference to the adjusted basis of the first interest, then the second interest is treated as having been purchased on the date the first interest was purchased. The rule in this paragraph (e)(3) applies only to exchanges that are not other-

wise treated as purchases under section 355(d)(5) and paragraph (d) of this section. The rule in this paragraph (e)(3) applies, for example, where stock of a corporation acquired by purchase is subsequently exchanged for other stock in a section 351, 354, or 1036(a) exchange. But see paragraph (d)(2)(i)(A)(2) of this section for situations where the stock is treated as purchased on the date of an exchange or distribution.

(ii) Example. The following example illustrates this paragraph (e)(3):

Example. A purchases 50 percent of the stock of T on Date 1. On Date 2, T merges into D in a section 368(a)(1)(A) reorganization, with A exchanging all of the T stock solely for stock of D. Under section 358(a), A's basis in the D stock is determined by reference to the basis of the T stock it purchased. Accordingly, A is treated as having purchased the D stock on Date 1, and has a purchased basis in the D stock under paragraph (b)(3)(iii) of this section.

(4) Certain section 355 or section 305 distributions—(i) Section 355. If a distributing corporation distributes any stock of a controlled corporation with respect to recently purchased distributing stock in a distribution that qualifies under section 355 (or so much of section 356 as relates to section 355), such controlled corporation stock is deemed to be acquired by purchase by the distributee on the date the distributee acquired the recently purchased distributing stock. Recently purchased distributing stock is stock in the distributing corporation acquired by purchase (determined with regard to section 355(d)(5) and paragraphs (d) and (e)(2), (3), and (4) of this section, but without regard to section 355(d)(8) and paragraph (e)(1) of this section) by the distributee during the five-year period with respect to that distribution.

(ii) Section 305. If a corporation distributes its stock in a distribution that qualifies under section 305(a), the stock received in the distribution (to the extent section 307(a) applies to determine the recipient's basis) is deemed to be acquired by purchase by the recipient on the date (if any) that the recipient acquired by purchase (determined with regard to section 355(d)(5) and paragraphs (d) and (e)(2), (3), and (4) of this section), the stock with respect to which the distribution is made.

(5) Substantial diminution of risk—(i) In general. If section 355(d)(6) applies to any stock for any period, the running of any five-year period set forth in section 355(d)(3) is suspended during such period.

(ii) Property to which suspension applies. Section 355(d)(6) applies to any stock for any period during which the holder's risk of loss with respect to such stock, or with respect to any portion of the activities of the corporation, is (directly or indirectly) substantially diminished by an option, a short sale, any special class of stock, or any other device or transaction.

(iii) Risk of loss substantially diminished. Whether a holder's risk of loss is substantially diminished under section 355(d)(6) and paragraph (e)(5)(ii) of this section will be determined based on all facts and circumstances relating to the stock, the corporate activities, and arrangements for holding the stock.

(iv) Special class of stock. For purposes of section 355(d)(6) and paragraph (e)(5)(ii) of this section, the term special class of stock includes a class of stock that grants particular rights to, or bears particular risks for, the holder or the issuer with respect to the earnings, assets, or attributes of less than all the assets or activities of a corporation or any of its subsidiaries. The term includes, for example, tracking stock and stock (or any related instruments or arrangements) the terms of which provide for the distribution (whether or not at the option of any party or in the event of any contingency) of any controlled corporation or other specified assets to the holder or to one or more persons other than the holder.

(f) Duty to determine stockholders—(1) In general. In determining whether section 355(d) applies to a distribution of controlled corporation stock, a distributing corporation must determine whether a disqualified person holds its stock or the stock of any distributed controlled corporation. This paragraph (f) provides rules regarding this determination and the extent to which a distributing corporation must investigate whether a disqualified person holds stock.

(2) Deemed knowledge of contents of securities filings. A distributing corporation is deemed to have knowledge of the existence and contents of all schedules, forms, and other documents filed with or under the rules of the Securities and Exchange Commission, including without limitation any Schedule 13D or 13G (or any similar schedules) and amendments, with respect to any relevant corporation.

(3) Presumption as to securities filings. Absent actual knowledge to the contrary, in determining whether section 355(d) applies to a distribution, a distributing corporation may presume, with respect to stock that is reporting stock (while such stock is reporting stock), that every shareholder or other person required to file a schedule, form, or other document with or under the rules of the Securities and Exchange Commission as of a given date has filed the schedule, form, or other document as of that date and that the contents of filed schedules, forms, or other documents are accurate and complete. Reporting stock is stock that is described in Rule 13d–1(i) of Regulation 13D (17 CFR 240.13d–1(i)) (or any rule or regulation to generally the same effect) promulgated by the Securities and Exchange Commission under the Securities Exchange Act of 1934 (15 U.S.C. 78a *et seq.*).

(4) Presumption as to less-than-five-percent shareholders. Absent actual knowledge (or deemed knowledge under paragraph (f) (2) of this section) immediately after the distribution to the contrary with regard to a particular shareholder, a distributing corporation may presume that no less-than-five-percent shareholder of a corporation acquired stock or securities by purchase under section 355(d)(5) or (8) and paragraphs (d) and (e) of this section during the five-year period. For purposes of this paragraph (f), a less-than-five-percent shareholder is a person that, at no time during the five-year period, holds directly (or by application of paragraph (c)(3)(ii) of this section, but not by application of section 355(d)(7) or (8)) stock possessing five percent or more of the total combined voting power of all classes of stock entitled to vote or the total value of shares of all classes of stock of a corporation. However, this presumption does not apply to any less-than-five-percent shareholder that, at any time during the five-year period—

(i) Is related under section 355(d)(7)(A) to a shareholder in the corporation that is, at any time during the five-year period, not a less-than-five-percent shareholder;

(ii) Acted pursuant to a plan or arrangement, with respect to acquisitions of the corporation's stock or securities under section 355(d)(7)(B) and paragraph (c)(4) of this section, with a shareholder in the corporation that is, at any time during the five-year period, not a less-than-five-percent shareholder; or

(iii) Holds stock or securities that is attributed under section 355(d)(8)(A) to a shareholder in the corporation that is, at any time during the five-year period, not a less-than-five-percent shareholder.

* * *

§ 1.355–7 Recognition of gain on certain distributions of stock or securities in connection with an acquisition.

(a) In general. Except as provided in section 355(e) and in this section, section 355(e) applies to any distribution—

(1) To which section 355 (or so much of section 356 as relates to section 355) applies; and

(2) That is part of a plan (or series of related transactions) (hereinafter, plan) pursuant to which 1 or more persons acquire directly or indirectly stock representing a 50-percent or greater interest in the distributing corporation (Distributing) or any controlled corporation (Controlled).

(b) Plan—(1) In general. Whether a distribution and an acquisition are part of a plan is determined based on all the facts and circumstances. The facts and circumstances to be considered in demonstrating whether a distribution and an acquisition are part of a plan include, but are not limited to, the facts and circumstances set forth in paragraphs (b)(3) and (4) of this section. In general, the weight to be given each of the facts and circumstances depends on the particular case. Whether a distribution and an acquisition are part of a plan does not depend on the relative number of facts and circumstances set forth in paragraph (b)(3) that evidence that a distribution and an acquisition are part of a plan as compared to the relative number of facts and circumstances set forth in paragraph (b)(4) that evidence that a distribution and an acquisition are not part of a plan.

(2) Certain post-distribution acquisitions. In the case of an acquisition (other than involving a public offering) after a distribution, the distribution and the acquisition can be part of a plan only if there was an agreement, understanding, arrangement, or substantial negotiations regarding the acquisition or a similar acquisition at some time during the two-year period ending on the date of the distribution. In the case of an acquisition (other than involving a public offering) after a distribution, the existence of an agreement, understanding, arrangement, or substantial negotiations regarding the acquisition or a similar acquisition at some time during the two-year period ending on the date of the distribution tends to show that the distribution and the acquisition are part of a plan. See paragraph (b)(3)(i) of this section. However, all facts and circumstances must be considered to determine whether the distribution and the acquisition are part of a plan. For example, in the case of an acquisition (other than involving a public offering) after a distribution, if the distribution was motivated in whole or substantial part by a corporate business purpose (within the meaning of § 1.355–2(b)) other than a business purpose to facilitate the acquisition or a similar acquisition of Distributing or Controlled (see paragraph (b)(4)(v) of this section) and would have occurred at approximately the same time and in similar form regardless of whether the acquisition or a similar acquisition was effected (see paragraph (b)(4)(vi) of this section), the taxpayer may be able to establish that the distribution and the acquisition are not part of a plan.

(3) Plan factors. Among the facts and circumstances tending to show that a distribution and an acquisition are part of a plan are the following:

(i) In the case of an acquisition (other than involving a public offering) after a distribution, at some time during the two-year period ending on the date of the distribution, there was an agreement, understanding, arrangement, or substantial negotiations regarding the acquisition or a similar acquisition. The weight to be accorded this fact depends on the nature, extent, and timing of the agreement, understanding, arrangement, or substantial negotiations. The existence of an agreement, understanding, or arrangement at the time of the distribution is given substantial weight.

(ii) In the case of an acquisition involving a public offering after a distribution, at some time during the two-year period ending on the date of the distribution, there were discussions by Distributing or Controlled with an investment banker regarding the acquisition or a similar acquisition. The weight to be accorded this fact depends on the nature, extent, and timing of the discussions.

(iii) In the case of an acquisition (other than involving a public offering) before a distribu-

tion, at some time during the two-year period ending on the date of the acquisition, there were discussions by Distributing or Controlled with the acquirer regarding a distribution. The weight to be accorded this fact depends on the nature, extent, and timing of the discussions. In addition, in the case of an acquisition (other than involving a public offering) before a distribution, the acquirer intends to cause a distribution and, immediately after the acquisition, can meaningfully participate in the decision regarding whether to make a distribution.

(iv) In the case of an acquisition involving a public offering before a distribution, at some time during the two-year period ending on the date of the acquisition, there were discussions by Distributing or Controlled with an investment banker regarding a distribution. The weight to be accorded this fact depends on the nature, extent, and timing of the discussions.

(v) In the case of an acquisition either before or after a distribution, the distribution was motivated by a business purpose to facilitate the acquisition or a similar acquisition.

(4) Non-plan factors. Among the facts and circumstances tending to show that a distribution and an acquisition are not part of a plan are the following:

(i) In the case of an acquisition involving a public offering after a distribution, during the two-year period ending on the date of the distribution, there were no discussions by Distributing or Controlled with an investment banker regarding the acquisition or a similar acquisition.

(ii) In the case of an acquisition after a distribution, there was an identifiable, unexpected change in market or business conditions occurring after the distribution that resulted in the acquisition that was otherwise unexpected at the time of the distribution.

(iii) In the case of an acquisition (other than involving a public offering) before a distribution, during the two-year period ending on the date of the earlier to occur of the acquisition or the first public announcement regarding the distribution, there were no discussions by Distributing or Controlled with the acquirer regarding a distribution. Paragraph (b)(4)(iii) of this section does not apply to an acquisition where the acquirer intends to cause a distribution and, immediately after the acquisition, can meaningfully participate in the decision regarding whether to make a distribution.

(iv) In the case of an acquisition before a distribution, there was an identifiable, unexpected change in market or business conditions occurring after the acquisition that resulted in a distribution that was otherwise unexpected.

(v) In the case of an acquisition either before or after a distribution, the distribution was motivated in whole or substantial part by a corporate business purpose (within the meaning of § 1.355–2(b)) other than a business purpose to facilitate the acquisition or a similar acquisition.

(vi) In the case of an acquisition either before or after a distribution, the distribution would have occurred at approximately the same time and in similar form regardless of the acquisition or a similar acquisition.

(c) Operating rules. The operating rules contained in this paragraph (c) apply for all purposes of this section.

(1) Internal discussions and discussions with outside advisors evidence of business purpose. Discussions by Distributing or Controlled with outside advisors and internal discussions may be indicative of one or more business purposes for the distribution and the relative importance of such purposes.

(2) Takeover defense. If Distributing engages in discussions with a potential acquirer regarding an acquisition of Distributing or Controlled and distributes Controlled stock intending, in whole or substantial part, to decrease the likelihood of the acquisition of Distributing or Controlled by separating it from another corporation that is likely to be acquired, Distributing will be treated as having a business purpose to facilitate the acquisition of the corporation that was likely to be acquired.

(3) Effect of distribution on trading in stock. The fact that the distribution made all or a part of the stock of Controlled available for trading or made Distributing's or Controlled's stock trade more actively is not taken into account in determining whether the distribution and an acquisition of Distributing or Controlled stock were part of a plan.

(4) Consequences of section 355(e) disregarded for certain purposes. For purposes of determining the intentions of the relevant parties under this section, the consequences of the application of section 355(e), and the existence of any contractual indemnity by Controlled for tax resulting from the application of section 355(e) caused by an acquisition of Controlled, are disregarded.

(5) Multiple acquisitions. All acquisitions of stock of Distributing or Controlled that are considered to be part of a plan with a distribution pursuant to paragraph (b) of this section will be aggregated for purposes of the 50-percent test of paragraph (a)(2) of this section.

(d) Safe harbors—(1) Safe Harbor I. A distribution and an acquisition occurring after the distribution will not be considered part of a plan if—

(i) The distribution was motivated in whole or substantial part by a corporate business purpose (within the meaning of § 1.355–2(b)), other than a business purpose to facilitate an acquisition of the acquired corporation (Distributing or Controlled); and

(ii) The acquisition occurred more than six months after the distribution and there was no agreement, understanding, arrangement, or substantial negotiations concerning the acquisition or a similar acquisition during the period that begins one year before the distribution and ends six months thereafter.

(2) Safe Harbor II—(i) In general. A distribution and an acquisition occurring after the distribution will not be considered part of a plan if—

(A) The distribution was not motivated by a business purpose to facilitate the acquisition or a similar acquisition;

(B) The acquisition occurred more than six months after the distribution and there was no agreement, understanding, arrangement, or substantial negotiations concerning the acquisition or a similar acquisition during the period that begins one year before the distribution and ends six months thereafter; and

(C) No more than 25 percent of the stock of the acquired corporation (Distributing or Controlled) was either acquired or the subject of an agreement, understanding, arrangement, or substantial negotiations during the period that begins one year before the distribution and ends six months thereafter.

(ii) Special rule. For purposes of paragraph (d)(2)(i)(C) of this section, acquisitions of stock that are treated as not part of a plan pursuant to Safe Harbor VII, Safe Harbor VIII, or Safe Harbor IX are disregarded.

(3) Safe Harbor III. If an acquisition occurs after a distribution, there was no agreement, understanding, or arrangement concerning the acquisition or a similar acquisition at the time of the distribution, and there was no agreement, understanding, arrangement, or substantial negotiations concerning the acquisition or a similar acquisition within one year after the distribution, the acquisition and the distribution will not be considered part of a plan.

(4) Safe Harbor IV—(i) In general. A distribution and an acquisition (other than involving a public offering) occurring before the distribution will not be considered part of a plan if the acquisition occurs before the date of the first disclosure event regarding the distribution.

(ii) Special rules. (A) Paragraph (d)(4)(i) of this section does not apply to a stock acquisition if the acquirer or a coordinating group of

which the acquirer is a member is a controlling shareholder or a ten-percent shareholder of the acquired corporation (Distributing or Controlled) at any time during the period beginning immediately after the acquisition and ending on the date of the distribution.

(B) Paragraph (d)(4)(i) of this section does not apply to an acquisition that occurs in connection with a transaction in which the aggregate acquisitions are of stock possessing 20 percent or more of the total voting power of the stock of the acquired corporation (Distributing or Controlled) or stock having a value of 20 percent or more of the total value of the stock of the acquired corporation (Distributing or Controlled).

(5) Safe Harbor V—(i) In general. A distribution that is *pro rata* among the Distributing shareholders and an acquisition (other than involving a public offering) of Distributing stock occurring before the distribution will not be considered part of a plan if—

(A) The acquisition occurs after the date of a public announcement regarding the distribution; and

(B) There were no discussions by Distributing or Controlled with the acquirer regarding a distribution on or before the date of the first public announcement regarding the distribution.

(ii) Special rules. (A) Paragraph (d)(5)(i) of this section does not apply to a stock acquisition if the acquirer or a coordinating group of which the acquirer is a member is a controlling shareholder or a ten-percent shareholder of Distributing at any time during the period beginning immediately after the acquisition and ending on the date of the distribution.

(B) Paragraph (d)(5)(i) of this section does not apply to an acquisition that occurs in connection with a transaction in which the aggregate acquisitions are of stock possessing 20 percent or more of the total voting power of the stock of Distributing or stock having a value of 20 percent or more of the total value of the stock of Distributing.

(6) Safe Harbor VI. A distribution and an acquisition involving a public offering occurring before the distribution will not be considered part of a plan if the acquisition occurs before the date of the first disclosure event regarding the distribution in the case of an acquisition of stock that is not listed on an established market immediately after the acquisition, or before the date of the first public announcement regarding the distribution in the case of an acquisition of stock that is listed on an established market immediately after the acquisition.

(7) Safe Harbor VII—(i) In general. An acquisition (other than involving a public offering) of Distributing or Controlled stock that is listed on an established market is not part of a plan if, immediately before or immediately after the transfer, none of the transferor, the transferee, and any coordinating group of which either the transferor or the transferee is a member is—

(A) The acquired corporation (Distributing or Controlled);

(B) A corporation that the acquired corporation (Distributing or Controlled) controls within the meaning of section 368(c);

(C) A member of a controlled group of corporations within the meaning of section 1563 of which the acquired corporation (Distributing or Controlled) is a member;

(D) A controlling shareholder of the acquired corporation (Distributing or Controlled); or

(E) A ten-percent shareholder of the acquired corporation (Distributing or Controlled).

(ii) Special rules. (A) Paragraph (d)(7)(i) of this section does not apply to a transfer of stock by or to a person if the corporation the stock of which is being transferred knows, or has reason to know, that the person or a coor-

dinating group of which such person is a member intends to become a controlling shareholder or a ten-percent shareholder of the acquired corporation (Distributing or Controlled) at any time after the acquisition and before the date that is two years after the distribution.

(B) If a transfer of stock to which paragraph (d)(7)(i) of this section applies results immediately, or upon a subsequent event or the passage of time, in an indirect acquisition of voting power by a person other than the transferee, paragraph (d)(7)(i) of this section does not prevent an acquisition of stock (with the voting power such stock represents after the transfer to which paragraph (d)(7)(i) of this section applies) by such other person from being treated as part of a plan.

(8) Safe Harbor VIII—(i) In general. If, in a transaction to which section 83 or section 421(a) or (b) applies, stock of Distributing or Controlled is acquired by a person in connection with such person's performance of services as an employee, director, or independent contractor for Distributing, Controlled, a related person, a corporation the assets of which Distributing, Controlled, or a related person acquires in a reorganization under section 368(a), or a corporation that acquires the assets of Distributing or Controlled in such a reorganization (and the stock acquired is not excessive by reference to the services performed), the acquisition and the distribution will not be considered part of a plan. For purposes of this paragraph (d)(8)(i), a related person is a person related to Distributing or Controlled under section 355(d)(7)(A).

(ii) Special rule. Paragraph (d)(8)(i) of this section does not apply to a stock acquisition if the acquirer or a coordinating group of which the acquirer is a member is a controlling shareholder or a ten-percent shareholder of the acquired corporation (Distributing or Controlled) immediately after the acquisition.

(9) Safe Harbor IX—(i) In general. If stock of Distributing or Controlled is acquired by a retirement plan of Distributing or Controlled (or a retirement plan of any other person that is treated as the same employer as Distributing or Controlled under section 414(b), (c), (m), or (*o*)) that qualifies under section 401(a) or 403(a), the acquisition and the distribution will not be considered part of a plan.

(ii) Special rule. Paragraph (d)(9)(i) of this section does not apply to the extent that the stock acquired pursuant to acquisitions by all of the qualified plans of the persons described in paragraph (d)(9)(i) of this section during the four-year period beginning two years before the distribution, in the aggregate, represents more than ten percent of the total combined voting power of all classes of stock entitled to vote, or more than ten percent of the total value of shares of all classes of stock, of the acquired corporation (Distributing or Controlled).

(e) Options, warrants, convertible obligations, and other similar interests — (1) Treatment of options — (i) General rule. For purposes of this section, if stock of Distributing or Controlled is acquired pursuant to an option that is written by Distributing, Controlled, or a person that is a controlling shareholder of Distributing or Controlled at the time the option is written, or that is acquired by a person that is a controlling shareholder of Distributing or Controlled immediately after the option is written, the option will be treated as an agreement, understanding, or arrangement to acquire the stock on the earliest of the following dates: the date that the option is written, if the option was more likely than not to be exercised as of such date; the date that the option is transferred if, immediately before or immediately after the transfer, the transferor or transferee was Distributing, Controlled, a corporation that Distributing or Controlled controls within the meaning of section 368(c), a member of a controlled group of corporations within the meaning of section 1563 of which Distributing or Controlled is a member, or a controlling shareholder or a ten-percent shareholder of Distributing or Controlled and the option was more likely than not to be exercised as of such

date; and the date that the option is modified in a manner that materially increases the likelihood of exercise, if the option was more likely than not to be exercised as of such date; provided, however, if the writing, transfer, or modification had a principal purpose of avoiding section 355(e), the option will be treated as an agreement, understanding, arrangement, or substantial negotiations to acquire the stock on the date of the distribution. The determination of whether an option was more likely than not to be exercised is based on all the facts and circumstances, taking control premiums and minority and blockage discounts into account in determining the fair market value of stock underlying an option.

(ii) Agreement, understanding, or arrangement to write, transfer, or modify an option. If there is an agreement, understanding, or arrangement to write an option, the option will be treated as written on the date of the agreement, understanding, or arrangement. If there is an agreement, understanding, or arrangement to transfer an option, the option will be treated as transferred on the date of the agreement, understanding, or arrangement. If there is an agreement, understanding, or arrangement to modify an option in a manner that materially increases the likelihood of exercise, the option will be treated as so modified on the date of the agreement, understanding, or arrangement.

(iii) Substantial negotiations related to options. If an option is treated as an agreement, understanding, or arrangement to acquire the stock on the date that the option is written, substantial negotiations to acquire the option will be treated as substantial negotiations to acquire the stock subject to such option. If an option is treated as an agreement, understanding, or arrangement to acquire the stock on the date that the option is transferred, substantial negotiations regarding the transfer of the option will be treated as substantial negotiations to acquire the stock subject to such option. If an option is treated as an agreement, understanding, or arrangement to acquire the stock on the date that the option is modified in a manner that materially increases the likelihood of exercise, substantial negotiations regarding such modifications to the option will be treated as substantial negotiations to acquire the stock subject to such option.

(2) Stock acquired pursuant to options. For purposes of this section, if an option is issued for cash, the terms of the acquisition of the option and the terms of the option are established by the corporation the stock of which is subject to the option (Distributing or Controlled) or the writer with the involvement of one or more investment bankers, and the potential acquirers of the option have no opportunity to negotiate the terms of the acquisition of the option or the terms of the option, then an acquisition pursuant to such option shall be treated as an acquisition involving a public offering occurring after the distribution if the option is exercised after the distribution or an acquisition involving a public offering before a distribution if the option is exercised before the distribution. Otherwise, an acquisition pursuant to an option shall be treated as an acquisition not involving a public offering.

(3) Instruments treated as options. For purposes of this section, except to the extent provided in paragraph (e)(4) of this section, call options, warrants, convertible obligations, the conversion feature of convertible stock, put options, redemption agreements (including rights to cause the redemption of stock), any other instruments that provide for the right or possibility to issue, redeem, or transfer stock (including an option on an option), or any other similar interests are treated as options.

(4) Instruments generally not treated as options. For purposes of this section, the following are not treated as options unless (in the case of paragraphs (e)(4)(i), (ii), and (iii) of this section) written, transferred (directly or indirectly), modified, or listed with a principal purpose of avoiding the application of section 355(e) or this section.

(i) Escrow, pledge, or other security agreements. An option that is part of a security arrangement in a typical lending transaction (including a purchase money loan), if the arrangement is subject to customary commercial conditions. For this purpose, a security arrangement includes, for example, an agreement for holding stock in escrow or under a pledge or other security agreement, or an option to acquire stock contingent upon a default under a loan.

(ii) Options exercisable only upon death, disability, mental incompetency, or separation from service. Any option entered into between shareholders of a corporation (or a shareholder and the corporation) that is exercisable only upon the death, disability, or mental incompetency of the shareholder, or, in the case of stock acquired in connection with the performance of services for the corporation or a person related to it under section 355(d)(7)(A) (and that is not excessive by reference to the services performed), the shareholder's separation from service.

(iii) Rights of first refusal. A *bona fide* right of first refusal regarding the corporation's stock with customary terms, entered into between shareholders of a corporation (or between the corporation and a shareholder).

(iv) Other enumerated instruments. Any other instrument the Commissioner may designate in revenue procedures, notices, or other guidance published in the Internal Revenue Bulletin (see § 601.601(d)(2) of this chapter).

(f) Multiple controlled corporations. Only the stock or securities of a controlled corporation in which one or more persons acquire directly or indirectly stock representing a 50-percent or greater interest as part of a plan involving the distribution of that corporation will be treated as not qualified property under section 355(e)(1) if—

(1) The stock or securities of more than one controlled corporation are distributed in distributions to which section 355 (or so much of section 356 as relates to section 355) applies; and

(2) One or more persons do not acquire, directly or indirectly, stock representing a 50-percent or greater interest in Distributing pursuant to a plan involving any of those distributions.

(g) Valuation. Except as provided in paragraph (e)(1)(i) of this section, for purposes of section 355(e) and this section, all shares of stock within a single class are considered to have the same value. Thus, control premiums and minority and blockage discounts within a single class are not taken into account.

(h) Definitions. For purposes of this section, the following definitions shall apply:

(1) Agreement, understanding, arrangement, or substantial negotiations. (i) An agreement, understanding, or arrangement generally requires either—

(A) an agreement, understanding, or arrangement by one or more officers or directors acting on behalf of Distributing or Controlled, by controlling shareholders of Distributing or Controlled, or by another person or persons with the implicit or explicit permission of one or more of such officers, directors, or controlling shareholders, with the acquirer or with a person or persons with the implicit or explicit permission of the acquirer; or

(B) an agreement, understanding, or arrangement by an acquirer that is a controlling shareholder of Distributing or Controlled immediately after the acquisition that is the subject of the agreement, understanding, or arrangement, or by a person or persons with the implicit or explicit permission of such acquirer, with the transferor or with a person or persons with the implicit or explicit permission of the transferor.

(ii) In the case of an acquisition by a corporation, an agreement, understanding, or arrangement with the acquiring corporation generally requires an agreement, understanding, or arrangement with one or more officers or

directors acting on behalf of the acquiring corporation, with controlling shareholders of the acquiring corporation, or with another person or persons with the implicit or explicit permission of one or more of such officers, directors, or controlling shareholders.

(iii) Whether an agreement, understanding, or arrangement exists depends on the facts and circumstances. The parties do not necessarily have to have entered into a binding contract or have reached agreement on all significant economic terms to have an agreement, understanding, or arrangement. However, an agreement, understanding, or arrangement clearly exists if a binding contract to acquire stock exists.

(iv) Substantial negotiations in the case of an acquisition (other than involving a public offering) generally require discussions of significant economic terms, *e.g.*, the exchange ratio in a reorganization, either—

(A) by one or more officers or directors acting on behalf of Distributing or Controlled, by controlling shareholders of Distributing or Controlled, or by another person or persons with the implicit or explicit permission of one or more of such officers, directors, or controlling shareholders, with the acquirer or with a person or persons with the implicit or explicit permission of the acquirer; or

(B) if the acquirer is a controlling shareholder of Distributing or Controlled immediately after the acquisition that is the subject of substantial negotiations, by the acquirer or by a person or persons with the implicit or explicit permission of the acquirer, with the transferor or with a person or persons with the implicit or explicit permission of the transferor.

(v) In the case of an acquisition (other than involving a public offering) by a corporation, substantial negotiations generally require discussions of significant economic terms with one or more officers or directors acting on behalf of the acquiring corporation, with controlling shareholders of the acquiring corporation, or with another person or persons with the implicit or explicit permission of one or more of such officers, directors, or controlling shareholders.

(vi) In the case of an acquisition involving a public offering, the existence of an agreement, understanding, arrangement, or substantial negotiations will be based on discussions by one or more officers or directors acting on behalf of Distributing or Controlled, by controlling shareholders of Distributing or Controlled, or by another person or persons with the implicit or explicit permission of one or more of such officers, directors, or controlling shareholders, with an investment banker.

(2) Controlled corporation. A controlled corporation is a corporation the stock of which is distributed in a distribution to which section 355 (or so much of section 356 as relates to section 355) applies.

(3) Controlling shareholder. (i) A controlling shareholder of a corporation the stock of which is listed on an established market is a five-percent shareholder who actively participates in the management or operation of the corporation. For purposes of this paragraph (h)(3)(i), a corporate director will be treated as actively participating in the management of the corporation.

(ii) A controlling shareholder of a corporation the stock of which is not listed on an established market is any person that owns stock possessing voting power representing a meaningful voice in the governance of the corporation. For purposes of determining whether a person owns stock possessing voting power representing a meaningful voice in the governance of the corporation, the person shall be treated as owning the stock that such person owns actually and constructively under the rules of section 318 (without regard to section 318(a)(4)). In addition, if the exercise of an option (whether by itself or in conjunction with the deemed exercise of one or more other options) would cause the holder to own stock possessing voting power representing

a meaningful voice in the governance of the corporation, then the option will be treated as exercised.

(iii) If a distribution precedes an acquisition, Controlled's controlling shareholders immediately after the distribution and Distributing are included among Controlled's controlling shareholders at the time of the distribution.

(4) Coordinating group. A coordinating group includes two or more persons that, pursuant to a formal or informal understanding, join in one or more coordinated acquisitions or dispositions of stock of Distributing or Controlled. A principal element in determining if such an understanding exists is whether the investment decision of each person is based on the investment decision of one or more other existing or prospective shareholders. A coordinating group is treated as a single shareholder for purposes of determining whether the coordinating group is treated as a controlling shareholder, a five-percent shareholder, or a ten-percent shareholder.

(5) Disclosure event. A disclosure event regarding the distribution means any communication by an officer, director, controlling shareholder, or employee of Distributing, Controlled, or a corporation related to Distributing or Controlled, or an outside advisor of any of those persons (where such advisor makes the communication on behalf of such person), regarding the distribution, or the possibility thereof, to the acquirer or any other person (other than an officer, director, controlling shareholder, or employee of Distributing, Controlled, or a corporation related to Distributing or Controlled, or an outside advisor of any of those persons). For purposes of this paragraph (h)(5), a corporation is related to Distributing or Controlled if it is a member of an affiliated group (as defined in section 1504(a) without regard to section 1504(b)) that includes either Distributing or Controlled or it is a member of a qualified group (as defined in § 1.368–1(d)

(4)(ii)) that includes either Distributing or Controlled.

(6) Discussions. Discussions by Distributing or Controlled generally require discussions by one or more officers or directors acting on behalf of Distributing or Controlled, by controlling shareholders of Distributing or Controlled, or by another person or persons with the implicit or explicit permission of one or more of such officers, directors, or controlling shareholders. Discussions with the acquirer generally require discussions with the acquirer or with a person or persons with the implicit or explicit permission of the acquirer. In the case of an acquisition by a corporation, discussions with the acquiring corporation generally require discussions with one or more officers or directors acting on behalf of the acquiring corporation, with controlling shareholders of the acquiring corporation, or with another person or persons with the implicit or explicit permission of one or more of such officers, directors, or controlling shareholders.

(7) Established market. An established market is—

(i) A national securities exchange registered under section 6 of the Securities Exchange Act of 1934 (15 U.S.C. 78f);

(ii) An interdealer quotation system sponsored by a national securities association registered under section 15A of the Securities Act of 1934 (15 U.S.C. 78o–3); or

(iii) Any additional market that the Commissioner may designate in revenue procedures, notices, or other guidance published in the Internal Revenue Bulletin (see § 601.601(d)(2) of this chapter).

(8) Five-percent shareholder. A person will be considered a five-percent shareholder of a corporation the stock of which is listed on an established market if the person owns five percent or more of any class of stock of the corporation whose stock is transferred. For purposes of determining whether a person owns five percent or more of any class of stock

of the corporation whose stock is transferred, the person shall be treated as owning the stock that such person owns actually and constructively under the rules of section 318 (without regard to section 318(a)(4)). In addition, if the exercise of an option (whether by itself or in conjunction with the deemed exercise of one or more other options) would cause the holder to become a five-percent shareholder, then the option will be treated as exercised. Absent actual knowledge that a person is a five-percent shareholder, a corporation can rely on Schedules 13D and 13G (or any similar schedules) filed with the Securities and Exchange Commission to identify its five-percent shareholders.

(9) Implicit permission. A corporation is treated as having the implicit permission of its shareholders when it engages in discussions or negotiations, or enters into an agreement, understanding, or arrangement.

(10) Public announcement. A public announcement regarding the distribution means any communication by Distributing or Controlled regarding Distributing's intention to effect the distribution where the communication is generally available to the public.

(11) Public offering. An acquisition involving a public offering means an acquisition of stock for cash where the terms of the acquisition are established by the acquired corporation (Distributing or Controlled) or the seller with the involvement of one or more investment bankers and the potential acquirers have no opportunity to negotiate the terms of the acquisition. For example, a public offering includes an underwritten offering of registered stock for cash.

(12) Similar acquisition (not involving a public offering). In general, an actual acquisition (other than involving a public offering) is similar to another potential acquisition if the actual acquisition effects a direct or indirect combination of all or a significant portion of the same business operations as the combination that would have been effected by such other potential acquisition. Thus, an actual acquisition may be similar to another acquisition even if the timing or terms of the actual acquisition are different from the timing or terms of the other acquisition. For example, an actual acquisition of Distributing by shareholders of another corporation in connection with a merger of such other corporation with and into Distributing is similar to another acquisition of Distributing by merger into such other corporation or into a subsidiary of such other corporation. However, in general, an actual acquisition (other than involving a public offering) is not similar to another acquisition if the ultimate owners of the business operations with which Distributing or Controlled is combined in the actual acquisition are substantially different from the ultimate owners of the business operations with which Distributing or Controlled was to be combined in such other acquisition.

(13) Similar acquisition involving a public offering—(i) One public offering. In general, an actual acquisition involving a public offering may be similar to a potential acquisition involving a public offering, even though there are changes in the terms of the stock, the class of stock being offered, the size of the offering, the timing of the offering, the price of the stock, or the participants in the offering.

(ii) More than one public offering. More than one actual acquisition involving a public offering may be similar to a potential acquisition involving a public offering. If there is an actual acquisition involving a public offering (the first public offering) that is the same as, or similar to, a potential acquisition involving a public offering, then another actual acquisition involving a public offering (the second public offering) cannot be similar to the potential acquisition unless the purpose of the second public offering is similar to that of the potential acquisition and occurs close in time to the first public offering.

(iii) Potential acquisition involving a public offering. For purposes of paragraph (h)

(13)(i) and (ii) of this section, as the context may require, a potential acquisition involving a public offering means a potential acquisition involving a public offering that was discussed by Distributing or Controlled with an investment banker, that motivated the distribution, or that was the subject of an agreement, understanding, arrangement, or substantial negotiations.

(14) Ten-percent shareholder. A person will be considered a ten-percent shareholder of a corporation the stock of which is listed on an established market if the person owns, actually or constructively under the rules of section 318 (without regard to section 318(a)(4)), ten percent or more of any class of stock of the corporation whose stock is transferred. A person will be considered a ten-percent shareholder of a corporation the stock of which is not listed on an established market if the person owns stock possessing ten percent or more of the total voting power of the stock of the corporation whose stock is transferred or stock having a value equal to ten percent or more of the total value of the stock of the corporation whose stock is transferred. For purposes of determining whether a person owns ten percent or more of the total voting power or value of the stock of the corporation whose stock is transferred, the person shall be treated as owning the stock that such person owns actually and constructively under the rules of section 318 (without regard to section 318(a)(4)). In addition, if the exercise of an option (whether by itself or in conjunction with the deemed exercise of one or more other options) would cause the holder to become a ten-percent shareholder, then the option will be treated as exercised. Absent actual knowledge that a person is a ten-percent shareholder, a corporation the stock of which is listed on an established market can rely on Schedules 13D and 13G (or any similar schedules) filed with the Securities and Exchange Commission to identify its ten-percent shareholders.

(i) [Reserved].

(j) Examples. The following examples illustrate paragraphs (a) through (h) of this section. Throughout these examples, assume that Distributing (D) owns all of the stock of Controlled (C). Assume further that D distributes the stock of C in a distribution to which section 355 applies and to which section 355(d) does not apply. Unless otherwise stated, assume the corporations do not have controlling shareholders. No inference should be drawn from any example concerning whether any requirements of section 355 other than those of section 355(e) are satisfied. The examples are as follows:

Example (1). Unwanted assets. (i) D is in business 1. C is in business 2. D is relatively small in its industry. D wants to combine with X, a larger corporation also engaged in business 1. X and D begin negotiating for X to acquire D, but X does not want to acquire C. To facilitate the acquisition of D by X, D agrees to distribute all the stock of C *pro rata* before the acquisition. Prior to the distribution, D and X enter into a contract for D to merge into X subject to several conditions. One month after D and X enter into the contract, D distributes C and, on the day after the distribution, D merges into X. As a result of the merger, D's former shareholders own less than 50 percent of the stock of X.

(ii) The issue is whether the distribution of C and the merger of D into X are part of a plan. No Safe Harbor applies to this acquisition. To determine whether the distribution of C and the merger of D into X are part of a plan, D must consider all the facts and circumstances, including those described in paragraph (b) of this section.

(iii) The following tends to show that the distribution of C and the merger of D into X are part of a plan: X and D had an agreement regarding the acquisition during the two-year period ending on the date of the distribution (paragraph (b)(3)(i) of this section), and the distribution was motivated by a business purpose to facilitate the merger (paragraph (b)(3)

(v) of this section). Because the merger was agreed to at the time of the distribution, the fact described in paragraph (b)(3)(i) of this section is given substantial weight.

(iv) None of the facts and circumstances listed in paragraph (b)(4) of this section, tending to show that a distribution and an acquisition are not part of a plan, exist in this case.

(v) The distribution of C and the merger of D into X are part of a plan under paragraph (b) of this section.

Example (2). Public offering. (i) D's managers, directors, and investment banker discuss the possibility of offering D stock to the public. They decide a public offering of 20 percent of D's stock with D as a stand-alone corporation would be in D's best interest. One month later, to facilitate a stock offering by D of 20 percent of its stock, D distributes all the stock of C *pro rata* to D's shareholders. D issues new shares amounting to 20 percent of its stock to the public in a public offering seven months after the distribution.

(ii) The issue is whether the distribution of C and the public offering by D are part of a plan. No Safe Harbor applies to this acquisition. Safe Harbor VII, relating to public trading, does not apply to public offerings (see paragraph (d)(7)(i) of this section). To determine whether the distribution of C and the public offering by D are part of a plan, D must consider all the facts and circumstances, including those described in paragraph (b) of this section.

(iii) The following tends to show that the distribution of C and the public offering by D are part of a plan: D discussed the public offering with its investment banker during the two-year period ending on the date of the distribution (paragraph (b)(3)(ii) of this section), and the distribution was motivated by a business purpose to facilitate the public offering (paragraph (b)(3)(v) of this section).

(iv) None of the facts and circumstances listed in paragraph (b)(4) of this section, tend-

ing to show that a distribution and an acquisition are not part of a plan, exist in this case.

(v) The distribution of C and the public offering by D are part of a plan under paragraph (b) of this section.

Example (3). Hot market. (i) D is a widely-held corporation the stock of which is listed on an established market. D announces a distribution of C and distributes C *pro rata* to D's shareholders. By contract, C agrees to indemnify D for any imposition of tax under section 355(e) caused by the acts of C. The distribution is motivated by a desire to improve D's access to financing at preferred customer interest rates, which will be more readily available if D separates from C. At the time of the distribution, although neither D nor C has been approached by any potential acquirer of C, it is reasonably certain that soon after the distribution either an acquisition of C will occur or there will be an agreement, understanding, arrangement, or substantial negotiations regarding an acquisition of C. Corporation Y acquires C in a merger described in section 368(a)(1)(A) by reason of section 368(a)(2)(E) within six months after the distribution. The C shareholders receive less than 50 percent of the stock of Y in the exchange.

(ii) The issue is whether the distribution of C and the acquisition of C by Y are part of a plan. No Safe Harbor applies to this acquisition. Under paragraph (b)(2) of this section, because prior to the distribution neither D nor C and Y had an agreement, understanding, arrangement, or substantial negotiations regarding the acquisition or a similar acquisition, the distribution of C by D and the acquisition of C by Y are not part of a plan under paragraph (b) of this section.

Example (4). Unexpected opportunity. (i) D, the stock of which is listed on an established market, makes a public announcement that it will distribute all the stock of C *pro rata* to D's shareholders. After the public announcement but before the distribution, widely-held X becomes available as an acquisition target.

There were no discussions by D or C with X before the date of the public announcement. D negotiates with X and X merges into D before the distribution. In the merger, X's shareholders receive ten percent of D's stock. D distributes the stock of C *pro rata* within six months after the acquisition of X. No shareholder of X was a controlling shareholder or a ten-percent shareholder of D at any time during the period beginning immediately after the merger and ending on the date of the distribution

(ii) The issue is whether the acquisition of X by D and the distribution of C are part of a plan. Safe Harbor V applies to this acquisition because the distribution is *pro rata* among D's shareholders, the acquisition occurs after the date of a public announcement regarding the distribution, there were no discussions by D or C with X on or before the date of the public announcement, no acquirer was a controlling shareholder or a ten-percent shareholder of D during the period beginning immediately after the merger and ending on the date of the distribution, and not more than 20 percent of D's stock was acquired by the X shareholders in the merger.

Example (5). Vote shifting transaction. (i) D is in business 1. C is in business 2. D wants to combine with X, which is also engaged in business 1. The stock of X is closely held. X and D begin negotiating for D to acquire X, but the X shareholders do not want to acquire an indirect interest in C. To facilitate the acquisition of X by D, D agrees to distribute all the stock of C *pro rata* before the acquisition of X. D and X enter into a contract for X to merge into D subject to several conditions. Among those conditions is that D will amend its corporate charter to provide for two classes of stock: Class A and Class B. Under all circumstances, each share of Class A stock will be entitled to ten votes in the election of each director on D's board of directors. Upon issuance, each share of Class B stock will be entitled to ten votes in the election of each director on D's board of directors; however, a disposition of such share by its original holder will result in such share being entitled to only one vote, rather than ten votes, in the election of each director. Immediately after the merger, the Class B shares will be listed on an established market. One month after D and X enter into the contract, D distributes C. Immediately after the distribution, the shareholders of D exchange their D stock for the new Class B shares. On the day after the distribution, X merges into D. In the merger, the former shareholders of X exchange their X stock for Class A shares of D. Immediately after the merger, D's historic shareholders own stock of D representing 51 percent of the total combined voting power of all classes of stock of D entitled to vote and more than 50 percent of the total value of all classes of stock of D. During the 30-day period following the merger, none of the Class A shares are transferred, but a number of D's historic shareholders sell their Class B stock of D in public trading with the result that, at the end of that 30-day period, the Class A shares owned by the former X shareholders represent 52 percent of the total combined voting power of all classes of stock of D entitled to vote.

(ii) X acquisition. (A) The issue is whether the distribution of C and the merger of X into D are part of a plan. No Safe Harbor applies to this acquisition. To determine whether the distribution of C and the merger of X into D are part of a plan, D must consider all the facts and circumstances, including those described in paragraph (b) of this section.

(B) The following tends to show that the distribution of C and the merger of X into D are part of a plan: X and D had an agreement regarding the acquisition during the two-year period ending on the date of the distribution (paragraph (b)(3)(i) of this section), and the distribution was motivated by a business purpose to facilitate the merger (paragraph (b)(3) (v) of this section). Because the merger was agreed to at the time of the distribution, the fact described in paragraph (b)(3)(i) of this section is given substantial weight.

(C) None of the facts and circumstances listed in paragraph (b)(4) of this section, tending to show that a distribution and an acquisition are not part of a plan, exist in this case.

(D) The distribution of C and the merger of X into D are part of a plan under paragraph (b) of this section.

(iii) Public trading of Class B shares. (A) Assuming that each of the transferors and the transferees of the Class B stock of D in public trading is not one of the prohibited transferors or transferees listed in paragraph (d)(7)(i), Safe Harbor VII will apply to the acquisitions of the Class B stock during the 30-day period following the merger such that the distribution and those acquisitions will not be treated as part of a plan. However, to the extent that those acquisitions result in an indirect acquisition of voting power by a person other than the acquirer of the transferred stock, Safe Harbor VII does not prevent the acquisition of the D stock (with the voting power such stock represents after those acquisitions) by the former X shareholders from being treated as part of a plan.

(B) To the extent that the transfer of the Class B shares causes the voting power of D to shift to the Class A stock acquired by the former X shareholders, such shifted voting power will be treated as attributable to the stock acquired by the former X shareholders as part of a plan that includes the distribution and the X acquisition.

Example (6). Acquisition not involving a public offering that is not similar. (i) D, X, and Y are each corporations the stock of which is publicly traded and widely held. Each of D, X, and Y is engaged in the manufacture and sale of trucks. C is engaged in the manufacture and sale of buses. D and X engage in substantial negotiations concerning X's acquisition of the stock of D from the D shareholders in exchange for stock of X. D and X do not reach an agreement regarding that acquisition. Three months after D and X first began negotiations regarding that acquisition, D distributes the stock of C *pro rata* to its shareholders. Three months after the distribution, Y acquires the stock of D from the D shareholders in exchange for stock of Y. The ultimate owners of Y are substantially different from the ultimate owners of X.

(ii) Although both X and Y engage in the manufacture and sale of trucks, X's truck business and Y's truck business are not the same business operations. Therefore, because Y's acquisition of D does not effect a combination of the same business operations as X's acquisition of D would have effected, and because the ultimate owners of Y are substantially different from the ultimate owners of X, Y's acquisition of D is not similar to X's potential acquisition of D that was the subject of earlier negotiations.

Example (7). Acquisition not involving a public offering that is similar. (i) D is engaged in the business of writing custom software for several industries (industries 1 through 6). The software business of D related to industries 4, 5, and 6 is significant relative to the software business of D related to industries 3, 4, 5, and 6. X, an unrelated corporation, is engaged in the business of writing software and the business of manufacturing and selling hardware devices. X's business of writing software is significant relative to its total businesses. X and D engage in substantial negotiations regarding X's acquisition of D stock from the D shareholders in exchange for stock of X. Because X does not want to acquire the software businesses related to industries 1 and 2, these negotiations relate to an acquisition of D stock where D owns the software businesses related only to industries 3, 4, 5, and 6. Thereafter, D concludes that the intellectual property licenses central to the software business related to industries 1 and 2 are not transferable and that a separation of the software business related to industry 3 from the software business related to industry 2 is not desirable. One month after D begins negotiating with X, D contributes the software businesses related to industries 4, 5,

and 6 to C, and distributes the stock of C *pro rata* to its shareholders. In addition, X sells its hardware businesses for cash. After the distribution, C and X negotiate for X's acquisition of the C stock from the C shareholders in exchange for X stock, and X acquires the stock of C.

(ii) Although D and C are different corporations, C does not own the custom software business related to industry 3, and X sold its hardware business prior to the acquisition of C, because X's acquisition of C involves a combination of a significant portion of the same business operations as the combination that would have been effected by the acquisition of D that was the subject of negotiations between D and X, X's acquisition of C is the same as, or similar to, X's potential acquisition of D that was the subject of earlier negotiations.

Example (8). Acquisitions involving public offerings with different purposes. (i) D's managers, directors, and investment banker discuss the possibility of offering D stock to the public for the purpose of funding the acquisition of the assets of X. They decide a public offering of 20 percent of D's stock with D as a stand-alone corporation would allow D to raise the capital needed to effect the acquisition of X's assets. One month later, to facilitate a stock offering by D of 20 percent of its stock, D distributes all the stock of C *pro rata* to D's shareholders. Two months after the distribution, D issues new shares amounting to 20 percent of its stock to the public in a public offering (the first public offering). Four months after the distribution, D acquires the assets of X. Seven months after the distribution, D's managers, directors, and investment banker discuss the possibility of offering D stock to the public solely for the purpose of funding the acquisition of the assets of Y, a corporation unrelated to X. One year after the distribution, D issues new shares amounting to 40 percent of its stock to the public in a public offering (the second public offering). One month after the second public offering, D acquires the assets of Y.

(ii) The first public offering is the same as the potential acquisition that D's managers, directors, and investment banker discussed prior to the distribution. The purpose of the second public offering (funding the acquisition of the assets of Y) is not similar to that of the potential acquisition (funding the acquisition of the assets of X). Therefore, the second public offering is not similar to the potential acquisition.

Example (9). Acquisitions involving public offerings that are close in time. (i) D's managers, directors, and investment banker discuss the possibility of offering D stock to the public for the purpose of raising funds for general corporate purposes. They decide a public offering of 20 percent of D's stock with D as a stand-alone corporation would allow D to raise such funds. One month later, to facilitate a stock offering by D of 20 percent of its stock, D distributes all the stock of C *pro rata* to D's shareholders. Two months after the distribution, D issues new shares amounting to 20 percent of its stock to the public in a public offering (the first public offering). After the first public offering, D's managers, directors, and investment banker discuss the possibility of another offering of D stock to the public for the purpose of raising additional funds for general corporate purposes. Eight months after the distribution, D issues new shares amounting to ten percent of its stock to the public in a public offering (the second public offering).

(ii) The first public offering is the same as the potential acquisition that D's managers, directors, and investment banker discussed prior to the distribution. The purpose of the second public offering (raising funds for general corporate purposes) is the same as that of the potential acquisition. In addition, the second public offering is close in time to the first public offering. Therefore, the second public offering is similar to the potential acquisition.

Example (10). Acquisitions involving public offerings that are not close in time. The facts are the same as those in *Example 9*, except that the second public offering occurs fourteen months after the distribution. Although the purpose of the second public offering is the same as that of the potential acquisition, the second public offering is not close in time to the first public offering. Therefore, the second public offering is not similar to the potential acquisition.

(k) Effective dates. This section applies to distributions occurring after April 19, 2005. For distributions occurring on or before April 19, 2005, and after April 26, 2002, see § 1.355–7T as contained in 26 CFR part 1 revised as of April 1, 2003; however, taxpayers may apply these regulations, in whole, but not in part, to such distributions. For distributions occurring on or before April 26, 2002, and after August 3, 2001, see § 1.355–7T as contained in 26 CFR part 1 revised as of April 1, 2002; however, taxpayers may apply, in whole, but not in part, either these regulations or § 1.355–7T as contained in 26 CFR part 1 revised as of April 1, 2003, to such distributions. For distributions occurring on or before August 3, 2001, and after April 16, 1997, taxpayers may apply, in whole, but not in part, either these regulations or § 1.355–7T as contained in 26 CFR part 1 revised as of April 1, 2003, to such distributions.

§ 1.356–1 Receipt of additional consideration in connection with an exchange.

(a) If in any exchange to which the provisions of section 354 or section 355 would apply except for the fact that there is received by the shareholders or security holders other property (in addition to property permitted to be received without recognition of gain by such sections) or money, then—

(1) The gain, if any, to the taxpayer shall be recognized in an amount not in excess of the sum of the money and the fair market value of the other property, but,

(2) The loss, if any, to the taxpayer from the exchange or distribution shall not be recognized to any extent.

(b) For purposes of computing the gain, if any, recognized pursuant to section 356 and paragraph (a)(1) of this section, to the extent the terms of the exchange specify the other property or money that is received in exchange for a particular share of stock or security surrendered or a particular class of stock or securities surrendered, such terms shall control provided that such terms are economically reasonable. To the extent the terms of the exchange do not specify the other property or money that is received in exchange for a particular share of stock or security surrendered or a particular class of stock or securities surrendered, a pro rata portion of the other property and money received shall be treated as received in exchange for each share of stock and security surrendered, based on the fair market value of such surrendered share of stock or security.

(c) If the distribution of such other property or money by or on behalf of a corporation has the effect of the distribution of a dividend, then there shall be chargeable to each distributee (either an individual or a corporation)—

(1) As a dividend, such an amount of the gain recognized as is not in excess of the distributee's ratable share of the undistributed earnings and profits of the corporation accumulated after February 28, 1913, and

(2) As a gain from the exchange of property, the remainder of the gain so recognized.

(d) The rules of this section may be illustrated by the following examples:

Example (1). In an exchange to which the provisions of section 356 apply and to which section 354 would apply but for the receipt of property not permitted to be received without the recognition of gain or loss, A (either an individual or a corporation), received the following in exchange for a share of stock having an adjusted basis to A of $85:

One share of stock worth	$100
Cash	25
Other property (basis $25)	
fair market value	50
Total fair market value of consideration received	175
Adjusted basis of stock surrendered in exchange	85
Total gain	90
Gain to be recognized, limited to cash and other property received	75
A's pro rata share of earnings and profits accumulated after February 28, 1913 (taxable dividend)	30
Remainder to be treated as a gain from the exchange of property	45

Example (2). If, in *Example 1*, A's stock had an adjusted basis to A of $200, A would have realized a loss of $25 on the exchange, which loss would not be recognized.

Example (3). (i) Facts. J, an individual, acquired 10 shares of Class A stock of Corporation X on Date 1 for $3 each and 10 shares of Class B stock of Corporation X on Date 2 for $9 each. On Date 3, Corporation Y acquires the assets of Corporation X in a reorganization under section 368(a)(1)(A). Pursuant to the terms of the plan of reorganization, J surrenders all of J's shares of Corporation X stock for 10 shares of Corporation Y stock and $100 of cash. On the date of the exchange, the fair market value of each share of Class A stock of Corporation X is $10, the fair market value of each share of Class B stock of Corporation X is $10, and the fair market value of each share of Corporation Y stock is $10. The terms of the exchange do not specify that shares of Corporation Y stock or cash are received in exchange for particular shares of Class A stock or Class B stock of Corporation X.

(ii) Analysis. Under paragraph (b) of this section, because the terms of the exchange do not specify that the cash is received in exchange for shares of Class A or Class B stock of Corporation X, a pro rata portion of the cash

received is treated as received in exchange for each share of Class A stock of Corporation X and each share of Class B stock of Corporation X based on the fair market value of the surrendered shares. Therefore, J is treated as receiving shares of Corporation Y stock with a fair market value of $50 and $50 of cash in exchange for its shares of Class A stock of Corporation X and shares of Corporation Y stock with a fair market value of $50 and $50 of cash in exchange for its shares of Class B stock of Corporation X. J realizes a gain of $70 on the exchange of shares of Class A stock, $50 of which is recognized under section 356 and paragraph (a) of this section, and J realizes a gain of $10 on the exchange of shares of Class B stock of Corporation X, all of which is recognized under section 356 and paragraph (a) of this section. Assuming that J's gain recognized is not treated as a dividend under section 356(a)(2), such gain shall be treated as gain from the exchange of property.

Example (4). *(i) Facts*. The facts are the same as in Example 3, except that the terms of the plan of reorganization specify that J receives 10 shares of stock of Corporation Y in exchange for J's shares of Class A stock of Corporation X and $100 of cash in exchange for J's shares of Class B stock of Corporation X.

(ii) Analysis. Under paragraph (b) of this section, because the terms of the exchange specify that J receives 10 shares of stock of Corporation Y in exchange for J's shares of Class A stock of Corporation X and $100 of cash in exchange for J's shares of Class B stock of Corporation X and such terms are economically reasonable, such terms control. J realizes a gain of $70 on the exchange of shares of Class A stock, none of which is recognized under section 356 and paragraph (a) of this section, and J realizes a gain of $10 on the exchange of shares of Class B stock of Corporation X, all of which is recognized under section 356 and paragraph (a) of this section.

(e) Section 301(b)(1)(B) and section 301(d)(2) do not apply to a distribution of "other property" to a corporate shareholder if such distribution is within the provisions of section 356.

(f) See paragraph (*l*) of § 1.301–1 for certain transactions which are not within the scope of section 356.

(g) This section applies to exchanges and distributions of stock and securities occurring on or after January 23, 2006.

§ 1.356–2 Receipt of additional consideration not in connection with an exchange.

(a) If, in a transaction to which section 355 would apply except for the fact that a shareholder (individual or corporate) receives property permitted by section 355 to be received without the recognition of gain, together with other property or money, without the surrender of any stock or securities of the distributing corporation, then the sum of the money and the fair market value of the other property as of the date of the distribution shall be treated as a distribution of property to which the rules of section 301 (other than section 301(b) and section 301(d)) apply. See section 358 for determination of basis of such other property.

(b) Paragraph (a) of this section may be illustrated by the following examples:

Example (1). Individuals A and B each own 50 of the 100 outstanding shares of common stock of Corporation X. Corporation X owns all of the stock of Corporation Y, 100 shares. Corporation X distributes to each shareholder 50 shares of the stock of Corporation Y plus $100 cash without requiring the surrender of any shares of its own stock. The $100 cash received by each is treated as a distribution of property to which the rules of section 301 apply.

Example (2). If, in the above example, Corporation X distributes 50 shares of stock of Corporation Y to A and 30 shares of such stock plus $100 cash to B without requiring the surrender of any of its own stock, the amount of cash received by B is treated as a distribution of property to which the rules of section 301 apply.

§ 1.356–3 Rules for treatment of securities as "other property".

(a) As a general rule, for purposes of section 356, the term "other property" includes securities. However, it does not include securities permitted under section 354 or section 355 to be received tax free. Thus, when securities are surrendered in a transaction to which section 354 or section 355 is applicable, the characterization of the securities received as "other property" does not include securities received where the principal amount of such securities does not exceed the principal amount of securities surrendered in the transaction. If a greater principal amount of securities is received in an exchange described in section 354 (other than subsection (c) or (d) thereof) or section 355 over the principal amount of securities surrendered, the term "other property" includes the fair market value of such excess principal amount as of the date of the exchange. If no securities are surrendered in exchange, the term "other property" includes the fair market value, as of the date of receipt, of the entire principal amount of the securities received.

(b) Except as provided in § 1.356–6, for purposes of this section, a right to acquire stock that is treated as a security for purposes of section 354 or 355 has no principal amount. Thus, such right is not other property when received in a transaction to which section 356 applies (regardless of whether securities are surrendered in the exchange).

(c) In the examples in this paragraph (c), stock means common stock and warrants means rights to acquire common stock. The following examples illustrate the rules of paragraph (a) of this section:

Example (1). A, an individual, exchanged 100 shares of stock for 100 shares of stock and a security in the principal amount of $1,000 with a fair market value of $990. The amount of $990 is treated as "other property."

Example (2). B, an individual, exchanged 100 shares of stock and a security in the principal amount of $1,000 for 300 shares of stock and a security in the principal amount of $1,500. The security had a fair market value on the date of receipt of $1,575. The fair market value of the excess principal amount, or $525, is treated as "other property."

Example (3). C, an individual, exchanged a security in the principal amount of $1,000 for 100 shares of stock and a security in the principal amount of $900. No part of the security received is treated as "other property."

Example (4). D, an individual, exchanged a security in the principal amount of $1,000 for 100 shares of stock and a security in the principal amount of $1,200 with a fair market value of $1,100. The fair market value of the excess principal amount, or $183.33, is treated as "other property."

Example (5). E, an individual, exchanged a security in the principal amount of $1,000 for another security in the principal amount of $1,200 with a fair market value of $1,080. The fair market value of the excess principal amount, or $180, is treated as "other property."

Example (6). F, an individual, exchanged a security in the principal amount of $1,000 for two different securities each in the principal amount of $750. One of the securities had a fair market value of $750, the other had a fair market value of $600. One-third of the fair market value of each security ($250 and $200) is treated as "other property."

Example (7). G, an individual, exchanged stock for stock and a warrant. The warrant had no principal amount. Thus, G received no excess principal amount within the meaning of section 356(d).

Example (8). H, an individual, exchanged a warrant for stock and a warrant. The warrants had no principal amount. Thus, H received no excess principal amount within the meaning of section 356(d).

Example (9). I, an individual, exchanged a warrant for stock and a debt security. The warrant had no principal amount. The debt security had a $100 principal amount. I received $100 of excess principal amount within the meaning of section 356(d).

§ 1.356–4 Exchanges for section 306 stock.

If, in a transaction to which section 356 is applicable, other property or money is received in exchange for section 306 stock, an amount equal to the fair market value of the property plus the money, if any, shall be treated as a distribution of property to which section 301 is applicable. The determination of whether section 306 stock is surrendered for other property (including money) is a question of fact to be decided under all of the circumstances of each case. Ordinarily, the other property (including money) received will first be treated as received in exchange for any section 306 stock owned by a shareholder prior to such transaction. For example, if a shareholder who owns a share of common stock (having a basis to him of $100) and a share of preferred stock which is section 306 stock (having a basis to him of $100) surrenders both shares in a transaction to which section 356 is applicable for one share of common stock having a fair market value of $80 and one $100 bond having a fair market value of $100, the bond will be deemed received in exchange for the section 306 stock and it will be treated as a distribution to which section 301 is applicable to the extent of its entire fair market value ($100).

§ 1.356–6 Rules for treatment of nonqualified preferred stock as other property.

(a) In general. For purposes of §§ 1.354–1(e), 1.355–1(c), and 1.356–3(b), the terms stock and securities do not include—

(1) Nonqualified preferred stock, as defined in section 351(g)(2), received in exchange for (or in a distribution with respect to) stock, or a

right to acquire stock, other than nonqualified preferred stock; or

(2) A right to acquire such nonqualified preferred stock, received in exchange for (or in a distribution with respect to) stock, or a right to acquire stock, other than nonqualified preferred stock.

(b) Exceptions. The following exceptions apply:

(1) Certain recapitalizations. Paragraph (a) of this section does not apply in the case of a recapitalization under section 368(a)(1)(E) of a family-owned corporation as described in section 354(a)(2)(C)(ii)(II).

* * *

§ 1.356–7 Rules for treatment of nonqualified preferred stock and other preferred stock received in certain transactions.

(a) Stock issued prior to effective date. Stock described in section 351(g)(2) is nonqualified preferred stock (NQPS) regardless of the date on which the stock is issued. However, sections 351(g), 354(a)(2)(C), 355(a)(3)(D), 356(e), and 1036(b) do not apply to any transaction occurring prior to June 9, 1997, or to any transaction occurring after June 8, 1997, that is described in section 1014(f)(2) of the Taxpayer Relief Act of 1997, Public Law 105–34 (111 Stat. 788, 921). For purposes of this section, preferred stock that is not NQPS is referred to as Qualified Preferred Stock (QPS).

(b) Receipt of preferred stock in exchange for (or distribution on) substantially identical preferred stock—(1) General rule. For purposes of sections 354(a)(2)(C)(i), 355(a)(3)(D), and 356(e)(2), preferred stock is QPS, even though it is described in section 351(g)(2), if it is received in exchange for (or in a distribution with respect to) preferred stock (the original preferred stock) that is QPS, provided—

(i) The original preferred stock is QPS solely because, on its issue date, either a right or obligation described in clause (i), (ii), or

(iii) of section 351(g)(2)(A) was not exercisable until after a 20-year period beginning on the issue date, or the right or obligation was exercisable within the 20-year period beginning on the issue date but was subject to a contingency which made remote the likelihood of the redemption or purchase, or the issuer's (or a related party's) right to redeem or purchase the stock was not more likely than not to be exercised within a 20-year period beginning on the issue date, or because of any combination of these reasons; and

(ii) The stock received is substantially identical to the original preferred stock.

(2) Substantially identical. The stock received is substantially identical to the original preferred stock if—

(i) The stock received does not contain any term or terms that, in relation to any term or terms of the original preferred stock, either decrease the period in which a right or obligation described in clause (i), (ii), or (iii) of section 351(g)(2)(A) can be exercised, or increase the likelihood that such a right or obligation will be exercised, or accelerate the timing of the returns from the stock instrument, including the timing of actual or deemed dividends or other distributions received on the stock; and

(ii) As a result of the exchange or distribution, exercise of the right or obligation does not become more likely than not to occur within a 20-year period beginning on the issue date of the original preferred stock.

(3) Treatment of stock received. The stock received will continue to be treated as QPS in subsequent transactions involving such stock, and the principles of this paragraph (b) apply to such transactions as though the stock received is the original preferred stock issued on the same date as the original preferred stock.

(c) Stock transferred for services. For purposes of sections 351(g)(1), 354(a)(2) (C)(i), 355(a)(3)(D), and 356(e)(2), preferred stock containing a right or obligation described in clause (i), (ii) or (iii) of section 351(g)(2)(A) that is exercisable only upon the holder's separation from service from the issuer or a related person (as described in section 351(g)(3)(B)) will be treated as transferred in connection with the performance of services (and representing reasonable compensation) within the meaning of section 351(g)(2)(C) (i)(II), if such preferred stock is received in exchange for (or in a distribution with respect to) existing stock containing a similar right or obligation (exercisable only upon separation from service) and the existing stock was transferred in connection with the performance of services for the issuer or a related person (and represented reasonable compensation when transferred). In applying the rules relating to NQPS, the preferred stock received will continue to be treated as transferred in connection with the performance of services (and representing reasonable compensation) in subsequent transactions involving such stock, and the principles of this paragraph (c) apply to such transactions.

(d) Rights to acquire stock. For purposes of § 1.356–6, the principles of paragraphs (a), (b), and (c) of this section apply.

(e) Examples. In the examples in this paragraph (e), T and P are corporations, A is a shareholder of T, and A surrenders and receives (in addition to the stock exchanged in the examples) common stock in the reorganizations described. The following examples illustrate paragraphs (a), (b), and (c) of this section:

Example (1). In 1995, A transfers property to T and receives T preferred stock that is described in section 351(g)(2) in a transaction under section 351. In 2002, pursuant to a reorganization under section 368(a)(1)(B), A surrenders the T preferred stock in exchange for P NQPS. Under paragraph (a) of this section, the T preferred stock issued to A in 1995 is NQPS. However, because section 351(g) does not apply to transactions occurring before June 9, 1997, the T NQPS was not "other property" within the meaning of section 351(b) when issued in 1995. Under sections 354(a)(2)(C) and 356(e)(2), the P NQPS received by A in 2002 is not "other property" within the meaning of section 356(a)(1)(B) because it is received in exchange for NQPS.

Example (2). T issues QPS to A on January 1, 2000 that is not NQPS solely because the holder cannot require T to redeem the stock until January 1, 2022. In 2007, pursuant to a reorganization under section 368(a)(1)(A) in which T merges into P, A surrenders the T preferred stock in exchange for P preferred stock with terms that are identical to the terms of the T preferred stock, including the term that the holder cannot require the redemption of the stock until January 1, 2022. Because the P stock and the T stock have identical terms, and because the redemption did not become more likely than not to occur within the 20-year period that begins on January 1, 2000 (which is the issue date of the T preferred stock) as a result of the exchange, under paragraph (b) of this section, the P preferred stock received by A is treated as QPS. Thus, the P preferred stock received is not "other property" within the meaning of section 356(a)(1)(B).

Example (3). The facts are the same as in *Example 2*, except that, in addition, in 2010, pursuant to a recapitalization of P under section 368(a)(1)(E), A exchanges the P preferred stock above for P NQPS that permits the holder to require P to redeem the stock in 2020. Under paragraph (b) of this section, the P preferred stock surrendered by A is treated as QPS. Because the P preferred stock received by A in the recapitalization is not substantially identical to the P preferred stock surrendered, the P preferred stock received by A is not treated as QPS. Thus, the P preferred stock received is "other property" within the meaning of section 356(a)(1)(B).

Example (4). T issues preferred stock to A on January 1, 2000 that permits the holder to require T to redeem the stock on January 1, 2018, or at any time thereafter, but which is not NQPS solely because, as of the issue date,

the holder's right to redeem is subject to a contingency that makes remote the likelihood of redemption on or before January 1, 2020. In 2007, pursuant to a reorganization under section 368(a)(1)(A) in which T merges into P, A surrenders the T preferred stock in exchange for P preferred stock with terms that are identical to the terms of the T preferred stock. Immediately before the exchange, the contingency to which the holder's right to cause redemption of the T stock is subject makes remote the likelihood of redemption before January 1, 2020, but the P stock, although subject to the same contingency, is more likely than not to be redeemed before January 1, 2020. Because, as a result of the exchange of T stock for P stock, the exercise of the redemption right became more likely than not to occur within the 20-year period beginning on the issue date of the T preferred stock, the P preferred stock received by A is not substantially identical to the T stock surrendered, and is not treated as QPS. Thus, the P preferred stock received is "other property" within the meaning of section 356(a)(1)(B).

Example (5). The facts are the same as in *Example 4*, except that, immediately before the merger of T into P in 2007, the contingency to which the holder's right to cause redemption of the T stock is subject makes it more likely than not that the T stock will be redeemed before January 1, 2020. Because exercise of the redemption right did not become more likely than not to occur within the 20-year period beginning on the issue date of the T preferred stock as a result of the exchange, the P preferred stock received by A is substantially identical to the T stock surrendered, and is treated as QPS. Thus, the P preferred stock received is not "other property" within the meaning of section 356(a)(1)(B).

Example (6). A is an employee of T. In connection with A's performance of services for T, T transfers to A in 2000 an amount of T common stock that represents reasonable compensation. The T common stock contains a term granting A the right to require T to redeem the common stock, but only upon A's separation from service from T. In 2005, pursuant to a reorganization under section 368(a)(1)(A) in which T merges into P, A receives, in exchange for A's T common stock, P preferred stock granting a similar redemption right upon A's separation from P's service. Under paragraph (c) of this section, the P preferred stock received by A is treated as transferred in connection with the performance of services (and representing reasonable compensation) within the meaning of section 351(g)(2)(C)(i)(II). Thus, the P preferred stock received by A is QPS.

(f) Effective dates. This section applies to transactions occurring on or after October 2, 2000.

§ 1.357–1 Assumption of liability.

(a) General rule. Section 357(a) does not affect the rule that liabilities assumed are to be taken into account for the purpose of computing the amount of gain or loss realized under section 1001 upon an exchange. Section 357(a) provides, subject to the exceptions and limitations specified in section 357(b) and (c), that—

(1) Liabilities assumed are not to be treated as "other property or money" for the purpose of determining the amount of realized gain which is to be recognized under section 351, or 361, if the transactions would, but for the receipt of "other property or money" have been exchanges of the type described in any one of such sections; and

(2) If the only type of consideration received by the transferor in addition to that permitted to be received by section 351, **[or]** 361, consists of an assumption of liabilities, the transaction, if otherwise qualified, will be deemed to be within the provisions of section 351 or 361.

(b) Application of general rule. The application of paragraph (a) of this section may be illustrated by the following example:

Example. A, an individual, transfers to a controlled corporation property with an adjusted basis of $10,000 in exchange for stock of the corporation with a fair market value of $8,000, $3,000 cash, and the assumption by the corporation of indebtedness of A amounting to $4,000. A's gain is $5,000, computed as follows:

Stock received, fair market value	$8,000
Cash received	3,000
Liability assumed by transferee	4,000
Total consideration received	15,000
Less: Adjusted basis of property transferred	10,000
Gain realized	5,000

Assuming that the exchange falls within section 351 as a transaction in which the gain to be recognized is limited to "other property or money" received, the gain recognized to A will be limited to the $3,000 cash received, since, under the general rule of section 357(a), the assumption of the $4,000 liability does not constitute "other property."

(c) Tax avoidance purpose. The benefits of section 357(a) do not extend to any exchange involving an assumption of liabilities where it appears that the principal purpose of the taxpayer with respect to such assumption was to avoid Federal income tax on the exchange, or, if not such purpose, was not a bona fide business purpose. In such cases, the total amount of liabilities assumed or acquired pursuant to such exchange (and not merely a particular liability with respect to which the tax avoidance purpose existed) shall, for the purpose of determining the amount of gain to be recognized upon the exchange in which the liabilities are assumed or acquired, be treated as money received by the taxpayer upon the exchange. Thus, if in the example set forth in paragraph (b) of this section, the principal purpose of the assumption of the $4,000 liability was to avoid tax on the exchange, or was not a bona fide business purpose, then the amount of gain recognized would be $5,000. In any suit or proceeding where the burden is on the taxpayer to prove that an assumption of liabilities is not to be treated as "other property or money" under section 357, which is the case if the Commissioner determines that the taxpayer's purpose with respect thereto was a purpose to avoid Federal income tax on the exchange or was not a bona fide business purpose, and the taxpayer contests such determination by litigation, the taxpayer must sustain such burden by the clear preponderance of the evidence. Thus, the taxpayer must prove his case by such a clear preponderance of all the evidence that the absence of a purpose to avoid Federal income tax on the exchange, or the presence of a bona fide business purpose, is unmistakable.

§ 1.357–2 Liabilities in excess of basis.

(a) Section 357(c) provides in general that in an exchange to which section 351 (relating to a transfer to a corporation controlled by the transferor) is applicable, or to which section 361 (relating to the nonrecognition of gain or loss to corporations) is applicable by reason of a section 368(a)(1)(D) reorganization, if the sum of the amount of liabilities assumed exceeds the total of the adjusted basis of the property transferred pursuant to such exchange, then such excess shall be considered as a gain from the sale or exchange of a capital asset or of property which is not a capital asset as the case may be. Thus, if an individual transfers, under section 351, properties having a total basis in his hands of $20,000, one of which has a basis of $10,000 but is subject to a mortgage of $30,000, to a corporation controlled by him, such individual will be subject to tax with respect to $10,000, the excess of the amount of the liability over the total adjusted basis of all the properties in his hands. The same result will follow whether or not the liability is assumed by the transferee. The determination of whether a gain resulting from the transfer of capital assets is long-term or short-term

capital gain shall be made by reference to the holding period to the transferor of the assets transferred. An exception to the general rule of section 357(c) is made (1) for any exchange as to which under section 357(b) (relating to assumption of liabilities for tax-avoidance purposes) the entire amount of the liabilities is treated as money received.

(b) The application of paragraph (a) of this section may be illustrated by the following examples:

Example (1). If all such assets transferred are capital assets and if half the assets (ascertained by reference to their fair market value at the time of the transfer) have been held for less than 1 year and the remaining half for more than 1 year, half the excess of the amount of the liability over the total of the adjusted basis of the property transferred pursuant to the exchange shall be treated as short-term capital gain, and the remaining half shall be treated as long-term capital gain.

Example (2). If half of the assets (ascertained by reference to their fair market value at the time of the transfer) transferred are capital assets and half are assets other than capital assets, then half of the excess of the amount of the liability over the total of the adjusted basis of the property transferred pursuant to the exchange shall be treated as capital gain, and the remaining half shall be treated as gain from the sale or exchange of assets other than capital assets.

§ 1.358–1 Basis to distributees.

(a) In the case of an exchange to which section 354 or 355 applies in which, under the law applicable to the year in which the exchange is made, only nonrecognition property is received, immediately after the transaction, the sum of the basis of all of the stock and securities received in the transaction shall be the same as the basis of all the stock and securities in such corporation surrendered in the transaction, allocated in the manner described in § 1.358–2. In the case of a distribution to which section 355 applies in which, under the law applicable to the year in which the distribution is made, only nonrecognition property is received, immediately after the transaction, the sum of the basis of all of the stock and securities with respect to which the distribution is made plus the basis of all stock and securities received in the distribution with respect to such stock and securities shall be the same as the basis of the stock and securities with respect to which the distribution is made immediately before the transaction, allocated in the manner described in § 1.358–2. In the case of an exchange to which section 351 or 361 applies in which, under the law applicable to the year in which the exchange was made, only nonrecognition property is received, the basis of all the stock and securities received in the exchange shall be the same as the basis of all property exchanged therefor. If in an exchange or distribution to which section 351, 356, or 361 applies both nonrecognition property and "other property" are received, the basis of all the property except "other property" held after the transaction shall be determined as described in the preceding three sentences decreased by the sum of the money and the fair market value of the "other property" (as of the date of the transaction) and increased by the sum of the amount treated as a dividend (if any) and the amount of the gain recognized on the exchange, but the term gain as here used does not include any portion of the recognized gain that was treated as a dividend. In any case in which a taxpayer transfers property with respect to which loss is recognized, such loss shall be reflected in determining the basis of the property received in the exchange. The basis of the "other property" is its fair market value as of the date of the transaction. See § 1.460–4(k)(3)(iv)(A) for rules relating to stock basis adjustments required where a contract accounted for using a long-term contract method of accounting is transferred in a transaction described in section 351 or a reorganization described in section 368(a)(1)(D) with respect to which the requirements of section 355 (or so much of section 356 as relates to section 355) are met.

(b) The application of paragraph (a) of this section may be illustrated by the following example:

Example. A purchased a share of stock in Corporation X in 1935 for $150. Since that date A has received distributions out of other than earnings and profits (as defined in section 316) totaling $60, so that A's adjusted basis for the stock is $90. In a transaction qualifying under section 356, A exchanged this share for one share in Corporation Y, worth $100, cash in the amount of $10, and other property with a fair market value of $30. The exchange had the effect of the distribution of a dividend. A's ratable share of the earnings and profits of Corporation X accumulated after February 28, 1913, was $5. A realized a gain of $50 on the exchange, but the amount recognized is limited to $40, the sum of the cash received and the fair market value of the other property. Of the gain recognized, $5 is taxable as a dividend, and $35 is taxable as a gain from the exchange of property. The basis to A of the one share of stock Corporation Y is $90, that is, the adjusted basis of the one share of stock of Corporation X ($90), decreased by the sum of the cash received ($10) and the fair market value of the other property received ($30) and increased by the sum of the amount treated as a dividend ($5) and the amount treated as a gain from the exchange of property ($35). The basis of the other property received is $30.

(c) This section applies to exchanges and distributions of stock and securities occurring on or after January 23, 2006.

§ 1.358–2 Allocation of basis among nonrecognition property.

(a) Allocation of basis in exchanges or distributions to which section 354, 355, or 356 applies. (1) As used in this paragraph the term *stock* means stock which is not "other property" under section 356. The term *securities* means securities (including, where appropriate, fractional parts of securities) which are not "other property" under section 356. Stock, or securities, as the case may be, which differ either because they are in different corporations or because the rights attributable to them differ (although they are in the same corporation) are considered different classes of stock or securities, as the case may be, for purposes of this section.

(2)(i) If a shareholder or security holder surrenders a share of stock or a security in an exchange under the terms of section 354, 355, or 356, the basis of each share of stock or security received in the exchange shall be the same as the basis of the share or shares of stock or security or securities (or allocable portions thereof) exchanged therefor (as adjusted under § 1.358–1). If more than one share of stock or security is received in exchange for one share of stock or one security, the basis of the share of stock or security surrendered shall be allocated to the shares of stock or securities received in the exchange in proportion to the fair market value of the shares of stock or securities received. If one share of stock or security is received in exchange for more than one share of stock or security or if a fraction of a share of stock or security is received, then the basis of the shares of stock or securities surrendered must be allocated to the shares of stock or securities (or allocable portions thereof) received in a manner that reflects, to the greatest extent possible, that a share of stock or security received is received in respect of shares of stock or securities that were acquired on the same date and at the same price. To the extent it is not possible to allocate basis in this manner, the basis of the shares of stock or securities surrendered must be allocated to the shares of stock or securities (or allocable portions thereof) received in a manner that minimizes the disparity in the holding periods of the surrendered shares of stock or securities whose basis is allocated to any particular share of stock or security received.

(ii) If a shareholder or security holder surrenders a share of stock or a security in an exchange under the terms of section 354, 355, or 356, and receives shares of stock or securities of more than one class, or receives "other property" or money in addition to shares of stock or securities, then, to the extent the terms of the exchange specify that shares of stock or securities of a particular class or "other property" or money is received in exchange for a particular share of stock or security or a particular class of stock or securities, for purposes of applying the rules of this section, such terms shall control provided such terms are economically reasonable. To the extent the terms of the exchange do not specify that shares of stock or securities of a particular class or "other property" or money is received in exchange for a particular share of stock or security or a particular class of stock or securities, then, for purposes of applying the rules of paragraph (a)(2)(i) of this section, a *pro rata* portion of the shares of stock and securities of each class received and a *pro rata* portion of the "other property" and money received shall be treated as received in exchange for each share of stock and security surrendered, based on the fair market value of the stock and securities surrendered.

(iii)(A) For purposes of this section, if a shareholder or security holder surrenders a share of stock or a security in a transaction under the terms of section 354 (or so much of section 356 as relates to section 354) in which the shareholder or security holder receives no property or property (including property permitted by section 354 to be received without the recognition of gain or "other property" or money) with a fair market value less than that of the stock or securities surrendered in the transaction:

(1) Such shareholder or security holder shall be treated as receiving the stock, securities, other property, and money actually received by the shareholder or security holder in the transaction and an amount of stock of the issuing corporation (as defined in § 1.368–

1(b)) that has a value equal to the excess of the value of the stock or securities the shareholder or security holder surrendered in the transaction over the value of the stock, securities, other property, and money the shareholder or security holder actually received in the transaction. If the shareholder owns only one class of stock of the issuing corporation the receipt of which would be consistent with the economic rights associated with each class of stock of the issuing corporation, the stock deemed received by the shareholder pursuant to the previous sentence shall be stock of such class. If the shareholder owns multiple classes of stock of the issuing corporation the receipt of which would be consistent with the economic rights associated with each class of stock of the issuing corporation, the stock deemed received by the shareholder shall be stock of each such class owned by the shareholder immediately prior to the transaction, in proportion to the value of the stock of each such class owned by the shareholder at that time. The basis of each share of stock or security of the issuing corporation deemed received and actually received shall be determined under the rules of this section. If and to the extent necessary to reflect the actual ownership of the issuing corporation immediately after the exchange to which section 354 (or so much of section 356 as relates to section 354) applies, an appropriate amount of the stock of the issuing corporation treated as issued to the shareholder or security holder in the exchange is deemed further transferred in accordance with § 1.368–2(l) to reflect the actual ownership of the issuing corporation. Paragraph (a)(2)(iii)(A)(2) of this section is only applied to any shareholder of the issuing corporation after all of the deemed transfers pursuant to § 1.368–2(l) are completed. The transferred shares' basis shall be adjusted for all deemed transfers required by § 1.368–2(l).

(2) A direct shareholder of the issuing corporation that receives the shares deemed issued as part of the transaction, as described in paragraph (a)(2)(iii)(A)(1) of this section, shall then be treated as surrendering all of its shares of stock and securities in the issuing corporation, including those shares of stock or securities held immediately prior to the transaction, those shares of stock or securities actually received in the transaction, and those shares of stock deemed received as described in paragraph (a)(2)(iii)(A)(1) of this section, in a reorganization under section 368(a)(1)(E) in exchange for the shares of stock and securities of the issuing corporation that the shareholder or security holder actually holds immediately after the transaction. The basis of each share of stock and security deemed received in the reorganization under section 368(a)(1)(E) shall be determined under the rules of this section.

(B) For purposes of this section, if an actual shareholder of the issuing corporation is deemed to receive a nominal share of stock of the issuing corporation as provided in § 1.368–2(l), then that shareholder must, after allocating and adjusting the basis of the nominal share in accordance with the rules of this section and § 1.358–1, designate the share of stock of the issuing corporation that it owns to which the basis, if any, of the nominal share will attach. If the shareholder does not actually own any shares of stock in the issuing corporation immediately after the exchange to which section 354 (or so much of section 356 as relates to section 354) applies, the nominal share of stock of the issuing corporation received by the shareholder in the exchange is deemed further transferred in accordance with § 1.368–2(l) without applying the designation rule set forth in the first sentence of this paragraph until it is transferred to a person that actually owns stock in the issuing corporation. The transferred share's basis shall be adjusted for all deemed transfers required by § 1.368–2(l).

(iv) If a shareholder or security holder receives one or more shares of stock or one or more securities in a distribution under the terms of section 355 (or so much of section 356 as relates to section 355), the basis of each share of stock or security of the distributing corporation (as defined in § 1.355–1(b)), as adjusted under § 1.358–1, shall be allocated between the share of stock or security of the distributing corporation with respect to which the distribution is made and the share or shares of stock or security or securities (or allocable portions thereof) received with respect to the share of stock or security of the distributing corporation in proportion to their fair market values. If one share of stock or security is received with respect to more than one share of stock or security or if a fraction of a share of stock or security is received, then the basis of each share of stock or security of the distributing corporation must be allocated to the shares of stock or securities (or allocable portions thereof) received in a manner that reflects that, to the greatest extent possible, a share of stock or security received is received with respect to shares of stock or securities acquired on the same date and at the same price. To the extent it is not possible to allocate basis in this manner, the basis of each share of stock or security of the distributing corporation must be allocated to the shares of stock or securities (or allocable portions thereof) received in a manner that minimizes the disparity in the holding periods of the shares of stock or securities with respect to which such shares of stock or securities are received.

(v) If a shareholder or security holder receives shares of stock or securities of more than one class, or receives "other property" or money in addition to stock or securities in a distribution under the terms of section 355 (or so much of section 356 as relates to section 355), then, to the extent the terms of the distribution specify that shares of stock or securities of a particular class or "other property" or money is received with respect to a particular share of stock or security of the distributing corporation or a particular class of stock or securities of the distributing corporation, for purposes of applying the rules of this section, such terms shall control provided that such terms are economically reasonable. To the extent the terms of the distribution do not specify that shares of stock or securities of a particular class or "oth-

er property" or money is received with respect to a particular share of stock or security of the distributing corporation or a particular class of stock or securities of the distributing corporation, then, for purposes of applying the rules of this section, a *pro rata* portion of the shares of stock and securities of each class received and a *pro rata* portion of the "other property" and money received shall be treated as received with respect to each share of stock and security of the distributing corporation with respect to which the distribution is made, based on the fair market value of each such share of stock or security.

(vi) If a share of stock or a security is received in exchange for, or with respect to, more than one share of stock or security and such shares or securities were acquired on different dates or at different prices, the share of stock or security received shall be divided into segments based on the relative fair market values of the shares of stock or securities surrendered in exchange for such share or security or the relative fair market values of the shares of stock or securities with respect to which the share of stock or security is received in a distribution under the terms of section 355 (or so much of section 356 as relates to section 355). Each segment shall have a basis determined under the rules of paragraph (a)(2) of this section and a corresponding holding period.

(vii) If a shareholder or security holder that purchased or acquired shares of stock or securities in a corporation on different dates or at different prices exchanges such shares of stock or securities under the terms of section 354, 355, or 356, or receives a distribution of shares of stock or securities under the terms of section 355 (or so much of section 356 as relates to section 355), and the shareholder or security holder is not able to identify which particular share of stock or security (or allocable portion of a share of stock or security) is received (or deemed received) in exchange for, or with respect to, a particular share of stock or security, the shareholder or security holder may designate which share of stock or security is received in exchange for, or with respect to, a particular share of stock or security, provided that such designation is consistent with the terms of the exchange or distribution (or an exchange deemed to have occurred pursuant to paragraph (a)(2)(iii) of this section), and the other rules of this section. In the case of an exchange under the terms of section 354 or 356 (including a deemed exchange as a result of the application of paragraph (a)(2)(iii) of this section), the designation must be made on or before the first date on which the basis of a share of stock or a security received (or deemed received in the reorganization under section 368(a)(1)(E) in the case of a transaction to which paragraph (a)(2)(iii) of this section applies) is relevant. In the case of an exchange or distribution under the terms of section 355 (or so much of section 356 as relates to section 355), the designation must be made on or before the first date on which the basis of a share of stock or a security of the distributing corporation or the controlled corporation (as defined in § 1.355–1(b)) is relevant. The basis of the shares or securities received in an exchange under the terms of section 354 or section 356, for example, is relevant when such shares or securities are sold or otherwise transferred. The designation will be binding for purposes of determining the Federal tax consequences of any sale or transfer of, or distribution with respect to, the shares or securities received. If the shareholder fails to make a designation in a case in which the shareholder is not able to identify which share of stock is received in exchange for, or with respect to, a particular share of stock, then the shareholder will not be able to identify which shares are sold or transferred for purposes of determining the basis of property sold or transferred under section 1012 and § 1.1012–1(c) and, instead, will be treated as selling or transferring the share received in respect of the earliest share purchased or acquired.

(viii) This paragraph (a)(2) shall not apply to determine the basis of a share of stock or security received by a shareholder or security holder in an exchange described in both section 351 and either section 354 or 356, if, in connection with the exchange—

(A) The shareholder or security holder exchanges property for stock or securities in an exchange to which neither section 354 nor section 356 applies;

(B) The shareholder or security holder exchanges property for stock or securities in a transaction for which an election to apply section 362(e)(2)(C) is in effect; or

(C) Liabilities of the shareholder or security holder are assumed.

* * *

(ix) This paragraph (a)(2) shall apply to determine the basis of a share of stock or security received by a shareholder or security holder in an exchange described in both section 1036 and section 354 or section 356.

(b) **Allocation of basis in exchanges to which section 351 or 361 applies.** (1) As used in this paragraph (b), the term *stock* refers only to stock which is not "other property" under section 351 or 361 and the term *securities* refers only to securities which are not "other property" under section 351 or 361.

(2) If in an exchange to which section 351 or 361 applies property is transferred to a corporation and the transferor receives stock or securities of more than one class or receives both stock and securities, then the basis of the property transferred (as adjusted under § 1.358–1) shall be allocated among all of the stock and securities received in proportion to the fair market values of the stock of each class and the securities of each class.

(c) **Examples.** The application of paragraphs (a) and (b) of this section is illustrated by the following examples:

Example (1). (i) Facts. J, an individual, acquired 20 shares of Corporation X stock on Date 1 for $3 each and 10 shares of Corporation X stock on Date 2 for $6 each. On Date

3, Corporation Y acquires the assets of Corporation X in a reorganization under section 368(a)(1)(A). Pursuant to the terms of the plan of reorganization, J receives 2 shares of Corporation Y stock in exchange for each share of Corporation X stock. Therefore, J receives 60 shares of Corporation Y stock. Pursuant to section 354, J recognizes no gain or loss on the exchange. J is not able to identify which shares of Corporation Y stock are received in exchange for each share of Corporation X stock.

(ii) Analysis. Under paragraph (a)(2)(ii) of this section and under § 1.356–1(b), because the terms of the exchange do not specify that shares of Corporation Y stock or cash are received in exchange for particular shares of Class A stock or Class B stock of Corporation X, a pro rata portion of the shares of Corporation Y stock and cash received will be treated as received in exchange for each share of Class A stock and Class B stock of Corporation X surrendered based on the fair market value of such stock. Therefore, J is treated as receiving one share of Corporation Y stock and $5 of cash in exchange for each share of Class A stock of Corporation X and one share of Corporation Y stock and $5 of cash in exchange for each share of Class B stock of Corporation X. J realizes a gain of $140 on the exchange of shares of Class A stock of Corporation X, $100 of which is recognized under § 1.356–1(a). J realizes a gain of $80 on the exchanges of Class B stock of Corporation X, all of which is recognized under § 1.356–1(a). Under paragraph (a)(2)(i) of this section, J has 10 shares of Corporation Y stock, each of which has a basis of $2 and is treated as having been acquired on Date 1, 10 shares of Corporation Y stock, each of which has a basis of $4 and is treated as having been acquired on Date 2, and 20 shares of Corporation Y stock, each of which has a basis of $5 and is treated as having been acquired on Date 3. Under paragraph (a)(2)(vii) of this section, on or before the date on which the basis of a share of Corporation Y stock received becomes relevant, J may des-

ignate which of the shares of Corporation Y stock received have a basis of $2, which have a basis of $4, and which have a basis of $5.

Example (2). (i) Facts. The facts are the same as in *Example 1*, except that instead of receiving 2 shares of Corporation Y stock in exchange for each share of Corporation X stock, J receives 1½ shares of Corporation Y stock in exchange for each share of Corporation X stock. Therefore, J receives 45 shares of Corporation Y stock. Again, J is not able to identify which shares (or portions of shares) of Corporation Y stock are received in exchange for each share of Corporation X stock.

(ii) Analysis. Under paragraph (a)(2)(i) of this section, J has 30 shares of Corporation Y stock each of which has a basis of $2 and is treated as having been acquired on Date 1 and 15 shares of Corporation Y stock each of which has a basis of $4 and is treated as having been acquired on Date 2. Under paragraph (a)(2)(vii) of this section, on or before the date on which the basis of a share of Corporation Y stock received becomes relevant, J may designate which of the shares of Corporation Y stock received have a basis of $2 and which have a basis of $4.

Example (3). (i) Facts. J, an individual, acquired 10 shares of Class A stock of Corporation X on Date 1 for $3 each, 10 shares of Class A stock of Corporation X on Date 2 for $9 each, and 10 shares of Class B stock of Corporation X on Date 3 for $3 each. On Date 4, J surrenders all of J's shares of Class A stock in exchange for 20 shares of new Class C stock and 20 shares of new Class D stock in a reorganization under section 368(a)(1)(E). Pursuant to section 354, J recognizes no gain or loss on the exchange. On the date of the exchange, the fair market value of each share of Class A stock is $6, the fair market value of each share of Class C stock is $2, and the fair market value of each share of Class D stock is $4. The terms of the exchange do not specify that shares of Class C stock or shares of Class D stock of Corporation X are received in exchange for particular shares of Class A stock of Corporation X.

(ii) Analysis. Under paragraph (a)(2)(ii) of this section, because the terms of the exchange do not specify that shares of Class C stock or shares of Class D stock of Corporation X are received in exchange for particular shares of Class A stock of Corporation X, a *pro rata* portion of the shares of Class C stock and shares of Class D stock received will be treated as received in exchange for each share of Class A stock based on the fair market value of the surrendered shares of Class A stock. Therefore, J is treated as receiving one share of Class C stock and one share of Class D stock in exchange for each share of Class A stock. Under paragraph (a)(2)(i) of this section, J has 10 shares of Class C stock, each of which has a basis of $1 and is treated as having been acquired on Date 1 and 10 shares of Class C stock, each of which has a basis of $3 and is treated as having been acquired on Date 2. In addition, J has 10 shares of Class D stock, each of which has a basis of $2 and is treated as having been acquired on Date 1 and 10 shares of Class D stock, each of which has a basis of $6 and is treated as having been acquired on Date 2. J's basis in each share of Class B stock remains $3. Under paragraph (a)(2)(vii) of this section, on or before the date on which the basis of a share of Class C stock or Class D stock received becomes relevant, J may designate which of the shares of Class C stock have a basis of $1 and which have a basis of $3, and which of the shares of Class D stock have a basis of $2 and which have a basis of $6.

Example (4). (i) Facts. J, an individual, acquired 10 shares of Class A stock of Corporation X on Date 1 for $2 each, 10 shares of Class A stock of Corporation X on Date 2 for $4 each, and 20 shares of Class B stock of Corporation X on Date 3 for $6 each. On Date 4, Corporation Y acquires the assets of Corporation X in a reorganization under section 368(a)(1)(A). Pursuant to the terms of the plan of reorganization, J surrenders all of J's shares of Corporation X stock for 40 shares of Corporation Y stock and $200 of cash. On the date of the exchange, the fair market value of each share of Class A stock of Corporation X is $10, the fair market value of each share of Class B stock of Corporation X is $10, and the fair market value of each share of Corporation Y stock is $5. The terms of the exchange do not specify that shares of Corporation Y stock or cash are received in exchange for particular shares of Class A stock or Class B stock of Corporation X.

(ii) Analysis. Under paragraph (a)(2)(ii) of this section and under § 1.356–1(b), because the terms of the exchange do not specify that shares of Corporation Y stock or cash are received in exchange for particular shares of Class A stock or Class B stock of Corporation X, a *pro rata* portion of the shares of Corporation Y stock and cash received will be treated as received in exchange for each share of Class A stock and Class B stock of Corporation X surrendered based on the fair market value of such stock. Therefore, J is treated as receiving one share of Corporation Y stock and $5 of cash in exchange for each share of Class A stock of Corporation X and one share of Corporation Y stock and $5 of cash in exchange for each share of Class B stock of Corporation X. J realizes a gain of $140 on the exchange of shares of Class A stock of Corporation X, $100 of which is recognized under § 1.356–1(a). J realizes a gain of $80 on the exchange of Class B stock of Corporation X, all of which is recognized under § 1.356–1(a). Under paragraph (a)(2)(i) of this section, J has 10 shares of Corporation Y stock, each of which has a basis of $2 and is treated as having been acquired on Date 1, 10 shares of Corporation Y stock, each of which has a basis of $4 and is treated as having been acquired on Date 2, and 20 shares of Corporation Y stock, each of which has a basis of $5 and is treated as having been acquired on Date 3. Under paragraph (a)(2)(vii) of this section, on or before the date on which the basis of a share of Corporation Y stock received becomes relevant, J may designate

which of the shares of Corporation Y stock received have a basis of $2, which have a basis of $4, and which have a basis of $5.

Example (5). (i) Facts. The facts are the same as in *Example 4*, except that the terms of the plan of reorganization specify that J receives 40 shares of stock of Corporation Y in exchange for J's shares of Class A stock of Corporation X and $200 of cash in exchange for J's shares of Class B stock of Corporation X.

(ii) Analysis. Under paragraph (a)(2)(ii) of this section and under § 1.356–1(b), because the terms of the exchange specify that J receives 40 shares of stock of Corporation Y in exchange for J's shares of Class A stock of Corporation X and $200 of cash in exchange for J's shares of Class B stock of Corporation X and such terms are economically reasonable, such terms control. J realizes a gain of $140 on the exchange of shares of Class A stock of Corporation X, none of which is recognized under § 1.356–1(a). J realizes a gain of $80 on the exchange of shares of Class B stock of Corporation X, all of which is recognized under § 1.356–1(a). Under paragraph (a)(2)(i) of this section, J has 20 shares of Corporation Y stock, each of which has a basis of $1 and is treated as having been acquired on Date 1, and 20 shares of Corporation Y stock, each of which has a basis of $2 and is treated as having been acquired on Date 2. Under paragraph (a)(2)(vii) of this section, on or before the date on which the basis of a share of Corporation Y stock received becomes relevant, J may designate which of the shares of Corporation Y stock received have a basis of $1 and which have a basis of $2.

Example (6). (i) Facts. J, an individual, acquired 10 shares of stock of Corporation X on Date 1 for $2 each, and a security issued by Corporation X to J on Date 2 with a principal amount of $100 and a basis of $100. On Date 3, Corporation Y acquires the assets of Corporation X in a reorganization under section 368(a)(1)(A). Pursuant to the terms of the plan

of reorganization, J surrenders all of J's shares of Corporation X stock in exchange for 10 shares of Corporation Y stock and surrenders J's Corporation X security in exchange for a Corporation Y security. On the date of the exchange, the fair market value of each share of stock of Corporation X is $10, the fair market value of J's Corporation X security is $100, the fair market value of each share of Corporation Y stock is $10, and the fair market value and principal amount of the Corporation Y security received by J is $100.

(ii) Analysis. Under paragraph (a)(2)(ii) of this section and under § 1.354–1(a), because the terms of the exchange specify that J receives 10 shares of stock of Corporation Y in exchange for J's shares of Class A stock of Corporation X and a Corporation Y security in exchange for its Corporation X security and such terms are economically reasonable, such terms control. Pursuant to section 354, J recognizes no gain on either exchange. Under paragraph (a)(2)(i) of this section, J has 10 shares of Corporation Y stock, each of which has a basis of $2 and is treated as having been acquired on Date 1, and a security that has a basis of $100 and is treated as having been acquired on Date 2.

Example (7). (i) Facts. J, an individual, acquired 10 shares of Corporation X stock on Date 1 for $2 each and 10 shares of Corporation X stock on Date 2 for $5 each. On Date 3, Corporation Y acquires the stock of Corporation X in a reorganization under section 368(a)(1)(B). Pursuant to the terms of the plan of reorganization, J receives one share of Corporation Y stock in exchange for every 2 shares of Corporation X stock. Pursuant to section 354, J recognizes no gain or loss on the exchange. J is not able to identify which portion of each share of Corporation Y stock is received in exchange for each share of Corporation X stock.

(ii) Analysis. Under paragraph (a)(2)(i) of this section, J has 5 shares of Corporation Y stock each of which has a basis of $4 and is treated as having been acquired on Date 1 and

5 shares of Corporation Y stock each of which has a basis of $10 and is treated as having been acquired on Date 2. Under paragraph (a)(2)(vii) of this section, on or before the date on which the basis of a share of Corporation Y stock received becomes relevant, J may designate which of the shares of Corporation Y stock received have a basis of $4 and which have a basis of $10.

Example (8). (i) Facts. The facts are the same as in *Example 7*, except that, in addition to transferring the stock of Corporation X to Corporation Y, J transfers land to Corporation Y. In addition, after the transaction, J owns stock of Corporation Y satisfying the requirements of section 368(c). J's transfer of the Corporation X stock to Corporation Y is an exchange described in sections 351 and 354. J's transfer of land to Corporation Y is an exchange described in section 351.

(ii) Analysis. Under paragraph (a)(2)(viii) of this section, because neither section 354 nor section 356 applies to the transfer of land to Corporation Y, the rules of paragraph (a)(2) of this section do not apply to determine J's basis in the Corporation Y stock received in the transaction.

Example (9). (i) Facts. J, an individual, acquired 10 shares of Corporation X stock on Date 1 for $3 each and 10 shares of Corporation X stock on Date 2 for $6 each. On Date 3, Corporation Z, a newly formed, wholly owned subsidiary of Corporation Y, merges with and into Corporation X with Corporation X surviving. As part of the plan of merger, J receives one share of Corporation Y stock in exchange for each share of Corporation X stock. In connection with the transaction, Corporation Y assumes a liability of J. In addition, after the transaction, J owns stock of Corporation Y satisfying the requirements of section 368(c). J's transfer of the Corporation X stock to Corporation Y is an exchange described in sections 351 and 354.

(ii) Analysis. Under paragraph (a)(2)(viii) of this section, because, in connection with the transfer of the Corporation X stock to Corporation Y, Corporation Y assumed a liability of J, the rules of paragraph (a)(2) of this section do not apply to determine J's basis in the Corporation Y stock received in the transaction.

Example (10). (i) Facts. Each of Corporation X and Corporation Y has a single class of stock outstanding, all of which is owned by J, an individual. J acquired 100 shares of Corporation X stock on Date 1 for $1 each and 100 shares of Corporation Y stock on Date 2 for $2 each. On Date 3, Corporation Y acquires the assets of Corporation X in a reorganization under section 368(a)(1)(D). Pursuant to the terms of the plan of reorganization, J surrenders J's 100 shares of Corporation X stock but does not receive any additional Corporation Y stock. Immediately before the effective time of the reorganization, the fair market value of each share of Corporation X stock and each share of Corporation Y stock is $1. Pursuant to section 354, J recognizes no gain or loss.

(ii) Analysis. Under paragraph (a)(2)(iii) of this section, J is deemed to have received shares of Corporation Y stock with an aggregate fair market value of $100 in exchange for J's Corporation X shares. Given the number of outstanding shares of stock of Corporation Y and their value immediately before the effective time of the reorganization, J is deemed to have received 100 shares of stock of Corporation Y in the reorganization. Under paragraph (a)(2)(i) of this section, each of those shares has a basis of $1 and is treated as having been acquired on Date 1. Then, the stock of Corporation Y is deemed to be recapitalized in a reorganization under section 368(a)(1)(E) in which J receives 100 shares of Corporation Y stock in exchange for those shares of Corporation Y stock that J held immediately prior to the reorganization and those shares J is deemed to have received in the reorganization. Under paragraph (a)(2)(i), immediately after the reorganization, J holds 50 shares of Corporation Y stock each of which has a basis of $2 and is treated as having been acquired on Date

1 and 50 shares of Corporation Y stock each of which has a basis of $4 and is treated as having been acquired on Date 2. Under paragraph (a) (2)(vii) of this section, on or before the date on which the basis of any share of J's Corporation Y stock becomes relevant, J may designate which of the shares of Corporation Y have a basis of $2 and which have a basis of $4.

Example (11). (i) Facts. Corporation X has a single class of stock outstanding, all of which is owned by J, an individual. J acquired 100 shares of Corporation X stock on Date 1 for $1 each. Corporation Y has two classes of stock outstanding, common stock and non-voting preferred stock. On Date 2, J acquired 100 shares of Corporation Y common stock for $2 each and 100 shares of Corporation Y preferred stock for $4 each. On Date 3, Corporation Y acquires the assets of Corporation X in a reorganization under section 368(a)(1) (D). Pursuant to the terms of the plan of reorganization, J surrenders J's 100 shares of Corporation X stock but does not receive any additional Corporation Y stock. Immediately before the effective time of the reorganization, the fair market value of each share of Corporation X stock is $10, the fair market value of each share of Corporation Y common stock is $10, and the fair market value of each share of Corporation Y preferred stock is $20. Pursuant to section 354, J recognizes no gain or loss.

(ii) Analysis. Under paragraph (a)(2)(iii) of this section, J is deemed to have received shares of Corporation Y stock with an aggregate fair market value of $1,000 in exchange for J's Corporation X shares. Consistent with the economics of the transaction and the rights associated with each class of stock of Corporation Y owned by J, J is deemed to receive additional shares of Corporation Y common stock. Because the value of the common stock indicates that the liquidation preference associated with the Corporation Y preferred stock could be satisfied even if the reorganization did not occur, it is not appropriate to deem the issuance of additional Corporation Y preferred stock.

Given the number of outstanding shares of common stock of Corporation Y and their value immediately before the effective time of the reorganization, J is deemed to have received 100 shares of common stock of Corporation Y in the reorganization. Under paragraph (a)(2) (i) of this section, each of those shares has a basis of $1 and is treated as having been acquired on Date 1. Then, the common stock of Corporation Y is deemed to be recapitalized in a reorganization under section 368(a)(1)(E) in which J receives 100 shares of Corporation Y common stock in exchange for those shares of Corporation Y common stock that J held immediately prior to the reorganization and those shares of Corporation Y common stock that J is deemed to have received in the reorganization. Under paragraph (a)(2)(i), immediately after the reorganization, J holds 50 shares of Corporation Y common stock, each of which has a basis of $2 and is treated as having been acquired on Date 1, and 50 shares of Corporation Y common stock, each of which has a basis of $4 and is treated as having been acquired on Date 2. Under paragraph (a)(2)(vii) of this section, on or before the date on which the basis of any share of J's Corporation Y common stock becomes relevant, J may designate which of those shares have a basis of $2 and which have a basis of $4.

Example (12). (i) Facts. J, an individual, acquired 5 shares of Corporation X stock on Date 1 for $4 each and 5 shares of Corporation X stock on Date 2 for $8 each. Corporation X owns all of the outstanding stock of Corporation Y. The fair market value of the stock of Corporation X is $1800. The fair market value of the stock of Corporation Y is $900. In a distribution to which section 355 applies, Corporation X distributes all of the stock of Corporation Y *pro rata* to its shareholders. No stock of Corporation X is surrendered in connection with the distribution. In the distribution, J receives 2 shares of Corporation Y stock with respect to each share of Corporation X stock. Pursuant to section 355, J recognizes no gain or loss on the receipt of the shares of Corporation Y stock. J is not able to identify which share of Corporation Y stock is received in respect of each share of Corporation X stock.

(ii) Analysis. Under paragraph (a)(2)(iv) of this section, because J receives 2 shares of Corporation Y stock with respect to each share of Corporation X stock, the basis of each share of Corporation X stock is allocated between such share of Corporation X stock and two shares of Corporation Y stock in proportion to the fair market value of those shares. Therefore, each of the 5 shares of Corporation X stock acquired on Date 1 will have a basis of $2 and each of the 10 shares of Corporation Y stock received with respect to those shares will have a basis of $1. In addition, each of the 5 shares of Corporation X stock acquired on Date 2 will have a basis of $4 and each of the 10 shares of Corporation Y stock received with respect to those shares will have a basis of $2. Under paragraph (a)(2)(vii) of this section, on or before the date on which the basis of a share of Corporation Y stock received becomes relevant, J may designate which of the shares of Corporation Y stock have a basis of $1 and which have a basis of $2.

Example (13). (i) Facts. J, an individual, acquired 20 shares of Corporation X stock on Date 1 for $2 each and 20 shares of Corporation X stock on Date 2 for $4 each. Corporation X has 80 shares of stock outstanding. Corporation X owns 40 shares of stock of Corporation Y, which represents all of the outstanding stock of Corporation Y. The fair market value of the stock of Corporation X is $80. The fair market value of the stock of Corporation Y is $40. Corporation X distributes all of the stock of Corporation Y in a transaction to which section 355 applies. In the transaction, J surrenders 20 shares of stock of Corporation X in exchange for 20 shares of stock of Corporation Y. J retains 20 shares of Corporation X stock. Pursuant to section 355, J recognizes no gain or loss on the receipt of the shares of Corporation Y stock. J is not able to identify which shares of Corporation X stock are sur-

rendered. In addition, J is not able to identify which shares of Corporation Y stock are received in exchange for each surrendered share of Corporation X stock.

(ii) Analysis. Under paragraph (a)(2)(i) of this section, J has 20 shares of Corporation Y stock each of which is treated as received in exchange for one share of Corporation X stock. The basis of the 20 shares of Corporation X stock that are retained by J will remain unchanged. Under paragraph (a)(2)(vii) of this section, on or before the date on which the basis of a share of Corporation X or Corporation Y stock becomes relevant, J may designate which shares of Corporation X stock J surrendered in the exchange and which share of the Corporation Y stock received is received for each share of Corporation X stock surrendered. Therefore, it is possible that a share of Corporation Y stock would have a basis of $2 and be treated as having been acquired on Date 1, or would have a basis of $4 and be treated as having been acquired on Date 2.

Example (14). (i) Facts. J, an individual, acquired 10 shares of Corporation X stock on Date 1 for $3 each, 10 shares of Corporation X stock on Date 2 for $18 each, 10 shares of Corporation X stock on Date 3 for $6 each, and 10 shares of Corporation X stock on Date 4 for $9 each. On Date 5, Corporation Y acquires the assets of Corporation X in a reorganization under section 368(a)(1)(A). Pursuant to the terms of the plan of reorganization, J receives a 3/4 share of Corporation Y stock in exchange for each share of Corporation X stock. Therefore, J receives 30 shares of Corporation X stock. Pursuant to section 354, J recognizes no gain or loss on the exchange. J is not able to identify which shares of Corporation Y stock are received in exchange for each share (or portions of shares) of Corporation X stock.

(ii) Analysis. Under paragraph (a)(2)(i) of this section, J has 7 shares of Corporation Y stock each of which has a basis of $4 and is treated as having been acquired on Date 1, 7 shares of Corporation Y stock each of which

has a basis of $24 and is treated as having been acquired on Date 2, 7 shares of Corporation Y stock each of which has a basis of $8 and is treated as having been acquired on Date 3, and 7 shares of Corporation Y stock each of which has a basis of $12 and is treated as having been acquired on Date 4. In addition, J has two shares of Corporation Y stock, each of which is divided into two equal segments under paragraph (a)(2)(vi) of this section. The first of those two shares has one segment with a basis of $2 that is treated as having been acquired on Date 1 and a second segment with a basis of $12 that is treated as having been acquired on Date 2. The second of those two shares has one segment with a basis of $4 that is treated as having been acquired on Date 3 and a second segment with a basis of $6 that is treated as having been acquired on Date 4. Under paragraph (a)(2)(vii), on or before the date on which a share of Corporation Y stock received becomes relevant, J may designate which of the shares of Corporation Y stock have a basis of $4, which have a basis of $24, which have a basis of $8, which have a basis of $12, and which share has a split basis of $2 and $12, and which share has a split basis of $4 and $6.

Example (15). (i) Facts. Each of Corporation X and Corporation Y has a single class of stock outstanding, all of which is owned by J, an individual. J purchased 100 shares of Corporation X stock on Date 1 for $1.50 each, resulting in J having an aggregate basis in the stock of Corporation X of $150. On Date 2, Corporation Y acquires the assets of Corporation X for $100 of cash, their fair market value, in a transaction described in § 1.368–2(*l*). Pursuant to the terms of the exchange, Corporation X does not receive any Corporation Y stock. Corporation X distributes the $100 of cash to J and retains no assets.

(ii) Analysis. Pursuant to § 1.368–2(*l*), Corporation Y will be deemed to issue a nominal share of Corporation Y stock to Corporation X in addition to the $100 of cash actually ex-

changed for the Corporation X assets. Corporation X will then be deemed to distribute the nominal share of Corporation Y stock to J in addition to the $100 of cash actually distributed to J. Pursuant to § 1.368–2(*l*), J, the actual shareholder of Corporation Y, the issuing corporation, is deemed to receive the nominal share of Corporation Y stock described in § 1.368–2(*l*). J will have a basis of $50 in the nominal share of Corporation Y stock under section 358(a)(1). Therefore, under paragraph (a)(2)(iii)(B) of this section, J must designate a share of Corporation Y stock to which J's basis of $50 in the nominal share of Corporation Y stock will attach.

Example (16). (i) Facts. Each of Corporation X and Corporation Y has a single class of stock outstanding, all of which is owned by Corporation P. Corporation T has a single class of stock outstanding, all of which is owned by Corporation X. The corporations do not join in the filing of a consolidated return. Corporation X purchased 100 shares of Corporation T stock on Date 1 for $1.50 each, resulting in Corporation X having an aggregate basis in the stock of Corporation T of $150. On Date 2, Corporation Y acquires the assets of Corporation T for $100 of cash, their fair market value, in a transaction described in § 1.368–2(*l*). Pursuant to the terms of the exchange, Corporation T does not receive any Corporation Y stock. Corporation T distributes the $100 of cash to Corporation X and retains no assets.

(ii) Analysis. Pursuant to § 1.368–2(*l*), Corporation Y will be deemed to issue a nominal share of Corporation Y stock to Corporation T in addition to the $100 of cash actually exchanged for the Corporation T assets. Corporation T will be deemed to distribute the nominal share of Corporation Y stock to Corporation X in addition to the $100 of cash actually distributed. Corporation X will have a basis of $50 in the nominal share of Corporation Y stock under section 358(a). However, Corporation X is not an actual shareholder of Corporation Y, the issuing corporation. Therefore, Corpora-

tion X cannot designate any share of Corporation Y stock under paragraph (a)(2)(iii)(B) of this section to which the basis of the nominal share of Corporation Y stock will attach and Corporation X will be deemed to distribute the nominal share of Corporation Y stock to Corporation P as required by § 1.368–2(*l*). Corporation X does not recognize the loss on the deemed distribution of the nominal share to Corporation P under section 311(a). Corporation P's basis in the nominal share it receives is zero, its fair market value, under section 301(d). Under paragraph (a)(2)(iii)(B) of this section, Corporation P must designate a share of Corporation Y stock to which the nominal share's zero basis will attach.

* * *

§ 1.358–3 Treatment of assumption of liabilities.

(a) For purposes of section 358, where a party to the exchange assumes a liability of a distributee, the amount of such liability is to be treated as money received by the distributee upon the exchange, whether or not the assumption of liabilities resulted in a recognition of gain or loss to the taxpayer under the law applicable to the year in which the exchange was made.

(b) The application of paragraph (a) of this section may be illustrated by the following examples:

Example (1). A, an individual, owns property with an adjusted basis of $100,000 on which there is a purchase money mortgage of $25,000. On December 1, 1945, A organizes Corporation X to which he transfers the property in exchange for all the stock of Corporation X and the assumption by Corporation X of the mortgage. The capital stock of the Corporation X has a fair market value of $150,000. Under sections 351 and 357, no gain or loss is recognized to A. The basis in A's hands of the stock of Corporation X is $75,000, computed as follows:

Adjusted basis of property transferred	$100,000
Less: Amount of money received (amount of liabilities assumed)	–25,000
Basis of Corporation X stock to A	75,000

Example (2). A, an individual, owns property with an adjusted basis of $25,000 on which there is a mortgage of $50,000. On December 1, 1954, A organizes Corporation X to which he transfers the property in exchange for all the stock of Corporation X and the assumption by Corporation X of the mortgage. The stock of Corporation X has a fair market value of $50,000. Under sections 351 and 357, gain is recognized to A in the amount of $25,000. The basis in A's hands of the stock of Corporation X is zero, computed as follows:

Adjusted basis of property transferred	$25,000
Less: Amount of money received (amount of liabilities)	–50,000
Plus: Amount of gain recognized to taxpayer	25,000
Basis of Corporation X stock to A	0

* * *

§ 1.358–5 Special rules for assumption of liabilities.

(a) In general. Section 358(h)(2)(B) does not apply to an exchange occurring on or after May 9, 2008.

* * *

§ 1.358–6 Stock basis in certain triangular reorganizations.

(a) Scope. This section provides rules for computing the basis of a controlling corporation in the stock of a controlled corporation as the result of certain reorganizations involving the stock of the controlling corporation as described in paragraph (b) of this section. The rules of this section are in addition to rules under other provisions of the Internal Revenue Code and principles of law. See, e.g., section 1001 for the recognition of gain or loss by the controlled corporation on the exchange of property for the assets or stock of a target corporation in a reorganization described in section 368. See also sections 362(e)(1) and 362(e)(2) for further adjustments to basis that may be necessary under either or both of those sections.

(b) Triangular reorganizations—(1) Nomenclature. For purposes of this section—

(i) P is a corporation—

(A) That is a party to a reorganization,

(B) That is in control (within the meaning of section 368(c)) of another party to the reorganization, and

(C) Whose stock is transferred pursuant to the reorganization.

(ii) S is a corporation—

(A) That is a party to the reorganization, and

(B) That is controlled by P.

(iii) T is a corporation that is another party to the reorganization.

(2) Definitions of triangular reorganizations. This section applies to the following reorganizations (which are referred to collectively as triangular reorganizations):

(i) Forward triangular merger. A forward triangular merger is a statutory merger of T and S, with S surviving, that qualifies as a reorganization under section 368(a)(1)(A) or (G) by reason of the application of section 368(a)(2)(D).

(ii) Triangular C reorganization. A triangular C reorganization is an acquisition by S of substantially all of T's assets in exchange for P stock in a transaction that qualifies as a reorganization under section 368(a)(1)(C).

(iii) Reverse triangular merger. A reverse triangular merger is a statutory merger of S and T, with T surviving, that qualifies as a reorganization under section 368(a)(1)(A) by reason of the application of section 368(a)(2)(E).

(iv) Triangular B reorganization. A triangular B reorganization is an acquisition by S of T stock in exchange for P stock in a transaction that qualifies as a reorganization under section 368(a)(1)(B).

(c) General rules. Subject to the special rule provided in paragraph (d) of this section, P's basis in the stock of S or T, as applicable, as a result of a triangular reorganization, is adjusted under the following rules—

(1) Forward triangular merger or triangular C reorganization—(i) In general. In a forward triangular merger or a triangular C reorganization, P's basis in its S stock is adjusted as if—

(A) P acquired the T assets acquired by S in the reorganization (and P assumed any liabilities which S assumed or to which the T assets acquired by S were subject) directly from T in a transaction in which P's basis in the T assets was determined under section 362(b); and

(B) P transferred the T assets (and liabilities which S assumed or to which the T assets acquired by S were subject) to S in a transaction in which P's basis in S stock was determined under section 358.

(ii) Limitation. If, in applying section 358, the amount of T liabilities assumed by S or to which the T assets acquired by S are subject equals or exceeds T's aggregate adjusted basis in its assets, the amount of the adjustment under paragraph (c)(1)(i) of this section is zero. P recognizes no gain under section 357(c) as a result of a triangular reorganization.

(2) Reverse triangular merger—(i) In general—(A) Treated as a forward triangular merger. Except as otherwise provided in this paragraph (c)(2), P's basis in its T stock acquired in a reverse triangular merger equals its basis in its S stock immediately before the transaction adjusted as if T had merged into S in a forward triangular merger to which paragraph (c)(1) of this section applies.

(B) Allocable share. If P acquires less than all of the T stock in the transaction, the basis adjustment described in paragraph (c)(2)(i)(A) of this section is reduced in proportion to the percentage of T stock not acquired in the transaction. The percentage of T stock not acquired in the transaction is determined by taking into account the fair market value of all classes of T stock.

(C) Special rule if P owns T stock before the transaction. Solely for purposes of paragraphs (c)(2)(i)(A) and (B) of this section, if P owns T stock before the transaction, P may treat that stock as acquired in the transaction or not, without regard to the form of the transaction.

(ii) Reverse triangular merger that qualifies as a section 351 transfer or section 368(a)(1)(B) reorganization. Notwithstanding paragraph (c)(2)(i) of this section, if a reorganization qualifies as both a reverse triangular merger and as a section 351 transfer or as both a reverse triangular merger and a reorganization under section 368(a)(1)(B), P can—

(A) Determine the basis in its T stock as if paragraph (c)(2)(i) of this section applies; or

(B) Determine the basis in the T stock acquired as if P acquired such stock from the former T shareholders in a transaction in which P's basis in the T stock was determined under section 362(b).

(3) Triangular B reorganization. In a triangular B reorganization, P's basis in its S stock is adjusted as if—

(i) P acquired the T stock acquired by S in the reorganization directly from the T shareholders in a transaction in which P's basis in the T stock was determined under section 362(b); and

(ii) P transferred the T stock to S in a transaction in which P's basis in its S stock was determined under section 358.

(4) Examples. The rules of this paragraph (c) are illustrated by the following examples. For purposes of these examples, P, S, and T are domestic corporations, the property trans-

ferred is not importation property within the meaning of § 1.362–3(c)(2) or loss duplication property within the meaning of § 1.362–4(g)(1), P and S do not file consolidated returns, P owns all of the shares of the only class of S stock, the P stock exchanged in the transaction satisfies the requirements of the applicable triangular reorganization provisions, and the facts set forth the only corporate activity.

Example (1). Forward triangular merger. (a) Facts. T has assets with an aggregate basis of $60 and fair market value of $100 and no liabilities. Pursuant to a plan, P forms S with $5 cash (which S retains), and T merges into S. In the merger, the T shareholders receive P stock worth $100 in exchange for their T stock. The transaction is a reorganization to which sections 368(a)(1)(A) and (a)(2)(D) apply.

(b) Basis adjustment. Under § 1.358–6(c)(1), P's $5 basis in its S stock is adjusted as if P acquired the T assets acquired by S in the reorganization directly from T in a transaction in which P's basis in the T assets was determined under section 362(b). Under section 362(b), P would have an aggregate basis of $60 in the T assets. P is then treated as if it transferred the T assets to S in a transaction in which P's basis in the S stock was determined under section 358. Under section 358, P's $5 basis in its S stock would be increased by the $60 basis in the T assets deemed transferred. Consequently, P has a $65 basis in its S stock as a result of the reorganization.

(c) Use of pre-existing S. The facts are the same as paragraph (a) of this Example 1, except that S is an operating company with substantial assets that has been in existence for several years. P has a $110 basis in the S stock. Under § 1.358–6(c)(1), P's $110 basis in its S stock is increased by the $60 basis in the T assets deemed transferred. Consequently, P has a $170 basis in its S stock as a result of the reorganization.

(d) Mixed consideration. The facts are the same as paragraph (a) of this Example 1, except that the T shareholders receive P stock

worth $80 and $20 cash from P. Under section 358, P's $5 basis in its S stock is increased by the $60 basis in the T assets deemed transferred. Consequently, P has a $65 basis in its S stock as a result of the reorganization.

(e) Liabilities. The facts are the same as paragraph (a) of this Example 1, except that T's assets are subject to $50 of liabilities, and the T shareholders receive $50 of P stock in exchange for their T stock. Under section 358, P's basis in its S stock is increased by the $60 basis in the T assets deemed transferred and decreased by the $50 of liabilities to which the T assets acquired by S are subject. Consequently, P has a net basis adjustment of $10, and a $15 basis in its S stock as a result of the reorganization.

(f) Liabilities in excess of basis. The facts are the same as in paragraph (a) of this Example 1, except that T's assets are subject to liabilities of $90, and the T shareholders receive $10 of P stock in exchange for their T stock in the reorganization. Under § 1.358–6(c)(1)(ii), the adjustment under § 1.358–6(c) is zero if the amount of the liabilities which S assumed or to which the T assets acquired by S are subject exceeds the aggregate adjusted basis in T's assets. Consequently, P has no adjustment in its S stock, and P has a $5 basis in its S stock as a result of the reorganization.

Example (2). Reverse triangular merger. (a) Facts. T has assets with an aggregate basis of $60 and a fair market value of $100 and no liabilities. P has a $110 basis in its S stock. Pursuant to a plan, S merges into T with T surviving. In the merger, the T shareholders receive $10 cash from P and P stock worth $90 in exchange for their T stock. The transaction is a reorganization to which sections 368(a)(1) (A) and (a)(2)(E) apply.

(b) Basis adjustment. Under § 1.358–6(c) (2)(i)(A), P's basis in the T stock acquired is P's $110 basis in its S stock before the transaction, adjusted as if T had merged into S in a forward triangular merger to which § 1.358–6(c)(1) applies. In such a case, P's $110 ba-

sis in its S stock before the transaction would have been increased by the $60 basis of the T assets deemed transferred. Consequently, P has a $170 basis in its T stock immediately after the transaction.

(c) Reverse triangular merger that also qualifies under section 368(a)(1)(B). The facts relating to T are the same as in paragraph (a) of this Example 2. P, however, forms S pursuant to the plan of reorganization. The T shareholders receive $100 worth of P stock (and no cash) in exchange for their T stock. The T shareholders have an aggregate basis in their T stock of $85 immediately before the reorganization. The reorganization qualifies as both a reverse triangular merger and a reorganization under section 368(a)(1)(B). Under § 1.358–6(c)(2) (ii), P may determine its basis in its T stock either as if § 1.358–6(c)(2)(i) applied to the T stock acquired, or as if P acquired the T stock from the former T shareholders in a transaction in which P's basis in the T stock was determined under section 362(b). Accordingly, P may determine a basis in its T stock of $60 (T's net asset basis) or $85 (the T shareholders' aggregate basis in the T stock immediately before the reorganization).

(d) Allocable share in a reverse triangular merger. The facts are the same as in paragraph (a) of this Example 2, except that X, a 10% shareholder of T, does not participate in the transaction. The remaining T shareholders receive $10 cash from P and P stock worth $80 for their T stock. P owns 90% of the T stock after the transaction. Under § 1.358–6(c)(2)(i) (A), P's basis in its T stock is P's $110 basis in its S stock before the reorganization, adjusted as if T had merged into S in a forward triangular merger. In such a case, P's basis would have been adjusted by the $60 basis in the T assets deemed transferred. Under § 1.358–6(c) (2)(i)(B), however, the basis adjustment determined under § 1.358–6(c)(2)(i)(A) is reduced in proportion to the percentage of T stock not acquired by P in the transaction. The percentage of T stock not acquired in the transaction is

10%. Therefore, P reduces its $60 basis adjustment by 10%, resulting in a net basis adjustment of $54. Consequently, P has a $164 basis in its T stock as a result of the transaction.

(e) P's ownership of T stock. The facts are the same as in paragraph (a) of this Example 2, except that P owns 10% of the T stock before the transaction. P's basis in that T stock is $8. All the T shareholders other than P surrender their T stock for $10 cash from P and P stock worth $80. P does not surrender the stock in the transaction. Under § 1.358–6(c)(2)(i)(C), P may treat its T stock owned before the transaction as acquired in the transaction or not. If P treats that T stock as acquired in the transaction, P's basis in that T stock and the T stock actually acquired in the transaction equals P's $110 basis in its S stock before the transaction, adjusted by the $60 basis of the T assets deemed transferred, for a total basis of $170. If P treats its T stock as not acquired, P retains its $8 pre-transaction basis in that stock. P's basis in its other T shares equals P's $110 basis in its S stock before the transaction, adjusted by $54 (the $60 basis in the T assets deemed transferred, reduced by 10%), for a total basis of $164 in those shares. See § 1.358–6(c)(2)(i)(A) and (B). Consequently, if P treats its T shares as not acquired, P's total basis in all of its T shares is $172.

Example (3). Triangular B reorganization.
(a) Facts. T has assets with a fair market value of $100 and no liabilities. The T shareholders have an aggregate basis in their T stock of $85 immediately before the reorganization. Pursuant to a plan, P forms S with $5 cash and S acquires all of the T stock in exchange for $100 of P stock. The transaction is a reorganization to which section 368(a)(1)(B) applies.

(b) Basis adjustment. Under § 1.358–6(c)(3), P adjusts its $5 basis in its S stock by treating P as if it acquired the T stock acquired by S in the reorganization directly from the T shareholders in exchange for the P stock in a transaction in which P's basis in the T stock was determined under section 362(b). Under

section 362(b), P would have an aggregate basis of $85 in the T stock received by S in the reorganization. P is then treated as if it transferred the T stock to S in a transaction in which P's basis in the S stock was determined under section 358. Under section 358, P's basis in its S stock would be increased by the $85 basis in the T stock deemed transferred. Consequently, P has a $90 basis in its S stock as a result of the reorganization.

(d) Special rule for consideration not provided by P—(1) In general. The amount of P's adjustment to basis in its S or T stock, as applicable, described in paragraph (c) of this section is decreased by the fair market value of any consideration (including P stock in which gain or loss is recognized, see § 1.1032–2(c)) that is exchanged in the reorganization and that is not provided by P pursuant to the plan of reorganization. This paragraph (d) does not apply to the amount of T liabilities assumed by S or to which the T assets acquired by S are subject under paragraph (c)(1) of this section (or deemed assumed or taken subject to by S under paragraph (c)(2)(i) of this section).

(2) Limitation. P makes no adjustment to basis under this section if the decrease required under paragraph (d)(1) of this section equals or exceeds the amount of the adjustment described in paragraph (c) of this section.

(3) Example. The rules of this paragraph (d) are illustrated by the following example. For purposes of this example, P, S, and T are domestic corporations, P and S do not file consolidated returns, P owns all of the only class of S stock, the P stock exchanged in the transaction satisfies the requirements of the applicable triangular reorganization provisions, and the facts set forth the only corporate activity.

Example. (a) Facts. T has assets with an aggregate basis of $60 and fair market value of $100 and no liabilities. S is an operating company with substantial assets that has been in existence for several years. P has a $100 basis in its S stock. Pursuant to a plan, T merges into S and the T shareholders receive $70 of P stock provided by P pursuant to the plan and $30 of cash provided by S in exchange for their T stock. The transaction is a reorganization to which sections 368(a)(1)(A) and (a)(2)(D) apply.

(b) Basis adjustment. Under § 1.358–6(c)(1), P's $100 basis in its S stock is increased by the $60 basis in the T assets deemed transferred. Under § 1.358–6(d)(1), the $60 adjustment is decreased by the $30 of cash provided by S in the reorganization. Consequently, P has a net adjustment of $30 in its S stock, and P has a $130 basis in its S stock as a result of the reorganization.

(c) Appreciated asset. The facts are the same as in paragraph (a) of this Example, except that in the reorganization S provides an asset with a $20 adjusted basis and $30 fair market value instead of $30 of cash. The basis results are the same as in paragraph (b) of this Example. In addition, S recognizes $10 of gain under section 1001 on its disposition of the asset in the reorganization.

(d) Depreciated asset. The facts are the same as in paragraph (c) of this Example, except that S has a $60 adjusted basis in the asset. The basis results are the same as in paragraph (b) of this Example. In addition, S recognizes $30 of loss under section 1001 on its disposition of the asset in the reorganization.

(e) P stock. The facts are the same as in paragraph (a) of this Example, except that in the reorganization S provides P stock with a fair market value of $30 instead of $30 of cash. S acquired the P stock in an unrelated transaction several years before the reorganization. S has a $20 adjusted basis in the P stock. The basis results are the same as in paragraph (b) of this Example. In addition, S recognizes $10 of gain on its disposition of the P stock in the reorganization. See § 1.1032–2(c).

* * *

§ 1.358–7 Transfers by partners and partnerships to corporations.

(a) Transfers by partners of partnership interests. For purposes of section 358(h), a transfer of a partnership interest to a corporation is treated as a transfer of the partner's share of each of the partnership's assets and an assumption by the corporation of the partner's share of partnership liabilities (including section 358(h) liabilities, as defined in paragraph (d) of this section). See paragraph (e) *Example 2* of this section.

(b) Transfers by partnerships. If a corporation assumes a section 358(h) liability from a partnership in an exchange to which section 358(a) applies, then, for purposes of applying section 705 (determination of basis of partner's interest) and § 1.704–1(b), any reduction, under section 358(h)(1), in the partnership's basis in corporate stock received in the transaction is treated as an expenditure of the partnership described in section 705(a)(2)(B). See paragraph (e) *Example 1* of this section. This expenditure must be allocated among the partners in accordance with section 704(b) and (c) and § 1.752–7(c). If a partner's share of the reduction, under section 358(h)(1), in the partnership's basis in corporate stock exceeds the partner's basis in the partnership interest, then the partner recognizes gain equal to the excess, which is treated as gain from the sale or exchange of a partnership interest. This paragraph does not apply to the extent that § 1.752–7(j)(4) applies to the assumption of the § 1.752–7 liability by the corporation.

(c) Assumption of section 358(h) liability by partnership followed by transfer of partnership interest or partnership property to a corporation—trade or business exception. Where a partnership assumes a section 358(h) liability from a partner and, subsequently, the partner transfers all or part of the partner's partnership interest to a corporation in an exchange to which section 358(a) applies, then, for purposes of applying section 358(h)(2), the section 358(h) liability is treated as associated only with the contribution made to the partnership by that partner. See paragraph (e) *Example 2* of this section. Similar rules apply where a partnership assumes a section 358(h) liability of a partner and a corporation subsequently assumes that section 358(h) liability from the partnership in an exchange to which section 358(a) applies.

(d) Section 358(h) liabilities defined. For purposes of this section, section 358(h) liabilities are liabilities described in section 358(h) (3).

(e) Examples. The following examples illustrate the provisions of this section. Assume, for purposes of these examples, that the obligation assumed by the corporation does not reduce the shareholder's basis in the corporate stock under section 358(d). The examples are as follows:

Example (1). Transfer of partnership property to corporation. In 2004, in an exchange to which section 351(a) applies, PRS, a cash basis taxpayer, transfers $2,000,000 cash to Corporation X, also a cash basis taxpayer, in exchange for Corporation X shares and the assumption by Corporation X of $1,000,000 of accounts payable incurred by PRS. At the time of the exchange, PRS has two partners, A, a 90% partner, who has a $2,000,000 basis in the PRS interest, and B, a 10% partner, who has a $50,000 basis in the PRS interest. Assume that, under section 358(h)(1), PRS's basis in the Corporation X stock is reduced by the accounts payable assumed by Corporation X ($1,000,000). Under paragraph (b) of this section, A's and B's bases in PRS must be reduced, but not below zero, by their respective shares of the section 358(h)(1) basis reduction. If either partner's share of the section 358(h)(1) basis reduction exceeds the partner's basis in the partnership interest, then the partner recognizes gain equal to the excess. A's share of the section 358(h) basis reduction is $900,000 (90% of $1,000,000). Therefore, A's basis in the PRS interest is reduced to $1,100,000 ($2,000,000 – $900,000). B's share of the sec-

tion 358(h) basis reduction is $100,000 (10% of $1,000,000). Because B's share of the section 358(h) basis reduction ($100,000) exceeds B's basis in the PRS interest ($50,000), B's basis in the PRS interest is reduced to $0 and B recognizes $50,000 of gain. This gain is treated as gain from the sale of the PRS interest.

Example (2). Transfer of partnership interest to corporation. In 2004, A contributes undeveloped land with a value and basis of $4,000,000 in exchange for a 50% interest in PRS and an assumption by PRS of $2,000,000 of pension liabilities from a separate business that A conducts. A's basis in the PRS interest immediately after the contribution is A's basis in the land, $4,000,000, unreduced by the amount of the pension liabilities. PRS develops the land as a landfill. Before PRS has economically performed with respect to the pension liabilities, A transfers A's interest in PRS to Corporation X, in an exchange to which section 351 applies. At the time of the exchange, the value of A's PRS interest is $2,000,000, A's basis in PRS is $4,000,000, and A has no share of partnership liabilities other than the pension liabilities. For purposes of applying section 358(h), the transfer of the PRS interest to Corporation X is treated as a transfer to Corporation X of A's share of PRS assets and an assumption by Corporation X of A's share of the pension liabilities of PRS ($2,000,000). Because the pension liabilities were not assumed by PRS from A in an exchange in which the trade or business associated with the liability was transferred to PRS, the transfer of the PRS interest to Corporation X is not excepted from section 358(h) under section 358(h) (2). See paragraph (c) of this section. Under section 358(h), A's basis in the Corporation X stock is reduced by the $2,000,000 of pension liabilities.

(f) Effective date. This section applies to assumptions of liabilities by a corporation occurring on or after June 24, 2003.

* * *

§ 1.362–3 Basis of importation property acquired in loss importation transaction.

(a) Purpose. The purpose of section 362(e)(1) and this section is to modify the application of section 362(a) (section 351 transfers, contributions to capital, or paid-in surplus) and section 362(b) (reorganizations) to prevent a corporation (Acquiring) from importing a net built-in loss in a transaction described in either section. See paragraph (c) of this section for definitions of terms used in this section.

(b) Basis determinations under this section—(1) Basis of importation property received in loss importation transaction. Notwithstanding the general rules of section 362(a) and (b), Acquiring's basis in importation property (as defined in paragraph (c)(2) of this section) acquired in a loss importation transaction (as defined in paragraph (c)(3) of this section) is equal to the value of the property immediately after the transaction.

(2) Adjustment to basis of subsidiary stock in triangular reorganizations. If a corporation (P) computes its basis in stock of a subsidiary (whether S or T) under § 1.358–6 (stock basis in certain triangular reorganizations), P's basis in property treated as acquired by P in § 1.358–6(c) is determined under section 362(e)(1) and this section to the extent such property, if actually acquired by P, would be importation property acquired in a loss importation transaction. See § 1.358–6(c)(1)(i)(A), (c)(2)(ii)(B), and (c)(3)(i). The subsidiary's basis in the property actually acquired in the transaction is determined under applicable law (including this section), without regard to the amount of any adjustment to P's basis in the subsidiary's stock. Thus, the basis of the property in S's or T's hands may differ from the amount of the adjustment to P's basis in its stock of S or T.

(3) Acquiring's basis in other property transferred. In general, Acquiring's basis in property received in a section 362 transaction (as defined in paragraph (c)(1) of this section) that is not determined under section 362(e)(1) and this section is determined under section 362(a) or section 362(b). However, if the transaction is described in section 362(a) (without regard to whether it is also described in any other section), further adjustment may be required under section 362(e)(2). See § 1.362–4.

(4) Other effects of basis determination under this section—(i) Determination by reference to transferor's basis. A determination of basis under this section is a determination by reference to the transferor's basis, including for purposes of sections 1223(2) and 7701(a)(43). However, solely for purposes of applying section 755, a determination of basis under this section is treated as a determination not by reference to the transferor's basis.

(ii) Not tax-exempt income or noncapital, nondeductible expense. The application of this section does not give rise to an item treated as tax-exempt income under § 1.1502–32(b)(2)(ii) or as a noncapital, nondeductible expense under § 1.1502–32(b)(2)(iii).

(iii) No effect on earnings and profits. Any determination of basis under this section does not reduce or otherwise affect the calculation of the all earnings and profits amount provided in § 1.367(b)–2(d).

(c) Definitions. For purposes of this section, the following definitions apply:

(1) Section 362 transaction. The term *section 362 transaction* means any transaction described in section 362(a) or in section 362(b).

(2) Importation property—(i) General rule. The term *importation property* means any property (including separate portions determined under paragraph (d)(4) of this section and separate portions of property tentatively divided under paragraph (e)(2) of this section) with respect to which—

(A) Any gain or loss that would be recognized on its sale by the transferor immediately before the transaction (the transferor's hypothetical sale) would not be subject to tax imposed under any provision of subtitle A of the Internal Revenue Code (federal income tax) (taking into account the provisions of paragraph (d) of this section); and

(B) Any gain or loss that would be recognized on its sale by Acquiring immediately after the transaction (Acquiring's hypothetical sale) would be subject to federal income tax (taking into account the provisions of paragraph (d) of this section).

(ii) Special rules for applying this paragraph (c)(2). See paragraph (d) of this section for rules for determining whether gain or loss on a hypothetical sale would be taken into account in determining a federal income tax liability and paragraph (e) of this section for rules applicable when more than one person would take such gain or loss into account.

(3) Loss importation transaction. The term *loss importation transaction* means any section 362 transaction in which Acquiring's aggregate basis in all importation property received from all transferors in the transaction would exceed the aggregate value of such property immediately after the transaction. For this purpose, Acquiring's basis in property received is determined without regard to this section or section 362(e)(2).

(4) Value—(i) General rule. The term *value* means fair market value.

(ii) Special rule for transfers of partnership interests. Notwithstanding the general rule in paragraph (c)(4)(i) of this section, when referring to a partnership interest, for purposes of this section, the term *value* means the sum of the cash that Acquiring would receive for the interest, assuming an exchange between a willing buyer and a willing seller (neither being under any compulsion to buy or sell and both having reasonable knowledge of relevant facts), increased by any § 1.752–1 liabilities (as defined in § 1.752–1(a)(4)) of the partnership allocated to Acquiring with regard to such transferred interest under section 752 immediately after the transfer to Acquiring. If a partnership has elected under section 754, or if section 743(b) would require a downward basis adjustment to the partnership property, the partnership must apply the rules of § 1.743–1 to determine the amount of the basis adjustment to the partnership property.

(d) Rules for determining whether gain or loss would be taken into account in determining a federal income tax liability—(1) General rule. In general, any gain or loss that would be recognized on a hypothetical sale described in paragraph (c)(2) of this section is considered to be subject to federal income tax if, taking into account all relevant facts and circumstances, such gain or loss would affect or be taken into account in determining the federal income tax liability of the transferor or Acquiring, respectively. This determination is made without regard to whether such person has or would have any actual federal income tax liability for the taxable year of the transaction.

(2) Look-through rule in the case of certain pass-through entities. Notwithstanding the general rule in paragraph (d)(1) of this section, the determination of whether any gain or loss on a hypothetical sale would be treated as subject to federal income tax is made by reference to the person that would be required to include such gain or loss in its taxable income if the hypothetical seller is—

(i) A trust treated as owned by its grantors or others (see section 671);

(ii) A partnership (see section 701); or

(iii) An S corporation (see sections 1363 and 1366).

(3) Controlled foreign corporation (CFC), passive foreign investment company (PFIC). For purposes of this section, gain or loss that would be recognized by a CFC (as defined in section 957(a)) or a PFIC (as defined in section 1297(a)) is not deemed taken into account in determining a federal income tax liability solely because it could affect an inclusion under section 951(a) or section 1293(a).

* * *

(5) Look-through treatment in the case of certain avoidance transactions—(i) Application of this paragraph (d)(5). This paragraph (d)(5) applies if—

(A) The transferor is a domestic entity that is a trust (other than a trust described in paragraph (d)(2)(i) of this section), estate, regulated investment company (as defined in section 851(a)), a real estate investment trust (as defined in section 856(a)), or a cooperative (as described in section 1381); and

(B) The transferor transfers, directly or indirectly, property that was transferred to or acquired by it as part of a plan (whether of transferor, Acquiring, or any other person) to avoid the application of section 362(e)(1) and this section to a section 362 transaction.

(ii) Effect of application of this paragraph (d)(5). Notwithstanding paragraph (d)(1) of this section, if a transferor is described in both paragraphs (d)(5)(i)(A) and (B) of this section—

(A) The transferor is treated as though it distributes the proceeds of the hypothetical sale (which, for this purpose, are presumed to be an amount greater than zero);

(B) To the fullest extent possible under the transferor's organizing instrument, the deemed distribution is treated as made to a distributee or distributees that would not take distributions from the transferor into account in determining a federal income tax liability; and

(C) The determination of whether the gain or loss on the hypothetical sale is treated as subject to federal income tax is made by reference to the deemed distributee or distributees.

(iii) Tiered entities. If a deemed distributee is an entity described in paragraph (d)(5)(i)(A) of this section, the determination of whether gain or loss on the hypothetical sale is taken into account in determining a federal income tax liability is made by treating the deemed distributee, and any successive such deemed distributees, as a transferor and applying the rules in paragraphs (d)(5)(i) and (ii) of this section to its deemed distribution (and to all successive deemed distributions), until no deemed distributee or successive deemed distributee is an entity described in paragraph (d)(5)(i)(A) of this section.

* * *

(f) Examples. The examples in this paragraph (f) illustrate the application of section 362(e)(1) and the provisions of this section. Unless otherwise indicated, the examples use the following nomenclature and assumptions: A and B are U.S. citizens. DC, DC1, and P are domestic corporations that have not elected to be S corporations within the meaning of section 1361(a)(1) and that are not members of a consolidated group. F is a foreign individual. FP is a foreign partnership. FC, FC1, and FC2 are foreign corporations. Unless the facts indicate otherwise, the foreign individuals, corporations, and partnerships are not engaged in a U.S. trade or business, have no U.S. real property interests, and have no other relationships, activities, or interests that would cause them, their shareholders, their partners, or their property to be subject to federal income tax. There is no applicable income tax treaty, all persons' tax years are calendar years, and all persons and transactions are unrelated unless the facts indicate otherwise.

Example (1). Basic application of section. (i) *Section 351 transfer of importation property in a loss importation transaction.* (A) *Facts.* FC owns three assets, A1 (basis $40, value $150), A2 (basis $120, value $30), and A3 (basis $140, value $20). On Date 1, FC transfers A1, A2, and A3 to DC in a transaction to which section 351 applies.

(B) Importation property. If FC had sold A1, A2, or A3 immediately before the transaction, no gain or loss recognized on the sale would have been taken into account in determining a federal income tax liability. Further, if DC had sold A1, A2, or A3 immediately after the transaction, DC would take into account any gain or loss recognized on the sale in determining its federal income tax liability.

Therefore, A1, A2, and A3 are all importation properties. See paragraph (c)(2) of this section.

(C) Loss importation transaction. FC's transfer of A1, A2, and A3 is a section 362 transaction. Furthermore, but for section 362(e)(1) and this section and section 362(e)(2), DC's aggregate basis in the importation properties, A1, A2, and A3, would be $300 ($40 + $120 + $140) under section 362(a) and the properties' aggregate value would be $200 ($150 + $30 + $20). Therefore, the importation properties' aggregate basis would exceed their aggregate value and the transaction is a loss importation transaction. See paragraph (c)(3) of this section.

(D) Application of section 362(e)(1) and this section to importation property received in loss importation transaction. Because the importation properties, A1, A2, and A3, were transferred in a loss importation transaction, paragraph (b)(1) of this section applies and DC's basis in A1, A2, and A3 will each be equal to the property's value ($150, $30, and $20, respectively) immediately after the transfer.

(E) Basis of property received in transaction. Following the application of section 362(e)(1) and this section, the provisions of section 362(e)(2) must be taken into account because the transfer is a section 362(a) transaction. Taking into account the application of section 362(e)(1) and this section, DC's aggregate basis in the transferred properties would not exceed their aggregate value immediately after the transfer. Therefore, FC does not have a net built-in loss, FC's transfer is not a loss duplication transaction, and section 362(e)(2) does not apply to this transaction. DC's bases in A1, A2, and A3, as determined under paragraph (i)(D) of this *Example 1*, are $150, $30, and $20, respectively. Under section 358(a), FC receives the DC stock with a basis of $300 (the sum of FC's bases in A1, A2, and A3 immediately before the exchange).

(ii) Reorganization. The facts are the same as in paragraph (i)(A) of this *Example 1* except

that, instead of transferring property to DC in a section 351 exchange, FC merges with and into DC in a transaction described in section 368(a)(1)(A). The analysis and results are the same as set forth in paragraphs (i)(B), (C), and (D) of this *Example 1*. However, the analysis in paragraph (i)(E) of this *Example 1* does not apply to these facts because the transaction is not subject to 362(e)(2) and § 1.362–4. Under section 358(a), FC's shareholders will take the DC stock with a basis determined by reference to their FC stock basis.

(iii) FC's property used in U.S. trade or business. (A) Facts. The facts are the same as in paragraph (i)(A) of this *Example 1*, except that FC is engaged in a U.S. trade or business and uses all the properties in that U.S. trade or business. In this case, none of the properties would be importation property because FC would take any gain or loss on the disposition of the properties into account in determining its federal income tax liability. Accordingly, this section does not apply to the transaction.

(B) Basis of property received in transaction. Following the application of section 362(e)(1) and this section, the provisions of section 362(e)(2) must be taken into account because the transfer is a section 362(a) transaction. Taking into account the application of section 362(e)(1) and this section but without taking into account the provisions of section 362(e)(2), DC's aggregate basis in the transferred properties would be $300 ($40 + $120 + $140) under section 362(a) and the properties' aggregate value immediately after the transfer would be $200 ($150 + $30 + $20). Therefore, FC has a net built-in loss and FC's transfer of A1, A2, and A3 is a loss duplication transaction. Accordingly, under the general rule of section 362(e)(2), FC's $100 net built-in loss ($300 aggregate basis over $200 aggregate value) would be allocated proportionately (by the amount of built-in loss in each property) to reduce DC's basis in the loss properties, A2 and A3. See § 1.362–4. As a result, DC's basis in A2 would be $77.14 ($120 basis under section 362(a) reduced by $42.86, A2's proportionate share of FC's net built-in loss, computed as $90/$210 × $100) and DC's basis in A3 would be $82.86 ($140 basis under section 362(a) reduced by $57.14, A3's proportionate share of FC's net built-in loss, computed as $120/$210 × $100). However, if FC and DC were to elect under section 362(e)(2) (C) to apply the $100 basis reduction to FC's basis in the DC stock received in the transaction, DC's bases in A2 and A3 would remain their section 362(a) bases of $120 and $140, respectively. Under section 362(a), DC's basis in A1 is $40 (irrespective of whether the section 362(e)(2)(C) election is made). If FC and DC do not make a section 362(e)(2)(C) election, FC's basis in the DC stock received in the exchange will be $300; if FC and DC do make the election, FC's basis in the DC stock will be $200 ($300 − $100 net built-in loss). See § 1.362–4(b).

* * *

§ 1.362–4 Limitations on built-in loss duplication.

(a) Purpose and scope—(1) In general. The purpose of section 362(e)(2) and this section is to prevent the duplication of net loss in transfers to which section 351 applies, capital contributions, and paid-in surplus (each, a section 362(a) transaction). See paragraph (g) of this section for definitions of terms used in this section.

* * *

(b) Basis determinations under section 362(e)(2) and this section. Notwithstanding section 362(a), if a corporation (Acquiring) receives loss duplication property (as defined in paragraph (g)(1) of this section) from a person (Transferor) in a loss duplication transaction (as defined in paragraph (g)(2) of this section), Acquiring's basis in such property is equal to the basis of the property determined without regard to section 362(e)(2) and this section (as described in paragraph (g)(1)(ii) of this section), reduced by the property's alloca-

ble portion of Transferor's net built-in loss (as defined in paragraph (g)(3) of this section). If more than one Transferor transfers property to a corporation in a section 362(a) transaction, whether and the extent to which section 362(e) (2) and this section apply is determined separately for each Transferor.

(c) Exceptions and special rules—(1) Transactions in which net built-in loss is eliminated without recognition. Section 362(e)(2) does not apply to a transaction to the extent that—

(i) Without recognizing gain or loss, Transferor distributes the Acquiring stock received in the transaction; and

(ii) Upon completion of the transaction, no person holds Acquiring stock or any other asset with a basis determined, in whole or in part, by reference to Transferor's basis in the distributed Acquiring stock.

(2) Certain transactions outside of the United States. Section 362(e)(2) does not apply to a transaction if—

(i) Neither Transferor nor Acquiring is a U.S. person (as defined in section 7701(a) (30)), a person otherwise required to file a U.S. return for the year of the transaction, a controlled foreign corporation (CFC, as defined in paragraph (g)(7) of this section), or a controlled foreign partnership (CFP, as defined in paragraph (g)(9) of this section) on the date of the transaction;

(ii) The transfer occurs more than two years prior to the date of any event described in paragraph (d)(3)(ii)(E), (F), or (G) of this section; and

(iii) The original transaction and the event or events described in paragraph (d)(3)(ii)(E), (F), or (G) of this section were not entered into with a view to reducing or avoiding the Federal income tax liability of any person by avoiding the application of section 362(e)(2) and this section to the original transaction.

* * *

(d) Election to reduce Transferor's stock basis instead of Acquiring's asset basis—(1) In general. In lieu of making the basis reductions otherwise required under paragraph (b) of this section, Transferor and Acquiring may elect to reduce Transferor's basis in Acquiring stock that is received in the transaction without the recognition of gain or loss (the section 362(e)(2)(C) election). The section 362(e)(2)(C) election may be made protectively and will have no effect to the extent that property transferred in the transaction is determined not to be subject to section 362(e)(2) and this section. However, the election is irrevocable once it is made. * * *

(2) Effect of section 362(e)(2)(C) election. If a section 362(e)(2)(C) election is made and in effect—

(i) An amount equal to the portion of Transferor's net built-in loss (as defined in paragraph (g)(3) of this section) that would otherwise be applied to reduce asset basis under paragraph (b) of this section is allocated among the Acquiring shares received or deemed received in the exchange (in proportion to the value of such shares) and applied to reduce Transferor's basis (determined without regard to section 362(e)(2) and this section) in each such share; and

(ii) Acquiring's basis in loss duplication property received from Transferor in the transaction is not determined under section 362(e)(2) and this section.

* * *

(e) Transfers by partnerships and S corporations—(1) Transfers by partnerships. If a partnership transfers property in a loss duplication transaction with respect to which a section 362(e)(2)(C) election is made, the resulting reduction to the partnership's basis in the Acquiring stock received in exchange for the loss duplication property is treated as an expenditure of the partnership described in section 705(a)(2)(B).

(2) Transfers by S corporations. If an S corporation transfers property in a loss duplication transaction with respect to which a section 362(e)(2)(C) election is made, the resulting reduction to the S corporation's basis in the Acquiring stock received in exchange for the loss duplication property is treated as an expense of the S corporation described in section 1367(a)(2)(D).

(f) Transfers to S corporations. If a person transfers property to an S corporation in a loss duplication transaction, any resulting reduction under section 362(e)(2) and this section to the S corporation's basis in the property received is not treated as an expense of the S corporation described in section 1367(a)(2)(D).

(g) Definitions. For purposes of section 362(e)(2) and this section—

(1) *Loss duplication property* is any property—

(i) That is transferred by Transferor to Acquiring in a loss duplication transaction (as defined in paragraph (g)(2) of this section); and

(ii) That Acquiring would take with a basis in excess of value immediately after the transaction; for this purpose, the basis Acquiring would take in the property is determined immediately after the transaction and without regard to section 362(e)(2) and this section, but otherwise taking into account all applicable provisions of law, including, without limitation, section 362(e)(1).

(2) A *loss duplication transaction* is a section 362(a) transaction in which Acquiring's aggregate basis in the property received from Transferor would, but for section 362(e)(2) and this section, exceed the aggregate value of such property immediately after the transaction. For this purpose—

(i) A transaction is a section 362(a) transaction if it is described in section 362(a) without regard to whether it is also described in any other provision of the Internal Revenue Code

(Code), including, without limitation, section 362(b); and

(ii) Acquiring's aggregate basis in the property received from Transferor is determined immediately after the transaction and without regard to section 362(e)(2) and this section, but otherwise taking into account all applicable provisions of law, including, without limitation, section 362(e)(1).

(3) *Transferor's net built-in loss* is the excess of—

(i) Acquiring's aggregate basis (determined under paragraph (g)(2)(ii) of this section) in all property received from Transferor in a loss duplication transaction, over

(ii) The aggregate value of such property immediately after the transaction.

(4) A property's *built-in loss* is the excess of Acquiring's basis in the property (determined as described in paragraph (g)(1)(ii) of this section) over the property's value (determined immediately after the transaction).

(5) A property's *allocable portion of Transferor's net built-in loss* is the portion of Transferor's net built-in loss that bears the same ratio to Transferor's net built-in loss that the property's built-in loss bears to the aggregate built-in losses reflected in the bases of loss duplication property transferred by Transferor in the transaction.

(6) A *U.S. return* is a return of income under section 6012 or an information return under Subtitle F, Chapter 61, Subchapter A, Part III of the Code (sections 6031 and following) or the regulations thereunder, that the taxpayer is unconditionally required to file. Thus, the term does not include elective forms or statements that are required to be filed only to obtain a particular tax treatment, including forms filed to make an election or to reduce or avoid withholding by a person not otherwise required to file a U.S. return (as described in this paragraph (g)(6)) (for example, a notice of nonrecognition under §1.1445–2(d)).

(7) A *controlled foreign corporation* (CFC) is any corporation described in section 957 or section 953(c).

(8) A *controlling U.S. shareholder* is any person that is treated as a controlling U.S. shareholder under §1.964–1(c)(5) because such person either owns a direct interest in the CFC or is treated as owning an interest in the CFC by reason of section 318(a)(2) (attribution from partnerships, estates, trusts, and corporations).

(9) A *controlled foreign partnership* (CFP) is any partnership treated as a controlled foreign partnership for purposes of section 6038.

* * *

(11) The term *stock* means both Acquiring stock and Acquiring securities received by Transferor in the transaction if gain or loss on the receipt of the stock or securities is not recognized in whole or in part.

(12) Value. (i) General rule. The term *value* means fair market value.

(ii) Special rule for transfers of partnership interests. Notwithstanding the general rule in paragraph (g)(12)(i) of this section, when referring to a partnership interest, for purposes of section 362(e)(2) and this section, the term *value* means the sum of the cash that Acquiring would receive for the interest, assuming an exchange between a willing buyer and a willing seller (neither being under any compulsion to buy or sell and both having reasonable knowledge of relevant facts), increased by any §1.752–1 liabilities (as defined in §1.752–1(a)(4)) of the partnership allocated to Acquiring with regard to such transferred interest under section 752 immediately after the transfer to Acquiring. See §1.743–1 regarding the application of section 743(b) following a section 362(e) basis reduction.

(h) Examples. The examples in this paragraph (h) illustrate the application of section 362(e)(2) and the provisions of this section. Unless the facts otherwise indicate, the examples use the following nomenclature and assumptions: X, Y, P, S, S1, and S2 are domestic corporations; A and B are U.S. individuals; FC1 and FC2 are foreign corporations and are not engaged in a U.S. trade or business, have no U.S. real property interests, and have no other relationships, activities, or interests that would cause them, their shareholders, or their property to be subject to tax imposed under any provision of subtitle A of the Internal Revenue Code (federal income tax); there is no applicable income tax treaty; PRS is a domestic partnership; no election is made under section 362(e)(2)(C); and the transferred property is not importation property (as defined in § 1.362–3(c)(2)) and the transfers are not loss importation transactions (as defined in § 1.362–3(c)(3)), so that the basis of no property is determined under section 362(e)(1). All persons and transactions are unrelated unless the facts indicate otherwise, all taxpayers are on a calendar tax year, and all other relevant facts are set forth in the examples. See § 1.362–3(f) for additional examples illustrating the application of section 362(e)(2) and this section, including to transactions that are subject to section 362(e)(2), and section 362(e)(1).

Example (1). Transfer described in section 351. (i) Basic application of section. (A) Facts. A owns Asset 1 (basis $90, value $60) and Asset 2 (basis $110, value $120). In a transaction to which section 351 applies, A transfers Asset 1 and Asset 2 to X in exchange for a single outstanding share of X stock representing all the outstanding X stock immediately after the transaction.

(B) Analysis. (1) Loss duplication transaction. A's transfer of Asset 1 and Asset 2 is a section 362(a) transaction. But for section 362(e)(2) and this section, X's aggregate basis in those assets would be $200 ($90 + $110), which would exceed the aggregate value of the assets $180 ($60 + $120) immediately after the transaction. Accordingly, the transfer is a loss duplication transaction and A has a net built-in loss of $20 ($200 – $180).

(2) Identifying loss duplication property. But for section 362(e)(2) and this section, X's basis in Asset 1 would be $90, which would exceed Asset 1's $60 value immediately after the transaction. Accordingly, Asset 1 is loss duplication property. But for section 362(e)(2) and this section, X's basis in Asset 2 would be $110, which would not exceed Asset 2's $120 value immediately after the transaction. Accordingly, Asset 2 is not loss duplication property.

(C) Basis in loss duplication property. X's basis in Asset 1 is $70, computed as its $90 basis under section 362(a) reduced by A's $20 net built-in loss.

(D) Basis in other property. Under section 362(a), X has a transferred basis of $110 in Asset 2. Under section 358(a), A has an exchanged basis of $200 in the X stock it receives in the transaction.

(ii) Section 362(e)(2)(C) election. The facts are the same as in paragraph (i)(A) of this *Example 1*, except that A and X make an election under section 362(e)(2)(C). Under paragraph (d)(2)(i) of this section, A reduces its basis in the X stock, as determined without regard to section 362(e)(2) and this section, by the amount of A's net built-in loss that would have been applied to reduce X's basis in Asset 1 had the section 362(e)(2)(C) election not been made. In addition, no reduction is made to X's basis in Asset 1, as determined without regard to section 362(e)(2) and this section. As a result, A's basis in the X stock is $180 ($200 – $20), X's basis in Asset 1 is $90, and X's basis in Asset 2 is $110.

Example (2). Transfer described in both section 351 and section 368(a)(1)(B). (i) Basic application of section. (A) Facts. P owns the sole outstanding share of S1 stock and the ten outstanding shares of S2 stock. In a transaction to which section 351 applies and that is described in section 368(a)(1)(B), P transfers its ten S2 shares to S1 in exchange for an additional ten shares of S1 voting stock. At the time of the transfer, P has a basis of $10 each in five of its S2 shares (Shares 1–5) and a basis of $5 each in its other five S2 shares (Shares 6–10), and the value of each share is $7.

(B) Analysis. (1) Loss duplication transaction. P's transfer of the S2 shares is a section 362(a) transaction notwithstanding that it is also a transaction described in section 368(a)(1)(B) and therefore section 362(b). But for section 362(e)(2) and this section, S1's aggregate basis in the S2 shares would be $75 ($10 × 5, or $50, for Shares 1–5 + $5 × 5, or $25, for Shares 6–10). Thus, S1's $75 aggregate basis in the shares would exceed the aggregate value of the shares, $70 ($7 × 10 shares), immediately after the transaction. Accordingly, the transfer is a loss duplication transaction and P has a net built-in loss of $5 ($75 – $70).

(2) Identifying loss duplication property. But for section 362(e)(2) and this section, S1's basis in each of Shares 1–5 would be $10, which would exceed each share's $7 value immediately after the transaction. Accordingly, Shares 1–5 are each loss duplication property. But for section 362(e)(2) and this section, S1's basis in each of Shares 6–10 would be $5, which would not exceed each share's $7 value immediately after the transaction. Accordingly, Shares 6–10 are not loss duplication property.

(C) Basis in loss duplication property. S1's basis in each of Shares 1–5 is $9, computed as its $10 basis (determined without regard to section 362(e)(2) and this section) reduced by $1, the share's allocable portion (1/5) of P's net built-in loss ($5).

(D) Basis in other property. Under section 362(a), S1 has a transferred basis of $5 in each of Shares 6–10. Under section 358(a), P has an exchanged basis in the ten S1 shares it receives in the exchange ($10 in each of the five S1 shares received in exchange for Shares 1–5 and $5 in each of the five S1 shares received in exchange for Shares 5–10).

(ii) Section 362(e)(2)(C) election. The facts are the same as in paragraph (i)(A) of this *Example 2*, except that an election under section 362(e)(2)(C) is made to reduce P's basis in the shares of S1 stock received in the exchange. Under paragraph (d)(2)(i) of this section, P reduces its basis in the S1 stock by $5, the amount of P's net built-in loss that S1's basis in the S2 shares would have been reduced under section 362(e)(2) and this section had the section 362(e)(2)(C) election not been made, and no reduction is made to S1's basis in the S2 stock (as determined without regard to section 362(e)(2) and this section). Because an election is being made under section 362(e)(2)(C), P's basis in the new S1 shares is not determined under the general rule of §1.358–2(a)(2)(i) (under which P's basis in each new S1 share would be equal to the basis of the S2 share transferred in exchange for the S1 share). Section 1.358–2(a)(2)(viii)(B). Accordingly, P's basis in each new S1 share will be $7, the share's allocable portion of P's $75 aggregate basis in the S2 shares transferred in the transaction (or, $7.50 per share), reduced under paragraph (d)(2)(i) of this section by the $5 that would have been applied to reduce S1's basis in the S2 shares had the section 362(e)(2)(C) election not been made (or $.50 per share). Under paragraph (d)(2)(ii) of this section and section 362(a), S1 receives five shares of the S2 stock with a basis of $10 each and five shares of the S2 stock with a basis of $5 each.

Example (3). Transfer described in both section 351 and section 368(a)(1)(A), multiple transferors, elimination of duplicated loss. (i) Facts. A owns Asset 1 (basis $120, value $130) and all the outstanding shares of X stock. B owns all the outstanding shares of Y stock (basis $150). Y owns Asset 2 (basis $250, value $210). Pursuant to a single plan, A transfers Asset 1 to X in exchange for additional X shares and, in a transaction qualifying as a reorganization described in section 368(a)(1)(A), Y merges with and into X. In the merger, B receives X stock with a basis equal to B's basis in its Y stock immediately before the merger. A's transfer of Asset 1 to X in exchange for X stock and Y's transfer of Asset

2 to X in the merger are both transactions to which section 351 applies. Notwithstanding that the transfers by A and Y are pursuant to a single plan forming one transaction, section 362(e)(2) and this section apply to each transferor separately.

(ii) Application of section to A's transfer of Asset 1. A's transfer of Asset 1 is a section 362(a) transaction. But for section 362(e)(2) and this section, X's basis in Asset 1 would be $120, which would not exceed Asset 1's $130 value immediately after the transaction. Accordingly, A's transfer of Asset 1 is not a loss duplication transaction notwithstanding that, taking both A's transfer and Y's transfer into account, X has an aggregate net loss in Asset 1 and Asset 2. Because Asset 1 is not received in a loss duplication transaction, it is not loss duplication property and section 362(e)(2) and this section do not apply to A's transfer of Asset 1.

(iii) Application of section to Y's transfer of Asset 2. (A) *Analysis.* (*1*) *Loss duplication transaction.* Y's transfer of Asset 2 to X is a section 362(a) transaction, notwithstanding that it is also a transaction described in section 368(a)(1)(A) and therefore section 362(b). But for section 362(e)(2) and this section, X's basis in Asset 2 would be $250, which would exceed Asset 2's $210 value immediately after the transaction. Accordingly, Y's transfer is a loss duplication transaction and Y has a net built-in loss of $40.

(2) Identifying loss duplication property. But for section 362(e)(2) and this section, X's basis in Asset 2 would be $250, which would exceed Asset 2's $210 value immediately after the transaction. Accordingly, Asset 2 is loss duplication property.

(B) Basis in loss duplication property. Although Asset 2 is loss duplication property, section 362(e)(2) does not apply to Y's transfer of Asset 2 to X because Y distributes all of the X stock received in the exchange without recognizing gain or loss, and, upon completion of the transaction, no person will hold the X stock

or any other asset with a basis determined in whole or in part by reference to Y's basis in such stock. Accordingly, under paragraph (c)(1) of this section, X's basis in Asset 2 is not determined under section 362(e)(2) and this section. Thus, under section 362(a), X's basis in Asset 2 is $250.

(iv) Basis in other property. Under section 358, A's basis in the X stock received in exchange for Asset 1 is $120 and B's basis in the X stock received in the merger is $150. Under section 362(a), X's basis in Asset 1 is $120.

Example (4). Transfer described in both section 351 and section 368(a)(1)(D), followed by a distribution qualifying under section 355. *(i) Basic transaction. (A) Facts.* A and B each own one of the two outstanding shares of X common stock. X's assets include Asset 1 (basis $120, value $70), Asset 2 (basis $160, value $110), and Asset 3 (basis $220, value $240). In a transaction to which section 351 applies and that is described in section 368(a)(1)(D), X transfers Asset 1, Asset 2, and Asset 3 to Y in exchange for all the Y stock; then, in a distribution that qualifies under section 355, X distributes all the Y stock received in the exchange to A in exchange for all of A's X stock. Under section 361(c)(1), X does not recognize gain or loss as a result of the distribution of all the Y stock.

(B) Analysis. (1) Loss duplication transaction. X's transfer of Asset 1, Asset 2, and Asset 3 is a section 362(a) transaction. But for section 362(e)(2) and this section, Y's aggregate basis in those assets would be $500 ($120 + $160 + $220). The aggregate value of the assets immediately after the transaction is $420 ($70 + $110 + $240). Thus, Y's aggregate basis in the assets would exceed the aggregate value of the assets immediately after the transaction. Accordingly, the transfer is a loss duplication transaction and X has a net built-in loss of $80 ($500 − $420).

(2) Identifying loss duplication property. But for section 362(e)(2) and this section, Y's basis in Asset 1 would be $120, which would

exceed Asset 1's $70 value immediately after the transaction. Accordingly, Asset 1 is loss duplication property. But for section 362(e)(2) and this section, Y's basis in Asset 2 would be $160, which would exceed Asset 2's $110 value immediately after the transaction. Accordingly, Asset 2 is also loss duplication property. But for section 362(e)(2) and this section, Y's basis in Asset 3 would be $220 and would therefore not exceed Asset 3's $240 value immediately after the transaction. Accordingly, Asset 3 is not loss duplication property.

(C) Basis in loss duplication property. Although Asset 1 and Asset 2 are each loss duplication property, X will distribute the Y stock received in exchange for Asset 1 and Asset 2 without recognition of gain or loss, and, upon completion of the transaction, no person will hold the Y stock received by X or any other asset with a basis determined in whole or in part by reference to X's basis in the Y stock received in the exchange. (A's basis in the Y stock will be determined by reference to his basis in his X stock.) Accordingly, under paragraph (c)(1) of this section, Y's bases in Asset 1 and Asset 2 are determined under section 362(a) and not under section 362(e)(2) and this section. Thus, Y's basis in Asset 1 is $120 and Y's basis in Asset 2 is $160.

(D) Basis in other property. Under section 358, A's basis in the Y stock received in exchange for his X stock is determined by reference to his basis in his X stock surrendered. Under section 362(a), Y's basis in Asset 3 is $220.

(ii) Section 355(e). (A) *Facts.* The facts are the same as in paragraph (i)(A) of this *Example 4*, except that, after the section 355 distribution, Y is acquired pursuant to a plan (within the meaning of §1.355–7), resulting in the application of section 355(e) to the transactions.

(B) Analysis. Because section 361(c)(2), and not section 361(c)(1), will apply to X's distribution of Y stock, X will not qualify for nonrecognition treatment on the distribution of the Y stock. As a result, paragraph (c)(1) of

this section does not apply to the transaction, and Y's bases in Asset 1 and Asset 2, the loss duplication property, are determined under section 362(e)(2) and this section. Asset 1 has a built-in loss of $50 ($120 – $70), and Asset 2 has a built-in loss of $50 ($160 – $110). Thus, Asset 1's allocable portion of X's net built-in loss is $40 ($50/$100 × $80), and Asset 2's allocable portion of X's net built-in loss is $40 ($50/$100 × $80). Accordingly, Y receives Asset 1 with a basis of $80 ($120 – $40) and Asset 2 with a basis of $120 ($160 – $40).

(iii) Retained stock and securities. (A) *Facts.* The facts are the same as in paragraph (i)(A) of this *Example 4*, except that X transfers Asset 1, Asset 2, and Asset 3 to Y in exchange for Y stock and Y securities, each constituting half of the consideration. In addition, for a valid business purpose, X retains Y stock and Y securities each worth 1 percent of the total consideration.

(B) Analysis. Paragraph (c)(1) of this section applies only to the extent that stock received in a transaction is distributed without recognition of gain or loss. Thus, section 362(e)(2) and this section apply to the extent that property was exchanged for the retained Y stock and Y securities (2 percent of the total). Accordingly, Y reduces its basis in Asset 1 and in Asset 2, the loss duplication property, by $1.60 (two percent of X's $80 net built-in loss). Asset 1 has a built-in loss of $50 ($120 – $70), and Asset 2 has a built-in loss of $50 ($160 – $110). Thus, Asset 1's allocable portion of X's net built-in loss is $.80 ($50/$100 × $1.60), and Asset 2's allocable portion of X's net built-in loss is $.80 ($50/$100 × $1.60). As a result, Y receives Asset 1 with a basis of $119.20 ($120 – $.80) and Asset 2 with a basis of $159.20 ($160 – $.80).

(iv) Retained stock and securities with a section 362(e)(2)(C) election. (A) *Facts.* The facts are the same as in paragraph (iii)(A) of this *Example 4*, except that an election under section 362(e)(2)(C) is made to reduce X's

bases in its retained Y stock and retained Y securities.

(B) Analysis. Under paragraph (d)(2)(i) of this section, X reduces its basis in the retained Y stock and the retained Y securities (determined without regard to section 362(e)(2) and this section) by $1.60, the portion of X's $80 net built-in loss that would have been applied to reduce Y's basis in the transferred assets had the election to apply section 362(e)(2)(C) not been made. (Because the value of the Y stock and the value of the Y securities are equal, X's $500 basis in the transferred property would be allocated equally between the Y stock and the Y securities, $250 to each, under §1.358–2(b)(2), and the retained Y stock and Y securities have a basis of $2.50 each (one percent of $250).) For the reasons set forth in paragraph (iii)(B) of this *Example 4*, Y would have been required to reduce its basis in the transferred assets by $1.60. Accordingly, X must reduce its aggregate basis in the retained Y stock and Y securities by $1.60. Under paragraph (d)(2)(i) of this section, the $1.60 basis reduction is allocated and applied to reduce X's bases in the retained Y stock and Y securities in proportion to the value of each. Because X retained Y stock and Y securities with equal values, X holds each of the retained Y stock and securities with an adjusted basis of $1.70 ($2.50 – $.80). Under paragraph (d)(2)(ii) of this section, Y receives Asset 1 with a basis of $120, Asset 2 with a basis of $160, and Asset 3 with a basis of $220.

Example (5). Transfer of liabilities. (i) Liabilities described in section 358(d)(1). (A) Basic application of section, no section 362(e)(2)(C) election. (1) Facts. A owns Asset 1 (basis $800, value $700). A also has a $200 liability that has been taken into account for tax purposes and is thus described in section 358(d)(1), and not in sections 357(c)(3), 358(d)(2), and 358(h)(1). A transfers Asset 1 to X in exchange for a single outstanding share of X stock representing all the outstanding X stock immediately after the transaction and X's assumption of the liability. The transfer is a transaction to which section 351 applies.

(2) Analysis. (i) Loss duplication transaction. A's transfer of Asset 1 is a section 362(a) transaction. But for section 362(e)(2) and this section, X's basis in Asset 1 would be $800, which would exceed Asset 1's $700 value immediately after the transaction. Accordingly, the transfer is a loss duplication transaction and A has a net built-in loss of $100 ($800 – $700).

(ii) Identifying loss duplication property. But for section 362(e)(2) and this section, X's basis in Asset 1 would be $800, which would exceed the $700 value of Asset 1 immediately after the transaction. Accordingly, Asset 1 is loss duplication property.

(3) Basis in loss duplication property. X's basis in Asset 1 is $700, computed as its $800 basis determined under section 362(a) reduced by A's $100 net built-in loss.

(4) Basis in other property. Under sections 358(a) and (d)(1), A's basis in the X stock is $600 ($800 basis in property transferred – $200 liability assumed).

(B) Section 362(e)(2)(C) election. The facts are the same as in paragraph (i)(A)(*1*) of this *Example 5*, except that A and X make an election under section 362(e)(2)(C). In this case, A's $100 net built-in loss that would have been applied to reduce X's basis in Asset 1 is applied to reduce A's basis in the X stock received. As a result, A's basis in the X stock is $500 ($600, as determined in paragraph (i)(A) (*4*) of this *Example 5*, reduced by $100) and X's basis in Asset 1 is $800.

(ii) Contingent liabilities described in section 358(h)(1), section 358(h)(2)(A) exception applies. (A) *Facts.* The facts are the same as in paragraph (i)(A)(*1*) of this *Example 5*, except that A's liability (valued at $200) has not been taken into account for tax purposes and is described in sections 358(d)(2) and 358(h)(1). However, Asset 1 is a trade or business and the liability is associated with the trade or

business; as a result, the liability is described in section 358(h)(2)(A) and is excepted from the general rule of section 358(h)(1).

(B) Analysis. For the reasons set forth in paragraph (i)(A)(*2*) of this *Example 5*, A's transfer of Asset 1 is a loss duplication transaction, A has a net built-in loss of $100, and Asset 1 is loss duplication property.

(C) Basis in loss duplication property. For the reasons set forth in paragraph (i)(A)(*3*) of this *Example 5*, X's basis in Asset 1 is $700.

(D) Basis in other property. A's basis in the X stock is $800 under sections 358(a), 358(d) (2), and 358(h)(2)(A).

(E) Section 362(e)(2)(C) election. The facts are the same as in paragraph (ii)(A) of this *Example 5*, except that A and X make an election under section 362(e)(2)(C). In this case, A's $100 net built-in loss that would have applied to reduce X's basis in Asset 1 is applied to reduce A's basis in the X stock received. As a result, A's basis in the X stock is $700 ($800, as determined in paragraph (ii)(D) of this *Example 5*, reduced by $100). X's basis in Asset 1 is $800.

Example (6). Section 351 transfer with boot. (i) Basic transaction. (A) Facts. A owns Asset 1 (basis $80, value $100) and Asset 2 (basis $30, value $25). In a transaction to which section 351 applies, A transfers Asset 1 and Asset 2 to X in exchange for 10 shares of X stock and $25.

(B) Analysis. (1) Loss duplication transaction. A's transfer of Asset 1 and Asset 2 is a section 362(a) transaction. But for section 362(e)(2) and this section, X's aggregate basis in those assets would be $130, computed as follows. Under section 362(a), a corporation's basis in property acquired in a transaction to which section 351 applies is the same as the property's basis in the hands of the transferor, increased by any gain recognized to the transferor on such transfer. Under section 351(b), gain (but not loss) is recognized to the extent a transferor in a section 351 exchange re-

ceives other property or money in addition to the stock permitted to be received without the recognition of gain. To determine the amount of gain recognized under section 351(b), the consideration is allocated proportionately (by value) among the transferred properties. A's gain on the transfer is therefore computed as follows: Asset 1 reflects 80 percent of the value transferred ($100/$125) and Asset 2 reflects 20 percent of the value transferred ($25/$125). Thus, 80 percent of the stock (eight shares) and the cash ($20) are treated as being received in exchange for Asset 1 and 20 percent of the stock (two shares) and the cash ($5) are treated as being received in exchange for Asset 2. Thus, under section 351(b), A recognizes $20 of gain for the cash received in exchange for Asset 1, but A recognizes no loss for the amount received for Asset 2. As a result, under section 362(a), X would have a basis of $100 in Asset 1 and $30 in Asset 2. Thus, X's aggregate basis in the assets would be $130, which exceeds the $125 aggregate value of the assets ($100 + $25)). The transfer is a loss duplication transaction and A has a net built-in loss of $5 ($130 – $125).

(2) Identifying loss duplication property. But for section 362(e)(2) and this section, X's basis in Asset 1 would be $100 (A's $80 basis increased by A's $20 gain recognized), which would not exceed Asset 1's $100 value immediately after the transaction. Accordingly, Asset 1 is not loss duplication property. But for section 362(e)(2) and this section, X's basis in Asset 2 would be $30, which would exceed Asset 2's $25 value immediately after the transaction. Accordingly, Asset 2 is loss duplication property.

(C) Basis in loss duplication property. X's basis in Asset 2 is $25, computed as its $30 basis under section 362(a) reduced by A's $5 net built-in loss.

(D) Basis in other property. Under section 362(a), X's basis in Asset 1 is $100 (A's $80 basis increased by the $20 gain recognized). Under section 358, A's basis in the X stock is

$105 (the sum of its $80 basis in Asset 1, its $30 basis in Asset 2, and its $20 gain recognized, reduced by the $25 cash received in the exchange).

(ii) Section 362(e)(2)(C) election. The facts are the same as in paragraph (i)(A) of this *Example 6*, except that A and X elect to reduce A's stock basis under section 362(e)(2)(C). Under paragraph (d)(2)(i) of this section, A reduces its $105 basis in the X stock by $5, the amount of A's net built-in loss of that would have been applied to reduce X's basis in Asset 2 had the section 362(e)(2)(C) election not been made. As a result, A's basis in the X stock is $100, and X's basis in Asset 2 is $30.

* * *

§ 1.368–1 Purpose and scope of exception of reorganization exchanges.

(a) Reorganizations. As used in the regulations under parts I, II, and III (section 301 and following), subchapter C, chapter 1 of the Code, the terms "reorganization" and "party to a reorganization" mean only a reorganization or a party to a reorganization as defined in subsections (a) and (b) of section 368. In determining whether a transaction qualifies as a reorganization under section 368(a), the transaction must be evaluated under relevant provisions of law, including the step transaction doctrine. But see §§ 1.368–2(f) and (k).

(b) Purpose. Under the general rule, upon the exchange of property, gain or loss must be accounted for if the new property differs in a material particular, either in kind or in extent, from the old property. The purpose of the reorganization provisions of the Code is to except from the general rule certain specifically described exchanges incident to such readjustments of corporate structures made in one of the particular ways specified in the Code, as are required by business exigencies and which effect only a readjustment of continuing interest in property under modified corporate forms. Requisite to a reorganization under the Internal Revenue Code are a continuity of the business enterprise through the issuing corporation under the modified corporate form as described in paragraph (d) of this section, and (except as provided in section 368(a)(1)(D)) a continuity of interest as described in paragraph (e) of this section. (For rules regarding the continuity of interest requirement under section 355, see § 1.355–2(c).) For purposes of this section, the term issuing corporation means the acquiring corporation (as that term is used in section 368(a)), except that, in determining whether a reorganization qualifies as a triangular reorganization (as defined in § 1.358–6(b)(2)), the issuing corporation means the corporation in control of the acquiring corporation. The continuity of business enterprise requirement is described in paragraph (d) of this section. The Code recognizes as a reorganization the amalgamation (occurring in a specified way) of two corporate enterprises under a single corporate structure if there exists among the holders of the stock and securities of either of the old corporations the requisite continuity of interest in the new corporation, but there is not a reorganization if the holders of the stock and securities of the old corporation are merely the holders of short-term notes in the new corporation. In order to exclude transactions not intended to be included, the specifications of the reorganization provisions of the law are precise. Notwithstanding the requirements of this paragraph (b), for transactions occurring on or after February 25, 2005, a continuity of the business enterprise and a continuity of interest are not required for the transaction to qualify as a reorganization under section 368(a)(1)(E) or (F). Both the terms of the specifications and their underlying assumptions and purposes must be satisfied in order to entitle the taxpayer to the benefit of the exception from the general rule. Accordingly, under the Code, a short-term purchase money note is not a security of a party to a reorganization, an ordinary dividend is to be treated as an ordinary dividend, and a sale is nevertheless to be treated as a sale even though the mechanics of a reorganization have been set up.

(c) Scope. The nonrecognition of gain or loss is prescribed for two specifically described types of exchanges, viz: The exchange that is provided for in section 354(a)(1) in which stock or securities in a corporation, a party to a reorganization, are, in pursuance of a plan of reorganization, exchanged for the stock or securities in a corporation, a party to the same reorganization; and the exchange that is provided for in section 361(a) in which a corporation, a party to a reorganization, exchanges property, in pursuance of a plan of reorganization, for stock or securities in another corporation, a party to the same reorganization. Section 368(a)(1) limits the definition of the term "reorganization" to six kinds of transactions and excludes all others. From its context, the term "a party to a reorganization" can only mean a party to a transaction specifically defined as a reorganization by section 368(a). Certain rules respecting boot received in either of the two types of exchanges provided for in section 354(a)(1) and section 361(a) are prescribed in sections 356, 357, and 361(b). A special rule respecting a transfer of property with a liability in excess of its basis is prescribed in section 357(c). The provisions of the Code referred to in this paragraph are inapplicable unless there is a plan of reorganization. A plan of reorganization must contemplate the bona fide execution of one of the transactions specifically described as a reorganization in section 368(a) and for the bona fide consummation of each of the requisite acts under which nonrecognition of gain is claimed. Such transaction and such acts must be an ordinary and necessary incident of the conduct of the enterprise and must provide for a continuation of the enterprise. A scheme, which involves an abrupt departure from normal reorganization procedure in connection with a transaction on which the imposition of tax is imminent, such as a mere device that puts on the form of a corporate reorganization as a disguise for concealing its real character, and the object and accomplishment of which is the consummation of a preconceived plan having no business or corporate purpose, is not a plan of reorganization.

(d) Continuity of business enterprise — (1) General rule. Continuity of business enterprise (COBE) requires that the issuing corporation (P), as defined in paragraph (b) of this section, either continue the target corporation's (T's) historic business or use a significant portion of T's historic business assets in a business. The application of this general rule to certain transactions, such as mergers of holding companies, will depend on all facts and circumstances. The policy underlying this general rule, which is to ensure that reorganizations are limited to readjustments of continuing interests in property under modified corporate form, provides the guidance necessary to make these facts and circumstances determinations.

(2) Business continuity. (i) The continuity of business enterprise requirement is satisfied if P continues T's historic business. The fact P is in the same line of business as T tends to establish the requisite continuity, but is not alone sufficient.

(ii) If T has more than one line of business, continuity of business enterprise requires only that P continue a significant line of business.

(iii) In general, a corporation's historic business is the business it has conducted most recently. However, a corporation's historic business is not one the corporation enters into as part of a plan of reorganization.

(iv) All facts and circumstances are considered in determining the time when the plan comes into existence and in determining whether a line of business is "significant".

(3) Asset continuity. (i) The continuity of business enterprise requirement is satisfied if P uses a significant portion of T's historic business assets in a business.

(ii) A corporation's historic business assets are the assets used in its historic business. Business assets may include stock and securities and intangible operating assets such as good will, patents, and trademarks, whether or not they have a tax basis.

(iii) In general, the determination of the portion of a corporation's assets considered "significant" is based on the relative importance of the assets to operation of the business. However, all other facts and circumstances, such as the net fair market value of those assets, will be considered.

(4) Acquired assets or stock held by members of the qualified group or partnerships. The following rules apply in determining whether the COBE requirement of paragraph (d)(1) of this section is satisfied:

(i) Businesses and assets of members of a qualified group. The issuing corporation is treated as holding all of the businesses and assets of all of the members of the qualified group, as defined in paragraph (d)(4)(ii) of this section.

(ii) Qualified group. A qualified group is one or more chains of corporations connected through stock ownership with the issuing corporation, but only if the issuing corporation owns directly stock meeting the requirements of section 368(c) in at least one other corporation, and stock meeting the requirements of section 368(c) in each of the corporations (except the issuing corporation) is owned directly (or indirectly as provided in paragraph (d)(4)(iii)(D) of this section) by one or more of the other corporations.

(iii) Partnerships—(A) Partnership assets. Each partner of a partnership will be treated as owning the T business assets used in a business of the partnership in accordance with that partner's interest in the partnership.

(B) Partnership businesses. The issuing corporation will be treated as conducting a business of a partnership if—

(1) Members of the qualified group, in the aggregate, own an interest in the partnership representing a significant interest in that partnership business; or

(2) One or more members of the qualified group have active and substantial management functions as a partner with respect to that partnership business.

(C) Conduct of the historic T business in a partnership. If a significant historic T business is conducted in a partnership, the fact that P is treated as conducting such T business under paragraph (d)(4)(iii)(B) of this section tends to establish the requisite continuity, but is not alone sufficient.

(D) Stock attributed from certain partnerships. Solely for purposes of paragraph (d)(4)(ii) of this section, if members of the qualified group own interests in a partnership meeting requirements equivalent to section 368(c) (a section 368(c) controlled partnership), any stock owned by the section 368(c) controlled partnership shall be treated as owned by members of the qualified group. Solely for purposes of determining whether a lower-tier partnership is a section 368(c) controlled partnership, any interest in a lower-tier partnership that is owned by a section 368(c) controlled partnership shall be treated as owned by members of the qualified group.

(iv) Effective/applicability dates. Paragraphs (d)(4)(i) and (d)(4)(iii) (other than paragraph (d)(4)(iii)(D)) of this section apply to transactions occurring after January 28, 1998, except that they do not apply to any transaction occurring pursuant to a written agreement which is binding on January 28, 1998, and at all times thereafter. Paragraphs (d)(4)(ii) and (d)(4)(iii)(D) of this section apply to transactions occurring on or after October 25, 2007, except that they do not apply to any transaction occurring pursuant to a written agreement which is binding before October 25, 2007, and at all times after that.

(5) Examples. The following examples illustrate this paragraph (d). All the corporations have only one class of stock outstanding. The preceding sentence and paragraph (d)(5) Example 6 and Example 8 through Example 13 apply to transactions occurring after January 28, 1998, except that they do not apply to any transaction occurring pursuant to a written agreement which is binding on January 28, 1998, and at all times thereafter. Paragraph (d) (5) Example 7, Example 14, and Example 15 apply to transactions occurring on or after October 25, 2007, except that they do not apply to any transaction occurring pursuant to a written agreement which is binding before October 25, 2007, and at all times after that. The examples read as follows:

Example (1). T conducts three lines of business: manufacture of synthetic resins, manufacture of chemicals for the textile industry, and distribution of chemicals. The three lines of business are approximately equal in value. On July 1, 1981, T sells the synthetic resin and chemicals distribution businesses to a third party for cash and marketable securities. On December 31, 1981, T transfers all of its assets to P solely for P voting stock. P continues the chemical manufacturing business without interruption. The continuity of business enterprise requirement is met. Continuity of business enterprise requires only that P continue one of T's three significant lines of business.

Example (2). P manufactures computers and T manufactures components for computers. T sells all of its output to P. On January 1, 1981, P decides to buy imported components only. On March 1, 1981, T merges into P. P continues buying imported components but retains T's equipment as a backup source of supply. The use of the equipment as a backup source of supply constitutes use of a significant portion of T's historic business assets, thus establishing continuity of business enterprise. P is not required to continue T's business.

Example (3). T is a manufacturer of boys' and men's trousers. On January 1, 1978, as part of a plan of reorganization, T sold all of its assets to a third party for cash and purchased a highly diversified portfolio of stocks and bonds. As part of the plan T operates an investment business until July 1, 1981. On that date, the plan of reorganization culminates in a transfer by T of all its assets to P, a regulated investment company, solely in exchange for P voting stock. The continuity of business enterprise requirement is not met. T's investment activity is not its historic business, and the stocks and bonds are not T's historic business assets.

Example (4). T manufactures children's toys and P distributes steel and allied products. On January 1, 1981, T sells all of its assets to a third party for $100,000 cash and $900,000 in notes. On March 1, 1981, T merges into P. Continuity of business enterprise is lacking. The use of the sales proceeds in P's business is not sufficient.

Example (5). T manufactures farm machinery and P operates a lumber mill. T merges into P. P disposes of T's assets immediately after the merger as part of the plan of reorganization. P does not continue T's farm machinery manufacturing business. Continuity of business enterprise is lacking.

Example (6). Use of a significant portion of T's historic business assets by the qualified group. (i) Facts. T operates an auto parts distributorship. P owns 80 percent of the stock of a holding company (HC). HC owns 80 percent of the stock of ten subsidiaries, S-1 through S-10. S-1 through S-10 each separately operate a full service gas station. Pursuant to a plan of reorganization, T merges into P and the T shareholders receive solely P stock. As part of the plan of reorganization, P transfers T's assets to HC, which in turn transfers some of the T assets to each of the ten subsidiaries. No one subsidiary receives a significant portion of T's historic business assets. Each of the subsidiaries will use the T assets in the operation of its full service gas station. No P subsidiary will be an auto parts distributor.

(ii) Continuity of business enterprise. Under paragraph (d)(4)(i) of this section, P is treated as conducting the ten gas station businesses of S-1 through S-10 and as holding the historic T assets used in those businesses. P is treated as holding all the assets and conducting the

businesses of all of the members of the qualified group, which includes S-1 through S-10 (paragraphs (d)(4)(i) and (ii) of this section). No member of the qualified group continues T's historic distributorship business. However, subsidiaries S-1 through S-10 continue to use the historic T assets in a business. Even though no one corporation of the qualified group is using a significant portion of T's historic business assets in a business, the COBE requirement of paragraph (d)(1) of this section is satisfied because, in the aggregate, the qualified group is using a significant portion of T's historic business assets in a business.

Example (7). Transfers of acquired stock to members of the qualified group—continuity of business enterprise satisfied. (i) Facts. The facts are the same as Example 6, except that, instead of P acquiring the assets of T, HC acquires all of the outstanding stock of T in exchange solely for stock of P. In addition, as part of the plan of reorganization, HC transfers 10 percent of the stock of T to each of subsidiaries S-1 through S-10. T will continue to operate an auto parts distributorship. Without regard to whether the transaction satisfies the COBE requirement, the transaction qualifies as a triangular B reorganization (as defined in § 1.358–6(b)(2)(iv)).

(ii) Continuity of business enterprise. Under paragraph (d)(4)(i) of this section, P is treated as holding the assets and conducting the business of T because T is a member of the qualified group (as defined in paragraph (d)(4)(ii) of this section). The COBE requirement of paragraph (d)(1) of this section is satisfied.

Example (8). Continuation of the historic T business in a partnership satisfies continuity of business enterprise. (i) Facts. T manufactures ski boots. P owns all of the stock of S-1. S-1 owns all of the stock of S-2, and S-2 owns all of the stock of S-3. T merges into P and the T shareholders receive consideration consisting of P stock and cash. The T ski boot business is to be continued and expanded. In anticipation of this expansion, P transfers all of the T assets

to S-1, S-1 transfers all of the T assets to S-2, and S-2 transfers all of the T assets to S-3. S-3 and X (an unrelated party) form a new partnership (PRS). As part of the plan of reorganization, S-3 transfers all the T assets to PRS, and S-3, in its capacity as a partner, performs active and substantial management functions for the PRS ski boot business, including making significant business decisions and regularly participating in the overall supervision, direction, and control of the employees of the ski boot business. S-3 receives a 20 percent interest in PRS. X transfers cash in exchange for an 80 percent interest in PRS.

(ii) Continuity of business enterprise. Under paragraph (d)(4)(iii)(B)(2) of this section, P is treated as conducting T's historic business because S-3 performs active and substantial management functions for the ski boot business in S-3's capacity as a partner. P is treated as holding all the assets and conducting the businesses of all of the members of the qualified group, which includes S-3 (paragraphs (d)(4)(i) and (ii) of this section). The COBE requirement of paragraph (d)(1) of this section is satisfied.

Example (9). Continuation of the historic T business in a partnership does not satisfy continuity of business enterprise. (i) Facts. The facts are the same as Example 8 except that S-3 transfers the historic T business to PRS in exchange for a 1 percent interest in PRS.

(ii) Continuity of business enterprise. Under paragraph (d)(4)(iii)(B)(2) of this section, P is treated as conducting T's historic business because S-3 performs active and substantial management functions for the ski boot business in S-3's capacity as a partner. The fact that a significant historic T business is conducted in PRS, and P is treated as conducting such T business under (d)(4)(iii)(B) tends to establish the requisite continuity, but is not alone sufficient (paragraph (d)(4)(iii)(C) of this section). The COBE requirement of paragraph (d)(1) of this section is not satisfied.

Example (10). Continuation of the T historic business in a partnership satisfies continuity of business enterprise. (i) Facts. The facts are the same as Example 8 except that S-3 transfers the historic T business to PRS in exchange for a 33 1/3 percent interest in PRS, and no member of P's qualified group performs active and substantial management functions for the ski boot business operated in PRS.

(ii) Continuity of business enterprise. Under paragraph (d)(4)(iii)(B)(1) of this section, P is treated as conducting T's historic business because S-3 owns an interest in the partnership representing a significant interest in that partnership business. P is treated as holding all the assets and conducting the businesses of all of the members of the qualified group, which includes S-3 (paragraphs (d)(4)(i) and (ii) of this section). The COBE requirement of paragraph (d)(1) of this section is satisfied.

Example (11). Use of T's historic business assets in a partnership business. (i) Facts. T is a fabric distributor. P owns all of the stock of S-1. T merges into P and the T shareholders receive solely P stock. S-1 and X (an unrelated party) own interests in a partnership (PRS). As part of the plan of reorganization, P transfers all of the T assets to S-1, and S-1 transfers all the T assets to PRS, increasing S-1's percentage interest in PRS from 5 to 33 1/3 percent. After the transfer, X owns the remaining 66 2/3 percent interest in PRS. Almost all of the T assets consist of T's large inventory of fabric, which PRS uses to manufacture sportswear. All of the T assets are used in the sportswear business. No member of P's qualified group performs active and substantial management functions for the sportswear business operated in PRS.

(ii) Continuity of business enterprise. Under paragraph (d)(4)(iii)(A) of this section, S-1 is treated as owning 33 1/3 percent of the T assets used in the PRS sportswear manufacturing business. Under paragraph (d)(4)(iii)(B)(1) of this section, P is treated as conducting the sportswear manufacturing business be-

cause S-1 owns an interest in the partnership representing a significant interest in that partnership business. P is treated as holding all the assets and conducting the businesses of all of the members of the qualified group, which includes S-1 (paragraphs (d)(4)(i) and (ii) of this section). The COBE requirement of paragraph (d)(1) of this section is satisfied.

Example (12). Aggregation of partnership interests among members of the qualified group: use of T's historic business assets in a partnership business. (i) Facts. The facts are the same as Example 11, except that S-1 transfers all the T assets to PRS, and P and X each transfer cash to PRS in exchange for partnership interests. After the transfers, P owns 11 percent, S-1 owns 22 1/3 percent, and X owns 66 2/3 percent of PRS.

(ii) Continuity of business enterprise. Under paragraph (d)(4)(iii)(B)(1) of this section, P is treated as conducting the sportswear manufacturing business because members of the qualified group, in the aggregate, own an interest in the partnership representing a significant interest in that business. P is treated as owning 11 percent of the assets directly, and S-1 is treated as owning 22 1/3 percent of the assets, used in the PRS sportswear business (paragraph (d)(4)(iii)(A) of this section). P is treated as holding all the assets of all of the members of the qualified group, which includes S-1, and thus in the aggregate, P is treated as owning 33 1/3 of the T assets (paragraphs (d)(4)(i) and (ii) of this section). The COBE requirement of paragraph (d)(1) of this section is satisfied because P is treated as using a significant portion of T's historic business assets in its sportswear manufacturing business.

Example (13). Tiered partnerships: use of T's historic business assets in a partnership business. (i) Facts. T owns and manages a commercial office building in state Z. Pursuant to a plan of reorganization, T merges into P, solely in exchange for P stock, which is distributed to the T shareholders. P transfers all of the T assets to a partnership, PRS-1, which owns and operates television stations nation-wide. After the transfer, P owns a 50 percent interest in PRS-1. P does not have active and substantial management functions as a partner with respect to the PRS-1 business. X, not a member of P's qualified group, owns the remaining 50 percent interest in PRS-1. PRS-1, in an effort to expand its state Z television operation, enters into a joint venture with U, an unrelated party. As part of the plan of reorganization, PRS-1 transfers all the T assets and its state Z television station to PRS-2, in exchange for a 75 percent partnership interest. U contributes cash to PRS-2 in exchange for a 25 percent partnership interest and oversees the management of the state Z television operation. PRS-1 does not actively and substantially manage PRS-2's business. PRS-2's state Z operations are moved into the acquired T office building. All of the assets that P acquired from T are used in PRS-2's business.

(ii) Continuity of business enterprise. Under paragraph (d)(4)(iii)(A) of this section, PRS-1 is treated as owning 75 percent of the T assets used in PRS-2's business. P, in turn, is treated as owning 50 percent of PRS-1's interest the T assets. Thus, P is treated as owning 37 1/2 percent (50 percent x 75 percent) of the T assets used in the PRS-2 business. Under paragraph (d)(4)(iii)(B)(1) of this section, P is treated as conducting PRS-2's business, the operation of the state Z television station, and under paragraph (d)(4)(iii)(A) of this section, P is treated as using 37 1/2 percent of the historic T business assets in that business. The COBE requirement of paragraph (d)(1) of this section is satisfied because P is treated as using a significant portion of T's historic business assets in its television business.

Example (14). Transfer of acquired stock to a partnership—continuity of business enterprise satisfied. (i) Facts. Pursuant to a plan of reorganization, the T shareholders transfer all of their T stock to a subsidiary of P, S-1, solely in exchange for P stock. In addition, as part of the plan of reorganization, S-1 transfers the

T stock to its subsidiary, S-2, and S-2 transfers the T stock to its subsidiary, S-3. S-2 and S-3 form a new partnership, PRS. Immediately thereafter, S-3 transfers all of the T stock to PRS in exchange for an 80 percent interest in PRS, and S-2 transfers cash to PRS in exchange for a 20 percent interest in PRS.

(ii) Continuity of business enterprise. Members of the qualified group, in the aggregate, own all of the interests in PRS. Because these interests in PRS meet requirements equivalent to section 368(c), under paragraph (d)(4)(iii)(D) of this section, the T stock owned by PRS is treated as owned by members of the qualified group. P is treated as holding all of the businesses and assets of T because T is a member of the qualified group (as defined in paragraph (d)(4)(ii) of this section). The COBE requirement of paragraph (d)(1) of this section is satisfied because P is treated as continuing T's business.

Example (15). Transfer of acquired stock to a partnership—continuity of business enterprise not satisfied. (i) Facts. The facts are the same as in Example 14, except that S-3 and U, an unrelated corporation, form a new partnership, PRS, and, immediately thereafter, S-3 transfers all of the T stock to PRS in exchange for a 50 percent interest in PRS, and U transfers cash to PRS in exchange for a 50 percent interest in PRS.

(ii) Continuity of business enterprise. Members of the qualified group, in the aggregate, own 50 percent of the interests in PRS. Because these interests in PRS do not meet requirements equivalent to section 368(c), the T stock owned by PRS is not treated as owned by members of the qualified group under paragraph (d)(4)(iii)(D) of this section. P is not treated as holding all of the businesses and assets of T because T has ceased to be a member of the qualified group (as defined in paragraph (d)(4)(ii) of this section). The COBE requirement of paragraph (d)(1) of this section is not satisfied because P is not treated as continuing

T's business or using T's historic business assets in a business.

(e) Continuity of interest—(1) General rule. (i) The purpose of the continuity of interest requirement is to prevent transactions that resemble sales from qualifying for nonrecognition of gain or loss available to corporate reorganizations. Continuity of interest requires that in substance a substantial part of the value of the proprietary interests in the target corporation be preserved in the reorganization. A proprietary interest in the target corporation is preserved if, in a potential reorganization, it is exchanged for a proprietary interest in the issuing corporation (as defined in paragraph (b) of this section), it is exchanged by the acquiring corporation for a direct interest in the target corporation enterprise, or it otherwise continues as a proprietary interest in the target corporation. However, a proprietary interest in the target corporation is not preserved if, in connection with the potential reorganization, it is acquired by the issuing corporation for consideration other than stock of the issuing corporation, or stock of the issuing corporation furnished in exchange for a proprietary interest in the target corporation in the potential reorganization is redeemed. All facts and circumstances must be considered in determining whether, in substance, a proprietary interest in the target corporation is preserved. See paragraph (e)(6) of this section for rules related to when a creditor's claim against a target corporation is a proprietary interest in the corporation. For purposes of the continuity of interest requirement, a mere disposition of stock of the target corporation prior to a potential reorganization to persons not related (as defined in paragraph (e)(4) of this section determined without regard to paragraph (e)(4)(i)(A) of this section) to the target corporation or to persons not related (as defined in paragraph (e)(4) of this section) to the issuing corporation is disregarded and a mere disposition of stock of the issuing corporation received in a potential reorganization to persons not related

(as defined in paragraph (e)(4) of this section) to the issuing corporation is disregarded.

(ii) For purposes of paragraph (e)(1)(i) of this section, a proprietary interest in the target corporation (other than one held by the acquiring corporation) is not preserved to the extent that consideration received prior to a potential reorganization, either in a redemption of the target corporation stock or in a distribution with respect to the target corporation stock, is treated as other property or money received in the exchange for purposes of section 356, or would be so treated if the target shareholder also had received stock of the issuing corporation in exchange for stock owned by the shareholder in the target corporation. A proprietary interest in the target corporation is not preserved to the extent that creditors (or former creditors) of the target corporation that own a proprietary interest in the corporation under paragraph (e)(6) of this section (or would be so treated if they had received the consideration in the potential reorganization) receive payment for the claim prior to the potential reorganization and such payment would be treated as other property or money received in the exchange for purposes of section 356 had it been a distribution with respect to stock.

(2) Measuring continuity of interest—(i) In general. In determining whether a proprietary interest in the target corporation is preserved, the consideration to be exchanged for the proprietary interests in the target corporation pursuant to a contract to effect the potential reorganization shall be valued on the last business day before the first date such contract is a binding contract (the pre-signing date), if such contract provides for fixed consideration. If a portion of the consideration provided for in such a contract consists of other property identified by value, then this specified value of such other property is used for purposes of determining the extent to which a proprietary interest in the target corporation is preserved. If the contract does not provide for fixed consideration, this paragraph (e)(2)(i) is not applicable.

(ii) Binding contract—(A) In general. A binding contract is an instrument enforceable under applicable law against the parties to the instrument. The presence of a condition outside the control of the parties (including, for example, regulatory agency approval) shall not prevent an instrument from being a binding contract. Further, the fact that insubstantial terms remain to be negotiated by the parties to the contract, or that customary conditions remain to be satisfied, shall not prevent an instrument from being a binding contract.

(B) Modifications—(1) In general. If a term of a binding contract that relates to the amount or type of the consideration the target shareholders will receive in a potential reorganization is modified before the closing date of the potential reorganization, and the contract as modified is a binding contract, the date of the modification shall be treated as the first date there is a binding contract.

(2) Modification of a transaction that preserves continuity of interest. Notwithstanding paragraph (e)(2)(ii)(B)(1) of this section, a modification of a term that relates to the amount or type of consideration the target shareholders will receive in a transaction that would have resulted in the preservation of a substantial part of the value of the target corporation shareholders' proprietary interests in the target corporation if there had been no modification will not be treated as a modification if—

(i) The modification has the sole effect of providing for the issuance of additional shares of issuing corporation stock to the target corporation shareholders;

(ii) The modification has the sole effect of decreasing the amount of money or other property to be delivered to the target corporation shareholders; or

(iii) The modification has the effect of decreasing the amount of money or other prop-

erty to be delivered to the target corporation shareholders and providing for the issuance of additional shares of issuing corporation stock to the target corporation shareholders.

(3) Modification of a transaction that does not preserve continuity of interest. Notwithstanding paragraph (e)(2)(ii)(B)(1) of this section, a modification of a term that relates to the amount or type of consideration the target shareholders will receive in a transaction that would not have resulted in the preservation of a substantial part of the value of the target corporation shareholders' proprietary interests in the target corporation if there had been no modification will not be treated as a modification if—

(i) The modification has the sole effect of providing for the issuance of fewer shares of issuing corporation stock to the target corporation shareholders;

(ii) The modification has the sole effect of increasing the amount of money or other property to be delivered to the target corporation shareholders; or

(iii) The modification has the effect of increasing the amount of money or other property to be delivered to the target corporation shareholders and providing for the issuance of fewer shares of issuing corporation stock to the target corporation shareholders.

(C) Tender offers. For purposes of this paragraph (e)(2), a tender offer that is subject to section 14(d) of the Securities and Exchange Act of 1934 [15 U.S.C. 78n(d)(1)] and Regulation 14D (17 CFR 240.14d–1 through 240.14d–101) and is not pursuant to a binding contract, is treated as a binding contract made on the date of its announcement, notwithstanding that it may be modified by the offeror or that it is not enforceable against the offerees. If a modification (not pursuant to a binding contract) of such a tender offer is subject to the provisions of Regulation 14d–6(c) (17 CFR 240.14d–6(c)) and relates to the amount or type of the consideration received in the tender offer, then the date of the modification shall be treated as the first date there is a binding contract.

(iii) Fixed consideration—(A) In general. A contract provides for fixed consideration if it provides the number of shares of each class of stock of the issuing corporation, the amount of money, and the other property (identified either by value or by specific description), if any, to be exchanged for all the proprietary interests in the target corporation, or to be exchanged for each proprietary interest in the target corporation. A shareholder's election to receive a number of shares of stock of the issuing corporation, money, or other property (or some combination of stock of the issuing corporation, money, or other property) in exchange for all of the shareholder's proprietary interests in the target corporation, or each of the shareholder's proprietary interests in the target corporation, will not prevent a contract from satisfying the definition of fixed consideration provided for in this paragraph (e)(2)(iii)(A).

(B) Shareholder elections. A contract that provides a target corporation shareholder with an election to receive a number of shares of stock of the issuing corporation, money, or other property (or some combination of stock of the issuing corporation, money, or other property) in exchange for all of the shareholder's proprietary interests in the target corporation, or each of the shareholder's proprietary interests in the target corporation, provides for fixed consideration if the determination of the number of shares of issuing corporation stock to be provided to the target corporation shareholder is determined using the value of the issuing corporation stock on the last business day before the first date there is a binding contract. This is the case even though the shareholder election may preclude a determination, prior to the closing date, of the number of shares of each class of the issuing corporation, the amount of money, and the other property (or the combination of shares, money and oth-

er property) to be exchanged for each proprietary interest in the target corporation.

(C) Contingent adjustments to the consideration—(1) In general. Except as provided in paragraph (e)(2)(iii)(C)(2) of this section, a contract that provides for contingent adjustments to the consideration will be treated as providing for fixed consideration if it would satisfy the requirements of paragraph (e)(2)(iii)(A) of this section without the contingent adjustment provision.

(2) Exceptions. A contract will not be treated as providing for fixed consideration if the contract provides for contingent adjustments to the consideration that prevent (to any extent) the target corporation shareholders from being subject to the economic benefits and burdens of ownership of the issuing corporation stock after the last business day before the first date the contract is a binding contract. For example, a contract will not be treated as providing for fixed consideration if the contract provides for contingent adjustments to the consideration in the event that the value of the stock of the issuing corporation, the value of the assets of the issuing corporation, or the value of any surrogate for either the value of the stock of the issuing corporation or the assets of the issuing corporation increases or decreases after the last business day before the first date there is a binding contract. Similarly, a contract will not be treated as providing for fixed consideration if the contract provides for contingent adjustments to the number of shares of the issuing corporation stock to be provided to the target corporation shareholders computed using any value of the issuing corporation shares after the last business day before the first date there is a binding contract.

(D) Escrows. Placing part of the consideration to be exchanged for proprietary interests in the target corporation in escrow to secure target's performance of customary pre-closing covenants or customary target representations and warranties will not prevent a contract from being treated as providing for fixed consideration.

(E) Anti-dilution clauses. The presence of a customary anti-dilution clause will not prevent a contract from being treated as providing for fixed consideration. However, the absence of such a clause will prevent a contract from being treated as providing for fixed consideration if the issuing corporation alters its capital structure between the first date there is an otherwise binding contract to effect the transaction and the effective date of the transaction in a manner that materially alters the economic arrangement of the parties to the binding contract. If the number of shares of the issuing corporation to be issued to the target corporation shareholders is altered pursuant to a customary anti-dilution clause, the value of the shares determined under paragraph (e)(2)(i) of this section must be adjusted accordingly.

(F) Dissenters' rights. The possibility that some shareholders may exercise dissenters' rights and receive consideration other than that provided for in the binding contract will not prevent the contract from being treated as providing for fixed consideration.

(G) Fractional shares. The fact that money may be paid in lieu of issuing fractional shares will not prevent a contract from being treated as providing for fixed consideration.

(iv) New issuances. For purposes of applying paragraph (e)(2)(i) of this section, any class of stock, securities, or indebtedness that the issuing corporation issues to the target corporation shareholders pursuant to the potential reorganization and that does not exist before the first date there is a binding contract to effect the potential reorganization is deemed to have been issued on the last business day before the first date there is a binding contract to effect the potential reorganization.

(v) Examples. For purposes of the examples in this paragraph (e)(2)(v), P is the issuing corporation, T is the target corporation, S is a wholly owned subsidiary of P, all corporations have only one class of stock outstanding, A is an individual, no transactions other than those described occur, and the transactions are not otherwise subject to recharacterization. The following examples illustrate the application of this paragraph (e)(2):

Example (1). Application of signing date rule. On January 3 of year 1, P and T sign a binding contract pursuant to which T will be merged with and into P on June 1 of year 1. Pursuant to the contract, the T shareholders will receive 40 P shares and $60 of cash in exchange for all of the outstanding stock of T. Twenty of the P shares, however, will be placed in escrow to secure customary target representations and warranties. The P stock is listed on an established market. On January 2 of year 1, the value of the P stock is $1 per share. On June 1 of year 1, T merges with and into P pursuant to the terms of the contract. On that date, the value of the P stock is $.25 per share. None of the stock placed in escrow is returned to P. Because the contract provides for the number of shares of P and the amount of money to be exchanged for all of the proprietary interests in T, under this paragraph (e)(2), there is a binding contract providing for fixed consideration as of January 3 of year 1. Therefore, whether the transaction satisfies the continuity of interest requirement is determined by reference to the value of the P stock on the pre-signing date. Because, for continuity of interest purposes, the T stock is exchanged for $40 of P stock and $60 of cash, the transaction preserves a substantial part of the value of the proprietary interest in T. Therefore, the transaction satisfies the continuity of interest requirement.

Example (2). Treatment of forfeited escrowed stock. (i) Escrowed stock. The facts are the same as in Example 1 except that T's breach of a representation results in the escrowed consideration being returned to P. Because the contract provides for the number of shares of P and the amount of money to be exchanged for all of the proprietary interests in T, under this paragraph (e)(2), there is a binding contract providing for fixed consideration as of January 3 of year 1. Therefore, whether the transaction satisfies the continuity of interest requirement is determined by reference to the value of the P stock on the pre-signing date. Pursuant to paragraph (e)(1)(i) of this section, for continuity of interest purposes, the T stock is exchanged for $20 of P stock and $60 of cash, and the transaction does not preserve a substantial part of the value of the proprietary interest in T. Therefore, the transaction does not satisfy the continuity of interest requirement.

(ii) Escrowed stock and cash. The facts are the same as in paragraph (i) of this Example 2 except that the consideration placed in escrow consists solely of eight of the P shares and $12 of the cash. Because the contract provides for the number of shares of P and the amount of money to be exchanged for all of the proprietary interests in T, under this paragraph (e) (2), there is a binding contract providing for fixed consideration as of January 3 of year 1. Therefore, whether the transaction satisfies the continuity of interest requirement is determined by reference to the value of the P stock on the pre-signing date. Pursuant to paragraph (e)(1)(i) of this section, for continuity of interest purposes, the T stock is exchanged for $32 of P stock and $48 of cash, and the transaction preserves a substantial part of the value of the proprietary interest in T. Therefore, the transaction satisfies the continuity of interest requirement.

Example (3). Redemption of stock received pursuant to binding contract. The facts are the same as in Example 1 except that A owns 50 percent of the outstanding stock of T immediately prior to the merger and receives 10 P shares and $30 in the merger and an additional 10 P shares upon the release of the stock placed in escrow. In connection with the merger, A and S agree that, immediately after the merger, S will purchase any P shares that A acquires in the merger for $1 per share. Shortly after the merger, S purchases A's P shares for $20. Because the contract provides for the number of shares of P and the amount of money to be exchanged for all of the proprietary interests in T, under this paragraph (e)(2), there is a binding contract providing for fixed consideration as of January 3 of year 1. Therefore, whether the transaction satisfies the continuity of interest requirement is determined by reference to the value of the P stock on the pre-signing date. In addition, S is a person related to P under paragraph (e)(4)(i)(A) of this section. Accordingly, A is treated as exchanging his T shares for $50 of cash. Because, for continuity of interest purposes, the T stock is exchanged for $20 of P stock and $80 of cash, the transaction does not preserve a substantial part of the value of the proprietary interest in T. Therefore, the transaction does not satisfy the continuity of interest requirement.

Example (4). Modification of binding contract—continuity not preserved. The facts are the same as in Example 1 except that on April 1 of year 1, the parties modify their contract. Pursuant to the modified contract, which is a binding contract, the T shareholders will receive 50 P shares (an additional 10 shares) and $75 of cash (an additional $15 of cash) in exchange for all of the outstanding T stock. On March 31 of year 1, the value of the P stock is $.50 per share. Under this paragraph (e)(2), although there was a binding contract providing for fixed consideration as of January 3 of year 1, terms of that contract relating to the consideration to be provided to the target shareholders were modified on April 1 of year 1. The execution of the transaction without modification would have resulted in the preservation of a substantial part of the value of the target corporation shareholders' proprietary interests in the target corporation if there had been no modification. However, because the modified contract provides for additional P stock and cash to be exchanged for all the proprietary interests in T, the exception in paragraph (e) (2)(ii)(B)(2) of this section does not apply to preserve the original signing date. Therefore, whether the transaction satisfies the continuity of interest requirement is determined by reference to the value of the P stock on March 31 of year 1. Because, for continuity of interest purposes, the T stock is exchanged for $25 of P stock and $75 of cash, the transaction does not preserve a substantial part of the value of the proprietary interest in T. Therefore, the transaction does not satisfy the continuity of interest requirement.

Example (5). Modification of binding contract disregarded—continuity preserved. The facts are the same as in Example 4 except that, pursuant to the modified contract, which is a binding contract, the T shareholders will receive 60 P shares (an additional 20 shares as compared to the original contract) and $60 of cash in exchange for all of the outstanding T stock. In addition, on March 31 of year 1, the value of the P stock is $.40 per share. Under this paragraph (e)(2), although there was a binding contract providing for fixed consideration as of January 3 of year 1, terms of that contract relating to the consideration to be provided to the target shareholders were modified on April 1 of year 1. Nonetheless, the modification has the sole effect of providing for the issuance of additional P shares to the T shareholders. In addition, the execution of the terms of the contract without regard to the modification would have resulted in the preservation of a substantial part of the value of the T shareholders' proprietary interest in T because, for continuity of interest purposes, the T stock would have been exchanged for $40 of P stock and $60 of cash. Pursuant to paragraph (e)(2)(ii)(B)(2) of this section, the modification is not treated as a modification for purposes of paragraph (e)(2)(ii)(B)(1) of this section. Accordingly, whether the transaction satisfies the continuity of interest requirement is determined by reference to the value of the P stock on the pre-signing date. Because, for continuity of interest purposes, the T stock is exchanged for $60 of P stock and $60 of cash, the transaction preserves a substantial part of the value of the proprietary

interest in T. Therefore the transaction satisfies the continuity of interest requirement.

Example (6). New issuance. The facts are the same as in Example 1, except that, instead of cash, the T shareholders will receive a new class of P securities that will be publicly traded. In the aggregate, the securities will have a stated principal amount of $60 and bear interest at the average LIBOR (London Interbank Offered Rates) during the 10 days prior to the potential reorganization. If the T shareholders had been issued the P securities on January 2 of year 1, the P securities would have had a value of $60 (determined by reference to the value of comparable publicly traded securities). Whether the transaction satisfies the continuity of interest requirement is determined by reference to the value of the P stock and the P securities to be issued to the T shareholders on January 2 of year 1. Under paragraph (e)(2)(iv) of this section, for purposes of valuing the new P securities, they will be treated as having been issued on the pre-signing date. Because, for continuity of interest purposes, the T stock is exchanged for $40 of P stock and $60 of other property, the transaction preserves a substantial part of the value of the proprietary interest in T. Therefore, the transaction satisfies the continuity of interest requirement.

Example (7). Fixed consideration—continuity not preserved. On January 3 of year 1, P and T sign a binding contract pursuant to which T will be merged with and into P on June 1 of year 1. Pursuant to the contract, 60 shares of the T stock will be exchanged for $80 of cash and 40 shares of the T stock will be exchanged for 20 shares of P stock. On January 2 of year 1, the value of the P stock is $1 per share. On June 1 of year 1, T merges with and into P pursuant to the terms of the contract. This contract provides for fixed consideration and therefore whether the transaction satisfies the continuity of interest requirement is determined by reference to the value of the P stock on the pre-signing date. However, applying the signing date rule, the P stock represents only

20 percent of the value of the total consideration to be received by the T shareholders. Accordingly, based on the economic realities of the exchange, the transaction does not preserve a substantial part of the value of the proprietary interest in T. Therefore, the transaction does not satisfy the continuity of interest requirement.

Example (8). Anti-dilution clause. (i) Absence of anti-dilution clause. On January 3 of year 1, P and T sign a binding contract pursuant to which T will be merged with and into P on June 1 of year 1. Pursuant to the contract, the T shareholders will receive 40 P shares and $60 of cash in exchange for all of the outstanding stock of T. The contract does not contain a customary anti-dilution provision. The P stock is listed on an established market. On January 2 of year 1, the value of the P stock is $1 per share. On April 10 of year 1, P issues its stock to effect a stock split; each shareholder of P receives an additional share of P for each P share that it holds. On April 11 of year 1, the value of the P stock is $.50 per share. Because P altered its capital structure between January 3 and June 1 of year 1 in a manner that materially alters the economic arrangement of the parties, under paragraph (e)(2)(iii)(E) of this section, the contract is not treated as a binding contract that provides for fixed consideration. Accordingly, whether the transaction satisfies the continuity of interest requirement cannot be determined by reference to the value of the P stock on January 2 of year 1.

(ii) Adjustment for anti-dilution clause. The facts are the same as in paragraph (i) of this Example 8 except that the contract contains a customary anti-dilution provision, and the T shareholders receive 80 P shares and $60 of cash in exchange for all of the outstanding stock of T. Under paragraph (e)(2)(iii)(E) of this section, the contract is treated as a binding contract that provides for fixed consideration as of January 3 of year 1. Therefore, whether the transaction satisfies the continuity of interest requirement is generally determined by reference to the value of the P stock on January 2 of year 1. However, under paragraph (e)(2)(iii)(E) of this section, the value of the P stock on the pre-signing date must be adjusted to take the stock split into account. For continuity of interest purposes, the T stock is exchanged for $40 of P stock (($1/2) x 80) and $60 of cash. Therefore, the transaction satisfies the continuity of interest requirement.

Example (9). Shareholder election. On January 3 of year 1, P and T sign a binding contract pursuant to which T will be merged with and into P on June 1 of year 1. On January 2 of year 1, the value of the P stock and the T stock is $1 per share. Pursuant to the contract, at the shareholders' election, each share of T's 100 shares will be exchanged for cash of $1, or alternatively, P stock. The contract provides that the determination of the number of shares of P stock to be exchanged for a share of T stock is made using the value of the P stock on the last business day before the first date there is a binding contract (that is, $1 per share). The contract further provides that, in the aggregate, 40 shares of P stock and $60 will be delivered, and contains a proration mechanism in the event that either item of consideration is oversubscribed. On the closing date, the value of the P stock is $.20 per share, and all target shareholders elect to receive cash. Pursuant to the proration provision, each target share is exchanged for $.60 of cash and $.08 of P stock. Pursuant to paragraph (e)(2)(iii)(A) of this section, the contract provides for fixed consideration because it provides for the number of shares of P stock and the amount of money to be exchanged for all the proprietary interests in the target corporation. Furthermore, pursuant to paragraph (e)(2)(iii)(B) of this section, the contract provides for fixed consideration because the number of shares of issuing corporation stock to be provided to the target corporation shareholders is determined using the pre-signing date value of P stock. Accordingly, whether the transaction satisfies the continuity of interest requirement is determined by reference to the value of the P stock on January 2 of year 1. Because, for continuity purposes, the T stock is exchanged for $40 of P stock and $60 of cash, the transaction preserves a substantial part of the value of the proprietary interest in T. Therefore, the transaction satisfies the continuity of interest requirement.

Example (10). Contingent adjustment based on the value of the issuing corporation stock—continuity not preserved. On January 3 of year 1, P and T sign a binding contract pursuant to which T will be merged with and into P on June 1 of year 1. On January 2 of year 1, the value of the P stock is $1 per share. Pursuant to the contract, if the value of the P stock does not decrease after January 2 of year 1, the T shareholders will receive 40 P shares and $60 of cash in exchange for all of the outstanding stock of T. Furthermore, the contract provides that the T shareholders will receive $.16 of additional P shares and $.24 for every $.01 decrease in the value of one share of P stock after January 2 of year 1. On June 1 of year 1, T merges with and into P pursuant to the terms of the contract. On that date, the value of the P stock is $.40 per share. Pursuant to the terms of the contract, the consideration is adjusted so that the T shareholders receive 24 more P shares ((60 × $.16)/$.40) and $14.40 more cash (60 × $.24) than they would absent an adjustment. Accordingly, at closing the T shareholders receive 64 P shares and $74.40 of cash. Because the contract provides that additional P shares and cash will be delivered to the T shareholders if the value of the stock of P decreases after January 2 of year 1, under paragraph (e)(2)(iii)(C)(2) of this section, the contract is not treated as providing for fixed consideration, and therefore whether the transaction satisfies the continuity of interest requirement cannot be determined by reference to the value of the P stock on January 2 of year 1. For continuity of interest purposes, the T stock is exchanged for $25.60 of P stock (64 × $.40) and $74.40 of cash and the transaction does not preserve a substantial part of the value of the proprietary interest in T. Therefore, the transaction does not satisfy the continuity of interest requirement.

Example (11). Contingent adjustment to boot based on the value of the target corporation stock—continuity not preserved. On January 3 of year 1, P and T sign a binding contract pursuant to which T will be merged with and into P on June 1 of year 1. On January 2 of year 1, T has 100 shares outstanding, and each T share is worth $1. On January 2 of year 1, each P share is worth $1. Pursuant to the contract, if the value of the T stock does not increase after January 3 of year 1, the T shareholders will receive 40 P shares and $60 of cash in exchange for all of the outstanding stock of T. Furthermore, the contract provides that the T shareholders will receive $1 of additional cash for every $.01 increase in the value of one share of T stock after January 3 of year 1. On June 1 of year 1, the value of the T stock is $1.40 per share and the value of the P stock is $.75 per share. Pursuant to the terms of the contract, the consideration is adjusted so that the T shareholders receive $40 more cash (40 × $1) than they would absent an adjustment. Accordingly, at closing the T shareholders receive 40 P shares and $100 of cash. Because the contract provides the number of shares of P stock and the amount of money to be exchanged for all the proprietary interests in T, and the contingent adjustment to the cash consideration is not based on changes in the value of the P stock, P assets, or any surrogate thereof, after January 2 of year 1, there is a binding contract providing for fixed consideration as of January 3 of year 1. Therefore, whether the transaction satisfies the continuity of interest requirement is determined by reference to the value of the P stock on January 2 of year 1. For continuity of interest purposes, the T stock is exchanged for $40 of P stock (40 × $1) and $100 of cash. Therefore, the transaction does not satisfy the continuity of interest requirement.

Example (12). Contingent adjustment to stock based on the value of the target corporation stock—continuity preserved. On January 3 of year 1, P and T sign a binding contract pursuant to which T will be merged with and into P on June 1 of year 1. On that date T has 100 shares outstanding, and each T share is worth $1. On January 2 of year 1, each P share is worth $1. Pursuant to the contract, if the value of the T stock does not decrease after January 3 of year 1, the T shareholders will receive 40 P shares and $60 of cash in exchange for all of the outstanding stock of T. Furthermore, the contract provides that the T shareholders will receive $.40 less P stock and $.60 less cash for every $.01 decrease in the value of one share of T stock after January 3 of year 1. The contract also provides that the number of P shares by which the consideration will be reduced as a result of this adjustment will be determined based on the value of the P stock on January 2 of year 1. On June 1 of year 1, T merges with and into P pursuant to the terms of the contract. On that date, the value of the T stock is $.70 per share and the value of the P stock is $.75 per share. Pursuant to the terms of the contract, the consideration is adjusted so that the T shareholders receive 12 fewer P shares ((30 × $.40)/$1) and $18 less cash (30 × $.60) than they would absent an adjustment. Accordingly, at closing the T shareholders receive 28 P shares and $42 of cash. Because the contract provides for the number of shares of P stock and the amount of money to be exchanged for all of the proprietary interests in T, the contract does not provide for contingent adjustments to the consideration based on a change in value of the P stock, P assets, or any surrogate thereof, after January 2 of year 1, and the adjustment to the number of P shares the T shareholders receive is determined based on the value of the P shares on January 2 of year 1, there is a binding contract providing for fixed consideration as of January 3 of year 1. Therefore, whether the transaction satisfies the continuity of interest requirement is determined by reference to the value of the P stock on January 2 of year 1. For continuity of interest purposes, the T stock is exchanged for $28 of P stock (28 × $1) and $42 of cash. Accordingly, the transaction satisfies the continuity of interest requirement.

(3) **Related persons acquisitions.** A proprietary interest in the target corporation is not preserved if, in connection with a potential reorganization, a person related (as defined in paragraph (e)(4) of this section) to the issuing corporation acquires, for consideration other than stock of the issuing corporation, either a proprietary interest in the target corporation or stock of the issuing corporation that was furnished in exchange for a proprietary interest in the target corporation. The preceding sentence does not apply to the extent those persons who were the direct or indirect owners of the target corporation prior to the potential reorganization maintain a direct or indirect proprietary interest in the issuing corporation.

(4) **Definition of related person—(i) In general.** For purposes of this paragraph (e), two corporations are related persons if either—

(A) The corporations are members of the same affiliated group as defined in section 1504 (determined without regard to section 1504(b)); or

(B) A purchase of the stock of one corporation by another corporation would be treated as a distribution in redemption of the stock of the first corporation under section 304(a)(2) (determined without regard to § 1.1502–80(b)).

(ii) **Special rules.** The following rules apply solely for purposes of this paragraph (e) (4):

(A) A corporation will be treated as related to another corporation if such relationship exists immediately before or immediately after the acquisition of the stock involved.

(B) A corporation, other than the target corporation or a person related (as defined in paragraph (e)(4) of this section determined without regard to paragraph (e)(4)(i)(A) of this section) to the target corporation, will be treated as related to the issuing corporation if the relationship is created in connection with the potential reorganization.

(5) **Acquisitions by partnerships.** For purposes of this paragraph (e), each partner

of a partnership will be treated as owning or acquiring any stock owned or acquired, as the case may be, by the partnership in accordance with that partner's interest in the partnership. If a partner is treated as acquiring any stock by reason of the application of this paragraph (e)(5), the partner is also treated as having furnished its share of any consideration furnished by the partnership to acquire the stock in accordance with that partner's interest in the partnership.

(6) Creditors' claims as proprietary interests—(i) In general. A creditor's claim against a target corporation may be a proprietary interest in the target corporation if the target corporation is in a title 11 or similar case (as defined in section 368(a)(3)) or the amount of the target corporation's liabilities exceeds the fair market value of its assets immediately prior to the potential reorganization. In such cases, if any creditor receives a proprietary interest in the issuing corporation in exchange for its claim, every claim of that class of creditors and every claim of all equal and junior classes of creditors (in addition to the claims of shareholders) is a proprietary interest in the target corporation immediately prior to the potential reorganization to the extent provided in paragraph (e)(6)(ii) of this section.

(ii) Value of proprietary interest—(A) Claims of most senior class of creditors receiving stock. A claim of the most senior class of creditors receiving a proprietary interest in the issuing corporation and a claim of any equal class of creditors will be treated as a proprietary interest in accordance with the rules of this paragraph (e)(6)(ii). For a claim of the most senior class of creditors receiving a proprietary interest in the issuing corporation, and a claim of any equal class of creditors, the value of the proprietary interest in the target corporation represented by the claim is determined by multiplying the fair market value of the claim by a fraction, the numerator of which is the fair market value of the proprietary interests in the issuing corporation that are received

in the aggregate in exchange for the claims of those classes of creditors, and the denominator of which is the sum of the amount of money and the fair market value of all other consideration (including the proprietary interests in the issuing corporation) received in the aggregate in exchange for such claims. If only one class (or one set of equal classes) of creditors receives stock, such class (or set of equal classes) is treated as the most senior class of creditors receiving stock. When only one class (or one set of equal classes) of creditors receives issuing corporation stock in exchange for a creditor's proprietary interest in the target corporation, such stock will be counted for measuring continuity of interest provided that the stock issued by the acquiring corporation is not de minimis in relation to the total consideration received by the insolvent target corporation, its shareholders, and its creditors.

(B) Claims of junior classes of creditor receiving stock. The value of a proprietary interest in the target corporation held by a creditor whose claim is junior to the claims of other classes of target claims which are receiving proprietary interests in the issuing corporation is the fair market value of the junior creditor's claim.

(iii) Bifurcated claims. If a creditor's claim is bifurcated into a secured claim and an unsecured claim pursuant to an order in a title 11 or similar case (as defined in section 368(a)(3)) or pursuant to an agreement between the creditor and the debtor, the bifurcation of the claim and the allocation of consideration to each of the resulting claims will be respected in applying the rules of this paragraph (e)(6).

(iv) Effect of treating creditors as proprietors. The treatment of a creditor's claim as a proprietary interest in the target corporation shall not preclude treating shares of the target corporation as proprietary interests in the target corporation.

(7) Successors and predecessors. For purposes of this paragraph (e), any reference to the issuing corporation or the target corporation includes a reference to any successor or predecessor of such corporation, except that the target corporation is not treated as a predecessor of the issuing corporation and the issuing corporation is not treated as a successor of the target corporation.

(8) **Examples.** For purposes of the examples in this paragraph (e)(7), P is the issuing corporation, T is the target corporation, S is a wholly owned subsidiary of P, all corporations have only one class of stock outstanding, A and B are individuals, PRS is a partnership, all reorganization requirements other than the continuity of interest requirement are satisfied, and the transaction is not otherwise subject to recharacterization. The following examples illustrate the application of this paragraph (e):

Example (1). Sale of stock to third party. (i) Sale of issuing corporation stock after merger. A owns all of the stock of T. T merges into P. In the merger, A receives P stock having a fair market value of $50x and cash of $50x. Immediately after the merger, and pursuant to a preexisting binding contract, A sells all of the P stock received by A in the merger to B. Assume that there are no facts and circumstances indicating that the cash used by B to purchase A's P stock was in substance exchanged by P for T stock. Under paragraphs (e)(1) and (3) of this section, the sale to B is disregarded because B is not a person related to P within the meaning of paragraph (e)(4) of this section. Thus, the transaction satisfies the continuity of interest requirement because 50 percent of A's T stock was exchanged for P stock, preserving a substantial part of the value of the proprietary interest in T.

(ii) Sale of target corporation stock before merger. The facts are the same as paragraph (i) of this Example 1, except that B buys A's T stock prior to the merger of T into P and then exchanges the T stock for P stock having a fair market value of $50x and cash of $50x. The sale by A is disregarded. The continuity of interest requirement is satisfied because B's T stock was exchanged for P stock, preserving a substantial part of the value of the proprietary interest in T.

Example (2). Relationship created in connection with potential reorganization. Corporation X owns 60 percent of the stock of P and 30 percent of the stock of T. A owns the remaining 70 percent of the stock of T. X buys A's T stock for cash in a transaction which is not a qualified stock purchase within the meaning of section 338. T then merges into P. In the merger, X exchanges all of its T stock for additional stock of P. As a result of the issuance of the additional stock to X in the merger, X s ownership interest in P increases from 60 to 80 percent of the stock of P. X is not a person related to P under paragraph (e)(4)(i)(B) of this section, because a purchase of stock of P by X would not be treated as a distribution in redemption of the stock of P under section 304(a)(2). However, X is a person related to P under paragraphs (e)(4)(i)(A) and (ii)(B) of this section, because X becomes affiliated with P in the merger. The continuity of interest requirement is not satisfied, because X acquired a proprietary interest in T for consideration other than P stock, and a substantial part of the value of the proprietary interest in T is not preserved. See paragraph (e)(3) of this section.

Example (3). Participation by issuing corporation in post-merger sale. A owns 80 percent of the T stock and none of the P stock, which is widely held. T merges into P. In the merger, A receives P stock. In addition, A obtains rights pursuant to an arrangement with P to have P register the P stock under the Securities Act of 1933, as amended. P registers A's stock, and A sells the stock shortly after the merger. No person who purchased the P stock from A is a person related to P within the meaning of paragraph (e)(4) of this section. Under paragraphs (e)(1) and (3) of this section, the sale of the P stock by A is disregarded because no person who purchased the P stock from A is a person related to P within the meaning of paragraph (e)(4) of this section. The transaction satisfies the continuity of interest requirement because A's T stock was exchanged for P stock, preserving a substantial part of the value of the proprietary interest in T.

Example (4). Redemptions and purchases by issuing corporation or related persons. (i) Redemption by issuing corporation. A owns 100 percent of the stock of T and none of the stock of P. T merges into S. In the merger, A receives P stock. In connection with the merger, P redeems all of the P stock received by A in the merger for cash. The continuity of interest requirement is not satisfied, because, in connection with the merger, P redeemed the stock exchanged for a proprietary interest in T, and a substantial part of the value of the proprietary interest in T is not preserved. See paragraph (e)(1) of this section.

(ii) Purchase of target corporation stock by issuing corporation. The facts are the same as paragraph (i) of this Example 4, except that, instead of P redeeming its stock, prior to and in connection with the merger of T into S, P purchases 90 percent of the T stock from A for cash. The continuity of interest requirement is not satisfied, because in connection with the merger, P acquired a proprietary interest in T for consideration other than P stock, and a substantial part of the value of the proprietary interest in T is not preserved. See paragraph (e)(1) of this section.

(iii) Purchase of issuing corporation stock by person related to issuing corporation. The facts are the same as paragraph (i) of this Example 4, except that, instead of P redeeming its stock, S buys all of the P stock received by A in the merger for cash. S is a person related to P under paragraphs (e)(4)(i)(A) and (B) of this section. The continuity of interest requirement is not satisfied, because S acquired P stock issued in the merger, and a substantial part of the value of the proprietary interest in T is not preserved. See paragraph (e)(3) of this section.

Example (5). Redemption in substance by issuing corporation. A owns 100 percent of the stock of T and none of the stock of P. T merges into P. In the merger, A receives P

stock. In connection with the merger, B buys all of the P stock received by A in the merger for cash. Shortly thereafter, in connection with the merger, P redeems the stock held by B for cash. Based on all the facts and circumstances, P in substance has exchanged solely cash for T stock in the merger. The continuity of interest requirement is not satisfied, because in substance P redeemed the stock exchanged for a proprietary interest in T, and a substantial part of the value of the proprietary interest in T is not preserved. See paragraph (e)(1) of this section.

Example (6). Purchase of issuing corporation stock through partnership. A owns 100 percent of the stock of T and none of the stock of P. S is an 85 percent partner in PRS. The other 15 percent of PRS is owned by unrelated persons. T merges into P. In the merger, A receives P stock. In connection with the merger, PRS purchases all of the P stock received by A in the merger for cash. Under paragraph (e)(5) of this section, S, as an 85 percent partner of PRS, is treated as having acquired 85 percent of the P stock exchanged for A's T stock in the merger, and as having furnished 85 percent of the cash paid by PRS to acquire the P stock. S is a person related to P under paragraphs (e)(4)(i)(A) and (B) of this section. The continuity of interest requirement is not satisfied, because S is treated as acquiring 85 percent of the P stock issued in the merger, and a substantial part of the value of the proprietary interest in T is not preserved. See paragraph (e)(3) of this section.

Example (7). Exchange by acquiring corporation for direct interest. A owns 30 percent of the stock of T. P owns 70 percent of the stock of T, which was not acquired by P in connection with the acquisition of T's assets. T merges into P. A receives cash in the merger. The continuity of interest requirement is satisfied, because P's 70 percent proprietary interest in T is exchanged by P for a direct interest in the assets of the target corporation enterprise.

Example (8). Maintenance of direct or indirect interest in issuing corporation. X, a corporation, owns all of the stock of each of corporations P and Z. Z owns all of the stock of T. T merges into P. Z receives P stock in the merger. Immediately thereafter and in connection with the merger, Z distributes the P stock received in the merger to X. X is a person related to P under paragraph (e)(4)(i)(A) of this section. The continuity of interest requirement is satisfied, because X was an indirect owner of T prior to the merger who maintains a direct or indirect proprietary interest in P, preserving a substantial part of the value of the proprietary interest in T. See paragraph (e)(3) of this section.

Example (9). Preacquisition redemption by target corporation. T has two shareholders, A and B. P expresses an interest in acquiring the stock of T. A does not wish to own P stock. T redeems A's shares in T in exchange for cash. No funds have been or will be provided by P for this purpose. P subsequently acquires all the outstanding stock of T from B solely in exchange for voting stock of P. The cash received by A in the prereorganization redemption is not treated as other property or money under section 356, and would not be so treated even if A had received some stock of P in exchange for his T stock. The prereorganization redemption by T does not affect continuity of interest, because B's proprietary interest in T is unaffected, and the value of the proprietary interest in T is preserved.

* * *

Example (10). Creditors treated as owning a proprietary interest. (i) More than one class of creditor receives issuing corporation stock. T has assets with a fair market value of $150x and liabilities of $200x. T has two classes of creditors: two senior creditors with claims of $25x each; and one junior creditor with a claim of $150x. T transfers all of its assets to P in exchange for $95x in cash and shares of P stock with a fair market value of $55x. Each T senior creditor receives $20x in cash and P stock with a fair market value of $5x in exchange for his claim. The T junior creditor receives $55x in

cash and P stock with a fair market value of $45x in exchange for his claim. The T shareholders receive no consideration in exchange for their T stock. Under paragraph (e)(6) of this section, because the amount of T's liabilities exceeds the fair market value of its assets immediately prior to the potential reorganization, the claims of the creditors of T may be proprietary interests in T. Because the senior creditors receive proprietary interests in P in the transaction in exchange for their claims, their claims and the claim of the junior creditor and the T stock are treated as proprietary interests in T immediately prior to the transaction. Under paragraph (e)(6)(ii)(A) of this section, the value of the proprietary interest of each of the senior creditors' claims is $5x (the fair market value of the senior creditor's claim, $25x, multiplied by a fraction, the numerator of which is $10x, the fair market value of the proprietary interests in the issuing corporation, P, received in the aggregate in exchange for the claims of all the creditors in the senior class, and the denominator of which is $50x, the sum of the amount of money and the fair market value of all other consideration (including the proprietary interests in P) received in the aggregate in exchange for such claims). Accordingly, $5x of the stock that each of the senior creditors receives is counted in measuring continuity of interest. Under paragraph (e)(6)(ii)(B) of this section, the value of the junior creditor's proprietary interest in T immediately prior to the transaction is $100x, the value of his claim. Thus, the value of the creditors' proprietary interests in total is $110x and the creditors received $55x worth of P stock in total in exchange for their proprietary interests. Therefore, P acquired 50 percent of the value of the proprietary interests in T in exchange for P stock. Because a substantial part of the value of the proprietary interests in T is preserved, the continuity of interest requirement is satisfied.

(ii) One class of creditor receives issuing corporation stock and cash in disproportionate amounts. T has assets with a fair market val-

ue of $80x and liabilities of $200x. T has one class of creditor with two creditors, A and B, each having a claim of $100x. T transfers all of its assets to P for $60x in cash and shares of P stock with a fair market value of $20x. A receives $40x in cash in exchange for its claim. B receives $20x in cash and P stock with a fair market value of $20x in exchange for its claim. The T shareholders receive no consideration in exchange for their T stock. The P stock is not de minimis in relation to the total consideration received. Under paragraph (e)(6) of this section, because the amount of T's liabilities exceeds the fair market value of its assets immediately prior to the potential reorganization, the claims of the creditors of T may be proprietary interests in T. Because the creditors of T received proprietary interests in P in the transaction in exchange for their claims, their claims and the T stock are treated as proprietary interests in T immediately prior to the transaction. Under paragraph (e)(6)(ii)(A) of this section, the value of the proprietary interest of each of the senior creditors is $10x (the fair market value of a senior creditor's claim, $40x, multiplied by a fraction, the numerator of which is $20x, the fair market value of the proprietary interests in the issuing corporation, P, received in the aggregate in exchange for the claims of all the creditors in the class, and the denominator of which is $80x, the sum of the amount of money and the fair market value of all other consideration (including the proprietary interests in P) received in the aggregate in exchange for such claims). Accordingly, $10x of the cash that was received by A and $10x of the P stock that was received by B are counted in measuring continuity of interest. Thus, the value of the creditors' proprietary interests in total is $20x and the creditors received $10x worth of P stock in total in exchange for their proprietary interests. Therefore, P acquired 50 percent of the value of the proprietary interests in T in exchange for P stock. Because a substantial part of the value of the proprietary interests in T is preserved, the continuity of interest requirement is satisfied.

* * *

§ 1.368–2 Definition of terms.

(a) The application of the term "reorganization" is to be strictly limited to the specific transactions set forth in section 368(a). The term does not embrace the mere purchase by one corporation of the properties of another corporation. If the properties are transferred for cash and deferred payment obligations of the transferee evidenced by short-term notes, the transaction is a sale and not an exchange in which gain or loss is not recognized.

(b)(1)(i) **Definitions.** For purposes of this paragraph (b)(1), the following terms shall have the following meanings:

(A) **Disregarded entity.** A disregarded entity is a business entity (as defined in § 301.7701–2(a) of this chapter) that is disregarded as an entity separate from its owner for Federal income tax purposes. Examples of disregarded entities include a domestic single member limited liability company that does not elect to be classified as a corporation for Federal income tax purposes, a corporation (as defined in § 301.7701–2(b) of this chapter) that is a qualified REIT subsidiary (within the meaning of section 856(i)(2)), and a corporation that is a qualified subchapter S subsidiary (within the meaning of section 1361(b)(3)(B)).

(B) **Combining entity.** A combining entity is a business entity that is a corporation (as defined in § 301.7701–2(b) of this chapter) that is not a disregarded entity.

(C) **Combining unit.** A combining unit is composed solely of a combining entity and all disregarded entities, if any, the assets of which are treated as owned by such combining entity for Federal income tax purposes.

(ii) Statutory merger or consolidation generally. For purposes of section 368(a)(1)(A), a statutory merger or consolidation is a transaction effected pursuant to the statute or statutes necessary to effect the merger or consolidation, in which transaction, as a result of the operation of such statute or statutes, the following events occur simultaneously at the effective time of the transaction—

(A) All of the assets (other than those distributed in the transaction) and liabilities (except to the extent such liabilities are satisfied or discharged in the transaction or are nonrecourse liabilities to which assets distributed in the transaction are subject) of each member of one or more combining units (each a transferor unit) become the assets and liabilities of one or more members of one other combining unit (the transferee unit); and

(B) The combining entity of each transferor unit ceases its separate legal existence for all purposes; provided, however, that this requirement will be satisfied even if, under applicable law, after the effective time of the transaction, the combining entity of the transferor unit (or its officers, directors, or agents) may act or be acted against, or a member of the transferee unit (or its officers, directors, or agents) may act or be acted against in the name of the combining entity of the transferor unit, provided that such actions relate to assets or obligations of the combining entity of the transferor unit that arose, or relate to activities engaged in by such entity, prior to the effective time of the transaction, and such actions are not inconsistent with the requirements of paragraph (b)(1)(ii)(A) of this section.

(iii) Examples. The following examples illustrate the rules of paragraph (b)(1) of this section. In each of the examples, except as otherwise provided, each of R, V, Y, and Z is a C corporation. X is a domestic limited liability company. Except as otherwise provided, X is wholly owned by Y and is disregarded as an entity separate from Y for Federal income tax purposes. The examples are as follows:

Example (1). Divisive transaction pursuant to a merger statute. (i) Facts. Under State W law, Z transfers some of its assets and liabilities to Y, retains the remainder of its assets and liabilities, and remains in existence for Federal income tax purposes following the transaction.

The transaction qualifies as a merger under State W corporate law.

(ii) Analysis. The transaction does not satisfy the requirements of paragraph (b)(1)(ii)(A) of this section because all of the assets and liabilities of Z, the combining entity of the transferor unit, do not become the assets and liabilities of Y, the combining entity and sole member of the transferee unit. In addition, the transaction does not satisfy the requirements of paragraph (b)(1)(ii)(B) of this section because the separate legal existence of Z does not cease for all purposes. Accordingly, the transaction does not qualify as a statutory merger or consolidation under section 368(a)(1)(A).

Example (2). Merger of a target corporation into a disregarded entity in exchange for stock of the owner. (i) Facts. Under State W law, Z merges into X. Pursuant to such law, the following events occur simultaneously at the effective time of the transaction: all of the assets and liabilities of Z become the assets and liabilities of X and Z's separate legal existence ceases for all purposes. In the merger, the Z shareholders exchange their stock of Z for stock of Y.

(ii) Analysis. The transaction satisfies the requirements of paragraph (b)(1)(ii) of this section because the transaction is effected pursuant to State W law and the following events occur simultaneously at the effective time of the transaction: all of the assets and liabilities of Z, the combining entity and sole member of the transferor unit, become the assets and liabilities of one or more members of the transferee unit that is comprised of Y, the combining entity of the transferee unit, and X, a disregarded entity the assets of which Y is treated as owning for Federal income tax purposes, and Z ceases its separate legal existence for all purposes. Accordingly, the transaction qualifies as a statutory merger or consolidation for purposes of section 368(a)(1)(A).

Example (3). Merger of a target S corporation that owns a QSub into a disregarded entity. (i) Facts. The facts are the same as in

Example 2, except that Z is an S corporation and owns all of the stock of U, a QSub.

(ii) Analysis. The deemed formation by Z of U pursuant to § 1.1361–5(b)(1) (as a consequence of the termination of U's QSub election) is disregarded for Federal income tax purposes. The transaction is treated as a transfer of the assets of U to X, followed by X's transfer of these assets to U in exchange for stock of U. See § 1.1361–5(b)(3) *Example 9*. The transaction will, therefore, satisfy the requirements of paragraph (b)(1)(ii) of this section because the transaction is effected pursuant to State W law and the following events occur simultaneously at the effective time of the transaction: all of the assets and liabilities of Z and U, the sole members of the transferor unit, become the assets and liabilities of one or more members of the transferee unit that is comprised of Y, the combining entity of the transferee unit, and X, a disregarded entity the assets of which Y is treated as owning for Federal income tax purposes, and Z ceases its separate legal existence for all purposes. Moreover, the deemed transfer of the assets of U in exchange for U stock does not cause the transaction to fail to qualify as a statutory merger or consolidation. See § 368(a)(2)(C). Accordingly, the transaction qualifies as a statutory merger or consolidation for purposes of section 368(a)(1)(A).

Example (4). Triangular merger of a target corporation into a disregarded entity. (i) Facts. The facts are the same as in *Example 2*, except that V owns 100 percent of the outstanding stock of Y and, in the merger of Z into X, the Z shareholders exchange their stock of Z for stock of V. In the transaction, Z transfers substantially all of its properties to X.

(ii) Analysis. The transaction is not prevented from qualifying as a statutory merger or consolidation under section 368(a)(1)(A), provided the requirements of section 368(a)(2)(D) are satisfied. Because the assets of X are treated for Federal income tax purposes as the assets of Y, Y will be treated as acquiring substantially all of the properties of Z in the

merger for purposes of determining whether the merger satisfies the requirements of section 368(a)(2)(D). As a result, the Z shareholders that receive stock of V will be treated as receiving stock of a corporation that is in control of Y, the combining entity of the transferee unit that is the acquiring corporation for purposes of section 368(a)(2)(D). Accordingly, the merger will satisfy the requirements of section 368(a)(2)(D).

Example (5). Merger of a target corporation into a disregarded entity owned by a partnership. (i) Facts. The facts are the same as in *Example 2*, except that Y is organized as a partnership under the laws of State W and is classified as a partnership for Federal income tax purposes.

(ii) Analysis. The transaction does not satisfy the requirements of paragraph (b)(1)(ii)(A) of this section. All of the assets and liabilities of Z, the combining entity and sole member of the transferor unit, do not become the assets and liabilities of one or more members of a transferee unit because neither X nor Y qualifies as a combining entity. Accordingly, the transaction cannot qualify as a statutory merger or consolidation for purposes of section 368(a)(1)(A).

Example (6). Merger of a disregarded entity into a corporation. (i) Facts. Under State W law, X merges into Z. Pursuant to such law, the following events occur simultaneously at the effective time of the transaction: all of the assets and liabilities of X (but not the assets and liabilities of Y other than those of X) become the assets and liabilities of Z and X's separate legal existence ceases for all purposes.

(ii) Analysis. The transaction does not satisfy the requirements of paragraph (b)(1)(ii)(A) of this section because all of the assets and liabilities of a transferor unit do not become the assets and liabilities of one or more members of the transferee unit. The transaction also does not satisfy the requirements of paragraph (b)(1)(ii)(B) of this section because X does not qualify as a combining entity. Accordingly, the

transaction cannot qualify as a statutory merger or consolidation for purposes of section 368(a)(1)(A).

Example (7). Merger of a corporation into a disregarded entity in exchange for interests in the disregarded entity. (i) Facts. Under State W law, Z merges into X. Pursuant to such law, the following events occur simultaneously at the effective time of the transaction: all of the assets and liabilities of Z become the assets and liabilities of X and Z's separate legal existence ceases for all purposes. In the merger of Z into X, the Z shareholders exchange their stock of Z for interests in X so that, immediately after the merger, X is not disregarded as an entity separate from Y for Federal income tax purposes. Following the merger, pursuant to § 301.7701–3(b)(1)(i) of this chapter, X is classified as a partnership for Federal income tax purposes.

(ii) Analysis. The transaction does not satisfy the requirements of paragraph (b)(1)(ii)(A) of this section because immediately after the merger X is not disregarded as an entity separate from Y and, consequently, all of the assets and liabilities of Z, the combining entity of the transferor unit, do not become the assets and liabilities of one or more members of a transferee unit. Accordingly, the transaction cannot qualify as a statutory merger or consolidation for purposes of section 368(a)(1)(A).

Example (8). Merger transaction preceded by distribution. (i) Facts. Z operates two unrelated businesses, Business P and Business Q, each of which represents 50 percent of the value of the assets of Z. Y desires to acquire and continue operating Business P, but does not want to acquire Business Q. Pursuant to a single plan, Z sells Business Q for cash to parties unrelated to Z and Y in a taxable transaction, and then distributes the proceeds of the sale pro rata to its shareholders. Then, pursuant to State W law, Z merges into Y. Pursuant to such law, the following events occur simultaneously at the effective time of the transaction: all of the assets and liabilities of Z related to

Business P become the assets and liabilities of Y and Z's separate legal existence ceases for all purposes. In the merger, the Z shareholders exchange their Z stock for Y stock.

(ii) Analysis. The transaction satisfies the requirements of paragraph (b)(1)(ii) of this section because the transaction is effected pursuant to State W law and the following events occur simultaneously at the effective time of the transaction: all of the assets and liabilities of Z, the combining entity and sole member of the transferor unit, become the assets and liabilities of Y, the combining entity and sole member of the transferee unit, and Z ceases its separate legal existence for all purposes. Accordingly, the transaction qualifies as a statutory merger or consolidation for purposes of section 368(a)(1)(A).

Example (9). State law conversion of target corporation into a limited liability company. (i) Facts. Y acquires the stock of V from the V shareholders in exchange for consideration that consists of 50 percent voting stock of Y and 50 percent cash. Immediately after the stock acquisition, V files the necessary documents to convert from a corporation to a limited liability company under State W law. Y's acquisition of the stock of V and the conversion of V to a limited liability company are steps in a single integrated acquisition by Y of the assets of V.

(ii) Analysis. The acquisition by Y of the assets of V does not satisfy the requirements of paragraph (b)(1)(ii)(B) of this section because V, the combining entity of the transferor unit, does not cease its separate legal existence. Although V is an entity disregarded from its owner for Federal income tax purposes, it continues to exist as a juridical entity after the conversion. Accordingly, Y's acquisition of the assets of V does not qualify as a statutory merger or consolidation for purposes of section 368(a)(1)(A).

Example (10). Dissolution of target corporation. (i) Facts. Y acquires the stock of Z from the Z shareholders in exchange for consideration that consists of 50 percent voting stock of Y and 50 percent cash. Immediately after the stock acquisition, Z files a certificate of dissolution pursuant to State W law and commences winding up its activities. Under State W dissolution law, ownership and title to Z's assets does not automatically vest in Y upon dissolution. Instead, Z transfers assets to its creditors in satisfaction of its liabilities and transfers its remaining assets to Y in the liquidation stage of the dissolution. Y's acquisition of the stock of Z and the dissolution of Z are steps in a single integrated acquisition by Y of the assets of Z.

(ii) Analysis. The acquisition by Y of the assets of Z does not satisfy the requirements of paragraph (b)(1)(ii) of this section because Y does not acquire all of the assets of Z as a result of Z filing the certificate of dissolution or simultaneously with Z ceasing its separate legal existence. Instead, Y acquires the assets of Z by reason of Z's transfer of its assets to Y. Accordingly, Y's acquisition of the assets of Z does not qualify as a statutory merger or consolidation for purposes of section 368(a)(1)(A).

Example (11). Merger of corporate partner into a partnership. (i) Facts. Y owns an interest in X, an entity classified as a partnership for Federal income tax purposes, that represents a 60 percent capital and profits interest in X. Z owns an interest in X that represents a 40 percent capital and profits interest. Under State W law, Z merges into X. Pursuant to such law, the following events occur simultaneously at the effective time of the transaction: all of the assets and liabilities of Z become the assets and liabilities of X and Z ceases its separate legal existence for all purposes. In the merger, the Z shareholders exchange their stock of Z for stock of Y. As a result of the merger, X becomes an entity that is disregarded as an entity separate from Y for Federal income tax purposes.

(ii) Analysis. The transaction satisfies the requirements of paragraph (b)(1)(ii) of this

section because the transaction is effected pursuant to State W law and the following events occur simultaneously at the effective time of the transaction: all of the assets and liabilities of Z, the combining entity and sole member of the transferor unit, become the assets and liabilities of one or more members of the transferee unit that is comprised of Y, the combining entity of the transferee unit, and X, a disregarded entity the assets of which Y is treated as owning for Federal income tax purposes immediately after the transaction, and Z ceases its separate legal existence for all purposes. Accordingly, the transaction qualifies as a statutory merger or consolidation for purposes of section 368(a)(1)(A).

Example (12). State law consolidation. (i) Facts. Under State W law, Z and V consolidate. Pursuant to such law, the following events occur simultaneously at the effective time of the transaction: all of the assets and liabilities of Z and V become the assets and liabilities of Y, an entity that is created in the transaction, and the existence of Z and V continues in Y. In the consolidation, the Z shareholders and the V shareholders exchange their stock of Z and V, respectively, for stock of Y.

(ii) Analysis. With respect to each of Z and V, the transaction satisfies the requirements of paragraph (b)(1)(ii) of this section because the transaction is effected pursuant to State W law and the following events occur simultaneously at the effective time of the transaction: all of the assets and liabilities of Z and V, respectively, each of which is the combining entity of a transferor unit, become the assets and liabilities of Y, the combining entity and sole member of the transferee unit, and Z and V each ceases its separate legal existence for all purposes. Accordingly, the transaction qualifies as the statutory merger or consolidation of each of Z and V into Y for purposes of section 368(a)(1)(A).

Example (13). Transaction effected pursuant to foreign statutes. (i) Facts. Z and Y are entities organized under the laws of Country Q and classified as corporations for Federal income tax purposes. Z and Y combine. Pursuant to statutes of Country Q the following events occur simultaneously: all of the assets and liabilities of Z become the assets and liabilities of Y and Z's separate legal existence ceases for all purposes.

(ii) Analysis. The transaction satisfies the requirements of paragraph (b)(1)(ii) of this section because the transaction is effected pursuant to statutes of Country Q and the following events occur simultaneously at the effective time of the transaction: all of the assets and liabilities of Z, the combining entity of the transferor unit, become the assets and liabilities of Y, the combining entity and sole member of the transferee unit, and Z ceases its separate legal existence for all purposes. Accordingly, the transaction qualifies as a statutory merger or consolidation for purposes of section 368(a)(1)(A).

Example (14). Foreign law amalgamation using parent stock. (i) Facts. Z and V are entities organized under the laws of Country Q and classified as corporations for Federal income tax purposes. Z and V amalgamate. Pursuant to statutes of Country Q, the following events occur simultaneously: all the assets and liabilities of Z and V become the assets and liabilities of R, an entity that is created in the transaction and that is wholly owned by Y immediately after the transaction, and Z's and V's separate legal existences cease for all purposes. In the transaction, the Z and V shareholders exchange their Z and V stock, respectively, for stock of Y.

(ii) Analysis. With respect to each of Z and V, the transaction satisfies the requirements of paragraph (b)(1)(ii) of this section because the transaction is effected pursuant to Country Q law and the following events occur simultaneously at the effective time of the transaction: all of the assets and liabilities of Z and V, respectively, each of which is the combining entity of a transferor unit, become the assets and liabilities of R, the combining entity and sole

member of the transferee unit, with regard to each of the above transfers, and Z and V each ceases its separate legal existence for all purposes. Because Y is in control of R immediately after the transaction, the Z shareholders and the V shareholders will be treated as receiving stock of a corporation that is in control of R, the combining entity of the transferee unit that is the acquiring corporation for purposes of section 368(a)(2)(D). Accordingly, the transaction qualifies as the statutory merger or consolidation of each of Z and V into R, a corporation controlled by Y, and is a reorganization under section 368(a)(1)(A) by reason of section 368(a)(2)(D).

* * *

(2) In order for the transaction to qualify under section 368(a)(1)(A) by reason of the application of section 368(a)(2)(D), one corporation (the acquiring corporation) must acquire substantially all of the properties of another corporation (the acquired corporation) partly or entirely in exchange for stock of a corporation which is in control of the acquiring corporation (the controlling corporation), provided that (i) the transaction would have qualified under section 368(a)(1)(A) if the merger had been into the controlling corporation, and (ii) no stock of the acquiring corporation is used in the transaction. The foregoing test of whether the transaction would have qualified under section 368(a)(1)(A) if the merger had been into the controlling corporation means that the general requirements of a reorganization under section 368(a)(1)(A) (such as a business purpose, continuity of business enterprise, and continuity of interest) must be met in addition to the special requirements of section 368(a)(2)(D). Under this test, it is not relevant whether the merger into the controlling corporation could have been effected pursuant to State or Federal corporation law. The term "substantially all" has the same meaning as it has in section 368(a)(1)(C). Although no stock of the acquiring corporation can be used in the transaction, there is no prohibition (other than the continuity of interest requirement) against using other property, such as cash or securities, of either the acquiring corporation or the parent or both. In addition, the controlling corporation may assume liabilities of the acquired corporation without disqualifying the transaction under section 368(a)(2)(D), and for purposes of section 357(a) the controlling corporation is considered a party to the exchange. For example, if the controlling corporation agrees to substitute its stock for stock of the acquired corporation under an outstanding employee stock option agreement, this assumption of liability will not prevent the transaction from qualifying as a reorganization under section 368(a)(2)(D) and the assumption of liability is not treated as money or other property for purposes of section 361(b). Section 368(a)(2)(D) applies whether or not the controlling corporation (or the acquiring corporation) is formed immediately before the merger, in anticipation of the merger, or after preliminary steps have been taken to merge directly into the controlling corporation.

* * *

(c) In order to qualify as a "reorganization" under section 368(a)(1)(B), the acquisition by the acquiring corporation of stock of another corporation must be in exchange solely for all or a part of the voting stock of the acquiring corporation (or, in the case of transactions occurring after December 31, 1963, solely for all or a part of the voting stock of a corporation which is in control of the acquiring corporation), and the acquiring corporation must be in control of the other corporation immediately after the transaction. If, for example, Corporation X in one transaction exchanges nonvoting preferred stock or bonds in addition to all or a part of its voting stock in the acquisition of stock of Corporation Y, the transaction is not a reorganization under section 368(a)(1)(B). Nor is a transaction a reorganization described in section 368(a)(1)(B) if stock is acquired in exchange for voting stock both of the acquiring corporation and of a corporation which is in control of the acquiring corporation. The acquisition of stock of another corporation by the acquiring corporation solely for its voting stock (or solely for voting stock of a corporation which is in control of the acquiring corporation) is permitted tax-free even though the acquiring corporation already owns some of the stock of the other corporation. Such an acquisition is permitted tax-free in a single transaction or in a series of transactions taking place over a relatively short period of time such as 12 months. For example, Corporation A purchased 30 percent of the common stock of Corporation W (the only class of stock outstanding) for cash in 1939. On March 1, 1955, Corporation A offers to exchange its own voting stock for all the stock of Corporation W tendered within 6 months from the date of the offer. Within the 6-months' period Corporation A acquires an additional 60 percent of stock of Corporation W solely for its own voting stock, so that it owns 90 percent of the stock of Corporation W. No gain or loss is recognized with respect to the exchanges of stock of Corporation A for stock of Corporation W. For this purpose, it is immaterial whether such exchanges occurred before Corporation A acquired control (80 percent) of Corporation W or after such control was acquired. If Corporation A had acquired 80 percent of the stock of Corporation W for cash in 1939, it could likewise acquire some or all of the remainder of such stock solely in exchange for its own voting stock without recognition of gain or loss.

(d) In order to qualify as a reorganization under section 368(a)(1)(C), the transaction must be one described in subparagraph (1) or (2) of this paragraph:

(1) One corporation must acquire substantially all the properties of another corporation solely in exchange for all or a part of its own voting stock, or solely in exchange for all or a part of the voting stock of a corporation which is in control of the acquiring corporation. For example, Corporation P owns all the stock of Corporation A. All the properties of Corpora-

tion W are transferred to Corporation A either solely in exchange for voting stock of Corporation P or solely in exchange for less than 80 percent of the voting stock of Corporation A. Either of such transactions constitutes a reorganization under section 368(a)(1)(C). However, if the properties of Corporation W are acquired in exchange for voting stock of both Corporation P and Corporation A, the transaction will not constitute a reorganization under section 368(a)(1)(C). In determining whether the exchange meets the requirement of "solely for voting stock", the assumption by the acquiring corporation of liabilities of the transferor corporation, or the fact that property acquired from the transferor corporation is subject to a liability, shall be disregarded. Though such an assumption does not prevent an exchange from being solely for voting stock for the purposes of the definition of a reorganization contained in section 368(a)(1)(C), it may in some cases, however, so alter the character of the transaction as to place the transaction outside the purposes and assumptions of the reorganization provisions. Section 368(a)(1)(C) does not prevent consideration of the effect of an assumption of liabilities on the general character of the transaction but merely provides that the requirement that the exchange be solely for voting stock is satisfied if the only additional consideration is an assumption of liabilities.

(2) One corporation:

(i) Must acquire substantially all of the properties of another corporation in such manner that the acquisition would qualify under (1) above, but for the fact that the acquiring corporation exchanges money, or other property in addition to such voting stock, and

(ii) Must acquire solely for voting stock (either of the acquiring corporation or of a corporation which is in control of the acquiring corporation) properties of the other corporation having a fair market value which is at least 80 percent of the fair market value of all the properties of the other corporation.

(3) For the purposes of subparagraph (2)(ii) only, a liability assumed or to which the properties are subject is considered money paid for the properties. For example, Corporation A has properties with a fair market value of $100,000 and liabilities of $10,000. In exchange for these properties, Corporation Y transfers its own voting stock, assumes the $10,000 liabilities, and pays $8,000 in cash. The transaction is a reorganization even though a part of the properties of Corporation A is acquired for cash. On the other hand, if the properties of Corporation A worth $100,000, were subject to $50,000 in liabilities, an acquisition of all the properties, subject to the liabilities, for any consideration other than solely voting stock would not qualify as a reorganization under this section since the liabilities alone are in excess of 20 percent of the fair market value of the properties. If the transaction would qualify under either subparagraph (1) or (2) of this paragraph and also under section 368(a)(1) (D), such transaction shall not be treated as a reorganization under section 368(a)(1)(C).

* * *

(4)(i) For purposes of paragraphs (d)(1) and (2)(ii) of this section, prior ownership of stock of the target corporation by an acquiring corporation will not by itself prevent the solely for voting stock requirement of such paragraphs from being satisfied. In a transaction in which the acquiring corporation has prior ownership of stock of the target corporation, the requirement of paragraph (d)(2)(ii) of this section is satisfied only if the sum of the money or other property that is distributed in pursuance of the plan of reorganization to the shareholders of the target corporation other than the acquiring corporation and to the creditors of the target corporation pursuant to section 361(b)(3), and all of the liabilities of the target corporation assumed by the acquiring corporation (including liabilities to which the properties of the target corporation are subject), does not exceed 20 percent of the value of all of the properties of the target corporation. If, in connection with a potential acquisition by an acquiring corporation of substantially all of a target corporation's properties, the acquiring corporation acquires the target corporation's stock for consideration other than the acquiring corporation's own voting stock (or voting stock of a corporation in control of the acquiring corporation if such stock is used in the acquisition of the target corporation's properties), whether from a shareholder of the target corporation or the target corporation itself, such consideration is treated, for purposes of paragraphs (d)(1) and (2) of this section, as money or other property exchanged by the acquiring corporation for the target corporation's properties. Accordingly, the transaction will not qualify under section 368(a)(1)(C) unless, treating such consideration as money or other property, the requirements of section 368(a)(2)(B) and paragraph (d)(2)(ii) of this section are met. The determination of whether there has been an acquisition in connection with a potential reorganization under section 368(a)(1)(C) of a target corporation's stock for consideration other than an acquiring corporation's own voting stock (or voting stock of a corporation in control of the acquiring corporation if such stock is used in the acquisition of the target corporation's properties) will be made on the basis of all of the facts and circumstances.

(ii) The following examples illustrate the principles of this paragraph (d)(4):

Example (1). Corporation P (P) holds 60 percent of the Corporation T (T) stock that P purchased several years ago in an unrelated transaction. T has 100 shares of stock outstanding. The other 40 percent of the T stock is owned by Corporation X (X), an unrelated corporation. T has properties with a fair market value of $110 and liabilities of $10. T transfers all of its properties to P. In exchange, P assumes the $10 of liabilities, and transfers to T $30 of P voting stock and $10 of cash. T distributes the P voting stock and $10 of cash to X and liquidates. The transaction satisfies the solely for voting stock requirement of

paragraph (d)(2)(ii) of this section because the sum of $10 of cash paid to X and the assumption by P of $10 of liabilities does not exceed 20% of the value of the properties of T.

Example (2). The facts are the same as in *Example 1* except that P purchased the 60 shares of T for $60 in cash in connection with the acquisition of T's assets. The transaction does not satisfy the solely for voting stock requirement of paragraph (d)(2)(ii) of this section because P is treated as having acquired all of the T assets for consideration consisting of $70 of cash, $10 of liability assumption and $30 of P voting stock, and the sum of $70 of cash and the assumption by P of $10 of liabilities exceeds 20% of the value of the properties of T.

(iii) This paragraph (d)(4) applies to transactions occurring after December 31, 1999, unless the transaction occurs pursuant to a written agreement that is (subject to customary conditions) binding on that date and at all times thereafter.

(e) A "recapitalization", and therefore a reorganization, takes place if, for example:

(1) A corporation with $200,000 par value of bonds outstanding, instead of paying them off in cash, discharges them by issuing preferred shares to the bondholders;

(2) There is surrendered to a corporation for cancellation 25 percent of its preferred stock in exchange for no par value common stock;

(3) A corporation issues preferred stock, previously authorized but unissued, for outstanding common stock;

(4) An exchange is made of a corporation's outstanding preferred stock, having certain priorities with reference to the amount and time of payment of dividends and the distribution of the corporate assets upon liquidation, for a new issue of such corporation's common stock having no such rights;

(5) An exchange is made of an amount of a corporation's outstanding preferred stock

with dividends in arrears for other stock of the corporation. However, if pursuant to such an exchange there is an increase in the proportionate interest of the preferred shareholders in the assets or earnings and profits of the corporation, then under § 1.305–7(c)(2), an amount equal to the lesser of (i) the amount by which the fair market value or liquidation preference, whichever is greater, of the stock received in the exchange (determined immediately following the recapitalization) exceeds the issue price of the preferred stock surrendered, or (ii) the amount of the dividends in arrears, shall be treated under section 305(c) as a deemed distribution to which sections 305(b)(4) and 301 apply.

(f) The term "a party to a reorganization" includes a corporation resulting from a reorganization, and both corporations, in a transaction qualifying as a reorganization where one corporation acquires stock or properties of another corporation. If a transaction otherwise qualifies as a reorganization, a corporation remains a party to the reorganization even though stock or assets acquired in the reorganization are transferred in a transaction described in paragraph (k) of this section. If a transaction otherwise qualifies as a reorganization, a corporation shall not cease to be a party to the reorganization solely by reason of the fact that part or all of the assets acquired in the reorganization are transferred to a partnership in which the transferor is a partner if the continuity of business enterprise requirement is satisfied. See § 1.368–1(d). A corporation controlling an acquiring corporation is a party to the reorganization when the stock of such controlling corporation is used in the acquisition of properties. Both corporations are parties to the reorganization if, under statutory authority, Corporation A is merged into Corporation B. All three of the corporations are parties to the reorganization if, pursuant to statutory authority, Corporation C and Corporation D are consolidated into Corporation E. Both corporations are parties to the reorganization if Corporation F transfers substantially all its

assets to Corporation G in exchange for all or a part of the voting stock of Corporation G. All three corporations are parties to the reorganization if Corporation H transfers substantially all its assets to Corporation K in exchange for all or a part of the voting stock of Corporation L, which is in control of Corporation K. Both corporations are parties to the reorganization if Corporation M transfers all or part of its assets to Corporation N in exchange for all or a part of the stock and securities of Corporation N, but only if (1) immediately after such transfer, Corporation M, or one or more of its shareholders (including persons who were shareholders immediately before such transfer), or any combination thereof, is in control of Corporation N, and (2) in pursuance of the plan, the stock and securities of Corporation N are transferred or distributed by Corporation M in a transaction in which gain or loss is not recognized under section 354 or 355, or is recognized only to the extent provided in section 356. Both Corporation O and Corporation P, but not Corporation S, are parties to the reorganization if Corporation O acquires stock of Corporation P from Corporation S in exchange solely for a part of the voting stock of Corporation O, if (1) the stock of Corporation P does not constitute substantially all of the assets of Corporation S, (2) Corporation S is not in control of Corporation O immediately after the acquisition, and (3) Corporation O is in control of Corporation P immediately after the acquisition. If a transaction otherwise qualifies as a reorganization under section 368(a)(1)(B) or as a reverse triangular merger (as defined in § 1.358–6(b)(2)(iii)), the target corporation (in the case of a transaction that otherwise qualifies as a reorganization under section 368(a) (1)(B)) or the surviving corporation (in the case of a transaction that otherwise qualifies as a reverse triangular merger) remains a party to the reorganization even though its stock or assets are transferred in a transaction described in paragraph (k) of this section. If a transaction otherwise qualifies as a forward triangular merger (as defined in § 1.358–6(b)(2)(i)), a triangular B reorganization (as defined in § 1.358–6(b)(2)(iv)), a triangular C reorganization (as defined in § 1.358–6(b)(2)(ii)), or a reorganization under section 368(a)(1)(G) by reason of section 368(a)(2)(D), the acquiring corporation remains a party to the reorganization even though its stock is transferred in a transaction described in paragraph (k) of this section. The two preceding sentences apply to transactions occurring on or after October 25, 2007, except that they do not apply to any transaction occurring pursuant to a written agreement which is binding before October 25, 2007, and at all times after that.

(g) The term "plan of reorganization" has reference to a consummated transaction specifically defined as a reorganization under section 368(a). The term is not to be construed as broadening the definition of "reorganization" as set forth in section 368(a), but is to be taken as limiting the nonrecognition of gain or loss to such exchanges or distributions as are directly a part of the transaction specifically described as a reorganization in section 368(a). Moreover, the transaction, or series of transactions, embraced in a plan of reorganization must not only come within the specific language of section 368(a), but the readjustments involved in the exchanges or distributions effected in the consummation thereof must be undertaken for reasons germane to the continuance of the business of a corporation a party to the reorganization. Section 368(a) contemplates genuine corporate reorganizations which are designed to effect a readjustment of continuing interests under modified corporate forms.

* * *

Example (4). On January 1, 1971, P purchased 201 shares of T's stock. On January 1, 1981, S merges into T. In the merger, T's shareholders (other than P) surrender 799 shares of T stock in exchange for P voting stock. Based on these facts, in the transaction, former shareholders of T do not surrender, in exchange for P voting stock, an amount of T stock which constitutes control of T (799/1,000 shares be-

ing less than 80 percent). Therefore, the transaction does not qualify under section 368(a)(1) (A). However, if S is a transitory corporation, formed solely for purposes of effectuating the transaction, the transaction may qualify as a reorganization described in section 368(a)(1) (B) provided all of the applicable requirements are satisfied.

Example (5). On January 1, 1971, P purchased 200 shares of T's stock. On January 1, 1981, S merges into T. Prior to the merger, as part of the transaction, T distributes its own cash in redemption of 1 share of T stock from a T shareholder other than P. In the merger, T's remaining shareholders (other than P) surrender 799 shares of T stock in exchange for P voting stock. Based on these facts, in the transaction, former shareholders of T do not surrender, in exchange for P voting stock, an amount of T stock which constitutes control of T (799/999 shares being less than 80 percent). Therefore, the transaction does not qualify under section 368(a)(1)(A). However, if S is a transitory corporation, formed for purposes of effectuating the transaction, the transaction may qualify as a reorganization described in section 368(a)(1)(B) provided all of the applicable requirements are satisfied.

* * *

(j)(1) This paragraph (j) prescribes rules relating to the application of section 368(a)(2) (E).

(2) Section 368(a)(2)(E) does not apply to a consolidation.

(3) A transaction otherwise qualifying under section 368(a)(1)(A) is not disqualified by reason of the fact that stock of a corporation (the controlling corporation) which before the merger was in control of the merged corporation is used in the transaction, if the conditions of section 368(a)(2)(E) are satisfied. Those conditions are as follows:

(i) In the transaction, shareholders of the surviving corporation must surrender stock in exchange for voting stock of the controlling corporation. Further, the stock so surrendered must constitute control of the surviving corporation. Control is defined in section 368(c). The amount of stock constituting control is measured immediately before the transaction. For purposes of this subdivision (i), stock in the surviving corporation which is surrendered in the transaction (by any shareholder except the controlling corporation) in exchange for consideration furnished by the surviving corporation (and not by the controlling corporation of the merged corporation) is considered not to be outstanding immediately before the transaction. For effect on "substantially all" test of consideration furnished by the surviving corporation, see paragraph (j)(3)(iii) of this section.

(ii) Except as provided in paragraph (k) of this section, the controlling corporation must control the surviving corporation immediately after the transaction.

(iii) After the transaction, the surviving corporation must hold substantially all of its own properties and substantially all of the properties of the merged corporation (other than stock of the controlling corporation distributed in the transaction). The surviving corporation may transfer such properties as provided in paragraph (k) of this section. The term *substantially all* has the same meaning as in section 368(a)(1)(C). The "substantially all" test applies separately to the merged corporation and to the surviving corporation. In applying the "substantially all" test to the surviving corporation, consideration furnished in the transaction by the surviving corporation in exchange for its stock is property of the surviving corporation which it does not hold after the transaction. In applying the "substantially all" test to the merged corporation, assets transferred from the controlling corporation to the merged corporation in pursuance of the plan of reorganization are not taken into account. Thus, for example, money transferred from the controlling corporation to the merged corporation to be used for the following pur-

poses is not taken into account for purposes of the "substantially all" test:

(A) To pay additional consideration to shareholders of the surviving corporation;

(B) To pay dissenting shareholders of the surviving corporation;

(C) To pay creditors of the surviving corporation;

(D) To pay reorganization expenses; or

(E) To enable the merged corporation to satisfy state minimum capitalization requirements (where the money is returned to the controlling corporation as part of the transaction).

(iv) Paragraph (j)(3)(ii) and the first two sentences of paragraph (j)(3)(iii) of this section apply to transactions occurring on or after October 25, 2007, except that they do not apply to any transaction occurring pursuant to a written agreement which is binding before October 25, 2007, and at all times thereafter. The remainder of paragraph (j)(3)(iii) of this section applies to transactions occurring after January 28, 1998, except that it does not apply to any transaction occurring pursuant to a written agreement which is binding on January 28, 1998, and at all times after that.

(4) The controlling corporation may assume liabilities of the surviving corporation without disqualifying the transaction under section 368(a)(2)(E). An assumption of liabilities of the surviving corporation by the controlling corporation is a contribution to capital by the controlling corporation to the surviving corporation. If, in pursuance of the plan of reorganization, securities of the surviving corporation are exchanged for securities of the controlling corporation, or for other securities of the surviving corporation, see sections 354 and 356.

(5) In applying section 368(a)(2)(E), it makes no difference if the merged corporation is an existing corporation, or is formed immediately before the merger, in anticipation of the merger, or after preliminary steps have been

taken to otherwise acquire control of the surviving corporation.

(6) The following examples illustrate the application of this paragraph (j). In each of the examples, Corporation P owns all of the stock of Corporation S and, except as otherwise stated, Corporation T has outstanding 1,000 shares of common stock and no shares of any other class. In each of the examples, it is also assumed that the transaction qualifies under section 368(a)(1)(A) if the conditions of section 368(a)(2)(E) are satisfied.

Example (1). P owns no T stock. On January 1, 1981, S merges into T. In the merger, T's shareholders surrender 950 shares of common stock in exchange for P voting stock. The holders of the other 50 shares (who dissent from the merger) are paid in cash with funds supplied by P. After the transaction, T holds all of its own assets and all of S's assets. Based on these facts, the transaction qualifies under section 368(a)(1)(A) by reason of the application of section 368(a)(2)(E). In the transaction, former shareholders of T surrender, in exchange for P voting stock, an amount of T stock (950/1,000 shares or 95 percent) which constitutes control of T.

Example (2). The facts are the same as in *Example (1)* except that holders of 100 shares in corporation T, who dissented from the merger, are paid in cash with funds supplied by T (and not by P or S) and in the merger, T's remaining shareholders surrender 720 shares of common stock in exchange for P voting stock and 180 shares of common stock for cash supplied by P. The requirements of section 368(a)(2)(E)(ii) are satisfied since, in the transaction, former shareholders of T surrender, in exchange for P voting stock, an amount of T stock (720/900 shares or 80 percent) which constitutes control of T. The T stock surrendered in exchange for consideration furnished by T is not considered outstanding for purposes of determining whether the amount of T stock surrendered by T shareholders for P stock constitutes control of T.

Example (3). T has outstanding 1,000 shares of common stock, 100 shares of nonvoting preferred stock, and no shares of any other class. On January 1, 1981, S merges into T. Prior to the merger, as part of the transaction, T distributes its own cash in redemption of the 100 shares of preferred stock. In the transaction, T's remaining shareholders surrender their 1,000 shares of common stock in exchange for P voting stock. The requirements of section 368(a)(2)(E)(ii) are satisfied since, in the transaction, former shareholders of T surrender, in exchange for P voting stock, an amount of T stock (1,000/1,000 shares or 100 percent) which constitutes control of T. The preferred stock surrendered in exchange for consideration furnished by T is not considered outstanding for purposes of determining whether the amount of T stock surrendered by T shareholders for P stock constitutes control of T. However, the consideration furnished by T for its stock is property of T which T does not hold after the transaction for purposes of the substantially all test in paragraph (j)(3)(iii) of this section.

Example (4). On January 1, 1971, P purchased 201 shares of T's stock. On January 1, 1981, S merges into T. In the merger, T's shareholders (other than P) surrender 799 shares of T stock in exchange for P voting stock. Based on these facts, in the transaction, former shareholders of T do not surrender, in exchange for P voting stock, an amount of T stock which constitutes control of T (799/1,000 shares being less than 80 percent). Therefore, the transaction does not qualify under section 368(a)(1)(A). However, if S is a transitory corporation, formed solely for purposes of effectuating the transaction, the transaction may qualify as a reorganization described in section 368(a)(1)(B) provided all of the applicable requirements are satisfied.

Example (5). On January 1, 1971, P purchased 200 shares of T's stock. On January 1, 1981, S merges into T. Prior to the merger, as part of the transaction, T distributes its own cash in redemption of 1 share of T stock from a T shareholder other than P. In the merger, T's remaining shareholders (other than P) surrender 799 shares of T stock in exchange for P voting stock. Based on these facts, in the transaction, former shareholders of T do not surrender, in exchange for P voting stock, an amount of T stock which constitutes control of T (799/999 shares being less than 80 percent). Therefore, the transaction does not qualify under section 368(a)(1)(A). However, if S is a transitory corporation, formed for purposes of effectuating the transaction, the transaction may qualify as a reorganization described in section 368(a)(1)(B) provided all of the applicable requirements are satisfied.

Example (6). The stock of S has a value of $25,000. The stock of T has a value of $75,000. On January 1, 1984, S merges into T. In the merger, T's shareholders surrender all of their T stock in exchange for P voting stock. After the transaction, T holds all of its own assets and all of S's assets. Based on these facts, the transaction qualifies under section 368(a)(1)(A) by reason of the application of section 368(a)(2)(E). In the transaction, former shareholders of T surrender, in exchange for P voting stock, an amount of T stock (1,000/1,000 shares or 100 percent) which constitutes control of T. The stock of T received by P in exchange for P's prior interest in S is not taken into account for purposes of section 368(a)(2)(E)(ii) since the amount of T stock constituting control of T is measured before the transaction.

Example (7). The stock of T has a value of $75,000. On January 1, 1984, S merges into T. In the merger, T's shareholders surrender all of their T stock in exchange for P voting stock. As part of the transaction, P contributes $25,000 to T in exchange for new shares of T stock. None of the cash received by T is distributed or otherwise paid out to former T shareholders. After the transaction, T holds all of its own assets and all of S's assets. Based on these facts, the transaction qualifies under section 368(a)(1)(A) by reason of the appli-

cation of section 368(a)(2)(E). In the transaction, former shareholders of T surrender, in exchange for P voting stock, an amount of T stock (1,000/1,000 shares or 100 percent) which constitutes control of T. The T stock received by P in exchange for its contribution to T is not taken into account for purposes of section 368(a)(2)(E)(ii) since the amount of T stock constituting control of T is measured before the transaction.

Example (8). The facts are the same as in *Example (7)* except that, as part of the transaction, corporation R, instead of P, contributes $25,000 to T in exchange for T stock. Based on these facts, the transaction does not qualify under section 368(a)(1)(A) by reason of section 368(a)(2)(E) since P does not control T immediately after the transaction.

Example (9). T stock has a value of $75,000. P owns 500 shares (1/2) of that stock with a value of $37,500. The stock of S has a value of $125,000. On January 1, 1984, S merges into T. In the merger, T's shareholders (other than P) surrender their T stock in exchange for P voting stock. Based on these facts, in the transaction, former shareholders of T do not surrender, in exchange for P voting stock, an amount of T stock which constitutes control of T (500/1,000 shares being less than 80 percent). Therefore, the transaction does not qualify under section 368(a)(1)(A). The stock of T received by P in exchange for P's prior interest in S does not contribute to satisfaction of the requirement of section 368(a)(2)(E)(ii).

(k) Certain transfers of assets or stock in reorganizations—(1) General rule. A transaction otherwise qualifying as a reorganization under section 368(a) shall not be disqualified or recharacterized as a result of one or more subsequent transfers (or successive transfers) of assets or stock, provided that the requirements of § 1.368–1(d) are satisfied and the transfer(s) are described in either paragraph (k)(1)(i) or (k)(1)(ii) of this section. However, this paragraph (k) shall not apply to a transfer to the former shareholders of the acquired corporation (other than a former shareholder that is also the acquiring corporation) or the surviving corporation, as the case may be, to the extent it constitutes the receipt of consideration for a proprietary interest in the acquired corporation or the surviving corporation, as the case may be. Similarly, this paragraph (k) shall not apply to a transfer by the former shareholders of the acquired corporation (other than a former shareholder that is also the acquiring corporation) or the surviving corporation, as the case may be, of consideration initially received in the potential reorganization to the issuing corporation or a person related to the issuing corporation (see definition of "related person" in § 1.368–1(e)).

(i) Distributions. One or more distributions to shareholders (including distribution(s) that involve the assumption of liabilities) are described in this paragraph (k)(1)(i) if—

(A) The property distributed consists of—

(1) Assets of the acquired corporation, the acquiring corporation, or the surviving corporation, as the case may be, or an interest in an entity received in exchange for such assets in a transfer described in paragraph (k)(1)(ii) of this section;

(2) Stock of the acquired corporation provided that such distribution(s) of stock do not cause the acquired corporation to cease to be a member of the qualified group (as defined in § 1.368–1(d)(4)(ii)); or

(3) A combination thereof; and

(B) The aggregate of such distributions does not consist of—

(1) An amount of assets of the acquired corporation, the acquiring corporation (disregarding assets held prior to the potential reorganization), or the surviving corporation (disregarding assets of the merged corporation), as the case may be, that would result in a liquidation of such corporation for Federal income tax purposes; or

(2) All of the stock of the acquired corporation that was acquired in the transaction.

(ii) Transfers other than distributions. One or more other transfers are described in this paragraph (k)(1)(ii) if—

(A) The transfer(s) do not consist of one or more distributions to shareholders;

(B) The property transferred consists of—

(1) Part or all of the assets of the acquired corporation, the acquiring corporation, or the surviving corporation, as the case may be;

(2) Part or all of the stock of the acquired corporation, the acquiring corporation, or the surviving corporation, as the case may be, provided that such transfer(s) of stock do not cause such corporation to cease to be a member of the qualified group (as defined in § 1.368–1(d)(4)(ii)); or

(3) A combination thereof; and

(C) The acquired corporation, the acquiring corporation, or the surviving corporation, as the case may be, does not terminate its corporate existence for Federal income tax purposes in connection with the transfer(s).

(2) Examples. The following examples illustrate the application of this paragraph (k). Except as otherwise noted, P is the issuing corporation, and T is an unrelated target corporation. All corporations have only one class of stock outstanding. T operates a bakery that supplies delectable pastries and cookies to local retail stores. The acquiring corporate group produces a variety of baked goods for nationwide distribution. Except as otherwise noted, P owns all of the stock of S-1 and 80 percent of the stock of S-4, S-1 owns 80 percent of the stock of S-2 and 50 percent of the stock of S-5, S-2 owns 80 percent of the stock of S-3, and S-4 owns the remaining 50 percent of the stock of S-5. The examples are as follows:

Example (1). Transfers of acquired assets to members of the qualified group after a reorganization under section 368(a)(1)(C). (i) Facts. Pursuant to a plan of reorganization, T

502

transfers all of its assets to S-1 solely in exchange for P stock, which T distributes to its shareholders, and S-1's assumption of T's liabilities. In addition, pursuant to the plan, S-1 transfers all of the T assets to S-2, and S-2 transfers all of the T assets to S-3.

(ii) Analysis. Under this paragraph (k), the transaction, which otherwise qualifies as a reorganization under section 368(a)(1)(C), is not disqualified by the successive transfers of all of the T assets to S-2 and from S-2 to S-3 because the transfers are not one or more distributions to shareholders, the transfers consist of part or all of the assets of the acquiring corporation, the acquiring corporation does not terminate its corporate existence for Federal income tax purposes in connection with the transfers, and the transaction satisfies the requirements of s 1.368–1(d).

Example (2). Distribution of acquired assets to a member of the qualified group after a reorganization under section 368(a)(1)(C). (i) Facts. Pursuant to a plan of reorganization, T transfers all of its assets to S-1 solely in exchange for P stock, which T distributes to its shareholders, and S-1's assumption of T's liabilities. In addition, pursuant to the plan, S-1 distributes half of the T assets to P, and P assumes half of the T liabilities.

(ii) Analysis. Under this paragraph (k), the transaction, which otherwise qualifies as a reorganization under section 368(a)(1)(C), is not disqualified by the distribution of half of the T assets from S-1 to P, or P's assumption of half of the T liabilities from S-1, because the distribution consists of assets of the acquiring corporation, the distribution does not consist of an amount of S-1's assets that would result in a liquidation of S-1 for Federal income tax purposes (disregarding S-1's assets held prior to the acquisition of T), and the transaction satisfies the requirements of s 1.368–1(d).

Example (3). Indirect distribution of acquired assets to a member of the qualified group after a reorganization under section 368(a)(1)(C). (i) Facts. The facts are the same

as Example 2, except that, instead of S-1 distributing half of the T assets to P and having P assume half of the T liabilities, S-1 contributes half of the T assets to newly formed S-6, S-6 assumes half of the T liabilities, and S-1 distributes all of the S-6 stock to P.

(ii) Analysis. Under this paragraph (k), the transaction, which otherwise qualifies as a reorganization under section 368(a)(1)(C), is not disqualified by the transfer of half of the T assets to S-6 and the distribution of the S-6 stock to P because the transfer of half of the T assets to S-6 is described in paragraph (k)(1) (ii) of this section, the distribution of the S-6 stock to P is an indirect distribution of assets of the acquiring corporation, the distribution does not consist of an amount of S-1's assets that would result in a liquidation of S-1 for Federal income tax purposes (disregarding S-1's assets held prior to the acquisition of T), and the transaction satisfies the requirements of s 1.368–1(d).

Example (4). Distribution of acquired stock to a controlled partnership after a reorganization under section 368(a)(1)(B). (i) Facts. P owns 80 percent of the stock of S-1, and an 80-percent interest in PRS, a partnership. S-4 owns the remaining 20-percent interest in PRS. PRS owns the remaining 20 percent of the stock of S-1. Pursuant to a plan of reorganization, the T shareholders transfer all of their T stock to S-1 solely in exchange for P stock. In addition, pursuant to the plan, S-1 distributes 90 percent of the T stock to PRS in redemption of 5 percent of the stock of S-1 owned by PRS.

(ii) Analysis. Under this paragraph (k), the transaction, which otherwise qualifies as a reorganization under section 368(a)(1)(B), is not disqualified by the distribution of 90 percent of the T stock from S-1 to PRS because the distribution consists of less than all of the stock of the acquired corporation that was acquired in the transaction, the distribution does not cause T to cease to be a member of the qualified group (as defined in § 1.368–1(d)(4)(ii)),

and the transaction satisfies the requirements of § 1.368–1(d).

Example (5). Transfer of acquired stock to a non-controlled partnership. (i) Facts. Pursuant to a plan, the T shareholders transfer all of their T stock to S-1 solely in exchange for P stock. In addition, as part of the plan, T distributes half of its assets to S-1, S-1 assumes half of the T liabilities, and S-1 transfers the T stock to S-2. S-2 and U, an unrelated corporation, form a new partnership, PRS. Immediately thereafter, S-2 transfers all of the T stock to PRS in exchange for a 50 percent interest in PRS, and U transfers cash to PRS in exchange for a 50 percent interest in PRS.

(ii) Analysis. Under this paragraph (k), the transaction, which otherwise qualifies as a reorganization under section 368(a)(1)(B), is not disqualified by the distribution of half of the T assets from T to S-1, or S-1's assumption of half of the T liabilities from T, because the distribution consists of assets of the acquired corporation, the distribution does not consist of an amount of T's assets that would result in a liquidation of T for Federal income tax purposes, and the transaction satisfies the requirements of § 1.368–1(d). Further, this paragraph (k) describes the transfer of the acquired stock from S-1 to S-2, but does not describe the transfer of the acquired stock from S-2 to PRS because such transfer causes T to cease to be a member of the qualified group (as defined in § 1.368–1(d)(4)(ii)). Therefore, the characterization of this transaction must be determined under the relevant provisions of law, including the step transaction doctrine. See § 1.368–1(a). The transaction fails to meet the control requirement of a reorganization described in section 368(a)(1)(B) because immediately after the acquisition of the T stock, the acquiring corporation does not have control of T.

Example (6). Transfers of acquired assets to members of the qualified group after a reorganization under section 368(a)(1)(D). (i) Facts. P owns all of the stock of T. Pursuant to a plan of reorganization, T transfers all of its assets to S-1 solely in exchange for S-1 stock, which T distributes to P, and S-1's assumption of T's liabilities. In addition, pursuant to the plan, S-1 transfers all of the T assets to S-2, and S-2 transfers all of the T assets to S-3.

(ii) Analysis. Under this paragraph (k), the transaction, which otherwise qualifies as a reorganization under section 368(a)(1)(D), is not disqualified by the successive transfers of all the T assets from S-1 to S-2 and from S-2 to S-3 because the transfers are not one or more distributions to shareholders, the transfers consist of part or all of the assets of the acquiring corporation, the acquiring corporation does not terminate its corporate existence for Federal income tax purposes in connection with the transfers, and the transaction satisfies the requirements of § 1.368–1(d).

Example (7). Transfer of stock of the acquiring corporation to a member of the qualified group after a reorganization under section 368(a)(1)(A) by reason of section 368(a)(2)(D). (i) Facts. Pursuant to a plan of reorganization, S-1 acquires all of the T assets in the merger of T into S-1. In the merger, the T shareholders receive solely P stock. Also, pursuant to the plan, P transfers all of the S-1 stock to S-4.

(ii) Analysis. Under this paragraph (k), the transaction, which otherwise qualifies as a reorganization under section 368(a)(1)(A) by reason of section 368(a)(2)(D), is not disqualified by the transfer of all of the S-1 stock to S-4 because the transfer is not a distribution to shareholders, the transfer consists of part or all of the stock of the acquiring corporation, the transfer does not cause S-1 to cease to be a member of the qualified group (as defined in § 1.368–1(d)(4)(ii)), the acquiring corporation does not terminate its corporate existence for Federal income tax purposes in connection with the transfer, and the transaction satisfies the requirements of § 1.368–1(d).

Example (8). Transfer of acquired assets to a partnership after a reorganization under section 368(a)(1)(A) by reason of section

368(a)(2)(D). (i) Facts. Pursuant to a plan of reorganization, S-1 acquires all of the T assets in the merger of T into S-1. In the merger, the T shareholders receive solely P stock. In addition, pursuant to the plan, S-1 transfers all of the T assets to PRS, a partnership in which S-1 owns a 33 1/3-percent interest. PRS continues T's historic business. S-1 does not perform active and substantial management functions as a partner with respect to PRS' business.

(ii) Analysis. Under this paragraph (k), the transaction, which otherwise qualifies as a reorganization under section 368(a)(1)(A) by reason of section 368(a)(2)(D), is not disqualified by the transfer of T assets from S-1 to PRS because the transfer is not a distribution to shareholders, the transfer consists of part or all of the assets of the acquiring corporation, the acquiring corporation does not terminate its corporate existence for Federal income tax purposes in connection with the transfers, and the transaction satisfies the requirements of § 1.368–1(d).

Example (9). Sale of acquired assets to a member of the qualified group after a reorganization under section 368(a)(1)(C). (i) Facts. Pursuant to a plan of reorganization, T transfers all of its assets to S-1 in exchange for P stock, which T distributes to its shareholders, and S-1's assumption of T's liabilities. In addition, pursuant to the plan, S-1 sells all of the T assets to S-5 for cash equal to the fair market value of those assets.

(ii) Analysis. Under this paragraph (k), the transaction, which otherwise qualifies as a reorganization under section 368(a)(1)(C), is not disqualified by the sale of all of the T assets from S-1 to S-5 because the transfer is not a distribution to shareholders, the transfer consists of part or all of the assets of the acquiring corporation, the acquiring corporation does not terminate its corporate existence for Federal income tax purposes in connection with the transfer, and the transaction satisfies the requirements of § 1.368–1(d).

* * *

(*l*) Certain transactions treated as reorganizations described in section 368(a) (1)(D)—(1) General rule. In order to qualify as a reorganization under section 368(a) (1)(D), a corporation (transferor corporation) must transfer all or part of its assets to another corporation (transferee corporation) and immediately after the transfer the transferor corporation, or one or more of its shareholders (including persons who were shareholders immediately before the transfer), or any combination thereof, must be in control of the transferee corporation; but only if, in pursuance of the plan, stock or securities of the transferee are distributed in a transaction which qualifies under section 354, 355, or 356.

(2) Distribution requirement—(i) In general. For purposes of paragraph (*l*)(1) of this section, a transaction otherwise described in section 368(a)(1)(D) will be treated as satisfying the requirements of sections 368(a)(1)(D) and 354(b)(1)(B) notwithstanding that there is no actual issuance of stock and/or securities of the transferee corporation if the same person or persons own, directly or indirectly, all of the stock of the transferor and transferee corporations in identical proportions. In cases where no consideration is received or the value of the consideration received in the transaction is less than the fair market value of the transferor corporation's assets, the transferee corporation will be treated as issuing stock with a value equal to the excess of the fair market value of the transferor corporation's assets over the value of the consideration actually received in the transaction. In cases where the value of the consideration received in the transaction is equal to the fair market value of the transferor corporation's assets, the transferee corporation will be deemed to issue a nominal share of stock to the transferor corporation in addition to the actual consideration exchanged for the transferor corporation's assets. The nominal share of stock in the transferee corporation will then be deemed distributed by the transferor corporation to the shareholders of the transferor corporation, as part of the exchange for the stock of such shareholders. Where appropriate, the nominal share will be further transferred through chains of ownership to the extent necessary to reflect the actual ownership of the transferor and transferee corporations. Similar treatment to that of the preceding two sentences shall apply where the transferee corporation is treated as issuing stock with a value equal to the excess of the fair market value of the transferor corporation's assets over the value of the consideration actually received in the transaction.

(ii) Attribution. For purposes of paragraph (*l*)(2)(i) of this section, ownership of stock will be determined by applying the principles of section 318(a)(2) without regard to the 50 percent limitation in section 318(a)(2)(C). In addition, an individual and all members of his family described in section 318(a)(1) shall be treated as one individual.

(iii) De minimis variations in ownership and certain stock not taken into account. For purposes of paragraph (*l*)(2)(i) of this section, the same person or persons will be treated as owning, directly or indirectly, all of the stock of the transferor and transferee corporations in identical proportions notwithstanding the fact that there is a de minimis variation in shareholder identity or proportionality of ownership. Additionally, for purposes of paragraph (*l*)(2)(i) of this section, stock described in section 1504(a)(4) is not taken into account.

(iv) Exception. Paragraph (*l*)(2) of this section does not apply to a transaction otherwise described in § 1.358–6(b)(2).

(3) Examples. The following examples illustrate the principles of paragraph (*l*) of this section. For purposes of these examples, each of A, B, C, and D is an individual, T is the acquired corporation, S is the acquiring corporation, P is the parent corporation, and each of S1, S2, S3, and S4 is a direct or indirect subsidiary of P. Further, all of the requirements of section 368(a)(1)(D) other than the requirement that stock or securities be distributed in a

transaction to which section 354 or 356 applies are satisfied. The examples are as follows:

Example (1). A owns all the stock of T and S. The T stock has a fair market value of $100x. T sells all of its assets to S in exchange for $100x of cash and immediately liquidates. Because there is complete shareholder identity and proportionality of ownership in T and S, under paragraph (*l*)(2)(i) of this section, the requirements of sections 368(a)(1)(D) and 354(b)(1)(B) are treated as satisfied notwithstanding the fact that no S stock is issued. Pursuant to paragraph (*l*)(2)(i) of this section, S will be deemed to issue a nominal share of S stock to T in addition to the $100x of cash actually exchanged for the T assets, and T will be deemed to distribute all such consideration to A. The transaction qualifies as a reorganization described in section 368(a)(1)(D).

Example (2). The facts are the same as in Example 1 except that C, A's son, owns all of the stock of S. Under paragraph (*l*)(2)(ii) of this section, A and C are treated as one individual. Accordingly, there is complete shareholder identity and proportionality of ownership in T and S. Therefore, under paragraph (*l*)(2)(i) of this section, the requirements of sections 368(a)(1)(D) and 354(b)(1)(B) are treated as satisfied notwithstanding the fact that no S stock is issued. Pursuant to paragraph (*l*)(2)(i) of this section, S will be deemed to issue a nominal share of S stock to T in addition to the $100x of cash actually exchanged for the T assets, and T will be deemed to distribute all such consideration to A. A will be deemed to transfer the nominal share of S stock to C. The transaction qualifies as a reorganization described in section 368(a)(1)(D).

Example (3). P owns all of the stock of S1 and S2. S1 owns all of the stock of S3, which owns all of the stock of T. S2 owns all of the stock of S4, which owns all of the stock of S. The T stock has a fair market value of $70x. T sells all of its assets to S in exchange for $70x of cash and immediately liquidates. Under paragraph (*l*)(2)(ii) of this section, there is indirect, complete shareholder identity and proportionality of ownership in T and S. Accordingly, the requirements of sections 368(a)(1)(D) and 354(b)(1)(B) are treated as satisfied notwithstanding the fact that no S stock is issued. Pursuant to paragraph (*l*)(2)(i) of this section, S will be deemed to issue a nominal share of S stock to T in addition to the $70x of cash actually exchanged for the T assets, and T will be deemed to distribute all such consideration to S3. S3 will be deemed to distribute the nominal share of S stock to S1, which, in turn, will be deemed to distribute the nominal share of S stock to P. P will be deemed to transfer the nominal share of S stock to S2, which, in turn, will be deemed to transfer such share of S stock to S4. The transaction qualifies as a reorganization described in section 368(a)(1)(D).

Example (4). A, B, and C own 34%, 33%, and 33%, respectively, of the stock of T. The T stock has a fair market value of $100x. A, B, and C each own 33% of the stock of S. D owns the remaining 1% of the stock of S. T sells all of its assets to S in exchange for $100x of cash and immediately liquidates. For purposes of determining whether the distribution requirement of sections 368(a)(1)(D) and 354(b)(1)(B) is met, under paragraph (*l*)(2)(iii) of this section, D's ownership of a de minimis amount of stock of S is disregarded and the transaction is treated as if there is complete shareholder identity and proportionality of ownership in T and S. Because there is complete shareholder identity and proportionality of ownership in T and S, under paragraph (*l*)(2)(i) of this section, the requirements of sections 368(a)(1)(D) and 354(b)(1)(B) are treated as satisfied notwithstanding the fact that no S stock is issued. Pursuant to paragraph (*l*)(2)(i) of this section, S will be deemed to issue a nominal share of S stock to T in addition to the $100x of cash actually exchanged for the T assets, T will be deemed to distribute all such consideration to A, B, and C, and the nominal S stock will be deemed transferred among the S shareholders to the extent necessary to reflect their actual ownership of S. The transac-

tion qualifies as a reorganization described in section 368(a)(1)(D).

Example (5). The facts are the same as in Example 4 except that A, B, and C own 34%, 33%, and 33%, respectively, of the common stock of T and S. D owns preferred stock in S described in section 1504(a)(4). For purposes of determining whether the distribution requirement of sections 368(a)(1)(D) and 354(b)(1)(B) is met, under paragraph (*l*)(2)(iii) of this section, D's ownership of S stock described in section 1504(a)(4) is ignored and the transaction is treated as if there is complete shareholder identity and proportionality of ownership in T and S. Because there is complete shareholder identity and proportionality of ownership in T and S, under paragraph (*l*)(2)(i) of this section, the requirements of sections 368(a)(1)(D) and 354(b)(1)(B) are treated as satisfied notwithstanding the fact that no S stock is issued. Pursuant to paragraph (*l*)(2)(i) of this section, S will be deemed to issue a nominal share of S stock to T in addition to the $100x of cash actually exchanged for the T assets, and T will be deemed to distribute all such consideration to A, B, and C. The transaction qualifies as a reorganization described in section 368(a)(1)(D).

Example (6). A and B each own 50% of the stock of T. The T stock has a fair market value of $100x. B and C own 90% and 10%, respectively, of the stock of S. T sells all of its assets to S in exchange for $100x of cash and immediately liquidates. Because complete shareholder identity and proportionality of ownership in T and S does not exist, paragraph (*l*)(2)(i) of this section does not apply. The requirements of sections 368(a)(1)(D) and 354(b)(1)(B) are not satisfied, and the transaction does not qualify as a reorganization described in section 368(a)(1)(D).

* * *

(m) Qualification as a reorganization under section 368(a)(1)(F)—(1) Mere change. To qualify as a reorganization under section 368(a)(1)(F), a transaction must result in a mere change in identity, form, or place of organization of one corporation, however effected (a mere change). A mere change can consist of a transaction that involves an actual or deemed transfer of property from one corporation (a transferor corporation) to one other corporation (a resulting corporation). Such a transaction is a mere change and qualifies as a reorganization under section 368(a)(1)(F) only if all the requirements set forth in paragraphs (m)(1)(i) through (vi) of this section are satisfied. For purposes of this paragraph (m), a transaction or a series of related transactions that can be tested against the requirements set forth in paragraphs (m)(1)(i) through (vi) of this section (a potential F reorganization) begins when the transferor corporation begins transferring (or is deemed to begin transferring) its assets, directly or indirectly, to the resulting corporation, and it ends when the transferor corporation has distributed (or is deemed to have distributed) to its shareholders the consideration it receives (or is deemed to receive) from the resulting corporation and has completely liquidated for federal income tax purposes. For purposes of this paragraph (m), deemed transfers include, for example, those provided in § 301.7701–3(g)(1)(iv) of this chapter (when an entity disregarded as separate from its owner elects under paragraph § 301.7701–3(c)(1)(i) of this chapter to be classified as an association, the owner of the entity is deemed to transfer all of the assets and liabilities of the entity to the association in exchange for stock of the association). Deemed transfers also include those resulting from the application of step transaction principles. For example, step transaction principles may disregard a transitory holding of property by an individual after a liquidation of the transferor corporation and before a subsequent transfer of the transferor corporation's property to the resulting corporation. Step transaction principles may also treat a contribution of all the stock of the transferor corporation to the resulting corporation, followed by a liquidation (or deemed liquidation) of the transferor corporation, as a deemed transfer of the transferor corporation's property to the resulting corporation, followed by a distribution of stock of the resulting corporation in complete liquidation of the transferor corporation.

(i) Resulting corporation stock distributed in exchange for transferor corporation stock. Immediately after the potential F reorganization, all the stock of the resulting corporation, including any stock of the resulting corporation issued before the potential F reorganization, must have been distributed (or deemed distributed) in exchange for stock of the transferor corporation in the potential F reorganization. However, for purposes of this paragraph (m)(1)(i) and paragraph (m)(1)(ii) of this section, a de minimis amount of stock issued by the resulting corporation other than in respect of stock of the transferor corporation to facilitate the organization of the resulting corporation or maintain its legal existence is disregarded.

(ii) Identity of stock ownership. The same person or persons must own all of the stock of the transferor corporation, determined immediately before the potential F reorganization, and of the resulting corporation, determined immediately after the potential F reorganization, in identical proportions. However, this requirement is not violated if one or more holders of stock in the transferor corporation exchange stock in the transferor corporation for stock of equivalent value in the resulting corporation, but having different terms from those of the stock in the transferor corporation, or receive a distribution of money or other property from either the transferor corporation or the resulting corporation, whether or not in exchange for stock in the transferor corporation or the resulting corporation.

(iii) Prior assets or attributes of resulting corporation. The resulting corporation may not hold any property or have any tax attributes (including those specified in section 381(c)) immediately before the potential F reorganization. However, this requirement is not violated if the resulting corporation holds or has held a de minimis amount of assets to facilitate its organization or maintain its legal existence, and has tax attributes related to holding those assets, or holds the proceeds of borrowings undertaken in connection with the potential F reorganization.

(iv) Liquidation of transferor corporation. The transferor corporation must completely liquidate, for federal income tax purposes, in the potential F reorganization. However, the transferor corporation is not required to dissolve under applicable law and may retain a de minimis amount of assets for the sole purpose of preserving its legal existence.

(v) Resulting corporation is the only acquiring corporation. Immediately after the potential F reorganization, no corporation other than the resulting corporation may hold property that was held by the transferor corporation immediately before the potential F reorganization, if such other corporation would, as a result, succeed to and take into account the items of the transferor corporation described in section 381(c).

(vi) Transferor corporation is the only acquired corporation. Immediately after the potential F reorganization, the resulting corporation may not hold property acquired from a corporation other than the transferor corporation if the resulting corporation would, as a result, succeed to and take into account the items of such other corporation described in section 381(c).

(2) Non-application of continuity of interest and continuity of business enterprise requirements. A continuity of the business enterprise and a continuity of interest are not required for a potential F reorganization to qualify as a reorganization under section 368(a)(1)(F). *See* § 1.368–1(b).

(3) Related transactions—(i) Series of transactions. A potential F reorganization consisting of a series of related transactions that together result in a mere change of one corporation may qualify as a reorganization under section 368(a)(1)(F), whether or not certain steps in the series, viewed in isolation, could be subject to other Code provisions, such as sections 304(a), 331, 332, or 351. However, *see* paragraph (k) of this section for transactions that qualify as reorganizations under section 368(a) and will not be recharacterized as a mere change as a result of one or more subsequent transfers of assets or stock.

(ii) Mere change within a larger transaction. A potential F reorganization that qualifies as a reorganization under section 368(a)(1)(F) may occur before, within, or after other transactions that effect more than a mere change, even if the resulting corporation has only transitory existence. Related events that precede or follow the potential F reorganization generally will not cause that potential F reorganization to fail to qualify as a reorganization under section 368(a)(1)(F). Qualification of a potential F reorganization as a reorganization under section 368(a)(1)(F) will not alter the character of other transactions for federal income tax purposes, and step transaction principles may be applied to other transactions without regard to whether certain steps qualify as a reorganization or part of a reorganization under section 368(a)(1)(F).

(iii) Distributions treated as separate transactions. As provided in paragraph (m)(1)(ii) of this section, a potential F reorganization may qualify as a mere change even though a holder of stock in the transferor corporation receives a distribution of money or other property from either the transferor corporation or the resulting corporation. If a shareholder receives money or other property (including in exchange for its shares) from the transferor corporation or the resulting corporation in a potential F reorganization that qualifies as a reorganization under section 368(a)(1)(F), then the receipt of money or other property (including any exchanged for shares) is treated as an unrelated, separate transaction from the reorganization, whether or not connected in a formal sense. *See* § 1.301–1(*l*).

(iv) Transactions also qualifying under other provisions of section 368(a)(1). In certain cases, a potential F reorganization would (but for this paragraph (m)(3)(iv)) qualify both as a reorganization under section 368(a)(1)(F) and as a reorganization or part of a reorganization under another provision of section 368(a)(1). The following rules determine which of these overlapping qualifications applies.

(A) If the potential F reorganization or a step thereof qualifies as a reorganization or part of a reorganization under another provision of section 368(a)(1), and if a corporation in control (within the meaning of section 368(c)) of the resulting corporation is a party to such other reorganization (within the meaning of section 368(b)), the potential F reorganization will not qualify as a reorganization under section 368(a)(1)(F).

(B) Except as provided in paragraph (m)(3)(iv)(A) of this section, if, but for this paragraph (m)(3)(iv)(B), the potential F reorganization would qualify as a reorganization under both section 368(a)(1)(F) and one or more of sections 368(a)(1)(A), 368(a)(1)(C), or 368(a)(1)(D), then for all federal income tax purposes the potential F reorganization will qualify as a reorganization only under section 368(a)(1)(F).

(4) Examples. The following examples illustrate the application of this paragraph (m). Unless the facts otherwise indicate, A, B, and C are domestic individuals; P, S, T, X, Y, and Z (and similar designations) are domestic corporations; each transaction is entered into for a valid business purpose; all persons and transactions are unrelated; and all other relevant facts are set forth in the examples.

Example (1). Cash contribution and redemption—no mere change. C owns all of the stock of X, a State A corporation. The net value of X's assets and liabilities is $1,000,000. Y, a State B corporation, seeks to acquire the assets

of X for cash. To effect the acquisition, Y and X enter into an agreement under which Y will contribute $1,000,000 to Z, a newly formed corporation of which Y is the sole shareholder, in exchange for Z stock and X will merge into Z. In the merger, C surrenders all of the X stock and receives the $1,000,000 Y contributed to Z. C receives no Z stock in the transaction. After the merger, Y holds all of the Z stock, and Z holds all of the assets and liabilities previously held by X. Z stock is not distributed to the shareholders of X in exchange for their stock in X as required by paragraph (m)(1)(i) of this section, and the transaction results in a change in the ownership of X that does not result from an exchange or distribution described in paragraph (m)(1)(ii) of this section. Therefore, the merger of X into Z is not a mere change of X and does not qualify as a reorganization under section 368(a)(1)(F).

Example (2). Cash redemption—mere change. A owns 75%, and B owns 25%, of the stock of X, a State A corporation. The management of X determines that it would be in the best interest of X to reorganize under the laws of State B. Accordingly, X forms Y, a State B corporation, and X and Y enter into an agreement under which X will merge into Y. A does not wish to own stock in Y. In the merger, A surrenders A's X stock and receives cash, and B surrenders all of B's X stock and receives all the stock of Y. The change in ownership caused by A's surrender of X stock results from a distribution and exchange described in paragraph (m)(1)(ii) of this section. Therefore, the merger of X into Y is a mere change of X and qualifies as a reorganization under section 368(a)(1)(F). Under paragraph (m)(3)(iii) of this section, A's surrender of X stock for cash is treated as a transaction, separate from the reorganization, to which section 302(a) applies.

Example (3). Pre-transaction de minimis stock issuance—mere change—other provisions of section 368(a)(1). P owns all of the stock of S, a Country A corporation. The management of P determines that it would be in the best interest of S to change its place of incorporation to Country B. Under Country B law, a corporation must have at least two shareholders to enjoy limited liability. P is advised by its Country B advisors that the new corporation should issue 1% of its stock to a shareholder that is not P's nominee to assure satisfaction of the two-shareholder requirement. As part of an integrated plan, C, an officer of S, organizes Y, a Country B corporation with 1,000 shares of common stock authorized, and contributes cash to Y in exchange for ten of the common shares. S then merges into Y under the laws of Country A and Country B. Pursuant to the plan of merger, P surrenders its shares of S stock and receives 990 shares of Y common stock. The ten shares of Y stock issued to C not in respect of the S stock are de minimis and are used to facilitate the organization of Y within the meaning of paragraph (m)(1)(i) of this section. Therefore, the issuance of this stock to a new shareholder does not prevent the merger of S into Y from qualifying as a mere change of S. Accordingly, the merger is a reorganization under section 368(a)(1)(F). Without regard to the merger's qualification under section 368(a)(1)(F), the merger would also qualify as a reorganization under both section 368(a)(1)(A) and section 368(a)(1)(D). Under paragraph (m)(3)(iv)(B) of this section, if a potential F reorganization qualifies as a reorganization under section 368(a)(1)(F), and would also qualify under one or more of sections 368(a)(1)(A) or 368(a)(1)(D), the potential F reorganization qualifies only as a reorganization under 368(a)(1)(F), and neither section 368(a)(1)(A) nor section 368(a)(1)(D) will apply.

Example (4). Pre-transaction assets, attributes—no mere change. A owns all of the stock of P, and P owns all of the stock of S, which is engaged in a manufacturing business. P has owned the stock of S for many years. P owns no assets other than the stock of S. A decides to eliminate the holding company structure by merging P into S. Because it operates a manufacturing business, the potential resulting corporation, S, holds property and has tax attributes immediately before the potential F reorganization. Therefore, under paragraph (m)(1)(iii) of this section, the merger of P into S is not a mere change of P and does not qualify as a reorganization under section 368(a)(1)(F). The same result would occur under paragraph (m)(1)(iii) of this section if, instead of P merging into S, S merged into P, because P, the potential resulting corporation, holds property (the stock of S) and has tax attributes immediately before the potential F reorganization.

Example (5). Series of related transactions—mere change. P owns all of the stock of S1, a State A corporation. The management of P determines that it would be in the best interest of S1 to change its place of incorporation to State B. Accordingly, under an integrated plan, P forms S2, a new State B corporation; P contributes the S1 stock to S2; and S1 merges into S2 under the laws of State A and State B. Under paragraph (m)(3)(i) of this section, a series of transactions that together result in a mere change of one corporation may qualify as a reorganization under section 368(a)(1)(F). The contribution of S1 stock to S2 and the merger of S1 into S2 together constitute a mere change of S1. Therefore, the potential F reorganization qualifies as a reorganization under section 368(a)(1)(F). Without regard to its qualification under section 368(a)(1)(F), the potential F reorganization would also qualify as a reorganization under both section 368(a)(1)(A) and section 368(a)(1)(D). Under paragraph (m)(3)(iv)(B) of this section, if a potential F reorganization qualifies as a reorganization under section 368(a)(1)(F) and would also qualify under one or more of sections 368(a)(1)(A) or 368(a)(1)(D), it qualifies only as a reorganization under 368(a)(1)(F), and neither section 368(a)(1)(A) nor section 368(a)(1)(D) will apply. The result would be the same with respect to qualification under section 368(a)(1)(F) if, instead of merging into S2, S1 completely liquidates or is deemed to liquidate by reason of a conversion into an entity disregarded as separate from its owner under § 301.7701–3(g)(1)(iii) of this chapter.

Example (6). Post-transaction stock sale— mere change. P owns all of the stock of S1, a State A corporation. The management of P determines that it would be in the best interest of S1 to change its place of incorporation to State B. Accordingly, P forms S2, a new State B corporation. S1 then merges into S2 under the laws of State A and State B. Immediately thereafter, and as part of the same plan, P sells all of its stock in S2 to an unrelated party. Without regard to P's sale of S2 stock, the merger of S1 into S2 is a potential F reorganization that qualifies as a mere change of S1 within the meaning of paragraph (m)(1) of this section. Under paragraph (m)(3)(ii) of this section, related events that occur before or after a potential F reorganization that qualifies as a mere change generally do not cause that potential F reorganization to fail to qualify as a reorganization under section 368(a)(1)(F). Therefore, P's sale of the S2 stock is disregarded in determining whether the merger of S1 into S2 is a mere change of S1. Accordingly, the merger of S1 into S2 qualifies as a reorganization under section 368(a)(1)(F). The result would be the same if, instead of the S2 stock being sold by P, S2 merges into a previously unrelated corporation and terminates its separate existence.

Example (7). Post-transaction redemption—mere change. A owns all of the stock of T. P owns all of the stock of S. Each of T, P, and S is a State A corporation engaged in a manufacturing business. The following transactions occur pursuant to a single plan. First, T merges into S with A receiving solely stock in P. Second, P changes its state of incorporation to State B by merging into newly incorporated New P under the laws of State A and State B. Third, New P redeems all the New P stock issued to A in respect of A's P stock (initially issued to A in respect of A's T stock) for cash. Without regard to the other steps, the merger of P into New P is a potential F reorganization that qualifies as a reorganization under section 368(a)(1)(F). Under paragraph (m)(3)(ii) of this section, related events that occur before or after a potential F reorganization that qualifies as a mere change generally do not prevent that potential F reorganization from qualifying as a reorganization under section 368(a)(1)(F). Therefore, the merger of P into New P qualifies as a reorganization under section 368(a)(1) (F). Under paragraph (m)(3)(ii) of this section, the qualification of the merger of P into New P as a reorganization under section 368(a)(1)(F) does not alter the tax treatment of the merger of T into S. Because the P shares received by A in respect of the T shares (exchanged for New P shares in the mere change of P into New P) are redeemed for cash pursuant to the plan, the merger of T into S does not satisfy the continuity of interest requirement of § 1.368–1(e) and therefore does not qualify as a reorganization under section 368(a).

Example (8). Series of related transactions—mere change. P owns all of the stock of S, a State A corporation. The management of P determines that it would be in the best interest of S to change its form from a State A corporation to a State A limited partnership but to continue to be treated as a corporation for federal tax purposes. Accordingly, P contributes 1% of the S stock to newly formed LLC, a limited liability company, in exchange for all of the membership interests in LLC. P is the sole member of LLC. Under § 301.7701–3 of this chapter, LLC is disregarded as an entity separate from its owner, P. Then, under a State A statute, S converts to a State A limited partnership. In the conversion, P's interest as a 99% shareholder of S is converted into a 99% limited partner interest, and LLC's interest as a 1% shareholder of S is converted into a 1% general partner interest. S also elects, under § 301.7701–3(c) of this chapter, to be classified as a corporation for federal income tax purposes, effective on the same day as the conversion. Under paragraph (m)(3)(i) of this section, the conversion of S from a State A corporation to a State A limited partnership, together with the election to treat S as a corporation for federal tax purposes, results in a mere change of S and qualifies as a reorganization under section 368(a)(1)(F).

Example (9). Other acquiring corporation—no mere change. P owns 80%, and A owns 20%, of the stock of S. A and the management of P determine that it would be in the best interest of S to completely liquidate while A continues to operate part of the business of S in corporate form. Accordingly, S distributes 80% of its assets to P and 20% of its assets to A; S dissolves; and A contributes the assets it receives from S to newly incorporated New S in exchange for all of the stock of New S. S's distribution of 80% of its property to P as part of the complete liquidation of S meets the requirements of section 332. Thus, section 381(a)(1) applies to P's acquisition of 80% of the property held by S immediately before the transaction. Under paragraph (m)(1)(v) of this section, the potential F reorganization in which 20% of the property held by S immediately before the transaction is transferred to New S cannot be a mere change of S, because section 381(a) applies to P's acquisition of property held by S immediately before the potential F reorganization. Accordingly, sections 331 and 336 apply to A's acquisition of property from S and S's distribution of property to A, and section 351 applies to A's contribution of that property to New S.

Example (10). Other acquiring corporation—no mere change. P owns all of the stock of S1. The management of P determines that it would be in the best interest of S1 to merge S1 into P. Accordingly, pursuant to a state merger statute, S1 merges into P. Immediately afterward and as part of the same plan, P contributes 50% of the former assets of S1 to newly incorporated S2 in exchange for all of the stock of S2. The transaction does not qualify as a complete liquidation of S1 under section 332 (because of the reincorporation of some of S1's assets) but does qualify as a reorganization under section 368(a)(1)(A) by reason of section 368(a)(2)(C) and paragraph (k) of this section. Under paragraph (m)(1)(v) of this section, the potential F reorganization in which some of the former assets of S1 are transferred (in form) first to P, and then to S2, is not a mere

change of S1, because section 381(a) applies to P's acquisition of property held by S1 immediately before the potential F reorganization. Furthermore, under paragraph (m)(3)(iv)(A) of this section, P, the corporation in control of S2 within the meaning of section 368(c), is a party to the reorganization within the meaning of section 368(b). Thus, the indirect transfer of property from S1 to S2 does not qualify under section 368(a)(1)(F).

Example (11). Other acquiring corporation—mere change. P owns all of the stock of S1. S1's only asset is all of the equity interest in LLC2, a domestic limited liability company. Under § 301.7701–3 of this chapter, LLC2 is disregarded as an entity separate from its owner, S1. Pursuant to an integrated plan to undergo a reorganization under 368(a)(1)(F), S1 and LLC2 undergo the following two state law conversions. First, under state law LLC2 converts into S2, a corporation. Second, under state law S1 converts into LLC1, a domestic limited liability company. Under § 301.7701–3 of this chapter, LLC1 is disregarded as an entity separate from its owner, P. As a result of the two conversions, S1 is deemed to transfer its assets to S2 in exchange for all of the stock in S2 and then distribute the S2 stock to P in complete liquidation of S1. The two conversions, viewed as a potential F reorganization, constitute a mere change of S1, and that potential F reorganization qualifies as a reorganization under section 368(a)(1)(F). The result would be the same if, instead of converting into S2 pursuant to state law, LLC2 elected under § 301.7701–3(c) to change its classification for federal tax purposes and be treated as an association taxable as a corporation, provided the effective date of the election (and its resulting deemed transactions) occurs before the conversion of S1.

Example (12). Other acquiring corporation—no mere change. The facts are the same facts as in *Example 11*, except that S1 converts into LLC1 prior to the conversion of LLC2 into S2. As a result of these conversions, S1 is deemed to distribute all of its assets to P in exchange for all of P's S1 stock, and P is deemed to transfer all of those assets to S2 in exchange for all of the stock in S2. The transaction does not qualify as a complete liquidation of S1 under section 332 (because of the reincorporation of S1's assets), but does qualify as a reorganization under section 368(a)(1)(C) by reason of section 368(a)(2)(C) and paragraph (k) of this section. Under paragraph (m)(1)(v) of this section, the potential F reorganization in which the former assets of S1 are deemed transferred, first by S1 to P, and then by P to S2, is not a mere change of S1 because section 381(a) applies to P's acquisition of property held by S1 immediately before the potential F reorganization. Furthermore, the corporation in control of S2, within the meaning of section 368(c), is a party to the reorganization within the meaning of section 368(b). Thus, the indirect transfer of property from S1 to S2 does not qualify under section 368(a)(1)(F).

Example (13). Series of related transactions—no mere change. X owns all of the stock of T. P acquires all of the stock of T in exchange for consideration consisting of $50 cash and P voting stock with $50 value. No election is made under section 338. Immediately thereafter and as part of the same plan, P forms S as a wholly-owned subsidiary, and T is merged into S. Viewed in isolation as a potential F reorganization, the merger of T into S appears to constitute a mere change of T. However, the acquisition of the T stock by P and the merger of T into S, viewed together, qualify as a reorganization under section 368(a)(1)(A) by reason of section 368(a)(2)(D). The step transaction doctrine is applied treat the transaction as a statutory merger of T into S in exchange for $50 cash and $50 of P's voting stock (and S's assumption of T's liabilities), P's momentary ownership of T stock is disregarded. Under paragraph (m)(3)(iv)(A) of this section, P, the corporation in control of S, is a party to the reorganization within the meaning of section 368(b). Thus, the transfer of property from T to S does not qualify under section 368(a)(1) (F).

Example (14). Multiple transferor corporations—no mere change. P owns all the stock of S1 and S2. The management of P determines it would be in the best interest of S1 and S2 to operate as a single corporation. P forms S3 and, under applicable corporate law, S1 and S2 simultaneously merge into S3. Immediately after the merger, P owns all the stock of S3. Each of the mergers can be tested as a potential F reorganization. However, immediately after the simultaneous mergers. the resulting corporation, S3, holds property acquired from a corporation other than the transferor corporation, and section 381(a) would apply to the acquisition of such property. Therefore, under paragraph (m)(1)(vi) of this section, neither potential F reorganization is a mere change, and neither merger into S3 qualifies as a reorganization under section 386(a)(1)(F). The result would be different if the mergers were not simultaneous. If S1 completed its merger into S3 before S2 began its merger into S3, the merger of S1 into S3 would qualify as a reorganization under section 368(a)(1)(F), but the merger of S2 into S3 would not so qualify (although it would qualify as a reorganization under sections 368(a)(1)(A) and 368(a)(1)(D)).

* * *

§ 1.381(a)–1 General rule relating to carryovers in certain corporate acquisitions.

(a) Allowance of carryovers. Section 381 provides that a corporation which acquires the assets of another corporation in certain liquidations and reorganizations shall succeed to, and take into account, as of the close of the date of distribution or transfer, the items described in section 381(c) of the distributor or transferor corporation. These items shall be taken into account by the acquiring corporation subject to the conditions and limitations specified in sections 381, 382(b), and 383 and the regulations thereunder.

(b) Determination of transactions and items to which section 381 applies—(1) Qualified transactions. The items described in section 381(c) are required by section 381 to be carried over to the acquiring corporation (as defined in subparagraph (2) of this paragraph) only in the following liquidations and reorganizations:

(i) The complete liquidation of a subsidiary corporation upon which no gain or loss is recognized in accordance with the provisions of section 332;

(ii) A statutory merger or consolidation qualifying under section 368(a)(1)(A) to which section 361 applies;

(iii) A reorganization qualifying under section 368(a)(1)(C);

(iv) A reorganization qualifying under section 368(a)(1)(D) if the requirements of section 354(b)(1)(A) and (B) are satisfied; and

(v) A mere change in identity, form, or place of organization qualifying under section 368(a)(1)(F).

(2) Acquiring corporation defined. (i) Only a single corporation may be an acquiring corporation for purposes of section 381 and the regulations thereunder. The corporation which acquires the assets of its subsidiary corporation in a complete liquidation to which section 381(a)(1) applies is the acquiring corporation for purposes of section 381. In a transaction to which section 381(a)(2) applies, the acquiring corporation is the corporation that, pursuant to the plan of reorganization, directly acquires the assets transferred by the transferor corporation, even if that corporation ultimately retains none of the assets so transferred.

(ii) The application of this subparagraph may be illustrated by the following examples:

Example (1). Y Corporation, a wholly-owned subsidiary of X Corporation, directly acquired all the assets of Z Corporation solely in exchange for voting stock of X Corporation in a transaction qualifying under section 368(a)(1)(C). Y Corporation is the acquiring corporation for purposes of section 381.

Example (2). X Corporation acquired all the assets of Z Corporation solely in exchange for voting stock of X Corporation in a transaction qualifying under section 368(a)(1)(C). Thereafter, pursuant to the plan of reorganization X Corporation transferred all the assets so acquired to Y Corporation, its wholly-owned subsidiary (see section 368(a)(2)(C)). X Corporation is the acquiring corporation for purposes of section 381.

Example (3). X Corporation acquired all the assets of Z Corporation solely in exchange for the voting stock of X Corporation in a transaction qualifying under section 368(a)(1)(C). Thereafter, pursuant to the plan of reorganization X Corporation transferred one-half of the assets so acquired to Y Corporation, its wholly-owned subsidiary, and retained the other half of such assets. X Corporation is the acquiring corporation for purposes of section 381.

Example (4). X Corporation acquired all the assets of Z Corporation solely in exchange for voting stock of X Corporation in a transaction qualifying under section 368(a)(1)(C). Thereafter, pursuant to the plan of reorganization X Corporation transferred one-half of the assets so acquired to Y Corporation, its wholly-owned subsidiary, and the other half of such assets to M Corporation, another wholly-owned subsidiary of X Corporation. X Corporation is the acquiring corporation for purposes of section 381.

(3) Transactions and items not covered by section 381. Section 381 does not apply to partial liquidations, divisive reorganizations, or other transactions not described in subparagraph (1) of this paragraph. Moreover, section 381 does not apply to the carryover of an item or tax attribute not specified in subsection (c) thereof. In a case where section 381 does not apply to a transaction, item, or tax attribute by reason of either of the preceding sentences, no inference is to be drawn from the provisions of section 381 as to whether any item or tax attribute shall be taken into account by the successor corporation.

* * *

§ 1.381(b)–1 Operating rules applicable to carryovers in certain corporate acquisitions.

(a) Closing of taxable year — (1) In general. Except in the case of certain reorganizations qualifying under section 368(a)(1)(F), the taxable year of the distributor or transferor corporation shall end with the close of the date of distribution or transfer. With regard to the closing of the taxable year of the transferor corporation in certain reorganizations under section 368(a)(1)(F) involving a foreign corporation after December 31, 1986, see §§ 1.367(a)–1T(e) and 1.367(b)–2(f).

(2) Reorganizations under section 368(a) (1)(F). In the case of a reorganization qualifying under section 368(a)(1)(F) (whether or not such reorganization also qualifies under any other provision of section 368(a)(1)), the acquiring corporation shall be treated (for purposes of section 381) just as the transferor corporation would have been treated if there had been no reorganization. Thus, the taxable year of the transferor corporation shall not end on the date of transfer merely because of the transfer; a net operating loss of the acquiring corporation for any taxable year ending after the date of transfer shall be carried back in accordance with section 172(b) in computing the taxable income of the transferor corporation for a taxable year ending before the date of transfer; and the tax attributes of the transferor corporation enumerated in section 381(c) shall be taken into account by the acquiring corporation as if there had been no reorganization.

(b) Date of distribution or transfer. (1) The date of distribution or transfer shall be that day on which are distributed or transferred all those properties of the distributor or transferor corporation which are to be distributed or transferred pursuant to a liquidation or reorganization described in paragraph (b)(1) of § 1.381(a)–1. If the distribution or transfer of all such properties is not made on one day, then, except as provided in subparagraph (2) of this paragraph, the date of distribution or transfer shall be that day on which the distribution or transfer of all such properties is completed.

(2) If the distributor or transferor and acquiring corporations file the statements described in subparagraph (3) of this paragraph, the date of distribution or transfer shall be that day as of which (i) substantially all of the properties to be distributed or transferred have been distributed or transferred, and (ii) the distributor or transferor corporation has ceased all operations (other than liquidating activities). Such day also shall be the date of distribution or transfer if the completion of the distribution or transfer is unreasonably postponed beyond the date as of which substantially all the properties to be distributed or transferred have been distributed or transferred and the distributor or transferor corporation has ceased all operations other than liquidating activities. A corporation shall be considered to have distributed or transferred substantially all of its properties to be distributed or transferred even though it retains money or other property in a reasonable amount to pay outstanding debts or preserve the corporation's legal existence. A corporation shall be considered to have ceased all operations, other than liquidating activities, when it ceases to be a going concern and its activities are merely for the purpose of winding up its affairs, paying its debts, and distributing any remaining balance of its money or other properties to its shareholders.

* * *

(4) If—

(i) The last day of the acquiring corporation's taxable year is a Saturday, Sunday, or legal holiday, and

(ii) The day specified in subparagraph (1) or (2) of this paragraph as the date of distribution or transfer is the last business day before such Saturday, Sunday, or holiday,

then the last day of the acquiring corporation's taxable year shall be the date of distribution or transfer for purposes of section 381(b) and this section. For purposes of this subparagraph, the term business day means a day which is not a Saturday, Sunday, or legal holiday, and also means a Saturday, Sunday, or legal holiday if the date of distribution or transfer determined under subparagraph (1) or (2) of this paragraph is such Saturday, Sunday, or holiday.

(c) Return of distributor or transferor corporation. The distributor or transferor corporation shall file an income tax return for the taxable year ending with the date of distribution or transfer described in paragraph (b) of this section. If the distributor or transferor corporation remains in existence after such date of distribution or transfer, it shall file an income tax return for the taxable year beginning on the day following the date of distribution or transfer and ending with the date on which the distributor or transferor corporation's taxable year would have ended if there had been no distribution or transfer.

(d) Carryback of net operating losses. For provisions relating to the carryback of net operating losses of the acquiring corporation, see paragraph (b) of § 1.381(c)(1)–1.

* * *

§ 1.381(c)(1)–1 Net operating loss carryovers in certain corporate acquisitions.

(a) Carryover requirement. (1) Section 381(c)(1) requires the acquiring corporation to succeed to, and take into account, the net operating loss carryovers of the distributor or transferor corporation. To determine the amount of these carryovers as of the close of the date of distribution or transfer, and to integrate them with any carryovers and carrybacks of the acquiring corporation for purposes of determining the taxable income of the acquiring corporation for taxable years ending after

the date of distribution or transfer, it is necessary to apply the provisions of section 172 in accordance with the conditions and limitations of section 381(c)(1) and this section. See also section 382(b) and the regulations thereunder.

(2) The net operating loss carryovers and carrybacks of the acquiring corporation determined as of the close of the date of distribution or transfer shall be computed without reference to any net operating loss of a distributor or transferor corporation. The net operating loss carryovers of a distributor or transferor corporation as of the close of the date of distribution or transfer shall be determined without reference to any net operating loss of the acquiring corporation.

(3) For purposes of the tax imposed under section 56, the acquiring corporation succeeding to and taking into account any net operating loss carryovers of the distributor or transferor corporation shall also succeed to and take into account along with such net operating loss carryforward any deferred tax liability under section 56(b) and the regulations thereunder attributable to such net operating loss carryover.

(b) Carryback of net operating losses. A net operating loss of the acquiring corporation for any taxable year ending after the date of distribution or transfer shall not be carried back in computing the taxable income of a distributor or transferor corporation. However, a net operating loss of the acquiring corporation for any such taxable year shall be carried back in accordance with section 172(b) in computing the taxable income of the acquiring corporation for a taxable year ending on or before the date of distribution or transfer. If a distributor or transferor corporation remains in existence after the date of distribution or transfer, a net operating loss sustained by it for any taxable year beginning after such date shall be carried back in accordance with section 172(b) in computing the taxable income of such corporation for a taxable year ending on or before that date, but may not be carried back or over in computing the taxable income of the acquiring corporation. This paragraph may be illustrated by the following examples:

Example (1). On December 31, 1954, X Corporation merged into Y Corporation in a statutory merger to which section 361 applies, and the charter of Y Corporation continued after the merger. Y Corporation sustained a net operating loss for the calendar year 1955. Y Corporation's net operating loss for 1955 may not be carried back in computing the taxable income of X Corporation but shall be carried back in computing the taxable income of Y Corporation.

Example (2). On December 31, 1954, X Corporation and Y Corporation transferred all their assets to Z Corporation in a statutory consolidation to which section 361 applies. Z Corporation sustained a net operating loss for the calendar year 1955. Z Corporation's net operating loss for 1955 may not be carried back in computing the taxable income of X Corporation or Y Corporation.

Example (3). On December 31, 1954, X Corporation ceased all operations (other than liquidating activities) and transferred substantially all its properties to Y Corporation in a reorganization qualifying under section 368(a)(1)(C). Such properties comprised all of X Corporation's properties which were to be transferred pursuant to the reorganization. In the process of liquidating its assets and winding up its affairs, X Corporation sustained a net operating loss for its taxable year beginning on January 1, 1955. This net operating loss of X Corporation shall be carried back in computing the taxable income of that corporation but may not be carried back or over in computing the taxable income of Y Corporation.

(c) First taxable year to which carryovers apply. (1) The net operating loss carryovers available to the distributor or transferor corporation as of the close of the date of distribution or transfer shall first be carried to the first taxable year of the acquiring corporation ending after that date. This rule applies irrespective of whether the date of distribution or transfer is on the last day, or any other day, of the acquiring corporation's taxable year. Thus, such net operating loss carryovers shall first be used by the acquiring corporation with respect to the computation of its net operating loss deduction under section 172(a), and its taxable income determined under the provisions of section 172(b)(2), for such first taxable year. However, see paragraph (f) of this section.

(2) The net operating loss carryovers available to the distributor or transferor corporation as of the close of the date of distribution or transfer shall be carried to the acquiring corporation without diminution by reason of the fact that the acquiring corporation does not acquire 100 percent of the assets of the distributor or transferor corporation. Thus, if a parent corporation owning 80 percent of all classes of stock of its subsidiary corporation were to acquire its share of the assets of the subsidiary corporation upon a complete liquidation described in paragraph (b)(1)(i) of § 1.381(a)–1, then, subject to the conditions and limitations of this section, 100 percent of the net operating loss carryovers available to the subsidiary corporation as of the close of the date of distribution would be carried over to the parent corporation.

(d) Limitation on net operating loss deduction for first taxable year ending after date of distribution or transfer. (1) That part of the acquiring corporation's net operating loss deduction, determined in accordance with sections 172(a) and 381(c)(1), for its first taxable year ending after the date of distribution or transfer which is attributable to the net operating loss carryovers of the distributor or transferor corporation, is limited by section 381(c)(1)(B) and this paragraph to an amount equal to the acquiring corporation's postacquisition part year taxable income. Such postacquisition part year taxable income is the amount which bears the same ratio to the acquiring corporation's taxable income for the first taxable year ending after the date of distribution or transfer (determined under section 63 without regard to any net operating loss deduction but taking into account other items to which the acquiring corporation succeeds under section 381) as the number of days in such first taxable year which follow the date of distribution or transfer bears to the total number of days in such taxable year. Thus, if the date of distribution or transfer is the last day of the acquiring corporation's taxable year, the net operating loss carryovers of the distributor or transferor are allowed in full in computing under section 172(a) the net operating loss deduction of the acquiring corporation for its first taxable year ending after that date. In such instance, the number of days in the first taxable year which follow the date of distribution or transfer is the total number of days in such taxable year.

(2) The limitation provided by section 381(c)(1)(B) applies solely for the purpose of computing the net operating loss deduction of the acquiring corporation under section 172(a) for the acquiring corporation's first taxable year ending after the date of distribution or transfer. The limitation does not apply for purposes of determining the portion of any net operating loss (whether of the distributor, transferor, or acquiring corporation) which may be carried to any taxable year of the acquiring corporation following its first taxable year ending after the date of distribution or transfer since such determination is made pursuant to section 172(b) and section 381(c)(1)(C). See paragraphs (e) and (f) of this section.

(3) The limitation provided by section 381(c)(1)(B) shall be applied to the aggregate of the allowable net operating loss carryovers of the distributor or transferor corporation without reference to the taxable years in which the net operating losses were sustained by such corporation. If the acquiring corporation has acquired the assets of two or more distributor or transferor corporations on the same date of distribution or transfer, then the limitation provided by section 381(c)(1)(B) shall be applied to the aggregate of the net operating loss carry-

overs from all of such distributor or transferor corporations.

* * *

(5) Illustrations. The application of this paragraph may be illustrated by the following examples:

Example (1). *(i)* X Corporation and Y Corporation were organized on January 1, 1956, and make their returns on the calendar year basis. On December 16, 1957, X Corporation transferred all its assets to Y Corporation in a statutory merger to which section 361 applies. The net operating losses and taxable income (computed without the net operating loss deduction) of the two corporations are as follows, the assumption being made that none of the modifications specified in section 172(b)(2)(A) apply to any taxable year:

Taxable	X Corporation (transferor)	Y Corporation (acquirer)
1956	($35,000)	($5,000)
Ending 12–16–57	(30,000)	xxx
1957	xxx	36,500

(ii) The aggregate of the net operating loss carryovers of X Corporation carried under section 381(c)(1)(A) to Y Corporation's taxable year ending December 31, 1957, is $65,000; but pursuant to section 381(c)(1)(B), only $1,500 of such aggregate amount ($36,500 × 15/365) may be used in computing the net operating loss deduction of Y Corporation for such taxable year under section 172(a). This limitation applies even though Y Corporation's own net operating loss carryover to such year is only $5,000, with the result that Y Corporation has taxable income under section 63 of $30,000 for its taxable year ending December 31, 1957, that is, $36,500 less the sum of $5,000 and $1,500.

(iii) For rules determining the portion of any given loss of X Corporation or Y Corporation which may be carried to a taxable year of Y Corporation following its taxable year ending December 31, 1957, see sections 172(b)

(2) and 381(c)(1)(C) and paragraph (f) of this section.

Example (2). *(i)* X Corporation was organized on January 1, 1954, and Y Corporation was organized on January 1, 1956. Each corporation makes its return on the basis of the calendar year. On December 31, 1956, X Corporation transferred all its assets to Y Corporation in a statutory merger to which section 361 applies. The net operating losses and the taxable income (computed without any net operating loss deduction) of the two corporations are as follows, the assumption being made that none of the modifications specified in section 172(b)(2)(A) apply to any taxable year:

Taxable	X Corporation (transferor)	Y Corporation (acquirer)
1954	($5,000)	xxx
1955	(15,000)	xxx
1956	(10,000)	$20,000
1957	xxx	40,000

(ii) The aggregate of the net operating loss carryovers of X Corporation carried under section 381(c)(1)(A) to Y Corporation's taxable year 1957 is $30,000, and the full amount of such carryovers is allowed in such taxable year to Y Corporation as a deduction under section 172(a), since such amount does not exceed the limitation ($40,000 × 365/365) for such taxable year under section 381(c)(1)(B).

Example (3). *(i)* X Corporation, Y Corporation, and Z Corporation were organized on January 1, 1954, and each corporation makes its return on the basis of the calendar year. On September 30, 1956, X Corporation and Y Corporation transferred all their assets to Z Corporation in a statutory merger to which section 361 applies. The net operating losses and the taxable income (computed without any net operating loss deduction) of the three corporations are as follows, the assumption being made that none of the modifications specified in section 172(b)(2)(A) apply to any taxable year:

Taxable year	X Corporation (transferor)	Y Corporation (transferor)	Z Corporation (acquirer)
1954	($5,000)	($3,000)	($40,000)
1955	(4,000)	(2,000)	10,000
Ending 9–30–56	(1,000)	(9,000)	xxx
1956	xxx	xxx	73,200

(ii) The aggregate of the net operating loss carryovers of X Corporation and Y Corporation carried under section 381(c)(1)(A) to Z Corporation's taxable year 1956 is $24,000; but, pursuant to section 381(c)(1)(B), only $18,400 of such aggregate amount ($73,200 × 92/366) may be used in computing the net operating loss deduction of Z Corporation for such taxable year under section 172(a). For this purpose, Z Corporation may not use the total of the aggregate carryovers ($10,000) from X Corporation plus the aggregate carryovers ($14,000) from Y Corporation, even though each such aggregate of carryovers is separately less than the limitation ($18,400) applicable under section 381(c)(1)(B) and this section.

(iii) For rules determining the portion of any given loss of X Corporation, Y Corporation, or Z Corporation which may be carried to a taxable year of Z Corporation following its taxable year ending December 31, 1956, see sections 172(b)(2) and 381(c)(1)(C) and paragraph (f) of this section.

(e) Computation of carryovers and carrybacks; general rule—(1) Sequence for applying losses and computation of taxable income. The portion of any net operating loss which is carried back or carried over to any taxable year is the excess, if any, of the amount of the loss over the sum of the taxable income for each of the prior taxable years to which the loss may be carried under sections 172(b)(1) and 381. In determining the taxable income for each such prior taxable year for this purpose, the various net operating loss carryovers and carrybacks to such prior taxable year are considered to be applied in reduction of the taxable income in the order of the taxable years in which the net operating losses are sustained, beginning with the loss for the earliest taxable year. The application of this rule to the taxable income of the acquiring corporation for any taxable year ending after the date of distribution or transfer involves the use of carryovers of the distributor or transfer corporation, and of carryovers and carrybacks of the acquiring corporation. In such instance, the sequence for the use of loss years remains the same, and the requirement is to begin with the net operating loss of the earliest taxable year, whether or not it is a loss of the distributor, transferor, or acquiring corporation. The taxable income of the acquiring corporation for any taxable year ending after the date of distribution or transfer shall be determined in the manner prescribed by section 172(b)(2), except that, if the date of distribution or transfer is on a day other than the last day of a taxable year of the acquiring corporation, the taxable income of such corporation for the taxable year which includes such date shall be computed in the special manner prescribed by section 381(c)(1)(C) and paragraph (f) of this section.

(2) Loss year of transferor or distributor considered prior taxable year. Section 381(c)(1)(C) provides that, for the purpose of determining the net operating loss carryovers under section 172(b)(2), a net operating loss for a loss year of a distributor or transferor corporation which ends on or before the last day of a loss year of the acquiring corporation shall be considered to be a net operating loss for a year prior to such loss year of the acquiring corporation. In a case where the acquiring corporation has acquired the assets of two or more distributor or transferor corporations on the same date of distribution or transfer, the loss years of the distributor or transferor corporations shall be taken into account in the order in which such loss years terminate; if any one of the loss years of a distributor or transferor corporation ends on the same day as the loss year of another distributor or transferor corporation, either loss year may be taken into account before the other.

(3) Years to which losses may be carried. The taxable years to which a net operating loss shall be carried back or carried over are prescribed by section 172(b)(1). Since the taxable year of the distributor or transferor corporation ends with the close of the date of distribution or transfer, such taxable year and the first taxable year of the acquiring corporation which ends after that date shall be considered two separate taxable years to which a net operating loss of the distributor or transferor corporation for any taxable year ending before that date may be carried over. This rule applies even though the taxable year of the distributor or transferor corporation which ends on the date of distribution or transfer is a period of less than twelve months. However, for the purpose of determining under section 172(b)(1) the taxable years to which a net operating loss of the acquiring corporation is carried over or carried back, the first taxable year of the acquiring corporation which ends after the date of distribution or transfer shall be treated as only one taxable year even though such taxable year is considered under section 381(c)(1)(C) and paragraph (f)(2) of this section as two taxable years. The application of this subparagraph may be illustrated by the following example:

Example. X Corporation was organized on January 1, 1954, and thereafter it sustained net operating losses in its calendar years 1954, 1955, and 1956. On June 30, 1957, X Corporation transferred all its assets to Y Corporation, which was organized on January 1, 1955, in a statutory merger to which section 361 applies. In its taxable year ending June 30, 1957, X Corporation sustained a net operating loss. Y Corporation sustained net operating losses in its calendar years 1955, 1956, and 1958, but had taxable income for the year 1957. The years to which these losses of X Corporation and Y Corporation shall be carried, and the sequence in which carried, are as follows:

Loss year	
X 1954	X 1955, X 1956, X 6/30/57, Y 1957, Y 1958.
X 1955	X 1954, X 1956, X 6/30/57, Y 1957, Y 1958, Y 1959.
Y 1955	Y 1956, Y 1957, Y 1958, Y 1959, Y 1960.
X 1956	X 1954, X 1955, X 6/30/57, Y 1957, Y 1958, Y 1959, Y 1960.
Y 1956	Y 1955, Y 1957, Y 1958, Y 1959, Y 1960, Y 1961.
X 6–30–57	X 1955, X 1956, Y 1957, Y 1958, Y 1959, Y 1960, Y 1961.
Y 1958	Y 1955, Y 1956, Y 1957, Y 1959, Y 1960, Y 1961, Y 1962, Y 1963.

* * *

§ 1.381(c)(2)–1 Earnings and profits.

(a) **In general.** (1) Section 381(c)(2) requires the acquiring corporation in a transaction to which section 381(a) applies to succeed to, and take into account, the earnings and profits, or deficit in earnings and profits, of the distributor or transferor corporation as of the close of the date of distribution or transfer. In determining the amount of such earnings and profits, or deficit, to be carried over, and the manner in which they are to be used by the acquiring corporation after such date, the provisions of section 381(c)(2) and this section shall apply. For purposes of section 381(c)(2) and this section, if the distributor or transferor corporation accumulates earnings and profits, or incurs a deficit in earnings and profits, after the date of distribution or transfer and before the completion of the reorganization or liquidation, such earnings and profits, or deficit, shall be deemed to have been accumulated or incurred as of the close of the date of distribution or transfer.

(2) If the distributor or transferor corporation has accumulated earnings and profits as of the close of the date of distribution or transfer, such earnings and profits shall (except as hereinafter provided in this section) be deemed to be received by, and to become a part of the accumulated earnings and profits of, the acquiring corporation as of such time. Similarly, if the distributor or transferor corporation has a deficit in accumulated earnings and profits as of the close of the date of distribution or transfer, such deficit shall (except as hereinafter provided in this section) be deemed to be incurred by the acquiring corporation as of such time. In no event, however, shall the accumulated earnings and profits, or deficit, of the distribution or transferor corporation be taken into account in determining earnings and profits of the acquiring corporation for the taxable year during which occurs the date of distribution or transfer.

* * *

(4) If the acquiring corporation and each distributor or transferor corporation has accumulated earnings and profits as of the close of the date of distribution or transfer, or if each of such corporations has a deficit in accumulated earnings and profits as of such time, then the accumulated earnings and profits (or deficit) of each such corporation shall be consolidated as of the close of the date of distribution or transfer in the accumulated earnings and profits account of the acquiring corporation. See subparagraph (6) of this paragraph for determination of the accumulated earnings and profits (or deficit) of the acquiring corporation as of the close of the date of distribution or transfer.

(5) If (i) one or more corporations a party to a distribution or transfer has accumulated earnings and profits as of the close of the date of distribution or transfer, and (ii) one or more of such corporations has a deficit in accumulated earnings and profits as of such time, the total of any such deficits shall be used only to offset earnings and profits accumulated, or deemed to have been accumulated under subparagraph (6) of this paragraph, by the acquiring corporation after the date of distribution or transfer. In such instance, the acquiring corporation will be considered as maintaining two separate earnings and profits accounts after the date of distribution or transfer. The first such

account shall contain the total of the accumulated earnings and profits as of the close of the date of distribution or transfer of each corporation which has accumulated earnings and profits as of such time, and the second such account shall contain the total of the deficits in accumulated earnings and profits of each corporation which has a deficit as of such time. The total deficit in the second account may not be used to reduce the accumulated earnings and profits in the first account (although such earnings and profits may be offset by deficits incurred, or deemed to have been incurred, after the date of distribution or transfer) but shall be used only to offset earnings and profits accumulated, or deemed to have been accumulated under subparagraph (6) of this paragraph, by the acquiring corporation after the date of distribution or transfer.

(6) In any case in which it is necessary to compute the accumulated earnings and profits, or the deficit in accumulated earnings and profits, of the acquiring corporation as of the close of the date of distribution or transfer and such date is a day other than the last day of a taxable year of the acquiring corporation—

(i) If the acquiring corporation has earnings and profits for its taxable year during which occurs the date of distribution or transfer, such earnings and profits (a) shall be deemed to have accumulated as of the close of such date in an amount which bears the same ratio to the undistributed earnings and profits of such corporation for such year as the number of days in the taxable year preceding the date following the date of distribution or transfer bears to the total number of days in the taxable year, and (b) shall be deemed to have accumulated after the date of distribution or transfer in an amount which bears the same ratio to the undistributed earnings and profits of such corporation for such year as the number of days in the taxable year following such date bears to the total number of days in such taxable year. For purposes of the preceding sentence, the undistributed earnings and profits of the ac-

quiring corporation for such taxable year shall be the earnings and profits for such taxable year reduced by any distributions made therefrom during such taxable year.

(ii) If the acquiring corporation has an operating deficit for its taxable year during which occurs the date of distribution or transfer, then, unless the actual accumulated earnings and profits, or deficit, as of such date can be shown, such operating deficit shall be deemed to have accumulated in a manner similar to that described in subdivision (i) of this subparagraph.

(7) This paragraph may be illustrated by the following examples.

Example (1). (i) M and N Corporations make their returns on the basis of the calendar year. On June 30, 1959, M Corporation transfers all its assets to N Corporation in a statutory merger to which section 361 applies. The books of the two corporations reveal the following information:

Description	M Corporation (transferor)	N Corporation (acquirer)
Accumulated earnings and profits at close of calendar year 1958	$100,000	$150,000
Earnings and profits of taxable year ending June 30, 1959	15,000	—
Earnings and profits of calendar year 1959	—	36,500
Distributions during calendar year 1959	0	0

(ii) As of the close of June 30, 1959, N acquires from M accumulated earnings and profits of $115,000. Since M and N each has accumulated earnings and profits as of the close of the date of transfer, M's accumulated earnings and profits are added to N's accumulated earnings and profits as of such time. However, no part of M's accumulated earnings and profits is taken into account in determining N's earnings and profits for the calendar year 1959. Therefore, N's earnings and profits for the calendar year 1959 are $36,500.

Example (2). (i) X and Y Corporations make their returns on the basis of the calendar year. On June 30, 1959, X Corporation transfers all its assets to Y Corporation in a statutory merger to which section 361 applies. The books of the two corporations reveal the following information:

Description	X Corporation (transferor)	Y Corporation (acquirer)
Accumulated earnings and profits at close of calendar year 1958	$20,000	$100,000
Deficit in earnings and profits for taxable year ending June 30, 1959	80,000	—
Earnings and profits of calendar year 1959	—	36,500
Distributions during calendar year 1959	0	0

(ii) As of the close of June 30, 1959, Y acquires from X a deficit in accumulated earnings and profits in the amount of $60,000. This deficit may be used only to reduce those earnings and profits of Y which are accumulated, or deemed to have accumulated, after June 30, 1959. Accordingly, as of December 31, 1959, the accumulated earnings and profits of Y amount to $118,100; at such time Y also has a separate deficit in accumulated earnings and profits in the amount of $41,600. These amounts are determined as follows:

Accumulated earnings and profits of Y as of the close of 1958 .... $100,000

Add:

Portion of undistributed earnings and profits of Y for 1959 deemed to have accumulated as of close of June 30, 1959 ($36,500 × 181/365) 18,100

Accumulated earnings and profits of Y as of close of June 30, 1959, and also as of Dec. 31, 1959 118,100

Portion of undistributed earnings and profits of Y for 1959 deemed to have accumulated after June 30, 1959 ($36,500 × 184/365) 18,400

Less:

Deficit in accumulated earnings and profits acquired by Y from X Corporation as of close of June 30, 1959 60,000

Separate deficit in accumulated earnings and profits of Y as of Dec. 31, 1959 41,600

Example (3). Assume the same facts as in example (2), except that on September 15, 1959, Y Corporation makes a cash distribution of $96,500. The entire distribution is a dividend: $36,500 from earnings and profits for the taxable year 1959 and $60,000 from earnings and profits accumulated as of December 31, 1958. Accordingly, as of December 31, 1959, Y has accumulated earnings and profits of $40,000, and also has a separate deficit in accumulated earnings and profits of $60,000. These amounts are determined as follows:

Earnings and profits of Y for calendar year 1959 .... $36,500

Accumulated earnings and profits of Y as of close of 1958 100,000

Total... 136,500

Less:

Distributions during 1959 96,500

Accumulated earnings and profits of Y as of Dec. 31, 1959 40,000

Deficit in accumulated earnings and profits acquired from X as of close of June 30, 1959 60,000

Less:

Portion of Y's undistributed earnings and profits for 1959 deemed to have accumulated after June 30, 1959 0

Separate deficit in accumulated earnings and profits of Y as of Dec. 31, 1959 60,000

Example (4). (i) M and N Corporations make their returns on the basis of the calendar year. On June 30, 1959, M Corporation transfers all its assets to N Corporation in a statutory merger to which section 361 applies. The books of the two corporations reveal the following information:

Description	M Corporation (transferor)	N Corporation (acquirer)
Accumulated earnings and profits at close of calendar year 1958	$100,000	$50,000
Earnings and profits for taxable year ending June 30, 1959	10,000	—
Deficit in earnings and profits for calendar year 1959	—	146,000
Distributions during calendar year 1959	0	0

(ii) Assuming that N has not shown its actual accumulated earnings and profits, or deficit, as of the close of June 30, 1959, N has a deficit in accumulated earnings and profits at such time which amounts to $22,400, determined as follows:

Accumulated earnings and profits of N as of close of 1958	$50,000

Less:

Portion of deficit in earnings and profits of N for 1959 deemed to have accumulated as of close of June 30, 1959	
($146,000 × 181/365)	72,400
Deficit in accumulated earnings and profits of N as of close of June 30, 1959, and also as of Dec. 31, 1959	22,400

As of the close of June 30, 1959, N acquires from M accumulated earnings and profits in the amount of $110,000, no part of which may be offset by N's own deficit of $22,400; however, such earnings and profits may be offset by deficits incurred, or deemed incurred, by N after June 30, 1959. Thus, as of December 31, 1959, N has the above-mentioned deficit of $22,400; at such time N also has accumulated earnings and profits in the amount of $36,400, determined as follows:

Accumulated earnings and profits acquired from M as of close of June 30, 1959	$110,000

Less:

Portion of deficit in earnings and profits of N for 1959 deemed to have accumulated after June 30, 1959 ($146,000 × 184/365)	73,600
Accumulated earnings and profits of N as of Dec. 31, 1959	36,400

Example (5). Assume the same facts as in example (4), except that on September 9, 1959, N Corporation makes a cash distribution of $100,000. The amount of $82,000 is a dividend from accumulated earnings and profits, computed as follows:

Accumulated earnings and profits acquired from M as of close of June 30, 1959	$110,000

Less:

Deficit in earnings and profits of N for 1959 deemed to have accumulated from June 30 through Sept. 8, 1959 ($146,000 × 70/365)	28,000
Accumulated earnings and profits as of close of Sept. 8, 1959	82,000

As of December 31, 1959, N Corporation has a deficit in accumulated earnings and profits of $68,000, computed as follows:

Deficit in accumulated earnings and profits of N as of close of June 30, 1959	$22,400

Add:

Portion of N's deficit in earnings and profits for 1959 deemed to have accumulated after Sept. 8, 1959 ($146,000 × 114/365)	45,600
Deficit in accumulated earnings and profits of N as of Dec. 31, 1959	68,000

Example (6). (i) X, Y, and Z Corporations make their returns on the basis of the calendar year. On June 30, 1959, X Corporation and Y Corporation transfer all their assets to Z Corporation in a statutory merger to which section 361 applies. The books of the three corporations reveal the following information:

Description	X Corporation (transferor)	Y Corporation (transferor)	Z Corporation (acquirer)
Accumulated earnings and profits (or deficit) at close of calendar year 1958	$35,000	($25,000)	($20,000)
Earnings and profits (or deficit) for taxable year ended June 30, 1959	5,000	(5,000)	—
Earnings and profits for calendar year 1959	—	—	36,500
Distributions during 1959	0	0	0

(ii) As of the close of June 30, 1959, Z acquires from Y a deficit in accumulated earnings and profits of $30,000. As of such time, Z's own deficit in accumulated earnings and profits amounts to $1,900, determined as follows:

Deficit in accumulated earnings and
    profits of Z as of close of 1958................ $20,000

Less:

        Portion of undistributed earnings
        and profits of Z for 1959
        deemed to have accumulated
        as of close of June 30, 1959
        ($36,500 × 181/365) 18,100

        Deficit in accumulated earnings
        and profits as of close of
        June 30, 1959............................. 1,900

The total deficit of $31,900 may be used only to offset earnings and profits of Z accumulated, or deemed to have accumulated, after June 30, 1959; such deficit may not be used to reduce the accumulated earnings and profits of $40,000 acquired from X as of the close of June 30, 1959. Thus, as of December 31, 1959, the accumulated earnings and profits of Z amount to $40,000; at such time Z Corporation also has a separate deficit in accumulated earnings and profits in the amount of $13,500, determined as follows:

Deficit in accumulated earnings
    and profits as of close of
    June 30, 1959 .... $31,900

Less:

        Portion of undistributed earnings
        and profits of Z for 1959
        deemed to have accumulated
        after June 30, 1959
        ($36,500 × 184/365) 18,400

        Separate deficit in accumulated
        earnings and profits as of
        Dec. 31, 1959............................. 13,500

Example (7). X and Y Corporations make their returns on the basis of the calendar year. On December 31, 1954, X transfers all its assets to Y in a statutory merger to which section 361 applies. The books of the two corporations reveal the following information:

Description	X Corporation (transferor)	Y Corporation (acquirer)
Accumulated earnings and profits (or deficit) at close of calendar year 1954	($50,000)	$210,000
Earnings and profits (or deficit) for calendar year:		
1955	—	5,000
1956	—	(20,000)
1957	—	70,000
1958	—	60,000
1959	—	55,000
Cash distributions on:		
Sept. 1, 1957	—	80,000
Sept. 1, 1958	—	40,000
Sept. 1, 1959	—	30,000

The balances in the accumulated earnings and profits account and the separate deficit account of Y Corporation at the close of the taxable year involved are as follows:

Year	Deficit acquired from X Corporation	Accumulated earnings and profits of Y Corporation
1954	$50,000	$210,000
1955	45,000	210,000

1956	45,000	190,000
1957	45,000	180,000
1958	25,000	180,000
1959	None	180,000

* * *

§ 1.381(c)(3)–1 Capital loss carryovers.

(a) Carryover requirement. (1) Section 381(c)(3) requires the acquiring corporation in a transaction to which section 381(a) applies to succeed to, and take into account, the capital loss carryovers of the distributor or transferor corporation. To determine the amount of these carryovers as of the close of the date of distribution or transfer, and to integrate them with the capital loss carryovers of the acquiring corporation for purposes of determining the taxable income of the acquiring corporation for taxable years ending after the date of distribution or transfer, it is necessary to apply the provisions of section 1212 in accordance with the conditions and limitations of section 381(c)(3) and this section.

(2) The capital loss carryovers of the acquiring corporation as of the close of the date of distribution or transfer shall be determined without reference to any capital gains or capital losses of the distributor or transferor corporation. The capital loss carryovers of a distributor or transferor corporation as of the close of the date of distribution or transfer shall be determined without reference to any capital gains or capital losses of the acquiring corporation.

(b) First taxable year to which carryovers apply. (1) The capital loss carryovers available to the distributor or transferor corporation as of the close of the date of distribution or transfer shall first be carried to the first taxable year of the acquiring corporation ending after that date. This rule applies irrespective of whether the date of distribution or transfer is on the last day, or any other day, of the acquiring corporation's taxable year.

(2) The capital loss carryovers available to the distributor or transferor corporation as of the close of the date of distribution or transfer shall be carried to the acquiring corporation without diminution by reason of the fact that the acquiring corporation does not acquire 100 percent of the assets of the distributor or transferor corporation.

(c) Limitation on capital loss carryovers for first taxable year ending after date of distribution or transfer. (1) Any capital loss carryover of a distributor or transferor corporation which is available to the acquiring corporation as of the close of the date of distribution or transfer shall be a short-term capital loss of the acquiring corporation in each of the taxable years to which the net capital loss giving rise to such carryover may be carried to the extent provided in this section. However, in the first taxable year of the acquiring corporation ending after the date of distribution or transfer, the total capital loss carryovers of the distributor or transferor corporation which may be treated in that year as short-term capital losses of the acquiring corporation is limited by section 381(c)(3)(B) to an amount which bears the same ratio to the acquiring corporation's capital gain net income for such first taxable year (determined without regard to any capital loss carryovers) as the number of days in such first taxable year which follow the date of distribution or transfer bears to the total number of days in such taxable year. Thus, if the date of distribution or transfer is the last day of the acquiring corporation's taxable year, there is no limitation under section 381(c)(3)(B) on the amount of such carryovers which may be treated as short-term capital losses of the acquiring corporation for its first taxable year ending after that date.

(2) The limitation provided by section 381(c)(3)(B) shall be applied to the aggregate of the capital loss carryovers of the distributor or transferor corporation without reference to the taxable years in which the net capital losses giving rise to the carryovers were sustained.

* * *

(4) The application of this paragraph may be illustrated by the following example:

Example. (i) X and Y Corporations are organized on January 1, 1954, and make their returns on the basis of the calendar year. On July 4, 1957, X Corporation transfers all its assets to Y Corporation in a statutory merger to which section 361 applies. The capital gain net income (computed without regard to any capital loss carryovers) of the two corporations are as follows:

Taxable year	X Corporation (transferor)	Y Corporation (acquirer)
1954	($5,000)	0
1955	(10,000)	$5,000
1956	(25,000)	(7,000)
Ending 7–4–57	(8,000)	—
1957	—	36,500

(ii) The capital loss carryovers of X Corporation which are available to Y Corporation as of the close of July 4, 1957, amount to $48,000 in the aggregate; but only $18,000 ($36,500 ×180/365) of such amount may be treated as short-term capital losses of Y Corporation for 1957.

(d) **Computation of carryovers; general rule—(1)** Sequence for applying losses and determination of capital gain net income. Section 1212 provides that a net capital loss sustained in any taxable year (hereinafter referred to as the "loss year") shall be carried over to each of the five succeeding taxable years and treated in each of such succeeding years as a short-term capital loss to the extent not allowed as a deduction against any capital gain net income of any taxable years intervening between the loss year and the taxable year to which such loss is carried. For this purpose, the capital gain net income of any intervening taxable year is determined without regard to the net capital loss for the loss year or for any taxable year thereafter, and the various capital loss carryovers from taxable years preceding the loss year to any such intervening taxable year are considered to be applied in reduction of the capital gain net income for such year in the order of the taxable years in which the losses were sustained, beginning with the loss for the earliest preceding taxable year. The application of these rules to the capital gain net income of the acquiring corporation for any taxable year ending after the date of distribution or transfer involves the use of carryovers of the distributor or transferor corporation and of the acquiring corporation. In determining the order in which the capital loss carryovers of the distributor or transferor and acquiring corporations from taxable years ending on or before the date of distribution or transfer are considered to be applied in reduction of the capital gain net income of the acquiring corporation for any intervening taxable year ending after such date, the following rules shall apply:

(i) Each taxable year of the distributor or transferor and acquiring corporations which, with respect to the first taxable year of the acquiring corporation ending after the date of distribution or transfer, constitutes a first preceding taxable year, shall be treated as if each such year ended on the same day, whether or not such taxable years actually end on the same day. In like manner, each taxable year of the distributor or transferor and acquiring corporations which, with respect to such first taxable year of the acquiring corporation ending after the date of distribution or transfer, constitutes a second preceding taxable year, shall be treated as if each such year ended on the same day (whether or not such taxable years actually end on the same day), and a similar rule shall be applied with respect to those taxable years of the distributor or transferor and acquiring corporations which constitute third, fourth, and fifth preceding taxable years;

(ii) If in the same preceding taxable year both the distributor or transferor and acquiring corporations incurred a net capital loss which is a carryover to an intervening taxable year of the acquiring corporation ending after the date of distribution or transfer, then in applying such losses in reduction of the capital gain net income for such an intervening year, either such loss may be taken into account before the other; and

(iii) The rules of subdivisions (i) and (ii) of this subparagraph shall apply regardless of the number of distributor or transferor corporations the assets of which are acquired by the acquiring corporation on the same date of distribution or transfer.

* * *

(4) Computation of carryovers in case where date of distribution or transfer occurs on last day of acquiring corporation's taxable year. The computation of the capital loss carryovers from the distributor or transferor corporation and from the acquiring corporation in a case where the date of distribution or transfer occurs on the last day of a taxable year of the acquiring corporation may be illustrated by the following example:

Example. X and Y Corporations are organized on January 1, 1955, and make their returns on the basis of the calendar year. On December 31, 1956, X Corporation transfers all its assets to Y Corporation in a statutory merger to which section 361 applies. The net capital losses and the net capital gains (capital gain net income for taxable years beginning after December 31, 1976) (computed without regard to any capital loss carryovers) of the two corporations are as follows:

Taxable year	X Corporation (transferor)	Y Corporation (acquirer)
1955	($20,000)	($2,000)
1956	(10,000)	(8,000)
1957		$25,000
1958		10,000

The sequence in which the net capital losses of X and Y Corporations are applied, and the computation of the capital loss carryovers to Y Corporation's taxable year 1959, may be illustrated as follows. (For purposes of this example, the carryover from a preceding taxable year of the transferor corporation will be applied before the carryover from the same preceding taxable year of the acquiring corporation):

(i) X Corporation's 1955 loss. The carryover to 1959 is $0, computed as follows:

Net capital loss	$20,000
Less: Y's 1957 net capital gain (computed without regard to any capital loss carryovers)	25,000
Carryover to Y 1958 and Y 1959	0

(ii) Y Corporation's 1955 loss. The carryover to 1959 is $0, computed as follows:

Net capital loss		$2,000
Less:		
Y's 1957 net capital gain (computed without regard to any capital loss carryovers)	$25,000	
Minus capital loss carryovers to Y 1957 (i.e., carryover of $20,000 from X 1955)	20,000	
—		5,000
Carryover to Y 1958 and Y 1959		0

(iii) X Corporation's 1956 loss. The carryover to 1959 is $0, computed as follows:

Net capital loss		$10,000
Less:		
Y's 1957 net capital gain (computed without regard to any capital loss carryovers)	$25,000	
Minus capital loss carryovers to Y 1957 (i.e., carryovers of $20,000 from X 1955 and $2,000 from Y 1955)	22,000	
—		3,000
Carryover to Y 1958		7,000
Less:		
Y's 1958 net capital gain (computed without regard to any capital loss carryovers)	$10,000	
Minus capital loss carryovers to Y 1958	0	
—	10,000	
Carryover to Y 1959		0

(iv) Y Corporation's 1956 loss. The carry-over to 1959 is $5,000, computed as follows:

Net capital loss	$8,000

Less:

Y's 1957 net capital gain (computed without regard to any capital loss carryovers) $25,000	
Minus capital loss carryovers to Y 1957 (i.e., carryovers of $20,000 from X 1955, $2,000 from Y 1955, and $10,000 from X 1956)	32,000
—	0
Carryover to Y 1958	8,000

Less:

Y's 1958 net capital gain (computed without regard to any capital loss carryovers)	$10,000
Minus capital loss carryovers to Y 1958 (i.e., carryover of $7,000 from X 1956)	7,000
—	3,000
Carryover to Y 1959	5,000

* * *

§ 1.382–2 General rules for ownership change.

(a) Certain definitions for purposes of sections 382 and 383 and the regulations thereunder. The following definitions apply for purposes of sections 382 and 383 and the regulations thereunder.

(1) Loss corporation—(i) In general. The term "loss corporation" means a corporation which—

(A) Is entitled to use a net operating loss carryforward, a capital loss carryover, a carryover of excess foreign taxes under section 904(c), a carryforward of a general business credit under section 39, or a carryover of a minimum tax credit under section 53,

(B) For the taxable year that includes a testing date, as defined in paragraph (a)(4) of this section or § 1.382–2T(a)(2)(i), whichever is applicable (determined for purposes of this

paragraph (a)(1) without regard to whether the corporation is a loss corporation), has a net operating loss, a net capital loss, excess foreign taxes under section 904(c), unused general business credits under section 38, or an unused minimum tax credit under section 53, or

(C) Has a net unrealized built-in loss (determined for purposes of this paragraph (a)(1) by treating the date on which such determination is made as the change date). See section 382(h)(3) for the definition of net unrealized built-in loss.

See section 383 and § 1.383–1 for rules relating to a loss corporation that has an ownership change and has capital losses, excess foreign taxes, general business credits or minimum tax credits. Any predecessor or successor to a loss corporation described in this paragraph (a)(1) is also a loss corporation.

(ii) Distributor or transferor loss corporation in a transaction under section 381. Notwithstanding that a loss corporation ceases to exist under state law, if its net operating loss carryforwards, excess foreign taxes, or other items described in section 381(c) are succeeded to and taken into account by an acquiring corporation in a transaction described in section 381(a), such loss corporation shall be treated as continuing in existence until—

(A) Any pre-change losses (excluding pre-change credits described in § 1.383–1(c)(3)), determined as if the date of such transaction were the change date, are fully utilized or expire under either section 172 or section 1212,

(B) Any net unrealized built-in losses, determined as if the date of such transaction were the change date, may no longer be treated as pre-change losses, and

(C) Any pre-change credits (described in § 1.383–1(c)(3)), determined as if the date of such transaction were the change date, are fully utilized or expire under sections 39, 53, or 904(c).

Following a transaction described in the preceding sentence, the stock of the acquiring corporation shall be treated as the stock of the loss corporation for purposes of determining whether an ownership change occurs with respect to the pre-change losses and net unrealized built-in losses that may be treated as pre-change losses of the distributor or transferor corporation.

(iii) *Separate accounting required for losses and credits of an acquiring corporation and a distributor or transferor loss corporation.* Except as provided in paragraph (a)(1)(iv) of this section, pre-change losses (determined as if the testing date were the change date and treating the amount of any net unrealized built-in loss as a pre-change loss), that are succeeded to and taken into account by an acquiring corporation in a transaction to which section 381(a) applies must be accounted for separately from losses and credits of the acquiring corporation for purposes of applying this section. See Example (2) of § 1.382–2T(e)(2)(iv) of this section.

(iv) *End of separate accounting for losses and credits of distributor or transferor loss corporation.* The separate tracking of owner shifts of the stock of an acquiring corporation required by paragraph (a)(1)(iii) of this section with respect to the net operating loss carryovers and other attributes described in paragraph (a)(1)(ii) of this section ends when a fold-in event occurs. A fold-in event is either an ownership change of the distributor or transferor corporation in connection with, or after, the transaction to which section 381(a) applies, or a period of 5 consecutive years following the section 381(a) transaction during which the distributor or transferor corporation has not had an ownership change. Starting on the day after the earlier of the change date (but not earlier than the day of the section 381(a) transaction) or the last day of the 5 consecutive year period, the losses and other attributes of the distributor or transferor corporation are treated as losses and attributes of the acquiring corporation for purposes of determining whether an ownership change occurs with respect to such losses. Also, for purposes of determining the

beginning of the acquiring corporation's testing period, such losses are considered to arise either in a taxable year that begins not earlier than the later of the day following the change date or the day of the section 381(a) transaction, or in a taxable year that begins 3 years before the end of the 5 consecutive year period. Pre-change losses of a distributor or transferor corporation that are subject to a limitation under section 382 continue to be subject to the limitation notwithstanding the occurrence of a fold-in event. Any ownership change that occurs in connection with, or subsequent to, the section 381 transaction may result in an additional, lesser limitation with respect to such pre-change losses. This paragraph (a)(1)(iv) applies to any testing date occurring on or after January 29, 1991.

(v) *Application to other successor corporations.* This paragraph (a)(1) also applies, as the context may require, to successor corporations other than successors in section 381(a) transactions. For example, if a corporation receives assets from the loss corporation that have basis in excess of value, the recipient corporation's basis for the assets is determined, directly or indirectly, in whole or in part, by reference to the loss corporation's basis, and the amount by which basis exceeds value is material, the recipient corporation is a successor corporation subject to this paragraph (a)(1). This paragraph (a)(1)(v) applies to any testing date occurring on or after January 1, 1997.

(2) **Pre-change loss.** The term pre-change loss means—

(i) Any net operating loss carryforward of the old loss corporation to the taxable year ending on the change date or in which the change date occurs,

(ii) Any net operating loss of the old loss corporation for the taxable year in which the ownership change occurs to the extent such loss is allocable to the period in such year on or before the change date,

(iii) Any recognized built-in loss for any recognition period taxable year (within the meaning of section 382(h)),

(iv) Any pre-change capital losses described in § 1.383–1T(c)(2)(i) and (ii), and

(v) Any pre-change credits described in § 1.383–1T(c)(3).

(3) Stock—(i) In general. Except as provided in this paragraph *(a)(3)(i) and § 1.382–2T(f)(18)(ii) and (iii),* the term stock means stock other than stock described in section 1504(a)(4). Notwithstanding the preceding sentence, stock that is not described in section 1504(a)(4) solely because it is entitled to vote as a result of dividend arrearages shall be treated as so described and thus shall not be considered stock. Stock described in section 1504(a)(4), however, is not excluded for purposes of determining the value of the loss corporation under section 382(e). The determination of the percentage of stock of any corporation owned by any person shall be made on the basis of the relative fair market value of the stock owned by such person to the total fair market value of the outstanding stock of the corporation. Solely for purposes of determining the percentage of stock owned by a person, each share of all the outstanding shares of stock that have the same material terms is treated as having the same value. Thus, for example, a control premium or blockage discount is disregarded in determining the percentage of stock owned by any person. The previous two sentences of this paragraph (a)(3)(i) apply to any testing date occurring on or after January 29, 1991.

(ii) Convertible stock. The term "stock" includes any convertible stock. For rules regarding the treatment of certain convertible stock as an option, see § 1.382–4(d)(9)(ii).

(4) Testing date—(i) In general. Except as provided in paragraph (a)(4)(ii) of this section, a loss corporation is required to determine whether an ownership change has occurred immediately after any owner shift, or issuance or transfer (including an issuance or transfer described in § 1.382–4(d)(8)(i) or (ii) of an option with respect to stock of the loss corporation that is treated as exercised under § 1.382–4(d)(2). Each date on which a loss corporation is required to make a determination of whether an ownership change has occurred is referred to as a testing date. All computations of increases in percentage ownership are to be made as of the close of the testing date and any transactions described in this paragraph (a)(4) that occur on that date are treated as occurring simultaneously at the close of the testing date. See § 1.382–2T(e)(1) for the definition of owner shift. The term option, as used in this paragraph (a)(4), includes interests that are treated as options under § 1.382–4(d)(9). For rules regarding the determination of whether dates prior to November 5, 1992, are testing dates, see § 1.382–2T(a)(2)(i).

(5) Successor corporation. A successor corporation is a distributee or transferee corporation that succeeds to and takes into account items described in section 381(c) from a corporation as the result of an acquisition of assets described in section 381(a). A successor corporation also includes, as the context may require, a corporation which receives an asset or assets from another corporation if the corporation's basis for the asset(s) is determined, directly or indirectly, in whole or in part, by reference to the other corporation's basis and the amount by which basis differs from value is, in the aggregate, material. The previous sentence of this paragraph (a)(5) applies to any testing date occurring on or after January 1, 1997.

(6) Predecessor corporation. A predecessor corporation is a distributor or transferor corporation that distributes or transfers its assets to an acquiring corporation in a transaction described in section 381(a). A predecessor corporation also includes, as the context may require, a corporation which transfers an asset or assets to another corporation if the transferee's basis for the asset(s) is determined, directly or indirectly, in whole or in part, by reference to the corporation's basis and the amount by which basis differs from value is, in the aggregate, material. The previous sentence of this paragraph (a)(6) applies to any testing date occurring on or after January 1, 1997.

§ 1.382–2T Definition of ownership change under section 382, as amended by the Tax Reform Act of 1986 (temporary).

(a) Ownership change—(1) In general. A corporation is a new loss corporation and thus subject to limitation under section 382 only if an ownership change has occurred with respect to such corporation. An ownership change occurs with respect to a corporation if it is a loss corporation on a testing date and, immediately after the close of the testing date, the percentage of stock of the corporation owned by one or more 5-percent shareholders has increased by more than 50 percentage points over the lowest percentage of stock of such corporation owned by such shareholders at any time during the testing period. See paragraph (a)(2) (i) of this section for the definition of testing date. See paragraph (d) of this section for the definition of testing period. See § 1.382–2(a) (1) and paragraph (f)(3) of this section for the respective definition of loss corporation and new loss corporation. See paragraph (g) of this section for the definition of 5-percent shareholder. See section 383 and § 1.383–1 for rules relating to loss corporations that have an ownership change and have capital loss carryovers, excess foreign taxes carried over under section 904(c), carryovers of general business credits under section 39, or unused minimum tax credits under section 53.

* * *

(b) Nomenclature and assumptions. For purposes of the example in this section—

(1) L is a loss corporation, and, if there is more than one loss corporation, they are designated as L_1, L_2, L_3, etc.

(2) P is a corporation that is not a loss corporation, and, if there is more than one such corporation, they are designated as P_1, P_2, P_3, etc.

(3) HC is a corporation whose assets consist solely of the stock of other corporations.

(4) E is an entity other than a corporation (e.g., a partnership), and, if there is more than one such entity, they are designated as E_1, E_2, E_3, etc.

(5) Unless otherwise stated—

(i) A, B, C, D, AA, BB, CC, and DD are unrelated individuals who own interests in corporations or other entities only to the extent expressly stated,

(ii) All corporations have one class of stock outstanding and each share of stock has the same fair market value as each other share,

(iii) The capital structure of the loss corporation and its business do not change over time, and

(iv) The rules of paragraphs (k)(2) and (4) of this section are not applicable.

(6) Public L represents a group of unrelated individuals and entities that own direct (and not indirect) stock ownership interests in loss corporation L, each of whom owns less than five percent of the stock of the loss corporation, and, if there is more than one loss corporation, such groups are designated as Public L_1, Public L_2, Public L_3, etc.

(7) Public P represents a group of unrelated individuals and entities that own direct (and not indirect) stock ownership interests in corporation P, each of whom owns less than five percent of the stock of the corporation, and, if there is more than one corporation, such groups are designated as Public P_1, P_2, P_3, etc.

(8) Public E represents a group of unrelated individuals and entities that own direct (and not indirect) ownership interests in entity E, each of whom owns less than five percent of the entity, and, if there is more than one entity, such groups are designated as Public E_1, Public E_2, Public E_3, etc.

(c) Computing the amount of increases in percentage ownership—(1) In general. In order to determine whether an ownership change has occurred on a testing date, the loss corporation must identify each 5-percent shareholder whose percentage of stock ownership in the loss corporation immediately after the close of the testing date has increased, compared to such shareholder's lowest percentage of stock ownership in such corporation at any time during the testing period. The amount of the increase in the percentage of stock ownership in the loss corporation of each 5-percent shareholder must be computed separately by comparing the percentage ownership of each such 5-percent shareholder immediately after the close of the testing date to such shareholder's lowest percentage ownership at any time during the testing period. Each such increase in the percentage ownership of a 5-percent shareholder is then added together with any other such increases of other 5-percent shareholders to determine whether an ownership change has occurred. Because only those 5-percent shareholders whose percentages of stock ownership have increased are taken into account, a 5-percent shareholder is disregarded if his percentage of stock ownership, immediately after the close of the testing date, has decreased (or has remained the same), compared to his lowest percentage ownership interest on any previous date during the testing period.

(2) Example.

(i) A and B each own 40 percent of the outstanding L stock. The remaining 20 percent of the L stock is owned by 100 unrelated individuals, none of whom own as much as five percent of L stock ("Public L"). C negotiates with A and B to purchase all their stock in L.

(ii) The acquisitions from both A and B are completed on September 13, 1990. C's acquisition of 80 percent of L stock results in an ownership change because C's percentage ownership has increased by 80 percentage points as of the testing date, compared to his

lowest percentage ownership in L at any time during the testing period (0 percent).

(3) Related and unrelated increases in percentage stock ownership. The determination whether an ownership change has occurred is made without regard to whether the changes in stock ownership of the loss corporation (by one or more 5-percent shareholders) result from related or unrelated events.

(4) Example.

(i) L has outstanding 200 shares of common stock. A, B and C respectively own 100, 50 and 50 shares of the L stock. On January 2, 1988, A sells 60 shares of L stock to B. Thus, B's percentage ownership interest in L increases by 30 percentage points, from 50 shares to 110 shares. On January 1, 1989, A purchases C's entire interest in L. Thus, A's percentage ownership interest in L increases by 25 percentage points, compared to his lowest percentage ownership interest in L, from 40 shares immediately following the January 2, 1988 sale to B to 90 shares. Even though A's ownership interest in L as of January 1, 1989 has decreased, compared to his 50 percent ownership interest at the beginning of the testing period, A is a 5-percent shareholder who must be taken into account for purposes of the computation required under paragraph (c)(1) of this section because his interest in L on that testing date (45 percent) has increased, compared to his lowest percentage ownership interest in L at any time during the testing period (20 percent following the sale to B).

(ii) Accordingly, although A and B jointly have increased their aggregate total ownership interest in L between January 2, 1988 and January 1, 1989 by only 25 percentage points (i.e., the total ownership interest in L held by A and B at all times is not less than a 75 percent interest), the total of their separate increases in the percentage stock ownership of L, compared to their respective lowest percentage ownership interests at any time during the testing period, is 55 percentage points. Thus, an ownership change occurs as a result of A's acquisition of L stock on January 1, 1989.

(d) Testing period—(1) In general. Except as otherwise provided in paragraphs (d) and (m) of this section, the testing period for any testing date is the three-year period ending on the testing date. See paragraph (a)(2)(i) of this section for the definition of testing date.

(2) Effect of a prior ownership change. Following an ownership change, the testing period for determining whether a subsequent ownership change has occurred shall begin no earlier than the first day following the change date of the most recent ownership change. See paragraph (f)(19) of this section for the definition of change date.

(3) Commencement of the testing period—(i) In general. Except as otherwise provided in paragraph (d)(3)(ii) of this section, the testing period for any loss corporation shall not begin before the earlier of the first day of either—

(A) The first taxable year from which there is a loss or excess credit carryforward to the first taxable year ending after the testing date, or

(B) The taxable year in which the testing date occurs.

(ii) Exception for corporations with net unrealized built-in loss. Paragraph (d)(3)(i) of this section shall not apply if the corporation has a net unrealized built-in loss (determined after application of section 382(h)(3)(B)) on the testing date, unless the loss corporation establishes the taxable year in which the net unrealized built-in loss first accrued. In that event, the testing period shall not begin before the earlier of—

(A) The first day of the taxable year in which the net unrealized built-in loss first accrued, or

(B) The day described in paragraph (d)(3)(i) of this section. See section 382(h) for the definition of net unrealized built-in loss.

(4) Disregarding testing dates. Any testing date that occurs before the beginning of the testing period shall be disregarded for purposes of this section.

(5) Example.

(i) A owns all 100 outstanding shares of L stock. A sells 40 shares to B on January 1, 1988. C purchases 20 shares of L stock from A on July 1, 1991. In determining if an ownership change occurs on the July 1, 1991 testing date, B's acquisition of L stock is disregarded because it occurred before the testing period that ends on such testing date. Thus, B's ownership interest in L does not increase during the testing period, and no ownership change results from C's acquisition.

(ii) The facts are the same as in (i), except that throughout the period during which B negotiated his stock purchase transaction with A, B knew that C intended to attempt to acquire a significant stock interest in L. Also, B and C have been partners in a number of significant business ventures. The result is the same as in (i).

(e) Owner shift and equity structure shift—(1) Owner shift—(i) Defined. For purposes of this section, an owner shift is any change in the ownership of the stock of a loss corporation that affects the percentage of such stock owned by any 5-percent shareholder. See paragraph (g) of this section for the definition of a 5-percent shareholder. An owner shift includes, but is not limited to, the following transactions:

(A) A purchase of disposition of loss corporation stock by a 5-percent shareholder,

(B) A section 351 exchange that affects the percentage of stock owned by a 5-percent shareholder,

(C) A redemption or a recapitalization that affects the percentage of stock owned by a 5-percent shareholder,

(D) An issuance of loss corporation stock that affects the percentage of stock owned by a 5-percent shareholder, and

(E) An equity structure shift that affects the percentage of stock owned by a 5-percent shareholder.

(ii) Transactions between persons who are not 5-percent shareholders disregarded. Transfers of loss corporation stock between persons who are not 5-percent shareholders of such corporation (and between members of separate public groups resulting from the application of the segregation rules of paragraphs (j)(2) and (3)(iii) of this section) are not owner shifts and thus are not taken into account. See paragraph (h)(4)(xi) of this section for a similar rule applicable to transfers of options.

(iii) Examples.

Example (1). A has owned all 1000 shares of outstanding L stock for more than three years. On June 15, 1988, A sells 300 of his L shares to B. This transaction is an owner shift. No other 5-percent shareholder has increased his percentage ownership of L stock during the testing period. Thus, the owner shift resulting from B's acquisition does not result in an ownership change, because B has increased his stock ownership in L by only 30 percentage points.

Example (2). The facts are the same as in Example (1). In addition, on June 15, 1989, L issues 100 shares to each of C, D and AA. The stock issuance is an owner shift. The transaction, however, does not result in an ownership change, because B, C, D and AA (the 5-percent shareholders whose stock ownership has increased as of the testing date, compared to any other time during the testing period) have increased their percentage of stock ownership in L by a total of only 46.2 percentage points during the testing period (by 23.1 percentage points [300 shares/1300 shares] for B, and 7.7 percentage points [100 shares/1300 shares] for each of C, D and AA).

Example (3). All 1000 shares of L stock are owned by a group of 100 unrelated individuals, none of whom own as much as five percent of L stock ("Public L"). Several of the members of Public L sell their L stock, amounting to a 30 percent ownership interest in L, to B on June 15, 1988. The sale of stock to B is an owner shift. Between June 16, 1988 and June 15, 1989, each of the remaining individuals in Public L sells his stock to another person who is not a 5-percent shareholder. Under paragraph (e)(1)(ii) of this section, trading activity among the members of Public L is disregarded and does not result in an owner shift. On June 15, 1989, L issues 100 shares to each of C, D and AA. The only sale transactions by members of Public L that are taken into account in determining whether an ownership change occurs on June 15, 1989 are the sales to B on June 15, 1988. Because B, C, D and AA together have increased their percentage ownership of L stock as a result of B's purchase and the stock issuance by an amount not in excess of 50 percentage points during the testing period ending on June 15, 1988, an ownership change does not occur on that date.

Example (4). The facts are the same as in Example (2). In addition, on December 15, 1989, L redeems 200 of the L shares from A. The redemption is an owner shift that results in an ownership change, because B, C, D and AA are 5-percent shareholders whose percentage ownership of L increase by a total of 54.6 percentage points during the testing period (by 27.3 percentage points [300 shares/1100 shares] for B and 9.1 percentage points [100 shares/1100 shares] for each of C, D and AA).

Example (5). L is owned entirely by 10,000 unrelated shareholders, none of whom owns as much as five percent of the stock of L ("Public L"). Accordingly, Public L is L's only 5-percent shareholder. See paragraph (j)(1) of this section. There are one million shares of common stock outstanding. On December 1, 1988, L issues two million new shares of its common stock to members of the public, none of whom owned any L stock prior to the issuance. Following the public offering, no shareholder of L owns, directly or indirectly, five percent or more of L stock. Under paragraph (j)(2) of this section, however, all of the newly issued stock is treated as acquired by a 5-percent shareholder ("Public NL") that is unrelated to Public L. Therefore, the public offering constitutes an owner shift that results in an ownership change because Public NL's percentage of stock ownership in L increased by 66 2/3 percentage points (two million shares acquired in the public offering/three million shares outstanding following the offering) over its lowest percentage ownership during the testing period (0 percent prior to the offering).

Example (6). The facts are the same as in Example (5), except that L issues only 500,000 new shares of L stock on December 1, 1988, and Public NL's percentage ownership interest in L increases by only 33 1/3 percentage points (500,000 shares acquired in the public offering/1.5 million shares outstanding following the offering). During the two years following December 2, 1988, 14 percent of the stock outstanding on that date is sold over a public stock exchange. On December 3, 1990, A purchases five percent of L stock (75,000 shares) over a public stock exchange. The purchase of five percent of L stock by A is an owner shift and is presumed to have been made proportionately from Public L and Public NL under paragraph (j)(1)(vi) of this section. Under paragraph (e)(1)(ii) of this section, transfers of L stock in transactions not involving A (i.e., in transactions among or between members of separate public groups resulting from the application of paragraphs (j)(2) and (3) of this section) are not taken into account, and do not constitute owner shifts. (Transfers between members of Public NL and Public L, which are treated as separate 5-percent shareholders solely by virtue of paragraph (j)(2) of this section, are disregarded even if L has actual knowledge of any such transfers.) A and Public NL, the only 5-percent shareholders whose interests in L have increased during the testing period, have increased there respective stock ownership by only 36 2/3 percentage points—five percentage points for A [75,000 shares/1.5 million shares outstanding] and 31 2/3 percentage points for Public NL [((500,000 shares issued

in the public offering)−(5 percent x 500,000 shares presumed to have been acquired by A))/1.5 million shares outstanding]. Accordingly, there is no ownership change with respect to L notwithstanding that, taking into account the public trading, a change of more than 50 percentage points in the ultimate beneficial ownership of L stock occurred during the three-year period ending on the December 3, 1990 testing date.

Example (7). The facts are the same as in Example 6, except that five percent of the L stock has always been owned by P which, in turn, has always been owned by Public P. On December 6, 1990, P sells all of its L stock over a public stock exchange. Although the trading of P stock among persons that are not 5-percent shareholders (without regard to the segregation rules of paragraph (j) of this section) are disregarded under paragraph (e)(1)(ii) of this section, the disposition of the L stock by P is not disregarded because the L stock is transferred in a transaction that is subject to paragraph (j)(3)(i) of this section.

(2) Equity structure shift—(i) Tax-free reorganizations. An equity structure shift is any reorganization within the meaning of section 368 with respect to which the loss corporation is a party to the reorganization, except that such term does not include a reorganization described in—

(A) Section 368(a)(1)(D) or (G) unless the requirements of section 354(b)(1) are met, or

(B) Section 368(a)(1)(F).

(ii) Transactions designated under section 382(g)(3)(B) treated as equity structure shifts. [Reserved]

(iii) Overlap of owner shift and equity structure shift. Any equity structure shift that affects the percentage of loss corporation stock owned by a 5-percent shareholder also constitutes an owner shift. See paragraph (e)(i)(E) of this section.

(iv) Examples.

Example (1). A owns all of the stock of L and B owns all of the stock of P. On October 13, 1988, L merges into P in a reorganization described in section 368a(1)(A). As a result of the merger, A and B own 25 and 75 percent, respectively, of the stock of P. The merger is an equity structure shift (and, because it affects the percentage of L stock owned by 5-percent shareholders, it also constitutes an owner shift). On the October 13, 1988 testing date, B is a 5-percent shareholder whose stock ownership in the loss corporation following the merger has increased by 75 percentage points over his lowest percentage of stock ownership in L at any time during the testing period (0 percent prior to the merger). Accordingly, an ownership change occurs as a result of the merger. P is thus a new loss corporation and L's pre-change losses are subject to limitation under section 382.

Example (2). (i) A owns 100 percent of L_1 stock and B owns 100 percent of L_2 stock. On January 1, 1988, L_1 merges into L_2 in a reorganization described in section 368(a)(1)(A). Immediately after the merger, A and B own 40 percent and 60 percent, respectively, of the L_2 stock. There is an equity structure shift (as well as an owner shift) with respect to both L_1 and L_2 on January 1, 1988.

(ii) Because the percentage of L_2 stock owned by B immediately after the merger (60 percent) increases by more than 50 percentage points over the lowest percentage of the stock of L_1 owned by B during the testing period (0 percent prior to the merger), there is an ownership change with respect to L_1. L_2 is a new loss corporation and thus, under § 1.382–2a(a)(1) (iii) of this section, the pre-change losses of L_1 must be accounted for separately by L_2 from the losses of L_2 (immediately before the ownership change) and are subject to limitation under section 382. See *§ 1.382–2(a)(1)(iv)* of this section for rules that end separate accounting for L_1's pre-change losses on any testing date occurring on or after January 29, 1991.

(iii) L_2 is a new loss corporation because it is a successor corporation to L_1. There is no ownership change with respect to L_2, however, because A's stock ownership in L_2 increased by only 40 percentage points (to 40 percent) over the amount owned by A prior to the merger (0 percent). Therefore, the pre-change losses of L_2 are not limited under section 382 as a result of the merger.

Example (3). The result in Example (2) would be the same if L_1 had survived the merger (i.e., L_2 merged into L_1) with A and B owning 40 and 60 percent, respectively, of L_1 stock. L_1's pre-change losses would be accounted for separately and limited under section 382 and the pre-change losses of L_2 would be accounted for separately under § 1.382–2a(a)(1)(iii) of this section, but would not be limited under section 382. See § 1.382–2a(a)(1)(ii) for the treatment of L_2 following the transaction.

Example (4). The facts are the same as Example (2), except, instead of acquiring L_1 in a merger, L_2 acquires all of the L_1 stock from A on January 1, 1988, solely in exchange for stock representing a 40 percent interest in L_2, in a reorganization described in section 368(a) (1)(B). The acquisition of stock by L_2 is an equity structure shift (as well as an owner shift) with respect to L_1 that results in an ownership change with respect to L_1 because the percentage of L_1 stock owned by B immediately after the reorganization (60 percent, by virtue of B's ownership of L_2, through the operation of the constructive ownership rules of paragraph (h) of this section) increases by more than 50 percentage points over the lowest percentage of L_1 stock owned by B at any time during the testing period (0 percent prior to the reorganization). The acquisition also results in an equity structure shift and an owner shift with respect to L_2, but L_2 incurs no ownership change, because A's stock ownership in L_2 increased by only 40 percentage points over the percentage of L_2 stock owned by A prior to the reorganization (0 percent).

* * *

§ 1.383–1 Special limitations on certain capital losses and excess credits.

* * *

(b) In general. Under section 383, if an ownership change occurs with respect to a loss corporation, the section 382 limitation and the section 383 credit limitation (as defined in paragraph (c)(6) of this section) for a post-change year shall apply to limit the amount of taxable income and regular tax liability, respectively, that can be offset by pre-change capital losses and pre-change credits of the new loss corporation. The section 383 credit limitation for a post-change year bears a direct relationship to the amount, if any, of the section 382 limitation that remains after taking into account the reduction in the loss corporation's taxable income during a post-change year as a result of its pre-change losses (as defined in paragraph (c)(4) of this section). In general, the section 383 credit limitation is an amount equal to the tax liability of the new loss corporation for the post-change year which is attributable to so much of the corporation's taxable income that would be reduced by allowing as a deduction its section 382 limitation remaining after accounting for the use of pre-change losses. As pre-change losses and pre-change credits of a corporation are used, they absorb the section 382 limitation and the section 383 credit limitation, respectively, in the manner prescribed by paragraph (d) of this section. See also section 382 and the regulations thereunder.

(c) Definitions—(1) Coordination with definitions and nomenclature used in section 382. Terms and nomenclature used in this section, and not otherwise defined herein, shall have the same respective meanings as in section 382 and the regulations thereunder, taking into account that the limitations of section 383 and this section apply to pre-change capital losses and pre-change credits.

(2) Pre-change capital loss. The term "pre-change capital loss" means—

(i) Any capital loss carryover under section 1212 of the old loss corporation to the taxable year ending on the change date or in which the change date occurs,

(ii) Any net capital loss of the old loss corporation for the taxable year in which the ownership change occurs, to the extent such loss is allocable to the period in such year ending on or before the change date, and

(iii) If the old loss corporation has a net unrealized built-in loss, any recognized built-in loss for any recognition period taxable year (within the meaning of section 382(h)) that is a capital loss.

(3) Pre-change credit. The term "pre-change credit" means—

(i) Any excess foreign taxes under section 904(c) of the old loss corporation—

(A) carried forward to the taxable year ending on the change date or in which the change date occurs, or

(B) carried forward from the taxable year that includes the change date, to the extent such credit is allocable to the period in such year ending on or before the change date,

(ii) Any credit under section 38 of the old loss corporation—

(A) carried forward to the taxable year ending on the change date or in which the change date occurs, or

(B) carried forward from a taxable year that includes the change date to the extent such credit is attributable to the period in such year ending on or before the change date, and

(iii) The available minimum tax credit of the old loss corporation under section 53 to the extent attributable to periods ending on or before the change date.

(4) Pre-change loss. Solely for purposes of this section, the term "pre-change loss" means any pre-change loss described in § 1.382–2(a)(2) other than pre-change credits described in paragraph (c)(3) of this section.

(5) Regular tax liability. For purposes of this section, the term "regular tax liability" has the same meaning as provided in section 26(b).

(6) Section 383 credit limitation—(i) Definition. The "section 383 credit limitation" for a post-change year of a new loss corporation is an amount equal to the excess of—

(A) The new loss corporation's regular tax liability for the post-change year, over

(B) The new loss corporation's regular tax liability for the post-change year computed, for this purpose, by allowing as an additional deduction an amount equal to the section 382 limitation remaining after the application of paragraphs (d)(2)(i) through (iv) of this section.

(ii) Example.

L, a new loss corporation, is a calendar year taxpayer. L has an ownership change on December 31, 1987. For 1988, L has taxable income (prior to the use of any pre-change losses) of $100,000. In addition, L has a section 382 limitation of $25,000, a pre-change net operating loss carryover of $12,000, a pre-change minimum tax credit of $50,000, and no pre-change capital losses. L's section 383 credit limitation is the excess of its regular tax liability computed after allowing a $12,000 net operating loss deduction (taxable income of $88,000; regular tax liability of $18,170), over its regular tax liability computed after allowing an additional deduction in the amount of L's section 382 limitation remaining after the application of paragraphs (d)(2)(i) through (iv) of this section, or $13,000 (taxable income of $75,000; regular tax liability of $13,750). L's section 383 credit limitation is therefore $4,420 ($18,170 minus $13,750).

(d) Limitation on use of pre-change losses and pre-change credits—(1) In general. The amount of taxable income of a new loss corporation for any post-change year that may be offset by pre-change losses shall not exceed the amount of the section 382 limitation for the post-change year. The amount of the regular tax liability of a new loss corporation for any post-change year that may be offset by pre-change credits shall not exceed the amount of the section 383 credit limitation for the post-change year.

(2) Ordering rules for utilization of pre-change losses and pre-change credits and for absorption of the section 382 limitation and the section 383 credit limitation. Pre-change losses described in any subdivision of this paragraph (d)(2) can offset taxable income in a post-change year only to the extent that the section 382 limitation for that year has not been absorbed by pre-change losses described in any lower-numbered subdivisions. Pre-change credits described in any subdivision of this paragraph (d)(2) can offset regular tax liability in a post-change year only to the extent that the section 383 credit limitation for that year has not been absorbed by pre-change credits described in any lower numbered subdivisions. The section 382 limitation is absorbed by one dollar for each dollar of pre-change loss that is used to offset taxable income. The section 383 credit limitation is absorbed by one dollar for each dollar of pre-change credit that is used to offset regular tax liability. For each post-change year, the section 382 limitation and the section 383 credit limitation of a new loss corporation are absorbed by such corporation's pre-change losses and pre-change credits in the following order:

(i) Pre-change capital losses described in paragraph (c)(2)(iii) of this section that are recognized and are subject to the section 382 limitation in such post-change year,

(ii) Pre-change capital losses described in paragraphs (c)(2)(i) and (ii) of this section,

(iii) Pre-change losses that are described in § 1.382–2(a)(2) (other than losses that are pre-change capital losses) that are recognized and are subject to the section 382 limitation in such post-change year,

(iv) Pre-change losses not described in paragraphs (d)(2)(i) through (iii) of this section,

(v) Pre-change credits described in paragraph (c)(3)(i) of this section (excess foreign taxes),

(vi) Pre-change credits described in paragraph (c)(3)(ii) of this section (business credits), and

(vii) Pre-change credits described in paragraph (c)(3)(iii) of this section (minimum tax credit).

(3) Coordination with other limitations—(i) In general. Paragraphs (d)(1) and (2) of this section shall be applied after the application of all other limitations contained in subtitle A which are applicable to the use of a pre-change loss or pre-change credit in a post-change year. Thus, only otherwise currently allowable pre-change losses and pre-change credits will result in the absorption of the section 382 limitation and the section 383 credit limitation.

(ii) Examples.

Example (1). L is a calendar year taxpayer and has an ownership change on December 31, 1987. For 1988, L has taxable income of $300,000, a regular tax liability of $100,250 and a tentative minimum tax of $90,000. L has no pre-change losses, but has a business credit carryforward from 1985 of $25,000, no portion of which is due to the regular percentage of the investment tax credit under section 46. L has a section 382 limitation for 1988 of $50,000. L's section 383 credit limitation is $19,500, i.e., an amount equal to the excess of L's regular tax liability ($100,250) over its regular tax liability calculated by allowing an additional deduction of $50,000. Pursuant to the limitation contained in section 38(c), however, L is entitled to use only $10,250 of its business credit carryforward in 1988. The unabsorbed portion of L's section 382 limitation (computed pursuant to paragraph (e) of this section) is carried forward under section 382(b)(2). The

unused portion of L's business credit carryforward, $14,750, is carried forward to the extent provided in section 39.

Example (2). Assume the same facts as in Example (1), except that L's tentative minimum tax is $70,000. L's use of its investment tax credit carryforward is no longer limited by section 38(c); however, pursuant to section 383 and this section, L is entitled to use only $19,500 of its business credit carryforward in 1988. The unused portion of L's business credit carryforward, $5,500, is carried forward to the extent provided in section 39. There is no unused section 382 limitation to be carried forward.

(e) Carryforward of unused section 382 limitation—(1) Computation of carryforward amount. The section 382 limitation that can be carried forward under section 382(b)(2) is the excess, if any, of (i) the section 382 limitation for the post-change year remaining after the application of paragraphs (d)(2)(i) through (iv) of this section, over (ii) the section 383 credit reduction amount for that post-change year.

(2) Section 383 credit reduction amount. The section 383 credit reduction amount for a post-change year is equal to the amount of taxable income attributable to the portion of the new loss corporation's regular tax liability for the year that is offset by pre-change credits. Each dollar of regular tax liability that is offset by a dollar of pre-change credit is divided by the effective marginal rate at which that dollar of tax was imposed to determine the amount of taxable income that resulted in that particular dollar of regular tax liability. The sum of these "grossed-up" amounts for the taxable year is the section 383 credit reduction amount. In determining the effective marginal rate at which a dollar of tax was imposed, special rules regarding rates of tax (e.g., sections 11(b)(2) and (15) or taxable income brackets (e.g., section 1561), or both, shall be taken into account. See Example (3) in paragraph (f) of this section illustrating the effect of section 1561(a). Paragraph (e)(3) of this section illustrates the gross-up computation of the section 383 credit reduction amount based on the tax table and the rates of tax prescribed by section 11(b) as in effect for taxable years beginning on January 1, 1988.

(3) Computation of section 383 credit reduction amount; illustration using tax rates and brackets in effect for calendar year 1988. (i) Assuming no special rules regarding rates of tax or taxable income brackets apply, the section 383 credit reduction amount for a new loss corporation is the sum of the amounts determined under paragraphs (e)(3)(ii), (iii), (iv), (v), and (vi) of this section.

(ii) The amount determined under this subdivision (ii) is the amount (if any) by which pre-change credits offset so much of the new loss corporation's regular tax liability as exceeds $113,900, divided by 0.34.

(iii) The amount determined under this subdivision (e)(3)(iii) is the amount (if any) by which pre-change credits offset so much of the new loss corporation's regular tax liability as exceeds $22,250 (but does not exceed $113,900), divided by 0.39.

(iv) The amount determined under this subdivision (e)(3)(iv) is the amount (if any) by which pre-change credits offset so much of the new loss corporation's regular tax liability as exceeds $13,750 (but does not exceed $22,250), divided by 0.34.

(v) The amount determined under this subdivision (e)(3)(v) is the amount (if any) by which pre-change credits offset so much of the new loss corporation's regular tax liability as exceeds $7,500 (but does not exceed $13,750), divided by 0.25.

(vi) The amount determined under this subdivision (e)(3)(vi) is the amount (if any) by which pre-change credits offset so much of the new loss corporation's regular tax liability as does not exceed $7,500, divided by 0.15.

(f) Examples. The following examples illustrate the operation of paragraphs (b) through (e) of this section. For purposes of these exam-

ples, the term "modified tax liability" means the amount determined under paragraph (c)(6)(i)(B) of this section.

Example (1). (i) L, a calendar year taxpayer, has an ownership change on December 31, 1987. Before the application of carryovers, L, a new loss corporation, has $60,000 of capital gain, $100,000 of ordinary taxable income and a section 382 limitation of $100,000 for its first post-change year beginning after the change date. L's only carryovers are an $80,000 capital loss carryover and a $100,000 net operating loss carryover. Both carryovers are from taxable years ending before the change date and thus are pre-change losses.

(ii) L first uses $60,000 of its pre-change capital loss carryover to offset its capital gain. This reduces its section 382 limitation to $40,000 (i.e., $100,000 − $60,000). L's pre-change net operating loss carryover can therefore be used only to the extent of $40,000. L's remaining $20,000 pre-change capital loss carryover and remaining $60,000 pre-change net operating loss carryover are carried to later years to the extent permitted under this section and sections 172, 382(*l*)(2) and 1212.

Example (2). (i) L, a calendar year taxpayer, has an ownership change on December 31, 1987. L has $750,000 of ordinary taxable income (before the application of carryovers) and a section 382 limitation of $1,500,000 for 1988. L's only carryovers are from pre-1987 taxable years and consist of a $500,000 net operating loss ("NOL") carryover and a $200,000 foreign tax credit carryover, all of which may be used under the section 904 limitation. The NOL carryover is a pre-change loss, and the foreign tax credit carryover is a pre-change credit. L has no other credits which can be used for 1988 and is not liable for an alternative minimum tax for 1988.

(ii) The following computation illustrates the application of this section for 1988:

1.	Taxable income before carryovers	$750,000
2.	Pre-change NOL carryover	500,000

3. Section 382 limitation   1,500,000

4. Amount of pre-change NOL
    carryover that can be used
    (lesser of line 1, 2, or 3)   500,000

5. Taxable income
    (line 1 minus line 4)   250,000

6. Section 382 limitation
    remaining (line 3 minus line 4)   1,000,000

7. Pre-change credit carryover   200,000

8. Regular tax liability
    (line 5 × section 11 rates):

    $50,000 × 0.15 = $7,500

    25,000 × 0.25 = 6,250

    25,000 × 0.34 = 8,500

    150,000 × 0.39 = 58,500   80,750

9. Modified tax liability
    (line 5 minus line 6 (but not
    less than zero) x section 11 rates)   0

10. Section 383 credit limitation
    (line 8 minus line 9)   80,750

11. Amount of pre-change
    credits that can be used
    (lesser of line 7 or line 10)   80,750

12. Amount of pre-change
    credits to be carried over to
    1989 under section 904(c)
    (line 7 minus line 11)   119,250

13. Section 383 credit reduction amount:

    ($80,750 minus $22,250)/0.39 = $150,000

    ($22,250 minus $13,750)/0.34 = 25,000

    ($13,750 minus $7,500)/0.25 = 25,000

    ($7,500/0.15 = 50,000 250,000

14. Section 382 limitation to be
    carried to 1989 under section
    382(b)(2) (line 6 minus line 13)   750,000

(g) Coordination with section 382 and the regulations thereunder. The rules and principles of section 382 (including, for example, section 382(b)(3) and section 382(*l*)(2)) and the regulations thereunder shall also apply with respect to section 383 and this section. To the extent section 382(h)(6) applies to credits, the principles of this section apply to such credits. In applying the rules and principles of section 382 and the regulations thereunder, appropriate adjustments shall be made to take into account that section 383 and this section apply to prechange capital losses and pre-change credits. For example, in applying § 1.382–2T(f)(18)(ii)(C), (f)(18)(iii)(C), and (h)(4)(ix), any pre-change credits, as defined in paragraph (c)(3) of this section, must be converted to a deduction equivalent by dividing the amount of such credits by the maximum effective rate of tax provided for under section 11 (e.g., 0.34 for taxable years beginning in 1989).

§ 1.385–1 General provisions.

(a) Overview of section 385 regulations. This section * * * provide rules under section 385 to determine the treatment of an interest in a corporation as stock or indebtedness (or as in part stock and in part indebtedness) in particular factual situations. Paragraph (b) of this section provides the general rule for determining the treatment of an interest based on provisions of the Internal Revenue Code and on common law, including the factors prescribed under common law.

* * *

(b) General rule. Except as otherwise provided in the Internal Revenue Code and the regulations thereunder, including the section 385 regulations, whether an interest in a corporation is treated for purposes of the Internal Revenue Code as stock or indebtedness (or as in part stock and in part indebtedness) is determined based on common law, including the factors prescribed under such common law.

* * *

Corporations Used to Avoid Income Tax on Shareholders

§ 1.532–1 Corporations subject to accumulated earnings tax.

* * *

(2) The tax imposed by section 531 may apply if the avoidance is accomplished through the formation or use of one corporation or a chain of corporations. For example, if the capital stock of the M Corporation is held by the N Corporation, the earnings and profits of the M Corporation would not be returned as income subject to the individual income tax until such earnings and profits of the M Corporation were distributed to the N Corporation and distributed in turn by the N Corporation to its shareholders. If either the M Corporation or the N Corporation was formed or is availed of for the purpose of avoiding or preventing the imposition of the individual income tax upon the shareholders of the N Corporation, the accumulated taxable income of the corporation so formed or availed of (M or N, as the case may be) is subject to the tax imposed by section 531.

(b) Exceptions. The accumulated earnings tax imposed by section 531 does not apply to a personal holding company (as defined in section 542) or to a corporation exempt from tax under subchapter F, chapter 1 of the Code.

§ 1.533–1 Evidence of purpose to avoid income tax.

(a) In general. (1) The Commissioner's determination that a corporation was formed or availed of for the purpose of avoiding income tax with respect to shareholders is subject to disproof by competent evidence. Section 533(a) provides that the fact that earnings and profits of a corporation are permitted to accumulate beyond the reasonable needs of the business shall be determinative of the purpose to avoid the income tax with respect to shareholders unless the corporation, by the preponderance of the evidence, shall prove to the contrary. The burden of proving that earnings and profits have been permitted to accumulate beyond the reasonable needs of the business may be shifted to the Commissioner under section 534. Section 533(b) provides that the fact that the taxpayer is a mere holding or investment company shall be prima facie evidence of the purpose to avoid income tax with respect to shareholders.

(2) The existence or nonexistence of the purpose to avoid income tax with respect to shareholders may be indicated by circumstances other than the conditions specified in section 533. Whether or not such purpose was present depends upon the particular circumstances of each case. All circumstances which might be construed as evidence of the purpose to avoid income tax with respect to shareholders cannot be outlined, but among other things, the following will be considered:

(i) Dealings between the corporation and its shareholders, such as withdrawals by the shareholders as personal loans or the expenditure of funds by the corporation for the personal benefit of the shareholders,

(ii) The investment by the corporation of undistributed earnings in assets having no reasonable connection with the business of the corporation (see § 1.537–3), and

(iii) The extent to which the corporation has distributed its earnings and profits. The fact that a corporation is a mere holding or investment company or has an accumulation of earnings and profits in excess of the reasonable needs of the business is not absolutely conclusive against it if the taxpayer satisfies the Commissioner that the corporation was neither formed nor availed of for the purpose of avoiding income tax with respect to shareholders.

(b) General burden of proof and statutory presumptions. The Commissioner may determine that the taxpayer was formed or availed of to avoid income tax with respect to shareholders through the medium of permitting earnings and profits to accumulate. In the case of litigation involving any such determination (except where the burden of proof is on the Commissioner under section 534), the burden of proving such determination wrong by a preponderance of the evidence, together with the corresponding burden of first going forward with the evidence, is on the taxpayer under principles applicable to income tax cases generally. For the burden of proof in a proceeding before the Tax Court with respect to the allegation that earnings and profits have been permitted to accumulate beyond the reasonable needs of the business, see section 534. For a definition of a holding or investment company, see paragraph (c) of this section. For determination of the reasonable needs of the business, see section 537 and §§ 1.537–1 through 1.537–3. If the taxpayer is a mere holding or investment company, and the Commissioner therefore determines that the corporation was formed or availed of for the purpose of avoiding income tax with respect to shareholders, then section 533(b) gives further weight to the presumption of correctness already arising from the Commissioner's determination by expressly providing an additional presumption of the existence of a purpose to avoid income tax with respect to shareholders. Further, if it is established (after complying with section 534 where applicable) that earnings and profits were permitted to accumulate beyond the reasonable needs of the business and the Commissioner has therefore determined that the corporation was formed or availed of for the purpose of avoiding income tax with respect to shareholders, then section 533(a) adds still more weight to the Commissioner's determination. Under such circumstances, the existence of such an accumulation is made determinative of the purpose to avoid income tax with respect to shareholders unless the taxpayer proves to the contrary by the preponderance of the evidence.

(c) **Holding or investment company.** A corporation having practically no activities except holding property and collecting the income therefrom or investing therein shall be considered a holding company within the meaning of section 533(b). If the activities further include, or consist substantially of, buying and selling stocks, securities, real estate, or other investment property (whether upon an outright or marginal basis) so that the income is derived not only from the investment yield but also from profits upon market fluctuations, the corporation shall be considered an invest-

ment company within the meaning of section 533(b).

§ 1.537–1 Reasonable needs of the business.

(a) **In general.** The term "reasonable needs of the business" includes (1) the reasonable anticipated needs of the business (including product liability loss reserves, as defined in paragraph (f) of this section), (2) the section 303 redemption needs of the business, as defined in paragraph (c) of this section, and (3) the excess business holdings redemption needs of the business as described in paragraph (d) of this section. See paragraph (E) of this section for additional rules relating to the section 303 redemption needs and the excess business holdings redemption needs of the business. An accumulation of the earnings and profits (including the undistributed earnings and profits of prior years) is in excess of the reasonable needs of the business if it exceeds the amount that a prudent businessman would consider appropriate for the present business purposes and for the reasonably anticipated future needs of the business. The need to retain earnings and profits must be directly connected with the needs of the corporation itself and must be for bona fide business purposes. For purposes of this paragraph the section 303 redemption needs of the business and the excess business holdings redemption needs of the business are deemed to be directly connected with the needs of the business and for a bona fide business purpose. See § 1.537–3 for a discussion of what constitutes the business of the corporation. The extent to which earnings and profits have been distributed by the corporation may be taken into account in determining whether or not retained earnings and profits exceed the reasonable needs of the business. See § 1.537–2, relating to grounds for accumulation of earnings and profits.

(b) **Reasonable anticipated needs. (1)** In order for a corporation to justify an accumulation of earnings and profits for reasonably anticipated future needs, there must be an indication that the future needs of the business require such accumulation, and the corporation must have specific, definite, and feasible plans for the use of such accumulation. Such an accumulation need not be used immediately, nor must the plans for its use be consummated within a short period after the close of the taxable year, provided that such accumulation will be used within a reasonable time depending upon all the facts and circumstances relating to the future needs of the business. Where the future needs of the business are uncertain or vague, where the plans for the future use of an accumulation are not specific, definite, and feasible, or where the execution of such a plan is postponed indefinitely, an accumulation cannot be justified on the grounds of reasonably anticipated needs of the business.

(2) Consideration shall be given to reasonably anticipated needs as they exist on the basis of the facts at the close of the taxable year. Thus, subsequent events shall not be used for the purpose of showing that the retention of earnings or profits was unreasonable at the close of the taxable year if all the elements of reasonable anticipation are present at the close of such taxable year. However, subsequent events may be considered to determine whether the taxpayer actually intended to consummate or has actually consummated the plans for which the earnings and profits were accumulated. In this connection, projected expansion or investment plans shall be reviewed in the light of the facts during each year and as they exist as of the close of the taxable year. If a corporation has justified an accumulation for future needs by plans never consummated, the amount of such an accumulation shall be taken into account in determining the reasonableness of subsequent accumulations.

(c) Section 303 redemption needs of the business. (1) The term "section 303 redemption needs" means, with respect to the taxable year of the corporation in which a shareholder of the corporation died or any taxable year thereafter, the amount needed (or reasonably

anticipated to be needed) to redeem stock included in the gross estate of such shareholder but not in excess of the amount necessary to effect a distribution to which section 303 applies. For purposes of this paragraph, the term "shareholder" includes an individual in whose gross estate stock of the corporation is includable upon his death for Federal estate tax purposes.

(2) This paragraph applies to a corporation to which section 303(c) would apply if a distribution described therein were made.

(3) If stock included in the gross estate of a decedent is stock of two or more corporations described in section 303(b)(2)(B), the amount needed by each such corporation for section 303 redemption purposes under this section shall, unless the particular facts and circumstances indicate otherwise, be that amount which bears the same ratio to the amount described in section 303(a) as the fair market value of such corporation's stock included in the gross estate of such decedent bears to the fair market value of all of the stock of such corporations included in the gross estate. For example, facts and circumstances indicating that the allocation prescribed by this subparagraph is not required would include notice given to the corporations by the executor or administrator of the decedent's estate that he intends to request the redemption of stock of only one of such corporations or the redemption of stock of such corporations in a ratio which is unrelated to the respective fair market values of the stock of the corporations included in the decedent's gross estate.

* * *

§ 1.537–2 Grounds for accumulation of earnings and profits.

(a) In general. Whether a particular ground or grounds for the accumulation of earnings and profits indicate that the earnings and profits have been accumulated for the reasonable needs of the business or beyond such needs is dependent upon the particular circumstances of the case. Listed below in paragraphs (b) and (c) of this section are some of the grounds which may be used as guides under ordinary circumstances.

(b) Reasonable accumulation of earnings and profits. Although the following grounds are not exclusive, one or more of such grounds, if supported by sufficient facts, may indicate that the earnings and profits of a corporation are being accumulated for the reasonable needs of the business provided the general requirements under §§ 1.537–1 and 1.537–3 are satisfied:

(1) To provide for bona fide expansion of business or replacement of plant;

(2) To acquire a business enterprise through purchasing stock or assets;

(3) To provide for the retirement of bona fide indebtedness created in connection with the trade or business, such as the establishment of a sinking fund for the purpose of retiring bonds issued by the corporation in accordance with contract obligations incurred on issue;

(4) To provide necessary working capital for the business, such as, for the procurement of inventories;

(5) To provide for investments or loans to suppliers or customers if necessary in order to maintain the business of the corporation; or

(6) To provide for the payment of reasonably anticipated product liability losses, as defined in section 172(j) * * *

(c) Unreasonable accumulations of earnings and profits. Although the following purposes are not exclusive, accumulations of earnings and profits to meet any one of such objectives may indicate that the earnings and profits of a corporation are being accumulated beyond the reasonable needs of the business:

(1) Loans to shareholders, or the expenditure of funds of the corporation for the personal benefit of the shareholders;

(2) Loans having no reasonable relation to the conduct of the business made to relatives or friends of shareholders, or to other persons;

(3) Loans to another corporation, the business of which is not that of the taxpayer corporation, if the capital stock of such other corporation is owned, directly or indirectly, by the shareholder or shareholders of the taxpayer corporation and such shareholder or shareholders are in control of both corporations;

(4) Investments in properties, or securities which are unrelated to the activities of the business of the taxpayer corporation; or

(5) Retention of earnings and profits to provide against unrealistic hazards.

§ 1.537–3 Business of the corporation.

(a) The business of a corporation is not merely that which it has previously carried on but includes, in general, any line of business which it may undertake.

(b) If one corporation owns the stock of another corporation and, in effect, operates the other corporation, the business of the latter corporation may be considered in substance, although not in legal form, the business of the first corporation. However, investment by a corporation of its earnings and profits in stock and securities of another corporation is not, of itself, to be regarded as employment of the earnings and profits in its business. Earnings and profits of the first corporation put into the second corporation through the purchase of stock or securities or otherwise, may, if a subsidiary relationship is established, constitute employment of the earnings and profits in its own business. Thus, the business of one corporation may be regarded as including the business of another corporation if such other corporation is a mere instrumentality of the first corporation; that may be established by showing that the first corporation owns at least 80 percent of the voting stock of the second corporation. If the taxpayer's ownership of stock is less than 80 percent in the other corporation, the determination of whether the funds are employed in a business operated by the taxpayer will depend upon the particular circumstances of the case. Moreover, the business of one corporation does not include the business of another corporation if such other corporation is a personal holding company, an investment company, or a corporation not engaged in the active conduct of a trade or business.

Partners and Partnerships

§ 1.701–1 Partners, not partnership, subject to tax.

Partners are liable for income tax only in their separate capacities. Partnerships as such are not subject to the income tax imposed by subtitle A but are required to make returns of income under the provisions of section 6031 and the regulations thereunder. For definition of the terms "partner" and "partnership", see sections 761 and 7701(a)(2), and the regulations thereunder. For provisions relating to the election of certain partnerships to be taxed as domestic corporations, see section 1361 and the regulations thereunder.

§ 1.701–2 Anti-abuse rule.

(a) Intent of subchapter K. Subchapter K is intended to permit taxpayers to conduct joint business (including investment) activities through a flexible economic arrangement without incurring an entity-level tax. Implicit in the intent of subchapter K are the following requirements —

(1) The partnership must be bona fide and each partnership transaction or series of related transactions (individually or collectively, the transaction) must be entered into for a substantial business purpose.

(2) The form of each partnership transaction must be respected under substance over form principles.

(3) Except as otherwise provided in this paragraph (a)(3), the tax consequences under subchapter K to each partner of partnership operations and of transactions between the partner and the partnership must accurately reflect the partners' economic agreement and clearly reflect the partner's income (collectively, proper reflection of income). However, certain provisions of subchapter K and the regulations thereunder were adopted to promote administrative convenience and other policy objectives, with the recognition that the application of those provisions to a transaction could, in some circumstances, produce tax results that do not properly reflect income. Thus, the proper reflection of income requirement of this paragraph (a)(3) is treated as satisfied with respect to a transaction that satisfies paragraphs (a)(1) and (2) of this section to the extent that the application of such a provision to the transaction and the ultimate tax results, taking into account all the relevant facts and circumstances, are clearly contemplated by that provision. See, for example, paragraph (d) Example 6 of this section (relating to the value-equals-basis rule in § 1.704–1(b)(2)(iii)(c)), paragraph (d) Example 9 of this section (relating to the election under section 754 to adjust basis in partnership property), and paragraph (d) Examples 10 and 11 of this section (relating to the basis in property distributed by a partnership under section 732). See also, for example, §§ 1.704–3(e)(1) and 1.752–2(e)(4) (providing certain de minimis exceptions).

(b) Application of subchapter K rules. The provisions of subchapter K and the regulations thereunder must be applied in a manner that is consistent with the intent of subchapter K as set forth in paragraph (a) of this section (intent of subchapter K). Accordingly, if a partnership is formed or availed of in connection with a transaction a principal purpose of which is to reduce substantially the present value of the partners' aggregate federal tax liability in a manner that is inconsistent with the intent of subchapter K, the Commissioner can recast the transaction for federal tax purposes, as appropriate to achieve tax results that are consistent with the intent of subchapter K, in light of the applicable statutory and regulatory provisions and the pertinent facts and circumstances. Thus, even though the transaction may fall within the literal words of a particular statutory or regulatory provision, the Commissioner can determine, based on the particular facts and circumstances, that to achieve tax results that are consistent with the intent of subchapter K—

(1) The purported partnership should be disregarded in whole or in part, and the partnership's assets and activities should be considered, in whole or in part, to be owned and conducted, respectively, by one or more of its purported partners;

(2) One or more of the purported partners of the partnership should not be treated as a partner;

(3) The methods of accounting used by the partnership or a partner should be adjusted to reflect clearly the partnership's or the partner's income;

(4) The partnership's items of income, gain, loss, deduction, or credit should be reallocated; or

(5) The claimed tax treatment should otherwise be adjusted or modified.

(c) **Facts and circumstances analysis; factors.** Whether a partnership was formed or availed of with a principal purpose to reduce substantially the present value of the partners' aggregate federal tax liability in a manner inconsistent with the intent of subchapter K is determined based on all of the facts and circumstances, including a comparison of the purported business purpose for a transaction and the claimed tax benefits resulting from the transaction. The factors set forth below may be indicative, but do not necessarily establish, that a partnership was used in such a manner. These factors are illustrative only, and therefore may not be the only factors taken into account in making the determination under this section. Moreover, the weight given to any factor (whether specified in this paragraph or otherwise) depends on all the facts and circumstances. The presence or absence of any factor described in this paragraph does not create a presumption that a partnership was (or was not) used in such a manner. Factors include:

(1) The present value of the partners' aggregate federal tax liability is substantially less than had the partners owned the partnership's assets and conducted the partnership's activities directly;

(2) The present value of the partners' aggregate federal tax liability is substantially less than would be the case if purportedly separate transactions that are designed to achieve a particular end result are integrated and treated as steps in a single transaction. For example, this analysis may indicate that it was contemplated that a partner who was necessary to achieve the intended tax results and whose interest in the partnership was liquidated or disposed of (in whole or in part) would be a partner only temporarily in order to provide the claimed tax benefits to the remaining partners;

(3) One or more partners who are necessary to achieve the claimed tax results either have a nominal interest in the partnership, are substantially protected from any risk of loss from the partnership's activities (through distribution preferences, indemnity or loss guaranty agreements, or other arrangements), or have little or no participation in the profits from the partnership's activities other than a preferred return that is in the nature of a payment for the use of capital;

(4) Substantially all of the partners (measured by number or interests in the partnership) are related (directly or indirectly) to one another;

(5) Partnership items are allocated in compliance with the literal language of §§ 1.704–1 and 1.704–2 but with results that are incon-

sistent with the purpose of section 704(b) and those regulations. In this regard, particular scrutiny will be paid to partnerships in which income or gain is specially allocated to one or more partners that may be legally or effectively exempt from federal taxation (for example, a foreign person, an exempt organization, an insolvent taxpayer, or a taxpayer with unused federal tax attributes such as net operating losses, capital losses, or foreign tax credits);

(6) The benefits and burdens of ownership of property nominally contributed to the partnership are in substantial part retained (directly or indirectly) by the contributing partner (or a related party); or

(7) The benefits and burdens of ownership of partnership property are in substantial part shifted (directly or indirectly) to the distributee partner before or after the property is actually distributed to the distributee partner (or a related party).

(d) Examples. The following examples illustrate the principles of paragraphs (a), (b), and (c) of this section. The examples set forth below do not delineate the boundaries of either permissible or impermissible types of transactions. Further, the addition of any facts or circumstances that are not specifically set forth in an example (or the deletion of any facts or circumstances) may alter the outcome of the transaction described in the example. Unless otherwise indicated, parties to the transactions are not related to one another.

Example (1). Choice of entity; avoidance of entity-level tax; use of partnership consistent with the intent of subchapter K. (i) A and B form limited partnership PRS to conduct a bona fide business. A, the corporate general partner, has a 1% partnership interest. B, the individual limited partner, has a 99% interest. PRS is properly classified as a partnership under §§ 301.7701–2 and 301.7701–3. A and B chose limited partnership form as a means to provide B with limited liability without subjecting the income from the business operations to an entity-level tax.

(ii) Subchapter K is intended to permit taxpayers to conduct joint business activity through a flexible economic arrangement without incurring an entity-level tax. See paragraph (a) of this section. Although B has retained, indirectly, substantially all of the benefits and burdens of ownership of the money or property B contributed to PRS (see paragraph (c)(6) of this section), the decision to organize and conduct business through PRS under these circumstances is consistent with this intent. In addition, on these facts, the requirements of paragraphs (a)(1), (2), and (3) of this section have been satisfied. The Commissioner therefore cannot invoke paragraph (b) of this section to recast the transaction.

Example (2). Choice of entity; avoidance of subchapter S shareholder requirements; use of partnership consistent with the intent of subchapter K. (i) A and B form partnership PRS to conduct a bona fide business. A is a corporation that has elected to be treated as an S corporation under subchapter S. B is a nonresident alien. PRS is properly classified as a partnership under §§ 301.7701–2 and 301.7701–3. Because section 1361(b) prohibits B from being a shareholder in A, A and B chose partnership form, rather than admit B as a shareholder in A, as a means to retain the benefits of subchapter S treatment for A and its shareholders.

(ii) Subchapter K is intended to permit taxpayers to conduct joint business activity through a flexible economic arrangement without incurring an entity-level tax. See paragraph (a) of this section. The decision to organize and conduct business through PRS is consistent with this intent. In addition, on these facts, the requirements of paragraphs (a)(1), (2), and (3) of this section have been satisfied. Although it may be argued that the form of the partnership transaction should not be respected because it does not reflect its substance (inasmuch as application of the substance over form doctrine arguably could result in B being treated as a shareholder of A, thereby invalidating A's subchapter S election), the facts indicate otherwise. The shareholders of

A are subject to tax on their pro rata shares of A's income (see section 1361 et seq.), and B is subject to tax on B's distributive share of partnership income (see sections 871 and 875). Thus, the form in which this arrangement is cast accurately reflects its substance as a separate partnership and S corporation. The Commissioner therefore cannot invoke paragraph (b) of this section to recast the transaction.

Example (3). Choice of entity; avoidance of more restrictive foreign tax credit limitation; use of partnership consistent with the intent of subchapter K. (i) X, a domestic corporation, and Y, a foreign corporation, form partnership PRS under the laws of foreign Country A to conduct a bona fide joint business. X and Y each owns a 50% interest in PRS. PRS is properly classified as a partnership under §§ 301.7701–2 and 301.7701–3. PRS pays income taxes to Country A. X and Y chose partnership form to enable X to qualify for a direct foreign tax credit under section 901, with look-through treatment under § 1.904–5(h)(1). Conversely, if PRS were a foreign corporation for U.S. tax purposes, X would be entitled only to indirect foreign tax credits under section 902 with respect to dividend distributions from PRS. The look-through rules, however, would not apply, and pursuant to section 904(d)(1)(E) and § 1.904–4(g), the dividends and associated taxes would be subject to a separate foreign tax credit limitation for dividends from PRS, a noncontrolled section 902 corporation.

(ii) Subchapter K is intended to permit taxpayers to conduct joint business activity through a flexible economic arrangement without incurring an entity-level tax. See paragraph (a) of this section. The decision to organize and conduct business through PRS in order to take advantage of the look-through rules for foreign tax credit purposes, thereby maximizing X's use of its proper share of foreign taxes paid by PRS, is consistent with this intent. In addition, on these facts, the requirements of paragraphs (a)(1), (2), and (3) of this section have been satisfied. The Commissioner

therefore cannot invoke paragraph (b) of this section to recast the transaction.

Example (4). Choice of entity; avoidance of gain recognition under sections 351(e) and 357(c); use of partnership consistent with the intent of subchapter K. (i) X, ABC, and DEF form limited partnership PRS to conduct a bona fide real estate management business. PRS is properly classified as a partnership under §§ 301.7701–2 and 301.7701–3. X, the general partner, is a newly formed corporation that elects to be treated as a real estate investment trust as defined in section 856. X offers its stock to the public and contributes substantially all of the proceeds from the public offering to PRS. ABC and DEF, the limited partners, are existing partnerships with substantial real estate holdings. ABC and DEF contribute all of their real property assets to PRS, subject to liabilities that exceed their respective aggregate bases in the real property contributed, and terminate under section 708(b)(1)(A). In addition, some of the former partners of ABC and DEF each have the right, beginning two years after the formation of PRS, to require the redemption of their limited partnership interests in PRS in exchange for cash or X stock (at X's option) equal to the fair market value of their respective interests in PRS at the time of the redemption. These partners are not compelled, as a legal or practical matter, to exercise their exchange rights at any time. X, ABC, and DEF chose to form a partnership rather than have ABC and DEF invest directly in X to allow ABC and DEF to avoid recognition of gain under sections 351(e) and 357(c). Because PRS would not be treated as an investment company within the meaning of section 351(e) if PRS were incorporated (so long as it did not elect under section 856), section 721(a) applies to the contribution of the real property to PRS. See section 721(b).

(ii) Subchapter K is intended to permit taxpayers to conduct joint business activity through a flexible economic arrangement without incurring an entity-level tax. See para-

graph (a) of this section. The decision to organize and conduct business through PRS, thereby avoiding the tax consequences that would have resulted from contributing the existing partnerships' real estate assets to X (by applying the rules of sections 721, 731, and 752 in lieu of the rules of sections 351(e) and 357(c)), is consistent with this intent. In addition, on these facts, the requirements of paragraphs (a)(1), (2), and (3) of this section have been satisfied. Although it may be argued that the form of the transaction should not be respected because it does not reflect its substance (inasmuch as the present value of the partners' aggregate federal tax liability is substantially less than would be the case if the transaction were integrated and treated as a contribution of the encumbered assets by ABC and DEF directly to X, see paragraph (c)(2) of this section), the facts indicate otherwise. For example, the right of some of the former ABC and DEF partners after two years to exchange their PRS interests for cash or X stock (at X's option) equal to the fair market value of their PRS interest at that time would not require that right to be considered as exercised prior to its actual exercise. Moreover, X may make other real estate investments and other business decisions, including the decision to raise additional capital for those purposes. Thus, although it may be likely that some or all of the partners with the right to do so will, at some point, exercise their exchange rights, and thereby receive either cash or X stock, the form of the transaction as a separate partnership and real estate investment trust is respected under substance over form principles (see paragraph (a)(2) of this section). The Commissioner therefore cannot invoke paragraph (b) of this section to recast the transaction.

Example (5). Special allocations; dividends received deductions; use of partnership consistent with the intent of subchapter K. (i) Corporations X and Y contribute equal amounts to PRS, a bona fide partnership formed to make joint investments. PRS pays $100x for a share of common stock of Z, an unrelated corporation, which has historically paid an annual dividend of $6x. PRS specially allocates the dividend income on the Z stock to X to the extent of the London Inter-Bank Offered Rate (LIBOR) on the record date, applied to X's contribution of $50x, and allocates the remainder of the dividend income to Y. All other items of partnership income and loss are allocated equally between X and Y. The allocations under the partnership agreement have substantial economic effect within the meaning of § 1.704–1(b)(2). In addition to avoiding an entity-level tax, a principal purpose for the formation of the partnership was to invest in the Z common stock and to allocate the dividend income from the stock to provide X with a floating-rate return based on LIBOR, while permitting X and Y to claim the dividends received deduction under section 243 on the dividends allocated to each of them.

(ii) Subchapter K is intended to permit taxpayers to conduct joint business activity through a flexible economic arrangement without incurring an entity-level tax. See paragraph (a) of this section. The decision to organize and conduct business through PRS is consistent with this intent. In addition, on these facts, the requirements of paragraphs (a)(1), (2), and (3) of this section have been satisfied. Section 704(b) and § 1.704–1(b)(2) permit income realized by the partnership to be allocated validly to the partners separate from the partners' respective ownership of the capital to which the allocations relate, provided that the allocations satisfy both the literal requirements of the statute and regulations and the purpose of those provisions (see paragraph (c)(5) of this section). Section 704(e)(2) is not applicable to the facts of this example (otherwise, the allocations would be required to be proportionate to the partners' ownership of contributed capital). The Commissioner therefore cannot invoke paragraph (b) of this section to recast the transaction.

Example (6). Special allocations; nonrecourse financing; low-income housing credit;

use of partnership consistent with the intent of subchapter K. (i) A and B, high-bracket taxpayers, and X, a corporation with net operating loss carryforwards, form general partnership PRS to own and operate a building that qualifies for the low-income housing credit provided by section 42. The project is financed with both cash contributions from the partners and nonrecourse indebtedness. The partnership agreement provides for special allocations of income and deductions, including the allocation of all depreciation deductions attributable to the building to A and B equally in a manner that is reasonably consistent with allocations that have substantial economic effect of some other significant partnership item attributable to the building. The section 42 credits are allocated to A and B in accordance with the allocation of depreciation deductions. PRS's allocations comply with all applicable regulations, including the requirements of §§ 1.704–1(b)(2)(ii) (pertaining to economic effect) and 1.704–2(e) (requirements for allocations of nonrecourse deductions). The nonrecourse indebtedness is validly allocated to the partners under the rules of § 1.752–3, thereby increasing the basis of the partners' respective partnership interests. The basis increase created by the nonrecourse indebtedness enables A and B to deduct their distributive share of losses from the partnership (subject to all other applicable limitations under the Internal Revenue Code) against their nonpartnership income and to apply the credits against their tax liability.

(ii) At a time when the depreciation deductions attributable to the building are not treated as nonrecourse deductions under § 1.704–2(c) (because there is no net increase in partnership minimum gain during the year), the special allocation of depreciation deductions to A and B has substantial economic effect because of the value-equals-basis safe harbor contained in § 1.704–1(b)(2)(iii)(c) and the fact that A and B would bear the economic burden of any decline in the value of the building (to the extent of the partnership's investment in the building), notwithstanding that A and B believe it is unlikely that the building will decline in value (and, accordingly, they anticipate significant timing benefits through the special allocation). Moreover, in later years, when the depreciation deductions attributable to the building are treated as nonrecourse deductions under § 1.704–2(c), the special allocation of depreciation deductions to A and B is considered to be consistent with the partners' interests in the partnership under § 1.704–2(e).

(iii) Subchapter K is intended to permit taxpayers to conduct joint business activity through a flexible economic arrangement without incurring an entity-level tax. See paragraph (a) of this section. The decision to organize and conduct business through PRS is consistent with this intent. In addition, on these facts, the requirements of paragraphs (a)(1), (2), and (3) of this section have been satisfied. Sections 704(b), 1.704–1(b)(2), and 1.704–2(e) allow partnership items of income, gain, loss, deduction, and credit to be allocated validly to the partners separate from the partners' respective ownership of the capital to which the allocations relate, provided that the allocations satisfy both the literal requirements of the statute and regulations and the purpose of those provisions (see paragraph (c)(5) of this section). Moreover, the application of the value-equals-basis safe harbor and the provisions of § 1.704–2(e) with respect to the allocations to A and B, and the tax results of the application of those provisions, taking into account all the facts and circumstances, are clearly contemplated. Accordingly, even if the allocations would not otherwise be considered to satisfy the proper reflection of income standard in paragraph (a)(3) of this section, that requirement will be treated as satisfied under these facts. Thus, even though the partners' aggregate federal tax liability may be substantially less than had the partners owned the partnership's assets directly (due to X's inability to use its allocable share of the partnership's losses and credits) (see paragraph (c)(1) of this section), the transaction is not inconsistent with the intent of subchapter K. The Commis-

sioner therefore cannot invoke paragraph (b) of this section to recast the transaction.

Example (7). Partner with nominal interest; temporary partner; use of partnership not consistent with the intent of subchapter K. (i) Pursuant to a plan a principal purpose of which is to generate artificial losses and thereby shelter from federal taxation a substantial amount of income, X (a foreign corporation), Y (a domestic corporation), and Z (a promoter) form partnership PRS by contributing $9,000x, $990x, and $10x, respectively, for proportionate interests (90.0%, 9.9%, and 0.1%, respectively) in the capital and profits of PRS. PRS purchases offshore equipment for $10,000x and validly leases the equipment offshore for a term representing most of its projected useful life. Shortly thereafter, PRS sells its rights to receive income under the lease to a third party for $9,000x, and allocates the resulting $9,000x of income $8,100x to X, $891x to Y, and $9x to Z. PRS thereafter makes a distribution of $9,000x to X in complete liquidation of its interest. Under § 1.704–1(b)(2)(iv) (f), PRS restates the partners' capital accounts immediately before making the liquidating distribution to X to reflect its assets consisting of the offshore equipment worth $1,000x and $9,000x in cash. Thus, because the capital accounts immediately before the distribution reflect assets of $19,000x (that is, the initial capital contributions of $10,000x plus the $9,000x of income realized from the sale of the lease), PRS allocates a $9,000x book loss among the partners (for capital account purposes only), resulting in restated capital accounts for X, Y, and Z of $9,000x, $990x, and $10x, respectively. Thereafter, PRS purchases real property by borrowing the $8,000x purchase price on a recourse basis, which increases Y's and Z's bases in their respective partnership interests from $1,881x and $19x, to $9,801x and $99x, respectively (reflecting Y's and Z's adjusted interests in the partnership of 99% and 1%, respectively). PRS subsequently sells the offshore equipment, subject to the lease, for $1,000x and allocates the $9,000x tax loss

$8,910x to Y and $90x to Z. Y's and Z's bases in their partnership interests are therefore reduced to $891x and $9x, respectively.

(ii) On these facts, any purported business purpose for the transaction is insignificant in comparison to the tax benefits that would result if the transaction were respected for federal tax purposes (see paragraph (c) of this section). Accordingly, the transaction lacks a substantial business purpose (see paragraph (a)(1) of this section). In addition, factors (1), (2), (3), and (5) of paragraph (c) of this section indicate that PRS was used with a principal purpose to reduce substantially the partners' tax liability in a manner inconsistent with the intent of subchapter K. On these facts, PRS is not bona fide (see paragraph (a)(1) of this section), and the transaction is not respected under applicable substance over form principles (see paragraph (a)(2) of this section) and does not properly reflect the income of Y (see paragraph (a)(3) of this section). Thus, PRS has been formed and availed of with a principal purpose of reducing substantially the present value of the partners' aggregate federal tax liability in a manner inconsistent with the intent of subchapter K. Therefore (in addition to possibly challenging the transaction under judicial principles or the validity of the allocations under § 1.704–1(b)(2) (see paragraph (h) of this section)), the Commissioner can recast the transaction as appropriate under paragraph (b) of this section.

Example (8). Plan to duplicate losses through absence of section 754 election; use of partnership not consistent with the intent of subchapter K. (i) A owns land with a basis of $100x and a fair market value of $60x. A would like to sell the land to B. A and B devise a plan a principal purpose of which is to permit the duplication, for a substantial period of time, of the tax benefit of A's built-in loss in the land. To effect this plan, A, C (A's brother), and W (C's wife) form partnership PRS, to which A contributes the land, and C and W each contribute $30x. All partnership items are shared in proportion to the partners' respective contributions to PRS. PRS invests the cash in an investment asset (that is not a marketable security within the meaning of section 731(c)). PRS also leases the land to B under a three-year lease pursuant to which B has the option to purchase the land from PRS upon the expiration of the lease for an amount equal to its fair market value at that time. All lease proceeds received are immediately distributed to the partners. In year 3, at a time when the values of the partnership's assets have not materially changed, PRS agrees with A to liquidate A's interest in exchange for the investment asset held by PRS. Under section 732(b), A's basis in the asset distributed equals $100x, A's basis in A's partnership interest immediately before the distribution. Shortly thereafter, A sells the investment asset to X, an unrelated party, recognizing a $40x loss.

(ii) PRS does not make an election under section 754. Accordingly, PRS's basis in the land contributed by A remains $100x. At the end of year 3, pursuant to the lease option, PRS sells the land to B for $60x (its fair market value). Thus, PRS recognizes a $40x loss on the sale, which is allocated equally between C and W. C's and W's bases in their partnership interests are reduced to $10x each pursuant to section 705. Their respective interests are worth $30x each. Thus, upon liquidation of PRS (or their interests therein), each of C and W will recognize $20x of gain. However, PRS's continued existence defers recognition of that gain indefinitely. Thus, if this arrangement is respected, C and W duplicate for their benefit A's built-in loss in the land prior to its contribution to PRS.

(iii) On these facts, any purported business purpose for the transaction is insignificant in comparison to the tax benefits that would result if the transaction were respected for federal tax purposes (see paragraph (c) of this section). Accordingly, the transaction lacks a substantial business purpose (see paragraph (a) (1) of this section). In addition, factors (1), (2),

and (4) of paragraph (c) of this section indicate that PRS was used with a principal purpose to reduce substantially the partners' tax liability in a manner inconsistent with the intent of subchapter K. On these facts, PRS is not bona fide (see paragraph (a)(1) of this section), and the transaction is not respected under applicable substance over form principles (see paragraph (a)(2) of this section). Further, the tax consequences to the partners do not properly reflect the partners' income; and Congress did not contemplate application of section 754 to partnerships such as PRS, which was formed for a principal purpose of producing a double tax benefit from a single economic loss (see paragraph (a)(3) of this section). Thus, PRS has been formed and availed of with a principal purpose of reducing substantially the present value of the partners' aggregate federal tax liability in a manner inconsistent with the intent of subchapter K. Therefore (in addition to possibly challenging the transaction under judicial principles or other statutory authorities, such as the substance over form doctrine or the disguised sale rules under section 707 (see paragraph (h) of this section)), the Commissioner can recast the transaction as appropriate under paragraph (b) of this section.

Example (9). Absence of section 754 election; use of partnership consistent with the intent of subchapter K. (i) PRS is a bona fide partnership formed to engage in investment activities with contributions of cash from each partner. Several years after joining PRS, A, a partner with a capital account balance and basis in its partnership interest of $100x, wishes to withdraw from PRS. The partnership agreement entitles A to receive the balance of A's capital account in cash or securities owned by PRS at the time of withdrawal, as mutually agreed to by A and the managing general partner, P. P and A agree to distribute to A $100x worth of non-marketable securities (see section 731(c)) in which PRS has an aggregate basis of $20x. Upon distribution, A's aggregate basis in the securities is $100x under section 732(b). PRS does not make an election to adjust the basis in its remaining assets under section 754. Thus, PRS's basis in its remaining assets is unaffected by the distribution. In contrast, if a section 754 election had been in effect for the year of the distribution, under these facts section 734(b) would have required PRS to adjust the basis in its remaining assets downward by the amount of the untaxed appreciation in the distributed property, thus reflecting that gain in PRS's retained assets. In selecting the assets to be distributed, A and P had a principal purpose to take advantage of the facts that A's basis in the securities will be determined by reference to A's basis in its partnership interest under section 732(b), and because PRS will not make an election under section 754, the remaining partners of PRS will likely enjoy a federal tax timing advantage (i.e., from the $80x of additional basis in its assets that would have been eliminated if the section 754 election had been made) that is inconsistent with proper reflection of income under paragraph (a)(3) of this section.

(ii) Subchapter K is intended to permit taxpayers to conduct joint business activity through a flexible economic arrangement without incurring an entity-level tax. See paragraph (a) of this section. The decision to organize and conduct business through PRS is consistent with this intent. In addition, on these facts, the requirements of paragraphs (a) (1) and (2) of this section have been satisfied. The validity of the tax treatment of this transaction is therefore dependent upon whether the transaction satisfies (or is treated as satisfying) the proper reflection of income standard under paragraph (a)(3) of this section. A's basis in the distributed securities is properly determined under section 732(b). The benefit to the remaining partners is a result of PRS not having made an election under section 754. Subchapter K is generally intended to produce tax consequences that achieve proper reflection of income. However, paragraph (a)(3) of this section provides that if the application of a provision of subchapter K produces tax results that do not properly reflect income, but application of that provision to the transaction and the ultimate tax results, taking into account all the relevant facts and circumstances, are clearly contemplated by that provision (and the transaction satisfies the requirements of paragraphs (a)(1) and (2) of this section), then the application of that provision to the transaction will be treated as satisfying the proper reflection of income standard.

(iii) In general, the adjustments that would be made if an election under section 754 were in effect are necessary to minimize distortions between the partners' bases in their partnership interests and the partnership's basis in its assets following, for example, a distribution to a partner. The electivity of section 754 is intended to provide administrative convenience for bona fide partnerships that are engaged in transactions for a substantial business purpose, by providing those partnerships the option of not adjusting their bases in their remaining assets following a distribution to a partner. Congress clearly recognized that if the section 754 election were not made, basis distortions may result. Taking into account all the facts and circumstances of the transaction, the electivity of section 754 in the context of the distribution from PRS to A, and the ultimate tax consequences that follow from the failure to make the election with respect to the transaction, are clearly contemplated by section 754. Thus, the tax consequences of this transaction will be treated as satisfying the proper reflection of income standard under paragraph (a)(3) of this section. The Commissioner therefore cannot invoke paragraph (b) of this section to recast the transaction.

Example (10). Basis adjustments under section 732; use of partnership consistent with the intent of subchapter K. (i) A, B, and C are partners in partnership PRS, which has for several years been engaged in substantial bona fide business activities. For valid business reasons, the partners agree that A's interest in PRS, which has a value and basis of $100x, will be liquidated with the following assets of PRS: a nondepreciable asset with a value of $60x and a basis to PRS of $40x, and related equipment with two years of cost recovery remaining and a value and basis to PRS of $40x. Neither asset is described in section 751 and the transaction is not described in section 732(d). Under section 732 (b) and (c), A's $100x basis in A's partnership interest will be allocated between the nondepreciable asset and the equipment received in the liquidating distribution in proportion to PRS's bases in those assets, or $50x to the nondepreciable asset and $50x to the equipment. Thus, A will have a $10x built-in gain in the nondepreciable asset ($60x value less $50x basis) and a $10x built-in loss in the equipment ($50x basis less $40x value), which it expects to recover rapidly through cost recovery deductions. In selecting the assets to be distributed to A, the partners had a principal purpose to take advantage of the fact that A's basis in the assets will be determined by reference to A's basis in A's partnership interest, thus, in effect, shifting a portion of A's basis from the nondepreciable asset to the equipment, which in turn would allow A to recover that portion of its basis more rapidly. This shift provides a federal tax timing advantage to A, with no offsetting detriment to B or C.

(ii) Subchapter K is intended to permit taxpayers to conduct joint business activity through a flexible economic arrangement without incurring an entity-level tax. See paragraph (a) of this section. The decision to organize and conduct business through PRS is consistent with this intent. In addition, on these facts, the requirements of paragraphs (a)(1) and (2) of this section have been satisfied. The validity of the tax treatment of this transaction is therefore dependent upon whether the transaction satisfies (or is treated as satisfying) the proper reflection of income standard under paragraph (a)(3) of this section. Subchapter K is generally intended to produce tax consequences that achieve proper reflection of income. However, paragraph (a)(3) of this section provides that if the application of a provision of subchapter K

produces tax results that do not properly reflect income, but the application of that provision to the transaction and the ultimate tax results, taking into account all the relevant facts and circumstances, are clearly contemplated by that provision (and the transaction satisfies the requirements of paragraphs (a)(1) and (2) of this section), then the application of that provision to the transaction will be treated as satisfying the proper reflection of income standard.

(iii) A's basis in the assets distributed to it was determined under section 732 (b) and (c). The transaction does not properly reflect A's income due to the basis distortions caused by the distribution and the shifting of basis from a nondepreciable to a depreciable asset. However, the basis rules under section 732, which in some situations can produce tax results that are inconsistent with the proper reflection of income standard (see paragraph (a)(3) of this section), are intended to provide simplifying administrative rules for bona fide partnerships that are engaged in transactions with a substantial business purpose. Taking into account all the facts and circumstances of the transaction, the application of the basis rules under section 732 to the distribution from PRS to A, and the ultimate tax consequences of the application of that provision of subchapter K, are clearly contemplated. Thus, the application of section 732 to this transaction will be treated as satisfying the proper reflection of income standard under paragraph (a)(3) of this section. The Commissioner therefore cannot invoke paragraph (b) of this section to recast the transaction.

Example (11). Basis adjustments under section 732; plan or arrangement to distort basis allocations artificially; use of partnership not consistent with the intent of subchapter K. (i) Partnership PRS has for several years been engaged in the development and management of commercial real estate projects. X, an unrelated party, desires to acquire undeveloped land owned by PRS, which has a value of $95x and a basis of $5x. X expects to hold the land indefinitely after its acquisition. Pursuant to a plan a principal purpose of which is to permit X to acquire and hold the land but nevertheless to recover for tax purposes a substantial portion of the purchase price for the land, X contributes $100x to PRS for an interest therein. Subsequently (at a time when the value of the partnership's assets have not materially changed), PRS distributes to X in liquidation of its interest in PRS the land and another asset with a value and basis to PRS of $5x. The second asset is an insignificant part of the economic transaction but is important to achieve the desired tax results. Under section 732 (b) and (c), X's $100x basis in its partnership interest is allocated between the assets distributed to it in proportion to their bases to PRS, or $50x each. Thereafter, X plans to sell the second asset for its value of $5x, recognizing a loss of $45x. In this manner, X will, in effect, recover a substantial portion of the purchase price of the land almost immediately. In selecting the assets to be distributed to X, the partners had a principal purpose to take advantage of the fact that X's basis in the assets will be determined under section 732 (b) and (c), thus, in effect, shifting a portion of X's basis economically allocable to the land that X intends to retain to an inconsequential asset that X intends to dispose of quickly. This shift provides a federal tax timing advantage to X, with no offsetting detriment to any of PRS's other partners.

(ii) Although section 732 recognizes that basis distortions can occur in certain situations, which may produce tax results that do not satisfy the proper reflection of income standard of paragraph (a)(3) of this section, the provision is intended only to provide ancillary, simplifying tax results for bona fide partnership transactions that are engaged in for substantial business purposes. Section 732 is not intended to serve as the basis for plans or arrangements in which inconsequential or immaterial assets are included in the distribution with a principal purpose of obtaining substantially favorable tax results by virtue of the statute's simplifying rules. The transaction does not properly reflect X's income due to the basis distortions caused by the distribution that result in shifting a significant portion of X's basis to this inconsequential asset. Moreover, the proper reflection of income standard contained in paragraph (a)(3) of this section is not treated as satisfied, because, taking into account all the facts and circumstances, the application of section 732 to this arrangement, and the ultimate tax consequences that would thereby result, were not clearly contemplated by that provision of subchapter K. In addition, by using a partnership (if respected), the partners' aggregate federal tax liability would be substantially less than had they owned the partnership's assets directly (see paragraph (c) (1) of this section). On these facts, PRS has been formed and availed of with a principal purpose to reduce the taxpayers' aggregate federal tax liability in a manner that is inconsistent with the intent of subchapter K. Therefore (in addition to possibly challenging the transaction under applicable judicial principles and statutory authorities, such as the disguised sale rules under section 707, see paragraph (h) of this section), the Commissioner can recast the transaction as appropriate under paragraph (b) of this section.

(e) Abuse of entity treatment—(1) General rule. The Commissioner can treat a partnership as an aggregate of its partners in whole or in part as appropriate to carry out the purpose of any provision of the Internal Revenue Code or the regulations promulgated thereunder.

(2) Clearly contemplated entity treatment. Paragraph (e)(1) of this section does not apply to the extent that—

(i) A provision of the Internal Revenue Code or the regulations promulgated thereunder prescribes the treatment of a partnership as an entity, in whole or in part, and

(ii) That treatment and the ultimate tax results, taking into account all the relevant facts and circumstances, are clearly contemplated by that provision.

(f) Examples. The following examples illustrate the principles of paragraph (e) of this section. The examples set forth below do not delineate the boundaries of either permissible or impermissible types of transactions. Further, the addition of any facts or circumstances that are not specifically set forth in an example (or the deletion of any facts or circumstances) may alter the outcome of the transaction described in the example. Unless otherwise indicated, parties to the transactions are not related to one another.

Example (1). Aggregate treatment of partnership appropriate to carry out purpose of section 163(e)(5). (i) Corporations X and Y are partners in partnership PRS, which for several years has engaged in substantial bona fide business activities. As part of these business activities, PRS issues certain high yield discount obligations to an unrelated third party. Section 163(e)(5) defers (and in certain circumstances disallows) the interest deductions on this type of obligation if issued by a corporation. PRS, X, and Y take the position that, because PRS is a partnership and not a corporation, section 163(e)(5) is not applicable.

(ii) Section 163(e)(5) does not prescribe the treatment of a partnership as an entity for purposes of that section. The purpose of section 163(e)(5) is to limit corporate-level interest deductions on certain obligations. The treatment of PRS as an entity could result in a partnership with corporate partners issuing those obligations and thereby circumventing the purpose of section (e)(5), because the corporate partner would deduct its distributive share of the interest on obligations that would have been deferred until paid or disallowed had the corporation issued its share of the obligation directly. Thus, under paragraph (e)(1) of this section, PRS is properly treated as an aggregate of its partners for purposes of applying section 163(e)(5) (regardless of whether any party had a tax avoidance purpose in having

PRS issue the obligation). Each partner of PRS will therefore be treated as issuing its share of the obligations for purposes of determining the deductibility of its distributive share of any interest on the obligations. See also section 163(i)(5)(B).

Example (2). Aggregate treatment of partnership appropriate to carry out purpose of section 1059. (i) Corporations X and Y are partners in partnership PRS, which for several years has engaged in substantial bona fide business activities. As part of these business activities, PRS purchases 50 shares of Corporation Z common stock. Six months later, Corporation Z announces an extraordinary dividend (within the meaning of section 1059). Section 1059(a) generally provides that if any corporation receives an extraordinary dividend with respect to any share of stock and the corporation has not held the stock for more than two years before the dividend announcement date, the basis in the stock held by the corporation is reduced by the nontaxed portion of the dividend. PRS, X, and Y take the position that section 1059(a) is not applicable because PRS is a partnership and not a corporation.

(ii) Section 1059(a) does not prescribe the treatment of a partnership as an entity for purposes of that section. The purpose of section 1059(a) is to limit the benefits of the dividends received deduction with respect to extraordinary dividends. The treatment of PRS as an entity could result in corporate partners in the partnership receiving dividends through partnerships in circumvention of the intent of section 1059. Thus, under paragraph (e)(1) of this section, PRS is properly treated as an aggregate of its partners for purposes of applying section 1059 (regardless of whether any party had a tax avoidance purpose in acquiring the Z stock through PRS). Each partner of PRS will therefore be treated as owning its share of the stock. Accordingly, PRS must make appropriate adjustments to the basis of the Corporation Z stock, and the partners must also make adjustments to the basis in their respective inter-

ests in PRS under section 705(a)(2)(B). See also section 1059(g)(1).

* * *

(h) Scope and application. This section applies solely with respect to taxes under subtitle A of the Internal Revenue Code, and for purposes of this section, any reference to a federal tax is limited to any tax imposed under subtitle A of the Internal Revenue Code.

(i) Application of nonstatutory principles and other statutory authorities. The Commissioner can continue to assert and to rely upon applicable nonstatutory principles and other statutory and regulatory authorities to challenge transactions. This section does not limit the applicability of those principles and authorities.

§ 1.702–1 Income and credits of partner.

(a) General rule. Each partner is required to take into account separately in his return his distributive share, whether or not distributed, of each class or item of partnership income, gain, loss, deduction, or credit described in subparagraphs (1) through (9) of this paragraph. (For the taxable year in which a partner includes his distributive share of partnership taxable income, see section 706(a) and § 1.706–1(a). Such distributive share shall be determined as provided in section 704 and § 1.704–1.) Accordingly, in determining his income tax:

(1) Each partner shall take into account, as part of his gains and losses from sales or exchanges of capital assets held for not more than 1 year . . . his distributive share of the combined net amount of such gains and losses of the partnership.

(2) Each partner shall take into account, as part of his gains and losses from sales or exchanges of capital assets held for more than 1 year . . . his distributive share of the combined net amount of such gains and losses of the partnership.

(3) Each partner shall take into account, as part of his gains and losses from sales or exchanges of property described in section 1231 (relating to property used in the trade or business and involuntary conversions), his distributive share of the combined net amount of such gains and losses of the partnership. The partnership shall not combine such items with items set forth in subparagraph (1) or (2) of this paragraph.

(4) Each partner shall take into account, as part of the charitable contributions paid by him, his distributive share of each class of charitable contributions paid by the partnership within the partnership's taxable year. Section 170 determines the extent to which such amount may be allowed as a deduction to the partner. For the definition of the term "charitable contribution", see section 170(c).

(5) Each partner shall take into account, as part of the dividends received by him from domestic corporations, his distributive share of dividends received by the partnership, with respect to which the partner is entitled to. an exclusion under section 116, or a deduction under part VIII, Subchapter B, Chapter 1 of the Code.

(6) Each partner shall take into account, as part of his taxes described in section 901 which have been paid or accrued to foreign countries or to possessions of the United States, his distributive share of such taxes which have been paid or accrued by the partnership, according to its method of treating such taxes. A partner may elect to treat his total amount of such taxes, including his distributive share of such taxes of the partnership, as a deduction under section 164 or as a credit under section 901, subject to the provisions of sections 901 through 905.

(7) Each partner shall take into account, as part of the partially tax-exempt interest received by him on obligations of the United States or on obligations of instrumentalities of the United States, as described in section 35 or section 242, his distributive share of such partially tax-exempt interest received by the partnership. However, if the partnership elects to amortize premiums on bonds as provided in section 171, the amount received on such obligations by the partnership shall be reduced by the amortizable bond premium applicable to such obligations as provided in section 171(a)(3).

(8)(i) Each partner shall take into account separately, as part of any class of income, gain, loss, deduction, or credit, his distributive share of the following items: Recoveries of bad debts, prior taxes, and delinquency amounts (section 111); gains and losses from wagering transactions (section 165(d)); soil and water conservation expenditures (section 175); non-business expenses as described in section 212; medical, dental, etc., expenses (section 213); expenses for care of certain dependents (section 214); alimony, etc., payments (section 215); amounts representing taxes and interest paid to cooperative housing corporations (section 216); intangible drilling and developments costs (section 263(c)); pre-1970 exploration expenditures (section 615); certain mining exploration expenditures (section 617); income, gain, or loss to the partnership under section 751(b); and any items of income, gain, loss, deduction, or credit subject to a special allocation under the partnership agreement which differs from the allocation of partnership taxable income or loss generally.

(ii) Each partner must also take into account separately his distributive share of any partnership item which if separately taken into account by any partner would result in an income tax liability for that partner different from that which would result if that partner did not take the item into account separately. Thus, if any partner would qualify for the retirement income credit under section 37 if the partnership pensions and annuities, interest, rents, dividends, and earned income were separately stated, such items must be separately stated for all partners. Under section 911(a), if any partner is a bona fide resident of a foreign country who may exclude from his gross income the

part of his distributive share which qualifies as earned income as defined in section 911(b), the earned income of the partnership for all partners must be separately stated. Similarly, all relevant items of income or deduction of the partnership must be separately stated for all partners in determining the applicability of section 270 (relating to "hobby losses") and the recomputation of tax thereunder for any partner.

(iii) Each partner shall aggregate the amount of his separate deductions or exclusions and his distributive share of partnership deductions or exclusions separately stated in determining the amount allowable to him of any deduction or exclusion under Subtitle A of the Code as to which a limitation is imposed. For example, partner A has individual domestic exploration expenditures of $300,000. He is also a member of the AB partnership which in 1971 in its first year of operation has foreign exploration expenditures of $400,000. A's distributable share of this item is $200,000. However, the total amount of his distributable share that A can deduct as exploration expenditures under section 617(a) is limited to $100,000 in view of the limitation provided in section 617(h). Therefore, the excess of $100,000 ($200,000 minus $100,000) is not deductible by A.

(9) Each partner shall also take into account separately his distributive share of the taxable income or loss of the partnership, exclusive of items requiring separate computations under subparagraphs (1) through (8) of this paragraph. For limitation on allowance of a partner's distributive share of partnership losses, see section 704(d) and paragraph (d) of § 1.704–1.

(b) Character of items constituting distributive share. The character in the hands of a partner of any item of income, gain, loss, deduction, or credit described in section 702(a) (1) through (8) shall be determined as if such item were realized directly from the source from which realized by the partnership or incurred in the same manner as incurred by the partnership. For example, a partner's distributive share of gain from the sale of depreciable property used in the trade or business of the partnership shall be considered as gain from the sale of such depreciable property in the hands of the partner. Similarly, a partner's distributive share of partnership "hobby losses" (section 270) or his distributive share of partnership charitable contributions to organizations qualifying under section 170(b)(1)(A) retains such character in the hands of the partner.

(c) Gross income of a partner. (1) Where it is necessary to determine the amount or character of the gross income of a partner, his gross income shall include the partner's distributive share of the gross income of the partnership, that is, the amount of gross income of the partnership from which was derived the partner's distributive share of partnership taxable income or loss (including items described in section 702(a)(1) through (8)). For example, a partner is required to include his distributive share of partnership gross income:

(i) In computing his gross income for the purpose of determining the necessity of filing a return (section 6012(a));

* * *

(2) In determining the applicability of the 6-year period of limitation on assessment and collection provided in section 6501(e) (relating to omission of more than 25 percent of gross income), a partner's gross income includes his distributive share of partnership gross income (as described in section 6501(e)(1)(A)(i)). In this respect, the amount of partnership gross income from which was derived the partner's distributive share of any item of partnership income, gain, loss, deduction, or credit (as included or disclosed in the partner's return) is considered as an amount of gross income stated in the partner's return for the purposes of section 6501(e). For example, A, who is entitled to one-fourth of the profits of the ABCD partnership, which has $10,000 gross income and $2,000 taxable income, reports only $300

as his distributive share of partnership profits. A should have shown $500 as his distributive share of profits, which amount was derived from $2,500 of partnership gross income. However, since A included only $300 on his return without explaining in the return the difference of $200, he is regarded as having stated in his return only $1,500 ($300/$500 of $2,500) as gross income from the partnership.

(d) Partners in community property States. If separate returns are made by a husband and wife domiciled in a community property State, and only one spouse is a member of the partnership, the part of his or her distributive share of any item or items listed in paragraph (a)(1) through (9) of this section which is community property, or which is derived from community property, should be reported by the husband and wife in equal proportions.

* * *

§ 1.702–2　Net operating loss deduction of partner.

For the purpose of determining a net operating loss deduction under section 172, a partner shall take into account his distributive share of items of income, gain, loss, deduction, or credit of the partnership. The character of any such item shall be determined as if such item were realized directly from the source from which realized by the partnership, or incurred in the same manner as incurred by the partnership. See section 702(b) and paragraph (b) of § 1.702–1. To the extent necessary to determine the allowance under section 172(d) (4) of the nonbusiness deductions of a partner (arising from both partnership and nonpartnership sources), the partner shall separately take into account his distributive share of the deductions of the partnership which are not attributable to a trade or business and combine such amount with his nonbusiness deductions from nonpartnership sources. Such partner shall also separately take into account his distributive share of the gross income of the partnership not derived from a trade or business and combine such amount with his nonbusiness income from nonpartnership sources. See section 172 and the regulations thereunder.

§1.703–1 Partnership computations.

(a) Income and deductions. (1) The taxable income of a partnership shall be computed in the same manner as the taxable income of an individual, except as otherwise provided in this section. A partnership is required to state separately in its return the items described in section 702(a)(1) through (7) and, in addition, to attach to its return a statement setting forth separately those items described in section 702(a)(8) which the partner is required to take into account separately in determining his income tax. See paragraph (a)(8) of § 1.702–1. The partnership is further required to compute and to state separately in its return:

(i) As taxable income under section 702(a)(9), the total of all other items of gross income (not separately stated) over the total of all other allowable deductions (not separately stated), or

(ii) As loss under section 702(a)(9), the total of all other allowable deductions (not separately stated) over the total of all other items of gross income (not separately stated).

The taxable income or loss so computed shall be accounted for by the partners in accordance with their partnership agreement.

(2) The partnership is not allowed the following deductions:

(i) The standard deduction provided in section 141.

(ii) The deduction for personal exemptions provided in section 151.

(iii) The deduction provided in section 164(a) for taxes, described in section 901, paid or accrued to foreign countries or possessions of the United States. Each partner's distributive share of such taxes shall be accounted for separately by him as provided in section 702(a)(6).

(iv) The deduction for charitable contributions provided in section 170. Each partner is considered as having paid within his taxable year his distributive share of any contribution or gift, payment of which was actually made by the partnership within its taxable year ending within or with the partner's taxable year. This item shall be accounted for separately by the partners as provided in section 702(a)(4). See also paragraph (b) of § 1.702–1.

(v) The net operating loss deduction provided in section 172. See § 1.702–2.

(vi) The additional itemized deductions for individuals provided in Part VII, Subchapter B, Chapter 1 of the Code, as follows: Expenses for production of income (section 212); medical, dental, etc., expenses (section 213); expenses for care of certain dependents (section 214); alimony, etc., payments (section 215); and amounts representing taxes and interest paid to cooperative housing corporation (section 216). However, see paragraph (a)(8) of § 1.702–1.

(vii) The deduction for depletion under section 611 with respect to domestic oil or gas which is produced after December 31, 1974, and to which gross income from the property is attributable after such year.

(viii) The deduction for capital gains provided by section 1202 and the deduction for capital loss carryover provided by section 1212.

(b) Elections of the partnership—(1) General rule. Any elections (other than those described in subparagraph (2) of this paragraph) affecting the computation of income derived from a partnership shall be made by the partnership. For example, elections of methods of accounting, of computing depreciation, of treating soil and water conservation expenditures, and the option to deduct as expenses intangible drilling and development costs, shall be made by the partnership and not by the partners separately. All partnership elections are applicable to all partners equally, but any election made by a partnership shall not apply to any partner's nonpartnership interests.

(2) Exceptions. (i) Each partner shall add his distributive share of taxes described in section 901 paid or accrued by the partnership to foreign countries or possessions of the United States (according to its method of treating such taxes) to any such taxes paid or accrued by him (according to his method of treating such taxes), and may elect to use the total amount either as a credit against tax or as a deduction from income.

(ii) Each partner shall add his distributive share of expenses described in section 615 or section 617 paid or accrued by the partnership to any such expenses paid or accrued by him and shall treat the total amount according to his method of treating such expenses, notwithstanding the treatment of the expenses by the partnership.

§ 1.704–1 Partner's distributive share.

[Caution: The Treasury has not yet amended Reg 1.704–1 to reflect changes made by P.L. 101–239, P.L. 98–369]

(a) Effect of partnership agreement. A partner's distributive share of any item or class of items of income, gain, loss, deduction, or credit of the partnership shall be determined by the partnership agreement, unless otherwise provided by section 704 and paragraphs (b) through (e) of this section. For definition of partnership agreement see section 761(c).

(b) Determination of partner's distributive share.

* * *

(1) In general.

(i) Basic principles. Under section 704(b) if a partnership agreement does not provide for the allocation of income, gain, loss, deduction, or credit (or item thereof) to a partner, or if the partnership agreement provides for the allocation of income, gain, loss, deduction, or credit

(or item thereof) to a partner but such allocation does not have substantial economic effect, then the partner's distributive share of such income, gain, loss, deduction, or credit (or item thereof) shall be determined in accordance with such partner's interest in the partnership (taking into account all facts and circumstances). If the partnership agreement provides for the allocation of income, gain, loss, deduction, or credit (or item thereof) to a partner, there are three ways in which such allocation will be respected under section 704(b) and this paragraph. First, the allocation can have substantial economic effect in accordance with paragraph (b)(2) of this section. Second, taking into account all facts and circumstances, the allocation can be in accordance with the partner's interest in the partnership. See paragraph (b)(3) of this section. Third, the allocation can be deemed to be in accordance with the partner's interest in the partnership pursuant to one of the special rules contained in paragraph (b) (4) of this section and § 1.704–2. To the extent an allocation under the partnership agreement of income, gain, loss, deduction, or credit (or item thereof) to a partner does not have substantial economic effect, is not in accordance with the partner's interest in the partnership, and is not deemed to be in accordance with the partner's interest in the partnership, such income, gain, loss, deduction, or credit (or item thereof) will be reallocated in accordance with the partner's interest in the partnership (determined under paragraph (b)(3) of this section).

* * *

(iii) Effect of other sections. The determination of a partner's distributive share of income, gain, loss, deduction, or credit (or item thereof) under section 704(b) and this paragraph is not conclusive as to the tax treatment of a partner with respect to such distributive share. For example, an allocation of loss or deduction to a partner that is respected under section 704(b) and this paragraph may not be deductible by such partner if the partner lacks the requisite motive for economic gain (see, e.g., Goldstein v. Commissioner, 364 F.2d 734 (2d Cir. 1966)), or may be disallowed for that taxable year (and held in suspense) if the limitations of section 465 or section 704(d) are applicable. Similarly, an allocation that is respected under section 704(b) and this paragraph nevertheless may be reallocated under other provisions, such as section 482, section 704(e)(2), section 706(d) (and related assignment of income principles), and paragraph (b)(2)(ii) of § 1.751–1. If a partnership has a section 754 election in effect, a partner's distributive share of partnership income, gain, loss, or deduction may be affected as provided in § 1.743–1 (see paragraph (b)(2)(iv)(m)(2) of this section). A deduction that appears to be a nonrecourse deduction deemed to be in accordance with the partners' interests in the partnership may not be such because purported nonrecourse liabilities of the partnership in fact constitute equity rather than debt. The examples in paragraph (b)(5) of this section concern the validity of allocations under section 704(b) and this paragraph and, except as noted, do not address the effect of other sections or limitations on such allocations.

(iv) Other possible tax consequences. Allocations that are respected under section 704(b) and this paragraph may give rise to other tax consequences, such as those resulting from the application of section 61, section 83, section 751, section 2501, paragraph (f) of § 1.46–3, § 1.47–6, paragraph (b)(1) of § 1.721–1 (and related principles), and paragraph (e) of § 1.752–1. The examples in paragraph (b)(5) of this section concern the validity of allocations under section 704(b) and this paragraph and, except as noted, do not address other tax consequences that may result from such allocations.

(v) Purported allocations. Section 704(b) and this paragraph do not apply to a purported allocation if it is made to a person who is not a partner of the partnership (see section 7701(a)(2) and paragraph (d) of § 301.7701–3) or to a person who is not receiving the purported allo-

cation in his capacity as a partner (see section 707(a) and paragraph (a) of § 1.707–1).

(vi) Section 704(c) determinations. Section 704(c) and § 1.704–3 generally require that if property is contributed by a partner to a partnership, the partners' distributive shares of income, gain, loss, and deduction, as computed for tax purposes, with respect to the property are determined so as to take account of the variation between the adjusted tax basis and fair market value of the property. Although section 704(b) does not directly determine the partners' distributive shares of tax items governed by section 704(c), the partners' distributive shares of tax items may be determined under section 704(c) and § 1.704–3 (depending on the allocation method chosen by the partnership under § 1.704–3) with reference to the partners' distributive shares of the corresponding book items, as determined under section 704(b) and this paragraph. (See paragraphs (b)(2)(iv)(d) and (b)(4)(i) of this section.) See § 1.704–3 for methods of making allocations under section 704(c), and § 1.704–3(d)(2) for a special rule in determining the amount of book items if the remedial allocation method is chosen by the partnership. See also paragraph (b)(5) Example (13)(i) of this section.

(vii) Bottom line allocations. Section 704(b) and this paragraph are applicable to allocations of income, gain, loss, deduction, and credit, allocations of specific items of income, gain, loss, deduction, and credit, and allocations of partnership net or "bottom line" taxable income and loss. An allocation to a partner of a share of partnership net or "bottom line" taxable income or loss shall be treated as an allocation to such partner of the same share of each item of income, gain, loss, and deduction that is taken into account in computing such net or "bottom line" taxable income or loss. See example (15)(i) of paragraph (b)(5) of this section.

(2) Substantial economic effect.

(i) Two-part analysis. The determination of whether an allocation of income, gain, loss, or deduction (or item thereof) to a partner has substantial economic effect involves a two-part analysis that is made as of the end of the partnership taxable year to which the allocation relates. First, the allocation must have economic effect (within the meaning of paragraph (b)(2)(ii) of this section). Second, the economic effect of the allocation must be substantial (within the meaning of paragraph (b)(2)(iii) of this section).

(ii) Economic effect.

(a) *Fundamental principles.* In order for an allocation to have economic effect, it must be consistent with the underlying economic arrangement of the partners. This means that in the event there is an economic benefit or economic burden that corresponds to an allocation, the partner to whom the allocation is made must receive such economic benefit or bear such economic burden.

(b) *Three requirements.* Based on the principles contained in paragraph (b)(2)(ii)(a) of this section, and except as otherwise provided in this paragraph, an allocation of income, gain, loss, or deduction (or item thereof) to a partner will have economic effect if, and only if, throughout the full term of the partnership, the partnership agreement provides—

(1) For the determination and maintenance of the partners' capital accounts in accordance with the rules of paragraph (b)(2)(iv) of this section,

(2) Upon liquidation of the partnership (or any partner's interest in the partnership), liquidating distributions are required in all cases to be made in accordance with the positive capital account balances of the partners, as determined after taking into account all capital account adjustments for the partnership taxable year during which such liquidation occurs (other than those made pursuant to this requirement (2) and requirement (3) of this paragraph (b)(2)(ii)(b)), by the end of such taxable year (or, if later, within 90 days after the date of such liquidation), and

(3) If such partner has a deficit balance in his capital account following the liquidation of his interest in the partnership, as determined after taking into account all capital account adjustments for the partnership taxable year during which such liquidation occurs (other than those made pursuant to this requirement (3)), he is unconditionally obligated to restore the amount of such deficit balance to the partnership by the end of such taxable year (or, if later, within 90 days after the date of such liquidation), which amount shall, upon liquidation of the partnership, be paid to creditors of the partnership or distributed to other partners in accordance with their positive capital account balances (in accordance with requirement (2) of this paragraph (b)(2)(ii)(b)).

For purposes of the preceding sentence, a partnership taxable year shall be determined without regard to section 706(c)(2)(A).

Requirements (2) and (3) of this paragraph (b)(2)(ii)(b) are not violated if all or part of the partnership interest of one or more partners is purchased (other than in connection with the liquidation of the partnership) by the partnership or by one or more partners (or one or more persons related, within the meaning of section 267(b) (without modification by section 267(e)(1)) or section 707(b)(1), to a partner) pursuant to an agreement negotiated at arm's length by persons who at the time such agreement is entered into have materially adverse interests and if a principal purpose of such purchase and sale is not to avoid the principles of the second sentence of paragraph (b)(2)(ii)(a) of this section. In addition, requirement (2) of this paragraph (b)(2)(ii)(b) is not violated if, upon the liquidation of the partnership, the capital accounts of the partners are increased or decreased pursuant to paragraph (b)(2)(iv)(f) of this section as of the date of such liquidation and the partnership makes liquidating distributions within the time set out in that requirement (2) in the ratios of the partners' positive capital accounts, except that it does not distribute reserves reasonably required to provide for liabilities (contingent or otherwise) of the partnership and installment obligations owed to the partnership, so long as such withheld amounts are distributed as soon as practicable and in the ratios of the partners' positive capital account balances. See examples (1)(i) and (ii), (4)(i), (8)(i), and (16)(i) of paragraph (b)(5) of this section.

(c) Obligation to restore deficit. If a partner is not expressly obligated to restore the deficit balance in his capital account, such partner nevertheless will be treated as obligated to restore the deficit balance in his capital account (in accordance with requirement (3) of paragraph (b)(2)(ii)(b) of this section) to the extent of—

(1) The outstanding principal balance of any promissory note (of which such partner is the maker) contributed to the partnership by such partner (other than a promissory note that is readily tradable on an established securities market), and

(2) The amount of any unconditional obligation of such partner (whether imposed by the partnership agreement or by State or local law) to make subsequent contributions to the partnership (other than pursuant to a promissory note of which such partner is the maker), provided that such note or obligation is required to be satisfied at a time no later than the end of the partnership taxable year in which such partner's interest is liquidated (or, if later, within 90 days after the date of such liquidation). If a promissory note referred to in the previous sentence is negotiable, a partner will be considered required to satisfy such note within the time period specified in such sentence if the partnership agreement provides that, in lieu of actual satisfaction, the partnership will retain such note and such partner will contribute to the partnership the excess, if any, of the outstanding principal balance of such note over its fair market value at the time of liquidation. See paragraph (b)(2)(iv)(d)(2) of this section. See examples (1)(ix) and (x) of paragraph (b)(5) of this section. A partner in no

event will be considered obligated to restore the deficit balance in his capital account to the partnership (in accordance with requirement (3) of paragraph (b)(2)(ii)(b) of this section) to the extent such partner's obligation is not legally enforceable, or the facts and circumstances otherwise indicate a plan to avoid or circumvent such obligation. See paragraphs (b)(2)(ii)(f), (b)(2)(ii)(h), and (b)(4)(vi) of this section for other rules regarding such obligation. For purposes of this paragraph (b)(2), if a partner contributes a promissory note to the partnership during a partnership taxable year beginning after December 29, 1988 and the maker of such note is a person related to such partner (within the meaning of § 1.752–1T(h), but without regard to subdivision (4) of that section), then such promissory note shall be treated as a promissory note of which such partner is the maker.

(d) Alternate test for economic effect. If—

(1) Requirements (1) and (2) of paragraph (b)(2)(ii)(b) of this section are satisfied, and

(2) The partner to whom an allocation is made is not obligated to restore the deficit balance in his capital account to the partnership (in accordance with requirement (3) of paragraph (b)(2)(ii)(b) of this section), or is obligated to restore only a limited dollar amount of such deficit balance, and

(3) The partnership agreement contains a qualified income offset,

such allocation will be considered to have economic effect under this paragraph (b)(2)(ii) (d) to the extent such allocation does not cause or increase a deficit balance in such partner's capital account (in excess of any limited dollar amount of such deficit balance that such partner is obligated to restore) as of the end of the partnership taxable year to which such allocation relates. In determining the extent to which the previous sentence is satisfied, such partner's capital account also shall be reduced for—

(4) Adjustments that, as of the end of such year, reasonably are expected to be made to such partner's capital account under paragraph (b)(2)(iv)(k) of this section for depletion allowances with respect to oil and gas properties of the partnership, and

(5) Allocations of loss and deduction that, as of the end of such year, reasonably are expected to be made to such partner pursuant to section 704(e)(2), section 706(d), and paragraph (b)(2)(ii) of § 1.751–1, and

(6) Distributions that, as of the end of such year, reasonably are expected to be made to such partner to the extent they exceed offsetting increases to such partner's capital account that reasonably are expected to occur during (or prior to) the partnership taxable years in which such distributions reasonably are expected to be made (other than increases pursuant to a minimum gain chargeback under paragraph (b)(4)(iv)(e) of this section or under § 1.704–2(f); however, increases to a partner's capital account pursuant to a minimum gain chargeback requirement are taken into account as an offset to distributions of nonrecourse liability proceeds that are reasonably expected to be made and that are allocable to an increase in partnership minimum gain.

For purposes of determining the amount of expected distributions and expected capital account increases described in (6) above, the rule set out in paragraph (b)(2)(iii)(c) of this section concerning the presumed value of partnership property shall apply. The partnership agreement contains a "qualified income offset" if, and only if, it provides that a partner who unexpectedly receives an adjustment, allocation, or distribution described in (4), (5), or (6) above, will be allocated items of income and gain (consisting of a pro rata portion of each item of partnership income, including gross income, and gain for such year) in an amount and manner sufficient to eliminate such deficit balance as quickly as possible. Allocations of items of income and gain made pursuant to the immediately preceding sentence shall

be deemed to be made in accordance with the partners' interests in the partnership if requirements (1) and (2) of paragraph (b)(2)(ii)(b) of this section are satisfied. See examples (1)(iii), (iv), (v), (vi), (vii), (ix), and (x), (15), and (16) (ii) of paragraph (b)(5) of this section.

(e) Partial economic effect. If only a portion of an allocation made to a partner with respect to a partnership taxable year has economic effect, both the portion that has economic effect and the portion that is reallocated shall consist of a proportionate share of all items that made up the allocation to such partner for such year. See examples (15)(ii) and (iii) of paragraph (b)(5) of this section.

(f) Reduction of obligation to restore. If requirements (1) and (2) of paragraph (b)(2)(ii)(b) of this section are satisfied, a partner's obligation to restore the deficit balance in his capital account (or any limited dollar amount thereof) to the partnership may be eliminated or reduced as of the end of a partnership taxable year without affecting the validity of prior allocations (see paragraph (b)(4)(vi) of this section) to the extent the deficit balance (if any) in such partner's capital account, after reduction for the items described in (4), (5), and (6) of paragraph (b)(2)(ii)(d) of this section, will not exceed the partner's remaining obligation (if any) to restore the deficit balance in his capital account. See example (1)(viii) of paragraph (b)(5) of this section.

(g) Liquidation defined. For purposes of this paragraph, a liquidation of a partner's interest in the partnership occurs upon the earlier of (1) the date upon which there is a liquidation of the partnership, or (2) the date upon which there is a liquidation of the partner's interest in the partnership under paragraph (d) of § 1.761–1. For purposes of this paragraph, the liquidation of a partnership occurs upon the earlier of (3) the date upon which the partnership is terminated under section 708(b)(1), or (4) the date upon which the partnership ceases to be a going concern (even though it may continue in existence for the purpose of

winding up its affairs, paying its debts, and distributing any remaining balance to its partners). Requirements (2) and (3) of paragraph (b)(2)(ii)(b) of this section will be considered unsatisfied if the liquidation of a partner's interest in the partnership is delayed after its primary business activities have been terminated (for example, by continuing to engage in a relatively minor amount of business activity, if such actions themselves do not cause the partnership to terminate pursuant to section 708(b)(1)) for a principal purpose of deferring any distribution pursuant to requirement (2) of paragraph (b)(2)(ii)(b) of this section or deferring any partner's obligations under requirement (3) of paragraph (b)(2)(ii)(b) of this section.

(h) Partnership agreement defined. For purposes of this paragraph, the partnership agreement includes all agreements among the partners, or between one or more partners and the partnership, concerning affairs of the partnership and responsibilities of partners, whether oral or written, and whether or not embodied in a document referred to by the partners as the partnership agreement. Thus, in determining whether distributions are required in all cases to be made in accordance with the partners' positive capital account balances (requirement (2) of paragraph (b)(2)(ii)(b) of this section), and in determining the extent to which a partner is obligated to restore a deficit balance in his capital account (requirement (3) of paragraph (b)(2)(ii)(b) of this section), all arrangements among partners, or between one or more partners and the partnership relating to the partnership, direct and indirect, including puts, options, and other buy-sell agreements, and any other "stop-loss" arrangement, are considered to be part of the partnership agreement. (Thus, for example, if one partner who assumes a liability of the partnership is indemnified by another partner for a portion of such liability, the indemnifying partner (depending upon the particular facts) may be viewed as in effect having a partial deficit makeup obligation as a result of such indemnity agreement.)

In addition, the partnership agreement includes provisions of Federal, State, or local law that govern the affairs of the partnership or are considered under such law to be a part of the partnership agreement (see the last sentence of paragraph (c) of § 1.761–1). For purposes of this paragraph (b)(2)(ii)(h), an agreement with a partner or a partnership shall include an agreement with a person related, within the meaning of section 267(b) (without modification by section 267(e)(1)) or section 707(b)(1), to such partner or partnership. For purposes of the preceding sentence, sections 267(b) and 707(b)(1) shall be applied for partnership taxable years beginning after December 29, 1988 by (1) substituting 80 percent or more, for more than 50 percent, each place it appears in such sections, (2) excluding brothers and sisters from the members of a person's family, and (3) disregarding section 267(f)(1)(A).

(i) Economic effect equivalence. Allocations made to a partner that do not otherwise have economic effect under this paragraph (b)(2)(ii) shall nevertheless be deemed to have economic effect, provided that as of the end of each partnership taxable year a liquidation of the partnership at the end of such year or at the end of any future year would produce the same economic results to the partners as would occur if requirements (1), (2), and (3) of paragraph (b)(2)(ii)(b) of this section had been satisfied, regardless of the economic performance of the partnership. See examples (4) (ii) and (iii) of paragraph (b)(5) of this section.

(iii) Substantiality.

(a) General rules. Except as otherwise provided in this paragraph (b)(2)(iii), the economic effect of an allocation (or allocations) is substantial if there is a reasonable possibility that the allocation (or allocations) will affect substantially the dollar amounts to be received by the partners from the partnership, independent of tax consequences. Notwithstanding the preceding sentence, the economic effect of an allocation (or allocations) is not substantial if, at the time the allocation becomes part of the

partnership agreement; (1) the after-tax economic consequences of at least one partner may, in present value terms, be enhanced compared to such consequences if the allocation (or allocations) were not contained in the partnership agreement, and (2) there is a strong likelihood that the after-tax economic consequences of no partner will, in present value terms, be substantially diminished compared to such consequences if the allocation (or allocations) were not contained in the partnership agreement. In determining the after-tax economic benefit or detriment to a partner, tax consequences that result from the interaction of the allocation with such partner's tax attributes that are unrelated to the partnership will be taken into account. See examples (5) and (9) of paragraph (b)(5) of this section. The economic effect of an allocation is not substantial in the two situations described in paragraphs (b)(2)(iii)(b) and (c) of this section. However, even if an allocation is not described therein, its economic effect may be insubstantial under the general rules stated in this paragraph (b)(2)(iii)(a). References in this paragraph (b)(2)(iii) to allocations includes capital account adjustments made pursuant to paragraph (b)(2)(iv)(k) of this section. References in this paragraph (b)(2)(iii) to a comparison to consequences arising if an allocation (or allocations) were not contained in the partnership agreement mean that the allocation (or allocations) is determined in accordance with the partners' interests in the partnership (within the meaning of paragraph (b)(3) of this section), disregarding the allocation (or allocations) being tested under this paragraph (b)(2)(iii).

(b) *Shifting tax consequences.* The economic effect of an allocation (or allocations) in a partnership taxable year is not substantial if, at the time the allocation (or allocations) becomes part of the partnership agreement, there is a strong likelihood that—

(1) The net increases and decreases that will be recorded in the partners' respective capital accounts for such taxable year will not differ substantially from the net increases and decreases that would be recorded in such partners' respective capital accounts for such year if the allocations were not contained in the partnership agreement, and

(2) The total tax liability of the partners (for their respective taxable years in which the allocations will be taken into account) will be less than if the allocations were not contained in the partnership agreement (taking into account tax consequences that result from the interaction of the allocation (or allocations) with partner tax attributes that are unrelated to the partnership). If, at the end of a partnership taxable year to which an allocation (or allocations) relates, the net increases and decreases that are recorded in the partners' respective capital accounts do not differ substantially from the net increases and decreases that would have been recorded in such partners' respective capital accounts had the allocation (or allocations) not been contained in the partnership agreement, and the total tax liability of the partners is (as described in (2) above) less than it would have been had the allocation (or allocations) not been contained in the partnership agreement, it will be presumed that, at the time the allocation (or allocations) became part of such partnership agreement, there was a strong likelihood that these results would occur. This presumption may be overcome by a showing of facts and circumstances that prove otherwise. See examples (6), (7)(ii) and (iii), and (10)(ii) of paragraph (b)(5) of this section.

(c) *Transitory allocations.* If a partnership agreement provides for the possibility that one or more allocations (the "original allocation(s)") will be largely offset by one or more other allocations (the "offsetting allocation(s)"), and, at the time the allocations become part of the partnership agreement, there is a strong likelihood that—

(1) The net increases and decreases that will be recorded in the partners' respective capital accounts for the taxable years to which the allocations relate will not differ substan-

tially from the net increases and decreases that would be recorded in such partners' respective capital accounts for such years if the original allocation(s) and offsetting allocation(s) were not contained in the partnership agreement, and

(2) The total tax liability of the partners (for their respective taxable years in which the allocations will be taken into account) will be less than if the allocations were not contained in the partnership agreement (taking into account tax consequences that result from the interaction of the allocation (or allocations) with partner tax attributes that are unrelated to the partnership) the economic effect of the original allocation(s) and offsetting allocation(s) will not be substantial. If, at the end of a partnership taxable year to which an offsetting allocation(s) relates, the net increases and decreases recorded in the partners' respective capital accounts do not differ substantially from the net increases and decreases that would have been recorded in such partners' respective capital accounts had the original allocation(s) and the offsetting allocation(s) not been contained in the partnership agreement, and the total tax liability of the partners is (as described in (2) above) less than it would have been had such allocations not been contained in the partnership agreement, it will be presumed that, at the time the allocations became part of the partnership agreement, there was a strong likelihood that these results would occur. This presumption may be overcome by a showing of facts and circumstances that prove otherwise. See examples (1)(xi), (2), (3), (7), (8)(ii), and (17) of paragraph (b)(5) of this section. Notwithstanding the foregoing, the original allocation(s) and the offsetting allocation(s) will not be insubstantial (under this paragraph (b)(2)(iii)(c)) and, for purposes of paragraph (b)(2)(iii)(a), it will be presumed that there is a reasonable possibility that the allocations will affect substantially the dollar amounts to be received by the partners from the partnership if, at the time the allocations become part of the partnership agreement, there is a strong likeli-

hood that the offsetting allocation(s) will not, in large part, be made within five years after the original allocation(s) is made (determined on a first-in, first-out basis). See example (2) of paragraph (b)(5) of this section. For purposes of applying the provisions of this paragraph (b)(2)(iii) (and paragraphs (b)(2)(ii)(d)(6) and (b)(3)(iii) of this section), the adjusted tax basis of partnership property (or, if partnership property is properly reflected on the books of the partnership at a book value that differs from its adjusted tax basis, the book value of such property) will be presumed to be the fair market value of such property, and adjustments to the adjusted tax basis (or book value) of such property will be presumed to be matched by corresponding changes in such property's fair market value. Thus, there cannot be a strong likelihood that the economic effect of an allocation (or allocations) will be largely offset by an allocation (or allocations) of gain or loss from the disposition of partnership property. See examples (1)(vi) and (xi) of paragraph (b)(5) of this section.

(d) Partners that are look-through entities or members of a consolidated group—**(1) In general.** For purposes of applying paragraphs (b)(2)(iii)(a), (b), and (c) of this section to a partner that is a look-through entity, the tax consequences that result from the interaction of the allocation with the tax attributes of any person that is an owner, or in the case of a trust or estate, the beneficiary, of an interest in such a partner, whether directly or indirectly through one or more look-through entities, must be taken into account. For purposes of applying paragraphs (b)(2)(iii)(a), (b), and (c) of this section to a partner that is a member of a consolidated group (within the meaning of § 1.1502–1(h)), the tax consequences that result from the interaction of the allocation with the tax attributes of the consolidated group and with the tax attributes of another member with respect to a separate return year must be taken into account. See paragraph (b)(5) Example 29 of this section.

(2) Look-through entity. For purposes of this paragraph (b)(2)(iii)(d), a look-through entity means—

(**i**) A partnership;

(**ii**) A subchapter S corporation;

(**iii**) A trust or an estate;

(**iv**) An entity that is disregarded for Federal tax purposes, such as a qualified subchapter S subsidiary under section 1361(b)(3), an entity that is disregarded as an entity separate from its owner under §§ 301.7701–1 through 301.7701–3 of this chapter, or a qualified REIT subsidiary within the meaning of section 856(i)(2); or

(**v**) A controlled foreign corporation if United States shareholders of the controlled foreign corporation in the aggregate own, directly or indirectly, at least 10 percent of the capital or profits of the partnership on any day during the partnership's taxable year. In such case, the controlled foreign corporation shall be treated as a look-through entity, but only with respect to allocations of income, gain, loss, or deduction (or items thereof) that enter into the computation of a United States shareholder's inclusion under section 951(a) with respect to the controlled foreign corporation, enter into any person's income attributable to a United States shareholder's inclusion under section 951(a) with respect to the controlled foreign corporation, or would enter into the computations described in this paragraph if such items were allocated to the controlled foreign corporation. See paragraph (b)(2)(iii)(d)(6) for the definition of indirect ownership.

(3) Controlled foreign corporations. For purposes of this section, the term controlled foreign corporation means a controlled foreign corporation as defined in section 957(a) or section 953(c). In the case of a controlled foreign corporation that is a look-through entity, the tax attributes to be taken into account are those of any person that is a United States shareholder (as defined in paragraph (b)(2)(iii)(d)(5) of this section) of the controlled foreign corpo-

ration, or, if the United States shareholder is a look-through entity, a United States person that owns an interest in such shareholder directly or indirectly through one or more look-through entities.

(4) United States person. For purposes of this section, a United States person is a person described in section 7701(a)(30).

(5) United States shareholder. For purposes of this section, a United States shareholder is a person described in section 951(b) or section 953(c).

(6) Indirect ownership. For purposes of this section, indirect ownership of stock or another equity interest (such as an interest in a partnership) shall be determined in accordance with the principles of section 318, substituting the phrase "10 percent" for the phrase "50 percent" each time it appears.

(e) De minimis rule—(**1**) **Partnership taxable years beginning after May 19, 2008 and beginning before December 28, 2012.** Except as provided in paragraph (b)(2)(iii)(e)(2) of this section, for purposes of applying this paragraph (b)(2)(iii), for partnership taxable years beginning after May 19, 2008 and beginning before December 28, 2012, the tax attributes of de minimis partners need not be taken into account. For purposes of this paragraph (b)(2)(iii)(e)(1), a de minimis partner is any partner, including a look-through entity that owns, directly or indirectly, less than 10 percent of the capital and profits of a partnership, and who is allocated less than 10 percent of each partnership item of income, gain, loss, deduction, and credit. See paragraph (b)(2)(iii)(d)(6) of this section for the definition of indirect ownership.

(2) Nonapplicability of de minimis rule. *(i) Allocations that become part of the partnership agreement on or after December 28, 2012.* Paragraph (b)(2)(iii)(e)(1) of this section does not apply to allocations that become part of the partnership agreement on or after December 28, 2012.

(ii) Retest for allocations that become part of the partnership agreement prior to December 28, 2012. If the de minimis partner rule of paragraph (b)(2)(iii)(e)(1) of this section was relied upon in testing the substantiality of allocations that became part of the partnership agreement before December 28, 2012, such allocations must be retested on the first day of the first partnership taxable year beginning on or after December 28, 2012, without regard to paragraph (b)(2)(iii)(e)(1) of this section.

(iv) Maintenance of capital accounts.

(a) In general. The economic effect test described in paragraph (b)(2)(ii) of this section requires an examination of the capital accounts of the partners of a partnership, as maintained under the partnership agreement. Except as otherwise provided in paragraph (b)(2)(ii)(i) of this section, an allocation of income, gain, loss, or deduction will not have economic effect under paragraph (b)(2)(ii) of this section, and will not be deemed to be in accordance with a partner's interest in the partnership under paragraph (b)(4) of this section, unless the capital accounts of the partners are determined and maintained throughout the full term of the partnership in accordance with the capital accounting rules of this paragraph (b)(2)(iv).

(b) Basic rules. Except as otherwise provided in this paragraph (b)(2)(iv), the partners' capital accounts will be considered to be determined and maintained in accordance with the rules of this paragraph (b)(2)(iv) if, and only if, each partner's capital account is increased by (1) the amount of money contributed by him to the partnership, (2) the fair market value of property contributed by him to the partnership (net of liabilities that the partnership is considered to assume or take subject to), and (3) allocations to him of partnership income and gain (or items thereof), including income and gain exempt from tax and income and gain described in paragraph (b)(2)(iv)(g) of this section, but excluding income and gain described in paragraph (b)(4)(i) of this section; and is decreased by (4) the amount of money distributed to him by the partnership, (5) the fair market value of property distributed to him by the partnership (net of liabilities that such partner is considered to assume or take subject to), (6) allocations to him of expenditures of the partnership described in section 705(a)(2)(B), and (7) allocations of partnership loss and deduction (or item thereof), including loss and deduction described in paragraph (b)(2)(iv)(g) of this section, but excluding items described in (6) above and loss or deduction described in paragraphs (b)(4)(i) or (b)(4)(iii) of this section; and is otherwise adjusted in accordance with the additional rules set forth in this paragraph (b)(2)(iv). For purposes of this paragraph, a partner who has more than one interest in a partnership shall have a single capital account that reflects all such interests, regardless of the class of interests owned by such partner (e.g., general or limited) and regardless of the time or manner in which such interests were acquired. For liabilities assumed before June 24, 2003, references to liabilities in this paragraph (b)(2)(iv)(b) shall include only liabilities secured by the contributed or distributed property that are taken into account under section 752(a) and (b).

(c) Treatment of liabilities. For purposes of this paragraph (b)(2)(iv), (1) money contributed by a partner to a partnership includes the amount of any partnership liabilities that are assumed by such partner (other than liabilities described in paragraph (b)(2)(iv)(b)(5) of this section that are assumed by a distributee partner) but does not include increases in such partner's share of partnership liabilities (see section 752(a)), and (2) money distributed to a partner by a partnership includes the amount of such partner's individual liabilities that are assumed by the partnership (other than liabilities described in paragraph (b)(2)(iv)(b)(2) of this section that are assumed by the partnership) but does not include decreases in such partner's share of partnership liabilities (see section 752(b)). For purposes of this paragraph (b)(2)(iv)(c), liabilities are considered assumed only to the extent the assuming party

is thereby subjected to personal liability with respect to such obligation, the obligee is aware of the assumption and can directly enforce the assuming party's obligation, and, as between the assuming party and the party from whom the liability is assumed, the assuming party is ultimately liable.

(d) Contributed property.

(1) In general. The basic capital accounting rules contained in paragraph (b)(2)(iv)(b) of this section require that a partner's capital account be increased by the fair market value of property contributed to the partnership by such partner on the date of contribution. See example (13)(i) of paragraph (b)(5) of this section. Consistent with section 752(c), section 7701(g) does not apply in determining such fair market value.

(2) Contribution of promissory notes. Notwithstanding the general rule of paragraph (b)(2)(iv)(b)(2) of this section, except as provided in this paragraph (b)(2)(iv)(d)(2), if a promissory note is contributed to a partnership by a partner who is the maker of such note, such partner's capital account will be increased with respect to such note only when there is a taxable disposition of such note by the partnership or when the partner makes principal payments on such note. See example (1)(ix) of paragraph (b)(5) of this section. The first sentence of this paragraph (b)(2)(iv)(d)(2) shall not apply if the note referred to therein is readily tradable on an established securities market. See also paragraph (b)(2)(ii)(c) of this section. Furthermore, a partner whose interest is liquidated will be considered as satisfying his obligation to restore the deficit balance in his capital account to the extent of (i) the fair market value, at the time of contribution, of any negotiable promissory note (of which such partner is the maker) that such partner contributes to the partnership on or after the date his interest is liquidated and within the time specified in paragraph (b)(2)(ii)(b)(3) of this section, and (ii) the fair market value, at the time of liquidation, of the unsatisfied portion of any negotiable promissory note (of which such partner is the maker) that such partner previously contributed to the partnership. For purposes of the preceding sentence, the fair market value of a note will be no less than the outstanding principal balance of such note, provided that such note bears interest at a rate no less than the applicable federal rate at the time of valuation.

(3) Section 704(c) considerations. Section 704(c) and § 1.704–3 govern the determination of the partners' distributive shares of income, gain, loss, and deduction, as computed for tax purposes, with respect to property contributed to a partnership (see paragraph (b)(1)(vi) of this section). In cases where section 704(c) and § 1.704–3 apply to partnership property, the capital accounts of the partners will not be considered to be determined and maintained in accordance with the rules of this paragraph (b)(2)(iv) unless the partnership agreement requires that the partners' capital accounts be adjusted in accordance with paragraph (b)(2)(iv)(g) of this section for allocations to them of income, gain, loss, and deduction (including depreciation, depletion, amortization, or other cost recovery) as computed for book purposes, with respect to the property. See, however, § 1.704–3(d)(2) for a special rule in determining the amount of book items if the partnership chooses the remedial allocation method. See also Example (13)(i) of paragraph (b)(5) of this section. Capital accounts are not adjusted to reflect allocations under section 704(c) and § 1.704–3 (e.g., tax allocations of precontribution gain or loss).

(4) Exercise of noncompensatory options. Solely for purposes of paragraph (b)(2)(iv)(b)(2) of this section, the fair market value of the property contributed on the exercise of a noncompensatory option (as defined in § 1.721–2(f)) does not include the fair market value of the option privilege, but does include the consideration paid to the partnership to acquire the option and the fair market value of any property (other than the option) contributed to the partnership on the exercise of the option. With respect to convertible debt, the fair market value of the property contributed on the exercise of the option is the adjusted issue price of the debt and the accrued but unpaid qualified stated interest (as defined in § 1.1273–1(c)) on the debt immediately before the conversion, plus the fair market value of any property (other than the convertible debt) contributed to the partnership on the exercise of the option. See Examples 31 through 35 of paragraph (b)(5) of this section.

* * *

(e) Distributed property.

(1) In general. The basic capital accounting rules contained in paragraph (b)(2)(iv)(b) of this section require that a partner's capital account be decreased by the fair market value of property distributed by the partnership (without regard to section 7701(g)) to such partner (whether in connection with a liquidation or otherwise). To satisfy this requirement, the capital accounts of the partners first must be adjusted to reflect the manner in which the unrealized income, gain, loss, and deduction inherent in such property (that has not been reflected in the capital accounts previously) would be allocated among the partners if there were a taxable disposition of such property for the fair market value of such property (taking section 7701(g) into account) on the date of distribution. See example (14)(v) of paragraph (b)(5) of this section.

(2) Distribution of promissory notes. Notwithstanding the general rule of paragraph (b)(2)(iv)(b)(5), except as provided in this paragraph (b)(2)(iv)(e)(2), if a promissory note is distributed to a partner by a partnership that is the maker of such note, such partner's capital account will be decreased with respect to such note only when there is a taxable disposition of such note by the partner or when the partnership makes principal payments on the note. The previous sentence shall not apply if a note distributed to a partner by a partnership who is the maker of such note is readily tradable on an established securities market. Furthermore, the capital account of a partner whose interest in a partnership is liquidated will be reduced to the extent of (i) the fair market value, at the time of distribution, of any negotiable promissory note (of which such partnership is the maker) that such partnership distributes to the partner on or after the date such partner's interest is liquidated and within the time specified in paragraph (b)(2)(ii)(b)(2) of this section, and (ii) the fair market value, at the time of liquidation, of the unsatisfied portion of any negotiable promissory note (of which such partnership is the maker) that such partnership previously distributed to the partner. For purposes of the preceding sentence, the fair market value of a note will be no less than the outstanding principal balance of such note, provided that such note bears interest at a rate no less than the applicable federal rate at time of valuation.

(f) Revaluations of property. A partnership agreement may, upon the occurrence of certain events, increase or decrease the capital accounts of the partners to reflect a revaluation of partnership property (including intangible assets such as goodwill) on the partnership's books. Capital accounts so adjusted will not be considered to be determined and maintained in accordance with the rules of this paragraph (b)(2)(iv) unless—

(1) The adjustments are based on the fair market value of partnership property (taking section 7701(g) into account) on the date of adjustment, as determined under paragraph (b)(2)(iv)(h) of this section. See Example 33 of paragraph (b)(5) of this section. * * *

(2) The adjustments reflect the manner is which the unrealized income, gain, loss, or deduction inherent in such property (that has not been reflected in the capital accounts previously) would be allocated among the partners if there were a taxable disposition of such property for such fair market value on that date, and

(3) The partnership agreement requires that the partners' capital accounts be adjusted in accordance with paragraph (b)(2)(iv)(g) of this section for allocations to them of depreciation, depletion, amortization, and gain or loss, as computed for book purposes, with respect to such property, and

(4) The partnership agreement requires that the partners' distributive shares of depreciation, depletion, amortization, and gain or loss, as computed for tax purposes, with respect to such property be determined so as to take account of the variation between the adjusted tax basis and book value of such property in the same manner as under section 704(c) (see paragraph (b)(4)(i) of this section), and

(5) The adjustments are made principally for a substantial non-tax business purpose—

(i) In connection with a contribution of money or other property (other than a de minimis amount) to the partnership by a new or existing partner as consideration for an interest in the partnership, or

(ii) In connection with the liquidation of the partnership or a distribution of money or other property (other than a de minimis amount) by the partnership to a retiring or continuing partner as consideration for an interest in the partnership, or

(iii) In connection with the grant of an interest in the partnership (other than a de minimis interest) on or after May 6, 2004, as consideration for the provision of services to or for the benefit of the partnership by an existing partner acting in a partner capacity, or by a new partner acting in a partner capacity or in anticipation of being a partner.

(iv) In connection with the issuance by the partnership of a noncompensatory option (other than an option for a *de minimis* partnership interest), or under generally accepted industry accounting practices, provided substantially all of the partnership's property (excluding money) consists of stock, securities, commodities, options, warrants, futures, or similar instruments that are readily tradable on an established securities market.

See example (14) and (18) of paragraph (b)(5) of this section. If the capital accounts of the partners are not adjusted to reflect the fair market value of partnership property when an interest in the partnership is acquired from or relinquished to the partnership, paragraphs (b)(1)(iii) and (b)(1)(iv) of this section should be consulted regarding the potential tax consequences that may arise if the principles of section 704(c) are not applied to determine the partners' distributive shares of depreciation, depletion, amortization, and gain or loss as computed for tax purposes, with respect to such property.

(g) Adjustments to reflect book value.

(1) In general. Under paragraphs (b)(2)(iv)(d) and (b)(2)(iv)(f) of this section, property may be properly reflected on the books of the partnership at a book value that differs from the adjusted tax basis of such property. In these circumstances, paragraphs (b)(2)(iv)(d)(3) and (b)(2)(iv)(f)(3) of this section provide that the capital accounts of the partners will not be considered to be determined and maintained in accordance with the rules of this paragraph (b)(2)(iv) unless the partnership agreement requires the partners' capital accounts to be adjusted in accordance with this paragraph (b)(2)(iv)(g) for allocations to them of depreciation, depletion, amortization, and gain or loss, as computed for book purposes, with respect to such property. In determining whether the economic effect of an allocation of book items is substantial, consideration will be given to the effect of such allocation on the determination of the partners' distributive shares of corresponding tax items under section 704(c) and paragraph (b)(4)(i) of this section. See example (17) of paragraph (b)(5) of this section. If an allocation of book items under the partnership agreement does not have substantial economic effect (as determined under paragraphs (b)(2)(ii) and (b)(2)(iii) of this section), or is not otherwise respected under this paragraph, such items will be reallocated in accordance with the partners' interests in the partnership, and such reallocation will be the basis upon which the partners' distributive shares of the corresponding tax items are determined under section 704(c) and paragraph (b)(4)(i) of this section. See examples (13), (14), and (18) of paragraph (b)(5) of this section.

(2) Payables and receivables. References in this paragraph (b)(2)(iv) and paragraph (b)(4)(i) of this section to book and tax depreciation, depletion, amortization, and gain or loss with respect to property that has an adjusted tax basis that differs from book value include, under analogous rules and principles, the unrealized income or deduction with respect to accounts receivable, accounts payable, and other accrued but unpaid items.

(3) Determining amount of book items. The partners' capital accounts will not be considered adjusted in accordance with this paragraph (b)(2)(iv)(g) unless the amount of book depreciation, depletion, or amortization for a period with respect to an item of partnership property is the amount that bears the same relationship to the book value of such property as the depreciation (or cost recovery deduction), depletion, or amortization computed for tax purposes with respect to such property for such period bears to the adjusted tax basis of such property. If such property has a zero adjusted tax basis, the book depreciation, depletion, or amortization may be determined under any reasonable method selected by the partnership.

(h) Determinations of fair market value. **(1) In general.** For purposes of this paragraph (b)(2)(iv), the fair market value assigned to property contributed to a partnership, property distributed by a partnership, or property otherwise revalued by a partnership, will be regarded as correct, provided that (1) such value is reasonably agreed to among the partners in arm's-length negotiations, and (2) the partners have sufficiently adverse interests. If, however, these conditions are not satisfied and the value assigned to such property is overstated or understated (by more than an insignificant amount), the capital accounts of the partners will not be considered to be determined and maintained in accordance with the rules of this paragraph (b)(2)(iv). Valuation of property contributed to the partnership, distributed by the partnership, or otherwise revalued by the partnership shall be on a property-by-property basis, except to the extent the regulations under section 704(c) permit otherwise.

(2) Adjustments for noncompensatory options. The value of partnership property as reflected on the books of the partnership must be adjusted to account for any outstanding noncompensatory options (as defined in § 1.721–2(f)) at the time of a revaluation of partnership property under paragraph (b)(2)(iv)(f) or (s) of this section. If the fair market value of outstanding noncompensatory options (as defined in § 1.721–2(f)) as of the date of the adjustment exceeds the consideration paid to the partnership to acquire the options, then the value of partnership property as reflected on the books of the partnership must be reduced by that excess to the extent of the unrealized income or gain in partnership property (that has not been reflected in the capital accounts previously). This reduction is allocated only to properties with unrealized appreciation in proportion to their respective amounts of unrealized appreciation. If the consideration paid to the partnership to acquire the outstanding noncompensatory options (as defined in § 1.721–2(f)) exceeds the fair market value of such options as of the date of the adjustment, then the value of partnership property as reflected on the books of the partnership must be increased by that excess to the extent of the unrealized loss in partnership property (that has not been reflected in the capital accounts previously). This increase is allocated only to properties with unrealized loss in proportion to their respective amounts of unrealized loss. However, any reduction or increase shall take into account the economic arrangement of the partners with respect to the property.

* * *

(i) Section 705(a)(2)(B) expenditures.

(1) In general. The basic capital accounting rules contained in paragraph (b)(2)(iv)(b) of this section require that a partner's capital account be decreased by allocations made to such partner of expenditures described in section 705(a)(2)(B). See example (11) of paragraph (b)(5) of this section. If an allocation of these expenditures under the partnership agreement does not have substantial economic effect (as determined under paragraphs (b) (2)(ii) and (b)(2)(iii) of this section), or is not otherwise respected under this paragraph, such expenditures will be reallocated in accordance with the partners' interest in the partnership.

(2) Expenses described in section 709. Except for amounts with respect to which an election is properly made under section 709(b), amounts paid or incurred to organize a partnership or to promote the sale of (or to sell) an interest in such a partnership shall, solely for purposes of this paragraph, be treated as section 705(a)(2)(B) expenditures, and upon liquidation of the partnership no further capital account adjustments will be made in respect thereof.

(3) Disallowed losses. If a deduction for a loss incurred in connection with the sale or exchange of partnership property is disallowed to the partnership under section 267(a)(1) or section 707(b), that deduction shall, solely for purposes of this paragraph, be treated as a section 705(a)(2)(B) expenditure.

* * *

(l) Transfers of partnership interests. The capital accounts of the partners will not be considered to be determined and maintained in accordance with the rules of this paragraph (b)(2)(iv) unless, upon the transfer of all or a part of an interest in the partnership, the capital account of the transferor that is attributable to the transferred interest carries over to the transferee partner. (See paragraph (b)(2)(iv) (m) of this section for rules concerning the effect of a section 754 election on the capital accounts of the partners.) If the transfer of an interest in a partnership causes a termination of the partnership under section 708(b)(1)(B), the capital account of the transferee partner and the capital accounts of the other partners of the terminated partnership carry over to the new partnership that is formed as a result of the termination of the partnership under § 1.708–1(b)(1)(iv). Moreover, the deemed contribution of assets and liabilities by the terminated partnership to a new partnership and the deemed liquidation of the terminated partnership that occur under § 1.708–1(b)(1) (iv) are disregarded for purposes of paragraph (b)(2)(iv) of this section. See Example 13 of paragraph (b)(5) of this section and the example in § 1.708–1(b)(1)(iv). The previous three sentences apply to terminations of partnerships under section 708(b)(1)(B) occurring on or after May 9, 1997; however, the sentences may be applied to terminations occurring on or after May 9, 1996, provided that the partnership and its partners apply the sentences to the termination in a consistent manner.

(m) Section 754 elections.

(1) In general. The capital accounts of the partners will not be considered to be determined and maintained in accordance with the rules of this paragraph (b)(2)(iv) unless, upon adjustment to the adjusted tax basis of partnership property under section 732, 734, or 743, the capital accounts of the partners are adjusted as provided in this paragraph (b)(2)(iv)(m).

(2) Section 743 adjustments. In the case of a transfer of all or a part of an interest in a partnership that has a section 754 election in effect for the partnership taxable year in which such transfer occurs, adjustments to the adjusted tax basis of partnership property under section 743 shall not be reflected in the capital account of the transferee partner or on the books of the partnership, and subsequent capital account adjustments for distributions (see paragraph (b)(2)(iv)(e)(1) of this section) and for depreciation, depletion, amortization, and gain or loss with respect to such property will disregard the effect of such basis adjustment. The preceding sentence shall not apply to the extent such basis adjustment is allocated to the common basis of partnership property under paragraph (b)(1) of § 1.734–2; in these cases, such basis adjustment shall, except as provided in paragraph (b)(2)(iv)(m)(5) of this section, give rise to adjustments to the capital accounts of the partners in accordance with their interests in the partnership under paragraph (b)(3) of this section. See examples (13) (iii) and (iv) of paragraph (b)(5) of this section.

(3) Section 732 adjustments. In the case of a transfer of all or a part of an interest in a partnership that does not have a section 754 election in effect for the partnership taxable year in which such transfer occurs, adjustments to the adjusted tax basis of partnership property under section 732(d) will be treated in the capital accounts of the partners in the same manner as section 743 basis adjustments are treated under paragraph (b)(2)(iv)(m)(2) of this section.

(4) Section 734 adjustments. Except as provided in paragraph (b)(2)(iv)(m)(5) of this section, in the case of a distribution of property in liquidation of a partner's interest in the partnership by a partnership that has a section 754 election in effect for the partnership taxable year in which the distribution occurs, the partner who receives the distribution that gives rise to the adjustment to the adjusted tax basis of partnership property under section 734 shall have a corresponding adjustment made to his capital account. If such distribution is made other than in liquidation of a partner's interest in the partnership, however, except as provided in paragraph (b)(2)(iv)(m)(5) of this section, the capital accounts of the partners shall be adjusted by the amount of the adjustment to the adjusted tax basis of partnership property under section 734, and such capital account adjustment shall be shared among the partners in the manner in which the unrealized income and gain that is displaced by such adjustment would have been shared if the property whose

basis is adjusted were sold immediately prior to such adjustment for its recomputed adjusted tax basis.

(5) Limitations on adjustments. Adjustments may be made to the capital account of a partner (or his successor in interest) in respect of basis adjustments to partnership property under sections 732, 734, and 743 only to the extent that such basis adjustments (i) are permitted to be made to one or more items of partnership property under section 755, and (ii) result in an increase or a decrease in the amount at which such property is carried on the partnership's balance sheet, as computed for book purposes. For example, if the book value of partnership property exceeds the adjusted tax basis of such property, a basis adjustment to such property may be reflected in a partner's capital account only to the extent such adjustment exceeds the difference between the book value of such property and the adjusted tax basis of such property prior to such adjustment.

(n) Partnership level characterization. Except as otherwise provided in paragraph (b)(2)(iv)(k) of this section, the capital accounts of the partners will not be considered to be determined and maintained in accordance with the rules of this paragraph (b)(2)(iv) unless adjustments to such capital accounts in respect of partnership income, gain, loss, deduction, and section 705(a)(2)(B) expenditures (or item thereof) are made with reference to the Federal tax treatment of such items (and in the case of book items, with reference to the Federal tax treatment of the corresponding tax items) at the partnership level, without regard to any requisite or elective tax treatment of such items at the partner level (for example, under section 58(i)). However, a partnership that incurs mining exploration expenditures will determine the Federal tax treatment of income, gain, loss, and deduction with respect to the property to which such expenditures relate at the partnership level only after first taking into account the elections made by its partners under section 617 and section 703(b)(4).

(o) Guaranteed payments. Guaranteed payments to a partner under section 707(c) cause the capital account of the recipient partner to be adjusted only to the extent of such partner's distributive share of any partnership deduction, loss, or other downward capital account adjustment resulting from such payment.

(p) Minor discrepancies. Discrepancies between the balances in the respective capital accounts of the partners and the balances that would be in such respective capital accounts if they had been determined and maintained in accordance with this paragraph (b)(2)(iv) will not adversely affect the validity of an allocation, provided that such discrepancies are minor and are attributable to good faith error by the partnership.

(q) Adjustments where guidance is lacking. If the rules of this paragraph (b)(2)(iv) fail to provide guidance on how adjustments to the capital accounts of the partners should be made to reflect particular adjustments to partnership capital on the books of the partnership, such capital accounts will not be considered to be determined and maintained in accordance with those rules unless such capital account adjustments are made in a manner that (1) maintains equality between the aggregate governing capital accounts of the partners and the amount of partnership capital reflected on the partnership's balance sheet, as computed for book purposes, (2) is consistent with the underlying economic arrangement of the partners, and (3) is based, wherever practicable, on Federal tax accounting principles.

* * *

(3) Partner's interest in the partnership.

(i) In general. References in section 704(b) and this paragraph to a partner's interest in the partnership, or to the partner's interests in the partnership, signify the manner in which the partners have agreed to share the economic benefit or burden (if any) corresponding to the income, gain, loss, deduction, or credit (or item thereof) that is allocated. Except with respect to partnership items that cannot have economic effect (such as nonrecourse deductions of the partnership), this sharing arrangement may or may not correspond to the overall economic arrangement of the partners. Thus, a partner who has a 50 percent overall interest in the partnership may have a 90 percent interest in a particular item of income or deduction. (For example, in the case of an unexpected downward adjustment to the capital account of a partner who does not have a deficit make-up obligation that causes such partner to have a negative capital account, it may be necessary to allocate a disproportionate amount of gross income of the partnership to such partner for such year so as to bring that partner's capital account back up to zero.) The determination of a partner's interest in a partnership shall be made by taking into account all facts and circumstances relating to the economic arrangement of the partners.

(ii) Factors considered. In determining a partner's interest in the partnership, the following factors are among those that will be considered:

(a) The partners' relative contributions to the partnership,

(b) The interests of the partners in economic profits and losses (if different than that in taxable income or loss),

(c) The interests of the partners in cash flow and other non-liquidating distributions, and

(d) The rights of the partners to distributions of capital upon liquidation.

The provisions of this subparagraph (b)(3) are illustrated by examples (1)(i) and (ii), (4)(i), (5)(i) and (ii), (6), (7), (8), (10)(ii), 16(i), and (19)(iii) of paragraph (b)(5) of this section. See paragraph (b)(4)(i) of this section concerning rules for determining the partners' interests in the partnership with respect to certain tax items.

(iii) Certain determinations. If—

(a) Requirements (1) and (2) of paragraph (b)(2)(ii)(b) of this section are satisfied, and

(b) All or a portion of an allocation of income, gain, loss, or deduction made to a partner for a partnership taxable year does not have economic effect under paragraph (b)(2)(ii) of this section, the partners' interests in the partnership with respect to the portion of the allocation that lacks economic effect will be determined by comparing the manner in which distributions (and contributions) would be made if all partnership property were sold at book value and the partnership were liquidated immediately following the end of the taxable year to which the allocation relates with the manner in which distributions (and contributions) would be made if all partnership property were sold at book value and the partnership were liquidated immediately following the end of the prior taxable year, and adjusting the result for the items described in (4), (5), and (6) of paragraph (b)(2)(ii)(d) of this section. A determination made under this paragraph (b)(3)(iii) will have no force if the economic effect of valid allocations made in the same manner is insubstantial under paragraph (b)(2)(iii) of this section. See examples (1)(iv), (v), and (vi), and (15)(ii) and (iii) of paragraph (b)(5) of this section.

(4) Special rules.

(i) Allocations to reflect revaluations. If partnership property is, under paragraphs (b)(2)(iv)(d) or (b)(2)(iv)(f) of this section, properly reflected in the capital accounts of the partners and on the books of the partnership at a book value that differs from the adjusted tax basis of such property, then depreciation, depletion, amortization, and gain or loss, as computed for book purposes, with respect to such property will be greater or less than the depreciation, depletion, amortization, and gain or loss, as computed for tax purposes, with respect to such property. In these cases the capital accounts of the partners are required to be adjusted solely for allocations of the book items to such partners (see paragraph (b)(2)(iv)(g)

of this section), and the partners' shares of the corresponding tax items are not independently reflected by further adjustments to the partners' capital accounts. Thus, separate allocations of these tax items cannot have economic effect under paragraph (b)(2)(ii)(b)(1) of this section, and the partners' distributive shares of such tax items must (unless governed by section 704(c)) be determined in accordance with the partners' interests in the partnership. These tax items must be shared among the partners in a manner that takes account of the variation between the adjusted tax basis of such property and its book value in the same manner as variations between the adjusted tax basis and fair market value of property contributed to the partnership are taken into account in determining the partners' shares of tax items under section 704(c). See examples (14) and (18) of paragraph (b)(5) of this section.

* * *

(vi) Amendments to partnership agreement. If an allocation has substantial economic effect under paragraph (b)(2) of this section or is deemed to be made in accordance with the partners' interests in the partnership under paragraph (b)(4) of this section under the partnership agreement that is effective for the taxable year to which such allocation relates, and such partnership agreement thereafter is modified, both the tax consequences of the modification and the facts and circumstances surrounding the modification will be closely scrutinized to determine whether the purported modification was part of the original agreement. If it is determined that the purported modification was part of the original agreement, prior allocations may be reallocated in a manner consistent with the modified terms of the agreement, and subsequent allocations may be reallocated to take account of such modified terms. For example, if a partner is obligated by the partnership agreement to restore the deficit balance in his capital account (or any limited dollar amount thereof) in accordance with requirement (3) of paragraph (b)(2)(ii)(b) of this section and, thereafter, such obligation is eliminated or reduced (other than as provided in paragraph (b)(2)(ii)(f) of this section), or is not complied with in a timely manner, such elimination, reduction, or noncompliance may be treated as if it always were part of the partnership agreement for purposes of making any reallocations and determining the appropriate limitations period.

(5) Examples. The operation of the rules in this paragraph is illustrated by the following examples:

Example (1). (i) A and B form a general partnership with cash contributions of $40,000 each, which cash is used to purchase depreciable personal property at a cost of $80,000. The partnership elects under section 48(q)(4) to reduce the amount of investment tax credit in lieu of adjusting the tax basis of such property. The partnership agreement provides that A and B will have equal shares of taxable income and loss (computed without regard to cost recovery deductions) and cash flow and that all cost recovery deductions on the property will be allocated to A. The agreement further provides that the partners' capital accounts will be determined and maintained in accordance with paragraph (b)(2)(iv) of the section, but that upon liquidation of the partnership, distributions will be made equally between the partners (regardless of capital account balances) and no partner will be required to restore the deficit balance in his capital account for distribution to partners with positive capital accounts balances. In the partnership's first taxable year, it recognizes operating income equal to its operating expenses and has an additional $20,000 cost recovery deduction, which is allocated entirely to A. That A and B will be entitled to equal distributions on liquidation, even through A is allocated the entire $20,000 cost recovery deduction, indicates A will not bear the full risk of the economic loss corresponding to such deduction if such loss occurs. Under paragraph (b)(2)(ii) of this section, the allocation lacks economic effect and

will be disregarded. The partners made equal contributions to the partnership, share equally in other taxable income and loss and in cash flow, and will share equally in liquidation proceeds, indicating that their actual economic arrangement is to bear the risk imposed by the potential decrease in the value of the property equally. Thus, under paragraph (b)(3) of this section the partners' interests in the partnership are equal, and the cost recovery deduction will be reallocated equally between A and B.

(ii) Assume the same facts as in (i) except that the partnership agreement provides that liquidation proceeds will be distributed in accordance with capital account balances if the partnership is liquidated during the first five years of its existence but that liquidation proceeds will be distributed equally if the partnership is liquidated thereafter. Since the partnership agreement does not provide for the requirement contained in paragraph (b)(2)(ii) (b)(2) of this section to be satisfied throughout the term of the partnership, the partnership allocations do not have economic effect. Even if the partnership agreement provided for the requirement contained in paragraph (b)(2)(ii) (b)(2) to be satisfied throughout the term of the partnership, such allocations would not have economic effect unless the requirement contained in paragraph (b)(2)(ii)(b)(3) of this section or the alternate economic effect test contained in paragraph (b)(2)(ii)(d) of this section were satisfied.

(iii) Assume the same facts as in (i) except that distributions in liquidation of the partnership (or any partner's interest) are to be made in accordance with the partners' positive capital account balances throughout the term of the partnership (as set forth in paragraph (b)(2) (ii)(b)(2) of this section). Assume further that the partnership agreement contains a qualified income offset (as defined in paragraph (b)(2) (ii)(d) of this section) and that, as of the end of each partnership taxable year, the items described in paragraphs (b)(2)(ii)(d)(4), (5), and (6) of this section are not reasonably expect-

ed to cause or increase a deficit balance in A's capital account.

	A	B
Capital account upon formation	$40,000	$40,000
Less: year 1 cost recovery deduction	(20,000)	0
Capital account at end of year 1	$20,000	$40,000

Under the alternate economic effect test contained in paragraph (b)(2)(ii)(d) of this section, the allocation of the $20,000 cost recovery deduction to A has economic effect.

(iv) Assume the same facts as in (iii) and that in the partnership's second taxable year it recognizes operating income equal to its operating expenses and has a $25,000 cost recovery deduction which, under the partnership agreement, is allocated entirely to A.

	A	B
Capital account at beginning of year 2	$20,000	$40,000
Less: year 2 cost recovery deduction	(25,000)	0
Capital account at end of year 2	($5,000)	$40,000

The allocation of the $25,000 cost recovery deduction to A satisfics that alternate economic effect test contained in paragraph (b)(2)(ii)(d) of this section only to the extent of $20,000. Therefore, only $20,000 of such allocation has economic effect, and the remaining $5,000 must be reallocated in accordance with the partners' interests in the partnership. Under the partnership agreement, if the property were sold immediately following the end of the partnership's second taxable year for $35,000 (its adjusted tax basis), the $35,000 would be distributed to B. Thus, B, and not A, bears the economic burden corresponding to $5,000 of the $25,000 cost recovery deduction allocated to A. Under paragraph (b)(3)(iii) of this section, $5,000 of such cost recovery deduction will be reallocated to B.

(v) Assume the same facts as in (iv) except that the cost recovery deduction for the partnership's second taxable year is $20,000 instead of $25,000. The allocation of such cost recovery deduction to A has economic effect under the alternate economic effect test contained in paragraph (b)(2)(ii)(d) of this section. Assume further that the property is sold for $35,000 immediately following the end of the partnership's second taxable year, resulting in a $5,000 taxable loss ($40,000 adjusted tax basis less $35,000 sales price), and the partnership is liquidated.

	A	B
Capital account at beginning of year 2	$20,000	$40,000
Less: year 2 cost recovery deduction	(20,000)	0
Capital account at end of year 2	0	$40,000
Less: loss on sale	(2,500)	(2,500)
Capital account before liquidation	($2,500)	$37,500

Under the partnership agreement the $35,000 sales proceeds are distributed to B. Since B bears the entire economic burden corresponding to the $5,000 taxable loss from the sale of the property, the allocation of $2,500 of such loss to A does not have economic effect and must be reallocated in accordance with the partners' interests in the partnership. Under paragraph (b)(3)(iii) of this section, such $2,500 loss will be reallocated to B.

(vi) Assume the same facts as in (iv) except that the cost recovery deduction for the partnership's second taxable year is $20,000 instead of $25,000, and that as of the end of the partnership's second taxable year it is reasonably expected that during its third taxable year the partnership will (1) have operating income equal to its operating expenses (but will have no cost recovery deductions), (2) borrow $10,000 (recourse) and distribute such amount $5,000 to A and $5,000 to B, and (3) thereafter sell the partnership property, repay the $10,000 liability, and liquidate. In determin-

ing the extent to which the alternate economic effect test contained in paragraph (b)(2)(ii)(d) of this section is satisfied as of the end of the partnership's second taxable year, the fair market value of partnership property is presumed to be equal to its adjusted tax basis (in accordance with paragraph (b)(2)(iii)(c) of this section). Thus, it is presumed that the selling price of such property during the partnership's third taxable year will be its $40,000 adjusted tax basis. Accordingly, there can be no reasonable expectation that there will be increases to A's capital account in the partnership's third taxable year that will offset the expected $5,000 distribution to A. Therefore, the distribution of the loan proceeds must be taken into account in determining to what extent the alternate economic effect test contained in paragraph (b)(2)(ii)(d) is satisfied.

	A	B
Capital account at beginning of year 2	$20,000	$40,000
Less: expected future distribution	(5,000)	(5,000)
Less: year 2 cost recovery deduction	(20,000)	(0)
Hypothetical capital account at end of year 2	($5,000)	$35,000

Upon sale of the partnership property, the $40,000 presumed sales proceeds would be used to repay the $10,000 liability, and the remaining $30,000 would be distributed to B. Under these circumstances the allocation of the $20,000 cost recovery deduction to A in the partnership's second taxable year satisfies the alternate economic effect test contained in paragraph (b)(2)(ii)(d) of this section only to the extent of $15,000. Under paragraph (b)(3)(iii) of this section, the remaining $5,000 of such deduction will be reallocated to B. The results in this example would be the same even if the partnership agreement also provided that any gain (whether ordinary income or capital gain) upon the sale of the property would be allocated to A to the extent of the prior allocations of cost recovery deductions to him, and,

at end of the partnership's second taxable year, the partners were confident that the gain on the sale of the property in the partnership's third taxable year would be sufficient to offset the expected $5,000 distribution to A.

(vii) Assume the same facts as in (iv) except that the partnership agreement also provides that any partner with a deficit balance in his capital account following the liquidation of his interest must restore that deficit to the partnership (as set forth in paragraph (b)(2)(ii)(b)(3) of this section). Thus, if the property were sold for $35,000 immediately after the end of the partnership's second taxable year, the $35,000 would be distributed to B, A would contribute $5,000 (the deficit balance in his capital account) to the partnership, and that $5,000 would be distributed to B. The allocation of the entire $25,000 cost recovery deduction to A in the partnership's second taxable year has economic effect.

(viii) Assume the same facts as in (vii) except that A's obligation to restore the deficit balance in his capital account is limited to a maximum of $5,000. The allocation of the $25,000 cost recovery deduction to A in the partnership's second taxable year has economic effect under the alternate economic effect test contained in paragraph (b)(2)(ii)(d) of this section. At the end of such year, A makes an additional $5,000 contribution to the partnership (thereby eliminating the $5,000 deficit balance in his capital account). Under paragraph (b)(2)(ii)(f) of this section, A's obligation to restore up to $5,000 of the deficit balance in his capital account may be eliminated after he contributes the additional $5,000 without affecting the validity of prior allocations.

(ix) Assume the same facts as in (iv) except that upon formation of the partnership A also contributes to the partnership his negotiable promissory note with a $5,000 principal balance. The note unconditionally obligates A to pay an additional $5,000 to the partnership at the earlier of (a) the beginning of the partnership's fourth taxable year, or (b) the end of

the partnership taxable year in which A's interest is liquidated. Under paragraph (b)(2)(ii)(c) of this section, A is considered obligated to restore up to $5,000 of the deficit balance in his capital account to the partnership. Accordingly, under the alternate economic effect test contained in partnership (b)(2)(ii)(d) of this section, the allocation of the $25,000 cost recovery deduction to A in the partnership's second taxable year has economic effect. The results in this example would be the same if (1) the note A contributed to the partnership were payable only at the end of the partnership's fourth taxable year (so that A would not be required to satisfy the note upon liquidation of his interest in the partnership), and (2) the partnership agreement provided that upon liquidation of A's interest, the partnership would retain A's note, and A would contribute to the partnership the excess of the outstanding principal balance of the note over its then fair market value.

(x) Assume the same facts as in (ix) except that A's obligation to contribute an additional $5,000 to the partnership is not evidenced by a promissory note. Instead, the partnership agreement imposes upon A the obligation to make an additional $5,000 contribution to the partnership at the earlier of (a) the beginning of the partnership's fourth taxable year, or (b) the end of the partnership taxable year in which A's interest is liquidated. Under paragraph (b)(2)(ii)(c) of this section, as a result of A's deferred contribution requirement, A is considered obligated to restore up to $5,000 of the deficit balance in his capital account to the partnership. Accordingly, under the alternate economic effect test contained in paragraph (b)(2)(ii)(d) of this section, the allocation of the $25,000 cost recovery deduction to A in the partnership's second taxable year has economic effect.

(xi) Assume the same facts as in (vii) except that the partnership agreement also provides that any gain (whether ordinary income or capital gain) upon the sale of the property will be allocated to A to the extent of the prior allocations to A of cost recovery deductions from such property, and additional gain will be allocated equally between A and B. At the time the allocations of cost recovery deductions were made to A, the partners believed there would be gain on the sale of the property in an amount sufficient to offset the allocations of cost recovery deductions to A. Nevertheless, the existence of the gain chargeback provision will not cause the economic effect of the allocations to be insubstantial under paragraph (b)(2)(iii)(c) of this section, since in testing whether the economic effect of such allocations is substantial, the recovery property is presumed to decrease in value by the amount of such deductions.

Example (2). C and D form a general partnership solely to acquire and lease machinery that is 5-year recovery property under section 168. Each contributes $100,000, and the partnership obtains an $800,000 recourse loan to purchase the machinery. The partnership elects under section 48(q)(4) to reduce the amount of investment tax credit in lieu of adjusting the tax basis of such machinery. The partnership, C, and D have calendar taxable years. The partnership agreement provides that the partners' capital accounts will be determined and maintained in accordance with paragraph (b)(2)(iv) of this section, distributions in liquidation of the partnership (or any partner's interest) will be made in accordance with the partners' positive capital account balances, and any partner with a deficit balance in his capital account following the liquidation of his interest must restore that deficit to the partnership (as set forth in paragraphs (b)(2)(ii)(b)(2) and (3) of this section). The partnership agreement further provides that (a) partnership net taxable loss will be allocated 90 percent to C and 10 percent to D until such time as there is partnership net taxable income, and therefore C will be allocated 90 percent of such taxable income until he has been allocated partnership net taxable income equal to the partnership net taxable loss previously allocated to him, (b) all further partnership net taxable income or loss will be allocated equally between C and D, and (c) distributions of operating cash flow will be made equally between C and D. The partnership enters into a 12-year lease with a financially secure corporation under which the partnership expects to have a net taxable loss in each of its first 5 partnership taxable years due to cost recovery deductions with respect to the machinery and net taxable income in each of its following 7 partnership taxable years, in part due to the absence of such cost recovery deductions. There is a strong likelihood that the partnership's net taxable loss in partnership taxable years 1 through 5 will be $100,000, $90,000, $80,000, $70,000, and $60,000, respectively, and the partnership's net taxable income in partnership taxable years 6 through 12 will be $40,000, $50,000, $60,000, $70,000, $80,000, $90,000, and $100,000, respectively. Even though there is a strong likelihood that the allocations of net taxable loss in years 1 through 5 will be largely offset by other allocations in partnership taxable years 6 through 12, and even if it is assumed that the total tax liability of the partners in years 1 through 12 will be less than if the allocations had not been provided in the partnership agreement, the economic effect of the allocations will not be insubstantial under paragraph (b)(2)(iii)(c) of this section. This is because at the time such allocations became part of the partnership agreement, there was a strong likelihood that the allocations of net taxable loss in years 1 through 5 would not be largely offset by allocations of income within 5 years (determined on a first-in, first-out basis). The year 1 allocation will not be offset until years 6, 7, and 8, the year 2 allocation will not be offset until years 8 and 9, the year 3 allocation will not be offset until years 9 and 10, the year 4 allocation will not be offset until years 10 and 11, and the year 5 allocation will not be offset until years 11 and 12.

Example (3). E and F enter into a partnership agreement to develop and market experimental electronic devices. E contributes $2,500 cash and agrees to devote his full-time services to the partnership. F contributes $100,000 cash and agrees to obtain a loan for the partnership for any additional capital needs. The partnership agreement provides that all deductions for research and experimental expenditures and interest on partnership loans are to be allocated to F. In addition, F will be allocated 90 percent, and E 10 percent, of partnership taxable income or loss, computed net of the deductions for such research and experimental expenditures and interest, until F has received allocations of such taxable income equal to the sum of such research and experimental expenditures, such interest expense, and his share of such taxable loss. Thereafter, E and F will share all taxable income and loss equally. Operating cash flow will be distributed equally between E and F. The partnership agreement also provides that E's and F's capital accounts will be determined and maintained in accordance with paragraph (b)(2)(iv) of this section, distributions in liquidation of the partnership (or any partner's interest) will be made in accordance with the partners' positive capital account balances, and any partner with a deficit balance in his capital account following the liquidation of his interest must restore that deficit to the partnership (as set forth in paragraphs (b)(2)(ii)(b)(2) and (3) of this section). These allocations have economic effect. In addition, in view of the nature of the partnership's activities, there is not a strong likelihood at the time the allocations become part of the partnership agreement that the economic effect of the allocations to F of deductions for research and experimental expenditures and interest on partnership loans will be largely offset by allocations to F of partnership net taxable income. The economic effect of the allocations is substantial.

Example (4). (i) G and H contribute $75,000 and $25,000, respectively, in forming a general partnership. The partnership agreement provides that all income, gain, loss, and deduction will be allocated equally between the partners, that the partners' capital accounts will be determined and maintained in accordance with paragraph (b)(2)(iv) of this section, but that all partnership distributions will, regardless of capital account balances, be made 75 percent to G and 25 percent to H. Following the liquidation of the partnership, neither partner is required to restore the deficit balance in his capital account to the partnership for distribution to partners with positive capital account balances. The allocations in the partnership agreement do not have economic effect. Since contributions were made in a 75/25 ratio and the partnership agreement indicates that all economic profits and losses of the partnership are to be shared in a 75/25 ratio, under paragraph (b)(3) of this section, partnership income, gain, loss, and deduction will be reallocated 75 percent to G and 25 percent to H.

(ii) Assume the same facts as in (i) except that the partnership maintains no capital accounts and the partnership agreement provides that all income, gain, loss, deduction, and credit will be allocated 75 percent to G and 25 percent to H. G and H are ultimately liable (under a State law right of contribution) for 75 percent and 25 percent, respectively, of any debts of the partnership. Although the allocations do not satisfy the requirements of paragraph (b)(2)(ii)(b) of this section, the allocations have economic effect under the economic effect equivalence test of paragraph (b)(2)(ii)(i) of this section.

(iii) Assume the same facts as in (i) except that the partnership agreement provides that any partner with a deficit balance in his capital account must restore that deficit to the partnership (as set forth in paragraph (b)(2)(ii)(b)(2) of this section). Although the allocations do not satisfy the requirements of paragraph (b)(2)(ii)(b) of this section, the allocations have economic effect under the economic effect equivalence test of paragraph (b)(2)(ii)(i) of this section.

Example (5). (i) Individuals I and J are the only partners of an investment partnership. The partnership owns corporate stocks, corporate debt instruments, and tax-exempt debt instruments. Over the next several years, I expects to be in the 50 percent marginal tax bracket, and J expects to be in the 15 percent marginal tax bracket. There is a strong likelihood that in each of the next several years the partnership will realize between $450 and $550 of tax-exempt interest and between $450 and $550 of a combination of taxable interest and dividends from its investments. I and J made equal capital contributions to the partnership, and they have agreed to share equally in gains and losses from the sale of the partnership's investment securities. I and J agree, however, that rather than share interest and dividends of the partnership equally, they will allocate the partnership's tax-exempt interest 80 percent to I and 20 percent to J and will distribute cash derived from interest received on the tax-exempt bonds in the same percentages. In addition, they agree to allocate 100 percent of the partnership's taxable interest and dividends to J and to distribute cash derived from interest and dividends received on the corporate stocks and debt instruments 100 percent to J. The partnership agreement further provides that the partners' capital accounts will be determined and maintained in accordance with paragraph (b)(2)(iv) of this section, distributions in liquidation of the partnership (or any partner's interest) will be made in accordance with the partner's positive capital account balances, and any partner with a deficit balance in his capital account following the liquidation of his interest must restore that deficit to the partnership (as set forth in paragraphs (b)(2)(ii)(b) (2) and (3) of this section). The allocation of taxable interest and dividends and tax-exempt interest has economic effect, but that economic effect is not substantial under the general rules set forth in paragraph (b)(2)(iii) of this section. Without the allocation I would be allocated between $225 and $275 of tax-exempt interest and between $225 and $275 of a combination of taxable interest and dividends, which (net of Federal income taxes he would owe on such income) would give I between $337.50 and $412.50 after tax. With the allocation, however, I will be allocated between $360 and $440 of tax-exempt interest and no taxable interest and dividends, which (net of Federal income taxes) will give I between $360 and $440 after tax. Thus, at the time the allocations became part of the partnership agreement, I is expected to enhance his after-tax economic consequences as a result of the allocations. On the other hand, there is a strong likelihood that neither I nor J will substantially diminish his after-tax economic consequences as a result of the allocations. Under the combination of likely investment outcomes least favorable for J, the partnership would realize $550 of tax-exempt interest and $450 of taxable interest and dividends, giving J $492.50 after tax (which is more than the $466.25 after tax J would have received if each of such amounts had been allocated equally between the partners). Under the combination of likely investment outcomes least favorable for I, the partnership would realize $450 of tax-exempt interest and $550 of taxable interest and dividends, giving I $360 after tax (which is not substantially less than the $362.50 he would have received if each of such amounts had been allocated equally between the partners). Accordingly, the allocations in the partnership agreement must be reallocated in accordance with the partners' interests in the partnership under paragraph (b)(3) of this section.

(ii) Assume the same facts as in (i). In addition, assume that in the first partnership taxable year in which the allocation arrangement described in (i) applies, the partnership realizes $450 of tax-exempt interest and $550 of taxable interest and dividends, so that, pursuant to the partnership agreement, I's capital account is credited with $360 (80 percent of the tax-exempt interest), and J's capital account is credited with $640 (20 percent of the tax-exempt interest and 100 percent of the taxable interest and dividends). The allocations of tax-exempt interest and taxable interest and dividends (which do not have substantial economic effect for the reasons stated in (i)) will be disregarded and will be reallocated. Since

under the partnership agreement I will receive 36 percent (360/1,000) and J will receive 64 percent (640/1,000) of the partnership's total investment income in such year, under paragraph (b)(3) of this section the partnership's tax-exempt interest and taxable interest and dividends each will be reallocated 36 percent to I and 64 percent to J.

Example (6). K and L are equal partners in a general partnership formed to acquire and operate property described in section 1231(b). The partnership, K, and L have calendar taxable years. The partnership agreement provides that the partners' capital accounts will be determined and maintained in accordance with paragraph (b)(2)(iv) of this section, that distributions in liquidation of the partnership (or any partner's interest) will be made in accordance with the partners' positive capital account balances, and that any partner with a deficit balance in his capital account following the liquidation of his interest must restore that deficit to the partnership (as set forth in paragraphs (b)(2)(ii)(b)(2) and (3) of this section). For a taxable year in which the partnership expects to incur a loss on the sale of a portion of such property, the partnership agreement is amended (at the beginning of the taxable year) to allocate such loss to K, who expects to have no gains from the sale of depreciable property described in section 1231(b) in that taxable year, and to allocate an equivalent amount of partnership loss and deduction for that year of a different character to L, who expects to have such gains. Any partnership loss and deduction in excess of these allocations will be allocated equally between K and L. The amendment is effective only for that taxable year. At the time the partnership agreement is amended, there is a strong likelihood that the partnership will incur deduction or loss in the taxable year other than loss from the sale of property described in section 1231(b) in an amount that will substantially equal or exceed the expected amount of the section 1231(b) loss. The allocations in such taxable year have economic effect. However, the economic effect of the allocations is insubstantial under the test described in paragraph (b)(2)(iii)(b) of this section because there is a strong likelihood, at the time the allocations become part of the partnership agreement, that the net increases and decreases to K's and L's capital accounts will be the same at the end of the taxable year to which they apply with such allocations in effect as they would have been in the absence of such allocations, and that the total taxes of K and L for such year will be reduced as a result of such allocations. If in fact the partnership incurs deduction or loss, other than loss from the sale of property described in section 1231(b), in an amount at least equal to the section 1231(b) loss, the loss and deduction in such taxable year will be reallocated equally between K and L under paragraph (b)(3) of this section. If not, the loss from the sale of property described in section 1231(b) and the items of deduction and other loss realized in such year will be reallocated between K and L in proportion to the net decreases in their capital accounts due to the allocation of such items under the partnership agreement.

Example (7). (i) M and N are partners in the MN general partnership, which is engaged in an active business. Income, gain, loss, and deduction from MN's business is allocated equally between M and N. The partnership, M, and N have calendar taxable years. Under the partnership agreement the partners' capital accounts will be determined and maintained in accordance with paragraph (b)(2)(iv) of this section, distributions in liquidation of the partnership (or any partner's interest) will be made in accordance with the partner's positive capital account balances, and any partner with a deficit balance in his capital account following the liquidation of his interest must restore that deficit to the partnership (as set forth in paragraphs (b)(2)(ii)(b)(2) and (3) of this section). In order to enhance the credit standing of the partnership, the partners contribute surplus funds to the partnership, which the partners agree to invest in equal dollar amounts of tax-exempt bonds and corporate stock for

the partnership's first 3 taxable years. M is expected to be in a higher marginal tax bracket than N during those 3 years. At the time the decision to make these investments is made, it is agreed that, during the 3-year period of the investment, M will be allocated 90 percent and N 10 percent of the interest income from the tax-exempt bonds as well as any gain or loss from the sale thereof, and that M will be allocated 10 percent and N 90 percent of the dividend income from the corporate stock as well as any gain or loss from the sale thereof. At the time the allocations concerning the investments become part of the partnership agreement, there is not a strong likelihood that the gain or loss from the sale of the stock will be substantially equal to the gain or loss from the sale of the tax-exempt bonds, but there is a strong likelihood that the tax-exempt interest and the taxable dividends realized from these investments during the 3-year period will not differ substantially. These allocations have economic effect, and the economic effect of the allocations of the gain or loss on the sale of the tax-exempt bonds and corporate stock is substantial. The economic effect of the allocations of the tax-exempt interest and the taxable dividends, however, is not substantial under the test described in paragraph (b)(2)(iii)(c) of this section because there is a strong likelihood, at the time the allocations become part of the partnership agreement, that at the end of the 3-year period to which such allocations relate, the net increases and decreases to M's and N's capital accounts will be the same with such allocations as they would have been in the absence of such allocations, and that the total taxes of M and N for the taxable years to which such allocations relate will be reduced as a result of such allocations. If in fact the amounts of the tax-exempt interest and taxable dividends earned by the partnership during the 3-year period are equal, the tax-exempt interest and taxable dividends will be reallocated to the partners in equal shares under paragraph (b)(3) of this section. If not, the tax-exempt interest and taxable dividends will be reallocated between M and N in proportion to the net increases in their capital accounts during such 3-year period due to the allocation of such items under the partnership agreement.

(ii) Assume the same facts as in (i) except that gain or loss from the sale of the tax-exempt bonds and corporate stock will be allocated equally between M and N and the partnership agreement provides that the 90/10 allocation arrangement with respect to the investment income applies only to the first $10,000 of interest income from the tax-exempt bonds and the first $10,000 of dividend income from the corporate stock, and only to the first taxable year of the partnership. There is a strong likelihood at the time the 90/10 allocation of the investment income became part of the partnership agreement that in the first taxable year of the partnership, the partnership will earn more than $10,000 of tax-exempt interest and more than $10,000 of taxable dividends. The allocations of tax-exempt interest and taxable dividends provided in the partnership agreement have economic effect, but under the test contained in paragraph (b)(2)(iii) (b) of this section, such economic effect is not substantial for the same reasons stated in (i) (but applied to the 1 taxable year, rather than to a 3-year period). If in fact the partnership realizes at least $10,000 of tax-exempt interest and at least $10,000 of taxable dividends in such year, the allocations of such interest income and dividend income will be reallocated equally between M and N under paragraph (b)(3) of this section. If not, the tax-exempt interest and taxable dividends will be reallocated between M and N in proportion to the net increases in their capital accounts due to the allocations of such items under the partnership agreement.

(iii) Assume the same facts as in (ii) except that at the time the 90/10 allocation of investment income becomes part of the partnership agreement, there is not a strong likelihood that (1) the partnership will earn $10,000 or more of tax-exempt interest and $10,000 or more of taxable dividends in the partnership's first tax-

able year, and (2) the amount of tax-exempt interest and taxable dividends earned during such year will be substantially the same. Under these facts the economic effect of the allocations generally will be substantial. (Additional facts may exist in certain cases, however, so that the allocation is insubstantial under the second sentence of paragraph (b)(2)(iii). See example (5) above.)

Example (8). (i) O and P are equal partners in the OP general partnership. The partnership, O, and P have calendar taxable years. Partner O has a net operating loss carryover from another venture that is due to expire at the end of the partnership's second taxable year. Otherwise, both partners expect to be in the 50 percent marginal tax bracket in the next several taxable years. The partnership agreement provides that the partners' capital accounts will be determined and maintained in accordance with paragraph (b)(2)(iv) of this section, distributions in liquidation of the partnership (or any partner's interest) will be made in accordance with the partners' positive capital account balances, and any partner with a deficit balance in his capital account following the liquidation of his interest must restore that deficit to the partnership (as set forth in paragraphs (b)(2)(ii) (b)(2) and (3) of this section). The partnership agreement is amended (at the beginning of the partnership's second taxable year) to allocate all the partnership net taxable income for that year to O. Future partnership net taxable loss is to be allocated to O, and future partnership net taxable income to P, until the allocation of income to O in the partnership's second taxable year is offset. It is further agreed orally that in the event the partnership is liquidated prior to completion of such offset, O's capital account will be adjusted downward to the extent of one-half of the allocations of income to O in the partnership's second taxable year that have not been offset by other allocations, P's capital account will be adjusted upward by a like amount, and liquidation proceeds will be distributed in accordance with the partners' adjusted capital account balances. As a result of this oral amendment, all allocations of partnership net taxable income and net taxable loss made pursuant to the amendment executed at the beginning of the partnership's second taxable year lack economic effect and will be disregarded. Under the partnership agreement other allocations are made equally to O and P, and O and P will share equally in liquidation proceeds, indicating that the partners' interests in the partnership are equal. Thus, the disregarded allocations will be reallocated equally between the partners under paragraph (b)(3) of this section.

(ii) Assume the same facts as in (i) except that there is no agreement that O's and P's capital accounts will be adjusted downward and upward, respectively, to the extent of one-half of the partnership net taxable income allocated to O in the partnership's second taxable year that is not offset subsequently by other allocations. The income of the partnership is generated primarily by fixed interest payments received with respect to highly rated corporate bonds, which are expected to produce sufficient net taxable income prior to the end of the partnership's seventh taxable year to offset in large part the net taxable income to be allocated to O in the partnership's second taxable year. Thus, at the time the allocations are made part of the partnership agreement, there is a strong likelihood that the allocation of net taxable income to be made to O in the second taxable year will be offset in large part within 5 taxable years thereafter. These allocations have economic effect. However, the economic effect of the allocation of partnership net taxable income to O in the partnership's second taxable year, as well as the offsetting allocations to P, is not substantial under the test contained in paragraph (b)(2)(iii)(c) of this section because there is a strong likelihood that the net increases or decreases in O's and P's capital accounts will be the same at the end of the partnership's seventh taxable year with such allocations as they would have been in the absence of such allocations, and the total taxes of O and P for the taxable years to which such allocations relate will be reduced as a result of such allocations. If in fact the partnership, in its taxable years 3 through 7, realizes sufficient net taxable income to offset the amount allocated to O in the second taxable year, the allocations provided in the partnership agreement will be reallocated equally between the partners under paragraph (b)(3) of this section.

Example (9). Q and R form a limited partnership with contributions of $20,000 and $180,000, respectively. Q, the limited partner, is a corporation that has $2,000,000 of net operating loss carryforwards that will not expire for 8 years. Q does not expect to have sufficient income (apart from the income of the partnership) to absorb any of such net operating loss carryforwards. R, the general partner, is a corporation that expects to be in the 46 percent marginal tax bracket for several years. The partnership agreement provides that the partners' capital accounts will be determined and maintained in accordance with paragraph (b)(2)(iv) of this section, distributions in liquidation of the partnership (or any partner's interest) will be made in accordance with the partners' positive capital account balances, and any partner with a deficit balance in his capital account following the liquidation of his interest must restore that deficit to the partnership (as set forth in paragraphs (b)(2)(ii)(b)(2) and (3) of this section). The partnership's cash, together with the proceeds of an $800,000 loan, are invested in assets that are expected to produce taxable income and cash flow (before debt service) of approximately $150,000 a year for the first 8 years of the partnership's operations. In addition, it is expected that the partnership's total taxable income in its first 8 taxable years will not exceed $2,000,000. The partnership's $150,000 of cash flow in each of its first 8 years will be used to retire the $800,000 loan. The partnership agreement provides that partnership net taxable income will be allocated 90 percent to Q and 10 percent to R in the first through eighth partnership taxable years, and 90 percent to R and 10 percent to Q in all subsequent partnership taxable years. Net taxable loss will be allocated 90 percent to R and 10 percent to Q in all partnership taxable years. All distributions of cash from the partnership to partners (other than the priority distributions to Q described below) will be made 90 percent to R and 10 percent to Q. At the end of the partnership's eighth taxable year, the amount of Q's capital account in excess of one-ninth of R's capital account on such date will be designated as Q's "excess capital account." Beginning in the ninth taxable year of the partnership, the undistributed portion of Q's excess capital account will begin to bear interest which will be paid and deducted under section 707(c) at a rate of interest below the rate that the partnership can borrow from commercial lenders, and over the next several years (following the eighth year) the partnership will make priority cash distributions to Q in prearranged percentages of Q's excess capital account designed to amortize Q's excess capital account and the interest thereon over a prearranged period. In addition, the partnership's agreement prevents Q from causing his interest in the partnership from being liquidated (and thereby receiving the balance in his capital account) without R's consent until Q's excess capital account has been eliminated. The below market rate of interest and the period over which the amortization will take place are prescribed such that, as of the end of the partnership's eighth taxable year, the present value of Q's right to receive such priority distributions is approximately 46 percent of the amount of Q's excess capital account as of such date. However, because the partnership's income for its first 8 taxable years will be realized approximately ratably over that period, the present value of Q's right to receive the priority distributions with respect to its excess capital account is, as of the date the partnership agreement is entered into, less than the present value of the additional Federal income taxes for which R would be liable if, during the partnership's first 8 taxable years, all partnership income were to be allocated 90 percent to R and 10 to Q. The allocations of partnership taxable income to Q and R in the first through eighth partnership taxable years have economic effect. However, such economic effect is not substantial under the general rules set forth in paragraph (b)(2)(iii) of this section. This is true because R may enhance his after-tax economic consequences, on a present value basis, as a result of the allocations to Q of 90 percent of partnership's income during taxable years 1 through 8, and there is a strong likelihood that neither R nor Q will substantially diminish its after-tax economic consequences, on a present value basis, as a result of such allocation. Accordingly, partnership taxable income for partnership taxable years 1 through 8 will be reallocated in accordance with the partners' interests in the partnership under paragraph (b)(3) of this section.

Example (10). (i) S and T form a general partnership to operate a travel agency. The partnership agreement provides that the partners' capital accounts will be determined and maintained in accordance with paragraph (b)(2)(iv) of this section, distributions in liquidation of the partnership (or any partner's interest) will be made in accordance with the partners' positive capital account balances, and any partner with a deficit balance in his capital account following the liquidation of his interest must restore that deficit to the partnership (as set forth in paragraphs (b)(2)(ii)(b)(2) and (3) of this section). The partnership agreement provides that T, a resident of a foreign country, will be allocated 90 percent, and S 10 percent, of the income, gain, loss, and deduction derived from operations conducted by T within his country, and all remaining income, gain, loss, and deduction will be allocated equally. The amount of such income, gain, loss, or deduction cannot be predicted with any reasonable certainty. The allocations provided by the partnership agreement have substantial economic effect.

(ii) Assume the same facts as in (i) except that the partnership agreement provides that all income, gain, loss, and deduction of the

partnership will be shared equally, but that T will be allocated all income, gain, loss, and deduction derived from operations conducted by him within his country as a part of his equal share of partnership income, gain, loss, and deduction, upto to the amount of such share. Assume the total tax liability of S and T for each year to which these allocations relate will be reduced as a result of such allocation. These allocations have economic effect. However, such economic effect is not substantial under the test stated in paragraph (b)(2)(iii)(b) of this section because, at the time the allocations became part of the partnership agreement, there is a strong likelihood that the net increases and decreases to S's and T's capital accounts will be the same at the end of each partnership taxable year with such allocations as they would have been in the absence of such allocations, and that the total tax liability of S and T for each year to which such allocations relate will be reduced as a result of such allocations. Thus, all items of partnership income, gain, loss, and income, gain, loss, and deduction will be reallocated equally between S and T under paragraph (b)(3) of this section.

* * *

Example (13). (i) Y and Z form a brokerage general partnership for the purpose of investing and trading in marketable securities. Y contributes cash of $10,000, and Z contributes securities of P corporation, which have an adjusted basis of $3,000 and a fair market value of $10,000. The partnership would not be an investment company under section 351(e) if it were incorporated. The partnership agreement provides that the partners' capital accounts will be determined and maintained in accordance with paragraph (b)(2)(iv) of this section, distributions in liquidation of the partnership (or any partner's interest) will be made in accordance with the partners' positive capital account balances, and any partner with a deficit balance in his capital account following the liquidation of his interest must restore that deficit to the partnership (as set forth in paragraphs (b)(2)(ii)(b)(2) and (3) of this section). The partnership uses the interim closing of the books method for purposes of section 706. The initial capital accounts of Y and Z are fixed at $10,000 each. The agreement further provides that all partnership distributions, income, gain, loss, deduction, and credit will be shared equally between Y and Z, except that the taxable gain attributable to the precontribution appreciation in the value of the securities of P corporation will be allocated to Z in accordance with section 704(c). During the partnership's first taxable year, it sells the securities of P corporation for $12,000, resulting in a $2,000 book gain ($12,000 less $10,000 book value) and a $9,000 taxable gain ($12,000 less $3,000 adjusted tax basis). The partnership has no other income, gain, loss, or deductions for the taxable year. The gain from the sale of the securities is allocated as follows:

	Tax	Book	Tax	Book
		Y		Z
Capital account upon formation	$10,000	$10,000	$3,000	$10,000
Plus: gain	1,000	1,000	8,000	1,000
Capital account at end of year 1	$11,000	$11,000	$11,000	$11,000

The allocation of the $2,000 book gain, $1,000 each to Y and Z, has substantial economic effect. Furthermore, under section 704(c) the partners' distributive shares of the $9,000 taxable gain are $1,000 to Y and $8,000 to Z.

(ii) Assume the same facts as in (i) and that at the beginning of the partnership's second taxable year, it invests its $22,000 of cash in securities of G Corp. The G Corp. securities increase in value to $40,000, at which time Y sells 50 percent of his partnership interest

(i.e., a 25 percent interest in the partnership) to LK for $10,000. The partnership does not have a section 754 election in effect for the partnership taxable year during which such sale occurs. In accordance with paragraph (b)(2)(iv)(*l*) of this section, the partnership agreement provides that LK inherits 50 percent of Y's $11,000 capital account balance. Thus, following the sale, LK and Y each have a capital account of $5,500, and Z's capital account remains at $11,000. Prior to the end of the partnership's second taxable year, the securities are sold for their $40,000 fair market value, resulting in an $18,000 taxable gain ($40,000 less $22,000 adjusted tax basis). The partnership has no other income, gain, loss, or deduction in such taxable year. Under the partnership agreement the $18,000 taxable gain is allocated as follows:

	Y	Z	LK
Capital account before sale of securities	$5,500	$11,000	$5,500
Plus gain	4,500	9,000	4,500
Capital account at end of year 2	$10,000	$20,000	$10,000

The allocation of the $18,000 taxable gain has substantial economic effect.

(iii) Assume the same facts as in (ii) except that the partnership has a section 754 election in effect for the partnership taxable year during which Y sells 50 percent of his interest to LK. Accordingly, under § 1.743–1 there is a $4,500 basis increase to the G Corp. securities with respect to LK. Notwithstanding this basis adjustment, as a result of the sale of the G Corp. securities, LK's capital account is, as in (ii), increased by $4,500. The fact that LK recognizes no taxable gain from such sale (due to his $4,500 section 743 basis adjustment) is irrelevant for capital accounting purposes since, in accordance with paragraph (b)(2)(iv)(m)(2) of this section, that basis adjustment is disregarded in the maintenance and computation of the partners' capital accounts.

(iv) Assume the same facts as in (iii) except that immediately following Y's sale of 50 percent of this interest to LK, the G Corp. securities decrease in value to $32,000 and are sold. The $10,000 taxable gain ($32,000 less $22,000 adjusted tax basis) is allocated as follows:

	Y	Z	LK
Capital account before sale of securities	$5,500	$11,000	$5,500
Plus: gain	2,500	5,000	2,500
Capital account at end of year 2	$8,000	$16,000	$8,000

The fact that LK recognizes a $2,000 taxable loss from the sale of the G Corp. securities (due to his $4,500 section 743 basis adjustment) is irrelevant for capital accounting purposes since, in accordance with paragraph (b)(2)(iv)(m)(2) of this section, that basis adjustment is disregarded in the maintenance and computation of the partners' capital accounts.

(v) Assume the same facts as in (ii) except that Y sells 100 percent of his partnership interest (i.e., a 50 percent interest in the partnership) to LK for $20,000. Under section 708(b) (1)(B) the partnership terminates. Under paragraph (b)(1)(iv) of § 1.708–1, there is a constructive liquidation of the partnership. Immediately preceding the constructive liquidation, the capital accounts of Z and LK equal $11,000 each (LK having inherited Y's $11,000 capital account) and the book value of G Corp. securities is $22,000 (original purchase price of securities). Under paragraph (b)(2)(iv)(*l*) of this section, the deemed contribution of assets and liabilities by the terminated partnership to the new partnership and the deemed liquidation of the terminated partnership that occur under § 1.708–1(b)(1)(iv) in connection with the constructive liquidation of the terminated partnership are disregarded in the maintenance and computation of the partners' capital accounts. As a result, the capital accounts of Z and LK in the new partnership equal $11,000 each (their capital accounts in the terminated partnership

immediately prior to the termination), and the book value of the G Corp. securities remains $22,000 (its book value immediately prior to the termination). This Example 13(v) may be applied to terminations occurring on or after May 9, 1996, provided that the partnership and its partners apply this Example 13(v) to the termination in a consistent manner.

* * *

Example (15). *(i)* JB and DK form a limited partnership for the purpose of purchasing residential real estate to lease. JB, the limited partner, contributes $13,500, and DK, the general partner, contributes $1,500. The partnership, which uses the cash receipts and disbursements method of accounting, purchases a building for $100,000 (on leased land), incurring a recourse mortgage of $85,000 that requires the payment of interest only for a period of 3 years. The partnership agreement provides that partnership net taxable income and loss will be allocated 90 percent to JB and 10 percent to DK, the partners' capital accounts will be determined and maintained in accordance with paragraph (b)(2)(iv) of this section, distributions in liquidation of the partnership (or any partner's interest) will be made in accordance with the partners' positive capital account balances (as set forth in paragraph (b)(2)(ii)(b)(2) of this section), and JB is not required to restore any deficit balance in his capital account, but DK is so required. The partnership agreement contains a qualified income offset (as defined in paragraph (b)(2) (ii)(d) of this section). As of the end of each of the partnership's first 3 taxable years, the items described in paragraphs (b)(2)(ii)(d)(4), (5), and (6) of this section are not reasonably expected to cause or increase a deficit balance in JB's capital account: In the partnership's first taxable year, it has rental income of $10,000, operating expenses of $2,000, interest expense of $8,000, and cost recovery deductions of $12,000. Under the partnership agreement JB and DK are allocated $10,800 and $1,200, re-

spectively, of the $12,000 net taxable loss incurred in the partnership's first taxable year.

	JB	DK
Capital account upon formation	$13,500	$1,500
Less year 1 net loss	(10,800)	(1,200)
Capital account at end of year 1	$2,700	$300

The alternate economic effect test contained in paragraph (b)(2)(ii)(d) of this section is satisfied as of the end of the partnership's first taxable year. Thus, the allocation made in the partnership's first taxable year has economic effect.

(ii) Assume the same facts as in (i) and that in the partnership's second taxable year it again has rental income of $10,000, operating expenses of $2,000, interest expense of $8,000, and cost recovery deductions of $12,000. Under the partnership agreement JB and DK are allocated $10,800 and $1,200, respectively, of the $12,000 net taxable loss incurred in the partnership's second taxable year.

	JB	DK
Capital account at beginning of year 1	$2,700	$300
Less: year 2 net loss	(10,800)	(1,200)
Capital account at end of year 2	($8,100)	($900)

Only $2,700 of the $10,800 net taxable loss allocated to JB satisfies the alternate economic effect test contained in paragraph (b)(2)(ii) (d) of this section as of the end of the partnership's second taxable year. The allocation of such $2,700 net taxable loss to JB (consisting of $2,250 of rental income, $450 of operating expenses, $1,800 of interest expense, and $2,700 of cost recovery deductions) has economic effect. The remaining $8,100 of net taxable loss allocated by the partnership agreement to JB must be reallocated in accordance with the partners' interests in the partnership. Under paragraph (b)(3)(iii) of this section, the determination of the partners' interests in the remaining $8,100 net taxable loss is made by comparing how distributions (and contributions) would be made if the partnership sold its property at its adjusted tax basis and liquidated immediately following the end of the partnership's first taxable year with the results of such a sale and liquidation immediately following the end of the partnership's second taxable year. If the partnership's real property were sold for its $88,000 adjusted tax basis and the partnership were liquidated immediately following the end of the partnership's first taxable year, the $88,000 sales proceeds would be used to repay the $85,000 note, and there would be $3,000 remaining in the partnership, which would be used to make liquidating distributions to DK and JB of $300 and $2,700, respectively. If such property were sold for its $76,000 adjusted tax basis and the partnership were liquidated immediately following the end of the partnership's second taxable year, DK would be required to contribute $9,000 to the partnership in order for the partnership to repay the $85,000 note, and there would be no assets remaining in the partnership to distribute. A comparison of these outcomes indicates that JB bore $2,700 and DK $9,300 of the economic burden that corresponds to the $12,000 net taxable loss. Thus, in addition to the $1,200 net taxable loss allocated to DK under the partnership agreement, $8,100 of net taxable loss will be reallocated to DK under paragraph (b)(3)(iii) of this section. Similarly, for subsequent taxable years, absent an increase in JB's capital account, all net taxable loss allocated to JB under the partnership agreement will be reallocated to DK.

(iii) Assume the same facts as in (ii) and that in the partnership's third taxable year there is rental income of $35,000, operating expenses of $2,000, interest expense of $8,000, and cost recovery deductions of $10,000. The capital accounts of the partners maintained on the books of the partnership do not take into account the reallocation to DK of the $8,100 net taxable loss in the partnership's second taxable year. Thus, an allocation of the $15,000 net taxable income $13,500 to JB and $1,500 to DK (as dictated by the partnership agree-

ment and as reflected in the capital accounts of the partners) does not have economic effect. The partners' interests in the partnership with respect to such $15,000 taxable gain again is made in the manner described in paragraph (b)(3)(iii) of this section. If the partnership's real property were sold for its $76,000 adjusted tax basis and the partnership were liquidated immediately following the end of the partnership's second taxable year, DK would be required to contribute $9,000 to the partnership in order for the partnership to repay the $85,000 note, and there would be no assets remaining to distribute. If such property were sold for its $66,000 adjusted tax basis and the partnership were liquidated immediately following the end of the partnership's third taxable year, the $91,000 ($66,000 sales proceeds plus $25,000 cash on hand) would be used to repay the $85,000 note and there would be $6,000 remaining in the partnership, which would be used to make liquidating distributions to DK and JB of $600 and $5,400, respectively. Accordingly, under paragraph (b)(3)(iii) of this section the $15,000 net taxable income in the partnership's third taxable year will be reallocated $9,600 to DK (minus $9,000 at end of the second taxable year to positive $600 at end of the third taxable year) and $5,400 to JB (zero at end of the second taxable year to positive $5,400 at end of the third taxable year).

Example (16). (i) KG and WN form a limited partnership for the purpose of investing in improved real estate. KG, the general partner, contributes $10,000 to the partnership, and WN, the limited partner, contributes $990,000 to the partnership. The $1,000,000 is used to purchase an apartment building on leased land. The partnership agreement provides that (1) the partners' capital accounts will be determined and maintained in accordance with paragraph (b)(2)(iv) of this section; (2) cash will be distributed first to WN until such time as he has received the amount of his original capital contribution ($990,000), next to KG until such time as he has received the amount of his original capital contribution ($10,000), and thereafter equally between WN and KG; (3) partnership net taxable income will be allocated 99 percent to WN 1 percent to KG until the cumulative net taxable income allocated for all taxable years is equal to the cumulative net taxable loss previously allocated to the partners, and thereafter equally between WN and KG; (4) partnership net taxable loss will be allocated 99 percent to WN and 1 percent to KG, unless net taxable income has previously been allocated equally between WN and KG, in which case such net taxable loss first will be allocated equally until the cumulative net taxable loss allocated for all taxable years is equal to the cumulative net taxable income previously allocated to the partners; and (5) upon liquidation, WN is not required to restore any deficit balance in his capital account, but KG is so required. Since distributions in liquidation are not required to be made in accordance with the partners' positive capital account balances, and since WN is not required, upon the liquidation of his interest, to restore the deficit balance in his capital account to the partnership, the allocations provided by the partnership agreement do not have economic effect and will be reallocated in accordance with the partners' interests in the partnership under paragraph (b)(3) of this section.

(ii) Assume the same facts as in (i) except that the partnership agreement further provides that distributions in liquidation of the partnership (or any partner's interest) are to be made in accordance with the partners' positive capital account balances (as set forth in paragraph (b)(2)(ii)(b)(2) of this section). Assume further that the partnership agreement contains a qualified income offset (as defined in paragraph (b)(2)(ii)(d) of this section) and that, as of the end of each partnership taxable year, the items described in paragraphs (b)(2)(iii)(d)(4), (5), and (6) of this section are not reasonably expected to cause or increase a deficit balance in WN's capital account. The allocations provided by the partnership agreement have economic effect.

Example (17). FG and RP form a partnership with FG contributing cash of $100 and RP contributing property, with 2 years of cost recovery deductions remaining, that has an adjusted tax basis of $80 and a fair market value of $100. The partnership, FG, and RP have calendar taxable years. The partnership agreement provides that the partners' capital accounts will be determined and maintained in accordance with paragraph (b)(2)(iv) of this section, liquidation proceeds will be made in accordance with capital account balances, and each partner is liable to restore the deficit balance in his capital account to the partnership upon liquidation of his interest (as set forth in paragraphs (b)(2)(ii)(b)(2) and (3) of this section). FG expects to be in a substantially higher tax bracket than RP in the partnership's first taxable year. In the partnership's second taxable year, and in subsequent taxable years, it is expected that both will be in approximately equivalent tax brackets. The partnership agreement allocates all items equally except that all $50 of book depreciation is allocated to FG in the partnership's first taxable year and all $50 of book depreciation is allocated to RP in the partnership's second taxable year. If the allocation to FG of all book depreciation in the partnership's first taxable year is respected, FG would be entitled under section 704(c) to the entire cost recovery deduction ($40) for such year. Likewise, if the allocation to RP of all the book depreciation in the partnership's second taxable year is respected, RP would be entitled under section 704(c) to the entire cost recovery deduction ($40) for such year. The allocation of book depreciation to FG and RP in the partnership's first 2 taxable years has economic effect within the meaning of paragraph (b)(2)(ii) of this section. However, the economic effect of these allocations is not substantial under the test described in paragraph (b)(2)(iii)(c) of this section since there is a strong likelihood at the time such allocations became part of the partnership agreement that at the end of the 2-year period to which such allocations relate, the net increases and decreases to FG's and RP's capital accounts will be the same with such allocations as they would have been in the absence of such allocation, and the total tax liability of FG and RP for the taxable years to which the section 704(c) determinations relate would be reduced as a result of the allocations of book depreciation. As a result the allocations of book depreciation in the partnership agreement will be disregarded. FG and RP will be allocated such book depreciation in accordance with the partners' interests in the partnership under paragraph (b)(3) of this section. Under these facts the book depreciation deductions will be reallocated equally between the partners, and section 704(c) will be applied with reference to such reallocation of book depreciation.

* * *

(c) Contributed property; cross reference. See § 1.704–3 for methods of making allocations that take into account precontribution appreciation or diminution in value of property contributed by a partner to a partnership.

(d) Limitation on allowance of losses.

(1) A partner's distributive share of partnership loss will be allowed only to the extent of the adjusted basis (before reduction by current year's losses) of such partner's interest in the partnership at the end of the partnership taxable year in which such loss occurred. A partner's share of loss in excess of his adjusted basis at the end of the partnership taxable year will not be allowed for that year. However, any loss so disallowed shall be allowed as a deduction at the end of the first succeeding partnership taxable year, and subsequent partnership taxable years, to the extent that the partner's adjusted basis for his partnership interest at the end of any such year exceeds zero (before reduction by such loss for such year).

(2) In computing the adjusted basis of a partner's interest for the purpose of ascertaining the extent to which a partner's distributive share of partnership loss shall be allowed as a deduction for the taxable year, the basis shall first be increased under section 705(a)(1) and decreased under section 705(a)(2), except for losses of the taxable year and losses previously disallowed. If the partner's distributive share of the aggregate of items of loss specified in section 702(a)(1), (2), (3), (8), and (9) exceeds the basis of the partner's interest computed under the preceding sentence, the limitation on losses under section 704(d) must be allocated to his distributive share of each such loss. This allocation shall be determined by taking the proportion that each loss bears to the total of all such losses. For purposes of the preceding sentence, the total losses for the taxable year shall be the sum of his distributive share of losses for the current year and his losses disallowed and carried forward from prior years.

(3) For the treatment of certain liabilities of the partner or partnership, see section 752 and § 1.752–1.

(4) The provisions of this paragraph may be illustrated by the following examples:

Example (1). At the end of the partnership taxable year 1955, partnership AB has a loss of $20,000. Partner A's distributive share of this loss is $10,000. At the end of such year, A's adjusted basis for his interest in the partnership (not taking into account his distributive share of the loss) is $6,000. Under section 704(d), A's distributive share of partnership loss is allowed to him (in his taxable year within or with which the partnership taxable year ends) only to the extent of his adjusted basis of $6,000. The $6,000 loss allowed for 1955 decreases the adjusted basis of A's interest to zero. Assume that, at the end of partnership taxable year 1956, A's share of partnership income has increased the adjusted basis of A's interest in the partnership to $3,000 (not taking into account the $4,000 loss disallowed in 1955). Of the $4,000 loss disallowed for the partnership taxable year 1955, $3,000 is allowed A for the partnership taxable year 1956, thus again decreasing the adjusted basis of his interest to zero. If, at the end of partnership taxable year 1957, A has an adjusted basis of his interest of at least $1,000 (not taking into account the disallowed loss of $1,000), he will be allowed the $1,000 loss previously disallowed.

Example (2). At the end of partnership taxable year 1955, partnership CD has a loss of $20,000. Partner C's distributive share of this loss is $10,000. The adjusted basis of his interest in the partnership (not taking into account his distributive share of such loss) is $6,000. Therefore, $4,000 of the loss is disallowed. At the end of partnership taxable year 1956, the partnership has no taxable income or loss, but owes $8,000 to a bank for money borrowed. Since C's share of this liability is $4,000, the basis of his partnership interest is increased from zero to $4,000. (See sections 752 and 722, and §§ 1.752–1 and 1.722–1.) C is allowed the $4,000 loss, disallowed for the preceding year under section 704(d), for his taxable year within or with which partnership taxable year 1956 ends.

Example (3). At the end of partnership taxable year 1955, partner C has the following distributive share of partnership items described in section 702(a): long-term capital loss, $4,000; short-term capital loss, $2,000; income as described in section 702(a)(9), $4,000. Partner C's adjusted basis for his partnership interest at the end of 1955, before adjustment for any of the above items, is $1,000. As adjusted under section 705(a)(1)(A), C's basis is increased from $1,000 to $5,000 at the end of the year. C's total distributive share of partnership loss is $6,000. Since without regard to losses, C has a basis of only $5,000, C is allowed only $5,000/$6,000 of each loss, that is, $3,333 of his long-term capital loss, and $1,667 of his short-term capital loss. C must carry forward to succeeding taxable years $667 as a long-term capital loss and $333 as a short-term capital loss.

(e) Family partnerships.

(1) In general.

(i) Introduction. The production of income by a partnership is attributable to the capital or services, or both, contributed by the partners. The provisions of subchapter K, chapter 1 of the Code, are to be read in the light of their relationship to section 61, which requires, inter alia, that income be taxed to the person who earns it through his own labor and skill and the utilization of his own capital.

(ii) Recognition of donee as partner. With respect to partnerships in which capital is a material income-producing factor, section 704(e)(1) provides that a person shall be recognized as a partner for income tax purposes if he owns a capital interest in such a partnership whether or not such interest is derived by purchase or gift from any other person. If a capital interest in a partnership in which capital is a material income-producing factor is created by gift, section 704(e)(2) provides that the distributive share of the donee under the partnership agreement shall be includible in his gross income, except to the extent that such distributive share is determined without allowance of reasonable compensation for services rendered to the partnership by the donor, and except to the extent that the portion of such distributive share attributable to donated capital is proportionately greater than the share of the donor attributable to the donor's capital. For rules of allocation in such cases, see subparagraph (3) of this paragraph.

(iii) Requirement of complete transfer to donee. A donee or purchaser of a capital interest in a partnership is not recognized as a partner under the principles of section 704(e)(1) unless such interest is acquired in a bona fide transaction, not a mere sham for tax avoidance or evasion purposes, and the donee or purchaser is the real owner of such interest. To be recognized, a transfer must vest dominion and control of the partnership interest in the transferee. The existence of such dominion and control in the donee is to be determined from all the facts and circumstances. A transfer is not recognized if the transferor retains such incidents of ownership that the transferee has not acquired full and complete ownership of the partnership interest. Transactions between members of a family will be closely scrutinized, and the circumstances, not only at the time of the purported transfer but also during the periods preceding and following it, will be taken into consideration in determining the bona fides or lack of bona fides of the purported gift or sale. A partnership may be recognized for income tax purposes as to some partners but not as to others.

(iv) Capital as a material income-producing factor. For purposes of section 704(e) (1), the determination as to whether capital is a material income-producing factor must be made by reference to all the facts of each case. Capital is a material income-producing factor if a substantial portion of the gross income of the business is attributable to the employment of capital in the business conducted by the partnership. In general, capital is not a material income-producing factor where the income of the business consists principally of fees, commissions, or other compensation for personal services performed by members or employees of the partnership. On the other hand, capital is ordinarily a material income-producing factor if the operation of the business requires substantial inventories or a substantial investment in plant, machinery, or other equipment.

(v) Capital interest in a partnership. For purposes of section 704(e), a capital interest in a partnership means an interest in the assets of the partnership, which is distributable to the owner of the capital interest upon his withdrawal from the partnership or upon liquidation of the partnership. The mere right to participate in the earnings and profits of a partnership is not a capital interest in the partnership.

(2) Basic tests as to ownership.

(i) In general. Whether an alleged partner who is a donee of a capital interest in a partnership is the real owner of such capital interest, and whether the donee has dominion and control over such interest, must be ascertained from all the facts and circumstances of the

particular case. Isolated facts are not determinative; the reality of the donee's ownership is to be determined in the light of the transaction as a whole. The execution of legally sufficient and irrevocable deeds or other instruments of gift under State law is a factor to be taken into account but is not determinative of ownership by the donee for the purposes of section 704(e). The reality of the transfer and of the donee's ownership of the property attributed to him are to be ascertained from the conduct of the parties with respect to the alleged gift and not by any mechanical or formal test. Some of the more important factors to be considered in determining whether the donee has acquired ownership of the capital interest in a partnership are indicated in subdivisions (ii) to (x), inclusive, of this subparagraph.

(ii) Retained controls. The donor may have retained such controls of the interest which he has purported to transfer to the donee that the donor should be treated as remaining the substantial owner of the interest. Controls of particular significance include, for example, the following:

(a) Retention of control of the distribution of amounts of income or restrictions on the distributions of amounts of income (other than amounts retained in the partnership annually with the consent of the partners, including the donee partner, for the reasonable needs of the business). If there is a partnership agreement providing for a managing partner or partners, then amounts of income may be retained in the partnership without the acquiescence of all the partners if such amounts are retained for the reasonable needs of the business.

(b) Limitation of the right of the donee to liquidate or sell his interest in the partnership at his discretion without financial detriment.

(c) Retention of control of assets essential to the business (for example, through retention of assets leased to the alleged partnership).

(d) Retention of management powers inconsistent with normal relationships among

partners. Retention by the donor of control of business management or of voting control, such as is common in ordinary business relationships, is not by itself to be considered as inconsistent with normal relationships among partners, provided the donee is free to liquidate his interest at his discretion without financial detriment. The donee shall not be considered free to liquidate his interest unless, considering all the facts, it is evident that the donee is independent of the donor and has such maturity and understanding of his rights as to be capable of deciding to exercise, and capable of exercising, his right to withdraw his capital interest from the partnership.

The existence of some of the indicated controls, though amounting to less than substantial ownership retained by the donor, may be considered along with other facts and circumstances as tending to show the lack of reality of the partnership interest of the donee.

(iii) Indirect controls. Controls inconsistent with ownership by the donee may be exercised indirectly as well as directly, for example, through a separate business organization, estate, trust, individual, or other partnership. Where such indirect controls exist, the reality of the donee's interest will be determined as if such controls were exercisable directly.

(iv) Participation in management. Substantial participation by the donee in the control and management of the business (including participation in the major policy decisions affecting the business) is strong evidence of a donee partner's exercise of dominion and control over his interest. Such participation presupposes sufficient maturity and experience on the part of the donee to deal with the business problems of the partnership.

(v) Income distributions. The actual distribution to a donee partner of the entire amount or a major portion of his distributive share of the business income for the sole benefit and use of the donee is substantial evidence of the reality of the donee's interest, provided the donor has not retained controls inconsistent with

real ownership by the donee. Amounts distributed are not considered to be used for the donee's sole benefit if, for example, they are deposited, loaned, or invested in such manner that the donor controls or can control the use or enjoyment of such funds.

(vi) Conduct of partnership business. In determining the reality of the donee's ownership of a capital interest in a partnership, consideration shall be given to whether the donee is actually treated as a partner in the operation of the business. Whether or not the donee has been held out publicly as a partner in the conduct of the business, in relations with customers, or with creditors or other sources of financing, is of primary significance. Other factors of significance in this connection include:

(a) Compliance with local partnership, fictitious names, and business registration statutes.

(b) Control of business bank accounts.

(c) Recognition of the donee's rights in distributions of partnership property and profits.

(d) Recognition of the donee's interest in insurance policies, leases, and other business contracts and in litigation affecting business.

(e) The existence of written agreements, records, or memoranda, contemporaneous with the taxable year or years concerned, establishing the nature of the partnership agreement and the rights and liabilities of the respective partners.

(f) Filing of partnership tax returns as required by law.

However, despite formal compliance with the above factors, other circumstances may indicate that the donor has retained substantial ownership of the interest purportedly transferred to the donee.

(vii) Trustees as partners. A trustee may be recognized as a partner for income tax purposes under the principles relating to family partnerships generally as applied to the particular facts of the trust-partnership arrangement.

A trustee who is unrelated to and independent of the grantor, and who participates as a partner and receives distribution of the income distributable to the trust, will ordinarily be recognized as the legal owner of the partnership interest which he holds in trust unless the grantor has retained controls inconsistent with such ownership. However, if the grantor is the trustee, or if the trustee is amenable to the will of the grantor, the provisions of the trust instrument (particularly as to whether the trustee is subject to the responsibilities of a fiduciary), the provisions of the partnership agreement, and the conduct of the parties must all be taken into account in determining whether the trustee in a fiduciary capacity has become the real owner of the partnership interest. Where the grantor (or person amenable to his will) is the trustee, the trust may be recognized as a partner only if the grantor (or such other person) in his participation in the affairs of the partnership actively represents and protects the interests of the beneficiaries in accordance with the obligations of a fiduciary and does not subordinate such interests to the interests of the grantor. Furthermore, if the grantor (or person amenable to his will) is the trustee, the following factors will be given particular consideration:

(*a*) Whether the trust is recognized as a partner in business dealings with customers and creditors, and

(*b*) Whether, if any amount of the partnership income is not properly retained for the reasonable needs of the business, the trust's share of such amount is distributed to the trust annually and paid to the beneficiaries or reinvested with regard solely to the interests of the beneficiaries.

(viii) Interests (not held in trust) of minor children. Except where a minor child is shown to be competent to manage his own property and participate in the partnership activities in accordance with his interest in the property, a minor child generally will not be recognized as a member of a partnership unless control of the property is exercised by another person as fiduciary for the sole benefit of the child, and unless there is such judicial supervision of the conduct of the fiduciary as is required by law. The use of the child's property or income for support for which a parent is legally responsible will be considered a use for the parent's benefit. "Judicial supervision of the conduct of the fiduciary" includes filing of such accountings and reports as are required by law of the fiduciary who participates in the affairs of the partnership on behalf of the minor. A minor child will be considered as competent to manage his own property if he actually has sufficient maturity and experience to be treated by disinterested persons as competent to enter business dealings and otherwise to conduct his affairs on a basis of equality with adult persons, notwithstanding legal disabilities of the minor under State law.

(ix) Donees as limited partners. The recognition of a donee's interest in a limited partnership will depend, as in the case of other donated interests, on whether the transfer of property is real and on whether the donee has acquired dominion and control over the interest purportedly transferred to him. To be recognized for Federal income tax purposes, a limited partnership must be organized and conducted in accordance with the requirements of the applicable State limited-partnership law. The absence of services and participation in management by a donee in a limited partnership is immaterial if the limited partnership meets all the other requirements prescribed in this paragraph. If the limited partner's right to transfer or liquidate his interest is subject to substantial restrictions (for example, where the interest of the limited partner is not assignable in a real sense or where such interest may be required to be left in the business for a long term of years), or if the general partner retains any other control which substantially limits any of the rights which would ordinarily be exercisable by unrelated limited partners in normal business relationships, such restrictions on the right to transfer or liquidate, or retention of other control, will be considered strong evidence as to the lack of reality of ownership by the donee.

(x) Motive. If the reality of the transfer of interest is satisfactorily established, the motives for the transaction are generally immaterial. However, the presence or absence of a tax-avoidance motive is one of many factors to be considered in determining the reality of the ownership of a capital interest acquired by gift.

(3) Allocation of family partnership income.

(i) In general. *(a)* Where a capital interest in a partnership in which capital is a material income-producing factor is created by gift, the donee's distributive share shall be includible in his gross income, except to the extent that such share is determined without allowance of reasonable compensation for services rendered to the partnership by the donor, and except to the extent that the portion of such distributive share attributable to donated capital is proportionately greater than the distributive share attributable to the donor's capital. For the purpose of section 704, a capital interest in a partnership purchased by one member of a family from another shall be considered to be created by gift from the seller, and the fair market value of the purchased interest shall be considered to be donated capital. The "family" of any individual, for the purpose of the preceding sentence, shall include only his spouse, ancestors, and lineal descendants, and any trust for the primary benefit of such persons.

(b) To the extent that the partnership agreement does not allocate the partnership income in accordance with (a) of this subdivision, the distributive shares of the partnership income of the donor and donee shall be reallocated by making a reasonable allowance for the services of the donor and by attributing the balance of such income (other than a reasonable allowance for the services, if any, rendered by the donee) to the partnership capital of the donor and donee. The portion of income, if any, thus attributable to partnership capital for the taxable year shall be allocated between the donor and donee in accordance with their respective interests in partnership capital.

(c) In determining a reasonable allowance for services rendered by the partners, consideration shall be given to all the facts and circumstances of the business, including the fact that some of the partners may have greater managerial responsibility than others. There shall also be considered the amount that would ordinarily be paid in order to obtain comparable services from a person not having an interest in the partnership.

(d) The distributive share of partnership income, as determined under (b) of this subdivision, of a partner who rendered services to the partnership before entering the Armed Forces of the United States shall not be diminished because of absence due to military service. Such distributive share shall be adjusted to reflect increases or decreases in the capital interest of the absent partner. However, the partners may by agreement allocate a smaller share to the absent partner due to his absence.

(ii) Special rules.

(a) The provisions of subdivision (i) of this subparagraph, relating to allocation of family partnership income, are applicable where the interest in the partnership is created by gift, indirectly or directly. Where the partnership interest is created indirectly, the term "donor" may include persons other than the nominal transferor. This rule may be illustrated by the following examples:

Example (1). A father gives property to his son who shortly thereafter conveys the property to a partnership consisting of the father and the son. The partnership interest of the son may be considered created by gift and the father may be considered the donor of the son's partnership interest.

Example (2). A father, the owner of a business conducted as a sole proprietorship, transfers the business to a partnership consisting of his wife and himself. The wife subsequently conveys her interest to their son. In such case, the father, as well as the mother, may be considered the donor of the son's partnership interest.

Example (3). A father makes a gift to his son of stock in the family corporation. The corporation is subsequently liquidated. The son later contributes the property received in the liquidation of the corporation to a partnership consisting of his father and himself. In such case, for purposes of section 704, the son's partnership interest may be considered created by gift and the father may be considered the donor of his son's partnership interest.

(b) The allocation rules set forth in section 704(e) and subdivision (i) of this subparagraph apply in any case in which the transfer or creation of the partnership interest has any of the substantial characteristics of a gift. Thus, allocation may be required where transfer of a partnership interest is made between members of a family (including collaterals) under a purported purchase agreement, if the characteristics of a gift are ascertained from the terms of the purchase agreement, the terms of any loan or credit arrangements made to finance the purchase, or from other relevant data.

(c) In the case of a limited partnership, for the purpose of the allocation provisions of subdivision (i) of this subparagraph, consideration shall be given to the fact that a general partner, unlike a limited partner, risks his credit in the partnership business.

(4) Purchased interest.

(i) In general. If a purported purchase of a capital interest in a partnership does not meet the requirements of subdivision (ii) of this subparagraph, the ownership by the transferee of such capital interest will be recognized only if it qualifies under the requirements applicable to a transfer of a partnership interest by gifts. In a case not qualifying under subdivision (ii) of this subparagraph, if payment of any part of the purchase price is made out of partner-

ship earnings, the transaction may be regarded in the same light as a purported gift subject to deferred enjoyment of income. Such a transaction may be lacking in reality either as a gift or as a bona fide purchase.

(ii) Tests as to reality of purchased interests. A purchase of a capital interest in a partnership, either directly or by means of a loan or credit extended by a member of the family, will be recognized as bona fide if:

(a) It can be shown that the purchase has the usual characteristics of an arm's-length transaction, considering all relevant factors, including the terms of the purchase agreement (as to price, due date of payment, rate of interest, and security, if any) and the terms of any loan or credit arrangement collateral to the purchase agreement; the credit standing of the purchaser (apart from relationship to the seller) and the capacity of the purchaser to incur a legally binding obligation; or

(b) It can be shown, in the absence of characteristics of an arm's-length transaction, that the purchase was genuinely intended to promote the success of the business by securing participation of the purchaser in the business or by adding his credit to that of the other participants.

However, if the alleged purchase price or loan has not been paid or the obligation otherwise discharged, the factors indicated in (a) and (b) of this subdivision shall be taken into account only as an aid in determining whether a bona fide purchase or loan obligation existed.

§ 1.704–2 Allocations attributable to nonrecourse liabilities.

(a) Table of contents. * * *

(b) General principles and definitions.

(1) Definition of and allocations of nonrecourse deductions. Allocations of losses, deductions, or section 705(a)(2)(B) expenditures attributable to partnership nonrecourse liabilities (nonrecourse deductions) cannot have economic effect because the creditor alone bears any economic burden that corresponds to those allocations. Thus, nonrecourse deductions must be allocated in accordance with the partners' interests in the partnership. Paragraph (e) of this section provides a test that deems allocations of nonrecourse deductions to be in accordance with the partners' interests in the partnership. If that test is not satisfied, the partners' distributive shares of nonrecourse deductions are determined under § 1.704–1(b)(3), according to the partners' overall economic interests in the partnership. See also paragraph (i) of this section for special rules regarding the allocation of deductions attributable to nonrecourse liabilities for which a partner bears the economic risk of loss (as described in paragraph (b)(4) of this section).

(2) Definition of and allocations pursuant to a minimum gain chargeback. To the extent a nonrecourse liability exceeds the adjusted tax basis of the partnership property it encumbers, a disposition of that property will generate gain that at least equals that excess (partnership minimum gain). An increase in partnership minimum gain is created by a decrease in the adjusted tax basis of property encumbered by a nonrecourse liability below the amount of that liability and by a partnership nonrecourse borrowing that exceeds the adjusted tax basis of the property encumbered by the borrowing. Partnership minimum gain decreases as reductions occur in the amount by which the nonrecourse liability exceeds the adjusted tax basis of the property encumbered by the liability. Allocations of gain attributable to a decrease in partnership minimum gain (a "minimum gain chargeback," as required under paragraph (f) of this section) cannot have economic effect because the gain merely offsets nonrecourse deductions previously claimed by the partnership. Thus, to avoid impairing the economic effect of other allocations, allocations pursuant to a minimum gain chargeback must be made to the partners that either were allocated nonrecourse deductions or received distributions of proceeds attributable to a nonrecourse borrowing. Paragraph (e) of this section provides a test that, if met, deems allocations of partnership income pursuant to a minimum gain chargeback to be in accordance with the partners' interests in the partnership if property encumbered by a nonrecourse liability is reflected on the partnership's books at a value that differs from its adjusted tax basis paragraph (d)(3) of this section provides that minimum gain is determined with reference to the property's book basis. See also paragraph (i)(4) of this section for special rules regarding the minimum gain chargeback requirement for partner nonrecourse debt.

(3) Definition of nonrecourse liability. Nonrecourse liability, means a nonrecourse liability as defined in § 1.752–1(a)(2) or § 1.752.7 liability (as defined in § 1.752.7(b)(3)(i)) assumed by the partnership from a partner on or after June 24, 2003.

(4) Definition of partner nonrecourse debt. Partner nonrecourse debt, or, partner nonrecourse liability, means any partnership liability to the extent the liability is nonrecourse for purposes of § 1.1001–2, and a partner or related person (within the meaning of § 1.752–4(b)) bears the economic risk of loss under § 1.752–2 because, for example, the partner or related person is the creditor or a guarantor.

(c) Amount of nonrecourse deductions. The amount of nonrecourse deductions for a partnership taxable year equals the net increase in partnership minimum gain during the year (determined under paragraph (d) of this section), reduced (but not below zero) by the aggregate distributions made during the year of proceeds of a nonrecourse liability that are allocable to an increase in partnership minimum gain (determined under paragraph (h) of this section). See paragraph (m), Examples (1)(i) and (vi), (2), and (3) of this section. However, increases in partnership minimum gain resulting from conversions, refinancings, or other changes to a debt instrument (as described in paragraph (g)(3)) do not generate nonrecourse deductions. Generally, nonrecourse deductions consist first of certain depreciation or cost recovery deductions and then, if necessary, a pro rata portion of other partnership losses, deductions, and section 705(a)(2)(B) expenditures for that year; excess nonrecourse deductions are carried over. See paragraphs (j)(1)(ii) and (iii) of this section for more specific ordering rules. See also paragraph (m), Example (1)(iv) of this section.

(d) Partnership minimum gain.

(1) Amount of partnership minimum gain. The amount of partnership minimum gain is determined by first computing for each partnership nonrecourse liability any gain the partnership would realize if it disposed of the property subject to that liability for no consideration other than full satisfaction of the liability, and then aggregating the separately computed gains. The amount of partnership minimum gain includes minimum gain arising from a conversion, refinancing, or other change to a debt instrument, as described in paragraph (g)(3) of this section, only to the extent a partner is allocated a share of that minimum gain. For any partnership taxable year, the net increase or decrease in partnership minimum gain is determined by comparing the partnership minimum gain on the last day of the immediately preceding taxable year with the partnership minimum gain on the last day of the current taxable year. See paragraph (m), Examples (1)(i) and (iv), (2), and (3) of this section.

(2) Property subject to more than one liability.

(i) In general. If property is subject to more than one liability, only the portion of the property's adjusted tax basis that is allocated to a nonrecourse liability under paragraph (d)(2)(ii) of this section is used to compute minimum gain with respect to that liability.

(ii) Allocating liabilities. If property is subject to two or more liabilities of equal priority, the property's adjusted tax basis is allocated among the liabilities In proportion to

their outstanding balances. If property is subject to two or more liabilities of unequal priority, the adjusted tax basis is allocated first to the liability of the highest priority to the extent of its outstanding balance and then to each liability in descending order of priority to the extent of its outstanding balance, until fully allocated. See paragraph (m), Example (1)(v) of this section.

(3) Partnership minimum gain if there is a book/tax disparity. If partnership property subject to one or more nonrecourse liabilities is, under § 1.704–1(b)(2)(iv)(d), (f), or (r), reflected on the partnership's books at a value that differs from its adjusted tax basis, the determinations under this section are made with reference to the property's book value. See section 704(c) and § 1.704–1(b)(4)(i) for principles that govern the treatment of a partner's share of minimum gain that is eliminated by the revaluation. See also paragraph (m), Example (3) of this section.

(4) Special rule for year of revaluation. If the partners' capital accounts are increased pursuant to § 1.704–1(b)(2)(iv)(d), (f), or (r) to reflect a revaluation of partnership property subject to a nonrecourse liability, the net increase or decrease in partnership minimum gain for the partnership taxable year of the revaluation is determined by:

(i) First calculating the net decrease or increase in partnership minimum gain using the current year's book values and the prior year's partnership minimum gain amount; and

(ii) Then adding back any decrease in minimum gain arising solely from the revaluation.

See paragraph (m), Example (3)(iii) of this section. If the partners' capital accounts are decreased to reflect a revaluation, the net increases or decreases in partnership minimum gain are determined in the same manner as in the year before the revaluation, but by using book values rather than adjusted tax bases. See section 7701(g) and § 1.704–1(b)(2)(iv)(f)(1) (property being revalued cannot be booked down below the amount of any nonrecourse liability to which the property is subject).

(e) Requirements to be satisfied. Allocations of nonrecourse deductions are deemed to be in accordance with the partners' interests in the partnership only if—

(1) Throughout the full term of the partnership requirements (1) and (2) of § 1.704–1(b) (2)(ii)(b) are satisfied (i.e., capital accounts are maintained in accordance with § 1.704–1(b)(2) (iv) and liquidating distributions are required to be made in accordance with positive capital account balances), and requirement (3) of either § 1.704–1(b)(2)(ii)(b) or § 1.704–1(b) (2)(ii)(d) is satisfied (i.e., partners with deficit capital accounts have an unconditional deficit restoration obligation or agree to a qualified income offset);

(2) Beginning in the first taxable year of the partnership in which there are nonrecourse deductions and thereafter throughout the full term of the partnership, the partnership agreement provides for allocations of nonrecourse deductions in a manner that is reasonably consistent with allocations that have substantial economic effect of some other significant partnership item attributable to the property securing the nonrecourse liabilities;

(3) Beginning in the first taxable year of the partnership that it has nonrecourse deductions or makes a distribution of proceeds of a nonrecourse liability that are allocable to an increase in partnership minimum gain, and thereafter throughout the full term of the partnership, the partnership agreement contains a provision that complies with the minimum gain chargeback requirement of paragraph (f) of this section; and

(4) All other material allocations and capital account adjustments under the partnership agreement are recognized under § 1.704–1(b) (without regard to whether allocations of adjusted tax basis and amount realized under section 613A(c)(7)(D) are recognized under § 1.704–1(b)(4)(v)).

(f) Minimum gain chargeback requirement.

(1) In general. If there is a net decrease in partnership minimum gain for a partnership taxable year, the minimum gain chargeback requirement applies and each partner must be allocated items of partnership income and gain for that year equal to that partner's share of the net decrease in partnership minimum gain (within the meaning of paragraph (g)(2)).

(2) Exception for certain conversions and refinancings. A partner is not subject to the minimum gain chargeback requirement to the extent the partner's share of the net decrease in partnership minimum gain is caused by a recharacterization of nonrecourse partnership debt as partially or wholly recourse debt or partner nonrecourse debt, and the partner bears the economic risk of loss (within the meaning of § 1.752–2) for the liability.

(3) Exception for certain capital contributions. A partner is not subject to the minimum gain chargeback requirement to the extent the partner contributes capital to the partnership that is used to repay the nonrecourse liability or is used to increase the basis of the property subject to the nonrecourse liability, and the partner's share of the net decrease in partnership minimum gain results from the repayment or the increase to the property's basis. See paragraph (m), Example (1) (iv) of this section.

(4) Waiver for certain income allocations that fail to meet minimum chargeback requirement if minimum gain chargeback distorts economic arrangement. In any taxable year that a partnership has a net decrease in partnership minimum gain, if the minimum gain chargeback requirement would cause a distortion in the economic arrangement among the partners and it is not expected that the partnership will have sufficient other income to correct that distortion, the Commissioner has the discretion, if requested by the partnership, to waive the minimum gain chargeback requirement. The following facts must be demonstrated in order for a request for a waiver to be considered:

(i) The partners have made capital contributions or received net income allocations that have restored the previous nonrecourse deductions and the distributions attributable to proceeds of a nonrecourse liability; and

(ii) The minimum gain chargeback requirement would distort the partners' economic arrangement as reflected in the partnership agreement and as evidenced over the term of the partnership by the partnership's allocations and distributions and the partners' contributions.

(5) Additional exceptions. The Commissioner may, by revenue ruling, provide additional exceptions to the minimum gain chargeback requirement.

(6) Partnership items subject to the minimum gain chargeback requirement. Any minimum gain chargeback required for a partnership taxable year consists first of certain gains recognized from the disposition of partnership property subject to one or more partnership nonrecourse liabilities and then if necessary consists of a pro rata portion of the partnership's other items of income and gain for that year. If the amount of the minimum gain chargeback requirement exceeds the partnership's income and gains for the taxable year, the excess carries over. See paragraphs (j)(2)(i) and (iii) of this section for more specific ordering rules.

(7) Examples. The following examples illustrate the provisions in § 1.704–2(f).

Example (1). Partnership AB consists of two partners, limited partner A and general partner B. Partner A contributes $90 and Partner B contributes $10 to the partnership. The partnership agreement has a minimum gain chargeback provision and provides that, except as otherwise required by section 704(c), all losses will be allocated 90 percent to A and 10 percent to B; and that all income will be allocated first to restore previous losses and thereafter 50 percent to A and 50 percent to B. Distributions are made first to return initial capital to the partners and then 50 percent to A and 50 percent to B. Final distributions are made in accordance with capital account balances. The partnership borrows $200 on a nonrecourse basis from an unrelated third party and purchases an asset for $300. The partnership's only tax item for each of the first three years is $100 of depreciation on the asset. A's and B's shares of minimum gain (under paragraph (g) of this section) and deficit capital account balances are $180 and $20 respectively at the end of the third year. In the fourth year, the partnership earns $400 of net operating income and allocates the first $300 to restore the previous losses (i.e., $270 to A and $30 to B); the last $100 is allocated $50 each. The partnership distributes $200 of the available cash that same year; the first $100 is distributed $90 to A and $10 to B to return their capital contributions; the last $100 is distributed $50 each to reflect their ratio for sharing profits.

	A	B
Capital account on formation	$90	$10
Less: net loss in years 1–3	($270)	($30)
Capital account at end of year 3	($180)	($20)
Allocation of operating income to restore nonrecourse deductions	$180	20
Allocation of operating income to restore capital contributions	$90	$10
Allocation of operating income to reflect profits	$50	$50

	A	B
Capital accounts after allocation of operating income	$140	$60
Distribution reflecting capital contribution	($90)	($10)
Distribution in profit-sharing ratio	($50)	($50)
Capital accounts following distribution	($0)	($0)

In the fifth year, the partnership sells the property for $300 and realizes $300 of gain. $200 of the proceeds are used to pay the nonrecourse lender. The partnership has $300 to distribute, and the partners expect to share that equally. Absent a waiver under paragraph (f)(4) of this section, the minimum gain chargeback would require the partnership to allocate the first $200 of the gain $180 to A and $20 to B, which would distort their economic arrangement. This allocation, together with the allocation of the $100 profit $50 to each partner, would result in A having a positive capital account balance of $230 and B having a positive capital account balance of $70. The allocation of income in year 4 in effect anticipated the minimum gain charge-back that did not occur until year 5. Assuming the partnership would not have sufficient other income to correct the distortion that would otherwise result, the partnership may request that the Commissioner exercise his or her discretion to waive the minimum gain chargeback requirement and recognize allocations that would allow A and B to share equally the gain on the sale of the property. These allocations would bring the partners' capital accounts to $150 each, allowing them to share the last $300 equally. The Commissioner may in his or her discretion, permit this allocation pursuant to paragraph (f)(4) of this section because the minimum gain chargeback would distort the partners' economic arrangement over the term of the partnership as reflected in the partnership agreement and as evidenced by the partners' contributions and the partnership's allocations and distributions.

Example (2). A and B form a partnership, contribute $25 each to the partnership's capital, and agree to share all losses and profits 50 percent each. Neither partner has an unconditional deficit restoration obligation and all the requirements in paragraph (e) of this section are met. The partnership obtains a nonrecourse loan from an unrelated third party of $100 and purchases two assets, stock for $50 and depreciable property for $100. The nonrecourse loan is secured by the partnership's depreciable property. The partnership generates $20 of depreciation in each of the first five years as its only tax item. These deductions are properly treated as nonrecourse deductions and the allocation of these deductions 50 percent to A and 50 percent to B is deemed to be in accordance with the partners' interests in the partnership. At the end of year five, A and B each have a $25 deficit capital account and a $50 share of partnership minimum gain. In the beginning of year six, (at the lender's request), A guarantees the entire nonrecourse liability. Pursuant to paragraph (d)(1) of this section, the partnership has a net decrease in minimum gain of $100 and under paragraph (g)(2) of this section. A's and B's shares of that net decrease are $50 each. Under paragraph (f)(1) of this section (the minimum gain chargeback requirement), B is subject to a $50 minimum gain chargeback. Because the partnership has no gross income in year six, the entire $50 carries over as a minimum gain chargeback requirement to succeeding taxable years until their is enough income to cover the minimum gain chargeback requirement. Under the exception to the minimum gain chargeback in paragraph (f)(2) of this section. A is not subject to a minimum gain chargeback for A's $50 share of the net decrease because A bears the economic risk of loss for the liability. Instead, A's share of partner nonrecourse debt minimum gain is

$50 pursuant to paragraph (i)(3) of this section. In year seven, the partnership earns $100 of net operating income and uses the money to repay the entire $100 nonrecourse debt (that A has guaranteed). Under paragraph (i)(3) of this section, the partnership has a net decrease in partner nonrecourse debt minimum gain of $50. B must be allocated $50 of the operating income pursuant to the carried over minimum gain chargeback requirement: pursuant to paragraph (i)(4) of this section, the other $50 of operating income must be allocated to A as a partner nonrecourse debt minimum gain chargeback.

(g) Shares of partnership minimum gain.

(1) Partner's share of partnership minimum gain. Except as increased in paragraph (g)(3) of this section, a partner's share of partnership minimum gain at the end of any partnership taxable year equals:

(i) The sum of nonrecourse deductions allocated to that partner (and to that partner's predecessors in interest) up to that time and the distributions made to that partner (and to that partner's predecessors in interest) up to that time of proceeds of a nonrecourse liability allocable to an increase in partnership minimum gain (see paragraph (h)(1) of this section); minus

(ii) The sum of that partner's (and that partner's predecessors in interest) aggregate share of the net decreases in partnership minimum gain plus their aggregate share of decreases resulting from revaluations of partnership property subject to one or more partnership nonrecourse liabilities.

For purposes of § 1.704–1(b)(2)(ii)(d), a partner's share of partnership minimum gain is added to the limited dollar amount, if any, of the deficit balance in the partner's capital account that the partner is obligated to restore. See paragraph (m), Examples (1)(i) and (3)(i) of this section.

(2) Partner's share of the net decrease in partnership minimum gain. A partner's share of the net decrease in partnership minimum gain is the amount of the total net decrease multiplied by the partner's percentage share of the partnership's minimum gain at the end of the immediately preceding taxable year. A partner's share of any decrease in partnership minimum gain resulting from a revaluation of partnership property equals the increase in the partner's capital account attributable to the revaluation to the extent the reduction in minimum gain is caused by the revaluation. See paragraph (m), Example (3)(ii) of this section.

(3) Conversions of recourse or partner nonrecourse debt into nonrecourse debt. A partner's share of partnership minimum gain is increased to the extent provided in this paragraph (g)(3) if a recourse or partner nonrecourse liability becomes partially or wholly nonrecourse. If a recourse, liability becomes a nonrecourse liability, a partner has a share of the partnership's minimum gain that results from the conversion equal to the partner's deficit capital account (determined under § 1.704–1(b)(2)(iv)) to the extent the partner no longer bears the economic burden for the entire deficit capital account as a result of the conversion. For purposes of the preceding sentence, the determination of the extent to which a partner bears the economic burden for a deficit capital account is made by determining the consequences to the partner in the case of a complete liquidation of the partnership immediately after the conversion applying the rules described in § 1.704–1(b)(2)(iii)(c) that deem the value of partnership property to equal its basis, taking into account section 7701(g) in the case of property that secures nonrecourse indebtedness. If a partner nonrecourse debt becomes a nonrecourse liability, the partner's share of partnership minimum gain is increased to the extent the partner is not subject to the minimum gain chargeback requirement under paragraph (i)(4) of this section.

(h) Distribution of nonrecourse liability proceeds allocable to an increase in partnership minimum gain.

(1) In general. If during its taxable year a partnership makes a distribution to the partners allocable to the proceeds of a nonrecourse liability, the distribution is allocable to an increase in partnership minimum gain to the extent the increase results from encumbering partnership property with aggregate nonrecourse liabilities that exceed the property's adjusted tax basis. See paragraph (m), Example (1)(vi) of this section. If the net increase in partnership minimum gain for a partnership taxable year is allocable to more than one nonrecourse liability, the net increase is allocated among the liabilities in proportion to the amount each liability contributed to the increase in minimum gain.

(2) Distribution allocable to nonrecourse liability proceeds. A partnership may use any reasonable method to determine whether a distribution by the partnership to one or more partners is allocable to proceeds of a nonrecourse liability. The rules prescribed under § 1.163–8T for allocating debt proceeds among expenditures (applying those rules to the partnership as if it were an individual) constitute a reasonable method for determining whether the nonrecourse liability proceeds are distributed to the partners and the partners to whom the proceeds are distributed.

(3) Option when there is an obligation to restore. A partnership may treat any distribution to a partner of the proceeds of a nonrecourse liability (that would otherwise be allocable to an increase in partnership minimum gain) as a distribution that is not allocable to an increase in partnership minimum gain to the extent the distribution does not cause or increase a deficit balance in the partner's capital account that exceeds the amount the partner is otherwise obligated to restore (within the meaning of § 1.704–1(b)(2)(ii)(c)) as of the end of the partnership taxable year in which the distribution occurs.

(4) Carryover to immediately succeeding taxable year. The carryover rule of this paragraph applies if the net increase in partnership minimum gain for a partnership taxable year that is allocable to a nonrecourse liability under paragraph (h)(2) of this section exceeds the distributions allocable to the proceeds of the liability (excess allocable amount), and all or part of the net increase in partnership minimum gain for the year is carried over as an increase in partnership minimum gain for the immediately succeeding taxable year (pursuant to paragraph (j)(1)(iii) of this section). If the carryover rule of this paragraph applies, the excess allocable amount (or the amount carried over under paragraph (j)(1)(iii) of this section, if less) is treated in the succeeding taxable year as an increase in partnership minimum gain that arose in that year as a result of incurring the nonrecourse liability to which the excess allocable amount is attributable. See paragraph (m), Example (1)(vi) of this section. If for a partnership taxable year there is an excess allocable amount with respect to more than one partnership nonrecourse liability, the excess allocable amount is allocated to each liability in proportion to the amount each liability contributed to the increase in minimum gain.

(i) Partnership nonrecourse liabilities where a partner bears the economic risk of loss.

(1) In general. Partnership losses, deductions, or section 705(a)(2)(B) expenditures that are attributable to a particular partner nonrecourse liability (partner nonrecourse deductions, as defined in paragraph (i)(2) of this section) must be allocated to the partner that bears the economic risk of loss for the liability. If more than one partner bears the economic risk of loss for a partner nonrecourse liability, any partner nonrecourse deductions attributable to that liability must be allocated among the partners according to the ratio in which they bear the economic risk of loss. If partners bear the economic risk of loss for different portions of a liability, each portion is treated as a separate partner nonrecourse liability.

(2) Definition of and determination of partner nonrecourse deductions. For any partnership taxable year the amount of partner nonrecourse deductions with respect to a partner nonrecourse debt equals the net increase during the year in minimum gain attributable to the partner nonrecourse debt (partner nonrecourse debt minimum gain), reduced (but not below zero) by proceeds of the liability distributed during the year to the partner bearing the economic risk of loss for the liability that are both attributable to the liability and allocable to an increase in the partner nonrecourse debt minimum gain. See paragraph (m), Example (1)(vii) and (viii) of this section The determination of which partnership items constitute the partner nonrecourse deductions with respect to a partner nonrecourse debt must be made in a manner consistent with the provisions of paragraphs (c) and (j)(1)(i) and (iii) of this section.

(3) Determination of partner nonrecourse debt minimum gain. For any partnership taxable year, the determination of partner nonrecourse debt minimum gain and the net increase or decrease in partner nonrecourse debt minimum gain must be made in a manner consistent with the provisions of paragraphs (d) and (g)(3) of this section.

(4) Chargeback of partner nonrecourse debt minimum gain. If during a partnership taxable year there is a net decrease in partner nonrecourse debt minimum gain, any partner with a share of that partner nonrecourse debt minimum gain (determined under paragraph (i)(5) of this section) as of the beginning of the year must be allocated items of income and gain for the year (and, if necessary, for succeeding years) equal to that partner's share of the net decrease in the partner nonrecourse debt minimum gain is determined in a manner consistent with the provisions of paragraph (g) (2) of this section. A partner is not subject to this minimum gain chargeback, however, to

the extent the net decrease in partner nonrecourse debt minimum gain arises because a partner nonrecourse liability becomes partially or wholly a nonrecourse liability. The amount that would otherwise be subject to the partner nonrecourse debt minimum gain chargeback is added to the partner's share of partnership minimum gain under paragraph (g)(3) of this section. In addition, rules consistent with the provisions of paragraphs (f)(2),(3),(4), and (5) of this section apply with respect to partner nonrecourse debt in appropriate circumstances. The determination of which items of partnership income and gain must be allocated pursuant to this paragraph (i)(4) is made in a manner that is consistent with the provisions of paragraph (f)(6) of this section. See paragraph (j)(2)(ii) and (iii) of this section for more specific rules.

(5) Partner's share of partner nonrecourse debt minimum gain. A partner's share of partner nonrecourse debt minimum gain at the end of any partnership taxable year is determined in a manner consistent with the provisions of paragraphs (g)(1) and (g)(3) of this section with respect to each particular partner nonrecourse debt for which the partner bears the economic risk of loss. For purposes of § 1.704–1(b)(2)(ii)(d), a partner's share of partner nonrecourse debt minimum gain is added to the limited dollar amount, if any, of the deficit balance in the partner's capital account that the partner is obligated to restore, and the partner is not otherwise considered to have a deficit restoration obligation as a result of bearing the economic risk of loss for any partner nonrecourse debt. See paragraph (m), Example (1)(vii) of this section.

(6) Distribution of partner nonrecourse debt proceeds allocable to an increase in partner nonrecourse debt minimum gain. Rules consistent with the provisions of paragraph (h) of this section apply to distributions of the proceeds of partner nonrecourse debt.

(j) Ordering rules. For purposes of this section, the following ordering rules apply to partnership items. Notwithstanding any other provision in this section and § 1.704–1, allocations of partner nonrecourse deductions, nonrecourse deductions, and minimum gain chargebacks are made before any other allocations.

(1) Treatment of partnership losses and deductions.

(i) Partner nonrecourse deductions. Partnership losses, deductions, and section 705(a)(2)(B) expenditures are treated as partner nonrecourse deductions in the amount determined under paragraph (i)(2) of this section (determining partner nonrecourse deductions) in the following order:

(A) First, depreciation or cost recovery deductions with respect to property that is subject to partner nonrecourse debt;

(B) Then, if necessary, a pro rata portion of the partnership's other deductions, losses, and section 705(a)(2)(B) items.

Depreciation or cost recovery deductions with respect to property that is subject to a partnership nonrecourse liability is first treated as a partnership nonrecourse deduction and any excess is treated as a partner nonrecourse deduction under this paragraph (j)(1)(i).

(ii) Partnership nonrecourse deductions. Partnership losses, deductions, and section 705(a)(2)(B) expenditures are treated as partnership nonrecourse deductions in the amount determined under paragraph (c) of this section (determining nonrecourse deductions) in the following order:

(A) First, depreciation or cost recovery deductions with respect to property that is subject to partnership nonrecourse liabilities;

(B) Then, if necessary, a pro rata portion of the partnership's other deductions, losses, and section 705(a)(2)(B) items.

Depreciation or cost recovery deductions with respect to property that is subject to partner nonrecourse debt is first treated as a partner nonrecourse deduction and any excess is

treated as a partnership nonrecourse deduction under this paragraph (j)(1)(ii). Any other item that is treated as a partner nonrecourse deduction will in no event be treated as a partnership nonrecourse deduction.

(iii) Carryover to succeeding taxable year. If the amount of partner nonrecourse deductions or nonrecourse deductions exceeds the partnership's losses, deductions, and section 705(a)(2)(B) expenditures for the taxable year (determined under paragraphs (j)(1)(i) and (ii) of this section), the excess is treated as an increase in partner nonrecourse debt minimum gain or partnership minimum gain in the immediately succeeding partnership taxable year. See paragraph (m), Example (1)(vi) of this section.

(2) Treatment of partnership income and gains.

(i) Minimum gain chargeback. Items of partnership income and gain equal to the minimum gain chargeback requirement (determined under paragraph (f) of this section) are allocated as a minimum gain chargeback in the following order:

(A) First, gain from the disposition of property subject to partnership nonrecourse liabilities;

(B) Then, if necessary, a pro rata portion of the partnership's other items of income and gain for that year.

Gain from the disposition of property subject to partner nonrecourse debt is allocated to satisfy a minimum gain chargeback requirement for partnership nonrecourse debt only to the extent not allocated under paragraph (j)(2)(ii) of this section.

(ii) Chargeback attributable to decrease in partner nonrecourse debt minimum gain. Items of partnership income and gain equal to the partner nonrecourse debt minimum gain chargeback (determined under paragraph (i)(4) of this section) are allocated to satisfy a partner nonrecourse debt minimum gain chargeback in the following order:

(A) First, gain from the disposition of property subject to partner nonrecourse debt;

(B) Then, if necessary, a pro rata portion of the partnership's other items of income and gain for that year.

Gain from the disposition of property subject to a partnership nonrecourse liability is allocated to satisfy a partner nonrecourse debt minimum gain chargeback only to the extent not allocated under paragraph (j)(2)(i) of this section. An item of partnership income and gain that is allocated to satisfy a minimum gain chargeback under paragraph (f) of this section is not allocated to satisfy a minimum gain chargeback under paragraph (i)(4).

(iii) Carryover to succeeding taxable year. If a minimum gain chargeback requirement (determined under paragraphs (f) and (i)(4) of this section) exceeds the partnership's income and gains for the taxable year, the excess is treated as a minimum gain chargeback requirement in the immediately succeeding partnership taxable years until fully charged back.

(k) Tiered partnerships. For purposes of this section, the following rules determine the effect on partnership minimum gain when a partnership (upper-tier partnership) is a partner in another partnership (lower-tier partnership).

(1) Increase in upper-tier partnership's minimum gain. The sum of the nonrecourse deductions that the lower-tier partnership allocates to the upper-tier partnership for any taxable year of the upper-tier partnership, and the distributions made during that taxable year from the lower-tier partnership to the upper-tier partnership of proceeds of nonrecourse debt that are allocable to an increase in the lower-tier partnership's minimum gain, is treated as an increase in the upper-tier partnership's minimum gain.

(2) Decrease in upper-tier partnership's minimum gain. The upper-tier partnership's share for its taxable year of the lower-tier partnership's net decrease in its minimum gain is treated as a decrease in the upper-tier partnership's minimum gain for that taxable year.

(3) Nonrecourse debt proceeds distributed from the lower-tier partnership to the uppertier partnership. All distributions from the lower-tier partnership to the upper-tier partnership during the upper-tier partnership's taxable year of proceeds of a nonrecourse liability allocable to an increase in the lower-tier partnership's minimum gain are treated as proceeds of a nonrecourse liability of the upper-tier partnership. The increase in the upper-tier partnership's minimum gain (under paragraph (k)(1) of this section) attributable to the receipt of those distributions is, for purposes of paragraph (h) of this section, treated as an increase in the upper-tier partnership's minimum gain arising from encumbering property of the upper-tier partnership with a nonrecourse liability of the upper-tier partnership.

(4) Nonrecourse deductions of lower-tier partnership treated as depreciation by uppertier partnership. For purposes of paragraph (c) of this section, all nonrecourse deductions allocated by the lower-tier partnership to the upper-tier partnership for the upper-tier partnership's taxable year are treated as depreciation or cost recovery deductions with respect to property owned by the upper-tier partnership and subject to a nonrecourse liability of the upper-tier partnership with respect to which minimum gain increased during the year by the amount of the nonrecourse deductions.

(5) Coordination with partner nonrecourse debt rules. The lower-tier partnership's liabilities that are treated as the upper-tier partnership's liabilities under § 1.752–4(a) are treated as the upper-tier partnership's liabilities for purposes of applying paragraph (i) of this section. Rules consistent with the provisions of paragraphs (k)(1) through (k)(4) of this section apply to determine the allocations that the upper-tier partnership must make with respect to any liability that constitutes a nonrecourse debt for which one or more partners of the upper-tier partnership bear the economic risk of loss.

* * *

(m) Examples. The principles of this section are illustrated by the following examples:

Example (1). Nonrecourse deductions and partnerships minimum gain. For Example 1, unless otherwise provided, the following facts are assumed. LP, the limited partner, and GP, the general partner, form a limited partnership to acquire and operate a commercial office building. LP contributes $180,000, and GP contributes $20,000. The partnership obtains an $800,000 nonrecourse loan and purchases the building (on leased land) for $1,000,000. The nonrecourse loan is secured only by the building, and no principal payments are due for 5 years. The partnership agreement provides that GP will be required to restore any deficit balance in GP's capital account following the liquidation of GP's interest (as set forth in § 1.704–1(b)(2)(ii)(b)(3)), and LP will not be required to restore any deficit balance in LP's capital account following the liquidation of LP's interest. The partnership agreement contains the following provisions required by paragraph (e) of this section: a qualified income offset (as defined in § 1.704–1(b)(2)(ii)(d)); a minimum gain chargeback (in accordance with paragraph (f) of this section); a provision that the partners' capital accounts will be determined and maintained in accordance with § 1.704–1(b)(2)(ii)(b)(1); and a provision that distributions will be made in accordance with partners' positive capital account balances (as set forth in § 1.704–1(b)(2)(ii)(b)(2)). In addition, as of the end of each partnership taxable year discussed herein, the items described in § 1.704–1(b)(2)(ii)(d)(4), (5), and (6) are not reasonably expected to cause or increase a deficit balance in LP's capital account. The partnership agreement provides that, except as otherwise required by its qualified income offset and minimum gain chargeback provisions, all partnership items will be allocated 90 percent to LP and 10 percent to GP until the first time when the partnership has recognized items of income and gain that exceed the items of loss and deduction it has recognized over its life, and all further partnership items will be allocated equally between LP and GP. Finally, the partnership agreement provides that all distributions, other than distributions in liquidation of the partnership or of a partner's interest in the partnership, will be made 90 percent to LP and 10 percent to GP until a total of $200,000 has been distributed, and thereafter all the distributions will be made equally to LP and GP. In each of the partnership's first 2 taxable years, it generates rental income of $95,000, operating expenses (including land lease payments) of $10,000, interest expense of $80,000, and a depreciation deduction of $90,000, resulting in a net taxable loss of $85,000 in each of those years. The allocations of these losses 90 percent to LP and 10 percent to GP have substantial economic effect.

	LP	GP
Capital account on formation	$180,000	$20,000
Less: net loss in years 1 and 2	(153,000)	(17,000)
Capital account at end of year 2	$27,000	$3,000

In the partnership's third taxable year, it again generates rental income of $95,000, operating expenses of $10,000, interest expense of $80,000, and a depreciation deduction of $90,000, resulting in net taxable loss of $85,000. The partnership makes no distributions.

(i) Calculation of nonrecourse deductions and partnership minimum gain. If the partnership were to dispose of the building in full satisfaction of the nonrecourse liability at the end of the third year, it would realize $70,000 of gain ($800,000 amount realized less $730,000 adjusted tax basis). Because the amount of partnership minimum gain at the end of the third year (and the net increase in partnership minimum gain during the year) is $70,000, there are partnership nonrecourse deductions

for that year of $70,000, consisting of depreciation deductions allowable with respect to the building of $70,000. Pursuant to the partnership agreement, all partnership items comprising the net taxable loss of $85,000, including the $70,000 nonrecourse deduction, are allocated 90 percent to LP and 10 percent to GP. The allocation of these items, other than the nonrecourse deductions, has substantial economic effect.

	LP	GP
Capital account at end of year 2	$27,000	$3,000
Less: net loss in year 3 (without nonrecourse deductions)	(13,500)	(1,500)
Less nonrecourse deductions in year 3	(63,000)	(7,000)
Capital account at end of year 3	($49,500)	($5,500)

The allocation of the $70,000 nonrecourse deduction satisfies requirement (2) of paragraph (e) of this section because it is consistent with allocations having substantial economic effect of other significant partnership items attributable to the building. Because the remaining requirements of paragraph (e) of this section are satisfied, the allocation of nonrecourse deductions is deemed to be in accordance with the partners' interests in the partnership. At the end of the partnership's third taxable year, LP's and GP's shares of partnership minimum gain are $63,000 and $7,000, respectively. Therefore, pursuant to paragraph (g)(1) of this section, LP is treated as obligated to restore a deficit capital account balance of $63,000, so that in the succeeding year LP could be allocated up to an additional $13,500 of partnership deductions, losses, and section 705(a)(2)(B) items that are not nonrecourse deductions. Even though this allocation would increase a deficit capital account balance, it would be considered to have economic effect under the alternate economic effect test contained in § 1.704–1(b)(2)(ii)(d). If the partnership were to dispose of the building in full satisfaction

of the nonrecourse liability at the beginning of the partnership's fourth taxable year (and had no other economic activity in that year), the partnership minimum gain would be decreased from $70,000 to zero, and the minimum gain chargeback would require that LP and GP be allocated $63,000 and $7,000, respectively, of the gain from that disposition.

(ii) Illustration of reasonable consistency requirement. Assume instead that the partnership agreement provides that all nonrecourse deductions of the partnership will be allocated equally between LP and GP. Furthermore, at the time the partnership agreement is entered into, there is a reasonable likelihood that over the partnership's life it will realize amounts of income and gain significantly in excess of amounts of loss and deduction (other than nonrecourse deductions). The equal allocation of excess income and gain has substantial economic effect.

	LP	GP
Capital account on formation	$180,000	$20,000
Less: net loss in years 1 and 2	(153,000)	(17,000)
Less: net loss in year (without nonrecourse deductions	(13,500)	(1,500)
Less: nonrecourse deductions in year 3	(35,000)	(35,000)
Capital account at end of year 3	($21,500)	($33,500)

The allocation of the $70,000 nonrecourse deduction equally between LP and GP satisfies requirement (2) of paragraph (e) of his section because the allocation is consistent with allocations, which will have substantial economic effect, of other significant partnership items attributable to the building. Because the remaining requirements of paragraph (e) of this section are satisfied, the allocation of nonrecourse deductions is deemed to be in accordance with the partners' interests in the partnership. The allocation of the nonrecourse deductions 75 percent to LP and 25 percent to GP (or in any other ratio between 90 percent to LP/10 percent to GP and 50 percent to LP/50 percent to GP) also would satisfy requirement (2) of paragraph (e) of this section.

(iii) Allocation of nonrecourse deductions that fails reasonable consistency requirement. Assume instead that the partnership agreement provides that LP will be allocated 99 percent, and GP 1 percent, of all nonrecourse deductions of the partnership. Allocating nonrecourse deductions this way does not satisfy requirement (2) of paragraph (e) of this section because the allocations are not reasonably consistent with allocations, having substantial economic effect, of any other significant partnership item attributable to the building. Therefore, the allocation of nonrecourse deductions will be disregarded, and the nonrecourse deductions of the partnership will be reallocated according to the partners' overall economic interests in the partnership, determined under § 1.704–1(b)(3)(ii).

(iv) Capital contribution to pay down nonrecourse debt. At the beginning of the partnership's fourth taxable year. LP contributes $144,000 and GP contributes $16,000 of addition capital to the partnership, which the partnership immediately uses to reduce the amount of its nonrecourse liability from $800,000 to $640,000. In addition, in the partnership's fourth taxable year, it generates rental income of $95,000, operating expenses of $10,000, interest expense of $64,000 (consistent with the debt reduction), and a depreciation deduction of $90,000, resulting in a net taxable loss of $69,000. If the partnership were to dispose of the building in full satisfaction of the nonrecourse liability at the end of that year, it would realize no gain ($640,000 amount realized less $640,000 adjusted tax basis). Therefore, the amount of partnership minimum gain at the end of the year is zero, which represents a net decrease in partnership minimum gain of $70,000 during the year. LP's and GP's shares of this net decrease are $63,000 and $7,000 respectively, so that at the end of the partnership's fourth taxable year, LP's and GP's

shares of partnership minimum gain are zero. Although there has been a net decrease in partnership minimum gain, pursuant to paragraph (f)(3) of this section LP and GP are not subject to a minimum gain chargeback.

	LP	GP
Capital account at end of year 3	($49,500)	($5,500)
Plus: contribution	144,000	16,000
Less: net loss in year 4	(62,100)	(6,900)
Capital account at end of year 4	32,400	(3,600)
Minimum gain chargeback carryforward	$0	$0

(v) Loans of unequal priority. Assume instead that the building acquired by the partnership is secured by a $700,000 nonrecourse loan and a $100,000 recourse loan, subordinate in priority to the nonrecourse loan. Under paragraph (d)(2) of this section, $700,000 of the adjusted basis of the building at the end of the partnership's third taxable year is allocated to the nonrecourse liability (with the remaining $30,000 allocated to the recourse liability) so that if the partnership disposed of the building in full satisfaction of the nonrecourse liability at the end of that year, it would realize no gain ($700,000 amount realized less $700,000 adjusted tax basis). Therefore, there is no minimum gain (or increase in minimum gain) at the end of the partnership's third taxable year. If, however, the $700,000 nonrecourse loan were subordinate in priority to the $100,000 recourse loan, under paragraph (d)(2) of this section, the first $100,000 of adjusted tax basis in the building would be allocated to the recourse liability, leaving only $630,000 of the adjusted basis of the building to be allocated to the $700,000 nonrecourse loan. In that case, the balance of the $700,000 nonrecourse liability would exceed the adjusted tax basis of the building by $70,000, so that there would be $70,000 of minimum gain (and a $70,000 increase in partnership minimum gain) in the partnership's third taxable year.

(vi) Nonrecourse borrowing; distribution of proceeds in subsequent year. The partnership obtains an additional nonrecourse loan of $200,000 at the end of its fourth taxable year, secured by a second mortgage on the building, and distributes $180,000 of this cash to its partners at the beginning of its fifth taxable year. In addition, in its fourth and fifth taxable years, the partnership again generates rental income of $95,000, operating expenses of $10,000, interest expense of $80,000 ($100,000 in the fifth taxable year reflecting the interest paid on both liabilities), and a depreciation deduction of $90,000, resulting in a net taxable loss of $85,000 ($105,000 in the fifth taxable year reflecting the interest paid on both liabilities). The partnership has distributed its $5,000 of operating cash flow in each year ($95,000 of rental income less $10,000 of operating expense and $80,000 of interest expense) to LP and GP at the end of each year. If the partnership were to dispose of the building in full satisfaction of both nonrecourse liabilities at the end of its fourth taxable year, the partnership would realize $360,000 of gain ($1,000,000 amount realized less $640,000 adjusted tax basis). Thus, the net increase in partnership minimum gain during the partnership's fourth taxable year is $290,000 ($360,000 of minimum gain at the end of the fourth year less $70,000 of minimum gain at the end of the third year). Because the partnership did not distribute any of the proceeds of the loan it obtained in its fourth year during that year, the potential amount of partnership nonrecourse deductions for that year is $290,000. Under paragraph (c) of this section, if the partnership had distributed the proceeds of that loan to its partners at the end of its fourth year, the partnership's nonrecourse deductions for that year would have been reduced by the amount of that distribution because the proceeds of that loan are allocable to an increase in partnership minimum gain under paragraph (h)(1) of this section. Because the nonrecourse deductions of $290,000 for the partnership's fourth taxable year exceed its total deductions for that

year, all $180,000 of the partnership's deductions for that year are treated as nonrecourse deductions, and the $110,000 excess nonrecourse deductions are treated as an increase in partnership minimum gain in the partnership's fifth taxable year under paragraph (c) of this section.

	LP	GP
Capital account at end of year 3 (including cash flow distributions)	($63,000)	($7,000)
Plus: rental income in year 4	85,500	9,500
Less: nonrecourse deductions in year 4	(162,000)	(18,000)
Less: cash flow distribution in year 4	(4,500)	(500)
Capital account at end of year 4	($144,000)	($16,000)

At the end of the partnership's fourth taxable year, LP's and GP's shares of partnership minimum gain are $225,000 and $25,000, respectively (because the $110,000 excess of nonrecourse deductions is carried forward to the next year). If the partnership were to dispose of the building in full satisfaction of the nonrecourse liabilities at the end of its fifth taxable year, the partnership would realize $450,000 of gain ($1,000,000 amount realized less $550,000 adjusted tax basis). Therefore, the net increase in partnership minimum gain during the partnership's fifth taxable year is $200,000 ($110,000 deemed increase plus the $90,000 by which minimum gain at the end of the fifth year exceeds minimum gain at the end of the fourth year ($450,000 less $360,000)). At the beginning of its fifth year, the partnership distributes $180,000 of the loan proceeds (retaining $20,000 to pay the additional interest expense). Under paragraph (h) of this section, the first $110,000 of this distribution (an amount equal to the deemed increase in partnership minimum gain for the year) is considered allocable to an increase in partnership minimum gain for the year. As a result, the amount of nonrecourse deductions for the partnership's fifth taxable year is $90,000 ($200,000 net increase in minimum gain less $110,000 distribution of nonrecourse liability proceeds allocable to an increase in partnership minimum gain), and the nonrecourse deductions consist solely of the $90,000 depreciation deduction allowable with respect to the building. As a result of the distributions during the partnership's fifth taxable year, the total distributions to the partners over the partnership's life equal $205,000. Therefore, the last $5,000 distributed to the partners during the fifth year will be divided equally between them under the partnership agreement. Thus, out of the $185,000 total distribution during the partnership's fifth taxable year, the first $180,000 is distributed 90 percent to LP and 10 percent to GP, and the last $5,000 is divided equally between them.

	LP	GP
Capital account at end of year 4	($144,000)	($16,000)
Less: net loss in year 5 (without nonrecourse deductions)	(13,500)	(1,500)
Less: nonrecourse deductions in year 5	(81,000)	(9,000)
Less: distribution of loan proceeds	(162,000)	(18,000)
Less: cash flow distribution in year 5	(2,500)	(2,500)
Capital account at end of year 5	($403,000)	($47,000)

At the end of the partnership's fifth taxable year, LP's share of partnership minimum gain is $405,000 ($225,000 share of minimum gain at the end of the fourth year plus $81,000 of nonrecourse deductions for the fifth year and a $99,000 distribution of nonrecourse liability proceeds that are allocable to an increase in minimum gain) and GP's share of partnership minimum gain is $45,000 ($25,000 share of minimum gain at the end of the fourth year plus $9,000 of nonrecourse deductions for the fifth year and an $11,000 distribution of nonrecourse liability proceeds that are allocable to an increase in minimum gain).

(vii) Partner nonrecourse debt. Assume instead that the $800,000 loan is made by LP, the limited partner. Under paragraph (b)(4) of this section, the $800,000 obligation does not constitute a nonrecourse liability of the partnership for purposes of this section because LP, a partner, bears the economic risk of loss for that loan within the meaning of § 1.752–2. Instead, the $800,000 loan constitutes a partner nonrecourse debt under paragraph (b)(4) of this section. In the partnership's third taxable year, partnership minimum gain would have increased by $70,000 if the debt were a nonrecourse liability of the partnership. Thus, under paragraph (i)(3) of this section, there is a net increase of $70,000 in the minimum gain attributable to the $800,000 partner nonrecourse debt for the partnership's third taxable year, and $70,000 of the $90,000 depreciation deduction from the building for the partnership's third taxable year constitutes a partner nonrecourse deduction with respect to the debt. See paragraph (i)(4) of this section. Under paragraph (i)(2) of this section, this partner nonrecourse deduction must be allocated to LP, the partner that bears the economic risk of loss for that liability.

(viii) Nonrecourse debt and partner nonrecourse debt of differing priorities. As in Example 1 (vii) of this paragraph (m), the $800,000 loan is made to the partnership by LP, the limited partner, but the loan is a purchase money loan that, wraps around, a $700,000 underlying nonrecourse note (also secured by the building) issued by LP to an unrelated person in connection with LP's acquisition of the building. Under these circumstances, LP bears the economic risk of loss with respect to only $100,000 of the liability within the meaning of § 1.752–2. See § 1.752–2(f) (Example 6). Therefore, for purposes of paragraph (d) of this section, the $800,000 liability is treated as a $700,000 nonrecourse liability of the partnership and a $100,000 partner nonrecourse debt (inferior in priority to the $700,000 liability) of the partnership for which LP bears the economic risk of loss. Under paragraph (i)(2)

of this section, $70,000 of the $90,000 depreciation deduction realized in the partnership's third taxable year constitutes a partner nonrecourse deduction that must be allocated to LP.

Example (2). Netting of increases and decreases in partnership minimum gain. For Example 2 unless otherwise provided, the following facts are assumed. X and Y form a general partnership to acquire and operate residential real properties. Each partner contributes $150,000 to the partnership. The partnership obtains a $1,500,000 nonrecourse loan and purchases 3 apartment buildings (on leased land) for $720,000 (Property A), $540,000 (Property B), and $540,000 (Property C). The nonrecourse loan is secured only by the 3 buildings, and no principal payments are due for 5 years. In each of the partnership's first 3 taxable years, it generates rental income of $225,000, operating expenses (including land lease payments) of $50,000, interest expense of $175,000, and depreciation deductions on the 3 properties of $150,000 ($60,000 on Property A and $45,000 on each of Property B end Property C), resulting in a net taxable loss of $150,000 in each of those years he partnership makes no distributions to X or Y.

(i) Calculation of net increases and decreases in partnership minimum gain. If the partnership were to dispose of the 3 apartment buildings in full satisfaction of its nonrecourse liability at the end of its third taxable year, it would realize $150,000 of gain ($1,500,000 amount realized less $1,350,000 adjusted tax basis), Because the amount of partnership minimum gain at the end of that year (and the net increase in partnership minimum gain during that year) is $150,000, the amount of partnership nonrecourse deductions for that year is $150,000, consisting of depreciation deductions allowable with respect to the 3 apartment buildings of $150,000. The result would be the same if the partnership obtained 3 separate nonrecourse loans that were cross-collateralized, (i.e., if each separate loan were secured by all 3 of the apartment buildings).

(ii) Netting of increases and decreases in partnership minimum gain when there is a disposition. At the beginning of the partnership's fourth taxable year, the partnership (with the permission of the nonrecourse lender) disposes of Property A for $835,000 and uses a portion of the proceeds to repay $600,000 of the nonrecourse liability (the principal amount attributable to Property A), reducing the balance to $900,000. As a result of the disposition, the partnership realizes gain of $295,000 ($835,000 amount realized less $540,000 adjusted tax basis). If the disposition is viewed in isolation, the partnership has generated minimum gain of $60,000 on the sale of Property A ($600,000 of debt reduction less $540,000 adjusted tax basis). However, during the partnership's fourth taxable year it also generates rental income of $135,000, operating expenses of $30,000, interest expense of $105,000, and depreciation deductions of $90,000 ($45,000 on each remaining building). If the partnership were to dispose of the remaining two buildings in full satisfaction of its nonrecourse liability at the end of the partnership's fourth taxable year, it would realize gain of $180,000 ($900,000 amount realized less $720,000 aggregate adjusted tax basis), which is the amount of partnership minimum gain at the end of the year. Because the partnership minimum gain increased from $150,000 to $180,000 during the partnership's Fourth taxable year, the amount of partnership nonrecourse deductions for that year is $30,000, consisting of a ratable portion of depreciation deductions allowable with respect to the two remaining apartment buildings. No minimum gain chargeback is required for the taxable year, even through the partnership disposed of one of the properties subject to the nonrecourse liability during the year, because there is no net decrease in partnership minimum gain for the year. See paragraph (f) (1) of this section.

Example (3). Nonrecourse deductions and partnership minimum gain before third partner is admitted. For purposes of Example 3, unless otherwise provided, the following facts are assumed. Additional facts are given in each of Examples 3(ii), (iii), and (iv). A and B form a limited partnership to acquire and lease machinery that is 5-year recovery property. A, the limited partner, and B, the general partner, contribute $100,000 each to the partnership, which obtains an $800,000 nonrecourse loan and purchases the machinery for $1,000,000. The nonrecourse loan is secured only by the machinery. The principal amount of the loan is to be repaid $50,000 per year during each of the partnership's first 5 taxable years, with the remaining $550,000 of unpaid principal due on the first day of the partnership's sixth taxable year. The partnership agreement contains all of the provisions required by paragraph (e) of this section, and, as of the end of each partnership taxable year discussed herein, the items described in § 1.704–1(b)(2)(ii)(d)(4), (5), and (6) are not reasonably expected to cause or increase a deficit balance in A's or B's capital account. The partnership agreement provides that, except as otherwise required by its qualified income offset and minimum gain chargeback provisions, all partnership items will be allocated equally between A and B. Finally, the partnership agreement provides that all distributions, other than distributions in liquidation of the partnership or of a partner's interest in the partnership, will be made equally between A and B. In the partnership's first taxable year it generates rental income of $130,000, interest expense of $80,000, and a depreciation deduction of $150,000, resulting in a net taxable loss of $100,000. In addition, the partnership repays $50,000 of the nonrecourse liability, reducing that liability to $750,000. Allocations of these losses equally between A and B have substantial economic effect.

	A	B
Capital account on formation	$100,000	$100,000
Less: net loss in year 1	(50,000)	(50,000)
Capital account at end of year 1	$50,000	$50,000

In the partnership's second taxable year, it generates rental income of $130,000, interest expense of $75,000, and a depreciation deduction of $220,000, resulting in a net taxable loss of $165,000. In addition, the partnership repays $50,000 of the nonrecourse liability, reducing that liability to $700,000, and distributes $2,500 of cash to each partner. If the partnership were to dispose of the machinery in full satisfaction of the nonrecourse liability at the end of that year, it would realize $70,000 of gain ($700,000 amount realized less $630,000 adjusted tax basis). Therefore, the amount of partnership minimum gain at the end of that year (and the net increase in partnership minimum gain during the year) is $70,000, and the amount of partnership nonrecourse deductions for the year is $70,000. The partnership nonrecourse deductions for its second taxable year consist of $70,000 of the depreciation deductions allowable with respect to the machinery. Pursuant to the partnership agreement, all partnership items comprising the net taxable loss of $165,000, including the $70,000 nonrecourse deduction, are allocated equally between A and B. The allocation of these items, other than the nonrecourse deductions, has substantial economic effect.

	A	B
Capital account at end of year 1	$50,000	$50,000
Less: net loss in year 2 (without nonrecourse deductions)	(47,500)	(47,500)
Less: nonrecourse deductions in year 2	($35,000)	($35,000)
Less: distribution	(2,500)	(2,500)
Capital account at end of year 2	($35,000)	($35,000)

(i) Calculation of nonrecourse deductions and partnership minimum gain. Because all of the requirements of paragraph (e) of this section are satisfied, the allocation of nonrecourse deductions is deemed to be made in accordance with the partners' interests in the partnership. At the end of the partnership's second taxable year, A's and B's shares of partnership minimum gain are $35,000 each. Therefore, pursuant to paragraph (g)(1) of this section, A and B are treated as obligated to restore deficit balances in their capital accounts of $35,000 each. If the partnership were to dispose of the machinery in full satisfaction of the nonrecourse liability at the beginning of the partnership's third taxable year (and had no other economic activity in that year), the partnership minimum gain would be decreased from $70,000 to zero. A's and B's shares of that net decrease would be $35,000 each. Upon that disposition, the minimum gain chargeback would require that A and B each be allocated $35,000 of that gain before any other allocation is made under section 704(b) with respect to partnership items for the partnership's third taxable year.

(ii) Nonrecourse deductions and restatement of capital accounts.

(a) Additional facts. C is admitted to the partnership at the beginning of the partnership's third taxable year. At the time of C's admission, the fair market value of the machinery is $900,000. C contributes $100,000 to the partnership (the partnership invests $95,000 of this in undeveloped land and holds the other $5,000 in cash) in exchange for an interest in the partnership. In connection with C's admission to the partnership, the partnership's machinery is revalued on the partnership's books to reflect its fair market value of $900,000. Pursuant to § 1.704–1(b)(2)(iv)(f), the capital accounts of A and B are adjusted upwards to $100,000 each to reflect the revaluation of the partnership's machinery. This adjustment reflects the manner in which the partnership gain of $270,000 ($900,000 fair market value minus $630,000 adjusted tax basis) would be shared if the machinery were sold for its fair market value immediately prior to C's admission to the partnership.

	A	B
Capital account before C's admission	($35,000)	($35,000)
Deemed sale adjustment	135,000	135,000
Capital account adjusted for C's admission	$100,000	$100,000

The partnership agreement is modified to provide that, except as otherwise required by its qualified income offset and minimum gain chargeback provisions, partnership income, gain, loss, and deduction, as computed for book purposes, are allocated equally among the partners, and those allocations are reflected in the partners' capital accounts. The partnership agreement also is modified to provide that depreciation and gain or loss, as computed for tax purposes, with respect to the machinery will be shared among the partners in a manner that takes account of the variation between the property's $630,000 adjusted tax basis and its $900,000 book value, in accordance with § 1.704–1(b)(2)(iv)(f) and the special rule contained in § 1.704–1(b)(4)(i).

(b) Effect of revaluation. Because the requirements of § 1.704–1(b)(2)(iv)(g) are satisfied, the capital accounts of the partners (as adjusted) continue to be maintained in accordance with § 1.704–1(b)(2)(iv). If the partnership were to dispose of the machinery in full satisfaction of the nonrecourse liability immediately following the revaluation of the machinery, it would realize no book gain ($700,000 amount realized less $900,000 book value). As a result of the revaluation of the machinery upward by $270,000, under part of paragraph (d)(4) of this section, the partnership minimum gain is reduced from $70,000 immediately prior to the revaluation to zero; but under part (ii) of paragraph (d)(4) of this section, the partnership minimum gain is increased by the $70,000 decrease arising solely from the revaluation. Accordingly, there is no net increase or decrease solely on account of the revaluation, and so no minimum gain chargeback is triggered. All future nonrecourse deductions that occur will be the nonrecourse

deductions as calculated for book purposes, and will be charged to all 3 partners in accordance with the partnership agreement. For purposes of determining the partners' shares of minimum gain under paragraph (g) of this section, A's and B's shares of the decrease resulting from the revaluation are $35,000 each. However, as illustrated below, under section 704(c) principles, the tax capital accounts of A and B will eventually be charged $35,000 each, reflecting their 50 percent shares of the decrease in partnership minimum gain that resulted from the revaluation.

(iii) Allocation of nonrecourse deductions following restatement of capital accounts.

(a) Additional facts. During the partnership's third taxable year, the partnership generates rental income of $130,000, interest expense of $70,000, a tax depreciation deduction of $210,000, and a book depreciation deduction (attributable to the machinery) of $300,000. As a result, the partnership has a net taxable loss of $150,000 and a net book loss of $240,000. In addition, the partnership repays $50,000 of the nonrecourse liability (after the data of C's admission), reducing the liability to $650,000 and distributes $5,000 of cash to each partner.

(b) Allocations. If the partnership were to dispose of the machinery in full satisfaction of the nonrecourse liability at the end of the year, $50,000 of book gain would result ($650,000 amount realized less $600,000 book basis). Therefore, the amount of partner-

ship minimum gain at the end of the year is $50,000, which represents a net decrease in partnership minimum gain of $20,000 during the year. (This is so even though there would be an increase in partnership minimum gain in the partnership's third taxable year if minimum gain were computed with reference to the adjusted tax basis of the machinery.) Nevertheless, pursuant to paragraph (d)(4) of this section, the amount of nonrecourse deductions of the partnership for its third taxable year is $50,000 (the net increase in partnership minimum gain during the year determined by adding back the $70,000 decrease in partnership minimum gain attributable to the revaluation of the machinery to the $20,000 net decrease in partnership minimum gain during the year). The $50,000 of partnership nonrecourse deductions for the year consist of book depreciation deductions allowable with respect to the machinery of $50,000. Pursuant to the partnership agreement, all partnership items comprising the net book loss of $240,000, including the $50,000 nonrecourse deduction, are allocated equally among the partners. The allocation of these items, other than the nonrecourse deductions, has substantial economic effect. Consistent with the special partners' interests in the partnership rate contained in § 1.704–1(b)(4)(i), the partnership agreement provides that the depreciation deduction for tax purposes of $210,000 for the partnership's third taxable year is, in accordance with section 704(c) principles, shared $55,000 to A, $55,000 to B, and $100,000 to C.

	A		B		C	
	Tax	Book	Tax	Book	Tax	Book
Capital account at beginning of year 3	($35,000)	$100,000	($35,000)	$100,000	$100,000	$100,000
Less: nonrecourse deductions	(9,166)	(16,666)	(9,166)	(16,666)	(16,666)	(16,666)
Less: items other than nonrecourse deductions in year 3	(25,834)	(63,334)	(25,834)	(63,334)	(63,334)	(63,334)
Less: distribution	(5,000)	(5,000)	(5,000)	(5,000)	(5,000)	(5,000)
Capital account at end of year 3	($75,000)	$15,000	($75,000)	$15,000	$15,000	$15,000

Because the requirements of paragraph (e) of this section are satisfied, the allocation of the nonrecourse deduction is deemed to be made in accordance with the partners' interests in the partnership. At the end of the partnership's third taxable year. A's, B's, and C's shares of partnership minimum gain are $16,666 each.

(iv) Subsequent allocation of nonrecourse deductions following restatement of capital accounts.

(a) Additional facts. The partners' capital accounts at the end of the second and third taxable years of the partnership are as stated in Example 3(iii) of this paragraph (m). In addition, during the partnership's fourth taxable year the partnership generates rental income of $130,000, interest expense of $65,000, a tax depreciation deduction of $210,000, and a book depreciation deduction (attributable to the machinery) of $300,000. As a result the partnership has a net taxable loss of $145,000 and a net book loss of $235,000. In addition, the partnership repays $50,000 of the non-recourse liability, reducing that liability to $600,000, and distributes $5,000 of cash to each partner.

(b) Allocations. If the partnership were to dispose of the machinery in full satisfaction of the nonrecourse liability at the end of the fourth year, $300,000 of book gain would result ($600,000 amount realized less $300,000 book value). Therefore, the amount of partnership minimum gain as of the end of the year is $300,000, which represents a net increase in partnership minimum gain during the year of $250,000. Thus, the amount of partnership nonrecourse deductions for that year equals $250,000, consisting of book depreciation deductions of $250,000. Pursuant to the partnership agreement, all partnership items comprising the net book loss of $235,000, including the $250,000 nonrecourse deduction, are allocated equally among the partners. That allocation of all items, other than the nonrecourse deductions, has substantial economic effect. Consistent with the special partners' interests in the partnership rule contained in § 1.704–1(b)(4)(i), the partnership agreement provides that the depreciation deduction for tax purposes of $210,000 in the partnership's fourth taxable year is, in accordance with section 704(c) principles, allocated $55,000 to A, $55,000 to B, and $100,000 to C.

	A		B		C	
	Tax	*Book*	*Tax*	*Book*	*Tax*	*Book*
Capital account at end of year 3	0.5625 in	$15,000	($75,000)	$15,000	$15,000	$15,000
Less: nonrecourse deductions	(45,833)	(83,333)	(45,833)	(83,333)	(83,333)	(83,333)
Plus: items other than nonrecourse deductions in year 4	12,499	5,000	12,499	5,000	5,000	5,000
Less: distribution	(5,000)	(5,000)	(5,000)	(5,000)	(5,000)	(5,000)
Capital account at end of year 4	($113,334)	($68,333)	($113,333)	($68,333)	($68,333)	($68,333)

The allocation of the $250,000 nonrecourse deduction equally among A, B, and C satisfies requirement (2) of paragraph (e) of this section. Because all of the requirements of paragraph (e) of this section are satisfied, the allocation is deemed to be in accordance with the partners' interests in the partnership. At the end of the partnership's fourth taxable year, A's, B's, and C's shares of partnership minimum gain are $100,000 each.

(v) Disposition of partnership property following restatement of capital accounts.

(a) Additional facts. The partners' capital accounts at the end of the fourth taxable year of the partnership are as stated above in (iv). In addition, at the beginning of the partnership's fifth taxable year it sells the machinery for $650,000 (using $600,000 of the proceeds to repay the nonrecourse liability), resulting in a taxable gain of $440,000 ($650,000 amount realized less $210,000 adjusted tax basis) and a book gain of $350,000 ($650,000 amount realized less $300,000 book basis). The partner-

ship has no other items of income, gain, loss, or deduction for the year.

(b) Effect of disposition. As a result of the sale, partnership minimum gain is reduced from $300,000 to zero, reducing A's, B's, and C's shares of partnership minimum gain to zero from $100,000 each. The minimum gain chargeback requires that A, B, and C each be allocated $100,000 of that gain (an amount equal to each partner's share of the net decrease in partnership minimum gain resulting from the sale) before any allocation is made to them under section 704(b) with respect to part-

nership items for the partnership's fifth taxable year. Thus, the allocation of the first $300,000 of book gain $100,000 to each of the partners is deemed to be in accordance with the partners' interests in the partnership under paragraph (e) of this section. The allocation of the remaining $50,000 of book gain equally among the partners has substantial economic effect. Consistent with the special partners' interests in the partnership rule contained in § 1.704–1(b)(4)(i), the partnership agreement provides that the $440,000 taxable gain is, in accordance with section 704(c) principles, allocated $161,667 to A, $161,667 to B, and $116,666 to C.

	A		B		C	
	Tax	Book	Tax	Book	Tax	Book
Capital account at end of year 4	($113,334)	($68,333)	($113,334)	($68,333)	($68,333)	($68,333)
Plus: minimum gain chargeback	138,573	100,000	138,573	100,000	100,000	100,000
Plus: additional gain	23,094	16,666	23,094	16,666	16,666	16,666
Capital account before liquidation	$48,333	$48,333	$48,333	$48,333	$48,333	$48,333

Example (4). Allocations of increase in partnership minimum gain among partnership properties. For Example 4, unless otherwise provided, the following facts are assumed. A partnership owns 4 properties, each of which is subject to a nonrecourse liability of the partnership. During a taxable year of the partnership, the following events take place. First, the partnership generates a depreciation deduction (for both book and tax purposes) with respect to Property W of $10,000 and repays $5,000 of the nonrecourse liability secured only by that property, resulting in an increase in minimum gain with respect to that liability of $5,000. Second, the partnership generates a depreciation deduction (for both book and tax purposes) with respect to Property X of $10,000 and repays none of the nonrecourse liability secured by that property, resulting in an increase in minimum gain with respect to that liability of $10,000. Third, the partnership generates a depreciation deduction (for both book and tax purposes) of $2,000 with respect to Property Y and repays $11,000 of the nonrecourse liability secured only by that property, resulting in a

decrease in minimum gain with respect to that liability of $9,000 (although at the end of that year, there remains minimum gain with respect to that liability). Finally, the partnership borrows $5,000 on a nonrecourse basis, giving as the only security for that liability Property Z, a parcel of undeveloped land with an adjusted tax basis (and book value) of $2,000, resulting in a net increase in minimum gain with respect to that liability of $3,000.

(i) Allocation of increase in partnership minimum gain. The net increase in partnership minimum gain during that partnership taxable year is $9,000, so that the amount of nonrecourse deductions of the partnership for that taxable year is $9,000. Those nonrecourse deductions consist of $3,000 of depreciation deductions with respect to Property W and $6,000 of depreciation deductions with respect to Property X. See paragraph (c) of this section. The amount of nonrecourse deductions consisting of depreciation deductions is determined as follows. With respect to the nonrecourse liability secured by Property Z, for which there is no depreciation deduction,

the amount of depreciation deductions that constitutes nonrecourse deductions is zero. Similarly, with respect to the nonrecourse liability secured by Property Y, for which there is no increase in minimum gain, the amount of depreciation deductions that constitutes nonrecourse deductions is zero. With respect to each of the nonrecourse liabilities secured by Properties W and X, which are secured by property for which there are depreciation deductions and for which there is an increase in minimum gain, the amount of depreciation deductions that constitutes nonrecourse deductions is determined by the following formula:

net increase in the partnership minimum gain for that taxable year x total depreciation deductions for that taxable year on the specific property securing the nonrecourse liability to the extent minimum gain increased on that liability (divided by) total depreciation deductions for that taxable year on all properties securing nonrecourse liabilities to the extent of the aggregate increase in minimum gain on all those liabilities.

Thus, for the liability secured by Property W, the amount is $9,000 times $5,000/$15,000, or $3,000. For the liability secured by Property X, the amount is $9,000 times $10,000/$15,000, or $6,000. (If one depreciable property secured two partnership nonrecourse liabilities, the amount of depreciation or book depreciation with respect to that property would be allocated among those liabilities in accordance with the method by which adjusted basis is allocated under paragraph (d)(2) of this section.)

(ii) Alternative allocation of increase in partnership minimum gain among partnership properties. Assume instead that the loan secured by Property Z is $15,000 (rather than $5,000), resulting in a net increase in minimum gain with respect to that liability of $13,000. Thus, the net increase in partnership minimum gain is $19,000, and the amount of nonrecourse deductions of the partnership for that taxable year is $19,000. Those nonrecourse deductions

consist of $5,000 of depreciation deductions with respect to Property W, $10,000 of depreciation deductions with respect to Property X, and a pro rata portion of the partnership's other items of deduction, loss, and section 705(a)(2)(B) expenditure for that year. The method for computing the amounts of depreciation deductions that constitute nonrecourse deductions is the same as in (i) of this Example 4 for the liabilities secured by Properties Y and Z. With respect to each of the nonrecourse liabilities secured by Properties W and X, the amount of depreciation deductions that constitutes nonrecourse deductions equals the total depreciation deductions with respect to the partnership property securing that particular liability to the extent of the increase in minimum gain with respect to that liability.

§ 1.704–3 Contributed property.

(a) In general.

(1) General principles. The purpose of section 704(c) is to prevent the shifting of tax consequences among partners with respect to precontribution gain or loss. Under section 704(c), a partnership must allocate income, gain, loss, and deduction with respect to property contributed by a partner to the partnership so as to take into account any variation between the adjusted tax basis of the property and its fair market value at the time of contribution. Notwithstanding any other provision of this section, the allocations must be made using a reasonable method that is consistent with the purpose of section 704(c). For this purpose, an allocation method includes the application of all of the rules of this section (e.g., aggregation rules). An allocation method is not necessarily unreasonable merely because another allocation method would result in a higher aggregate tax liability. Paragraphs (b), (c), and (d) of this section describe allocation methods that are generally reasonable. Other methods may be reasonable in appropriate circumstances. Nevertheless, in the absence of specific published guidance, it is not reasonable to use an allocation method in which the basis of property contributed to the partnership is increased (or decreased) to reflect built-in gain (or loss), or a method under which the partnership creates tax allocations of income, gain, loss, or deduction independent of allocations affecting book capital accounts. See § 1.704–3(d). Paragraph (e) of this section contains special rules and exceptions. The principles of this paragraph (a)(1), together with the methods described in paragraphs (b), (c) and (d) of this section, apply only to contributions of property that are otherwise respected. See for example § 1.701–2. Accordingly, even though a partnership's allocation method may be described in the literal language of paragraphs (b), (c) or (d) of this section, based on the particular facts and circumstances, the Commissioner can recast the contribution as appropriate to avoid tax results inconsistent with the intent of subchapter K. One factor that may be considered by the Commissioner is the use of the remedial allocation method by related partners in which allocations of remedial items of income, gain, loss or deduction are made to one partner and the allocations of offsetting remedial items are made to a related partner.

(2) Operating rules. Except as provided in paragraphs (e)(2) and (e)(3) of this section, section 704(c) and this section apply on a property-by-property basis. Therefore, in determining whether there is a disparity between adjusted tax basis and fair market value, the built-in gains and built-in losses on items of contributed property cannot be aggregated. A partnership may use different methods with respect to different items of contributed property, provided that the partnership and the partners consistently apply a single reasonable method for each item of contributed property and that the overall method or combination of methods are reasonable based on the facts and circumstances and consistent with the purpose of section 704(c). It may be unreasonable to use one method for appreciated property and another method for depreciated property. Similarly, it may be unreasonable

to use the traditional method for built-in gain property contributed by a partner with a high marginal tax rate while using curative allocations for built-in gain property contributed by a partner with a low marginal tax rate. A new partnership formed as the result of the termination of a partnership under section 708(b)(1)(B) is not required to use the same method as the terminated partnership with respect to section 704(c) property deemed contributed to the new partnership by the terminated partnership under § 1.708–1(b)(1)(iv). The previous sentence applies to terminations of partnerships under section 708(b)(1)(B) occurring on or after May 9, 1997; however, the sentence may be applied to terminations occurring on or after May 9, 1996, provided that the partnership and its partners apply the sentence to the termination in a consistent manner.

(3) Definitions.

(i) Section 704(c) Property. Property contributed to a partnership is section 704(c) property if at the time of contribution its book value differs from the contributing partner's adjusted tax basis. For purposes of this section, book value is determined as contemplated by § 1.704–1(b). Therefore, book value is equal to fair market value at the time of contribution and is subsequently adjusted for cost recovery and other events that affect the basis of the property. For a partnership that maintains capital accounts in accordance with § 1.704–1(b)(2)(iv), the book value of property is initially the value used in determining the contributing partner's capital account under § 1.704–1(b)(2)(iv)(d), and is appropriately adjusted thereafter (e.g., for book cost recovery under §§ 1.704–1(b)(2)(iv)(g)(3) and 1.704–3(d)(2) and other events that affect the basis of the property). A partnership that does not maintain capital accounts under § 1.704–1(b)(2)(iv) must comply with this section using a book capital account based on the same principles (i.e., a book capital account that reflects the fair market value of property at the time of contribution and that is subsequently adjusted for cost recovery and other events that affect the basis of the property). Property deemed contributed to a new partnership as the result of the termination of a partnership under section 708(b)(1)(B) is treated as section 704(c) property in the hands of the new partnership only to the extent that the property was section 704(c) property in the hands of the terminated partnership immediately prior to the termination. See § 1.708–1(b)(1)(iv) for an example of the application of this rule. The previous two sentences apply to terminations of partnerships under section 708(b)(1)(B) occurring on or after May 9, 1997; however, the sentences may be applied to terminations occurring on or after May 9, 1996, provided that the partnership and its partners apply the sentences to the termination in a consistent manner.

(ii) **Built-in gain and built-in loss.** The built-in gain on section 704(c) property is the excess of the property's book value over the contributing partner's adjusted tax basis upon contribution. The built-in gain is thereafter reduced by decreases in the difference between the property's book value and adjusted tax basis. The built-in loss on section 704(c) property is the excess of the contributing partner's adjusted tax basis over the property's book value upon contribution. The built-in loss is thereafter reduced by decreases in the difference between the property's adjusted tax basis and book value.

(4) **Accounts payable and other accrued but unpaid items.** Accounts payable and other accrued but unpaid items contributed by a partner using the cash receipts and disbursements method of accounting are treated as section 704(c) property for purposes of applying the rules of this section.

(5) **Other provisions of the Internal Revenue Code.** Section 704(c) and this section apply to a contribution of property to the partnership only if the contribution is governed by section 721, taking into account other provisions of the Internal Revenue Code. For example, to the extent that a transfer of property to a partnership is a sale under section 707, the transfer is not a contribution of property to which section 704(c) applies.

(6) **Other applications of section 704(c) principles.**

(i) **Revaluations under section 704(b).** The principles of this section apply to allocations with respect to property for which differences between book value and adjusted tax basis are created when a partnership revalues partnership property pursuant to § 1.704–1(b)(2)(iv)(f) or 1.704–1(b)(2)(iv)(s) (reverse section 704(c) allocations). Partnerships are not required to use the same allocation method for reverse section 704(c) allocations as for contributed property, even if at the time of revaluation the property is already subject to section 704(c) and paragraph (a) of this section. In addition, partnerships are not required to use the same allocation method for reverse section 704(c) allocations each time the partnership revalues its property. A partnership that makes allocations with respect to revalued property must use a reasonable method that is consistent with the purposes of section 704(b) and (c).

(ii) **Basis adjustments.** A partnership making adjustments under § 1.743–1(b) or 1.751–1(a)(2) must account for built-in gain or loss under section 704(c) in accordance with the principles of this section.

(7) **Transfers of a partnership interest.** If a contributing partner transfers a partnership interest, built-in gain or loss must be allocated to the transferee partner as it would have been allocated to the transferor partner. If the contributing partner transfers a portion of the partnership interest, the share of built-in gain or loss proportionate to the interest transferred must be allocated to the transferee partner. This rule does not apply to any person who acquired a partnership interest from a § 1.752–7 liability partner in a transaction to which paragraph (e)(1) of § 1.752–7 applies. See § 1.752–7(c)(1).

(8) Disposition of property in nonrecognition transaction.

(i) If a partnership disposes of section 704(c) property in a nonrecognition transaction in which no gain or loss is recognized, the substituted basis property (within the meaning of section 7701(a)(42)) is treated as section 704(c) property with the same amount of built-in gain or loss as the section 704(c) property disposed of by the partnership. If gain or loss is recognized in such a transaction, appropriate adjustments must be made. The allocation method for the substituted basis property must be consistent with the allocation method chosen for the original property. If a partnership transfers an item of section 704(c) property together with other property to a corporation under section 351, in order to preserve that item's built-in gain or loss, the basis in the stock received in exchange for the section 704(c) property is determined as if each item of section 704(c) property had been the only property transferred to the corporation by the partnership.

(ii) Disposition in an installment sale. If a partnership disposes of section 704(c) property in an installment sale as defined in section 453(b), the installment obligation received by the partnership is treated as the section 704(c) property with the same amount of built-in gain as the section 704(c) property disposed of by the partnership (with appropriate adjustments for any gain recognized on the installment sale). The allocation method for the installment obligation must be consistent with the allocation method chosen for the original property.

(iii) Contributed contracts. If a partner contributes to a partnership a contract that is section 704(c) property, and the partnership subsequently acquires property pursuant to the contract in a transaction in which less than all of the gain or loss is recognized, then the acquired property is treated as the section 704(c) property with the same amount of built-in gain or loss as the contract (with appropriate adjustments for any gain or loss recognized on the acquisition). For this purpose, the term contract includes, but is not limited to, options, forward contracts, and futures contracts. The allocation method for the acquired property must be consistent with the allocation method chosen for the contributed contract.

(iv) Capitalized amounts. To the extent that a partnership properly capitalizes all or a portion of an item as described in paragraph (a)(12) of this section, then the item or items to which such cost is properly capitalized is treated as section 704(c) property with the same amount of built-in loss as corresponds to the amount capitalized.

(9) Tiered partnerships. If a partnership contributes section 704(c) property to a second partnership (the lower-tier partnership), or if a partner that has contributed section 704(c) property to a partnership contributes that partnership interest to a second partnership (the upper-tier partnership), the upper-tier partnership must allocate its distributive share of lower-tier partnership items with respect to that section 704(c) property in a manner that takes into account the contributing partner's remaining built-in gain or loss. Allocations made under this paragraph will be considered to be made in a manner that meets the requirements of § 1.704 1(b)(2)(iv)(q) (relating to capital account adjustments where guidance is lacking).

(10) Anti-abuse rule. (i) In general. An allocation method (or combination of methods) is not reasonable if the contribution of property (or event that results in reverse section 704(c) allocations) and the corresponding allocation of tax items with respect to the property are made with a view to shifting the tax consequences of built-in gain or loss among the partners in a manner that substantially reduces the present value of the partners' aggregate tax liability. For purposes of this paragraph (a)(10), all references to the partners shall include both direct and indirect partners.

(ii) Definition of indirect partner. An *indirect partner* is any direct or indirect owner of a partnership, S corporation, or controlled foreign corporation (as defined in section 957(a) or 953(c)), or direct or indirect beneficiary of a trust or estate, that is a partner in the partnership, and any consolidated group of which the partner in the partnership is a member (within the meaning of § 1.1502–1(h)). An owner (whether directly or through tiers of entities) of a controlled foreign corporation is treated as an indirect partner only with respect to allocations of items of income, gain, loss, or deduction that enter into the computation of a United States shareholder's inclusion under section 951(a) with respect to the controlled foreign corporation, enter into any person's income attributable to a United States shareholder's inclusion under section 951(a) with respect to the controlled foreign corporation, or would enter into the computations described in this sentence if such items were allocated to the controlled foreign corporation.

(11) Contributing and noncontributing partners' recapture shares. For special rules applicable to the allocation of depreciation recapture with respect to property contributed by a partner to a partnership, see §§ 1.1245–1(e)(2) and 1.1250–1(f).

(12) § 1.752–7 liabilities. Except as otherwise provided in § 1.752–7, § 1.752–7 liabilities (within the meaning of § 1.752–7(b)(2)) are section 704(c) property (built-in loss property that at the time of contribution has a book value that differs from the contributing partner's adjusted tax basis) for purposes of applying the rules of this section. See § 1.752–7(c). To the extent that the built-in loss associated with the § 1.752–7 liability exceeds the cost of satisfying the § 1.752–7 liability (as defined in § 1.752–7(b)(3)), the excess creates a "ceiling rule" limitation, within the meaning of § 1.704–3(b)(1), subject to the methods of allocation set forth in § 1.704–3(b), (c) and (d).

(b) Traditional method.

(1) In general. This paragraph (b) describes the traditional method of making section 704(c) allocations. In general, the traditional method requires that when the partnership has income, gain, loss, or deduction attributable to section 704(c) property, it must make appropriate allocations to the partners to avoid shifting the tax consequences of the built-in gain or loss. Under this rule, if the partnership sells section 704(c) property and recognizes gain or loss, built-in gain or loss on the property is allocated to the contributing partner. If the partnership sells a portion of, or an interest in, section 704(c) property, a proportionate part of the built-in gain or loss is allocated to the contributing partner. For section 704(c) property subject to amortization, depletion, depreciation, or other cost recovery, the allocation of deductions attributable to these items takes into account built-in gain or loss on the property. For example, tax allocations to the noncontributing partners of cost recovery deductions with respect to section 704(c) property generally must, to the extent possible, equal book allocations to those partners. However, the total income, gain, loss, or deduction allocated to the partners for a taxable year with respect to a property cannot exceed the total partnership income, gain, loss, or deduction with respect to that property for the taxable year (the ceiling rule). If a partnership has no property the allocations from which are limited by the ceiling rule, the traditional method is reasonable when used for all contributed property.

(2) Examples. The following examples illustrate the principles of the traditional method.

Example (1). Operation of the traditional method. (i) Calculation of built-in gain on contribution. A and B form partnership AB and agree that each will be allocated a 50 percent share of all partnership items and that AB will make allocations under section 704(c) using the traditional method under paragraph (b) of this section. A contributes depreciable property with an adjusted tax basis of $4,000 and a book value of $10,000, and B contributes $10,000 cash. Under paragraph (a)(3) of this section, A has built-in gain of $6,000, the excess of the partnership's book value for the property ($10,000) over A's adjusted tax basis in the property at the time of contribution ($4,000).

(ii) Allocation of tax depreciation. The property is depreciated using the straight-line method over a 10-year recovery period. Because the property depreciates at an annual rate of 10 percent, B would have been entitled to a depreciation deduction of $500 per year for both book and tax purposes if the adjusted tax basis of the property equaled its fair market value at the time of contribution. Although each partner is allocated $500 of book depreciation per year, the partnership is allowed a tax depreciation deduction of only $400 per year (10 percent of $4,000). The partnership can allocate only $400 of tax depreciation under the ceiling rule of paragraph (b)(1) of this section, and it must be allocated entirely to B. In AB's first year, the proceeds generated by the equipment exactly equal AB's operating expenses. At the end of that year, the book value of the property is $9,000 ($10,000 less the $1,000 book depreciation deduction), and the adjusted tax basis is $3,600 ($4,000 less the $400 tax depreciation deduction). A's built-in gain with respect to the property decreases to $5,400 ($9,000 book value less $3,600 adjusted tax basis). Also, at the end of AB's first year, A has a $9,500 book capital account and a $4,000 tax basis in A's partnership interest. B has a $9,500 book capital account and a $9,600 adjusted tax basis in B's partnership interest.

(iii) Sale of the property. If AB sells the property at the beginning of AB's second year for $9,000, AB realizes tax gain of $5,400 ($9,000, the amount realized, less the adjusted tax basis of $3,600). Under paragraph (b)(1) of this section, the entire $5,400 gain must be allocated to A because the property A contributed has that much built-in gain remaining. If AB sells the property at the beginning of AB's

second year for $10,000, AB realizes tax gain of $6,400 ($10,000, the amount realized, less the adjusted tax basis of $3,600). Under paragraph (b)(1) of this section, only $5,400 of gain must be allocated to A to account for A's built-in gain. The remaining $1,000 of gain is allocated equally between A and B in accordance with the partnership agreement. If AB sells the property for less than the $9,000 book value, AB realizes tax gain of less than $5,400, and the entire gain must be allocated to A.

(iv) Termination and liquidation of partnership. If AB sells the property at the beginning of AB's second year for $9,000, and AB engages in no other transactions that year, A will recognize a gain of $5,400, and B will recognize no income or loss. A's adjusted tax basis for A's interest in AB will then be $9,400 ($4,000, A's original tax basis, increased by the gain of $5,400). B's adjusted tax basis for B's interest in AB will be $9,600 ($10,000, B's original tax basis, less the $400 depreciation deduction in the first partnership year). If the partnership then terminates and distributes its assets ($19,000 in cash) to A and B in proportion to their capital account balances, A will recognize a capital gain of $100 ($9,500, the amount distributed to A, less $9,400, the adjusted tax basis of A's interest). B will recognize a capital loss of $100 (the excess of B's adjusted tax basis, $9,600, over the amount received, $9,500).

Example (2). Unreasonable use of the traditional method. (i) Facts. C and D form partnership CD and agree that each will be allocated a 50 percent share of all partnership items and that CD will make allocations under section 704(c) using the traditional method under paragraph (b) of this section. C contributes equipment with an adjusted tax basis of $1,000 and a book value of $10,000, with a view to taking advantage of the fact that the equipment has only one year remaining on its cost recovery schedule although its remaining economic life is significantly longer. At the time of contribution, C has a built-in gain of $9,000 and the equipment is section 704(c) property. D contributes $10,000 of cash, which CD uses to buy securities. D has substantial net operating loss carryforwards that D anticipates will otherwise expire unused. Under § 1.704–1(b)(2)(iv)(g)(3), the partnership must allocate the $10,000 of book depreciation to the partners in the first year of the partnership. Thus, there is $10,000 of book depreciation and $1,000 of tax depreciation in the partnership's first year. CD sells the equipment during the second year for $10,000 and recognizes a $10,000 gain ($10,000, the amount realized, less the adjusted tax basis of $0).

(ii) Unreasonable use of method. (A) At the beginning of the second year, both the book value and adjusted tax basis of the equipment are $0. Therefore, there is no remaining built-in gain. The $10,000 gain on the sale of the equipment in the second year is allocated $5,000 each to C and D. The interaction of the partnership's one-year write-off of the entire book value of the equipment and the use of the traditional method results in a shift of $4,000 of the precontribution gain in the equipment from C to D (D's $5,000 share of CD's $10,000 gain, less the $1,000 tax depreciation deduction previously allocated to D).

(B) The traditional method is not reasonable under paragraph (a)(10) of this section because the contribution of property is made, and the traditional method is used, with a view to shifting a significant amount of taxable income to a partner with a low marginal tax rate and away from a partner with a high marginal tax rate.

(C) Under these facts, if the partnership agreement in effect for the year of contribution had provided that tax gain from the sale of the property (if any) would always be allocated first to C to offset the effect of the ceiling rule limitation, the allocation method would not violate the anti-abuse rule of paragraph (a)(10) of this section. See paragraph (c)(3) of this section. Under other facts, (for example, if the partnership holds multiple section 704(c) properties and either uses multiple allocation methods or uses a single allocation method where one or more of the properties are subject to the ceiling rule) the allocation to C may not be reasonable.

(c) Traditional method with curative allocations.

(1) In general. To correct distortions created by the ceiling rule, a partnership using the traditional method under paragraph (b) of this section may make reasonable curative allocations to reduce or eliminate disparities between book and tax items of noncontributing partners. A curative allocation is an allocation of income, gain, loss, or deduction for tax purposes that differs from the partnership's allocation of the corresponding book item. For example, if a noncontributing partner is allocated less tax depreciation than book depreciation with respect to an item of section 704(c) property, the partnership may make a curative allocation to that partner of tax depreciation from another item of partnership property to make up the difference, notwithstanding that the corresponding book depreciation is allocated to the contributing partner. A partnership may limit its curative allocations to allocations of one or more particular tax items (e.g., only depreciation from a specific property or properties) even if the allocation of those available items does not offset fully the effect of the ceiling rule.

(2) Consistency. A partnership must be consistent in its application of curative allocations with respect to each item of section 704(c) property from year to year.

(3) Reasonable curative allocations.

(i) Amount. A curative allocation is not reasonable to the extent it exceeds the amount necessary to offset the effect of the ceiling rule for the current taxable year or, in the case of a curative allocation upon disposition of the property, for prior taxable years.

(ii) Timing. The period of time over which the curative allocations are made is a factor in determining whether the allocations are reasonable. Notwithstanding paragraph (c)(3)(i) of this section, a partnership may make curative allocations in a taxable year to offset the effect of the ceiling rule for a prior taxable year if those allocations are made over a reasonable period of time, such as over the property's economic life, and are provided for under the partnership agreement in effect for the year of contribution. See paragraph (c)(4) Example 3(ii)(C) of this section.

(iii) Type.

(A) In general. To be reasonable, a curative allocation of income, gain, loss, or deduction must be expected to have substantially the same effect on each partner's tax liability as the tax item limited by the ceiling rule. The expectation must exist at the time the section 704(c) property is obligated to be (or is) contributed to the partnership and the allocation with respect to that property becomes part of the partnership agreement. However, the expectation is tested at the time the allocation with respect to that property is actually made if the partnership agreement is not sufficiently specific as to the precise manner in which allocations are to be made with respect to that property. Under this paragraph (c), if the item limited by the ceiling rule is loss from the sale of property, a curative allocation of gain must be expected to have substantially the same effect as would an allocation to that partner of gain with respect to the sale of the property. If the item limited by the ceiling rule is depreciation or other cost recovery, a curative allocation of income to the contributing partner must be expected to have substantially the same effect as would an allocation to that partner of partnership income with respect to the contributed property. For example, if depreciation deductions with respect to leased equipment contributed by a tax-exempt partner are limited by the ceiling rule, a curative allocation of dividend or interest income to that partner generally is not reasonable, although a curative allocation of depreciation deductions from

other leased equipment to the noncontributing partner is reasonable. Similarly, under this rule, if depreciation deductions apportioned to foreign source income in a particular statutory grouping under section 904(d) are limited by the ceiling rule, a curative allocation of income from another statutory grouping to the contributing partner generally is not reasonable, although a curative allocation of income from the same statutory grouping and of the same character is reasonable.

(B) Exception for allocation from disposition of contributed property. If cost recovery has been limited by the ceiling rule, the general limitation on character does not apply to income from the disposition of contributed property subject to the ceiling rule, but only if properly provided for in the partnership agreement in effect for the year of contribution or revaluation. For example, if allocations of depreciation deductions to a noncontributing partner have been limited by the ceiling rule, a curative allocation to the contributing partner of gain from the sale of that property, if properly provided for in the partnership agreement, is reasonable for purposes of paragraph (c)(3)(iii)(A) of this section even if not of the same character.

(4) Examples. The following examples illustrate the principles of this paragraph (c).

Example (1). Reasonable and unreasonable curative allocations. (i) Facts. E and F form partnership EF and agree that each will be allocated a 50 percent share of all partnership items and that EF will make allocations under section 704(c) using the traditional method with curative allocations under paragraph (c) of this section. E contributes equipment with an adjusted tax basis of $4,000 and a book value of $10,000. The equipment has 10 years remaining on its cost recovery schedule and is depreciable using the straight-line method. At the time of contribution, E has a built-in gain of $6,000, and therefore, the equipment is section 704(c) property. F contributes $10,000 of cash, which EF uses to buy inventory for resale. In

EF's first year, the revenue generated by the equipment equals EF's operating expenses. The equipment generates $1,000 of book depreciation and $400 of tax depreciation for each of 10 years. At the end of the first year EF sells all the inventory for $10,700, recognizing $700 of income. The partners anticipate that the inventory income will have substantially the same effect on their tax liabilities as income from E's contributed equipment. Under the traditional method of paragraph (b) of this section, E and F would each be allocated $350 of income from the sale of inventory for book and tax purposes and $500 of depreciation for book purposes. The $400 of tax depreciation would all be allocated to F. Thus, at the end of the first year, E and F's book and tax capital accounts would be as follows:

E		F		
Book	Tax	Book	Tax	
$10,000	$4,000	$10,000	$10,000	Initial contribution
<500>	<0>	<500>	<400>	Depreciation
350	350	350	350	Sales income
$9,850	$4,350	$9,850	$9,950	

(ii) Reasonable curative allocation. Because the ceiling rule would cause a disparity of $100 between F's book and tax capital accounts, EF may properly allocate to E under paragraph (c) of this section an additional $100 of income from the sale of inventory for tax purposes. This allocation results in capital accounts at the end of EF's first year as follows:

E		F		
Book	Tax	Book	Tax	
$10,000	$4,000	$10,000	$10,000	Initial contribution
<500>	<0>	<500>	<400>	Depreciation
350	450	350	250	Sales income
$9,850	$4,450	$ 9,850	$ 9,850	

(iii) Unreasonable curative allocation. (A) The facts are the same as in paragraphs (i) and (ii) of this Example 1, except that E and F choose to allocate all the income from the sale of the inventory to E for tax purposes, although they share it equally for book purposes. This allocation results in capital accounts at the end of EF's first year as follows:

E		F		
Book	Tax	Book	Tax	
$10,000	$4,000	$10,000	$10,000	Initial contribution
<500>	<0>	<500>	<400>	Depreciation
350	700	350	0	Sales income
$9,850	$4,700	$9,850	$9,600	

(B) This curative allocation is not reasonable under paragraph (c)(3)(i) of this section because the allocation exceeds the amount necessary to offset the disparity caused by the ceiling rule.

Example (2). Curative allocations limited to depreciation. (i) Facts. G and H form partnership GH and agree that each will be allocated a 50 percent share of all partnership items and that GH will make allocations under section 704(c) using the traditional method with curative allocations under paragraph (c) of this section, but only to the extent that the partnership has sufficient tax depreciation deductions. G contributes property G1, with an adjusted tax basis of $3,000 and a fair market value of $10,000, and H contributes property H1, with an adjusted tax basis of $6,000 and a fair market value of $10,000. Both properties have 5 years remaining on their cost recovery schedules and are depreciable using the straight-line method. At the time of contribution, G1 has a built-in gain of $7,000 and H1 has a built-in gain of $4,000, and therefore, both properties are section 704(c) property. G1 generates $600 of tax depreciation and $2,000 of book depreciation for each of five years. H1 generates $1,200 of tax depreciation and $2,000 of book depreciation for each of 5 years. In addition, the properties each generate $500 of operating income annually. G and H are each allocated $1,000 of book depreciation for each property. Under the traditional method of paragraph (b) of this section, G would be allocated $0 of tax depreciation for G1 and $1,000 for H1, and H would be allocated $600 of tax depreciation for G1 and $200 for H1. Thus, at the end of the first year, G and H's book and tax capital accounts would be as follows:

G		H		
Book	Tax	Book	Tax	
$10,000	$3,000	$10,000	$6,000	Initial contribution
<1,000>	<0>	<1,000>	<600>	G1 depreciation
<1,000>	<1,000>	<1,000>	<200>	H1 depreciation
500	500	500	500	Operating income
$8,500	$2,500	$8,500	$ 5,700	

(ii) Curative allocations. Under the traditional method, G is allocated more depreciation deductions than H, even though H contributed property with a smaller disparity reflected on GH's book and tax capital accounts. GH makes curative allocations to H of an additional $400 of tax depreciation each year, which reduces the disparities between G and H's book and tax capital accounts ratably each year. These allocations are reasonable provided the allocations meet the other requirements of this section. As a result of their agreement, at the end of the first year, G and H's capital accounts are as follows:

G		H		
Book	Tax	Book	Tax	
$10,000	$3,000	$10,000	$6,000	Initial contribution
<1,000>	<0>	<1,000>	<600>	G1 depreciation
<1,000>	<600>	<1,000>	<600>	H1 depreciation
500	500	500	500	Operating income
$8,500	$2,900	$8,500	$5,300	

Example (3). Unreasonable use of curative allocations. (i) Facts. J and K form partnership JK and agree that each will receive a 50 percent share of all partnership items and that JK will make allocations under section 704(c) using the traditional method with curative allocations under paragraph (c) of this section. J contributes equipment with an adjusted tax basis of $1,000 and a book value of $10,000, with a view to taking advantage of the fact that the equipment has only one year remaining on its cost recovery schedule although it has an estimated remaining economic life of 10 years. J has substantial net operating loss carryforwards that J anticipates will otherwise expire unused. At the time of contribution, J has a built-in gain of $9,000, and therefore, the equipment is section 704(c) property. K contributes $10,000 of cash, which JK uses to buy inventory for resale. In JK's first year, the revenues generated by the equipment exactly equal JK's operating expenses. Under § 1.704–1(b)(2)(iv)(g)(3), the partnership must allocate the $10,000 of book depreciation to the partners in the first year of the partnership. Thus, there is $10,000 of book depreciation and $1,000 of tax depreciation in the partnership's first year. In addition, at the end of the first year JK sells all of the inventory for $18,000, recognizing $8,000 of income. The partners anticipate that the inventory income will have substantially the same effect on their tax liabilities as income from J's contributed equipment. Under the traditional method of paragraph (b) of this section, J and K's book and tax capital accounts at the end of the first year would be as follows:

J		K		
Book	Tax	Book	Tax	
$10,000	$1,000	$10,000	$10,000	Initial contribution
<5,000>	<0>	<5,000>	<1,000>	Depreciation
4,000	4,000	4,000	4,000	Sales income
$9,000	$5,000	$9,000	$13,000	

(ii) Unreasonable use of method. (A) The use of curative allocations under these facts to offset immediately the full effect of the ceiling rule would result in the following book and tax capital accounts at the end of JK's first year:

J		K		
Book	Tax	Book	Tax	
$10,000	$1,000	$10,000	$10,000	Initial contribution
<5,000>	<0>	<5,000>	<1,000>	Depreciation
4,000	8,000	4,000	0	Sales income
$9,000	$9,000	$9,000	$9,000	

(B) This curative allocation is not reasonable under paragraph (a)(10) of this section because the contribution of property is made and the curative allocation method is used with a view to shifting a significant amount of partnership taxable income to a partner with a low marginal tax rate and away from a partner with a high marginal tax rate, within a period of time significantly shorter than the economic life of the property.

(C) The property has only one year remaining on its cost recovery schedule even though its economic life is considerably longer. Under these facts, if the partnership agreement had provided for curative allocations over a reasonable period of time, such as over the property's economic life, rather than over its remaining cost recovery period, the allocations would have been reasonable. See paragraph (c)(3)(ii) of this section. Thus, in this example, JK would make a curative allocation of $400 of sales income to J in the partnership's first year (10 percent of $4,000). J and K's book and tax capital accounts at the end of the first year would be as follows:

	J		K		
	Book	Tax	Book	Tax	
	$10,000	$1,000	$10,000	$10,000	Initial contribution
	<5,000>	<0>	<5,000>	<1,000>	Depreciation
	4,000	4,400	4,000	3,600	Sales income
	$9,000	$5,400	$9,000	$12,600	

(d) Remedial allocation method.

(1) In general. A partnership may adopt the remedial allocation method described in this paragraph to eliminate distortions caused by the ceiling rule. A partnership adopting the remedial allocation method eliminates those distortions by creating remedial items and allocating those items to its partners. Under the remedial allocation method, the partnership first determines the amount of book items under paragraph (d)(2) of this section and the partners' distributive shares of these items under section 704(b). The partnership then allocates the corresponding tax items recognized by the partnership, if any, using the traditional method described in paragraph (b)(1) of this section. If the ceiling rule (as defined in paragraph (b)(1) of this section) causes the book allocation of an item to a noncontributing partner to differ from the tax allocation of the same item to the noncontributing partner, the partnership creates a remedial item of income, gain, loss, or deduction equal to the full amount of the difference and allocates it to the noncontributing partner. The partnership simultaneously creates an offsetting remedial item in an identical amount and allocates it to the contributing partner.

(2) Determining the amount of book items. Under the remedial allocation method, a partnership determines the amount of book items attributable to contributed property in the following manner rather than under the rules of § 1.704–1(b)(2)(iv)(g)(3). The portion of the partnership's book basis in the property equal to the adjusted tax basis in the property at the time of contribution is recovered in the same manner as the adjusted tax basis in the property is recovered (generally, over the prop-

erty's remaining recovery period under section 168(i)(7) or other applicable Internal Revenue Code section). The remainder of the partnership's book basis in the property (the amount by which book basis exceeds adjusted tax basis) is recovered using any recovery period and depreciation (or other cost recovery) method (including first-year conventions) available to the partnership for newly purchased property (of the same type as the contributed property) that is placed in service at the time of contribution.

(3) Type. Remedial allocations of income, gain, loss, or deduction to the noncontributing partner have the same tax attributes as the tax item limited by the ceiling rule. The tax attributes of offsetting remedial allocations of income, gain, loss, or deduction to the contributing partner are determined by reference to the item limited by the ceiling rule. Thus, for example, if the ceiling rule limited item is loss from the sale of contributed property, the offsetting remedial allocation to the contributing partner must be gain from the sale of that property. Conversely, if the ceiling rule limited item is gain from the sale of contributed property, the offsetting remedial allocation to the contributing partner must be loss from the sale of that property. If the ceiling rule limited item is depreciation or other cost recovery from the contributed property, the offsetting remedial allocation to the contributing partner must be income of the type produced (directly or indirectly) by that property. Any partner level tax attributes are determined at the partner level. For example, if the ceiling rule limited item is depreciation from property used in a rental activity, the remedial allocation to the noncontributing partner is depreciation from property used in a rental activity and the offsetting remedial allocation to the contributing partner is ordinary income from that rental activity. Each partner then applies section 469 to the allocations as appropriate.

(4) Effect of remedial items.

(i) Effect on partnership. Remedial items do not affect the partnership's computation of its taxable income under section 703 and do not affect the partnership's adjusted tax basis in partnership property.

(ii) Effect on partners. Remedial items are notional tax items created by the partnership solely for tax purposes and do not affect the partners' book capital accounts. Remedial items have the same effect as actual tax items on a partner's tax liability and on the partner's adjusted tax basis in the partnership interest.

(5) Limitations on use of methods involving remedial allocations.

(i) Limitation on taxpayers. In the absence of published guidance, the remedial allocation method described in this paragraph (d) is the only reasonable section 704(c) method permitting the creation of notional tax items.

(ii) Limitation on internal revenue service. In exercising its authority under paragraph (a)(10) of this section to make adjustments if a partnership's allocation method is not reasonable, the Internal Revenue Service will not require a partnership to use the remedial allocation method described in this paragraph (d) or any other method involving the creation of notional tax items.

(6) Adjustments to application of method. The Commissioner may, by published guidance, prescribe adjustments to the remedial allocation method under this paragraph (d) as necessary or appropriate. This guidance may, for example, prescribe adjustments to the remedial allocation method to prevent the duplication or omission of items of income or deduction or to reflect more clearly the partners' income or the income of a transferee of a partner.

(7) Examples. The following examples illustrate the principles of this paragraph (d).

Example (1). Remedial allocation method. (i) Facts. On January 1, L and M form partnership LM and agree that each will be allocated a 50 percent share of all partnership items. The partnership agreement provides that LM will make allocations under section 704(c) using the remedial allocation method under this paragraph (d) and that the straight-line method will be used to recover excess book basis. L contributes depreciable property with an adjusted tax basis of $4,000 and a fair market value of $10,000. The property is depreciated using the straightline method with a 10-year recovery period and has 4 years remaining on its recovery period. M contributes $10,000, which the partnership uses to purchase land. Except for the depreciation deductions, LM's expenses equal its income in each year of the 10 years commencing with the year the partnership is formed.

(ii) Years 1 through 4. Under the remedial allocation method of this paragraph (d), LM has book depreciation for each of its first 4 years of $1,600 [$1,000 ($4,000 adjusted tax basis divided by the 4-year remaining recovery period) plus $600 ($6,000 excess of book value over tax basis, divided by the NEW 10-year recovery period)]. (For the purpose of simplifying the example, the partnership's book depreciation is determined without regard to any first-year depreciation conventions.) Under the partnership agreement, L and M are each allocated 50 percent ($800) of the book depreciation. M is allocated $800 of tax depreciation and L is allocated the remaining $200 of tax depreciation ($1,000 – $800). See paragraph (d)(1) of this section. No remedial allocations are made because the ceiling rule does not result in a book allocation of depreciation to M different from the tax allocation. The allocations result in capital accounts at the end of LM's first 4 years as follows:

L		M		
Book	Tax	Book	Tax	
$10,000	$4,000	$10,000	$10,000	Initial contribution
<3,200>	<800>	<3,200>	<3,200>	Depreciation
$6,800	$3,200	$6,800	$6,800	

(iii) Subsequent years. (A) For each of years 5 through 10, LM has $600 of book depreciation ($6,000 excess of initial book value over adjusted tax basis divided by the 10-year recovery period that commenced in year 1), but no tax depreciation. Under the partnership agreement, the $600 of book depreciation is allocated equally to L and M. Because of the application of the ceiling rule in year 5, M would be allocated $300 of book depreciation, but no tax depreciation. Thus, at the end of LM's fifth year L's and M's book and tax capital accounts would be as follows:

L		M		
Book	Tax	Book	Tax	
$6,800	$3,200	$6,800	$6,800	End of year 4
<300>		<300>		Depreciation
$6,500	$3,200	$6,500	$6,800	

(B) Because the ceiling rule would cause an annual disparity of $300 between M's allocations of book and tax depreciation, LM must make remedial allocations of $300 of tax depreciation deductions to M under the remedial allocation method for each of years 5 through 10. LM must also make an offsetting remedial allocation to L of $300 of taxable income, which must be of the same type as income produced by the property. At the end of year 5, LM's capital accounts are as follows:

L		M		
Book	Tax	Book	Tax	
$6,800	$3,200	$6,800	$6,800	End of year 4
<300>		<300>		Depreciation
	300		<300>	Remedial allocations
$6,500	$3,500	$6,500	$6,500	

(C) At the end of year 10, LM's capital accounts are as follows:

L		M		
Book	Tax	Book	Tax	
$6,500	$3,500	$6,500	$6,500	End of year 5
<1,500>		<1,500>		Depreciation
	1,500		<1,500>	Remedial allocations
$5,000	$5,000	$5,000	$5,000	

Example (2). Remedial allocations on sale.
(i) Facts. N and P form partnership NP and agree that each will be allocated a 50 percent share of all partnership items. The partnership

agreement provides that NP will make allocations under section 704(c) using the remedial allocation method under this paragraph (d). N contributes Blackacre (land) with an adjusted tax basis of $4,000 and a fair market value of $10,000. Because N has a built-in gain of $6,000, Blackacre is section 704(c) property. P contributes Whiteacre (land) with an adjusted tax basis and fair market value of $10,000. At the end of NP's first year, NP sells Blackacre to Q for $9,000 and recognizes a capital gain

of $5,000 ($9,000 amount realized less $4,000 adjusted tax basis) and a book loss of $1,000 ($9,000 amount realized less $10,000 book basis). NP has no other items of income, gain, loss, or deduction. If the ceiling rule were applied, N would be allocated the entire $5,000 of tax gain and N and P would each be allocated $500 of book loss. Thus, at the end of NP's first year N's and P's book and tax capital accounts would be as follows:

N		P		
Book	Tax	Book	Tax	
$10,000	$4,000	$10,000	$10,000	Initial contribution
<500>	5,000	<500>		Sale of Blackacre
$9,500	$9,000	$9,500	$10,000	

(ii) Remedial allocation. Because the ceiling rule would cause a disparity of $500 between P's allocation of book and tax loss, NP must make a remedial allocation of $500

of capital loss to P and an offsetting remedial allocation to N of an additional $500 of capital gain. These allocations result in capital accounts at the end of NP's first year as follows:

N		P		
Book	Tax	Book	Tax	
$10,000	$4,000	$10,000	$10,000	Initial contribution
<500>	5,000	<500>		Sale of Blackacre
	500		<500>	Remedial allocations
$9,500	$9,500	$9,500	$ 9,500	

Example (3). Remedial allocation where built-in gain property sold for book and tax loss. (i) Facts. The facts are the same as in Example 2, except that at the end of NP's first year, NP sells Blackacre to Q for $3,000 and recognizes a capital loss of $1,000 ($3,000 amount realized less $4,000 adjusted tax ba-

sis) and a book loss of $7,000 ($3,000 amount realized less $10,000 book basis). If the ceiling rule were applied, P would be allocated the entire $1,000 of tax loss and N and P would each be allocated $3,500 of book loss. Thus, at the end of NP's first year, N's and P's book and tax capital accounts would be as follows:

N		P		
Book	Tax	Book	Tax	
$10,000	$4,000	$10,000	$10,000	Initial contribution
<3,500>	0	<3,500>	<1,000>	Sale of Blackacre
$6,500	$4,000	$6,500	$9,000	

(ii) Remedial allocation. Because the ceiling rule would cause a disparity of $2,500 between P's allocation of book and tax loss on

the sale of Blackacre, NP must make a remedial allocation of $2,500 of capital loss to P and an offsetting remedial allocation to N of

$2,500 of capital gain. These allocations result in capital accounts at the end of NP's first year as follows:

	N		P		
	Book	Tax	Book	Tax	
	$10,000	$4,000	$10,000	$10,000	Initial contribution
	<3,500>	0	<3,500>	<1,000>	Sale of Blackacre
		2,500		<2,500>	Remedial allocations
	$6,500	$6,500	$6,500	$6,500	

(e) Exceptions and special rules.

(1) Small disparities.

(i) General rule. If a partner contributes one or more items of property to a partnership within a single taxable year of the partnership, and the disparity between the book value of the property and the contributing partner's adjusted tax basis in the property is a small disparity, the partnership may—

(A) Use a reasonable section 704(c) method;

(B) Disregard the application of section 704(c) to the property; or

(C) Defer the application of section 704(c) to the property until the disposition of the property.

(ii) Definition of small disparity. A disparity between book value and adjusted tax basis is a small disparity if the book value of all properties contributed by one partner during the partnership taxable year does not differ from the adjusted tax basis by more than 15 percent of the adjusted tax basis, and the total gross disparity does not exceed $20,000.

(2) Aggregation. Each of the following types of property may be aggregated for purposes of making allocations under section 704(c) and this section if contributed by one partner during the partnership taxable year.

(i) Depreciable property. All property, other than real property, that is included in the same general asset account of the contributing partner and the partnership under section 168.

(ii) Zero-basis property. All property with a basis equal to zero, other than real property.

(iii) Inventory. For partnerships that do not use a specific identification method of accounting, each item of inventory, other than qualified financial assets (as defined in paragraph (e)(3)(ii) of this section.).

(3) Special aggregation rule for securities partnerships.

(i) General rule. For purposes of making reverse section 704(c) allocations, a securities partnership may aggregate gains and losses from qualified financial assets using any reasonable approach that is consistent with the purpose of section 704(c). Notwithstanding paragraphs (a)(2) and (a)(6)(i) of this section, once a partnership adopts an aggregate approach, that partnership must apply the same aggregate approach to all of its qualified financial assets for all taxable years in which the partnership qualifies as a securities partnership. Paragraphs (e)(3)(iv) and (e)(3)(v) of this section describe approaches for aggregating reverse section 704(c) gains and losses that are generally reasonable. Other approaches may be reasonable in appropriate circumstances. See, however, paragraph (a)(10) of this section, which describes the circumstances under which section 704(c) methods, including the aggregate approaches described in this paragraph (e)(3), are not reasonable. A partnership using an aggregate approach must separately account for any built-in gain or loss from contributed property.

(ii) Qualified financial assets.

(A) In general. A qualified financial asset is any personal property (including stock) that is actively traded. Actively traded means actively traded as defined in § 1.1092(d)–1 (defining actively traded property for purposes of the straddle rules).

(B) Management companies. For a management company, qualified financial assets also include the following, even if not actively traded: shares of stock in a corporation; notes, bonds, debentures, or other evidences of indebtedness; interest rate, currency, or equity notional principal contracts; evidences of an interest in, or derivative financial instruments in, any security, currency, or commodity, including any option, forward or futures contract, or short position; or any similar financial instrument.

(C) Partnership interests. An interest in a partnership is not a qualified financial asset for purposes of this paragraph (e)(3)(ii). However, for purposes of this paragraph (e)(3), a partnership (upper-tier partnership) that holds an interest in a securities partnership (lower-tier partnership) must take into account the lower-tier partnership's assets and qualified financial assets as follows:

(1) In determining whether the upper-tier partnership qualifies as an investment partnership, the upper-tier partnership must treat its proportionate share of the lower-tier securities partnership's assets as assets of the upper-tier partnership; and

(2) If the upper-tier partnership adopts an aggregate approach under this paragraph (e)(3), the upper-tier partnership must aggregate the gains and losses from its directly held qualified financial assets with its distributive share of the gains and losses from the qualified financial assets of the lower-tier securities partnership.

(iii) Securities partnership.

(A) In general. A partnership is a securities partnership if the partnership is either a management company or an investment partnership, and the partnership makes all of its book allocations in proportion to the partners' relative book capital accounts (except for reasonable special allocations to a partner that provides management services or investment advisory services to the partnership).

(B) Definitions.

(1) Management company. A partnership is a management company if it is registered with the Securities and Exchange Commission as a management company under the Investment Company Act of 1940, as amended (15 U.S.C. 80a).

(2) Investment partnership. A partnership is an investment partnership if:

(i) On the date of each capital account restatement, the partnership holds qualified financial assets that constitute at least 90 percent of the fair market value of the partnership's non-cash assets; and

(ii) The partnership reasonably expects, as of the end of the first taxable year in which the partnership adopts an aggregate approach under this paragraph (e)(3), to make revaluations at least annually.

(iv) Partial netting approach.

This paragraph (e)(3)(iv) describes the partial netting approach of making reverse section 704(c) allocations. See Example 1 of paragraph (e)(3)(ix) of this section for an illustration of the partial netting approach. To use the partial netting approach, the partnership must establish appropriate accounts for each partner for the purpose of taking into account each partner's share of the book gains and losses and determining each partner's share of the tax gains and losses. Under the partial netting approach, on the date of each capital account restatement, the partnership:

(A) Nets its book gains and book losses from qualified financial assets since the last capital account restatement and allocates the net amount to its partners;

(B) Separately aggregates all tax gains and all tax losses from qualified financial assets since the last capital account restatement; and

(C) Separately allocates the aggregate tax gain and aggregate tax loss to the partners in a manner that reduces the disparity between the book capital account balances and the tax capital account balances (book-tax disparities) of the individual partners.

(v) Full netting approach. This paragraph (e)(3)(v) describes the full netting approach of making reverse section 704(c) allocations on an aggregate basis. See Example 2 of paragraph (e)(3)(ix) of this section for an illustration of the full netting approach. To use the full netting approach, the partnership must establish appropriate accounts for each partner for the purpose of taking into account each partner's share of the book gains and losses and determining each partner's share of the tax gains and losses. Under the full netting approach, on the date of each capital account restatement, the partnership:

(A) Nets its book gains and book losses from qualified financial assets since the last capital account restatement and allocates the net amount to its partners;

(B) Nets tax gains and tax losses from qualified financial assets since the last capital account restatement; and

(C) Allocates the net tax gain (or net tax loss) to the partners in a manner that reduces the book-tax disparities of the individual partners.

(vi) Type of tax gain or loss. The character and other tax attributes of gain or loss allocated to the partners under this paragraph (e)(3) must:

(A) Preserve the tax attributes of each item of gain or loss realized by the partnership;

(B) Be determined under an approach that is consistently applied; and

(C) Not be determined with a view to reducing substantially the present value of the partners' aggregate tax liability.

(vii) Disqualified securities partnerships. A securities partnership that adopts an aggregate approach under this paragraph (e)(3) and subsequently fails to qualify as a securities partnership must make reverse section 704(c) allocations on an asset-by-asset basis after the date of disqualification. The partnership, however, is not required to disaggregate the book gain or book loss from qualified asset revaluations before the date of disqualification when making reverse section 704(c) allocations on or after the date of disqualification.

(viii) Transitional rule for qualified financial assets revalued after effective date. A securities partnership revaluing its qualified financial assets pursuant to § 1.704–1(b)(2)(iv)(f) on or after the effective date of this section may use any reasonable approach to coordinate with revaluations that occurred prior to the effective date of this section.

(ix) Examples. The following examples illustrate the principles of this paragraph (e)(3).

Example (1). Operation of the partial netting approach. (i) Facts. Two regulated investment companies, X and Y, each contribute $150,000 in cash to form PRS, a partnership that registers as a management company. The partnership agreement provides that book items will be allocated in accordance with the partners' relative book capital accounts, that book capital accounts will be adjusted to reflect daily revaluations of property pursuant to § 1.704–1(b)(2)(iv)(f)(5)(iii), and that reverse section 704(c) allocations will be made using the partial netting approach described in paragraph (e)(3)(iv) of this section. X and Y each have an initial book capital account of $150,000. In addition, the partnership establishes for each of X and Y a revaluation account with a beginning balance of $0. On Day 1, PRS buys Stock 1, Stock 2, and Stock 3 for $100,000 each. On Day 2, Stock 1 increases in value from $100,000 to $102,000, Stock 2 increases in value from \$100,000 to \$105,000, and Stock 3 declines in value from \$100,000 to \$98,000. At the end of Day 2, Z, a regulated investment company, joins PRS by contributing \$152,500 in cash for a one-third interest in the partnership [\$152,500 divided by \$300,000 (initial values of stock) \$5,000 (net gain at end of Day 2) \$152,500]. PRS uses this cash to purchase Stock 4. PRS establishes a revaluation account for Z with a \$0 beginning balance. As of the close of Day 3, Stock 1 increases in value from \$102,000 to \$105,000, and Stocks 2, 3, and 4 decrease in value from \$105,000 to \$102,000, from \$98,000 to \$96,000, and from \$152,500 to \$151,500, respectively. At the end of Day 3, PRS sells Stocks 2 and 3.

(ii) Book allocations. Day 2. At the end of Day 2, PRS revalues the partnership's qualified financial assets and increases X's and Y's book capital accounts by each partner's 50 percent share of the \$5,000 (\$2,000 \$5,000 – \$2,000) net increase in the value of the partnership's assets during Day 2. PRS increases X's and Y's respective revaluation account balances by \$2,500 each to reflect the amount by which each partner's book capital account increased on Day 2. Z's capital account is not affected because Z did not join PRS until the end of Day 2. At the beginning of Day 3, the partnership's accounts are as follows:

	Stock 1	Stock 2	Stock 3	Stock 4
Opening Balance	\$100,000	\$100,000	\$100,000	—
Day 2 Adjustment	2,000	5,000	(2,000)	—
Total	\$102,000	\$105,000	\$98,000	\$152,500

	X		
	Book	Tax	Revaluation Account
Opening Balance	\$150,000	\$150,000	\$0
Day 2 Adjustment	2,500	0	2,500
Closing Balance	\$152,500	\$150,000	\$2,500

	Y		
	Book	Tax	Revaluation Account
Opening Balance	\$150,000	\$150,000	\$0
Day 2 Adjustment	2,500	0	2,500
Closing Balance	\$152,500	\$150,000	\$2,500

	Z		
	Book	Tax	Revaluation Account
Opening Balance	—	—	—
Day 2 Adjustment	—	—	—
Closing Balance	\$152,500	\$152,500	\$0

(iii) Book and tax allocations. Day 3. At the end of Day 3, PRS decreases the book capital accounts of X, Y, and Z by \$1,000 to reflect each partner's share of the \$3,000 (\$3,000 – \$3,000 – \$2,000 – \$1,000) net decrease in the value of the partnership's qualified financial assets. PRS also reduces each partner's revaluation account balance by \$1,000. Accordingly, X's and Y's revaluation account balances are reduced to \$1,500 each and Z's revaluation account balance is (\$1,000). PRS then separately allocates the tax gain from the sale of Stock 2 and the tax loss from the sale of Stock 3. The \$2,000 of tax gain recognized on the sale of Stock 2 (\$102,000 – \$100,000) is allocated among the partners with positive revaluation

account balances in accordance with the relative balances of those revaluation accounts. X's and Y's revaluation accounts have equal positive balances; thus, PRS allocates $1,000 of the gain from the sale of Stock 2 to X and $1,000 of that gain to Y. PRS allocates none of the gain from the sale to Z because Z's revaluation account balance is negative. The $4,000 of tax loss recognized from the sale of Stock 3 ($96,000 – $100,000) is allocated first to the partners with negative revaluation account balances to the extent of those balances. Because Z is the only partner with a negative revaluation account balance, the tax loss is allocated first to Z to the extent of Z's ($1,000) balance.

The remaining $3,000 of tax loss is allocated among the partners in accordance with their distributive shares of the loss. Accordingly, PRS allocates $1,000 of tax loss from the sale of Stock 3 to each of X and Y. PRS also allocates an additional $1,000 of the tax loss to Z, so that Z's total share of the tax loss from the sale of Stock 3 is $2,000. PRS then reduces each partner's revaluation account balance by the amount of any tax gain allocated to that partner and increases each partner's revaluation account balance by the amount of any tax loss allocated to that partner. At the beginning of Day 4, the partnership's accounts are as follows:

	Stock 1	Stock 2	Stock 3	Stock 4
Opening Balance	$100,000	$100,000	$100,000	$152,500
Day 2 Adjustment	2,000	5,000	(2,000)	—
Day 3 Adjustment	3,000	(3,000)	(2,000)	(1,000)
Total	$105,000	$102,000	$96,000	$151,500

	X and Y		
	Book	Tax	Revaluation Account
Opening Balance	$150,000	$150,000	$0
Day 2 Adjustment	2,500	0	2,500
Day 3 Adjustment	(1,000)	0	(1,000)
Total	$151,500	$150,000	$1,500
Gain from Stock 2	0	1,000	(1,000)
Loss from Stock 3	0	(1,000)	1,000
Closing Balance	$151,500	$150,000	$1,500

	Z		
	Book	Tax	Revaluation Account
Opening Balance	$152,500	$152,500	$0
Day 3 Adjustment	(1,000)	0	(1,000)
Total	$151,500	$152,500	($1,000)
Gain from Stock 2	0	0	0
Loss from Stock 3	0	(2,000)	2,000
Closing Balance	$151,500	$150,500	$1,000

Example (2). Operation of the full netting approach. (i) Facts. The facts are the same as in Example 1, except that the partnership agreement provides that PRS will make reverse section 704(c) allocations using the full netting approach described in paragraph (e)(3) (v) of this section.

(ii) Book allocations. Days 2 and 3. PRS allocates its book gains and losses in the manner described in paragraphs (ii) and (iii) of Ex-

ample 1 (the partial netting approach). Thus, at the end of Day 2, PRS increases the book capital accounts of X and Y by $2,500 to reflect the appreciation in the partnership's assets from the close of Day 1 to the close of Day 2 and records that increase in the revaluation account created for each partner. At the end of Day 3, PRS decreases the book capital accounts of X, Y, and Z by $1,000 to reflect each partner's share of the decline in value of the partnership's assets from Day 2 to Day 3 and reduces each partner's revaluation account by a corresponding amount.

(iii) Tax allocations. Day 3. After making the book adjustments described in the previous paragraph, PRS allocates its net tax gain (or net tax loss) from its sales of qualified financial assets during Day 3. To do so, PRS first determines its net tax gain (or net tax loss)

recognized from its sales of qualified financial assets for the day. There is a $2,000 net tax loss ($2,000 gain from the sale of Stock 2 less $4,000 loss from the sale of Stock 3) on the sale of PRS's qualified financial assets. Because Z is the only partner with a negative revaluation account balance, the partnership's net tax loss is allocated first to Z to the extent of Z's ($1,000) revaluation account balance. The remaining net tax loss is allocated among the partners in accordance with their distributive shares of loss. Thus, PRS allocates $333.33 of the $2,000 net tax loss to each of X and Y. PRS also allocates an additional $333.33 of the net tax loss to Z, so that the total net tax loss allocation to Z is $1,333.33. PRS then increases each partner's revaluation account balance by the amount of net tax loss allocated to that partner. At the beginning of Day 4, the partnership's accounts are as follows:

	Stock 1	Stock 2	Stock 3	Stock 4
Opening Balance	$100,000	$100,000	$100,000	$152,500
Day 2 Adjustment	2,000	5,000	(2,000)	—
Day 3 Adjustment	3,000	(3,000)	(2,000)	(1,000)
Total	$105,000	$102,000	$96,000	$151,500

X and Y			
	Book	Tax	Revaluation Account
Opening Balance	$150,000	$150,000	$0
Day 2 Adjustment	2,500	0	2,500
Day 3 Adjustment	(1,000)	0	(1,000)
Total	$151,500	$150,000	$1,500
Net Tax Loss—Stocks 2&3	0	(333)	333
Closing Balance	$151,500	$149,667	$1,833

Z			
	Book	Tax	Revaluation Account
Opening Balance	$152,500	$152,500	$0
Day 3 Adjustment	(1,000)	0	(1,000)
Total	$151,500	$152,500	($1,000)
Net Tax Loss—Stocks 2&3	0	(1,333)	1,333
Closing Balance	$151,500	$151,167	$333

(4) Aggregation as permitted by the commissioner. The Commissioner may, by published guidance or by letter ruling, permit:

(i) Aggregation of properties other than those described in paragraphs (e)(2) and (e)(3) of this section;

(ii) Partnerships and partners not described in paragraph (e)(3) of this section to aggregate gain and loss from qualified financial assets; and

(iii) Aggregation of qualified financial assets for purposes of making section 704(c) allocations in the same manner as that described in paragraph (e)(3) of this section.

(f) Effective/applicability dates. With the exception of paragraphs (a)(1), (a)(8)(ii), (a)(8)(iii), (a)(10), and (a)(11) of this section, this section applies to properties contributed to a partnership and to restatements pursuant to § 1.704–1(b)(2)(iv)(f) on or after December 21, 1993. Paragraph (a)(11) of this section applies to properties contributed by a partner to a partnership on or after August 20, 1997. However, partnerships may rely on paragraph (a)(11) of this section for properties contributed before August 20, 1997, and disposed of on or after August 20, 1997. Except as otherwise provided in § 1.752–7(k), paragraphs (a)(8)(iv) and (a)(12) apply to § 1.752–7 liability transfers, as defined in § 1.752–7(b)(4), occurring on or after June 24, 2003. See § 1.752–7(k). Paragraphs (a)(1) and (a)(10) of this section are applicable for taxable years beginning after June 9, 2010.

§ 1.704–4 Distribution of contributed property.

[Caution: The Treasury has not yet amended Reg 1.704–4 to reflect changes made by P.L. 105–34]

(a) Determination of gain and loss.

(1) In general. A partner that contributes section 704(c) property to a partnership must recognize gain or loss under section 704(c)(1)(B) and this section on the distribution of such property to another partner within five years of its contribution to the partnership in an amount equal to the gain or loss that would have been allocated to such partner under section 704(c)(1)(A) and § 1.704–3 if the distributed property had been sold by the partnership to the distributee partner for its fair market value at the time of the distribution. See § 1.704–3(a)(3)(i) for a definition of section 704(c) property.

(2) Transactions to which section 704(c)(1)(B) applies. Section 704(c)(1)(B) and this section apply only to the extent that a distribution by a partnership is a distribution to a partner acting in the capacity of a partner within the meaning of section 731.

(3) Fair market value of property. The fair market value of the distributed section 704(c) property is the price at which the property would change hands between a willing buyer and a willing seller at the time of the distribution, neither being under any compulsion to buy or sell and both having reasonable knowledge of the relevant facts. The fair market value that a partnership assigns to distributed section 704(c) property will be regarded as correct, provided that the value is reasonably agreed to among the partners in an arm's-length negotiation and the partners have sufficiently adverse interests.

(4) Determination of five-year period.

(i) General rule. The five-year period specified in paragraph (a)(1) of this section begins on and includes the date of contribution.

(ii) Section 708(b)(1)(B) terminations. A termination of the partnership under section 708(b)(1)(B) does not begin a new five-year period for each partner with respect to the built-in gain and built-in loss property that the terminated partnership is deemed to contribute to the new partnership under § 1.708–1(b)(1)(iv). See § 1.704–3(a)(3)(ii) for the definitions of built-in gain and built-in loss on section 704(c) property. This paragraph (a)(4)(ii) applies to terminations of partnerships under section 708(b)(1)(B) occurring on or after May 9, 1997; however, this paragraph (a)(4)(ii) may be applied to terminations occurring on or after May 9, 1996, provided that the partnership and its partners apply this paragraph (a)(4)(ii) to the termination in a consistent manner.

(5) Examples. The following examples illustrate the rules of this paragraph (a). Unless otherwise specified, partnership income equals partnership expenses (other than depreciation deductions for contributed property) for each year of the partnership, the fair market value of partnership property does not change, all distributions by the partnership are subject to section 704(c)(1)(B), and all partners are unrelated.

Example (1). Recognition of gain. (i) On January 1, 1995, A, B, and C form partnership ABC as equal partners. A contributes $10,000 cash and Property A, nondepreciable real property with a fair market value of $10,000 and an adjusted tax basis of $4,000. Thus, there is a built-in gain of $6,000 on Property A at the time of contribution. B contributes $10,000 cash and Property B, nondepreciable real property with a fair market value and adjusted tax basis of $10,000. C contributes $20,000 cash.

(ii) On December 31, 1998, Property A and Property B are distributed to C in complete liquidation of C's interest in the partnership.

(iii) A would have recognized $6,000 of gain under section 704(c)(1)(A) and § 1.704–3 on the sale of Property A at the time of the distribution ($10,000 fair market value less $4,000 adjusted tax basis). As a result, A must recognize $6,000 of gain on the distribution of Property A to C. B would not have recognized any gain or loss under section 704(c)(1)(A) and § 1.704–3 on the sale of Property B at the time of distribution because Property B was not section 704(c) property. As a result, B does not recognize any gain or loss on the distribution of Property B.

Example (2). Effect of post-contribution depreciation deductions. (i) On January 1, 1995, A, B, and C form partnership ABC as equal partners. A contributes Property A, depreciable property with a fair market value of $30,000 and an adjusted tax basis of $20,000. Therefore, there is a built-in gain of $10,000 on Property A. B and C each contribute $30,000

cash. ABC uses the traditional method of making section 704(c) allocations described in § 1.704–3(b) with respect to Property A.

(ii) Property A is depreciated using the straight-line method over its remaining 10-year recovery period. The partnership has book depreciation of $3,000 per year (10 percent of the $30,000 book basis), and each partner is allocated $1,000 of book depreciation per year (one-third of the total annual book depreciation of $3,000). The partnership has a tax depreciation deduction of $2,000 per year (10 percent of the $20,000 tax basis in Property A). This $2,000 tax depreciation deduction is allocated equally between B and C, the noncontributing partners with respect to Property A.

(iii) At the end of the third year, the book value of Property A is $21,000 ($30,000 initial book value less $9,000 aggregate book depreciation) and the adjusted tax basis is $14,000 ($20,000 initial tax basis less $6,000 aggregate tax depreciation). A's remaining section 704(c)(1)(A) built-in gain with respect to Property A is $7,000 ($21,000 book value less $14,000 adjusted tax basis).

(iv) On December 31, 1997, Property A is distributed to B in complete liquidation of B's interest in the partnership. If Property A had been sold for its fair market value at the time of the distribution, A would have recognized $7,000 of gain under section 704(c)(1)(A) and § 1.704–3(b). Therefore, A recognizes $7,000 of gain on the distribution of Property A to B.

Example (3). Effect of remedial method. (i) On January 1, 1995, A, B, and C form partnership ABC as equal partners. A contributes Property A1, nondepreciable real property with a fair market value of $10,000 and an adjusted tax basis of $5,000, and Property A2, nondepreciable real property with a fair market value and adjusted tax basis of $10,000. B and C each contribute $20,000 cash. ABC uses the remedial method of making section 704(c) allocations described in § 1.704–3(d) with respect to Property A1.

(ii) On December 31, 1998, when the fair market value of Property A1 has decreased to $7,000, Property A1 is distributed to C in a current distribution. If Property A1 had been sold by the partnership at the time of the distribution, ABC would have recognized the $2,000 of remaining built-in gain under section 704(c) (1)(A) on the sale (fair market value of $7,000 less $5,000 adjusted tax basis). All of this gain would have been allocated to A. ABC would also have recognized a book loss of $3,000 ($10,000 original book value less $7,000 current fair market value of the property). Book loss in the amount of $2,000 would have been allocated equally between B and C. Under the remedial method, $2,000 of tax loss would also have been allocated equally to B and C to match their share of the book loss. As a result, $2,000 of gain would also have been allocated to A as an offsetting remedial allocation. A would have recognized $4,000 of total gain under section 704(c)(1)(A) on the sale of Property A1 ($2,000 of section 704(c) recognized gain plus $2,000 remedial gain). Therefore, A recognizes $4,000 of gain on the distribution of Property A1 to C under this section.

(b) Character of gain or loss.

(1) General rule. Gain or loss recognized by the contributing partner under section 704(c)(1)(B) and this section has the same character as the gain or loss that would have resulted if the distributed property had been sold by the partnership to the distributee partner at the time of the distribution.

(2) Example. The following example illustrates the rule of this paragraph (b). Unless otherwise specified, partnership income equals partnership expenses (other than depreciation deductions for contributed property) for each year of the partnership, the fair market value of partnership property does not change, all distributions by the partnership are subject to section 704(c)(1)(B), and all partners are unrelated.

Example. Character of gain. (i) On January 1, 1995, A and B form partnership AB. A contributes $10,000 and Property A, nondepreciable real property with a fair market value of $10,000 and an adjusted tax basis of $4,000, in exchange for a 25 percent interest in partnership capital and profits. B contributes $60,000 cash for a 75 percent interest in partnership capital and profits.

(ii) On December 31, 1998, Property A is distributed to B in a current distribution. Property A is used in a trade or business of B.

(iii) A would have recognized $6,000 of gain under section 704(c)(1)(A) on a sale of Property A at the time of the distribution (the difference between the fair market value ($10,000) and the adjusted tax basis ($4,000) of the property at that time). Because Property A is not a capital asset in the hands of Partner B and B holds more than 50 percent of partnership capital and profits, the character of the gain on a sale of Property A to B would have been ordinary income under section 707(b)(2). Therefore, the character of the gain to A on the distribution of Property A to B is ordinary income.

(c) Exceptions.

(1) Property contributed on or before October 3, 1989. Section 704(c)(1)(B) and this section do not apply to property contributed to the partnership on or before October 3, 1989.

(2) Certain liquidations. Section 704(c) (1)(B) and this section do not apply to a distribution of an interest in section 704(c) property to a partner other than the contributing partner in a liquidation of the partnership if—

(i) The contributing partner receives an interest in the section 704(c) property contributed by that partner (and no other property); and

(ii) The built-in gain or loss in the interest distributed to the contributing partner, determined immediately after the distribution, is equal to or greater than the built-in gain or loss on the property that would have been allocated to the contributing partner under section 704(c)(1)(A) and § 1.704–3 on a sale of the contributed property to an unrelated party immediately before the distribution.

(3) Section 708(b)(1)(B) terminations. Section 704(c)(1)(B) and this section do not apply to the deemed distribution of interests in a new partnership caused by the termination of a partnership under section 708(b)(1)(B). A subsequent distribution of section 704(c) property by the new partnership to a partner of the new partnership is subject to section 704(c)(1)(B) to the same extent that a distribution by the terminated partnership would have been subject to section 704(c)(1)(B). See also § 1.737–2(a) for a similar rule in the context of section 737. This paragraph (c)(3) applies to terminations of partnerships under section 708(b)(1)(B) occurring on or after May 9, 1997; however, this paragraph (c)(3) may be applied to terminations occurring on or after May 9, 1996, provided that the partnership and its partners apply this paragraph (c)(3) to the termination in a consistent manner.

(4) Complete transfer to another partnership. Section 704(c)(1)(B) and this section do not apply to a transfer by a partnership (transferor partnership) of all of its assets and liabilities to a second partnership (transferee partnership) in an exchange described in section 721, followed by a distribution of the interest in the transferee partnership in liquidation of the transferor partnership as part of the same plan or arrangement. A subsequent distribution of section 704(c) property by the transferee partnership to a partner of the transferee partnership is subject to section 704(c)(1)(B) to the same extent that a distribution by the transferor partnership would have been subject to section 704(c)(1)(B). See § 1.737–2(b) for a similar rule in the context of section 737.

(5) Incorporation of a partnership. Section 704(c)(1)(B) and this section do not apply to an incorporation of a partnership by any method of incorporation (other than a method involving an actual distribution of partnership property to the partners followed by a contribution of that property to a corporation), pro-

vided that the partnership is liquidated as part of the incorporation transaction. See § 1.737–2(c) for a similar rule in the context of section 737.

(6) Undivided interests. Section 704(c)(1)(B) and this section do not apply to a distribution of an undivided interest in property to the extent that the undivided interest does not exceed the undivided interest, if any, contributed by the distributee partner in the same property. See § 1.737–2(d)(4) for the application of section 737 in a similar context. The portion of the undivided interest in property retained by the partnership after the distribution, if any, that is treated as contributed by the distributee partner, is reduced to the extent of the undivided interest distributed to the distributee partner.

(7) Example. The following example illustrates the rule of paragraph (c)(2) of this section. Unless otherwise specified, partnership income equals partnership expenses (other than depreciation deductions for contributed property) for each year of the partnership, the fair market value of partnership property does not change, all distributions by the partnership are subject to section 704(c)(1)(B), and all partners are unrelated.

Example. (i) On January 1, 1995, A and B form partnership AB, as equal partners. A contributes Property A, nondepreciable real property with a fair market value and adjusted tax basis of $20,000. B contributes Property B, nondepreciable real property with a fair market value of $20,000 and an adjusted tax basis of $10,000. Property B therefore has a built-in gain of $10,000 at the time of contribution.

(ii) On December 31, 1998, the partnership liquidates when the fair market value of Property A has not changed, but the fair market value of Property B has increased to $40,000.

(iii) In the liquidation, A receives Property A and a 25 percent interest in Property B. This interest in Property B has a fair market value of $10,000 to A, reflecting the fact that A was entitled to 50 percent of the $20,000 post-contribution appreciation in Property B. The partnership distributes to B a 75 percent interest in Property B with a fair market value of $30,000. B's basis in this portion of Property B is $10,000 under section 732(b). As a result, B has a built-in gain of $20,000 in this portion of Property B immediately after the distribution ($30,000 fair market value less $10,000 adjusted tax basis). This built-in gain is greater than the $10,000 of built-in gain in Property B at the time of contribution to the partnership. B therefore does not recognize any gain on the distribution of a portion of Property B to A under this section.

(d) Special rules—(1) Nonrecognition transactions, installment obligations, contributed contracts, and capitalized costs— (i) Nonrecognition transactions. Property received by the partnership in exchange for section 704(c) property in a nonrecognition transaction is treated as the section 704(c) property for purposes of section 704(c)(1)(B) and this section to the extent that the property received is treated as section 704(c) property under § 1.704–3(a)(8). See § 1.737–2(d)(3) for a similar rule in the context of section 737.

(ii) [Reserved].

(iii) [Reserved].

(iv) Capitalized costs. Property to which the cost of section 704(c) property is properly capitalized is treated as section 704(c) property for purposes of section 704(c)(1)(B) and this section to the extent that such property is treated as section 704(c) property under § 1.704–3(a)(8)(iv). See § 1.737–2(d)(3) for a similar rule in the context of section 737.

(2) Transfers of a partnership interest. The transferee of all or a portion of the partnership interest of a contributing partner is treated as the contributing partner for purposes of section 704(c)(1)(B) and this section to the extent of the share of built-in gain or loss allocated to the transferee partner. See § 1.704–3(a)(7).

(3) Distributions of like-kind property. If section 704(c) property is distributed to a partner other than the contributing partner and like-kind property (within the meaning of section 1031) is distributed to the contributing partner no later than the earlier of (i) 180 days following the date of the distribution to the non-contributing partner, or (ii) the due date (determined with regard to extensions) of the contributing partner's income tax return for the taxable year of the distribution to the noncontributing partner, the amount of gain or loss, if any, that the contributing partner would otherwise have recognized under section 704(c)(1) (B) and this section is reduced by the amount of built-in gain or loss in the distributed like-kind property in the hands of the contributing partner immediately after the distribution. The contributing partner's basis in the distributed like-kind property is determined as if the like-kind property were distributed in an unrelated distribution prior to the distribution of any other property distributed as part of the same distribution and is determined without regard to the increase in the contributing partner's adjusted tax basis in the partnership interest under section 704(c)(1)(B) and this section. See § 1.707–3 for provisions treating the distribution of the likekind property to the contributing partner as a disguised sale in certain situations.

(4) Example. The following example illustrates the rules of this paragraph (d). Unless otherwise specified, partnership income equals partnership expenses (other than depreciation deductions for contributed property) for each year of the partnership, the fair market value of partnership property does not change, all distributions by the partnership are subject to section 704(c)(1)(B), and all partners are unrelated.

Example. Distribution of like-kind property. (i) On January 1, 1995, A, B, and C form partnership ABC as equal partners. A contributes Property A, nondepreciable real property with a fair market value of $20,000 and an adjusted tax basis of $10,000. B and C each contribute $20,000 cash. The partnership subsequently buys Property X, nondepreciable real property of a like-kind to Property A with a fair market value and adjusted tax basis of $8,000. The fair market value of Property X subsequently increases to $10,000.

(ii) On December 31, 1998, Property A is distributed to B in a current distribution. At the same time, Property X is distributed to A in a current distribution. The distribution of Property X does not result in the contribution of Property A being properly characterized as a disguised sale to the partnership under § 1.707–3. A's basis in Property X is $8,000 under section 732(a)(1). A therefore has $2,000 of built-in gain in Property X ($10,000 fair market value less $8,000 adjusted tax basis).

(iii) A would generally recognize $10,000 of gain under section 704(c)(1)(B) on the distribution of Property A, the difference between the fair market value ($20,000) of the property and its adjusted tax basis ($10,000). This gain is reduced, however, by the amount of the built-in gain of Property X in the hands of A. As a result, A recognizes only $8,000 of gain on the distribution of Property A to B under section 704(c)(1)(B) and this section.

(e) Basis adjustments.

(1) Contributing partner's basis in the partnership interest. The basis of the con-tributing partner's interest in the partnership is increased by the amount of the gain, or decreased by the amount of the loss, recognized by the partner under section 704(c) (1)(B) and this section. This increase or decrease is taken into account in determining (i) the contributing partner's adjusted tax basis under section 732 for any property distributed to the partner in a distribution that is part of the same distribution as the distribution of the contributed property, other than like-kind property described in paragraph (d)(3) of this section (pertaining to the special rule for distributions of like-kind property), and (ii) the amount of the gain recognized by the contributing partner under section 731 or section 737,

if any, on a distribution of money or property to the contributing partner that is part of the same distribution as the distribution of contributed property. For a determination of basis in a distribution subject to section 737, see § 1.737–3(a).

(2) Partnership's basis in partnership property. The partnership's adjusted tax basis in the distributed section 704(c) property is increased or decreased immediately before the distribution by the amount of gain or loss recognized by the contributing partner under section 704(c)(1)(B) and this section. Any increase or decrease in basis is therefore taken into account in determining the distributee partner's adjusted tax basis in the distributed property under section 732. For a determination of basis in a distribution subject to section 737, see § 1.737–3(b).

(3) Section 754 adjustments. The basis adjustments to partnership property made pursuant to paragraph (e)(2) of this section are not elective and must be made regardless of whether the partnership has an election in effect under section 754. Any adjustments to the bases of partnership property (including the distributed section 704(c) property) under section 734(b) pursuant to a section 754 election must be made after (and must take into account) the adjustments to basis made under paragraph (e)(2) of this section. See § 1.737–3(c)(4) for a similar rule in the context of section 737.

(4) Example. The following example illustrates the rules of this paragraph (e). Unless otherwise specified, partnership income equals partnership expenses (other than depreciation deductions for contributed property) for each year of the partnership, the fair market value of partnership property does not change, all distributions by the partnership are subject to section 704(c)(1)(B), and all partners are unrelated.

Example. Basis adjustment. (i) On January 1, 1995, A, B, and C form partnership ABC as equal partners. A contributes $10,000 cash and

Property A, nondepreciable real property with a fair market value of $10,000 and an adjusted tax basis of $4,000. B and C each contribute $20,000 cash.

(ii) On December 31, 1998, Property A is distributed to B in a current distribution.

(iii) Under paragraph (a) of this section, A recognizes $6,000 of gain on the distribution of Property A because that is the amount of gain that would have been allocated to A under section 704(c)(1)(A) and § 1.704–3 on a sale of Property A for its fair market value at the time of the distribution (fair market value of Property A ($10,000) less its adjusted tax basis at the time of distribution ($4,000)). The adjusted tax basis of A's partnership interest is increased from $14,000 to $20,000 to reflect this gain. The partnership's adjusted tax basis in Property A is increased from $4,000 to $10,000 immediately prior to its distribution to B. B's adjusted tax basis in Property A is therefore $10,000 under section 732(a)(1).

(f) Anti-abuse rule.

(1) In general. The rules of section 704(c)(1)(B) and this section must be applied in a manner consistent with the purpose of section 704(c)(1)(B). Accordingly, if a principal purpose of a transaction is to achieve a tax result that is inconsistent with the purpose of section 704(c)(1)(B), the Commissioner can recast the transaction for federal tax purposes as appropriate to achieve tax results that are consistent with the purpose of section 704(c)(1)(B) and this section. Whether a tax result is inconsistent with the purpose of section 704(c)(1)(B) and this section must be determined based on all the facts and circumstances. See § 1.737–4 for an anti-abuse rule and examples in the context of section 737.

(2) Examples. The following examples illustrate the anti-abuse rule of this paragraph (f). The examples set forth below do not delineate the boundaries of either permissible or impermissible types of transactions. Further, the addition of any facts or circumstances that are not specifically set forth in an example (or the deletion of any facts or circumstances) may alter the outcome of the transaction described in the example. Unless otherwise specified, partnership income equals partnership expenses (other than depreciation deductions for contributed property) for each year of the partnership, the fair market value of partnership property does not change, all distributions by the partnership are subject to section 704(c)(1)(B), and all partners are unrelated.

Example (1). Distribution in substance made within five-year period; results inconsistent with the purpose of section 704(c)(1)(B). (i) On January 1, 1995, A, B, and C form partnership ABC as equal partners. A contributes Property A, nondepreciable real property with a fair market value of $10,000 and an adjusted tax basis of $1,000. B and C each contributes $10,000 cash.

(ii) On December 31, 1998, the partners desire to distribute Property A to B in complete liquidation of B's interest in the partnership. If Property A were distributed at that time, however, A would recognize $9,000 of gain under section 704(c)(1)(B), the difference between the $10,000 fair market value and the $1,000 adjusted tax basis of Property A, because Property A was contributed to the partnership less than five years before December 31, 1998. On becoming aware of this potential gain recognition, and with a principal purpose of avoiding such gain, the partners amend the partnership agreement on December 31, 1998, and take any other steps necessary to provide that substantially all of the economic risks and benefits of Property A are borne by B as of December 31, 1998, and that substantially all of the economic risks and benefits of all other partnership property are borne by A and C. The partnership holds Property A until January 5, 2000, at which time it is distributed to B in complete liquidation of B's interest in the partnership.

(iii) The actual distribution of Property A occurred more than five years after the contri-

bution of the property to the partnership. The steps taken by the partnership on December 31, 1998, however, are the functional equivalent of an actual distribution of Property A to B in complete liquidation of B's interest in the partnership as of that date. Section 704(c)(1)(B) requires recognition of gain when contributed section 704(c) property is in substance distributed to another partner within five years of its contribution to the partnership. Allowing a contributing partner to avoid section 704(c)(1)(B) through arrangements such as those in this Example 1 that have the effect of a distribution of property within five years of the date of its contribution to the partnership would effectively undermine the purpose of section 704(c)(1)(B) and this section. As a result, the steps taken by the partnership on December 31, 1998, are treated as causing a distribution of Property A to B for purposes of section 704(c)(1)(B) on that date, and A recognizes gain of $9,000 under section 704(c)(1)(B) and this section at that time.

(iv) Alternatively, if on becoming aware of the potential gain recognition to A on a distribution of Property A on December 31, 1998, the partners had instead agreed that B would continue as a partner with no changes to the partnership agreement or to B's economic interest in partnership operations, the distribution of Property A to B on January 5, 2000, would not have been inconsistent with the purpose of section 704(c)(1)(B) and this section. In that situation, Property A would not have been distributed until after the expiration of the five-year period specified in section 704(c)(1)(B) and this section. Deferring the distribution of Property A until the end of the five-year period for a principal purpose of avoiding the recognition of gain under section 704(c)(1)(B) and this section is not inconsistent with the purpose of section 704(c)(1)(B). Therefore, A would not have recognized gain on the distribution of Property A in that case.

Example (2). Suspension of five-year period in manner consistent with the purpose

of section 704(c)(1)(B). (i) A, B, and C form partnership ABC on January 1, 1995, to conduct bona fide business activities. A contributes Property A, nondepreciable real property with a fair market value of $10,000 and an adjusted tax basis of $1,000, in exchange for a 49.5 percent interest in partnership capital and profits. B contributes $10,000 in cash for a 49.5 percent interest in partnership capital and profits. C contributes cash for a 1 percent interest in partnership capital and profits. A and B are wholly owned subsidiaries of the same affiliated group and continue to control the management of Property A by virtue of their controlling interests in the partnership. The partnership is formed pursuant to a plan a principal purpose of which is to minimize the period of time that A would have to remain a partner with a potential acquiror of Property A.

(ii) On December 31, 1997, D is admitted as a partner to the partnership in exchange for $10,000 cash.

(iii) On January 5, 2000, Property A is distributed to D in complete liquidation of D's interest in the partnership.

(iv) The distribution of Property A to D occurred more than five years after the contribution of the property to the partnership. On these facts, however, a principal purpose of the transaction was to minimize the period of time that A would have to remain partners with a potential acquiror of Property A, and treating the five-year period of section 704(c)(1)(B) as running during a time when Property A was still effectively owned through the partnership by members of the contributing affiliated group of which A is a member is inconsistent with the purpose of section 704(c)(1)(B). Prior to the admission of D as a partner, the pooling of assets between A and B, on the one hand, and C, on the other hand, although sufficient to constitute ABC as a valid partnership for federal income tax purposes, is not a sufficient pooling of assets for purposes of running the five-year period with respect to the distribution of Property A to D. Allowing a contrib-

uting partner to avoid section 704(c)(1)(B) through arrangements such as those in this Example 2 would have the effect of substantially nullifying the five-year requirement of section 704(c)(1)(B) and this section and elevating the form of the transaction over its substance. As a result, with respect to the distribution of Property A to D, the five-year period of section 704(c)(1)(B) is tolled until the admission of D as a partner on December 31, 1997. Therefore, the distribution of Property A occurred before the end of the five-year period of section 704(c)(1)(B), and A recognizes gain of $9,000 under section 704(c)(1)(B) on the distribution.

(g) Effective date. This section applies to distributions by a partnership to a partner on or after January 9, 1995, except that paragraph (d)(1)(iv) applies to distributions by a partnership to a partner on or after June 24, 2003.

§ 1.705–1 Determination of basis of partner's interest.

(a) General rule. (1) Section 705 and this section provide rules for determining the adjusted basis of a partner's interest in a partnership. A partner is required to determine the adjusted basis of his interest in a partnership only when necessary for the determination of his tax liability or that of any other person. The determination of the adjusted basis of a partnership interest is ordinarily made as of the end of a partnership taxable year. Thus, for example, such year-end determination is necessary in ascertaining the extent to which a partner's distributive share of partnership losses may be allowed. See section 704(d). However, where there has been a sale or exchange of all or a part of a partnership interest or a liquidation of a partner's entire interest in a partnership, the adjusted basis of the partner's interest should be determined as of the date of sale or exchange or liquidation. The adjusted basis of a partner's interest in a partnership is determined without regard to any amount shown in the partnership books as the partner's "capital", "equity", or similar account. For example, A contributes property with an adjusted basis to him of $400 (and a value of $1,000) to a partnership. B contributes $1,000 cash. While under their agreement each may have a "capital account" in the partnership of $1,000, the adjusted basis of A's interest is only $400 and B's interest $1,000.

(2) The original basis of a partner's interest in a partnership shall be determined under section 722 (relating to contributions to a partnership) or section 742 (relating to transfers of partnership interests). Such basis shall be increased under section 722 by any further contributions to the partnership and by the sum of the partner's distributive share for the taxable year and prior taxable years of:

(i) Taxable income of the partnership as determined under section 703(a),

(ii) Tax-exempt receipts of the partnership, and

(iii) The excess of the deductions for depletion over the basis of the depletable property, unless the property is an oil or gas property the basis of which has been allocated to partners under section 613A(c)(7)(D).

(3) The basis shall be decreased (but not below zero) by distributions from the partnership as provided in section 733 and by the sum of the partner's distributive share for the taxable year and prior taxable years of:

(i) Partnership losses (including capital losses), and

(ii) Partnership expenditures which are not deductible in computing partnership taxable income or loss and which are not capital expenditures.

(4) The basis shall be decreased (but not below zero) by the amount of the partner's deduction for depletion allowable under section 611 for any partnership oil and gas property to the extent the deduction does not exceed the proportionate share of the adjusted basis of the property allocated to the partner under section 613A(c)(7)(D).

(5) The basis shall be adjusted (but not below zero) to reflect any gain or loss to the partner resulting from a disposition by the partnership of a domestic oil or gas property after December 31, 1974.

(6) For the effect of liabilities in determining the amount of contributions made by a partner to a partnership or the amount of distributions made by a partnership to a partner, see section 752 and § 1.752–1, relating to the treatment of certain liabilities. In determining the basis of a partnership interest on the effective date of Subchapter K, Chapter 1 of the Code, or any of the sections thereof, the partner's share of partnership liabilities on that date shall be included.

(7) For basis adjustments necessary to coordinate sections 705 and 1032 in certain situations in which a partnership disposes of stock of a corporation that holds a direct or indirect interest in the partnership, see § 1.705–2.

(8) For basis adjustments necessary to coordinate sections 705 and 358(h), see § 1.358–7(b). For certain basis adjustments with respect to a § 1.752–7 liability assumed by a partnership from a partner, see § 1.752–7.

(9) For basis adjustments necessary to coordinate sections 705 and 362(e)(2), see §1.362–4(e)(i).

(b) Alternative rule. In certain cases, the adjusted basis of a partner's interest in a partnership may be determined by reference to the partner's share of the adjusted basis of partnership property which would be distributable upon termination of the partnership. The alternative rule may be used to determine the adjusted basis of a partner's interest where circumstances are such that the partner cannot practicably apply the general rule set forth in section 705(a) and paragraph (a) of this section, or where, from a consideration of all the facts, it is, in the opinion of the Commissioner, reasonable to conclude that the result produced will not vary substantially from the result obtainable under the general rule. Where

the alternative rule is used, adjustments may be necessary in determining the adjusted basis of a partner's interest in a partnership. Adjustments would be required, for example, in order to reflect in a partner's share of the adjusted basis of partnership property any significant discrepancies arising as a result of contributed property, transfers of partnership interests, or distributions of property to the partners. The operation of the alternative rules may be illustrated by the following examples:

Example (1). The ABC partnership, in which A, B, and C are equal partners, owns various properties with a total adjusted basis of $1,500 and has earned and retained an additional $1,500. The total adjusted basis of partnership property is thus $3,000. Each partner's share in the adjusted basis of partnership property is one-third of this amount, or $1,000. Under the alternative rule, this amount represents each partner's adjusted basis for his partnership interest.

Example (2). Assume that partner A in example (1) of this paragraph sells his partnership interest to D for $1,250 at a time when the partnership property with an adjusted basis of $1,500 had appreciated in value to $3,000, and when the partnership also had $750 in cash. The total adjusted basis of all partnership property is $2,250 and the value of such property is $3,750. D's basis for his partnership interest is his cost, $1,250. However, his one-third share of the adjusted basis of partnership property is only $750. Therefore, for the purposes of the alternative rule, D has an adjustment of $500 in determining the basis of his interest. This amount represents the difference between the cost of his partnership interest and his share of partnership basis at the time of his purchase. If the partnership subsequently earns and retains an additional $1,500, its property will have an adjusted basis of $3,750. D's adjusted basis for his interest under the alternative rule is $1,750, determined by adding $500, his basis adjustment to $1,250 (his one-third share of the $3,750 adjusted basis of partnership property). If the partnership distributes $250 to each partner in a current distribution, D's adjusted basis for his interest will be $1,500 ($1,000, his one-third share of the remaining basis of partnership property, $3,000, plus his basis adjustment of $500).

Example (3). Assume that BCD partnership in example (2) of this paragraph continues to operate. In 1960, D proposes to sell his partnership interest and wishes to evaluate the tax consequences of such sale. It is necessary, therefore, to determine the adjusted basis of his interest in the partnership. Assume further that D cannot determine the adjusted basis of his interest under the general rule. The balance sheet of the BCD partnership is as follows:

Assets	Adjusted basis per books	Market value
Cash	$3,000	$3,000
Receivables	4,000	4,000
Depreciable property	5,000	5,000
Land held for investment	18,000	30,000
Total	30,000	42,000
Liabilities and capital		Per books
Liabilities		$6,000
Capital accounts:		
B		4,500
C		4,500
D		15,000
Total		30,000

The $15,000 representing the amount of D's capital account does not reflect the $500 basis adjustment arising from D's purchase of his interest. See example (2) of this paragraph. The adjusted basis of D's partnership interest determined under the alternative rule is as follows:

D's share of the adjusted basis of partnership property (reduced by the amount of liabilities) at time of proposed sale...................................... $15,000

D's share of partnership liabilities (under the partnership agreement liabilities are shared equally)... 2,000

D's basis adjustment from example (2) 500

Adjusted basis of D's interest at the time of proposed sale, as determined under alternative rule 17,500

§ 1.705–2. Basis adjustments coordinating sections 705 and 1032.

(a) Purpose. This section coordinates the application of sections 705 and 1032 and is intended to prevent inappropriate increases or decreases in the adjusted basis of a corporate partner's interest in a partnership resulting from the partnership's disposition of the corporate partner's stock. The rules under section 705 generally are intended to preserve equality between the adjusted basis of a partner's interest in a partnership (outside basis) and such partner's share of the adjusted basis in partnership assets (inside basis). However, in situations where a section 754 election was not in effect for the year in which a partner acquired its interest, the partner's inside basis and outside basis may not be equal. Similarly, in situations where a section 754 election was not in effect for the year in which a partnership distributes money or other property to another partner and that partner recognizes gain or loss on the distribution or the basis of the property distributed to that partner is adjusted, the remaining partners' inside basis and outside basis may not be equal. In these situations, gain or loss allocated to the partner upon disposition of the partnership assets that is attributable to the difference between the adjusted basis of the partnership assets absent the section 754 election and the adjusted basis of the partnership assets had a section 754 election been in effect generally will result in an adjustment to the basis of the partner's interest in the partnership under section 705(a). Such gain (or loss) therefore generally will be offset by a corresponding decrease in the gain or increase in the loss (or increase in the gain or decrease in the loss) upon the subsequent disposition by the partner of its interest in the partnership. Where such a difference exists with respect to stock of a corporate partner that is held by the partnership, gain or loss from the disposition of corporate partner stock attributable to the difference is not recognized by the corporate partner under section 1032. To adjust the basis of the corporate partner's interest in the partnership for this unrecognized gain or loss would not be appropriate because it would create an opportunity for the recognition of taxable gain or loss on a subsequent disposition of the partnership interest where no economic gain or loss has been incurred by the corporate partner and no corresponding taxable gain or loss had previously been allocated to the corporate partner by the partnership.

(b) Single partnership—(1) Required adjustments relating to acquisitions of partnership interest—(i) This paragraph (b)(1) applies in situations where a corporation acquires an interest in a partnership that holds stock in that corporation (or the partnership subsequently acquires stock in that corporation in an exchanged basis transaction), the partnership does not have an election under section 754 in effect for the year in which the corporation acquires the interest, and the partnership later sells or exchanges the stock. In these situations, the increase (or decrease) in the corporation's adjusted basis in its partnership interest resulting from the sale or exchange of the stock equals the amount of gain (or loss) that the corporate partner would have recognized (absent the application of section 1032) if, for the year in which the corporation acquired the interest, a section 754 election had been in effect.

(ii) The provisions of this paragraph (b)(1) are illustrated by the following example:

Example. (i) A, B, and C form equal partnership PRS. Each partner contributes $30,000 in exchange for its partnership interest. PRS has no liabilities. PRS purchases stock in corporation X for $30,000, which appreciates in value to $120,000. PRS also purchases inventory for $60,000, which appreciates in value to $150,000. A sells its interest in PRS to corporation X for $90,000 in a year for which an election under section 754 is not in effect. PRS later sells the X stock for $150,000. PRS realizes a gain of $120,000 on the sale of the X stock. X's share of the gain is $40,000. Under section 1032, X does not recognize its share of the gain.

(ii) Normally, X would be entitled to a $40,000 increase in the basis of its PRS interest for its allocable share of PRS's gain from the sale of the X stock, but a special rule applies in this situation. If a section 754 election had been in effect for the year in which X acquired its interest in PRS, X would have been entitled to a basis adjustment under section 743(b) of $60,000 (the excess of X's basis for the transferred partnership interest over X's share of the adjusted basis to PRS of PRS's property). See § 1.743–1(b). Under § 1.755–1(b), the basis adjustment under section 743(b) would have been allocated $30,000 to the X stock (the amount of the gain that would have been allocated to X from the hypothetical sale of the stock), and $30,000 to the inventory (the amount of the gain that would have been allocated to X from the hypothetical sale of the inventory).

(iii) If a section 754 election had been in effect for the year in which X acquired its interest in PRS, the amount of gain that X would have recognized upon PRS's disposition of X stock (absent the application of section 1032) would be $10,000 (X's share of PRS's gain from the stock sale, $40,000, minus the amount of X's basis adjustment under section 743(b), $30,000). See § 1.743–1(j). Accordingly, the increase in the basis of X's interest in PRS is $10,000.

(2) Required adjustments relating to distributions—(i) This paragraph (b)(2) applies in situations where a corporation owns a direct or indirect interest in a partnership that owns stock in that corporation, the partnership distributes money or other property to another partner and that partner recognizes gain or loss on the distribution or the basis of the property distributed to that partner is adjusted during a

year in which the partnership does not have an election under section 754 in effect, and the partnership subsequently sells or exchanges the stock. In these situations, the increase (or decrease) in the corporation's adjusted basis in its partnership interest resulting from the sale or exchange of the stock equals the amount of gain (or loss) that the corporate partner would have recognized (absent the application of section 1032) if, for the year in which the partnership made the distribution, a section 754 election had been in effect.

(ii) The provisions of this paragraph (b)(2) are illustrated by the following example:

Example. (i) A, B, and corporation C form partnership PRS. A and B each contribute $10,000 and C contributes $20,000 in exchange for a partnership interest. PRS has no liabilities. PRS purchases stock in corporation C for $10,000, which appreciates in value to $70,000. PRS distributes $25,000 to A in complete liquidation of A's interest in PRS in a year for which an election under section 754 is not in effect. PRS later sells the C stock for $70,000. PRS realizes a gain of $60,000 on the sale of the C stock. C's share of the gain is $40,000. Under section 1032, C does not recognize its share of the gain.

(ii) Normally, C would be entitled to a $40,000 increase in the basis of its PRS interest for its allocable share of PRS's gain from the sale of the C stock, but a special rule applies in this situation. If a section 754 election had been in effect for the year in which PRS made the distribution to A, PRS would have been entitled to adjust the basis of partnership property under section 734(b)(1)(A) by $15,000 (the amount of gain recognized by A with respect to the distribution to A under section 731(a) (1)). See § 1.734–1(b). Under § 1.755–1(c)(1) (ii), the basis adjustment under section 734(b) would have been allocated to the C stock, increasing its basis to $25,000 (where there is a distribution resulting in an adjustment under section 734(b)(1)(A) to the basis of undistrib-

uted partnership property, the adjustment is allocated only to capital gain property).

(iii) If a section 754 election had been in effect for the year in which PRS made the distribution to A, the amount of gain that PRS would have recognized upon PRS's disposition of C stock would be $45,000 ($70,000 minus $25,000 basis in the C stock), and the amount of gain C would have recognized upon PRS's disposition of the C stock (absent the application of section 1032) would be $30,000 (C's share of PRS's gain of $45,000 from the stock sale). Accordingly, upon PRS's sale of the C stock, the increase in the basis of C's interest in PRS is $30,000.

(c) Tiered partnerships and other arrangements—(1) Required adjustments. The purpose of these regulations as set forth in paragraph (a) of this section cannot be avoided through the use of tiered partnerships or other arrangements. For example, if a corporation acquires an indirect interest in its own stock through a chain of two or more partnerships (either where the corporation acquires a direct interest in a partnership or where one of the partnerships in the chain acquires an interest in another partnership), and gain or loss from the sale or exchange of the stock is subsequently allocated to the corporation, then the bases of the interests in the partnerships included in the chain shall be adjusted in a manner that is consistent with the purpose of this section. Similarly, if a corporation owns an indirect interest in its own stock through a chain of two or more partnerships, and a partnership in the chain distributes money or other property to another partner and that partner recognizes gain or loss on the distribution or the basis of the property distributed to that partner is adjusted during a year in which the partnership does not have an election under section 754 in effect, then upon any subsequent sale or exchange of the stock, the bases of the interests in the partnerships included in the chain shall be adjusted in a manner that is consistent with the purpose of this section.

(2) Examples. The provisions of this paragraph (c) are illustrated by the following examples:

Example (1). Acquisition of upper-tier partnership interest by corporation. (i) A, B, and C form a partnership (UTP), with each partner contributing $25,000. UTP and D form a partnership (LTP). UTP contributes $75,000 in exchange for its interest in LTP, and D contributes $25,000 in exchange for D's interest in LTP. Neither UTP nor LTP has any liabilities. LTP purchases stock in corporation E for $100,000, which appreciates in value to $1,000,000. C sells its interest in UTP to corporation E for $250,000 in a year for which an election under section 754 is not in effect for UTP or LTP. LTP later sells the E stock for $2,000,000. LTP realizes a $1,900,000 gain on the sale of the E stock. UTP's share of the gain is $1,425,000, and E's share of the gain is $475,000. Under section 1032, E does not recognize its share of the gain.

(ii) With respect to the basis of UTP's interest in LTP, if all of the gain from the sale of the E stock (including E's share) were to increase the basis of UTP's interest in LTP, UTP's basis in such interest would be $1,500,000 ($75,000 + $1,425,000). The fair market value of UTP's interest in LTP is $1,500,000. Because UTP did not have a section 754 election in effect for the taxable year in which E acquired its interest in UTP, UTP's basis in the LTP interest does not reflect the purchase price paid by E for its interest. Increasing the basis of UTP's interest in LTP by the full amount of the gain that would be recognized (in the absence of section 1032) on the sale of the E stock preserves the conformity between UTP's inside basis and outside basis with respect to LTP (i.e., UTP's share of LTP's cash is equal to $1,500,000, and UTP's basis in the LTP interest is $1,500,000) and appropriately would cause UTP to recognize no gain or loss on the sale of UTP's interest in LTP immediately after the sale of the E stock. Accordingly, increasing the basis of UTP's interest in LTP by the entire amount of gain allocated to UTP (including E's share) from LTP's sale of the E stock is consistent with the purpose of this section. The $1,425,000 of gain allocated by LTP to UTP will increase the adjusted basis of UTP's interest in LTP under section 705(a)(1). The basis of UTP's interest in LTP immediately after the sale of the E stock is $1,500,000.

(iii) With respect to the basis of E's interest in UTP, if E's share of the gain allocated to UTP and then to E were to increase the basis of E's interest in UTP, E's basis in such interest would be $725,000 ($250,000 + $475,000) and the fair market value of such interest would be $500,000, so that E would recognize a loss of $225,000 if E sold its interest in UTP immediately after LTP's disposition of the E stock. It would be inappropriate for E to recognize a taxable loss of $225,000 upon a disposition of its interest in UTP because E would not incur an economic loss in the transaction, and E did not recognize a taxable gain upon LTP's disposition of the E stock that appropriately would be offset by a taxable loss on the disposition of its interest in UTP. Accordingly, increasing E's basis in its UTP interest by the entire amount of gain allocated to E from the sale of the E stock is not consistent with the purpose of this section. (Conversely, because A and B were allocated taxable gain on the disposition of the E stock, it would be appropriate to increase A's and B's bases in their respective interests in UTP by the full amount of the gain allocated to them.)

(iv) The appropriate basis adjustment for E's interest in UTP upon the disposition of the E stock by LTP can be determined as the amount of gain that E would have recognized (in the absence of section 1032) upon the sale by LTP of the E stock if both UTP and LTP had made section 754 elections for the taxable year in which E acquired the interest in UTP. If section 754 elections had been in effect for UTP and LTP for the year in which E acquired E's interest in UTP, the following would occur. E would be entitled to a $225,000 positive

basis adjustment under section 743(b) with respect to the property of UTP. The entire basis adjustment would be allocated to UTP's only asset, its interest in LTP. In addition, the sale of C's interest in UTP would be treated as a deemed sale of E's share of UTP's interest in LTP for purposes of sections 754 and 743. The deemed selling price of E's share of UTP's interest in LTP would be $250,000 (E's share of UTP's adjusted basis in LTP, $25,000, plus E's basis adjustment under section 743(b) with respect to the assets of UTP, $225,000). The deemed sale of E's share of UTP's interest in LTP would trigger a basis adjustment under section 743(b) of $225,000 with respect to the assets of LTP (the excess of E's share of UTP's adjusted basis in LTP, including E's basis adjustment ($225,000), $250,000, over E's share of the adjusted basis of LTP's property, $25,000). This $225,000 adjustment by LTP would be allocated to LTP's only asset, the E stock, and would be segregated and allocated solely to E. The amount of LTP's gain from the sale of the E stock (before considering section 743(b)) would be $1,900,000. E's share of this gain, $475,000, would be offset in part by the $225,000 basis adjustment under section 743(b), so that E would recognize gain equal to $250,000 in the absence of section 1032.

(v) If the basis of E's interest in UTP were increased by $250,000, the total basis of E's interest would equal $500,000. This would conform to E's share of UTP's basis in the LTP interest ($1,500,000 × 1/3 = $500,000) as well as E's indirect share of the cash held by LTP ((1/3 × 3/4) × $2,000,000 = $500,000). Such a basis adjustment does not create the opportunity for the recognition of an inappropriate loss by E on a subsequent disposition of E's interest in UTP and is consistent with the purpose of this section. Accordingly, under this paragraph (c), of the $475,000 gain allocated to E, only $250,000 will apply to increase the adjusted basis of E in UTP under section 705(a)(1). E's adjusted basis in its UTP interest following the sale of the E stock is $500,000.

Example (2). Acquisition of lower-tier partnership interest by upper-tier partnership. (i) A, corporation B, and C form an equal partnership (UTP), with each partner contributing $100,000. D, E, and F also form an equal partnership (LTP), with each partner contributing $30,000. LTP purchases stock in corporation B for $90,000, which appreciates in value to $900,000. LTP has no liabilities. UTP purchases D's interest in LTP for $300,000. LTP does not have an election under section 754 in effect for the taxable year of UTP's purchase. LTP later sells the B stock for $900,000. UTP's share of the gain is $270,000, and B's share of that gain is $90,000. Under section 1032, B does not recognize its share of the gain.

(ii) With respect to the basis of UTP's interest in LTP, if all of the gain from the sale of the B stock (including B's share) were to increase the basis of UTP's interest in LTP, UTP's basis in the LTP interest would be $570,000 ($300,000 + $270,000), and the fair market value of such interest would be $300,000, so that B would be allocated a loss of $90,000 (($570,000 – $300,000) × 1/3) if UTP sold its interest in LTP immediately after LTP's disposition of the B stock. It would be inappropriate for B to recognize a taxable loss of $90,000 upon a disposition of UTP's interest in LTP. B would not incur an economic loss in the transaction, and B was not allocated a taxable gain upon LTP's disposition of the B stock that appropriately would be offset by a taxable loss on the disposition of UTP's interest in LTP. Accordingly, increasing UTP's basis in its LTP interest by the gain allocated to B from the sale of the B stock is not consistent with the purpose of this section. (Conversely, because E and F were allocated taxable gain on the disposition of the B stock, it would be appropriate to increase E's and F's bases in their respective interests in LTP by the full amount of such gain.)

(iii) The appropriate basis adjustment for UTP's interest in LTP upon the disposition of the B stock by LTP can be determined as the amount of gain that UTP would have recognized (in the absence of section 1032) upon the sale by LTP of the B stock if the portion of the gain allocated to UTP that subsequently is allocated to B were determined as if LTP had made an election under section 754 for the taxable year in which UTP acquired its interest in LTP. If a section 754 election had been in effect for LTP for the year in which UTP acquired its interest in LTP, then with respect to B, the following would occur. UTP would be entitled to a $90,000 positive basis adjustment under section 743(b), allocable to B, in the property of LTP. The entire basis adjustment would be allocated to LTP's only asset, its B stock. The amount of LTP's gain from the sale of the B stock (before considering section 743(b)) would be $810,000. UTP's share of this gain, $270,000, would be offset, in part, by the basis adjustment under section 743(b), so that UTP would recognize gain equal to $180,000.

(iv) If the basis of UTP's interest in LTP were increased by $180,000, the total basis of UTP's partnership interest would equal $480,000. This would conform to the sum of UTP's share of the cash held by LTP (1/3 × $900,000 = $300,000) and the taxable gain recognized by A and C on the disposition of the B stock that appropriately may be offset on the disposition of their interests in UTP ($90,000 + $90,000 = $180,000). Such a basis adjustment does not inappropriately create the opportunity for the allocation of a loss to B on a subsequent disposition of UTP's interest in LTP and is consistent with the purpose of this section. Accordingly, of the $270,000 gain allocated to UTP, only $180,000 will apply to increase the adjusted basis of UTP in LTP under section 705(a)(1). Such $180,000 basis increase must be segregated and allocated $90,000 each to solely A and C. UTP's adjusted basis in its LTP interest following the sale of the B stock is $480,000.

(v) With respect to B's interest in UTP, if B's share of the gain allocated to UTP and then to B were to increase the basis of B's inter-

est in UTP, B would have a UTP partnership interest with an adjusted basis of $190,000 ($100,000 + $90,000) and a value of $100,000, so that B would recognize a loss of $90,000 if B sold its interest in UTP immediately after LTP's disposition of the B stock. It would be inappropriate for B to recognize a taxable loss of $90,000 upon a disposition of its interest in UTP because B would not incur an economic loss in the transaction, and B did not recognize a taxable gain upon LTP's disposition of the B stock that appropriately would be offset by a taxable loss on the disposition of its interest in UTP. Accordingly, increasing B's basis in its UTP interest by the gain allocated to B from the sale of the B stock is not consistent with the purpose of this section. (Conversely, because A and C were allocated taxable gain on the disposition of the B stock that is a result of LTP not having a section 754 election in effect, it would be appropriate for A and C to recognize an offsetting taxable loss on the disposition of A's and C's interests in UTP. Accordingly, it would be appropriate to increase A's and C's bases in their respective interests in UTP by the amount of gain recognized by A and C.)

(vi) The appropriate basis adjustment for B's interest in UTP upon the disposition of the B stock by LTP can be determined as the amount of gain that B would have recognized (in the absence of section 1032) upon the sale by LTP of the B stock if the portion of the gain allocated to UTP that is subsequently allocated to B were determined as if LTP had made an election under section 754 for the taxable year in which UTP acquired its interest in LTP. If a section 754 election had been in effect for LTP for the year in which UTP acquired its interest in LTP, then with respect to B, the following would occur. UTP would be entitled to a basis adjustment under section 743(b) in the property of LTP of $90,000 with respect to B. The entire basis adjustment would be allocated to LTP's only asset, its B stock. The amount of LTP's gain from the sale of the B stock (before considering section 743(b)) would be

$810,000. UTP's share of this gain, $270,000, would be offset, in part, by the $90,000 basis adjustment under section 743(b), so that UTP would recognize gain equal to $180,000. The $90,000 basis adjustment would completely offset the gain that otherwise would be allocated to B.

(vii) If no gain were allocated to B so that the basis of B's interest in UTP was not increased, the total basis of B's interest would equal $100,000. This would conform to B's share of UTP's basis in the LTP interest (($480,000 – $180,000 (i.e., A's and C's share of the basis that should offset taxable gain recognized as a result of LTP's failure to have a section 754 election)) × 1/3 = $100,000) as well as B's indirect share of the cash held by LTP ((1/3 × 1/3) × $900,000 = $100,000). Such a basis adjustment does not create the opportunity for the recognition of an inappropriate loss by B on a subsequent disposition of B's interest in UTP and is consistent with the purpose of this section. Accordingly, under this paragraph (c), of the $90,000 gain allocated to B, none will apply to increase the adjusted basis of B in UTP under section 705(a)(1). B's adjusted basis in its UTP interest following the sale of the B stock is $100,000.

(viii) Immediately after LTP's disposition of the B stock, UTP sells its interest in LTP for $300,000. UTP's adjusted basis in its LTP interest is $480,000, $180,000 of which must be allocated $90,000 each to A and C. Accordingly, upon UTP's sale of its interest in LTP, UTP realizes $180,000 of loss, and A and C in turn each realize $90,000 of loss.

(d) Positions in Stock. For purposes of this section, stock includes any position in stock to which section 1032 applies.

* * *

§ 1.706–1 Taxable years of partner and partnership.

(a) Year in which partnership income is includible. (1) In computing taxable income for a taxable year, a partner is required to include the partner's distributive share of partnership items set forth in section 702 and the regulations thereunder for any partnership taxable year ending within or with the partner's taxable year. A partner must also include in taxable income for a taxable year guaranteed payments under section 707(c) that are deductible by the partnership under its method of accounting in the partnership taxable year ending within or with the partner's taxable year.

(2) The rules of this paragraph (a)(1) may be illustrated by the following example:

Example. Partner A reports income using a calendar year, while the partnership of which A is a member reports its income using a fiscal year ending May 31. The partnership reports its income and deductions under the cash method of accounting. During the partnership taxable year ending May 31, 2002, the partnership makes guaranteed payments of $ 120,000 to A for services and for the use of capital. Of this amount, $ 70,000 was paid to A between June 1 and December 31, 2001, and the remaining $ 50,000 was paid to A between January 1 and May 31, 2002. The entire $ 120,000 paid to A is includible in A's taxable income for the calendar year 2002 (together with A's distributive share of partnership items set forth in section 702 for the partnership taxable year ending May 31, 2002).

(3) If a partner receives distributions under section 731 or sells or exchanges all or part of a partnership interest, any gain or loss arising therefrom does not constitute partnership income.

(b) Taxable year—(1) Partnership treated as a taxpayer. The taxable year of a partnership must be determined as though the partnership were a taxpayer.

(2) Partnership's taxable year—(i) Required taxable year. Except as provided in paragraph (b)(2)(ii) of this section, the taxable year of a partnership must be—

(A) The majority interest taxable year, as defined in section 706(b)(4);

(B) If there is no majority interest taxable year, the taxable year of all of the principal partners of the partnership, as defined in 706(b)(3) (the principal partners' taxable year); or

(C) If there is no majority interest taxable year or principal partners' taxable year, the taxable year that produces the least aggregate deferral of income as determined under paragraph (b)(3) of this section.

(ii) Exceptions. A partnership may have a taxable year other than its required taxable year if it makes an election under section 444, elects to use a 52–53-week taxable year that ends with reference to its required taxable year or a taxable year elected under section 444, or establishes a business purpose for such taxable year and obtains approval of the Commissioner under section 442.

(3) Least aggregate deferral — (i) Taxable year that results in the least aggregate deferral of income. The taxable year that results in the least aggregate deferral of income will be the taxable year of one or more of the partners in the partnership which will result in the least aggregate deferral of income to the partners. The aggregate deferral for a particular year is equal to the sum of the products determined by multiplying the month(s) of deferral for each partner that would be generated by that year and each partner's interest in partnership profits for that year. The partner's taxable year that produces the lowest sum when compared to the other partner's taxable years is the taxable year that results in the least aggregate deferral of income to the partners. If the calculation results in more than one taxable year qualifying as the taxable year with the least aggregate deferral, the partnership may select any one of those taxable years as its taxable year. However, if one of the qualifying taxable years is also the partnership's existing taxable year, the partnership must maintain its existing taxable year. The determination of the taxable year that results in the least aggregate deferral

of income generally must be made as of the beginning of the partnership's current taxable year. The director, however, may determine that the first day of the current taxable year is not the appropriate testing day and require the use of some other day or period that will more accurately reflect the ownership of the partnership and thereby the actual aggregate deferral to the partners where the partners engage in a transaction that has as its principal purpose the avoidance of the principles of this section. Thus, for example the preceding sentence would apply where there is a transfer of an interest in the partnership that results in a temporary transfer of that interest principally for purposes of qualifying for a specific taxable year under the principles of this section. For purposes of this section, deferral to each partner is measured in terms of months from the end of the partnership's taxable year forward to the end of the partner's taxable year.

(ii) Determination of the taxable year of a partner or partnership that uses a 52–53-week taxable year. For purposes of the calculation described in paragraph (b)(3)(i) of this section, the taxable year of a partner or partnership that uses a 52–53-week taxable year must be the same year determined under the rules of section 441(f) and the regulations thereunder with respect to the inclusion of income by the partner or partnership.

(iii) Special de minimis rule. If the taxable year that results in the least aggregate deferral produces an aggregate deferral that is less than. 5 when compared to the aggregate deferral of the current taxable year, the partnership's current taxable year will be treated as the taxable year with the least aggregate deferral. Thus, the partnership will not be permitted to change its taxable year.

* * *

(c) Closing of partnership year — (1) General rule. Section 706(c) and this paragraph provide rules governing the closing of partnership years. The closing of a partnership taxable year or a termination of a partnership for Federal income tax purposes is not necessarily governed by the "dissolution", "liquidation", etc., of a partnership under State or local law. The taxable year of a partnership shall not close as the result of the death of a partner, the entry of a new partner, the liquidation of a partner's entire interest in the partnership (as defined in section 761(d)), or the sale or exchange of a partner's interest in the partnership, except in the case of a termination of a partnership and except as provided in subparagraph (2) of this paragraph. In the case of termination, the partnership taxable year closes for all partners as of the date of termination. See section 708(b) and paragraph (b) of § 1.708–1.

(2) Disposition of entire interest — (i) In general. A partnership taxable year shall close with respect to a partner who sells or exchanges his entire interest in the partnership, with respect to a partner whose entire interest in the partnership is liquidated, and with respect to a partner who dies. In the case of a death, liquidation, or sale or exchange of a partner's entire interest in the partnership, the partner shall include in his taxable income for his taxable year within or with which the partner's interest in the partnership ends the partner's distributive share of items described in section 702(a) and any guaranteed payments under section 707(c) for the partnership taxable year ending with the date of such termination. If the decedent partner's estate or other successor sells or exchanges its entire interest in the partnership, or if its entire interest is liquidated, the partnership taxable year with respect to the estate or other successor in interest shall close on the date of such sale or exchange, or the date of the completion of the liquidation. The sale or exchange of a partnership interest does not, for the purpose of this rule, include any transfer of a partnership interest which occurs at death as a result of inheritance or any testamentary disposition.

(ii) Example. H is a partner of a partnership having a taxable year ending December 31. Both H and his wife W are on a calendar year and file joint returns. H dies on March 31, 2015. Administration of the estate is completed and the estate, including the partnership interest, is distributed to W as legatee on November 30, 2015. Such distribution by the estate is not a sale or exchange of H's partnership interest. The taxable year of the partnership will close with respect to H on March 31, 2015, and H will include in his final return for his final taxable year (January 1, 2015, through March 31, 2015) his distributive share of partnership items for that period under the rules of sections 706(d)(2), 706(d)(3), and § 1.706–4. W will include in her return for the taxable year ending December 31, 2015, her distributive share of partnership items for the period of April 1, 2015, through December 31, 2015, under the rules of sections 706(d)(2), 706(d)(3), and § 1.706–4.

(iii) Deemed dispositions. A deemed disposition of the partner's interest pursuant to § 1.1502–76(b)(2)(vi) (relating to corporate partners that become or cease to be members of a consolidated group within the meaning of §§ 1.1502–1(h)), 1.1362–3(c)(1) (relating to the termination of the subchapter S election of an S corporation partner), or 1.1377–1(b)(3) (iv) (regarding an election to terminate the taxable year of an S corporation partner), shall be treated as a disposition of the partner's entire interest in the partnership solely for purposes of section 706.

(3) Partner who dies. (i) When a partner dies, the partnership taxable year shall not close with respect to such partner prior to the end of the partnership taxable year. The partnership taxable year shall continue both for the remaining partners and the decedent partner. Where the death of a partner results in the termination of the partnership, the partnership taxable year shall close for all partners on the date of such termination under section 708(b) (1)(A). See also paragraph (b)(1)(i)(b) of § 1.708–1 for the continuation of a 2-member partnership under certain circumstances after the death of a partner. However, if the decedent partner's estate or other successor sells or exchanges its entire interest in the partnership, or if its entire interest is liquidated, the partnership taxable year with respect to the estate or other successor in interest shall close on the date of such sale or exchange, or the date of completion of the liquidation.

(ii) The last return of a decedent partner shall include only his share of partnership taxable income for any partnership taxable year or years ending within or with the last taxable year for such decedent partner (i. e., the year ending with the date of his death). The distributive share of partnership taxable income for a partnership taxable year ending after the decedent's last taxable year is includible in the return of his estate or other successor in interest. If the estate or other successor in interest of a partner continues to share in the profits or losses of the partnership business, the distributive share thereof is includible in the taxable year of the estate or other successor in interest within or with which the taxable year of the partnership ends. See also paragraph (a)(1)(ii) of § 1.736–1. Where the estate or other successor in interest receives distributions, any gain or loss on such distributions is includible in its gross income for its taxable year in which the distribution is made.

(iii) If a partner (or a retiring partner), in accordance with the terms of the partnership agreement, designates a person to succeed to his interest in the partnership after his death, such designated person shall be regarded as a successor in interest of the deceased for purposes of this chapter. Thus, where a partner designates his widow as the successor in interest, her distributive share of income for the taxable year of the partnership ending within or with her taxable year may be included in a joint return in accordance with the provisions of sections 2 and 6013(a)(2) and (3).

(iv) If, under the terms of an agreement existing at the date of death of a partner, a sale or exchange of the decedent partner's interest in the partnership occurs upon that date, then the taxable year of the partnership with respect to such decedent partner shall close upon the date of death. See section 706(c)(2)(A)(i). The sale or exchange of a partnership interest does not, for the purpose of this rule, include any transfer of a partnership interest which occurs at death as a result of inheritance or any testamentary disposition.

(v) To the extent that any part of a distributive share of partnership income of the estate or other successor in interest of a deceased partner is attributable to the decedent for the period ending with the date of his death, such part of the distributive share is income in respect of the decedent under section 691. See section 691 and the regulations thereunder.

(vi) The provisions of this subparagraph may be illustrated by the following examples:

Example (1). B has a taxable year ending December 31 and is a member of partnership ABC, the taxable year of which ends on June 30. B dies on October 31, 1955. His estate (which as a new taxpayer may, under section 441 and the regulations thereunder, adopt any taxable year) adopts a taxable year ending October 31. The return of the decedent for the period January 1 to October 31, 1955, will include only his distributive share of taxable income of the partnership for its taxable year ending June 30, 1955. The distributive share of taxable income of the partnership for its taxable year ending June 30, 1956, arising from the interest of the decedent, will be includible in the return of the estate for its taxable year ending October 31, 1956. That part of the distributive share attributable to the decedent for the period ending with the date of his death (July 1 through October 31, 1955) is income in respect of a decedent under section 691.

(4) Determination of distributive shares. See section 706(d)(2), 706(d)(3), and § 1.706–4 for rules regarding the methods to be used in determining the distributive shares of items described in section 702(a) for partners whose interests in the partnership vary during the partnership's taxable year as a result of a disposition of a partner's entire interest in a partnership as described in paragraph (c)(2) of this section or as a result of a disposition of less than a partner's entire interest as described in paragraph (c)(3) of this section.

(5) Transfer of interest by gift. The transfer of a partnership interest by gift does not close the partnership taxable year with respect to the donor. However, the income up to the date of gift attributable to the donor's interest shall be allocated to him under section 704(e)(2).

* * *

§ 1.706–4 Determination of distributive share when a partner's interest varies.

(a) General rule — (1) Variations subject to this section. Except as provided in paragraph (a)(2) of this section, this section provides rules for determining the partners' distributive shares of partnership items when a partner's interest in a partnership varies during the taxable year as a result of the disposition of a partial or entire interest in a partnership as described in § 1.706–1(c)(2) and (3), or with respect to a partner whose interest in a partnership is reduced as described in § 1.706–1(c)(3), including by the entry of a new partner (collectively, a "variation").

(2) Coordination with sections 706(d)(2) and 706(d)(3) and other Code sections. Items subject to allocation under other rules, including sections 108(e)(8) and 108(i) (which provide special allocation rules for certain items from the discharge or retirement of indebtedness), section 706(d)(2) (relating to the determination of partners' distributive shares of allocable cash basis items) and section 706(d)(3) (relating to the determination of partners' distributive share of any item of an upper tier partnership attributable to a lower tier partnership), are not subject to the rules of this section. In all cases, all partnership items for each taxable year must be allocated among the partners, and no partnership items may be duplicated, regardless of the particular provision of section 706 (or other Code section) which applies, and regardless of the method or convention adopted by the partnership.

(3) Allocation of items subject to this section. In determining the distributive share under section 702(a) of partnership items subject to this section, the partnership shall follow the steps described in this paragraph (a)(3)(i) through (x).

(i) First, determine whether either of the exceptions in paragraph (b) of this section (regarding certain changes among contemporaneous partners and partnerships for which capital is not a material income-producing factor) applies.

(ii) Second, determine which of its items are subject to allocation under the special rules for extraordinary items in paragraph (e) of this section, and allocate those items accordingly.

(iii) Third, determine with respect to each variation whether it will apply the interim closing method or the proration method. Absent an agreement of the partners (within the meaning of paragraph (f) of this section) to use the proration method, the partnership shall use the interim closing method. The partnership may use different methods (interim closing or proration) for different variations within each partnership taxable year; however, the Commissioner may place restrictions on the ability of partnerships to use different methods during the same taxable year in guidance published in the Internal Revenue Bulletin.

(iv) Fourth, determine when each variation is deemed to have occurred under the partnership's selected convention (as described in paragraph (c) of this section).

(v) Fifth, determine whether there is an agreement of the partners (within the meaning of paragraph (f) of this section) to perform regular monthly or semi-monthly interim closings (as described in paragraph (d) of this section). If so, then the partnership will perform an interim closing of its books at the end of each month (in the case of an agreement to perform monthly closings) or at the end and middle of each month (in the case of an agreement to perform semi-monthly closings), regardless of whether any variation occurs. Absent an agreement of the partners to perform regular monthly or semi-monthly interim closings, the only interim closings during the partnership's taxable year will be at the deemed time of the occurrence of variations for which the partnership uses the interim closing method.

(vi) Sixth, determine the partnership's segments, which are specific periods of the partnership's taxable year created by interim closings of the partnership's books. The first segment shall commence with the beginning of the taxable year of the partnership and shall end at the time of the first interim closing. Any additional segment shall commence immediately after the closing of the prior segment and shall end at the time of the next interim closing. However, the last segment of the partnership's taxable year shall end no later than the close of the last day of the partnership's taxable year. If there are no interim closings, the partnership has one segment, which corresponds to its entire taxable year.

(vii) Seventh, apportion the partnership's items for the year among its segments. The partnership shall determine the items of income, gain, loss, deduction, and credit of the partnership for each segment. In general, a partnership shall treat each segment as though the segment were a separate distributive share period. For example, a partnership may compute a capital loss for a segment of a taxable year even though the partnership has a net capital gain for the entire taxable year. For purposes of determining allocations to segments, any special limitation or requirement relating to the timing or amount of income, gain, loss, deduction, or credit applicable to the entire partnership taxable year will be applied based upon the partnership's satisfaction of the limitation or requirement as of the end of the partnership's taxable year. For example,

the expenses related to the election to expense a section 179 asset must first be calculated (and limited if applicable) based on the partnership's full taxable year, and then the effect of any limitation must be apportioned among the segments in accordance with the interim closing method or the proration method using any reasonable method.

(viii) Eighth, determine the partnership's proration periods, which are specific portions of a segment created by a variation for which the partnership chooses to apply the proration method. The first proration period in each segment begins at the beginning of the segment, and ends at the time of the first variation within the segment for which the partnership selects the proration method. The next proration period begins immediately after the close of the prior proration period and ends at the time of the next variation for which the partnership selects the proration method. However, each proration period shall end no later than the close of the segment.

(ix) Ninth, prorate the items of income, gain, loss, deduction, and credit in each segment among the proration periods within the segment.

(x) Tenth, determine the partners' distributive shares of partnership items under section 702(a) by taking into account the partners' interests in such items during each segment and proration period.

(4) Example. At the beginning of 2015, PRS, a calendar year partnership, has three equal partners, A, B, and C. On April 16, 2015, A sells 50% of its interest in PRS to new partner D. On August 6, 2015, B sells 50% of its interest in PRS to new partner E. During 2015, PRS earned $75,000 of ordinary income, incurred $33,000 of ordinary deductions, earned $12,000 of capital gain in the ordinary course of its business, and sustained $9,000 of capital loss in the ordinary course of its business. Within that year, PRS earned $60,000 of ordinary income, incurred $24,000 of ordinary deductions, earned $12,000 of capital gain,

and sustained $6,000 of capital loss between January 1, 2015, and July 31, 2015, and PRS earned $15,000 of gross ordinary income, incurred $9,000 of gross ordinary deductions, and sustained $3,000 of capital loss between August 1, 2015, and December 31, 2015. None of PRS's items are extraordinary items within the meaning of paragraph (e)(2) of this section. Capital is a material income-producing factor for PRS. For 2015, PRS determines the distributive shares of A, B, C, D, and E as follows.

(i) First, PRS determines that none of the exceptions in paragraph (b) of this section apply because capital is a material-income producing factor and no variation is the result of a change in allocations among contemporaneous partners.

(ii) Second, PRS determines that none of its items are extraordinary items subject to allocation under paragraph (e) of this section.

(iii) Third, the partners of PRS agree (within the meaning of paragraph (f) of this section) to apply the proration method to the April 16, 2015, variation, and PRS accepts the default application of the interim closing method to the August 6, 2015, variation.

(iv) Fourth, PRS determines the deemed date of the variations for purposes of this section based upon PRS's selected convention. Because PRS applied the proration method to the April 16, 2015, variation, PRS must use the calendar day convention with respect to the April 16, 2015, variation pursuant to paragraph (c) of this section. Therefore, the variation that resulted from A's sale to D on April 16, 2015, is deemed to occur for purposes of this section at the end of the day on April 16, 2015. Further, the partners of PRS agree (within the meaning of paragraph (f) of this section) to apply the semi-monthly convention to the August 6, 2015, variation. Therefore, the August 6, 2015, variation is deemed to occur at the end of the day on July 31, 2015.

(v) Fifth, the partners of PRS do not agree to perform regular semi-monthly or monthly closings as described in paragraph (d) of this section. Therefore, PRS will have only one interim closing for 2015, occurring at the end of the day on July 31.

(vi) Sixth, PRS determines that it has two segments for 2015. The first segment commences January 1, 2015, and ends at the close of the day on July 31, 2015. The second segment commences at the beginning of the day on August 1, 2015, and ends at the close of the day on December 31, 2015.

(vii) Seventh, PRS determines that during the first segment of its taxable year (beginning January 1, 2015, and ending July 31, 2015), it had $60,000 of ordinary income, $24,000 of ordinary deductions, $12,000 of capital gain, and $6,000 of capital loss. PRS determines that during the second segment of its taxable year (beginning August 1, 2015, and ending December 31, 2015), it had $15,000 of gross ordinary income, $9,000 of gross ordinary deductions, and $3,000 of capital loss.

(viii) Eighth, PRS determines that it has two proration periods. The first proration period begins January 1, 2015, and ends at the close of the day on April 16, 2015; the second proration period begins April 17, 2015, and ends at the close of the day on July 31, 2015.

(ix) Ninth, PRS prorates its income from the first segment of its taxable year among the two proration periods. Because each proration period has 106 days, PRS allocates 50% of its items from the first segment to each proration period. Thus, each proration period contains $30,000 gross ordinary income, $12,000 gross ordinary deductions, $6,000 capital gain, and $3,000 capital loss.

(x) Tenth, PRS calculates each partner's distributive share. Because A, B, and C were equal partners during the first proration period, each is allocated one-third of the partnership's items attributable to that proration period. Thus, A, B, and C are each allocated $10,000 gross ordinary income, $4,000 gross ordinary deductions, $2,000 capital gain, and

$1,000 capital loss for the first proration period. For the second proration period, A and D each had a one-sixth interest in PRS and B and C each had a one-third interest in PRS. Thus, A and D are each allocated $5,000 gross ordinary income, $2,000 gross ordinary deductions, $1,000 capital gain, and $500 capital loss, and B and C are each allocated $10,000 gross ordinary income, $4,000 gross ordinary deductions, $2,000 capital gain, and $1,000 capital loss for the second proration period. For the second segment of PRS's taxable year, A, B, D, and E each had a one-sixth interest in PRS and C had a one-third interest in PRS. Thus, A, B, D, and E are each allocated $2,500 gross ordinary income, $1,500 gross ordinary deductions, and $500 capital loss, and C is allocated $5,000 gross ordinary income, $3,000 gross ordinary deductions, and $1,000 capital loss for the second segment.

(b) Exceptions—(1) Permissible changes among contemporaneous partners. The general rule of paragraph (a)(3) of this section, with respect to the varying interests of a partner described in § 1.706–1(c)(3), will not preclude changes in the allocations of the distributive share of items described in section 702(a) among contemporaneous partners for the entire partnership taxable year (or among contemporaneous partners for a segment if the item is entirely attributable to a segment), provided that—

(i) Any variation in a partner's interest is not attributable to a contribution of money or property by a partner to the partnership or a distribution of money or property by the partnership to a partner; and

(ii) The allocations resulting from the modification satisfy the provisions of section 704(b) and the regulations promulgated thereunder.

(2) Safe harbor for partnerships for which capital is not a material income-producing factor. Notwithstanding paragraph (a) (3) of this section, with respect to any taxable year in which there is a change in any part-

ner's interest in a partnership for which capital is not a material income-producing factor, the partnership and such partner may choose to determine the partner's distributive share of partnership income, gain, loss, deduction, and credit using any reasonable method to account for the varying interests of the partners in the partnership during the taxable year provided that the allocations satisfy the provisions of section 704(b).

(c) Conventions—(1) *In general.* Conventions are rules of administrative convenience that determine when each variation is deemed to occur for purposes of this section. Because the timing of each variation is necessary to determine the partnership's segments and proration periods, which are used to determine the partners' distributive shares, the convention used by the partnership with respect to a variation will generally affect the allocation of partnership items. However, see paragraph (e) of this section for special rules regarding extraordinary items, which generally must be allocated without regard to the partnership's convention. Subject to the limitations set forth in paragraphs (c)(2) and (3) of this section, partnerships may generally choose from the following three conventions:

(i) *Calendar day convention.* Under the calendar day convention, each variation is deemed to occur for purposes of this section at the end of the day on which the variation occurs.

(ii) *Semi-monthly convention.* Under the semi-monthly convention, each variation is deemed to occur for purposes of this section either:

(A) In the case of a variation occurring on the 1st through the 15th day of a calendar month, at the end of the last day of the immediately preceding calendar month; or

(B) In the case of a variation occurring on the 16th through the last day of a calendar month, at the end of the 15th calendar day of that month.

(iii) *Monthly convention.* Under the monthly convention, each variation is deemed to occur for purposes of this section either:

(A) In the case of a variation occurring on the 1st through the 15th day of a calendar month, at the end of the last day of the immediately preceding calendar month; or

(B) In the case of a variation occurring on the 16th through the last day of a calendar month, at the end of the last day of that calendar month.

(2) *Exceptions.* (i) Notwithstanding paragraph (c)(1) of this section, all variations within a taxable year shall be deemed to occur no earlier than the first day of the partnership's taxable year, and no later than the close of the final day of the partnership's taxable year. Thus, in the case of a calendar year partnership applying either the semi-monthly or monthly convention to a variation occurring on January 1st through January 15th, the variation will be deemed to occur for purposes of this section at the beginning of the day on January 1st.

(ii) In the case of a partner who becomes a partner during the partnership's taxable year as a result of a variation, and ceases to be a partner as a result of another variation, if both such variations would be deemed to occur at the same time under the rules of paragraph (c)(1) of this section, then the variations with respect to that partner's interest will instead be treated as occurring on the dates each variation actually occurred. Thus, the partnership must treat such a partner as a partner for the entire portion of its taxable year during which the partner actually owned an interest. See *Example 2* of paragraph (c)(4) of this section. However, this paragraph (c)(2)(ii) does not apply to publicly traded partnerships (as defined in section 7704(b)) that are treated as partnerships with respect to holders of publicly traded units (as described in § 1.7704–1(b) or 1.7704–1(c)(1)).

(iii) Notwithstanding paragraph (c)(1)(iii) of this section, a publicly traded partnership (as defined in section 7704(b)) that is treated as a partnership may consistently treat all variations occurring during each month as occurring at the end of the last day of that calendar month if the publicly traded partnership uses the monthly convention for those variations.

(3) **Permissible conventions for each variation—(i) Rules applicable to all partnerships.** A partnership generally shall use the calendar day convention for each variation; however, for all variations during a taxable year for which the partnership uses the interim closing method, the partnership may instead use the semi-monthly or monthly convention by agreement of the partners (within the meaning of paragraph (f) of this section). The partnership must use the same convention for all variations for which the partnership uses the interim closing method.

(ii) *Publicly traded partnerships.* A publicly traded partnership (as defined in section 7704(b)) that is treated as a partnership may, by agreement of the partners (within the meaning of paragraph (f) of this section) use any of the calendar day, the semi-monthly, or the monthly conventions with respect to all variations during the taxable year relating to its publicly-traded units (as described in § 1.7704–1(b) or (c)(1)), regardless of whether the publicly traded partnership uses the proration method with respect to those variations. A publicly traded partnership must use the same convention for all variations during the taxable year relating to its publicly traded units. A publicly traded partnership must use the calendar day convention with respect to all variations relating to its non-publicly traded units for which the publicly traded partnership uses the proration method.

(4) **Examples.** The following examples illustrate the principles in this paragraph (c).

Example (1). PRS is a calendar year partnership with four equal partners A, B, C, and D. PRS is not a publicly traded partnership. PRS has the following three variations that occur during its 2015 taxable year: on March 11, A sells its entire interest in PRS to new partner E;

on June 12, PRS partially redeems B's interest in PRS with a distribution comprising a partial return of B's capital; on October 21, C sells part of C's interest in PRS to new partner E. These transfers do not result in a termination of PRS under section 708. Pursuant to paragraph (a)(3)(iii) of this section, the partners of PRS agree (within the meaning of paragraph (f) of this section) to use the interim closing method with respect to the variations occurring on March 11 and October 21 and agree to use the proration method with respect to the variation occurring on June 12. Pursuant to paragraph (c)(3) of this section, the partners of PRS may agree (within the meaning of paragraph (f) of this section) to use any of the calendar day, semi-monthly, or monthly conventions with respect to the March 11 and October 21 variations, but must use the same convention for both variations. If the partners of PRS agree to use the calendar day convention, the March 11 and October 21 variations will be deemed to occur for purposes of this section at the end of the day on March 11, 2015, and October 21, 2015, respectively. If the partners of PRS agree to use the semi-monthly convention, the March 11 and October 21 variations will be deemed to occur for purposes of this section at the end of the day on February 28, 2015, and October 15, 2015, respectively. If the partners of PRS agree to use the monthly convention, the March 11 and October 21 variations will be deemed to occur for purposes of this section at the end of the day on February 28, 2015, and October 31, 2015, respectively. Pursuant to paragraph (c)(3) of this section PRS must use the calendar day convention with respect to the June 12 variation; thus, the June 12 variation is deemed to occur for purposes of this section at the end of the day on June 12, 2015.

Example (2). PRS is a calendar year partnership that uses the interim closing method and monthly convention to account for variations during its taxable year. PRS is not a publicly traded partnership. On January 20, 2015, new partner A purchases an interest in PRS from one of PRS's existing partners. On February 14, 2015, A sells its entire interest in PRS. These transfers do not result in a termination of PRS under section 708. Under the rules of paragraph (c)(1)(iii) of this section, the January 20, 2015, variation and the February 14, 2015, variation would both be deemed to occur at the same time: the end of the day on January 31, 2015. Therefore, under the exception in paragraph (c)(2)(ii) of this section, the rules of paragraph (c)(1) of this section do not apply, and instead the January 20, 2015, variation and the February 14 variation are considered to occur on January 20, 2015, and February 14, 2015, respectively. PRS must perform a closing of the books on both January 20, 2015, and February 14, 2015, and allocate A a share of PRS's items attributable to that segment.

(d)(1) Optional regular monthly or semi-monthly interim closings. Under the rules of this section, a partnership is not required to perform an interim closing of its books except at the time of any variation for which the partnership uses the interim closing method (taking into account the applicable convention). However, a partnership may, by agreement of the partners (within the meaning of paragraph (f) of this section) perform regular monthly or semi-monthly interim closings of its books, regardless of whether any variation occurs. Regardless of whether the partners agree to perform these regular interim closings, the partnership must continue to apply the interim closing or proration method to its variations according to the rules of this section.

(2) Example. The following example illustrates the principles in this paragraph (d).

Example. (i) PRS is a calendar year partnership with five equal partners A, B, C, D, and E. PRS has the following two variations that occur during its 2015 taxable year: on August 29, A sells its entire interest in PRS to new partner F; on December 27, PRS completely liquidates B's interest in PRS with a distribution. These variations do not result in a termination of PRS under section 708.

(ii) The partners of PRS agree (within the meaning of paragraph (f) of this section) to use the interim closing method and the semi-monthly convention with respect to the variation occurring on August 29. Thus, the August variation is deemed to occur for purposes of this section at the end of the day on August 15, 2015. The partners of PRS agree (within the meaning of paragraph (f) of this section) to use the proration method with respect to the December 27 variation. Therefore, PRS must use the calendar day convention with respect to the December variation pursuant to paragraph (c) of this section. Thus, the December variation is deemed to occur for purposes of this section at the end of the day on December 27, 2015.

(iii) Pursuant to paragraph (d)(1) of this section, the partners of PRS agree (within the meaning of paragraph (f) of this section) to perform regular monthly interim closings. Therefore, PRS will have twelve interim closings for its 2015 taxable year, one at the end of every month and one at the end of the day on August 15. Therefore, PRS will have thirteen segments for 2015, one corresponding to each month from January through July, one segment from August 1 through August 15, one segment from August 16 through August 31, and one corresponding to each month from September through December. PRS must apportion its items among these segments under the rules of paragraph (a)(3) of this section.

(iv) PRS will have two proration periods for 2015, one from December 1 through December 27, and one from December 28 through December 31. Pursuant to the rules of paragraph (a)(3) of this section, PRS will prorate the items in its December segment among these two proration periods. Therefore, PRS will apportion 27/31 of all items in its December segment to the proration period from December 1 through December 27, and 4/31 of all items in its December segment to the proration period from December 28 through December 31.

(v) Pursuant to the rules of paragraph (a)(3)(x) of this section, PRS determines the partners' distributive shares of partnership items under section 702(a) by taking into account the partners' interests in such items during each of the thirteen segments and two proration periods. Thus, A, B, C, D, and E will each be allocated one-fifth of all items in the following segments: January, February, March, April, May, June, July, and August 1 through August 15. B, C, D, E, and F will each be allocated one-fifth of all items in the following segments: August 16 through August 31, September, October, and November. B, C, D, E, and F will each be allocated one-fifth of all items in the proration period from December 1 through December 27. C, D, E, and F will each be allocated one-quarter of all items in the proration period from December 28 through December 31.

(e) **Extraordinary items—(1) General principles.** Extraordinary items may not be prorated. The partnership must allocate extraordinary items among the partners in proportion to their interests in the partnership item at the time of day on which the extraordinary item occurred, regardless of the method (interim closing or proration method) and convention (daily, semi-monthly, or monthly) otherwise used by the partnership. These rules require the allocation of extraordinary items as an exception to the proration method, which would otherwise ratably allocate the extraordinary items across the segment, and the conventions, which could otherwise inappropriately shift extraordinary items between a transferor and transferee. However, publicly traded partnerships (as defined in section 7704(b)) that are treated as partnerships may, but are not required to, apply their selected convention in determining who held publicly traded units (as described in § 1.7704–1(b) or (c)(1)) at the time of the occurrence of an extraordinary item. Extraordinary items continue to be subject to any special limitation or requirement relating to the timing or amount of income, gain, loss, deduction, or credit applicable to the entire partnership taxable year (for example, the limitation for section 179 expenses).

(2) Definition. Except as provided in paragraph (e)(3) of this section, an extraordinary item is:

(i) Any item from the disposition or abandonment (other than in the ordinary course of business) of a capital asset as defined in section 1221 (determined without the application of any other rules of law);

(ii) Any item from the disposition or abandonment (other than in the ordinary course of business) of property used in a trade or business as defined in section 1231(b) (determined without the application of any holding period requirement);

(iii) Any item from the disposition or abandonment of an asset described in section 1221(a)(1), (a)(3), (a)(4), or (a)(5) if substantially all the assets in the same category from the same trade or business are disposed of or abandoned in one transaction (or series of related transactions);

(iv) Any item from assets disposed of in an applicable asset acquisition under section 1060(c);

(v) Any item resulting from any change in accounting method initiated by the filing of the appropriate form after a variation occurs;

(vi) Any item from the discharge or retirement of indebtedness (except items subject to section 108(e)(8) or 108(i), which are subject to special allocation rules provided in section 108(e)(8) and 108(i));

(vii) Any item from the settlement of a tort or similar third-party liability or payment of a judgment;

(viii) Any credit, to the extent it arises from activities or items that are not ratably allocated (for example, the rehabilitation credit under section 47, which is based on placement in service);

(ix) For all partnerships, any additional item if, the partners agree (within the meaning of paragraph (f) of this section) to consistently treat such item as an extraordinary item for that taxable year; however, this rule does not apply if treating that additional item as an extraordinary item would result in a substantial distortion of income in any partner's return; any additional extraordinary items continue to be subject to any special limitation or requirement relating to the timing or amount of income, gain, loss, deduction, or credit applicable to the entire partnership taxable year (for example, the limitation for section 179 expenses);

(x) Any item which, in the opinion of the Commissioner, would, if ratably allocated, result in a substantial distortion of income in any return in which the item is included;

(xi) Any item identified as an additional class of extraordinary item in guidance published in the Internal Revenue Bulletin.

(3) Small item exception. A partnership may treat an item described in paragraph (e)(2) of this section as other than an extraordinary item for purposes of this paragraph (e) if, for the partnership's taxable year the total of all items in the particular class of extraordinary items (as enumerated in paragraphs (e)(2)(i) through (xi) of this section, for example, all tort or similar liabilities, but in no event counting an extraordinary item more than once) is less than five percent of the partnership's gross income, including tax-exempt income described in section 705(a)(1)(B), in the case of income or gain items, or gross expenses and losses, including section 705(a)(2)(B) expenditures, in the case of losses and expense items; and the total amount of the extraordinary items from all classes of extraordinary items amounting to less than five percent of the partnership's gross income, including tax-exempt income described in section 705(a)(1)(B), in the case of income or gain items, or gross expenses and losses, including section 705(a)(2)(B) expenditures, in the case of losses and expense items, does not exceed $10 million in the taxable year, determined by treating all such extraordinary items as positive amounts.

(4) Examples. The following examples illustrate the provisions of this paragraph (e).

Example (1). PRS, a calendar year partnership, uses the proration method and calendar day convention to account for varying interests of the partners. At 3:15 p.m. on December 7, 2015, PRS recognizes an extraordinary item within the meaning of paragraph (e)(2) of this section. On December 12, 2015, A, a partner in PRS, disposes of its entire interest in PRS. PRS does not experience a termination under section 708 during 2015. PRS has no other extraordinary items for the taxable year, the small item exception of paragraph (e)(3) of this section does not apply, the exceptions in paragraph (b) of this section do not apply, and PRS is not a publicly traded partnership. Pursuant to paragraph (e)(1) of this section, the item of income, gain, loss, deduction, or credit attributable to the extraordinary item will be allocated in accordance with the partners' interests in the extraordinary item at 3:15 p.m. on December 7, 2015. The remaining partnership items of PRS that are subject to this section must be prorated across the partnership's taxable year in accordance with paragraph (a) (3) of this section.

Example (2). Assume the same facts as in Example 1, except that PRS uses the interim closing method and monthly convention to account for varying interests of the partners. Pursuant to paragraph (c)(1)(iii) of this section, the December 12 variation is deemed to have occurred for purposes of this section at the end of the day on November 30, 2015. Thus, A will not generally be allocated any items of PRS attributable to the segment between December 1, 2015, and December 31, 2015; however, pursuant to paragraph (e)(1) of this section, PRS must allocate the item of income, gain, loss, deduction, or credit attributable to the ex-

traordinary item in accordance with the partners' interests in the extraordinary item at the time of day on which the extraordinary item occurred, regardless of the convention used by PRS. Thus, because A was a partner in PRS at 3:15 p.m. on December 7, 2015 (ignoring application of PRS's convention), A must be allocated a share of the extraordinary item.

Example (3). Assume the same facts as in *Example 2*, except that PRS is a publicly traded partnership (within the meaning of section 7704(b)) and A held a publicly traded unit (as described in § 1.7704–1(b) or 1.7704–1(c) (1)) in PRS. Under PRS's monthly convention, the December 12 variation is deemed to have occurred for purposes of this section at the end of the day on November 30, 2015. Pursuant to paragraph (e)(1) of this section, a publicly traded partnership (as defined in section 7704(b)) may choose to respect its conventions in determining who held its publicly traded units (as described in § 1.7704–1(b) or § 1.7704–1(c)(1)) at the time of the occurrence of an extraordinary item. Therefore, PRS may choose to treat A as not having been a partner in PRS for purposes of this paragraph (e) at the time the extraordinary item arose, and thus PRS may choose not to allocate A any share of the extraordinary item.

Example (4). A and B each own a 15 percent interest in PRS, a partnership that is not a publicly traded partnership and for which capital is a material income-producing factor. At 9:00 a.m. on April 25, 2015, A sells its entire interest in PRS to new partner D. At 3:00 p.m. on April 25, 2015, PRS incurs an extraordinary item (within the meaning of paragraph (e)(2) of this section). At 5:00 p.m. on April 25, 2015, B sells its entire interest in PRS to new partner E. Under paragraph (e)(1) of this section, PRS must allocate the extraordinary item in accordance with the partners' interests at 3:00 p.m. on April 25, 2015. Accordingly, a portion of the extraordinary item will be allocated to each of B and D, but no portion will be allocated to A or E.

Example (5). PRS, a calendar year partnership that is not a publicly traded partnership, has a variation in a partner's interest during 2015 and the exceptions in paragraph (b) of this section do not apply. During 2015 PRS has two extraordinary items: PRS recognizes $8 million of gross income on the sale outside the ordinary course of business of an asset described in paragraph (e)(2)(ii) of this section, and PRS also recognizes $12 million of gross income from a tort settlement as described in paragraph (e)(2)(vii) of this section. PRS's gross income (including the gross income from the extraordinary items) for the taxable year is $200 million. The gain from all items described in paragraph (e)(2)(ii) of this section is less than five percent of PRS's gross income ($8 million gross income from the asset sale divided by $200 million total gross income, or four percent) and all of the extraordinary items of PRS from classes that are less than five percent of PRS's gross income ($8 million), in the aggregate, do not exceed $10 million for the taxable year. Thus, the $8 million gain recognized on the asset sale is considered a small item under paragraph (e)(3) of this section and is therefore excepted from the rules of paragraph (e)(1) of this section. Because the gross income attributable to the tort settlement exceeds five percent of PRS's gross income (six percent), the tort settlement gross income is not considered a small item under paragraph (e)(3) of this section. Therefore, the $12 million gross income attributable to the tort settlement must be allocated according to the rules of paragraph (e)(1) of this section in accordance with PRS's partners' interests in the item at the time of the day that the tort settlement income arose.

Example (6). Assume the same facts as Example 5, except that during the year, PRS also recognizes two additional extraordinary items: $2 million of gross income from the sale of a capital asset described in paragraph (e)(2)(i) of this section, and $1 million of gross income from discharge of indebtedness described in paragraph (e)(2)(vi) of this section. Although the gain from items described in each of paragraphs (e)(2)(i), (e)(2)(ii), and (e)(2)(vi) of this section is each less than five percent of PRS's gross income, the extraordinary items of PRS from classes that are less than five percent of PRS's gross income ($11 million), in the aggregate, exceeds $10 million for the taxable year. Thus, none of the items are considered a small item under paragraph (e)(3) of this section. Therefore, the items attributable to the sale of the capital asset, the sale of the trade or business asset, the discharge of indebtedness income, and the tort settlement must each be allocated according to the rules of paragraph (e)(1) of this section in accordance with PRS's partners' interests in the items at the time of the day that the items arose.

(f) Agreement of the partners. For purposes of paragraphs (a)(3)(iii) (relating to selection of the proration method), (c)(3) (relating to selection of the semi-monthly or monthly convention), (d) (relating to performance of regular monthly or semi-monthly interim closings), and (e)(2)(ix) (relating to selection of additional extraordinary items) of this section, the term agreement of the partners means either an agreement of all the partners to select the method, convention, or extraordinary item in a dated, written statement maintained with the partnership's books and records, including, for example, a selection that is included in the partnership agreement, or a selection of the method, convention, or extraordinary item made by a person authorized to make that selection, including under a grant of general authority provided for by either state law or in the partnership agreement, if that person's selection is in a dated, written statement maintained with the partnership's books and records. In either case, the dated written agreement must be maintained with the partnership's books and records by the due date, including extension, of the partnership's tax return.

* * *

§ 1.707–1 Transactions between partner and partnership.

(a) Partner not acting in capacity as partner. A partner who engages in a transaction with a partnership other than in his capacity as a partner shall be treated as if he were not a member of the partnership with respect to such transaction. Such transactions include, for example, loans of money or property by the partnership to the partner or by the partner to the partnership, the sale of property by the partner to the partnership, the purchase of property by the partner from the partnership, and the rendering of services by the partnership to the partner or by the partner to the partnership. Where a partner retains the ownership of property but allows the partnership to use such separately owned property for partnership purposes (for example, to obtain credit or to secure firm creditors by guaranty, pledge, or other agreement) the transaction is treated as one between a partnership and a partner not acting in his capacity as a partner. However, transfers of money or property by a partner to a partnership as contributions, or transfers of money or property by a partnership to a partner as distributions, are not transactions included within the provisions of this section. In all cases, the substance of the transaction will govern rather than its form. See paragraph (c) (3) of § 1.731–1.

(b) Certain sales or exchanges of property with respect to controlled partnerships — (1) Losses disallowed. (i) No deduction shall be allowed for a loss on a sale or exchange of property (other than an interest in the partnership), directly or indirectly, between a partnership and a partner who owns, directly or indirectly, more than 50 percent of the capital interest or profits interest in such partnership. A loss on a sale or exchange of property, directly or indirectly, between two partnerships in which the same persons own, directly or indirectly, more than 50 percent of the capital interest or profits interest in each partnership shall not be allowed.

(ii) If a gain is realized upon the subsequent sale or exchange by a transferee of property with respect to which a loss was disallowed under the provisions of subdivision (i) of this subparagraph, section 267(d) (relating to amount of gain where loss previously disallowed) shall apply as though the loss were disallowed under section 267(a)(1).

(2) Gains treated as ordinary income. Any gain recognized upon the sale or exchange, directly or indirectly, of property which, in the hands of the transferee immediately after the transfer, is property other than a capital asset, as defined in section 1221, shall be ordinary income if the transaction is between a partnership and a partner who owns, directly or indirectly, more than 80 percent of the capital interest or profits interest in the partnership. This rule also applies where such a transaction is between partnerships in which the same persons own, directly or indirectly, more than 80 percent of the capital interest or profits interest in each partnership. The term "property other than a capital asset" includes (but is not limited to) trade accounts receivable, inventory, stock in trade, and depreciable or real property used in the trade or business.

(3) Ownership of a capital or profits interest. In determining the extent of the ownership by a partner, as defined in section 761(b), of his capital interest or profits interest in a partnership, the rules for constructive ownership of stock provided in section 267(c) (1), (2), (4), and (5) shall be applied for the purpose of section 707(b) and this paragraph. Under these rules, ownership of a capital or profits interest in a partnership may be attributed to a person who is not a partner as defined in section 761(b) in order that another partner may be considered the constructive owner of such interest under section 267(c). However, section 707(b)(1)(A) does not apply to a constructive owner of a partnership interest since he is not a partner as defined in section 761(b). For example, where trust T is a partner in the partnership ABT, and AW, A's wife, is the sole beneficiary of the trust, the ownership of a capital and profits interest in the partnership by T will be attributed to AW only for the purpose of further attributing the ownership of such interest to A. See section 267(c)(1) and (5). If A, B, and T are equal partners, then A will be considered as owning more than 50 percent of the capital and profits interest in the partnership, and losses on transactions between him and the partnership will be disallowed by section 707(b)(1)(A). However, a loss sustained by AW on a sale or exchange of property with the partnership would not be disallowed by section 707, but will be disallowed to the extent provided in paragraph (b) of § 1.267(b)–1. See section 267(a) and (b), and the regulations thereunder.

(c) **Guaranteed payments.** Payments made by a partnership to a partner for services or for the use of capital are considered as made to a person who is not a partner, to the extent such payments are determined without regard to the income of the partnership. However, a partner must include such payments as ordinary income for his taxable year within or with which ends the partnership taxable year in which the partnership deducted such payments as paid or accrued under its method of accounting. See section 706(a) and paragraph (a) of § 1.706–1. Guaranteed payments are considered as made to one who is not a member of the partnership only for the purposes of section 61(a) (relating to gross income) and section 162(a) (relating to trade or business expenses). For a guaranteed payment to be a partnership deduction, it must meet the same tests under section 162(a) as it would if the payment had been made to a person who is not a member of the partnership, and the rules of section 263 (relating to capital expenditures) must be taken into account. This rule does not affect the deductibility to the partnership of a payment described in section 736(a)(2) to a retiring partner or to a deceased partner's successor in interest. Guaranteed payments do not constitute an interest in partnership profits for purposes of sections 706(b)(3), 707(b), and

708(b). For the purposes of other provisions of the internal revenue laws, guaranteed payments are regarded as a partner's distributive share of ordinary income. Thus, a partner who receives guaranteed payments for a period during which he is absent from work because of personal injuries or sickness is not entitled to exclude such payments from his gross income under section 105(d). Similarly, a partner who receives guaranteed payments is not regarded as an employee of the partnership for the purposes of withholding of tax at source, deferred compensation plans, etc. The provisions of this paragraph may be illustrated by the following examples:

Example (1). Under the ABC partnership agreement, partner A is entitled to a fixed annual payment of $10,000 for services, without regard to the income of the partnership. His distributive share is 10 percent. After deducting the guaranteed payment, the partnership has $50,000 ordinary income. A must include $15,000 as ordinary income for his taxable year within or with which the partnership taxable year ends ($10,000 guaranteed payment plus $5,000 distributive share).

Example (2). Partner C in the CD partnership is to receive 30 percent of partnership income as determined before taking into account any guaranteed payments, but not less than $10,000. The income of the partnership is $60,000, and C is entitled to $18,000 (30 percent of $60,000) as his distributive share. No part of this amount is a guaranteed payment. However, if the partnership had income of $20,000 instead of $60,000, $6,000 (30 percent of $20,000) would be partner C's distributive share, and the remaining $4,000 payable to C would be a guaranteed payment.

Example (3). Partner X in the XY partnership is to receive a payment of $10,000 for services, plus 30 percent of the taxable income or loss of the partnership. After deducting the payment of $10,000 to partner X, the XY partnership has a loss of $9,000. Of this amount, $2,700 (30 percent of the loss) is X's distributive share of partnership loss and, subject to section 704(d), is to be taken into account by him in his return. In addition, he must report as ordinary income the guaranteed payment of $10,000 made to him by the partnership.

Example (4). Assume the same facts as in example (3) of this paragraph, except that, instead of a $9,000 loss, the partnership has $30,000 in capital gains and no other items of income or deduction except the $10,000 paid X as a guaranteed payment. Since the items of partnership income or loss must be segregated under section 702(a), the partnership has a $10,000 ordinary loss and $30,000 in capital gains. X's 30 percent distributive shares of these amounts are $3,000 ordinary loss and $9,000 capital gain. In addition, X has received a $10,000 guaranteed payment which is ordinary income to him.

§ 1.707–2 Disguised payments for services. [Reserved.]

§ 1.707–3 Disguised sales of property to partnership; general rules.

(a) Treatment of transfers as a sale — (1) In general. Except as otherwise provided in this section, if a transfer of property by a partner to a partnership and one or more transfers of money or other consideration by the partnership to that partner are described in paragraph (b)(1) of this section, the transfers are treated as a sale of property, in whole or in part, to the partnership.

(2) Definition and timing of sale. For purposes of § § 1.707–3 through 1.707–5, the use of the term sale (or any variation of that word) to refer to a transfer of property by a partner to a partnership and a transfer of consideration by a partnership to a partner means a sale or exchange of that property, in whole or in part, to the partnership by the partner acting in a capacity other than as a member of the partnership, rather than a contribution and distribution to which sections 721 and 731, respectively, apply. A transfer that is treated as a sale under

paragraph (a)(1) this section is treated as a sale for all purposes of the Internal Revenue Code (e.g., sections 453, 483, 1001, 1012, 1031 and 1274). The sale is considered to take place on the date that, under general principles of Federal tax law, the partnership is considered the owner of the property. If the transfer of money or other consideration from the partnership to the partner occurs after the transfer of property to the partnership; the partner and the partnership are treated as if, on the date of the sale, the partnership transferred to the partner an obligation to transfer to the partner money or other consideration.

(3) Application of disguised sale rules. If a person purports to transfer property to a partnership in a capacity as a partner, the rules of this section apply for purposes of determining whether the property was transferred in a disguised sale, even if it is determined after the application of the rules of this section that such person is not a partner. If after the application of the rules of this section to a purported transfer of property to a partnership, it is determined that no partnership exists because the property was actually sold, or it is otherwise determined that the contributed property is not owned by the partnership for tax purposes, the transferor of the property is treated as having sold the property to the person (or persons) that acquired ownership of the property for tax purposes.

(4) Deemed terminations under section 708. In applying the rules of this section, transfers resulting from a termination of a partnership under section 708(b)(1)(B) are disregarded.

(b) Transfers treated as a sale — (1) In general. A transfer of property (excluding money or an obligation to contribute money) by a partner to a partnership and a transfer of money or other consideration (including the assumption of or the taking subject to a liability) by the partnership to the partner constitute a sale of property, in whole or in part, by the partner to the partnership only if based on all the facts and circumstances—

(i) The transfer of money or other consideration would not have been made but for the transfer of property; and

(ii) In cases in which the transfers are not made simultaneously, the subsequent transfer is not dependent on the entrepreneurial risks of partnership operations.

(2) Facts and circumstances. The determination of whether a transfer of property by a partner to the partnership and a transfer of money or other consideration by the partnership to the partner constitute a sale, in whole or in part, under paragraph (b)(1) of this section is made based on all the facts and circumstances in each case. The weight to be given each of the facts and circumstances will depend on the particular case. Generally, the facts and circumstances existing on the date of the earliest of such transfers are the ones considered in determining whether a sale exists under paragraph (b)(1) of this section. Among the facts and circumstances that may tend to prove the existence of a sale under paragraph (b)(1) of this section are the following:

(i) That the timing and amount of a subsequent transfer are determinable with reasonable certainty at the time of an earlier transfer;

(ii) That the transferor has a legally enforceable right to the subsequent transfer;

(iii) That the partner's right to receive the transfer of money or other consideration is secured in any manner, taking into account the period during which it is secured;

(iv) That any person has made or is legally obligated to make contributions to the partnership in order to permit the partnership to make the transfer of money or other consideration;

(v) That any person has loaned or has agreed to loan the partnership the money or other consideration required to enable the partnership to make the transfer, taking into account whether any such lending obligation

is subject to contingencies related to the results of partnership operations;

(vi) That a partnership has incurred or is obligated to incur debt to acquire the money or other consideration necessary to permit it to make the transfer, taking into account the likelihood that the partnership will be able to incur that debt (considering such factors as whether any person has agreed to guarantee or otherwise assume personal liability for that debt);

(vii) That the partnership holds money or other liquid assets, beyond the reasonable needs of the business, that are expected to be available to make the transfer (taking into account the income that will be earned from those assets);

(viii) That partnership distributions, allocation or control of partnership operations is designed to effect an exchange of the burdens and benefits of ownership of property;

(ix) That the transfer of money or other consideration by the partnership to the partner is disproportionately large in relationship to the partner's general and continuing interest in partnership profits; and

(x) That the partner has no obligation to return or repay the money or other consideration to the partnership, or has such an obligation but it is likely to become due at such a distant point in the future that the present value of that obligation is small in relation to the amount of money or other consideration transferred by the partnership to the partner.

(c) Transfers made within two years presumed to be a sale—(1) In general. For purposes of this section, if within a two-year period a partner transfers property to a partnership and the partnership transfers money or other consideration to the partner (without regard to the order of the transfers), the transfers are presumed to be a sale of the property to the partnership unless the facts and circumstances clearly establish that the transfers do not constitute a sale.

(2) Disclosure of transfers made within two years. Disclosure to the Internal Revenue Service in accordance with § 1.707–8 is required if—

(i) A partner transfers property to a partnership and the partnership transfers money or other consideration to the partner with a two-year period (without regard to the order of the transfers);

(ii) The partner treats the transfers other than as a sale for tax purposes; and

(iii) The transfer of money or other consideration to the partner is not presumed to be a guaranteed payment for capital under § 1.707–4(a)(1)(ii), is not a reasonable preferred return within the meaning of § 1.707–4(a)(3), and is not an operating cash flow distribution within the meaning of § 1.707–4(b)(2).

(d) Transfers made more than two years apart presumed not to be a sale. For purposes of this section, if a transfer of money or other consideration to a partner by a partnership and the transfer of property to the partnership by that partner are more than two years apart, the transfers are presumed not to be a sale of the property to the partnership unless the facts and circumstances clearly establish that the transfers constitute a sale.

(e) Scope. This section and § § 1.707–4 through 1.707–9 apply to contributions and distributions of property described in section 707(a)(2)(A) and transfers described in section 707(a)(2)(B) of the Internal Revenue Code.

(f) Examples. The following examples illustrate the application of this section.

Example (1). Treatment of simultaneous transfers as a sale. A transfers property X to partnership AB on April 9, 1992, in exchange for an interest in the partnership. At the time of the transfer, property X has a fair market value of $4,000,000 and an adjusted tax basis of $1,200,000. Immediately after the transfer, the partnership transfers $3,000,000 in cash to A. Assume that, under this section, the partnership's transfer of cash to A is treated as part of a sale of property X to the partnership. Because the amount of cash A receives on April 9, 1992, does not equal the fair market value of the property, A is considered to have sold a portion of property X with a value of $3,000,000 to the partnership in exchange for the cash. Accordingly, A must recognize $2,100,000 of gain ($3,000,000 amount realized less $900,000 adjusted tax basis ($1,200,000 multiplied by $3,000,000/$4,000,000)). Assuming A receives no other transfers that are treated as consideration for the sale of the property under this section, A is considered to have contributed to the partnership, in A's capacity as a partner, $1,000,000 of the fair market value of the property with an adjusted tax basis of $300,000.

Example (2). Treatment of transfers at different times as a sale. (i) The facts are the same as in Example 1, except that the $3,000,000 is transferred to A one year after A's transfer of property X to the partnership. Assume that under this section the partnership's transfer of cash to A is treated as part of a sale of property X to the partnership. Assume also that the applicable Federal short-term rate for April, 1992, is 10 percent, compounded semiannually.

(ii) Under paragraph (a)(2) of this section, A and the partnership are treated as if, on April 9, 1992, A sold a portion of property X to the partnership in exchange for an obligation to transfer $3,000,000 to A one year later. Section 1274 applies to this obligation because it does not bear interest and is payable more than six months after the date of the sale. As a result, A's amount realized from the receipt of the partnership's obligation will be the imputed principal amount of the partnership's obligation to transfer $3,000,000 to A, which equals $2,721,088 (the present value on April 9, 1992, of a $3,000,000 payment due one year later, determined using a discount rate of 10 percent, compounded semiannually). Therefore, A's amount realized from the receipt of the partnership's obligation is

$2,721,088 (without regard to whether the sale is reported under the installment method). A is therefore considered to have sold only $2,721,088 of the fair market value of property X. The remainder of the $3,000,000 payment ($278,912) is characterized in accordance with the provisions of section 1272. Accordingly, A must recognize $1,904,761 of gain ($2,721,088 amount realized less $816,327 adjusted tax basis ($1,200,000 multiplied by $2,721,088/$4,000,000)) on the sale of property X to the partnership. The gain is reportable under the installment method of section 453 if the sale is otherwise eligible. Assuming A receives no other transfers that are treated as consideration for the sale of property under this section, A is considered to have contributed to the partnership, in A's capacity as a partner, $1,278,912 of the fair market value of property X with an adjusted tax basis of $383,673.

Example (3). Operation of presumption for transfers within two years. (i) C transfers undeveloped land to the CD partnership in exchange for an interest in the partnership. The partnership intends to construct a building on the land. At the time the land is transferred to the partnership, it is unencumbered and has an adjusted tax basis of $500,000 and a fair market value of $1,000,000. The partnership agreement provides that upon completing construction of the building the partnership will distribute $900,000 to C.

(ii) If, within two years of C's transfer of land to the partnership, a transfer is made to C pursuant to the provision requiring a distribution upon completion of the building, the transfer is presumed to be, under paragraph (c) of this section, part of a sale of the land to the partnership. C may rebut the presumption that the transfer is part of a sale if the facts and circumstances clearly establish that—

(A) The transfer to C would have been made without regard to C's transfer of land to the partnership; or

(B) The partnership's obligation or ability to make this transfer to C depends, at the time of the transfer to the partnership, on the entrepreneurial risks of partnership operations.

(iii) For example, if the partnership will be able to fund the transfer of cash to C only to the extent that permanent loan proceeds exceed the cost of constructing the building, the fact that excess permanent loan proceeds will be available only if the cost to complete the building is significantly less than the amount projected by a reasonable budget would be evidence that the transfer to C is not part of a sale. Similarly, a condition that limits the amount of the permanent loan to the cost of constructing the building (and thereby limits the partnership's ability to make a transfer to C) unless all or a substantial portion of the building is leased would be evidence that the transfer to C is not part of a sale, if a significant risk exists that the partnership may not be able to lease the building to that extent. Another factor that may prove that the transfer of cash to C is not part of a sale would be that, at the time the land is transferred to the partnership, no lender has committed to make a permanent loan to fund the transfer of cash to C.

(iv) Facts indicating that the transfer of cash to C is not part of a sale, however, may be offset by other factors. An offsetting factor to restrictions on the permanent loan proceeds may be that the permanent loan is to be a recourse loan and certain conditions to the loan are likely to be waived by the lender because of the creditworthiness of the partners or the value of the partnership's other assets. Similarly, the factor that no lender has committed to fund the transfer of cash to C may be offset by facts establishing that the partnership is obligated to attempt to obtain such a loan and that its ability to obtain such a loan is not significantly dependent on the value that will be added by successful completion of the building, or that the partnership reasonably anticipates that it will have (and will utilize) an alternative

source to fund the transfer of cash to C if the permanent loan proceeds are inadequate.

Example (4). Operation of presumption for transfers within two years. E is a partner in the equal EF partnership. The partnership owns two parcels of unimproved real property (parcels 1 and 2). Parcels 1 and 2 are unencumbered. Parcel 1 has a fair market value of $500,000, and parcel 2 has a fair market value of $1,500,000. E transfers additional unencumbered, unimproved real property (parcel 3) with a fair market value of $1,000,000 to the partnership in exchange for an increased interest in partnership profits of 66 $^2/_3$ percent. Immediately after this transfer, the partnership sells parcel 1 for $500,000 in a transaction not in the ordinary course of business. The partnership transfers the proceeds of the sale $333,333 to E and $166,667 to F in accordance with their respective partnership interests. The transfer of $333,333 to E is presumed to be, in accordance with paragraph (c) of this section, a sale, in part, of parcel 3 to the partnership. However, the facts of this example clearly establish that $250,000 of the transfer to E is not part of a sale of parcel 3 to the partnership because E would have been distributed $250,000 from the sale of parcel 1 whether or not E had transferred parcel 3 to the partnership. The transfer to E exceeds by $83,333 ($333,333 minus $250,000) the amount of the distribution that would have been made to E if E had not transferred parcel 3 to the partnership. Therefore, $83,333 of the transfer is presumed to be part of a sale of a portion of parcel 3 to the partnership by E.

Example (5). Operation of presumption for transfers more than two years apart. (i) G transfers undeveloped land to the GH partnership in exchange for an interest in the partnership. At the time the land is transferred to the partnership, it is unencumbered and has an adjusted tax basis of $500,000 and a fair market value of $1,000,000. H contributes $1,000,000 in cash in exchange for an interest in the partnership. Under the partnership agreement, the partnership is obligated to construct a building on the land. The projected construction cost is $5,000,000, which the partnership plans to fund with its $1,000,000 in cash and the proceeds of a construction loan secured by the land and improvements.

(ii) Shortly before G's transfer of the land to the partnership, the partnership secures commitments from lending institutions for construction and permanent financing. To obtain the construction loan, H guarantees completion of the building for a cost of $5,000,000. The partnership is not obligated to reimburse or indemnify H if H must make payment on the completion guarantee. The permanent loan will be funded upon completion of the building, which is expected to occur two years after G's transfer of the land. The amount of the permanent loan is to equal the lesser of $5,000,000 or 80 percent of the appraised value of the improved property at the time the permanent loan is closed. Under the partnership agreement, the partnership is obligated to apply the proceeds of the permanent loan to retire the construction loan and to hold any excess proceeds for transfer to G 25 months after G's transfer of the land to the partnership. The appraised value of the improved property at the time the permanent loan is closed is expected to exceed $5,000,000 only if the partnership is able to lease a substantial portion of the improvements by that time, and there is a significant risk that the partnership will not be able to achieve a satisfactory occupancy level. The partnership completes construction of the building for the projected cost of $5,000,000 approximately two years after G's transfer of the land. Shortly thereafter, the permanent loan is funded in the amount of $5,000,000. At the time of funding the land and building have an appraised value of $7,000,000. The partnership transfers the $1,000,000 excess permanent loan proceeds to G 25 months after G's transfer of the land to the partnership.

(iii) G's transfer of the land to the partnership and the partnership's transfer of

$1,000,000 to G occurred more than two years apart. In accordance with paragraph (d) of this section, those transfers are presumed not to be a sale unless the facts and circumstances clearly establish that the transfers constitute a sale of the property, in whole or part, to the partnership. The transfer of $1,000,000 to G would not have been made but for G's transfer of the land to the partnership. In addition, at the time G transferred the land to the partnership, G had a legally enforceable right to receive a transfer from the partnership at a specified time an amount that equals the excess of the permanent loan proceeds over $4,000,000. In this case, however, there was a significant risk that the appraised value of the property would be insufficient to support a permanent loan in excess of $4,000,000 because of the risk that the partnership would not be able to achieve a sufficient occupancy level. Therefore, the facts of this example indicate that at the time G transferred the land to the partnership the subsequent transfer of $1,000,000 to G depended on the entrepreneurial risks of partnership operations. Accordingly, G's transfer of the land to the partnership is not treated as part of a sale.

Example (6). Rebuttal of presumption for transfers more than two years apart. The facts are the same as in Example 5, except that the partnership is able to secure a commitment for a permanent loan in the amount of $5,000,000 without regard to the appraised value of the improved property at the time the permanent loan is funded. Under these facts, at the time that G transferred the land to the partnership the subsequent transfer of $1,000,000 to G was not dependent on the entrepreneurial risks of partnership operations, because during the period before the permanent loan is funded, the permanent lender's obligation to make a loan in the amount necessary to fund the transfer is not subject to the contingencies related to the risks of partnership operations, and after the permanent loan is funded, the partnership holds liquid assets sufficient to make the transfer. Therefore, the facts and circumstances

clearly establish that G's transfer of the land to the partnership is part of a sale.

Example (7). Operation of presumption for transfers more than two years apart. The facts are the same as in Example 6, except that H does not guarantee either that the improvements will be completed or that the cost to the partnership of completing the improvements will not exceed $5,000,000. Under these facts, if there is a significant risk that the improvements will not be completed, G's transfer of the land to the partnership will not be treated as part of a sale because the lender is required to make the permanent loan if the improvements are not completed. Similarly, the transfers will not be treated as a sale to the extent that there is a significant risk that the cost of constructing the improvements will exceed $5,000,000, because, in the absence of a guarantee of the cost of the improvements by H, the $5,000,000 proceeds of the permanent loan might not be sufficient to retire the construction loan and fund the transfer to G. In either case, the transfer of cash to G would be dependent on the entrepreneurial risks of partnership operations.

Example (8). Rebuttal of presumption for transfers more than two years apart. (i) On February 1, 1992, I, J, and K form partnership IJK. On formation of the partnership, I transfers an unencumbered office building with a fair market value of $50,000,000 and an adjusted tax basis of $20,000,000 to the partnership, and J and K each transfer United States government securities with a fair market value and an adjusted tax basis of $25,000,000 to the partnership. Substantially all of the rentable space in the office building is leased on a long-term basis. The partnership agreement provides that all items of income, gain, loss, and deduction from the office building are to be allocated 45 percent to J, 45 percent to K, and 10 percent to I. The partnership agreement also provides that all items of income, gain, loss, and deduction from the government securities are to be allocated 90 percent to I, 5 percent to J, and 5 percent to K. The partnership agreement requires that cash flow from the office building and government securities be allocated between partners in the same manner as the items of income, gain, loss, and deduction from those properties are allocated between them. The partnership agreement complies with the requirements of § 1.704–1(b)(2)(ii)(b). It is not expected that the partnership will need to resort to the government securities or the cash flow therefrom to operate the office building. At the time the partnership is formed, I, J, and K contemplated that I's interest in the partnership would be liquidated sometime after January 31, 1994, in exchange for a transfer of the government securities and cash (if necessary). On March 1, 1995, the partnership transfers cash and the government securities to I in liquidation of I's interest in the partnership. The cash transferred to I represents the excess of I's share of the appreciation in the office building since the formation of the partnership over J's and K's share of the appreciation in the government securities since they are acquired by the partnership.

(ii) I's transfer of the office building to the partnership and the partnership's transfer of the government securities and cash to I occurred more than two years apart. Therefore, those transfers are presumed not to be a sale unless the facts and circumstances clearly establish that the transfers constitute a sale. Absent I's transfer of the office building to the (partnership, I would not have received the government securities from the partnership. The facts including the amount and nature of partnership assets) indicate that, at the time that I transferred the office building to the partnership, the timing of the transfer of the government securities to I was anticipated and was not dependent on the entrepreneurial risks of partnership operations. Moreover, the facts indicate that the partnership allocations were designed to effect an exchange of the burdens and benefits of ownership of the government securities in anticipation of the transfer of those securities to I and those burdens and benefits were effectively shifted to I on formation

of the partnership. Accordingly, the facts and circumstances clearly establish that I sold the office building to the partnership on February 1, 1992, in exchange for the partnership's obligation to transfer the government securities to I and to make certain other cash transfers to I.

§ 1.707–4 Disguised sales of property to partnership; special rules applicable to guaranteed payments, preferred returns, operating cash flow distributions, and reimbursements of preformation expenditures.

(a) Guaranteed payments and preferred returns—(1) Guaranteed payment not treated as part of a sale—(i) In general. A guaranteed payment for capital made to a partner is not treated as part of a sale of property under § 1.707–3(a) (relating to treatment of transfers as a sale). A party's characterization of a payment as a guaranteed payment for capital will not control in determining whether a payment is, in fact, a guaranteed payment for capital. The term guaranteed payment for capital means any payment to a partner by a partnership that is determined without regard to partnership income and is for the use of that partner's capital. See section 707(c). For this purpose, one or more payments are not made for the use of a partner's capital if the payments are designed to liquidate all or part of the partner's interest in property contributed to the partnership rather than to provide the partner with a return on an investment in the partnership.

(ii) Reasonable guaranteed payments. Notwithstanding the presumption set forth in § 1.707–3(c) (relating to transfers made within two years of each other), for purposes of section 707(a)(2) and the regulations thereunder a transfer of money to a partner that is characterized by the parties as a guaranteed payment for capital, is determined without regard to the income of the partnership and is reasonable (within the meaning of paragraph (a)(3) of this section) is presumed to be a guaranteed payment for capital unless the facts and circumstances clearly establish that the transfer is not a guaranteed payment for capital and is part of a sale.

(iii) Unreasonable guaranteed payments. A transfer of money to a partner that is characterized by the parties as a guaranteed payment for capital but that is not reasonable (within the meaning of paragraph (a)(3) of this section) is presumed not to be a guaranteed payment for capital unless the facts and circumstances clearly establish that the transfer is a guaranteed payment for capital. A transfer that is not a guaranteed payment for capital is subject to the rules of § 1.707–3.

(2) Presumption regarding reasonable preferred returns. Notwithstanding the presumption set forth in § 1.707–3(c) (relating to transfers made within two years of each other), a transfer of money to a partner that is characterized by the parties as a preferred return and that is reasonable (within the meaning of paragraph (a)(3) of this section) is presumed not to be part of a sale of property to the partnership unless the facts and circumstances (including the likelihood and expected timing of the subsequent allocation of income or gain to support the preferred return) clearly establish that the transfer is part of a sale. The term preferred return means a preferential distribution of partnership cash flow to a partner with respect to capital contributed to the partnership by the partner that will be matched, to the extent available, by an allocation of income or gain.

(3) Definition of reasonable preferred returns and guaranteed payments—(i) In general. A transfer of money to a partner that is characterized as a preferred return or guaranteed payment for capital is reasonable only to the extent that the transfer is made to the partner pursuant to a written provision of a partnership agreement that provides for payment for the use of capital in a reasonable amount, and only to the extent that the payment is made for the use of capital after the date on which that provision is added to the partnership agreement.

(ii) Reasonable amount. A transfer of money that is made to a partner during any partnership taxable year and is characterized as a preferred return or guaranteed payment for capital is reasonable in amount if the sum of any preferred return and any guaranteed payment for capital that is payable for that year does not exceed the amount determined by multiplying either the partner's unreturned capital at the beginning of the year or, at the partner's option, the partner's weighted average capital balance for the year (with either amount appropriately adjusted, taking into account the relevant compounding periods, to reflect any unpaid preferred return or guaranteed payment for capital that is payable to the partner) by the safe harbor interest rate for that year. The safe harbor interest rate for a partnership's taxable year equals 150 percent of the highest applicable Federal rate, at the appropriate compounding period or periods, in effect at any time from the time that the right to the preferred return or guaranteed payment for capital is first established pursuant to a binding, written agreement among the partners through the end of the taxable year. A partner's unreturned capital equals the excess of the aggregate amount of money and the fair market value of other consideration (net of liabilities) contributed by the partner to the partnership over the aggregate amount of money and the fair market value of other consideration (net of liabilities) distributed by the partnership to the partner other than transfers of money that are presumed to be guaranteed payments for capital under paragraph (a)(1)(ii) of this section, transfers of money that are reasonable preferred returns within the meaning of this paragraph (a)(3), and operating cash flow distributions within the meaning of paragraph (b)(2) of this section.

(4) Examples. The following examples illustrate the application of paragraph (a) of this section:

Example (1). Transfer presumed to be a guaranteed payment. (i) A transfers property with a fair market value of $100,000 to partnership AB. At the time of A's transfer, the partnership agreement is amended to provide that A is to receive a guaranteed payment for the use of A's capital of 10 percent (compounded annually) of the fair market value of the transferred property in each of the three years following the transfer. The partnership agreement provides that partnership net taxable income and loss will be allocated equally between partners A and B, and that partnership cash flow will be distributed in accordance with the allocation of partnership net taxable income and loss. The partnership would be allowed a deduction in the year paid if the transfers made to A are treated as guaranteed payments under section 707(c). Under the partnership agreement, that deduction would be allocated in the same manner as any other item of partnership deduction. The partnership agreement complies with the requirements of § 1.704–1(b)(2)(ii)(b). The partnership agreement does not provide for the payment of a preferred return and, other than the guaranteed payment to be paid to A, no transfer is expected to be made during the three year period following A's transfer that is not an operating cash flow distribution (within the meaning of paragraph (b)(2) of this section). Assume that the highest applicable Federal rate in effect at the time of A's transfer is eight percent compounded annually.

(ii) The transfer of money to be made to A under the partnership agreement is characterized by the parties as a guaranteed payment for capital and is determined without regard to the income of the partnership. The transfer is also reasonable within the meaning of § 1.707–4(a) (3). The transfer, therefore, is presumed to be a guaranteed payment for capital. The presumption set forth in § 1.707–3(c) (relating to transfers made within two years of each other) thus does not apply to this transfer. The transfer will not be treated as part of a sale of property to the partnership unless the facts and circumstances clearly establish that the transfer is not a guaranteed payment for capital but is part of a sale.

(iii) The presumption that the transfer is a guaranteed payment for capital is not rebutted, because there are no facts indicating that the transfer is not a guaranteed payment for the use of capital.

Example (2). Transfers characterized as guaranteed payments treated as part of a sale. *(i)* C and D form partnership CD. C transfers property with a fair market value of $100,000 and an adjusted tax basis of $20,000 in exchange for a partnership interest. D is responsible for managing the day-to-day operations of the partnership and makes no capital contribution to the partnership upon its formation. The partnership agreement provides that C is to receive payments characterized as guaranteed payments and determined without regard to partnership income of $8,333 per year for the first four years of partnership operations for the use of C's capital. In addition, the partnership agreement provides that—

(A) Partnership net taxable income and loss will be allocated 75 percent to C and 25 percent to D; and

(B) All partnership cash flow (determined prior to consideration of the guaranteed payment) will be distributed 75 percent to C and 25 percent to D except that guaranteed payments that the partnership is obligated to make to C are payable solely out of D's share of the partnership's cash flow.

(ii) If D's share of the partnership's cash flow is not sufficient to make the guaranteed payment to C, then D is obligated to contribute any shortfall to the partnership, even in the event the partnership is liquidated. Thus, the effect of the guaranteed payment arrangement is that the guaranteed payment to C is funded entirely by D. The partnership agreement complies with the requirements of § 1.704–1(b)(2) (ii)(b). Assume that, at the time the partnership is formed, the partnership or D could borrow $25,000 pursuant to a loan requiring equal payments of principal and interest over a four-year term at the current market interest rate of approximately 12 percent (compounded annu-

ally). Assume that the highest applicable Federal rate in effect at the time the partnership is formed is 10 percent compounded annually.

(iii) The transfer of money to be made to C under the partnership agreement is characterized by the parties as a guaranteed payment for capital and is determined without regard to the income of the partnership. The transfer is also reasonable within the meaning of § 1.707–4(a)(3). The transfer, therefore, is presumed to be a guaranteed payment for capital. The presumption set forth in § 1.707–3(c) (relating to transfers made within two years of each other) thus does not apply to this transfer. The transfer will not be treated as part of a sale of property to the partnership unless the facts and circumstances clearly establish that the transfer is not a guaranteed payment for capital and is part of a sale.

(iv) For the first four years of partnership operations, the total guaranteed payments made to C under the partnership agreement will equal $33,332. If the characterization of those payments as guaranteed payments for capital within the meaning of section 707(c) were respected, C would be allocated $24,999 of the deductions that would be claimed by the partnership for those payments, thereby leaving the balance in C's capital account approximately $25,000 less than it would have been if the guaranteed payments had not been made. The guaranteed payments thus have the effect of offsetting approximately $25,000 of the credit made to C's capital account for the property transferred to the partnership by C. C's resulting capital account is approximately equivalent to the capital account C would have had if C had only contributed 75 percent of the property to the partnership. Furthermore, the effect of D's funding the guaranteed payment to C (either through reduced distributions of cash flow to D or additional contributions) is that D's capital account is approximately equivalent to the capital account D would have had if D had contributed 25 percent of the property (or contributed cash so that the part-

nership could purchase the 25 percent). Moreover, a $25,000 loan requiring equal payments of principal and interest over a four-year term at the current market interest rate of 12 percent (compounded annually), would have resulted in annual payments of principal and interest of $8,230.86. Consequently, the guaranteed payments effectively place the partners in the same economic position that they would have been in had D purchased a one-quarter interest in the property from C financed at the current market rate of interest, and then C and D each contributed their share of the property to the partnership. In view of the burden the guaranteed payments place on D's right to transfers of partnership cash flow and D's legal obligation to make contributions to the partnership to the extent necessary to fund the guaranteed payments, D has effectively purchased through the partnership a one-quarter interest in the property from C.

(v) Under these facts, the presumption that the transfers to C are guaranteed payments for capital is rebutted, because the facts and circumstances clearly establish that the transfers are part of a sale and not guaranteed payments for capital. Under § 1.707–3(a), C and the partnership are treated as if C sold a one-quarter interest in the property to the partnership in exchange for a promissory note evidencing the partnership's obligation to make the guaranteed payments.

(b) Presumption regarding operating cash flow distributions—(1) In general. Notwithstanding the presumption set forth in § 1.707–3(c) (relating to transfers made within two years of each other), an operating cash flow distribution is presumed not to be part of a sale of property to the partnership unless the facts and circumstances clearly establish that the transfer is part of a sale.

(2) Operating cash flow distributions— (i) In general. One or more transfers of money by the partnership to a partner during a taxable year of the partnership are operating cash flow distributions for purposes of paragraph (b)(1) of this section to the extent that those transfers are not presumed to be guaranteed payments for capital under paragraph (a)(1)(ii) of this section, are not reasonable preferred returns within the meaning of paragraph (a)(3) of this section, are not characterized by the parties as distributions to the partner acting in a capacity other than as a partner, and to the extent they do not exceed the product of the net cash flow of the partnership from operations for the year multiplied by the lesser of the partner's percentage interest in overall partnership profits for that year or the partner's percentage interest in overall partnership profits for the life of the partnership. For purposes of the preceding sentence, the net cash flow of the partnership from operations for a taxable year is an amount equal to the taxable income or loss of the partnership arising in the ordinary course of the partnership's business and investment activities, increased by tax exempt interest, depreciation, amortization, cost recovery allowances and other noncash charges deducted in determining such taxable income and decreased by—

(A) Principal payments made on any partnership indebtedness;

(B) Property replacement or contingency reserves actually established by the partnership;

(C) Capital expenditures when made other than from reserves or from borrowings the proceeds of which are not included in operating cash flow; and

(D) Any other cash expenditures (including preferred returns) not deducted in determining such taxable income or loss.

(ii) Operating cash flow safe harbor. For any taxable year, in determining a partner's operating cash flow distributions for the year, the partner may use the partner's smallest percentage interest under the terms of the partnership agreement in any material item of partnership income or gain that may be realized by the partnership in the three-year period beginning with such taxable year. This provision is merely intended to provide taxpayers with a safe harbor and is not intended to preclude a taxpayer from using a different percentage under the rules of paragraph (b)(2)(i) of this section.

(iii) Tiered partnerships. In the case of tiered partnerships, the upper-tier partnership must take into account its share of the net cash flow from operations of the lower-tier partnership applying principles similar to those described in paragraph (b)(2)(i) of this section, so that the amount of the upper-tier partnership's operating cash flow distributions is neither overstated nor understated.

(c) Accumulation of guaranteed payments, preferred returns, and operating cash flow distributions. Guaranteed payments for capital, preferred returns, and operating cash flow distributions presumed not to be part of a sale under the rules of paragraphs (a) and (b) of this section do not lose the benefit of the presumption by reason of being retained for distribution in a later year.

(d) Exception for reimbursements of pre-formation expenditures. (1) In general. A transfer of money or other consideration by the partnership to a partner is not treated as part of a sale of property by the partner to the partnership under § 1.707–3(a) (relating to treatment of transfers as a sale) to the extent that the transfer to the partner by the partnership is made to reimburse the partner for, and does not exceed the amount of, capital expenditures that—

(i) Are incurred during the two-year period preceding the transfer by the partner to the partnership; and

(ii) Are incurred by the partner with respect to—

(A) Partnership organization and syndication costs described in section 709; or

(B) Property transferred to the partnership by the partner, but only to the extent the reimbursed capital expenditures do not exceed 20 percent of the fair market value of such property at the time of the transfer (the 20-percent limitation). However, the 20-percent limitation of this paragraph (d)(1)(ii)(B) does not apply if the fair market value of the transferred property does not exceed 120 percent of the partner's adjusted basis in the transferred property at the time of the transfer (the 120-percent test). This paragraph (d)(1)(ii)(B) shall be applied on a property-by-property basis, except that a partner may aggregate any of the transferred property under this paragraph (d)(1) to the extent—

(1) The total fair market value of such aggregated property (of which no single property's fair market value exceeds 1 percent of the total fair market value of such aggregated property) is not greater than the lesser of 10 percent of the total fair market value of all property, excluding money and marketable securities (as defined under section 731(c)), transferred by the partner to the partnership, or $1,000,000;

(2) The partner uses a reasonable aggregation method that is consistently applied; and

(3) Such aggregation of property is not part of a plan a principal purpose of which is to avoid §§ 1.707–3 through 1.707–5.

(C) [Reserved].

(2) Capital expenditures incurred by another person. For purposes of paragraph (d)(1) of this section, a partner steps in the shoes of a person (to the extent the person was not previously reimbursed under paragraph (d)(1) of this section) with respect to capital expenditures the person incurred with respect to property transferred to the partnership by the partner to the extent the partner acquired the property from the person in a nonrecognition transaction described in section 351, 381(a), 721, or 731.

(3) Contribution of a partnership interest with capital expenditures property. If a person transfers property with respect to which the person incurred capital expenditures (capital expenditures property) to a partnership (lower-tier partnership) and, within the two-year period beginning on the date upon which the person incurred the capital expenditures, transfers an interest in the lower-tier partnership to another partnership (upper-tier partnership) in a nonrecognition transaction under section 721, the upper-tier partnership steps in the shoes of the person who transferred the capital expenditures property to the lower-tier partnership with respect to the capital expenditures that are not otherwise reimbursed to the person. The upper-tier partnership may be reimbursed by the lower-tier partnership under paragraph (d)(1) of this section to the extent the person could have been reimbursed for the capital expenditures by the lower-tier partnership under paragraph (d)(1) of this section. In addition, for purposes of paragraph (d)(1) of this section, the person is deemed to have transferred the capital expenditures property to the upper-tier partnership and may be reimbursed by the upper-tier partnership under paragraph (d)(1) of this section to the extent the person could have been reimbursed for the capital expenditures by the lower-tier partnership under paragraph (d)(1) of this section and has not otherwise been previously reimbursed. The aggregate reimbursements for capital expenditures under this paragraph (d)(3) shall not exceed the amount that the person could have been reimbursed for such capital expenditures under paragraph (d)(1) of this section.

(4) Special rule for qualified liabilities— (i) In general. For purposes of paragraph (d)(1) of this section, if capital expenditures were funded by the proceeds of a qualified liability defined in § 1.707–5(a)(6)(i) that a partnership assumes or takes property subject to in connection with a transfer of property to the partnership by a partner, a transfer of money or other consideration by the partnership to the partner is not treated as made to reimburse the partner for such capital expenditures to the extent the transfer of money or other consideration by the partnership to the partner exceeds the partner's share of the qualified liability (as determined under § 1.707–5(a)(2), (3), and (4)). Capital expenditures are treated as fund-

ed by the proceeds of a qualified liability to the extent the proceeds are either traceable to the capital expenditures under § 1.163–8T or were actually used to fund the capital expenditures, irrespective of the tracing requirements under § 1.163–8T.

(ii) Anti-abuse rule. If capital expenditures and a qualified liability are incurred under a plan a principal purpose of which is to avoid the requirements of paragraph (d)(4)(i) of this section, the capital expenditures are deemed funded by the qualified liability.

(5) Scope of capital expenditures. For purposes of this section and § 1.707–5, the term *capital expenditures* has the same meaning as the term *capital expenditures* has under the Internal Revenue Code and applicable regulations, except that it includes capital expenditures taxpayers elect to deduct, and does not include deductible expenses taxpayers elect to treat as capital expenditures.

(6) Example. The following example illustrates the application of paragraph (d) of this section:

Example. Intangible treated as separate property. (i) Z transfers to a partnership a business the material assets of which include a tangible asset and goodwill from the reputation of the business. At the time Z transfers the business to the partnership, the tangible asset has a fair market value of $550,000 and an adjusted basis of $450,000. The goodwill is a section 197 intangible with a fair market value of $100,000 and an adjusted basis of $0. Z incurred $130,000 of capital expenditures with respect to improvements to the tangible asset (which amount is reflected in its adjusted basis) one year preceding the transfer. Z would like to be reimbursed by the partnership for the capital expenditures with an amount that qualifies for the exception for reimbursement of preformation expenditures under paragraph (d)(1) of this section.

(ii) Under paragraph (d)(1)(ii)(B) of this section, the 20-percent limitation on reim-

bursed capital expenditures applies on a property-by-property basis. The 120-percent test also applies on a property-by-property basis. Accordingly, the tangible asset and the goodwill each constitutes a separate property. Z incurred the capital expenditures with respect to the tangible asset only. The $550,000 fair market value of the tangible asset exceeds 120 percent of Z's $450,000 adjusted basis in the asset at the time of the transfer (120 percent × $450,000 = $540,000). Thus, the 20-percent limitation applies so that the reimbursement of Z's $130,000 of capital expenditures is limited to 20 percent of the fair market value of the tangible asset, or $110,000 (20 percent × $550,000).

(e) Other exceptions. The Commissioner may provide by guidance published in the Internal Revenue Bulletin that other payments or transfers to a partner are not treated as part of a sale for purposes of section 707(a)(2) and the regulations thereunder.

(f) Ordering rule cross reference. For payments or transfers by a partnership to a partner to which the rules under this section and § 1.707–5(b) apply, see the ordering rule under § 1.707–5(b)(3).

§ 1.707–5 Disguised sales of property to partnership; special rules relating to liabilities.

(a) Liability assumed or taken subject to by partnership—(1) In general. For purposes of this section and §§ 1.707–3 and 1.707–4, if a partnership assumes or takes property subject to a qualified liability (as defined in paragraph (a)(6) of this section) of a partner, the partnership is treated as transferring consideration to the partner only to the extent provided in paragraph (a)(5) of this section. By contrast, if the partnership assumes or takes property subject to a liability of the partner other than a qualified liability, the partnership is treated as transferring consideration to the partner to the extent that the amount of the liability exceeds the partner's share of that liability immediately after the partnership assumes or takes subject to the liability as provided in paragraphs (a) (2), (3) and (4) of this section.

(2) Partner's share of liability. A partner's share of any liability of the partnership is determined under the following rules:

(i) Recourse liability. A partner's share of a recourse liability of the partnership equals the partner's share of the liability under the rules of section 752 and the regulations thereunder. A partnership liability is a recourse liability to the extent that the obligation is a recourse liability under § 1.752–1(a)(1) or would be treated as a recourse liability under that section if it were treated as a partnership liability for purposes of that section.

(ii) Nonrecourse liability. A partner's share of a nonrecourse liability of the partnership is determined by applying the same percentage used to determine the partner's share of the excess nonrecourse liability under § 1.752–3(a)(3). A partnership liability is a nonrecourse liability of the partnership to the extent that the obligation is a nonrecourse liability under § 1.752–1(a)(2) or would be a nonrecourse liability of the partnership under § 1.752–1(a)(2) if it were treated as a partnership liability for purposes of that section.

(3) Reduction of partner's share of liability. For purposes of this section, a partner's share of a liability, immediately after a partnership assumes or takes property subject to the liability, is determined by taking into account a subsequent reduction in the partner's share if—

(i) At the time that the partnership assumes or takes property subject to the liability, it is anticipated that the transferring partner's share of the liability will be subsequently reduced;

(ii) The anticipated reduction is not subject to the entrepreneurial risks of partnership operations; and

(iii) The reduction of the partner's share of the liability is part of a plan that has as one of its principal purposes minimizing the extent to which the assumption of or taking property subject to the liability is treated as part of a sale under § 1.707–3.

(4) Special rule applicable to transfers of encumbered property to a partnership by more than one partner pursuant to a plan. For purposes of paragraph (a)(1) of this section, if the partnership assumes or takes property or properties subject to the liabilities of more than one partner pursuant to a plan, a partner's share of the liabilities assumed or taken subject to by the partnership pursuant to that plan immediately after the transfers equals the sum of that partner's shares of the liabilities (other than that partner's qualified liabilities, as defined in paragraph (a)(6) of this section) assumed or taken subject to by the partnership pursuant to the plan. This paragraph (a)(4) does not apply to any liability assumed or taken subject to by the partnership with a principal purpose of reducing the extent to which any other liability assumed or taken subject to by the partnership is treated as a transfer of consideration under paragraph (a) (1) of this section.

(5) Special rule applicable to qualified liabilities. (i) If a transfer of property by a partner to a partnership is not otherwise treated as part of a sale, the partnership's assumption of or taking subject to a qualified liability in connection with a transfer of property is not treated as part of a sale. If a transfer of property by a partner to the partnership is treated as part of a sale without regard to the partnership's assumption of or taking subject to a qualified liability (as defined in paragraph (a)(6) of this section) in connection with the transfer of property, the partnership's assumption of or taking subject to that liability is treated as a transfer of consideration made pursuant to a sale of such property to the partnership only to the extent of the lesser of—

(A) The amount of consideration that the partnership would be treated as transferring to the partner under paragraph (a)(1) of this section if the liability were not a qualified liability; or

(B) The amount obtained by multiplying the amount of the qualified liability by the partner's net equity percentage with respect to that property.

(ii) A partner's net equity percentage with respect to an item of property equals the percentage determined by dividing—

(A) The aggregate transfers of money or other consideration to the partner by the partnership (other than any transfer described in this paragraph (a)(5)) that are treated as proceeds realized from the sale of the transferred property; by

(B) The excess of the fair market value of the property at the time it is transferred to the partnership over any qualified liability encumbering the property or, in the case of any qualified liability described in paragraph (a)(6)(i)(C) or (D) of this section, that is properly allocable to the property.

(iii) Notwithstanding paragraph (a)(5)(i) of this section, in connection with a transfer of property by a partner to a partnership that is treated as a sale due solely to the partnership's assumption of or taking property subject to a liability other than a qualified liability, the partnership's assumption of or taking property subject to a qualified liability is not treated as a transfer of consideration made pursuant to the sale if the total amount of all liabilities other than qualified liabilities that the partnership assumes or takes subject to is the lesser of 10 percent of the total amount of all qualified liabilities the partnership assumes or takes subject to, or $1,000,000.

(6) Qualified liability of a partner defined. A liability assumed or taken subject to by a partnership in connection with a transfer of property to the partnership by a partner is qualified liability of the partner only to the extent—

(i) The liability is—

(A) A liability that was incurred by the partner more than two years prior to the earlier of the date the partner agrees in writing to transfers the property or the date the partner transfers the property to the partnership and that has encumbered the transferred property throughout that two-year period;

(B) A liability that was not incurred in anticipation of the transfer of the property to a partnership, buy that was incurred by the partner within the two-year period prior to the earlier of the date the partner agrees in writing to transfer the property or the date the partner transfers the property to the partnership and that has encumbered the transferred property since it was incurred (see paragraph (a)(7) of this section for further rules regarding a liability incurred within two years of a property transfer or of a written agreement to transfer);

(C) A liability that is allocable under the rules of § 1.163–8T to capital expenditures (as described under § 1.707–4(d)(5)) with respect to the property; or

(D) A liability that was incurred in the ordinary course of the trade or business in which property transferred to the partnership was used or held but only if all the assets related to that trade or business are transferred other than assets that are not material to a continuation of the trade or business; or

(E) A liability that was not incurred in anticipation of the transfer of the property to a partnership, but that was incurred in connection with a trade or business in which property transferred to the partnership was used or held but only if all the assets related to that trade or business are transferred other than assets that are not material to a continuation of the trade or business (see paragraph (a)(7) of this section for further rules regarding a liability incurred within two years of a transfer presumed to be in anticipation of the transfer); and

(ii) If the liability is a recourse liability, the amount of the liability does not exceed the fair market value of the transferred property (less the amount of any other liabilities that are senior in priority and that either encumber such property or are liabilities described in paragraph (a)(6)(i)(C) or (D) of this section) at the time of the transfer.

(7) Liability incurred within two years of transfer presumed to be in anticipation of the transfer—(i) In general. For purposes of this section, if within a two-year period a partner incurs a liability (other than a liability described in paragraph (a)(6)(i)(C) or (D) of this section) and transfers property to a partnership or agrees in writing to transfer the property, and in connection with the transfer the partnership assumes or takes the property subject to the liability, the liability is presumed to be incurred in anticipation of the transfer unless the facts and circumstances clearly establish that the liability was not incurred in anticipation of the transfer.

(ii) Disclosure of transfers of property subject to liabilities incurred within two years of the transfer. A partner that treats a liability assumed or taken subject to by a partnership in connection with a transfer of property as a qualified liability under paragraph (a)(6)(i)(B) of this section or under paragraph (a)(6)(i)(E) of this section (if the liability was incurred by the partner within the two-year period prior to the earlier of the date the partner agrees in writing to transfer the property or the date the partner transfers the property to the partnership) must disclose such treatment to the Internal Revenue Service in accordance with § 1.707–8.

(8) Liability incurred by another person. Except as provided in paragraph (e)(2) of this section, a partner steps in the shoes of a person for purposes of paragraph (a) of this section with respect to a liability the person incurred or assumed to the extent the partner assumed or took property subject to the liability from the person in a nonrecognition transaction described in section 351, 381(a), 721, or 731.

(b) Treatment of debt-financed transfers of consideration by partnerships—(1) In general. For purposes of § 1.707–3, if a partner transfers property to a partnership, and the partnership incurs a liability and all or a portion of the proceeds of that liability are allocable under § 1.163–8T to a transfer of money or other consideration to the partner made within 90 days of incurring the liability, the transfer of money or other consideration to the partner is taken into account only to the extent that the amount of money or the fair market value of the other consideration transferred exceeds that partner's allocable share of the partnership liability.

For purposes of paragraph (b) of this section, an upper-tier partnership's share of the liability of a lower-tier partnership as described under § 1.707–5(a)(2) that is treated as a liability of the upper-tier partnership under § 1.752–4(a) shall be treated as a liability of the upper-tier partnership incurred on the same day the liability was incurred by the lower-tier partnership.

(2) Partner's allocable share of liability—(i) In general. A partner's allocable share of a partnership liability for purposes of paragraph (b)(1) of this section equals the amount obtained by multiplying the partner's share of the liability as described in paragraph (a)(2) of this section by the fraction determined by dividing—

(A) The portion of the liability that is allocable under § 1.163–8T to the money or other consideration transferred to the partner; by

(B) The total amount of the liability.

(ii) Debt-financed transfers made pursuant to a plan—(A) In general. Except as provided in paragraph (b)(2)(iii) of this section, if a partnership transfers to more than one partner pursuant to a plan all or a portion of the proceeds of one or more partnership liabilities, paragraph (b)(1) of this section is applied by treating all of the liabilities incurred pursuant to the plan as one liability, and each partner's allocable share of those liabilities equals the amount obtained by multiplying the sum of the partner's shares of each of the respective liabilities (as defined in paragraph (a)(2) of this section) by the fraction obtained by dividing —

(1) The portion of those liabilities that is allocable under § 1.163–8T to the money or other consideration transferred to the partners pursuant to the plan; by

(2) The total amount of those liabilities.

(B) Special rule. Paragraph (b)(2)(ii)(A) of this section does not apply to any transfer of money or other property to a partner that is made with a principal purpose of reducing the extent to which any transfer is taken into account under paragraph (b)(1) of this section.

(iii) Reduction of partner's share of liability. For purposes of paragraph (b)(2) of this section, a partner's share of a liability immediately after a partnership incurs the liability is determined by taking into account a subsequent reduction in the partner's share if —

(A) At the time that the partnership incurs the liability, it is anticipated that the partner's share of the liability that is allocable to a transfer of money or other consideration to the partner will be reduced subsequent to the transfer;

(B) The anticipated reduction is not subject to the entrepreneurial risks of partnership operations; and

(C) The reduction of the partner's share of the liability is part of a plan that has as one of its principal purposes minimizing the extent to which the partnership's distribution of the proceeds of the borrowing is treated as part of a sale.

(3) Ordering rule. The treatment of a transfer of money or other consideration under paragraph (b) of this section is determined before applying the rules under § 1.707–4.

(c) Refinancings. To the extent that the proceeds of a partner or partnership liability (the refinancing debt) are allocable under the rules of § 1.163–8T to payments discharging all or part of any other liability of that partner or of the partnership, as the case may be, the refinancing debt is treated as the other liability for purposes of applying the rules of this section.

(d) Share of liability where assumption accompanied by transfer of money. For purposes of §§ 1.707–3 through 1.707–5, if pursuant to a plan a partner pays or contributes money to the partnership and the partnership assumes or takes subject to one or more liabilities (other than qualified liabilities) of the partner, the amount of those liabilities that the partnership is treated as assuming or taking subject to is reduced (but not below zero) by the money transferred.

(e) Tiered partnerships and other related persons.—(1) If a lower-tier partnership succeeds to a liability of an upper-tier partnership, the liability in the lower-tier partnership retains the characterization as qualified or nonqualified that it had under these rules in the upper-tier partnership. A similar rule applies to other related party transactions involving liabilities to the extent provided by guidance published in the Internal Revenue Bulletin.

(2) If an interest in a partnership that has one or more liabilities (the lower-tier partnership) is transferred to another partnership (the upper-tier partnership), the upper-tier partnership's share of any liability of the lower-tier partnership that is treated as a liability of the upper-tier partnership under § 1.752–4(a) is treated as a qualified liability under paragraph (a)(6)(i) of this section to the extent the liability would be a qualified liability under paragraph (a)(6)(i) of this section had the liability been assumed or taken subject to by the upper-tier partnership in connection with a transfer of all of the lower-tier partnership's property to the upper-tier partnership by the lower-tier partnership. For purposes of determining whether the liability constitutes a qualified liability under paragraphs (a)(6)(i)(B) and (E) of this section, a determination that the liability was not incurred in anticipation of the transfer of property to the upper-tier partnership is based on whether the partner in the lower-tier partnership anticipated transferring its interest in the lower-tier partnership to the upper-tier partnership at the time the liability was incurred by the lower-tier partnership.

(f) Examples. The following examples illustrate the application of this section.

Example (1). Partnership's assumption of nonrecourse liability encumbering transferred property. (i) A and B form partnership AB, which will engage in renting office space. A transfers $500,000 in cash to the partnership, and B transfers an office building to the partnership. At the time it is transferred to the partnership, the office building has a fair market value of $1,000,000, has an adjusted basis of $400,000, and is encumbered by a $500,000 nonrecourse liability, which B incurred 12 months earlier to finance the acquisition of other property and which the partnership assumed. No facts rebut the presumption that the liability was incurred in anticipation of the transfer of the property to the partnership. Assume that this liability is a nonrecourse liability of the partnership within the meaning of section 752 and the regulations thereunder. The partnership agreement provides that partnership items will be allocated equally between A and B, including excess nonrecourse liabilities under § 1.752–3(a)(3). The partnership agreement complies with the requirements of § 1.704–1(b)(2)(ii)(*b*).

(ii) The nonrecourse liability secured by the office building is not a qualified liability within the meaning of paragraph (a)(6) of this section. B would be allocated 50 percent of the excess nonrecourse liability under the partnership agreement. Accordingly, immediately after the partnership's assumption of that liability, B's share of the liability as determined under paragraph (a)(2) of this section is $250,000 (B's 50 percent share of the partnership's excess nonrecourse liability as determined in accordance with B's share of partnership profits under § 1.752–3(a)(3)).

(iii) The partnership's assumption of the liability encumbering the office building is treat-

ed as a transfer of $250,000 of consideration to B (the amount by which the liability ($500,000) exceeds B's share of that liability immediately after the partnership's assumption of the liability ($250,000)). B is treated as having sold $250,000 of the fair market value of the office building to the partnership in exchange for the partnership's assumption of a $250,000 liability. This results in a gain of $150,000 ($250,000 minus ($250,000/$1,000,000 multiplied by $400,000)).

Example (2). Partnership's assumption of recourse liability encumbering transferred property. (i) C transfers property Y to a partnership. At the time of its transfer to the partnership, property Y has a fair market value of $10,000,000 and is subject to an $8,000,000 liability that C incurred, immediately before transferring property Y to the partnership, in order to finance other expenditures. Upon the transfer of property Y to the partnership, the partnership assumed the liability encumbering that property. The partnership assumed this liability solely to acquire property Y. Under section 752 and the regulations thereunder, immediately after the partnership's assumption of the liability encumbering property Y, the liability is a recourse liability of the partnership and C's share of that liability is $7,000,000.

(ii) Under the facts of this example, the liability encumbering property Y is not a qualified liability.

Accordingly, the partnership's assumption of the liability results in a transfer of consideration to C in connection with C's transfer of property Y to the partnership in the amount of $1,000,000 (the excess of the liability assumed by the partnership ($8,000,000) over C's share of the liability immediately after the assumption ($7,000,000)). See paragraphs (a)(1) and (2) of this section.

Example (3). Subsequent reduction of transferring partner's share of liability. (i) The facts are the same as in Example 2. In addition, property Y is a fully leased office building, the rental income from property Y is sufficient to meet debt service, and the remaining term of the liability is ten years. It is anticipated that, three years after the partnership's assumption of the liability, C's share of the liability under section 752 will be reduced to zero because of a shift in the allocation of partnership losses pursuant to the terms of the partnership agreement. Under the partnership agreement, this shift in the allocation of partnership losses is dependent solely on the passage of time.

(ii) Under paragraph (a)(3) of this section, if the reduction in C's share of the liability was anticipated at the time of C's transfer, and the reduction was part of a plan that has as one of its principal purposes minimizing the extent of sale treatment under § 1.707–3 (i.e., a principal purpose of allocating a large percentage of losses to C in the first three years when losses were not likely to be realized was to minimize the extent to which C's transfer would be treated as part of a sale), C's share of the liability immediately after the assumption is treated as equal to C's reduced share.

Example (4). Trade payables as qualified liabilities. *(i)* D and E form partnership DE which will engage in a consulting business that requires no overhead and minimal cash on hand for daily operating expenses. Previously, D and E, as individual sole proprietors, operated separate consulting businesses. D and E each transfer to the partnership sufficient cash to cover daily operating expenses together with the goodwill and trade payables related to each sole proprietorship. Due to uncertainty over the collection rate on the trade receivables related to their sole proprietorships, D and E agree that none of the trade receivables will be transferred to the partnership.

(ii) Under the facts of this example, all the assets related to the consulting business (other than the trade receivables) together with the trade payables were transferred to partnership DE. The trade receivables retained by D and E are not material to a continuation of the trade or business by the partnership because D and E contributed sufficient cash to cover daily op-

erating expenses. Accordingly, the trade payables transferred to the partnership constitute qualified liability under paragraph (a)(6) of this section.

Example (5). Partnership's assumption of a qualified liability as sole consideration. (i) F purchases property Z in 2012. In 2017, F transfers property Z to a partnership. At the time of its transfer to the partnership, property Z has a fair market value of $165,000 and an adjusted tax basis of $75,000. Also, at the time of the transfer, property Z is subject to a $75,000 nonrecourse liability that F incurred more than two years before transferring property Z to the partnership. The liability has been secured by property Z since it was incurred by F. Upon the transfer of property Z to the partnership, the partnership assumed the liability encumbering that property. The partnership made no other transfers to F in consideration for the transfer of property Z to the partnership. Assume that immediately after the partnership's assumption of the liability encumbering property Z, F's share of that liability for disguised sale purposes is $25,000 in accordance with § 1.707–5(a)(2).

(ii) The $75,000 liability secured by property Z is a qualified liability of F because F incurred the liability more than two years prior to the partnership's assumption of the liability and the liability has encumbered property Z for more than two years prior to F's transfer. See paragraph (a)(6) of this section. Therefore, since no other transfer to F was made as consideration for the transfer of property Z, under paragraph (a)(5) of this section, the partnership's assumption of the qualified liability of F encumbering property Z is not treated as part of a sale.

Example (6). Partnership's assumption of a qualified liability in addition to other consideration. (i) The facts are the same as in *Example 5*, except that the partnership makes a transfer to F of $30,000 in money that is consideration for F's transfer of property Z to the partnership under § 1.707–3.

(ii) As in *Example 5*, the $75,000 liability secured by property Z is a qualified liability of F. Since the partnership transferred $30,000 to F in addition to assuming the qualified liability under paragraph (a)(5) of this section, assuming no other exception to disguised sale treatment applies to the transfer of the $30,000, the partnership's assumption of this qualified liability is treated as a transfer of additional consideration to F to the extent of the lesser of—

(A) The amount that the partnership would be treated as transferring to F if the liability were not a qualified liability ($50,000 (that is, the excess of the $75,000 qualified liability over F's $25,000 share of that liability)); or

(B) The amount obtained by multiplying the qualified liability ($75,000) by F's net equity percentage with respect to property Z (one-third).

(iii) F's net equity percentage with respect to property Z equals the fraction determined by dividing—

(A) The aggregate amount of money or other consideration (other than the qualified liability) transferred to F and treated as part of a sale of property Z under § 1.707–3(a) ($30,000 transfer of money); by

(B) F's net equity in property Z ($90,000 (that is, the excess of the $165,000 fair market value over the $75,000 qualified liability)).

(iv) Accordingly, the partnership's assumption of the qualified liability of F encumbering property Z is treated as a transfer of $25,000 (one-third of $75,000) of consideration to F pursuant to a sale. Therefore, F is treated as having sold $55,000 of the fair market value of property Z to the partnership in exchange for $30,000 in money and the partnership's assumption of $25,000 of the qualified liability. Accordingly, F must recognize $30,000 of gain on the sale (the excess of the $55,000 amount realized over $25,000 of F's adjusted basis for property Z (that is, one-third of F's adjusted basis for the property, because F is

treated as having sold one-third of the property to the partnership)).

Example (7). *Partnership's assumptions of liabilities encumbering properties transferred pursuant to a plan.* *(i)* Pursuant to a plan, G and H transfer property 1 and property 2, respectively, to an existing partnership in exchange for interests in the partnership. At the time the properties are transferred to the partnership, property 1 has a fair market value of $10,000 and an adjusted tax basis of $6,000, and property 2 has a fair market value of $10,000 and an adjusted tax basis of $4,000. At the time properties 1 and 2 are transferred to the partnership, a $6,000 nonrecourse liability (liability 1) is secured by property 1 and a $7,000 recourse liability of F (liability 2) is secured by property 2. Properties 1 and 2 are transferred to the partnership, and the partnership takes subject to liability 1 and assumes liability 2. G and H incurred liabilities 1 and 2 immediately prior to transferring properties 1 and 2 to the partnership and used the proceeds for personal expenditures. The liabilities are not qualified liabilities. Assume that G and H are each allocated $2,000 of liability 1 in accordance with § 1.707–5(a)(2)(ii) (which determines a partner's share of a nonrecourse liability). Assume further that G's share of liability 2 is $3,500 and H's share is $0 in accordance with § 1.707–5(a)(2)(i) (which determines a partner's share of a recourse liability).

(ii) G and H transferred properties 1 and 2 to the partnership pursuant to a plan. Accordingly, the partnership's taking subject to liability 1 is treated as a transfer of only $500 of consideration to G, (the amount by which liability 1 ($6,000) exceeds G's share of liabilities 1 and 2 ($5,500)), and the partnership's assumption of liability 2 is treated as a transfer of only $5,000 of consideration to H (the amount by which liability 2 ($7,000) exceeds H's share of liabilities 1 and 2 ($2,000)). G is treated under the rule in § 1.707–3 as having sold $500 of the fair market value of property 1 in exchange for the partnership's taking subject to liability

1 and H is treated as having sold $5,000 of the fair market value of property 2 in exchange for the assumption of liability 2.

Example (8). Partnership's assumption of liability pursuant to a plan to avoid sale treatment of partnership assumption of another liability. (i) The facts are the same as in Example 7, except that—

(A) H transferred the proceeds of liability 2 to the partnership; and

(B) H incurred liability 2 in an attempt to reduce the extent to which the partnership's taking subject to liability 1 would be treated as a transfer of consideration to G (and thereby reduce the portion of G's transfer of property 1 to the partnership that would be treated as part of a sale).

(ii) Because the partnership assumed liability 2 with a principal purpose of reducing the extent to which the partnership's taking subject to liability 1 would be treated as a transfer of consideration to G, liability 2 is ignored in applying paragraph (a)(3) of this section. Accordingly, the partnership's taking subject to liability 1 is treated as a transfer of $4,000 of consideration to G (the amount by which liability 1 ($6,000) exceeds G's share of liability 1 ($2,000)). On the other hand, the partnership's assumption of liability 2 is not treated as a transfer of any consideration to H because H's share of that liability equals $7,000 as a result of H's transfer of $7,000 in money to the partnership.

Example (9). Partnership's assumptions of qualified liabilities encumbering properties transferred pursuant to a plan in addition to other consideration. (i) Pursuant to a plan, I transfers property 1 and J transfers property 2 plus $10,000 in cash to partnership IJ in exchange for equal interests in the partnership. At the time the properties are transferred to the partnership, property 1 has a fair market value of $100,000, an adjusted tax basis of $5,000, and is encumbered by a qualified liability of $50,000 (liability 1). Property 2 has a fair mar-

ket value of $100,000, an adjusted tax basis of $5,000, and is encumbered by a qualified liability of $70,000 (liability 2). Pursuant to the plan, the partnership transferred to I $10,000 in cash. That amount is consideration for I's transfer of property 1 to the partnership under § 1.707–3. In accordance with § 1.707–5(a)(2), I and J are each allocated $25,000 of liability 1 and $35,000 of liability 2.

(ii) Because the partnership transferred $10,000 to I as consideration for the transfer of property, under § 1.707–5(a)(5), the partnership's assumption of liability 1 is treated as a transfer of additional consideration to I, even though liability 1 is a qualified liability, to the extent of the lesser of—

(A) The amount that the partnership would be treated as transferring to I if the liability were not a qualified liability; or

(B) The amount obtained by multiplying the qualified liability by I's net equity percentage with respect to property 1.

(iii) Because I and J transferred properties 1 and 2 to the partnership pursuant to a plan, treating I's qualified liability as a nonqualified liability under § 1.707–5(a)(5)(i)(A) enables I to apply the special rule applicable to transfers of encumbered property to a partnership by more than one partner pursuant to a plan under § 1.707–5(a)(4). Under this alternative test, the partnership's assumption of liability 1 encumbering property 1 is treated as a transfer of zero ($0) additional consideration to I pursuant to a sale. This is because the amount of liability 1 ($50,000) does not exceed the sum of I's share of liability 1 treated as a nonqualified liability ($25,000) and I's share of liability 2 ($35,000).

(iv) The alternative under § 1.707–5(a)(5)(i)(B) is the amount obtained by multiplying the qualified liability ($50,000) by I's net equity percentage with respect to property 1. I's net equity percentage with respect to property 1 equals one-fifth, the fraction determined by dividing—

(A) The aggregate amount of money or other consideration (other than the qualified liability) transferred to I and treated as part of a sale of property 1 under § 1.707–3(a) (the $10,000 transfer of money); by

(B) I's net equity in property 1 ($50,000 i.e., the excess of the $100,000 fair market value over the $50,000 qualified liability).

(v) Under this alternative test, the partnership's assumption of the qualified liability encumbering property 1 is treated as a transfer of $10,000 (one-fifth of the $50,000 qualified liability) of additional consideration to I pursuant to a sale.

(vi) Applying § 1.707–5(a)(5) to these facts, the partnership's assumption of liability 1 is treated as a transfer of additional consideration to I to the extent of the lesser of—

(A) zero; or

(B) $10,000.

(vii) Therefore, the partnership's assumption of I's qualified liability encumbering property 1 is not treated as a transfer of any additional consideration to I pursuant to a sale, and I is treated as having only received $10,000 of the fair market value of property 1 to the partnership in exchange for $10,000 in cash. Accordingly, I must recognize $9,500 of gain on the sale, that is, the excess of the $10,000 amount realized over $500 of I's adjusted tax basis for property 1 (one-tenth of I's adjusted tax basis for the property, because I is treated as having sold one-tenth of the property to the partnership). Since no other transfer to J was made as consideration for the transfer of property 2, the partnership's assumption of the qualified liability of J encumbering property 2 is not treated as part of a sale.

Example (10). Treatment of debt-financed transfers of consideration by partnership. (i) K transfers property Z to partnership KL in exchange for a 50 percent interest therein on April 9, 2017. On September 13, 2017, the partnership incurs a nonrecourse liability of $20,000. On November 17, 2017, the part-

nership transfers $20,000 to K, and $10,000 of this transfer is allocable under the rules of § 1.163–8T to proceeds of the partnership liability incurred on September 13, 2017. The remaining $10,000 is paid from other partnership funds. Assume that on November 17, 2017, for disguised sale purposes, K's share of the $20,000 liability incurred on September 13, 2017, is $10,000 in accordance with § 1.707–5(a)(2).

(ii) Because a portion of the transfer made to K on November 17, 2017, is allocable under § 1.163–8T to proceeds of a partnership liability that was incurred by the partnership within 90 days of that transfer, K is required to take the transfer into account in applying the rules of this section and § 1.707–3 only to the extent that the amount of the transfer exceeds K's allocable share of the liability used to fund the transfer. K's allocable share of the $20,000 liability used to fund $10,000 of the transfer to K is $5,000 (K's share of the liability ($10,000) multiplied by the fraction obtained by dividing—

(A) The amount of the liability that is allocable to the distribution to K ($10,000); by

(B) The total amount of such liability ($20,000)).

(iii) Therefore, K is required to take into account $15,000 of the $20,000 partnership transfer to K for purposes of this section and § 1.707–3. Under these facts, assuming no other exception applies and the within-two-year presumption is not rebutted, this $15,000 transfer will be treated under the rule in § 1.707–3 as part of a sale by K of property Z to the partnership.

Example (11). Treatment of debt-financed transfers of consideration and transfers characterized as guaranteed payments by a partnership. (i) The facts are the same as in *Example 10*, except that the entire $20,000 transfer to K is allocable under the rules of § 1.163–8T to proceeds of the partnership liability incurred on September 13, 2017. In addition, the partnership agreement provides that K is to receive a guaranteed payment for the use of K's capital in the amount of $10,000 in each of the three years following the transfer of property Z. Ten thousand dollars of the transfer made to K on November 17, 2017, is pursuant to this provision of the partnership agreement. Assume that the guaranteed payment to K constitutes a reasonable guaranteed payment within the meaning of § 1.707–4(a)(3).

(ii) Under these facts, the rules under both § 1.707–4(a) and § 1.707–5(b) apply to the November 17, 2017 transfer to K by the partnership. Thus, the ordering rule in § 1.707–5(b)(3) requires that the § 1.707–5(b) debt-financed distribution rules apply first to determine the treatment of the $20,000 transfer. Because the entire transfer made to K on November 17, 2017, is allocable under § 1.163–8T to proceeds of a partnership liability that was incurred by the partnership within 90 days of that transfer, K is required to take the transfer into account in applying the rules of this section and § 1.707–3 only to the extent that the amount of the transfer exceeds K's allocable share of the liability used to fund the transfer. K's allocable share of the $20,000 liability used to fund the transfer to K is $10,000 (K's share of the liability ($10,000) multiplied by the fraction obtained by dividing—

(A) The amount of the liability that is allocable to the distribution to K ($20,000); by

(B) The total amount of such liability ($20,000)).

(iii) The remaining $10,000 amount of the transfer to K that exceeds K's allocable share of the liability is tested to determine whether an exception under § 1.707–4 applies. Because $10,000 of the payment to K is a reasonable guaranteed payment for capital under § 1.707–4(a)(1)(ii), the $10,000 transfer will not be treated as part of a sale by K of property Z to the partnership under § 1.707–3.

Example (12). Treatment of debt-financed transfers of consideration by partnership made pursuant to plan. (i) O transfers property X, and P transfers property Y, to partnership OP in exchange for equal interests therein on June 1, 2017. On October 1, 2017, the partnership incurs two nonrecourse liabilities: Liability 1 of $8,000 and Liability 2 of $4,000. On December 15, 2017, the partnership transfers $2,000 to each of O and P pursuant to a plan. The transfers made to O and P on December 15, 2017 are allocable under § 1.163–8T to the proceeds of either Liability 1 or Liability 2. Assume that under § 1.707–5(a)(2), O's and P's share of Liability 1 is $4,000 each and of Liability 2 is $2,000 each on December 15, 2017.

(ii) Because the partnership transferred pursuant to a plan a portion of the proceeds of the two liabilities to O and P, paragraph (b)(1) of this section is applied by treating Liability 1 and Liability 2 as a single $12,000 liability. Pursuant to paragraph (b)(2)(ii)(A) of this section, each partner's allocable share of the $12,000 liability equals the amount obtained by multiplying the sum of the partner's share of Liability 1 and Liability 2 ($6,000) ($4,000 for Liability 1 plus $2,000 for Liability 2) by the fraction obtained by dividing—

(A) The amount of the liability that is allocable to the distribution to O and P pursuant to the plan ($4,000); by

(B) The total amount of such liability ($12,000).

(iii) Therefore, O's and P's allocable share of the $12,000 liability is $2,000 each. Accordingly, because a portion of the proceeds of the $12,000 liability are allocable under § 1.163–8T to the $2,000 transfer made to each of O and P within 90 days of incurring the liability, and the $2,000 transfer does not exceed O's or P's $2,000 allocable share of that liability, each is required to take into account $0 of the $2,000 transfer for purposes of this section and § 1.707–3. Under these facts, no part of the transfers to O and P will be treated as part of a sale of property X by O or of property Y by P.

Example (13). Borrowing against pool of receivables. (i) M generates receivables which have an adjusted basis of zero in the ordinary course of its business. For M to use receivables as security for a loan, a commercial lender requires M to transfer the receivables to a partnership in which M has a 90 percent interest. In January, 1992, M transfers to the partnership receivables with a face value of $100,000. N (who is not related to M) transfers $10,000 cash to the partnership in exchange for a 10 percent interest. The partnership borrows $80,000, secured by the receivables, and makes a distribution of $72,000 of the proceeds to M and $8,000 of the proceeds to N within 90 days of incurring the liability. M's share of the liability under § 1.707–5(a)(2) is $72,000 (90 percent × $80,000).

(ii) Because the transfer of the loan proceeds to M is allocable under § 1.163–8T to proceeds of a partnership loan that was incurred by the partnership within 90 days of that transfer, M is required to take the transfer into account in applying the rules of this section and § 1.707–3 only to the extent that the amount of the transfer ($72,000) exceeds M's allocable share of the liability used to fund the transfer. Because the distribution was a debt-financed transfer pursuant to a plan, M's allocable share of the liability is $72,000 ($72,000 × $80,000/80,000) under § 1.707–5(b)(2)(ii). Therefore, M is not required to take into account any of the loan proceeds for purposes of this section and § 1.707–3.

(iii) When the receivables are collected, M must be allocated the gain on the contributed receivables under section 704(c). However, the lender permits the partnership to distribute cash to the partners only to the extent of the value of new receivables contributed to the partnership. In 1993, M contributes additional receivables and receives a distribution of cash. The taxable income recognized by the partnership on the receivables is taxable income of the partnership arising in the ordinary course of the partnership's activities. To the extent the distribution does not exceed 90 percent (M's percentage interest in overall partnership profits) of the partnership's operating cash flow under § 1.707–4(b), the distribution to M is presumed not to be a part of a sale of receivables by M to the partnership, and the presumption is not rebutted under these facts.

§ 1.707–5T Disguised sales of property to partnership; special rules relating to liabilities (temporary).

(a)(1) [Reserved]. For further guidance, see § 1.707–5(a)(1).

(2) Partner's share of liability—(i) In general. For purposes of § 1.707–5, a partner's share of a liability of a partnership, as defined in § 1.752–1(a) (whether a recourse liability or a nonrecourse liability) is determined by applying the same percentage used to determine the partner's share of the excess nonrecourse liability under § 1.752–3(a)(3) (as limited in its application to this paragraph (a)(2)), but such share shall not exceed the partner's share of the partnership liability under section 752 and applicable regulations (as limited in the application of § 1.752–3(a)(3) to this paragraph (a)(2)).

(ii) Partner's share of § 1.752–7 liability. [Reserved].

(a)(3) through (e) [Reserved]. For further guidance, see § 1.707–5(a)(3) through (e).

(f) Example 1 [Reserved]. For further guidance, see § 1.707–5(f) *Example 1.*

§ 1.707–6 Disguised sales of property by partnership to partner; general rules.

(a) In general. Rules similar to those provided in § 1.707–3 apply in determining whether a transfer of property by a partnership to a partner and one or more transfers of money or other consideration by that partner to the partnership are treated as a sale of property, in whole or in part, to the partner.

(b) Special rules relating to liabilities—(1) In general. Rules similar to those provided in § 1.707–5 apply to determine the extent to which an assumption of or taking subject to a liability by a partner, in connection with a transfer of property by a partnership, is considered part of a sale. Accordingly, if a partner assumes or takes property subject to a qualified liability (as defined in paragraph (b)(2) of this section) of a partnership, the partner is treated as transferring consideration to the partnership only to the extent provided in paragraph (b). If the partner assumes or takes subject to a liability that is not a qualified liability, the amount treated as consideration transferred to the partnership is the amount that the liability assumed or taken subject to by the partner exceeds the partner's share of that liability (determined under the rules of § 1.707–5(a)(2)) immediately before the transfer. Similar to the rules provided in § 1.707–5(a)(4), if more than one partner assumes or takes subject to a liability pursuant to a plan, the amount that is treated as a transfer of consideration by each partner is the amount by which all of the liabilities (other than qualified liabilities) assumed or taken subject to by the partner pursuant to the plan exceed the partner's share of all of those liabilities immediately before the assumption or taking subject to. This paragraph (b)(1) does not apply to any liability assumed or taken subject to by a partner with a principal purpose of reducing the extent to which any other liability assumed or taken subject to by a partner is treated as a transfer of consideration under this paragraph (b).

(2) **Qualified liabilities.** (i) If a transfer of property by a partnership to a partner is not otherwise treated as part of a sale, the partner's assumption of or taking subject to a qualified liability is not treated as part of a sale. If a transfer of property by a partnership to the partner is treated as part of a sale without regard to the partner's assumption of or taking subject to a qualified liability, the partner's assumption of or taking subject to that liability is treated as a transfer of consideration made pursuant to a sale of such property to the partner only to the extent of the lesser of—

(A) The amount of consideration that the partner would be treated as transferring to the partnership under paragraph (b) of this section if the liability were not a qualified liability; or

(B) The amount obtained by multiplying the amount of the liability at the time of its assumption or taking subject to by the partnership's net equity percentage with respect to that property.

(ii) A partnership's net equity percentage with respect to an item of property encumbered by a qualified liability equals the percentage determined by dividing—

(A) The aggregate transfers to the partnership from the partner (other than any transfer described in this paragraph (b)(2) that are treated as the proceeds realized from the sale of the transferred property to the partner; by

(B) The excess of the fair market value of the property at the time it is transferred to the partner over any qualified liabilities of the partnership that are assumed or taken subject to by the partner at that time.

(iii) For purposes of this section, the definition of a qualified liability is that provided in § 1.707–5(a)(6) with the following exceptions—

(A) In applying the definition, the qualified liability is one that is originally an obligation of the partnership and is assumed or taken subject to by the partner in connection with a transfer of property to the partner; and

(B) If the liability was incurred by the partnership more than two years prior to the earlier of the date the partnership agrees in writing to transfer the property or the date the partnership transfers the property to the partner, that liability is a qualified liability whether or not it has encumbered the transferred property throughout the two-year period.

(c) **Disclosure rules.** Similar to the rules provided in §§ 1.707–3(c)(2) and 1.707–5(a)(7)(ii), a partnership is to disclose to the Internal Revenue Service, in accordance with

§ 1.707–8, the facts in the following circumstances:

(1) When a partnership transfers property to a partner and the partner transfers money or other consideration to the partnership within a two-year period (without regard to the order of the transfers) and the partnership treats the transfers as other than a sale for tax purposes; and

(2) When a partner assumes or takes subject to a liability of a partnership in connection with a transfer of property by the partnership to the partner, and the partnership incurred the liability within the two-year period prior to the earlier of the date the partnership agrees in writing to the transfer of property or the date the partnership transfers the property, and the partnership treats the liability as a qualified liability under rules similar to § 1.707–5(a)(6)(i)(B).

(d) Examples. The following examples illustrate the rules of this section.

Example (1). Sale of property by partnership to partner. (i) A is a member of a partnership. The partnership transfers property X to A. At the time of the transfer, property X has a fair market value of $1,000,000. One year after the transfer, A transfers $1,100,000 to the partnership. Assume that under the rules of section 1274 the imputed principal amount of an obligation to transfer $1,100,000 one year after the transfer of property X is $1,000,000 on the date of the transfer.

(ii) Since the transfer of $1,100,000 to the partnership by A is made within two years of the transfer of property X to A, under rules similar to those provided in § 1.707–3(c), the transfers are presumed to be a sale unless the facts and circumstances clearly establish otherwise. If no facts exist that would rebut this presumption, on the date that the partnership transfers property X to A, the partnership is treated as having sold property X to A in exchange for A's obligation to transfer $1,100,000 to the partnership one year later.

Example (2). Assumption of liability by partner. (i) B is a member of an existing partnership. The partnership transfers property Y to B. On the date of the transfer, property Y has a fair market value of $1,000,000 and is encumbered by a nonrecourse liability of $600,000. B takes the property subject to the liability. The partnership incurred the nonrecourse liability six months prior to the transfer of property Y to B and used the proceeds to purchase an unrelated asset. Assume that under § 1.707–5(a)(2), B's share of the nonrecourse liability immediately before the transfer of property Y was $100,000.

(ii) The liability is not allocable under the rules of § 1.163–8T to capital expenditures with respect to the property transferred to B and was not incurred in the ordinary course of the trade or business in which the property transferred to the partner was used or held. Since the partnership incurred the nonrecourse liability within two years of the transfer to B, under rules similar to those provided in § 1.707–5(a)(5), the liability is presumed to be incurred in anticipation of the transfer unless the facts and circumstances clearly establish the contrary. Assuming no facts exist to rebut this presumption, the liability taken subject to by B is not a qualified liability. The partnership is treated as having received, on the date of the transfer of property Y to B, $500,000 ($600,000 liability assumed by B less B's share of the $100,000 liability immediately prior to the transfer) as consideration for the sale of one-half ($500,000/$1,000,000) of property Y to B. The partnership is also treated as having distributed to B, in B's capacity as a partner, the other one-half of property Y.

§ 1.707–7 Disguised sales of partnership interests. [Reserved]

§ 1.708–1 Continuation of partnership.

(a) General rule. For purposes of subchapter K, chapter 1 of the Code, an existing partnership shall be considered as continuing if it is not terminated.

(b) Termination—(1) General rule. A partnership shall terminate when the operations of the partnership are discontinued and no part of any business, financial operation, or venture of the partnership continues to be carried on by any of its partners in a partnership. For example, on November 20, 1956, A and B, each of whom is a 20-percent partner in partnership ABC, sell their interests to C, who is a 60-percent partner. Since the business is no longer carried on by any of its partners in a partnership, the ABC partnership is terminated as of November 20, 1956. However, where partners DEF agree on April 30, 1957, to dissolve their partnership, but carry on the business through a winding up period ending September 30, 1957, when all remaining assets, consisting only of cash, are distributed to the partners, the partnership does not terminate because of cessation of business until September 30, 1957.

(i) Upon the death of one partner in a 2-member partnership, the partnership shall not be considered as terminated if the estate or other successor in interest of the deceased partner continues to share in the profits or losses of the partnership business.

(ii) For the continuation of a partnership where payments are being made under section 736 (relating to payments to a retiring partner or a deceased partner's successor in interest), see paragraph (a)(6) of §1.736–1.

* * *

(3) For purposes of subchapter K, chapter 1 of the Code, a partnership taxable year closes with respect to all partners on the date on which the partnership terminates. See section 706(c)(1) and paragraph (c)(1) of §1.706–1. The date of termination is:

(i) For purposes of section 708(b)(1)(A), the date on which the winding up of the partnership affairs is completed.

* * *

(c) Merger or consolidation—(1) General rule. If two or more partnerships merge or consolidate into one partnership, the resulting partnership shall be considered a continuation of the merging or consolidating partnership the members of which own an interest of more than 50 percent in the capital and profits of the resulting partnership. If the resulting partnership can, under the preceding sentence, be considered a continuation of more than one of the merging or consolidating partnerships, it shall, unless the Commissioner permits otherwise, be considered the continuation solely of that partnership which is credited with the contribution of assets having the greatest fair market value (net of liabilities) to the resulting partnership. Any other merging or consolidating partnerships shall be considered as terminated. If the members of none of the merging or consolidating partnerships have an interest of more than 50 percent in the capital and profits of the resulting partnership, all of the merged or consolidated partnerships are terminated, and a new partnership results.

(2) Tax returns. The taxable years of any merging or consolidating partnerships which are considered terminated shall be closed in accordance with the provisions of section 706(c) and the regulations thereunder, and such partnerships shall file their returns for a taxable year ending upon the date of termination, i.e., the date of merger or consolidation. The resulting partnership shall file a return for the taxable year of the merging or consolidating partnership that is considered as continuing. The return shall state that the resulting partnership is a continuation of such merging or consolidating partnership, shall retain the employer identification number (EIN) of the partnership that is continuing, and shall include the names, addresses, and EINs of the other merged or consolidated partnerships. The respective distributive shares of the partners for the periods prior to and including the date of the merger or consolidation and subsequent to the date of merger or consolidation shall be shown as a part of the return.

(3) Form of a merger or consolidation—(i) Assets-over form. When two or more partner ships merge or consolidate into one partnership under the applicable jurisdictional law without undertaking a form for the merger or consolidation, or undertake a form for the merger or consolidation that is not described in paragraph (c)(3)(ii) of this section, any merged or consolidated partnership that is considered terminated under paragraph (c)(1) of this section is treated as undertaking the assets-over form for Federal income tax purposes. Under the assets-over form, the merged or consolidated partnership that is considered terminated under paragraph (c)(1) of this section contributes all of its assets and liabilities to the resulting partnership in exchange for an interest in the resulting partnership, and immediately thereafter, the terminated partnership distributes interests in the resulting partnership to its partners in liquidation of the terminated partnership.

(ii) **Assets-up form.** Despite the partners' transitory ownership of the terminated partnership's assets, the form of a partnership merger or consolidation will be respected for Federal income tax purposes if the merged or consolidated partnership that is considered terminated under paragraph (c)(1) of this section distributes all of its assets to its partners (in a manner that causes the partners to be treated, under the laws of the applicable jurisdiction, as the owners of such assets) in liquidation of the partners' interests in the terminated partnership, and immediately thereafter, the partners in the terminated partnership contribute the distributed assets to the resulting partnership in exchange for interests in the resulting partnership.

(4) **Sale of an interest in the merging or consolidating partnership.** In a transaction characterized under the assets-over form, a sale of all or part of a partner's interest in the terminated partnership to the resulting partnership that occurs as part of a merger or consolidation under section 708(b)(2)(A), as described in paragraph (c)(3)(i) of this section, will be respected as a sale of a partnership interest if the merger agreement (or another document) specifies that the resulting partnership is purchasing interests from a particular partner in the merging or consolidating partnership and the consideration that is transferred for each interest sold, and if the selling partner in the terminated partnership, either prior to or contemporaneous with the transaction, consents to treat the transaction as a sale of the partnership interest. See section 741 and § 1.741–1 for determining the selling partner's gain or loss on the sale or exchange of the partnership interest.

(5) **Examples.** The following examples illustrate the rules in paragraphs (c)(1) through (4) of this section:

Example (1). Partnership AB, in whose capital and profits A and B each own a 50-percent interest, and partnership CD, in whose capital and profits C and D each own a 50-percent interest, merge on September 30, 1999, and form partnership ABCD. Partners A, B, C, and D are on a calendar year, and partnership AB and partnership CD also are on a calendar year. After the merger, the partners have capital and profits interests as follows: A, 30 percent; B, 30 percent; C, 20 percent; and D, 20 percent. Since A and B together own an interest of more than 50 percent in the capital and profits of partnership ABCD, such partnership shall be considered a continuation of partnership AB and shall continue to file returns on a calendar year basis. Since C and D own an interest of less than 50 percent in the capital and profits of partnership ABCD, the taxable year of partnership CD closes as of September 30, 1999, the date of the merger, and partnership CD is terminated as of that date. Partnership ABCD is required to file a return for the taxable year January 1 to December 31, 1999, indicating thereon that, until September 30, 1999, it was partnership AB. Partnership CD is required to file a return for its final taxable year, January 1 through September 30, 1999.

Example (2). (i) Partnership X, in whose capital and profits A owns a 40-percent interest and B owns a 60-percent interest, and partnership Y, in whose capital and profits B owns a 60-percent interest and C owns a 40-percent interest, merge on September 30, 1999. The fair market value of the partnership X assets (net of liabilities) is $100X, and the fair market value of the partnership Y assets (net of liabilities) is $200X. The merger is accomplished under state law by partnership Y contributing its assets and liabilities to partnership X in exchange for interests in partnership X, with partnership Y then liquidating, distributing interests in partnership X to B and C.

(ii) B, a partner in both partnerships prior to the merger, owns a greater than 50-percent interest in the resulting partnership following the merger. Accordingly, because the fair market value of partnership Y's assets (net of liabilities) was greater than that of partnership X's, under paragraph (c)(1) of this section, partnership X will be considered to terminate in the merger. As a result, even though, for state law purposes, the transaction was undertaken with partnership Y contributing its assets and liabilities to partnership X and distributing interests in partnership X to its partners, pursuant to paragraph (c)(3)(i) of this section, for Federal income tax purposes, the transaction will be treated as if partnership X contributed its assets to partnership Y in exchange for interests in partnership Y and then liquidated, distributing interests in partnership Y to A and B.

Example (3). (i) The facts are the same as in Example 2, except that partnership X is engaged in a trade or business and has, as one of its assets, goodwill. In addition, the merger is accomplished under state law by having partnership X convey an undivided 40-percent interest in each of its assets to A and an undivided 60-percent interest in each of its assets to B, with A and B then contributing their interests in such assets to partnership Y. Partnership Y also assumes all of the liabilities of partnership X.

(ii) Under paragraph (c)(3)(ii) of this section, the form of the partnership merger will be respected so that partnership X will be treated

as following the assets-up form for Federal income tax purposes.

Example (4). (i) Partnership X and partnership Y merge when the partners of partnership X transfer their partnership X interests to partnership Y in exchange for partnership Y interests. Immediately thereafter, partnership X liquidates into partnership Y. The resulting partnership is considered a continuation of partnership Y, and partnership X is considered terminated.

(ii) The partnerships are treated as undertaking the assets-over form described in paragraph (c)(3)(i) of this section because the partnerships undertook a form that is not the assets-up form described in paragraph (c)(3)(ii) of this section. Accordingly, for Federal income tax purposes, partnership X is deemed to contribute its assets and liabilities to partnership Y in exchange for interests in partnership Y, and, immediately thereafter, partnership X is deemed to have distributed the interests in partnership Y to its partners in liquidation of their interests in partnership X.

Example (5). (i) A, B, and C are partners in partnership X. D, E, and F are partners in Partnership Y. Partnership X and partnership Y merge, and the resulting partnership is considered a continuation of partnership Y. Partnership X is considered terminated. Under state law, partnerships X and Y undertake the assets-over form of paragraph (c)(3)(i) of this section to accomplish the partnership merger. C does not want to become a partner in partnership Y, and partnership X does not have the resources to buy C's interest before the merger. C, partnership X, and partnership Y enter into an agreement specifying that partnership Y will purchase C's interest in partnership X for $150 before the merger, and as part of the agreement, C consents to treat the transaction in a manner that is consistent with the agreement. As part of the merger, partnership X receives from partnership Y $150 that will be distributed to C immediately before the merger, and interests in partnership Y in exchange for partnership X's assets and liabilities.

(ii) Because the merger agreement satisfies the requirements of paragraph (c)(4) of this section and C provides the necessary consent, C will be treated as selling its interest in partnership X to partnership Y for $150 before the merger. See section 741 and § 1.741–1 to determine the amount and character of C's gain or loss on the sale or exchange of its interest in partnership X.

(iii) Because the merger agreement satisfies the requirements of paragraph (c)(4) of this section, partnership Y is considered to have purchased C's interest in partnership X for $150 immediately before the merger. See § 1.704–1(b)(2)(iv)(*l*) for determining partnership Y's capital account in partnership X. Partnership Y's adjusted basis of its interest in partnership X is determined under section 742 and § 1.742–1. To the extent any built-in gain or loss on section 704(c) property in partnership X would have been allocated to C (including any allocations with respect to property revaluations under section 704(b) (reverse section 704(c) allocations)), see section 704 and § 1.704–3(a)(7) for determining the built-in gain or loss or reverse section 704(c) allocations apportionable to partnership Y. Similarly, after the merger is completed, the built-in gain or loss and reverse section 704(c) allocations attributable to C's interest are apportioned to D, E, and F under section 704(c) and § 1.704–3(a)(7).

(iv) Under paragraph (c)(3)(i) of this section, partnership X contributes its assets and liabilities attributable to the interests of A and B to partnership Y in exchange for interests in partnership Y; and, immediately thereafter, partnership X distributes the interests in partnership Y to A and B in liquidation of their interests in partnership X. At the same time, partnership X distributes assets to partnership Y in liquidation of partnership Y's interest in partnership X. Partnership Y's bases in the distributed assets are determined under section 732(b).

(6) Prescribed form not followed in certain circumstances. (i) If any transactions described in paragraph (c)(3) or (4) of this section are part of a larger series of transactions, and the substance of the larger series of transactions is inconsistent with following the form prescribed in such paragraph, the Commissioner may disregard such form, and may recast the larger series of transactions in accordance with their substance.

(ii) Example. The following example illustrates the rules in paragraph (c)(6) of this section:

Example. A, B, and C are equal partners in partnership ABC. ABC holds no section 704(c) property. D and E are equal partners in partnership DE. B and C want to exchange their interests in ABC for all of the interests in DE. However, rather than exchanging partnership interests, DE merges with ABC by undertaking the assets-up form described in paragraph (c)(3)(ii) of this section, with D and E receiving title to the DE assets and then contributing the assets to ABC in exchange for interests in ABC. As part of a prearranged transaction, the assets acquired from DE are contributed to a new partnership, and the interests in the new partnership are distributed to B and C in complete liquidation of their interests in ABC. The merger and division in this example represent a series of transactions that in substance are an exchange of interests in ABC for interests in DE. Even though paragraph (c)(3)(ii) of this section provides that the form of a merger will be respected for Federal income tax purposes if the steps prescribed under the assets-up form are followed, and paragraph (d)(3)(i) of this section provides a form that will be followed for Federal income tax purposes in the case of partnership divisions, these forms will not be respected for Federal income tax purposes under these facts, and the transactions will be recast in accordance with their substance as a taxable exchange of interests in ABC for interests in DE.

* * *

(d) Division of a partnership—(1) General rule. Upon the division of a partnership into two or more partnerships, any resulting partnership (as defined in paragraph (d)(4)(iv) of this section) or resulting partnerships shall be considered a continuation of the prior partnership (as defined in paragraph (d)(4)(ii) of this section) if the members of the resulting partnership or partnerships had an interest of more than 50 percent in the capital and profits of the prior partnership. Any other resulting partnership will not be considered a continuation of the prior partnership but will be considered a new partnership. If the members of none of the resulting partnerships owned an interest of more than 50 percent in the capital and profits of the prior partnership, none of the resulting partnerships will be considered a continuation of the prior partnership, and the prior partnership will be considered to have terminated. Where members of a partnership which has been divided into two or more partnerships do not become members of a resulting partnership which is considered a continuation of the prior partnership, such members' interests shall be considered liquidated as of the date of the division.

(2) Tax consequences—(i) Tax returns. The resulting partnership that is treated as the divided partnership (as defined in paragraph (d)(4)(i) of this section) shall file a return for the taxable year of the partnership that has been divided and retain the employer identification number (EIN) of the prior partnership. The return shall include the names, addresses, and EINs of all resulting partnerships that are regarded as continuing. The return shall also state that the partnership is a continuation of the prior partnership and shall set forth separately the respective distributive shares of the partners for the periods prior to and including the date of the division and subsequent to the date of division. All other resulting partnerships that are regarded as continuing and new partnerships shall file separate returns for the taxable year beginning on the day after the date of the division with new EINs for each

partnership. The return for a resulting partnership that is regarded as continuing and that is not the divided partnership shall include the name, address, and EIN of the prior partnership.

(ii) Elections. All resulting partnerships that are regarded as continuing are subject to preexisting elections that were made by the prior partnership. A subsequent election that is made by a resulting partnership does not affect the other resulting partnerships.

(3) Form of a division—(i) Assets-over form. When a partnership divides into two or more partnerships under applicable jurisdictional law without undertaking a form for the division, or undertakes a form that is not described in paragraph (d)(3)(ii) of this section, the transaction will be characterized under the assets-over form for Federal income tax purposes.

(A) Assets-over form where at least one resulting partnership is a continuation of the prior partnership. In a division under the assets-over form where at least one resulting partnership is a continuation of the prior partnership, the divided partnership (as defined in paragraph (d)(4)(i) of this section) contributes certain assets and liabilities to a recipient partnership (as defined in paragraph (d)(4) (iii) of this section) or recipient partnerships in exchange for interests in such recipient partnership or partnerships; and, immediately thereafter, the divided partnership distributes the interests in such recipient partnership or partnerships to some or all of its partners in partial or complete liquidation of the partners' interests in the divided partnership.

(B) Assets-over form where none of the resulting partnerships is a continuation of the prior partnership. In a division under the assets-over form where none of the resulting partnerships is a continuation of the prior partnership, the prior partnership will be treated as contributing all of its assets and liabilities to new resulting partnerships in exchange for interests in the resulting partnerships; and, immediately thereafter, the prior partnership will be treated as liquidating by distributing the interests in the new resulting partnerships to the prior partnership's partners.

(ii) Assets-up form—(A) Assets-up form where the partnership distributing assets is a continuation of the prior partnership. Despite the partners' transitory ownership of some of the prior partnership's assets, the form of a partnership division will be respected for Federal income tax purposes if the divided partnership (which, pursuant to § 1.708–1(d) (4)(i), must be a continuing partnership) distributes certain assets (in a manner that causes the partners to be treated, under the laws of the applicable jurisdiction, as the owners of such assets) to some or all of its partners in partial or complete liquidation of the partners' interests in the divided partnership, and immediately thereafter, such partners contribute the distributed assets to a recipient partnership or partnerships in exchange for interests in such recipient partnership or partnerships. In order for such form to be respected for transfers to a particular recipient partnership, all assets held by the prior partnership that are transferred to the recipient partnership must be distributed to, and then contributed by, the partners of the recipient partnership.

(B) Assets-up form where none of the resulting partnerships are a continuation of the prior partnership. If none of the resulting partnerships are a continuation of the prior partnership, then despite the partners' transitory ownership of some or all of the prior partnership's assets, the form of a partnership division will be respected for Federal income tax purposes if the prior partnership distributes certain assets (in a manner that causes the partners to be treated, under the laws of the applicable jurisdiction, as the owners of such assets) to some or all of its partners in partial or complete liquidation of the partners' interests in the prior partnership, and immediately thereafter, such partners contribute the distributed assets to a resulting partnership or partnerships

in exchange for interests in such resulting partnership or partnerships. In order for such form to be respected for transfers to a particular resulting partnership, all assets held by the prior partnership that are transferred to the resulting partnership must be distributed to, and then contributed by, the partners of the resulting partnership. If the prior partnership does not liquidate under the applicable jurisdictional law, then with respect to the assets and liabilities that, in form, are not transferred to a new resulting partnership, the prior partnership will be treated as transferring these assets and liabilities to a new resulting partnership under the assets-over form described in paragraph (d)(3) (i)(B) of this section.

(4) Definitions—(i) Divided partnership. For purposes of paragraph (d) of this section, the divided partnership is the continuing partnership which is treated, for Federal income tax purposes, as transferring the assets and liabilities to the recipient partnership or partnerships, either directly (under the assets-over form) or indirectly (under the assets-up form). If the resulting partnership that, in form, transferred the assets and liabilities in connection with the division is a continuation of the prior partnership, then such resulting partnership will be treated as the divided partnership. If a partnership divides into two or more partnerships and only one of the resulting partnerships is a continuation of the prior partnership, then the resulting partnership that is a continuation of the prior partnership will be treated as the divided partnership. If a partnership divides into two or more partnerships without undertaking a form for the division that is recognized under paragraph (d)(3) of this section, or if the resulting partnership that had, in form, transferred assets and liabilities is not considered a continuation of the prior partnership, and more than one resulting partnership is considered a continuation of the prior partnership, the continuing resulting partnership with the assets having the greatest fair market value (net of liabilities) will be treated as the divided partnership.

(ii) Prior partnership. For purposes of paragraph (d) of this section, the prior partnership is the partnership subject to division that exists under applicable jurisdictional law before the division.

(iii) Recipient partnership. For purposes of paragraph (d) of this section, a recipient partnership is a partnership that is treated as receiving, for Federal income tax purposes, assets and liabilities from a divided partnership, either directly (under the assets-over form) or indirectly (under the assets-up form).

(iv) Resulting partnership. For purposes of paragraph (d) of this section, a resulting partnership is a partnership resulting from the division that exists under applicable jurisdictional law after the division and that has at least two partners who were partners in the prior partnership. For example, where a prior partnership divides into two partnerships, both partnerships existing after the division are resulting partnerships.

(5) Examples. The following examples illustrate the rules in paragraphs (d)(1), (2), (3), and (4) of this section:

Example (1). Partnership ABCD is in the real estate and insurance businesses. A owns a 40-percent interest, and B, C, and D each owns a 20-percent interest, in the capital and profits of the partnership. The partnership and the partners report their income on a calendar year. On November 1, 1999, they separate the real estate and insurance businesses and form two partnerships. Partnership AB takes over the real estate business, and partnership CD takes over the insurance business. Because members of resulting partnership AB owned more than a 50-percent interest in the capital and profits of partnership ABCD (A, 40 percent, and B, 20 percent), partnership AB shall be considered a continuation of partnership ABCD. Partnership AB is required to file a return for the taxable year January 1 to December 31, 1999, indicating thereon that until November 1, 1999, it was partnership ABCD. Partnership CD is considered a new partnership formed at the be-

ginning of the day on November 2, 1999, and is required to file a return for the taxable year it adopts pursuant to section 706(b) and the applicable regulations.

Example (2). (i) Partnership ABCD owns properties W, X, Y, and Z, and divides into partnership AB and partnership CD. Under paragraph (d)(1) of this section, partnership AB is considered a continuation of partnership ABCD and partnership CD is considered a new partnership. Partnership ABCD distributes property Y to C and titles property Y in C's name. Partnership ABCD distributes property Z to D and titles property Z in D's name. C and D then contribute properties Y and Z, respectively, to partnership CD in exchange for interests in partnership CD. Properties W and X remain in partnership AB.

(ii) Under paragraph (d)(3)(ii) of this section, partnership ABCD will be treated as following the assets-up form for Federal income tax purposes.

Example (3). (i) The facts are the same as in Example 2, except partnership ABCD distributes property Y to C and titles property Y in C's name. C then contributes property Y to partnership CD. Simultaneously, partnership ABCD contributes property Z to partnership CD in exchange for an interest in partnership CD. Immediately thereafter, partnership ABCD distributes the interest in partnership CD to D in liquidation of D's interest in partnership ABCD.

(ii) Under paragraph (d)(3)(i) of this section, because partnership ABCD did not undertake the assets-up form with respect to all of the assets transferred to partnership CD, partnership ABCD will be treated as undertaking the assets-over form in transferring the assets to partnership CD. Accordingly, for Federal income tax purposes, partnership ABCD is deemed to contribute property Y and property Z to partnership CD in exchange for interests in partnership CD, and immediately thereafter, partnership ABCD is deemed to distribute the interests in partnership CD to partner C and

partner D in liquidation of their interests in partnership ABCD.

Example (4). *(i)* Partnership ABCD owns three parcels of property: property X, with a value of $500; property Y, with a value of $300; and property Z, with a value of $200. A and B each own a 40-percent interest in the capital and profits of partnership ABCD, and C and D each own a 10 percent interest in the capital and profits of partnership ABCD. On November 1, 1999, partnership ABCD divides into three partnerships (AB1, AB2, and CD) by contributing property X to a newly formed partnership (AB1) and distributing all interests in such partnership to A and B as equal partners, and by contributing property Z to a newly formed partnership (CD) and distributing all interests in such partnership to C and D as equal partners in exchange for all of their interests in partnership ABCD. While partnership ABCD does not transfer property Y, C and D cease to be partners in the partnership. Accordingly, after the division, the partnership holding property Y is referred to as partnership AB2.

(ii) Partnerships AB1 and AB2 both are considered a continuation of partnership ABCD, while partnership CD is considered a new partnership formed at the beginning of the day on November 2, 1999. Under paragraph (d)(3)(i)(A) of this section, partnership ABCD will be treated as following the assets-over form, with partnership ABCD contributing property X to partnership AB1 and property Z to partnership CD, and distributing the interests in such partnerships to the designated partners.

Example (5). *(i)* The facts are the same as in Example 4, except that partnership ABCD divides into three partnerships by operation of state law, without undertaking a form.

(ii) Under the last sentence of paragraph (d) (4)(i) of this section, partnership AB1 will be treated as the resulting partnership that is the divided partnership. Under paragraph (d)(3)(i) (A) of this section, partnership ABCD will be treated as following the assets-over form, with partnership ABCD contributing property Y to partnership AB2 and property Z to partnership CD, and distributing the interests in such partnerships to the designated partners.

Example (6). *(i)* The facts are the same as in Example 4, except that partnership ABCD divides into three partnerships by contributing property X to newly-formed partnership AB1 and property Y to newly-formed partnership AB2 and distributing all interests in each partnership to A and B in exchange for all of their interests in partnership ABCD.

(ii) Because resulting partnership CD is not a continuation of the prior partnership (partnership ABCD), partnership CD cannot be treated, for Federal income tax purposes, as the partnership that transferred assets (i.e., the divided partnership), but instead must be treated as a recipient partnership. Under the last sentence of paragraph (d)(4)(i) of this section, partnership AB1 will be treated as the resulting partnership that is the divided partnership. Under paragraph (d)(3)(i)(A) of this section, partnership ABCD will be treated as following the assets-over form, with partnership ABCD contributing property Y to partnership AB2 and property Z to partnership CD, and distributing the interests in such partnerships to the designated partners.

Example (7). *(i)* Partnership ABCDE owns Blackacre, Whiteacre, and Redacre, and divides into partnership AB, partnership CD, and partnership DE. Under paragraph (d)(1) of this section, partnership ABCDE is considered terminated (and, hence, none of the resulting partnerships are a continuation of the prior partnership) because none of the members of the new partnerships (partnership AB, partnership CD, and partnership DE) owned an interest of more than 50 percent in the capital and profits of partnership ABCDE.

(ii) Partnership ABCDE distributes Blackacre to A and B and titles Blackacre in the names of A and B. A and B then contribute Blackacre to partnership AB in exchange for

interests in partnership AB. Partnership ABC-DE will be treated as following the assets-up form described in paragraph (d)(3)(ii)(B) of this section for Federal income tax purposes.

(iii) Partnership ABCDE distributes White-acre to C and D and titles Whiteacre in the names of C and D. C and D then contribute Whiteacre to partnership CD in exchange for interests in partnership CD. Partnership ABC-DE will be treated as following the assets-up form described in paragraph (d)(3)(ii)(B) of this section for Federal income tax purposes.

(iv) Partnership ABCDE does not liquidate under state law so that, in form, the assets in new partnership DE are not considered to have been transferred under state law. Partnership ABCDE will be treated as undertaking the assets-over form described in paragraph (d)(3)(i)(B) of this section for Federal income tax purposes with respect to the assets of partnership DE. Thus, partnership ABCDE will be treated as contributing Redacre to partnership DE in exchange for interests in partnership DE; and, immediately thereafter, partnership ABCDE will be treated as distributing interests in partnership DE to D and E in liquidation of their interests in partnership ABCDE. Partnership ABCDE then terminates.

(6) Prescribed form not followed in certain circumstances. If any transactions described in paragraph (d)(3) of this section are part of a larger series of transactions, and the substance of the larger series of transactions is inconsistent with following the form prescribed in such paragraph, the Commissioner may disregard such form, and may recast the larger series of transactions in accordance with their substance.

* * *

§ 1.709–1 Treatment of organization and syndication costs.

(a) General rule. Except as provided in paragraph (b) of this section, no deduction shall be allowed under Chapter 1 of the Code to a partnership or to any partner for any

amounts paid or incurred, directly or indirectly, in partnership taxable years beginning after December 31, 1975, to organize a partnership, or to promote the sale of, or to sell, an interest in the partnership.

* * *

(c) Time and manner of making election. The election to amortize organizational expenses provided by section 709(b) shall be made by attaching a statement to the partnership's return of income for the taxable year in which the partnership begins business. The statement shall set forth a description of each organizational expense incurred (whether or not paid) with the amount of the expense, the date each expense was incurred, the month in which the partnership began business, and the number of months (not less than 60) over which the expenses are to be amortized. A taxpayer on the cash receipts and disbursements method of accounting shall also indicate the amount paid before the end of the taxable year with respect to each such expense. Expenses less than $10 need not be separately listed, provided the total amount of these expenses is listed with the dates on which the first and last of such expenses were incurred, and, in the case of a taxpayer on the cash receipts and disbursements method of accounting, the aggregate amount of such expenses that was paid by the end of the taxable year is stated. In the case of a partnership which begins business in a taxable year that ends after March 31, 1983, the original return and statement must be filed (and the election made) not later than the date prescribed by law for filing the return (including any extensions of time) for that taxable year. Once an election has been made, an amended return (or returns) and statement (or statements) may be filed to include any organizational expenses not included in the partnership's original return and statement.

§ 1.709–2 Definitions.

(a) Organizational expenses. Section 709(b)(2) of the Internal Revenue Code defines organizational expenses as expenses which:

(1) Are incident to the creation of the partnership;

(2) Are chargeable to capital account; and

(3) Are of a character which, if expended incident to the creation of a partnership having an ascertainable life, would (but for section 709(a)) be amortized over such life.

An expenditure which fails to meet one or more of these three tests does not qualify as an organizational expense for purposes of section 709(b) and this section. To satisfy the statutory requirement described in paragraph (a)(1) of this section, the expense must be incurred during the period beginning at a point which is a reasonable time before the partnership begins business and ending with the date prescribed by law for filing the partnership return (determined without regard to any extensions of time) for the taxable year the partnership begins business. In addition, the expenses must be for creation of the partnership and not for operation or starting operation of the partnership trade or business. To satisfy the statutory requirement described in paragraph (a)(3) of this section, the expense must be for an item of a nature normally expected to benefit the partnership throughout the entire life of the partnership. The following are examples of organizational expenses within the meaning of section 709 and this section: Legal fees for services incident to the organization of the partnership, such as negotiation and preparation of a partnership agreement; accounting fees for services incident to the organization of the partnership; and filing fees. The following are examples of expenses that are not organizational expenses within the meaning of section 709 and this section (regardless of how the partnership characterizes them): Expenses connected with acquiring assets for the partnership or transferring assets to the partnership; expenses connected with the admission or removal of partners other than at the time the partnership is first organized; expenses connected with a contract relating to the operation of the partnership trade or business (even where the contract is between the partnership and one of its members); and syndication expenses.

(b) Syndication expenses. Syndication expenses are expenses connected with the issuing and marketing of interests in the partnership. Examples of syndication expenses are brokerage fees; registration fees; legal fees of the underwriter or placement agent and the issuer (the general partner or the partnership) for securities advice and for advice pertaining to the adequacy of tax disclosures in the prospectus or placement memorandum for securities law purposes; accounting fees for preparation of representations to be included in the offering materials; and printing costs of the prospectus, placement memorandum, and other selling and promotional material. These expenses are not subject to the election under section 709(b) and must be capitalized.

(c) Beginning business. The determination of the date a partnership begins business for purposes of section 709 presents a question of fact that must be determined in each case in light of all the circumstances of the particular case. Ordinarily, a partnership begins business when it starts the business operations for which it was organized. The mere signing of a partnership agreement is not alone sufficient to show the beginning of business.

If the activities of the partnership have advanced to the extent necessary to establish the nature of its business operations, it will be deemed to have begun business. Accordingly, the acquisition of operating assets which are necessary to the type of business contemplated may constitute beginning business for these purposes. The term "operating assets", as used herein, means assets that are in a state of readiness to be placed in service within a reasonable period following their acquisition.

§ 1.721–1 Nonrecognition of gain or loss on contribution.

(a) No gain or loss shall be recognized either to the partnership or to any of its partners upon a contribution of property, including installment obligations, to the partnership in exchange for a partnership interest. This rule applies whether the contribution is made to a partnership in the process of formation or to a partnership which is already formed and operating. Section 721 shall not apply to a transaction between a partnership and a partner not acting in his capacity as a partner since such a transaction is governed by section 707. Rather than contributing property to a partnership, a partner may sell property to the partnership or may retain the ownership of property and allow the partnership to use it. In all cases, the substance of the transaction will govern, rather than its form. See paragraph (c)(3) of § 1.731–1. Thus, if the transfer of property by the partner to the partnership results in the receipt by the partner of money or other consideration, including a promissory obligation fixed in amount and time for payment, the transaction will be treated as a sale or exchange under section 707 rather than as a contribution under section 721. For the rules governing the treatment of liabilities to which contributed property is subject, see section 752 and § 1.752–1.

(b)(1) Normally, under local law, each partner is entitled to be repaid his contributions of money or other property to the partnership (at the value placed upon such property by the partnership at the time of the contribution) whether made at the formation of the partnership or subsequent thereto. To the extent that any of the partners gives up any part of his right to be repaid his contributions (as distinguished from a share in partnership profits) in favor of another partner as compensation for services (or in satisfaction of an obligation), section 721 does not apply. The value of an interest in such partnership capital so transferred to a partner as compensation for services constitutes income to the partner under section 61. The amount of such income is the fair market value of the interest in capital so transferred, either at the time the transfer is made for past services, or at the time the services have been rendered where the transfer is conditioned on the completion of the transferee's future services. The time when such income is realized depends on all the facts and circumstances, including any substantial restrictions or conditions on the compensated partner's right to withdraw or otherwise dispose of such interest. To the extent that an interest in capital representing compensation for services rendered by the decedent prior to his death is transferred after his death to the decedent's successor in interest, the fair market value of such interest is income in respect of a decedent under section 691.

(2) To the extent that the value of such interest is: (i) Compensation for services rendered to the partnership, it is a guaranteed payment for services under section 707(c); (ii) compensation for services rendered to a partner, it is not deductible by the partnership, but is deductible only by such partner to the extent allowable under this chapter.

(c) Underwritings of partnership interests—(1) In general. For the purpose of section 721, if a person acquires a partnership interest from an underwriter in exchange for cash in a qualified underwriting transaction, the person who acquires the partnership interest is treated as transferring cash directly to the partnership in exchange for the partnership interest and the underwriter is disregarded. A qualified underwriting transaction is a transaction in which a partnership issues partnership interests for cash in an underwriting in which either the underwriter is an agent of the partnership or the underwriter's ownership of the partnership interests is transitory.

* * *

§ 1.721–2 Noncompensatory options.

(a) Exercise of a noncompensatory option—(1) In general. Notwithstanding § 1.721–1(b)(1), section 721 applies to the exercise (as defined in paragraph (g)(4) of this section) of a noncompensatory option (as defined in paragraph (f) of this section). Except as provided in paragraph (a)(2) of this section, section 721 applies to the exercise of a noncompensatory option when the holder pays the exercise price with either property or cash, regardless of whether the terms of the option require or permit cash payment. However, if the exercise price (as defined in paragraph (g)(5) of this section) of a noncompensatory option exceeds the capital account received by the option holder on the exercise of the option, then general tax principles will apply to determine the tax consequences of the transaction.

(2) Exception. Section 721 does not apply to the exercise of a noncompensatory option to the extent that the exercise price is satisfied with the partnership's obligation to the option holder for unpaid rent, royalties, or interest (including accrued original issue discount) that accrued on or after the beginning of the option holder's holding period for the obligation. The issuing partnership will not recognize gain or loss upon the transfer of a partnership interest to an exercising option holder in satisfaction of such unpaid rent, royalties, or interest (including accrued original issue discount).

(b) Transfer of property or satisfaction of an obligation in exchange for a noncompensatory option—(1) In general. Except as provided in paragraph (b)(2) of this section, section 721 does not apply to a transfer of property to a partnership in exchange for a noncompensatory option, or to the satisfaction of a partnership obligation with a noncompensatory option.

(2) Exception. Section 721 does apply to a transfer of property to a partnership in exchange for convertible equity (as defined in paragraph (g)(3) of this section).

(c) Lapse of a noncompensatory option. Section 721 does not apply to the lapse of a noncompensatory option.

(d) Cash settlement of a noncompensatory option. Section 721 does not apply to the settlement of a noncompensatory option in cash or property other than a partnership interest in the issuing partnership.

(e) Issuance of a partnership interest in satisfaction of indebtedness for interest on convertible debt. Section 721 does not apply to the transfer of a partnership interest to a noncompensatory option holder upon conversion of convertible debt in the partnership to the extent that the transfer is in satisfaction of the partnership's indebtedness for unpaid interest (including accrued original issue discount) on the convertible debt that accrued on or after the beginning of the convertible debt holder's holding period for the indebtedness. The debtor partnership will not, however, recognize gain or loss upon such conversion. For rules in determining whether a partnership interest transferred to a creditor is treated as payment of interest or accrued original issue discount, see §§ 1.446–2 and 1.1275–2, respectively.

(f) Scope. The provisions of this section apply only to noncompensatory options. For purposes of this section, the term noncompensatory option means an option (as defined in paragraph (g)(1) of this section) issued by a partnership (the issuing partnership), other than an option issued in connection with the performance of services.

(g) Definitions. The following definitions apply for the purposes of this section:

(1) Option means a contractual right to acquire an interest in the issuing partnership, including a call option, warrant, or other similar arrangement, the conversion feature of convertible debt (as defined in paragraph (g) (2) of this section), or the conversion feature of convertible equity (as defined in paragraph (g)(3) of this section). To achieve the purposes of this section, the Commissioner can treat other contractual agreements, including a futures contract, a forward contract, or a notional principal contract, as an option. A contract that otherwise constitutes an option will not fail to be treated as an option for purposes of this section merely because it may or must be settled in cash or property other than a partnership interest.

(2) Convertible debt is any indebtedness of a partnership that is convertible into an interest in the partnership that issued the debt.

(3) Convertible equity is equity in a partnership that is convertible into a different equity interest in the partnership that issued the convertible equity.

(4) Exercise means the exercise of an option in exchange for an interest in the issuing partnership or the conversion of convertible debt or convertible equity into an interest in the issuing partnership.

(5) Exercise price means, in the case of a call option, the exercise price of the call option; in the case of convertible equity, the converting partner's capital account with respect to that convertible equity, increased by the fair market value of cash or other property contributed to the partnership in connection with the conversion; and, in the case of convertible debt, the adjusted issue price (within the meaning of § 1.1275–1(b)) of the debt converted, increased by accrued but unpaid qualified stated interest on the debt and by the fair market value of cash or other property contributed to the partnership in connection with the conversion.

(h) Example. The following example illustrates the provisions of this section:

Example. In Year 1, L and M form general partnership LM with cash contributions of $5,000 each, which are used to purchase land, Property D, for $10,000. In that same year, LM issues an option to N to buy a one-third interest in LM at any time before the end of Year 3. The exercise price of the option is $5,000, payable in either cash or property. N transfers Property

E with a basis of $600 and a value of $1,000 to the partnership in exchange for the option. N provides no other consideration for the option. Assume that N's option is a noncompensatory option under paragraph (f) of this section and that N is not treated as a partner with respect to the option. Under paragraph (b) of this section, section 721(a) does not apply to N's transfer of Property E to LM in exchange for the option. In accordance with § 1.1001–1, upon N's transfer of Property E to the partnership in exchange for the option, N recognizes $400 of gain. Under open transaction principles applicable to noncompensatory options, the partnership does not recognize any income for the premium (the property received in exchange for the option). The partnership has a basis of $1,000 in Property E. In Year 3, when the partnership property is valued at $16,000, N exercises the option, contributing Property F with a basis of $3,000 and a fair market value of $5,000 to the partnership. Under paragraph (a) of this section, neither the partnership nor N recognizes gain upon N's contribution of property to the partnership upon the exercise of the option. Under section 723, the partnership has a basis of $3,000 in Property F. The partnership does not recognize income for the premium (Property E) upon exercise of the option. See § 1.704–1(b)(2)(iv)(d)(4) and (s) for special rules applicable to capital account adjustments on the exercise of a noncompensatory option.

* * *

§ 1.722–1 Basis of contributing partner's interest.

The basis to a partner of a partnership interest acquired by a contribution of property, including money, to the partnership shall be the amount of money contributed plus the adjusted basis at the time of contribution of any property contributed. If the acquisition of an interest in partnership capital results in taxable income to a partner, such income shall constitute an addition to the basis of the partner's interest. See paragraph (b) of § 1.721–1. If the contributed property is subject to indebtedness or if liabilities of the partner are assumed by the partnership, the basis of the contributing partner's interest shall be reduced by the portion of the indebtedness assumed by the other partners, since the partnership's assumption of his indebtedness is treated as a distribution of money to the partner. Conversely, the assumption by the other partners of a portion of the contributor's indebtedness is treated as a contribution of money by them. See section 752 and § 1.752–1. The provisions of this section may be illustrated by the following examples:

Example (1). A acquired a 20-percent interest in a partnership by contributing property. At the time of A's contribution, the property had a fair market value of $10,000, an adjusted basis to A of $4,000, and was subject to a mortgage of $2,000. Payment of the mortgage was assumed by the partnership. The basis of A's interest in the partnership is $2,400, computed as follows:

Adjusted basis to A of property contributed..	$4,000
Less portion of mortgage assumed by other partners which must be treated as a distribution (80 percent of $2,000)	1,600
Basis of A's interest	2,400

Example (2). If, in example 1 of this section, the property contributed by A was subject to a mortgage of $6,000, the basis of A's interest would be zero, computed as follows:

Adjusted basis to A of property contributed..	$4,000
Less portion of mortgage assumed by other partners which must be treated as a distribution (80 percent of $6,000)	4,800
	(800)

Since A's basis cannot be less than zero, the $800 in excess of basis, which is considered as a distribution of money under section 752(b), is treated as capital gain from the sale or exchange or a partnership interest. See section 731(a).

§ 1.723–1 Basis of property contributed to partnership.

The basis to the partnership of property contributed to it by a partner is the adjusted basis of such property to the contributing partner at the time of the contribution. Since such property has the same basis in the hands of the partnership as it had in the hands of the contributing partner, the holding period of such property for the partnership includes the period during which it was held by the partner. See section 1223(2). For elective adjustments to the basis of partnership property arising from distributions or transfers of partnership interests, see sections 732(d), 734(b), and 743(b).

§ 1.731–1 Extent of recognition of gain or loss on distribution.

(a) **Recognition of gain or loss to partner**—(1) **Recognition of gain.** (i) Where money is distributed by a partnership to a partner, no gain shall be recognized to the partner except to the extent that the amount of money distributed exceeds the adjusted basis of the partner's interest in the partnership immediately before the distribution. This rule is applicable both to current distributions (i.e., distributions other than in liquidation of an entire interest) and to distributions in liquidation of a partner's entire interest in a partnership. Thus, if a partner with a basis for his interest of $10,000 receives a distribution of cash of $8,000 and property with a fair market value of $3,000, no gain is recognized to him. If $11,000 cash were distributed, gain would be recognized to the extent of $1,000. No gain shall be recognized to a distributee partner with respect to a distribution of property (other than money) until he sells or otherwise disposes of such property, except to the extent otherwise provided by section 736 (relating to payments to a retiring partner or a deceased partner's successor in interest) and section 751 (relating to unrealized receivables and inventory items). See section 731(c) and paragraph (c) of this section.

(ii) For the purposes of sections 731 and 705, advances or drawings of money or property against a partner's distributive share of income shall be treated as current distributions made on the last day of the partnership taxable year with respect to such partner.

(2) Recognition of loss. Loss is recognized to a partner only upon liquidation of his entire interest in the partnership, and only if the property distributed to him consists solely of money, unrealized receivables (as defined in section 751(c)), and inventory items (as defined in section 751(d)(2)). The term liquidation of a partner's interest, as defined in section 761(d), is the termination of the partner's entire interest in the partnership by means of a distribution or a series of distributions. Loss is recognized to the distributee partner in such cases to the extent of the excess of the adjusted basis of such partner's interest in the partnership at the time of the distribution over the sum of:

(i) Any money distributed to him, and

(ii) The basis to the distributee, as determined under section 732, of any unrealized receivables and inventory items that are distributed to him.

If the partner whose interest is liquidated receives any property other than money, unrealized receivables, or inventory items, then no loss will be recognized. Application of the provisions of this subparagraph may be illustrated by the following examples:

Example (1). Partner A has a partnership interest in partnership ABC with an adjusted basis to him of $10,000. He retires from the partnership and receives, as a distribution in liquidation of his entire interest, his share of partnership property. This share is $5,000 cash and inventory with a basis to him (under section 732) of $3,000. Partner A realizes a capital loss of $2,000, which is recognized under section 731(a)(2).

Example (2). Partner B has a partnership interest in partnership BCD with an adjusted basis to him of $10,000. He retires from the partnership and receives, as a distribution in liquidation of his entire interest, his share of partnership property. This share is $4,000 cash, real property (used in the trade or business) with an adjusted basis to the partnership of $2,000, and unrealized receivables having a basis to him (under section 732) of $3,000. No loss will be recognized to B on the transaction because he received property other than money, unrealized receivables, and inventory items. As determined under section 732, the basis to B for the real property received is $3,000.

(3) Character of gain or loss. Gain or loss recognized under section 731(a) on a distribution is considered gain or loss from the sale or exchange of the partnership interest of the distributee partner, that is, capital gain or loss.

(b) Gain or loss recognized by partnership. A distribution of property (including money) by a partnership to a partner does not result in recognized gain or loss to the partnership under section 731. However, recognized gain or loss may result to the partnership from certain distributions which, under section 751(b), must be treated as a sale or exchange of property between the distributee partner and the partnership.

(c) Exceptions. (1) Section 731 does not apply to the extent otherwise provided by:

(i) Section 736 (relating to payments to a retiring partner or to a deceased partner's successor in interest) and

(ii) Section 751 (relating to unrealized receivables and inventory items).

For example, payments under section 736(a), which are considered as a distributive share or guaranteed payment, are taxable as such under that section.

(2) The receipt by a partner from the partnership of money or property under an obligation to repay the amount of such money or to return such property does not constitute a distribution subject to section 731 but is a loan governed by section 707(a). To the extent that such an obligation is canceled, the obligor partner will be considered to have received a distribution of money or property at the time of cancellation.

(3) If there is a contribution of property to a partnership and within a short period:

(i) Before or after such contribution other property is distributed to the contributing partner and the contributed property is retained by the partnership, or

(ii) After such contribution the contributed property is distributed to another partner, such distribution may not fall within the scope of section 731. Section 731 does not apply to a distribution of property, if, in fact, the distribution was made in order to effect an exchange of property between two or more of the partners or between the partnership and a partner. Such a transaction shall be treated as an exchange of property.

§ 1.731–2 Partnership distributions of marketable securities.

(a) Marketable securities treated as money. Except as otherwise provided in section 731(c) and this section, for purposes of sections 731(a)(1) and 737, the term money includes marketable securities and such securities are taken into account at their fair market value as of the date of the distribution.

(b) Reduction of amount treated as money—(1) Aggregation of securities. For purposes of section 731(c)(3)(B) and this paragraph (b), all marketable securities held by a partnership are treated as marketable securities of the same class and issuer as the distributed security.

(2) Amount of reduction. The amount of the distribution of marketable securities that is treated as a distribution of money under section 731(c) and paragraph (a) of this section is reduced (but not below zero) by the excess, if any, of—

(i) The distributee partner's distributive share of the net gain, if any, which would be recognized if all the marketable securities held by the partnership were sold (immediately before the transaction to which the distribution relates) by the partnership for fair market value; over

(ii) The distributee partner's distributive share of the net gain, if any, which is attributable to the marketable securities held by the partnership immediately after the transaction, determined by using the same fair market value as used under paragraph (b)(2)(i) of this section.

(3) Distributee partner's share of net gain. For purposes of section 731(c)(3)(B) and paragraph (b)(2) of this section, a partner's distributive share of net gain is determined—

(i) By taking into account any basis adjustments under section 743(b) with respect to that partner;

(ii) Without taking into account any special allocations adopted with a principal purpose of avoiding the effect of section 731(c) and this section; and

(iii) Without taking into account any gain or loss attributable to a distributed security to which paragraph (d)(1) of this section applies.

(c) Marketable securities—(1) In general. For purposes of section 731(c) and this section, the term marketable securities is defined in section 731(c)(2).

(2) Actively traded. For purposes of section 731(c) and this section, a financial instrument is actively traded (and thus is a marketable security) if it is of a type that is, as of the date of distribution, actively traded within the meaning of section 1092(d)(1). Thus, for example, if XYZ common stock is listed on a national securities exchange, particular shares of XYZ common stock that are distributed by a partnership are marketable securities even if those particular shares cannot be resold by the distributee partner for a designated period of time.

(3) Interests in an entity—(i) Substantially all. For purposes of section 731(c)(2)(B)(v) and this section, substantially all of the assets of an entity consist (directly or indirectly) of marketable securities, money, or both only if 90 percent or more of the assets of the entity (by value) at the time of the distribution of an interest in the entity consist (directly or indirectly) of marketable securities, money, or both.

(ii) Less than substantially all. For purposes of section 731(c)(2)(B)(vi) and this section, an interest in an entity is a marketable security to the extent that the value of the interest is attributable (directly or indirectly) to marketable securities, money, or both, if less than 90 percent but 20 percent or more of the assets of the entity (by value) at the time of the distribution of an interest in the entity consist (directly or indirectly) of marketable securities, money, or both.

(4) Value of assets. For purposes of section 731(c) and this section, the value of the assets of an entity is determined without regard to any debt that may encumber or otherwise be allocable to those assets, other than debt that is incurred to acquire an asset with a principal purpose of avoiding or reducing the effect of section 731(c) and this section.

(d) Exceptions—(1) In general. Except as otherwise provided in paragraph (d)(2) of this section, section 731(c) and this section do not apply to the distribution of a marketable security if—

(i) The security was contributed to the partnership by the distributee partner;

(ii) The security was acquired by the partnership in a nonrecognition transaction, and the following conditions are satisfied—

(A) The value of any marketable securities and money exchanged by the partnership in the nonrecognition transaction is less than 20 percent of the value of all the assets exchanged by the partnership in the nonrecognition transaction; and

(B) The partnership distributed the security within five years of either the date the security was acquired by the partnership or, if later, the date the security became marketable; or

(iii) The security was not a marketable security on the date acquired by the partnership, and the following conditions are satisfied—

(A) The entity that issued the security had no outstanding marketable securities at the time the security was acquired by the partnership;

(B) The security was held by the partnership for at least six months before the date the security became marketable; and

(C) The partnership distributed the security within five years of the date the security became marketable.

(2) Anti-stuffing rule. Paragraph (d)(1) of this section does not apply to the extent that 20 percent or more of the value of the distributed security is attributable to marketable securities or money contributed (directly or indirectly) by the partnership to the entity to which the distributed security relates after the security was acquired by the partnership (other than marketable securities contributed by the partnership that were originally contributed to the partnership by the distributee partner). For purposes of this paragraph (d)(2), money contributed by the distributing partnership does not include any money deemed contributed by the partnership as a result of section 752.

(3) Successor security. Section 731(c) and this section apply to the distribution of a marketable security acquired by the partnership in a nonrecognition transaction in exchange for a security the distribution of which immediately prior to the exchange would have been excepted under this paragraph (d) only to the extent that section 731(c) and this section otherwise would have applied to the exchanged security.

(e) Investment partnerships—(1) In general. Section 731(c) and this section do not apply to the distribution of marketable securities by an investment partnership (as defined in section 731(c)(3)(C)(i)) to an eligible partner (as defined in section 731(c)(3)(C)(iii)).

(2) Eligible partner—(i) Contributed services. For purposes of section 731(c)(3)(C)(iii) and this section, a partner is not treated as a partner other than an eligible partner solely because the partner contributed services to the partnership.

(ii) Contributed partnership interests. For purposes of determining whether a partner is an eligible partner under section 731(c)(3)(C), if the partner has contributed to the investment partnership an interest in another partnership that meets the requirements of paragraph (e)(4)(i) of this section after the contribution, the contributed interest is treated as property specified in section 731(c)(3)(C)(i).

(3) Trade or business activities. For purposes of section 731(c)(3)(C) and this section, a partnership is not treated as engaged in a trade or business by reason of—

(i) Any activity undertaken as an investor, trader, or dealer in any asset described in section 731(c)(3)(C)(i), including the receipt of commitment fees, break-up fees, guarantee fees, director's fees, or similar fees that are customary in and incidental to any activities of the partnership as an investor, trader, or dealer in such assets;

(ii) Reasonable and customary management services (including the receipt of reasonable and customary fees in exchange for such management services) provided to an investment partnership (within the meaning of section 731(c)(3)(C)(i)) in which the partnership holds a partnership interest; or

(iii) Reasonable and customary services provided by the partnership in assisting the formation, capitalization, expansion, or offering of interests in a corporation (or other entity) in which the partnership holds or acquires a significant equity interest (including the provision of advice or consulting services, bridge loans, guarantees of obligations, or service on a company's board of directors), provided that the anticipated receipt of compensation for the services, if any, does not represent a significant purpose for the partnership's investment in the entity and is incidental to the investment in the entity.

(4) Partnership tiers. For purposes of section 731(c)(3)(C)(iv) and this section, a partnership (upper-tier partnership) is not treated as engaged in a trade or business engaged in by, or as holding (instead of a partnership interest) a proportionate share of the assets of, a partnership (lower-tier partnership) in which the partnership holds a partnership interest if—

(i) The upper-tier partnership does not actively and substantially participate in the management of the lower-tier partnership; and

(ii) The interest held by the upper-tier partnership is less than 20 percent of the total profits and capital interests in the lower-tier partnership.

(f) Basis rules—(1) Partner's basis—(i) Partner's basis in distributed securities. The distributee partner's basis in distributed marketable securities with respect to which gain is recognized by reason of section 731(c) and this section is the basis of the security determined under section 732, increased by the amount of such gain. Any increase in the basis of the marketable securities attributable to gain recognized by reason of section 731(c) and this section is allocated to marketable securities in proportion to their respective amounts of unrealized appreciation in the hands of the partner before such increase.

(ii) Partner's basis in partnership interest. The basis of the distributee partner's interest in the partnership is determined under section 733 as if no gain were recognized by the partner on the distribution by reason of section 731(c) and this section.

(2) Basis of partnership property. No adjustment is made to the basis of partnership property under section 734 as a result of any gain recognized by a partner, or any step-up in the basis in the distributed marketable securities in the hands of the distributee partner, by reason of section 731(c) and this section.

(g) Coordination with other sections— (1) Sections 704(c)(1)(B) and 737—(i) In general. If a distribution results in the application of sections 731(c) and one or both of sections 704(c)(1)(B) and 737, the effect of the distribution is determined by applying section 704(c)(1)(B) first, section 731(c) second, and finally section 737.

(ii) Section 704(c)(1)(B). The basis of the distributee partner's interest in the partnership for purposes of determining the amount of gain, if any, recognized by reason of section 731(c) (and for determining the basis of the marketable securities in the hands of the distributee partner) includes the increase or decrease, if any, in the partner's basis that occurs under section 704(c)(1)(B)(iii) as a result of a distribution to another partner of property contributed by the distributee partner in a distribution that is part of the same distribution as the marketable securities.

(iii) Section 737—(A) Marketable securities as other property. A distribution of marketable securities is treated as a distribution of property other than money for purposes of section 737 to the extent that the marketable securities are not treated as money under section 731(c). In addition, marketable securities contributed to the partnership are treated as property other than money in determining the contributing partner's net precontribution gain under section 737(b).

(B) Basis increase under section 737. The basis of the distributee partner's interest in the partnership for purposes of determining the amount of gain, if any, recognized by reason of section 731(c) (and for determining the basis of the marketable securities in the hands of the distributee partner) does not include the increase, if any, in the partner's basis that occurs under section 737(c)(1) as a result of a distribution of property to the distributee partner in a distribution that is part of the same distribution as the marketable securities.

(2) Section 708(b)(1)(B). If a partnership termination occurs under section 708(b)(1)(B), the successor partnership will be treated as if there had been no termination for purposes of section 731(c) and this section. Accordingly, a section 708(b)(1)(B) termination will not affect whether a partnership qualifies for any of the exceptions in paragraphs (d) and (e) of this section. In addition, a deemed distribution that may occur as a result of a section 708(b)(1) (B) termination will not be subject to section 731(c) and this section.

(h) Anti-abuse rule. The provisions of section 731(c) and this section must be applied in a manner consistent with the purpose of section 731(c) and the substance of the transaction. Accordingly, if a principal purpose of a transaction is to achieve a tax result that is inconsistent with the purpose of section 731(c) and this section, the Commissioner can recast the transaction for Federal tax purposes as appropriate to achieve tax results that are consistent with the purpose of section 731(c) and this section. Whether a tax result is inconsistent with the purpose of section 731(c) and this section must be determined based on all the facts and circumstances. For example, under the provisions of this paragraph (h)—

(1) A change in partnership allocations or distribution rights with respect to marketable securities may be treated as a distribution of the marketable securities subject to section 731(c) if the change in allocations or distribution rights is, in substance, a distribution of the securities;

(2) A distribution of substantially all of the assets of the partnership other than marketable securities and money to some partners may also be treated as a distribution of marketable securities to the remaining partners if the distribution of the other property and the withdrawal of the other partners is, in substance, equivalent to a distribution of the securities to the remaining partners; and

(3) The distribution of multiple properties to one or more partners at different times may also be treated as part of a single distribution if the distributions are part of a single plan of distribution.

(i) [Reserved.]

(j) Examples. The following examples illustrate the rules of this section. Unless otherwise specified, all securities held by a partnership are marketable securities within the meaning of section 731(c); the partnership holds no marketable securities other than the securities described in the example; all distributions by the partnership are subject to section 731(a) and are not subject to sections 704(c)(1)(B), 707(a)(2)(B), 751(b), or 737; and no securities are eligible for an exception to section 731(c). The examples are as follows:

Example (1). Recognition of gain. (i) A and B form partnership AB as equal partners. A contributes property with a fair market value of $1,000 and an adjusted tax basis of $250. B contributes $1,000 cash. AB subsequently purchases Security X for $500 and immediately distributes the security to A in a current distribution. The basis in A's interest in the partnership at the time of distribution is $250.

(ii) The distribution of Security X is treated as a distribution of money in an amount equal to the fair market value of Security X on the date of distribution ($500). (The amount of the distribution that is treated as money is not reduced under section 731(c)(3)(B) and paragraph (b) of this section because, if Security X had been sold immediately before the distribution, there would have been no gain recognized by AB and A's distributive share of the gain would therefore have been zero.) As a result, A recognizes $250 of gain under section 731(a)(1) on the distribution ($500 distribution of money less $250 adjusted tax basis in A's partnership interest).

Example (2). Reduction in amount treated as money—in general. (i) A and B form partnership AB as equal partners. AB subsequently distributes Security X to A in a current distribution. Immediately before the distribution, AB held securities with the following fair market values, adjusted tax bases, and unrecognized gain or loss:

	Value	Basis	Gain (Loss)
Security X	100	70	30
Security Y	100	80	20
Security Z	100	110	(10)

(ii) If AB had sold the securities for fair market value immediately before the distribution to A, the partnership would have recognized $40 of net gain ($30 gain on Security X plus $20 gain on Security Y minus $10 loss on Security Z). A's distributive share of this gain would have been $20 (one-half of $40 net gain). If AB had sold the remaining securities immediately after the distribution of Security X to A, the partnership would have $10 of net gain ($20 of gain on Security Y minus $10 loss on Security Z). A's distributive share of this gain would have been $5 (one-half of $10 net gain). As a result, the distribution resulted in a decrease of $15 in A's distributive share of the net gain in AB's securities ($20 net gain before distribution minus $5 net gain after distribution).

(iii) Under paragraph (b) of this section, the amount of the distribution of Security X that is treated as a distribution of money is reduced by $15. The distribution of Security X is therefore treated as a distribution of $85 of money to A ($100 fair market value of Security X minus $15 reduction).

Example (3). Reduction in amount treated as money-carried interest. (i) A and B form partnership AB. A contributes $1,000 and provides substantial services to the partnership in exchange for a 60 percent interest in partnership profits. B contributes $1,000 in exchange for a 40 percent interest in partnership profits. AB subsequently distributes Security X to A in a current distribution. Immediately before the distribution, AB held securities with the following fair market values, adjusted tax bases, and unrecognized gain:

	Value	Basis	Gain
Security X	100	80	20
Security Y	100	90	10

	Value	Basis	Gain (Loss)
Security X	1,000	500	500
Security Y	1,000	800	200
Security Z	1,000	1,100	(100)

(ii) If AB had sold the securities for fair market value immediately before the distribution to A, the partnership would have recognized $30 of net gain ($20 gain on Security X plus $10 gain on Security Y). A's distributive share of this gain would have been $18 (60 percent of $30 net gain). If AB had sold the remaining securities immediately after the distribution of Security X to A, the partnership would have $10 of net gain ($10 gain on Security Y). A's distributive share of this gain would have been $6 (60 percent of $10 net gain). As a result, the distribution resulted in a decrease of $12 in A's distributive share of the net gain in AB's securities ($18 net gain before distribution minus $6 net gain after distribution).

(iii) Under paragraph (b) of this section, the amount of the distribution of Security X that is treated as a distribution of money is reduced by $12. The distribution of Security X is therefore treated as a distribution of $88 of money to A ($100 fair market value of Security X minus $12 reduction).

Example (4). Reduction in amount treated as money-change in partnership allocations.

(i) A is admitted to partnership ABC as a partner with a 1 percent interest in partnership profits. At the time of A's admission, ABC held no securities. ABC subsequently acquires Security X. A's interest in partnership profits is subsequently increased to 2 percent for securities acquired after the increase. A retains a 1 percent interest in all securities acquired before the increase. ABC then acquires Securities Y and Z and later distributes Security X to A in a current distribution. Immediately before the distribution, the securities held by ABC had the following fair market values, adjusted tax bases, and unrecognized gain or loss:

(ii) If ABC had sold the securities for fair market value immediately before the distribution to A, the partnership would have recognized $600 of net gain ($500 gain on Security X plus $200 gain on Security Y minus $100 loss on Security Z). A's distributive share of this gain would have been $7 (1 percent of $500 gain on Security X plus 2 percent of $200 gain on Security Y minus 2 percent of $100 loss on Security Z).

(iii) If ABC had sold the remaining securities immediately after the distribution of Security X to A, the partnership would have $100 of net gain ($200 gain on Security Y minus $100 loss on Security Z). A's distributive share of this gain would have been $2 (2 percent of $200 gain on Security Y minus 2 percent of $100 loss on Security Z). As a result, the distribution resulted in a decrease of $5 in A's distributive share of the net gain in ABC's securities ($7 net gain before distribution minus $2 net gain after distribution).

(iv) Under paragraph (b) of this section, the amount of the distribution of Security X that is treated as a distribution of money is reduced by $5. The distribution of Security X is therefore treated as a distribution of $995 of money to A ($1000 fair market value of Security X minus $5 reduction).

Example (5). Basis consequences-distribution of marketable security. (i) A and B form partnership AB as equal partners. A contributes nondepreciable real property with a fair market value and adjusted tax basis of $100.

(ii) AB subsequently distributes Security X with a fair market value of $120 and an adjusted tax basis of $90 to A in a current distribution. At the time of distribution, the basis in A's interest in the partnership is $100. The amount of the distribution that is treated as money is

reduced under section 731(c)(3)(B) and paragraph (b)(2) of this section by $15 (one-half of $30 net gain in Security X). As a result, A recognizes $5 of gain under section 731(a) on the distribution (excess of $105 distribution of money over $100 adjusted tax basis in A's partnership interest).

(iii) A's adjusted tax basis in Security X is $95 ($90 adjusted basis of Security X determined under section 732(a)(1) plus $5 of gain recognized by A by reason of section 731(c)). The basis in A's interest in the partnership is $10 as determined under section 733 ($100 pre-distribution basis minus $90 basis allocated to Security X under section 732).

Example (6). Basis consequences-distribution of marketable security and other property. (i) A and B form partnership AB as equal partners. A contributes nondepreciable real property, with a fair market value of $100 and an adjusted tax basis of $10.

(ii) AB subsequently distributes Security X with a fair market value and adjusted tax basis of $40 to A in a current distribution and, as part of the same distribution, AB distributes Property Z to A with an adjusted tax basis and fair market value of $40. At the time of distribution, the basis in A's interest in the partnership is $10. A recognizes $30 of gain under section 731(a) on the distribution (excess of $40 distribution of money over $10 adjusted tax basis in A's partnership interest).

(iii) A's adjusted tax basis in Security X is $35 ($5 adjusted basis determined under section 732(a)(2) plus $30 of gain recognized by A by reason of section 731(c)). A's basis in Property Z is $5, as determined under section 732(a)(2). The basis in A's interest in the partnership is $0 as determined under section 733 ($10 predistribution basis minus $10 basis allocated between Security X and Property Z under section 732).

(iv) AB's adjusted tax basis in the remaining partnership assets is unchanged unless the partnership has a section 754 election in effect.

If AB made such an election, the aggregate basis of AB's assets would be increased by $70 (the difference between the $80 combined basis of Security X and Property Z in the hands of the partnership before the distribution and the $10 combined basis of the distributed property in the hands of A under section 732 after the distribution). Under section 731(c)(5), no adjustment is made to partnership property under section 734 as a result of any gain recognized by A by reason of section 731(c) or as a result of any step-up in basis in the distributed marketable securities in the hands of A by reason of section 731(c).

Example (7). Coordination with section 737. (i) A and B form partnership AB. A contributes Property A, nondepreciable real property with a fair market value of $200 and an adjusted basis of $100 in exchange for a 25 percent interest in partnership capital and profits. AB owns marketable Security X.

(ii) Within five years of the contribution of Property A, AB subsequently distributes Security X, with a fair market value of $120 and an adjusted tax basis of $100, to A in a current distribution that is subject to section 737. As part of the same distribution, AB distributes Property Y to A with a fair market value of $20 and an adjusted tax basis of $0. At the time of distribution, there has been no change in the fair market value of Property A or the adjusted tax basis in A's interest in the partnership.

(iii) If AB had sold Security X for fair market value immediately before the distribution to A, the partnership would have recognized $20 of gain. A's distributive share of this gain would have been $5 (25 percent of $20 gain). Because AB has no other marketable securities, A's distributive share of gain in partnership securities after the distribution would have been $0. As a result, the distribution resulted in a decrease of $5 in A's share of the net gain in AB's securities ($5 net gain before distribution minus $0 net gain after distribution). Under paragraph (b)(2) of this section, the amount of the distribution of Security X

that is treated as a distribution of money is reduced by $5. The distribution of Security X is therefore treated as a distribution of $115 of money to A ($120 fair market value of Security X minus $5 reduction). The portion of the distribution of the marketable security that is not treated as a distribution of money ($5) is treated as other property for purposes of section 737.

(iv) A recognizes total gain of $40 on the distribution. A recognizes $15 of gain under section 731(a)(1) on the distribution of the portion of Security X treated as money ($115 distribution of money less $100 adjusted tax basis in A's partnership interest). A recognizes $25 of gain under section 737 on the distribution of Property Y and the portion of Security X that is not treated as money. A's section 737 gain is equal to the lesser of (i) A's precontribution gain ($100) or (ii) the excess of the fair market value of property received ($20 fair market value of Property Y plus $5 portion of Security X not treated as money) over the adjusted basis in A's interest in the partnership immediately before the distribution ($100) reduced (but not below zero) by the amount of money received in the distribution ($115).

(v) A's adjusted tax basis in Security X is $115 ($100 basis of Security X determined under section 732(a) plus $15 of gain recognized by reason of section 731(c)). A's adjusted tax basis in Property Y is $0 under section 732(a). The basis in A's interest in the partnership is $25 ($100 basis before distribution minus $100 basis allocated to Security X under section 732(a) plus $25 gain recognized under section 737).

* * *

§1.732–1 Basis of distributed property other than money.

(a) Distributions other than in liquidation of a partner's interest. The basis of property (other than money) received by a partner in a distribution from a partnership, other than in liquidation of his entire interest, shall be its adjusted basis to the partnership immediately before such distribution. However, the basis of the property to the partner shall not exceed the adjusted basis of the partner's interest in the partnership, reduced by the amount of any money distributed to him in the same transaction. The provisions of this paragraph may be illustrated by the following examples:

Example (1). Partner A, with an adjusted basis of $15,000 for his partnership interest, receives in a current distribution property having an adjusted basis of $10,000 to the partnership immediately before distribution, and $2,000 cash. The basis of the property in A's hands will be $10,000. Under sections 733 and 705, the basis of A's partnership interest will be reduced by the distribution to $3,000 ($15,000 less $2,000 cash, less $10,000, the basis of the distributed property to A).

Example (2). Partner R has an adjusted basis of $10,000 for his partnership interest. He receives a current distribution of $4,000 cash and property with an adjusted basis to the partnership of $8,000. The basis of the distributed property to partner R is limited to $6,000 ($10,000, the adjusted basis of his interest, reduced by $4,000, the cash distributed).

(b) Distribution in liquidation. Where a partnership distributes property (other than money) in liquidation of a partner's entire interest in the partnership, the basis of such property to the partner shall be an amount equal to the adjusted basis of his interest in the partnership reduced by the amount of any money distributed to him in the same transaction. Application of this rule may be illustrated by the following example:

Example. Partner B, with a partnership interest having an adjusted basis to him of $12,000, retires from the partnership and receives cash of $2,000, and real property with an adjusted basis to the partnership of $6,000 and a fair market value of $14,000. The basis of the real property to B is $10,000 (B's basis for his partnership interest, $12,000, reduced by $2,000, the cash distributed).

(c) Allocation of basis among properties distributed to a partner — (1) General rule — (i) Unrealized receivables and inventory items. The basis to be allocated to properties distributed to a partner under section 732(a)(2) or (b) is allocated first to any unrealized receivables (as defined in section 751(c)) and inventory items (as defined in section 751(d)(2)) in an amount equal to the adjusted basis of each such property to the partnership immediately before the distribution. If the basis to be allocated is less than the sum of the adjusted bases to the partnership of the distributed unrealized receivables and inventory items, the adjusted basis of the distributed property must be decreased in the manner provided in paragraph (c)(2)(i) of this section.

(ii) Other distributed property. Any basis not allocated to unrealized receivables or inventory items under paragraph (c)(1)(i) of this section is allocated to any other property distributed to the partner in the same transaction by assigning to each distributed property an amount equal to the adjusted basis of the property to the partnership immediately before the distribution. However, if the sum of the adjusted bases to the partnership of such other distributed property does not equal the basis to be allocated among the distributed property, any increase or decrease required to make the amounts equal is allocated among the distributed property as provided in paragraph (c)(2) of this section.

(2) Adjustment to basis allocation — (i) Decrease in basis. Any decrease to the basis of distributed property required under paragraph (c)(1) of this section is allocated first to distributed property with unrealized depreciation in proportion to each property's respective amount of unrealized depreciation before any decrease (but only to the extent of each property's unrealized depreciation). If the required decrease exceeds the amount of unrealized depreciation in the distributed property, the excess is allocated to the distributed property in proportion to the adjusted bases of the dis-

tributed property, as adjusted pursuant to the immediately preceding sentence.

(ii) Increase in basis. Any increase to the basis of distributed property required under paragraph (c)(1)(ii) of this section is allocated first to distributed property (other than unrealized receivables and inventory items) with unrealized appreciation in proportion to each property's respective amount of unrealized appreciation before any increase (but only to the extent of each property's unrealized appreciation). If the required increase exceeds the amount of unrealized appreciation in the distributed property, the excess is allocated to the distributed property (other than unrealized receivables or inventory items) in proportion to the fair market value of the distributed property.

(3) Unrealized receivables and inventory items. If the basis to be allocated upon a distribution in liquidation of the partner's entire interest in the partnership is greater than the adjusted basis to the partnership of the unrealized receivables and inventory items distributed to the partner, and if there is no other property distributed to which the excess can be allocated, the distributee partner sustains a capital loss under section 731(a)(2) to the extent of the unallocated basis of the partnership interest.

(4) Examples. The provisions of this paragraph (c) are illustrated by the following examples:

Example (1). A is a one-fourth partner in partnership PRS and has an adjusted basis in its partnership interest of $650. PRS distributes inventory items and Assets X and Y to A in liquidation of A's entire partnership interest. The distributed inventory items have a basis to the partnership of $100 and a fair market value of $200. Asset X has an adjusted basis to the partnership of $50 and a fair market value of $400. Asset Y has an adjusted basis to the partnership and a fair market value of $100. Neither Asset X nor Asset Y consists of inventory items or unrealized receivables. Under this paragraph (c), A's basis in its partnership interest is allocated first to the inventory items in an amount equal to their adjusted basis to the partnership. A, therefore, has an adjusted basis in the inventory items of $100. The remaining basis, $550, is allocated to the distributed property first in an amount equal to the property's adjusted basis to the partnership. Thus, Asset X is allocated $50 and Asset Y is allocated $100. Asset X is then allocated $350, the amount of unrealized appreciation in Asset X. Finally, the remaining basis, $50, is allocated to Assets X and Y in proportion to their fair market values: $40 to Asset X (400/500 × $50), and $10 to Asset Y (100/500 × $50). Therefore, after the distribution, A has an adjusted basis of $440 in Asset X and $110 in Asset Y.

Example (2). B is a one-fourth partner in partnership PRS and has an adjusted basis in its partnership interest of $200. PRS distributes Asset X and Asset Y to B in liquidation of its entire partnership interest. Asset X has an adjusted basis to the partnership and fair market value of $150. Asset Y has an adjusted basis to the partnership of $150 and a fair market value of $50. Neither of the assets consists of inventory items or unrealized receivables. Under this paragraph (c), B's basis is first assigned to the distributed property to the extent of the partnership's basis in each distributed property. Thus, Asset X and Asset Y are each assigned $150. Because the aggregate adjusted basis of the distributed property, $300, exceeds the basis to be allocated, $200, a decrease of $100 in the basis of the distributed property is required. Assets X and Y have unrealized depreciation of zero and $100, respectively. Thus, the entire decrease is allocated to Asset Y. After the distribution, B has an adjusted basis of $150 in Asset X and $50 in Asset Y.

Example (3). C, a partner in partnership PRS, receives a distribution in liquidation of its entire partnership interest of $6,000 cash, inventory items having an adjusted basis to the partnership of $6,000, and real property having an adjusted basis to the partnership of

$4,000. C's basis in its partnership interest is $9,000. The cash distribution reduces C's basis to $3,000, which is allocated entirely to the inventory items. The real property has a zero basis in C's hands. The partnership bases not carried over to C for the distributed properties are lost unless an election under section 754 is in effect requiring the partnership to adjust the bases of remaining partnership properties under section 734(b).

Example (4). Assume the same facts as in Example 3 of this paragraph except C receives a distribution in liquidation of its entire partnership interest of $1,000 cash and inventory items having a basis to the partnership of $6,000. The cash distribution reduces C's basis to $8,000, which can be allocated only to the extent of $6,000 to the inventory items. The remaining $2,000 basis, not allocable to the distributed property, constitutes a capital loss to partner C under section 731(a)(2). If the election under section 754 is in effect, see section 734(b) for adjustment of the basis of undistributed partnership property.

(d) Special partnership basis to transferee under section 732(d). (1)(i) A transfer of a partnership interest occurs upon a sale or exchange of an interest or upon the death of a partner. Section 732(d) provides a special rule for the determination of the basis of property distributed to a transferee partner who acquired any part of his partnership interest in a transfer with respect to which the election under section 754 (relating to the optional adjustment to basis of partnership property) was not in effect.

(ii) Where an election under section 754 is in effect, see section 743(b) and § 1.743–1 and § 1.732–2.

(iii) If a transferee partner receives a distribution of property (other than money) from the partnership within 2 years after he acquired his interest or part thereof in the partnership by a transfer with respect to which the election under section 754 was not in effect, he may elect to treat as the adjusted partnership basis of such property the adjusted basis such property would have if the adjustment provided in section 743(b) were in effect.

(iv) If an election under section 732(d) is made upon a distribution of property to a transferee partner, the amount of the adjustment with respect to the transferee partner is not diminished by any depletion or depreciation of that portion of the basis of partnership property which arises from the special basis adjustment under section 732(d), since depletion or depreciation on such portion for the period prior to distribution is allowed or allowable only if the optional adjustment under section 743(b) is in effect.

(v) If property is distributed to a transferee partner who elects under section 732(d), and if such property is not the same property which would have had a special basis adjustment, then such special basis adjustment shall apply to any like property received in the distribution, provided that the transferee, in exchange for the property distributed, has relinquished his interest in the property with respect to which he would have had a special basis adjustment. This rule applies whether the property in which the transferee has relinquished his interest is retained or disposed or by the partnership. (For shift of transferee's special basis adjustment to like property, see paragraph (b) (2)(ii) of § 1.743–1.)

(vi) The provisions of this paragraph (d)(1) may be illustrated by the following example:

Example. *(i)* Transferee partner, T, purchased a one-fourth interest in partnership PRS for $17,000. At the time T purchased the partnership interest, the election under section 754 was not in effect and the partnership inventory had a basis to the partnership of $14,000 and a fair market value of $16,000. T's purchase price reflected $500 of this difference. Thus, $4,000 of the $17,000 paid by T for the partnership interest was attributable to T's share of partnership inventory with a basis of $3,500. Within 2 years after T acquired the partnership interest, T retired from the partnership and received in liquidation of its entire partnership interest the following property:

	Assets	
	Adjusted basis to PRS	*Fair market value*
Cash	$1,500	$1,500
Inventory	3,500	4,000
Asset X	2,000	4,000
Asset Y	4,000	5,000

(ii) The fair market value of the inventory received by T was one-fourth of the fair market value of all partnership inventory and was T's share of such property. It is immaterial whether the inventory T received was on hand when T acquired the interest. In accordance with T's election under section 732(d), the amount of T's share of partnership basis that is attributable to partnership inventory is increased by $500 (one-fourth of the $2,000 difference between the fair market value of the property, $16,000, and its $14,000 basis to the partnership at the time T purchased its interest). This adjustment under section 732(d) applies only for purposes of distributions to T, and not for purposes of partnership depreciation, depletion, or gain or loss on disposition. Thus, the amount to be allocated among the properties received by T in the liquidating distribution is $15,500 ($17,000, T's basis for the partnership interest, reduced by the amount of cash received, $1,500). This amount is allocated as follows: The basis of the inventory items received is $4,000, consisting of the $3,500 common partnership basis, plus the basis adjustment of $500 which T would have had under section 743(b). The remaining basis of $11,500 ($15,500 minus $4,000) is allocated among the remaining property distributed to T by assigning to each property the adjusted basis to the partnership of such property and adjusting that basis by any required increase or decrease. Thus, the adjusted basis to T of Asset X is $5,111 ($2,000, the adjusted basis of Asset X to the partnership, plus $2,000, the amount of unrealized appreciation in Asset

X, plus $1,111 ($4,000/$9,000 multiplied by $2,500)). Similarly, the adjusted basis of Asset Y to T is $6,389 ($4,000, the adjusted basis of Asset Y to the partnership, plus $1,000, the amount of unrealized appreciation in Asset Y, plus, $1,389 ($5,000/$9,000 multiplied by $2,500)).

(2) A transferee partner who wishes to elect under section 732(d) shall make the election with his tax return:

(i) For the year of the distribution, if the distribution includes any property subject to the allowance for depreciation, depletion, or amortization, or

(ii) For any taxable year no later than the first taxable year in which the basis of any of the distributed property is pertinent in determining his income tax, if the distribution does not include any such property subject to the allowance for depreciation, depletion or amortization.

(3) A taxpayer making an election under section 732(d) shall submit with the return in which the election is made a schedule setting forth the following:

(i) That under section 732(d) he elects to adjust the basis of property received in a distribution; and

(ii) The computation of the special basis adjustment for the property distributed and the properties to which the adjustment has been allocated. For rules of allocation, see section 755.

(4) A partner who acquired any part of his partnership interest in a transfer to which the election provided in section 754 was not in effect, is required to apply the special basis rule contained in section 732(d) to a distribution to him, whether or not made within 2 years after the transfer, if at the time of his acquisition of the transferred interest:

(i) The fair market value of all partnership property (other than money) exceeded 110 percent of its adjusted basis to the partnership.

(ii) An allocation of basis under section 732(c) upon a liquidation of his interest immediately after the transfer of the interest would have resulted in a shift of basis from property not subject to an allowance for depreciation, depletion, or amortization, to property subject to such an allowance, and

(iii) A basis adjustment under section 743(b) would change the basis to the transferee partner of the property actually distributed.

* * *

(e) Exception. When a partnership distributes unrealized receivables (as defined in section 751(c)) or substantially appreciated inventory items (as defined in section 751(d)) in exchange for any part of a partner's interest in other partnership property (including money), or, conversely, partnership property (including money) other than unrealized receivables or substantially appreciated inventory items in exchange for any part of a partner's interest in the partnership's unrealized receivables or substantially appreciated inventory items, the distribution will be treated as a sale or exchange of property under the provisions of section 751(b). In such case, section 732 (including subsection (d) thereof) applies in determining the partner's basis of the property which he is treated as having sold to or exchanged with the partnership (as constituted after the distribution). The partner is considered as having received such property in a current distribution and, immediately thereafter, as having sold or exchanged it. See section 751(b) and paragraph (b) of § 1.751–1. However, section 732 does not apply in determining the basis of that part of property actually distributed to a partner which is treated as received by him in a sale or exchange under section 751(b). Consequently, the basis of such property shall be its cost to the partner.

§ 1.732–2 Special partnership basis of distributed property.

(a) Adjustments under section 734(b). In the case of a distribution of property to a partner, the partnership bases of the distributed properties shall reflect any increases or decreases to the basis of partnership property which have been made previously under section 734(b) (relating to the optional adjustment to basis of undistributed partnership property) in connection with previous distributions.

(b) Adjustments under section 743(b). In the case of a distribution of property to a partner who acquired any part of his interest in a transfer as to which an election under section 754 was in effect, then, for the purposes of section 732 (other than subsection (d) thereof), the adjusted partnership bases of the distributed property shall take into account, in addition to any adjustments under section 734(b), the transferee's special basis adjustment for the distributed property under section 743(b). The application of this paragraph may be illustrated by the following example:

Example. Partner D acquired his interest in partnership ABD from a previous partner. Since the partnership had made an election under section 754, a special basis adjustment with respect to D is applicable to the basis of partnership property in accordance with section 743(b). One of the assets of the partnership at the time D acquired his interest was property X, which is later distributed to D in a current distribution. Property X has an adjusted basis to the partnership of $1,000 and with respect to D it has a special basis adjustment of $500. Therefore, for purposes of section 732(a)(1), the adjusted basis of such property to the partnership with respect to D immediately before its distribution is $1,500. However, if property X is distributed to partner A, a nontransferee partner, its adjusted basis to the partnership for purposes of section 732(a)(1) is only $1,000. In such case, D's $500 special basis adjustment may shift over to other property. See § 1.743–1(g).

(c) Adjustments to basis of distributed inventory and unrealized receivables. Under section 732, the basis to be allocated to distributed properties shall be allocated first to any unrealized receivables and inventory items. If the distributee partner is a transferee of a partnership interest and has a special basis adjustment for unrealized receivables or inventory items under either section 743(b) or section 732(d), then the partnership adjusted basis immediately prior to distribution of any unrealized receivables or inventory items distributed to such partner shall be determined as follows: If the distributee partner receives his entire share of the fair market value of the inventory items or unrealized receivables of the partnership, the adjusted basis of such distributed property to the partnership, for the purposes of section 732, shall take into account the entire amount of any special basis adjustment which the distributee partner may have for such assets. If the distributee partner receives less than his entire share of the fair market value of partnership inventory items or unrealized receivables, then, for purposes of section 732, the adjusted basis of such distributed property to the partnership shall take into account the same proportion of the distributee's special basis adjustment for unrealized receivables or inventory items as the value of such items distributed to him bears to his entire share of the total value of all such items of the partnership. The provisions of this paragraph may be illustrated by the following example:

Example. Partner C acquired his 40-percent interest in partnership AC from a previous partner. Since the partnership had made an election under section 754, C has a special basis adjustment to partnership property under section 743(b). C retires from the partnership when the adjusted basis of his partnership interest is $3,000. He receives from the partnership in liquidation of his entire interest, $1,000 cash, certain capital assets, depreciable property, and certain inventory items and unrealized receivables. C has a special basis adjustment of $800 with respect to partnership inventory items and of $200 with respect to unrealized receivables. The common partnership basis for the inventory items distributed to him is $500 and for the unrealized receivables is zero. If the value of inventory items and the unrealized receivables distributed to C in his 40 percent share of the total value of all partnership inventory items and unrealized receivables, then, for purposes of section 732, the adjusted basis of such property in C's hands will be $1,300 for the inventory items ($500 plus $800) and $200 for the unrealized receivables (zero plus $200). The remaining basis of $500, which constitutes the basis of the capital assets and depreciable property distributed to C, is determined as follows: $3,000 (total basis) less $1,000 cash, or $2,000 (the amount to be allocated to the basis of all distributed property), less $1,500 ($800 and $200 special basis adjustments, plus $500 common partnership basis, the amount allocated to inventory items and unrealized receivables). However, if the value of the inventory items and unrealized receivables distributed to C consisted of only 20 percent of the total fair market value of such property (i.e., only one-half of C's 40-percent share), then only one-half of C's special basis adjustment of $800 for partnership inventory items and $200 for unrealized receivables would be taken into account. In that case, the basis of the inventory items in C's hands would be $650 ($250, the common partnership basis for inventory items distributed to him, plus $400, one-half of C's special basis adjustment for inventory items). The basis of the unrealized receivables in C's hands would be $100 (zero plus $100, one-half of C's special basis adjustment for unrealized receivables).

§ 1.733–1 Basis of distributee partner's interest.

In the case of a distribution by a partnership to a partner other than in liquidation of a partner's entire interest, the adjusted basis to such partner of his interest in the partnership shall be reduced (but not below zero) by the amount of any money distributed to such partner and by the amount of the basis to him of distributed property other than money as determined under section 732 and §§ 1.732–1 and 1.732–2.

§ 1.734–1 Optional adjustment to basis of undistributed partnership property.

(a) General rule. A partnership shall not adjust the basis of partnership property as the result of a distribution of property to a partner, unless the election provided in section 754 (relating to optional adjustment to basis of partnership property) is in effect.

(b) Method of adjustment—(1) Increase in basis. Where an election under section 754 is in effect and a distribution of partnership property is made, whether or not in liquidation of the partner's entire interest in the partnership, the adjusted basis of the remaining partnership assets shall be increased by:

(i) The amount of any gain recognized under section 731(a)(1) to the distributee partner, or

(ii) The excess of the adjusted basis to the partnership immediately before the distribution of any property distributed (including adjustments under section 743(b) or section 732(d) when applied) over the basis under section 732 (including such special basis adjustments) of such property to the distributee partner. The provisions of this subparagraph may be illustrated by the following examples:

Example (1). Partner A has a basis of $10,000 for his one-third interest in partnership ABC. The partnership has no liabilities and has assets consisting of cash of $11,000 and property with a partnership basis of $19,000 and a value of $22,000. A receives $11,000 in cash in liquidation of his entire interest in the partnership. He has a gain of $1,000 under section 731(a)(1). If the election under section 754 is in effect, the partnership basis for the property becomes $20,000 ($19,000 plus $1,000).

Example (2). Partner D has a basis of $10,000 for his one-third interest in partnership DEF. The partnership balance sheet before the distribution shows the following:

Assets		
	Adjusted basis	Value
Cash	$4,000	$4,000
Property X	11,000	11,000
Property Y	15,000	18,000
Total	30,000	33,000

Liabilities and Capital		
	Adjusted basis	Value
Liabilities Capital:	$0	$0
D	10,000	11,000
E	10,000	11,000
F	10,000	11,000
Total	30,000	33,000

In liquidation of his entire interest in the partnership, D received property X with a partnership basis of $11,000. D's basis for property X is $10,000 under section 732(b). Where the election under section 754 is in effect, the excess of $1,000 (the partnership basis before the distribution less D's basis for property X after distribution) is added to the basis of property Y. The basis of property Y becomes $16,000 ($15,000 plus $1,000). If the distribution is made to a transferee partner who elects under section 732(d), see § 1.734–2.

(2) Decrease in basis. Where the election provided in section 754 is in effect and a distribution is made in liquidation of a partner's entire interest, the partnership shall decrease the adjusted basis of the remaining partnership property by:

(i) The amount of loss, if any, recognized under section 731(a)(2) to the distributee partner, or

(ii) The excess of the basis of the distributed property to the distributee, as determined under section 732 (including adjustments under section 743(b) or section 732(d) when applied) over the adjusted basis of such property to the partnership (including such special basis adjustments) immediately before such distribution.

The provisions of this subparagraph may be illustrated by the following examples:

Example (1). Partner G has a basis of $11,000 for his one-third interest in partnership GHI. Partnership assets consist of cash of $10,000 and property with a basis of $23,000 and a value of $20,000. There are no partnership liabilities. In liquidation of his entire interest in the partnership, G receives $10,000 in cash. He has a loss of $1,000 under section 731(a)(2). If the election under section 754 is in effect, the partnership basis for the property becomes $22,000 ($23,000 less $1,000).

Example (2). Partner J has a basis of $11,000 for his one-third interest in partnership JKL. The partnership balance sheet before the distribution shows the following:

Assets		
	Adjusted basis	Value
Cash	$5,000	$5,000
Property X	10,000	10,000
Property Y	18,000	15,000
Total	33,000	30,000

Liabilities and Capital		
	Adjusted basis	Value
Liabilities Capital:	$0	$0
J	11,000	10,000
K	11,000	10,000
L	11,000	10,000
Total	33,000	30,000

In liquidation of his entire interest in the partnership, J receives property X with a partnership basis of $10,000. J's basis for property X under section 732(b) is $11,000. Where the election under section 754 is in effect, the excess of $1,000 ($11,000 basis of property X to J, the distributee, less its $10,000 adjusted basis to the partnership immediately before the distribution) decreases the basis of property Y in the partnership. Thus, the basis of property Y becomes $17,000 ($18,000 less $1,000). If the distribution is made to a transferee partner who elects under section 732(d), see § 1.734–2.

(c) Allocation of basis. For allocation among the partnership properties of basis adjustments under section 734(b) and paragraph (b) of this section, see section 755 and § 1.755–1.

(d) Returns. A partnership which must adjust the bases of partnership properties under section 734 shall attach a statement to the partnership return for the year of the distribution setting forth the computation of the adjustment and the partnership properties to which the adjustment has been allocated.

(e) Recovery of adjustments to basis of partnership property—(1) Increases in basis. For purposes of section 168, if the basis of a partnership's recovery property is increased as a result of the distribution of property to a partner, then the increased portion of the basis must be taken into account as if it were newly-purchased recovery property placed in service when the distribution occurs. Consequently, any applicable recovery period and method may be used to determine the recovery allowance with respect to the increased portion of the basis. However, no change is made for purposes of determining the recovery allowance under section 168 for the portion of the basis for which there is no increase.

(2) Decreases in basis. For purposes of section 168, if the basis of a partnership's recovery property is decreased as a result of the distribution of property to a partner, then the decrease in basis must be accounted for over the remaining recovery period of the property beginning with the recovery period in which the basis is decreased.

* * *

§ 1.734–2 Adjustment after distribution to transferee partner.

(a) In the case of a distribution of property by the partnership to a partner who has obtained all or part of his partnership interest by transfer, the adjustments to basis provided in section 743(b) and section 732(d) shall be taken into account in applying the rules under section 734(b). For determining the adjusted basis of distributed property to the partnership immediately before the distribution where there has been a prior transfer of a partnership interest with respect to which the election provided in section 754 or section 732(d) is in effect, see §§ 1.732–1 and 1.732–2.

(b)(1) If a transferee partner, in liquidation of his entire partnership interest, receives a distribution of property (including money) with respect to which he has no special basis adjustment, in exchange for his interest in property with respect to which he has a special basis adjustment, and does not utilize his entire special basis adjustment in determining the basis of the distributed property to him under section 732, the unused special basis adjustment of the distributee shall be applied as an adjustment to the partnership basis of the property retained by the partnership and as to which the distributee did not use his special basis adjustment. The provisions of this subparagraph may be illustrated by the following example:

Example. Upon the death of his father, partner S acquires by inheritance a half-interest in partnership ACS. Partners A and C each have a one-quarter interest. The assets of the partnership consist of $10,000 cash and land used in farming worth $10,000 with a basis of $1,000 to the partnership. Since the partnership had made the election under section 754 at the time of transfer, partner S had a special basis adjustment of $4,500 under section 743(b) with respect to his undivided half-interest in the real estate. The basis of S's partnership interest, in accordance with section 742, is $10,000. S retires from the partnership and receives $10,000 in cash in exchange for his entire interest. Since S has received no part of the real estate, his special basis adjustment of $4,500 will be allocated to the real estate, the remaining partnership property, and will increase its basis to the partnership to $5,500.

(2) The provisions of this paragraph do not apply to the extent that certain distributions are treated as sales or exchanges under section 751(b) (relating to unrealized receivables and substantially appreciated inventory items). See section 751(b) and paragraph (b) of § 1.751–1.

§ 1.735–1 Character of gain or loss on disposition of distributed property.

(a) Sale or exchange of distributed property—(1) Unrealized receivables. Any gain realized or loss sustained by a partner on a sale or exchange or other disposition of unrealized receivables (as defined in paragraph (c)(1) of § 1.751–1) received by him in a distribution from a partnership shall be considered gain or loss from the sale or exchange of property other than a capital asset.

(2) Inventory items. Any gain realized or loss sustained by a partner on a sale or exchange of inventory items (as defined in section 751(d)(2)) received in a distribution from a partnership shall be considered gain or loss from the sale or exchange of property other than a capital asset if such inventory items are sold or exchanged within 5 years from the date of the distribution by the partnership. The character of any gain or loss from a sale or exchange by the distributee partner of such inventory items after 5 years from the date of distribution shall be determined as of the date of such sale or exchange by reference to the character of the assets in his hands at that date (inventory items, capital assets, property used in a trade or business, etc.).

(b) Holding period for distributed property. A partner's holding period for property distributed to him by a partnership shall include the period such property was held by the partnership. The provisions of this paragraph do not apply for the purpose of determining the 5-year period described in section 735(a)(2) and paragraph (a)(2) of this section. If the property has been contributed to the partnership by a partner, then the period that the property was held by such partner shall also be included. See section 1223(2). For a partnership's holding period for contributed property, see § 1.723–1.

* * *

§ 1.736–1 Payments to a retiring partner or a deceased partner's successor in interest.

(a) Payments considered as distributive share or guaranteed payment. (1)(i) Section 736 and this section apply only to payments made to a retiring partner or to a deceased partner's successor in interest in liquidation of such partner's entire interest in the partnership. See section 761(d). Section 736 and this section do not apply if the estate or other successor in interest of a deceased partner continues as a partner in its own right under local law. Section 736 and this section apply only to payments made by the partnership and not to transactions between the partners. Thus, a sale by partner A to partner B of his entire one-fourth interest in partnership ABCD would not come within the scope of section 736.

(ii) A partner retires when he ceases to be a partner under local law. However, for the purposes of subchapter K, chapter 1 of the Code, a retired partner or a deceased partner's successor will be treated as a partner until his interest in the partnership has been completely liquidated.

(2) When payments (including assumption of liabilities treated as a distribution of money under section 752) are made to a withdrawing partner, that is, a retiring partner or the estate or other successor in interest of a deceased partner, the amounts paid may represent several items. In part, they may represent the fair market value at the time of his death or retirement of the withdrawing partner's interest in all the assets of the partnership (including inventory) unreduced by partnership liabilities. Also, part of such payments may be attributable to his interest in unrealized receivables and part to an arrangement among the partners in the nature of mutual insurance. When a partnership makes such payments, whether or not related to partnership income, to retire the withdrawing partner's entire interest in the partnership, the payments must be allocated between (i) payments for the value of his interest in assets, except unrealized receivables and, under some circumstances, good will (section 736(b)), and (ii) other payments (section 736(a)). The amounts paid for his interest in assets are treated in the same manner as a distribution in complete liquidation under sections 731, 732, and, where applicable, 751. See paragraph (b) (4)(ii) of § 1.751–1. The remaining partners are allowed no deduction for these payments since they represent either a distribution or a purchase of the withdrawing partner's capital interest by the partnership (composed of the remaining partners).

(3) Under section 736(a), the portion of the payments made to a withdrawing partner for his share of unrealized receivables, good will (in the absence of an agreement to the contrary), or otherwise not in exchange for his interest in assets under the rules contained in paragraph (b) of this section will be considered either:

(i) A distributive share of partnership income, if the amount of payment is determined with regard to income of the partnership; or

(ii) A guaranteed payment under section 707(c), if the amount of the payment is determined without regard to income of the partnership.

(4) Payments, to the extent considered as a distributive share of partnership income under section 736(a)(1), are taken into account under section 702 in the income of the withdrawing partner and thus reduce the amount of the distributive shares of the remaining partners. Payments, to the extent considered as guaranteed payments under section 736(a)(2), are deductible by the partnership under section 162(a) and are taxable as ordinary income to the recipient under section 61(a). See section 707(c).

(5) The amount of any payments under section 736(a) shall be included in the income of the recipient for his taxable year with or within which ends the partnership taxable year for which the payment is a distributive share, or in which the partnership is entitled to deduct such amount as a guaranteed payment. On the other hand, payments under section 736(b) shall be taken into account by the recipient for his taxable year in which such payments are made. See paragraph (b)(4) of this section.

(6) A retiring partner or a deceased partner's successor in interest receiving payments under section 736 is regarded as a partner until the entire interest of the retiring or deceased partner is liquidated. Therefore, if one of the members of a 2-man partnership retires under a plan whereby he is to receive payments under section 736, the partnership will not be considered terminated, nor will the partnership year close with respect to either partner, until the retiring partner's entire interest is liquidated, since the retiring partner continues to hold a partnership interest in the partnership until that time. Similarly, if a partner in a 2-man partnership dies, and his estate or other successor in interest receives payments under section 736, the partnership shall not be considered to have terminated upon the death of the partner but shall terminate as to both partners only when the entire interest of the decedent is liquidated. See section 708(b).

(b) **Payments for interest in partnership.** (1) Payments made in liquidation of the entire interest of a retiring partner or deceased partner shall, to the extent made in exchange for such partner's interest in partnership property (except for unrealized receivables and good will as provided in subparagraphs (2) and (3) of this paragraph), be considered as a distribution by the partnership (and not as a distributive share or guaranteed payment under section 736(a)). Generally, the valuation placed by the partners upon a partner's interest in partnership property in an arm's length agreement will be regarded as correct. If such valuation reflects only the partner's net interest in the property (i.e., total assets less liabilities), it must be adjusted so that both the value of the partner's interest in property and the basis for his interest take into account the partner's share of partnership liabilities. Gain or loss with respect to distributions under section 736(b) and this paragraph will be recognized to the distributee to the extent provided in section 731 and, where applicable, section 751.

(2) Payments made to a retiring partner or to the successor in interest of a deceased partner for his interest in unrealized receivables of the partnership in excess of their partnership basis, including any special basis adjustment for them to which such partner is entitled, shall not be considered as made in exchange for such partner's interest in partnership property. Such payments shall be treated as payments under section 736(a) and paragraph (a) of this section. For definition of unrealized receivables, see section 751(c).

(3) For the purposes of section 736(b) and this paragraph, payments made to a retiring partner or to a successor in interest of a deceased partner in exchange for the interest of such partner in partnership property shall not include any amount paid for the partner's share of good will of the partnership in excess of its partnership basis, including any special basis adjustments for it to which such partner is entitled, except to the extent that the partnership agreement provides for a reasonable payment with respect to such good will. Such payments shall be considered as payments under section 736(a). To the extent that the partnership agreement provides for a reasonable payment with respect to good will, such payments shall be treated under section 736(b) and this paragraph. Generally, the valuation placed upon good will by an arm's length agreement of the partners, whether specific in amount or determined by a formula, shall be regarded as correct.

(4) Payments made to a retiring partner or to a successor in interest of a deceased partner for his interest in inventory shall be considered as made in exchange for such partner's interest in partnership property for the purposes of section 736(b) and this paragraph. However, payments for an interest in substantially appreciated inventory items, as defined in section 751(d), are subject to the rules provided in section 751(b) and paragraph (b) of § 1.751–1. The partnership basis in inventory items as to a deceased partner's successor in interest does not change because of the death of the partner unless the partnership has elected the optional basis adjustment under section 754. But see paragraph (b)(3)(iii) of § 1.751–1.

(5) Where payments made under section 736 are received during the taxable year, the recipient must segregate that portion of each such payment which is determined to be in exchange for the partner's interest in partnership property and treated as a distribution under section 736(b) from that portion treated as a distributive share or guaranteed payment under section 736(a). Such allocation shall be made as follows:

(i) If a fixed amount (whether or not supplemented by any additional amounts) is to be received over a fixed number of years, the portion of each payment to be treated as a distribution under section 736(b) for the taxable year shall bear the same ratio to the total fixed agreed payments for such year (as distinguished from the amount actually received) as the total fixed agreed payments under section 736(b) bear to the total fixed agreed payments under section 736 (a) and (b). The balance, if any, of such amount received in the same taxable year shall be treated as a distributive share or a guaranteed payment under section 736(a) (1) or (2). However, if the total amount received in any one year is less than the amount considered as a distribution under section 736(b) for that year, then any unapplied portion shall be added to the portion of the payments for the following year or years which are to be treated as a distribution under section 736(b). For example, retiring partner W who is entitled to an annual payment of $6,000 for 10 years for his interest in partnership property, receives only $3,500 in 1955. In 1956, he receives $10,000. Of this amount, $8,500 ($6,000 plus $2,500 from 1955) is treated as a distribution under section 736 (b) for 1956; $1,500, as a payment under section 736(a).

(ii) If the retiring partner or deceased partner's successor in interest receives payments which are not fixed in amount, such payments shall first be treated as payments in exchange for his interest in partnership property under section 736(b) to the extent of the value of that interest and, thereafter, as payments under section 736(a).

(iii) In lieu of the rules provided in subdivisions (i) and (ii) of this subparagraph, the allocation of each annual payment between section 736 (a) and (b) may be made in any manner to which all the remaining partners and the withdrawing partner or his successor in interest agree, provided that the total amount allocated to property under section 736(b) does not exceed the fair market value of such property at the date of death or retirement.

(6) Except to the extent section 751(b) applies, the amount of any gain or loss with respect to payments under section 736(b) for a retiring or deceased partner's interest in property for each year of payment shall be determined under section 731. However, where the total of section 736(b) payments is a fixed sum, a retiring partner or a deceased partner's successor in interest may elect (in his tax return for the first taxable year for which he receives such payments), to report and to measure the amount of any gain or loss by the difference between:

(i) The amount treated as a distribution under section 736(b) in that year, and

(ii) The portion of the adjusted basis of the partner for his partnership interest attributable to such distribution (i.e., the amount which bears the same proportion to the partner's total adjusted basis for his partnership interest as

the amount distributed under section 736(b) in that year bears to the total amount to be distributed under section 736(b)).

A recipient who elects under this subparagraph shall attach a statement to his tax return for the first taxable year for which he receives such payments, indicating his election and showing the computation of the gain included in gross income.

(7) The provisions of this paragraph may be illustrated by the following examples:

Example (1). Partnership ABC is a personal service partnership and its balance sheet is as follows:

Assets		
	Adjusted basis per books	Market value
Cash	$13,000	$13,000
Unrealized receivables	0	30,000
Capital and section 1231 assets	20,000	23,000
Total	33,000	66,000
Liabilities and Capital		
	Per books	Value
Liabilities Capital:	$3,000	$3,000
A	10,000	21,000
B	10,000	21,000
C	10,000	21,000
Total	33,000	66,000

Partner A retires from the partnership in accordance with an agreement whereby his share of liabilities ($1,000) is assumed. In addition he is to receive $9,000 in the year of retirement plus $10,000 in each of the two succeeding years. Thus, the total that A receives for his partnership interest is $30,000 ($29,000 in cash and $1,000 in liabilities assumed). Under the agreement terminating A's interest, the value of A's interest in section 736(b) partnership property is $12,000 (one-third of $36,000, the sum of $13,000 cash and $23,000, the fair market value of capital and section 1231 assets). A's share in unrealized receivables is not included in his interest in partnership property described in section 736(b). Since the basis of A's interest is $11,000 ($10,000 plus $1,000, his share of partnership liabilities), he will realize a capital gain of $1,000 ($12,000 minus $11,000) from the disposition of his interest in partnership property. The remaining $18,000 ($30,000 minus $12,000) will constitute payments under section 736(a)(2) which are taxable to A as guaranteed payments under section 707(c). The payment for the first year is $10,000, consisting of $9,000 in cash, plus $1,000 in liability assumed (section 752(b)). Thus, unless the partners agree otherwise under subparagraph (5)(iii) of this paragraph, each annual payment of $10,000 will be allocated as follows: $6,000 (18,000/30,000 of $10,000) is a section 736(a)(2) payment and $4,000 (12,000/30,000 of $10,000) is a payment for an interest in section 736(b) partnership property. (The partnership may deduct the $6,000 guaranteed payment made to A in each of the 3 years.) The gain on the payments for partnership property will be determined under section 731, as provided in subparagraph (6) of this paragraph. A will treat only $4,000 of each payment as a distribution in a series in liquidation of his entire interest and, under section 731, will have a capital gain of $1,000 when the last payment is made. However, if A so elects, as provided in subparagraph (6) of this paragraph, he may treat such gain as follows: Of each $4,000 payment attributable to A's interest in partnership property, $333 is capital gain (one-third of the total capital gain of $1,000), and $3,667 is a return of capital.

Example (2). Assume the same facts as in example 1 of this subparagraph except that the agreement between the partners provides for payments to A for 3 years of a percentage of annual income instead of a fixed amount. Unless the partners agree otherwise under subparagraph (5)(iii) of this paragraph, all payments received by A up to $12,000 shall be treated under section 736(b) as payments for A's interest in partnership property. His gain

of $1,000 will be taxed only after he has received his full basis under section 731. Since the payments are not fixed in amount, the election provided in subparagraph (6) of this paragraph is not available. Any payments in excess of $12,000 shall be treated as a distributive share of partnership income to A under section 736(a)(1).

Example (3). Assume the same facts as in example 1 of this subparagraph except that the partnership agreement provides that the payment for A's interest in partnership property shall include payment for his interest in the good will of the partnership. At the time of A's retirement, the partners determine the value of partnership good will to be $9,000. The value of A's interest in partnership property described in section 736(b) is thus $15,000 (one-third of $45,000, the sum of $13,000 cash, plus $23,000, the value of capital and section 1231 assets, plus $9,000 good will). From the disposition of his interest in partnership property, A will realize a capital gain of $4,000 ($15,000, minus $11,000) the basis of his interest. The remaining $15,000 ($30,000 minus $15,000) will constitute payments under section 736(a)(2) which are taxable to A as guaranteed payments under section 707(c).

Example (4). Assume the same facts as in example 1 of this subparagraph except that the capital and section 1231 assets consist of an item of section 1245 property (as defined in section 1245(a)(3)). Assume further that under paragraph (c)(4) of § 1.751–1 the section 1245 property is an unrealized receivable to the extent of $2,000. Therefore, the value of A's interest in section 736(b) partnership property is only $11,333 (one-third of $34,000, the sum of $13,000 cash and $21,000, the fair market value of section 1245 property to the extent not an unrealized receivable). From the disposition of his interest in partnership property, A will realize a capital gain of $333 ($11,333 minus $11,000, the basis of his interest). The remaining $18,667 ($30,000 minus $11,333) will constitute payments under section 736(a)

(2) which are taxable to A as guaranteed payments under section 707(c).

(c) Cross reference. See section 753 for treatment of payments under section 736(a) as income in respect of a decedent under section 691.

§ 1.737–1 Recognition of precontribution gain.

(a) Determination of gain—(1) In general. A partner that receives a distribution of property (other than money) must recognize gain under section 737 and this section in an amount equal to the lesser of the excess distribution (as defined in paragraph (b) of this section) or the partner's net precontribution gain (as defined in paragraph (c) of this section). Gain recognized under section 737 and this section is in addition to any gain recognized under section 731.

(2) Transactions to which section 737 applies. Section 737 and this section apply only to the extent that a distribution by a partnership is a distribution to a partner acting in the capacity of a partner within the meaning of section 731, except that section 737 and this section do not apply to the extent that section 751(b) applies to the distribution.

(b) Excess distribution—(1) Definition. The excess distribution is the amount (if any) by which the fair market value of the distributed property (other than money) exceeds the distributee partner's adjusted tax basis in the partner's partnership interest.

(2) Fair market value of property. The fair market value of the distributed property is the price at which the property would change hands between a willing buyer and a willing seller at the time of the distribution, neither being under any compulsion to buy or sell and both having reasonable knowledge of the relevant facts. The fair market value that a partnership assigns to distributed property will be regarded as correct, provided that the value is reasonably agreed to among the partners in an arm's-length negotiation and the partners have sufficiently adverse interests.

(3) Distributee partner's adjusted tax basis—(i) General rule. In determining the amount of the excess distribution, the distributee partner's adjusted tax basis in the partnership interest includes any basis adjustment resulting from the distribution that is subject to section 737 (for example, adjustments required under section 752) and from any other distribution or transaction that is part of the same distribution, except for—

(A) The increase required under section 737(c)(1) for the gain recognized by the partner under section 737; and

(B) The decrease required under section 733(2) for any property distributed to the partner other than property previously contributed to the partnership by the distributee partner. See § 1.704–4(e)(1) for a rule in the context of section 704(c)(1)(B). See also § 1.737–3(b)(2) for a special rule for determining a partner's adjusted tax basis in distributed property previously contributed by the partner to the partnership.

(ii) Advances or drawings. The distributee partner's adjusted tax basis in the partnership interest is determined as of the last day of the partnership's taxable year if the distribution to which section 737 applies is properly characterized as an advance or drawing against the partner's distributive share of income. See § 1.731–1(a)(1)(ii).

(c) Net precontribution gain—(1) General rule. The distributee partner's net precontribution gain is the net gain (if any) that would have been recognized by the distributee partner under section 704(c)(1)(B) and § 1.704–4 if all property that had been contributed to the partnership by the distributee partner within five years of the distribution and is held by the partnership immediately before the distribution had been distributed by the partnership to another partner other than a partner who owns, directly or indirectly, more than 50 percent of the capital or profits interest in the partnership. See § 1.704–4 for provisions determining a contributing partner's gain or loss under section 704(c)(1)(B) on an actual distribution of contributed section 704(c) property to another partner.

(2) Special rules—(i) Property contributed on or before October 3, 1989. Property contributed to the partnership on or before October 3, 1989, is not taken into account in determining a partner's net precontribution gain. See § 1.704–4(c)(1) for a similar rule in the context of section 704(c)(1)(B).

(ii) Section 734(b)(1)(A) adjustments. For distributions to a distributee partner of money by a partnership with a section 754 election in effect that are part of the same distribution as the distribution of property subject to section 737, for purposes of paragraph (a) and (c)(1) of this section the distributee partner's net precontribution gain is reduced by the basis adjustments (if any) made to section 704(c) property contributed by the distributee partner under section 734(b)(1)(A). See § 1.737–3(c)(4) for rules regarding basis adjustments for partnerships with a section 754 election in effect.

(iii) Transfers of a partnership interest. The transferee of all or a portion of a contributing partner's partnership interest succeeds to the transferor's net precontribution gain, if any, in an amount proportionate to the interest transferred. See § 1.704–3(a)(7) and § 1.704–4(d)(2) for similar provisions in the context of section 704(c)(1)(A) and section 704(c)(1)(B).

(iv) Section 704(c)(1)(B) gain recognized in related distribution. A distributee partner's net precontribution gain is determined after taking into account any gain or loss recognized by the partner under section 704(c)(1)(B) and § 1.704–4 (or that would have been recognized by the partner except for the like-kind exception in section 704(c)(2) and § 1.704–4(d)(3)) on an actual distribution to another partner of section 704(c) property contributed by the distributee partner that is part of the same dis-

tribution as the distribution to the distributee partner.

(v) Section 704(c)(2) disregarded. A distributee partner's net precontribution gain is determined without regard to the provisions of section 704(c)(2) and § 1.704–4(d)(3) in situations in which the property contributed by the distributee partner is not actually distributed to another partner in a distribution related to the section 737 distribution.

(d) Character of gain. The character of the gain recognized by the distributee partner under section 737 and this section is determined by, and is proportionate to, the character of the partner's net precontribution gain. For this purpose, all gains and losses on section 704(c) property taken into account in determining the partner's net precontribution gain are netted according to their character. Character is determined at the partnership level for this purpose, and any character with a net negative amount is disregarded. The character of the partner's gain under section 737 is the same as, and in proportion to, any character with a net positive amount. Character for this purpose is determined as if the section 704(c) property had been sold by the partnership to an unrelated third party at the time of the distribution and includes any item that would have been taken into account separately by the contributing partner under section 702(a) and § 1.702–1(a).

(e) Examples. The following examples illustrate the provisions of this section. Unless otherwise specified, partnership income equals partnership expenses (other than depreciation deductions for contributed property) for each year of the partnership, the fair market value of partnership property does not change, all distributions by the partnership are subject to section 737, and all partners are unrelated.

Example (1). Calculation of excess distribution and net precontribution gain. (i) On January 1, 1995, A, B, and C form partnership ABC as equal partners. A contributes Property A, depreciable real property with a fair market value of $30,000 and an adjusted tax basis of

$20,000. B contributes Property B, nondepreciable real property with a fair market value and adjusted tax basis of $30,000. C contributes $30,000 cash.

(ii) Property A has 10 years remaining on its cost recovery schedule and is depreciated using the straight-line method. The partnership uses the traditional method for allocating items under section 704(c) described in § 1.704–3(b)(1) for Property A. The partnership has book depreciation of $3,000 per year (10 percent of the $30,000 book basis in Property A) and each partner is allocated $1,000 of book depreciation per year (one-third of the total annual book depreciation of $3,000). The partnership also has tax depreciation of $2,000 per year (10 percent of the $20,000 adjusted tax basis in Property A). This $2,000 tax depreciation is allocated equally between B and C, the noncontributing partners with respect to Property A.

(iii) At the end of 1997, the book value of Property A is $21,000 ($30,000 initial book value less $9,000 aggregate book depreciation) and its adjusted tax basis is $14,000 ($20,000 initial tax basis less $6,000 aggregate tax depreciation).

(iv) On December 31, 1997, Property B is distributed to A in complete liquidation of A's partnership interest. The adjusted tax basis of A's partnership interest at that time is $20,000. The amount of the excess distribution is $10,000, the difference between the fair market value of the distributed Property B ($30,000) and A's adjusted tax basis in A's partnership interest ($20,000). A's net precontribution gain is $7,000, the difference between the book value of Property A ($21,000) and its adjusted tax basis at the time of the distribution ($14,000). A recognizes gain of $7,000 on the distribution, the lesser of the excess distribution and the net precontribution gain.

Example (2). Determination of distributee partner's basis. (i) On January 1, 1995, A, B, and C form general partnership ABC as equal partners. A contributes Property A, nondepreciable real property with a fair market value of

$10,000 and an adjusted tax basis of $4,000. B and C each contributes $10,000 cash.

(ii) The partnership purchases Property B, nondepreciable real property with a fair market value of $9,000, subject to a $9,000 nonrecourse liability. This nonrecourse liability is allocated equally among the partners under section 752, increasing A's adjusted tax basis in A's partnership interest from $4,000 to $7,000.

(iii) On December 31, 1998, A receives $2,000 cash and Property B, subject to the $9,000 liability, in a current distribution.

(iv) In determining the amount of the excess distribution, the adjusted tax basis of A's partnership interest is adjusted to take into account the distribution of money and the shift in liabilities. A's adjusted tax basis is therefore increased to $11,000 for this purpose ($7,000 initial adjusted tax basis, less $2,000 distribution of money, less $3,000 (decrease in A's share of the $9,000 partnership liability), plus $9,000 (increase in A's individual liabilities)). As a result of this basis adjustment, the adjusted tax basis of A's partnership interest ($11,000) is greater than the fair market value of the distributed property ($9,000) and therefore, there is no excess distribution. A recognizes no gain under section 737.

Example (3). Net precontribution gain reduced for gain recognized under section 704(c)(1)(B). (i) On January 1, 1995, A, B, and C form partnership ABC as equal partners. A contributes Properties A1 and A2, nondepreciable real properties located in the United States each with a fair market value of $10,000 and an adjusted tax basis of $6,000. B contributes Property B, nondepreciable real property located outside the United States, with a fair market value and adjusted tax basis of $20,000. C contributes $20,000 cash.

(ii) On December 31, 1998, Property B is distributed to A in complete liquidation of A's interest and, as part of the same distribution, Property A1 is distributed to B in a current distribution.

(iii) A's net precontribution gain before the distribution is $8,000 ($20,000 fair market value of Properties A1 and A2 less $12,000 adjusted tax basis of such properties). A recognizes $4,000 of gain under section 704(c)(1)(B) and § 1.704–4 on the distribution of Property A1 to B ($10,000 fair market value of Property A1 less $6,000 adjusted tax basis of Property A1). This gain is taken into account in determining A's excess distribution and net precontribution gain. As a result, A's net precontribution gain is reduced from $8,000 to $4,000, and the adjusted tax basis in A's partnership interest is increased by $4,000 to $16,000.

(iv) A recognizes gain of $4,000 on the receipt of Property B under section 737, an amount equal to the lesser of the excess distribution of $4,000 ($20,000 fair market value of Property B less $16,000 adjusted tax basis of A's interest in the partnership) and A's remaining net precontribution gain of $4,000.

Example (4). Character of gain. (i) On January 1, 1995, A, B, and C form partnership ABC as equal partners. A contributes the following nondepreciable property to the partnership:

	Fair market value	Adjusted tax basis
Property A1	$ 30,000	$ 20,000
Property A2	30,000	38,000
Property A3	10,000	9,000

(ii) The character of gain or loss on Property A1 and Property A2 is long-term, U.S.-source capital gain or loss. The character of gain on Property A3 is long-term, foreign-source capital gain. B contributes Property B, nondepreciable real property with a fair market value and adjusted tax basis of $70,000. C contributes $70,000 cash.

(iii) On December 31, 1998, Property B is distributed to A in complete liquidation of A's interest in the partnership. A recognizes $3,000 of gain under section 737, an amount equal to the excess distribution of $3,000

($70,000 fair market value of Property B less $67,000 adjusted tax basis in A's partnership interest) and A's net precontribution gain of $3,000 ($70,000 aggregate fair market value of properties contributed by A less $67,000 aggregate adjusted tax basis of such properties).

(iv) In determining the character of A's gain, all gains and losses on property taken into account in determining A's net precontribution gain are netted according to their character and allocated to A's recognized gain under section 737 based on the relative proportions of the net positive amounts. U.S.-source and foreign-source gains must be netted separately because A would have been required to take such gains into account separately under section 702. As a result, A's net precontribution gain of $3,000 consists of $2,000 of net long-term, U.S.-source capital gain ($10,000 gain on Property A1 and $8,000 loss on Property A2) and $1,000 of net long-term, foreign-source capital gain ($1,000 gain on Property A3).

(v) The character of A's gain under paragraph (d) of this section is therefore $2,000 long-term, U.S.-source capital gain ($3,000 gain recognized under section 737 × $2,000 net long-term, U.S.-source capital gain/$3,000 total net precontribution gain) and $1,000 long-term, foreign-source capital gain ($3,000 gain recognized under section 737 × $1,000 net long-term, foreign-source capital gain/$3,000 total net precontribution gain).

§ 1.737–2 Exceptions and special rules.

(a) Section 708(b)(1)(B) terminations. Section 737 and this section do not apply to the deemed distribution of interests in a new partnership caused by the termination of a partnership under section 708(b)(1)(B). A subsequent distribution of property by the new partnership to a partner of the new partnership that was formerly a partner of the terminated partnership is subject to section 737 to the same extent that a distribution from the terminated partnership would have been subject to section 737. See also § 1.704–4(c)(3) for a similar rule in the context of section 704(c)(1)(B). This paragraph (a) applies to terminations of partnerships under section 708(b)(1)(B) occurring on or after May 9, 1997; however, this paragraph (a) may be applied to terminations occurring on or after May 9, 1996, provided that the partnership and its partners apply this paragraph (a) to the termination in a consistent manner.

(b) Transfers to another partnership— (1) Complete transfer. Section 737 and this section do not apply to a transfer by a partnership (transferor partnership) of all of its assets and liabilities to a second partnership (transferee partnership) in an exchange described in section 721, followed by a distribution of the interest in the transferee partnership in liquidation of the transferor partnership as part of the same plan or arrangement. See § 1.704–4(c)(4) for a similar rule in the context of section 704(c)(1)(B).

(2) Certain divisive transactions. Section 737 and this section do not apply to a transfer by a partnership (transferor partnership) of all of the section 704(c) property contributed by a partner to a second partnership (transferee partnership) in an exchange described in section 721, followed by a distribution as part of the same plan or arrangement of an interest in the transferee partnership (and no other property) in complete liquidation of the interest of the partner that originally contributed the section 704(c) property to the transferor partnership.

(3) Subsequent distributions. A subsequent distribution of property by the transferee partnership to a partner of the transferee partnership that was formerly a partner of the transferor partnership is subject to section 737 to the same extent that a distribution from the transferor partnership would have been subject to section 737.

(c) Incorporation of a partnership. Section 737 and this section do not apply to an incorporation of a partnership by any method of incorporation (other than a method involving an actual distribution of partnership property to the partners followed by a contribution of that property to a corporation), provided that the partnership is liquidated as part of the incorporation transaction. See § 1.704–4(c)(5) for a similar rule in the context of section 704(c)(1)(B).

(d) Distribution of previously contributed property—(1) General rule. Any portion of the distributed property that consists of property previously contributed by the distributee partner (previously contributed property) is not taken into account in determining the amount of the excess distribution or the partner's net precontribution gain. The previous sentence applies on or after May 9, 1997. See § 1.737–3(b)(2) for a special rule for determining the basis of previously contributed property in the hands of a distributee partner who contributed the property to the partnership.

(2) Limitation for distribution of previously contributed interest in an entity. An interest in an entity previously contributed to the partnership is not treated as previously contributed property to the extent that the value of the interest is attributable to property contributed to the entity after the interest was contributed to the partnership. The preceding sentence does not apply to the extent that the property contributed to the entity was contributed to the partnership by the partner that also contributed the interest in the entity to the partnership.

(3) Nonrecognition transactions, installment sales, contributed contracts, and capitalized costs—(i) Nonrecognition transactions. Property received by the partnership in exchange for contributed section 704(c) property in a nonrecognition transaction is treated as the contributed property with regard to the contributing partner for purposes of section 737 to the extent that the property received is treated as section 704(c) property under § 1.704–3(a)(8). See § 1.704–4(d)(1) for a similar rule in the context of section 704(c)(1)(B).

(ii) Installment sales. An installment obligation received by the partnership in an installment sale (as defined in section 453(b)) of section 704(c) property is treated as the contributed property with regard to the contributing partner for purposes of section 737 to the extent that the installment obligation received is treated as section 704(c) property under § 1.704–3(a)(8). See § 1.704–4(d)(1) for a similar rule in the context of section 704(c)(1)(B).

(iii) Contributed contracts. Property acquired by a partnership pursuant to a contract that is section 704(c) property is treated as the contributed property with regard to the contributing partner for purposes of section 737 to the extent that the acquired property is treated as section 704(c) property under § 1.704–3(a)(8). See § 1.704–4(d)(1) for a similar rule in the context of section 704(c)(1)(B).

(iv) Capitalized costs. Property to which the cost of section 704(c) property is properly capitalized is treated as section 704(c) property for purposes of section 737 to the extent that such property is treated as section 704(c) property under § 1.704–3(a)(8)(iv). See § 1.704–4(d)(1) for a similar rule in the context of section 704(c)(1)(B).

(4) Undivided interests. The distribution of an undivided interest in property is treated as the distribution of previously contributed property to the extent that the undivided interest does not exceed the undivided interest, if any, contributed by the distributee partner in the same property. See § 1.704–4(c)(6) for the application of section 704(c)(1)(B) in a similar context. The portion of the undivided interest in property retained by the partnership after the distribution, if any, that is treated as contributed by the distributee partner, is reduced to the extent of the undivided interest distributed to the distributee partner.

(e) Examples. The following examples illustrate the rules of this section. Unless otherwise specified, partnership income equals partnership expenses (other than depreciation deductions for contributed property) for each year of the partnership, the fair market value of partnership property does not change, all distributions by the partnership are subject to section 737, and all partners are unrelated.

Example (1). Distribution of previously contributed property. (i) On January 1, 1995, A, B, and C form partnership ABC as equal partners. A contributes the following nondepreciable real property to the partnership:

	Fair market value	Adjusted tax basis
Property A1	$20,000	$10,000
Property A2	10,000	6,000

(ii) A's total net precontribution gain on the contributed property is $14,000 ($10,000 on Property A1 plus $4,000 on Property A2). B contributes $10,000 cash and Property B, nondepreciable real property with a fair market value and adjusted tax basis of $20,000. C contributes $30,000 cash.

(iii) On December 31, 1998, Property A2 and Property B are distributed to A in complete liquidation of A's interest in the partnership. Property A2 was previously contributed by A and is therefore not taken into account in determining the amount of the excess distribution or A's net precontribution gain. The adjusted tax basis of Property A2 in the hands of A is also determined under section 732 as if that property were the only property distributed to A.

(iv) As a result of excluding Property A2 from these determinations, the amount of the excess distribution is $10,000 ($20,000 fair market value of distributed Property B less $10,000 adjusted tax basis in A's partnership interest). A's net precontribution gain is also $10,000 ($14,000 total net precontribution gain less $4,000 gain with respect to previ-

ously contributed Property A2). A therefore recognizes $10,000 of gain on the distribution, the lesser of the excess distribution and the net precontribution gain.

Example (2). Distribution of a previously contributed interest in an entity. (i) On January 1, 1995, A, B, and C form partnership ABC as equal partners. A contributes Property A, nondepreciable real property with a fair market value of $10,000 and an adjusted tax basis of $5,000, and all of the stock of Corporation X with a fair market value and adjusted tax basis of $500. B contributes $500 cash and Property B, nondepreciable real property with a fair market value and adjusted tax basis of $10,000. Partner C contributes $10,500 cash. On December 31, 1996, ABC contributes Property B to Corporation X in a nonrecognition transaction under section 351.

(ii) On December 31, 1998, all of the stock of Corporation X is distributed to A in complete liquidation of A's interest in the partnership. The stock is treated as previously contributed property with respect to A only to the extent of the $500 fair market value of the Corporation X stock contributed by A. The fair market value of the distributed stock for purposes of determining the amount of the excess distribution is therefore $10,000 ($10,500 total fair market value of Corporation X stock less $500 portion treated as previously contributed property). The $500 fair market value and adjusted tax basis of the Corporation X stock is also not taken into account in determining the amount of the excess distribution and the net precontribution gain.

(iii) A recognizes $5,000 of gain under section 737, the amount of the excess distribution ($10,000 fair market value of distributed property less $5,000 adjusted tax basis in A's partnership interest) and A's net precontribution gain ($10,000 fair market value of Property A less $5,000 adjusted tax basis in Property A).

Example (3). Distribution of undivided interest in property. (i) On January 1, 1995, A and B form partnership AB as equal partners.

A contributes $500 cash and an undivided one-half interest in Property X. B contributes $500 cash and an undivided one-half interest in Property X.

(ii) On December 31, 1998, an undivided one-half interest in Property X is distributed to A in a current distribution. The distribution of the undivided one-half interest in Property X is treated as a distribution of previously contributed property because A contributed an undivided one-half interest in Property X. As a result, A does not recognize any gain under section 737 on the distribution.

§ 1.737–3 Basis adjustments; Recovery rules.

(a) Distributee partner's adjusted tax basis in the partnership interest. The distributee partner's adjusted tax basis in the partnership interest is increased by the amount of gain recognized by the distributee partner under section 737 and this section. This increase is not taken into account in determining the amount of gain recognized by the partner under section 737(a)(1) and this section or in determining the amount of gain recognized by the partner under section 731(a) on the distribution of money in the same distribution or any related distribution. See § 1.704–4(e)(1) for a determination of the distributee partner's adjusted tax basis in a distribution subject to section 704(c)(1)(B).

(b) Distributee partner's adjusted tax basis in distributed property—(1) In general. The distributee partner's adjusted tax basis in the distributed property is determined under section 732 (a) or (b) as applicable. The increase in the distributee partner's adjusted tax basis in the partnership interest under paragraph (a) of this section is taken into account in determining the distributee partner's adjusted tax basis in the distributed property other than property previously contributed by the partner. See § 1.704–4(e)(2) for a determination of basis in a distribution subject to section 704(c)(1)(B).

(2) Previously contributed property. The distributee partner's adjusted tax basis in distributed property that the partner previously contributed to the partnership is determined as if it were distributed in a separate and independent distribution prior to the distribution that is subject to section 737 and § 1.737–1.

(c) Partnership's adjusted tax basis in partnership property—(1) Increase in basis. The partnership's adjusted tax basis in eligible property is increased by the amount of gain recognized by the distributee partner under section 737.

(2) Eligible property. Eligible property is property that—

(i) Entered into the calculation of the distributee partner's net precontribution gain;

(ii) Has an adjusted tax basis to the partnership less than the property's fair market value at the time of the distribution;

(iii) Would have the same character of gain on a sale by the partnership to an unrelated party as the character of any of the gain recognized by the distributee partner under section 737; and

(iv) Was not distributed to another partner in a distribution subject to section 704(c)(1) (B) and § 1.704–4 that was part of the same distribution as the distribution subject to section 737.

(3) Method of adjustment. For the purpose of allocating the basis increase under paragraph (c)(2) of this section among the eligible property, all eligible property of the same character is treated as a single group. Character for this purpose is determined in the same manner as the character of the recognized gain is determined under § 1.737–1(d). The basis increase is allocated among the separate groups of eligible property in proportion to the character of the gain recognized under section 737. The basis increase is then allocated among property within each group in the order in which the property was contributed to the partnership by the partner, starting with the property contributed first, in an amount equal to the difference between the property's fair market value and its adjusted tax basis to the partnership at the time of the distribution. For property that has the same character and was contributed in the same (or a related) transaction, the basis increase is allocated based on the respective amounts of unrealized appreciation in such properties at the time of the distribution.

(4) Section 754 adjustments. The basis adjustments to partnership property made pursuant to paragraph (c)(1) of this section are not elective and must be made regardless of whether the partnership has an election in effect under section 754. Any adjustments to the bases of partnership property (including eligible property as defined in paragraph (c)(2) of this section) under section 734(b) pursuant to a section 754 election (other than basis adjustments under section 734(b)(1)(A) described in the following sentence) must be made after (and must take into account) the adjustments to basis made under paragraph (a) and paragraph (c)(1) of this section. Basis adjustments under section 734(b)(1)(A) that are attributable to distributions of money to the distributee partner that are part of the same distribution as the distribution of property subject to section 737 are made before the adjustments to basis under paragraph (a) and paragraph (c) (1) of this section. See § 1.737–1(c)(2)(ii) for the effect, if any, of basis adjustments under section 734(b)(1)(A) on a partner's net precontribution gain. See also § 1.704–4(e)(3) for a similar rule regarding basis adjustments pursuant to a section 754 election in the context of section 704(c)(1)(B).

(d) Recovery of increase to adjusted tax basis. Any increase to the adjusted tax basis of partnership property under paragraph (c)(1) of this section is recovered using any applicable recovery period and depreciation (or other cost recovery) method (including first-year conventions) available to the partnership for newly purchased property (of the type adjusted) placed in service at the time of the distribution.

(e) Examples. The following examples illustrate the rules of this section. Unless otherwise specified, partnership income equals partnership expenses (other than depreciation deductions for contributed property) for each year of the partnership, the fair market value of partnership property does not change, all distributions by the partnership are subject to section 737, and all partners are unrelated.

Example (1). Partner's basis in distributed property. (i) On January 1, 1995, A, B, and C form partnership ABC as equal partners. A contributes Property A, nondepreciable real property with a fair market value of $10,000 and an adjusted tax basis of $5,000. B contributes Property B, nondepreciable real property with a fair market value and adjusted tax basis of $10,000. C contributes $10,000 cash.

(ii) On December 31, 1998, Property B is distributed to A in complete liquidation of A's interest in the partnership. A recognizes $5,000 of gain under section 737, an amount equal to the excess distribution of $5,000 ($10,000 fair market value of Property B less $5,000 adjusted tax basis in A's partnership interest) and A's net precontribution gain of $5,000 ($10,000 fair market value of Property A less $5,000 adjusted tax basis of such property).

(iii) A's adjusted tax basis in A's partnership interest is increased by the $5,000 of gain recognized under section 737. This increase is taken into account in determining A's basis in the distributed property. Therefore, A's adjusted tax basis in distributed Property B is $10,000 under section 732(b).

Example (2). Partner's basis in distributed property in connection with gain recognized under section 704(c)(1)(B). (i) On January 1, 1995, A, B, and C form partnership ABC as equal partners. A contributes the following nondepreciable real property located in the United States to the partnership:

	Fair market value	Adjusted tax basis
Property A1	$10,000	5,000
Property A2	10,000	2,000

(ii) B contributes $10,000 cash and Property B, nondepreciable real property located outside the United States, with a fair market value and adjusted tax basis of $10,000. C contributes $20,000 cash.

(iii) On December 31, 1998, Property B is distributed to A in a current distribution and Property A1 is distributed to B in a current distribution. A recognizes $5,000 of gain under section 704(c)(1)(B) and § 1.704–4 on the distribution of Property A1 to B, the difference between the fair market value of such property ($10,000) and the adjusted tax basis in distributed Property A1 ($5,000). The adjusted tax basis of A's partnership interest is increased by this $5,000 of gain under section 704(c)(1)(B) and § 1.704–4(e)(1).

(iv) The increase in the adjusted tax basis of A's partnership interest is taken into account in determining the amount of the excess distribution. As a result, there is no excess distribution because the fair market value of Property B ($10,000) is less than the adjusted tax basis of A's interest in the partnership at the time of distribution ($12,000). A therefore recognizes no gain under section 737 on the receipt of Property B. A's adjusted tax basis in Property B is $10,000 under section 732(a)(1). The adjusted tax basis of A's partnership interest is reduced from $12,000 to $2,000 under section 733. See Example 3 of § 1.737–1(e).

Example (3). Partnership's basis in partnership property after a distribution with section 737 gain. (i) On January 31, 1995, A, B, and C form partnership ABC as equal partners. A contributes the following nondepreciable property to the partnership:

	Fair market value	Adjusted tax basis
Property A1	$1,000	$500
Property A2	4,000	1,500
Property A3	4,000	6,000
Property A4	6,000	4,000

(ii) The character of gain or loss on Properties A1, A2, and A3 is long-term, U.S.-source capital gain or loss. The character of gain on Property A4 is long-term, foreign-source capital gain. B contributes Property B, nondepreciable real property with a fair market value and adjusted tax basis of $15,000. C contributes $15,000 cash.

(iii) On December 31, 1998, Property B is distributed to A in complete liquidation of A's interest in the partnership. A recognizes gain of $3,000 under section 737, an amount equal to the excess distribution of $3,000 ($15,000 fair market value of Property B less $12,000 adjusted tax basis in A's partnership interest) and A's net precontribution gain of $3,000 ($15,000 aggregate fair market value of the property contributed by A less $12,000 aggregate adjusted tax basis of such property).

(iv) $2,000 of A's gain is long-term, foreign-source capital gain ($3,000 total gain under section 737 × $2,000 net long-term, foreign-source capital gain/$3,000 total net precontribution gain). $1,000 of A's gain is long-term, U.S.-source capital gain ($3,000 total gain under section 737 × $1,000 net long-term, U.S.-source capital gain/$3,000 total net precontribution gain).

(v) The partnership must increase the adjusted tax basis of the property contributed by A by $3,000. All property contributed by A is eligible property. Properties A1, A2, and A3 have the same character and are grouped into a single group for purposes of allocating this basis increase. Property A4 is in a separate character group.

(vi) $2,000 of the basis increase must be allocated to long-term, foreign-source capital as-sets because $2,000 of the gain recognized by A was long-term, foreign-source capital gain. The adjusted tax basis of Property A4 is therefore increased from $4,000 to $6,000. $1,000 of the increase must be allocated to Properties A1 and A2 because $1,000 of the gain recognized by A is long-term, U.S.-source capital gain. No basis increase is allocated to Property A3 because its fair market value is less than its adjusted tax basis. The $1,000 basis increase is allocated between Properties A1 and A2 based on the unrealized appreciation in each asset before such basis adjustment. As a result, the adjusted tax basis of Property A1 is increased by $167 ($1,000 × $500/$3,000) and the adjusted tax basis of Property A2 is increased by $833 ($1,000 × $2,500/3,000).

§ 1.737–4 Anti-abuse rule.

(a) In general. The rules of section 737 and §§ 1.737–1, 1.737–2, and 1.737–3 must be applied in a manner consistent with the purpose of section 737. Accordingly, if a principal purpose of a transaction is to achieve a tax result that is inconsistent with the purpose of section 737, the Commissioner can recast the transaction for federal tax purposes as appropriate to achieve tax results that are consistent with the purpose of section 737. Whether a tax result is inconsistent with the purpose of section 737 must be determined based on all the facts and circumstances. See § 1.704–4(f) for an anti-abuse rule and examples in the context of section 704(c)(1)(B). The anti-abuse rule and examples under section 704(c)(1)(B) and § 1.704–4(f) are relevant to section 737 and §§ 1.737–1, 1.737–2, and 1.737–3 to the extent that the net precontribution gain for purposes of section 737 is determined by reference to section 704(c)(1)(B).

(b) Examples. The following examples illustrate the rules of this section. The examples set forth below do not delineate the boundaries of either permissible or impermissible types of transactions. Further, the addition of any facts or circumstances that are not specifically set forth in an example (or the deletion of any facts or circumstances) may alter the outcome of the transaction described in the example. Unless otherwise specified, partnership income equals partnership expenses (other than depreciation deductions for contributed property) for each year of the partnership, the fair market value of partnership property does not change, all distributions by the partnership are subject to section 737, and all partners are unrelated.

Example (1). Increase in distributee partner's basis by temporary contribution; results inconsistent with the purpose of section 737. (i) On January 1, 1995, A, B, and C form partnership ABC as equal partners. A contributes Property A1, nondepreciable real property with a fair market value of $10,000 and an adjusted tax basis of $1,000. B contributes Property B, nondepreciable real property with a fair market value of $10,000 and an adjusted tax basis of $10,000. C contributes $10,000 cash.

(ii) On January 1, 1999, pursuant to a plan a principal purpose of which is to avoid gain under section 737, A transfers to the partnership Property A2, nondepreciable real property with a fair market value and adjusted tax basis of $9,000. A treats the transfer as a contribution to the partnership pursuant to section 721 and increases the adjusted tax basis of A's partnership interest from $1,000 to $10,000. On January 1, 1999, the partnership agreement is amended and all other necessary steps are taken so that substantially all of the economic risks and benefits of Property A2 are retained by A. On February 1, 1999, Property B is distributed to A in a current distribution. If the contribution of Property A2 is treated as a contribution to the partnership for purposes of section 737, there is no excess distribution because the fair market value of distributed Property B ($10,000) does not exceed the adjusted tax basis of A's interest in the partnership ($10,000), and therefore section 737 does not apply. A's adjusted tax basis in distributed Property B is $10,000 under section 732(a)(1)

and the adjusted tax basis of A's partnership interest is reduced to zero under section 733.

(iii) On March 1, 2000, A receives Property A2 from the partnership in complete liquidation of A's interest in the partnership. A recognizes no gain on the distribution of Property A2 because the property was previously contributed property. See § 1.737–2(d).

(iv) Although A has treated the transfer of Property A2 as a contribution to the partnership that increased the adjusted tax basis of A's interest in the partnership, it would be inconsistent with the purpose of section 737 to recognize the transfer as a contribution to the partnership. Section 737 requires recognition of gain when the value of distributed property exceeds the distributee partner's adjusted tax basis in the partnership interest. Section 737 assumes that any contribution or other transaction that affects a partner's adjusted tax basis in the partnership interest is a contribution or transaction in substance and is not engaged in with a principal purpose of avoiding recognition of gain under section 737. Because the transfer of Property A2 to the partnership was not a contribution in substance and was made with a principal purpose of avoiding recognition of gain under section 737, the Commissioner can disregard the contribution of Property A2 for this purpose. As a result, A recognizes gain of $9,000 under section 737 on the receipt of Property B, an amount equal to the lesser of the excess distribution of $9,000 ($10,000 fair market value of distributed Property B less the $1,000 adjusted tax basis of A's partnership interest, determined without regard to the transitory contribution of Property A2) or A's net precontribution gain of $9,000 on Property A1.

Example (2). Increase in distributee partner's basis; section 752 liability shift; results consistent with the purpose of section 737. (i) On January 1, 1995, A and B form general partnership AB as equal partners. A contributes Property A, nondepreciable real property with a fair market value of $10,000 and an adjusted tax basis of $1,000. B contributes Property B, nondepreciable real property with a fair market value and adjusted tax basis of $10,000. The partnership also borrows $10,000 on a recourse basis and purchases Property C. The $10,000 liability is allocated equally between A and B under section 752, thereby increasing the adjusted tax basis in A's partnership interest to $6,000.

(ii) On December 31, 1998, the partners agree that A is to receive Property B in a current distribution. If A were to receive Property B at that time, A would recognize $4,000 of gain under section 737, an amount equal to the lesser of the excess distribution of $4,000 ($10,000 fair market value of Property B less $6,000 adjusted tax basis in A's partnership interest) or A's net precontribution gain of $9,000 ($10,000 fair market value of Property A less $1,000 adjusted tax basis of Property A).

(iii) With a principal purpose of avoiding such gain, A and B agree that A will be solely liable for the repayment of the $10,000 partnership liability and take the steps necessary so that the entire amount of the liability is allocated to A under section 752. The adjusted tax basis in A's partnership interest is thereby increased from $6,000 to $11,000 to reflect A's share of the $5,000 of liability previously allocated to B. As a result of this increase in A's adjusted tax basis, there is no excess distribution because the fair market value of distributed Property B ($10,000) is less than the adjusted tax basis of A's partnership interest. Recognizing A's increased adjusted tax basis as a result of the shift in liabilities is consistent with the purpose of section 737 and this section. Section 737 requires recognition of gain only when the value of the distributed property exceeds the distributee partner's adjusted tax basis in the partnership interest. The $10,000 recourse liability is a bona fide liability of the partnership that was undertaken for a substantial business purpose and A's and B's agreement that A will assume responsibility for

repayment of that debt has substance. Therefore, the increase in A's adjusted tax basis in A's interest in the partnership due to the shift in partnership liabilities under section 752 is respected, and A recognizes no gain under section 737.

§ 1.741–1 Recognition and character of gain or loss on sale or exchange.

(a) The sale or exchange of an interest in a partnership shall, except to the extent section 751(a) applies, be treated as the sale or exchange of a capital asset, resulting in capital gain or loss measured by the difference between the amount realized and the adjusted basis of the partnership interest, as determined under section 705. For treatment of selling partner's distributive share up to date of sale, see section 706(c)(2). Where the provisions of section 751 require the recognition of ordinary income or loss with respect to a portion of the amount realized from such sale or exchange, the amount realized shall be reduced by the amount attributable under section 751 to unrealized receivables and substantially appreciated inventory items, and the adjusted basis of the transferor partner's interest in the partnership shall be reduced by the portion of such basis attributable to such unrealized receivables and substantially appreciated inventory items. See section 751 and § 1.751–1.

(b) Section 741 shall apply whether the partnership interest is sold to one or more members of the partnership or to one or more persons who are not members of the partnership. Section 741 shall also apply even though the sale of the partnership interest results in a termination of the partnership under section 708(b). Thus, the provisions of section 741 shall be applicable (1) to the transferor partner in a 2-man partnership when he sells his interest to the other partner, and (2) to all the members of a partnership when they sell their interests to one or more persons outside the partnership.

(c) See section 351 for nonrecognition of gain or loss upon transfer of a partnership interest to a corporation controlled by the transferor.

(d) For rules relating to the treatment of liabilities on the sale or exchange of interests in a partnership see §§ 1.752–1 and 1.1001–2.

(e) For rules relating to the capital gain or loss recognized when a partner sells or exchanges an interest in a partnership that holds appreciated collectibles or section 1250 property with section 1250 capital gain, see § 1.1(h)–1. This paragraph (e) applies to transfers of interests in partnerships that occur on or after September 21, 2000.

(f) For rules relating to dividing the holding period of an interest in a partnership, see § 1.1223–3. This paragraph (f) applies to transfers of partnership interests and distributions of property from a partnership that occur on or after September 21, 2000.

§ 1.742–1 Basis of transferee partner's interest.

The basis to a transferee partner of an interest in a partnership shall be determined under the general basis rules for property provided by part II (section 1011 and following), subchapter O, chapter 1 of the Code. Thus, the basis of a purchased interest will be its cost. The basis of a partnership interest acquired from a decedent is the fair market value of the interest at the date of his death or at the alternate valuation date, increased by his estate's or other successor's share of partnership liabilities, if any, on that date, and reduced to the extent that such value is attributable to items constituting income in respect of a decedent (see section 753 and paragraph (c)(3)(v) of § 1.706–1 and paragraph (b) of § 1.753–1) under section 691. See section 1014(c). For basis of contributing partner's interest, see section 722. The basis so determined is then subject to the adjustments provided in section 705.

§ 1.743–1 Optional adjustment to basis of partnership property.

(a) Generally. The basis of partnership property is adjusted as a result of the transfer of an interest in a partnership by sale or exchange or on the death of a partner only if the election provided by section 754 (relating to optional adjustments to the basis of partnership property) is in effect with respect to the partnership. Whether or not the election provided in section 754 is in effect, the basis of partnership property is not adjusted as the result of a contribution of property, including money, to the partnership.

(b) Determination of adjustment. In the case of the transfer of an interest in a partnership, either by sale or exchange or as a result of the death of a partner, a partnership that has an election under section 754 in effect—

(1) Increases the adjusted basis of partnership property by the excess of the transferee's basis for the transferred partnership interest over the transferee's share of the adjusted basis to the partnership of the partnership's property; or

(2) Decreases the adjusted basis of partnership property by the excess of the transferee's share of the adjusted basis to the partnership of the partnership's property over the transferee's basis for the transferred partnership interest.

(c) Determination of transferee's basis in the transferred partnership interest. In the case of the transfer of a partnership interest by sale or exchange or as a result of the death of a partner, the transferee's basis in the transferred partnership interest is determined under section 742 and § 1.742–1. See also section 752 and §§ 1.752–1 through 1.752–5.

(d) Determination of transferee's share of the adjusted basis to the partnership of the partnership's property—(1) Generally. A transferee's share of the adjusted basis to the partnership of partnership property is equal to the sum of the transferee's interest as a partner in the partnership's previously taxed capital, plus the transferee's share of partnership liabilities. Generally, a transferee's interest as a partner in the partnership's previously taxed capital is equal to—

(i) The amount of cash that the transferee would receive on a liquidation of the partnership following the hypothetical transaction, as defined in paragraph (d)(2) of this section (to the extent attributable to the acquired partnership interest); increased by

(ii) The amount of tax loss (including any remedial allocations under § 1.704–3(d)), that would be allocated to the transferee from the hypothetical transaction (to the extent attributable to the acquired partnership interest); and decreased by

(iii) The amount of tax gain (including any remedial allocations under § 1.704–3(d)), that would be allocated to the transferee from the hypothetical transaction (to the extent attributable to the acquired partnership interest).

(2) Hypothetical transaction defined. For purposes of paragraph (d)(1) of this section, the hypothetical transaction means the disposition by the partnership of all of the partnership's assets, immediately after the transfer of the partnership interest, in a fully taxable transaction for cash equal to the fair market value of the assets.

(3) Examples. The provisions of this paragraph (d) are illustrated by the following examples:

Example (1). (i) A is a member of partnership PRS in which the partners have equal interests in capital and profits. The partnership has made an election under section 754, relating to the optional adjustment to the basis of partnership property. A sells its interest to T for $22,000. The balance sheet of the partnership at the date of sale shows the following:

Assets		
	Adjusted basis	Fair market value
Cash	$5,000	$5,000
Accounts receivable	10,000	10,000
Inventory	20,000	21,000
Depreciable assets	20,000	40,000
Total	55,000	76,000

Liabilities and Capital		
	Adjusted per books	Fair market value
Liabilities	$10,000	$10,000
Capital:		
A	15,000	22,000
B	15,000	22,000
C	15,000	22,000
Total	55,000	76,000

(ii) The amount of the basis adjustment under section 743(b) is the difference between the basis of T's interest in the partnership and T's share of the adjusted basis to the partnership of the partnership's property. Under section 742, the basis of T's interest is $25,333 (the cash paid for A's interest, $22,000, plus $3,333, T's share of partnership liabilities). T's interest in the partnership's previously taxed capital is $15,000 ($22,000, the amount of cash T would receive if PRS liquidated immediately after the hypothetical transaction, decreased by $7,000, the amount of tax gain allocated to T from the hypothetical transaction). T's share of the adjusted basis to the partnership of the partnership's property is $18,333 ($15,000 share of previously taxed capital, plus $3,333 share of the partnership's liabilities). The amount of the basis adjustment under section 743(b) to partnership property therefore, is $7,000, the difference between $25,333 and $18,333.

Example (2). A, B, and C form partnership PRS, to which A contributes land (Asset 1) with a fair market value of $1,000 and an adjusted basis to A of $400, and B and C each contribute $1,000 cash. Each partner has $1,000 credited to it on the books of the partnership as its capital contribution. The partners share in profits equally. During the partnership's first taxable year, Asset 1 appreciates in value to $1,300. A sells its one-third interest in the partnership to T for $1,100, when an election under section 754 is in effect. The amount of tax gain that would be allocated to T from the hypothetical transaction is $700 ($600 section 704(c) built-in gain, plus one-third of the additional gain). Thus, T's interest in the partnership's previously taxed capital is $400 ($1,100, the amount of cash T would receive if PRS liquidated immediately after the hypothetical transaction, decreased by $700, T's share of gain from the hypothetical transaction). The amount of T's basis adjustment under section 743(b) to partnership property is $700 (the excess of $1,100, T's cost basis for its interest, over $400, T's share of the adjusted basis to the partnership of partnership property).

(e) Allocation of basis adjustment. For the allocation of the basis adjustment under this section among the individual items of partnership property, see section 755 and the regulations thereunder.

(f) Subsequent transfers. Where there has been more than one transfer of a partnership interest, a transferee's basis adjustment is determined without regard to any prior transferee's basis adjustment. In the case of a gift of an interest in a partnership, the donor is treated as transferring, and the donee as receiving, that portion of the basis adjustment attributable to the gifted partnership interest. The provisions of this paragraph (f) are illustrated by the following example:

Example. (*i*) A, B, and C form partnership PRS. A and B each contribute $1,000 cash, and C contributes land with a basis and fair market value of $1,000. When the land has appreciated in value to $1,300, A sells its interest to T1 for $1,100 (one-third of $3,300, the fair market value of the partnership property). An

election under section 754 is in effect; therefore, T1 has a basis adjustment under section 743(b) of $100.

(*ii*) After the land has further appreciated in value to $1,600, T1 sells its interest to T2 for $1,200 (one-third of $3,600, the fair market value of the partnership property). T2 has a basis adjustment under section 743(b) of $200. This amount is determined without regard to any basis adjustment under section 743(b) that T1 may have had in the partnership assets.

(*iii*) During the following year, T2 makes a gift to T3 of fifty percent of T2's interest in PRS. At the time of the transfer, T2 has a $200 basis adjustment under section 743(b). T2 is treated as transferring $100 of the basis adjustment to T3 with the gift of the partnership interest.

(g) Distributions—(1) Distribution of adjusted property to the transferee—(i) Coordination with section 732. If a partnership distributes property to a transferee and the transferee has a basis adjustment for the property, the basis adjustment is taken into account under section 732. See § 1.732–2(b).

(ii) Coordination with section 734. For certain adjustments to the common basis of remaining partnership property after the distribution of adjusted property to a transferee, see § 1.734–2(b).

(2) Distribution of adjusted property to another partner—(i) Coordination with section 732. If a partner receives a distribution of property with respect to which another partner has a basis adjustment, the distributee does not take the basis adjustment into account under section 732.

(ii) Reallocation of basis. A transferee with a basis adjustment in property that is distributed to another partner reallocates the basis adjustment among the remaining items of partnership property under § 1.755–1(c).

(3) Distributions in complete liquidation of a partner's interest. If a transferee receives a distribution of property (whether or not the transferee has a basis adjustment in such property) in liquidation of its interest in the partnership, the adjusted basis to the partnership of the distributed property immediately before the distribution includes the transferee's basis adjustment for the property in which the transferee relinquished an interest (either because it remained in the partnership or was distributed to another partner). Any basis adjustment for property in which the transferee is deemed to relinquish its interest is reallocated among the properties distributed to the transferee under § 1.755–1(c).

(4) Coordination with other provisions. The rules of sections 704(c)(1)(B), 731, 737, and 751 apply before the rules of this paragraph (g).

(5) Example. The provisions of this paragraph (g) are illustrated by the following example:

Example. (i) A, B, and C are equal partners in partnership PRS. Each partner originally contributed $10,000 in cash, and PRS used the contributions to purchase five nondepreciable capital assets. PRS has no liabilities. After five years, PRS's balance sheet appears as follows:

Assets		
	Adjusted basis	Fair market value
Asset 1	$10,000	$10,000
Asset 2	4,000	6,000
Asset 3	6,000	6,000
Asset 4	7,000	4,000
Asset 5	3,000	13,000
Total	30,000	39,000

Capital		
	Adjusted per books	Fair market value
Partner A	$10,000	$13,000
Partner B	10,000	13,000
Partner C	10,000	13,000
Total	30,000	39,000

(ii) A sells its interest to T for $13,000 when PRS has an election in effect under section 754. T receives a basis adjustment under section 743(b) in the partnership property that is equal to $3,000 (the excess of T's basis in the partnership interest, $13,000, over T's share of the adjusted basis to the partnership of partnership property, $10,000). The basis adjustment is allocated under section 755, and the partnership's balance sheet appears as follows:

Assets			
	Adjusted basis	Fair market value	Basis adjustment
Asset 1	$10,000	$10,000	$0.00
Asset 2	4,000	6,000	666.67
Asset 3	6,000	6,000	0.00
Asset 4	7,000	4,000	(1,000.00)
Asset 5	3,000	13,000	3,333.33
Total	30,000	39,000	3,000.000

Capital			
	Adjusted per books	Fair market value	Special basis
Partner T	$10,000	$13,000	$3,000
Partner B	10,000	13,000	0
Partner C	10,000	13,000	0
Total	30,000	39,000	3,000

(iii) Assume that PRS distributes Asset 2 to T in partial liquidation of T's interest in the partnership. T has a basis adjustment under section 743(b) of $666.67 in Asset 2. Under paragraph (g)(1)(i) of this section, T takes the basis adjustment into account under section 732. Therefore, T will have a basis in Asset 2 of $4,666.67 following the distribution.

(iv) Assume instead that PRS distributes Asset 5 to C in complete liquidation of C's interest in PRS. T has a basis adjustment under section 743(b) of $3,333.33 in Asset 5. Under paragraph (g)(2)(i) of this section, C does not take T's basis adjustment into account under section 732. Therefore, the partnership's basis for purposes of sections 732 and 734 is $3,000.

Under paragraph (g)(2)(ii) of this section, T's $3,333.33 basis adjustment is reallocated among the remaining partnership assets under § 1.755–1(c).

(v) Assume instead that PRS distributes Asset 5 to T in complete liquidation of its interest in PRS. Under paragraph (g)(3) of this section, immediately prior to the distribution of Asset 5 to T, PRS must adjust the basis of Asset 5. Therefore, immediately prior to the distribution, PRS's basis in Asset 5 is equal to $6,000, which is the sum of (A) $3,000, PRS's common basis in Asset 5, plus (B) $3,333.33, T's basis adjustment to Asset 5, plus (C) ($333.33), the sum of T's basis adjustments in Assets 2 and 4. For purposes of sections 732 and 734, therefore, PRS will be treated as having a basis in Asset 5 equal to $6,000.

(h) Contributions of adjusted property—(1) Section 721(a) transactions. If, in a transaction described in section 721(a), a partnership (the upper tier) contributes to another partnership (the lower tier) property with respect to which a basis adjustment has been made, the basis adjustment is treated as contributed to the lower-tier partnership, regardless of whether the lower-tier partnership makes a section 754 election. The lower tier's basis in the contributed assets and the upper tier's basis in the partnership interest received in the transaction are determined with reference to the basis adjustment. However, that portion of the basis of the upper tier's interest in the lower tier attributable to the basis adjustment must be segregated and allocated solely to the transferee partner for whom the basis adjustment was made. Similarly, that portion of the lower tier's basis in its assets attributable to the basis adjustment must be segregated and allocated solely to the upper tier and the transferee. A partner with a basis adjustment in property held by a partnership that terminates under section 708(b)(1)(B) will continue to have the same basis adjustment with respect to property deemed contributed by the terminated partnership to the new partnership under § 1.708–1(b)

(1)(iv), regardless of whether the new partnership makes a section 754 election.

(2) Section 351 transactions—(i) Basis in transferred property. A corporation's adjusted tax basis in property transferred to the corporation by a partnership in a transaction described in section 351 is determined with reference to any basis adjustments to the property under section 743(b) (other than any basis adjustment that reduces a partner's gain under paragraph (h)(2)(ii) of this section).

(ii) Partnership gain. The amount of gain, if any, recognized by the partnership on a transfer of property by the partnership to a corporation in a transfer described in section 351 is determined without reference to any basis adjustment to the transferred property under section 743(b). The amount of gain, if any, recognized by the partnership on the transfer that is allocated to a partner with a basis adjustment in the transferred property is adjusted to reflect the partner's basis adjustment in the transferred property.

(iii) Basis in stock. The partnership's adjusted tax basis in stock received from a corporation in a transfer described in section 351 is determined without reference to the basis adjustment in property transferred to the corporation in the section 351 exchange. A partner with a basis adjustment in property transferred to the corporation, however, has a basis adjustment in the stock received by the partnership in the section 351 exchange in an amount equal to the partner's basis adjustment in the transferred property, reduced by any basis adjustment that reduced the partner's gain under paragraph (h)(2)(ii) of this section.

(iv) Example. The following example illustrates the principles of this paragraph (h):

Example. (i) A, B, and C are equal partners in partnership PRS. The partnership's only asset, Asset 1, has an adjusted tax basis of $60 and a fair market value of $120. Asset 1 is a nondepreciable capital asset and is not section 704(c) property. A has a basis in its partnership interest of $40, and a positive section 743(b) adjustment of $20 in Asset 1. In a transaction to which section 351 applies, PRS contributes Asset 1 to X, a corporation, in exchange for $15 in cash and X stock with a fair market value of $105.

(ii) Under paragraph (h)(2)(ii) of this section, PRS realizes $60 of gain on the transfer of Asset 1 to X ($120, its amount realized, minus $60, its adjusted basis), but recognizes only $15 of that gain under section 351(b)(1). Of this amount, $5 is allocated to each partner. A must use $5 of its basis adjustment in Asset 1 to offset A's share of PRS's gain. Under paragraph (h)(2)(iii) of this section, PRS's basis in the stock received from X is $60. However, A has a basis adjustment in the stock received by PRS equal to $15 (its basis adjustment in Asset 1, $20, reduced by the portion of the adjustment which reduced A's gain, $5). Under paragraph (h)(2)(i) of this section, X's basis in Asset 1 equals $75 (PRS's common basis in the asset, $60, plus A's basis adjustment under section 743(b), $20, less the portion of the adjustment which reduced A's gain, $5).

(i) [Reserved].

(j) Effect of basis adjustment—(1) In general. The basis adjustment constitutes an adjustment to the basis of partnership property with respect to the transferee only. No adjustment is made to the common basis of partnership property. Thus, for purposes of calculating income, deduction, gain, and loss, the transferee will have a special basis for those partnership properties the bases of which are adjusted under section 743(b) and this section. The adjustment to the basis of partnership property under section 743(b) has no effect on the partnership's computation of any item under section 703.

(2) Computation of partner's distributive share of partnership items. The partnership first computes its items of income, deduction, gain, or loss at the partnership level under section 703. The partnership then allocates the partnership items among the partners, includ-

ing the transferee, in accordance with section 704, and adjusts the partners' capital accounts accordingly. The partnership then adjusts the transferee's distributive share of the items of partnership income, deduction, gain, or loss, in accordance with paragraphs (j)(3) and (4) of this section, to reflect the effects of the transferee's basis adjustment under section 743(b). These adjustments to the transferee's distributive shares must be reflected on Schedules K and K-1 of the partnership's return (Form 1065). These adjustments to the transferee's distributive shares do not affect the transferee's capital account.

(3) Effect of basis adjustment in determining items of income, gain, or loss—(i) In general. The amount of a transferee's income, gain, or loss from the sale or exchange of a partnership asset in which the transferee has a basis adjustment is equal to the transferee's share of the partnership's gain or loss from the sale of the asset (including any remedial allocations under § 1.704–3(d)), minus the amount of the transferee's positive basis adjustment for the partnership asset (determined by taking into account the recovery of the basis adjustment under paragraph (j)(4)(i)(B) of this section) or plus the amount of the transferee's negative basis adjustment for the partnership asset (determined by taking into the account the recovery of the basis adjustment under paragraph (j)(4)(ii)(B) of this section).

(ii) Examples. The following examples illustrate the principles of this paragraph (j)(3):

Example (1). A and B form equal partnership PRS. A contributes nondepreciable property with a fair market value of $50 and an adjusted tax basis of $100. PRS will use the traditional allocation method under § 1.704–3(b). B contributes $50 cash. A sells its interest to T for $50. PRS has an election in effect to adjust the basis of partnership property under section 754. T receives a negative $50 basis adjustment under section 743(b) that, under section 755, is allocated to the nondepreciable property. PRS then sells the property for $60.

PRS recognizes a book gain of $10 (allocated equally between T and B) and a tax loss of $40. T will receive an allocation of $40 of tax loss under the principles of section 704(c). However, because T has a negative $50 basis adjustment in the nondepreciable property, T recognizes a $10 gain from the partnership's sale of the property.

Example (2). A and B form equal partnership PRS. A contributes nondepreciable property with a fair market value of $100 and an adjusted tax basis of $50. B contributes $100 cash. PRS will use the traditional allocation method under § 1.704–3(b). A sells its interest to T for $100. PRS has an election in effect to adjust the basis of partnership property under section 754. Therefore, T receives a $50 basis adjustment under section 743(b) that, under section 755, is allocated to the nondepreciable property. PRS then sells the nondepreciable property for $90. PRS recognizes a book loss of $10 (allocated equally between T and B) and a tax gain of $40. T will receive an allocation of the entire $40 of tax gain under the principles of section 704(c). However, because T has a $50 basis adjustment in the property, T recognizes a $10 loss from the partnership's sale of the property.

Example (3). A and B form equal partnership PRS. PRS will make allocations under section 704(c) using the remedial allocation method described in § 1.704–3(d). A contributes nondepreciable property with a fair market value of $100 and an adjusted tax basis of $150. B contributes $100 cash. A sells its partnership interest to T for $100. PRS has an election in effect to adjust the basis of partnership property under section 754. T receives a negative $50 basis adjustment under section 743(b) that, under section 755, is allocated to the property. The partnership then sells the property for $120. The partnership recognizes a $20 book gain and a $30 tax loss. The book gain will be allocated equally between the partners. The entire $30 tax loss will be allocated to T under the principles of section

704(c). To match its $10 share of book gain, B will be allocated $10 of remedial gain, and T will be allocated an offsetting $10 of remedial loss. T was allocated a total of $40 of tax loss with respect to the property. However, because T has a negative $50 basis adjustment to the property, T recognizes a $10 gain from the partnership's sale of the property.

(4) Effect of basis adjustment in determining items of deduction—(i) Increases—(A) Additional deduction. The amount of any positive basis adjustment that is recovered by the transferee in any year is added to the transferee's distributive share of the partnership's depreciation or amortization deductions for the year. The basis adjustment is adjusted under section 1016(a)(2) to reflect the recovery of the basis adjustment.

(B) Recovery period—(1) In general. Except as provided in paragraph (j)(4)(i)(B)(2) of this section, for purposes of section 168, if the basis of a partnership's recovery property is increased as a result of the transfer of a partnership interest, then the increased portion of the basis is taken into account as if it were newly-purchased recovery property placed in service when the transfer occurs. Consequently, any applicable recovery period and method may be used to determine the recovery allowance with respect to the increased portion of the basis. However, no change is made for purposes of determining the recovery allowance under section 168 for the portion of the basis for which there is no increase.

(2) Remedial allocation method. If a partnership elects to use the remedial allocation method described in § 1.704–3(d) with respect to an item of the partnership's recovery property, then the portion of any increase in the basis of the item of the partnership's recovery property under section 743(b) that is attributable to section 704(c) built-in gain is recovered over the remaining recovery period for the partnership's excess book basis in the property as determined in the final sentence of § 1.704–3(d)(2). Any remaining portion of the basis increase is recovered under paragraph (j) (4)(i)(B)(1) of this section.

(C) Examples. The provisions of this paragraph (j)(4)(i) are illustrated by the following examples:

Example (1). (i) A, B, and C are equal partners in partnership PRS, which owns Asset 1, an item of depreciable property that has a fair market value in excess of its adjusted tax basis. C sells its interest in PRS to T while PRS has an election in effect under section 754. PRS, therefore, increases the basis of Asset 1 with respect to T.

(ii) Assume that in the year following the transfer of the partnership interest to T, T's distributive share of the partnership's common basis depreciation deductions from Asset 1 is $1,000. Also assume that, under paragraph (j)(4)(i)(B) of this section, the amount of the basis adjustment under section 743(b) that T recovers during the year is $500. The total amount of depreciation deductions from Asset 1 reported by T is equal to $1,500.

Example (2). (i) A and B form equal partnership PRS. A contributes property with an adjusted basis of $100,000 and a fair market value of $500,000. B contributes $500,000 cash. When PRS is formed, the property has five years remaining in its recovery period. The partnership's adjusted basis of $100,000 will, therefore, be recovered over the five years remaining in the property's recovery period. PRS elects to use the remedial allocation method under § 1.704–3(d) with respect to the property. If PRS had purchased the property at the time of the partnership's formation, the basis of the property would have been recovered over a 10-year period. The $400,000 of section 704(c) built-in gain will, therefore, be amortized under § 1.704–3(d) over a 10-year period beginning at the time of the partnership's formation.

(ii)(A) Except for the depreciation deductions, PRS's expenses equal its income in each year of the first two years commencing with the year the partnership is formed. After two years, A's share of the adjusted basis of partnership property is $120,000, while B's is $440,000:

| | Capital accounts | | | |
| | A | | B | |
	Book	Tax	Book	Tax
Initial Contribution	$500,000	$100,000	$500,000	$500,000
Depreciation Year 1	(30,000)		(30,000)	(20,000)
Remedial		10,000		(10,000)
	470,000	110,000	470,000	470,000
Depreciation Year 2	(30,000)		(30,000)	(20,000)
Remedial		10,000		(10,000)
	440,000	120,000	440,000	440,000

(B) A sells its interest in PRS to T for its fair market value of $440,000. A valid election under section 754 is in effect with respect to the sale of the partnership interest. Accordingly, PRS makes an adjustment, pursuant to section 743(b), to increase the basis of partnership property. Under section 743(b), the amount of the basis adjustment is equal to $320,000. Under section 755, the entire basis adjustment is allocated to the property.

(iii) At the time of the transfer, $320,000 of section 704(c) built-in gain from the property was still reflected on the partnership's books, and all of the basis adjustment is attributable to section 704(c) built-in gain. Therefore, the basis adjustment will be recovered over the re-

maining recovery period for the section 704(c) built-in gain under § 1.704–3(d).

(ii) Decreases—(A) Reduced deduction. The amount of any negative basis adjustment allocated to an item of depreciable or amortizable property that is recovered in any year first decreases the transferee's distributive share of the partnership's depreciation or amortization deductions from that item of property for the year. If the amount of the basis adjustment recovered in any year exceeds the transferee's distributive share of the partnership's depreciation or amortization deductions from the item of property, then the transferee's distributive share of the partnership's depreciation or amortization deductions from other items of partnership property is decreased. The transferee then recognizes ordinary income to the extent of the excess, if any, of the amount of the basis adjustment recovered in any year over the transferee's distributive share of the partnership's depreciation or amortization deductions from all items of property.

(B) Recovery period. For purposes of section 168, if the basis of an item of a partnership's recovery property is decreased as the result of the transfer of an interest in the partnership, then the decrease is recovered over the remaining useful life of the item of the partnership's recovery property. The portion of the decrease that is recovered in any year during the recovery period is equal to the product of—

(1) The amount of the decrease to the item's adjusted basis (determined as of the date of the transfer); multiplied by

(2) A fraction, the numerator of which is the portion of the adjusted basis of the item recovered by the partnership in that year, and the denominator of which is the adjusted basis of the item on the date of the transfer (determined prior to any basis adjustments).

(C) Examples. The provisions of this paragraph (j)(4)(ii) are illustrated by the following examples:

Example (1). (i) A, B, and C are equal partners in partnership PRS, which owns Asset 2, an item of depreciable property that has a fair market value that is less than its adjusted tax basis. C sells its interest in PRS to T while PRS has an election in effect under section 754. PRS, therefore, decreases the basis of Asset 2 with respect to T.

(ii) Assume that in the year following the transfer of the partnership interest to T, T's distributive share of the partnership's common basis depreciation deductions from Asset 2 is $1,000. Also assume that, under paragraph (j)(4)(ii)(B) of this section, the amount of the basis adjustment under section 743(b) that T recovers during the year is $500. The total amount of depreciation deductions from Asset 2 reported by T is equal to $500.

Example (2). (i) A and B form equal partnership PRS. A contributes property with an adjusted basis of $100,000 and a fair market value of $50,000. B contributes $50,000 cash. When PRS is formed, the property has five years remaining in its recovery period. The partnership's adjusted basis of $100,000 will, therefore, be recovered over the five years remaining in the property's recovery period. PRS uses the traditional allocation method under § 1.704–3(b) with respect to the property. As a result, B will receive $5,000 of depreciation deductions from the property in each of years 1–5, and A, as the contributing partner, will receive $15,000 of depreciation deductions in each of these years.

(ii) Except for the depreciation deductions, PRS's expenses equal its income in each of the first two years commencing with the year the partnership is formed. After two years, A's share of the adjusted basis of partnership property is $70,000, while B's is $40,000. A sells its interest in PRS to T for its fair market value of $40,000. A valid election under section 754 is in effect with respect to the sale of the partnership interest. Accordingly, PRS makes an adjustment, pursuant to section 743(b), to decrease the basis of partnership property. Under

section 743(b), the amount of the adjustment is equal to ($30,000). Under section 755, the entire adjustment is allocated to the property.

(iii) The basis of the property at the time of the transfer of the partnership interest was $60,000. In each of years 3 through 5, the partnership will realize depreciation deductions of $20,000 from the property. Thus, one third of the negative basis adjustment ($10,000) will be recovered in each of years 3 through 5. Consequently, T will be allocated, for tax purposes, depreciation of $15,000 each year from the partnership and will recover $10,000 of its negative basis adjustment. Thus, T's net depreciation deduction from the partnership in each year is $5,000.

Example (3). (i) A, B, and C are equal partners in partnership PRS, which owns Asset 2, an item of depreciable property that has a fair market value that is less than its adjusted tax basis. C sells its interest in PRS to T while PRS has an election in effect under section 754. PRS, therefore, decreases the basis of Asset 2 with respect to T.

(ii) Assume that in the year following the transfer of the partnership interest to T, T's distributive share of the partnership's common basis depreciation deductions from Asset 2 is $500. PRS allocates no other depreciation to T. Also assume that, under paragraph (j)(4)(ii)(B) of this section, the amount of the negative basis adjustment that T recovers during the year is $1,000. T will report $500 of ordinary income because the amount of the negative basis adjustment recovered during the year exceeds T's distributive share of the partnership's common basis depreciation deductions from Asset 2.

(5) Depletion. Where an adjustment is made under section 743(b) to the basis of partnership property subject to depletion, any depletion allowance is determined separately for each partner, including the transferee partner, based on the partner's interest in such property. See § 1.702–1(a)(8). For partnerships that hold oil and gas properties that are depleted at the partner level under section 613A(c)(7)(D), the transferee partner (and not the partnership) must make the basis adjustments, if any, required under section 743(b) with respect to such properties. See § 1.613A–3(e)(6)(iv).

(6) Example. The provisions of paragraph (j)(5) of this section are illustrated by the following example:

Example. A, B, and C each contributes $5,000 cash to form partnership PRS, which purchases a coal property for $15,000. A, B, and C have equal interests in capital and profits. C subsequently sells its partnership interest to T for $100,000 when the election under section 754 is in effect. T has a basis adjustment under section 743(b) for the coal property of $95,000 (the difference between T's basis, $100,000, and its share of the basis of partnership property, $5,000). Assume that the depletion allowance computed under the percentage method would be $21,000 for the taxable year so that each partner would be entitled to $7,000 as its share of the deduction for depletion. However, under the cost depletion method, at an assumed rate of 10 percent, the allowance with respect to T's one-third interest which has a basis to him of $100,000 ($5,000, plus its basis adjustment of $95,000) is $10,000, although the cost depletion allowance with respect to the one-third interest of A and B in the coal property, each of which has a basis of $5,000, is only $500. For partners A and B, the percentage depletion is greater than cost depletion and each will deduct $7,000 based on the percentage depletion method. However, as to T, the transferee partner, the cost depletion method results in a greater allowance and T will, therefore, deduct $10,000 based on cost depletion. See section 613(a).

(k) Returns—(1) Statement of adjustments—(i) In general. A partnership that must adjust the bases of partnership properties under section 743(b) must attach a statement to the partnership return for the year of the transfer setting forth the name and taxpayer identification number of the transferee as well as the computation of the adjustment and the partnership properties to which the adjustment has been allocated.

(ii) Special rule. Where an interest is transferred in a partnership which holds oil and gas properties that are depleted at the partner level under section 613A(c)(7)(D), the transferee must attach a statement to the transferee's return for the year of the transfer, setting forth the computation of the basis adjustment under section 743(b) which is allocable to such properties and the specific properties to which the adjustment has been allocated.

(iii) Example. The provisions of paragraph (k)(1)(ii) of this section are illustrated by the following example:

Example. (i) Partnership XYZ owns a single section 613A(c)(7)(D) domestic oil and gas property (Property) and other non-depletable assets. A, a partner in XYZ with an adjusted tax basis in Property of $100 (excluding any prior adjustments under section 743(b)), sells its partnership interest to B for $800 cash. Under § 1.613A–3(e)(6)(iv), A's adjusted basis of $100 in Property carries over to B.

(ii) Under section 755, XYZ determines that Property accounts for 50% of the fair market value of all partnership assets. The remaining 50% of B's purchase price ($400) is attributable to non-depletable property. XYZ must provide a statement to B containing the portion of B's adjusted basis attributable to non-depletable property ($400). Under this paragraph (k)(1), XYZ must report basis adjustments under section 743(b) to non-depletable property. B must report basis adjustments under section 743(b) to Property.

(2) Requirement that transferee notify partnership—(i) Sale or exchange. A transferee that acquires, by sale or exchange, an interest in a partnership with an election under section 754 in effect for the taxable year of the transfer, must notify the partnership, in writing, within 30 days of the sale or exchange. The written notice to the partnership must be

signed under penalties of perjury and must include the names and addresses of the transferee and (if ascertainable) of the transferor, the taxpayer identification numbers of the transferee and (if ascertainable) of the transferor, the relationship (if any) between the transferee and the transferor, the date of the transfer, the amount of any liabilities assumed or taken subject to by the transferee, and the amount of any money, the fair market value of any other property delivered or to be delivered for the transferred interest in the partnership, and any other information necessary for the partnership to compute the transferee's basis.

(ii) Transfer on death. A transferee that acquires, on the death of a partner, an interest in a partnership with an election under section 754 in effect for the taxable year of the transfer, must notify the partnership, in writing, within one year of the death of the deceased partner. The written notice to the partnership must be signed under penalties of perjury and must include the names and addresses of the deceased partner and the transferee, the taxpayer identification numbers of the deceased partner and the transferee, the relationship (if any) between the transferee and the transferor, the deceased partner's date of death, the date on which the transferee became the owner of the partnership interest, the fair market value of the partnership interest on the applicable date of valuation set forth in section 1014, and the manner in which the fair market value of the partnership interest was determined.

(iii) Nominee reporting. If a partnership interest is transferred to a nominee which is required to furnish the statement under section 6031(c)(1) to the partnership, the nominee may satisfy the notice requirement contained in this paragraph (k)(2) by providing the statement required under § 1.6031(c)–1T, provided that the statement satisfies all requirements of § 1.6031(c)–1T and this paragraph (k)(2).

(3) Reliance. In making the adjustments under section 743(b) and any statement or return relating to such adjustments under this section, a partnership may rely on the written notice provided by a transferee pursuant to paragraph (k)(2) of this section to determine the transferee's basis in a partnership interest. The previous sentence shall not apply if any partner who has responsibility for federal income tax reporting by the partnership has knowledge of facts indicating that the statement is clearly erroneous.

(4) Partnership not required to make or report adjustments under section 743(b) until it has notice of the transfer. A partnership is not required to make the adjustments under section 743(b) (or any statement or return relating to those adjustments) with respect to any transfer until it has been notified of the transfer. For purposes of this section, a partnership is notified of a transfer when either—

(i) The partnership receives the written notice from the transferee required under paragraph (k)(2) of this section; or

(ii) Any partner who has responsibility for federal income tax reporting by the partnership has knowledge that there has been a transfer of a partnership interest.

(5) Effect on partnership of the failure of the transferee to comply. If the transferee fails to provide the partnership with the written notice required by paragraph (k)(2) of this section, the partnership must attach a statement to its return in the year that the partnership is otherwise notified of the transfer. This statement must set forth the name and taxpayer identification number (if ascertainable) of the transferee. In addition, the following statement must be prominently displayed in capital letters on the first page of the partnership's return for such year, and on the first page of any schedule or information statement relating to such transferee's share of income, credits, deductions, etc.: "RETURN FILED PURSUANT TO § 1.743–1(k)(5)." The partnership will then be entitled to report the transferee's share of partnership items without adjustment to reflect the transferee's basis adjustment in partnership property. If, following the filing

of a return pursuant to this paragraph (k)(5), the transferee provides the applicable written notice to the partnership, the partnership must make such adjustments as are necessary to adjust the basis of partnership property (as of the date of the transfer) in any amended return otherwise to be filed by the partnership or in the next annual partnership return of income to be regularly filed by the partnership. At such time, the partnership must also provide the transferee with such information as is necessary for the transferee to amend its prior returns to properly reflect the adjustment under section 743(b).

* * *

§ 1.751–1 Unrealized receivables and inventory items.

(a) Sale or exchange of interest in a partnership—(1) Character of amount realized. To the extent that money or property received by a partner in exchange for all or part of his partnership interest is attributable to his share of the value of partnership unrealized receivables or substantially appreciated inventory items, the money or fair market value of the property received shall be considered as an amount realized from the sale or exchange of property other than a capital asset. The remainder of the total amount realized on the sale or exchange of the partnership interest is realized from the sale or exchange of a capital asset under section 741. For definition of "unrealized receivables" and "inventory items which have appreciated substantially in value", see section 751 (c) and (d). Unrealized receivables and substantially appreciated inventory items are hereafter in this section referred to as "section 751 property". See paragraph (e) of this section.

(2) Determination of gain or loss. The income or loss realized by a partner upon the sale or exchange of its interest in section 751 property is the amount of income or loss from section 751 property (including any remedial allocations under § 1.704–3(d)) that would have been allocated to the partner (to the extent attributable to the partnership interest sold or exchanged) if the partnership had sold all of its property in a fully taxable transaction for cash in an amount equal to the fair market value of such property (taking into account section 7701(g)) immediately prior to the partner's transfer of the interest in the partnership. Any gain or loss recognized that is attributable to section 751 property will be ordinary gain or loss. The difference between the amount of capital gain or loss that the partner would realize in the absence of section 751 and the amount of ordinary income or loss determined under this paragraph (a)(2) is the transferor's capital gain or loss on the sale of its partnership interest. See § 1.460–4(k)(2)(iv)(E) for rules relating to the amount of ordinary income or loss attributable to a contract accounted for under a long-term contract method of accounting.

(3) Statement required. A partner selling or exchanging any part of an interest in a partnership that has any section 751 property at the time of sale or exchange must submit with its income tax return for the taxable year in which the sale or exchange occurs a statement setting forth separately the following information—

(i) The date of the sale or exchange;

(ii) The amount of any gain or loss attributable to the section 751 property; and

(iii) The amount of any gain or loss attributable to capital gain or loss on the sale of the partnership interest.

(b) Certain distributions treated as sales or exchanges—(1) In general. (i) Certain distributions to which section 751(b) applies are treated in part as sales or exchanges of property between the partnership and the distributee partner, and not as distributions to which sections 731 through 736 apply. A distribution treated as a sale or exchange under section 751(b) is not subject to the provisions of section 707(b). Section 751(b) applies whether or not the distribution is in liquidation of the distributee partner's entire interest in the partner-

ship. However, section 751(b) applies only to the extent that a partner either receives section 751 property in exchange for his relinquishing any part of his interest in other property, or receives other property in exchange for his relinquishing any part of his interest in section 751 property.

(ii) Section 751(b) does not apply to a distribution to a partner which is not in exchange for his interest in other partnership property. Thus, section 751(b) does not apply to the extent that a distribution consists of the distributee partner's share of section 751 property or his share of other property. Similarly, section 751(b) does not apply to current drawings or to advances against the partner's distributive share, or to a distribution which is, in fact, a gift or payment for services or for the use of capital. In determining whether a partner has received only his share of either section 751 property or of other property, his interest in such property remaining in the partnership immediately after a distribution must be taken into account. For example, the section 751 property in partnership ABC has a fair market value of $100,000 in which partner A has an interest of 30 percent, or $30,000. If A receives $20,000 of section 751 property in a distribution, and continues to have a 30-percent interest in the $80,000 of section 751 property remaining in the partnership after the distribution, only $6,000 ($30,000 minus $24,000 (30 percent of $80,000)) of the section 751 property received by him will be considered to be his share of such property. The remaining $14,000 ($20,000 minus $6,000) received is in excess of his share.

(iii) If a distribution is, in part, a distribution of the distributee partner's share of section 751 property, or of other property (including money) and, in part, a distribution in exchange of such properties, the distribution shall be divided for the purpose of applying section 751(b). The rules of section 751(b) shall first apply to the part of the distribution treated as a sale or exchange of such properties, and then the rules of sections 731 through 736 shall apply to the part of the distribution not treated as a sale or exchange. See paragraph (b)(4)(ii) of this section for treatment of payments under section 736(a).

(2) Distribution of section 751 property (unrealized receivables or substantially appreciated inventory items). (i) To the extent that a partner receives section 751 property in a distribution in exchange for any part of his interest in partnership property (including money) other than section 751 property, the transaction shall be treated as a sale or exchange of such properties between the distributee partner and the partnership (as constituted after the distribution).

(ii) At the time of the distribution, the partnership (as constituted after the distribution) realizes ordinary income or loss on the sale or exchange of the section 751 property. The amount of the income or loss to the partnership will be measured by the difference between the adjusted basis to the partnership of the section 751 property considered as sold to or exchanged with the partner, and the fair market value of the distributee partner's interest in other partnership property which he relinquished in the exchange. In computing the partners' distributive shares of such ordinary income or loss, the income or loss shall be allocated only to partners other than the distributee and separately taken into account under section 702(a)(8).

(iii) At the time of the distribution, the distributee partner realizes gain or loss measured by the difference between his adjusted basis for the property relinquished in the exchange (including any special basis adjustment which he may have) and the fair market value of the section 751 property received by him in exchange for his interest in other property which he has relinquished. The distributee's adjusted basis for the property relinquished is the basis such property would have had under section 732 (including subsection (d) thereof) if the distributee partner had received such property in a current distribution immediately before

the actual distribution which is treated wholly or partly as a sale or exchange under section 751(b). The character of the gain or loss to the distributee partner shall be determined by the character of the property in which he relinquished his interest.

(3) Distribution of partnership property other than section 751 property. (i) To the extent that a partner receives a distribution of partnership property (including money) other than section 751 property in exchange for any part of his interest in section 751 property of the partnership, the distribution shall be treated as a sale or exchange of such properties between the distributee partner and the partnership (as constituted after the distribution).

(ii) At the time of the distribution, the partnership (as constituted after the distribution) realizes gain or loss on the sale or exchange of the property other than section 751 property. The amount of the gain to the partnership will be measured by the difference between the adjusted basis to the partnership of the distributed property considered as sold to or exchanged with the partner, and the fair market value of the distributee partner's interest in section 751 property which he relinquished in the exchange. The character of the gain or loss to the partnership is determined by the character of the distributed property treated as sold or exchanged by the partnership. In computing the partners' distributive shares of such gain or loss, the gain or loss shall be allocated only to partners other than the distributee and separately taken into account under section 702(a)(8).

(iii) At the time of the distribution, the distributee partner realizes ordinary income or loss on the sale or exchange of the section 751 property. The amount of the distributee partner's income or loss shall be measured by the difference between his adjusted basis for the section 751 property relinquished in the exchange (including any special basis adjustment which he may have), and the fair market value of other property (including money) received by him in exchange for his interest in the section 751 property which he has relinquished. The distributee partner's adjusted basis for the section 751 property relinquished is the basis such property would have had under section 732 (including subsection (d) thereof) if the distributee partner had received such property in a current distribution immediately before the actual distribution which is treated wholly or partly as a sale or exchange under section 751(b).

(4) Exceptions. (i) Section 751(b) does not apply to the distribution to a partner of property which the distributee partner contributed to the partnership. The distribution of such property is governed by the rules set forth in sections 731 through 736, relating to distributions by a partnership.

(ii) Section 751(b) does not apply to payments made to a retiring partner or to a deceased partner's successor in interest to the extent that, under section 736(a), such payments constitute a distributive share of partnership income or guaranteed payments. Payments to a retiring partner or to a deceased partner's successor in interest for his interest in unrealized receivables of the partnership in excess of their partnership basis, including any special basis adjustment for them to which such partner is entitled, constitute payments under section 736(a) and, therefore, are not subject to section 751(b). However, payments under section 736(b) which are considered as made in exchange for an interest in partnership property are subject to section 751(b) to the extent that they involve an exchange of substantially appreciated inventory items for other property. Thus, payments to a retiring partner or to a deceased partner's successor in interest under section 736 must first be divided between payments under section 736(a) and section 736(b). The section 736(b) payments must then be divided, if there is an exchange of substantially appreciated inventory items for other property, between the payments treated as a sale or exchange under section 751(b) and payments

treated as a distribution under sections 731 through 736. See subparagraph (1)(iii) of this paragraph, and section 736 and § 1.736–1.

(5) Statement required. A partnership which distributes section 751 property to a partner in exchange for his interest in other partnership property, or which distributes other property in exchange for any part of the partner's interest in section 751 property, shall submit with its return for the year of the distribution a statement showing the computation of any income, gain, or loss to the partnership under the provisions of section 751(b) and this paragraph. The distributee partner shall submit with his return a statement showing the computation of any income, gain, or loss to him. Such statement shall contain information similar to that required under paragraph (a)(3) of this section.

(c) Unrealized receivables. (1) The term unrealized receivables, as used in subchapter K, chapter 1 of the Code, means any rights (contractual or otherwise) to payment for:

(i) Goods delivered or to be delivered (to the extent that such payment would be treated as received for property other than a capital asset), or

(ii) Services rendered or to be rendered, to the extent that income arising from such rights to payment was not previously includible in income under the method of accounting employed by the partnership. Such rights must have arisen under contracts or agreements in existence at the time of sale or distribution, although the partnership may not be able to enforce payment until a later time. For example, the term includes trade accounts receivable of a cash method taxpayer, and rights to payment for work or goods begun but incomplete at the time of the sale or distribution.

(2) The basis for such unrealized receivables shall include all costs or expenses attributable thereto paid or accrued but not previously taken into account under the partnership method of accounting.

(3) In determining the amount of the sale price attributable to such unrealized receivables, or their value in a distribution treated as a sale or exchange, full account shall be taken not only of the estimated cost of completing performance of the contract or agreement, but also of the time between the sale or distribution and the time of payment.

(4)(i) With respect to any taxable year of a partnership ending after September 12, 1966 (but only in respect of expenditures paid or incurred after that date), the term unrealized receivables, for purposes of this section and sections 731, 736, 741, and 751, also includes potential gain from mining property defined in section 617(f)(2). With respect to each item of partnership mining property so defined, the potential gain is the amount that would be treated as gain to which section 617(d)(1) would apply if (at the time of the transaction described in section 731, 736, 741, or 751, as the case may be) the item were sold by the partnership at its fair market value.

(ii) With respect to sales, exchanges, or other dispositions after December 31, 1975, in any taxable year of a partnership ending after that date, the term unrealized receivables, for purposes of this section and sections 731, 736, 741, and 751, also includes potential gain from stock in a DISC as described in section 992(a). With respect to stock in such a DISC, the potential gain is the amount that would be treated as gain to which section 995(c) would apply if (at the time of the transaction described in section 731, 736, 741, or 751, as the case may be) the stock were sold by the partnership at its fair market value.

(iii) With respect to any taxable year of a partnership beginning after December 31, 1962, the term unrealized receivables, for purposes of this section and sections 731, 736, 741, and 751, also includes potential gain from section 1245 property. With respect to each item of partnership section 1245 property (as defined in section 1245(a)(3)), potential gain from section 1245 property is the amount

that would be treated as gain to which section 1245(a)(1) would apply if (at the time of the transaction described in section 731, 736, 741, or 751, as the case may be) the item of section 1245 property were sold by the partnership at its fair market value. See § 1.1245–1(e)(1). For example, if a partnership would recognize under section 1245(a)(1) gain of $600 upon a sale of one item of section 1245 property and gain of $300 upon a sale of its only other item of such property, the potential section 1245 income of the partnership would be $900.

(iv) With respect to transfers after October 9, 1975, and to sales, exchanges, and distributions taking place after that date, the term unrealized receivables, for purposes of this section and sections 731, 736, 741, and 751, also includes potential gain from stock in certain foreign corporations as described in section 1248. With respect to stock in such a foreign corporation, the potential gain is the amount that would be treated as gain to which section 1248(a) would apply if (at the time of the transaction described in section 731, 736, 741, or 751, as the case may be) the stock were sold by the partnership at its fair market value.

(v) With respect to any taxable year of a partnership ending after December 31, 1963, the term unrealized receivables, for purposes of this section and sections 731, 736, 741, and 751, also includes potential gain from section 1250 property. With respect to each item of partnership section 1250 property (as defined in section 1250(c)), potential gain from section 1250 property is the amount that would be treated as gain to which section 1250(a) would apply if (at the time of the transaction described in section 731, 736, 741, or 751, as the case may be) the item of section 1250 property were sold by the partnership at its fair market value. See § 1.1250–1(f)(1).

(vi) With respect to any taxable year of a partnership beginning after December 31, 1969, the term unrealized receivables, for purposes of this section and sections 731, 736, 741, and 751, also includes potential gain from farm recapture property as defined in section 1251(e)(1) (as in effect before enactment of the Tax Reform Act of 1984). With respect to each item of partnership farm recapture property so defined, the potential gain is the amount which would be treated as gain to which section 1251(c) (as in effect before enactment of the Tax Reform Act of 1984) would apply if (at the time of the transaction described in section 731, 736, 741, or 751, as the case may be) the item were sold by the partnership at its fair market value.

(vii) With respect to any taxable year of a partnership beginning after December 31, 1969, the term unrealized receivables, for purposes of this section and sections 731, 736, 741, and 751, also includes potential gain from farm land as defined in section 1252(a)(2). With respect to each item of partnership farm land so defined, the potential gain is the amount that would be treated as gain to which section 1252(a)(1) would apply if (at the time of the transaction described in section 731, 736, 741, or 751, as the case may be) the item were sold by the partnership at its fair market value.

(viii) With respect to transactions which occur after December 31, 1976, in any taxable year of a partnership ending after that date, the term unrealized receivables, for purposes of this section and sections 731, 736, 741, and 751, also includes potential gain from franchises, trademarks, or trade names referred to in section 1253(a). With respect to each such item so referred to in section 1253(a), the potential gain is the amount that would be treated as gain to which section 1253(a) would apply if (at the time of the transaction described in section 731, 736, 741, or 751, as the case may be) the items were sold by the partnership at its fair market value.

(ix) With respect to any taxable year of a partnership ending after December 31, 1975, the term unrealized receivables, for purposes of this section and sections 731, 736, 741, and 751, also includes potential gain under sec-

tion 1254(a) from natural resource recapture property as defined in § 1.1254–1(b)(2). With respect to each separate partnership natural resource recapture property so described, the potential gain is the amount that would be treated as gain to which section 1254(a) would apply if (at the time of the transaction described in section 731, 736, 741, or 751, as the case may be) the property were sold by the partnership at its fair market value.

(5) For purposes of subtitle A of the Internal Revenue Code, the basis of any potential gain described in paragraph (c)(4) of this section is zero.

(6)(i) If (at the time of any transaction referred to in paragraph (c)(4) of this section) a partnership holds property described in paragraph (c)(4) of this section and if—

(A) A partner had a special basis adjustment under section 743(b) in respect of the property;

(B) The basis under section 732 of the property if distributed to the partner would reflect a special basis adjustment under section 732(d); or

(C) On the date a partner acquired a partnership interest by way of a sale or exchange (or upon the death of another partner) the partnership owned the property and an election under section 754 was in effect with respect to the partnership, the partner's share of any potential gain described in paragraph (c)(4) of this section is determined under paragraph (c)(6)(ii) of this section.

(ii) The partner's share of the potential gain described in paragraph (c)(4) of this section in respect of the property to which this paragraph (c)(6)(ii) applies is that amount of gain that the partner would recognize under section 617(d)(1), 995(c), 1245(a), 1248(a), 1250(a), 1251(c) (as in effect before the Tax Reform Act of 1984), 1252(a), 1253(a), or 1254(a) (as the case may be) upon a sale of the property by the partnership, except that, for purposes of this paragraph (c)(6) the partner's share of such gain is determined in a manner that is consistent with the manner in which the partner's share of partnership property is determined; and the amount of a potential special basis adjustment under section 732(d) is treated as if it were the amount of a special basis adjustment under section 743(b). For example, in determining, for purposes of this paragraph (c)(6), the amount of gain that a partner would recognize under section 1245 upon a sale of partnership property, the items allocated under § 1.1245–1(e)(3)(ii) are allocated to the partner in the same manner as the partner's share of partnership property is determined. See § 1.1250–1(f) for rules similar to those contained in § 1.1245–1(e)(3)(ii).

(d) Inventory items which have substantially appreciated in value—(1) Substantial appreciation. Partnership inventory items shall be considered to have appreciated substantially in value if, at the time of the sale or distribution, the total fair market value of all the inventory items of the partnership exceeds 120 percent of the aggregate adjusted basis for such property in the hands of the partnership (without regard to any special basis adjustment of any partner) and, in addition, exceeds 10 percent of the fair market value of all partnership property other than money. The terms "inventory items which have appreciated substantially in value" or "substantially appreciated inventory items" refer to the aggregate of all partnership inventory items. These terms do not refer to specific partnership inventory items or to specific groups of such items. For example, any distribution of inventory items by a partnership the inventory items of which as a whole are substantially appreciated in value shall be a distribution of substantially appreciated inventory items for the purposes of section 751(b), even though the specific inventory items distributed may not be appreciated in value. Similarly, if the aggregate of partnership inventory items are not substantially appreciated in value, a distribution of specific inventory items, the value of which is more than 120 percent of their adjusted basis, will not

constitute a distribution of substantially appreciated inventory items. For the purpose of this paragraph, the "fair market value" of inventory items has the same meaning as "market" value in the regulations under section 471, relating to general rule for inventories.

(2) Inventory items. The term inventory items as used in subchapter K, chapter 1 of the Code, includes the following types of property:

(i) Stock in trade of the partnership, or other property of a kind which would properly be included in the inventory of the partnership if on hand at the close of the taxable year, or property held by the partnership primarily for sale to customers in the ordinary course of its trade or business. See section 1221(1).

(ii) Any other property of the partnership which, on sale or exchange by the partnership, would be considered property other than a capital asset and other than property described in section 1231. Thus, accounts receivable acquired in the ordinary course of business for services or from the sale of stock in trade constitute inventory items (see section 1221(4)), as do any unrealized receivables.

(iii) Any other property retained by the partnership which, if held by the partner selling his partnership interest or receiving a distribution described in section 751(b), would be considered property described in subdivision (i) or (ii) of this subparagraph. Property actually distributed to the partner does not come within the provisions of section 751(d)(2)(C) and this subdivision.

(e) Section 751 property and other property. For the purposes of this section, section 751 property means unrealized receivables or substantially appreciated inventory items, and other property means all property (including money) except section 751 property.

* * *

(g) Examples. Application of the provisions of section 751 may be illustrated by the following examples:

Example (1). (i)(A) A and B are equal partners in personal service partnership PRS. B transfers its interest in PRS to T for $15,000 when PRS's balance sheet (reflecting a cash receipts and disbursements method of accounting) is as follows:

Assets		
	Adjusted basis	*Fair market value*
Cash	$3,000	$3,000
Loans Receivable	10,000	10,000
Capital Assets	7,000	5,000
Unrealized Receivables	0	14,000
Total	20,000	32,000

Liabilities and Capital		
	Adjusted per books	*Fair market value*
Liabilities	$2,000	$2,000
Capital:		
A	9,000	15,000
B	9,000	15,000
Total	20,000	32,000

(B) None of the assets owned by PRS is section 704(c) property, and the capital assets are nondepreciable. The total amount realized by B is $16,000, consisting of the cash received, $15,000, plus $1,000, B's share of the partnership liabilities assumed by T. See section 752. B's undivided half-interest in the partnership property includes a half-interest in the partnership's unrealized receivables items. B's basis for its partnership interest is $10,000 ($9,000, plus $1,000, B's share of partnership liabilities). If section 751(a) did not apply to the sale, B would recognize $6,000 of capital gain from the sale of the interest in PRS. However, section 751(a) does apply to the sale.

(ii) If PRS sold all of its section 751 property in a fully taxable transaction immediately prior to the transfer of B's partnership interest to T, B would have been allocated $7,000 of ordinary income from the sale of PRS's un-

realized receivables. Therefore, B will recognize $7,000 of ordinary income with respect to the unrealized receivables. The difference between the amount of capital gain or loss that the partner would realize in the absence of section 751 ($6,000) and the amount of ordinary income or loss determined under paragraph (a)(2) of this section ($7,000) is the transferor's capital gain or loss on the sale of its partnership interest. In this case, B will recognize a $1,000 capital loss.

Example (2). (a) Facts. Partnership ABC makes a distribution to partner C in liquidation of his entire one-third interest in the partnership. At the time of the distribution, the balance sheet of the partnership, which uses the accrual method of accounting, is as follows:

Assets		
	Adjusted basis per books	*Market value*
Cash	$15,000	$15,000
Accounts receivable	9,000	9,000
Inventory	21,000	30,000
Depreciable property	42,000	48,000
Land	9,000	9,000
Total	96,000	11,000

Liabilities and Capital		
	Per books	*Value*
Current liabilities	$15,000	$15,000
Mortgage payable	21,000	21,000
Capital:		
A	20,000	25,000
B	20,000	25,000
C	20,000	25,000
Total	96,000	111,000

The distribution received by C consists of $10,000 cash and depreciable property with a fair market value of $15,000 and an adjusted basis to the partnership of $15,000.

(b) Presence of section 751 property. The partnership has no unrealized receivables, but the dual test provided in section 751(d)

(1) must be applied to determine whether the inventory items of the partnership, in the aggregate, have appreciated substantially in value. The fair market value of all partnership inventory items, $39,000 (inventory $30,000, and accounts receivable $9,000), exceeds 120 percent of the $30,000 adjusted basis of such items to the partnership. The fair market value of the inventory items, $39,000, also exceeds 10 percent of the fair market value of all partnership property other than money (10 percent of $96,000 or $9,600). Therefore, the partnership inventory items have substantially appreciated in value.

(c) The properties exchanged. Since C's entire partnership interest is to be liquidated, the provisions of section 736 are applicable. No part of the payment, however, is considered as a distributive share or as a guaranteed payment under section 736(a) because the entire payment is made for C's interest in partnership property. Therefore, the entire payment is for an interest in partnership property under section 736(b), and, to the extent applicable, subject to the rules of section 751. In the distribution, C received his share of cash ($5,000) and $15,000 in depreciable property ($1,000 less than his $16,000 share). In addition, he received other partnership property ($5,000 cash and $12,000 liabilities assumed, treated as money distributed under section 752(b)) in exchange for his interest in accounts receivable ($3,000), inventory ($10,000), land ($3,000), and the balance of his interest in depreciable property ($1,000). Section 751(b) applies only to the extent of the exchange of other property for section 751 property (i.e., inventory items, which include trade accounts receivable). The section 751 property exchanged has a fair market value of $13,000 ($3,000 in accounts receivable and $10,000 in inventory). Thus, $13,000 of the total amount C received is considered as received for the sale of section 751 property.

(d) Distributee partner's tax consequences. C's tax consequences on the distribution are as follows:

(1) The section 751(b) sale or exchange. C's share of the inventory items is treated as if he received them in a current distribution, and his basis for such items is $10,000 ($7,000 for inventory and $3,000 for accounts receivable) as determined under paragraph (b)(3)(iii) of this section. Then C is considered as having sold his share of inventory items to the partnership for $13,000. Thus, on the sale of his share of inventory items, C realizes $3,000 of ordinary income.

(2) The part of the distribution not under section 751(b). Section 751(b) does not apply to the balance of the distribution. Before the distribution, C's basis for his partnership interest was $32,000 ($20,000 plus $12,000, his share of partnership liabilities). See section 752(a). This basis is reduced by $10,000, the basis attributed to the section 751 property treated as distributed to C and sold by him to the partnership. Thus, C has a basis of $22,000 for the remainder of his partnership interest. The total distribution to C was $37,000 ($22,000 in cash and liabilities assumed, and $15,000 in depreciable property). Since C received no more than his share of the depreciable property, none of the depreciable property constitutes proceeds of the sale under section 751(b). C did receive more than his share of money. Therefore, the sale proceeds, treated separately in subparagraph (1) of this paragraph of this example, must consist of money and therefore must be deducted from the money distribution. Consequently, in liquidation of the balance of C's interest, he receives depreciable property and $9,000 in money ($22,000 less $13,000). Therefore, no gain or loss is recognized to C on the distribution. Under section 732(b), C's basis for the depreciable property is $13,000 (the remaining basis of his partnership interest, $22,000, reduced by $9,000, the money received in the distribution).

(e) Partnership's tax consequences. The tax consequences to the partnership on the distribution are as follows:

(1) The section 751(b) sale or exchange. The partnership consisting of the remaining members has no ordinary income on the distribution since it did not give up any section 751 property in the exchange. Of the $22,000 money distributed (in cash and the assumption of C's share of liabilities), $13,000 was paid to acquire C's interest in inventory ($10,000 fair market value) and in accounts receivable ($3,000). Since under section 751(b) the partnership is treated as buying these properties, it has a new cost basis for the inventory and accounts receivable acquired from C. Its basis for C's share of inventory and accounts receivable is $13,000, the amount which the partnership is considered as having paid C in the exchange. Since the partnership is treated as having distributed C's share of inventory and accounts receivable to him, the partnership must decrease its basis for inventory and accounts receivable ($30,000) by $10,000, the basis of C's share treated as distributed to him, and then increase the basis for inventory and accounts receivable by $13,000 to reflect the purchase prices of the items acquired. Thus, the basis of the partnership inventory is increased from $21,000 to $24,000 in the transaction. (Note that the basis of property acquired in a section 751(b) exchange is determined under section 1012 without regard to any elections of the partnership. See paragraph (e) of § 1.732–1.) Further, the partnership realizes no capital gain or loss on the portion of the distribution treated as a sale under section 751(b) since, to acquire C's interest in the inventory and accounts receivable, it gave up money and assumed C's share of liabilities.

(2) The part of the distribution not under section 751(b). In the remainder of the distribution to C which was not in exchange for C's interest in section 751 property, C received only other property as follows: $15,000 in depreciable property (with a basis to the partnership of $15,000) and $9,000 in money ($22,000 less $13,000 treated under subparagraph (1) of this paragraph of this example). Since this part of the distribution is not an exchange of section 751 property for other property, section 751(b) does not apply. Instead, the provisions which apply are sections 731 through 736, relating to distributions by a partnership. No gain or loss is recognized to the partnership on the distribution. (See section 731(b).) Further, the partnership makes no adjustment to the basis of remaining depreciable property unless an election under section 754 is in effect. (See section 734(a).) Thus, the basis of the depreciable property before the distribution, $42,000, is reduced by the basis of the depreciable property distributed, $15,000, leaving a basis for the depreciable property in the partnership of $27,000. However, if an election under section 754 is in effect, the partnership must make the adjustment required under section 734(b) as follows: Since the adjusted basis of the distributed property to the partnership had been $15,000, and is only $13,000 in C's hands (see paragraph (d)(2) of this example), the partnership will increase the basis of the depreciable property remaining in the partnership by $2,000 (the excess of the adjusted basis to the partnership of the distributed depreciable property immediately before the distribution over its basis to the distributee). Whether or not an election under section 754 is in effect, the basis for each of the remaining partner's partnership interests will be $38,000 ($20,000 original contribution, plus $12,000, each partner's original share of the liabilities, plus $6,000, the share of C's liabilities each assumed).

(f) Partnership trial balance. A trial balance of the AB partnership after the distribution in liquidation of C's entire interest would reflect the results set forth in the schedule below. Column I shows the amounts to be reflected in the records if an election is in effect under section 754 with respect to an optional adjustment under section 734(b) to the basis of undistributed partnership property. Column II shows the

amounts to be reflected in the records where an election under section 754 is not in effect. Note that in column II, the total bases for the partnership assets do not equal the total of the bases for the partnership interests.

Example (3). (a) Facts. Assume that the distribution to partner C in example 2 of this paragraph in liquidation of his entire interest in partnership ABC consists of $5,000 in cash and $20,000 worth of partnership inventory with a basis of $14,000.

| | I | | II | |
| | Sec.754, Election in effect | | Sec.754, Election not in effect | |
	Basis	Fair market value	Basis	Fair market value
Cash	$5,000	$5,000	$5,000	$5,000
Accounts receivable	9,000	9,000	9,000	9,000
Inventory	24,000	30,000	24,000	30,000
Depreciable property	29,000	33,000	27,000	33,000
Land	9,000	9,000	9,000	9,000
	76,000	86,000	74,000	86,000
Current liabilities	15,000	15,000	15,000	15,000
Mortgage	21,000	21,000	21,000	21,000
Capital:				
	20,000	25,000	20,000	25,000
	20,000	25,000	20,000	25,000
	76,000	86,000	76,000	86,000

(b) Presence of section 751 property. For the same reason as stated in paragraph (b) of example 2, the partnership inventory items have substantially appreciated in value.

(c) The properties exchanged. In the distribution, C received his share of cash ($5,000) and his share of appreciated inventory items ($13,000). In addition, he received appreciated inventory with a fair market value of $7,000 (and with an adjusted basis to the partnership of $4,900) and $12,000 in money (liabilities assumed). C has relinquished his interest in $16,000 of depreciable property and $3,000 of land. Although C relinquished his interest in $3,000 of accounts receivable, such accounts receivable are inventory items and, therefore, that exchange was not an exchange of section 751 property for other property. Section 751(b) applies only to the extent of the exchange of other property for section 751 property (i.e.,

depreciable property or land for inventory items). Assume that the partners agree that the $7,000 of inventory in excess of C's share was received by him in exchange for $7,000 of depreciable property.

(d) Distributee partner's tax consequences. C's tax consequence on the distributions are as follows:

(1) The section 751(b) sale or exchange. C is treated as if he had received his 7/16ths share of the depreciable property in a current distribution. His basis for that share is $6,125 (42,000/48,000 of $7,000), as determined under paragraph (b)(2)(iii) of this section. Then C is considered as having sold his 7/16ths share of depreciable property to the partnership for $7,000, realizing a gain of $875.

(2) The part of the distribution not under section 751(b). Section 751(b) does not ap-

ply to the balance of the distribution. Before the distribution, C's basis for his partnership interest was $32,000 ($20,000, plus $12,000, his share of partnership liabilities). See section 752(a). This basis is reduced by $6,125, the basis of property treated as distributed to C and sold by him to the partnership. Thus, C will have a basis of $25,875 for the remainder of his partnership interest. Of the $37,000 total distribution to C, $30,000 ($17,000 in money, including liabilities assumed, and $13,000 in inventory) is not within section 751(b). Under section 732(b), C's basis for the inventory with a fair market value of $13,000 (which had an adjusted basis to the partnership of $9,100) is limited to $8,875, the amount of the remaining basis for his partnership interest, $25,875, reduced by $17,000, the money received. Thus, C's total aggregate basis for the inventory received is $15,875 ($7,000 plus $8,875), and not its $14,000 basis in the hands of the partnership.

(e) Partnership's tax consequences. The tax consequences to the partnership on the distribution are as follows:

(1) The section 751(b) sale or exchange. The partnership consisting of the remaining members has $2,100 of ordinary income on the sale of the $7,000 of inventory which had a basis to the partnership of $4,900 (21,000/30,000 of $7,000). This $7,000 of inventory was paid to acquire 7/16ths of C's interest in the depreciable property. Since, under section 751(b), the partnership is treated as buying this property from C, it has a new cost basis for such property. Its basis for the depreciable property is $42,875 ($42,000 less $6,125, the basis of the 7/16ths share considered as distributed to C, plus $7,000, the partnership purchase price for this share).

(2) The part of the distribution not under section 751(b). In the remainder of the distribution to C which was not a sale or exchange of section 751 property for other property, the partnership realizes no gain or loss. See section 731(b). Further, under section 734(a), the

partnership makes no adjustment to the basis of the accounts receivable or the 9/16ths interest in depreciable property which C relinquished. However, if an election under section 754 is in effect, the partnership must make the adjustment required under section 734(b) since the adjusted basis to the partnership of the inventory distributed had been $9,100, and C's basis for such inventory after distribution is only $8,875. The basis of the inventory remaining in the partnership must be increased by $225. Whether or not an election under section 754 is in effect, the basis for each of the remaining partnership interests will be $39,050 ($20,000 original contribution, plus $12,000, each partner's original share of the liabilities, plus $6,000, the share of C's liabilities now assumed, plus $1,050, each partner's share of ordinary income realized by the partnership upon that part of the distribution treated as a sale or exchange).

Example (4). (a) Facts. Assume the same facts as in example 3 of this paragraph, except that the partners did not identify the property which C relinquished in exchange for the $7,000 of inventory which he received in excess of his share.

(b) Presence of section 751 property. For the same reasons stated in paragraph (b) of example 2 of this paragraph, the partnership inventory items have substantially appreciated in value.

(c) The properties exchanged. The analysis stated in paragraph (c) of example 3 of this paragraph is the same in this example, except that, in the absence of a specific agreement among the partners as to the properties exchanged, C will be presumed to have sold to the partnership a proportionate amount of each property in which he relinquished an interest. Thus, in the absence of an agreement, C has received $7,000 of inventory in exchange for his release of 7/19ths of the depreciable property and 7/19ths of the land. ($7,000, fair market value of property released, over $19,000, the sum of the fair market values of C's interest

in the land and C's interest in the depreciable property.)

(d) Distributee partner's tax consequences. C's tax consequences on the distribution are as follows:

(1) The section 751(b) sale or exchange. C is treated as if he had received his 7/19ths shares of the depreciable property and land in a current distribution. His basis for those shares is $6,263 (51,000/57,000 of $7,000, their fair market value), as determined under paragraph (b)(2)(iii) of this section. Then C is considered as having sold his 7/19ths shares of depreciable property and land to the partnership for $7,000, realizing a gain of $737.

(2) The part of the distribution not under section 751(b). Section 751(b) does not apply to the balance of the distribution. Before the distribution C's basis for his partnership interest was $32,000 ($20,000 plus $12,000, his share of partnership liabilities). See section 752(a). This basis is reduced by $6,263, the bases of C's shares of depreciable property and land treated as distributed to him and sold by him to the partnership. Thus, C will have a basis of $25,737 for the remainder of his partnership interest. Of the total $37,000 distributed to C, $30,000 ($17,000 in money, including liabilities assumed, and $13,000 in inventory) is not within section 751(b). Under section 732(b), C's basis for the inventory (with a fair market value of $13,000 and an adjusted basis to the partnership of $9,100) is limited to $8,737, the amount of the remaining basis for his partnership interest ($25,737 less $17,000, money received. Thus, C's total aggregate basis for the inventory he received is $15,737 ($7,000 plus $8,737), and not the $14,000 basis it had in the hands of the partnership.

(e) Partnership's tax consequences. The tax consequences to the partnership on the distribution are as follows:

(1) The section 751(b) sale or exchange. The partnership consisting of the remaining members has $2,100 of ordinary income on the sale of $7,000 of inventory which had a basis to the partnership of $4,900 (21,000/30,000 of $7,000). This $7,000 of inventory was paid to acquire 7/19ths of C's interest in the depreciable property and land. Since, under section 751(b), the partnership is treated as buying this property from C, it has a new cost basis for such property. The bases of the depreciable property and land would be $42,737 and $9,000, respectively. The basis for the depreciable property is computed as follows: The common partnership basis of $42,000 is reduced by the $5,158 basis (42,000/48,000 of $5,895) for C's 7/19ths interest constructively distributed and increased by $5,895 (16,000/19,000 of $7,000), the part of the purchase price allocated to the depreciable property. The basis of the land would be computed in the same way. The $9,000 original partnership basis is reduced by $1,105 basis ($9,000/9,000 of $1,105) of land constructively distributed to C, and increased by $1,105 (3,000/19,000 of $7,000), the portion of the purchase price allocated to the land.

(2) The part of the distribution not under section 751(b). In the remainder of the distribution to C which was not a sale or exchange of section 751 property for other property, the partnership realizes no gain or loss. See section 731(b). Further, under section 734(a), the partnership makes no adjustment to the basis of the accounts receivable or the 12/19ths interests in depreciable property and land which C relinquished. However, if an election under section 754 is in effect, the partnership must make the adjustment required under section 734(b) since the adjusted basis to the partnership of the inventory distributed had been $9,100 and C's basis for such inventory after the distribution is only $8,737. The basis of the inventory remaining in the partnership must be increased by the difference of $363. Whether or not an election under section 754 is in effect, the basis for each of the remaining partnership interests will be $39,050 ($20,000 original contribution plus $12,000, each partner's original share of the liabilities, plus $6,000, the

share of C's liabilities assumed, plus $1,050, each partner's share of ordinary income realized by the partnership upon the part of the distribution treated as a sale or exchange).

Example (5). (a) Facts. Assume that partner C in example 2 of this paragraph agrees to reduce his interest in capital and profits from one-third to one-fifth for a current distribution consisting of $5,000 in cash, and $7,500 of accounts receivable with a basis to the partnership of $7,500. At the same time, the total liabilities of the partnership are not reduced. Therefore, after the distribution, C's share of the partnership liabilities has been reduced by $4,800 from $12,000 (1/3 of $36,000) to $7,200 (1/5 of $36,000).

(b) Presence of section 751 property. For the same reasons as stated in paragraph (b) of example 2 of this paragraph, the partnership inventory items have substantially appreciated in value.

(c) The properties exchanged. C's interest in the fair market value of the partnership properties before and after the distribution can be illustrated by the following table:

| Item | C's interest Fair Market Value | | C received | | |
	One-third before	One-fifth after	Distribution of share	In excess of share	C relinquished
Cash	$5,000	$2,000	$3,000	$2,000	—
Liabilities assumed	(12,000)	(7,200)	—	4,800	—
Inventory items:					
Accounts receivable	3,000	300	2,700	4,800	—
Inventory	10,000	6,000	—	—	$4,000
Depreciable property	16,000	9,600	—	—	6,400
Land	3,000	1,800	—	—	1,200
Total	25,000	12,500	5,700	11,600	11,600

Although C relinquished his interest in $4,000 of inventory and received $4,800 of accounts receivable, both items constitute section 751 property and C has received only $800 of accounts receivable for $800 worth of depreciable property or for an $800 undivided interest in land. In the absence of an agreement identifying the properties exchanged, it is presumed C received $800 for proportionate shares of his interests in both depreciable property and land. To the extent that inventory was exchanged for accounts receivable, or to the extent cash was distributed for the release of C's interest in the balance of the depreciable property and land, the transaction does not fall within section 751(b) and is a current distribution under section 732(a). Thus, the remaining $6,700 of accounts receivable are received in a current distribution.

(d) Distributee partner's tax consequences. C's tax consequences on the distribution are as follows:

(1) The section 751(b) sale or exchange. Assuming that the partners paid $800 worth of accounts receivable for $800 worth of depreciable property, C is treated as if he received the depreciable property in a current distribution, and his basis for the $800 worth of depreciable property is $700 (42,000/48,000 of $800, its fair market value), as determined under paragraph (b)(2)(iii) of this section. Then C is considered as having sold his $800 share of depreciable property to the partnership for $800. On the sale of the depreciable property, C realizes a gain of $100. If, on the other hand, the partners had agreed that C exchanged an $800 interest in the land for $800 worth of accounts receivable, C would realize no gain

or loss, because under paragraph (b)(2)(iii) of this section his basis for the land sold would be $800. In the absence of an agreement, the basis for the depreciable property and land (which C is considered as having received in a current distribution and then sold back to the partnership) would be $716 (51,000/57,000 of $800). In that case, on the sale of the balance of the $800 share of depreciable property and land, C would realize $84 of gain ($800 less $716).

(2) The part of the distribution not under section 751(b). Section 751(b) does not apply to the balance of the distribution. Under section 731, C does not realize either gain or loss on the balance of the distribution. The adjustments to the basis of C's interest are illustrated in the following table:

	If accounts receivable received for depreciable property	If accounts receivable received for land	If there is no agreement
Original basis for C's interest	$32,000	$32,000	$32,000
Less basis of property distributed prior to sec. 751 (b) sale or exchange	–700	–800	–716
	31,300	31,200	31,284
Less money received in distribution	–9,800	–9,800	–9,800
	21,500	21,400	21,484
Less basis of property received in a current distribution under sec. 732	–6,700	–6,700	–6,700
Resulting basis for C's interest	14,800	14,700	14,784

C's basis for the $1,500 worth of accounts receivable which he received in the distribution will be $7,500, composed of $800 for the portion purchased in the section 751(b) exchange, plus $6,700, the basis carried over under section 732(a) for the portion received in the current distribution.

(e) Partnership's tax consequences. The tax consequences to the partnership on the distribution are as follows:

(1) The section 751(b) sale or exchange. The partnership realizes no gain or loss in the section 751 sale or exchange because it had a basis of $800 for the accounts receivable for which it received $800 worth of other property. If the partnership agreed to purchase $800 worth of depreciable property, the partnership basis of depreciable property becomes $42,100 ($42,000 less $700 basis of property constructively distributed to C, plus $800, price of property purchased). If the partnership purchased land with the accounts receivable, there would be no change in the basis of

the land to the partnership because the basis of land distributed was equal to its purchase price. If there were no agreement, the basis of the depreciable property and land would be $51,084 (depreciable property, $42,084 and land $9,000). The basis for the depreciable property is computed as follows: The common partnership basis of $42,000 is reduced by the $590 basis (42,000/48,000 of $674) for C's $674 interest constructively distributed, and increased by $674 (6,400/7,600 of $800), the part of the purchase price allocated to the depreciable property. The basis of the land would be computed in the same way. The $9,000 original partnership basis is reduced by $126 basis (9,000/9,000 of $126) of the land constructively distributed to C, and increased by $126 (1,200/7,600 of $800), the portion of the purchase price allocated to the land.

(2) The part of the distribution not under section 751(b). The partnership will realize no gain or loss in the balance of the distribution under section 731. Since the property in

C's hands after the distribution will have the same basis it had in the partnership, the basis of partnership property remaining in the partnership after the distribution will not be adjusted (whether or not an election under 754 is in effect).

Example (6). (a) Facts. Partnership ABC distributes to partner C, in liquidation of his entire one-third interest in the partnership, a machine which is section 1245 property with a recomputed basis (as defined in section 1245(a)(2)) of $18,000. At the time of the distribution, the balance sheet of the partnership is as follows:

Assets

	Adjusted basis per books	Market value
Cash	$3,000	$3,000
Machine (sec 1245 property)	9,000	15,000
Land	18,000	27,000
Total	30,000	45,000

Liabilities and Capital

	Per books	Value
Liabilities	$0	$0
Capital:		
A	10,000	15,000
B	10,000	15,000
C	10,000	15,000
Total	30,000	45,000

(b) Presence of section 751 property. The section 1245 property is an unrealized receivable of the partnership to the extent of the potential section 1245 income in respect of the property. Since the fair market value of the property ($15,000) is lower than its recomputed basis ($18,000), the excess of the fair market value over its adjusted basis ($9,000), or $6,000, is the potential section 1245 income of the partnership in respect of the property. The partnership has no other section 751 property.

(c) The properties exchanged. In the distribution C received his share of section 751 property (potential section 1245 income of $2,000, i.e., 1/3 of $6,000) and his share of section 1245 property (other than potential section 1245 income) with a fair market value of $3,000, i.e., 1/3 of ($15,000 minus $6,000), and an adjusted basis of $3,000, i.e., 1/3 of $9,000. In addition he received $4,000 of section 751 property (consisting of $4,000 ($6,000 minus $2,000) of potential section 1245 income) and section 1245 property (other than potential section 1245 income) with a fair market value of $6,000 ($9,000 minus $3,000) and an adjusted basis of $6,000 ($9,000 minus $3,000). C relinquished his interest in $1,000 of cash and $9,000 of land. Assume that the partners agree that the $4,000 of section 751 property in excess of C's share was received by him in exchange for $4,000 of land.

(d) Distributee partner's tax consequences. C's tax consequences on the distributions are as follows:

(1) The section 751(b) sale or exchange. C is treated as if he received in a current distribution 4/9ths of his share of the land with a basis of $2,667 (18,000/27,000 × $4,000). Then C is considered as having sold his 4/9ths share of the land to the partnership for $4,000, realizing a gain of $1,333. C's basis for the remainder of his partnership interest after the current distribution is $7,333, i.e., the basis of his partnership interest before the current distribution ($10,000) minus the basis of the land treated as distributed to him ($2,667).

(2) The part of the distribution not under section 751(b). Of the $15,000 total distribution to C, $11,000 ($2,000 of potential section 1245 income and $9,000 section 1245 property other than potential section 1245 income) is not within section 751(b). Under section 732(b) and (c), C's basis for his share of potential section 1245 income is zero (see paragraph (c)(5) of this section) and his basis for $9,000 of section 1245 property (other than potential section 1245 income) is $7,333, i.e., the amount of the remaining basis for his partnership interest ($7,333) reduced by the basis

for his share of potential section 1245 income (zero). Thus C's total aggregate basis for the section 1245 property (fair market value of $15,000) distributed to him is $11,333 ($4,000 plus $7,333). For an illustration of the computation of his recomputed basis for the section 1245 property immediately after the distribution, see example 2 of paragraph (f)(3) of § 1.1245–4.

(e) Partnership's tax consequences. The tax consequences to the partnership on the distribution are as follows:

(1) The section 751(b) sale or exchange. Upon the sale of $4,000 potential section 1245 income, with a basis of zero, for 4/9ths of C's interest in the land, the partnership consisting of the remaining members has $4,000 ordinary income under sections 751(b) and 1245(a)(1). See section 1245(b)(3) and (6)(A). The partnership's new basis for the land is $19,333, i.e., $18,000, less the basis of the 4/9ths share considered as distributed to C ($2,667), plus the partnership purchase price for this share ($4,000).

(2) The part of the distribution not under section 751(b). The analysis under this subparagraph should be made in accordance with the principles illustrated in paragraph (e)(2) of examples 3, 4, and 5 of this paragraph.

§ 1.752–1 Treatment of partnership liabilities.

(a) Definitions. For purposes of section 752, the following definitions apply:

(1) Recourse liability defined. A partnership liability is a recourse liability to the extent that any partner or related person bears the economic risk of loss for that liability under § 1.752–2.

(2) Nonrecourse liability defined. A partnership liability is a nonrecourse liability to the extent that no partner or related person bears the economic risk of loss for that liability under § 1.752–2.

(3) Related person. Related person means a person having a relationship to a partner that is described in § 1.752–4(b).

(4) Liability defined—(i) In general. An obligation is a liability for purposes of section 752 and the regulations thereunder (§ 1.752–1 liability), only if, when, and to the extent that incurring the obligation—

(A) Creates or increases the basis of any of the obligor's assets (including cash);

(B) Gives rise to an immediate deduction to the obligor; or

(C) Gives rise to an expense that is not deductible in computing the obligor's taxable income and is not properly chargeable to capital.

(ii) Obligation. For purposes of this paragraph and § 1.752–7, an obligation is any fixed or contingent obligation to make payment without regard to whether the obligation is otherwise taken into account for purposes of the Internal Revenue Code. Obligations include, but are not limited to, debt obligations, environmental obligations, tort obligations, contract obligations, pension obligations, obligations under a short sale, and obligations under derivative financial instruments such as options, forward contracts, futures contracts, and swaps.

(iii) Other liabilities. For obligations that are not § 1.752–1 liabilities, see §§ 1.752–6 and 1.752–7.

(iv) Effective date. Except as otherwise provided in § 1.752–7(k), this paragraph (a) (4) applies to liabilities that are incurred or assumed by a partnership on or after June 24, 2003.

(b) Increase in partner's share of liabilities. Any increase in a partner's share of partnership liabilities, or any increase in a partner's individual liabilities by reason of the partner's assumption of partnership liabilities, is treated as a contribution of money by that partner to the partnership.

(c) Decrease in partner's share of liabilities. Any decrease in a partner's share of partnership liabilities, or any decrease in a partner's individual liabilities by reason of the partnership's assumption of the individual liabilities of the partner, is treated as a distribution of money by the partnership to that partner.

(d) Assumption of liability. Except as otherwise provided in paragraph (e) of this section, a person is considered to assume a liability only to the extent that:

(1) The assuming person is personally obligated to pay the liability; and

(2) If a partner or related person assumes a partnership liability, the person to whom the liability is owed knows of the assumption and can directly enforce the partner's or related person's obligation for the liability, and no other partner or person that is a related person to another partner would bear the economic risk of loss for the liability immediately after the assumption.

(e) Property subject to a liability. If property is contributed by a partner to the partnership or distributed by the partnership to a partner and the property is subject to a liability of the transferor, the transferee is treated as having assumed the liability, to the extent that the amount of the liability does not exceed the fair market value of the property at the time of the contribution or distribution.

(f) Netting of increases and decreases in liabilities resulting from same transaction. If, as a result of a single transaction, a partner incurs both an increase in the partner's share of the partnership liabilities (or the partner's individual liabilities) and a decrease in the partner's share of the partnership liabilities (or the partner's individual liabilities), only the net decrease is treated as a distribution from the partnership and only the net increase is treated as a contribution of money to the partnership. Generally, the contribution to or distribution from a partnership of property subject to a liability or the termination of the partnership under section 708(b) will require that increases and decreases in liabilities associated with the transaction be netted to determine if a partner will be deemed to have made a contribution or received a distribution as a result of the transaction. When two or more partnerships merge or consolidate under section 708(b)(2)(A), as described in § 1.708–1(c)(3)(i), increases and decreases in partnership liabilities associated with the merger or consolidation are netted by the partners in the terminating partnership and the resulting partnership to determine the effect of the merger under section 752.

(g) Example. The following example illustrates the principles of paragraphs (b), (c), (e), and (f) of this section.

Example (1). Property contributed subject to a liability; netting of increase and decrease in partner's share of liability. B contributes property with an adjusted basis of $1,000 to a general partnership in exchange for a one-third interest in the partnership. At the time of the contribution, the partnership does not have any liabilities outstanding and the property is subject to a recourse debt of $150 and has a fair market value in excess of $150. After the contribution, B remains personally liable to the creditor and none of the other partners bears any of the economic risk of loss for the liability under state law or otherwise. Under paragraph (e) of this section, the partnership is treated as having assumed the $150 liability. As a result, B's individual liabilities decrease by $150. At the same time, however, B's share of liabilities of the partnership increases by $150. Only the net increase or decrease in B's share of the liabilities of the partnership and B's individual liabilities is taken into account in applying section 752. Because there is no net change, B is not treated as having contributed money to the partnership or as having received a distribution of money from the partnership under paragraph (b) or (c) of this section. Therefore B's basis for B's partnership interest is $1,000 (B's basis for the contributed property).

Example (2). Merger or consolidation of partnerships holding property encumbered by liabilities. (i) B owns a 70 percent interest in partnership T. Partnership T's sole asset is property X, which is encumbered by a $900 liability. Partnership T's adjusted basis in property X is $600, and the value of property X is $1,000. B's adjusted basis in its partnership T interest is $420. B also owns a 20 percent interest in partnership S. Partnership S's sole asset is property Y, which is encumbered by a $100 liability. Partnership S's adjusted basis in property Y is $200, the value of property Y is $1,000, and B's adjusted basis in its partnership S interest is $40.

(ii) Partnership T and partnership S merge under section 708(b)(2)(A). Under section 708(b)(2)(A) and § 1.708–1(c)(1), partnership T is considered terminated and the resulting partnership is considered a continuation of partnership S. Partnerships T and S undertake the form described in § 1.708–1(c)(3)(i) for the partnership merger. Under § 1.708–1(c)(3)(i), partnership T contributes property X and its $900 liability to partnership S in exchange for an interest in partnership S. Immediately thereafter, partnership T distributes the interests in partnership S to its partners in liquidation of their interests in partnership T. B owns a 25 percent interest in partnership S after partnership T distributes the interests in partnership S to B.

(iii) Under paragraph (f) of this section, B nets the increases and decreases in its share of partnership liabilities associated with the merger of partnership T and partnership S. Before the merger, B's share of partnership liabilities was $650 (B had a $630 share of partnership liabilities in partnership T and a $20 share of partnership liabilities in partnership S immediately before the merger). B's share of S's partnership liabilities after the merger is $250 (25 percent of S's total partnership liabilities of $1,000). Accordingly, B has a $400 net decrease in its share of S's partnership liabilities. Thus, B is treated as receiving a $400 distribu-tion from partnership S under section 752(b). Because B's adjusted basis in its partnership S interest before the deemed distribution under section 752(b) is $460 ($420 + $40), B will not recognize gain under section 731. After the merger, B's adjusted basis in its partnership S interest is $60.

(h) Sale or exchange of a partnership interest. If a partnership interest is sold or exchanged, the reduction in the transferor partner's share of partnership liabilities is treated as an amount realized under section 1001 and the regulations thereunder. For example, if a partner sells an interest in a partnership for $750 cash and transfers to the purchaser the partner's share of partnership liabilities in the amount of $250, the seller realizes $1,000 on the transaction.

(i) Bifurcation of partnership liabilities. If one or more partners bears the economic risk of loss as to part, but not all, of a partnership liability represented by a single contractual obligation, that liability is treated as two or more separate liabilities for purposes of section 752. The portion of the liability as to which one or more partners bear the economic risk of loss is a recourse liability and the remainder of the liability, if any, is a nonrecourse liability.

§ 1.752–2 Partner's share of recourse liabilities.

(a) In general. A partner's share of a recourse partnership liability equals the portion of that liability, if any, for which the partner or related person bears the economic risk of loss. The determination of the extent to which a partner bears the economic risk of loss for a partnership liability is made under the rules in paragraphs (b) through (k) of this section.

(b) Obligation to make a payment. (1) In general. Except as otherwise provided in this section, a partner bears the economic risk of loss for a partnership liability to the extent that, if the partnership constructively liquidated, the partner or related person would be obligated to make a payment to any person (or a contribution to the partnership) because that liability becomes due and payable and the partner or related person would not be entitled to reimbursement from another partner or person that is a related person to another partner. Upon a constructive liquidation, all of the following events are deemed to occur simultaneously:

(i) All of the partnership's liabilities become payable in full;

(ii) With the exception of property contributed to secure a partnership liability (see § 1.752–2(h)(2)), all of the partnership's assets, including cash, have a value of zero;

(iii) The partnership disposes of all of its property in a fully taxable transaction for no consideration (except relief from liabilities for which the creditors's right to repayment is limited solely to one or more assets of the partnership);

(iv) All items of income, gain, loss, or deduction are allocated among the partners; and

(v) The partnership liquidates.

(2) **Treatment upon deemed disposition.** For purposes of paragraph (b)(1) of this section, gain or loss on the deemed disposition of the partnership's assets is computed in accordance with the following:

(i) If the creditor's right to repayment of a partnership liability is limited solely to one or more assets of the partnership, gain or loss is recognized in an amount equal to the difference between the amount of the liability that is extinguished by the deemed disposition and the tax basis (or book value to the extent section 704(c) or § 1.704–1(b)(4)(i) applies) in those assets.

(ii) A loss is recognized equal to the remaining tax basis (or book value to the extent section 704(c) or § 1.704–1(b)(4)(i) applies) of all the partnership's assets not taken into account in paragraph (b)(2)(i) of this section.

(3) **Obligations recognized.** The determination of the extent to which a partner or related person has an obligation to make a payment

under paragraph (b)(1) of this section is based on the facts and circumstances at the time of the determination. All statutory and contractual obligations relating to the partnership liability are taken into account for purposes of applying this section, including:

(i) Contractual obligations outside the partnership agreement such as guarantees, indemnifications, reimbursement agreements, and other obligations running directly to creditors or to other partners, or to the partnership;

(ii) Obligations to the partnership that are imposed by the partnership agreement, including the obligation to make a capital contribution and to restore a deficit capital account upon liquidation of the partnership; and

(iii) Payment obligations (whether in the form of direct remittances to another partner or a contribution to the partnership) imposed by state law, including the governing state partnership statute.

To the extent that the obligation of a partner to make a payment with respect to a partnership liability is not recognized under this paragraph (b)(3), paragraph (b) of this section is applied as if the obligation did not exist.

(4) **Contingent obligations.** A payment obligation is disregarded if, taking into account all the facts and circumstances, the obligation is subject to contingencies that make it unlikely that the obligation will ever be discharged. If a payment obligation would arise at a future time after the occurrence of an event that is not determinable with reasonable certainty, the obligation is ignored until the event occurs.

(5) **Reimbursement rights.** A partner's or related person's obligation to make a payment with respect to a partnership liability is reduced to the extent that the partner or related person is entitled to reimbursement from another partner or a person who is a related person to another partner.

(6) **Deemed satisfaction of obligation.** For purposes of determining the extent to which a partner or related person has a payment ob-

ligation and the economic risk of loss, it is assumed that all partners and related persons who have obligations to make payments actually perform those obligations, irrespective of their actual net worth, unless the facts and circumstances indicate a plan to circumvent or avoid the obligation. See paragraphs (j) and (k) of this section.

(c) Partner or related person as lender—(1) In general. A partner bears the economic risk of loss for a partnership liability to the extent that the partner or a related person makes (or acquires an interest in) a nonrecourse loan to the partnership and the economic risk of loss for the liability is not borne by another partner.

(2) Wrapped debt. If a partnership liability is owed to a partner or related person and that liability includes (i.e., is "wrapped" around) a nonrecourse obligation encumbering partnership property that is owed to another person, the partnership liability will be treated as two separate liabilities. The portion of the partnership liability corresponding to the wrapped debt is treated as a liability owed to another person.

(d) De minimis exceptions—(1) Partner as lender. The general rule contained in paragraph (c)(1) of this section does not apply if a partner or related person whose interest (directly or indirectly through one or more partnerships including the interest of any related person) in each item of partnership income, gain, loss, deduction, or credit for every taxable year that the partner is a partner in the partnership is 10 percent or less, makes a loan to the partnership which constitutes qualified nonrecourse financing within the meaning of section 465(b)(6) (determined without regard to the type of activity financed).

(2) Partner as guarantor. The general rule contained in paragraph (b)(1) of this section does not apply if a partner or related person whose interest (directly or indirectly through one or more partnerships including the interest of any related person) in each item of partnership income, gain, loss, deduction, or

credit for every taxable year that the partner is a partner in the partnership is 10 percent or less, guarantees a loan that would otherwise be a nonrecourse loan of the partnership and which would constitute qualified nonrecourse financing within the meaning of section 465(b)(6) (without regard to the type of activity financed) if the guarantor had made the loan to the partnership.

(e) Special rule for nonrecourse liability with interest guaranteed by a partner—(1) In general. For purposes of this section, if one or more partners or related persons have guaranteed the payment of more than 25 percent of the total interest that will accrue on a partnership nonrecourse liability over its remaining term, and it is reasonable to expect that the guarantor will be required to pay substantially all of the guaranteed future interest if the partnership fails to do so, then the liability is treated as two separate partnership liabilities. If this rule applies, the partner or related person that has guaranteed the payment of interest is treated as bearing the economic risk of loss for the partnership liability to the extent of the present value of the guaranteed future interest payments. The remainder of the stated principal amount of the partnership liability constitutes a nonrecourse liability. Generally, in applying this rule, it is reasonable to expect that the guarantor will be required to pay substantially all of the guaranteed future interest if, upon a default in payment by the partnership, the lender can enforce the interest guaranty without foreclosing on the property and thereby extinguishing the underlying debt. The guarantee of interest rule continues to apply even after the point at which the amount of guaranteed interest that will accrue is less than 25 percent of the total interest that will accrue on the liability.

(2) Computation of present value. The present value of the guaranteed future interest payments is computed using a discount rate equal to either the interest rate stated in the loan documents, or if interest is imputed under either section 483 or section 1274, the applicable federal rate, compounded semi-annually. The computation takes into account any payment of interest that the partner or related person may be required to make only to the extent that the interest will accrue economically (determined in accordance with section 446 and the regulations thereunder) after the date of the interest guarantee. If the loan document contains a variable rate of interest that is an interest rate based on current values of an objective interest index, the present value is computed on the assumption that the interest determined under the objective interest index on the date of the computation will remain constant over the term of the loan. The term "objective interest index" has the meaning given to it in section 1275 and the regulations thereunder (relating to variable rate debt instruments). Examples of an objective interest index include the prime rate of a designated financial institution, LIBOR (London Interbank Offered Rate), and the applicable federal rate under section 1274(d).

(3) Safe harbor. The general rule contained in paragraph (e)(1) of this section does not apply to a partnership nonrecourse liability if the guarantee of interest by the partner or related person is for a period not in excess of the lesser of five years or one-third of the term of the liability.

(4) De minimis exception. The general rule contained in paragraph (e)(1) of this section does not apply if a partner or related person whose interest (directly or indirectly through one or more partnerships including the interest of any related person) in each item of partnership income, gain, loss, deduction, or credit for every taxable year that the partner is a partner in the partnership is 10 percent of less, guarantees the interest on a loan to that partnership which constitutes qualified nonrecourse financing within the meaning of section 465(b)(6) (determined without regard to the type of activity financed). An allocation of interest to the extent paid by the guarantor is

not treated as a partnership item of deduction or loss subject to the 10 percent or less rule.

(f) Examples. The following examples illustrate the principles of paragraphs (a) through (e) of this section.

Example (1). Determining when a partner bears the economic risk of loss. A and B form a general partnership with each contributing $100 in cash. The partnership purchases an office building on leased land for $1,000 from an unrelated seller, paying $200 in cash and executing a note to the seller for the balance of $800. The note is a general obligation of the partnership, i.e., no partner has been relieved from personal liability. The partnership agreement provides that all items are allocated equally except that tax losses are specially allocated 90% to A and 10% to B and that capital accounts will be maintained in accordance with the regulations under section 704(b), including a deficit capital account restoration obligation on liquidation. In a constructive liquidation, the $800 liability becomes due and payable. All of the partnership's assets, including the building, are deemed to be worthless. The building is deemed sold for a value of zero. Capital accounts are adjusted to reflect the loss on the hypothetical disposition, as follows:

	A	B
Initial contribution	$100	$100
Loss on hypothetical sale	(900)	(100)
	($800)	$0

Other than the partners' obligation to fund negative capital accounts on liquidation, there are no other contractual or statutory payment obligations existing between the partners, the partnership and the lender. Therefore, $800 of the partnership liability is classified as a recourse liability because one or more partners bears the economic risk of loss for non-payment. B has no share of the $800 liability since the constructive liquidation produces no payment obligation for B. A's share of the partnership liability is $800 because A would have an obligation in that amount to make a contribution to the partnership.

Example (2). Recourse liability; deficit restoration obligation. C and D each contribute $500 in cash to the capital of a new general partnership, CD. CD purchases property from an unrelated seller for $1,000 in cash and a $9,000 mortgage note. The note is a general obligation of the partnership, i.e., no partner has been relieved from personal liability. The partnership agreement provides that profits and losses are to be divided 40% to C and 60% to D. C and D are required to make up any deficit in their capital accounts. In a constructive liquidation, all partnership assets are deemed to become worthless and all partnership liabilities become due and payable in full. The partnership is deemed to dispose of all its assets in a fully taxable transaction for no consideration. Capital accounts are adjusted to reflect the loss on the hypothetical disposition, as follows:

	C	D
Initial contribution	$500	$500
Loss on hypothetical sale	(4,000)	(6,000)
	($3,500)	($5,500)

C's capital account reflects a deficit that C would have to make up to $3,500 and D's capital account reflects a deficit that D would have to make up of $5,500. Therefore, the $9,000 mortgage note is a recourse liability because one or more partners bear the economic risk of loss for the liability. C's share of the recourse liability is $3,500 and D's share is $5,500.

Example (3). Guarantee by limited partner; partner deemed to satisfy obligation. E and F form a limited partnership. E, the general partner, contributes $2,000 and F, the limited partner, contributes $8,000 in cash to the partnership. The partnership agreement allocates losses 20% to E and 80% to F until F's capital account is reduced to zero, after which all losses are allocated to E. The partnership purchases depreciable property for $25,000 using its $10,000 cash and a $15,000 recourse

loan from a bank. F guarantee payment of the $15,000 loan to the extent the loan remains unpaid after the bank has exhausted its remedies against the partnership. In a constructive liquidation, the $15,000 liability becomes due and payable. All of the partnership's assets, including the depreciable property, are deemed to be worthless. The depreciable property is deemed sold for a value of zero. Capital accounts are adjusted to reflect the loss on the hypothetical disposition, as follows:

	E	F
Initial contribution	$2,000	$8,000
Loss on hypothetical sale	(17,000)	(8,000)
	($15,000)	$0

E, as a general partner, would be obligated by operation of law to make a net contribution to the partnership of $15,000. Because E is assumed to satisfy that obligation, it is also assumed that F would not have to satisfy F's guarantee. The $15,000 mortgage is treated as a recourse liability because one or more partners bear the economic risk of loss. E's share of the liability is $15,000, and F's share is zero. This would be so even if E's net worth at the time of the determination is less than $15,000, unless the facts and circumstances indicate a plan to circumvent or avoid E's obligation to contribute to the partnership.

Example (4). Partner guarantee with right of subrogation. G, a limited partner in the GH partnership, guarantees a portion of a partnership liability. The liability is a general obligation of the partnership, i.e., no partner has been relieved from personal liability. If under state law G is subrogated to the rights of the lender, G would have the right to recover the amount G paid to the recourse lender from the general partner. Therefore, G does not bear the economic risk of loss for the partnership liability.

Example (5). Bifurcation of partnership liability; guarantee of part of nonrecourse liability. A partnership borrows $10,000, secured by a mortgage on real property. The mortgage note contains an exoneration clause which provides that in the event of default, the holder's only remedy is to foreclose on the property. The holder may not look to any other partnership asset or to any partner to pay the liability. However, to induce the lender to make the loan, a partner guarantees payment of $200 of the loan principal. The exoneration clause does not apply to the partner's guarantee. If the partner paid pursuant to the guarantee, the partner would be subrogated to the rights of the lender with respect to $200 of the mortgage debt, but the partner is not otherwise entitled to reimbursement from the partnership or any partner. For purposes of section 752, $200 of the $10,000 mortgage liability is treated as a recourse liability of the partnership and $9,800 is treated as a nonrecourse liability of the partnership. The partner's share of the recourse liability of the partnership is $200.

Example (6). Wrapped debt. I, an individual, purchases real estate from an unrelated seller for $10,000, paying $1,000 in cash and giving a $9,000 purchase mortgage note on which I has no personal liability and as to which the seller can look only to the property for satisfaction. At a time when the property is worth $15,000, I sells the property to a partnership in which I is a general partner. The partnership pays for the property with a partnership purchase money mortgage note of $15,000 on which neither the partnership nor any partner (or person related to a partner) has personal liability. The $15,000 mortgage note is a wrapped debt that includes the $9,000 obligation to the original seller. The liability is a recourse liability to the extent of $6,000 because I is the creditor with respect to the loan and I bears the economic risk of loss for $6,000. I's share of the recourse liability is $6,000. The remaining $9,000 is treated as a partnership nonrecourse liability that is owed to the unrelated seller.

Example (7). Guarantee of interest by partner treated as part recourse and part nonrecourse. On January 1, 1992, a partnership obtains a $4,000,000 loan secured by a shopping center owned by the partnership. Neither the partnership nor any partner has any personal liability under the loan documents for repayment of the stated principal amount. Interest accrues at a 15 percent annual rate and is payable on December 31 of each year. The principal is payable in a lump sum on December 31, 2006. A partner guarantees payment of 50 percent of each interest payment required by the loan. The guarantee can be enforced without first foreclosing on the property. When the partnership obtains the loan, the present value (discounted at 15 percent, compounded annually) of the future interest payments is $3,508,422, and of the future principal payment is $491,578. If tested on that date, the loan would be treated as a partnership liability of $1,754,211 ($3,508,422.5) for which the guaranteeing partner bears the economic risk of loss and a partnership nonrecourse liability of $2,245,789 ($1,754,211 + $491,578).

Example (8). Contingent obligation not recognized. J and K form a general partnership with cash contributions of $2,500 each. J and K share partnership profits and losses equally. The partnership purchases an apartment building for its $5,000 of cash and a $20,000 nonrecourse loan from a commercial bank. The nonrecourse loan is secured by a mortgage on the building. The loan documents provide that the partnership will be liable for the outstanding balance of the loan on a recourse basis to the extent of any decrease in the value of the apartment building resulting from the partnership's failure properly to maintain the property. There are no facts that establish with reasonable certainty the existence of any liability on the part of the partnership (and its partners) for damages resulting from the partnership's failure properly to maintain the building. Therefore, no partner bears the economic risk of loss, and the liability constitutes a nonrecourse liability. Under § 1.752–3, J and K share this nonrecourse liability equally because they share all profits and losses equally.

(g) Time-value-of-money considerations—(1) In general. The extent to which a partner or related person bears the economic risk of loss is determined by taking into account any delay in the time when a payment or contribution obligation with respect to a partnership liability is to be satisfied. If a payment obligation with respect to a partnership liability is not required to be satisfied within a reasonable time after the liability becomes due and payable, or if the obligation to make a contribution to the partnership is not required to be satisfied before the later of—

(i) The end of the year in which the partner's interest is liquidated, or

(ii) 90 days after the liquidation, the obligation is recognized only to the extent of the value of the obligation.

(2) Valuation of an obligation. The value of a payment or contribution obligation that is not required to be satisfied within the time period specified in paragraph (g)(1) of this section equals the entire principal balance of the obligation only if the obligation bears interest equal to or greater than the applicable federal rate under section 1274(d) at the time of valuation, commencing on—

(i) In the case of a payment obligation, the date that the partnership liability to a creditor or other person to whom the obligation relates becomes due and payable, or

(ii) In the case of a contribution obligation, the date of the liquidation of the partner's interest in the partnership.

If the obligation does not bear interest at a rate at least equal to the applicable federal rate at the time of valuation, the value of the obligation is discounted to the present value of all payments due from the partner or related person (i.e., the imputed principal amount computed under section 1274(b)). For purposes of making this present value determination, the partnership is deemed to have constructively liquidated as of the date on which the payment obligation is valued and the payment

obligation is assumed to be a debt instrument subject to the rules of section 1274 (i.e., the debt instrument is treated as if it were issued for property at the time of the valuation).

(3) Satisfaction of obligation with partner's promissory note. An obligation is not satisfied by the transfer to the obligee of a promissory note by a partner or related person unless the note is readily tradeable on an established securities market.

(4) Example. The following example illustrates the principle of paragraph (g) of this section.

Example. Value of obligation not required to be satisfied within specified time period. A, the general partner, and B, the limited partner, each contributes $10,000 to partnership AB. AB purchases property from an unrelated seller for $20,000 in cash and a $70,000 recourse purchase money note. The partnership agreement provides that profits and losses are to be divided equally. A and B are required to make up any deficit in their capital accounts. While A is required to restore any deficit balance in A's capital account within 90 days after the date of liquidation of the partnership, B is not required to restore any deficit for two years following the date of liquidation. The deficit in B's capital account will not bear interest during that two-year period. In a constructive liquidation, all partnership assets are deemed to become worthless and all partnership liabilities become due and payable in full. The partnership is deemed to dispose of all its assets in a fully taxable transaction for no consideration. Capital accounts are adjusted to reflect the loss on the hypothetical disposition, as follows:

	A	B
Initial contribution	$10,000	$10,000
Loss on hypothetical	(45,000)	(45,000)
sale	(35,000)	(35,000)

A's and B's capital accounts each reflect deficits of $35,000. B's obligation to make a contribution pursuant to B's deficit restoration obligation is recognized only to the extent of the fair market value of that obligation at the time of the constructive liquidation because B is not required to satisfy that obligation by the later of the end of the partnership taxable year in which B's interest is liquidated or within 90 days after the date of the liquidation. Because B's obligation does not bear interest, the fair market value is deemed to equal the imputed principal amount under section 1274(b). Under section 1274(b), the imputed principal amount of a debt instrument equals the present value of all payments due under the debt instrument. Assume the applicable federal rate with respect to B's obligation is 10 percent compounded semiannually. Using this discount rate, the present value of the $35,000 payment that B would be required to make two years after the constructive liquidation to restore the deficit balance in B's capital account equals $28,795. To the extent that B's deficit restoration obligation is not recognized, it is assumed that B's obligation does not exist. Therefore, A, as the sole general partner, would be obligated by operation of law to contribute an additional $6,205 of capital to the partnership. Accordingly, under paragraph (g) of this section, B bears the economic risk of loss for $28,795 and A bears the economic risk of loss for $41,205 ($35,000 + $6,205).

(h) Partner providing property as security for partnership liability—(1) Direct pledge. A partner is considered to bear the economic risk of loss for a partnership liability to the extent of the value of any the partner's or related person's separate property (other than a direct or indirect interest in the partnership) that is pledged as security for the partnership liability.

(2) Indirect pledge. A partner is considered to bear the economic risk of loss for a partnership liability to the extent of the value of any property that the partner contributes to the partnership solely for the purpose of securing a partnership liability. Contributed property is not treated as contributed solely for the purpose of securing a partnership liability unless substantially all of the items of income, gain, loss, and deduction attributable to the contributed property are allocated to the contributing partner, and this allocation is generally greater than the partner's share of other significant items of partnership income, gain, loss, or deduction.

(3) Valuation. The extent to which a partner bears the economic risk of loss for a partnership liability as a result of a direct pledge described in paragraph (h)(1) of this section or an indirect pledge described in paragraph (h)(2) of this section is limited to the net fair market value of the property (pledged property) at the time of the pledge or contribution. If a partner provides additional pledged property, the addition is treated as a new pledge and the net fair market value of the pledged property (including but not limited to the additional property) must be determined at that time. For purposes of this paragraph (h), if pledged property is subject to one or more other obligations, those obligations must be taken into account in determining the net fair market value of pledged property at the time of the pledge or contribution.

(4) Partner's promissory note. For purposes of paragraph (h)(2) of this section, a promissory note of the partner or related person that is contributed to the partnership shall not be taken into account unless the note is readily tradeable on an established securities market.

(i) Treatment of recourse liabilities in tiered partnerships. If a partnership (the "upper-tier partnership") owns (directly or indirectly through one or more partnerships) an interest in another partnership (the "lower-tier partnership"), the liabilities of the lower-tier partnership are allocated to the upper-tier partnership in an amount equal to the sum of the following—

(1) The amount of the economic risk of loss that the upper-tier partnership bears with respect to the liabilities; and

(2) Any other amount of the liabilities with respect to which partners of the upper-tier partnership bear the economic risk of loss.

(j) Anti-abuse rules—(1) In general. An obligation of a partner or related person to make a payment may be disregarded or treated as an obligation of another person for purposes of this section if facts and circumstances indicate that a principal purpose of the arrangement between the parties is to eliminate the partner's economic risk of loss with respect to that obligation or create the appearance of the partner or related person bearing the economic risk of loss when, in fact, the substance of the arrangement is otherwise. Circumstances with respect to which a payment obligation may be disregarded include, but are not limited to, the situations described in paragraphs (j)(2) and (j)(3) of this section.

(2) Arrangements tantamount to a guarantee. Irrespective of the form of a contractual obligation, a partner is considered to bear the economic risk of loss with respect to a partnership liability, or a portion thereof, to the extent that:

(i) The partner or related person undertakes one or more contractual obligations so that the partnership may obtain a loan;

(ii) The contractual obligations of the partner or related person eliminate substantially all the risk to the lender that the partnership will not satisfy its obligations under the loan; and

(iii) One of the principal purposes of using the contractual obligations is to attempt to permit partners (other than those who are directly or indirectly liable for the obligation) to include a portion of the loan in the basis of their partnership interests.

The partners are considered to bear the economic risk of loss for the liability in accordance with their relative economic burdens for the liability pursuant to the contractual obligations. For example, a lease between a partner and a partnership which is not on commercially reasonable terms may be tantamount

to a guarantee by the partner of a partnership liability.

(3) Plan to circumvent or avoid the obligation. An obligation of a partner to make a payment is not recognized if the facts and circumstances evidence a plan to circumvent or avoid the obligation.

(4) Example. The following example illustrates the principle of paragraph (j)(3) of this section.

Example. Plan to circumvent or avoid obligation. A and B form a general partnership. A, a corporation, contributes $20,000 and B contributes $80,000 to the partnership. A is obligated to restore any deficit in its partnership capital account. The partnership agreement allocates losses 20% to A and 80% to B until B's capital account is reduced to zero, after which all losses are allocated to A. The partnership purchases depreciable property for $250,000 using its $100,000 cash and a $150,000 recourse loan from a bank. B guarantees payment of the $150,000 loan to the extent the loan remains unpaid after the bank has exhausted its remedies against the partnership. A is a subsidiary, formed by a parent of a consolidated group, with capital limited to $20,000 to allow the consolidated group to enjoy the tax losses generated by the property while at the same time limiting its monetary exposure for such losses. These facts, when considered together with B's guarantee, indicate a plan to circumvent or avoid A's obligation to contribute to the partnership. The rules of section 752 must be applied as if A's obligation to contribute did not exist. Accordingly, the $150,000 liability is a recourse liability that is allocated entirely to B.

(k) Effect of a disregarded entity—(1) In general. In determining the extent to which a partner bears the economic risk of loss for a partnership liability, an obligation under paragraph (b)(1) of this section (§ 1.752–2(b)(1) payment obligation) of a business entity that is disregarded as an entity separate from its owner under sections 856(i) or 1361(b)(3) or

§§ 301.7701–1 through 301.7701–3 of this chapter (disregarded entity) is taken into account only to the extent of the net value of the disregarded entity as of the allocation date (as defined in paragraph (k)(2)(iv) of this section) that is allocated to the partnership liability as determined under the rules of this paragraph (k). The rules of this paragraph (k) do not apply to a § 1.752–2(b)(1) payment obligation of a disregarded entity to the extent that the owner of the disregarded entity is otherwise required to make a payment (that satisfies the requirements of paragraph (b)(1) of this section) with respect to the obligation of the disregarded entity.

(2) Net value of a disregarded entity—(i) Definition. For purposes of this paragraph (k), the net value of a disregarded entity equals the following—

(A) The fair market value of all assets owned by the disregarded entity that may be subject to creditors' claims under local law (including the disregarded entity's enforceable rights to contributions from its owner and the fair market value of an interest in any partnership other than the partnership for which net value is being determined, but excluding the disregarded entity's interest in the partnership for which the net value is being determined and the net fair market value of property pledged to secure a liability of the partnership under paragraph (h)(1) of this section); less

(B) All obligations of the disregarded entity that do not constitute § 1.752–2(b)(1) payment obligations of the disregarded entity.

(ii) Timing of the net value determination—(A) Initial determination. If a partnership interest is held by a disregarded entity, and the partnership has or incurs a liability, all or a portion of which may be allocable to the owner of the disregarded entity under this paragraph (k), the disregarded entity's net value must be initially determined on the allocation date described in paragraph (k)(2)(iv) of this section.

(B) Other events. If a partnership interest is held by a disregarded entity, and the partnership has or incurs a liability, all or a portion of which may be allocable to the owner of the disregarded entity under this paragraph (k), then, if one or more valuation events (as defined in paragraph (k)(2)(iii) of this section) occur during the partnership taxable year, except as provided in paragraph (k)(2)(iii)(E) of this section, the net value of the disregarded entity is determined on the allocation date described in paragraph (k)(2)(iv) of this section.

(iii) Valuation events. The following are valuation events for purposes of this paragraph (k):

(A) A more than *de minimis* contribution to a disregarded entity of property other than property pledged to secure a partnership liability under paragraph (h)(1) of this section, unless the contribution is followed immediately by a contribution of equal net value by the disregarded entity to the partnership for which the net value of the disregarded entity otherwise would be determined, taking into account any obligations assumed or taken subject to in connection with such contributions.

(B) A more than *de minimis* distribution from a disregarded entity of property other than property pledged to secure a partnership liability under paragraph (h)(1) of this section, unless the distribution immediately follows a distribution of equal net value to the disregarded entity by the partnership for which the net value of the disregarded entity otherwise would be determined, taking into account any obligations assumed or taken subject to in connection with such distributions.

(C) A change in the legally enforceable obligation of the owner of the disregarded entity to make contributions to the disregarded entity.

(D) The incurrence, refinancing, or assumption of an obligation of the disregarded entity that does not constitute a § 1.752–2(b)(1) payment obligation of the disregarded entity.

(E) The sale or exchange of a non-*de minimis* asset of the disregarded entity (in a transaction that is not in the ordinary course of business). In this case, the net value of the disregarded entity may be adjusted only to reflect the difference, if any, between the fair market value of the asset at the time of the sale or exchange and the fair market value of the asset when the net value of the disregarded entity was last determined. The adjusted net value is taken into account for purposes of § 1.752–2(k)(1) as of the allocation date.

(iv) Allocation Date. For purposes of this paragraph (k), the allocation date is the earlier of—

(A) The first date occurring on or after the date on which the requirement to determine the net value of a disregarded entity arises under paragraph (k)(2)(ii)(A) or (B) of this section on which the partnership otherwise determines a partner's share of partnership liabilities under §§ 1.705–1(a) and 1.752–4(d); or

(B) The end of the partnership's taxable year in which the requirement to determine the net value of a disregarded entity arises under paragraph (k)(2)(ii)(A) or (B) of this section.

(3) Multiple liabilities. If one or more disregarded entities have § 1.752–2(b)(1) payment obligations with respect to one or more liabilities of a partnership, the partnership must allocate the net value of each disregarded entity among partnership liabilities in a reasonable and consistent manner, taking into account the relative priorities of those liabilities.

(4) Reduction in net value of a disregarded entity. For purposes of this paragraph (k), the net value of a disregarded entity is determined by taking into account a subsequent reduction in the net value of the disregarded entity if, at the time the net value of the disregarded entity is determined, it is anticipated that the net value of the disregarded entity will subsequently be reduced and the reduction is part of a plan that has as one of its principal purposes creating the appearance that a partner bears the economic risk of loss for a partnership liability.

(5) Information to be provided by the owner of a disregarded entity. A partner that may be treated as bearing the economic risk of loss for a partnership liability based upon a § 1.752–2(b)(1) payment obligation of a disregarded entity must provide information to the partnership as to the entity's tax classification and the net value of the disregarded entity that is appropriately allocable to the partnership's liabilities on a timely basis.

(6) Examples. The following examples illustrate the rules of this paragraph (k):

Example (1). Disregarded entity with net value of zero. (i) In 2007, A forms a wholly owned domestic limited liability company, LLC, with a contribution of $100,000. A has no liability for LLC's debts, and LLC has no enforceable right to contribution from A. Under § 301.7701–3(b)(1)(ii) of this chapter, LLC is a disregarded entity. Also in 2007, LLC contributes $100,000 to LP, a limited partnership with a calendar year taxable year, in exchange for a general partnership interest in LP, and B and C each contributes $100,000 to LP in exchange for a limited partnership interest in LP. The partnership agreement provides that only LLC is required to make up any deficit in its capital account. On January 1, 2008, LP borrows $300,000 from a bank and uses $600,000 to purchase nondepreciable property. The $300,000 debt is secured by the property and is also a general obligation of LP. LP makes payments of only interest on its $300,000 debt during 2008. LP has a net taxable loss in 2008, and under §§ 1.705–1(a) and 1.752–4(d), LP determines its partners' shares of the $300,000 debt at the end of its taxable year, December 31, 2008. As of that date, LLC holds no assets other than its interest in LP.

(ii) Because LLC is a disregarded entity, A is treated as the partner in LP for Federal tax purposes. Only LLC has an obligation to make a payment on account of the $300,000 debt if LP were to constructively liquidate as

described in paragraph (b)(1) of this section. Therefore, under this paragraph (k), A is treated as bearing the economic risk of loss for LP's $300,000 debt only to the extent of LLC's net value. Because that net value is $0 on December 31, 2008, when LP determines its partners' shares of its $300,000 debt, A is not treated as bearing the economic risk of loss for any portion of LP's $300,000 debt. As a result, LP's $300,000 debt is characterized as nonrecourse under § 1.752–1(a) and is allocated as required by § 1.752–3.

Example (2). Disregarded entity with positive net value. (i) The facts are the same as in *Example 1* except that on January 1, 2009, A contributes $250,000 to LLC. On January 5, 2009, LLC borrows $100,000 and LLC shortly thereafter uses the $350,000 to purchase unimproved land. LP makes payments of only interest on its $300,000 debt during 2009. As of December 31, 2009, LLC holds its interest in LP and the land, the value of which has declined to $275,000. LP has a net taxable loss in 2009, and under §§ 1.705–1(a) and 1.752–4(d), LP determines its partners' shares of the $300,000 debt at the end of its taxable year, December 31, 2009.

(ii) A's contribution of $250,000 to LLC on January 1, 2009, constitutes a more than *de minimis* contribution of property to LLC under paragraph (k)(2)(iii)(A) of this section and the debt incurred by LLC on January 5, 2009, is a valuation event under paragraph (k)(2)(iii)(D) of this section. Accordingly, under paragraph (k)(2)(ii) of this section, LLC's value must be redetermined as of the end of the partnership's taxable year. At that time LLC's net value is $175,000 ($275,000 land – $100,000 debt). Accordingly, $175,000 of LP's $300,000 debt will be recharacterized as recourse under § 1.752–1(a) and allocated to A under this section, and the remaining $125,000 of LP's $300,000 debt will remain characterized as nonrecourse under § 1.752–1(a) and is allocated as required by § 1.752–3.

Example (3). Multiple partnership liabilities. (i) The facts are the same as in *Example 2* except that on January 1, 2010, A forms another wholly owned domestic limited liability company, LLC2, with a contribution of $120,000. Shortly thereafter, LLC2 uses the $120,000 to purchase stock in X corporation. A has no liability for LLC2's debts, and LLC2 has no enforceable right to contribution from A. Under § 301.7701–3(b)(1)(ii) of this chapter, LLC2 is a disregarded entity. On July 1, 2010, LP borrows $100,000 from a bank and uses the $100,000 to purchase nondepreciable property. The $100,000 debt is secured by the property and is also a general obligation of LP. The $100,000 debt is senior in priority to LP's existing $300,000 debt. Also, on July 1, 2010, LLC2 agrees to guarantee both LP's $100,000 and $300,000 debts. LP makes payments of only interest on both its $100,000 and $300,000 debts during 2010. LP has a net taxable loss in 2010 and, under §§ 1.705–1(a) and 1.752–4(d), must determine its partners' shares of its $100,000 and $300,000 debts at the end of its taxable year, December 31, 2010. As of that date, LLC holds its interest in LP and the land, and LLC2 holds the X corporation stock which has appreciated in value to $140,000.

(ii) Both LLC and LLC2 have obligations to make a payment on account of LP's debts if LP were to constructively liquidate as described in paragraph (b)(1) of this section. Therefore, under paragraph (k)(1) of this section, A is treated as bearing the economic risk of loss for LP's $100,000 and $300,000 debts only to the extent of the net values of LLC and LLC2, as allocated among those debts in a reasonable and consistent manner pursuant to paragraph (k)(3) of this section.

(iii) No events have occurred that would allow a valuation of LLC under paragraph (k)(2)(iii) of this section. Therefore, LLC's net value remains $175,000. LLC2's net value as of December 31, 2010, when LP determines its partners' shares of its liabilities, is $140,000. Under paragraph (k)(3) of this section, LP

must allocate the net values of LLC and LLC2 between its $100,000 and $300,000 debts in a reasonable and consistent manner. Because the $100,000 debt is senior in priority to the $300,000 debt, LP first allocates the net values of LLC and LLC2, *pro rata*, to its $100,000 debt. Thus, LP allocates $56,000 of LLC's net value and $44,000 of LLC2's net value to its $100,000 debt, and A is treated as bearing the economic risk of loss for all of LP's $100,000 debt. As a result, all of LP's $100,000 debt is characterized as recourse under § 1.752–1(a) and is allocated to A under this section. LP then allocates the remaining $119,000 of LLC's net value and LLC2's $96,000 net value to its $300,000 debt, and A is treated as bearing the economic risk of loss for a total of $215,000 of the $300,000 debt. As a result, $215,000 of LP's $300,000 debt is characterized as recourse under § 1.752–1(a) and is allocated to A under this section, and the remaining $85,000 of LP's $300,000 debt is characterized as nonrecourse under § 1.752–1(a) and is allocated as required by § 1.752–3. This example illustrates one reasonable method of allocating net values of disregarded entities among multiple partnership liabilities.

Example (4). Disregarded entity with interests in two partnerships. (i) In 2007, B forms a wholly owned domestic limited liability company, LLC, with a contribution of $175,000. B has no liability for LLC's debts and LLC has no enforceable right to contribution from B. Under § 301.7701–3(b)(1)(ii) of this chapter, LLC is a disregarded entity. LLC contributes $50,000 to LP1 in exchange for a general partnership interest in LP1, and $25,000 to LP2 in exchange for a general partnership interest in LP2. LLC retains the $100,000 in cash. Both LP1 and LP2 have taxable years that end on December 31 and, under both LP1's and LP2's partnership agreements, only LLC is required to make up any deficit in its capital account. During 2007, LP1 and LP2 incur partnership liabilities that are general obligations of the partnership. LP1 borrows $300,000 (Debt 1), and LP2 borrows $60,000 (Debt 2) and

$40,000 (Debt 3). Debt 2 is senior in priority to Debt 3. LP1 and LP2 make payments of only interest on Debts 1, 2, and 3 during 2007. As of the end of taxable year 2007, LP1 and LP2 each have a net taxable loss and must determine its partners' shares of partnership liabilities under §§ 1.705–1(a) and 1.752–4(d) as of December 31, 2007. As of that date, LLC's interest in LP1 has a fair market value of $45,000, and LLC's interest in LP2 has a fair market value of $15,000.

(ii) Because LLC is a disregarded entity, B is treated as the partner in LP1 and LP2 for federal tax purposes. Only LLC has an obligation to make a payment on account of Debts 1, 2, and 3 if LP1 and LP2 were to constructively liquidate as described in paragraph (b)(1) of this section. Therefore, under this paragraph (k), B is treated as bearing the economic risk of loss for LP1's and LP2's liabilities only to the extent of LLC's net value as of the allocation date, December 31, 2007.

(iii) LLC's net value with respect to LP1 is $115,000 ($100,000 cash + $15,000 interest in LP2). Therefore, under paragraph (k)(1) of this section, B is treated as bearing the economic risk of loss for $115,000 of Debt 1. Accordingly, $115,000 of LP1's $300,000 debt is characterized as recourse under § 1.752–1(a) and is allocated to B under this section. The balance of Debt 1 ($185,000) is characterized as nonrecourse under § 1.752–1(a) and is allocated as required by § 1.752–3.

(iv) LLC's net value with respect to LP2 is $145,000 ($100,000 cash + $45,000 interest in LP1). Therefore, under paragraph (k)(1) of this section, B is treated as bearing the economic risk of loss with respect to Debts 2 and 3 only to the extent of $145,000. Because Debt 2 is senior in priority to Debt 3, LP2 first allocates $60,000 of LLC's net value to Debt 2. LP2 then allocates $40,000 of LLC's net value to Debt 3. As a result, both Debts 2 and 3 are characterized as recourse under § 1.752–1(a) and allocated to B. This example illustrates one reasonable method of allocating the net

value of a disregarded entity among multiple partnership liabilities.

§ 1.752–2T Partner's share of recourse liabilities (temporary).

(a) through **(b)(2)** **[Reserved].** For further guidance, see § 1.752–2(a) through (b)(2).

(3) Obligations recognized—(i) In general. The determination of the extent to which a partner or related person has an obligation to make a payment under § 1.752–2(b)(1) is based on the facts and circumstances at the time of the determination. To the extent that the obligation of a partner or related person to make a payment with respect to a partnership liability is not recognized under this paragraph (b)(3), § 1.752–2(b) is applied as if the obligation did not exist. All statutory and contractual obligations relating to the partnership liability are taken into account for purposes of applying this section, including—

(A) Contractual obligations outside the partnership agreement such as guarantees, indemnifications, reimbursement agreements, and other obligations running directly to creditors, to other partners, or to the partnership;

(B) Obligations to the partnership that are imposed by the partnership agreement, including the obligation to make a capital contribution and to restore a deficit capital account upon liquidation of the partnership as described in § 1.704–1(b)(2)(ii)(*b*)(*3*) (taking into account § 1.704–1(b)(2)(ii)(*c*)); and

(C) Payment obligations (whether in the form of direct remittances to another partner or a contribution to the partnership) imposed by state or local law, including the governing state or local law partnership statute.

(ii) Special rules for bottom dollar payment obligations—(A) In general. For purposes of § 1.752–2, a bottom dollar payment obligation (as defined in paragraph (b)(3)(ii)(C) of this section) is not recognized under this paragraph (b)(3).

(B) Exception. If a partner or related person has a payment obligation that would be recognized under this paragraph (b)(3) (initial payment obligation) but for the effect of an indemnity, reimbursement agreement, or similar arrangement, such bottom dollar payment obligation is recognized under this paragraph (b)(3) if, taking into account the indemnity, reimbursement agreement, or similar arrangement, the partner or related person is liable for at least 90 percent of the partner's or related person's initial payment obligation.

(C) Definition of bottom dollar payment obligation—(1) In general. Except as provided in paragraph (b)(3)(ii)(C)(2) of this section, a *bottom dollar payment obligation* is a payment obligation that is the same as or similar to a payment obligation or arrangement described in this paragraph (b)(3)(ii)(C)(*1*).

(i) With respect to a guarantee or similar arrangement, any payment obligation other than one in which the partner or related person is or would be liable up to the full amount of such partner's or related person's payment obligation if, and to the extent that, any amount of the partnership liability is not otherwise satisfied.

(ii) With respect to an indemnity or similar arrangement, any payment obligation other than one in which the partner or related person is or would be liable up to the full amount of such partner's or related person's payment obligation, if, and to the extent that, any amount of the indemnitee's or benefited party's payment obligation that is recognized under this paragraph (b)(3) is satisfied.

(iii) An arrangement with respect to a partnership liability that uses tiered partnerships, intermediaries, senior and subordinate liabilities, or similar arrangements to convert what would otherwise be a single liability into multiple liabilities if, based on the facts and circumstances, the liabilities were incurred pursuant to a common plan, as part of a single transaction or arrangement, or as part of a series of related transactions or arrangements, and with a principal purpose of avoiding having at least one of such liabilities or payment obligations with respect to such liabilities being treated as a bottom dollar payment obligation as described in paragraph (b)(3)(ii)(C)(*1*) (*i*) or (*ii*) of this section.

(2) Exceptions. A payment obligation is not a bottom dollar payment obligation merely because a maximum amount is placed on the partner's or related person's payment obligation, a partner's or related person's payment obligation is stated as a fixed percentage of every dollar of the partnership liability to which such obligation relates, or there is a right of proportionate contribution running between partners or related persons who are co-obligors with respect to a payment obligation for which each of them is jointly and severally liable.

(3) Benefited party defined. For purposes of § 1.752–2, a *benefited party* is the person to whom a partner or related person has the payment obligation.

(D) Disclosure of bottom dollar payment obligations. A partnership must disclose to the Internal Revenue Service a bottom dollar payment obligation (including a bottom dollar payment obligation that is recognized under paragraph (b)(3)(ii)(B) of this section) with respect to a partnership liability on a completed Form 8275, Disclosure Statement, or successor form, attached to the return of the partnership for the taxable year in which the bottom dollar payment obligation is undertaken or modified, that includes all of the following information:

(1) A caption identifying the statement as a disclosure of a bottom dollar payment obligation under section 752.

(2) An identification of the payment obligation with respect to which disclosure is made.

(3) The amount of the payment obligation.

(4) The parties to the payment obligation.

(5) A statement of whether the payment obligation is treated as recognized for purposes of this paragraph (b)(3).

(6) If the payment obligation is recognized under paragraph (b)(3)(ii)(B) of this section, the facts and circumstances that clearly establish that a partner or related person is liable for up to 90 percent of the partner's or related person's initial payment obligation and, but for an indemnity, reimbursement agreement, or similar arrangement, the partner's or related person's initial payment obligation would have been recognized under this paragraph (b)(3).

(iii) Special rule for indemnities and reimbursement agreements. An indemnity, reimbursement agreement, or similar arrangement will be recognized under this paragraph (b)(3) only if, before taking into account the indemnity, reimbursement agreement, or similar arrangement, the indemnitee's or other benefited party's payment obligation is recognized under this paragraph (b)(3), or would be recognized under this paragraph (b)(3) if such person were a partner or related person.

(b)(4) through (e) [Reserved]. For further guidance, see § 1.752–2(b)(4) through (e).

(f) Examples 1 through 9 [Reserved]. For further guidance, see § 1.752–2(f) *Examples 1 through 9.*

Example (10). Guarantee of first and last dollars. (i) A, B, and C are equal members of a limited liability company, ABC, that is treated as a partnership for federal tax purposes. ABC borrows $1,000 from Bank. A guarantees payment of up to $300 of the ABC liability if any amount of the full $1,000 liability is not recovered by Bank. B guarantees payment of up to $200, but only if the Bank otherwise recovers less than $200. Both A and B waive their rights of contribution against each other.

(ii) Because A is obligated to pay up to $300 if, and to the extent that, any amount of the $1,000 partnership liability is not recovered by Bank, A's guarantee is not a bottom dollar payment obligation under paragraph (b)(3)(ii) (C) of this section. Therefore, A's payment obligation is recognized under paragraph (b)(3)

of this section. The amount of A's economic risk of loss under § 1.752–2(b)(1) is $300.

(iii) Because B is obligated to pay up to $200 only if and to the extent that the Bank otherwise recovers less than $200 of the $1,000 partnership liability, B's guarantee is a bottom dollar payment obligation under paragraph (b)(3)(ii)(C) of this section and, therefore, is not recognized under paragraph (b)(3)(ii)(A) of this section. Accordingly, B bears no economic risk of loss under § 1.752–2(b)(1) for ABC's liability.

(iv) In sum, $300 of ABC's liability is allocated to A under § 1.752–2(a), and the remaining $700 liability is allocated to A, B, and C under § 1.752–3.

Example (11). Indemnification of guarantees. (i) The facts are the same as in *Example 10*, except that, in addition, C agrees to indemnify A up to $100 that A pays with respect to its guarantee and agrees to indemnify B fully with respect to its guarantee.

(ii) The determination of whether C's indemnity is recognized under paragraph (b)(3) of this section is made without regard to whether C's indemnity itself causes A's guarantee not to be recognized. Because A's obligation would be recognized but for the effect of C's indemnity and C is obligated to pay A up to the full amount of C's indemnity if A pays any amount on its guarantee of ABC's liability, C's indemnity of A's guarantee is not a bottom dollar payment obligation under paragraph (b)(3)(ii)(C) of this section and, therefore, is recognized under paragraph (b)(3) of this section. The amount of C's economic risk of loss under § 1.752–2(b)(1) for its indemnity of A's guarantee is $100.

(iii) Because C's indemnity is recognized under paragraph (b)(3) of this section, A is treated as liable for $200 only to the extent any amount beyond $100 of the partnership liability is not satisfied. Thus, A is not liable if, and to the extent, any amount of the partnership liability is not otherwise satisfied, and

the exception in paragraph (b)(3)(ii)(B) of this section does not apply. As a result, A's guarantee is a bottom dollar payment obligation under paragraph (b)(3)(ii)(C) of this section and is not recognized under paragraph (b)(3)(ii)(A) of this section. Therefore, A bears no economic risk of loss under § 1.752–2(b)(1) for ABC's liability.

(iv) Because B's obligation is not recognized under paragraph (b)(3)(ii) of this section independent of C's indemnity of B's guarantee, C's indemnity is not recognized under paragraph (b)(3)(iii) of this section. Therefore, C bears no economic risk of loss under § 1.752–2(b)(1) for its indemnity of B's guarantee.

(v) In sum, $100 of ABC's liability is allocated to C under § 1.752–2(a) and the remaining $900 liability is allocated to A, B, and C under § 1.752–3.

(g) through (j)(1) [Reserved]. For further guidance, see § 1.752–2(g) through (j)(1).

(2) Arrangements tantamount to a guarantee—(i) In general. Irrespective of the form of a contractual obligation, the Commissioner may treat a partner as bearing the economic risk of loss with respect to a partnership liability, or a portion thereof, to the extent that—

(A) The partner or related person undertakes one or more contractual obligations so that the partnership may obtain or retain a loan;

(B) The contractual obligations of the partner or related person significantly reduce the risk to the lender that the partnership will not satisfy its obligations under the loan, or a portion thereof; and

(C) With respect to the contractual obligations described in paragraphs (j)(2)(i)(A) and (B) of this section—

(1) One of the principal purposes of using the contractual obligations is to attempt to permit partners (other than those who are directly or indirectly liable for the obligation) to include a portion of the loan in the basis of their partnership interests; or

(2) Another partner, or a person related to another partner, enters into a payment obligation and a principal purpose of the arrangement is to cause the payment obligation described in paragraphs (j)(2)(i)(A) and (B) of this section to be disregarded under paragraph (b)(3) of this section.

(ii) Economic risk of loss. For purposes of this paragraph (j)(2), partners are considered to bear the economic risk of loss for a liability in accordance with their relative economic burdens for the liability pursuant to the contractual obligations. For example, a lease between a partner and a partnership that is not on commercially reasonable terms may be tantamount to a guarantee by the partner of the partnership liability.

(j)(3) through (*l*)(1) [Reserved]. For further guidance, see § 1.752–2(j)(3) through (*l*) (1).

(2) Paragraph (b)(3), paragraph (f) *Examples 10* and *11*, and paragraph (j)(2) of this section apply to liabilities incurred or assumed by a partnership and payment obligations imposed or undertaken with respect to a partnership liability on or after October 5, 2016, other than liabilities incurred or assumed by a partnership and payment obligations imposed or undertaken pursuant to a written binding contract in effect prior to that date. Partnerships may apply paragraph (b)(3), paragraph (f) *Examples 10* and *11*, and paragraph (j)(2) of this section to all of their liabilities as of the beginning of the first taxable year of the partnership ending on or after October 5, 2016. The rules applicable to liabilities incurred or assumed (or subject to a written binding contract in effect) prior to October 5, 2016 are contained in § 1.752–2 in effect prior to October 5, 2016 (see 26 CFR part 1 revised as of April 1, 2016).

(3) If a partner has a share of a recourse partnership liability under § 1.752–2(a) as a result of bearing the economic risk of loss

under § 1.752–2(b) immediately prior to October 5, 2016 (Transition Partner), the partnership (Transition Partnership) may choose not to apply paragraph (b)(3), paragraph (f) *Examples 10* and *11*, and paragraph (j)(2)(i) (C)(2) of this section to the extent the amount of the Transition Partner's share of liabilities under § 1.752–2(a) as a result of bearing the economic risk of loss under § 1.752–2(b) immediately prior to October 5, 2016 exceeds the amount of the Transition Partner's adjusted basis in its partnership interest as determined under § 1.705–1 at such time (Grandfathered Amount). A Transition Partner that is a partnership, S corporation, or a business entity disregarded as an entity separate from its owner under section 856(i) or 1361(b)(3) or §§ 301.7701–1 through 301.7701–3 of this chapter ceases to qualify as a Transition Partner if the direct or indirect ownership of that Transition Partner changes by 50 percent or more. The Transition Partnership may continue to apply the rules under § 1.752–2 in effect prior to October 5, 2016, with respect to a Transition Partner for payment obligations described in § 1.752–2(b) to the extent of the Transition Partner's adjusted Grandfathered Amount for the seven-year period beginning October 5, 2016. The termination of a Transition Partnership under section 708(b)(1)(B) and applicable regulations does not affect the Grandfathered Amount of a Transition Partner that remains a partner in the new partnership (as described in § 1.708–1(b)(4)), and the new partnership is treated as a continuation of the Transition Partnership for purposes of this paragraph (*l*)(3). However, a Transition Partner's Grandfathered Amount is reduced (not below zero), but never increased by—

(i) Upon the sale of any property by the Transition Partnership, an amount equal to the excess of any gain allocated for federal income tax purposes to the Transition Partner by the Transition Partnership (including amounts allocated under section 704(c) and applicable regulations) over the product of the total amount realized by the Transition Partnership from the property sale multiplied by the Transition Partner's percentage interest in the partnership; and

(ii) An amount equal to any decrease in the Transition Partner's share of liabilities to which the rules of this paragraph (*l*)(3) apply, other than by operation of paragraph (*l*)(3)(i) of this section.

§ 1.752–3 Partner's share of nonrecourse liabilities.

(a) In general. A partner's share of the nonrecourse liabilities of a partnership equals the sum of paragraphs (a)(1) through (a)(3) of this section as follows—

(1) The partner's share of partnership minimum gain determined in accordance with the rules of section 704(b) and the regulations thereunder;

(2) The amount of any taxable gain that would be allocated to the partner under section 704(c) (or in the same manner as section 704(c) in connection with a revaluation of partnership property) if the partnership disposed of (in a taxable transaction) all partnership property subject to one or more nonrecourse liabilities of the partnership in full satisfaction of the liabilities and for no other consideration; and

(3) The partner's share of the excess nonrecourse liabilities (those not allocated under paragraphs (a)(1) and (a)(2) of this section) of the partnership as determined in accordance with the partner's share of partnership profits. The partner's interest in partnership profits is determined by taking into account all facts and circumstances relating to the economic arrangement of the partners. The partnership agreement may specify the partners' interests in partnership profits for purposes of allocating excess nonrecourse liabilities provided the interests so specified are reasonably consistent with allocations (that have substantial economic effect under the section 704(b) regulations) of some other significant item of partnership income or gain (significant item method). Al-ternatively, excess nonrecourse liabilities may be allocated among the partners in accordance with the manner in which it is reasonably expected that the deductions attributable to those nonrecourse liabilities will be allocated (alternative method). Additionally, the partnership may first allocate an excess nonrecourse liability to a partner up to the amount of built-in gain that is allocable to the partner on section 704(c) property (as defined under § 1.704–3(a)(3)(ii)) or property for which reverse section 704(c) allocations are applicable (as described in § 1.704–3(a)(6)(i)) where such property is subject to the nonrecourse liability to the extent that such built-in gain exceeds the gain described in paragraph (a)(2) of this section with respect to such property (additional method). The significant item method, alternative method, and additional method do not apply for purposes of § 1.707–5(a)(2). To the extent that a partnership uses this additional method and the entire amount of the excess nonrecourse liability is not allocated to the contributing partner, the partnership must allocate the remaining amount of the excess nonrecourse liability under one of the other methods in this paragraph (a)(3). Excess nonrecourse liabilities are not required to be allocated under the same method each year.

(b) Allocation of a single nonrecourse liability among multiple properties—(1) In general. For purposes of determining the amount of taxable gain under paragraph (a)(2) of this section, if a partnership holds multiple properties subject to a single nonrecourse liability, the partnership may allocate the liability among the multiple properties under any reasonable method. A method is not reasonable if it allocates to any item of property an amount of the liability that, when combined with any other liabilities allocated to the property, is in excess of the fair market value of the property at the time the liability is incurred. The portion of the nonrecourse liability allocated to each item of partnership property is then treated as a separate loan under paragraph (a)(2) of this section. In general, a partnership may not change the method of allocating a single nonrecourse liability under this paragraph (b) while any portion of the liability is outstanding. However, if one or more of the multiple properties subject to the liability is no longer subject to the liability, the portion of the liability allocated to that property must be reallocated among the properties still subject to the liability so that the amount of the liability allocated to any property does not exceed the fair market value of such property at the time of reallocation.

(2) Reductions in principal. For purposes of this paragraph (b), when the outstanding principal of a partnership liability is reduced, the reduction of outstanding principal is allocated among the multiple properties in the same proportion that the partnership liability originally was allocated to the properties under paragraph (b)(1) of this section.

(c) Examples. The following examples illustrate the principles of paragraph (a) of this section.

Example (1). Partner's share of nonrecourse liabilities. The AB partnership purchases depreciable property for a $1,000 purchase money note that is nonrecourse liability under the rules of this section. Assume that this is the only nonrecourse liability of the partnership, and that no principal payments are due on the purchase money note for a year. The partnership agreement provides that all items of income, gain, loss, and deduction are allocated equally. Immediately after purchasing the depreciable property, the partners share the nonrecourse liability equally because they have equal interests in partnership profits. A and B are each treated as if they contributed $500 to the partnership to reflect each partner's increase in his or her share of partnership liabilities (from $0 to $500). The minimum gain with respect to an item of partnership property subject to a nonrecourse liability equals the amount of gain that would be recognized if the partnership disposed of the property in full satisfaction of the nonrecourse liability and

for no other consideration. Therefore, if the partnership claims a depreciation deduction of $200 for the depreciable property for the year it acquires that property, partnership minimum gain for the year will increase by $200 (the excess of the $1,000 nonrecourse liability over the $800 adjusted tax basis of the property). See section 704(b) and the regulations thereunder. A and B each have a $100 share of partnership minimum gain at the end of that year because the depreciation deduction is treated as a nonrecourse deduction. See section 704(b) and the regulation thereunder. Accordingly, at the end of that year, A and B are allocated $100 each of the nonrecourse liability to match their shares of partnership minimum gain. The remaining $800 of the nonrecourse liability will be allocated equally between A and B ($400 each).

Example (2). Excess nonrecourse liabilities allocated consistently with reasonably expected deductions. The facts are the same as in Example 1 except that the partnership agreement provides that depreciation deductions will be allocated to A. The partners agree to allocate excess nonrecourse liabilities in accordance with the manner in which it is reasonably expected that the deductions attributable to those nonrecourse liabilities will be allocated. Assuming that the allocation of all of the depreciation deductions to A is valid under section 704(b), immediately after purchasing the depreciable property, A's share of the nonrecourse liability is $1,000. Accordingly, A is treated as if A contributed $1,000 to the partnership.

Example (3). Allocation of liability among multiple properties. (i) A and B are equal partners in a partnership (PRS). A contributes $70 of cash in exchange for a 50-percent interest in PRS. B contributes two items of property, X and Y, in exchange for a 50-percent interest in PRS. Property X has a fair market value (and book value) of $70 and an adjusted basis of $40, and is subject to a nonrecourse liability of $50. Property Y has a fair market value (and book value) of $120, an adjusted basis of $40, and is subject to a nonrecourse liability of $70. Immediately after the initial contributions, PRS refinances the two separate liabilities with a single $120 nonrecourse liability. All of the built-in gain attributable to Property X ($30) and Property Y ($80) is section 704(c) gain allocable to B.

(ii) The amount of the nonrecourse liability ($120) is less than the total book value of all of the properties that are subject to such liability ($70 + $120 = $190), so there is no partnership minimum gain. § 1.704–2(d). Accordingly, no portion of the liability is allocated pursuant to paragraph (a)(1) of this section.

(iii) Pursuant to paragraph (b)(1) of this section, PRS decides to allocate the nonrecourse liability evenly between the Properties X and Y. Accordingly, each of Properties X and Y are treated as being subject to a separate $60 nonrecourse liability for purposes of applying paragraph (a)(2) of this section. Under paragraph (a)(2) of this section, B will be allocated $20 of the liability for each of Properties X and Y (in each case, $60 liability minus $40 adjusted basis). As a result, a portion of the liability is allocated pursuant to paragraph (a)(2) of this section as follows:

Partner	Property	Tier 1	Tier 2
A	X	$0	$0
....	Y	0	0
B	X	0	20
....	Y	0	20

(iv) PRS has $80 of excess nonrecourse liability that it may allocate in any manner consistent with paragraph (a)(3) of this section. PRS determines to allocate the $80 of excess nonrecourse liabilities to the partners up to their share of the remaining section 704(c) gain on the properties, with any remaining amount of liabilities being allocated equally to A and B consistent with their equal interests in partnership profits. B has $70 of remaining section 704(c) gain ($10 on Property X and $60 on

Property Y), and thus will be allocated $70 of the liability in accordance with this gain.

The remaining $10 is divided equally between A and B. Accordingly, the overall allocation of the $120 nonrecourse liability is as follows:

Partner	Tier 1	Tier 2	Tier 3	Total
A	$0	$0	$5	$5
B	0	40	75	115

§ 1.752–4 Special rules.

(a) Tiered partnerships. An upper-tier partnership's share of the liabilities of a lower-tier partnership (other than any liability of the lower-tier partnership that is owed to the upper-tier partnership) is treated as a liability of the upper-tier partnership for purposes of applying section 752 and the regulations thereunder to the partners of the upper-tier partnership.

(b) Related person definition—(1) In general. A person is related to a partner if the person and the partner bear a relationship to each other that is specified in section 267(b) or 707(b)(1), subject to the following modifications:

(i) Substitute "80 percent or more" for "more than 50 percent" each place it appears in those sections;

(ii) A person's family is determined by excluding brothers and sisters; and

(iii) Disregard sections 267(e)(1) and 267(f)(1)(A).

(2) Person related to more than one partner—(i) In general. If, in applying the related person rules in paragraph (b)(1) of this section, a person is related to more than one partner, paragraph (b)(1) of this section is applied by treating the person as related only to the partner with whom there is the highest percentage of related ownership. If two or more partners have the same percentage of related ownership and no other partner has a greater percentage, the liability is allocated equally among the partners having the equal percentages of related ownership.

(ii) Natural persons. For purposes of determining the percentage of related ownership between a person and a partner, natural persons who are related by virtue of being members of the same family are treated as having a percentage relationship of 100 percent with respect to each other.

(iii) Related partner exception. Notwithstanding paragraph (b)(1) of this section (which defines related person), persons owning interests directly or indirectly in the same partnership are not treated as related persons for purposes of determining the economic risk of loss borne by each of them for the liabilities of the partnership. This paragraph (iii) does not apply when determining a partner's interest under the de minimis rules in §§ 1.752–2 (d) and (e).

(iv) Special rule where entity structured to avoid related person status—(A) In general. If—

(1) A partnership liability is owed to or guaranteed by another entity that is a partnership, an S corporation, a C corporation, or a trust;

(2) A partner or related person owns (directly or indirectly) a 20 percent or more ownership interest in the other entity; and

(3) A principal purpose of having the other entity act as a lender or guarantor of the liability was to avoid the determination that the partner that owns the interest bears the economic risk of loss for federal income tax purposes for all or part of the liability; then the partner is treated as holding the other entity's interest as a creditor or guarantor to the extent of the partner's or related person's ownership interest in the entity.

(B) Ownership interest. For purposes of paragraph (b)(2)(iv)(A) of this section, a person's ownership interest in:

(1) A partnership equals the partner's highest percentage interest in any item of partnership loss or deduction for any taxable year;

(2) An S corporation equals the percentage of the outstanding stock in the S corporation owned by the shareholder;

(3) A C corporation equals the percentage of the fair market value of the issued and outstanding stock owned by the shareholder; and

(4) A trust equals the percentage of the actuarial interests owned by the beneficial owner of the trust.

(C) Example. Entity structured to avoid related person status. A, B, and C form a general partnership, ABC. A, B, and C are equal partners, each contributing $1,000 to the partnership. A and B want to loan money to ABC and have the loan treated as nonrecourse for purposes of section 752. A and B form partnership AB to which each contributes $50,000. A and B share losses equally in partnership AB. Partnership AB loans partnership ABC $100,000 on a nonrecourse basis secured by the property ABC buys with the loan. Under these facts and circumstances, A and B bear the economic risk of loss with respect to the partnership liability equally based on their percentage interest in losses of partnership AB.

(c) Limitation. The amount of an indebtedness is taken into account only once, even though a partner (in addition to the partner's liability for the indebtedness as a partner) may be separately liable therefor in a capacity other than as a partner.

(d) Time of determination. A partner's share of partnership liabilities must be determined whenever the determination is necessary in order to determine the tax liability of the partner or any other person. See § 1.705–1(a) for rules regarding when the adjusted basis of a partner's interest in the partnership must be determined.

* * *

§1.753–1 Partner receiving income in respect of decedent.

(a) Income in respect of a decedent under section 736(a). All payments coming within the provisions of section 736(a) made by a partnership to the estate or other successor in interest of a deceased partner are considered income in respect of the decedent under section 691. The estate or other successor in interest of a deceased partner shall be considered to have received income in respect of a decedent to the extent that amounts are paid by a third person in exchange for rights to future payments from the partnership under section 736(a). When a partner who is receiving payments under section 736(a) dies, section 753 applies to any remaining payments under section 736(a) made to his estate or other successor in interest.

(b) Other income in respect of a decedent. When a partner dies, the entire portion of the distributive share which is attributable to the period ending with the date of his death and which is taxable to his estate or other successor constitutes income in respect of a decedent under section 691. This rule applies even though that part of the distributive share for the period before death which the decedent withdrew is not included in the value of the decedent's partnership interest for estate tax purposes. See paragraph (c)(3) of §1.706–1.

(c) Example. The provisions of this section may be illustrated by the following example:

Example. A and the decedent B were equal partners in a business having assets (other than money) worth $40,000 with an adjusted basis of $10,000. Certain partnership business was well advanced towards completion before B's death and, after B's death but before the end of the partnership year, payment of $10,000 was made to the partnership for such work. The partnership agreement provided that, upon the death of one of the partners, all partnership property, including unfinished work, would pass to the surviving partner, and that the surviving partner would pay the estate of the decedent the undrawn balance of his share of partnership earnings to the date of death, plus $10,000 in each of the three years after death. B's share of earnings to the date of his death was $4,000, of which he had withdrawn $3,000. B's distributive share of partnership income of $4,000 to the date of his death is income in respect of a decedent (although only the $1,000 undrawn at B's death will be reflected in the value of B's partnership interest on B's estate tax return). Assume that the value of B's interest in partnership property at the date of his death was $22,000, composed of the following items: B's one-half share of the assets of $40,000, plus $2,000, B's interest in partnership cash. It should be noted that B's $1,000 undrawn share of earnings to the date of his death is not a separate item but will be paid from partnership assets. Under the partnership agreement, A is to pay B's estate a total of $31,000. The difference of $9,000 between the amount to be paid by A ($31,000) and the value of B's interest in partnership property ($22,000) comes within section 736(a) and, thus, also constitutes income in respect of a decedent. (However, the $17,000 difference between the $5,000 basis for B's share of the partnership property and its $22,000 value at the date of his death does not constitute income in respect of a decedent.) If, before the close of the partnership taxable year, A pays B's estate $11,000, of which they agree to allocate $3,000 as the payment under section 736(a), B's estate will include $7,000 in its gross income (B's $4,000 distributive share plus $3,000 payment under section 736(a)). In computing the deduction under section 691(c), this $7,000 will be considered as the value for estate tax purposes of such income in respect of a decedent, even though only $4,000 ($1,000 of distributive share not withdrawn, plus $3,000, payment under section 736(a)) of this amount can be identified on the estate tax return as part of the partnership interest.

§ 1.754–1 Time and manner of making election to adjust basis of partnership property.

(a) In general. A partnership may adjust the basis of partnership property under sections 734(b) and 743(b) if it files an election in accordance with the rules set forth in paragraph (b) of this section. An election may not be filed to make the adjustments provided in either section 734(b) or section 743(b) alone, but such an election must apply to both sections. An election made under the provisions of this section shall apply to all property distributions and transfers of partnership interests taking place in the partnership taxable year for which the election is made and in all subsequent partnership taxable years unless the election is revoked pursuant to paragraph (c) of this section.

(b) Time and method of making election. (1) An election under section 754 and this section to adjust the basis of partnership property under sections 734(b) and 743(b), with respect to a distribution of property to a partner or a transfer of an interest in a partnership, shall be made in a written statement filed with the partnership return for the taxable year during which the distribution or transfer occurs. For the election to be valid, the return must be filed not later than the time prescribed by paragraph (e) of § 1.6031–1 (including extensions thereof) for filing the return for such taxable year . . . . Notwithstanding the preceding two sentences, if a valid election has been made under section 754 and this section for a preceding taxable year and not revoked pursuant to paragraph (c) of this section, a new election is not required to be made. The statement required by this subparagraph shall (i) set forth the name and address of the partnership making the election, (ii) be signed by any one of the partners, and (iii) contain a declaration that the partnership elects under section 754 to apply the provisions of section 734(b) and section 743(b). For rules regarding extensions of time for filing elections, see § 1.9100–1.

(2) The principles of this paragraph may be illustrated by the following example:

Example. A, a U.S. citizen, is a member of partnership ABC, which has not previously made an election under section 754 to adjust the basis of partnership property. The partnership and the partners use the calendar year as the taxable year. A sells his interest in the partnership to D on January 1, 1971. The partnership may elect under section 754 and this section to adjust the basis of partnership property under sections 734(b) and 743(b). Unless an extension of time to make the election is obtained under the provisions of § 1.9100–1, the election must be made in a written statement filed with the partnership return for 1971 and must contain the information specified in subparagraph (1) of this paragraph. Such return must be filed by April 17, 1972 (unless an extension of time for filing the return is obtained). The election will apply to all distributions of property to a partner and transfers of an interest in the partnership occurring in 1971 and subsequent years, unless revoked pursuant to paragraph (c) of this section.

(c) Revocation of election. (1) In general. A partnership having an election in effect under this section may revoke such election with the approval of the district director for the internal revenue district in which the partnership return is required to be filed. A partnership which wishes to revoke such an election shall file with the district director for the internal revenue district in which the partnership return is required to be filed an application setting forth the grounds on which the revocation is desired. The application shall be filed not later than 30 days after the close of the partnership taxable year with respect to which revocation is intended to take effect and shall be signed by any one of the partners. Examples of situations which may be considered sufficient reason for approving an application for revocation include a change in the nature of the partnership business, a substantial increase in the assets of the partnership, a change in the character of partnership assets, or an increased frequency of retirements or shifts of partnership interests, so that an increased administrative burden would result to the partnership from the election. However, no application for revocation of an election shall be approved when the purpose of the revocation is primarily to avoid stepping down the basis of partnership assets upon a transfer or distribution.

(2) Revocations made for first taxable year ending after December 15, 1999. Notwithstanding paragraph (c)(1) of this section, any partnership having an election in effect under this section for its taxable year that includes December 15, 1999 may revoke such election by attaching a statement to the partnership's return for such year. For the revocation to be valid, the statement must be filed not later than the time prescribed by § 1.6031(a)–1(e) (including extensions thereof) for filing the return for such taxable year, and must set forth the name and address of the partnership revoking the election, be signed by any one of the partners who is authorized to sign the partnership's federal income tax return, and contain a declaration that the partnership revokes its election under section 754 to apply the provisions of section 734(b) and 743(b). In addition, the following statement must be prominently displayed in capital letters on the first page of the partnership's return for such year: "RETURN FILED PURSUANT TO 1.754–1(c)(2)."

§ 1.755–1 Rules for allocation of basis.

(a) In general.

(1) Scope.

This section provides rules for allocating basis adjustments under sections 743(b) and 734(b) among partnership property. If there is a basis adjustment to which this section applies, the basis adjustment is allocated among the partnership's assets as follows. First, the partnership must determine the value of each of its assets under paragraphs (a)(2) through (5) of this section. Second, the basis adjustment is allocated between the two classes of property described in section 755(b). These classes of property consist of capital assets and section 1231(b) property (capital gain property), and any other property of the partnership (ordinary income property). For purposes of this section, properties and potential gain treated as unrealized receivables under section 751(c) and the regulations thereunder shall be treated as separate assets that are ordinary income property. Third, the portion of the basis adjustment allocated to each class is allocated among the items within the class. Basis adjustments under section 743(b) are allocated among partnership assets under paragraph (b) of this section. Basis adjustments under section 734(b) are allocated among partnership assets under paragraph (c) of this section.

(2) Coordination of sections 755 and 1060.

If there is a basis adjustment to which this section applies, and the assets of the partnership constitute a trade or business (as described in § 1.1060–1(b)(2)), then the partnership is required to use the residual method to assign values to the partnership's section 197 intangibles. To do so, the partnership must, first, determine the value of partnership assets other than section 197 intangibles under paragraph (a)(3) of this section. The partnership then must determine partnership gross value under paragraph (a)(4) of this section. Last, the partnership must assign values to the partnership's section 197 intangibles under paragraph (a)(5) of this section. For purposes of this section, the term section 197 intangibles includes all section 197 intangibles (as defined in section 197), as well as any goodwill or going concern value that would not qualify as a section 197 intangible under section 197.

(3) Values of properties other than section 197 intangibles.

For purposes of this section, the fair market value of each item of partnership property other than section 197 intangibles shall be determined on the basis of all the facts and circumstances, taking into account section 7701(g).

(4) Partnership gross value.

(i) Basis adjustments under section 743(b).

(A) In general. Except as provided in paragraph (a)(4)(ii) of this section, in the case of a basis adjustment under section 743(b), partnership gross value generally is equal to the amount that, if assigned to all partnership property, would result in a liquidating distribution to the partner equal to the transferee's basis in the transferred partnership interest immediately following the relevant transfer (reduced by the amount, if any, of such basis that is attributable to partnership liabilities).

(B) Special situations. In certain circumstances, such as where income or loss with respect to particular section 197 intangibles are allocated differently among partners, partnership gross value may vary depending on the values of particular section 197 intangibles held by the partnership. In these special situations, the partnership must assign value, first, among section 197 intangibles (other than goodwill and going concern value) in a reasonable manner that is consistent with the ordering rule in paragraph (a)(5) of this section and would cause the appropriate liquidating distribution under paragraph (a)(4)(i)(A) of this section. If the actual fair market values, determined on the basis of all the facts and circumstances, of all section 197 intangibles (other than goodwill and going concern value) is not sufficient to cause the appropriate liquidating distribution, then the fair market value of goodwill and going concern value shall be presumed to equal an amount that if assigned to goodwill and going concern value would cause the appropriate liquidating distribution.

(C) Income in respect of a decedent. Solely for the purpose of determining partnership gross value under this paragraph (a)(4) (i), where a partnership interest is transferred as a result of the death of a partner, the transferee's basis in its partnership interest is deter-

mined without regard to section 1014(c), and is deemed to be adjusted for that portion of the interest, if any, that is attributable to items representing income in respect of a decedent under section 691.

(ii) Basis adjustments under section 743(b) resulting from substituted basis transactions. This paragraph (a)(4)(ii) applies to basis adjustments under section 743(b) that result from exchanges in which the transferee's basis in the partnership interest is determined in whole or in part by reference to the transferor's basis in the interest or to the basis of other property held at any time by the transferee (substituted basis transactions). In the case of a substituted basis transaction, partnership gross value equals the value of the entire partnership as a going concern, increased by the amount of partnership liabilities at the time of the exchange giving rise to the basis adjustment.

(iii) Basis adjustments under section 734(b). In the case of a basis adjustment under section 734(b), partnership gross value equals the value of the entire partnership as a going concern immediately following the distribution causing the adjustment, increased by the amount of partnership liabilities immediately following the distribution.

(5) Determining the values of section 197 intangibles.

(i) Two classes. If the aggregate value of partnership property other than section 197 intangibles (as determined in paragraph (a)(3) of this section) is equal to or greater than partnership gross value (as determined in paragraph (a)(4) of this section), then all section 197 intangibles are deemed to have a value of zero for purposes of this section. In all other cases, the aggregate value of the partnership's section 197 intangibles (the residual section 197 intangibles value) is deemed to equal the excess of partnership gross value over the aggregate value of partnership property other than section 197 intangibles. The residual section 197 intangibles value must be allocated between two asset classes in the following order—

(A) Among section 197 intangibles other than goodwill and going concern value; and

(B) To goodwill and going concern value.

(ii) Values assigned to section 197 intangibles other than goodwill and going concern value. The fair market value assigned to a section 197 intangible (other than goodwill and going concern value) shall not exceed the actual fair market value (determined on the basis of all the facts and circumstances) of that asset on the date of the relevant transfer. If the residual section 197 intangibles value is less than the sum of the actual fair market values (determined on the basis of all the facts and circumstances) of all section 197 intangibles (other than goodwill and going concern value) held by the partnership, then the residual section 197 intangibles value must be allocated among the individual section 197 intangibles (other than goodwill and going concern value) as follows. The residual section 197 intangibles value is assigned first to any section 197 intangibles (other than goodwill and going concern value) having potential gain that would be treated as unrealized receivables under the flush language of section 751(c) (flush language receivables) to the extent of the basis of those section 197 intangibles and the amount of income arising from the flush language receivables that the partnership would recognize if the section 197 intangibles were sold for their actual fair market values (determined based on all the facts and circumstances) (collectively, the flush language receivables value). If the value assigned to section 197 intangibles (other than goodwill and going concern value) is less than the flush language receivables value, then the assigned value is allocated among the properties giving rise to the flush language receivables in proportion to the flush language receivables value in those properties. Any remaining residual section 197 intangibles value is allocated among the remaining portions of the section 197 intangibles (other than goodwill and going concern value) in proportion to the actual fair market values of such portions (determined based on all the facts and circumstances).

(iii) Value assigned to goodwill and going concern value. The fair market value of goodwill and going concern value is the amount, if any, by which the residual section 197 intangibles value exceeds the aggregate value of the partnership's section 197 intangibles (other than goodwill and going concern value).

(6) Examples.

The provisions of paragraphs (a)(2) through (5) are illustrated by the following examples, which assume that the partnerships have an election in effect under section 754 at the time of the transfer and that the assets of each partnership constitute a trade or business (as described in § 1.1060–1(b)(2)). Except as provided, no partnership asset (other than inventory) is property described in section 751(a), and partnership liabilities are secured by all partnership assets. The examples are as follows:

Example (1). (i) A is the sole general partner in PRS, a limited partnership having three equal partners. PRS has goodwill and going concern value, two section 197 intangibles other than goodwill and going concern value (Intangible 1 and Intangible 2), and two other assets with fair market values (determined using all the facts and circumstances) as follows: inventory worth $1,000,000 and a building (a capital asset) worth $2,000,000. The fair market value of each of Intangible 1 and Intangible 2 is $50,000. PRS has one liability of $1,000,000, for which A bears the entire risk of loss under section 752 and the regulations thereunder. D purchases A's partnership interest for $650,000, resulting in a basis adjustment under section 743(b). After the purchase, D bears the entire risk of loss for PRS's liability under section 752 and the regulations thereunder. Therefore, D's basis in its interest in PRS is $1,650,000.

(ii) D's basis in the transferred partnership interest (reduced by the amount of such basis

that is attributable to partnership liabilities) is $650,000 ($1,650,000–$1,000,000). Under paragraph (a)(4)(i) of this section, partnership gross value is $2,950,000 (the amount that, if assigned to all partnership property, would result in a liquidating distribution to D equal to $650,000).

(iii) Under paragraph (a)(3) of this section, the inventory has a fair market value of $1,000,000, and the building has a fair market value of $2,000,000. Thus, the aggregate value of partnership property other than section 197 intangibles, $3,000,000, is equal to or greater than partnership gross value, $2,950,000. Accordingly, under paragraphs (a)(3) and (5) of this section, the value assigned to each of the partnership's assets is as follows: inventory, $1,000,000; building, $2,000,000; Intangibles 1 and 2, $0; and goodwill and going concern value, $0. D's section 743(b) adjustment must be allocated under paragraph (b) of this section using these assigned fair market values.

Example (2). (i) Assume the same facts as in Example 1, except that the fair market values of Intangible 1 and Intangible 2 are each $300,000, and that D purchases A's interest in PRS for $1,000,000. After the purchase, D's basis in its interest in PRS is $2,000,000.

(ii) D's basis in the transferred partnership interest (reduced by the amount of such basis that is attributable to partnership liabilities) is $1,000,000 ($2,000,000–$1,000,000). Under paragraph (a)(4)(i) of this section, partnership gross value is $4,000,000 (the amount that, if assigned to all partnership property, would result in a liquidating distribution to D equal to $1,000,000).

(iii) Under paragraph (a)(5) of this section, the residual section 197 intangibles value is $1,000,000 (the excess of partnership gross value, $4,000,000, over the aggregate value of assets other than section 197 intangibles, $3,000,000 (the sum of the value of the inventory, $1,000,000, and the value of the building, $2,000,000)). The partnership must determine the values of section 197 assets by allocat-

ing the residual section 197 intangibles value among the partnership's assets. The residual section 197 intangibles value is assigned first to section 197 intangibles other than goodwill and going concern value, and then to goodwill and going concern value. Thus, $300,000 is assigned to each of Intangible 1 and Intangible 2, and $400,000 is assigned to goodwill and going concern value (the amount by which the residual section 197 intangibles value, $1,000,000, exceeds the fair market value of section 197 intangibles other than goodwill and going concern value, $600,000). D's section 743(b) adjustment must be allocated under paragraph (b) of this section using these assigned fair market values.

Example (3). (i) Assume the same facts as in Example 1, except that the fair market values of Intangible 1 and Intangible 2 are each $300,000, and that D purchases A's interest in PRS for $750,000. After the purchase, D's basis in its interest in PRS is $1,750,000. Also assume that Intangible 1 was originally purchased for $300,000, and that its adjusted basis has been decreased to $50,000 as a result of amortization. Assume that, if PRS were to sell Intangible 1 for $300,000, it would recognize $250,000 of gain that would be treated as an unrealized receivable under the flush language in section 751(c).

(ii) D's basis in the transferred partnership interest (reduced by the amount of such basis that is attributable to partnership liabilities) is $750,000 ($1,750,000–$1,000,000). Under paragraph (a)(4)(i) of this section, partnership gross value is $3,250,000 (the amount that, if assigned to all partnership property, would result in a liquidating distribution to D equal to $750,000).

(iii) Under paragraph (a)(5) of this section, the residual section 197 intangibles value is $250,000 (the amount by which partnership gross value, $3,250,000, exceeds the aggregate value of partnership property other than section 197 intangibles, $3,000,000). Intangible 1 has potential gain that would be treated as unre-

alized receivables under the flush language of section 751(c). The flush language receivables value in Intangible 1 is $300,000 (the sum of PRS's basis in Intangible 1, $50,000, and the amount of ordinary income, $250,000, that the partnership would recognize if Intangible 1 were sold for its actual fair market value). Because the residual section 197 intangibles value, $250,000, is less than the flush language receivables value of Intangible 1, Intangible 1 is assigned a value of $250,000, and Intangible 2 and goodwill and going concern value are assigned a value of zero. D's section 743(b) adjustment must be allocated under paragraph (b) of this section using these assigned fair market values.

Example (4). Assume the same facts as in Example 1, except that the fair market values of Intangible 1 and Intangible 2 are each $300,000, and that A does not sell its interest in PRS. Instead, A contributes its interest in PRS to E, a newly formed corporation wholly-owned by A, in a transaction described in section 351. Assume that the contribution results in a basis adjustment under section 743(b) (other than zero). PRS determines that its value as a going concern immediately following the contribution is $3,000,000. Under paragraph (a)(4)(ii) of this section, partnership gross value is $4,000,000 (the value of PRS as a going concern, $3,000,000, increased by the partnership's liability, $1,000,000, immediately after the contribution). Under paragraph (a)(5) of this section, the residual section 197 intangibles value is $1,000,000 (the amount by which partnership gross value, $4,000,000, exceeds the aggregate value of partnership property other than section 197 intangibles, $3,000,000). Of the residual section 197 intangibles value, $300,000 is assigned to each of Intangible 1 and Intangible 2, and $400,000 is assigned to goodwill and going concern value (the amount by which the residual section 197 intangibles value, $1,000,000, exceeds the fair market value of section 197 intangibles other than goodwill and going concern value, $600,000). E's section 743(b) adjustment must

be allocated under paragraph (b)(5) of this section using these assigned fair market values.

Example (5). G is the sole general partner in PRS, a limited partnership having three equal partners (G, H, and I). PRS has goodwill and going concern value, two section 197 intangibles other than goodwill and going concern value (Intangible 1 and Intangible 2), and two capital assets with fair market values (determined using all the facts and circumstances) as follows: Vacant land worth $1,000,000, and a building worth $2,000,000. The fair market value of each of Intangible 1 and Intangible 2 is $300,000. PRS has one liability of $1,000,000, for which G bears the entire risk of loss under section 752 and the regulations thereunder. PRS distributes the land to H in liquidation of H's interest in PRS. Immediately prior to the distribution, PRS's basis in the land is $800,000, and H's basis in its interest in PRS is $750,000. The distribution causes the partnership to increase the basis of its remaining property by $50,000 under section 734(b)(1)(B). PRS determines that its value as a going concern immediately following the distribution is $2,000,000. Under paragraph (a)(4)(iii) of this section, partnership gross value is $3,000,000 (the value of PRS as a going concern, $2,000,000, increased by the partnership's liability, $1,000,000, immediately after the distribution). Under paragraph (a)(5) of this section, the residual section 197 intangibles value of PRS's section 197 intangibles is $1,000,000 (the amount by which partnership gross value, $3,000,000, exceeds the aggregate value of partnership property other than section 197 intangibles, $2,000,000). Of the residual section 197 intangibles value, $300,000 is assigned to each of Intangible 1 and Intangible 2, and $400,000 is assigned to goodwill and going concern value (the amount by which the residual section 197 intangibles value, $1,000,000, exceeds the fair market value of section 197 intangibles other than goodwill and going concern value, $600,000). PRS's section 734(b) adjustment must be allocated under paragraph (c) of this section using these assigned fair market values.

(b) Adjustments under section 743(b).

(1) Generally.

(i) Application. For basis adjustments under section 743(b) resulting from substituted basis transactions, paragraph (b)(5) of this section shall apply. For basis adjustments under section 743(b) resulting from all other transfers, paragraphs (b)(2) through (4) of this section shall apply. For transfers subject to section 334(b)(1)(B), see § 1.334–1(b)(3)(iii)(C)(1) (treating a determination of basis under § 1.334–1(b)(3) as a determination not by reference to the transferor's basis solely for purposes of applying section 755); for transfers subject to section 362(e)(1), see § 1.362–3(b)(4)(i) (treating a determination of basis under § 1.362–3 as a determination not by reference to the transferor's basis solely for purposes of applying section 755); for transfers subject to section 362(e)(2), see § 1.362–4(c)(3)(i) (treating a determination of basis under § 1.362–4 as a determination by reference to the transferor's basis for all purposes). Except as provided in paragraph (b)(5) of this section, the portion of the basis adjustment allocated to one class of property may be an increase while the portion allocated to the other class is a decrease. This would be the case even though the total amount of the basis adjustment is zero. Except as provided in paragraph (b)(5) of this section, the portion of the basis adjustment allocated to one item of property within a class may be an increase while the portion allocated to another is a decrease. This would be the case even though the basis adjustment allocated to the class is zero.

(ii) Hypothetical transaction. For purposes of paragraphs (b)(2) through (b)(4) of this section, the allocation of the basis adjustment under section 743(b) between the classes of property and among the items of property within each class are made based on the allocations of income, gain, or loss (including remedial allocations under § 1.704–3(d)) that

the transferee partner would receive (to the extent attributable to the acquired partnership interest) if, immediately after the transfer of the partnership interest, all of the partnership's property were disposed of in a fully taxable transaction for cash in an amount equal to the fair market value of such property (the hypothetical transaction).

(2) Allocations between classes of property.

(i) In general. The amount of the basis adjustment allocated to the class of ordinary income property is equal to the total amount of income, gain, or loss (including any remedial allocations under § 1.704–3(d)) that would be allocated to the transferee (to the extent attributable to the acquired partnership interest) from the sale of all ordinary income property in the hypothetical transaction. The amount of the basis adjustment to capital gain property is equal to—

(A) The total amount of the basis adjustment under section 743(b); less

(B) The amount of the basis adjustment allocated to ordinary income property under the preceding sentence; provided, however, that in no event may the amount of any decrease in basis allocated to capital gain property exceed the partnership's basis (or in the case of property subject to the remedial allocation method, the transferee's share of any remedial loss under § 1.704–3(d) from the hypothetical transaction) in capital gain property. In the event that a decrease in basis allocated to capital gain property would otherwise exceed the partnership's basis in capital gain property, the excess must be applied to reduce the basis of ordinary income property.

(ii) Examples. The provisions of this paragraph (b)(2) are illustrated by the following examples:

Example (1). (i) A and B form equal partnership PRS. A contributes $50,000 and Asset 1, a nondepreciable capital asset with a fair market value of $50,000 and an adjusted tax basis of $25,000. B contributes $100,000. PRS uses the cash to purchase Assets 2, 3, and 4. After a year, A sells its interest in PRS to T for $120,000. At the time of the transfer, A's share of the partnership's basis in partnership assets is $75,000. Therefore, T receives a $45,000 basis adjustment.

(ii) Immediately after the transfer of the partnership interest to T, the adjusted basis and fair market value of PRS's assets are as follows:

Assets		
	Adjusted Basis	Fair Market Value
Capital Gain Property:		
Asset 1	$25,000	$75,000
Asset 2	100,000	117,500
Ordinary Income Property:		
Asset 3	40,000	45,000
Asset 4	10,000	2,500
Total	175,000	240,000

(iii) If PRS sold all of its assets in a fully taxable transaction at fair market value immediately after the transfer of the partnership interest to T, the total amount of capital gain that would be allocated to T is equal to $46,250 ($25,000 section 704(c) built-in gain from Asset 1, plus fifty percent of the $42,500 appreciation in capital gain property). T would also be allocated a $1,250 ordinary loss from the sale of the ordinary income property.

(iv) The amount of the basis adjustment that is allocated to ordinary income property is equal to ($1,250) (the amount of the loss allocated to T from the hypothetical sale of the ordinary income property).

(v) The amount of the basis adjustment that is allocated to capital gain property is equal to $46,250 (the amount of the basis adjustment, $45,000, less ($1,250), the amount of loss allocated to T from the hypothetical sale of the ordinary income property).

Example (2). (i) A and B form equal partnership PRS. A and B each contribute $1,000 cash which the partnership uses to purchase Assets 1, 2, 3, and 4. After a year, A sells its partnership interest to T for $1,000. T's basis adjustment under section 743(b) is zero.

(ii) Immediately after the transfer of the partnership interest to T, the adjusted basis and fair market value of PRS's assets are as follows:

Assets		
	Adjusted Basis	Fair Market Value
Capital Gain Property:		
Asset 1	$500	$750
Asset 2	500	500
Ordinary Income Property:		
Asset 3	500	250
Asset 4	500	500
Total	2,000	2,000

(iii) If, immediately after the transfer of the partnership interest to T, PRS sold all of its assets in a fully taxable transaction at fair market value, T would be allocated a loss of $125 from the sale of the ordinary income property. Thus, the amount of the basis adjustment to ordinary income property is ($125). The amount of the basis adjustment to capital gain property is $125 (zero, the amount of the basis adjustment under section 743(b), less ($125), the amount of the basis adjustment allocated to ordinary income property).

(3) Allocation within the class.

(i) Ordinary income property. The amount of the basis adjustment to each item of property within the class of ordinary income property is equal to—

(A) The amount of income, gain, or loss (including any remedial allocations under § 1.704–3(d)) that would be allocated to the transferee (to the extent attributable to the acquired partnership interest) from the hypothetical sale of the item; reduced by

(B) The product of—

(1) Any decrease to the amount of the basis adjustment to ordinary income property required pursuant to the last sentence of paragraph (b)(2)(i) of this section; multiplied by

(2) A fraction, the numerator of which is the fair market value of the item of property to the partnership and the denominator of which is the total fair market value of all of the partnership's items of ordinary income property.

(ii) Capital gain property. The amount of the basis adjustment to each item of property within the class of capital gain property is equal to—

(A) The amount of income, gain, or loss (including any remedial allocations under § 1.704–3(d)) that would be allocated to the transferee (to the extent attributable to the acquired partnership interest) from the hypothetical sale of the item; minus

(B) The product of—

(1) The total amount of gain or loss (including any remedial allocations under § 1.704–3(d)) that would be allocated to the transferee (to the extent attributable to the acquired partnership interest) from the hypothetical sale of all items of capital gain property, minus the amount of the positive basis adjustment to all items of capital gain property or plus the amount of the negative basis adjustment to capital gain property; multiplied by

(2) A fraction, the numerator of which is the fair market value of the item of property to the partnership, and the denominator of which is the fair market value of all of the partnership's items of capital gain property.

(iii) Special rules.

(A) Assets in which partner has no interest. An asset with respect to which the transferee partner has no interest in income, gain, losses, or deductions shall not be taken into account

in applying paragraph (b)(3)(ii)(B) of this section.

(B) Limitation in decrease of basis. In no event may the amount of any decrease in basis allocated to an item of capital gain property under paragraph (b)(3)(ii)(B) of this section exceed the partnership's adjusted basis in that item (or in the case of property subject to the remedial allocation method, the transferee's share of any remedial loss under § 1.704–3(d) from the hypothetical transaction). In the event that a decrease in basis allocated under paragraph (b)(3)(ii)(B) of this section to an item of capital gain property would otherwise exceed the partnership's adjusted basis in that item, the excess must be applied to reduce the remaining basis, if any, of other capital gain assets pro rata in proportion to the bases of such assets (as adjusted under this paragraph (b)(3)).

(iv) Examples. The provisions of this paragraph (b)(3) are illustrated by the following examples:

Example (1). (i) Assume the same facts as Example 1 in paragraph (b)(2)(ii) of this section. Of the $45,000 basis adjustment, $46,250 was allocated to capital gain property. The amount allocated to ordinary income property was ($1,250).

(ii) Asset 1 is a capital gain asset, and T would be allocated $37,500 from the sale of Asset 1 in the hypothetical transaction. Therefore, the amount of the adjustment to Asset 1 is $37,500.

(iii) Asset 2 is a capital gain asset, and T would be allocated $8,750 from the sale of Asset 2 in the hypothetical transaction. Therefore, the amount of the adjustment to Asset 2 is $8,750.

(iv) Asset 3 is ordinary income property, and T would be allocated $2,500 from the sale of Asset 3 in the hypothetical transaction. Therefore, the amount of the adjustment to Asset 3 is $2,500.

(v) Asset 4 is ordinary income property, and T would be allocated ($3,750) from the sale of Asset 4 in the hypothetical transaction. Therefore, the amount of the adjustment to Asset 4 is ($3,750).

Example (2). (i) Assume the same facts as Example 1 in paragraph (b)(2)(ii) of this section, except that A sold its interest in PRS to T for $110,000 rather than $120,000. T, therefore, receives a basis adjustment under section 743(b) of $35,000. Of the $35,000 basis adjustment, ($1,250) is allocated to ordinary income property, and $36,250 is allocated to capital gain property.

(ii) Asset 3 is ordinary income property, and T would be allocated $2,500 from the sale of Asset 3 in the hypothetical transaction. Therefore, the amount of the adjustment to Asset 3 is $2,500.

(iii) Asset 4 is ordinary income property, and T would be allocated ($3,750) from the sale of Asset 4 in the hypothetical transaction. Therefore, the amount of the adjustment to Asset 4 is ($3,750).

(iv) Asset 1 is a capital gain asset, and T would be allocated $37,500 from the sale of Asset 1 in the hypothetical transaction. Asset 2 is a capital gain asset, and T would be allocated $8,750 from the sale of Asset 2 in the hypothetical transaction. The total amount of gain that would be allocated to T from the sale of the capital gain assets in the hypothetical transaction is $46,250, which exceeds the amount of the basis adjustment allocated to capital gain property by $10,000. The amount of the adjustment to Asset 1 is $33,604 ($37,500 minus $3,896 ($10,000 × $75,000/192,500)). The amount of the basis adjustment to Asset 2 is $2,646 ($8,750 minus $6,104 ($10,000 × $117,500/192,500)).

(4) Income in respect of a decedent.

(i) In general. Where a partnership interest is transferred as a result of the death of a partner, under section 1014(c) the transferee's basis in its partnership interest is not adjusted

for that portion of the interest, if any, which is attributable to items representing income in respect of a decedent under section 691. See §1.742–1. Accordingly, if a partnership interest is transferred as a result of the death of a partner, and the partnership holds assets representing income in respect of a decedent, no part of the basis adjustment under section 743(b) is allocated to these assets. See §1.743–1(b).

(ii) The provisions of this paragraph (b)(4) are illustrated by the following example:

Example. (i) A and B are equal partners in personal service partnership PRS. In 2004, as a result of B's death, B's partnership interest is transferred to T when PRS's balance sheet (reflecting a cash receipts and disbursements method of accounting) is as follows (based on all the facts and circumstances):

Assets		
	Adjusted Basis	Fair Market Value
Section 197		
Intangible	$2,000	$5,000
Unrealized		
Receivables	0	15,000
Total	2,000	20,000

Liabilities and Capital		
	Adjusted per Books	Fair Market Value
Capital:		
A	1,000	10,000
B	1,000	10,000
Total	2,000	20,000

(ii) None of the assets owned by PRS is section 704(c) property, and the section 197 intangible is not amortizable. The fair market value of T's partnership interest on the applicable date of valuation set forth in section 1014 is $10,000. Of this amount, $2,500 is attributable to T's 50% share of the partnership's section 197 intangible, and $7,500 is attributable to T's 50% share of the partnership's unreal-

ized receivables. The partnership's unrealized receivables represent income in respect of a decedent. Accordingly, under section 1014(c), T's basis in its partnership interest is not adjusted for that portion of the interest which is attributable to the unrealized receivables. Therefore, T's basis in its partnership interest is $2,500.

(iii) Under paragraph (a)(4)(i)(C) of this section, solely for purposes of determining partnership gross value, T's basis in its partnership interest is deemed to be $10,000. Under paragraph (a)(4)(i) of this section, partnership gross value is $20,000 (the amount that, if assigned to all partnership property, would result in a liquidating distribution to T equal to $10,000).

(iv) Under paragraph (a)(5) of this section, the residual section 197 intangibles value is $5,000 (the excess of partnership gross value, $20,000, over the aggregate value of assets other than section 197 intangibles, $15,000). The residual section 197 intangibles value is assigned first to section 197 intangibles other than goodwill and going concern value, and then to goodwill and going concern value. Thus, $5,000 is assigned to the section 197 intangible, and $0 is assigned to goodwill and going concern value. T's section 743(b) adjustment must be allocated using these assigned fair market values.

(v) At the time of the transfer, B's share of the partnership's basis in partnership assets is $1,000. Accordingly, T receives a $1,500 basis adjustment under section 743(b). Under this paragraph (b)(4), the entire basis adjustment is allocated to the partnership's section 197 intangible.

(5) Substituted basis transactions.

(i) In general. This paragraph (b)(5) applies to basis adjustments under section 743(b) that result from exchanges in which the transferee's basis in the partnership interest is determined in whole or in part by reference to the transferor's basis in that interest. For exchang-

es on or after June 9, 2003, this paragraph (b)(5) also applies to basis adjustments under section 743(b) that result from exchanges in which the transferee's basis in the partnership interest is determined by reference to other property held at any time by the transferee. For example, this paragraph (b)(5) applies if a partnership interest is contributed to a corporation in a transaction to which section 351 applies, if a partnership interest is contributed to a partnership in a transaction to which section 721(a) applies, or if a partnership interest is distributed by a partnership in a transaction to which section 731(a) applies.

(ii) Allocations between classes of property. If the total amount of the basis adjustment under section 743(b) is zero, then no adjustment to the basis of partnership property will be made under this paragraph (b)(5). If there is an increase in basis to be allocated to partnership assets, such increase must be allocated to capital gain property or ordinary income property, respectively, only if the total amount of gain or loss (including any remedial allocations under § 1.704–3(d)) that would be allocated to the transferee (to the extent attributable to the acquired partnership interest) from the hypothetical sale of all such property would result in a net gain or net income, as the case may be, to the transferee. Where, under the preceding sentence, an increase in basis may be allocated to both capital gain assets and ordinary income assets, the increase shall be allocated to each class in proportion to the net gain or net income, respectively, which would be allocated to the transferee from the sale of all assets in each class. If there is a decrease in basis to be allocated to partnership assets, such decrease must be allocated to capital gain property or ordinary income property, respectively, only if the total amount of gain or loss (including any remedial allocations under § 1.704–3(d)) that would be allocated to the transferee (to the extent attributable to the acquired partnership interest) from the hypothetical sale of all such property would result in a net loss to the transferee. Where, under the preceding sentence, a decrease in basis may be allocated to both capital gain assets and ordinary income assets, the decrease shall be allocated to each class in proportion to the net loss which would be allocated to the transferee from the sale of all assets in each class.

(iii) Allocations within the classes.

(A) Increases. If there is an increase in basis to be allocated within a class, the increase must be allocated first to properties with unrealized appreciation in proportion to the transferee's share of the respective amounts of unrealized appreciation before such increase (but only to the extent of the transferee's share of each property's unrealized appreciation). Any remaining increase must be allocated among the properties within the class in proportion to the transferee's share of the amount that would be realized by the partnership upon the hypothetical sale of each asset in the class.

(B) Decreases. If there is a decrease in basis to be allocated within a class, the decrease must be allocated first to properties with unrealized depreciation in proportion to the transferee's shares of the respective amounts of unrealized depreciation before such decrease (but only to the extent of the transferee's share of each property's unrealized depreciation). Any remaining decrease must be allocated among the properties within the class in proportion to the transferee's shares of their adjusted bases (as adjusted under the preceding sentence).

(C) Limitation in decrease of basis. Where, as the result of a transaction to which this paragraph (b)(5) applies, a decrease in basis must be allocated to capital gain assets, ordinary income assets, or both, and the amount of the decrease otherwise allocable to a particular class exceeds the transferee's share of the adjusted basis to the partnership of all depreciated assets in that class, the transferee's negative basis adjustment is limited to the transferee's share of the partnership's adjusted basis in all depreciated assets in that class.

(D) Carryover adjustment. Where a transferee's negative basis adjustment under section 743(b) cannot be allocated to any asset, because the adjustment exceeds the transferee's share of the adjusted basis to the partnership of all depreciated assets in a particular class, the adjustment is made when the partnership subsequently acquires property of a like character to which an adjustment can be made.

(iv) Examples. The provisions of this paragraph (b)(5) are illustrated by the following examples:

Example (1). A is a member of partnership LTP, which has made an election under section 754. The three partners in LTP have equal interests in capital and profits. Solely in exchange for a partnership interest in UTP, A contributes its interest in LTP to UTP in a transaction described in section 721. At the time of the transfer, A's basis in its partnership interest ($5,000) equals its share of inside basis (also $5,000). Under section 723, UTP's basis in its interest in LTP is $5,000. LTP's only two assets on the date of contribution are inventory with a basis of $5,000 and a fair market value of $7,500, and a nondepreciable capital asset with a basis of $10,000 and a fair market value of $7,500. The amount of the basis adjustment under section 743(b) to partnership property is $0 ($5,000, UTP's basis in its interest in LTP, minus $5,000, UTP's share of LTP's basis in partnership assets). Because UTP acquired its interest in LTP in a substituted basis transaction, and the total amount of the basis adjustment under section 743(b) is zero, UTP receives no special basis adjustments under section 743(b) with respect to the partnership property of LTP.

Example (2). (i) A purchases a partnership interest in LTP at a time when an election under section 754 is not in effect. The three partners in LTP have equal interests in capital and profits. During a later year for which LTP has an election under section 754 in effect, and in a transaction that is unrelated to A's purchase of the LTP interest, A contributes its interest in LTP to UTP in a transaction described in section 721 (solely in exchange for a partnership interest in UTP). At the time of the transfer, A's adjusted basis in its interest in LTP is $20,433. Under section 721, A recognizes no gain or loss as a result of the contribution of its partnership interest to UTP. Under section 723, UTP's basis in its partnership interest in LTP is $20,433. The balance sheet of LTP on the date of the contribution shows the following:

Assets

	Adjusted Basis	Fair Market Value
Cash	$5,000	$5,000
Accounts Receivable	10,000	10,000
Inventory	20,000	21,000
Nondepreciable capital asset	20,000	40,000
Total	55,000	76,000

Liabilities and Capital

	Adjusted per Books	Fair Market Value
Liabilities Capital:	$10,000	$10,000
A	15,000	22,000
B	15,000	22,000
C	15,000	22,000
Total	55,000	76,000

(ii) The amount of the basis adjustment under section 743(b) is the difference between the basis of UTP's interest in LTP and UTP's share of the adjusted basis to LTP of partnership property. UTP's interest in the previously taxed capital of LTP is $15,000 ($22,000, the amount of cash UTP would receive if LTP liquidated immediately after the hypothetical transaction, decreased by $7,000, the amount of tax gain allocated to UTP from the hypothetical transaction). UTP's share of the adjusted basis to LTP of partnership property is $18,333 ($15,000 share of previously taxed capital, plus $3,333 share of LTP's liabilities). The amount of the basis adjustment under sec-

tion 743(b) to partnership property therefore, is $2,100 ($20,433 minus $18,333).

(iii) The total amount of gain that would be allocated to UTP from the hypothetical sale of capital gain property is $6,666.67 (one-third of the excess of the fair market value of LTP's nondepreciable capital asset, $40,000, over its basis, $20,000). The total amount of gain that would be allocated to UTP from the hypothetical sale of ordinary income property is $333.33 (one-third of the excess of the fair market value of LTP's inventory, $21,000, over its basis, $20,000). Under this paragraph (b)(5), LTP must allocate $2,000 ($6,666.67 divided by $7,000 times $2,100) of UTP's basis adjustment to the nondepreciable capital asset. LTP must allocate $100 ($333.33 divided by $7,000 times $2,100) of UTP's basis adjustment to the inventory.

(c) Adjustments under section 734(b).

(1) Allocations between classes of property.

(i) General rule. Where there is a distribution of partnership property resulting in an adjustment to the basis of undistributed partnership property under section 734(b)(1)(B) or (b)(2)(B), the adjustment must be allocated to remaining partnership property of a character similar to that of the distributed property with respect to which the adjustment arose. Thus, when the partnership's adjusted basis of distributed capital gain property immediately prior to distribution exceeds the basis of the property to the distributee partner (as determined under section 732), the basis of the undistributed capital gain property remaining in the partnership is increased by an amount equal to the excess. Conversely, when the basis to the distributee partner (as determined under section 732) of distributed capital gain property exceeds the partnership's adjusted basis of such property immediately prior to the distribution, the basis of the undistributed capital gain property remaining in the partnership is decreased by an amount equal to such excess. Similarly, where there is a distribution of ordinary income property, and the basis of the property to the distributee partner (as determined under section 732) is not the same as the partnership's adjusted basis of the property immediately prior to distribution, the adjustment is made only to undistributed property of the same class remaining in the partnership.

(ii) Special rule. Where there is a distribution resulting in an adjustment under section 734(b)(1)(A) or (b)(2)(A) to the basis of undistributed partnership property, the adjustment is allocated only to capital gain property.

(2) Allocations within the classes.

(i) Increases. If there is an increase in basis to be allocated within a class, the increase must be allocated first to properties with unrealized appreciation in proportion to their respective amounts of unrealized appreciation before such increase (but only to the extent of each property's unrealized appreciation). Any remaining increase must be allocated among the properties within the class in proportion to their fair market values.

(ii) Decreases. If there is a decrease in basis to be allocated within a class, the decrease must be allocated first to properties with unrealized depreciation in proportion to their respective amounts of unrealized depreciation before such decrease (but only to the extent of each property's unrealized depreciation). Any remaining decrease must be allocated among the properties within the class in proportion to their adjusted bases (as adjusted under the preceding sentence).

(3) Limitation in decrease of basis.

Where a decrease in the basis of partnership assets is required under section 734(b)(2) and the amount of the decrease exceeds the adjusted basis to the partnership of property of the required character, the basis of such property is reduced to zero (but not below zero).

(4) Carryover adjustment.

Where, in the case of a distribution, an increase or a decrease in the basis of undistributed property cannot be made because the partnership owns no property of the character required to be adjusted, or because the basis of all the property of a like character has been reduced to zero, the adjustment is made when the partnership subsequently acquires property of a like character to which an adjustment can be made.

(5) Example.

The following example illustrates this paragraph (c):

(i) A, B, and C form equal partnership PRS. A contributes $50,000 and Asset 1, nondepreciable capital gain property with a fair market value of $50,000 and an adjusted tax basis of $25,000. B and C each contributes $100,000. PRS uses the cash to purchase Assets 2, 3, 4, 5, and 6. Assets 2 and 3 are nondepreciable capital assets, and Assets 4, 5, and 6 are inventory that has not appreciated substantially in value within the meaning of section 751(b)(3). Assets 4, 5, and 6 are the only assets held by the partnership that are subject to section 751. The partnership has an election in effect under section 754. After seven years, the adjusted basis and fair market value of PRS's assets are as follows:

	Assets	
	Adjusted Basis	Fair Market Value
Capital Gain Property:		
Asset 1	$25,000	$75,000
Asset 2	100,000	117,500
Asset 3	50,000	60,000
Ordinary Income Property:		
Asset 4	0,000	45,000
Asset 5	50,000	60,000
Asset 6	10,000	2,500
Total	275,000	360,000

(ii) Allocation between classes. Assume that PRS distributes Assets 3 and 5 to A in complete liquidation of A's interest in the partnership. A's basis in the partnership interest

was $75,000. The partnership's basis in Assets 3 and 5 was $50,000 each. A's $75,000 basis in its partnership interest is allocated between Assets 3 and 5 under sections 732(b) and (c). A will, therefore, have a basis of $25,000 in Asset 3 (capital gain property), and a basis of $50,000 in Asset 5 (section 751 property). The distribution results in a $25,000 increase in the basis of capital gain property. There is no change in the basis of ordinary income property.

(iii) Allocation within class. The amount of the basis increase to capital gain property is $25,000 and must be allocated among the remaining capital gain assets in proportion to the difference between the fair market value and basis of each. The fair market value of Asset 1 exceeds its basis by $50,000. The fair market value of Asset 2 exceeds its basis by $17,500. Therefore, the basis of Asset 1 will be increased by $18,519 ($25,000, multiplied by $50,000, divided by $67,500), and the basis of Asset 2 will be increased by $6,481 ($25,000 multiplied by $17,500, divided by $67,500).

(d) Required statements.

See § 1.743–1(k)(2) for provisions requiring the transferee of a partnership interest to provide information to the partnership relating to the transfer of an interest in the partnership. See § 1.743–1(k)(1) for a provision requiring the partnership to attach a statement to the partnership return showing the computation of a basis adjustment under section 743(b) and the partnership properties to which the adjustment is allocated under section 755 See § 1.732–1(d)(3) for a provision requiring a transferee partner to attach a statement to its return showing the computation of a basis adjustment under section 732(d) and the partnership properties to which the adjustment is allocated under section 755. See § 1.732–1(d) (5) for a provision requiring the partnership to provide information to a transferee partner reporting a basis adjustment under section 732(d).

* * *

§ 1.761–1 Terms defined.

(a) Partnership. The term partnership means a partnership as determined under §§ 301.7701–1, 301.7701–2, and 301.7701–3 of this chapter.

(b) Partner. The term partner means a member of a partnership.

(c) Partnership agreement. For the purposes of subchapter K, a partnership agreement includes the original agreement and any modifications thereof agreed to by all the partners or adopted in any other manner provided by the partnership agreement. Such agreement or modifications can be oral or written. A partnership agreement may be modified with respect to a particular taxable year subsequent to the close of such taxable year, but not later than the date (not including any extension of time) prescribed by law for the filing of the partnership return. As to any matter on which the partnership agreement, or any modification thereof, is silent, the provisions of local law shall be considered to constitute a part of the agreement.

(d) Liquidation of partner's interest. The term liquidation of a partner's interest means the termination of a partner's entire interest in a partnership by means of a distribution, or a series of distributions, to the partner by the partnership. A series of distributions will come within the meaning of this term whether they are made in one year or in more than one year. Where a partner's interest is to be liquidated by a series of distributions, the interest will not be considered as liquidated until the final distribution has been made. For the basis of property distributed in one liquidating distribution, or in a series of distributions in liquidation, see section 732(b). A distribution which is not in liquidation of a partner's entire interest, as defined in this paragraph, is a current distribution. Current distributions, therefore, include distributions in partial liquidation of a partner's interest, and distributions of the partner's distributive share. See paragraph (a) (1)(ii) of § 1.731–1.

(e) Distribution of partnership interest. For purposes of section 708(b)(1)(B) and § 1.708–1(b)(1)(iv), the deemed distribution of an interest in a new partnership by a partnership that terminates under section 708(b)(1)(B) is not a sale or exchange of an interest in the new partnership. However, the deemed distribution of an interest in a new partnership by a partnership that terminates under section 708(b)(1)(B) is treated as an exchange of the interest in the new partnership for purposes of section 743. This paragraph (e) applies to terminations of partnerships under section 708(b)(1)(B) occurring on or after May 9, 1997; however, this paragraph (e) may be applied to terminations occurring on or after May 9, 1996, provided that the partnership and its partners apply this paragraph (e) to the termination in a consistent manner.

§ 1.761–2 Exclusion of certain unincorporated organizations from the application of all or part of subchapter K of chapter 1 of the Internal Revenue Code.

(a) Exclusion of eligible unincorporated organizations—(1) In general. Under conditions set forth in this section, an unincorporated organization described in subparagraph (2) or (3) of this paragraph may be excluded from the application of all or a part of the provisions of subchapter K of chapter 1 of the Code. Such organization must be availed of (i) for investment purposes only and not for the active conduct of a business, or (ii) for the joint production, extraction, or use of property, but not for the purpose of selling services or property produced or extracted. The members of such organization must be able to compute their income without the necessity of computing partnership taxable income. Any syndicate, group, pool, or joint venture which is classifiable as an association, or any group operating under an agreement which creates an organization classifiable as an association, does not fall within these provisions.

(2) Investing partnership. Where the participants in the joint purchase, retention, sale, or exchange of investment property:

(i) Own the property as coowners,

(ii) Reserve the right separately to take or dispose of their shares of any property acquired or retained, and

(iii) Do not actively conduct business or irrevocably authorize some person or persons acting in a representative capacity to purchase, sell, or exchange such investment property, although each separate participant may delegate authority to purchase, sell, or exchange his share of any such investment property for the time being for his account, but not for a period of more than a year, then

such group may be excluded from the application of the provisions of subchapter K under the rules set forth in paragraph (b) of this section.

(3) Operating agreements. Where the participants in the joint production, extraction, or use of property:

(i) Own the property as coowners, either in fee or under lease or other form of contract granting exclusive operating rights, and

(ii) Reserve the right separately to take in kind or dispose of their shares of any property produced, extracted, or used, and

(iii) Do not jointly sell services or the property produced or extracted, although each separate participant may delegate authority to sell his share of the property produced or extracted for the time being for his account, but not for a period of time in excess of the minimum needs of the industry, and in no event for more than 1 year, then such group may be excluded from the application of the provisions of subchapter K under the rules set forth in paragraph (b) of this section. However, the preceding sentence does not apply to any unincorporated organization one of whose principal purposes is cycling, manufacturing, or processing for persons who are not members of the organization.

In addition, except as provided in paragraph (d)(2)(i) of this section, this paragraph (a)(3) does not apply to any unincorporated organization that produces natural gas under a joint operating agreement, unless all members of the unincorporated organization comply with paragraph (d) of this section.

§ 1.761–3 Certain option holders treated as partners.

(a) Noncompensatory option treated as a partnership interest—(1) General rule. A noncompensatory option (as defined in paragraph (b)(2) of this section) is treated as a partnership interest for all Federal tax purposes if, on the date of a measurement event (as defined in paragraph (c) of this section) with respect to the option—

(i) The noncompensatory option (and any agreements associated with it) provides the option holder with rights that are substantially similar to the rights afforded a partner (as determined under paragraph (d) of this section); and

(ii) There is a strong likelihood that the failure to treat the holder of the noncompensatory option as a partner would result in a substantial reduction in the present value of the partners' and noncompensatory option holder's aggregate Federal tax liabilities (as determined under paragraph (e) of this section).

(2) Continuing applicability of general principles of law. The fact that an option is not treated as a partnership interest under this section does not prevent the option from being treated as a partnership interest under general principles of Federal tax law.

(3) Timing of characterization. If a noncompensatory option is treated under this section as a partnership interest, that treatment applies, as the case may be, upon the issuance of the option, or immediately before any other measurement event that gave rise to the characterization under paragraph (a)(1) of this section.

(4) Effect of characterization. If a noncompensatory option is treated as a partnership interest under this section or under general principles of law, the option holder will be treated as a partner with respect to the partnership interest and will receive a distributive share of the partnership's income, gain, loss, deduction, or credit (or items thereof), as determined in accordance with that partner's interest in the partnership (taking into account all facts and circumstances) in accordance with § 1.704–1(b)(3). Once a noncompensatory option is treated as a partnership interest, in no event may it be characterized as an option thereafter.

(b) Definitions. For purposes of this section:

(1) Look-through entity. Look-through entity means an entity described in § 1.704–1(b)(2)(iii)(d)(2).

(2) Noncompensatory option. Noncompensatory option means an option (as defined in paragraph (b)(3) of this section) issued by a partnership, other than an option issued in connection with the performance of services. For purposes of applying this section, an option that would be a noncompensatory option under this paragraph if it had been issued by a partnership is a noncompensatory option if the option was issued by an eligible entity (as defined in § 301.7701–3(a)) that would become a partnership under § 301.7701–3(f)(2) if the noncompensatory option holder were treated as a partner. Also for purposes of applying this section, if a noncompensatory option is issued by such an eligible entity, then the eligible entity is treated as a partnership.

(3) Option. An option is a contractual right to acquire an interest in the issuing partnership, including a call option, warrant, or other similar arrangement. In addition, an option includes convertible debt (as defined in § 1.721–2(g)(2)) and convertible equity (as defined in § 1.721–2(g)(3)). To achieve the purposes of this section, the Commissioner can treat other contractual agreements, including a forward contract, a futures contract, or a notional principal contract, as an option. A contract that otherwise constitutes an option will not fail to be treated as an option for purposes of this section merely because it may or must be settled in cash or property other than a partnership interest.

(4) Underlying partnership interest. Underlying partnership interest means the interest in the issuing partnership that would be acquired by the noncompensatory option holder upon exercise of the noncompensatory option.

(c) Measurement event—(1) General rule. Except as provided in paragraph (c)(2) of this section, a measurement event with respect to a noncompensatory option is any of the following events:

(i) Issuance of the noncompensatory option;

(ii) An adjustment of the terms (modification) of the noncompensatory option or of the underlying partnership interest (as defined in paragraph (b)(4) of this section) (including an adjustment pursuant to the terms of the noncompensatory option or the underlying partnership interest);

(iii) Transfer of the noncompensatory option if either:

(A) The option may be exercised (or settled) more than 12 months after its issuance, or

(B) The transfer is pursuant to a plan in existence at the time of the issuance or modification of the noncompensatory option that has as a principal purpose the substantial reduction of the present value of the aggregate Federal tax liabilities of the partners and the noncompensatory option holder (under paragraph (a)(1)(ii) of this section);

(2) Events not treated as measurement events. A measurement event does not include the following events:

(i) A transfer of the noncompensatory option at death, between spouses or former

spouses under section 1041, or in a transaction that is disregarded for Federal tax purposes;

(ii) A modification that neither materially increases the likelihood that the noncompensatory option will be exercised (as described in paragraph (d)(2) of this section) nor provides the noncompensatory option holder with partner attributes (as described in paragraph (d)(3) of this section);

(iii) A change in the strike price of a noncompensatory option or in the interests in the issuing partnership that may be issued or transferred pursuant to the noncompensatory option, made pursuant to a bona fide, reasonable adjustment formula that has the intended effect of preventing dilution of the interests of the noncompensatory option holder;

(iv) Any other event as provided in guidance published in the Internal Revenue Bulletin.

(d) Rights substantially similar to partner rights—(1) In general. A noncompensatory option provides the holder with rights that are substantially similar to the rights afforded to a partner if either the option is reasonably certain to be exercised or the option holder possesses partner attributes.

(2) Reasonable certainty of exercise—(i) General rule. The determination of whether a noncompensatory option is reasonably certain to be exercised at the time of a measurement event is based on all the facts and circumstances, including—

(A) The fair market value of the partnership interest that is the subject of the noncompensatory option;

(B) The strike price of the noncompensatory option;

(C) The term of the noncompensatory option;

(D) The volatility of the value or income of the issuing partnership or the underlying partnership interest;

(E) Anticipated distributions by the partnership during the term of the noncompensatory option;

(F) Any other special option features, such as a strike price that fluctuates;

(G) The existence of related options, including reciprocal options; and

(H) Any other arrangements affecting or undertaken with a principal purpose of affecting the likelihood that the noncompensatory option will be exercised.

(ii) Safe harbors—(A) General rule. Except as provided in paragraph (d)(2)(ii)(C) of this section, a noncompensatory option is not considered reasonably certain to be exercised if, as of the date of a measurement event with respect to the noncompensatory option—

(1) The option may be exercised no more than 24 months after the date of the measurement event and the strike price is equal to or greater than 110 percent of the fair market value of the underlying partnership interest on the date of the measurement event; or

(2) The terms of the option provide that the strike price of the option is equal to or greater than the fair market value of the underlying partnership interest on the exercise date.

(B) Options exercisable at fair market value. For purposes of paragraph (d)(2)(ii)(A) of this section, an option whose strike price is determined by a formula is considered to have a strike price equal to or greater than the fair market value of the underlying partnership interest on the exercise date if the formula is agreed upon by the parties when the option is issued in a bona fide attempt to arrive at the fair market value on the exercise date and is to be applied based on the facts and circumstances in existence on the exercise date.

(C) Exception. The safe harbors of paragraph (d)(2)(ii)(A) of this section do not apply if the parties to the noncompensatory option had a principal purpose described in paragraph (c)(1)(iii)(B) of this section with respect to a measurement event for that option (or, if multiple options were issued pursuant to a plan, a measurement event with respect to any option issued pursuant to that plan).

(D) Failure to satisfy safe harbor. Failure of an option to satisfy one of the safe harbors of paragraph (d)(2)(ii)(A) does not affect the determination of whether an option is treated as reasonably certain to be exercised.

(3) Partner attributes—(i) General rule. The determination of whether a holder of a noncompensatory option possesses partner attributes is based on all the facts and circumstances, including whether the option holder, directly or indirectly, through the option agreement or a related agreement, is provided with voting rights or managerial rights in the partnership.

(ii) Certain factors that conclusively establish partner attributes. For purposes of this section, a noncompensatory option holder has partner attributes if, based on all the facts and circumstances—

(A) The option holder is provided with rights (through the option agreement or a related agreement) that are similar to rights ordinarily afforded to a partner to participate in partnership profits through present possessory rights to share in current operating or liquidating distributions with respect to the underlying partnership interests; or

(B) The option holder, directly or indirectly, undertakes obligations (through the option agreement or a related agreement) that are similar to obligations undertaken by a partner to bear partnership losses.

(iii) Special rules. The following rules apply for purposes of paragraphs (d)(3)(i) and (d)(3)(ii) of this section:

(A) Rights in the issuing partnership possessed by a noncompensatory option holder solely by virtue of owning an interest in the issuing partnership are not taken into account, provided that those rights are no greater than the rights granted to other partners owning substantially similar interests in the partnership and who do not hold noncompensatory options in the partnership.

(B) If all of the partners owning substantially similar interests in the issuing partnership also hold noncompensatory options in the partnership, or if none of the other partners owns substantially similar interests in the partnership, then all facts and circumstances will be considered in determining whether the rights in the partnership possessed by the option holder are possessed solely by virtue of owning a partnership interest. If those rights are possessed solely by virtue of owning a partnership interest, they are not taken into account.

(C) A noncompensatory option holder will not ordinarily be considered to possess partner attributes solely because the noncompensatory option agreement significantly controls or restricts, or the noncompensatory option holder has the ability to significantly control or restrict, a partnership decision that could substantially affect the value of the underlying partnership interest. In particular, the following abilities of the option holder will not be treated as partner attributes:

(1) The ability to impose reasonable restrictions on partnership distributions or dilutive issuances of partnership equity or options while the noncompensatory option is outstanding.

(2) The ability to choose the partnership's section 704(c) method for partnership properties.

(D) When the applicable measurement event is a transfer described in paragraph (c)(1) of this section, the partner attributes of the transferee, not the transferor, are taken into account.

(E) The option holder will be treated as owning all partnership interests and noncompensatory options issued by the partnership that are owned by any person related to the option holder. For purposes of the preceding sentence, a person related to the option holder is defined as any person bearing a relationship to the option holder described in section 267(b) or 707(b).

(e) Substantial tax reduction requirement—(1) General rule. The determination of whether there is a strong likelihood that the failure to treat a noncompensatory option holder as a partner would result in a substantial reduction in the present value of the partners' and the noncompensatory option holder's aggregate Federal tax liabilities is based on all the facts and circumstances, including—

(i) The interaction of the allocations of the issuing partnership and the partners' and noncompensatory option holder's Federal tax attributes (taking into account tax consequences that result from the interaction of the allocations with the partners' and noncompensatory option holder's Federal tax attributes that are unrelated to the partnership);

(ii) The absolute amount of the Federal tax reduction;

(iii) The amount of the reduction relative to overall Federal tax liability; and

(iv) The timing of items of income and deductions.

(2) Special rules. For purposes of applying paragraph (e)(1) of this section to a partner or noncompensatory option holder that is—

(i) A look-through entity (as defined in paragraph (b)(1) of this section), the Federal tax consequences that result from the interaction of allocations of the partnership and the Federal tax attributes of any person that is an owner, or in the case of a trust or estate, the beneficiary, of an interest in such a partner or noncompensatory option holder, whether directly, or indirectly through one or more look-through entities, must be taken into account; or

(ii) A member of a consolidated group (within the meaning of § 1.1502–1(h)), the tax consequences that result from the interaction of the issuing partnership's allocations and the tax attributes of the consolidated group and the tax attributes of another member with respect to a separate return year must be taken into account.

(f) Example. The following example illustrates the provisions of this section. For purposes of the example, assume that PRS is a partnership for Federal tax purposes, none of the noncompensatory option holders or partners are related persons, and that general principles of law do not apply to treat the noncompensatory option as a partnership interest. The example reads as follows:

Example. Active trade or business. PRS is engaged in an active real estate business, the amount of income, gain, loss, and deductions from which cannot be predicted with any reasonable certainty. In exchange for a premium of $10x, PRS issues a noncompensatory option to A to acquire a 10 percent interest in PRS for $110x at any time during a 3-year period commencing on the date on which the option is issued. At the time of the issuance of the noncompensatory option, a 10 percent interest in PRS has a fair market value of $100x. Due to the nature of PRS's business, the value of a 10 percent PRS interest in 3 years is not reasonably predictable as of the time the noncompensatory option is issued. Assuming there are no other facts affecting the certainty of the option's exercise, it is not reasonably certain that A's option will be exercised. Therefore, assuming that A does not possess partner attributes as described in paragraph (d) (3) of this section, A's noncompensatory option is not treated as a partnership interest under paragraph (a)(1) of this section.

(g) Effective/applicability date. This section applies to noncompensatory options issued on or after February 5, 2013

Gain or Loss on Disposition of Property

§ 1.1032–1 Disposition by a corporation of its own capital stock.

(a) The disposition by a corporation of shares of its own stock (including treasury stock) for money or other property does not give rise to taxable gain or deductible loss to the corporation regardless of the nature of the transaction or the facts and circumstances involved. For example, the receipt by a corporation of the subscription price of shares of its stock upon their original issuance gives rise to neither taxable gain nor deductible loss, whether the subscription or issue price be equal to, in excess of, or less than, the par or stated value of such stock. Also, the exchange or sale by a corporation of its own shares for money or other property does not result in taxable gain or deductible loss, even though the corporation deals in such shares as it might in the shares of another corporation. A transfer by a corporation of shares of its own stock (including treasury stock) as compensation for services is considered, for purposes of section 1032(a), as a disposition by the corporation of such shares for money or other property.

(b) Section 1032(a) does not apply to the acquisition by a corporation of shares of its own stock except where the corporation acquires such shares in exchange for shares of its own stock (including treasury stock). See paragraph (e) of § 1.311–1, relating to treatment of acquisitions of a corporation's own stock. Section 1032(a) also does not relate to the tax treatment of the recipient of a corporation's stock.

(c) Where a corporation acquires shares of its own stock in exchange for shares of its own stock (including treasury stock) the transaction may qualify not only under section 1032(a), but also under section 368(a)(1)(E) (recapitalization) or section 305(a) (distribution of stock and stock rights).

(d) For basis of property acquired by a corporation in connection with a transaction to which section 351 applies or in connection with a reorganization, see section 362. For basis of property acquired by a corporation in a transaction to which section 1032 applies but which does not qualify under any other nonrecognition provision, see section 1012.

* * *

§ 1.1032–2 Disposition by a corporation of stock of a controlling corporation in certain triangular reorganizations.

(a) **Scope.** This section provides rules for certain triangular reorganizations described in § 1.358–6(b) when the acquiring corporation (S) acquires property or stock of another corporation (T) in exchange for stock of the corporation (P) in control of S.

(b) **General nonrecognition of gain or loss.** For purposes of § 1.1032–1(a), in the case of a forward triangular merger, a triangular C reorganization, or a triangular B reorganization (as described in § 1.358–6(b)), P stock provided by P to S, or directly to T or T's shareholders on behalf of S, pursuant to the plan of reorganization is treated as a disposition by P of shares of its own stock for T's assets or stock, as applicable. For rules governing the use of P stock in a reverse triangular merger, see section 361.

(c) **Treatment of S.** S must recognize gain or loss on its exchange of P stock as consideration in a forward triangular merger, a triangular C reorganization, or a triangular B reorganization (as described in § 1.358–6(b)), if S did not receive the P stock from P pursuant to the plan of reorganization. See § 1.358–6(d) for the effect on P's basis in its S or T stock, as applicable. For rules governing S's use of P stock in a reverse triangular merger, see section 361.

(d) **Examples.** The rules of this section are illustrated by the following examples. For purposes of these examples, P, S, and T are domestic corporations, P and S do not file consolidated returns, P owns all of the only class of S stock, the P stock exchanged in the transaction satisfies the requirements of the applicable re-organization provisions, and the facts set forth the only corporate activity.

Example (1). Forward triangular merger solely for P stock. (a) Facts. T has assets with an aggregate basis of $60 and fair market value of $100 and no liabilities. Pursuant to a plan, P forms S by transferring $100 of P stock to S and T merges into S. In the merger, the T shareholders receive, in exchange for their T stock, the P stock that P transferred to S. The transaction is a reorganization to which sections 368(a)(1)(A) and (a)(2)(D) apply.

(b) No gain or loss recognized on the use of P stock. Under paragraph (b) of this section, the P stock provided by P pursuant to the plan of reorganization is treated for purposes of § 1.1032–1(a) as disposed of by P for the T assets acquired by S in the merger. Consequently, neither P nor S has taxable gain or deductible loss on the exchange.

Example (2). Forward triangular merger solely for P stock provided in part by S. (a) Facts. T has assets with an aggregate basis of $60 and fair market value of $100 and no liabilities. S is an operating company with substantial assets that has been in existence for several years. S also owns P stock with a $20 adjusted basis and $30 fair market value. S acquired the P stock in an unrelated transaction several years before the reorganization. Pursuant to a plan, P transfers additional P stock worth $70 to S and T merges into S. In the merger, the T shareholders receive $100 of P stock ($70 of P stock provided by P to S as part of the plan and $30 of P stock held by S previously). The transaction is a reorganization to which sections 368(a)(1)(A) and (a)(2)(D) apply.

(b) Gain or loss recognized by S on the use of its P stock. Under paragraph (b) of this section, the $70 of P stock provided by P pursuant to the plan of reorganization is treated as disposed of by P for the T assets acquired by S in the merger. Consequently, neither P nor S has taxable gain or deductible loss on the exchange of those shares. Under paragraph (c) of this section, however, S recognizes $10 of gain

on the exchange of its P stock in the reorganization because S did not receive the P stock from P pursuant to the plan of reorganization. See § 1.358–6(d) for the effect on P's basis in its S stock.

§ 1.1036–1 Stock for stock of the same corporation.

(a) Section 1036 permits the exchange, without the recognition of gain or loss, of common stock for common stock, or of preferred stock for preferred stock, in the same corporation. Section 1036 applies even though voting stock is exchanged for nonvoting stock or nonvoting stock is exchanged for voting stock. It is not limited to an exchange between two individual stockholders; it includes a transaction between a stockholder and the corporation. However, a transaction between a stockholder

and the corporation may qualify not only under section 1036(a), but also under section 368(a)(1)(E) (recapitalization) or section 305(a) (distribution of stock and stock rights). The provisions of section 1036(a) do not apply if stock is exchanged for bonds, or preferred stock is exchanged for common stock, or common stock is exchanged for preferred stock, or common stock in one corporation is exchanged for common stock in another corporation.

* * *

(c) A transfer is not within the provisions of section 1036(a) if as part of the consideration the other party to the exchange assumes a liability of the taxpayer (or if the property transferred is subject to a liability), but the transfer, if otherwise qualified, will be within the provisions of section 1031(b).

S Corporations

§ 1.1361–1 S corporation defined.

(a) In general. For purposes of this title, with respect to any taxable year—(1) The term S corporation means a small business corporation (as defined in paragraph (b) of this section) for which an election under section 1362(a) is in effect for that taxable year.

(2) The term C corporation means a corporation that is not an S corporation for that taxable year.

(b) Small business corporation defined—(1) In general. For purposes of subchapter S, chapter 1 of the Code and the regulations thereunder, the term small business corporation means a domestic corporation that is not an ineligible corporation (as defined in section 1361(b)(2)) and that does not have—

(i) More than the number of shareholders provided in section 1361(b)(1)(A);

(ii) As a shareholder, a person (other than an estate, a trust described in section 1361(c)(2), or, for taxable years beginning after De-

cember 31, 1997, an organization described in section 1361(c)(6)) who is not an individual;

(iii) A nonresident alien as a shareholder; or

(iv) More than one class of stock.

(2) Estate in bankruptcy. The term estate, for purposes of this paragraph, includes the estate of an individual in a case under title 11 of the United States Code.

(3) Treatment of restricted stock. For purposes of subchapter S, stock that is issued in connection with the performance of services (within the meaning of § 1.83–3(f)) and that is substantially nonvested (within the meaning of § 1.83–3(b)) is not treated as outstanding stock of the corporation, and the holder of that stock is not treated as a shareholder solely by reason of holding the stock, unless the holder makes an election with respect to the stock under section 83(b). In the event of such an election, the stock is treated as outstanding stock of the corporation, and the holder of the stock is treated as a shareholder for purposes of subchapter S.

See paragraphs (*l*)(1) and (3) of this section for rules for determining whether substantially nonvested stock with respect to which an election under section 83(b) has been made is treated as a second class of stock.

(4) Treatment of deferred compensation plans. For purposes of subchapter S, an instrument, obligation, or arrangement is not outstanding stock if it—

(i) Does not convey the right to vote;

(ii) Is an unfunded and unsecured promise to pay money or property in the future;

(iii) Is issued to an individual who is an employee in connection with the performance of services for the corporation or to an individual who is an independent contractor in connection with the performance of services for the corporation (and is not excessive by reference to the services performed); and

(iv) Is issued pursuant to a plan with respect to which the employee or independent contractor is not taxed currently on income.

A deferred compensation plan that has a current payment feature (e.g., payment of dividend equivalent amounts that are taxed currently as compensation) is not for that reason excluded from this paragraph (b)(4).

(5) Treatment of straight debt. For purposes of subchapter S, an instrument or obligation that satisfies the definition of straight debt in paragraph (*l*)(5) of this section is not treated as outstanding stock.

* * *

(c) Domestic corporation. For purposes of paragraph (b) of this section, the term domestic corporation means a domestic corporation as defined in Sec. 301.7701–5 of this chapter, and the term corporation includes an entity that is classified as an association taxable as a corporation under Sec. 301.7701–2 of this chapter.

* * *

(e) Number of shareholders—(1) General rule. A corporation does not qualify as a small business corporation if it has more than the number of shareholders provided in section 1361(b)(1)(A). Ordinarily, the person who would have to include in gross income dividends distributed with respect to the stock of the corporation (if the corporation were a C corporation) is considered to be the shareholder of the corporation. For example, if stock (owned other than by a husband and wife or members of a family described in section 1361(c)(1)) is owned by tenants in common or joint tenants, each tenant in common or joint tenant is generally considered to be a shareholder of the corporation. (For special rules relating to stock owned by husband and wife or members of a family, see paragraphs (e)(2) and (3) of this section, respectively; for special rules relating to restricted stock, see paragraphs (b)(3) and (6) of this section.) The person for whom stock of a corporation is held by a nominee, guardian, custodian, or an agent is considered to be the shareholder of the corporation for purposes of this paragraph (e) and paragraphs (f) and (g) of this section. For example, a partnership may be a nominee of S corporation stock for a person who qualifies as a shareholder of an S corporation. However, if the partnership is the beneficial owner of the stock, then the partnership is the shareholder, and the corporation does not qualify as a small business corporation. In addition, in the case of stock held for a minor under a uniform transfers to minors act or similar statute, the minor and not the custodian is the shareholder. Except as otherwise provided in paragraphs (h) and (j) of this section, and for purposes of this paragraph (e) and paragraphs (f) and (g) of this section, if stock is held by a decedent's estate or a trust described in section 1361(c)(2)(A)(ii) or (iii), the estate or trust (and not the beneficiaries of the estate or trust) is considered to be the shareholder; however, if stock is held by a subpart E trust (which includes a voting trust) or an electing QSST described in section 1361(d)(1), the deemed owner of the trust is considered to be the shareholder. If stock is held by an ESBT described in section 1361(c)(2)(A)(v), each potential current beneficiary of the trust shall be treated as a shareholder, except that the trust shall be treated as the shareholder during any period in which there is no potential current beneficiary of the trust. If stock is held by a trust described in section 1361(c)(2)(A)(vi), the individual for whose benefit the trust was created shall be treated as the shareholder. See paragraph (h) of this section for special rules relating to trusts.

(2) Special rules relating to stock owned by husband and wife. For purposes of paragraph (e)(1) of this section, stock owned by a husband and wife (or by either or both of their estates) is treated as if owned by one shareholder, regardless of the form in which they own the stock. For example, if husband and wife are owners of a subpart E trust, they will be treated as one individual. Both husband and wife must be U.S. citizens or residents, and a decedent spouse's estate must not be a foreign estate as defined in section 7701(a)(31). The treatment described in this paragraph (e)(2) will cease upon dissolution of the marriage for any reason other than death.

(3) Special rules relating to stock owned by members of a family—(i) In general. For purposes of paragraph (e)(1) of this section, stock owned by members of a family is treated as owned by one shareholder. Members of a family include a common ancestor, any lineal descendant of the common ancestor (without any generational limit), and any spouse (or former spouse) of the common ancestor or of any lineal descendants of the common ancestor. An individual shall not be considered to be a common ancestor if, on the applicable date, the individual is more than six generations removed from the youngest generation of shareholders who would be members of the family determined by deeming that individual as the common ancestor. For purposes of this six-generation test, a spouse (or former spouse) is treated as being of the same generation as the individual to whom the spouse is or was married. This test is applied on the latest of the date the election under section 1362(a) is made for the corporation, the earliest date that a member of the family (determined by deeming that individual as the common ancestor) holds stock in the corporation, or October 22, 2004. For this purpose, the date the election under section 1362(a) is made for the corporation is the effective date of the election, not the date it is signed or received by any person. The test is only applied as of the applicable date, and lineal descendants (and spouses) more than six generations removed from the common ancestor will be treated as members of the family even if they acquire stock in the corporation after that date. The members of a family are treated as one shareholder under this paragraph (e)(3) solely for purposes of section 1361(b)(1)(A), and not for any other purpose, whether under section 1361 or any other provision. Specifically, each member of the family who owns or is deemed to own stock must meet the requirements of sections 1361(b)(1)(B) and (C) (regarding permissible shareholders) and section 1362(a)(2) (regarding shareholder consents to an S corporation election). Although a person may be a member of more than one family under this paragraph (e)(3), each family (not all of whose members are also members of the other family) will be treated as one shareholder. For purposes of this paragraph (e)(3), any legally adopted child of an individual, any child who is lawfully placed with an individual for legal adoption by that individual, and any eligible foster child of an individual (within the meaning of section 152(f)(1)(C)), shall be treated as a child of such individual by blood.

(ii) Certain entities treated as members of a family. For purposes of this paragraph (e)(3), the estate or trust (described in section 1361(c)(2)(A)(ii) or (iii)) of a deceased member of the family will be considered to be a member of the family during the period in which the estate or such trust (if the trust is described in section 1361(c)(2)(A)(ii) or (iii)), holds stock in the S corporation. The members of the family also will include—

(A) In the case of an ESBT, each potential current beneficiary who is a member of the family;

(B) In the case of a QSST, the income beneficiary who makes the QSST election, if that income beneficiary is a member of the family;

(C) In the case of a trust created primarily to exercise the voting power of stock transferred to it, each beneficiary who is a member of the family;

(D) The individual for whose benefit a trust described in section 1361(c)(2)(A)(vi) was created, if that individual is a member of the family;

(E) The deemed owner of a trust described in section 1361(c)(2)(A)(i) if that deemed owner is a member of the family; and

(F) The owner of an entity disregarded as an entity separate from its owner under § 301.7701–3 of this chapter, if that owner is a member of the family.

(f) Shareholder must be an individual or estate. Except as otherwise provided in paragraph (e)(1) of this section (relating to nominees), paragraph (h) of this section (relating to certain trusts), and, for taxable years beginning after December 31, 1997, section 1361(c)(6) (relating to certain exempt organizations), a corporation in which any shareholder is a corporation, partnership, or trust does not qualify as a small business corporation.

(g) Nonresident alien shareholder—(1) General rule. (i) A corporation having a shareholder who is a nonresident alien as defined in section 7701(b)(1)(B) does not qualify as a small business corporation. If a U.S. shareholder's spouse is a nonresident alien who has a current ownership interest (as opposed, for example, to a survivorship interest) in the stock of the corporation by reason of any applicable law, such as a state community property law of a foreign country's law, the corporation

does not qualify as a small business corporation from the time the nonresident alien spouse acquires the interest in the stock. If a corporation's S election is inadvertently terminated as a result of a nonresident alien spouse being considered a shareholder, the corporation may request relief under section 1362(f).

* * *

(l) Classes of stock—(1) General rule. A corporation that has more than one class of stock does not qualify as a small business corporation. Except as provided in paragraph (l)(4) of this section (relating to instruments, obligations, or arrangements treated as a second class of stock), a corporation is treated as having only one class of stock if all outstanding shares of stock of the corporation confer identical rights to distribution and liquidation proceeds. Differences in voting rights among shares of stock of a corporation are disregarded in determining whether a corporation has more than one class of stock. Thus, if all shares of stock of an S corporation have identical rights to distribution and liquidation proceeds, the corporation may have voting and nonvoting common stock, a class of stock that may vote only on certain issues, irrevocable proxy agreements, or groups of shares that differ with respect to rights to elect members of the board of directors.

(2) Determination of whether stock confers identical rights to distribution and liquidation proceeds—(i) In general. The determination of whether all outstanding shares of stock confer identical rights to distribution and liquidation proceeds is made based on the corporate charter, articles of incorporation, bylaws, applicable state law, and binding agreements relating to distribution and liquidation proceeds (collectively, the governing provisions). A commercial contractual agreement, such as a lease, employment agreement, or loan agreement, is not a binding agreement relating to distribution and liquidation proceeds and thus is not a governing provision unless a principal purpose of the agreement is to circumvent the one class of stock requirement of section 1361(b)(1)(D) and this paragraph (*l*). Although a corporation is not treated as having more than one class of stock so long as the governing provisions provide for identical distribution and liquidation rights, any distributions (including actual, constructive, or deemed distributions) that differ in timing or amount are to be given appropriate tax effect in accordance with the facts and circumstances.

(ii) State law requirements for payment and withholding of income tax. State laws may require a corporation to pay or withhold state income taxes on behalf of some or all of the corporation's shareholders. Such laws are disregarded in determining whether all outstanding shares of stock of the corporation confer identical rights to distribution and liquidation proceeds, within the meaning of paragraph (*l*)(1) of this section, provided that, when the constructive distributions resulting from the payment or withholding of taxes by the corporation are taken into account, the outstanding shares confer identical rights to distribution and liquidation proceeds. A difference in timing between the constructive distributions and the actual distributions to the other shareholders does not cause the corporation to be treated as having more than one class of stock.

(iii) Buy-sell and redemption agreements—(A) In general. Buy-sell agreements among shareholders, agreements restricting the transferability of stock, and redemption agreements are disregarded in determining whether a corporation's outstanding shares of stock confer identical distribution and liquidation rights unless—

(1) A principal purpose of the agreement is to circumvent the one class of stock requirement of section 1361(b)(1)(D) and this paragraph (*l*), and

(2) The agreement establishes a purchase price that, at the time the agreement is entered into, is significantly in excess of or below the fair market value of the stock.

Agreements that provide for the purchase or redemption of stock at book value or at a price between fair market value and book value are not considered to establish a price that is significantly in excess of or below the fair market value of the stock and, thus, are disregarded in determining whether the outstanding shares of stock confer identical rights. For purposes of this paragraph (*l*)(2)(iii)(A), a good faith determination of fair market value will be respected unless it can be shown that the value was substantially in error and the determination of the value was not performed with reasonable diligence. Although an agreement may be disregarded in determining whether shares of stock confer identical distribution and liquidation rights, payments pursuant to the agreement may have income or transfer tax consequences.

(B) Exception for certain agreements. Bona fide agreements to redeem or purchase stock at the time of death, divorce, disability, or termination of employment are disregarded in determining whether a corporation's shares of stock confer identical rights. In addition, if stock that is substantially nonvested (within the meaning of § 1.83–3(b)) is treated as outstanding under these regulations, the forfeiture provisions that cause the stock to be substantially nonvested are disregarded. Furthermore, the Commissioner may provide by Revenue Ruling or other published guidance that other types of bona fide agreements to redeem or purchase stock are disregarded.

(C) Safe harbors for determinations of book value. A determination of book value will be respected if—

(1) The book value is determined in accordance with Generally Accepted Accounting Principles (including permitted optional adjustments); or

(2) The book value is used for any substantial nontax purpose.

(iv) Distributions that take into account varying interests in stock during a taxable year. A governing provision does not, within the meaning of paragraph (*l*)(2)(i) of this section, alter the rights to liquidation and distribution proceeds conferred by an S corporation's stock merely because the governing provision provides that, as a result of a change in stock ownership, distributions in a taxable year are to be made on the basis of the shareholders' varying interests in the S corporation's income in the current or immediately preceding taxable year. If distributions pursuant to the provision are not made within a reasonable time after the close of the taxable year in which the varying interests occur, the distributions may be recharacterized depending on the facts and circumstances, but will not result in a second class of stock.

(v) Examples. The application of paragraph (*l*)(2) of this section may be illustrated by the following examples. In each of the examples, the S corporation requirements of section 1361 are satisfied except as otherwise stated, the corporation has in effect an S election under section 1362, and the corporation has only the shareholders described.

Example (1). Determination of whether stock confers identical rights to distribution and liquidation proceeds. (i) The law of State A requires that permission be obtained from the State Commissioner of Corporations before stock may be issued by a corporation. The Commissioner grants permission to S, a corporation, to issue its stock subject to the restriction that any person who is issued stock in exchange for property, and not cash, must waive all rights to receive distributions until the shareholders who contributed cash for stock have received distributions in the amount of their cash contributions.

(ii) The condition imposed by the Commissioner pursuant to state law alters the rights to distribution and liquidation proceeds conferred by the outstanding stock of S so that those rights are not identical. Accordingly,

under paragraph (*l*)(2)(i) of this section, S is treated as having more than one class of stock and does not qualify as a small business corporation.

Example (2). Distributions that differ in timing. (i) S, a corporation, has two equal shareholders, A and B. Under S's bylaws, A and B are entitled to equal distributions. S distributes $50,000 to A in the current year, but does not distribute $50,000 to B until one year later. The circumstances indicate that the difference in timing did not occur by reason of a binding agreement relating to distribution or liquidation proceeds.

(ii) Under paragraph (*l*)(2)(i) of this section, the difference in timing of the distributions to A and B does not cause S to be treated as having more than one class of stock. However, section 7872 or other recharacterization principles may apply to determine the appropriate tax consequences.

Example (3). Treatment of excessive compensation. (i) S, a corporation, has two equal shareholders, C and D, who are each employed by S and have binding employment agreements with S. The compensation paid by S to C under C's employment agreement is reasonable. The compensation paid by S to D under D's employment agreement, however, is found to be excessive. The facts and circumstances do not reflect that a principal purpose to D's employment agreement is to circumvent the one class of stock requirement of section 1361(b)(1)(D) and this paragraph (*l*).

(ii) Under paragraph (*l*)(2)(i) of this section, the employment agreements are not governing provisions. Accordingly, S is not treated as having more than one class of stock by reason of the employment agreements, even though S is not allowed a deduction for the excessive compensation paid to D.

Example (4). Agreement to pay fringe benefits. (i) S, a corporation, is required under binding agreements to pay accident and health insurance premiums on behalf of certain of its employees who are also shareholders. Different premium amounts are paid by S for each employee-shareholder. The facts and circumstances do not reflect that a principal purpose of the agreements is to circumvent the one class of stock requirement of section 1361(b)(1)(D) and this paragraph (*l*).

(ii) Under paragraph (*l*)(2)(i) of this section, the agreements are not governing provisions. Accordingly, S is not treated as having more than one class of stock by reason of the agreements. In addition, S is not treated as having more than one class of stock by reason of the payment of fringe benefits.

Example (5). Below-market corporation-shareholder loan. (i) E is a shareholder of S, a corporation. S makes a below-market loan to E that is a corporation-shareholder loan to which section 7872 applies. Under section 7872, E is deemed to receive a distribution with respect to S stock by reason of the loan. The facts and circumstances do not reflect that a principal purpose of the loan is to circumvent the one class of stock requirement of section 1361(b)(1)(D) and this paragraph (*l*).

(ii) Under paragraph (*l*)(2)(i) of this section, the loan agreement is not a governing provision. Accordingly, S is not treated as having more than one class of stock by reason of the below-market loan to E.

Example (6). Agreement to adjust distributions for state tax burdens. (i) S, a corporation, executes a binding agreement with its shareholders to modify its normal distribution policy by making upward adjustments of its distributions to those shareholders who bear heavier state tax burdens. The adjustments are based on a formula that will give the shareholders equal after-tax distributions.

(ii) The binding agreement relates to distribution or liquidation proceeds. The agreement is thus a governing provision that alters the rights conferred by the outstanding stock of S to distribution proceeds so that those rights are not identical. Therefore, under paragraph

(*l*)(2)(i) of this section, S is treated as having more than one class of stock.

Example (7). State law requirements for payment and withholding of income tax. (i) The law of State X requires corporations to pay state income taxes on behalf of nonresident shareholders. The law of State X does not require corporations to pay state income taxes on behalf of resident shareholders. S is incorporated in State X. S's resident shareholders have the right (for example, under the law of State X or pursuant to S's bylaws or a binding agreement) to distributions that take into account the payments S makes on behalf of its nonresident shareholders.

(ii) The payment by S of state income taxes on behalf of its nonresident shareholders are generally treated as constructive distributions to those shareholders. Because S's resident shareholders have the right to equal distributions, taking into account the constructive distributions to the nonresident shareholders, S's shares confer identical rights to distribution proceeds. Accordingly, under paragraph (*l*)(2)(ii) of this section, the state law requiring S to pay state income taxes on behalf of its nonresident shareholders is disregarded in determining whether S has more than one class of stock.

(iii) The same result would follow if the payments of state income taxes on behalf of nonresident shareholders are instead treated as advances to those shareholders and the governing provisions require the advances to be repaid or offset by reductions in distributions to those shareholders.

Example (8). Redemption agreements. (i) F, G, and H are shareholders of S, a corporation. F is also an employee of S. By agreement, S is to redeem F's shares on the termination of F's employment.

(ii) On these facts, under paragraph (*l*)(2)(iii)(B) of this section, the agreement is disregarded in determining whether all outstanding

shares of S's stock confer identical rights to distribution and liquidation proceeds.

Example (9). Analysis of redemption agreements. (i) J, K, and L are shareholders of S, a corporation. L is also an employee of S. L's shares were not issued to L in connection with the performance of services. By agreement, S is to redeem L's shares for an amount significantly below their fair market value on the termination of L's employment or if S's sales fall below certain levels.

(ii) Under paragraph (*l*)(2)(iii)(B) of this section, the portion of the agreement providing for redemption of L's stock on termination of employment is disregarded. Under paragraph (*l*)(2)(iii)(A), the portion of the agreement providing for redemption of L's stock if S's sales fall below certain levels is disregarded unless a principal purpose of that portion of the agreement is to circumvent the one class of stock requirement of section 1361(b)(1)(D) and this paragraph (*l*).

(3) Stock taken into account. Except as provided in paragraphs (b)(3), (4), and (5) of this section (relating to restricted stock, deferred compensation plans, and straight debt), in determining whether all outstanding shares of stock confer identical rights to distribution and liquidation proceeds, all outstanding shares of stock of a corporation are taken into account. For example, substantially nonvested stock with respect to which an election under section 83(b) has been made is taken into account in determining whether a corporation has a second class of stock, and such stock is not treated as a second class of stock if the stock confers rights to distribution and liquidation proceeds that are identical, within the meaning of paragraph (*l*)(1) of this section, to the rights conferred by the other outstanding shares of stock.

(4) Other instruments, obligations, or arrangements treated as a second class of stock—(i) In general. Instruments, obligations, or arrangements are not treated as a second class of stock for purposes of this paragraph (*l*) unless they are described in paragraph (*l*)(5)(ii) or (iii) of this section. However, in no event are instruments, obligations, or arrangements described in paragraph (b) (4) of this section (relating to deferred compensation plans), paragraphs (*l*)(4)(iii)(B) and (C) of this section (relating to the exceptions and safe harbor for options), paragraph (*l*)(4) (ii)(B) of this section (relating to the safe harbors for certain short-term unwritten advances and proportionally-held debt), or paragraph (*l*) (5) of this section (relating to the safe harbor for straight debt), treated as a second class of stock for purposes of this paragraph (*l*).

(ii) Instruments, obligations, or arrangements treated as equity under general principles—(A) In general. Except as provided in paragraph (*l*)(4)(i) of this section, any instrument, obligation, or arrangement issued by a corporation (other than outstanding shares of stock described in paragraph (*l*)(3) of this section), regardless of whether designated as debt, is treated as a second class of stock of the corporation—

(1) If the instrument, obligation, or arrangement constitutes equity or otherwise results in the holder being treated as the owner of stock under general principles of Federal tax law; and

(2) A principal purpose of issuing or entering into the instrument, obligation, or arrangement is to circumvent the rights to distribution or liquidation proceeds conferred by the outstanding shares of stock or to circumvent the limitation on eligible shareholders contained in paragraph (b)(1) of this section.

(B) Safe harbor for certain short-term unwritten advances and proportionately held obligations—(1) Short-term unwritten advances. Unwritten advances from a shareholder that do not exceed $10,000 in the aggregate at any time during the taxable year of the corporation, are treated as debt by the parties, and are expected to be repaid within a reasonable time are not treated as a second class of stock for that taxable year, even if the advances are considered equity under general principles of Federal tax law. The failure of an unwritten advance to meet this safe harbor will not result in a second class of stock unless the advance is considered equity under paragraph (*l*)(4)(ii)(A)(*1*) of this section and a principal purpose of the advance is to circumvent the rights of the outstanding shares of stock or the limitation on eligible shareholders under paragraph (*l*)(4)(ii)(A)(*2*) of this section.

(2) Proportionately-held obligations. Obligations of the same class that are considered equity under general principles of Federal tax law, but are owned solely by the owners of, and in the same proportion as, the outstanding stock of the corporation, are not treated as a second class of stock. Furthermore, an obligation or obligations owned by the sole shareholder of a corporation are always held proportionately to the corporation's outstanding stock. The obligations that are considered equity that do not meet this safe harbor will not result in a second class of stock unless a principal purpose of the obligations is to circumvent the rights of the outstanding shares of stock or the limitation on eligible shareholders under paragraph (*l*)(4)(ii)(A)(*2*) of this section.

(iii) Certain call options, warrants or similar instruments—(A) In general. Except as otherwise provided in this paragraph (*l*)(4)(iii), a call option, warrant, or similar instrument (collectively, call option) issued by a corporation is treated as a second class of stock of the corporation if, taking into account all the facts and circumstances, the call option is substantially certain to be exercised (by the holder or a potential transferee) and has a strike price substantially below the fair market value of the underlying stock on the date that the call option is issued, transferred by a person who is an eligible shareholder under paragraph (b)(1) of this section to a person who is not an eligible shareholder under paragraph (b)(1) of this section, or materially modified. For purposes of this paragraph (*l*)(4)(iii), if an option is issued in connection with a loan and the time

period in which the option can be exercised is extended in connection with (and consistent with) a modification of the terms of the loan, the extension of the time period in which the option may be exercised is not considered a material modification. In addition, a call option does not have a strike price substantially below fair market value if the price at the time of exercise cannot, pursuant to the terms of the instrument, be substantially below the fair market value of the underlying stock at the time of exercise.

(B) Certain exceptions. (1) A call option is not treated as a second class of stock for purposes of this paragraph (*l*) if it is issued to a person that is actively and regularly engaged in the business of lending and issued in connection with a commercially reasonable loan to the corporation. This paragraph (*l*)(4)(iii) (B)(1) continues to apply if the call option is transferred with the loan (or if a portion of the call option is transferred with a corresponding portion of the loan). However, if the call option is transferred without a corresponding portion of the loan, this paragraph (*l*)(4)(iii)(B) (1) ceases to apply. Upon that transfer, the call option is tested under paragraph (*l*)(4)(iii)(A) (notwithstanding anything in that paragraph to the contrary) if, but for this paragraph, the call option would have been treated as a second class of stock on the date it was issued.

(2) A call option that is issued to an individual who is either an employee or an independent contractor in connection with the performance of services for the corporation or a related corporation (and that is not excessive by reference to the services performed) is not treated as a second class of stock for purposes of this paragraph (*l*) if—

(i) The call option is nontransferable within the meaning of § 1.83–3(d); and

(ii) The call option does not have a readily ascertainable fair market value as defined in § 1.83–7(b) at the time the option is issued.

If the call option becomes transferable, this paragraph (*l*)(4)(iii)(B)(2) ceases to apply. Solely for purposes of this paragraph (*l*)(4)(iii) (B)(2), a corporation is related to the issuing corporation if more than 50 percent of the total voting power and total value of its stock is owned by the issuing corporation.

(3) The Commissioner may provide other exceptions by Revenue Ruling or other published guidance.

(C) **Safe harbor for certain options.** A call option is not treated as a second class of stock if, on the date the call option is issued, transferred by a person who is an eligible shareholder under paragraph (b)(1) of this section to a person who is not an eligible shareholder under paragraph (b)(1) of this section, or materially modified, the strike price of the call option is at least 90 percent of the fair market value of the underlying stock on that date. For purposes of this paragraph (*l*)(4)(iii)(C), a good faith determination of fair market value by the corporation will be respected unless it can be shown that the value was substantially in error and the determination of the value was not performed with reasonable diligence to obtain a fair value. Failure of an option to meet this safe harbor will not necessarily result in the option being treated as a second class of stock.

(iv) **Convertible debt.** A convertible debt instrument is considered a second class of stock if—

(A) It would be treated as a second class of stock under paragraph (*l*)(4)(ii) of this section (relating to instruments, obligations, or arrangements treated as equity under general principles); or

(B) It embodies rights equivalent to those of a call option that would be treated as a second class of stock under paragraph (*l*)(4)(iii) of this section (relating to certain call options, warrants, and similar instruments).

(v) **Examples.** The application of this paragraph (*l*)(4) may be illustrated by the following examples. In each of the examples, the S corporation requirements of section 1361 are satisfied except as otherwise stated, the corporation has in effect an S election under section 1362, and the corporation has only the shareholders described.

Example (1). Transfer of call option by eligible shareholder to ineligible shareholder. (i) S, a corporation, has 10 shareholders. S issues call options to A, B, and C, individuals who are U.S. residents. A, B, and C are not shareholders, employees, or independent contractors of S. The options have a strike price of $40 and are issued on a date when the fair market value of S stock is also $40. A year later, P, a partnership, purchases A's option. On the date of transfer, the fair market value of S stock is $80.

(ii) On the date the call option is issued, its strike price is not substantially below the fair market value of the S stock. Under paragraph (*l*)(4)(iii)(A) of this section, whether a call option is a second class of stock must be redetermined if the call option is transferred by a person who is an eligible shareholder under paragraph (b)(1) of this section to a person who is not an eligible shareholder under paragraph (b)(1) of this section. In this case, A is an eligible shareholder of S under paragraph (b)(1) of this section, but P is not. Accordingly, the option is retested on the date it is transferred to D.

(iii) Because on the date the call option is transferred to P its strike price is 50% of the fair market value, the strike price is substantially below the fair market value of the S stock. Accordingly, the call option is treated as a second class of stock as of the date it is transferred to P if, at that time, it is determined that the option is substantially certain to be exercised. The determination of whether the option is substantially certain to be exercised is made on the basis of all the facts and circumstances.

Example (2). Call option issued in connection with the performance of services. (i) E is a bona fide employee of S, a corporation.

S issues to E a call option in connection with E's performance of services. At the time the call option is issued, it is not transferable and does not have a readily ascertainable fair market value. However, the call option becomes transferable before it is exercised by E.

(ii) While the option is not transferable, under paragraph (*l*)(4)(iii)(B)(2) of this section it is not treated as a second class of stock, regardless of its strike price. When the option becomes transferable, that paragraph ceases to apply, and the general rule of paragraph (*l*)(4)(iii)(A) of this section applies. Accordingly, if the option is materially modified or is transferred to a person who is not an eligible shareholder under paragraph (b)(1) of this section, and on the date of such modification or transfer, the option is substantially certain to be exercised and has a strike price substantially below the fair market value of the underlying stock, the option is treated as a second class of stock.

(iii) If E left S's employment before the option became transferable, the exception provided by paragraph (*l*)(4)(iii)(B)(2) would continue to apply until the option became transferable.

(5) Straight debt safe harbor—(i) In general. Notwithstanding paragraph (*l*)(4) of this section, straight debt is not treated as a second class of stock. For purposes of section 1361(c)(5) and this section, the term straight debt means a written unconditional obligation, regardless of whether embodied in a formal note, to pay a sum certain on demand, or on a specified due date, which—

(A) Does not provide for an interest rate or payment dates that are contingent on profits, the borrower's discretion, the payment of dividends with respect to common stock, or similar factors;

(B) Is not convertible (directly or indirectly) into stock or any other equity interest of the S corporation; and

(C) Is held by an individual (other than a nonresident alien), an estate, or a trust described in section 1361(c)(2).

(ii) Subordination. The fact that an obligation is subordinated to other debt of the corporation does not prevent the obligation from qualifying as straight debt.

(iii) Modification or transfer. An obligation that originally qualifies as straight debt ceases to so qualify if the obligation—

(A) Is materially modified so that it no longer satisfies the definition of straight debt; or

(B) Is transferred to a third party who is not an eligible shareholder under paragraph (b)(1) of this section.

(iv) Treatment of straight debt for other purposes. An obligation of an S corporation that satisfies the definition of straight debt in paragraph (*l*)(5)(i) of this section is not treated as a second class of stock even if it is considered equity under general principles of Federal tax law. Such an obligation is generally treated as debt and when so treated is subject to the applicable rules governing indebtedness for other purposes of the Code. Accordingly, interest paid or accrued with respect to a straight debt obligation is generally treated as interest by the corporation and the recipient and does not constitute a distribution to which section 1368 applies. However, if a straight debt obligation bears a rate of interest that is unreasonably high, an appropriate portion of the interest may be recharacterized and treated as a payment that is not interest. Such a recharacterization does not result in a second class of stock.

(v) Treatment of C corporation debt upon conversion to S status. If a C corporation has outstanding an obligation that satisfies the definition of straight debt in paragraph (*l*)(5)(i) of this section, but that is considered equity under general principles of Federal tax law, the obligation is not treated as a second class of stock for purposes of this section if the C corporation converts to S status. In addition, the conversion from C corporation status to S corporation status is not treated as an exchange of debt for stock with respect to such an instrument.

(6) Inadvertent terminations. See section 1362(f) and the regulations thereunder for rules relating to inadvertent terminations in cases where the one class of stock requirement has been inadvertently breached.

(7) Effective date. Section 1.1361–1(*l*) generally applies to taxable years of a corporation beginning on or after May 28, 1992. However, § 1.1361–1(*l*) does not apply to: an instrument, obligation, or arrangement issued or entered into before May 28, 1992 and not materially modified after that date; a buy-sell agreement, redemption agreement, or agreement restricting transferability entered into before May 28, 1992 and not materially modified after that date; or a call option or similar instrument issued before May 28, 1992 and not materially modified after that date. In addition, a corporation and its shareholders may apply this § 1.1361–1(*l*) to prior taxable years.

§ 1.1361–2 Definitions relating to S corporation subsidiaries.

(a) In general. The term qualified subchapter S subsidiary (QSub) means any domestic corporation that is not an incligible corporation (as defined in section 1361(b)(2) and the regulations thereunder), if—

(1) 100 percent of the stock of such corporation is held by an S corporation; and

(2) The S corporation properly elects to treat the subsidiary as a QSub under § 1.1361–3.

(b) Stock treated as held by S corporation. For purposes of satisfying the 100 percent stock ownership requirement in section 1361(b)(3)(B)(i) and paragraph (a)(1) of this section—

(1) Stock of a corporation is treated as held by an S corporation if the S corporation is the owner of that stock for Federal income tax purposes; and

(2) Any outstanding instruments, obligations, or arrangements of the corporation which would not be considered stock for purposes of section 1361(b)(1)(D) if the corporation were an S corporation are not treated as outstanding stock of the QSub.

(c) Straight debt safe harbor. Section 1.1361–1(*l*)(5)(iv) and (v) apply to an obligation of a corporation for which a QSub election is made if that obligation would satisfy the definition of straight debt in § 1.1361–1(*l*)(5) if issued by the S corporation.

(d) Examples. The following examples illustrate the application of this section:

Example (1). X, an S corporation, owns 100 percent of Y, a corporation for which a valid QSub election is in effect for the taxable year. Y owns 100 percent of Z, a corporation otherwise eligible for QSub status. X may elect to treat Z as a QSub under section 1361(b)(3)(B)(ii).

Example (2). Assume the same facts as in Example 1, except that Y is a business entity that is disregarded as an entity separate from its owner under § 301.7701–2(c)(2) of this chapter. X may elect to treat Z as a QSub.

Example (3). Assume the same facts as in Example 1, except that Y owns 50 percent of Z, and X owns the other 50 percent. X may elect to treat Z as a QSub.

Example (4). Assume the same facts as in Example 1, except that Y is a C corporation. Although Y is a domestic corporation that is otherwise eligible to be a QSub, no QSub election has been made for Y. Thus, X is not treated as holding the stock of Z. Consequently, X may not elect to treat Z as a QSub.

Example (5). Individuals A and B own 100 percent of the stock of corporation X, an S corporation, and, except for C's interest (described below), X owns 100 percent of corporation Y, a C corporation. Individual C holds an instrument issued by Y that is considered to be equity under general principles of tax law but would satisfy the definition of straight debt under § 1.1361–1(*l*)(5) if Y were an S corporation. In determining whether X owns 100 percent of Y for purposes of making the QSub election, the instrument held by C is not considered outstanding stock. In addition, under § 1.1361–1(*l*)(5)(v), the QSub election is not treated as an exchange of debt for stock with respect to such instrument, and § 1.1361–1(*l*)(5)(iv) applies to determine the tax treatment of payments on the instrument while Y's QSub election is in effect.

§ 1.1361–3 QSub election.

(a) **Time and manner of making election—(1) In general.** The corporation for which the QSub election is made must meet all the requirements of section 1361(b)(3)(B) at the time the election is made and for all periods for which the election is to be effective.

(2) **Manner of making election.** Except as provided in section 1361(b)(3)(D) and § 1.1361–5(c) (five-year prohibition on re-election), an S corporation may elect to treat an eligible subsidiary as a QSub by filing a completed form to be prescribed by the IRS. The election form must be signed by a person authorized to sign the S corporation's return required to be filed under section 6037. Unless the election form provides otherwise, the election must be submitted to the service center where the subsidiary filed its most recent tax return (if applicable), and, if an S corporation forms a subsidiary and makes a valid QSub election (effective upon the date of the subsidiary's formation) for the subsidiary, the election should be submitted to the service center where the S corporation filed its most recent return.

(3) **Time of making election.** A QSub election may be made by the S corporation parent at any time during the taxable year.

* * *

(5) **Example.** The following example illustrates the application of paragraph (a)(4) of this section:

Example. X has been a calendar year S corporation engaged in a trade or business for several years. X acquires the stock of Y, a calendar year C corporation, on April 1, 2002. On August 10, 2002, X makes an election to treat Y as a QSub. Unless otherwise specified on the election form, the election will be effective as of August 10, 2002. If specified on the election form, the election may be effective on some other date that is not more than two months and 15 days prior to August 10, 2002, and not more than 12 months after August 10, 2002.

(6) **Extension of time for making a QSub election.** An extension of time to make a QSub election may be available under the procedures applicable under §§ 301.9100–1 and 301.9100–3 of this chapter.

(b) **Revocation of QSub election—(1) Manner of revoking QSub election.** An S corporation may revoke a QSub election under section 1361 by filing a statement with the service center where the S corporation's most recent tax return was properly filed. The revocation statement must include the names, addresses, and taxpayer identification numbers of both the parent S corporation and the QSub, if any. The statement must be signed by a person authorized to sign the S corporation's return required to be filed under section 6037.

(2) **Effective date of revocation.** The revocation of a QSub election is effective on the date specified on the revocation statement or on the date the revocation statement is filed if no date is specified. The effective date specified on the revocation statement cannot be more than two months and 15 days prior to the date on which the revocation statement is filed and cannot be more than 12 months after the date on which the revocation statement is filed. If a revocation statement specifies an effective date more than two months and 15 days prior to the date on which the statement is filed, it will be effective two months and 15 days pri-

or to the date it is filed. If a revocation statement specifies an effective date more than 12 months after the date on which the statement is filed, it will be effective 12 months after the date it is filed.

(3) Revocation after termination. A revocation may not be made after the occurrence of an event that renders the subsidiary ineligible for QSub status under section 1361(b)(3)(B).

(4) Revocation before QSub election effective. For purposes of Section 1361(b)(3)(D) and § 1.1361–5(c) (five-year prohibition on re-election), a revocation effective on the first day the QSub election was to be effective will not be treated as a termination of a QSub election.

§ 1.1361–4 Effect of QSub election.

(a) Separate existence ignored—(1) In general. Except as otherwise provided in paragraphs (a)(3), (a)(6), (a)(7), (a)(8), and (a)(9) of this section, for Federal tax purposes—

(i) A corporation that is a QSub shall not be treated as a separate corporation; and

(ii) All assets, liabilities, and items of income, deduction, and credit of a QSub shall be treated as assets, liabilities, and items of income, deduction, and credit of the S corporation.

(2) Liquidation of subsidiary—(i) In general. If an S corporation makes a valid QSub election with respect to a subsidiary, the subsidiary is deemed to have liquidated into the S corporation. Except as provided in paragraph (a)(5) of this section, the tax treatment of the liquidation or of a larger transaction that includes the liquidation will be determined under the Internal Revenue Code and general principles of tax law, including the step transaction doctrine. Thus, for example, if an S corporation forms a subsidiary and makes a valid QSub election (effective upon the date of the subsidiary's formation) for the subsidiary, the transfer of assets to the subsidiary and the deemed liquidation are disregarded, and the

corporation will be deemed to be a QSub from its inception.

(ii) Examples. The following examples illustrate the application of this paragraph (a)(2) (i) of this section:

Example (1). Corporation X acquires all of the outstanding stock of solvent corporation Y from an unrelated individual for cash and short-term notes. Thereafter, as part of the same plan, X immediately makes an S election and a QSub election for Y. Because X acquired all of the stock of Y in a qualified stock purchase within the meaning of section 338(d)(3), the liquidation described in paragraph (a)(2) of this section is respected as an independent step separate from the stock acquisition, and the tax consequences of the liquidation are determined under sections 332 and 337.

Example (2). Corporation X, pursuant to a plan, acquires all of the outstanding stock of corporation Y from the shareholders of Y solely in exchange for 10 percent of the voting stock of X. Prior to the transaction, Y and its shareholders are unrelated to X. Thereafter, as part of the same plan, X immediately makes an S election and a QSub election for Y. The transaction is a reorganization described in section 368(a)(1)(C), assuming the other conditions for reorganization treatment (e.g., continuity of business enterprise) are satisfied.

Example (3). After the expiration of the transition period provided in paragraph (a)(5) (i) of this section, individual A, pursuant to a plan, contributes all of the outstanding stock of Y to his wholly owned S corporation, X, and immediately causes X to make a QSub election for Y. The transaction is a reorganization under section 368(a)(1)(D), assuming the other conditions for reorganization treatment (e.g., continuity of business enterprise) are satisfied. If the sum of the amount of liabilities of Y treated as assumed by X exceeds the total of the adjusted basis of the property of Y, then section 357(c) applies and such excess is considered as gain from the sale or exchange of a capital asset or of property which is not a capital asset, as the case may be.

(iii) Adoption of plan of liquidation. For purposes of satisfying the requirement of adoption of a plan of liquidation under section 332, unless a formal plan of liquidation that contemplates the QSub election is adopted on an earlier date, the making of the QSub election is considered to be the adoption of a plan of liquidation immediately before the deemed liquidation described in paragraph (a)(2)(i) of this section.

(iv) Example. The following example illustrates the application of paragraph (a)(2) (iii) of this section:

Example. Corporation X owns 75 percent of a solvent corporation Y, and individual A owns the remaining 25 percent of Y. As part of a plan to make a QSub election for Y, X causes Y to redeem A's 25 percent interest on June 1 for cash and makes a QSub election for Y effective on June 3. The making of the QSub election is considered to be the adoption of a plan of liquidation immediately before the deemed liquidation. The deemed liquidation satisfies the requirements of section 332.

(v) Stock ownership requirements of section 332. The deemed exercise of an option under § 1.1504–4 and any instruments, obligations, or arrangements that are not considered stock under § 1.1361–2(b)(2) are disregarded in determining if the stock ownership requirements of section 332(b) are met with respect to the deemed liquidation provided in paragraph (a)(2)(i) of this section.

* * *

(4) Treatment of stock of QSub. Except for purposes of section 1361(b)(3)(B)(i) and § 1.1361–2(a)(1), the stock of a QSub shall be disregarded for all Federal tax purposes.

(5) Transitional relief—(i) General rule. If an S corporation and another corporation (the related corporation) are persons specified in section 267(b) prior to an acquisition by the S corporation of some or all of the stock of the related corporation followed by a QSub election for the related corporation, the step transaction doctrine will not apply to determine the tax consequences of the acquisition. This paragraph (a)(5) shall apply to QSub elections effective before January 1, 2001.

(ii) Examples. The following examples illustrate the application of this paragraph (a)(5):

Example (1). Individual A owns 100 percent of the stock of X, an S corporation. X owns 79 percent of the stock of Y, a solvent corporation, and A owns the remaining 21 percent. On May 4, 1998, A contributes its Y stock to X in exchange for X stock. X makes a QSub election with respect to Y effective immediately following the transfer. The liquidation described in paragraph (a)(2) of this section is respected as an independent step separate from the stock acquisition, and the tax consequences of the liquidation are determined under sections 332 and 337. The contribution by A of the Y stock qualifies under section 351, and no gain or loss is recognized by A, X, or Y.

Example (2). Individual A owns 100 percent of the stock of two solvent S corporations, X and Y. On May 4, 1998, A contributes the stock of Y to X. X makes a QSub election with respect to Y immediately following the transfer. The liquidation described in paragraph (a) (2) of this section is respected as an independent step separate from the stock acquisition, and the tax consequences of the liquidation are determined under sections 332 and 337. The contribution by A of the Y stock to X qualifies under section 351, and no gain or loss is recognized by A, X, or Y. Y is not treated as a C corporation for any period solely because of the transfer of its stock to X, an ineligible shareholder. Compare Example 3 of § 1.1361–4(a)(2)(ii).

(6) Treatment of certain QSubs—(i) In general. A QSub, even though it is generally not treated as a corporation separate from the S corporation, is treated as a separate corporation for purposes of:

(A) Federal tax liabilities of the QSub with respect to any taxable period for which the QSub was treated as a separate corporation.

(B) Federal tax liabilities of any other entity for which the QSub is liable.

(C) Refunds or credits of Federal tax.

(ii) Examples. The following examples illustrate the application of paragraph (a)(6)(i) of this section:

Example (1). X has owned all of the outstanding stock of Y, a domestic corporation that reports its taxes on a calendar year basis, since 2001. X and Y do not report their taxes on a consolidated basis. For 2003, X makes a timely S election and simultaneously makes a QSub election for Y. In 2004, the Internal Revenue Service ("IRS") seeks to extend the period of limitations on assessment for Y's 2001 taxable year. Because Y was treated as a separate corporation for its 2001 taxable year, Y is the proper party to sign the consent to extend the period of limitations.

Example (2). The facts are the same as in *Example 1,* except that in 2004, the IRS determines that Y miscalculated and underreported its income tax liability for 2001. Because Y was treated as a separate corporation for its 2001 taxable year, the deficiency for Y's 2001 taxable year may be assessed against Y and, in the event that Y fails to pay the liability after notice and demand, a general tax lien will arise against all of Y's property and rights to property.

Example (3). X is a QSub of Y. In 2001, Z, a domestic corporation that reports its taxes on a calendar year basis, merges into X in a state law merger. Z was not a member of a consolidated group at any time during its taxable year ending in December 2000. Under the applicable state law, X is the successor to Z and is liable for all of Z's debts. In 2003, the IRS seeks to extend the period of limitations on assessment for Z's 2000 taxable year. Because X is the successor to Z and is liable for Z's 2000 taxes that remain unpaid, X is the proper party

to execute the consent to extend the period of limitations on assessment.

(iii) Effective date. This paragraph (a)(6) applies on or after April 1, 2004.

* * *

(b) Timing of the liquidation—(1) In general. Except as otherwise provided in paragraph (b)(3) or (4) of this section, the liquidation described in paragraph (a)(2) of this section occurs at the close of the day before the QSub election is effective. Thus, for example, if a C corporation elects to be treated as an S corporation and makes a QSub election (effective the same date as the S election) with respect to a subsidiary, the liquidation occurs immediately before the S election becomes effective, while the S electing parent is still a C corporation.

(2) Application to elections in tiered situations. When QSub elections for a tiered group of subsidiaries are effective on the same date, the S corporation may specify the order of the liquidations. If no order is specified, the liquidations that are deemed to occur as a result of the QSub elections will be treated as occurring first for the lowest tier entity and proceed successively upward until all of the liquidations under paragraph (a)(2) of this section have occurred. For example, S, an S corporation, owns 100 percent of C, the common parent of an affiliated group of corporations that includes X and Y. C owns all of the stock of X and X owns all of the stock of Y. S elects under § 1.1361–3 to treat C, X and Y as QSubs effective on the same date. If no order is specified for the elections, the following liquidations are deemed to occur as a result of the elections, with each successive liquidation occurring on the same day immediately after the preceding liquidation: Y is treated as liquidating into X, then X is treated as liquidating into C, and finally C is treated as liquidating into S.

(3) Acquisitions. (i) In general. If an S corporation does not own 100 percent of the stock of the subsidiary on the day before the

QSub election is effective, the liquidation described in paragraph (a)(2) of this section occurs immediately after the time at which the S corporation first owns 100 percent of the stock.

(ii) Special rules for acquired S corporations. Except as provided in paragraph (b)(4) of this section, if a corporation (Y) for which an election under section 1362(a) was in effect is acquired, and a QSub election is made effective on the day Y is acquired, Y is deemed to liquidate into the S corporation at the beginning of the day the termination of its S election is effective. As a result, if corporation X acquires Y, an S corporation, and makes an S election for itself and a QSub election for Y effective on the day of acquisition, Y liquidates into X at the beginning of the day when X's S election is effective, and there is no period between the termination of Y's S election and the deemed liquidation of Y during which Y is a C corporation. Y's taxable year ends for all Federal income tax purposes at the close of the preceding day. Furthermore, if Y owns Z, a corporation for which a QSub election was in effect prior to the acquisition of Y by X, and X makes QSub elections for Y and Z, effective on the day of acquisition, the transfer of assets to Z and the deemed liquidation of Z are disregarded. See §§ 1.1361–4(a)(2) and 1.1361–5(b)(1)(i).

(4) Coordination with section 338 election. An S corporation that makes a qualified stock purchase of a target may make an election under section 338 with respect to the acquisition if it meets the requirements for the election, and may make a QSub election with respect to the target. If an S corporation makes an election under section 338 with respect to a subsidiary acquired in a qualified stock purchase, a QSub election made with respect to that subsidiary is not effective before the day after the acquisition date (within the meaning of section 338(h)(2)). If the QSub election is effective on the day after the acquisition date, the liquidation under paragraph (a)(2) of this section occurs immediately after the deemed asset purchase by the new target corporation under section 338. If an S corporation makes an election under section 338 (without a section 338(h)(10) election) with respect to a target, the target must file a final or deemed sale return as a C corporation reflecting the deemed sale. See § 1.338–10T(a).

(c) Carryover of disallowed losses and deductions. If an S corporation (S1) acquires the stock of another S corporation (S2), and S1 makes a QSub election with respect to S2 effective on the day of the acquisition, see § 1.1366–2(c)(1) for provisions relating to the carryover of losses and deductions with respect to a former shareholder of S2 that may be available to that shareholder as a shareholder of S1.

(d) Examples. The following examples illustrate the application of this section:

Example (1). X, an S corporation, owns 100 percent of the stock of Y, a C corporation. On June 2, 2002, X makes a valid QSub election for Y, effective June 2, 2002. Assume that, under general principles of tax law, including the step transaction doctrine, X's acquisition of the Y stock and the subsequent QSub election would not be treated as related. The liquidation described in paragraph (a)(2) of this section occurs at the close of the day on June 1, 2002, the day before the QSub election is effective, and the plan of liquidation is considered adopted on that date. Y's taxable year and separate existence for Federal tax purposes end at the close of June 1, 2002.

Example (2). X, a C corporation, owns 100 percent of the stock of Y, another C corporation. On December 31, 2002, X makes an election under section 1362 to be treated as an S corporation and a valid QSub election for Y, both effective January 1, 2003. Assume that, under general principles of tax law, including the step transaction doctrine, X's acquisition of the Y stock and the subsequent QSub election would not be treated as related. The liquidation described in paragraph (a)(2) of this section occurs at the close of December

31, 2002, the day before the QSub election is effective. The QSub election for Y is effective on the same day that X's S election is effective, and the deemed liquidation is treated as occurring before the S election is effective, when X is still a C corporation. Y's taxable year ends at the close of December 31, 2002. See § 1.381(b)–1.

Example (3). On June 1, 2002, X, an S corporation, acquires 100 percent of the stock of Y, an existing S corporation, for cash in a transaction meeting the requirements of a qualified stock purchase (QSP) under section 338. X immediately makes a QSub election for Y effective June 2, 2002, and also makes a joint election under section 338(h)(10) with the shareholder of Y. Under section 338(a) and § 1.338(h)(10)–1T(d)(3), Y is treated as having sold all of its assets at the close of the acquisition date, June 1, 2002. Y is treated as a new corporation which purchased all of those assets as of the beginning of June 2, 2000, the day after the acquisition date. Section 338(a)(2). The QSub election is effective on June 2, 2002, and the liquidation under paragraph (a)(2) of this section occurs immediately after the deemed asset purchase by the new corporation.

Example (4). X, an S corporation, owns 100 percent of Y, a corporation for which a QSub election is in effect. On May 12, 2002, a date on which the QSub election is in effect, X issues Y a $10,000 note under state law that matures in ten years with a market rate of interest. Y is not treated as a separate corporation, and X's issuance of the note to Y on May 12, 2002, is disregarded for Federal tax purposes.

Example (5). X, an S corporation, owns 100 percent of the stock of Y, a C corporation. At a time when Y is indebted to X in an amount that exceeds the fair market value of Y's assets, X makes a QSub election effective on the date it is filed with respect to Y. The liquidation described in paragraph (a)(2) of this section does not qualify under sections 332 and 337 and, thus, Y recognizes gain or loss on the assets distributed, subject to the limitations of section 267.

§ 1.1361–5 Termination of QSub election.

(a) In general—(1) Effective date. The termination of a QSub election is effective—

(i) On the effective date contained in the revocation statement if a QSub election is revoked under § 1.1361–3(b);

(ii) At the close of the last day of the parent's last taxable year as an S corporation if the parent's S election terminates under § 1.1362–2; or

(iii) At the close of the day on which an event (other than an event described in paragraph (a)(1)(ii) of this section) occurs that renders the subsidiary ineligible for QSub status under section 1361(b)(3)(B).

(2) Information to be provided upon termination of QSub election by failure to qualify as a QSub. If a QSub election terminates because an event renders the subsidiary ineligible for QSub status, the S corporation must attach to its return for the taxable year in which the termination occurs a notification that a QSub election has terminated, the date of the termination, and the names, addresses, and employer identification numbers of both the parent corporation and the QSub.

(3) QSub joins a consolidated group. If a QSub election terminates because the S corporation becomes a member of a consolidated group (and no election under section 338(g) is made) the principles of § 1.1502–76(b)(1)(ii)(A)(2) (relating to a special rule for S corporations that join a consolidated group) apply to any QSub of the S corporation that also becomes a member of the consolidated group at the same time as the S corporation. See Example 4 of paragraph (a)(4) of this section.

(4) Examples. The following examples illustrate the application of this paragraph (a):

Example (1). Termination because parent's S election terminates. X, an S corporation, owns 100 percent of Y. A QSub election is in effect with respect to Y for 2001. Effective on January 1, 2002, X revokes its S election. Because X is no longer an S corporation, Y no longer qualifies as a QSub at the close of December 31, 2001.

Example (2). Termination due to transfer of QSub stock. X, an S corporation, owns 100 percent of Y. A QSub election is in effect with respect to Y. On December 10, 2002, X sells one share of Y stock to A, an individual. Because X no longer owns 100 percent of the stock of Y, Y no longer qualifies as a QSub. Accordingly, the QSub election made with respect to Y terminates at the close of December 10, 2002.

Example (3). No termination on stock transfer between QSub and parent. X, an S corporation, owns 100 percent of the stock of Y, and Y owns 100 percent of the stock of Z. QSub elections are in effect with respect to both Y and Z. Y transfers all of its Z stock to X. Because X is treated as owning the stock of Z both before and after the transfer of stock solely for purposes of determining whether the requirements of section 1361(b)(3)(B)(i) and § 1.1361–2(a)(1) have been satisfied, the transfer of Z stock does not terminate Z's QSub election. Because the stock of Z is disregarded for all other Federal tax purposes, no gain is recognized under section 311.

Example (4). Termination due to acquisition of S parent by a consolidated group. X, an S corporation, owns 100 percent of Y, a corporation for which a QSub election is in effect. Z, the common parent of a consolidated group of corporations, acquires 80 percent of the stock of X on June 1, 2002. Z does not make an election under section 338(g) with respect to the purchase of X stock. X's S election terminates as of the close of the preceding day, May 31, 2002. Y's QSub election also terminates at the close of May 31, 2002. Under § 1.1502–76(b)(1)(ii)(A)(2) and paragraph (a)(3) of this section, X and Y become members of Z's consol-

idated group of corporations as of the beginning of the day June 1, 2002.

Example (5). Termination due to acquisition of QSub by a consolidated group. The facts are the same as in Example 4, except that Z acquires 80 percent of the stock of Y (instead of X) on June 1, 2002. In this case, Y's QSub election terminates as of the close of June 1, 2002, and, under § 1.1502–76(b)(1)(ii)(A)(1), Y becomes a member of the consolidated group at that time.

(b) Effect of termination of QSub election—(1) Formation of new corporation—(i) In general. If a QSub election terminates under paragraph (a) of this section, the former QSub is treated as a new corporation acquiring all of its assets (and assuming all of its liabilities) immediately before the termination from the S corporation parent in exchange for stock of the new corporation. The tax treatment of this transaction or of a larger transaction that includes this transaction will be determined under the Internal Revenue Code and general principles of tax law, including the step transaction doctrine. For purposes of determining the application of section 351 with respect to this transaction, instruments, obligations, or other arrangements that are not treated as stock of the QSub under § 1.1361–2(b) are disregarded in determining control for purposes of section 368(c) even if they are equity under general principles of tax law.

(ii) Termination for tiered QSubs. If QSub elections terminate for tiered QSubs on the same day, the formation of any higher tier subsidiary precedes the formation of its lower tier subsidiary. See Example 6 in paragraph (b)(3) of this section.

(2) Carryover of disallowed losses and deductions. If a QSub terminates because the S corporation distributes the QSub stock to some or all of the S corporation's shareholders in a transaction to which section 368(a)(1)(D) applies by reason of section 355 (or so much of section 356 as relates to section 355), see § 1.1366–2(c)(2) for provisions relating to the carryover of disallowed losses and deductions that may be available.

(3) Examples. The following examples illustrate the application of this paragraph (b):

Example (1). X, an S corporation, owns 100 percent of the stock of Y, a corporation for which a QSub election is in effect. X sells 21 percent of the Y stock to Z, an unrelated corporation, for cash, thereby terminating the QSub election. Y is treated as a new corporation acquiring all of its assets (and assuming all of its liabilities) in exchange for Y stock immediately before the termination from the S corporation. The deemed exchange by X of assets for Y stock does not qualify under section 351 because X is not in control of Y within the meaning of section 368(c) immediately after the transfer as a result of the sale of stock to Z. Therefore, X must recognize gain, if any, on the assets transferred to Y in exchange for its stock. X's losses, if any, on the assets transferred are subject to the limitations of section 267.

Example (2). (i) X, an S corporation, owns 100 percent of the stock of Y, a corporation for which a QSub election is in effect. As part of a plan to sell a portion of Y, X causes Y to merge into T, a limited liability company wholly owned by X that is disregarded as an entity separate from its owner for Federal tax purposes. X then sells 21 percent of T to Z, an unrelated corporation, for cash. Following the sale, no entity classification election is made under § 301.7701–3(c) of this chapter to treat the limited liability company as an association for Federal tax purposes.

(ii) The merger of Y into T causes a termination of Y's QSub election. The new corporation (Newco) that is formed as a result of the termination is immediately merged into T, an entity that is disregarded for Federal tax purposes. Because, at the end of the series of transactions, the assets continue to be held by X for Federal tax purposes, under step transaction principles, the formation of Newco and the transfer of assets pursuant to the merger of

Newco into T are disregarded. The sale of 21 percent of T is treated as a sale of a 21 percent undivided interest in each of T's assets. Immediately thereafter, X and Z are treated as contributing their respective interests in those assets to a partnership in exchange for ownership interests in the partnership.

(iii) Under section 1001, X recognizes gain or loss from the deemed sale of the 21 percent interest in each asset of the limited liability company to Z. Under section 721(a), no gain or loss is recognized by X and Z as a result of the deemed contribution of their respective interests in the assets to the partnership in exchange for ownership interests in the partnership.

Example (3). Assume the same facts as in Example 1, except that, instead of purchasing Y stock, Z contributes to Y an operating asset in exchange for 21 percent of the Y stock. Y is treated as a new corporation acquiring all of its assets (and assuming all of its liabilities) in exchange for Y stock immediately before the termination. Because X and Z are co-transferors that control the transferee immediately after the transfer, the transaction qualifies under section 351.

Example (4). X, an S corporation, owns 100 percent of the stock of Y, a corporation for which a QSub election is in effect. X distributes all of the Y stock pro rata to its shareholders, and the distribution terminates the QSub election. The transaction can qualify as a distribution to which sections 368(a)(1)(D) and 355 apply if the transaction otherwise satisfies the requirements of those sections.

Example (5). X, an S corporation, owns 100 percent of the stock of Y, a corporation for which a QSub election is in effect. X subsequently revokes the QSub election. Y is treated as a new corporation acquiring all of its assets (and assuming all of its liabilities) immediately before the revocation from its S corporation parent in a deemed exchange for Y stock. On a subsequent date, X sells 21 percent of the stock of Y to Z, an unrelated corporation, for cash. Assume that under general principles of tax law including the step transaction doctrine, the sale is not taken into account in determining whether X is in control of Y immediately after the deemed exchange of assets for stock. The deemed exchange by X of assets for Y stock and the deemed assumption by Y of its liabilities qualify under section 351 because, for purposes of that section, X is in control of Y within the meaning of section 368(c) immediately after the transfer.

Example (6). (i) X, an S corporation, owns 100 percent of the stock of Y, and Y owns 100 percent of the stock of Z. Y and Z are corporations for which QSub elections are in effect. X subsequently revokes the QSub elections and the effective date specified on each revocation statement is June 26, 2002, a date that is less than 12 months after the date on which the revocation statements are filed.

(ii) Immediately before the QSub elections terminate, Y is treated as a new corporation acquiring all of its assets (and assuming all of its liabilities) directly from X in exchange for the stock of Y. Z is treated as a new corporation acquiring all of its assets (and assuming all of its liabilities) directly from Y in exchange for the stock of Z.

Example (7). (i) The facts are the same as in Example 6, except that, prior to June 26, 2002 (the effective date of the revocations), Y distributes the Z stock to X under state law.

(ii) Immediately before the QSub elections terminate, Y is treated as a new corporation acquiring all of its assets (and assuming all of its liabilities) directly from X in exchange for the stock of Y. Z is also treated as a new corporation acquiring all of its assets (and assuming all of its liabilities) directly from X in exchange for the stock of Z.

Example (8). Merger of parent into QSub. X, an S corporation, owns 100 percent of the stock of Y, a corporation for which a QSub election is in effect. X merges into Y under state law, causing the QSub election for Y

to terminate, and Y survives the merger. The formation of the new corporation, Y, and the merger of X into Y can qualify as a reorganization described in section 368(a)(1)(F) if the transaction otherwise satisfies the requirements of that section.

Example (9). Transfer of 100 percent of QSub. X, an S corporation, owns 100 percent of the stock of Y, a corporation for which a QSub election is in effect. Z, an unrelated C corporation, acquires 100 percent of the stock of Y. The deemed formation of Y by X (as a consequence of the termination of Y's QSub election) is disregarded for Federal income tax purposes. The transaction is treated as a transfer of the assets of Y to Z, followed by Z's transfer of these assets to the capital of Y in exchange for Y stock. Furthermore, if Z is an S corporation and makes a QSub election for Y effective as of the acquisition, Z's transfer of the assets of Y in exchange for Y stock, followed by the immediate liquidation of Y as a consequence of the QSub election are disregarded for Federal income tax purposes.

(c) Election after QSub termination—(1) In general. Absent the Commissioner's consent, and except as provided in paragraph (c)(2) of this section, a corporation whose QSub election has terminated under paragraph (a) of this section (or a successor corporation as defined in paragraph (b) of this section) may not make an S election under section 1362 or have a QSub election under section 1361(b)(3)(B)(ii) made with respect to it for five taxable years (as described in section 1361(b)(3)(D)). The Commissioner may permit an S election by the corporation or a new QSub election with respect to the corporation before the five-year period expires. The corporation requesting consent to make the election has the burden of establishing that, under the relevant facts and circumstances, the Commissioner should consent to a new election.

(2) Exception. In the case of S and QSub elections effective after December 31, 1996, if a corporation's QSub election terminates, the corporation may, without requesting the Commissioner's consent, make an S election or have a QSub election made with respect to it before the expiration of the five-year period described in section 1361(b)(3)(D) and paragraph (c)(1) of this section, provided that—

(i) Immediately following the termination, the corporation (or its successor corporation) is otherwise eligible to make an S election or have a QSub election made for it; and

(ii) The relevant election is made effective immediately following the termination of the QSub election.

(3) Examples. The following examples illustrate the application of this paragraph (c):

Example (1). Termination upon distribution of QSub stock to shareholders of parent. X, an S corporation, owns Y, a QSub. X distributes all of its Y stock to X's shareholders. The distribution terminates the QSub election because Y no longer satisfies the requirements of a QSub. Assuming Y is otherwise eligible to be treated as an S corporation, Y's shareholders may elect to treat Y as an S corporation effective on the date of the stock distribution without requesting the Commissioner's consent.

Example (2). Sale of 100 percent of QSub stock. X, an S corporation, owns Y, a QSub. X sells 100 percent of the stock of Y to Z, an unrelated S corporation. Z may elect to treat Y as a QSub effective on the date of purchase without requesting the Commissioner's consent.

* * *

§ 1.1362–1 Election to be an S corporation.

(a) In general. Except as provided in § 1.1362–5, a small business corporation as defined in section 1361 may elect to be an S corporation under section 1362(a). An election may be made only with the consent of all of the shareholders of the corporation at the time of the election. See § 1.1362–6(a) for rules concerning the time and manner of making this election.

(b) Years for which election is effective. An election under section 1362(a) is effective for the entire taxable year of the corporation for which it is made and for all succeeding taxable years of the corporation, until the election is terminated.

§ 1.1362–2 Termination of election.

(a) Termination by revocation—(1) In general. An election made under section 1362(a) is terminated if the corporation revokes the election for any taxable year of the corporation for which the election is effective, including the first taxable year. A revocation may be made only with the consent of shareholders who, at the time the revocation is made, hold more than one-half of the number of issued and outstanding shares of stock (including non-voting stock) of the corporation. See § 1.1362–6(a) for rules concerning the time and manner of revoking an election made under section 1362(a).

(2) When effective—(i) In general. Except as provided in paragraph (a)(2)(ii) of this section, a revocation made during the taxable year and before the 16th day of the third month of the taxable year is effective on the first day of the taxable year and a revocation made after the 15th day of the third month of the taxable year is effective for the following taxable year. If a corporation makes an election to be an S corporation that is to be effective beginning with the next taxable year and revokes its election on or before the first day of the next taxable year, the corporation is deemed to have revoked its election on the first day of the next taxable year.

(ii) Revocations specifying a prospective revocation date. If a corporation specifies a date for revocation and the date is expressed in terms of a stated day, month, and year that is on or after the date the revocation is filed, the revocation is effective on and after the date so specified.

(3) Effect on taxable year of corporation. In the case of a corporation that revokes its election to be an S corporation effective on the first day of the first taxable year for which its election is to be effective, any statement made with the election regarding a change in the corporation's taxable year has no effect.

(4) Rescission of a revocation. A corporation may rescind a revocation made under paragraph (a)(2) of this section at any time before the revocation becomes effective. A rescission may be made only with the consent of each person who consented to the revocation and by each person who became a shareholder of the corporation within the period beginning on the first day after the date the revocation was made and ending on the date on which the rescission is made. See § 1.1362–6(a) for rules concerning the time and manner of rescinding a revocation.

(b) Termination by reason of corporation ceasing to be a small business corporation—(1) In general. If a corporation ceases to be a small business corporation, as defined in section 1361(b), at any time on or after the first day of the first taxable year for which its election under section 1362(a) is effective, the election terminates. In the event of a termination under this paragraph (b)(1), the corporation should attach to its return for the taxable year in which the termination occurs a notification that a termination has occurred and the date of the termination.

(2) When effective. If an election terminates because of a specific event that causes the corporation to fail to meet the definition of a small business corporation, the termination is effective as of the date on which the event occurs. If a corporation makes an election to be an S corporation that is effective beginning with the following taxable year and is not a small business corporation on the first day of that following taxable year, the election is treated as having terminated on that first day. If a corporation is a small business corporation on the first day of the taxable year for which its election is effective, its election does not terminate even if the corporation was not a

small business corporation during all or part of the period beginning after the date the election was made and ending before the first day of the taxable year for which the election is effective.

(3) Effect on taxable year of corporation. In the case of a corporation that fails to meet the definition of a small business corporation on the first day of the first taxable year for which its election to be an S corporation is to be effective, any statement made with the election regarding a change in the corporation's taxable year has no effect.

(c) Termination by reason of excess passive investment income—(1) In general. A corporation's election under section 1362(a) terminates if the corporation has subchapter C earnings and profits at the close of each of three consecutive taxable years and, for each of those taxable years, has passive investment income in excess of 25 percent of gross receipts. See section 1375 for the tax imposed on excess passive investment income.

(2) When effective. A termination under this paragraph (c) is effective on the first day of the first taxable year beginning after the third consecutive year in which the S corporation had excess passive investment income.

(3) Subchapter C earnings and profits. For purposes of this paragraph (c), subchapter C earnings and profits of a corporation are the earnings and profits of any corporation, including the S corporation or an acquired or predecessor corporation, for any period with respect to which an election under section 1362(a) (or under section 1372 of prior law) was not in effect. The subchapter C earnings and profits of an S corporation are modified as required by section 1371(c).

* * *

§ 1.1362–3 Treatment of S termination year.

(a) In general. If an S election terminates under section 1362(d) on a date other than the first day of a taxable year of the corporation, the corporation's taxable year in which the termination occurs is an S termination year. The portion of the S termination year ending at the close of the day prior to the termination is treated as a short taxable year for which the corporation is an S corporation (the S short year). The portion of the S termination year beginning on the day the termination is effective is treated as a short taxable year for which the corporation is a C corporation (the C short year). Except as provided in paragraphs (b) and (c)(1) of this section, the corporation allocates income or loss for the entire year on a pro rata basis as described in section 1362(e)(2). To the extent that income or loss is not allocated on a pro rata basis under this section, items of income, gain, loss, deduction, and credit are assigned to each short taxable year on the basis of the corporation's normal method of accounting as determined under section 446.

(b) Allocations other than pro rata—(1) Elections under section 1362(e)(3). The pro rata allocation rules of section 1362(e)(2) do not apply if the corporation elects to allocate its S termination year income on the basis of its normal tax accounting method. This election may be made only with the consent of each person who is a shareholder in the corporation at any time during the S short year and of each person who is a shareholder in the corporation on the first day of the C short year. See § 1.1362–6(a) for rules concerning the time and manner of making this election.

(2) Purchase of stock treated as an asset purchase. The pro rata allocation rules of section 1362(e)(2) do not apply with respect to any item resulting from the application of section 338.

(3) 50 percent change in ownership during S termination year. The pro rata allocation rules of section 1362(e)(2) do not apply if at any time during the S termination year, as a result of sales or exchanges of stock in the corporation during that year, there is a change in ownership of 50 percent or more of the issued and outstanding shares of stock of the corporation. If stock has already been sold or exchanged during the S termination year, subsequent sales or exchanges of that stock are not taken into account for purposes of this paragraph (b)(3).

(c) Special rules—(1) S corporation that is a partner in a partnership. For purposes of section 706(c) only, the termination of the election of an S corporation that is a partner in a partnership during any portion of the S short year under § 1.1362–2 (a) or (b), is treated as a sale or exchange of the corporation's entire interest in the partnership on the last day of the S short year, if—

(i) The pro rata allocation rules do not apply to the corporation; and

(ii) Any taxable year of the partnership ends with or within the C short year.

(2) Tax for the C short year. The taxable income for the C short year is determined on an annualized basis as described in section 1362(e)(5).

(3) Each short year treated as taxable year. Except as otherwise provided in paragraph (c)(4) of this section, the S and C short years are treated as two separate years for purposes of all provisions of the Internal Revenue Code.

(4) Year for carryover purposes. The S and C short years are treated as one year for purposes of determining the number of taxable years to which any item may be carried back or forward by the corporation.

(5) Due date for S short year return. The date by which the return for the S short year must be filed is the same as the date by which the return for the C short year must be filed (including extensions).

(6) Year in which income from S short year is includible. A shareholder must include in taxable income the shareholder's pro rata share of the items described in section 1366(a) for the S short year for the taxable year with or within which the S termination year ends.

(d) Examples. The provisions of this section are illustrated by the following examples:

Example (1). S termination year not created. (i) On January 1, 1993, the first day of its taxable year, a subchapter C corporation had three eligible shareholders. During 1993, the corporation properly elected to be treated as an S corporation effective January 1, 1994, the first day of the succeeding taxable year. Subsequently, a transfer of some of the stock in the corporation was made to an ineligible shareholder. The ineligible shareholder still holds the stock on January 1, 1994.

(ii) The corporation fails to meet the definition of a small business corporation on January 1, 1994, and its election is treated as having terminated on that date. See § 1.1362–2(b)(2) for the termination rules. Because the corporation ceases to be a small business corporation on the first day of a taxable year, an S termination year is not created. In addition, if the corporation in the future meets the definition of a small business corporation and desires to elect to be treated as an S corporation, the corporation is automatically granted consent to reelect before the expiration of the 5-year waiting period. See § 1.1362–5 for special rules concerning automatic consent to reelect.

Example (2). More than 50 percent change in ownership during S short year. A, an individual, owns all 100 outstanding shares of stock of S, a calendar year S corporation. On January 31, 1993, A sells 60 shares of S stock to B, an individual. On June 1, 1993, A sells 5 shares of S stock to PRS, a partnership. S ceases to be a small business corporation on June 1, 1993, and pursuant to section 1362(d)(2), its election terminates on that date. Because there was a more than 50 percent change in ownership of the issued and outstanding shares of S stock, S must assign the items of income, loss, deduction, or credit for the S termination year to the two short taxable years on the basis of S's normal method of accounting under the rules of paragraph (b)(3) of this section.

Example (3). More than 50 percent change in ownership during C short year. A, an individual, owns all 100 outstanding shares of stock of S, a calendar year S corporation. On June 1, 1993, A sells 5 shares of S stock to PRS, a partnership. S ceases to be a small business corporation on that date and pursuant to section 1362(d)(3), its election terminates on that date. On July 1, 1993, A sells 60 shares of S stock to B, an individual. Since there was a more than 50 percent change in ownership of the issued and outstanding shares of S stock during the S termination year, S must assign the items of income, loss, deduction, or credit for the S termination year to the two short taxable years on the basis of S's normal method of accounting under the rules of paragraph (b)(3) of this section.

Example (4). Stock acquired other than by sale or exchange. C and D are shareholders in S, a calendar year S corporation. Each owns 50 percent of the issued and outstanding shares of the corporation on December 31, 1993. On March 1, 1994, C makes a gift of his entire shareholder interest to T, a trust not permitted as a shareholder under section 1361(c)(2). S ceases to be a small business corporation on March 1, 1994, and pursuant to section 1362(d)(2), its S corporation election terminates effective on that date. As a result of the gift, T owns 50 percent of S's issued and outstanding stock. However, because T acquired the stock by gift from C rather than by sale or exchange, there has not been a more than 50 percent change in ownership by sale or exchange of S that would cause the rules of paragraph (b)(3) of this section to apply.

§ 1.1362–4 Inadvertent terminations and inadvertently invalid elections.

(a) In general. A corporation is treated as continuing to be an S corporation or a QSub (or, an invalid election to be either an S corporation or a QSub is treated as valid) during the period specified by the Commissioner if—

(1) The corporation made a valid election under section 1362(a) or section 1361(b)(3) and the election terminated or the corporation made an election under section 1362(a) or section 1361(b)(3) that was invalid;

(2) The Commissioner determines that the termination or invalidity was inadvertent;

(3) Within a reasonable period of time after discovery of the terminating event or invalid election, steps were taken so that the corporation for which the election was made or the termination occurred is a small business corporation or a QSub, as the case may be, or to acquire the required shareholder consents; and

(4) The corporation and shareholders agree to adjustments that the Commissioner may require for the period.

* * *

§ 1.1362–6 Elections and consents.

(a) Time and manner of making elections—(1) In general. An election statement made under this section must identify the election being made, set forth the name, address, and taxpayer identification number of the corporation, and be signed by a person authorized to sign the return required to be filed under section 6037.

(2) Election to be an S corporation—(i) Manner of making election. A small business corporation makes an election under section 1362(a) to be an S corporation by filing a completed Form 2553. The election form must be filed with the service center designated in the instructions applicable to Form 2553. The election is not valid unless all shareholders of the corporation at the time of the election consent to the election in the manner provided in paragraph (b) of this section. However, once a valid election is made, new shareholders need not consent to that election.

(ii) Time of making election—(A) In general. The election described in paragraph (a)(2)(i) of this section may be made by a small business corporation at any time during the taxable year that immediately precedes the taxable year for which the election is to be effective, or during the taxable year for which the election is to be effective provided that the election is made before the 16th day of the third month of the year. If a corporation makes an election for a taxable year, and the election meets all the requirements of this section but is made during the period beginning after the 15th day of the third month of the taxable year, the election is treated as being made for the following taxable year provided that the corporation meets all the requirements of section 1361(b) at the time the election is made. For taxable years of 2 1/2 months or less, an election made before the 16th day of the third month after the first day of the taxable year is treated as made during that year.

(B) Elections made during the first 2 1/2 months treated as made for the following taxable year. A timely election made by a small business corporation during the taxable year for which it is intended to be effective is nonetheless treated as made for the following taxable year if—

(1) The corporation is not a small business corporation during the entire portion of the taxable year which occurs before the date the election is made; or

(2) Any person who held stock in the corporation at any time during the portion of the taxable year which occurs before the time the election is made, and who does not hold stock at the time the election is made, does not consent to the election.

(C) Definition of month and beginning of the taxable year. Month means a period commencing on the same numerical day of any calendar month as the day of the calendar month on which the taxable year began and ending with the close of the day preceding the numerically corresponding day of the succeeding calendar month or, if there is no corresponding day, with the close of the last day of the succeeding calendar month. In addition, the taxable year of a new corporation begins on the date that the corporation has shareholders, acquires assets, or begins doing business, whichever is the first to occur. The existence of incorporators does not necessarily begin the taxable year of a new corporation.

(iii) Examples. The provisions of this section are illustrated by the following examples:

Example (1). Effective election; no prior taxable year. A calendar year small business corporation begins its first taxable year on January 7, 1993. To be an S corporation beginning with its first taxable year, the corporation must make the election set forth in this section during the period that begins January 7, 1993, and ends before March 22, 1993. Because the corporation had no taxable year immediately preceding the taxable year for which the election is to be effective, an election made earlier than January 7, 1993, will not be valid.

* * *

Example (3). Election effective for the following taxable year; ineligible shareholder. On January 1, 1993, two individuals and a partnership own all of the stock of a calendar year subchapter C corporation. On January 31, 1993, the partnership dissolved and distributed its shares in the corporation to its five partners, all individuals. On February 28, 1993, the seven shareholders of the corporation consented to the corporation's election of subchapter S status. The corporation files a properly completed Form 2553 on March 2, 1993. The corporation is not eligible to be a subchapter S corporation for the 1993 taxable year because during the period of the taxable year prior to the election it had an ineligible shareholder. However, under paragraph (a)(2)(ii)(B) of this section, the election is treated as made for the corporation's 1994 taxable year.

(3) Revocation of S election.

(i) Manner of revoking election. To revoke an election, the corporation files a statement that the corporation revokes the election made under section 1362(a). The statement must be filed with the service center where the election was properly filed. The revocation statement must include the number of shares of stock (including non-voting stock) issued and outstanding at the time the revocation is made. A revocation may be made only with the consent of shareholders who, at the time the revocation is made, hold more than one-half of the number of issued and outstanding shares of stock (including non-voting stock) of the corporation. Each shareholder who consents to the revocation must consent in the manner required under paragraph (b) of this section. In addition, each consent should indicate the number of issued and outstanding shares of stock (including non-voting stock) held by each shareholder at the time of the revocation.

(ii) Time of revoking election. For rules concerning when a revocation is effective, see § 1.1362–2(a)(2).

(iii) Examples. The principles of this paragraph (a)(3) are illustrated by the following examples:

Example (1). Revocation; consent of shareholders owning more than one-half of issued and outstanding shares. A calendar year S corporation has issued and outstanding 40,000 shares of class A voting common stock and 20,000 shares of class B non-voting common stock. The corporation wishes to revoke its election of subchapter S status. Shareholders owning 11,000 shares of class A stock sign revocation consents. Shareholders owning 20,000 shares of class B stock sign revocation consents. The corporation has obtained the required shareholder consent to revoke its subchapter S election because shareholders owning more than one-half of the total number of issued and outstanding shares of stock of the corporation consented to the revocation.

Example (2). Effective prospective revocation. In June 1993, a calendar year S corporation determines that it will revoke its subchapter S election effective August 1, 1993. To do so it must file its revocation statement with consents attached on or before August 1, 1993, and the statement must indicate that the revocation is intended to be effective August 1, 1993.

(4) Rescission of a revocation.

(i) Manner of rescinding a revocation. To rescind a revocation, the corporation files a statement that the corporation rescinds the revocation made under section 1362(d)(1). The statement must be filed with the service center where the revocation was properly filed. A rescission may be made only with the consent (in the manner required under paragraph (b)(1) of this section) of each person who consented to the revocation and of each person who became a shareholder of the corporation within the period beginning on the first day after the date the revocation was made and ending on the date on which the rescission is made.

(ii) Time of rescinding a revocation. If the rescission statement is filed before the revocation becomes effective and is filed with proper service center, the rescission is effective on the date it is so filed.

(5) Election not to apply pro rata allocation. To elect not to apply the pro rata allocation rules to an S termination year, a corporation files a statement that it elects under section 1362(e)(3) not to apply the rules provided in section 1362(e)(2). In addition to meeting the requirements of paragraph (a)(1) of this section, the statement must set forth the cause of the termination and the date thereof. The statement must be filed with the corporation's return for the C short year. This election may be made only with the consent of all persons who are shareholders of the corporation at any time during the S short year and all persons who are shareholders of the corporation on the first day of the C short year (in the manner required under paragraph (b)(1) of this section).

(b) Shareholders' consents.

(1) Manner of consents in general. A shareholder's consent required under paragraph (a) of this section must be in the form of a written statement that sets forth the name, address, and taxpayer identification number of the shareholder, the number of shares of stock owned by the shareholder, the date (or dates) on which the stock was acquired, the date on which the shareholder's taxable year ends, the name of the S corporation, the corporation's taxpayer identification number, and the election to which the shareholder consents. The statement must be signed by the shareholder under penalties of perjury. Except as provided in paragraph (b)(3)(iii) of this section, the election of the corporation is not valid if any required consent is not filed in accordance with the rules contained in this paragraph (b). The consent statement should be attached to the corporation's election statement.

(2) Persons required to consent. The following rules apply in determining persons required to consent:

(i) Community interest in stock. When stock of the corporation is owned by husband and wife as community property (or the income from the stock is community property), or is owned by tenants in common, joint tenants, or tenants by the entirety, each person having a community interest in the stock or income therefrom and each tenant in common, joint tenant and tenant by the entirety must consent to the election.

(ii) Minor. The consent of a minor must be made by the minor or by the legal representative of the minor (or by a natural or an adoptive parent of the minor if no legal representative has been appointed).

(iii) Estate. The consent of an estate must be made by an executor or administrator thereof, or by any other fiduciary appointed by testamentary instrument or appointed by the court having jurisdiction over the administration of the estate.

(iv) Trust. In the case of a trust described in section 1361(c)(2)(A) (including a trust treated under section 1361(d)(1)(A) as a trust described in section 1361(c)(2)(A)(i)), only the person treated as the shareholder for purposes of section 1361(b)(1) must consent to the election. When stock of the corporation is held by a trust, both husband and wife must consent to any election if the husband and wife have a community interest in the trust property. See paragraph (b)(2)(i) of this section for rules concerning community interests in S corporation stock.

(3) Special rules for consent of shareholder to election to be an S corporation.

(i) In general. The consent of a shareholder to an election by a small business corporation under section 1362(a) may be made on Form 2553 or on a separate statement in the manner described in paragraph (b)(1) of this section. In addition, the separate statement must set forth the name, address, and taxpayer identification number of the corporation. A shareholder's consent is binding and may not be withdrawn after a valid election is made by the corporation. Each person who is a shareholder (including any person who is treated as a shareholder under section 1361(c)(2)(B)) at the time the election is made) must consent to the election. If the election is made before the 16th day of the third month of the taxable year and is intended to be effective for that year, each person who was a shareholder (including any person who was treated as a shareholder under section 1361(c)(2)(B)) at any time during the portion of that year which occurs before the time the election is made, and who is not a shareholder at the time the election is made, must also consent to the election. If the election is to be effective for the following taxable year, no consent need be filed by any shareholder who is not a shareholder on the date of the election. Any person who is considered to be a shareholder under applicable state law solely by virtue of his or her status as an incorporator is not treated as a shareholder for purposes of this paragraph (b)(3)(i).

(ii) Examples. The principles of this section are illustrated by the following examples:

Example (1). Effective election; shareholder consents. On January 1, 1993, the first day of its taxable year, a subchapter C corporation

had 15 shareholders. On January 30, 1993, two of the C corporation's shareholders, A and B, both individuals, sold their shares in the corporation to P, Q, and R, all individuals. On March 1, 1993, the corporation filed its election to be an S corporation for the 1993 taxable year. The election will be effective (assuming the other requirements of section 1361(b) are met) provided that all of the shareholders as of March 1, 1993, as well as former shareholders A and B, consent to the election.

Example (2). Consent of new shareholder unnecessary. On January 1, 1993, three individuals own all of the stock of a calendar year subchapter C corporation. On April 15, 1993, the corporation, in accordance with paragraph (a)(2) of this section, files a properly completed Form 2553. The corporation anticipates that the election will be effective beginning January 1, 1994, the first day of the succeeding taxable year. On October 1, 1993, the three shareholders collectively sell 75% of their shares in the corporation to another individual. On January 1, 1994, the corporation's shareholders are the three original individuals and the new shareholder. Because the election was valid and binding when made, it is not necessary for the new shareholder to consent to the election. The corporation's subchapter S election is effective on January 1, 1994 (assuming the other requirements of section 1361(b) are met).

(iii) Extension of time for filing consents to an election.

(A) In general. An election that is timely filed for any taxable year and that would be valid except for the failure of any shareholder to file a timely consent is not invalid if consents are filed as required under paragraph (b)(3)(iii)(B) of this section and it is shown to the satisfaction of the district director or director of the service center with which the corporation files its income tax return that—

(1) There was reasonable cause for the failure to file the consent;

(2) The request for the extension of time to file a consent is made within a reasonable time under the circumstances; and

(3) The interests of the Government will not be jeopardized by treating the election as valid.

(B) Required consents. Consents must be filed within the extended period of time as may be granted by the Internal Revenue Service, by all persons who—

(1) Were shareholders of the corporation at any time during the period beginning as of the date of the invalid election and ending on the date on which an extension of time is granted in accordance with this paragraph (b)(3)(iii); and

(2) Have not previously consented to the election.

§ 1.1363–1 Effect of election on corporation.

(a) Exemption of corporation from income tax—(1) In general. Except as provided in this paragraph (a), a small business corporation that makes a valid election under section 1362(a) is exempt from the taxes imposed by chapter 1 of the Internal Revenue Code with respect to taxable years of the corporation for which the election is in effect.

(2) Corporate level taxes. An S corporation is not exempt from the tax imposed by section 1374 (relating to the tax imposed on certain built-in gains), or section 1375 (relating to the tax on excess passive investment income). See also section 1363(d) (relating to the recapture of LIFO benefits) for the rules regarding the payment by an S corporation of LIFO recapture amounts.

(b) Computation of corporate taxable income. The taxable income of an S corporation is computed as described in section 1363(b).

(c) Elections of the S corporation—(1) In general. Any elections (other than those described in paragraph (c)(2) of this section) affecting the computation of items derived from an S corporation are made by the corporation. For example, elections of methods of accounting, of computing depreciation, of treating soil and water conservation expenditures, and the option to deduct as expenses intangible drilling and development costs, are made by the corporation and not by the shareholders separately. All corporate elections are applicable to all shareholders.

(2) Exceptions. (i) Each shareholder's pro rata share of expenses described in section 617 paid or accrued by the S corporation is treated according to the shareholder's method of treating those expenses, notwithstanding the treatment of the expenses by the corporation.

(ii) Each shareholder may elect to amortize that shareholder's pro rata share of any qualified expenditure described in section 59(e) paid or accrued by the S corporation.

(iii) Each shareholder's pro rata share of taxes described in section 901 paid or accrued by the S corporation to foreign countries or possessions of the United States (according to its method of treating those taxes) is treated according to the shareholder's method of treating those taxes, and each shareholder may elect to use the total amount either as a credit against tax or as a deduction from income.

* * *

§ 1.1366–1 Shareholder's share of items of an S corporation.

(a) Determination of shareholder's tax liability—(1) In general. An S corporation must report, and a shareholder is required to take into account in the shareholder's return, the shareholder's pro rata share, whether or not distributed, of the S corporation's items of income, loss, deduction, or credit described in paragraphs (a)(2), (3), and (4) of this section. A shareholder's pro rata share is determined in accordance with the provisions of section 1377(a) and the regulations thereunder. The shareholder takes these items into account in determining the shareholder's taxable income and tax liability for the shareholder's taxable year with or within which the taxable year of the corporation ends. If the shareholder dies (or if the shareholder is an estate or trust and the estate or trust terminates) before the end of the taxable year of the corporation, the shareholder's pro rata share of these items is taken into account on the shareholder's final return. For the limitation on allowance of a shareholder's pro rata share of S corporation losses or deductions, see section 1366(d) and § 1.1366–2.

(2) Separately stated items of income, loss, deduction, or credit. Each shareholder must take into account separately the shareholder's pro rata share of any item of income (including tax-exempt income), loss, deduction, or credit of the S corporation that if separately taken into account by any shareholder could affect the shareholder's tax liability for that taxable year differently than if the shareholder did not take the item into account separately. The separately stated items of the S corporation include, but are not limited to, the following items—

(i) The corporation's combined net amount of gains and losses from sales or exchanges of capital assets grouped by applicable holding periods, by applicable rate of tax under section 1(h), and by any other classification that may be relevant in determining the shareholder's tax liability;

(ii) The corporation's combined net amount of gains and losses from sales or exchanges of property described in section 1231 (relating to property used in the trade or business and involuntary conversions), grouped by applicable holding periods, by applicable rate of tax under section 1(h), and by any other classification that may be relevant in determining the shareholder's tax liability;

(iii) Charitable contributions, grouped by the percentage limitations of section 170(b), paid by the corporation within the taxable year of the corporation;

(iv) The taxes described in section 901 that have been paid (or accrued) by the corporation to foreign countries or to possessions of the United States;

(v) Each of the corporation's separate items involved in the determination of credits against tax allowable under part IV of subchapter A (section 21 and following) of the Internal Revenue Code, except for any credit allowed under section 34 (relating to certain uses of gasoline and special fuels);

(vi) Each of the corporation's separate items of gains and losses from wagering transactions (section 165(d)); soil and water conservation expenditures (section 175); deduction under an election to expense certain depreciable business expenses (section 179); medical, dental, etc., expenses (section 213); the additional itemized deductions for individuals provided in part VII of subchapter B (section 212 and following) of the Internal Revenue Code; and any other itemized deductions for which the limitations on itemized deductions under sections 67 or 68 applies;

(vii) Any of the corporation's items of portfolio income or loss, and expenses related thereto, as defined in the regulations under section 469;

(viii) The corporation's tax-exempt income. For purposes of subchapter S, tax-exempt income is income that is permanently excludible from gross income in all circumstances in which the applicable provision of the Internal Revenue Code applies. For example, income that is excludible from gross income under section 101 (certain death benefits) or section 103 (interest on state and local bonds) is tax-exempt income, while income that is excludible from gross income under section 108 (income from discharge of indebtedness) or section 109 (improvements by lessee on lessor's property) is not tax-exempt income;

(ix) The corporation's adjustments described in sections 56 and 58, and items of tax preference described in section 57; and

(x) Any item identified in guidance (including forms and instructions) issued by the Commissioner as an item required to be separately stated under this paragraph (a)(2).

(3) Nonseparately computed income or loss. Each shareholder must take into account separately the shareholder's pro rata share of the nonseparately computed income or loss of the S corporation. For this purpose, nonseparately computed income or loss means the corporation's gross income less the deductions allowed to the corporation under chapter 1 of the Internal Revenue Code, determined by excluding any item requiring separate computation under paragraph (a)(2) of this section.

(4) Separate activities requirement. An S corporation must report, and each shareholder must take into account in the shareholder's return, the shareholder's pro rata share of an S corporation's items of income, loss, deduction, or credit described in paragraphs (a)(2) and (3) of this section for each of the corporation's activities as defined in section 469 and the regulations thereunder.

(5) Aggregation of deductions or exclusions for purposes of limitations — (i) In general. A shareholder aggregates the shareholder's separate deductions or exclusions with the shareholder's pro rata share of the S corporation's separately stated deductions or exclusions in determining the amount of any deduction or exclusion allowable to the shareholder under subtitle A of the Internal Revenue Code as to which a limitation is imposed.

(ii) Example. The provisions of paragraph (a)(5)(i) of this section are illustrated by the following example:

Example. In 1999, Corporation M, a calendar year S corporation, purchases and places in service section 179 property costing $10,000. Corporation M elects to expense the entire cost of the property. Shareholder A owns 50 percent of the stock of Corporation M. Shareholder A's pro rata share of this item after Corporation M applies the section 179(b) limitations is $5,000. Because the aggregate amount of Shareholder A's pro rata share and separately acquired section 179 expense may not exceed $19,000 (the aggregate maximum cost that may be taken into account under section 179(a) for the applicable taxable year), Shareholder A may elect to expense up to $14,000 of separately acquired section 179 property that is purchased and placed in service in 1999, subject to the limitations of section 179(b).

(b) Character of items constituting pro rata share — (1) In general. Except as provided in paragraph (b)(2) or (3) of this section, the character of any item of income, loss, deduction, or credit described in section 1366(a)(1)(A) or (B) and paragraph (a) of this section is determined for the S corporation and retains that character in the hands of the shareholder. For example, if an S corporation has capital gain on the sale or exchange of a capital asset, a shareholder's pro rata share of that gain will also be characterized as a capital gain regardless of whether the shareholder is otherwise a dealer in that type of property. Similarly, if an S corporation engages in an activity that is not for profit (as defined in section 183), a shareholder's pro rata share of the S corporation's deductions will be characterized as not for profit. Also, if an S corporation makes a charitable contribution to an organization qualifying under section 170(b)(1)(A), a shareholder's pro rata share of the S corporation's charitable contribution will be characterized as made to an organization qualifying under section 170(b)(1)(A).

(2) Exception for contribution of non-capital gain property. If an S corporation is formed or availed of by any shareholder or group of shareholders for a principal purpose of selling or exchanging contributed property that in the hands of the shareholder or shareholders would not have produced capital gain if sold or exchanged by the shareholder or shareholders, then the gain on the sale or exchange of the property recognized by the corporation is not treated as a capital gain.

(3) Exception for contribution of capital loss property. If an S corporation is formed or availed of by any shareholder or group of shareholders for a principal purpose of selling or exchanging contributed property that in the hands of the shareholder or shareholders would have produced capital loss if sold or exchanged by the shareholder or shareholders, then the loss on the sale or exchange of the property recognized by the corporation is treated as a capital loss to the extent that, immediately before the contribution, the adjusted basis of the property in the hands of the shareholder or shareholders exceeded the fair market value of the property.

(c) Gross income of a shareholder — (1) In general. Where it is necessary to determine the amount or character of the gross income of a shareholder, the shareholder's gross income includes the shareholder's pro rata share of the gross income of the S corporation. The shareholder's pro rata share of the gross income of the S corporation is the amount of gross income of the corporation used in deriving the shareholder's pro rata share of S corporation taxable income or loss (including items described in section 1366(a)(1)(A) or (B) and paragraph (a) of this section). For example, a shareholder is required to include the shareholder's pro rata share of S corporation gross income in computing the shareholder's gross income for the purposes of determining the necessity of filing a return (section 6012(a)) and the shareholder's gross income derived from farming (sections 175 and 6654(i)).

(2) Gross income for substantial omission of items — (i) In general. For purposes of determining the applicability of the 6-year period of limitation on assessment and collection provided in section 6501(e) (relating to omission of more than 25 percent of gross income), a shareholder's gross income includes the shareholder's pro rata share of S corporation gross income (as described in section 6501(e)(1)(A)(i)). In this respect, the amount of S corporation gross income used in deriving the shareholder's pro rata share of any item of S corporation income, loss, deduction, or credit (as included or disclosed in the shareholder's return) is considered as an amount of gross income stated in the shareholder's return for purposes of section 6501(e).

(ii) Example. The following example illustrates the provisions of paragraph (c)(2)(i) of this section:

Example. Shareholder A, an individual, owns 25 percent of the stock of Corporation N, an S corporation that has $10,000 gross income and $2,000 taxable income. A reports only $300 as A's pro rata share of N's taxable income. A should have reported $500 as A's pro rata share of taxable income, derived from A's pro rata share, $2,500, of N's gross income. Because A's return included only $300 without a disclosure meeting the requirements of section 6501(e)(1)(A)(ii) describing the difference of $200, A is regarded as having reported on the return only $1,500 ($300/$500 of $2,500) as gross income from N.

(d) Shareholders holding stock subject to community property laws. If a shareholder holds S corporation stock that is community property, then the shareholder's pro rata share of any item or items listed in paragraphs (a) (2), (3), and (4) of this section with respect to that stock is reported by the husband and wife in accordance with community property rules.

(e) Net operating loss deduction of shareholder of S corporation. For purposes of determining a net operating loss deduction under section 172, a shareholder of an S corporation must take into account the shareholder's pro rata share of items of income, loss, deduction, or credit of the corporation. See section 1366(b) and paragraph (b) of this section for rules on determining the character of the items. In determining under section 172(d) (4) the nonbusiness deductions allowable to a shareholder of an S corporation (arising from both corporation sources and any other sources), the shareholder separately takes into account the shareholder's pro rata share of the deductions of the corporation that are not attributable to a trade or business and combines this amount with the shareholder's nonbusiness deductions from any other sources. The shareholder also separately takes into account the shareholder's pro rata share of the gross income of the corporation not derived from a trade or business and combines this amount with the shareholder's nonbusiness income from all other sources. See section 172 and the regulations thereunder.

(f) Cross-reference. For rules relating to the consistent tax treatment of subchapter S items, see section 6037(c).

§1.1366–2 Limitations on deduction of passthrough items of an S corporation to its shareholders.

(a) In general—(1) Limitation on losses and deductions. The aggregate amount of losses and deductions taken into account by a shareholder under §1.1366–1(a)(2), (3), and (4) for any taxable year of an S corporation cannot exceed the sum of—

(i) The adjusted basis of the shareholder's stock in the corporation (as determined under paragraph (a)(4)(i) of this section); and

(ii) The adjusted basis of any indebtedness of the corporation to the shareholder (as determined under paragraphs (a)(2) and (a)(4)(ii) of this section).

(2) Basis of indebtedness—(i) In general. The term basis of any indebtedness of the S corporation to the shareholder means the shareholder's adjusted basis (as defined in §1.1011–1 and as specifically provided in section 1367(b)(2)) in any bona fide indebtedness of the S corporation that runs directly to the shareholder. Whether indebtedness is bona fide indebtedness to a shareholder is determined under general Federal tax principles and depends upon all of the facts and circumstances.

(ii) Special rule for guarantees. A shareholder does not obtain basis of indebtedness in the S corporation merely by guaranteeing a loan or acting as a surety, accommodation party, or in any similar capacity relating to a loan. When a shareholder makes a payment on bona fide indebtedness of the S corporation for which the shareholder has acted as guarantor or in a similar capacity, then the shareholder may increase the shareholder's basis of indebtedness to the extent of that payment.

(iii) Examples. The following examples illustrate the provisions of paragraph (a)(2)(i) and (ii) of this section:

Example (1). Shareholder loan transaction. A is the sole shareholder of S, an S corporation. S received a loan from A. Whether the loan from A to S constitutes bona fide indebtedness from S to A is determined under general Federal tax principles and depends upon all of the facts and circumstances. See paragraph (a)(2)(i) of this section. If the loan constitutes bona fide indebtedness from S to A, A's loan to S increases A's basis of indebtedness under paragraph (a)(2)(i) of this section. The result is the same if A made the loan to S through an entity that is disregarded as an entity separate from A under §301.7701–3 of this chapter.

Example (2). Back-to-back loan transaction. A is the sole shareholder of two S corporations, S1 and S2. S1 loaned $200,000 to A. A then loaned $200,000 to S2. Whether the loan from A to S2 constitutes bona fide indebtedness from S2 to A is determined under general Federal tax principles and depends upon all of the facts and circumstances. See paragraph (a)(2)(i) of this section. If A's loan to S2 constitutes bona fide indebtedness from S2 to A, A's back-to-back loan increases A's basis of indebtedness in S2 under paragraph (a)(2)(i) of this section.

Example (3). Loan restructuring through distributions. A is the sole shareholder of two S corporations, S1 and S2. In May 2014, S1 made a loan to S2. In December 2014, S1 assigned its creditor position in the note to A by making a distribution to A of the note. Under local law, after S1 distributed the note to A,

S2 was relieved of its liability to S1 and was directly liable to A. Whether S2 is indebted to A rather than S1 is determined under general Federal tax principles and depends upon all of the facts and circumstances. See paragraph (a)(2)(i) of this section. If the note constitutes bona fide indebtedness from S2 to A, the note increases A's basis of indebtedness in S2 under paragraph (a)(2)(i) of this section.

Example (4). Guarantee. A is a shareholder of S, an S corporation. In 2014, S received a loan from Bank. Bank required A's guarantee as a condition of making the loan to S. Beginning in 2015, S could no longer make payments on the loan and A made payments directly to Bank from A's personal funds until the loan obligation was satisfied. For each payment A made on the note, A obtains basis of indebtedness under paragraph (a)(2)(ii) of this section. Thus, A's basis of indebtedness is increased during 2015 under paragraph (a)(2)(ii) of this section to the extent of A's payments to Bank pursuant to the guarantee agreement.

(3) Carryover of disallowance. A shareholder's aggregate amount of losses and deductions for a taxable year in excess of the sum of the adjusted basis of the shareholder's stock in an S corporation and of any indebtedness of the S corporation to the shareholder is not allowed for the taxable year. However, any disallowed loss or deduction retains its character and is treated as incurred by the corporation in the corporation's first succeeding taxable year, and subsequent taxable years, with respect to the shareholder. For rules on determining the adjusted bases of stock of an S corporation and indebtedness of the corporation to the shareholder, see paragraphs (a)(4)(i) and (ii) of this section.

(4) Basis limitation amount—(i) Stock portion. A shareholder generally determines the adjusted basis of stock for purposes of paragraphs (a)(1)(i) and (3) of this section (limiting losses and deductions) by taking into account only increases in basis under section 1367(a)(1) for the taxable year and decreases in basis under section 1367(a)(2)(A), (D) and (E) (relating to distributions, noncapital, nondeductible expenses, and certain oil and gas depletion deductions) for the taxable year. In so determining this loss limitation amount, the shareholder disregards decreases in basis under section 1367(a)(2)(B) and (C) (for losses and deductions, including losses and deductions previously disallowed) for the taxable year. However, if the shareholder has in effect for the taxable year an election under § 1.1367–1(g) to decrease basis by items of loss and deduction prior to decreasing basis by noncapital, nondeductible expenses and certain oil and gas depletion deductions, the shareholder also disregards decreases in basis under section 1367(a)(2)(D) and (E). This basis limitation amount for stock is determined at the time prescribed under § 1.1367–1(d)(1) for adjustments to the basis of stock.

(ii) Indebtedness portion. A shareholder determines the shareholder's adjusted basis in indebtedness of the corporation for purposes of paragraphs (a)(1)(ii) and (3) of this section (limiting losses and deductions) without regard to any adjustment under section 1367(b)(2)(A) for the taxable year. This basis limitation amount for indebtedness is determined at the time prescribed under § 1.1367–2(d)(1) for adjustments to the basis of indebtedness.

(5) Limitation on losses and deductions allocated to each item. If a shareholder's pro rata share of the aggregate amount of losses and deductions specified in § 1.1366–1(a)(2), (3), and (4) exceeds the sum of the adjusted basis of the shareholder's stock in the corporation (determined in accordance with paragraph (a)(4)(i) of this section) and the adjusted basis of any indebtedness of the corporation to the shareholder (determined in accordance with paragraph (a)(4)(ii) of this section), then the limitation on losses and deductions under section 1366(d)(1) must be allocated among the shareholder's pro rata share of each loss or deduction. The amount of the limitation allocated to any loss or deduction is an amount that bears the same ratio to the amount of the limitation as the loss or deduction bears to the total of the losses and deductions. For this purpose, the total of losses and deductions for the taxable year is the sum of the shareholder's pro rata share of losses and deductions for the taxable year, and the losses and deductions disallowed and carried forward from prior years pursuant to section 1366(d)(2).

(6) Nontransferability of losses and deductions—(i) In general. Except as provided in paragraph (a)(6)(ii) of this section, any loss or deduction disallowed under paragraph (a)(1) of this section is personal to the shareholder and cannot in any manner be transferred to another person. If a shareholder transfers some but not all of the shareholder's stock in the corporation, the amount of any disallowed loss or deduction under this section is not reduced and the transferee does not acquire any portion of the disallowed loss or deduction. If a shareholder transfers all of the shareholder's stock in the corporation, any disallowed loss or deduction is permanently disallowed.

(ii) Exceptions for transfers of stock under section 1041(a). If a shareholder transfers stock of an S corporation after December 31, 2004, in a transfer described in section 1041(a), any loss or deduction with respect to the transferred stock that is disallowed to the transferring shareholder under paragraph (a)(1) of this section shall be treated as incurred by the corporation in the following taxable year with respect to the transferee spouse or former spouse. The amount of any loss or deduction with respect to the stock transferred shall be determined by prorating any losses or deductions disallowed under paragraph (a)(1) of this section for the year of the transfer between the transferor and the spouse or former spouse based on the stock ownership at the beginning of the following taxable year. If a transferor claims a deduction for losses in the taxable year of transfer, then under paragraph (a)(5) of this section, if the transferor's pro rata share of the losses and deductions in the year of transfer exceeds the transferor's basis in stock and the indebtedness of the corporation to the transferor, then the limitation must be allocated among the transferor spouse's pro rata share of each loss or deduction, including disallowed losses and deductions carried over from the prior year.

(iii) Examples. The following examples illustrates the provisions of paragraph (a)(6)(ii) of this section:

Example (1). A owns all 100 shares in X, a calendar year S corporation. For X's taxable year ending December 31, 2006, A has zero basis in the shares and X does not have any indebtedness to A. For the 2006 taxable year, X had $100 in losses that A cannot use because of the basis limitation in section 1366(d)(1) and that are treated as incurred by the corporation with respect to A in the following taxable year. Halfway through the 2007 taxable year, A transfers 50 shares to B, A's former spouse in a transfer to which section 1041(a) applies. In the 2007 taxable year, X has $80 in losses. On A's 2007 individual income tax return, A may use the entire $100 carryover loss from 2006, as well as A's share of the $80 2007 loss determined under section 1377(a) ($60), assuming A acquires sufficient basis in the X stock. On B's 2007 individual income tax return, B may use B's share of the $80 2007 loss determined under section 1377(a) ($20), assuming B has sufficient basis in the X stock. If any disallowed 2006 loss is disallowed to A under section 1366(d)(1) in 2007, that loss is prorated between A and B based on their stock ownership at the beginning of 2008. On B's 2008 individual income tax return, B may use that loss, assuming B acquires sufficient basis in the X stock. If neither A nor B acquires any basis during the 2007 taxable year, then as of the beginning of 2008, the corporation will be treated as incurring $50 of loss with respect to A and $50 of loss with respect to B for the $100 of disallowed 2006 loss, and the corporation will be treated as incurring $60 of loss with respect to A and $20 with respect to B for the $80 of disallowed 2007 loss.

Example (2). Assume the same facts as Example 1, except that during the 2007 taxable year, A acquires $10 of basis in A's shares in X. For the 2007 taxable year, A may claim a $10 loss deduction, which represents $6.25 of the disallowed 2006 loss of $100 and $3.75 of A's 2007 loss of $60. The disallowed 2006 loss is reduced to $93.75. As of the beginning of 2008, the corporation will be treated as incurring half of the remaining $93.75 of loss with respect to A and half of that loss with respect to B for the remaining $93.75 of disallowed 2006 loss, and if B does not acquire any basis during 2007, the corporation will be treated as incurring $56.25 of loss with respect to A and $20 with respect to B for the remaining disallowed 2007 loss.

(7) Basis of stock acquired by gift. For purposes of section 1366(d)(1)(A) and paragraphs (a)(1)(i) and (3) of this section, the basis of stock in a corporation acquired by gift is the basis of the stock that is used for purposes of determining loss under section 1015(a).

(b) Special rules for carryover of disallowed losses and deductions to post-termination transition period described in section 1377(b)—(1) In general. If, for the last taxable year of a corporation for which it was an S corporation, a loss or deduction was disallowed to a shareholder by reason of the limitation in paragraph (a) of this section, the loss or deduction is treated under section 1366(d)(3) as incurred by that shareholder on the last day of any post-termination transition period (within the meaning of section 1377(b)).

(2) Limitation on losses and deductions. The aggregate amount of losses and deductions taken into account by a shareholder under paragraph (b)(1) of this section cannot exceed the adjusted basis of the shareholder's stock in the corporation determined at the close of the last day of the post-termination transition period. For this purpose, the adjusted basis of a shareholder's stock in the corporation is determined at the close of the last day of the post-termination transition period without regard to any reduction required under paragraph (b)(4) of this section. If a shareholder disposes of a share of stock prior to the close of the last day of the post-termination transition period, the adjusted basis of that share is its basis as of the close of the day of disposition. Any losses and deductions in excess of a shareholder's adjusted stock basis are permanently disallowed. For purposes of section 1366(d)(3)(B) and this paragraph (b)(2), the basis of stock in a corporation acquired by gift is the basis of the stock that is used for purposes of determining loss under section 1015(a).

(3) Limitation on losses and deductions allocated to each item. If the aggregate amount of losses and deductions treated as incurred by the shareholder under paragraph (b)(1) of this section exceeds the adjusted basis of the shareholder's stock determined under paragraph (b)(2) of this section, the limitation on losses and deductions under section 1366(d)(3)(B) must be allocated among each loss or deduction. The amount of the limitation allocated to each loss or deduction is an amount that bears the same ratio to the amount of the limitation as the amount of each loss or deduction bears to the total of all the losses and deductions.

(4) Adjustment to the basis of stock. The shareholder's basis in the stock of the corporation is reduced by the amount allowed as a deduction by reason of this paragraph (b). For rules regarding adjustments to the basis of a shareholder's stock in an S corporation, see § 1.1367–1.

(c) Carryover of disallowed losses and deductions in the case of liquidations, reorganizations, and divisions—(1) Liquidations and reorganizations. If a corporation acquires the assets of an S corporation in a transaction to which section 381(a) applies, any loss or deduction disallowed under paragraph (a) of this section with respect to a shareholder of the distributor or transferor S corporation is available to that shareholder as a shareholder of the acquiring corporation.

Thus, where the acquiring corporation is an S corporation, a loss or deduction of a shareholder of the distributor or transferor S corporation disallowed prior to or during the taxable year of the transaction is treated as incurred by the acquiring S corporation with respect to that shareholder if the shareholder is a shareholder of the acquiring S corporation after the transaction. Where the acquiring corporation is a C corporation, a post-termination transition period arises the day after the last day that an S corporation was in existence and the rules provided in paragraph (b) of this section apply with respect to any shareholder of the acquired S corporation that is also a shareholder of the acquiring C corporation after the transaction. See the special rules under section 1377 for the availability of the post-termination transition period if the acquiring corporation is a C corporation.

(2) Corporate separations to which section 368(a)(1)(D) applies. If an S corporation transfers a portion of its assets constituting an active trade or business to another corporation in a transaction to which section 368(a)(1)(D) applies, and immediately thereafter the stock and securities of the controlled corporation are distributed in a distribution or exchange to which section 355 (or so much of section 356 as relates to section 355) applies, any loss or deduction disallowed under paragraph (a) of this section with respect to a shareholder of the distributing S corporation immediately before the transaction is allocated between the distributing corporation and the controlled corporation with respect to the shareholder. Such allocation shall be made according to any reasonable method, including a method based on the relative fair market value of the shareholder's stock in the distributing and controlled corporations immediately after the distribution, a method based on the relative adjusted basis of the assets in the distributing and controlled corporations immediately after the distribution, or, in the case of losses and deductions clearly attributable to either the distributing or controlled corporation, any

method that allocates such losses and deductions accordingly.

§1.1366–3 Treatment of family groups.

(a) In general. Under section 1366(e), if an individual, who is a member of the family of one or more shareholders of an S corporation, renders services for, or furnishes capital to, the corporation without receiving reasonable compensation, the Commissioner shall prescribe adjustments to those items taken into account by the individual and the shareholders as may be necessary to reflect the value of the services rendered or capital furnished. For these purposes, in determining the reasonable value for services rendered, or capital furnished, to the corporation, consideration will be given to all the facts and circumstances, including the amount that ordinarily would be paid in order to obtain comparable services or capital from a person (other than a member of the family) who is not a shareholder in the corporation. In addition, for purposes of section 1366(e), if a member of the family of one or more shareholders of the S corporation holds an interest in a passthrough entity (e.g., a partnership, S corporation, trust, or estate), that performs services for, or furnishes capital to, the S corporation without receiving reasonable compensation, the Commissioner shall prescribe adjustments to the passthrough entity and the corporation as may be necessary to reflect the value of the services rendered or capital furnished. For purposes of section 1366(e), the term family of any shareholder includes only the shareholder's spouse, ancestors, lineal descendants, and any trust for the primary benefit of any of these persons.

(b) Examples. The provisions of this section may be illustrated by the following examples:

Example (1). The stock of an S corporation is owned 50 percent by F and 50 percent by T, the minor son of F. For the taxable year, the corporation has items of taxable income equal to $70,000. Compensation of $10,000 is paid by the corporation to F for services rendered during the taxable year, and no compensation is paid to T, who rendered no services. Based on all the relevant facts and circumstances, reasonable compensation for the services rendered by F would be $30,000. In the discretion of the Internal Revenue Service, up to an additional $20,000 of the $70,000 of the corporation's taxable income, for tax purposes, may be allocated to F as compensation for services rendered. If the Internal Revenue Service allocates $20,000 of the corporation's taxable income to F as compensation for services, taxable income of the corporation would be reduced by $20,000 to $50,000, of which F and T each would be allocated $25,000. F would have $30,000 of total compensation paid by the corporation for services rendered.

Example (2). The stock of an S corporation is owned by A and B. For the taxable year, the corporation has paid compensation to a partnership that rendered services to the corporation during the taxable year. The spouse of A is a partner in that partnership. Consequently, if based on all the relevant facts and circumstances the partnership did not receive reasonable compensation for the services rendered to the corporation, the Internal Revenue Service, in its discretion, may make adjustments to those items taken into account by the partnership and the corporation as may be necessary to reflect the value of the services rendered.

§ 1.1366–4 Special rules limiting the passthrough of certain items of an S corporation to its shareholders.

(a) Passthrough inapplicable to section 34 credit. Section 1.1366–1(a) does not apply to any credit allowable under section 34 (relating to certain uses of gasoline and special fuels).

(b) Reduction in passthrough for tax imposed on built-in gains. For purposes of § 1.1366–1(a), if for any taxable year of the S corporation a tax is imposed on the corporation under section 1374, the amount of the

tax imposed is treated as a loss sustained by the S corporation during the taxable year. The character of the deemed loss is determined by allocating the loss proportionately among the net recognized built-in gains giving rise to the tax and attributing the character of each net recognized built-in gain to the allocable portion of the loss.

(c) Reduction in passthrough for tax imposed on excess net passive income. For purposes of § 1.1366–1(a), if for any taxable year of the S corporation a tax is imposed on the corporation under section 1375, each item of passive investment income shall be reduced by an amount that bears the same ratio to the amount of the tax as the amount of the item bears to the total net passive investment income for that taxable year.

* * *

§ 1.1367–1 Adjustments to basis of shareholder's stock in an S corporation.

(a) In general—(1) Adjustments under section 1367.

This section provides rules relating to adjustments required by section 1367 to the basis of a shareholder's stock in an S corporation. Paragraph (b) of this section provides rules concerning increases in the basis of a shareholder's stock, and paragraph (c) of this section provides rules concerning decreases in the basis of a shareholder's stock.

(2) Applicability of other Internal Revenue Code provisions. In addition to the adjustments required by section 1367 and this section, the basis of stock is determined or adjusted under other applicable provisions of the Internal Revenue Code.

(b) Increase in basis of stock—(1) In general. Except as provided in § 1.1367–2(c) (relating to restoration of basis of indebtedness to the shareholder), the basis of a shareholder's stock in an S corporation is increased by the sum of the items described in section 1367(a)(1). The increase in basis described in section

1367(a)(1)(C) for the excess of the deduction for depletion over the basis of the property subject to depletion does not include the depletion deduction attributable to oil or gas property. See section 613(A)(c)(11).

(2) Amount of increase in basis of individual shares. The basis of a shareholder's share of stock is increased by an amount equal to the shareholder's pro rata portion of the items described in section 1367(a)(1) that is attributable to that share, determined on a per share, per day basis in accordance with section 1377(a).

(c) Decrease in basis of stock—(1) In general. The basis of a shareholder's stock in an S corporation is decreased (but not below zero) by the sum of the items described in section 1367(a)(2).

(2) Noncapital, nondeductible expenses. For purposes of section 1367(a)(2)(D), expenses of the corporation not deductible in computing its taxable income and not properly chargeable to a capital account (noncapital, nondeductible expenses) are only those items for which no loss or deduction is allowable and do not include items the deduction for which is deferred to a later taxable year. Examples of noncapital, nondeductible expenses include (but are not limited to) the following: illegal bribes, kickbacks, and other payments not deductible under section 162(c); fines and penalties not deductible under section 162(f); expenses and interest relating to tax-exempt income under section 265; losses for which the deduction is disallowed under section 267(a)(1); the portion of meals and entertainment expenses disallowed under section 274; and the two-thirds portion of treble damages paid for violating antitrust laws not deductible under section 162. (2) * * * For basis adjustments necessary to coordinate sections 1367 and 362(e)(2), see §1.362–4(e)(2).

(3) Amount of decrease in basis of individual shares. The basis of a shareholder's share of stock is decreased by an amount equal to the shareholder's pro rata portion of the passthrough items and distributions described in section 1367(a)(2) attributable to that share, determined on a per share, per day basis in accordance with section 1377(a). If the amount attributable to a share exceeds its basis, the excess is applied to reduce (but not below zero) the remaining bases of all other shares of stock in the corporation owned by the shareholder in proportion to the remaining basis of each of those shares.

(d) Time at which adjustments to basis of stock are effective—(1) In general. The adjustments described in section 1367(a) to the basis of a shareholder's stock are determined as of the close of the corporation's taxable year, and the adjustments generally are effective as of that date. However, if a shareholder disposes of stock during the corporation's taxable year, the adjustments with respect to that stock are effective immediately prior to the disposition.

(2) Adjustment for nontaxable item. An adjustment for a nontaxable item is determined for the taxable year in which the item would have been includible or deductible under the corporation's method of accounting for federal income tax purposes if the item had been subject to federal income taxation.

(3) Effect of election under section 1377(a)(2) or §1.1368–1(g)(2). If an election under section 1377(a)(2) (to terminate the year in the case of the termination of a shareholder's interest) or under §1.1368–1(g)(2) (to terminate the year in the case of a qualifying disposition) is made with respect to the taxable year of a corporation, this paragraph (d) applies as if the taxable year consisted of separate taxable years, the first of which ends at the close of the day on which either the shareholder's interest is terminated or a qualifying disposition occurs, whichever the case may be.

* * *

(f) Ordering rules for taxable years beginning on or after August 18, 1998. For any taxable year of a corporation beginning on or after August 18, 1998, except as provided in paragraph (g) of this section, the adjustments required by section 1367(a) are made in the following order—

(1) Any increase in basis attributable to the income items described in section 1367(a)(1)(A) and (B), and the excess of the deductions for depletion described in section 1367(a)(1)(C);

(2) Any decrease in basis attributable to a distribution by the corporation described in section 1367(a)(2)(A);

(3) Any decrease in basis attributable to noncapital, nondeductible expenses described in section 1367(a)(2)(D), and the oil and gas depletion deduction described in section 1367(a)(2)(E); and

(4) Any decrease in basis attributable to items of loss or deduction described in section 1367(a)(2)(B) and (C).

(g) Elective ordering rule. A shareholder may elect to decrease basis under paragraph (e)(3) or (f)(4) of this section, whichever applies, prior to decreasing basis under paragraph (e)(2) or (f)(3) of this section, whichever applies. If a shareholder makes this election, any amount described in paragraph (e)(2) or (f)(3) of this section, whichever applies, that is in excess of the shareholder's basis in stock and indebtedness is treated, solely for purposes of this section, as an amount described in paragraph (e)(2) or (f)(3) of this section, whichever applies, in the succeeding taxable year. A shareholder makes the election under this paragraph by attaching a statement to the shareholder's timely filed original or amended return that states that the shareholder agrees to the carryover rule of the preceding sentence. Once a shareholder makes an election under this paragraph with respect to an S corporation, the shareholder must continue to use the rules of this paragraph for that S corporation in future taxable years unless the shareholder receives the permission of the Commissioner.

(h) Examples. The following examples illustrate the principles of § 1.1367–1. In each example, the corporation is a calendar year S corporation:

* * *

Example (2). Adjustments to basis of stock for taxable years beginning on or after August 18, 1998. (i) On December 31, 2001, A owns a block of 50 shares of stock with an adjusted basis per share of $6 in Corporation S. On December 31, 2001, A purchases for $400 an additional block of 50 shares of stock with an adjusted basis of $8 per share. Thus, A holds 100 shares of stock for each day of the 2002 taxable year. For S's 2002 taxable year, A's pro rata share of the amount of items described in section 1367(a)(1)(A) (relating to increases in basis of stock) is $300, A's pro rata share of the amount of the items described in section 1367(a)(2)(B) (relating to decreases in basis of stock attributable to items of loss and deduction) is $300, and A's pro rata share of the amount of the items described in section 1367(a)(2)(D) (relating to decreases in basis of stock attributable to noncapital, nondeductible expenses) is $200. S makes a distribution to A in the amount of $100 during 2002.

(ii) Pursuant to the ordering rules of paragraph (f) of this section, A first increases the basis of each share of stock by $3 ($300/100 shares) and then decreases the basis of each share by $1 ($100/100 shares) for the distribution. A next decreases the basis of each share by $2 ($200/100 shares) for the noncapital, nondeductible expenses and then decreases the basis of each share by $3 ($300/100 shares) for the items of loss. Thus, on January 1, 2003, A has a basis of $3 per share in the original block of 50 shares ($6 + $3 − $1 − $2 − $3) and a basis of $5 per share in the second block of 100 shares ($8 + $3 − $1 − $2 − $3).

Example (5). Effects of section 1377(a)(2) election and distribution on basis of stock for taxable years beginning on or after August 18, 1998. (i) The facts are the same as in Example 4, except that all of the events occur in 2001 rather than in 1994 and except as follows: On June 30, 2001, B sells 25 shares of her stock for $5,000 to D and 25 shares back to Corporation S for $5,000. Under section 1377(a)(2)(B) and § 1.1377–1(b)(2), B and C are affected shareholders because B has transferred shares to Corporation S. Pursuant to section 1377(a)(2)(A) and § 1.1377–1(b)(1), B and C, the affected shareholders, and Corporation S agree to treat the taxable year 2001 as if it consisted of two separate taxable years for all affected shareholders for the purposes set forth in § 1.1377–1(b)(3)(i).

(ii) On June 30, 2001, B and C, pursuant to the ordering rules of paragraph (f)(1) of this section, increase the basis of each share by $60 ($6,000/100 shares) for the nonseparately computed income. Then B and C reduce the basis of each share by $120 ($12,000/100 shares) for the distribution. Finally, B and C decrease the basis of each share by $40 ($4,000/100 shares) for the separately stated deduction item.

(iii) The basis of the stock of B is reduced from $120 to $20 per share ($120 + $60 – $120 – $40). Prior to accounting for the separately stated deduction item, the basis of the stock of C is reduced from $80 to $20 ($80 + $60 – $120). Finally, because the period from January 1 through June 30, 2001 is treated under § 1.1377–1(b)(3)(i) as a separate taxable year for purposes of making adjustments to the basis of stock, under section 1366(d) and § 1.1366–2(a)(3), C may deduct only $20 per share of the remaining $40 of the separately stated deduction item, and the basis of the stock of C is reduced from $20 per share to $0 per share. Under section 1366 and § 1.1366–2(a)(3), C's remaining separately stated deduction item of $20 per share is treated as having been incurred in the first succeeding taxable year of Corporation S, which, for this purpose, begins on July 1, 2001.

§ 1.1367–2 Adjustments to basis of indebtedness to shareholder.

(a) In general—(1) Adjustments under section 1367. This section provides rules relating to adjustments required by subchapter S to the basis of indebtedness (including open account debt as described in paragraph (a)(2) of this section) of an S corporation to a shareholder. The basis of indebtedness of the S corporation to a shareholder is reduced as provided in paragraph (b) of this section and restored as provided in paragraph (c) of this section in accordance with the timing rules in paragraph (d) of this section.

(2) Open account debt—(i) General rule. The term open account debt means shareholder advances not evidenced by separate written instruments and repayments on the advances, the aggregate outstanding principal of which does not exceed $25,000 of indebtedness of the S corporation to the shareholder at the close of the S corporation's taxable year. Advances and repayments on open account debt are treated as a single indebtedness.

(ii) Exception. If the shareholder advances not evidenced by a separate written instrument, net of repayments, exceeds an aggregate outstanding principal amount of $25,000 at the close of the S corporation's taxable year, for any subsequent taxable year the aggregate principal amount of that indebtedness is treated in the same manner as indebtedness evidenced by a separate written instrument for purposes of this section. For any subsequent taxable year, that indebtedness is not open account debt and is subject to all basis adjustment rules applicable to basis of indebtedness of an S corporation to a shareholder in this section.

(b) Reduction in basis of indebtedness—(1) General rule. If, after making the adjustments required by section 1367(a)(1) for any taxable year of the S corporation, the amounts specified in section 1367(a)(2)(B), (C), (D), and (E) (relating to losses, deductions, noncapital, nondeductible expenses, and certain oil and gas depletion deductions) exceed the basis of a shareholder's stock in the corporation, the excess is applied to reduce (but not below zero) the basis of any indebtedness of the S corporation to the shareholder held by the shareholder at the close of the corporation's taxable year. Any such indebtedness that has been satisfied by the corporation, or disposed of or forgiven by the shareholder, during the taxable year, is not held by the shareholder at the close of that year and is not subject to basis reduction.

(2) Termination of shareholder's interest in corporation during taxable year. If a shareholder terminates his or her interest in the corporation during the taxable year, the rules of this paragraph (b) are applied with respect to any indebtedness of the S corporation held by the shareholder immediately prior to the termination of the shareholder's interest in the corporation.

(3) Multiple indebtedness. If a shareholder holds more than one indebtedness at the close of the corporation's taxable year or, if applicable, immediately prior to the termination of the shareholder's interest in the corporation, the reduction in basis is applied to each indebtedness in the same proportion that the basis of each indebtedness bears to the aggregate bases of the indebtedness to the shareholder.

(c) Restoration of basis—(1) General rule. If, for any taxable year of an S corporation beginning after December 31, 1982, there has been a reduction in the basis of an indebtedness of the S corporation to a shareholder under section 1367(b)(2)(A), any net increase in any subsequent taxable year of the corporation is applied to restore that reduction. For purposes of this section, net increase with respect to a shareholder means the amount by which the shareholder's pro rata share of the items described in section 1367(a)(1) (relating to income items and excess deduction for depletion) exceed the items described in section 1367(a)(2) (relating to losses, deductions, noncapital, nondeductible expenses, certain oil and gas depletion deductions, and certain

distributions) for the taxable year. These restoration rules apply only to indebtedness held by a shareholder as of the beginning of the taxable year in which the net increase arises. The reduction in basis of indebtedness must be restored before any net increase is applied to restore the basis of a shareholder's stock in an S corporation. In no event may the shareholder's basis of indebtedness be restored above the adjusted basis of the indebtedness under section 1016(a), excluding any adjustments under section 1016(a)(17) for prior taxable years, determined as of the beginning of the taxable year in which the net increase arises.

(2) Multiple indebtedness. If a shareholder holds more than one indebtedness (including any open account debt and any debt treated as a single indebtedness under paragraph (a)(2)(ii) of this section) as of the beginning of an S corporation's taxable year, any net increase is applied first to restore the reduction of basis in any indebtedness repaid (in whole or in part) in that taxable year to the extent necessary to offset any gain that would otherwise be realized on the repayment. Any remaining net increase is applied to restore each outstanding indebtedness (including any open account debt and any debt treated as a single indebtedness under paragraph (a)(2)(ii) of this section) in proportion to the amount that the basis of each outstanding indebtedness has been reduced under section 1367(b)(2)(A) and paragraph (b) of this section and not restored under section 1367(b)(2)(B) and this paragraph (c).

(d) Time at which adjustments to basis of indebtedness are effective—

(1) In general. The amounts of the adjustments to basis of indebtedness (including open account debt) provided in section 1367(b)(2) and this section are determined as of the close of the S corporation's taxable year, and the adjustments are generally effective as of the close of the S corporation's taxable year. However, if the shareholder is not a shareholder in the S corporation at that time, these adjustments are effective immediately before the shareholder terminates his or her interest in the S corporation. Except as provided in paragraph (d)(2) of this section, if a debt is disposed of or repaid in whole or in part before the close of the taxable year, the basis of that indebtedness is restored under paragraph (c) of this section, effective immediately before the disposition or the first repayment on the debt during the taxable year. To the extent any indebtedness of the S corporation to the shareholder is disposed of or repaid (in whole or in part) during the taxable year and the shareholder's basis in that indebtedness has been reduced under paragraph (b) of this section and is not restored completely under paragraph (c) of this section, the disposition or repayment is a recognition event effective immediately before the indebtedness is disposed of or repaid (in whole or in part).

(2) Open account debt—(i) In general. All advances and repayments on open account debt (as described in paragraph (a)(2)(i) of this section) during the S corporation's taxable year are netted at the close of the S corporation's taxable year to determine the amount of any net advance or net repayment. The net advance or net repayment is combined with the outstanding aggregate principal balance of the existing open account debt and that amount is carried forward to the beginning of the subsequent taxable year as the outstanding aggregate principal amount of the open account debt (unless the aggregate principal amount meets the exception defined in paragraph (a)(2)(ii) of this section at the close of the taxable year). However, if the shareholder in the S corporation is not a shareholder of the S corporation at the close of the S corporation's taxable year, such advances and repayments on open account debt are netted, and the basis of that indebtedness is restored under paragraph (c) of this section, effective immediately before the shareholder terminates his or her interest in the S corporation. If any open account debt is disposed of before or upon the close of the taxable year, the disposition is effective at the close of the S corporation's taxable year, and all advances and repayments are netted immediately prior to the disposition and the basis of that indebtedness is restored under paragraph (c) of this section, effective at the close of the S corporation's taxable year.

(ii) Exception. Shareholder indebtedness that is open account debt at the beginning of the taxable year but meets the exception defined in paragraph (a)(2)(ii) of this section at the close of the taxable year, adjustments to the basis of the indebtedness for that taxable year follow the provisions for open account debt. The resulting aggregate principal amount of indebtedness is treated as the principal amount of a debt evidenced by a separate written instrument for any subsequent taxable year, and is no longer subject to the open account debt provisions of this section.

(3) Effect of election under section 1377(a)(2) or § 1.1368–1(g)(2). If an election is made under section 1377(a)(2) (to terminate the year in the case of the termination of a shareholder's interest) or under § 1.1368–1(g) (2) (to terminate the year in the case of a qualifying disposition), this paragraph (d) applies as if the taxable year consisted of separate taxable years, the first of which ends at the close of the day on which the shareholder either terminates his or her interest in the corporation or disposes of a substantial amount of stock, whichever the case may be.

(e) Examples. The following examples illustrate the principles of § 1.1367–2. In each example, the corporation is a calendar year S corporation. The lending transactions described in the examples do not result in foregone interest (within the meaning of section 7872(e)(2)), original issue discount (within the meaning of section 1273), or total unstated interest (within the meaning of section 483(b)).

Example (1). Reduction in basis of indebtedness. (i) A has been the sole shareholder in Corporation S since 1992. In 1993, A loans S $1,000 (Debt No. 1), which is evidenced by a ten-year promissory note in the face amount of $1,000. In 1996, A loans S $5,000 (Debt No. 2), which is evidenced by a demand promissory note. On December 31, 1996, the basis of A's stock is zero; the basis of Debt No. 1 has been reduced under paragraph (b) of this section to $0; and the basis of Debt No. 2 has been reduced to $1,000. On January 1, 1997, A loans S $4,000 (Debt No. 3), which is evidenced by a demand promissory note. For S's 1997 taxable year, the sum of the amounts specified in section 1367(a)(1) (in this case, nonseparately computed income and the excess deduction for depletion) is $6,000, and the sum of the amounts specified in section 1367(a)(2)(B), (D), and (E) (in this case, items of separately stated deductions and losses, noncapital, nondeductible expenses, and certain oil and gas depletion deductions—there is no nonseparately computed loss) is $10,000. Corporation S makes no payments to A on any of the loans during 1997.

(ii) The $4,000 excess of loss and deduction items is applied to reduce the basis of each indebtedness in proportion to the basis of that indebtedness over the aggregate bases of the indebtedness to the shareholder (determined immediately before any adjustment under section 1367(b)(2)(A) and paragraph (b) of this section is effective for the taxable year). Thus, the basis of Debt No. 2 is reduced in an amount equal to $800 ($4,000 (excess) x $1,000 (basis of Debt No. 2)/$5,000 (total basis of all debt)). Similarly, the basis in Debt No. 3 is reduced in an amount equal to $3,200 ($4,000 × $4,000/$5,000). Accordingly, on December 31, 1997, A's basis in his stock is zero and his bases in the three debts are as follows:

Debt	1/1/96 basis	12/31/96 reduction	1/1/97 basis	12/31/97 reduction	1/1/98 basis
No. 1	$1,000	$1,000	$0	$0	$0
No. 2	5,000	4,000	1,000	800	200
No. 3			4,000	3,200	800

Example (2). Restoration of basis of indebtedness. (i) The facts are the same as in Example 1. On July 1, 1998, S completely repays Debt No. 3, and, for S's 1998 taxable year, the net increase (within the meaning of paragraph (c) of this section) with respect to A equals $4,500.

(ii) The net increase is applied first to restore the bases in the debts held on January 1, 1998, before any of the net increase is applied to increase A's basis in his shares of S stock. The net increase is applied to restore first the reduction of basis in indebtedness repaid in 1998. Any remaining net increase is applied to restore the bases of the outstanding debts in proportion to the amount that each of these outstanding debts have been reduced previously under paragraph (b) of this section and have not been restored. As of December 31, 1998, the total reduction in A's debts held on January 1, 1998 equals $9,000. Thus, the basis of Debt No. 3 is restored by $3,200 (the amount of the previous reduction) to $4,000. A's basis in Debt No. 3 is treated as restored immediately before that debt is repaid. Accordingly, A does not realize any gain on the repayment. The remaining net increase of $1,300 ($4,500 – $3,200) is applied to restore the bases of Debt No. 1 and Debt No. 2. As of December 31, 1998, the total reduction in these outstanding debts is $5,800 ($9,000 – $3,200). The basis of Debt No. 1 is restored in an amount equal to $224 ($1,300 × $1,000/$5,800). Similarly, the basis in Debt No. 2 is restored in an amount equal to $1,076 ($1,300 × $4,800/$5,800). On December 31, 1998, A's basis in his S stock is zero and his bases in the two remaining debts are as follows:

Original basis	Amount reduced	1/1/98 basis	Amount restored	12/31/98 basis
$1,000	$1,000	$ 0	$ 224	$ 224
5,000	4,800	200	1,076	1,276

Example (3). Full restoration of basis in indebtedness when debt is repaid in part during the taxable year. (i) C has been a shareholder in Corporation S since 1992. In 1997, C loans S $1,000. S issues its note to C in the amount of $1,000, of which $950 is payable on March 1, 1998, and $50 is payable on March 1, 1999. On December 31, 1997, C's basis in all her shares of S stock is zero and her basis in the note has been reduced under paragraph (b) of this section to $900. For 1998, the net increase (within the meaning of paragraph (c) of this section) with respect to C is $300.

(ii) Because C's basis of indebtedness was reduced in a prior taxable year under § 1.1367–2(b), the net increase for 1998 is applied to restore this reduction. The restored basis cannot exceed the adjusted basis of the debt as of the beginning of the first day of 1998, excluding prior adjustments under section 1367, or $1,000. Therefore, $100 of the $300 net increase is applied to restore the basis of the debt from $900 to $1,000 effective immediately before the repayment on March 1, 1998. The remaining net increase of $200 increases C's basis in her stock.

Example (4). Determination of net increase-distribution in excess of increase in basis. (i) D has been the sole shareholder in Corporation S since 1990. On January 1, 1996, D loans S $10,000 in return for a note from S in the amount of $10,000 of which $5,000 is payable on each of January 1, 2000, and January 1, 2001. On December 31, 1997, the basis of D's shares of S stock is zero, and his basis in the note has been reduced under paragraph (b) of this section to $8,000. During 1998, the sum of the items under section 1367(a)(1) (relating to increases in basis of stock) with respect to D equals $10,000 (in this case, nonseparately computed income), and the sum of the items under section 1367(a)(2)(B), (C), (D), and (E) (relating to decreases in basis of stock) with respect to D equals $0. During 1998, S also makes distributions to D totaling $11,000. This distribution is an item that reduces basis of stock under section 1367(a)(2)(A) and must be taken into account for purposes of determining whether there is a net increase for the taxable year. Thus, for 1998, there is no net increase with respect to D because the amount of the items provided in section 1367(a)(1) do not exceed the amount of the items provided in section 1367(a)(2).

(ii) Because there is no net increase with respect to D for 1998, none of the 1997 reduction in D's basis in the indebtedness is restored.

The $10,000 increase in basis under section 1367(a)(1) is applied to increase D's basis in his S stock. Under section 1367(a)(2)(A), the $11,000 distribution with respect to D's stock reduces D's basis in his shares of S stock to $0. See section 1368 and § 1.1368–1(c) and (d) for the tax treatment of the $1,000 distribution in excess of D's basis.

Example (5). Distributions less than increase in basis. (i) The facts are the same as in Example 4, except that in 1998 S makes distributions to D totaling $8,000. On these facts, for 1998, there is a net increase with respect to D of $2,000 (the amount by which the items provided in section 1367(a)(1) exceed the amount of the items provided in section 1367(a)(2)).

(ii) Because there is a net increase of $2,000 with respect to D for 1998, $2,000 of the $10,000 increase in basis under section 1367(a)(1) is first applied to restore D's basis in the indebtedness to $10,000 ($8,000 + $2,000). Accordingly, on December 31, 1998, D has a basis in his shares of S stock of $0 ($0 + $8,000 (increase in basis remaining after restoring basis in indebtedness) – $8,000 (distribution)) and a basis in the note of $10,000.

Example (6). The $25,000 Aggregate Principal Amount Applies to Each Shareholder. (i) A and B have been the two shareholders in Corporation S since 2000. As of the end of the 2008 taxable year, the bases of A's and B's stock are both zero. On June 1, 2009, A advances S $16,000, which is not evidenced by a written instrument. On August 1, 2009, B advances S $22,000, which is not evidenced by a written instrument. Both the $16,000 advance and the $22,000 advance are open account debt and remain outstanding at those amounts during 2009. There is no net increase under paragraph (c) of this section in year 2009.

(ii) At the close of the 2009 taxable year, A's open account debt does not exceed $25,000. A therefore carries forward to the beginning of the 2010 taxable year the $16,000 as open account debt.

(iii) At the close of the 2009 taxable year, B's open account debt does not exceed $25,000. B therefore carries forward to the beginning of the 2010 taxable year the $22,000 as open account debt.

Example (7). Treatment of open account debt. (i) The facts are the same as in Example 6, in addition to which, on December 31, 2009, A's basis in the open account debt is reduced under paragraph (b) of this section to $8,000. On April 1, 2010, S repays A $4,000 of the open account indebtedness. On September 1, 2010, A advances S an additional $1,000, which is not evidenced by a written instrument. There is no net increase under paragraph (c) of this section in year 2010.

(ii) The $4,000 April repayment S makes to A and A's $1,000 September advance are netted to result in a net repayment of $3,000 for the taxable year on A's $16,000 open account debt carried forward from 2009. Because there is no net increase in 2010, no basis of indebtedness is restored for the 2010 taxable year, and A realizes $1,500 of income on the $3,000 net repayment at the close of the 2010 taxable year.

(iii) At close of the 2010 taxable year, A's open account debt does not exceed $25,000. The net repayment of $3,000 for the taxable year on A's $16,000 open account debt carried forward from 2009, leaves A with an open account debt of $13,000 to carry forward as open account debt to the beginning of the 2011 taxable year.

Example (8). Treatment of shareholder indebtedness not evidenced by a written instrument which exceeds $25,000. (i) The facts are the same as in Example 7, in addition to which, on February 1, 2011, S repays $5,000 of the open account debt and on March 1, 2011, A advances S $20,000, which is not evidenced by a written instrument.

(ii) At the close of the 2010 taxable year, A has an open account debt of $13,000 to carry forward as open account debt to the beginning of the 2011 taxable year.

(iii) The 2011 advances and repayments are netted to result in a net advance of $15,000 on A's $13,000 open account debt carried forward from 2010, increasing A's open account debt to $28,000 as of the close of the 2011 taxable year. Because A's open account debt exceeds $25,000, for any subsequent taxable year the $28,000 indebtedness will be treated in the same manner as indebtedness evidenced by a separate written instrument for the purposes of this section. Because there is no net increase in 2011, no basis of indebtedness is restored for the 2011 taxable year.

* * *

§ 1.1368–1 Distributions by S corporations.

(a) In general. This section provides rules for distributions made by an S corporation with respect to its stock which, but for section 1368(a) and this section, would be subject to section 301(c) and other rules of the Internal Revenue Code that characterize a distribution as a dividend.

(b) Date distribution made. For purposes of section 1368, a distribution is taken into account on the date the corporation makes the distribution, regardless of when the distribution is treated as received by the shareholder.

(c) S corporation with no earnings and profits. A distribution made by an S corporation that has no accumulated earnings and profits as of the end of the taxable year of the S corporation in which the distribution is made is treated in the manner provided in section 1368(b).

(d) S corporation with earnings and profits—(1) General treatment of distribution. Except as provided in paragraph (d)(2) of this section, a distribution made with respect to its stock by an S corporation that has accumulated earnings and profits as of the end of the taxable year of the S corporation in which the distribution is made is treated in the manner provided in section 1368(c). See section 316 and § 1.316–2 for provisions relating to the allocation of earnings and profits among distributions.

(2) Previously taxed income. This paragraph (d)(2) applies to distributions by a corporation that has both accumulated earnings and profits and previously taxed income (within the meaning of section 1375(d)(2), as in effect prior to its amendment by the Subchapter S Revision Act of 1982, and the regulations thereunder) with respect to one or more shareholders. In the case of such a distribution, that portion remaining after the application of section 1368(c)(1) (relating to distributions from the accumulated adjustments account (AAA) as defined in § 1.1368–2(a)) is treated in the manner provided in section 1368(b) (relating to S corporations without earnings and profits) to the extent that portion is a distribution of money and does not exceed the shareholder's net share immediately before the distribution of the corporation's previously taxed income. The AAA and the earnings and profits of the corporation are not decreased by that portion of the distribution. Any distribution remaining after the application of this paragraph (d) (2) is treated in the manner provided in section 1368(c)(2) and (3).

(e) Certain adjustments taken into account—(1) Taxable years beginning before January 1, 1997. For any taxable year of the corporation beginning before January 1, 1997, paragraphs (c) and (d) of this section are applied only after taking into account—

(i) The adjustments to the basis of the shares of a shareholder's stock described in section 1367 (without regard to section 1367(a)(2)(A) (relating to decreases attributable to distributions not includible in income)) for the S corporation's taxable year; and

(ii) The adjustments to the AAA required by section 1368(e)(1)(A) (but without regard to the adjustments for distributions under § 1.1368–2(a)(3)(iii)) for the S corporation's taxable year.

(2) Taxable years beginning on or after August 18, 1998. For any taxable year of the corporation beginning on or after August 18, 1998, paragraphs (c) and (d) of this section are applied only after taking into account—

(i) The adjustments to the basis of the shares of a shareholder's stock described in section 1367(a)(1) (relating to increases in basis of stock) for the S corporation's taxable year; and

(ii) The adjustments to the AAA required by section 1368(e)(1)(A) (but without regard to the adjustments for distributions under § 1.1368–2(a)(3)(iii)) for the S corporation's taxable year. Any net negative adjustment (as defined in section 1368(e)(1)(C)(ii)) for the taxable year shall not be taken into account.

(f) Elections relating to source of distributions—(1) In general. An S corporation may modify the application of paragraphs (c) and (d) of this section by electing (pursuant to paragraph (f)(5) of this section)—

(i) To distribute earnings and profits first as described in paragraph (f)(2) of this section;

(ii) To make a deemed dividend as described in paragraph (f)(3) of this section; or

(iii) To forego previously taxed income as described in paragraph (f)(4) of this section.

(2) Election to distribute earnings and profits first—(i) In general. An S corporation with accumulated earnings and profits may elect under this paragraph (f)(2) for any taxable year to distribute earnings and profits first as provided in section 1368(e)(3). Except as provided in paragraph (f)(2)(ii) of this section, distributions made by an S corporation making this election are treated as made first from earnings and profits under section 1368(c) (2) and second from the AAA under section 1368(c)(1). Any remaining portion of the distribution is treated in the manner provided in section 1368(b). This election is effective for all distributions made during the year for which the election is made.

(ii) Previously taxed income. If a corporation to which paragraph (d)(2) of this section (relating to corporations with previously taxed income) applies makes the election provided in this paragraph (f)(2) for the taxable year, and does not make the election to forego previously taxed income under paragraph (f)(4) of this section, distributions by the S corporation during the taxable year are treated as made first, from previously taxed income under paragraph (d)(2) of this section; second, from earnings and profits under section 1368(c)(2); and third, from the AAA under section 1368(c)(1). Any portion of a distribution remaining after the previously taxed income, earnings and profits, and the AAA are exhausted is treated in the manner provided in section 1368(b).

(iii) Corporation with subchapter C and subchapter S earnings and profits. If an S corporation that makes the election provided in this paragraph (f)(2) has both subchapter C earnings and profits (as defined in section 1362(d)(3)(B)) and subchapter S earnings and profits in a taxable year of the corporation in which the distribution is made, the distribution is treated as made first from subchapter C earnings and profits, and second from subchapter S earnings and profits. Subchapter S earnings and profits are earnings and profits accumulated in a taxable year beginning before January 1, 1983 (or in the case of a qualified casualty insurance electing small business corporation or a qualified oil corporation, earnings and profits accumulated in any taxable year), for which an election under subchapter S of chapter 1 of the Internal Revenue Code was in effect.

(3) Election to make a deemed dividend. An S corporation may elect under this paragraph (f)(3) to distribute all or part of its subchapter C earnings and profits through a deemed dividend. If an S corporation makes the election provided in this paragraph (f)(3), the S corporation will be considered to have made the election provided in paragraph (f)(2) of this section (relating to the election to dis-

tribute earnings and profits first). The amount of the deemed dividend may not exceed the subchapter C earnings and profits of the corporation on the last day of the taxable year, reduced by any actual distributions of subchapter C earnings and profits made during the taxable year. The amount of the deemed dividend is considered, for all purposes of the Internal Revenue Code, as if it were distributed in money to the shareholders in proportion to their stock ownership, received by the shareholders, and immediately contributed by the shareholders to the corporation, all on the last day of the corporation's taxable year.

(4) Election to forego previously taxed income. An S corporation may elect to forego distributions of previously taxed income. If such an election is made, paragraph (d)(2) of this section (relating to corporations with previously taxed income) does not apply to any distribution made during the taxable year. Thus, distributions by a corporation that makes the election to forego previously taxed income for a taxable year under this paragraph (f)(4) and does not make the election to distribute earnings and profits first under paragraph (f)(2) of this section are treated in the manner provided in section 1368(c) (relating to distributions by corporations with earnings and profits). Distributions by a corporation that makes both the election to distribute earnings and profits first under paragraph (f)(2) of this section and the election to forego previously taxed income under this paragraph (f)(4), are treated in the manner provided in paragraph (f)(2)(i) of this section.

(5) Time and manner of making elections—(i) For earnings and profits. If an election is made under paragraph (f)(2) of this section to distribute earnings and profits first, see section 1368(e)(3) regarding the consent required by shareholders.

(ii) For previously taxed income and deemed dividends. If an election is made to forego previously taxed income under paragraph (f)(4) of this section or to make a deemed dividend under paragraph (f)(3) of this section, consent by each "affected shareholder," as defined in section 1368(e)(3)(B), is required.

(iii) Corporate statement regarding elections. A corporation makes an election for a taxable year under this paragraph (f) by attaching a statement to a timely filed original or amended return required to be filed under section 6037 for that taxable year. In the statement, the corporation must identify the election it is making under § 1.1368–1(f) and must state that each shareholder consents to the election. An officer of the corporation must sign under penalties of perjury the statement on behalf of the corporation. A statement of election to make a deemed dividend under this paragraph must include the amount of the deemed dividend that is distributed to each shareholder.

(iv) Irrevocable elections. The elections under this paragraph (f) are irrevocable and are effective only for the taxable year for which they are made. In applying the preceding sentence to elections under this paragraph (f), an election to terminate the taxable year under section 1377(a)(2) or § 1.1368–1(g)(2) is disregarded.

(g) Special rules—(1) Election to terminate year under section 1377 or § 1.1368–1(g)(2). If an election is made under section 1377(a)(2) (to terminate the year when a shareholder terminates his or her interest in the corporation) or under paragraph (g)(2) of this section (to terminate the year when there is a qualifying disposition), this section applies as if the taxable year consisted of separate taxable years, the first of which ends at the close of the day on which the shareholder terminates his or her interest in the corporation or on which there is a qualifying disposition of stock, whichever the case may be.

(2) Election in case of a qualifying disposition—(i) In general. In the case of a qualifying disposition, a corporation may elect under this paragraph (g)(2)(i) to treat the year as if it consisted of separate taxable years, the first

of which ends at the close of the day on which the qualifying disposition occurs. A qualifying disposition is—

(A) A disposition by a shareholder of 20 percent or more of the outstanding stock of the corporation in one or more transactions during any thirty-day period during the corporation's taxable year;

(B) A redemption treated as an exchange under section 302(a) or section 303(a) of 20 percent or more of the outstanding stock of the corporation from a shareholder in one or more transactions during any thirty-day period during the corporation's taxable year; or

(C) An issuance of an amount of stock equal to or greater than 25 percent of the previously outstanding stock to one or more new shareholders during any thirty-day period during the corporation's taxable year.

(ii) Effect of the election. A corporation making an election under paragraph (g)(2)(i) of this section must treat the taxable year as separate taxable years for purposes of allocating items of income and loss; making adjustments to the AAA, earnings and profits, and basis; and determining the tax effect of distributions under section 1368(b) and (c). An election made under paragraph (g)(2)(i) of this section may be made upon the occurrence of any qualifying disposition. Dispositions of stock that are taken into account as part of a qualifying disposition are not taken into account in determining whether a subsequent qualifying disposition has been made.

(iii) Time and manner of making election. A corporation makes an election under paragraph (g)(2)(i) of this section for a taxable year by attaching a statement to a timely filed original or amended return required to be filed under section 6037 for a taxable year (without regard to the election under paragraph (g)(2)(i) of this section). In the statement, the corporation must state that it is electing for the taxable year under § 1.1368–1(g)(2)(i) to treat the taxable year as if it consisted of separate taxable years. The corporation also must set forth facts in the statement relating to the qualifying disposition (e.g., sale, gift, stock issuance, or redemption), and state that each shareholder who held stock in the corporation during the taxable year (without regard to the election under paragraph (g)(2)(i) of this section) consents to this election. An officer of the corporation must sign under penalties of perjury the statement on behalf of the corporation. For purposes of this election, a shareholder of the corporation for the taxable year is a shareholder as described in section 1362(a)(2). A single election statement may be filed for all elections made under paragraph (g)(2)(i) of this section for the taxable year. An election made under paragraph (g)(2)(i) of this section is irrevocable.

§ 1.1368–2 Accumulated adjustments account (AAA).

(a) Accumulated adjustments account—(1) In general. The accumulated adjustments account is an account of the S corporation and is not apportioned among shareholders. The AAA is relevant for all taxable year beginning on or after January 1, 1983, for which the corporation is an S corporation. On the first day of the first year for which the corporation is an S corporation, the balance of the AAA is zero. The AAA is increased in the manner provided in paragraph (a)(2) of this section and is decreased in the manner provided in paragraph (a)(3) of this section. For the adjustments to the AAA in the case of redemptions, reorganizations, and corporate separations, see paragraph (d) of this section.

(2) Increases to the AAA. The AAA is increased for the taxable year of the corporation by the sum of the following items with respect to the corporation for the taxable year:

(i) The items of income described in section 1366(a)(1)(A) other than income that is exempt from tax;

(ii) Any nonseparately computed income determined under section 1366(a)(1)(B); and

(iii) The excess of the deductions for depletion over the basis of property subject to depletion unless the property is an oil or gas property the basis of which has been allocated to shareholders under section 613A(c)(11).

(3) Decreases to the AAA—(i) In general. The AAA is decreased for the taxable year of the corporation by the sum of the following items with respect to the corporation for the taxable year—

(A) The items of loss or deduction described in section 1366(a)(1)(A);

(B) Any nonseparately computed loss determined under section 1366(a)(1)(B);

(C) Any expense of the corporation not deductible in computing its taxable income and not properly chargeable to a capital account, other than—

(1) Federal taxes attributable to any taxable year in which the corporation was a C corporation; and

(2) Expenses related to income that is exempt from tax; and

(D) The sum of the shareholders' deductions for depletion for any oil or gas property held by the corporation described in section 1367(a)(2)(E).

(ii) Extent of allowable reduction. The AAA may be decreased under paragraph (a)(3)(i) of this section below zero. The AAA is decreased by noncapital, nondeductible expenses under paragraph (a)(3)(i)(C) of this section even though a portion of the noncapital, nondeductible expenses is not taken into account by a shareholder under § 1.1367–1(g) (relating to the elective ordering rule). The AAA is also decreased by the entire amount of any loss or deduction even though a portion of the loss or deduction is not taken into account by a shareholder under section 1366(d) (1) or is otherwise not currently deductible under the Internal Revenue Code. However, in any subsequent taxable year in which the loss or deduction or noncapital, nondeductible expense is treated as incurred by the corporation with respect to the shareholder under section 1366(d)(2) or § 1.1367–1(g) (or in which the loss or deduction is otherwise allowed to the shareholder), no further adjustment is made to the AAA.

(iii) Decrease to the AAA for distributions. The AAA is decreased (but not below zero) by any portion of a distribution to which section 1368(b) or (c)(1) applies.

* * *

(5) Ordering rules for the AAA for taxable years beginning on or after August 18, 1998. For any taxable year of the S corporation beginning on or after August 18, 1998, the adjustments to the AAA are made in the following order—

(i) The AAA is increased under paragraph (a)(2) of this section before it is decreased under paragraph (a)(3)(i) of this section for the taxable year;

(ii) The AAA is decreased under paragraph (a)(3)(i) of this section (without taking into account any net negative adjustment (as defined in section 1368(e)(1)(C)(ii)) before it is decreased under paragraph (a)(3)(iii) of this section;

(iii) The AAA is decreased (but not below zero) by any portion of an ordinary distribution to which section 1368(b) or (c)(1) applies;

(iv) The AAA is decreased by any net negative adjustment (as defined in section 1368(e)(1)(C)(ii)); and

(v) The AAA is adjusted (whether negative or positive) for redemption distributions under paragraph (d)(1) of this section.

(b) Distributions in excess of the AAA—(1) In general. A portion of the AAA (determined under paragraph (b)(2) of this section) is allocated to each of the distributions made for the taxable year if—

(i) An S corporation makes more than one distribution of property with respect to its stock during the taxable year of the corporation (including an S short year as defined under section 1362(e)(1)(A));

(ii) The AAA has a positive balance at the close of the year; and

(iii) The sum of the distributions made during the corporation's taxable year exceeds the balance of the AAA at the close of the year.

(2) Amount of the AAA allocated to each distribution. The amount of the AAA allocated to each distribution is determined by multiplying the balance of the AAA at the close of the current taxable year by a fraction, the numerator of which is the amount of the distribution and the denominator of which is the amount of all distributions made during the taxable year. For purposes of this paragraph (b)(2), the term all distributions made during the taxable year does not include any distribution treated as from earnings and profits or previously taxed income pursuant to an election made under section 1368(e)(3) and § 1.1368–1(f)(2). See paragraph (d)(1) of this section for rules relating to the adjustments to the AAA for redemptions and distributions in the year of a redemption.

(c) Distribution of money and loss property—(1) In general. The amount of the AAA allocated to a distribution under this section must be further allocated (under paragraph (c)(2) of this section) if the distribution—

(i) Consists of property the adjusted basis of which exceeds its fair market value on the date of the distribution and money;

(ii) Is a distribution to which § 1.1368–1(d)(1) applies; and

(iii) Exceeds the amount of the corporation's AAA properly allocable to that distribution.

(2) Allocating the AAA to loss property. The amount of the AAA allocated to the property other than money is equal to the amount of the AAA allocated to the distribution multiplied by a fraction, the numerator of which is the fair market value of the property other than money on the date of distribution and the denominator of which is the amount of the distribution. The amount of the AAA allocated to the money is equal to the amount of the AAA allocated to the distribution reduced by the amount of the AAA allocated to the property other than money.

(d) Adjustment in the case of redemptions, liquidations, reorganizations, and divisions—(1) Redemptions—(i) General rule. In the case of a redemption distribution by an S corporation that is treated as an exchange under section 302(a) or section 303(a) (a redemption distribution), the AAA of the corporation is adjusted in an amount equal to the ratable share of the corporation's AAA (whether negative or positive) attributable to the redeemed stock as of the date of the redemption.

(ii) Special rule for years in which a corporation makes both ordinary and redemption distributions. In any year in which a corporation makes one or more distributions to which section 1368(a) applies (ordinary distributions) and makes one or more redemption distributions, the AAA of the corporation is adjusted first for any ordinary distributions and then for any redemption distributions.

(iii) Adjustments to earnings and profits. Earnings and profits are adjusted under section 312 independently of any adjustments made to the AAA.

(2) Reorganizations. An S corporation acquiring the assets of another S corporation in a transaction to which section 381(a)(2) applies will succeed to and merge its AAA (whether positive or negative) with the AAA (whether positive or negative) of the distributor or transferor S corporation as of the close of the date of distribution or transfer. Thus, the AAA of the acquiring corporation after the transaction is the sum of the AAAs of the corporations prior to the transaction.

(3) Corporate separations to which section 368(a)(l)(D) applies. If an S corporation with accumulated earnings and profits transfers a part of its assets constituting an active trade or business to another corporation in a transaction to which section 368(a)(l)(D) applies, and immediately thereafter the stock and securities of the controlled corporation are distributed in a distribution or exchange to which section 355 (or so much of section 356 as relates to section 355) applies, the AAA of the distributing corporation immediately before the transaction is allocated between the distributing corporation and the controlled corporation in a manner similar to the manner in which the earnings and profits of the distributing corporation are allocated under section 312 (h). See § 1.312–10(a).

(e) Election to terminate year under section 1377(a)(2) or § 1.1368–1(g)(2). If an election is made under section 1377(a)(2) (to terminate the year in the case of termination of a shareholder's interest) or § 1.1368–1(g) (2) (to terminate the year in the case of a qualifying disposition), this section applies as if the taxable year consisted of separate taxable years, the first of which ends at the close of the day on which the shareholder terminated his or her interest in the corporation or makes a substantial disposition of stock, whichever the case may be.

§ 1.1368–3 Examples.

The principles of § § 1.1368–1 and 1.1368–2 are illustrated by the examples below. In each example Corporation S is a calendar year corporation:

* * *

Example (2). Distributions by S corporations without earnings and profits for taxable years beginning on or after August 18, 1998. (i) Corporation S, an S corporation, has no earnings and profits as of January 1, 2001, the first day of its 2001 taxable year. S's sole shareholder, A, holds 10 shares of S stock with a basis of $1 per share as of that date. On March

1, 2001, S makes a distribution of $38 to A. The balance in Corporation S's AAA is $100. For S's 2001 taxable year, A's pro rata share of the amount of the items described in section 1367(a)(1) (relating to increases in basis of stock) is $50. A's pro rata share of the amount of the items described in sections 1367(a)(2) (B) through (D) (relating to decreases in basis of stock for items other than distributions) is $26, $20 of which is attributable to items described in section 1367(a)(2)(B) and (C) and $6 of which is attributable to items described in section 1367(a)(2)(D) (relating to decreases in basis attributable to noncapital, nondeductible expenses).

(ii) Under section 1368(d)(1) and § 1.1368–1(e)(1) and (2), the adjustments to the basis of A's stock in S described in sections 1367(a)(1) are made before the distribution rules of section 1368 are applied. Thus, A's basis per share in the stock is $6.00 ($1 + [$50/10]) before taking into account the distribution. Under section 1367(a)(2)(A), the basis of A's stock is decreased by distributions to A that are not includible in A's income. Under § 1.1367–1(c) (3), the amount of the distribution that is attributable to each share of A's stock is $3.80 ($38 distribution/10 shares). Thus, A's basis per share in the stock is $2.20 ($6.00–$3.80), after taking into account the distribution. Under section 1367(a)(2)(D), the basis of each share of A's stock in S after taking into account the distribution, $2.20, is decreased by $.60 ($6 noncapital, nondeductible expenses/10). Thus, A's basis per share after taking into account the nondeductible, noncapital expenses is $1.60. Under section 1367(a)(2)(B) and (C), A's basis per share is further decreased by $2 ($20 items described in section 1367(a)(2)(B) and (C)/10 shares). However, basis may not be reduced below zero. Therefore, the basis of each share of A's stock is reduced to zero. As of January 1, 2002, A has a basis of $0 in his shares of S stock. Pursuant to section 1366(d)(2), the $.40 of loss in excess of A's basis in each of his shares of S stock is treated as incurred by the corporation in the succeeding taxable year with respect to A.

* * *

Example (4). Distributions by S corporations with earnings and profits and no net negative adjustment for taxable years beginning on or after August 18, 1998. (i) Corporation S, an S corporation, has accumulated earnings and profits of $1,000 and a balance in the AAA of $2,000 on January 1, 2001. S's sole shareholder B holds 100 shares of stock with a basis of $20 per share as of January 1, 2001. On April 1, 2001, S makes a distribution of $1,500 to B. B's pro rata share of the income earned by S during 2001 is $2,000 and B's pro rata share of S's losses is $1,500. For the taxable year ending December 31, 2001, S does not have a net negative adjustment as defined in section 1368(e)(1)(C). S does not make the election under section 1368(e)(3) and § 1.1368–1(f)(2) to distribute its earnings and profits before its AAA.

(ii) The AAA is increased from $2,000 to $4,000 for the $2,000 of income earned during the 2001 taxable year. The AAA is decreased from $4,000 to $2,500 for the $1,500 of losses. The AAA is decreased from $2,500 to $1,000 for the portion of the distribution ($1,500) to B that does not exceed the AAA.

(iii) As of December 31, 2001, B's basis in his stock is $10 ($20 + $20 ($2,000 income/100 shares)—$15 ($1,500 distribution/100 shares)—$15 ($1,500 loss/100 shares).

Example (5). Distributions by S corporations with earnings and profits and net negative adjustment for taxable years beginning on or after August 18, 1998. (i) Corporation S, an S corporation, has accumulated earnings and profits of $1,000 and a balance in the AAA of $2,000 on January 1, 2001. S's sole shareholder B holds 100 shares of stock with a basis of $20 per share as of January 1, 2001. On April 1, 2001, S makes a distribution of $2,000 to B. B's pro rata share of the income earned by S during 2001 is $2,000 and B's pro rata share of S's losses is $3,500. For the taxable year ending December 31, 2001, S has a net negative adjustment as defined in section 1368(e)(1) (C). S does not make the election under section 1368(e)(3) and § 1.1368–1(f)(2) to distribute its earnings and profits before its AAA.

(ii) The AAA is increased from $2,000 to $4,000 for the $2,000 of income earned during the 2001 taxable year. Because under section 1368(e)(1)(C)(ii) and § 1.1368–2(a)(ii), the net negative adjustment is not taken into account, the AAA is decreased from $4,000 to $2,000 for the portion of the losses ($2,000) that does not exceed the income earned during the 2001 taxable year. The AAA is reduced from $2,000 to zero for the portion of the distribution to B ($2,000) that does not exceed the AAA. The AAA is decreased from zero to a negative $1,500 for the portion of the $3,500 of loss that exceeds the $2,000 of income earned during the 2001 taxable year.

(iii) Under § 1.1367–1(c)(1), the basis of a shareholder's share in an S corporation stock may not be reduced below zero. Accordingly, as of December 31, 2001, B's basis per share in his stock is zero ($20 + $20 income − $20 distribution − $ 35 loss). Pursuant to section 1366(d)(2), the $15 of loss in excess of B's basis in each of his shares of S stock is treated as incurred by the corporation in the succeeding taxable year with respect to B.

Example (6). Election in case of disposition of substantial amount of stock. (i) Corporation S, an S corporation, has earnings and profits of $3,000 and a balance in the AAA of $1,000 on January 1, 1997. C, an individual and the sole shareholder of Corporation S, has 100 shares of S stock with a basis of $10 per share. On July 3, 1997, C sells 50 shares of his S stock to D, an individual, for $250. For 1997, S has taxable income of $1,000, of which $500 was earned on or before July 3, 1997, and $500 earned after July 3, 1997. During its 1997 taxable year, S distributes $1,000 to C on February 1 and $1,000 to each of C and D on August

1. S does not make the election under section 1368(e)(3) and § 1.1368–1(f)(2) to distribute its earnings and profits before its AAA. S makes the election under § 1.1368–1(g)(2) to treat its taxable year as if it consisted of separate taxable years, the first of which ends at the close of July 3, 1997, the date of the qualifying disposition.

(ii) Under section § 1.1368–1(g)(2), for the period ending on July 3, 1997, S's AAA is $500 ($1,000 (AAA as of January 1, 1997) + $500 (income earned from January 1, 1997 through July 3, 1997) − $1,000 (distribution made on February 1, 1997)). C's bases in his shares of stock is decreased to $5 per share ($10 (original basis) + $5 (increase per share for income) − $10 (decrease per share for distribution)).

(iii) The AAA is adjusted at the end of the taxable year for the period July 4 through December 31, 1997. It is increased from $500 (AAA as of the close of July 3, 1997) to $1,000 for the income earned during this period and is decreased by $1,000, the portion of the distribution ($2,000 in total) made to C and D on August 1 that does not exceed the AAA. The $1,000 portion of the distribution that remains after the AAA is reduced to zero is attributable to earnings and profits. Therefore C and D each have a dividend of $500, which does not affect their basis or S's AAA. The earnings and profits account is reduced from $3,000 to $2,000.

(iv) As of December 31, 1997, C and D have bases in their shares of stock of zero ($5 (basis as of July 4) + $5 ($500 income/100 shares) − $10 ($1,000 distribution/100 shares)). C and D each will report $500 as dividend income, which does not affect their basis or S's AAA.

Example (7). Election to distribute earnings and profits first. (i) Corporation S has been a calendar year C corporation since 1975. For 1982, S elects for the first time to be taxed under subchapter S, and during 1982 has $60 of earnings and profits. As of December 31, 1995, S has an AAA of $10 and earnings and profits of $160, consisting of $100 of subchapter C earnings and profits and $60 of subchapter S earnings and profits. For 1996, S has $200 of taxable income and the AAA is increased to $210 (before taking distributions into account). During 1996, S distributes $240 to its shareholders. With its 1996 tax return, S properly elects under section 1368(e)(3) and § 1.1368–1(f)(2) to distribute its earnings and profits before its AAA.

(ii) Because S elected to distribute its earnings and profits before its AAA, the first $100 of the distribution is characterized as a distribution from subchapter C earnings and profits; the next $60 of the distribution is characterized as a distribution from subchapter S earnings and profits. Because $160 of the distribution is from earnings and profits, the shareholders of S have a $160 dividend. The remaining $80 of the distribution is a distribution from S's AAA and is treated by the shareholders as a return of capital or gain from the sale or exchange of property, as appropriate, under § 1.1368–1(d)(1). S's AAA, as of December 31, 1996, equals $130 ($210 – $80).

Example (8). Distributions in excess of the AAA. (i) On January 1, 1995, Corporation S has $40 of earnings and profits and a balance in the AAA of $100. S has two shareholders, E and F, each of whom own 50 shares of S's stock. For 1995, S has taxable income of $50, which increases the AAA to $150 as of December 31, 1995 (before taking into account distributions made during 1995). On February 1, 1995, S distributes $60 to each shareholder. On September 1, 1995, S distributes $30 to each shareholder. S does not make the election under section 1368(e)(3) and § 1.1368–1(f)(2) to distribute its earnings and profits before its AAA.

(ii) The sum of the distributions exceed S's AAA. Therefore, under § 1.1368–2(b), a portion of S's $150 balance in the AAA as of December 31, 1995, is allocated to each of the February 1 and September 1 distributions based on the respective sizes of the distribu-

tions. Accordingly, S must allocate $100 ($150 (AAA) × ($120 (February 1 distribution)/$180 (the sum of the distributions))) of the AAA to the February 1 distribution, and $50 ($150 × ($60/$180)) to the September 1 distribution. The portions of the distributions to which the AAA is allocated are treated by the shareholder as a return of capital or gain from the sale or exchange of property, as appropriate. The remainder of the two distributions is treated as a dividend to the extent that it does not exceed S's earnings and profits. E and F must each report $10 of dividend income for the February 1 distribution. For the September 1 distribution, E and F must each report $5 of dividend income.

Example (9). Ordinary and redemption distributions in the same taxable year. (i) On January 1, 1995, Corporation S, an S corporation, has $20 of earnings and profits and a balance in the AAA of $10. S has two shareholders, G and H, each of whom owns 50 shares of S's stock. For 1995, S has taxable income of $16, which increases the AAA to $26 as of December 31, 1995 (before taking into account distributions made during 1995). On February 1, 1995, S distributes $10 to each shareholder. On December 31, 1995, S redeems for $13 all of shareholder G's stock in a redemption that is treated as a sale or exchange under section 302(a).

(ii) The sum of the ordinary distributions does not exceed S's AAA. Therefore, S must reduce the $26 balance in the AAA by $20 for the February 1 ordinary distribution. The portions of the distribution by which the AAA is reduced are treated by the shareholders as a return of capital or gain from the sale or exchange of property. S must adjust the remaining AAA, $6, in an amount equal to the ratable share of the remaining AAA attributable to the redeemed stock, or $3 (50% × $6).

(iii) S also must adjust the earnings and profits of $20 in an amount equal to the ratable share of the earnings and profits attributable to the redeemed stock. Therefore, S adjusts the

earnings and profits by $10 (50% × $20), the ratable share of the earnings and profits attributable to the redeemed stock.

§ 1.1374–1 General rules and definitions.

(a) Computation of tax. The tax imposed on the income of an S corporation by section 1374(a) for any taxable year during the recognition period is computed as follows—

(1) Step One: Determine the net recognized built-in gain of the corporation for the taxable year under section 1374(d)(2) and § 1.1374–2;

(2) Step Two: Reduce the net recognized built-in gain (but not below zero) by any net operating loss and capital loss carryforward allowed under section 1374(b)(2) and § 1.1374–5;

(3) Step Three: Compute a tentative tax by applying the rate of tax determined under section 1374(b)(1) for the taxable year to the amount determined under paragraph (a)(2) of this section;

(4) Step Four: Compute the final tax by reducing the tentative tax (but not below zero) by any credit allowed under section 1374(b)(3) and § 1.1374–6.

(b) Anti-trafficking rules. If section 382, 383, or 384 would have applied to limit the use of a corporation's recognized built-in loss or section 1374 attributes at the beginning of the first day of the recognition period if the corporation had remained a C corporation, these sections apply to limit their use in determining the S corporation's pre-limitation amount, taxable income limitation, net unrealized built-in gain limitation, deductions against net recognized built-in gain, and credits against the section 1374 tax.

(c) Section 1374 attributes. Section 1374 attributes are the loss carryforwards allowed under section 1374(b)(2) as a deduction against net recognized built-in gain and the credit and credit carryforwards allowed under

section 1374(b)(3) as a credit against the section 1374 tax.

(d) Recognition period. The recognition period is the 10-year (120-month) period beginning on the first day the corporation is an S corporation or the day an S corporation acquires assets in a section 1374(d)(8) transaction. For example, if the first day of the recognition period is July 14, 1996, the last day of the recognition period is July 13, 2006. If the recognition period for certain assets ends during an S corporation's taxable year (for example, because the corporation was on a fiscal year as a C corporation and changed to a calendar year as an S corporation or because an S corporation acquired assets in a section 1374(d)(8) transaction during a taxable year), the S corporation must determine its pre-limitation amount (as defined in § 1.1374–2(a)(1)) for the year as if the corporation's books were closed at the end of the recognition period.

(e) Predecessor corporation. For purposes of section 1374(c)(1), if the basis of an asset of the S corporation is determined (in whole or in part) by reference to the basis of the asset (or any other property) in the hands of another corporation, the other corporation is a predecessor corporation of the S corporation.

§ 1.1374–2 Net recognized built-in gain.

(a) In general. An S corporation's net recognized built-in gain for any taxable year is the least of—

(1) Its taxable income determined by using all rules applying to C corporations and considering only its recognized built-in gain, recognized built-in loss, and recognized built-in gain carryover (pre-limitation amount);

(2) Its taxable income determined by using all rules applying to C corporations as modified by section 1375(b)(1)(B) (taxable income limitation); and

(3) The amount by which its net unrealized built-in gain exceeds its net recognized built-in gain for all prior taxable years (net unrealized built-in gain limitation).

(b) Allocation rule. If an S corporation's pre-limitation amount for any taxable year exceeds its net recognized built-in gain for that year, the S corporation's net recognized built-in gain consists of a ratable portion of each item of income, gain, loss, and deduction included in the pre-limitation amount.

(c) Recognized built-in gain carryover. If an S corporation's net recognized built-in gain for any taxable year is equal to its taxable income limitation, the amount by which its pre-limitation amount exceeds its taxable income limitation is a recognized built-in gain carryover included in its pre-limitation amount for the succeeding taxable year. The recognized built-in gain carryover consists of that portion of each item of income, gain, loss, and deduction not included in the S corporation's net recognized built-in gain for the year the carryover arose, as determined under paragraph (b) of this section.

(d) Accounting methods. In determining its taxable income for pre-limitation amount and taxable income limitation purposes, a corporation must use the accounting method(s) it uses for tax purposes as an S corporation.

(e) Example. The rules of this section are illustrated by the following example.

Example. Net recognized built-in gain. X is a calendar year C corporation that elects to become an S corporation on January 1, 1996. X has a net unrealized built-in gain of $50,000 and no net operating loss or capital loss carryforwards. In 1996, X has a pre-limitation amount of $20,000, consisting of ordinary income of $15,000 and capital gain of $5,000, a taxable income limitation of $9,600, and a net unrealized built-in gain limitation of $50,000. Therefore, X's net recognized built-in gain for 1996 is $9,600, because that is the least of the three amounts described in paragraph (a) of this section. Under paragraph (b) of this section, X's net recognized built-in gain con-

sists of recognized built-in ordinary income of $7,200 [$15,000 × ($9,600/$20,000) = $7,200] and recognized built-in capital gain of $2,400 [$5,000 × ($9,600/$20,000) = $2,400]. Under paragraph (c) of this section, X has a recognized built-in gain carryover to 1997 of $10,400 ($20,000 − $9,600 = $10,400), consisting of $7,800 ($15,000 − $7,200 = $7,800) of recognized built-in ordinary income and $2,600 ($5,000 − $2,400 = $2,600) of recognized built-in capital gain.

§ 1.1374–3 Net unrealized built-in gain.

(a) In general. An S corporation's net unrealized built-in gain is the total of the following—

(1) The amount that would be the amount realized if, at the beginning of the first day of the recognition period, the corporation had remained a C corporation and had sold all its assets at fair market value to an unrelated party that assumed all its liabilities; decreased by

(2) Any liability of the corporation that would be included in the amount realized on the sale referred to in paragraph (a)(1) of this section, but only if the corporation would be allowed a deduction on payment of the liability; decreased by

(3) The aggregate adjusted bases of the corporation's assets at the time of the sale referred to in paragraph (a)(1) of this section; increased or decreased by

(4) The corporation's section 481 adjustments that would be taken into account on the sale referred to in paragraph (a)(1) of this section; and increased by

(5) Any recognized built-in loss that would not be allowed as a deduction under section 382, 383, or 384 on the sale referred to in paragraph (a)(1) of this section.

(b) Example. The rules of this section are illustrated by the following example.

Example. Net unrealized built-in gain. (i) (a) X, a calendar year C corporation using the cash method, elects to become an S corporation on January 1, 1996. On December 31, 1995, X has assets and liabilities as follows:

	FMV	Basis
Assets:		
Factory	$500,000	$900,000
Accounts Receivable	300,000	0
Goodwill	250,000	0
Total	1,050,000	900,000
Liabilities	Amount	
Mortgage	$ 200,000	
Accounts Payable	100,000	
Total	300,000	

(b) Further, X must include a total of $60,000 in taxable income in 1996, 1997, and 1998 under section 481(a).

(ii) If, on December 31, 1995, X sold all its assets to a third party that assumed all its liabilities, X's amount realized would be $1,050,000 ($750,000 cash received + $300,000 liabilities assumed = $1,050,000). Thus, X's net unrealized built-in gain is determined as follows:

Amount realized...	$1,050,000
Deduction allowed	(100,000)
Basis of X's assets..	(900,000)
Section 481 adjustments	60,000
Net unrealized built-in gain	110,000

§ 1.1374–4 Recognized built-in gain or loss.

(a) Sales and exchanges—(1) In general. Section 1374(d)(3) or 1374(d)(4) applies to any gain or loss recognized during the recognition period in a transaction treated as a sale or exchange for federal income tax purposes.

(2) Oil and gas property. For purposes of paragraph (a)(1) of this section, an S corporation's adjusted basis in oil and gas property equals the sum of the shareholders' adjusted bases in the property as determined in section 613A(c)(11)(B).

(3) Examples. The rules of this paragraph (a) are illustrated by the following examples.

Example (1). Production and sale of oil. X is a C corporation that purchased a working interest in an oil and gas property for $100,000 on July 1, 1993. X elects to become an S corporation effective January 1, 1996. On that date, the working interest has a fair market value of $250,000 and an adjusted basis of $50,000, but no oil has as yet been extracted. In 1996, X begins production of the working interest, sells oil that it has produced to a refinery for $75,000, and includes that amount in gross income. Under paragraph (a)(1) of this section, the $75,000 is not recognized built-in gain because as of the beginning of the recognition period X held only a working interest in the oil and gas property (since the oil had not yet been extracted from the ground), and not the oil itself.

Example (2). Sale of oil and gas property. Y is a C corporation that elects to become an S corporation effective January 1, 1996. Y has two shareholders, A and B. A and B each own 50 percent of Y's stock. In addition, Y owns a royalty interest in an oil and gas property with a fair market value of $300,000 and an adjusted basis of $200,000. Under section 613A(c)(11)(B), Y's $200,000 adjusted basis in the royalty interest is allocated $100,000 to A and $100,000 to B. During 1996, A and B take depletion deductions with respect to the royalty interest of $10,000 and $15,000, respectively. As of January 1, 1997, A and B have a basis in the royalty interest of $90,000 and $85,000, respectively. On January 1, 1997, Y sells the royalty interest for $250,000. Under paragraph (a) (1) of this section, Y has gain recognized and recognized built-in gain of $75,000 ($250,000 − ($90,000 + $85,000) = $75,000) on the sale.

(b) Accrual method rule—(1) Income items. Except as otherwise provided in this section, any item of income properly taken into account during the recognition period is recognized built-in gain if the item would have been properly included in gross income before the beginning of the recognition period by an accrual method taxpayer (disregarding any method of accounting for which an election by the taxpayer must be made unless the taxpayer actually used the method when it was a C corporation).

(2) Deduction items. Except as otherwise provided in this section, any item of deduction properly taken into account during the recognition period is recognized built-in loss if the item would have been properly allowed as a deduction against gross income before the beginning of the recognition period to an accrual method taxpayer (disregarding any method of accounting for which an election by the taxpayer must be made unless the taxpayer actually used the method when it was a C corporation). In determining whether an item would have been properly allowed as a deduction against gross income by an accrual method taxpayer for purposes of this paragraph, section 461(h) (2)(C) and § 1.461–4(g) (relating to liabilities for tort, worker's compensation, breach of contract, violation of law, rebates, refunds, awards, prizes, jackpots, insurance contracts, warranty contracts, service contracts, taxes, and other liabilities) do not apply.

(3) Examples. The rules of this paragraph (b) are illustrated by the following examples.

Example (1). Accounts receivable. X is a C corporation using the cash method that elects to become an S corporation effective January 1, 1996. On January 1, 1996, X has $50,000 of accounts receivable for services rendered before that date. On that date, the accounts receivable have a fair market value of $40,000 and an adjusted basis of $0. In 1996, X collects $50,000 on the accounts receivable and includes that amount in gross income. Under paragraph (b)(1) of this section, the $50,000 included in gross income in 1996 is recognized built-in gain because it would have been included in gross income before the beginning of the recognition period if X had been an accrual method taxpayer. However, if X instead disposes of the accounts receivable for $45,000

on July 1, 1996, in a transaction treated as a sale or exchange for federal income tax purposes, X would have recognized built-in gain of $40,000 on the disposition.

Example (2). Contingent liability. Y is a C corporation using the cash method that elects to become an S corporation effective January 1, 1996. In 1995, a lawsuit was filed against Y claiming $1,000,000 in damages. In 1996, Y loses the lawsuit, pays a $500,000 judgment, and properly claims a deduction for that amount. Under paragraph (b)(2) of this section, the $500,000 deduction allowed in 1996 is not recognized built-in loss because it would not have been allowed as a deduction against gross income before the beginning of the recognition period if Y had been an accrual method taxpayer (even disregarding section 461(h) (2)(C) and § 1.461–4(g)).

Example (3). Deferred payment liabilities. X is a C corporation using the cash method that elects to become an S corporation on January 1, 1996. In 1995, X lost a lawsuit and became obligated to pay $150,000 in damages. Under section 461(h)(2)(C), this amount is not allowed as a deduction until X makes payment. In 1996, X makes payment and properly claims a deduction for the amount of the payment. Under paragraph (b)(2) of this section, the $150,000 deduction allowed in 1996 is recognized built-in loss because it would have been allowed as a deduction against gross income before the beginning of the recognition period if X had been an accrual method taxpayer (disregarding section 461(h)(2)(C) and § 1.461–4(g)).

Example (4). Deferred prepayment income. Y is a C corporation using an accrual method that elects to become an S corporation effective January 1, 1996. In 1995, Y received $2,500 for services to be rendered in 1996, and properly elected to include the $2,500 in gross income in 1996 under *Rev. Proc. 71–21, 1971–2 C.B. 549* (see § 601.601(d)(2)(ii)(b) of this chapter). Under paragraph (b)(1) of this section, the $2,500 included in gross income in

1996 is not recognized built-in gain because it would not have been included in gross income before the beginning of the recognition period by an accrual method taxpayer using the method that Y actually used before the beginning of the recognition period.

Example (5). Change in method. X is a C corporation using an accrual method that elects to become an S corporation effective January 1, 1996. In 1995, X received $5,000 for services to be rendered in 1996, and properly included the $5,000 in gross income. In 1996, X properly elects to include the $5,000 in gross income in 1996 under *Rev. Proc. 71–21, 1971– 2 C.B. 549* (see § 601.601(d)(2)(ii)(b) of this chapter). As a result of the change in method of accounting, X has a $5,000 negative section 481(a) adjustment. Under paragraph (b)(1) of this section, the $5,000 included in gross income in 1996 is recognized built-in gain because it would have been included in gross income before the beginning of the recognition period by an accrual method taxpayer using the method that X actually used before the beginning of the recognition period. In addition, the $5,000 negative section 481(a) adjustment is recognized built-in loss because it relates to an item (the $5,000 X received for services in 1995) attributable to periods before the beginning of the recognition period under the principles for determining recognized built-in gain or loss in this section. See paragraph (d) of this section for rules regarding section 481(a) adjustments.

(c) Section 267(a)(2) and 404(a)(5) deductions—(1) Section 267(a)(2). Notwithstanding paragraph (b)(2) of this section, any amount properly deducted in the recognition period under section 267(a)(2), relating to payments to related parties, is recognized built-in loss to the extent—

(i) All events have occurred that establish the fact of the liability to pay the amount, and the exact amount of the liability can be determined, as of the beginning of the recognition period; and

(ii) The amount is paid—

(A) In the first two and one-half months of the recognition period; or

(B) To a related party owning, under the attribution rules of section 267, less than 5 percent, by voting power and value, of the corporation's stock, both as of the beginning of the recognition period and when the amount is paid.

(2) Section 404(a)(5). Notwithstanding paragraph (b)(2) of this section, any amount properly deducted in the recognition period under section 404(a)(5), relating to payments for deferred compensation, is recognized built-in loss to the extent—

(i) All events have occurred that establish the fact of the liability to pay the amount, and the exact amount of the liability can be determined, as of the beginning of the recognition period; and

(ii) The amount is not paid to a related party to which section 267(a)(2) applies.

(3) Examples. The rules of this paragraph (c) are illustrated by the following examples.

Example (1). Fixed annuity. X is a C corporation that elects to become an S corporation effective January 1, 1996. On December 31, 1995, A is age 60, has provided services to X as an employee for 20 years, and is a vested participant in X's unfunded nonqualified retirement plan. Under the plan, A receives $1,000 per month upon retirement until death. The plan provides no additional benefits. A retires on December 31, 1997, after working for X for 22 years. A at no time is a shareholder of X. X's deductions under section 404(a)(5) in the recognition period on paying A the $1,000 per month are recognized built-in loss because all events have occurred that establish the fact of the liability to pay the amount, and the exact amount of the liability can be determined, as of the beginning of the recognition period.

Example (2). Increase in annuity for working beyond 20 years. The facts are the same as Example 1, except that under the plan A receives $1,000 per month, plus $100 per month for each year A works for X beyond 20 years, upon retirement until death. X's deductions on paying A the $1,000 per month are recognized built-in loss. However, X's deductions on paying A the $200 per month for the two years A worked for X beyond 20 years are not recognized built-in loss because all events have not occurred that establish the fact of the liability to pay the amount, and the exact amount of the liability cannot be determined, as of the beginning of the recognition period.

Example (3). Cost of living adjustment. The facts are the same as Example 1, except that under the plan A receives $1,000 per month, plus annual cost of living adjustments, upon retirement until death. X's deductions under section 404(a)(5) on paying A the $1,000 per month are recognized built-in loss. However, X's deductions under section 404(a)(5) on paying A the annual cost of living adjustment are not recognized built-in loss because all events have not occurred that establish the fact of the liability to pay the amount, and the exact amount of the liability cannot be determined, as of the beginning of the recognition period.

(d) Section 481(a) adjustments—(1) In general. Any section 481(a) adjustment taken into account in the recognition period is recognized built-in gain or loss to the extent the adjustment relates to items attributable to periods before the beginning of the recognition period under the principles for determining recognized built-in gain or loss in this section. The principles for determining recognized built-in gain or loss in this section include, for example, the accrual method rule under paragraph (b) of this section.

(2) Examples. The rules of this paragraph (d) are illustrated by the following examples.

Example (1). Omitted item attributable to prerecognition period. X is a C corporation that elects to become an S corporation effective January 1, 1996. X improperly capitalizes repair costs and recovers the costs through depreciation of the related assets. In 1999, X properly changes to deducting repair costs as they are incurred. Under section 481(a), the basis of the related assets are reduced by an amount equal to the excess of the repair costs incurred before the year of change over the repair costs recovered through depreciation before the year of change. In addition, X has a negative section 481(a) adjustment equal to the basis reduction. Under paragraph (d)(1) of this section, the portion of X's negative section 481(a) adjustment relating to the repair costs incurred before the recognition period is recognized built-in loss because those repair costs are items attributable to periods before the beginning of the recognition period under the principles for determining recognized built-in gain or loss in this section.

Example (2). Duplicated item attributable to prerecognition period. Y is a C corporation that elects to become an S corporation effective January 1, 1996. Y improperly uses an accrual method without regard to the economic performance rules of section 461(h) to account for worker's compensation claims. As a result, Y takes deductions when claims are filed. In 1999, Y properly changes to an accrual method with regard to the economic performance rules under section 461(h)(2)(C) for worker's compensation claims. As a result, Y takes deductions when claims are paid. The positive section 481(a) adjustment resulting from the change is equal to the amount of claims filed, but unpaid, before the year of change. Under paragraph (b)(2) of this section, the deduction allowed in the recognition period for claims filed, but unpaid, before the recognition period is recognized built-in loss because a deduction was allowed for those claims before the recognition period under an accrual method without regard to section 461(h)(2)(C). Under paragraph (d)(1) of this section, the portion of Y's positive section 481(a) adjustment relating to claims filed, but unpaid, before the recognition period is recognized built-in gain because those claims are items attributable to periods before the beginning of the recognition period under the principles for determining recognized built-in gain or loss in this section.

(e) Section 995(b)(2) deemed distributions. Any item of income properly taken into account during the recognition period under section 995(b)(2) is recognized built-in gain if the item results from a DISC termination or disqualification occurring before the beginning of the recognition period.

(f) Discharge of indebtedness and bad debts. Any item of income or deduction properly taken into account during the first year of the recognition period as discharge of indebtedness income under section 61(a)(12) or as a bad debt deduction under section 166 is recognized built-in gain or loss if the item arises from a debt owed by or to an S corporation at the beginning of the recognition period.

(g) Completion of contract. Any item of income properly taken into account during the recognition period under the completed contract method (as described in § 1.451–3(d)) where the corporation began performance of the contract before the beginning of the recognition period is recognized built-in gain if the item would have been included in gross income before the beginning of the recognition period under the percentage of completion method (as described in § 1.451–3(c)). Any similar item of deduction is recognized built-in loss if the item would have been allowed as a deduction against gross income before the beginning of the recognition period under the percentage of completion method.

(h) Installment method—(1) In general. If a corporation sells an asset before or during the recognition period and reports the income from the sale using the installment method under section 453 during or after the recognition period, that income is subject to tax under section 1374.

(2) Limitation on amount subject to tax. For purposes of paragraph (h)(1) of this section, the taxable income limitation under § 1.1374–2(a)(2) is equal to the amount by which the S corporation's net recognized built-in gain would have been increased from the year of the sale to the earlier of the year the income is reported under the installment method or the last year of the recognition period, assuming all income from the sale had been reported in the year of the sale and all provisions of section 1374 applied. For purposes of the preceding sentence, if the corporation sells the asset before the recognition period, the income from the sale that is not reported before the recognition period is treated as having been reported in the first year of the recognition period.

(3) Rollover rule. If the limitation in paragraph (h)(2) of this section applies, the excess of the amount reported under the installment method over the amount subject to tax under the limitation is treated as if it were reported in the succeeding taxable year(s), but only for succeeding taxable year(s) in the recognition period. The amount reported in the succeeding taxable year(s) under the preceding sentence is reduced to the extent that the amount not subject to tax under the limitation in paragraph (h)(2) of this section was not subject to tax because the S corporation had an excess of recognized built-in loss over recognized built-in gain in the taxable year of the sale and succeeding taxable year(s) in the recognition period.

(4) Use of losses and section 1374 attributes. If income is reported under the installment method by an S corporation for a taxable year after the recognition period and the income is subject to tax under paragraph (h)(1) of this section, the S corporation's section 1374 attributes may be used to the extent their use is allowed under all applicable provisions of the Code in determining the section 1374 tax. However, the S corporation's loss recognized for a taxable year after the recognition period that would have been recognized built-in loss if it had been recognized in the recognition period may not be used in determining the section 1374 tax.

(5) Examples. The rules of this paragraph (h) are illustrated by the following examples.

Example (1). Rollover rule. X is a C corporation that elects to become an S corporation effective January 1, 1996. On that date, X sells Blackacre with a basis of $0 and a value of $100,000 in exchange for a $100,000 note bearing a market rate of interest payable on January 1, 2001. X does not make the election under section 453(d) and, therefore, reports the $100,000 gain using the installment method under section 453. In the year 2001, X has income of $100,000 on collecting the note, unexpired C year attributes of $0, recognized built-in loss of $0, current losses of $100,000, and taxable income of $0. If X had reported the $100,000 gain in 1996, X's net recognized built-in gain from 1996 through 2001 would have been $75,000 greater than otherwise. Under paragraph (h) of this section, X has $75,000 net recognized built-in gain subject to tax under section 1374. X also must treat the $25,000 excess of the amount reported, $100,000, over the amount subject to tax, $75,000, as income reported under the installment method in the succeeding taxable year(s) in the recognition period, except to the extent X establishes that the $25,000 was not subject to tax under section 1374 in the year 2001 because X had an excess of recognized built-in loss over recognized built-in gain in the taxable year of the sale and succeeding taxable year(s) in the recognition period.

Example (2). Use of losses. Y is a C corporation that elects to become an S corporation effective January 1, 1996. On that date, Y sells Whiteacre with a basis of $0 and a value of $250,000 in exchange for a $250,000 note bearing a market rate of interest payable on January 1, 2006. Y does not make the election under section 453(d) and, therefore, reports the $250,000 gain using the installment method under section 453. In the year 2006, Y has income of $250,000 on collecting the note, unexpired C year attributes of $0, loss of $100,000 that would have been recognized

built-in loss if it had been recognized in the recognition period, current losses of $150,000, and taxable income of $0. If Y had reported the $250,000 gain in 1996, X's net recognized built-in gain from 1996 through 2005 (that is, during the recognition period) would have been $225,000 greater than otherwise. Under paragraph (h) of this section, X has $225,000 net recognized built-in gain subject to tax under section 1374.

Example (3). Use of section 1374 attribute. Z is a C corporation that elects to become an S corporation effective January 1, 1996. On that date, Z sells Greenacre with a basis of $0 and a value of $500,000 in exchange for a $500,000 note bearing a market rate of interest payable on January 1, 2011. Z does not make the election under section 453(d) and, therefore, reports the $500,000 gain using the installment method under section 453. In the year 2011, Z has income of $500,000 on collecting the note, loss of $0 that would have been recognized built-in loss if it had been recognized in the recognition period, current losses of $0, taxable income of $500,000, and a minimum tax credit of $60,000 arising in 1995. None of Z's minimum tax credit is limited under sections 53(c) or 383. If Z had reported the $500,000 gain in 1996, Z's net recognized built-in gain from 1996 through 2005 (that is, during the recognition period) would have been $350,000 greater than otherwise. Under paragraph (h) of this section, Z has $350,000 net recognized built-in gain subject to tax under section 1374, a tentative section 1374 tax of $122,500 ($350,000 × .35 = $122,500), and a section 1374 tax after using its minimum tax credit arising in 1995 of $62,250 ($122,500 − $60,000 = $62,250).

(i) Partnership interests—(1) In general. If an S corporation owns a partnership interest at the beginning of the recognition period or transfers property to a partnership in a transaction to which section 1374(d)(6) applies during the recognition period, the S corporation determines the effect on net recognized built-in gain from its distributive share of partnership items as follows—

(i) Step One: Apply the rules of section 1374(d) to the S corporation's distributive share of partnership items of income, gain, loss, or deduction included in income or allowed as a deduction under the rules of subchapter K to determine the extent to which it would have been treated as recognized built-in gain or loss if the partnership items had originated in and been taken into account directly by the S corporation (partnership 1374 items);

(ii) Step Two: Determine the S corporation's net recognized built-in gain without partnership 1374 items;

(iii) Step Three: Determine the S corporation's net recognized built-in gain with partnership 1374 items; and

(iv) Step Four: If the amount computed under Step Three (paragraph (i)(1)(iii) of this section) exceeds the amount computed under Step Two (paragraph (i)(1)(ii) of this section), the excess (as limited by paragraph (i)(2)(i) of this section) is the S corporation's partnership RBIG, and the S corporation's net recognized built-in gain is the sum of the amount computed under Step Two (paragraph (i)(1)(ii) of this section) plus the partnership RBIG. If the amount computed under Step Two (paragraph (i)(1)(ii) of this section) exceeds the amount computed under Step Three (paragraph (i)(1)(iii) of this section), the excess (as limited by paragraph (i)(2)(ii) of this section) is the S corporation's partnership RBIL, and the S corporation's net recognized built-in gain is the remainder of the amount computed under Step Two (paragraph (i)(1)(ii) of this section) after subtracting the partnership RBIL.

(2) Limitations—(i) Partnership RBIG. An S corporation's partnership RBIG for any taxable year may not exceed the excess (if any) of the S corporation's RBIG limitation over its partnership RBIG for prior taxable years. The preceding sentence does not apply if a corporation forms or avails of a partnership with a

principal purpose of avoiding the tax imposed under section 1374.

(ii) Partnership RBIL. An S corporation's partnership RBIL for any taxable year may not exceed the excess (if any) of the S corporation's RBIL limitation over its partnership RBIL for prior taxable years.

(3) Disposition of partnership interest. If an S corporation disposes of its partnership interest, the amount that may be treated as recognized built-in gain may not exceed the excess (if any) of the S corporation's RBIG limitation over its partnership RBIG during the recognition period. Similarly, the amount that may be treated as recognized built-in loss may not exceed the excess (if any) of the S corporation's RBIL limitation over its partnership RBIL during the recognition period.

(4) RBIG and RBIL limitations—(i) Sale of partnership interest. An S corporation's RBIG or RBIL limitation is the total of the following—

(A) The amount that would be the amount realized if, at the beginning of the first day of the recognition period, the corporation had remained a C corporation and had sold its partnership interest (and any assets the corporation contributed to the partnership during the recognition period) at fair market value to an unrelated party; decreased by

(B) The corporation's adjusted basis in the partnership interest (and any assets the corporation contributed to the partnership during the recognition period) at the time of the sale referred to in paragraph (i)(4)(i)(A) of this section; and increased or decreased by

(C) The corporation's allocable share of the partnership's section 481(a) adjustments at the time of the sale referred to in paragraph (i)(4)(i)(A) of this section.

(ii) Amounts of limitations. If the result in paragraph (i)(4)(i) of this section is a positive amount, the S corporation has a RBIG limitation equal to that amount and a RBIL limitation of $0, but if the result in paragraph (i)(4)

(i) of this section is a negative amount, the S corporation has a RBIL limitation equal to that amount and a RBIG limitation of $0.

(5) Small interest exception — (i) In general. Paragraph (i)(1) of this section does not apply to a taxable year in the recognition period if the S corporation's partnership interest represents less than 10 percent of the partnership's capital and profits at all times during the taxable year and prior taxable years in the recognition period, and the fair market value of the S corporation's partnership interest as of the beginning of the recognition period is less than $100,000.

(ii) Contributed assets. For purposes of paragraph (i)(5)(i) of this section, if the S corporation contributes any assets to the partnership during the recognition period and the S corporation held the assets as of the beginning of the recognition period, the fair market value of the S corporation's partnership interest as of the beginning of the recognition period is determined as if the assets were contributed to the partnership before the beginning of the recognition period (using the fair market value of each contributed asset as of the beginning of the recognition period). The contribution does not affect whether paragraph (i)(5)(i) of this section applies for taxable years in the recognition period before the taxable year in which the contribution was made.

(iii) Anti-abuse rule. Paragraph (i)(5)(i) of this section does not apply if a corporation forms or avails of a partnership with a principal purpose of avoiding the tax imposed under section 1374.

(6) Section 704(c) gain or loss. Solely for purposes of section 1374, an S corporation's section 704(c) gain or loss amount with respect to any asset is not reduced during the recognition period, except for amounts treated as recognized built-in gain or loss with respect to that asset under this paragraph.

(7) Disposition of distributed partnership asset. If on the first day of the recognition period an S corporation holds an interest in a partnership that holds an asset and during the recognition period the partnership distributes the asset to the S corporation that thereafter disposes of the asset, the asset is treated as having been held by the S corporation on the first day of the recognition period and as having the fair market value and adjusted basis in the hands of the S corporation that it had in the hands of the partnership on that day.

(8) Examples. The rules of this paragraph (i) are illustrated by the following examples.

Example (1). Pre-conversion partnership interest. X is a C corporation that elects to become an S corporation on January 1, 1996. On that date, X owns a 50 percent interest in partnership P and P owns (among other assets) Blackacre with a basis of $25,000 and a value of $45,000. In 1996, P buys Whiteacre for $50,000. In 1999, P sells Blackacre for $55,000 and recognizes a gain of $30,000 of which $15,000 is included in X's distributive share. P also sells Whiteacre in 1999 for $42,000 and recognizes a loss of $8,000 of which $4,000 is included in X's distributive share. Under this paragraph and section 1374(d)(3), X's $15,000 gain is presumed to be recognized built-in gain and thus treated as a partnership 1374 item, but this presumption is rebutted if X establishes that P's gain would have been only $20,000 ($45,000 − $25,000 = $ 20,000) if Blackacre had been sold on the first day of the recognition period. In such a case, only X's distributive share of the $20,000 built-in gain, $10,000, would be treated as a partnership 1374 item. Under this paragraph and section 1374(d)(4), X's $4,000 loss is not treated as a partnership 1374 item because P did not hold Whiteacre on the first day of the recognition period.

Example (2). Post-conversion contribution. Y is a C corporation that elects to become an S corporation on January 1, 1996. On that date, Y owns (among other assets) Blackacre with a basis of $100,000 and a value of $200,000. On January 1, 1998, when Blackacre has a basis of $100,000 and a value of $200,000, Y contributes Blackacre to partnership P for a 50 percent interest in P. On January 1, 2000, P sells Blackacre for $300,000 and recognizes a gain of $200,000 on the sale ($300,000 − $100,000 = $200,000). P is allocated $100,000 of the gain under section 704(c), and another $50,000 of the gain for its fifty percent share of the remainder, for a total of $150,000. Under this paragraph and section 1374(d)(3), if Y establishes that P's gain would have been only $100,000 ($200,000 − $100,000 = $100,000) if Blackacre had been sold on the first day of the recognition period, Y would treat only $100,000 as a partnership 1374 item.

Example (3). RBIG limitation of $100,000 or $50,000. X is a C corporation that elects to become an S corporation on January 1, 1996. On that date, X owns a 50 percent interest in partnership P with a RBIG limitation of $100,000 and a RBIL limitation of $0. P owns (among other assets) Blackacre with a basis of $50,000 and a value of $200,000. In 1996, P sells Blackacre for $200,000 and recognizes a gain of $150,000 of which $75,000 is included in X's distributive share and treated as a partnership 1374 item. X's net recognized built-in gain for 1996 computed without partnership 1374 items is $35,000 and with partnership 1374 items is $110,000. Thus, X has a partnership RBIG of $75,000 except as limited under paragraph (i)(2)(i) of this section. Because X's RBIG limitation is $100,000, X's partnership RBIG of $75,000 is not limited and X's net recognized built-in gain for the year is $110,000 ($35,000 + $75,000 = $110,000). However, if X had a RBIG limitation of $50,000 instead of $100,000, X's partnership RBIG would be limited to $50,000 under paragraph (i)(2)(i) of this section and X's net recognized built-in gain would be $85,000 ($35,000 + $50,000 = $85,000).

Example (4). RBIL limitation of $60,000 or $40,000. Y is a C corporation that elects to become an S corporation on January 1, 1996. On that date, Y owns a 50 percent interest in partnership P with a RBIG limitation of $0 and a RBIL limitation of $60,000. P owns (among other assets) Blackacre with a basis of $225,000 and a value of $125,000. In 1996, P sells Blackacre for $125,000 and recognizes a loss of $100,000 of which $50,000 is included in Y's distributive share and treated as a partnership 1374 item. Y's net recognized built-in gain for 1996 computed without partnership 1374 items is $75,000 and with partnership 1374 items is $25,000. Thus, Y has a partnership RBIL of $50,000 for the year except as limited under paragraph (i)(2)(ii) of this section. Because Y's RBIL limitation is $60,000, Y's partnership RBIL for the year is not limited and Y's net recognized built-in gain for the year is $25,000 ($75,000 − $50,000 = $25,000). However, if Y had a RBIL limitation of $40,000 instead of $60,000, Y's partnership RBIL would be limited to $40,000 under paragraph (i)(2)(ii) of this section and Y's net recognized built-in gain for the year would be $35,000 ($75,000 − $40,000 = $35,000).

Example (5). RBIG limitation of $0. *(i)* X is a C corporation that elects to become an S corporation on January 1, 1996. X owns a 50 percent interest in partnership P with a RBIG limitation of $0 and a RBIL limitation of $25,000.

(a) In 1996, P's partnership 1374 items are —

(1) Ordinary income of $25,000; and

(2) Capital gain of $75,000.

(b) X itself has —

(1) Recognized built-in ordinary income of $40,000; and

(2) Recognized built-in capital loss of $90,000.

(ii) X's net recognized built-in gain for 1996 computed without partnership 1374 items is $40,000 and with partnership 1374 items is $65,000 ($40,000 + $25,000 = $65,000). Thus, X's partnership RBIG is $25,000 for the year except as limited under paragraph (i)(2)(i) of this section. Because X's RBIG limitation is

$0, X's partnership RBIG of $25,000 is limited to $0 and X's net recognized built-in gain for the year is $40,000.

Example (6). RBIL limitation of $0. (i) Y is a C corporation that elects to become an S corporation on January 1, 1996. Y owns a 50 percent interest in partnership P with a RBIG limitation of $60,000 and a RBIL limitation of $0.

(a) In 1996, P's partnership 1374 items are—

(1) Ordinary income of $25,000; and

(2) Capital loss of $90,000.

(b) Y itself has—

(1) recognized built-in ordinary income of $40,000; and

(2) recognized built-in capital gain of $75,000.

(ii) Y's net recognized built-in gain for 1996 computed without partnership 1374 items is $115,000 ($40,000 + $75,000 = $115,000) and with partnership 1374 items is $65,000 ($40,000 + $25,000 = $65,000). Thus, Y's partnership RBIL is $50,000 for the year except as limited under paragraph (i)(2)(ii) of this section. Because Y's RBIL limitation is $0, Y's partnership RBIL of $50,000 is limited to $0 and Y's net recognized built-in gain is $115,000.

Example (7). Disposition of partnership interest. X is a C corporation that elects to become an S corporation on January 1, 1996. On that date, X owns a 50 percent interest in partnership P with a RBIG limitation of $200,000 and a RBIL limitation of $0. P owns (among other assets) Blackacre with a basis of $20,000 and a value of $140,000. In 1996, P sells Blackacre for $140,000 and recognizes a gain of $120,000 of which $60,000 is included in X's distributive share and treated as a partnership 1374 item. X's net recognized built-in gain for 1996 computed without partnership 1374 items is $95,000 and with partnership 1374 items is $155,000. Thus, X has a part-nership RBIG of $ 60,000. In 1999, X sells its entire interest in P for $350,000 and recogniz-es a gain of $250,000. Under paragraph (i)(3) of this section, X's recognized built-in gain on the sale is limited by its RBIG limitation to $140,000 ($200,000 – $60,000 = $140,000).

Example (8). Section 704(c) case. Y is a C corporation that elects to become an S cor-poration on January 1, 1996. On that date, Y contributes Asset 1, 5-year property with a value of $40,000 and a basis of $0, and an unrelated party contributes $40,000 in cash, each for a 50 percent interest in partnership P. The partnership adopts the traditional meth-od under § 1.704–3(b). If P sold Asset 1 for $40,000 immediately after it was contributed by Y, P's $40,000 gain would be allocated to Y under section 704(c). Instead, Asset 1 is sold by P in 1999 for $36,000 and P recognizes gain of $36,000 ($36,000 – $0 = $36,000) on the sale. However, because book depreciation of $8,000 per year has been taken on Asset 1 in 1996, 1997, and 1998, Y is allocated only $16,000 of P's $36,000 gain ($40,000 – (3 × $8,000) = ($16,000 – $0) = $16,000) under section 704(c). The remaining $20,000 of P's $36,000 gain ($36,000 – $16,000 = $20,000) is allocated 50 percent to each partner under sec-tion 704(b). Thus, a total of $26,000 ($16,000 + $10,000 = $26,000) of P's $36,000 gain is allocated to Y. However, under paragraph (i) (6) of this section, Y treats $36,000 as a part-nership 1374 item on P's sale of Asset 1.

Example (9). Disposition of distributed partnership asset. X is a C corporation that elects to become an S corporation on January 1, 1996. On that date, X owns a fifty percent interest in partnership P and P owns (among other assets) Blackacre with a basis of $20,000 and a value of $40,000. On January 1, 1998, P distributes Blackacre to X, when Blackacre has a basis of $20,000 and a value of $50,000. Under section 732(a)(1), X has a transferred basis of $20,000 in Blackacre. On January 1, 1999, X sells Blackacre for $60,000 and rec-ognizes a gain of $40,000. Under paragraph (i)

893

(7) of this section and section 1374(d)(3), X has recognized built-in gain from the sale of $20,000, the amount of built-in gain in Blackacre on the first day of the recognition period.

§ 1.1374–5 Loss carryforwards.

(a) **In general.** The loss carryforwards allowed as deductions against net recognized built-in gain under section 1374(b)(2) are allowed only to the extent their use is allowed under the rules applying to C corporations. Any other loss carryforwards, such as charitable contribution carryforwards under section 170(d)(2), are not allowed as deductions against net recognized built-in gain.

(b) **Example.** The rules of this section are illustrated by the following example.

Example. Section 382 limitation. X is a C corporation that has an ownership change under section 382(g)(1) on January 1, 1994. On that date, X has a fair market value of $500,000, NOL carryforwards of $400,000, and a net unrealized built-in gain under section 382(h)(3)(A) of $0. Assume X's section 382 limitation under section 382(b)(1) is $40,000. X elects to become an S corporation on January 1, 1998. On that date, X has NOL carryforwards of $240,000 (having used $160,000 of its pre-change net operating losses in its 4 preceding taxable years) and a section 1374 net unrealized built-in gain of $250,000. In 1998, X has net recognized built-in gain of $100,000. X may use $40,000 of its NOL carryforwards as a deduction against its $100,000 net recognized built-in gain, because X's section 382 limitation is $40,000.

§ 1.1374–6 Credits and credit carryforwards.

(a) **In general.** The credits and credit carryforwards allowed as credits against the section 1374 tax under section 1374(b)(3) are allowed only to the extent their use is allowed under the rules applying to C corporations. Any other credits or credit carryforwards, such as foreign tax credits under section 901, are not allowed as credits against the section 1374 tax.

(b) **Limitations.** The amount of business credit carryforwards and minimum tax credit allowed against the section 1374 tax are subject to the limitations described in section 38(c) and section 53(c), respectively, as modified by this paragraph. The tentative tax determined under paragraph (a)(3) of § 1.1374–1 is treated as the regular tax liability described in sections 38(c)(1) and 53(c)(1), and as the net income tax and net regular tax liability described in section 38(c)(1). The tentative minimum tax described in section 55(b) is determined using the rate of tax applicable to corporations and without regard to any alternative minimum tax foreign tax credit described in that section and by treating the net recognized built-in gain determined under § 1.1374–2, modified to take into account the adjustments of sections 56 and 58 applicable to corporations and the preferences of section 57, as the alternative minimum taxable income described in section 55(b)(2).

(c) **Examples.** The rules of this section are illustrated by the following examples.

Example (1). Business credit carryforward. X is a C corporation that elects to become an S corporation effective January 1, 1996. On that date, X has a $500,000 business credit carryforward from a C year and Asset # 1 with a fair market value of $400,000, a basis for regular tax purposes of $95,000, and a basis for alternative minimum tax purposes of $150,000. In 1996, X has net recognized built-in gain of $305,000 from selling Asset # 1 for $400,000. Thus, X's tentative tax under paragraph (a)(3) of § 1.1374–1 and regular tax liability under paragraph (b) of this section is $106,750 ($400,000 − $95,000 = $305,000 × .35 = $106,750, assuming a 35 percent tax rate). Also, X's tentative minimum tax determined under paragraph (b) of this section is $47,000 [$400,000 − $150,000 = $250,000 − $15,000 ($40,000 corporate exemption amount − $25,000 phase-out = $15,000) = $235,000 ×

.20 = $47,000, assuming a 20 percent tax rate]. Thus, the business credit limitation under section 38(c) is $59,750 [$106,750 – $47,000 (the greater of $47,000 or $20,438 (.25 × $81,750 ($106,750 – $25,000 = $81,750))) = $59,750]. As a result, X's section 1374 tax is $47,000 ($106,750 – $59,750 = $47,000) for 1996 and X has $440,250 ($500,000 – $59,750 = $440,250) of business credit carryforwards for succeeding taxable years.

Example (2). Minimum tax credit. Y is a C corporation that elects to become an S corporation effective January 1, 1996. On that date, Asset #1 has a fair market value of $5,000,000, a basis for regular tax purposes of $4,000,000, and a basis for alternative minimum tax purposes of $4,750,000. Y also has a minimum tax credit of $310,000 from 1995. Y has no other assets, no net operating or capital loss carryforwards, and no business credit carryforwards. In 1996, Y's only transaction is the sale of Asset #1 for $5,000,000. Therefore, Y has net recognized built-in gain in 1996 of $1,000,000 ($5,000,000 – $4,000,000 = $1,000,000) and a tentative tax under paragraph (a)(3) of § 1.1374–1 of $350,000 ($1,000,000 × .35 = $350,000, assuming a 35 percent tax rate). Also, Y's tentative minimum tax determined under paragraph (b) of this section is $47,000 [$5,000,000 – $4,750,000 = $250,000–$15,000 ($40,000 corporate exemption amount – $25,000 phase-out = $15,000) = $235,000x.20 = $47,000, assuming a 20 percent tax rate]. Thus, Y may use its minimum tax credit in the amount of $303,000 ($350,000–$47,000 = $303,000) to offset its section 1374 tentative tax. As a result, Y's section 1374 tax is $47,000 ($350,000–$303,000 = $47,000) in 1996 and Y has a minimum tax credit attributable to years for which Y was a C corporation of $7,000 ($310,000 – $303,000 = $7,000).

§ 1.1374–7 Inventory.

(a) Valuation. The fair market value of the inventory of an S corporation on the first day of the recognition period equals the amount that a willing buyer would pay a willing seller for the inventory in a purchase of all the S corporation's assets by a buyer that expects to continue to operate the S corporation's business. For purposes of the preceding sentence, the buyer and seller are presumed not to be under any compulsion to buy or sell and to have reasonable knowledge of all relevant facts.

(b) Identity of dispositions. The inventory method used by an S corporation for tax purposes must be used to identify whether the inventory it disposes of during the recognition period is inventory it held on the first day of that period. Thus, a corporation using the LIFO method does not dispose of inventory it held on the first day of the recognition period unless the carrying value of its inventory for a taxable year during that period is less than the carrying value of its inventory on the first day of the recognition period (determined using the LIFO method as described in section 472). However, if a corporation changes its method of accounting for inventory (for example, from the FIFO method to the LIFO method or from the LIFO method to the FIFO method) with a principal purpose of avoiding the tax imposed under section 1374, it must use its former method to identify its dispositions of inventory.

§ 1.1374–8 Section 1374(d)(8) transactions.

(a) In general. If any S corporation acquires any asset in a transaction in which the S corporation's basis in the asset is determined (in whole or in part) by reference to a C corporation's basis in the assets (or any other property) (a section 1374(d)(8) transaction), section 1374 applies to the net recognized built-in gain attributable to the assets acquired in any section 1374(d)(8) transaction.

(b) Effective date of section 1374(d)(8). Section 1374(d)(8) applies to any section 1374(d)(8) transaction, as defined in paragraph (a)(1) of this section, that occurs on or after December 27, 1994, without regard to the date of the corporation's election to be an S corporation under section 1362.

(c) Separate determination of tax. For purposes of the tax imposed under section 1374(d)(8), a separate determination of tax is made with respect to the assets the S corporation acquires in one section 1374(d)(8) transaction from the assets the S corporation acquires in another section 1374(d)(8) transaction and from the assets the corporation held when it became an S corporation. Thus, an S corporation's section 1374 attributes when it became an S corporation may only be used to reduce the section 1374 tax imposed on dispositions of assets the S corporation held at that time. Similarly, an S corporation's section 1374 attributes acquired in a section 1374(d) (8) transaction may only be used to reduce a section 1374 tax imposed on dispositions of assets the S corporation acquired in the same transaction.

(d) Taxable income limitation. For purposes of paragraph (a) of this section, an S corporation's taxable income limitation under § 1.1374–2(a)(2) for any taxable year is allocated between or among each of the S corporation's separate determinations of net recognized built-in gain for that year (determined without regard to the taxable income limitation) based on the ratio of each of those determinations to the sum of all of those determinations.

(e) Examples. The rules of this section are illustrated by the following examples.

Example (1). Separate determination of tax. (i) X is a C corporation that elected to become an S corporation effective January 1, 1986 (before section 1374 was amended in the Tax Reform Act of 1986). X has a net operating loss carryforward of $20,000 arising in 1985 when X was a C corporation. On January 1, 1996, Y (an unrelated C corporation) merges into X in a transaction to which section 368(a)(1)(A) applies. Y has no loss carryforwards, credits, or credit carryforwards. The assets X acquired from Y are subject to tax under section 1374 and have a net unrealized built-in gain of $150,000.

(ii) In 1996, X has a pre-limitation amount of $50,000 on dispositions of assets acquired from Y and a taxable income limitation of $100,000 (because only one group of assets is subject to section 1374, there is no allocation of the taxable income limitation). As a result, X has a net recognized built-in gain on those assets of $50,000. X's $20,000 net operating loss carryforward may not be used as a deduction against its $50,000 net recognized built-in gain on the assets X acquired from Y. Therefore, X has a section 1374 tax of $17,500 ($50,000 × .35 = $17,500, assuming a 35 percent tax rate) for its 1996 taxable year.

Example (2). Allocation of taxable income limitation. (i) Y is a C corporation that elects to become an S corporation effective January 1, 1996. The assets Y holds when it becomes an S corporation have a net unrealized built-in gain of $5,000. Y has no loss carryforwards, credits, or credit carryforwards. On January 1, 1997, Z (an unrelated C corporation) merges into Y in a transaction to which section 368(a) (1)(A) applies. Z has no loss carryforwards, credits, or credit carryforwards. The assets Y acquired from Z are subject to tax under section 1374 and have a net unrealized built-in gain of $80,000.

(ii) In 1997, Y has a pre-limitation amount on the assets it held when it became an S corporation of $15,000, a pre-limitation amount on the assets Y acquired from Z of $15,000, and a taxable income limitation of $10,000. However, because the assets Y held on becoming an S corporation have a net unrealized built-in gain of $5,000, its net recognized built-in gain on those assets is limited to $5,000 before taking into account the taxable income limitation. Y's taxable income limitation of $10,000 is allocated between the assets Y held on becoming an S corporation and the assets Y acquired from Z for purposes of determining the net recognized built-in gain from each pool of assets. Thus, Y's net recognized built-in gain on

the assets Y held on becoming an S corporation is $2,500 [$10,000 × ($5,000/$20,000) = $2,500]. Y's net recognized built-in gain on the assets Y acquired from Z is $7,500 [$10,000 × ($15,000/$20,000) = $7,500]. Therefore, Y has a section 1374 tax of $3,500 [($2,500 + $7,500) × .35 = $3,500, assuming a 35 percent tax rate] for its 1997 taxable year.

§ 1.1374–9 Anti-stuffing rule.

If a corporation acquires an asset before or during the recognition period with a principal purpose of avoiding the tax imposed under section 1374, the asset and any loss, deduction, loss carryforward, credit, or credit carryforward attributable to the asset is disregarded in determining the S corporation's pre-limitation amount, taxable income limitation, net unrealized built-in gain limitation, deductions against net recognized built-in gain, and credits against the section 1374 tax.

§ 1.1374–10 Effective date and additional rules.

(a) In general. Sections 1.1374–1 through 1.1374–9 apply for taxable years ending on or after December 27, 1994, but only in cases where the S corporation's return for the taxable year is filed pursuant to an S election or a section 1374(d)(8) transaction occurring on or after December 27, 1994.

(b) Additional rules. This paragraph (b) provides rules applicable to certain S corporations, assets, or transactions to which §§ 1.1374–1 through 1.1374–9 do not apply.

(1) Certain transfers to partnerships. If a corporation transfers an asset to a partnership in a transaction to which section 721(a) applies and the transfer is made in contemplation of an S election or during the recognition period, section 1374 applies on a disposition of the asset by the partnership as if the S corporation had disposed of the asset itself. This paragraph (b)(1) applies as of the effective date of section 1374, unless the recognition period with respect to the contributed asset is pursuant to an S election or a section 1374(d)(8) transaction occurring on or after December 27, 1994.

(2) Certain inventory dispositions. For purposes of section 1374(d)(2)(A), the inventory method used by the taxpayer for tax purposes (FIFO, LIFO, etc.) must be used to identify whether goods disposed of following conversion to S corporation status were held by the corporation at the time of conversion. Thus, for example, a corporation using the LIFO inventory method will not be subject to the built-in gain tax with respect to sales of inventory except to the extent that a LIFO layer existing prior to the beginning of the first taxable year as an S corporation is invaded after the beginning of that year. This paragraph (b) (2) applies as of the effective date of section 1374, unless the recognition period with respect to the inventory is pursuant to an S election or a section 1374(d)(8) transaction occurring on or after December 27, 1994.

(3) Certain contributions of built-in loss assets. If a built-in loss asset (that is, an asset with an adjusted tax basis in excess of its fair market value) is contributed to a corporation within 2 years before the earlier of the beginning of its first taxable year as an S corporation, or the filing of its S election, the loss inherent in the asset will not reduce net unrealized built-in gain, as defined in section 1374(d)(1), unless the taxpayer demonstrates a clear and substantial relationship between the contributed property and the conduct of the corporation's current or future business enterprises. This paragraph (b)(3) applies as of the effective date of section 1374, unless the recognition period with respect to the contributed asset is pursuant to an S election or a section 1374(d)(8) transaction occurring on or after December 27, 1994.

(4) Certain installment sales—(i) In general. If a taxpayer sells an asset either prior to or during the recognition period and recognizes income either during or after the recognition period from the sale under the installment method, the income will, when recognized, be taxed under section 1374 to the extent it would have been so taxed in prior taxable years if the selling corporation had made the election under section 453(d) not to report the income under the installment method. For purposes of determining the extent to which the income would have been subject to tax if the section 453(d) election had not been made, the taxable income limitation of section 1374(d)(2)(A)(ii) and the built-in gain carryover rule of section 1374(d)(2)(B) will be taken into account. This paragraph (b)(4) applies for installment sales occurring on or after March 26, 1990, and before December 27, 1994.

(ii) Examples. The rules of this paragraph (b)(4) are illustrated by the following examples.

Example (1). In year 1 of the recognition period under section 1374, a corporation realizes a gain of $100,000 on the sale of an asset with built-in gain. The corporation is to receive full payment for the asset in year 11. Because the corporation does not make an election under section 453(d), all $100,000 of the gain from the sale is reported under the installment method in year 11. If the corporation had made an election under section 453(d) with respect to the sale, the gain would have been recognized in year 1 and, taking into account the corporation's income and gains from other sources, application of the taxable income limitation of section 1374(d)(2)(A)(ii) and the built-in gain carryover rule of section 1374(d)(2)(B) would have resulted in $40,000 of the gain being subject to tax during the recognition period under section 1374. Therefore, $40,000 of the gain recognized in year 11 is subject to tax under section 1374.

Example (2). In year 1 of the recognition period under section 1374, a corporation realizes a gain of $100,000 on the sale of an asset with built-in gain. The corporation is to receive full payment for the asset in year 6. Because the corporation does not make an election under section 453(d), all $100,000 of the gain from the sale is reported under the installment meth-

od in year 6. If the corporation had made an election under section 453(d) with respect to the sale, the gain would have been recognized in year 1 and, taking into account the corporation's income and gains from other sources, application of the taxable income limitation of section 1374(d)(2)(A)(ii) and the built-in gain carryover rule of section 1374(d)(2)(B) would have resulted in all of the gain being subjected to tax under section 1374 in years 1 through 5. Therefore, notwithstanding that the taxable income limitation of section 1374(d)(2)(A)(ii) might otherwise limit the taxation of the gain recognized in year 6, the entire $100,000 of gain will be subject to tax under section 1374 when it is recognized in year 6.

(c) Termination and re-election of S corporation status—(1) In general. For purposes of section 633(d)(8) of the Tax Reform Act of 1986, as amended, any reference to an election to be an S corporation under section 1362 shall be treated as a reference to the corporation's most recent election to be an S corporation under section 1362. This paragraph (c) applies for taxable years beginning after December 22, 2004, without regard to the date of the corporation's most recent election to be an S corporation under section 1362.

(2) Example. The following example illustrates the rules of this paragraph (c):

Example. *(i)* Effective January 1, 1988, X, a C corporation that is a qualified corporation under section 633(d) of the Tax Reform Act of 1986, as amended, elects to be an S corporation under section 1362. Effective January 1, 1990, X revokes its S status and becomes a C corporation. On January 1, 2004, X again elects to be an S corporation under section 1362. X disposes of assets in 2006, 2007, and 2008, recognizing gain.

(ii) X is not eligible for treatment under the transition rule of section 633(d)(8) of the Tax Reform Act of 1986, as amended, with respect to these assets. Accordingly, X is subject to section 1374, as amended by the Tax Reform Act of 1986 and the Technical and Miscella-

neous Revenue Act of 1988, and the 10-year recognition period begins on January 1, 2004.

(iii) To the extent the gain that X recognizes on the asset sales in 2006, 2007, and 2008 reflects built-in gain inherent in such assets in X's hands on January 1, 2004, such gain is subject to tax under section 1374 as amended by the Tax Reform Act of 1986 and the Technical and Miscellaneous Revenue Act of 1988.

* * *

§ 1.1377–1 Pro rata share.

(a) Computation of pro rata shares—(1) In general. For purposes of subchapter S of chapter 1 of the Internal Revenue Code and this section, each shareholder's pro rata share of any S corporation item described in section 1366(a) for any taxable year is the sum of the amounts determined with respect to the shareholder by assigning an equal portion of the item to each day of the S corporation's taxable year, and then dividing that portion pro rata among the shares outstanding on that day. See paragraph (b) of this section for rules pertaining to the computation of each shareholder's pro rata share when an election is made under section 1377(a)(2) to treat the taxable year of an S corporation as if it consisted of two taxable years in the case of a termination of a shareholder's entire interest in the corporation.

(2) Special rules—(i) Days on which stock has not been issued. Solely for purposes of determining a shareholder's pro rata share of an item for a taxable year under section 1377(a) and this section, the beneficial owners of the corporation are treated as the shareholders of the corporation for any day on which the corporation has not issued any stock.

(ii) Determining shareholder for day of stock disposition. A shareholder who disposes of stock in an S corporation is treated as the shareholder for the day of the disposition. A shareholder who dies is treated as the shareholder for the day of the shareholder's death.

(b) Election to terminate year—(1) In general. If a shareholder's entire interest in an S corporation is terminated during the S corporation's taxable year and the corporation and all affected shareholders agree, the S corporation may elect under section 1377(a)(2) and this paragraph (b) (terminating election) to apply paragraph (a) of this section to the affected shareholders as if the corporation's taxable year consisted of two separate taxable years, the first of which ends at the close of the day on which the shareholder's entire interest in the S corporation is terminated. If the event resulting in the termination of the shareholder's entire interest also constitutes a qualifying disposition as described in § 1.1368–1(g)(2)(i), the election under § 1.1368–1(g)(2) cannot be made. An S corporation may not make a terminating election if the cessation of a shareholder's interest occurs in a transaction that results in a termination under section 1362(d)(2) of the corporation's election to be an S corporation. (See section 1362(e)(3) for an election to have items assigned to each short taxable year under normal tax accounting rules in the case of a termination of a corporation's election to be an S corporation.) A terminating election is irrevocable and is effective only for the terminating event for which it is made.

(2) Affected shareholders. For purposes of the terminating election under section 1377(a)(2) and paragraph (b) of this section, the term affected shareholders means the shareholder whose interest is terminated and all shareholders to whom such shareholder has transferred shares during the taxable year. If such shareholder has transferred shares to the corporation, the term affected shareholders includes all persons who are shareholders during the taxable year.

(3) Effect of the terminating election—(i) In general. An S corporation that makes a terminating election for a taxable year must treat the taxable year as separate taxable years for all affected shareholders for purposes of allocating items of income (including tax-exempt income), loss, deduction, and credit; making adjustments to the accumulated adjustments account, earnings and profits, and basis; and determining the tax effect of a distribution. An S corporation that makes a terminating election must assign items of income (including tax-exempt income), loss, deduction, and credit to each deemed separate taxable year using its normal method of accounting as determined under section 446(a).

(ii) Due date of S corporation return. A terminating election does not affect the due date of the S corporation's return required to be filed under section 6037(a) for a taxable year (determined without regard to a terminating election).

(iii) Taxable year of inclusion by shareholder. A terminating election does not affect the taxable year in which an affected shareholder must take into account the affected shareholder's pro rata share of the S corporation's items of income, loss, deduction, and credit.

(iv) S corporation that is a partner in a partnership. A terminating election by an S corporation that is a partner in a partnership is treated as a sale or exchange of the corporation's entire interest in the partnership for purposes of section 706(c) (relating to closing the partnership taxable year), if the taxable year of the partnership ends after the shareholder's interest is terminated and within the taxable year of the S corporation (determined without regard to any terminating election) for which the terminating election is made.

(4) Determination of whether an S shareholder's entire interest has terminated. For purposes of the terminating election under section 1377(a)(2) and paragraph (b) of this section, a shareholder's entire interest in an S corporation is terminated on the occurrence of any event through which a shareholder's entire stock ownership in the S corporation ceases, including a sale, exchange, or other disposition of all of the stock held by the shareholder; a gift under section 102(a) of all the share-

holder's stock; a spousal transfer under section 1041(a) of all the shareholder's stock; a redemption, as defined in section 317(b), of all the shareholder's stock, regardless of the tax treatment of the redemption under section 302; and the death of the shareholder. A shareholder's entire interest in an S corporation is not terminated if the shareholder retains ownership of any stock (including an interest treated as stock under § 1.1361–1(*l*)) that would result in the shareholder continuing to be considered a shareholder of the corporation for purposes of section 1362(a)(2). Thus, in determining whether a shareholder's entire interest in an S corporation has been terminated, any interest held by the shareholder as a creditor, employee, director, or in any other non-shareholder capacity is disregarded.

(5) Time and manner of making a terminating election—(i) In general. An S corporation makes a terminating election by attaching a statement to its timely filed original or amended return required to be filed under section 6037(a) (that is, a Form 1120S) for the taxable year during which a shareholder's entire interest is terminated. A single election statement may be filed by the S corporation for all terminating elections for the taxable year. The election statement must include—

(A) A declaration by the S corporation that it is electing under section 1377(a)(2) and this paragraph (b) to treat the taxable year as if it consisted of two separate taxable years;

(B) Information setting forth when and how the shareholder's entire interest was terminated (for example, a sale or gift);

(C) The signature on behalf of the S corporation of an authorized officer of the corporation under penalties of perjury; and

(D) A statement by the corporation that the corporation and each affected shareholder consent to the S corporation making the terminating election.

(ii) Affected shareholders required to consent. For purposes of paragraph (b)(5)(i)

(D) of this section, a shareholder of the S corporation for the taxable year is a shareholder as described in section 1362(a)(2). For example, the person who under § 1.1362–6(b)(2) must consent to a corporation's S election in certain special cases is the person who must consent to the terminating election. In addition, an executor or administrator of the estate of a deceased affected shareholder may consent to the terminating election on behalf of the deceased affected shareholder.

(iii) More than one terminating election. A shareholder whose entire interest in an S corporation is terminated in an event for which a terminating election was made is not required to consent to a terminating election made with respect to a subsequent termination within the same taxable year unless the shareholder is an affected shareholder with respect to the subsequent termination.

(c) Examples. The following examples illustrate the provisions of this section:

Example (1). Shareholder's pro rata share in the case of a partial disposition of stock. (i) On January 6, 1997, X incorporates as a calendar year corporation, issues 100 shares of common stock to each of A and B, and files an election to be an S corporation for its 1997 taxable year. On July 24, 1997, B sells 50 shares of X stock to C. Thus, in 1997, A owned 50 percent of the outstanding shares of X on each day of X's 1997 taxable year, B owned 50 percent on each day from January 6, 1997, to July 24, 1997 (200 days), and 25 percent from July 25, 1997, to December 31, 1997 (160 days), and C owned 25 percent from July 25, 1997, to December 31, 1997 (160 days).

(ii) Because B's entire interest in X is not terminated when B sells 50 shares to C on July 24, 1997, X cannot make a terminating election under section 1377(a)(2) and paragraph (b) of this section for B's sale of 50 shares to C. Although B's sale of 50 shares to C is a qualifying disposition under § 1.1368–1(g) (2)(i), X does not make an election to terminate its taxable year under § 1.1368–1(g)(2).

During its 1997 taxable year, X has nonseparately computed income of $720,000.

(iii) For each day in X's 1997 taxable year, A's daily pro rata share of X's nonseparately computed income is $1,000 ($720,000/360 days × 50%). Thus, A's pro rata share of X's nonseparately computed income for 1997 is $360,000 ($1,000 × 360 days). B's daily pro rata share of X's nonseparately computed income is $1,000 ($720,000/360 × 50%) for the first 200 days of X's 1997 taxable year, and $500 ($720,000/360 × 25%) for the following 160 days in 1997. Thus, B's pro rata share of X's nonseparately computed income for 1997 is $280,000 (($1,000 × 200 days) + ($500 × 160 days)). C's daily pro rata share of X's nonseparately computed income is $500 ($720,000/360 × 25%) for 160 days in 1997. Thus, C's pro rata share of X's nonseparately computed income for 1997 is $80,000 ($500 × 160 days).

Example (2). Shareholder's pro rata share when an S corporation makes a terminating election under section 1377(a)(2). (i) On January 6, 1997, X incorporates as a calendar year corporation, issues 100 shares of common stock to each of A and B, and files an election to be an S corporation for its 1997 taxable year. On July 24, 1997, B sells B's entire 100 shares of X stock to C. With the consent of B and C, X makes an election under section 1377(a)(2) and paragraph (b) of this section for the termination of B's entire interest arising from B's sale of 100 shares to C. As a result of the election, the pro rata shares of B and C are determined as if X's taxable year consisted of two separate taxable years, the first of which ends on July 24, 1997, the date B's entire interest in X terminates. Because A is not an affected shareholder as defined by section 1377(a)(2) (B) and paragraph (b)(2) of this section, the treatment as separate taxable years does not apply to A.

(ii) During its 1997 taxable year, X has nonseparately computed income of $720,000. Under X's normal method of accounting,

$200,000 of the $720,000 of nonseparately computed income is allocable to the period of January 6, 1997, through July 24, 1997 (the first deemed taxable year), and the remaining $520,000 is allocable to the period of July 25, 1997, through December 31, 1997 (the second deemed taxable year).

(iii) B's pro rata share of the $200,000 of nonseparately computed income for the first deemed taxable year is determined by assigning the $200,000 of nonseparately computed income to each day of the first deemed taxable year ($200,000/200 days = $1,000 per day). Because B held 50% of X's authorized and issued shares on each day of the first deemed taxable year, B's daily pro rata share for each day of the first deemed taxable year is $500 ($1,000 per day × 50%). Thus, B's pro rata share of the $200,000 of nonseparately computed income for the first deemed taxable year is $100,000 ($500 per day × 200 days). B must report this amount for B's taxable year with or within which X's full taxable year ends (December 31, 1997).

(iv) C's pro rata share of the $520,000 of nonseparately computed income for the second deemed taxable year is determined by assigning the $520,000 of nonseparately computed income to each day of the second deemed taxable year ($520,000/160 days = $3,250 per day). Because C held 50% of X's authorized and issued shares on each day of the second deemed taxable year, C's daily pro rata shares for each day of the second deemed taxable year is $1,625 ($3,250 per day × 50%). Therefore, C's pro rata share of the $520,000 of nonseparately computed income is $260,000 ($1,625 per day × 160 days). C must report this amount for C's taxable year with or within which X's full taxable year ends (December 31, 1997).

§ 1.1377–2 Post-termination transition period.

(a) In general. For purposes of subchapter S of chapter 1 of the Internal Revenue Code (Code) and this section, the term post-termination transition period means—

(1) The period beginning on the day after the last day of the corporation's last taxable year as an S corporation and ending on the later of—

(i) The day which is 1 year after such last day; or

(ii) The due date for filing the return for the last taxable year as an S corporation (including extensions);

(2) The 120-day period beginning on the date of any determination pursuant to an audit of the taxpayer which follows the termination of the corporation's election and which adjusts a subchapter S item of income, loss, or deduction of the corporation arising during the S period (as defined in section 1368(e)(2)); and

(3) The 120-day period beginning on the date of a determination that the corporation's election under section 1362(a) had terminated for a previous taxable year.

(b) Special rules for post-termination transition period. Pursuant to section 1377(b)(1) and paragraph (a)(1) of this section, a post-termination transition period arises the day after the last day that an S corporation was in existence if a C corporation acquires the assets of the S corporation in a transaction to which section 381(a)(2) applies. However, if an S corporation acquires the assets of another S corporation in a transaction to which section 381(a)(2) applies, a post-termination transition period does not arise. (See § 1.1368–2(d)(2) for the treatment of the acquisition of the assets of an S corporation by another S corporation in a transaction to which section 381(a)(2) applies.) The special treatment under section 1371(e)(1) of distributions of money by a corporation with respect to its stock during the post-termination transition period is available only to those shareholders who were shareholders in the S corporation at the time of the termination.

(c) Determination defined. For purposes of section 1377(b)(1) and paragraph (a) of this section, the term determination means—

(1) A determination as defined in section 1313(a);

(2) A written agreement between the corporation and the Commissioner (including a statement acknowledging that the corporation's election to be an S corporation terminated under section 1362(d)) that the corporation failed to qualify as an S corporation;

(3) For a corporation subject to the audit and assessment provisions of subchapter C of chapter 63 of subtitle A of the Code, the expiration of the period specified in section 6226 for filing a petition for readjustment of a final S corporation administrative adjustment finding that the corporation failed to qualify as an S corporation, provided that no petition was timely filed before the expiration of the period; and

(4) For a corporation not subject to the audit and assessment provisions of subchapter C of chapter 63 of subtitle A of the Code, the expiration of the period for filing a petition under section 6213 for the sharcholder's taxable year for which the Commissioner has made a finding that the corporation failed to qualify as an S corporation, provided that no petition was timely filed before the expiration of the period.

(d) Date a determination becomes effective—(1) Determination under section 1313(a). A determination under paragraph (c)(1) of this section becomes effective on the date prescribed in section 1313 and the regulations thereunder.

(2) Written agreement. A determination under paragraph (c)(2) of this section becomes effective when it is signed by the district director having jurisdiction over the corporation (or by another Service official to whom authority to sign the agreement is delegated) and by an officer of the corporation authorized to sign on its behalf. Neither the request for a written agreement nor the terms of the written agreement suspend the running of any statute of limitations.

(3) Implied agreement. A determination under paragraph (c)(3) or (4) of this section becomes effective on the day after the date of expiration of the period specified under section 6226 or 6213, respectively.

§1.1378–1 Taxable year of S corporation.

(a) In general. No corporation may make an election be an S corporation for any taxable year unless the taxable year is a permitted year. In addition, an S corporation shall not change its taxable year to any taxable year other than a permitted year. A permitted year is a taxable year ending on December 31 or is any other taxable year for which the corporation establishes a business purpose (within the meaning of §1.442–1(b)(1)) to the satisfaction of the Commissioner.

(b) Corporations qualifying for automatic change of taxable year to a taxable year ending December 31 and corporations adopting a taxable year ending December 31—(1) Qualification for automatic change. Notwithstanding section 442 (relating to change of taxable year) and the regulations thereunder, a corporation may automatically change its taxable year to a taxable year ending on December 31 to comply with the permitted year requirement if all of its principal shareholders have taxable years ending on December 31, or if all of its principal shareholders concurrently change to such taxable year. A shareholder may not change his or her taxable year without securing prior approval from the Commissioner. See section 442 and the regulations thereunder. For purposes of this paragraph, a principal shareholder is a shareholder having 5% or more of the issued and outstanding stock of the corporation. See paragraph (d) of this section in the case where a corporation does not qualify under this subparagraph for an automatic change of its taxable year to a taxable year ending on December 31.

§ 301.7701–1 Classification of organizations for federal tax purposes.

(a) Organizations for federal tax purposes.

(1) In general. The Internal Revenue Code prescribes the classification of various organizations for federal tax purposes. Whether an organization is an entity separate from its owners for federal tax purposes is a matter of federal tax law and does not depend on whether the organization is recognized as an entity under local law.

(2) Certain joint undertakings give rise to entities for federal tax purposes. A joint venture or other contractual arrangement may create a separate entity for federal tax purposes if the participants carry on a trade, business, financial operation, or venture and divide the profits therefrom. For example, a separate entity exists for federal tax purposes if co-owners of an apartment building lease space and in addition provide services to the occupants either directly or through an agent. Nevertheless, a joint undertaking merely to share expenses does not create a separate entity for federal tax purposes. For example, if two or more persons jointly construct a ditch merely to drain surface water from their properties, they have not created a separate entity for federal tax purposes. Similarly, mere coownership of property that is maintained, kept in repair, and rented or leased does not constitute a separate entity for federal tax purposes. For example, if an individual owner, or tenants in common, of farm property lease it to a farmer for a cash rental or a share of the crops, they do not necessarily create a separate entity for federal tax purposes.

(3) Certain local law entities not recognized. An entity formed under local law is not always recognized as a separate entity for federal tax purposes. For example, an organization wholly owned by a State is not recognized as a separate entity for federal tax purposes if it is an integral part of the State. Similarly, tribes incorporated under section 17 of the Indian Reorganization Act of 1934, as amended, 25 U.S.C. 477, or under section 3 of the Oklahoma Indian Welfare Act, as amended, 25 U.S.C. 503, are not recognized as separate entities for federal tax purposes.

(4) Single owner organizations. Under sections 301.7701–2 and 301.7701–3, certain organizations that have a single owner can choose to be recognized or disregarded as entities separate from their owners.

(b) Classification of organizations. The classification of organizations that are recognized as separate entities is determined under sections 301.7701–2, 301.7701–3, and 301.7701–4 unless a provision of the Internal Revenue Code (such as section 860A addressing Real Estate Mortgage Investment Conduits (REMICs)) provides for special treatment of that organization. For the classification of organizations as trusts, see section 301.7701–4. That section provides that trusts generally do not have associates or an objective to carry on business for profit. Sections 301.7701–2 and 301.7701–3 provide rules for classifying organizations that are not classified as trusts.

(c) Cost sharing arrangements. A cost sharing arrangement that is described in § 1.482–7 of this chapter, including any arrangement that the Commissioner treats as a CSA under § 1.482–7(b)(5) of this chapter, is not recognized as a separate entity for purposes of the Internal Revenue Code. See § 1.482–7 of this chapter for the rules regarding CSAs.

(d) Domestic and foreign business entities. See § 301.7701–5 for the rules that determine whether a business entity is domestic or foreign.

(e) State. For purposes of this section and section 301.7701–2, the term State includes the District of Columbia.

* * *

§ 301.7701–2 Business entities; definitions.

(a) Business entities. For purposes of this section and section 301.7701–3, a business entity is any entity recognized for federal tax purposes (including an entity with a single owner that may be disregarded as an entity separate from its owner under section 301.7701–3) that is not properly classified as a trust under section 301.7701–4 or otherwise subject to special treatment under the Internal Revenue Code. A business entity with two or more members is classified for federal tax purposes as either a corporation or a partnership. A business entity with only one owner is classified as a corporation or is disregarded; if the entity is disregarded, its activities are treated in the same manner as a sole proprietorship, branch, or division of the owner.

(b) Corporations. For federal tax purposes, the term corporation means—

(1) A business entity organized under a Federal or State statute, or under a statute of a federally recognized Indian tribe, if the statute describes or refers to the entity as incorporated or as a corporation, body corporate, or body politic;

(2) An association (as determined under section 301.7701–3);

(3) A business entity organized under a State statute, if the statute describes or refers to the entity as a joint-stock company or joint-stock association;

(4) An insurance company;

(5) A State-chartered business entity conducting banking activities, if any of its deposits are insured under the Federal Deposit Insurance Act, as amended, 12 U.S.C. 1811 et seq., or a similar federal statute;

(6) A business entity wholly owned by a State or any political subdivision thereof;

(7) A business entity that is taxable as a corporation under a provision of the Internal Revenue Code other than section 7701(a)(3);

(8) Certain foreign entities—

(i) In general. Except as provided in paragraphs (b)(8)(ii) and (d) of this section, the

following business entities formed in the following jurisdictions:

* * *

(c) Other business entities. For federal tax purposes—

(1) The term partnership means a business entity that is not a corporation under paragraph (b) of this section and that has at least two members.

(2) Wholly owned entities—

(i) In general. Except as otherwise provided in this paragraph (c), a business entity that has a single owner and is not a corporation under paragraph (b) of this section is disregarded as an entity separate from its owner.

(ii) Special rule for certain business entities. If the single owner of a business entity is a bank (as defined in section 581 * * *), then the special rules applicable to banks under the Internal Revenue Code will continue to apply to the single owner as if the wholly owned entity were a separate entity. * * *

(iii) Tax liabilities of certain disregarded entities—(A) In general. An entity that is disregarded as separate from its owner for any purpose under this section is treated as an entity separate from its owner for purposes of—

(1) Federal tax liabilities of the entity with respect to any taxable period for which the entity was not disregarded;

(2) Federal tax liabilities of any other entity for which the entity is liable; and

(3) Refunds or credits of Federal tax.

(B) Examples. The following examples illustrate the application of paragraph (c)(2)(iii)(A) of this section:

Example (1). In 2006, X, a domestic corporation that reports its taxes on a calendar year basis, merges into Z, a domestic LLC wholly owned by Y that is disregarded as an entity separate from Y, in a state law merger. X was not a member of a consolidated group at any time during its taxable year ending in December 2005. Under the applicable state law, Z is the successor to X and is liable for all of X's debts. In 2009, the Internal Revenue Service (IRS) seeks to extend the period of limitations on assessment for X's 2005 taxable year. Because Z is the successor to X and is liable for X's 2005 taxes that remain unpaid, Z is the proper party to sign the consent to extend the period of limitations.

Example (2). The facts are the same as in Example 1, except that in 2007, the IRS determines that X miscalculated and underreported its income tax liability for 2005. Because Z is the successor to X and is liable for X's 2005 taxes that remain unpaid, the deficiency may be assessed against Z and, in the event that Z fails to pay the liability after notice and demand, a general tax lien will arise against all of Z's property and rights to property.

* * *

§ 301.7701–3 Classification of certain business entities.

(a) In general. A business entity that is not classified as a corporation under section 301.7701–2(b)(1), (3), (4), (5), (6), (7), or (8) (an eligible entity) can elect its classification for federal tax purposes as provided in this section. An eligible entity with at least two members can elect to be classified as either an association (and thus a corporation under section 301.7701–2(b)(2)) or a partnership, and an eligible entity with a single owner can elect to be classified as an association or to be disregarded as an entity separate from its owner. Paragraph (b) of this section provides a default classification for an eligible entity that does not make an election. Thus, elections are necessary only when an eligible entity chooses to be classified initially as other than the default classification or when an eligible entity chooses to change its classification. An entity whose classification is determined under the default classification retains that classification (regardless of any changes in the members' liability that occurs at any time during the time

that the entity's classification is relevant as defined in paragraph (d) of this section) until the entity makes an election to change that classification under paragraph (c)(1) of this section. Paragraph (c) of this section provides rules for making express elections. Paragraph (d) of this section provides special rules for foreign eligible entities. Paragraph (e) of this section provides special rules for classifying entities resulting from partnership terminations and divisions under section 708(b). Paragraph (f) of this section sets forth the effective date of this section and a special rule relating to prior periods. . . .

(b) Classification of eligible entities that do not file an election—

(1) Domestic eligible entities. Except as provided in paragraph (b)(3) of this section, unless the entity elects otherwise, a domestic eligible entity is—

(i) A partnership if it has two or more members; or

(ii) Disregarded as an entity separate from its owner if it has a single owner.

(2) Foreign eligible entities—

(i) In general. Except as provided in paragraph (b)(3) of this section, unless the entity elects otherwise, a foreign eligible entity is—

(A) A partnership if it has two or more members and at least one member does not have limited liability;

(B) An association if all members have limited liability; or

(C) Disregarded as an entity separate from its owner if it has a single owner that does not have limited liability.

(ii) Definition of limited liability. For purposes of paragraph (b)(2)(i) of this section, a member of a foreign eligible entity has limited liability if the member has no personal liability for the debts of or claims against the entity by reason of being a member. This determination is based solely on the statute or law pursuant to which the entity is organized, except that if the underlying statute or law allows the entity to specify in its organizational documents whether the members will have limited liability, the organizational documents may also be relevant. For purposes of this section, a member has personal liability if the creditors of the entity may seek satisfaction of all or any portion of the debts or claims against the entity from the member as such. A member has personal liability for purposes of this paragraph even if the member makes an agreement under which another person (whether or not a member of the entity) assumes such liability or agrees to indemnify that member for any such liability.

(3) Existing eligible entities—

(i) In general. Unless the entity elects otherwise, an eligible entity in existence prior to the effective date of this section will have the same classification that the entity claimed under sections 301.7701–1 through 301.7701–3 as in effect on the date prior to the effective date of this section; except that if an eligible entity with a single owner claimed to be a partnership under those regulations, the entity will be disregarded as an entity separate from its owner under this paragraph (b)(3)(i). For special rules regarding the classification of such entities prior to the effective date of this section, see paragraph (h)(2) of this section.

(ii) Special rules. For purposes of paragraph (b)(3)(i) of this section, a foreign eligible entity is treated as being in existence prior to the effective date of this section only if the entity's classification was relevant (as defined in paragraph (d) of this section) at any time during the sixty months prior to the effective date of this section. If an entity claimed different classifications prior to the effective date of this section, the entity's classification for purposes of paragraph (b)(3)(i) of this section is the last classification claimed by the entity. If a foreign eligible entity's classification is relevant prior to the effective date of this section, but no federal tax or information return is filed or the federal tax or information return does

not indicate the classification of the entity, the entity's classification for the period prior to the effective date of this section is determined under the regulations in effect on the date prior to the effective date of this section.

(c) Elections—

(1) Time and place for filing—

(i) In general. Except as provided in paragraphs (c)(1)(iv) and (v) of this section, an eligible entity may elect to be classified other than as provided under paragraph (b) of this section, or to change its classification, by filing Form 8832, Entity Classification Election, with the service center designated on Form 8832. An election will not be accepted unless all of the information required by the form and instructions, including the taxpayer identifying number of the entity, is provided on Form 8832. See section 301.6109–1 for rules on applying for and displaying Employer Identification Numbers.

(ii) Further notification of elections. An eligible entity required to file a federal tax or information return for the taxable year for which an election is made under paragraph (c) (1)(i) of this section must attach a copy of its Form 8832 to its federal tax or information return for that year. If the entity is not required to file a return for that year, a copy of its Form 8832 must be attached to the federal income tax or information return of any direct or indirect owner of the entity for the taxable year of the owner that includes the date on which the election was effective. An indirect owner of the entity does not have to attach a copy of the Form 8832 to its return if an entity in which it has an interest is already filing a copy of the Form 8832 with its return. If an entity, or one of its direct or indirect owners, fails to attach a copy of a Form 8832 to its return as directed in this section, an otherwise valid election under paragraph (c)(1)(i) of this section will not be invalidated, but the non-filing party may be subject to penalties, including any applicable penalties if the federal tax or information returns are inconsistent with the entity's election under paragraph (c)(1)(i) of this section.

(iii) Effective date of election. An election made under paragraph (c)(1)(i) of this section will be effective on the date specified by the entity on Form 8832 or on the date filed if no such date is specified on the election form. The effective date specified on Form 8832 can not be more than 75 days prior to the date on which the election is filed and can not be more than 12 months after the date on which the election is filed. If an election specifies an effective date more than 75 days prior to the date on which the election is filed, it will be effective 75 days prior to the date it was filed. If an election specifies an effective date more than 12 months from the date on which the election is filed, it will be effective 12 months after the date it was filed. If an election specifies an effective date before January 1, 1997, it will be effective as of January 1, 1997. If a purchasing corporation makes an election under section 338 regarding an acquired subsidiary, an election under paragraph (c)(1)(i) of this section for the acquired subsidiary can be effective no earlier than the day after the acquisition date (within the meaning of section 338(h)(2)).

(iv) Limitation. If an eligible entity makes an election under paragraph (c)(1)(i) of this section to change its classification (other than an election made by an existing entity to change its classification as of the effective date of this section), the entity cannot change its classification by election again during the sixty months succeeding the effective date of the election. However, the Commissioner may permit the entity to change its classification by election within the sixty months if more than fifty percent of the ownership interests in the entity as of the effective date of the subsequent election are owned by persons that did not own any interests in the entity on the filing date or on the effective date of the entity's prior election. . . .

(v) Deemed elections—

(A) Exempt organizations. An eligible entity that has been determined to be, or claims to be, exempt from taxation under section 501(a) is treated as having made an election under this section to be classified as an association. Such election will be effective as of the first day for which exemption is claimed or determined to apply, regardless of when the claim or determination is made, and will remain in effect unless an election is made under paragraph (c)(1)(i) of this section after the date the claim for exempt status is withdrawn or rejected or the date the determination of exempt status is revoked.

(B) Real estate investment trusts. An eligible entity that files an election under section 856(c)(1) to be treated as a real estate investment trust is treated as having made an election under this section to be classified as an association. Such election will be effective as of the first day the entity is treated as a real estate investment trust.

(C) S corporations. An eligible entity that timely elects to be an S corporation under section 1362(a)(1) is treated as having made an election under this section to be classified as an association, provided that (as of the effective date of the election under section 1362(a)(1)) the entity meets all other requirements to qualify as a small business corporation under section 1361(b). Subject to § 301.7701–3(c)(1)(iv), the deemed election to be classified as an association will apply as of the effective date of the S corporation election and will remain in effect until the entity makes a valid election, under § 301.7701–3(c)(1)(i), to be classified as other than an association.

(vi) Examples. The following examples illustrate the rules of this paragraph (c)(1):

Example (1). On July 1, 1998, X, a domestic corporation, purchases a 10% interest in Y, an eligible entity formed under Country A law in 1990. The entity's classification was not relevant to any person for federal tax or information purposes prior to X's acquisition of an interest in Y. Thus, Y is not considered to be in existence on the effective date of this section for purposes of paragraph (b)(3) of this section. Under the applicable Country A statute, all members of Y have limited liability as defined in paragraph (b)(2)(ii) of this section. Accordingly, Y is classified as an association under paragraph (b)(2)(i)(B) of this section unless it elects under this paragraph (c) to be classified as a partnership. To be classified as a partnership as of July 1, 1998, Y must file a Form 8832 by September 14, 1998. See paragraph (c)(1)(i) of this section. Because an election cannot be effective more than 75 days prior to the date on which it is filed, if Y files its Form 8832 after September 14, 1998, it will be classified as an association from July 1, 1998, until the effective date of the election. In that case, it could not change its classification by election under this paragraph (c) during the sixty months succeeding the effective date of the election.

Example (2). (i) Z is an eligible entity formed under Country B law and is in existence on the effective date of this section within the meaning of paragraph (b)(3) of this section. Prior to the effective date of this section, Z claimed to be classified as an association. Unless Z files an election under this paragraph (c), it will continue to be classified as an association under paragraph (b)(3) of this section.

(ii) Z files a Form 8832 pursuant to this paragraph (c) to be classified as a partnership, effective as of the effective date of this section. Z can file an election to be classified as an association at any time thereafter, but then would not be permitted to change its classification by election during the sixty months succeeding the effective date of that subsequent election.

* * *

(2) Authorized signatures—

(i) In general. An election made under paragraph (c)(1)(i) of this section must be signed by—

(A) Each member of the electing entity who is an owner at the time the election is filed; or

(B) Any officer, manager, or member of the electing entity who is authorized (under local law or the entity's organizational documents) to make the election and who represents to having such authorization under penalties of perjury.

(ii) Retroactive elections. For purposes of paragraph (c)(2)(i) of this section, if an election under paragraph (c)(1)(i) of this section is to be effective for any period prior to the time that it is filed, each person who was an owner between the date the election is to be effective and the date the election is filed, and who is not an owner at the time the election is filed, must also sign the election.

(iii) Changes in classification. For paragraph (c)(2)(i) of this section, if an election under paragraph (c)(1)(i) of this section is made to change the classification of an entity, each person who was an owner on the date that any transactions under paragraph (g) of this section are deemed to occur, and who is not an owner at the time the election is filed, must also sign the election. This paragraph (c)(2)(iii) applies to elections filed on or after November 29, 1999.

(d) Special rules for foreign eligible entities.

(1) Definition of relevance.

(i) General rule. For purposes of this section, a foreign eligible entity's classification is relevant when its classification affects the liability of any person for federal tax or information purposes. For example, a foreign entity's classification would be relevant if U.S. income was paid to the entity and the determination by the withholding agent of the amount to be withheld under chapter 3 of the Internal Revenue Code (if any) would vary depending upon whether the entity is classified as a partnership or as an association. Thus, the classification might affect the documentation that the withholding agent must receive from the entity, the type of tax or information return to file, or how the return must be prepared. The date that the classification of a foreign eligible entity is relevant is the date an event occurs that creates an obligation to file a federal tax return, information return, or statement for which the classification of the entity must be determined. Thus, the classification of a foreign entity is relevant, for example, on the date that an interest in the entity is acquired which will require a U.S. person to file an information return on Form 5471.

(ii) Deemed relevance.

(A) General rule. For purposes of this section, except as provided in paragraph (d)(1)(ii)(B) of this section, the classification for Federal tax purposes of a foreign eligible entity that files Form 8832, "Entity Classification Election", shall be deemed to be relevant only on the date the entity classification election is effective.

(B) Exception. If the classification of a foreign eligible entity is relevant within the meaning of paragraph (d)(1)(i) of this section, then the rule in paragraph (d)(1)(ii)(A) of this section shall not apply.

(2) Entities the classification of which has never been relevant.

If the classification of a foreign eligible entity has never been relevant (as defined in paragraph (d)(1) of this section), then the entity's classification will initially be determined pursuant to the provisions of paragraph (b)(2) of this section when the classification of the entity first becomes relevant (as defined in paragraph (d)(1)(i) of this section).

(3) Special rule when classification is no longer relevant.

If the classification of a foreign eligible entity is not relevant (as defined in paragraph (d) (1) of this section) for 60 consecutive months, then the entity's classification will initially be determined pursuant to the provisions of paragraph (b)(2) of this section when the classification of the foreign eligible entity becomes relevant (as defined in paragraph (d)(1)(i) of this section). The date that the classification of

a foreign entity is not relevant is the date an event occurs that causes the classification to no longer be relevant, or, if no event occurs in a taxable year that causes the classification to be relevant, then the date is the first day of that taxable year.

* * *

(e) Coordination with section 708(b). Except as provided in section 301.7701–2(d)(3) (regarding termination of grandfather status for certain foreign business entities), an entity resulting from a transaction described in section 708(b)(1)(B) (partnership termination due to sales or exchanges) or section 708(b)(2)(B) (partnership division) is a partnership.

(f) Changes in number of members of an entity—

(1) Associations. The classification of an eligible entity as an association is not affected by any change in the number of members of the entity.

(2) Partnerships and single member entities. An eligible entity classified as a partnership becomes disregarded as an entity separate from its owner when the entity's membership is reduced to one member. A single member entity disregarded as an entity separate from its owner is classified as a partnership when the entity has more than one member. If an elective classification change under paragraph (c) of this section is effective at the same time as a membership change described in this paragraph (f)(2), the deemed transactions in paragraph (g) of this section resulting from the elective change preempt the transactions that would result from the change in membership.

(3) Effect on sixty month limitation. A change in the number of members of an entity does not result in the creation of a new entity for purposes of the sixty month limitation on elections under paragraph (c)(1)(iv) of this section.

(4) Examples. The following examples illustrate the application of this paragraph (f):

Example (1). A, a U.S. person, owns a domestic eligible entity that is disregarded as an entity separate from its owner. On January 1, 1998, B, a U.S. person, buys a 50 percent interest in the entity from A. Under this paragraph (f), the entity is classified as a partnership when B acquires an interest in the entity. However, A and B elect to have the entity classified as an association effective on January 1, 1998. Thus, B is treated as buying shares of stock on January 1, 1998. (Under paragraph (c)(1)(iv) of this section, this election is treated as a change in classification so that the entity generally cannot change its classification by election again during the sixty months succeeding the effective date of the election.) Under paragraph (g)(1) of this section, A is treated as contributing the assets and liabilities of the entity to the newly formed association immediately before the close of December 31, 1997. Because A does not retain control of the association as required by section 351, A's contribution will be a taxable event. Therefore, under section 1012, the association will take a fair market value basis in the assets contributed by A, and A will have a fair market value basis in the stock received. A will have no additional gain upon the sale of stock to B, and B will have a cost basis in the stock purchased from A.

Example (2). *(i)* On April 1, 1998, A and B, U.S. persons, form X, a foreign eligible entity. X is treated as an association under the default provisions of paragraph (b)(2)(i) of this section, and X does not make an election to be classified as a partnership. A subsequently purchases all of B's interest in X.

(ii) Under paragraph (f)(1) of this section, X continues to be classified as an association. X, however, can subsequently elect to be disregarded as an entity separate from A. The sixty month limitation of paragraph (c)(1)(iv) of this section does not prevent X from making an election because X has not made a prior election under paragraph (c)(1)(i) of this section.

Example (3). *(i)* On April 1, 1998, A and B, U.S. persons, form X, a foreign eligible entity. X is treated as an association under the default provisions of paragraph (b)(2)(i) of this section, and X does not make an election to be classified as a partnership. On January 1, 1999, X elects to be classified as a partnership effective on that date. Under the sixty month limitation of paragraph (c)(1)(iv) of this section, X cannot elect to be classified as an association until January 1, 2004 (i.e., sixty months after the effective date of the election to be classified as a partnership).

(ii) On June 1, 2000, A purchases all of B's interest in X. After A's purchase of B's interest, X can no longer be classified as a partnership because X has only one member. Under paragraph (f)(2) of this section, X is disregarded as an entity separate from A when A becomes the only member of X. X, however, is not treated as a new entity for purposes of paragraph (c)(1)(iv) of this section. As a result, the sixty month limitation of paragraph (c)(1)(iv) of this section continues to apply to X, and X cannot elect to be classified as an association until January 1, 2004 (i.e., sixty months after January 1, 1999, the effective date of the election by X to be classified as a partnership).

* * *

(g) Elective changes in classification—

(1) Deemed treatment of elective change—(i) Partnership to association. If an eligible entity classified as a partnership elects under paragraph (c)(1)(i) of this section to be classified as an association, the following is deemed to occur: The partnership contributes all of its assets and liabilities to the association in exchange for stock in the association, and immediately thereafter, the partnership liquidates by distributing the stock of the association to its partners.

(ii) Association to partnership. If an eligible entity classified as an association elects under paragraph (c)(1)(i) of this section to be classified as a partnership, the following is deemed to occur: The association distributes all of its assets and liabilities to its shareholders in liquidation of the association, and immediately thereafter, the shareholders contribute all of the distributed assets and liabilities to a newly formed partnership.

(iii) **Association to disregarded entity.** If an eligible entity classified as an association elects under paragraph (c)(1)(i) of this section to be disregarded as an entity separate from its owner, the following is deemed to occur: The association distributes all of its assets and liabilities to its single owner in liquidation of the association.

(iv) **Disregarded entity to an association.** If an eligible entity that is disregarded as an entity separate from its owner elects under paragraph (c)(1)(i) of this section to be classified as an association, the following is deemed to occur: The owner of the eligible entity contributes all of the assets and liabilities of the entity to the association in exchange for stock of the association.

(2) **Effect of elective changes. (i) In general.** The tax treatment of a change in the classification of an entity for federal tax purposes by election under paragraph (c)(1)(i) of this section is determined under all relevant provisions of the Internal Revenue Code and general principles of tax law, including the step transaction doctrine.

(ii) **Adoption of plan of liquidation.** For purposes of satisfying the requirement of adoption of a plan of liquidation under section 332, unless a formal plan of liquidation that contemplates the election to be classified as a partnership or to be disregarded as an entity separate from its owner is adopted on an earlier date, the making, by an association, of an election under paragraph (c)(1)(i) of this section to be classified as a partnership or to be disregarded as an entity separate from its owner is considered to be the adoption of a plan of liquidation immediately before the deemed liquidation described in paragraph (g)(1)(ii) or (iii) of this section. This paragraph (g)(2)(ii)

applies to elections filed on or after December 17, 2001. Taxpayers may apply this paragraph (g)(2)(ii) retroactively to elections filed before December 17, 2001, if the corporate owner claiming treatment under section 332 and its subsidiary making the election take consistent positions with respect to the federal tax consequences of the election.

(3) **Timing of election—(i) In general.** An election under paragraph (c)(1)(i) of this section that changes the classification of an eligible entity for federal tax purposes is treated as occurring at the start of the day for which the election is effective. Any transactions that are deemed to occur under this paragraph (g) as a result of a change in classification are treated as occurring immediately before the close of the day before the election is effective. For example, if an election is made to change the classification of an entity from an association to a partnership effective on January 1, the deemed transactions specified in paragraph (g)(1)(ii) of this section (including the liquidation of the association) are treated as occurring immediately before the close of December 31 and must be reported by the owners of the entity on December 31. Thus, the last day of the association's taxable year will be December 31 and the first day of the partnership's taxable year will be January 1.

(ii) **Coordination with section 338 election.** A purchasing corporation that makes a qualified stock purchase of an eligible entity taxed as a corporation may make an election under section 338 regarding the acquisition if it satisfies the requirements for the election, and may also make an election to change the classification of the target corporation. If a taxpayer makes an election under section 338 regarding its acquisition of another entity taxable as a corporation and makes an election under paragraph (c) of this section for the acquired corporation (effective at the earliest possible date as provided by paragraph (c)(1)(iii) of this section), the transactions under paragraph (g) of this section are deemed to occur immediately after the deemed asset purchase by the new target corporation under section 338.

(iii) Application to successive elections in tiered situations. When elections under paragraph (c)(1)(i) of this section for a series of tiered entities are effective on the same date, the eligible entities may specify the order of the elections on Form 8832. If no order is specified for the elections, any transactions that are deemed to occur in this paragraph (g) as a result of the classification change will be treated as occurring first for the highest tier entity's classification change, then for the next highest tier entity's classification change, and so forth down the chain of entities until all the transactions under this paragraph (g) have occurred. For example, Parent, a corporation, wholly owns all of the interest of an eligible entity classified as an association (S1), which wholly owns another eligible entity classified as an association (S2), which wholly owns another eligible entity classified as an association (S3). Elections under paragraph (c)(1)(i) of this section are filed to classify S1, S2, and S3 each as disregarded as an entity separate from its owner effective on the same day. If no order is specified for the elections, the following transactions are deemed to occur under this paragraph (g) as a result of the elections, with each successive transaction occurring on the same day immediately after the preceding transaction: S1 is treated as liquidating into Parent, then S2 is treated as liquidating into Parent, and finally S3 is treated as liquidating into Parent.

* * *

§ 301.7701–5 Domestic and foreign business entities

(a) Domestic and foreign entities. A business entity (including an entity that is disregarded as separate from its owner) is domestic if it is created or organized as any type of entity (including, but not limited to, a corporation, unincorporated association, general partnership, limited partnership, and limited liability company) in the United States, or under the law of the United States or of any State. Accordingly, a business entity that is created or organized both in the United States and in a foreign jurisdiction is a domestic entity. A business entity (including an entity that is disregarded as separate from its owner) is foreign if it is not domestic. (The determination of whether an entity is domestic is made independently of the determination of its classification for Federal tax purposes. See §§ 301.7701–2, 301.7701–2T, and 301.7701–3 for the rules governing the classification of entities.)

(b) Examples. The following examples illustrate the rules of this section:

Example (1). (i) Facts. Y is an entity that is created or organized under the laws of Country A as a public limited company. It is also an entity that is organized as a limited liability company (LLC) under the laws of State B. Y has been classified as a corporation for Federal tax purposes under the rules of §§ 301.7701–2, 301.7701–2T, and 301.7701–3.

(ii) Result. Y is a domestic corporation because it is an entity that is classified as a corporation and it is organized as an entity under the laws of State B.

Example (2). (i) Facts. P is an entity with more than one owner organized under the laws of Country A as an unlimited company. It is also an entity that is organized as a general partnership under the laws of State B. P has been classified as a partnership for Federal tax purposes under the rules of §§ 301.7701–2, and 301.7701–3.

(ii) Result. P is a domestic partnership because it is an entity that is classified as a partnership and it is organized as an entity under the laws of State B.

* * *